# ENCYCLOPEDIA OF
# Special Education

## THIRD EDITION

THIRD EDITION
VOLUME 2

# ENCYCLOPEDIA OF
# Special Education

## A Reference for the Education of Children, Adolescents, and Adults with Disabilities and Other Exceptional Individuals

Edited by

Cecil R. Reynolds

Elaine Fletcher-Janzen

BICENTENNIAL
1807
WILEY
2007
BICENTENNIAL

JOHN WILEY & SONS

Published by John Wiley & Sons, Inc., Hoboken, New Jersey.
Published simultaneously in Canada.

For general information on our other products and services please contact our Customer Care Department within the U.S. at (800) 762-2974, outside the United States at (317) 572-3993 or fax (317) 572-4002.

Wiley also publishes its books in a variety of electronic formats. Some content that appears in print may not be available in electronic books. For more information about Wiley products, visit our website at www.wiley.com.

ISBN-13: 978-0-471-67798-7 (VOL. 1); ISBN-10: 0-471-67798-1 (VOL. 1)
ISBN-13: 978-0-471-67799-4 (VOL. 2); ISBN-10: 0-471-67799-X (VOL. 2)
ISBN-13: 978-0-471-67801-4 (VOL. 3); ISBN-10: 0-471-67801-5 (VOL. 3)

ISBN-13: 978-0-471-67802-1 (SET); ISBN-10: 0-471-67802-3 (SET)
Printed in the United States of America.
10 9 8 7 6 5 4 3 2 1

# PREFACE TO THE THIRD EDITION

It has been 20 years since we first set foot on the journey that has become the third edition of the *Encyclopedia of Special Education*. If someone has told us then that we would end up chronicling the evolution of special education, we probably would not have believed him or her. It was enough, at that time, to have created the first *Encyclopedia of Special Education;* nearly 2,000 pages, thousands of entries, and more than 400 authors coming together to cement this fledgling field that was full of hope and imagination.

So, here we are more than 20 years later, near the end of our guardianship of the *Encyclopedia*. It is our old friend, and it has been our mentor, our judge, and our inspiration. During the editing of the second and third editions, we are well aware of how life, research, and standards have changed for those of us who practice in special education. It is an interesting process to look back and see how the *Encyclopedia* has changed over the years and how it has really provided a mirror of the zeitgeist of the times in which we live.

The first edition was full of new ideas such as profile analysis, direct instruction, and terms such as "trainable" and "educable." The field had license to imagine and try ways to rewire the brain that was having trouble in school. Not so now! The third edition clearly marks the federal and state demands for evidence-based practices, perhaps reflecting the end of imagination and the beginning of an era of proof or accountability. Hence, we see behavioral terms and behavioral-oriented credentials enjoying resurgence because they allow for documentation of behaviors that are easy to observe. Accountability is a force to be noticed as it infiltrates and guides current practice.

The first edition was full of laws that were still new and somewhat unexplored: We were still trying to interpret Public Law 94-142! Now we have visited those laws, reauthorized (and revised) them many times, and joined them with support such as the ADA and Technology acts. Individuals with disabilities have never enjoyed the protections of as many laws and regulations as we have today. There are also so many more consumer protection groups and organizations around today that fight for the rights of those who have disabilities. In fact, current beliefs about advocacy are also focusing on assisting full participation by the individual with the disability in planning and transitions. Years ago, parents got together and had to forge an

organization and eventually laws that gave their children the right to an appropriate education. Their voices were heard and their legacy has been grand indeed as we see the very same children advocating for themselves.

The advocacy network that surrounds special education students today is vast, connected, and accessible. The Internet has exponentially changed the individual's abilities to learn about support organizations and to reach out to others who have similar concerns and conditions. This movement is not just on a national level, the World Health Organization is rallying the international community to connect the daily living experiences of individuals with disabilities in the *International Classification of Functioning, Disability, and Health*. This classification system was designed to describe the *individual* with a disability, not just to classify the disability itself. Indeed, we remember that in the first edition of the *Encyclopedia,* it was acceptable to label individuals via the disability; therefore, individuals with Schizophrenia were schizophrenics and individuals with Mental Retardation were the mentally retarded. The disability came first and the individual came second. In the second edition of the *Encyclopedia,* we remember stressing heavily with all of our editors and authors that all language referring to clinical populations would have to reflect the individual first and his or her handicapping condition second. This was a major literary turn at the time!

Many years ago, special education students were all too often relegated to isolated classrooms in secluded areas of school buildings. Not so now. The third edition (and somewhat in the second edition) of the *Encyclopedia* fully reflects that concepts such as "mainstreaming" are now archaic. Inclusion is the rule unless it is not in the best interests of the student. Disability and ability now live side by side. Humanness is central and our similarities outweigh our differences, even in special education.

The three editions of the *Encyclopedia* have also reflected the evolution of test construction and interpretation. The level of psychometric design is outstanding right now. Consumers have come to enjoy new tests that have specificity, such as tests about executive functions, trauma, study skills, and so on. The major broadband assessment batteries that measure cognitive abilities and psychological constructs are excellent, theory-based measures that have imaginative and careful design. Therefore, our ability to include well-designed tools in the assessment process has never been better. The third edition of the *Encyclopedia* catalogues many new tests and revisions of old and true instruments.

The demand for "countable" accountability of special education outcomes is upon these days. For the past 20 years, the *Encyclopedia* reflected exploration, and now exploration is passé and counting and demanding results is the zeitgeist of the times. Renegades as we are, we have included more and more neuropsychological principles and terms into the various editions of the *Encyclopedia* as we have paid homage to the vast mystery of the human brain and personality that will most likely never be reduced down to accountable facts. Herein lies the rub for those with interests in brain-behavior relationships, the very thing that we seek is unattainable and therein provides continuous wonder, curiosity, and frustration! We are confident that the most important aspect of future research that seeks to improve the daily lives of children with disabilities lies in the study of the brain and its relationship to learning and daily living skills. This process will always be a study of one, and not given to group statistics. Therefore, regardless of the political zeitgeist, we have expressed our desire to support clinical excellence throughout the third edition of the *Encyclopedia* and minimize old ideas that have been parceled out as new and redesigned to fit ends that are not apolitical. The original *Encyclopedia* was bursting with curiosity and wonder about a new field. We wish to maintain this tribute in the current edition and support the continued innocence of true scientific exploration.

So, what is new in the third edition of the *Encyclopedia*? Very little information these days is entirely new; however, there are some entries that reflect a resurgence or future directions, such as Response to Intervention, Highly Qualified Teachers, Diffusion Tensor Imaging, and Positive Behavior Supports. Tom Oakland, our "International Special Education entries" Contributing Editor provided us with many entries from new areas of the world such as Estonia, Albania, sub-Saharan Africa, and other exciting places reflecting his expertise in international special education and the trend of professionals to think more globally these days.

All of the laws and legal entries were completely and competently updated by our Contributing Editor, Kimberly Applequist, JD. The final regulations for the Individuals with Disabilities Education Improvement Act of 2004 are not out at this time and so the exact nature of the guidelines is not known, but we look forward to seeing how they take shape. Randall DePry updated many entries related to teaching and behavioral supports and provided new entries on the exacting process of applied behavior analysis. Lee Swanson focused on entries pertaining to the latest developments in reading and reading remediation. These entries will provide the reader with the most up-to-date information on a topic that is being urgently stressed all over the United States at this time. His expertise is very evident in these entries.

Rachel Toplis spent many hours updating information on organizations and journals so the readers will be able to get current information that they can apply immediately. She also wrote to all of the biographees and asked what they had been up to for the past few years. It was nice to have contact with them again.

Ron Zellner and Cynthia Riccio were Contributing Editors hailing from Texas A&M University who provided us with current information on technology, assistive, devices, and current trends in special education guidelines. Contributing Editor Sam Goldstein brought us up to date on the latest imaging devices that are assisting in the investigation of autism spectrum disorders, reading interventions, and learning in general. In addition, James Kaufman had a very creative time refreshing entries on theories of creativity and intelligence; the reader will enjoy his unique perspectives on these topics. Last but not least, the Drs. Ron Dumont and John Willis provided a completely new thread of reviews of standardized assessments throughout the *Encyclopedia*; their expertise in assessment reviews are legendary and we are please to have them as part of our effort.

Please allow us to apologize to our authors if their affiliations or names have changed over the past 20 years and the most recent changes are not incorporated into the third edition. We have tried to keep up with the changes but are sure that we have missed a few and promise to remediate in future editions! We also had to make editorial decisions about giving credit where credit was due for updates of entries. Therefore, the reader will notice that we have taken painstaking efforts to list the authors and to which editions they contributed. In some cases, an entry needed some tiny editing and in that case, Cecil and Elaine took tiny liberties and corrected dates or added a current reference here and there. We, again, apologize if our tiny contributions were bigger than the author would wish. In most of these cases, the article was so well written it would have been a waste of time to try to rewrite.

There are, as usual, many individuals to thank for assisting with the creating and preparation of this volume of work. First, let us thank the contributing editors to the previous and current editions. These individuals took on the responsibilities of looking at where the field has been and where it is going in their respective areas of expertise. They then shepherded many authors into taking on smaller parts to reflect important aspects of the basics and documenting growth. Without their commitment and dedication, we would be bereft of hope for a renovation of this size of work! We would also like to thank the individual authors for their cheerful attitude and dedication to their contributions: They are representatives of the best the field has to offer and we are very grateful for their efforts.

Cecil would like to thank Julia, as he does so untiringly, for her support in so many ways, and his long-deceased Dad, who gave him the gift of a model of service. Elaine would like to take this opportunity to thank David, Emma, and Leif for putting up with her being obsessed one more time; and her father, Peter C. Fletcher, who has modeled insatiable curiosity and a love of life's work that will stay with her always.

Lastly, we would like to thank the editors at John Wiley & Sons, Inc., Tracey Belmont and Lisa Gebo for their supervision of the work, and publisher Peggy Alexander for making a lifetime commitment to this endeavor. What started as a description of the field of special education became a history of special education and a chronicle of its life and times. We have been honored to witness this process and, as always, look forward to future growth.

# E

## EAR AND HEARING

The ear is the sensory organ of hearing, and hearing is the sense by which sound waves are recognized and interpreted. The ear can be divided into four parts: the outer, middle, and inner ear, and central pathways. Sound waves enter the outer ear via the auricle (or pinna) on the side of the head and then go through the ear canal (external auditory meatus) to the middle ear. The middle ear consists of the eardrum (tympanic membrane) and three articulated bones (malleus, incus, and stapes), collectively called the ossicles, which extend from the eardrum to the inner ear. The middle ear transforms the acoustic energy of the sound waves impinging on the eardrum to mechanical energy.

The inner ear is divided into a vestibular (balance) and cochlear (hearing) section. The cochlea consists of three fluid-filled ducts. The middle duct contains the Organ of Corti, which houses the sensory nerve endings for hearing. The cochlea transforms the mechanical sound wave energy from the middle ear to electrical energy to initiate a neural response. The neural response of the cochlea is carried by the central auditory pathways to the brain. The central pathways consist of the auditory nerve (eighth cranial nerve), which starts in the inner ear, interacts with neural complexes in the brain stem, and terminates in Heschel's gyri, which is the primary auditory reception center in the temporal cortex on each side of the brain.

### REFERENCES

Moore, B. C. J. (1982). *An introduction to the psychology of hearing* (2nd ed.). New York: Academic.

Pickles, J. O. (1982). *An introduction to the physiology of hearing.* New York: Academic.

THOMAS A. FRANK
*Pennsylvania State University*

## DEAF
## DEAF EDUCATION

## EARLY CHILDHOOD, CULTURALLY AND LINGUISTICALLY DIVERSE ISSUES IN

Two important factors have increased professional awareness of the responsibility to better meet the needs of young children from culturally and linguistically diverse backgrounds. The first factor includes the group of dramatic demographic changes occurring in the United States (Lynch & Hanson, 1992). The second is the passage of the 1986 amendments to the Education of the Handicapped Act Amendments (EHA; Gettinger, Elliot, & Kratochwill, 1992).

Due to linguistic, cultural, and economic barriers, children from cultural and linguistically diverse backgrounds are at greater risk to experience difficulties and to be identified for intervention (Cook, Tessier, & Klein, 1992; National Information Center for Children and Youth with Handicaps, 1987). As the number of culturally and linguistically diverse children increases, early interventionists are faced with issues surrounding the delivery of comprehensive early intervention services to children and their families (Gettinger et al., 1992). Evaluation and assessment of infants, toddlers, and preschoolers who are culturally and linguistically diverse presents complex responsibilities to early childhood professionals. Determining eligibility for special education and related services for diverse children poses particular challenges to early interventionists. On the other hand, children who are culturally and linguistically diverse are overrepresented in special education (Yansen & Shulman, 1996). On the other hand, a genuine delay or disability may be overlooked if the child's cultural and/or linguistic context is poorly understood. The provision of early intervention services to young children who are culturally and linguistically diverse requires sensitivity to cultural and linguistic factors that may explain behaviors that might appear to indicate disability or delay.

Educational services to young children with special needs increased dramatically during the later 1980s and the 1990s. The considerable growth in the area of early childhood intervention is largely a result of the addition of the 1986 amendments to the EHA. Commonly known as Public Law 99-457, the amendments offered a strong impetus for expanding research, practice, and training in early childhood services. Public Law 99-457 mandated availability of early intervention programs for children from birth to 3 years of age, and free and appropriate public education for children from 3 to 5 years of age (Preator & McAllister,

1995). In 1991, PL 99-457 was combined with other legislation, passed as Public Law 102-119, and renamed the Individuals with Disabilities Education Act (IDEA). IDEA was reauthorized in 1997 and again in 2004.

As a result of the expansion of early childhood services and the increasing numbers of ethnic minority children requiring services, there is a growing need for professionals appropriately trained to address the needs of culturally and linguistically diverse children and their families. However, results of national surveys indicate a lack of trained bilingual, bicultural personnel among provider agencies (Delgado, Galarza, Ford, & Ochoa, 1992). Furthermore, enrollment of minority students in training programs is low (Delgado, Ochoa, Ford, & Galarza, 1993). Thus, early childhood programs will serve an increasing number of children from culturally and linguistically diverse groups and their families, yet services will be provided by interventionists of the mainstream culture. Averting the potential problems for cultural mismatch, it is imperative for early childhood service providers to become aware of the cultural similarities and differences of the families they serve (Hanson, 1990; Preator & McAllister, 1995).

Service delivery to families of children who are disabled or at risk for disabilities has moved toward a much more family-centered approach (Lynch & Hanson, 1990). Part H of PL 99-457 strongly emphasizes the involvement of families in the service delivery process. The Individualized Family Service Plan (IFSP), a key feature of Part H, must be designed to meet the developmental needs of the child and also the family's needs (Lynch & Hanson, 1990). Approaches to early childhood intervention with culturally and linguistically diverse children and families, therefore, require an understanding of the child within the family and cultural context. An understanding of the cultural beliefs and practices of families from diverse backgrounds is needed to develop and implement high quality services that are culturally appropriate and effective. For children and families from culturally and linguistically diverse backgrounds, critical issues including language learning and the impact of culture on early development and behaviors must be addressed (Bergeson, Gutting, Gill, & Shureen, 1997).

General considerations for evaluation and intervention with young children who are culturally or linguistically diverse include an effort to avoid mistaking differences in culture and language with genuine disabilities and delays in development (Bergeson et al., 1997). Comprehensive assessment of young culturally and linguistically diverse children must include a determination of language proficiency and dominance in order to assist early childhood specialists in deciding which language to use for evaluation and instruction (Yansen & Schulman, 1996). Alternative procedures, such as observations, interviews, profiles, and professional judgment, should be utilized due to the limited number of norm-referenced tests standardized to include specific cultural and linguistic factors. The results of the assessment must provide for appropriate interventions that honor the child's primary language and culture (Bergeson et al., 1997). Frisby and Reynolds (2005) have produced a volume that illuminates many current aspects of multicultural issues in education, and is an excellent resource.

## REFERENCES

Aponte, J. F., & Crouch, R. T. (1995). The changing ethnic profile of the United States. In J. F. Aponte, R. Y. Rivers, & J. Wohl (Eds.), *Psychological interventions and cultural diversity* (pp. 1–18). Boston: Allyn & Bacon.

Bergeson, T., Gutting, J. M., Gill, D. H., & Shureen, A. (1997). *Evaluation and assessment in early childhood special education: Children who are culturally and linguistically diverse.* Olympia, WA: State Superintendent of Public Instruction.

Chan, S. (1990). Early intervention with culturally diverse families of infants and toddlers with disabilities. *Infants and Young Children, 3,* 2, 78–87.

Children's Defense Fund. (1994). *State of the children report.* Washington, DC: Author.

Cook, R. E., Tessier, A., & Klein, M. D. (1992). *Adapting early childhood curricula for children with special needs* (3rd ed.). New York: Merrill.

Delgado, B. M., Galarza, A., Ford, L., & Ochoa, S. H. (1992). *Early intervention training with culturally and linguistically diverse populations: A national survey.* Paper presented at the meeting of the Council for Exceptional Children, Division for Culturally and Linguistically Diverse Exceptional Learners, Minneapolis, MN.

Delgado, B. M., Ochoa, S. H., Ford, L. A., & Galarza, A. (1993). *Current practices in training and service delivery for young culturally diverse children with disabilities.* Paper presented at the meeting of the Council for Exceptional Children, San Antonio, TX.

Frisby, C. L., & Reynolds, C. R. (2005). *The handbook of multicultural school psychology.* New York: Wiley.

Gettinger, M., Elliot, S. N., & Kratochwill, T. R. (1992). *Preschool and early childhood treatment directions.* New Jersey: Erlbaum.

Hanson, M. J., Lynch, E. W., & Wayman, K. I. (1990). Honoring the cultural diversity of families when gathering data. *Topics in Early Childhood Special Education, 10,* 112–131.

Hanson, M. J. (1992). Ethnic, cultural, and language diversity in intervention settings. In M. J. Hanson & E. W. Lynch (Eds.), *Developing cross-cultural competence: A guide for working with young children and their families* (pp. 3–18). Baltimore: Brookes.

Lynch, E. W. (1992). Developing cross-cultural competence. In E. W. Lynch & M. J. Hanson (Eds.), *Developing cross-cultural competence: A guide for working with young children and their families* (pp. 35–62). Baltimore: Brookes.

National Information Center for Children and Youth with Handicaps (NICHCY). (1990). *Individualized education programs.* Washington, DC: Author.

Preator, K. K., & McAllister, J. R. (1995). Best practices assessing infants and toddlers. In A. Thomas & J. Grimes (Eds.), *Best practices in school psychology III* (pp. 775–778). Washington, DC: National Association of School Psychologists.

U.S. Bureau of the Census. (1992). *Current population reports, P25-1092, population projections of the United States by age, sex, race, and Hispanic origin: 1992-2050.* Washington, DC: U.S. Government Printing Office.

Yansen, E., & Shulman, E. (1996). Language assessment: Multicultural considerations. In L. Suzuki, P. Meller, & J. Ponterotto (Eds.), *The handbook of multicultural assessment* (pp. 353–393). San Francisco: Jossey-Bass.

BERNADETTE M. DELGADO
*University of Nebraska*

# EARLY EXPERIENCE AND CRITICAL PERIODS

Early experience has long been presumed to have great impact on later development. Even into the beginning of the 20th century, many lay people and professionals believed that experiences, particularly traumatic ones, suffered by a pregnant woman could be transmitted to the embryo or fetus through a form of prenatal imprinting. In his autobiography, Joseph Merrick, the "Elephant Man," for example, attributed his gross deformities to his mother's being pushed under an elephant during a parade (Howell & Ford, 1980). In what may be the first book devoted to mental retardation and related conditions in children, Ireland (1898, p. 24) suggested that:

> In all ages women have believed that fright or extreme distress is dangerous to their offspring, causing weakness, deformities, or deafness. . . . Mr. Paget gave a case where a young girl bore a great resemblance to a monkey, and had a crop of brown, harsh, lank hair on the back and arms. The mother had in an early period of pregnancy been terrified by a monkey jumping on her back from a street organ.

Merrick was wrong in particular (see Elephant Man entry in this volume) and Ireland in general about the transmission of prenatal experiences to offspring; they were only among the first of many misclaims about the effects of early experience, as will be seen below.

Early experience and critical periods have traditionally been given important roles in intellective, personality, social, and emotional development. Briefly, early experience is viewed as having greater and more lasting impact on development than merely prior experience. Events that occur during certain discrete early critical periods, during which development is rapidly occurring, may have irreversible effects on later behavior. A partial list of proposed critical periods is in Table 1. Summaries of supporting research are in Denenberg (1972) and Scott (1978).

Persisting influence of early experience is implicit in the continuity position on development, which dominated both

Table 1 Some suggested behavioral critical periods

| Species | Early manipulation | Later effect |
|---|---|---|
| Precocial birds | Exposure to parent surrogate | Filial imprinting |
| Birds | Exposure to potential mate | Sexual imprinting |
| Mammals | Hormone presentation or removal | Sexual and agonistic behavior |
| Songbirds | Exposure to adult song; surgery | Acquisition of adult song |
| Mice | Exposure to noise | Susceptibility to audiogenic seizures |
| Cats and monkeys | Visual environment | Pattern vision; brain structure and function |
| Rats and mice | Mild stress | Resistance to stress |
| Rats | Rearing environment | Learning; brain structure and function |
| Dogs and monkeys | Social environment | Sexual and social behavior |
| Sheep and goats | Social environment | Mother-infant bond |
| Human infants and children | Exposure to toxins | Intellective and sensory functioning |
| Human children | Exposure to language; brain damage | Language acquisition |
| Humans | Social environment | Caretaker-infant bond |
| Human children | Rearing environment | Social, emotional, intellective functioning |

psychology and education for much of the twentieth century. It holds that later development is continuous with, and thus grows out of, earlier behavior, which in turn is molded by early experience. As an example, Pasamanick and Knoblock (1966) proposed a continuum of reproductive casualty: the degree of perinatal insult suffered by a newborn directly relates to the degree of later impairment it will show. Thus, early plasticity and response to stimulation is replaced by later rigidity and resistance to change. The proposed generality of the continuity view was well expressed by Kelly (1955): "Whether one is an extreme hereditarian, an environmentalist, a constitutionalist, or an orthodox psychoanalyst, he is not likely to anticipate major changes in personality after the first years of life" (p. 659).

Beginning in the 1950s and 1960s, however, and burgeoning in the 1970s and 1980s, a number of researchers and theorists began to produce data and reviews of previous research that supported the noncontinuity view that early experience and behavior did not necessarily predispose humans—or nonhumans for that matter—to particular later behavior (Brim & Kagan, 1980; Emde & Harmon, 1984; Erikson, 1950; Kagan, 1984; Kagan, Kearsley, & Zelazo,

1978; Kagan & Moss, 1962). As one example, Sameroff and Chandler (1975) found little evidence to suggest that degree of perinatal insult directly caused degree of later impairment. Most children who had suffered low or even moderate degrees of perinatal insult could not be differentiated from those who had suffered none. Problems were shown by children whose perinatal insult was combined with inadequate caretaking behavior. Sameroff and Chandler proposed a dynamic and interactive "continuum of caretaking casuality" to replace Pasamanick and Knoblock's linear "continuum of reproductive casualty." Lerner (1986) has provided a thoughtful discussion of the continuity-noncontinuity dispute.

Emphasis on early experience and critical periods initially came independently from two distinct disciplines, psychoanalysis and biology. In virtually all of his writings on psychoanalysis and the psychodynamic theory of personality development, Sigmund Freud proposed that traumatic emotional experiences in infancy and early childhood had lasting, usually permanent, effects on personality. Such experiences, often of a sexual nature and involving the parents, were repressed into the unconscious where they later manifested themselves as neurotic behaviors. Freud viewed personality development as essentially complete and set by 6 years of age (Freud, 1938). Freud's views persist in many contemporary psychodynamically oriented theorists and practitioners. Some in the Freudian tradition extended psychodynamic theory to account for psychoses. Bettelheim (1967), for example, proposed that autistic children withdraw into themselves and shut out others as a defense against their cold, hostile parents. Generations of parents were blamed for their children's schizophrenia and autism as well as other less disturbed behaviors. Others (Bowlby, 1951) proposed that early maternal deprivation would lead to later maladjusted behavior.

The biological concept of critical periods refers to times, generally in prenatal development, when organ systems are undergoing rapid differentiation. Early in embryonic development, tissue transplanted from a donor site to a host site develops as appropriate to the host site. If transplanted later, however, the tissue continues to develop as appropriate to the original donor site, demonstrating an irreversible loss of plasticity. Teratogens introduced during these critical periods activate irreversible changes in development, frequently producing gross abnormalities. Organ systems have individual, but largely overlapping, critical periods. Most end shortly after the embryonic period (8 weeks of gestation), but those for the central nervous system, eyes, and external genitalia extend well after birth (see Figure 1 in Etiology entry, this volume). The classic, if tragic, example of a brief critical period for teratogenic action is that of thalidomide, a mild tranquilizer. Depending on when it was taken by the pregnant woman, between days 34 and 50 past her last menstrual period, thalidomide produced various finger, limb, external ear, and other anomalies in the fetus. Ingestion before day 34 or after day 50 had essentially no effect.

Thus, outside of these critical periods, the developing embryo generally is well-buffered against adverse prenatal environmental influences through what Waddington (1962) called "canalization." In the absence of any adverse influence, the embryo is predicted to develop along its normal pathway. Gottlieb (1983) has cogently criticized the canalization concept as being little more than a new term for innate, and it indeed minimizes the role that a variety of experiences may play in pre- and postnatal development. However, canalization remains a useful descriptive term for biological influences, such as the thalidomide situation described above.

The importance of these biological influences cannot be exaggerated. The devastating and irreversible effects of numerous prenatal and postnatal experiences are well documented (e.g., Gandelman, 1992). Known prenatal teratogens include alcohol, antiseizure and anticancer medications, x-irradiation, maternal infections (toxoplasmosis, rubella, cytomegalovirus, herpes, syphilis, and HIV), and cocaine (Behnke & Eyler, 1993; Shriver & Piersel, 1994). Teratogens that can have major impact early in postnatal development include lead (e.g., Needleman, 1993). Also of concern are effects that may be seen as genetic in women but as prenatal environmental for embryos and fetuses. Consider women with phenylketonuria (PKU) who have received dietary treatment during their development. The diet largely prevents brain damage, and their IQs will approach normal. However, those with PKU have traditionally been taken off the diet no later than adolescence. Thus, when pregnant, women with PKU on normal diets transmit unmetabolized phenylalanine through the placenta, producing brain damage in their embryos and fetuses.

The ethologist Konrad Lorenz (1937) observed that newly hatched precocial birds such as ducklings and goslings appeared to form filial attachments that could not be reversed by later experiences only during short periods of time early in life. He thus provided evidence for a behavioral critical period. Later research (Hess, 1959) corroborated Lorenz's work. Further, particular experience seems to affect a variety of behaviors only if presented at particular times, and deprivation of experience beyond a certain point appears permanently to alter certain behaviors (see Table 1). Researchers proposed, for example, that (1) early, but not later, rearing in complex environments improves rats' problem-solving performance and increases their brain weight; (2) rearing monkeys in social isolation for 1 year hinders permanently their acquisition of appropriate social behavior; (3) exposure to particular auditory stimuli during certain early periods only primes mice to have audiogenic seizures in later life; (4) human infants become imprinted or attached to their mothers only in the first 6 months of life; and (5) mothers can become adequately attached to their infants only in the first few days of life.

In an important theoretical paper, Scott (1962) proposed a "general principle of organization" that integrated biological and psychological critical periods:

> Once a system becomes organized, whether it is the cells of the embryo that are multiplying and differentiating or the behavior patterns of a young animal that are becoming organized through learning, it becomes progressively more difficult to reorganize the system. That is, organization inhibits reorganization. Further, organization can be strongly modified only when active processes are still going on, and this accounts for critical periods of development. (p. 11)

Regardless of the wealth of evidence for the importance of early experience and critical periods in development and functioning of biological systems, research suggests that many purported permanent effects of early behavioral experiences are either transitory, reversible, not as time-limited as originally thought, or not due to experience at all.

Some areas where research questions a critical role of early experience are:

1. Early feeding, toilet-training, and other experiences are not correlated with later behavior. In addition, although a few behaviors are stable over age, little consistency in personality is seen from infancy or even early childhood to adulthood (Kagan & Moss, 1962).

2. No overall continuum of reproductive casualty exists. In addition to Sameroff and Chandler's emphasis on interaction between infant characteristics and caretakers' behavior, perinatal insult appears to affect development according to threshold, rather than continuous model. Most children appear to recover from mild perinatal insult; recovery from severe insult is much less likely.

3. Some types of early experiences thought to be permanent are reversible under certain conditions and do not operate in the restricted time frame once proposed. For example, ducklings will show strong imprinting long after the normal end of the critical period if allowed sufficient time to follow the object (Brown, 1975). Of particular interest, monkeys raised in isolation for a year will develop a considerable amount of normal social behavior if put in the unusual therapeutic context of living with a young monkey (Suomi & Harlow, 1972).

4. A number of severely deprived children have shown surprising degrees of intellective and social development after initiation of intensive therapy (Clarke & Clarke, 1976; Skuse, 1984). Genie, a severely deprived child, is of particular interest because of her acquisition of language long after the purported critical period had ended.

5. Proposed critical periods for attachment of infants to their caretakers, and vice versa, have not been found by a variety of researchers.

6. Virtually no evidence supports the claim that severe behavior disorders result from aberrant parental behavior. Parents were inappropriately blamed for their children's autism and schizophrenia for decades, regardless of evidence that the disorders have genetic or other organic origins (Torrey, 1977). However, children of schizophrenic mothers are themselves more likely to manifest schizophrenia if their adoptive parents are maladjusted than if their adoptive parents are normal.

7. As early deprivation does not necessarily produce irreversible deficits, so early enrichment does not necessarily produce lasting gains. Brief early intervention does not inoculate children against adverse environmental factors. On the other hand, programs such as Head Start do produce meaningful changes in children's behavior, and highly intrusive compensatory programs, such as the Abecedarian Project, have produced dramatic results.

8. Maternal deprivation, in and of itself, does not provide lasting deleterious effects on children (Rutter, 1981).

9. Children's personality characteristics once attributed to parental behavior (Baumrind, 1989; Kagan & Moss, 1962) are being reinterpreted. Directionality of relationships is questionable, since the data are largely correlational and could reflect children's influences on parents instead of parents' influences on children (Bell, 1968; Maccoby & Martin, 1983) or genetic influences (Plomin & McClearn, 1993). In very controversial reviews of the literature, Harris (1995) has suggested that parents influence their children's behavior largely only within the home context and that socialization in other situations is largely through peer interactions.

10. The oft-proposed theory that work-related separations between a mother and young child have negative effects on the child's personality or development does not have consistent support. In one follow-up study of 6–7 year old children whose mothers had worked during their first year of life, Barglow, Contreras, Kavesh, and Vaughn (1998) reported that maternal employment during their children's infancy had few adverse long-term consequences on the children's social behavior and none on IQ in children.

On the other hand, some early learning and other experiences may be necessary for appropriate later development or may predispose individuals to later inappropriate development. Indeed, Brown (1986) and Gottlieb (1991) proposed that behavioral canalization or experiential canalization, respectively, may to an extent parallel Waddington's biological canalization. Early learning experiences may predispose an infant or child to certain later behaviors that, in the absence of intense relearning, become highly prepotent in his or her repertoire. Further, the first three years of life are very important for brain development and differentiation. For decades, we have known that varied early environmental experiences increase brain development in animals (Bennett, Diamond, Krech, & Rosenzweig, 1964). More recently, evidence has accumulated supporting similar phenomena in humans (Schroeder, 1996; Store, 1997). Thus, we might expect early experiences to persist in the absence of some countering force. For example, parents of different socioeconomic status (SES) speak in very different amounts and ways to their children (Hart & Risley, 1995). Upper SES professional parents not only speak much more, but are more responsive, use more varied words and sentences, and use many more approvals and fewer prohibitions than do working-class or welfare parents. Of particular interest, overall family SES rating correlated positively with the children's IQs at 3 and 9 years of age. Unfortunately, interpretation is complicated by the fact that the authors did not statistically control for parents' IQs, leading to a confounding of environmental and possible genetic factors.

Early experience indeed plays an important role in development, but the degree of that role varies greatly with the type and timing of the experience. Evidence for critical periods in some areas of development is strong (Colombo, 1982; Gandelman, 1992). Further, evidence that change in normal development occurs throughout life and that effects of extreme deprivation can be partially countered with intensive therapy should not be misread as implying that plasticity is equivalent across life. Humans are more responsive to many types of experience at a relatively early age. Indeed, MacDonald (1985) suggests that plasticity declines with age and that more intense therapy may be necessary with older individuals. Similarly, Brown (1986) proposes a continuum of therapeutic environments, suggesting that the greater the degree of early impairment, the greater—and more unusual—may be the needed intervention. Recovery from some early experiences will occur only in response to therapies that are not part of the normal environment. Recovery from others that involve manifest brain damage may not be possible under any condition. A question of considerable current interest is whether recovery from early brain damage is more complete than recovery after later damage. Further, we need to distinguish between different types of early experiences and critical periods (Brown, 1981). Areas where adverse early experiences have disrupted a developing organic system will be more resistant to therapy than areas where the experiences have resulted in the learning of

particular behaviors. Early interference with organization of an organ system is likely to be permanent, whereas interference with the organization of behavior through learning can be overcome through relearning.

Parents should not be blamed for their children's autistic or schizophrenic behavior, nor should complete recovery of most such children, particularly autistic ones, be expected. Much recovery from early psychological deprivation or adverse conditions can be effected with sensitive and intensive therapy. Psychodynamic explanations of childhood and adult behavior in terms of infant experiences have little scientific support. Early intervention programs can be effective in increasing the intellective, emotional, and social development of high-risk infants and children, but they need to be intensive and long term (Bricker, Bailey, & Bruder, 1984; Ramey & Ramey, 1998). Finally, therapy or rehabilitation of children with manifest brain damage should be undertaken as soon as realistically possible in order to effect maximum recovery.

Those in special education should be aware of the varied ways in which prenatal and early postnatal experiences can affect children. Different educational approaches likely will be different owing not only to the types of experience children have had, but the way in which those experiences may have interacted with the children's own characteristics. Finally, and obviously, we should all be sensitive to the extent to which inappropriate behaviors children show in school are likely to persist.

## REFERENCES

Barglow, P., Contreras, J., Kavesh, L., & Vaughn, B. E. (1998). Developmental follow-up of 6–7 year old children of mothers employed during their infancies. *Child Psychiatry and Human Development, 29,* 3–19.

Baumrind, D. (1989). Rearing competent children. In W. Damon (Ed.), *Child development today and tomorrow* (pp. 349–378). San Francisco: Jossey-Bass.

Behnke, M., & Eyler, F. D. (1993). The consequences of prenatal substance use for the developing fetus, newborn, and young child. *International Journal of the Addictions, 28,* 1341–1391.

Bell, R. Q. (1968). A reinterpretation of the direction of effects in studies of socialization. *Psychological Review, 75,* 81–95.

Bennett, E. L., Diamond, M. C., Krech, D., & Rosenzweig, M. R. (1964). Chemical and anatomical plasticity of the brain. *Science, 146,* 610–619.

Bettelheim, B. (1967). *The empty fortress: Infantile autism and the birth of the self.* New York: Free Press.

Bowlby, J. (1951). Maternal care and child health. *Bulletin of the World Health Organization, 3,* 355–534.

Bricker, D., Bailey, E., & Bruder, M. B. (1984). The efficacy of early intervention and the handicapped infant: A wise or wasted resource. In M. Wolraich & D. K. Routh (Eds.), *Advances in developmental and behavioral pediatrics* (Vol. 5, pp. 331–371). Greenwich, CT: JAI.

Brim, O. G., Jr., & Kagan, J. (Eds.). (1980). *Constancy and change in human development.* Cambridge, MA: Harvard University Press.

Brown, R. T. (1975). Following and visual imprinting in ducklings across a wide age range. *Developmental Psychobiology, 8,* 187–191.

Brown, R. T. (1981). *Should we be sensitive about critical periods?* Annual meeting of the Psychonomic Society.

Brown, R. T. (1986). Etiology and development of exceptionality. In R. T. Brown & C. R. Reynolds (Eds.), *Psychological perspectives on childhood exceptionality: A handbook.* New York: Wiley.

Clarke, A. M., & Clarke, A. D. B. (Eds.). (1976). *Early experience: Myth and evidence.* New York: Free Press.

Colombo, J. (1982). The critical period concept: Research, methodology, and theoretical issues. *Psychological Bulletin, 91,* 260–275.

Denenberg, V. H. (Ed.). (1972). *The development of behavior.* Sunderland, MA: Sinauer.

Emde, R. N., & Harmon, R. J. (Eds.). (1984). *Continuities and discontinuities in development.* New York: Plenum.

Erikson, E. (1950). *Childhood and society.* New York: Norton.

Freud, S. (1938). *A general introduction to psychoanalysis.* New York: Garden City.

Gandelman, R. (1992). *Psychobiology of behavioral development.* New York: Oxford University Press.

Gottlieb, G. (1983). The psychobiological approach to developmental issues. In P. H. Mussen, M. M. Haith, & J. J. Campos (Eds.), *Handbook of child psychology* (4th ed., Vol. 2, pp. 1–26). New York: Wiley.

Gottlieb, G. (1991). Experiential canalization of behavioral development: Theory. *Developmental Psychology, 27,* 4–13.

Harris, J. R. (1995). Where is the child's environment? A group socialization theory of development. *Psychological Review, 102,* 458–489.

Hart, B., & Risley, T. R. (1995). *Meaningful differences in the everyday experience of young American children.* Baltimore: Brookes.

Howell, M., & Ford, P. (1980). *The true history of the Elephant Man.* London: Allison & Busby.

Ireland, W. W. (1898). *Mental affections of children, idiocy, imbecility, and insanity.* London: J. & A. Churchill.

Kagan, J., & Moss, H. A. (1962). *From birth to maturity.* New York: Wiley.

Kelly, E. L. (1955). Consistency of the adult personality. *American Psychologist, 10,* 659–681.

Lerner, R. M. (1986). *Concepts and theories of human development* (2nd ed.). New York: Random House.

Lorenz, K. (1937). The companion in the bird's world. *Auk, 54,* 245–273.

Maccoby, E. E., & Martin, J. A. (1983). Socialization in the context of the family: Parent-child relationships. In P. H. Mussen & E. M. Hetherington (Eds.), *Handbook of child development* (4th ed., Vol. 4, pp. 1–101). New York: Wiley.

MacDonald, K. (1985). Early experience, relative plasticity, and social development. *Developmental Review, 5,* 99–121.

Needleman, H. L. (Ed.). (1993). *Human lead exposure.* Boca Raton, FL: CRC.

Pasamanick, B., & Knoblock, H. (1966). Retrospective studies on the epidemiology of reproductive casualty: Old and new. *Merrill-Palmer Quarterly, 12,* 7–26.

Plomin, R., & McClearn, G. E. (Eds.). (1993). *Nature, nurture, & psychology.* Washington, DC: American Psychological Association.

Ramey, C. T., & Ramey, S. L. (1998). Early intervention and early experience. *American Psychologist, 53,* 109–120.

Rutter, M. (1981). *Maternal deprivation reassessed* (2nd ed.). New York: Penguin.

Sameroff, A. J., & Chandler, M. J. (1975). Reproductive risk and the continuum of caretaking casualty. In F. D. Horowitz, M. Hetherington, S. Scarr-Salapotek, & G. Siegel (Eds.), *Review of child development research* (Vol. 4). Chicago: University of Chicago Press.

Schroeder, S. R. (1996). *Cognitive and neurological importance of first and early experience.* Paper presented at annual convention of the American Psychological Association, Toronto, Canada.

Scott, J. P. (1952). Critical periods in behavioral development. *Science, 138,* 949–958.

Scott, J. P. (Ed.). (1978). *Critical periods.* Stroudsburg, PA: Dowden, Hutchinson, & Ross.

Shore, R. (1997). *Rethinking the brain: New insights into early development.* New York: Families and Work Institute.

Shriver, M. D., & Piersel, W. (1994). The long-term effects of intrauterine drug exposure: Review of recent research and implications for early childhood special education. *Topics in Early Childhood Special Education, 14,* 161–183.

Skuse, D. (1984). Extreme deprivation in early childhood-II. Theoretical issues and a comparative review. *Journal of Child Psychology & Psychiatry, 25,* 543–572.

Suomi, S., & Harlow, H. (1972). Social rehabilitation of isolate-reared monkeys. *Developmental Psychology, 6,* 487–496.

Torrey, E. F. (1977). A fantasy trial about a real issue. *Psychology Today, 10*(10), 24.

Waddington, C. H. (1962). *New patterns in genetics and development.* New York: Columbia University Press.

ROBERT T. BROWN
*University of North Carolina at Wilmington*
First edition

WENDY L. FLYNN
*Staffordshire University*
Second edition

**ABECEDARIAN PROJECT, THE**

**AUTISM**

**BRAIN DAMAGE**

**ETIOLOGY**

**GENIE**

**HEAD START**

**THALIDOMIDE**

# EARLY IDENTIFICATION OF CHILDREN WITH DISABILITIES

Early identification became a topic of increasing interest with the community mental health movement of the 1960s and again with the passage of the Education for All Handicapped Children Act of 1975 (PL 94-142). This law contained components requiring that schools take aggressive action to identify children with disabilities needing services; it recommended that such children be provided services from ages 4 through 19, and children with severe disabilities from birth through age 21. In addition, several early childhood intervention programs that targeted at-risk children began yielding impressive evidence by the late 1970s of the cost-effectiveness of early intervention (Edmiaston & Mowder, 1985). The Individuals with Disabilities Education Act (IDEA) and its implementing regulations carried forward and extended the requirements articulated in PL 94-142 with respect to state and local education agency responsibilities regarding the identification of children with disabilities (20 U.S.C. § 1412[a][3]).

Effective early intervention programs require identification methods with high predictive validity. Given possible undesirable outcomes (such as labeling effects) and the extensive costs of intervention programs, the number of false positives (students predicted to become disabled but who do not) should be kept low (Mercer, Algozzine, & Trifiletti, 1979b). The identification procedure must also be cost-efficient; screening procedures should use readily available information or tests that are quick and inexpensive to administer.

An example of a possible cost-efficient method is to use data contained on children's birth certificates. Finkelstein and Ramey (1985) used such data, including the mother's age, education, and previous live births now dead; the child's birth order, race, and birth weight; and the month in which prenatal care was begun. The data were used to predict which of 1,000 children would have disabilities at first grade. A disability was defined as having scores more than one standard deviation below the mean on the Peabody Picture Vocabulary Test and on the Myklebust Pupil Rating Scale. Although using birth certificate data correctly identified almost all (81 percent) of the actual students with disabilities, only 15 percent of the group predicted to have a disability actually did. This procedure cannot be used as the sole method of early identification, but it may represent a first screen in a series of ever more extensive screening tests. There appear to be many inexpensive techniques that can be used to identify the students most at risk, but most of these methods yield too many false positives (Mercer, Algozzine, & Trifiletti, 1979a).

There have been a large number of attempts to construct easily administered tests and test batteries that accurately identify children needing special services. Mercer et al. (1979a) reviewed 70 studies, only 15 of which allowed computation of false positives and false negatives. In these studies, screening instruments included the Evanston Early Identification Scale, the Wide Range Achievement Test (WRAT), the Metropolitan Reading Readiness Test, and the Bender-Gestalt, as well as batteries composed of visual-motor, language, gross motor, and cognitive measures. Intervals between administration of the screening and criterion measures ranged from 8 months to 7 years. Median accuracy rates (percentage of all subjects correctly identified) were 75 percent for single instruments, 79 percent for batteries, and 80 percent for teacher perceptions. Mercer et al. indicate that developmental history, socioeconomic status, and teacher perception of skill deficits are strong predictors of later learning difficulty. They suggest that screening should take place in mid-kindergarten, as this allows intervention to begin at the earliest time that teacher ratings become reliable as predictors. Share, Jorm, Maclean, and Matthews (1984) provide data indicating that more than half the variance in first-grade reading scores can be predicted by direct assessment of phonemic naming and letter copying in kindergarten; Mercer et al. suggest that useful ratings of these skills can be made by classroom teachers, freeing professional examiners' time.

## REFERENCES

Edmiaston, R. K., & Mowder, B. A. (1985). Early identification for handicapped children: Efficacy issues and data for school psychologists. *Psychology in the Schools, 22,* 171–178.

Finkelstein, N. W., & Ramey, C. T. (1985). Information from birth certificates as a risk index for educational handicap. *American Journal of Mental Deficiency, 84,* 546–552.

Meisels, S. J., Wiske, M. S., & Tivaran, T. (1984). Predicting school performance with the Early Screening Inventory. *Psychology in the Schools, 21,* 25–33.

Mercer, C. D., Algozzine, B., & Trifiletti, J. J. (1979a). Early identification—An analysis of the research. *Learning Disabilities Quarterly, 2*(2), 12–24.

Mercer, C. D., Algozzine, B., & Trifiletti, J. J. (1979b). Early identification: Issues and considerations. *Exceptional Children, 46,* 52–54.

Share, D. L., Jorm, A. F., Maclean, R., & Matthews, R. (1984). Sources of individual differences in reading acquisition. *Journal of Educational Psychology, 76,* 1309–1324.

JOHN MACDONALD
*Eastern Kentucky University*
Second edition

KIMBERLY F. APPLEQUIST
*University of Colorado at Colorado Springs*
Third edition

## ABECEDARIAN PROJECT, THE EARLY SCREENING PROFILES

PREREFERRAL INTERVENTIONS
PRESCHOOL ASSESSMENT
PRESCHOOL SCREENING

## EARLY INFANTILE AUTISM

See AUTISM.

## EARLY SCREENING PROFILES

The Early Screening Profiles (ESP; Harrison et al., 1990) is a developmental screening test of young children ages 2 years 0 months through 6 years 11 months of age. It is designed to identify children who require further testing or early intervention services. The ESP is comprised of seven components: the Cognitive/Language Profile, Motor Profile, Self-Help/Social Profile, Articulation Survey, Home Survey, Health History Survey, and Behavior Survey. The parts may be used independently or in combination with other parts. Only three components (Cognitive/Language Profile, Motor Profile, and Articulation Survey) are administered directly to the child. Test administration time for these three components ranges from 15 to 30 minutes. The Cognitive/Language Profile consists of 2 cognitive subtests that measure nonverbal reasoning (Visual Discrimination and Logical Relations) and two language subtests that measure receptive and expressive language (Verbal Concepts and Basic School Skills). The Motor Profile consists of two subtests, assessing gross motor and fine motor skills. The Articulation Survey measures the child's speech production. The Behavior Survey is completed by the examiner regarding the child's behaviors during the test administration. The Home Survey (assessing aspects of home environment and parent-child interactions) and Health History Survey (a list of past and present health problems) are both brief questionnaires completed by the parent. The Self-Help/Social Profile is also a questionnaire completed by the parent and/or the child's teacher. It measures the child's performance of everyday activities required to take care of oneself and interact with others. The parent and teacher questionnaires take 10 to 15 minutes to complete.

Scoring the ESP occurs in two levels: Level I and Level II. Level I scoring yields numerical values of 1 to 6, indicating from below average to above average performance, for three Profiles (Cognitive/Language, Motor, and Self-Help/Social) and for a composite or Total Screening. Scores can be obtained quickly and directly from the tables packaged with the components. Level II scoring yields more detailed normative scores for the three Profiles and Total Screening, providing standard scores (M = 100, SD = 15), national percentile ranks, normal curve equivalents, stanines and age equivalents. The Articulation, Home, and Behavior Surveys are scored only with descriptive categories (below average, average, or above average) and the Health History Survey is not scored.

The ESP was standardized on a sample of 1,149 children from 2 years 0 months through 6 years 11 months of age. The number of subjects in each of the five one-year intervals ranged from 163 to 303. There were approximately equal distributions of males and females per group. Data from the 1985 and 1990 U.S. Census Bureau was used to stratify the sample on variables including age, sex, parent education, geographic region, and race/ethnicity. The sample matches the U.S. population well on all variables, although there are slight differences in parental education. The manual contains specific characteristics of the sample. A high degree of reliability was found of the profiles and Total Screening, with the exception of the Motor Profile and Behavior Survey, which were less reliable, and the Home Survey, which was quite low, which the author notes may be due to the diverse items on the scale.

Critiques of the ESP have been mixed. Telzrow (1995) reveals a favorable impression. She notes that the manual is comprehensive and detailed in its discussion of its development, technical adequacy, and scoring, including limitations to using age equivalents, which makes the ESP a "comprehensive addition to a total program in early childhood identification and service delivery." However, Barnett (1995) criticizes that the ESP lacks ecological validity and does not improve on the limitations of most screening instruments.

### REFERENCES

Barnett, D. W. (1995). AGS Early Screening Profiles. In J. C. Conoley & J. C. Impara (Eds.), *The twelfth mental measurements yearbook*. Lincoln, NE: Buros Institute of Mental Measurements.

Harrison, P. L., Kaufman, A. S., Kaufman, N. L., Bruininks, R. H., Rynders, J., Ilmer, S., Sparrow, S. S., & Cicchetti, D. V. (1990). *Early Screening Profiles manual*. Circle Pines, MN: American Guidance Service.

Telzrow, C. (1995). AGS Early Screening Profiles. In J. C. Conoley & J. C. Impara (Eds.), *The twelfth mental measurements yearbook*. Lincoln, NE: Buros Institute of Mental Measurements.

DEBRA Y. BROADBOOKS
*California School of
Professional Psychology*

## EATING DISORDERS

Eating disorders involve some form of disturbance in regular eating behaviors that is characterized as severe. Such disturbances can involve either eating too much or too little food. In addition, individuals with eating disorders usually experience feelings of emotional distress concerning body weight and shape.

The *Diagnostic and Statistical Manual of Mental Disorders,* fourth edition, text revision (*DSM-IV-TR*) recognizes three specific categories of eating disorders, Anorexia Nervosa, Bulimia Nervosa, and Eating Disorder Not Otherwise Specified (American Psychiatric Association, 2000). Women who meet criteria for any of the three categories of eating disorder have higher rates of other psychopathologies than do women without eating disorders (Ekeroth, Broberg, & Nevonen, 2004).

Anorexia Nervosa, a disease in which a person willfully resists maintaining a body weight that is at or above the health limit, affects an estimated .5 to 3.7 percent of females some time in their lifetime (American Psychiatric Association Work Group on Eating Disorders, 2000). People with Anorexia Nervosa may attempt to control weight through caloric restriction, excessive exercise, and purging (e.g., vomiting, using laxatives or other diuretics). Despite being underweight, many persons who suffer from anorexia develop obsessive fears of weight gain. While many people recover from anorexia after receiving appropriate intervention services, mortality can result for those who do not seek or respond to treatment. Caucasian females constitute the most likely demographic group to report symptoms of Anorexia Nervosa.

Bulimia Nervosa is another eating disorder in which individuals experience an obsessive fear of weight gain. However, unlike individuals who suffer from Anorexia Nervosa, people with Bulimia Nervosa usually maintain or exceed a healthy body weight. Bulimia Nervosa is characterized by episodes of binge eating at least two times per week, in which a large amount of food is consumed in a small amount of time. During binge eating episodes, individuals frequently experience a lack of control and feelings of shame and guilt. In addition, people with Bulimia Nervosa attempt to compensate for their binge eating disorder through inappropriate behaviors, such as excessive exercise and/or purging.

Individuals whose eating disturbances that fall into the category of Eating Disorder Not Otherwise Specified may exhibit symptoms consistent with Anorexia Nervosa or Bulimia Nervosa but do not meet full criteria for either diagnosis.

All three categories of eating disorders are considered culture-bound disorders. Eating disorders are more common in women than in men. Three culture-related conditions seemingly influence prevalence rates of eating disorders: eating behaviors, body image ideals, and perceptions of health (Markey, 2004). Twin studies have revealed the existence of an underlying genetic component (Bulik, Sullivan, Wade, & Kendler, 2000).

**REFERENCES**

American Psychiatric Association. (2000). *Diagnostic and statistical manual of mental disorders* (4th ed., text revision). Washington, DC: Author.

American Psychiatric Association Work Group on Eating Disorders. (2000). Practice guideline for the treatment of patients with eating disorders (revision). *American Journal of Psychiatry, 157,* 1–39.

Bulik, C. M., Sullivan, P. F., Wade, T. D., & Kendler, K. S. (2000). Twin studies of eating disorders: A review. *International Journal of Eating Disorders, 27,* 2–20.

Ekeroth, K., Broberg, A. G., & Nevonen, L. (2004). Eating disorders and general psychopathology: A comparison between young adult patients and normal controls with and without self-reported eating problems. *European Eating Disorders Review, 12,* 208–216.

Markey, C. N. (2004). Culture and the development of eating disorders: A tripartite model. *Eating Disorders, 12,* 139–156.

ALLISON G. DEMPSEY
*University of Florida*

**ANOREXIA**
**BULIMIA NERVOSA**

# ECHOLALIA

Echolalia is a strong, almost mandatory, tendency to repeat spontaneously what has been said by another person (Benson & Ardila, 1996). Echolalia has been noted in those with degenerative brain disease, psychosis (both children and adults), Gilles de la Tourette syndrome, childhood dysphasia, severe mental retardation, and some forms of aphasia, as well as in some congenitally blind children (Cummings & Benson, 1989; Fay, 1980a). It is a prominent characteristic of all of these children's speech, with the vast majority who eventually acquire speech having a history of echoing. Many children who acquire normal speech and language practice some echolalia during the developmental speech and language period of infancy and early childhood, although these echolatic behaviors generally disappear by 2½ to 3 years of age (Fay, 1980a; Loveland, McEvoy, & Tunali, 1990). A message may be repeated in its entirety or partially, with repetition usually following immediately after the initial presentation. Delayed echolalia is the repetition of utterances made by oneself or others; the utterances are stored and repeated at a later time, ranging from minutes to weeks. Repetition of television commercials by autistic children is an example of delayed echolalia. Unlike immediate repetitions, delayed echolalia may serve a communicative purpose. Children have been reported to use stored utterances to express an intention or to verbalize a behavioral self-reminder (Fay, 1980b). An echoed utterance preceded or followed by an appropriate self-formulated comment evidences comprehension. The repetition seems to facilitate understanding in much the same manner as in normal adults and children when confronted with difficult messages.

## REFERENCES

Benson, D. F., & Ardila, A. (1996). *Aphasia: A clinical perspective.* New York: Oxford University Press.

Cummings, J. L., & Benson, D. F. (1989). Speech and language alterations in dementia syndromes. In A. Ardila & F. Ostrosky (Eds.), *Brain organization of language and cognitive processes* (pp. 107–120). New York: Plenum.

Fay, W. H. (1980a). Aspects of speech. In R. L. Schiefelbush (Ed.), *Language intervention series* (Vol. 5, pp. 21–50). Baltimore: University Park Press.

Fay, W. H. (1980b). Aspects of language. In R. L. Schiefelbush (Ed.), *Language intervention series* (Vol. 5, pp. 53–85). Baltimore: University Park Press.

Loveland, K. A., McEvoy, R. E., & Tunali, B. (1990). Narrative story telling in autism and Down's syndrome. *British Journal of Developmental Psychology, 8,* 9–23.

K. SANDRA VANTA
*Cleveland Public Schools,
Cleveland, Ohio*
First edition

ROBERT L. RHODES
*New Mexico State University*
Second edition

**AUTISM
AUTISTIC BEHAVIOR
COMMUNICATION DISORDERS
LANGUAGE DISORDERS**

# ECHOPRAXIA

Echopraxia can be defined as the involuntary and spasmodic imitation of movements made by another person (Goodwin, 1989). The echolalia of a child with autism, in which the child echo-speaks phrases and words, might be viewed as a specific kind of echopraxia. Another echo of movement that is specific to some hearing-impaired persons has been observed clinically. In this form, the individual imitates the facial and mouth movements of the speaker. These movements may be a means of reinforcing meaning and subsequent content for the hearing-impaired individual.

Clinical experience suggests that the neural mechanisms involved in these examples of echopraxia are different from true voluntary imitation. The latter represents a developmental landmark and has a voluntary quality that probably reflects the involvement of higher cortical centers. The phenomenon of echopraxia is also associated with different neural mechanisms than mirrored movements, which are observed when voluntary movements of one hand of an individual are accompanied by simultaneous identical movements of the opposite hand. This kind of movement may reflect a delay in inhibition related to specialization of one hand as a holder and the other hand as a doer. Young children with mirrored hand movements may find skilled motor tasks such as writing particularly difficult.

## REFERENCE

Goodwin, D. M. (1989). *A dictionary of neuropsychology.* New York: Springer-Verlag.

RACHAEL J. STEVENSON
*Bedford, Ohio*
First edition

ROBERT L. RHODES
*New Mexico State University*
Second edition

**CHILDHOOD SCHIZOPHRENIA
ECHOLALIA**

# ECOLOGICAL ASSESSMENT

The purpose of ecological assessment is to understand the complex interactions that occur between an individual who is the focus of assessment and his or her environment. Representing what is essentially an expansion of traditional behavior assessment techniques, ecological behavior assessment is similar to behavioral assessment with two important distinctions. First, in ecological behavior assessment, emphasis is placed on the quantification of behavior and its controlling environmental factors from a systems level perspective. That is, rather than focusing exclusively on molecular units of targeted behaviors and consequences directly responsible for their maintenance, the goal of ecological behavior assessment is to generate an understanding of the total behavior-environment system. This "system mapping" is typically accomplished through the measurement of behaviors and persons other than those to which an intervention is to be applied. For example, research conducted by Wahler (1975) in which observational data were taken on a variety of child behaviors suggested that behavioral interventions targeted at a single response are likely to result in complex patterns of collateral and inverse changes in behavior within a child's repertoire. Second, in ecological behavior assessment, emphasis is placed on the measurement of existing patterns of teacher and student behavior with the goal of using this information in the development of intervention alternatives.

Given the complexity of the classroom ecology, how then is it possible to adequately assess the myriad interactions among behaviors of students, behaviors of students and teachers, and behaviors of students and teachers and the physical environment? With the finite nature of the assessment process and the functionally infinite possibilities for behavior-setting interactions, such a task would indeed be formidable. Fortunately, by drawing on concepts employed in the area of statistical analysis, the task need not be that of documenting all interactions but merely of observing those that contribute to a significant proportion of variance in possible classroom behavior.

The following steps then are presented as suggestions in the ecological assessment of behavior in any classroom setting. First, it is important to assess teacher expectations for what constitutes "good" and "bad" regularities in classroom behavior. Because teachers are typically the rule makers for such behavior, and because they are the individuals most responsible for making decisions regarding behavior appropriateness, assessment of their expectations is likely to provide an important criterion by which to evaluate intervention success.

Second, once teacher expectations for student behavior have been identified, the next step is to assess regularities in student behavior that actually exist in the classroom setting. Here it is necessary to identify and observe multiple categories of student behavior at both the individual and group level. Because of the emphasis of ecological behavior assessment on molar units of student behavior (i.e., patterns of behavior that occur across students), techniques such as momentary time sampling, sequential interval time sampling of several students chosen at random, self-monitoring, and review of permanent products may be useful in obtaining frequency measures at the group level. Whatever the technique employed, one goal of ecological behavioral assessment is to identify relative frequencies of both appropriate and inappropriate classroom behaviors that are descriptive for the class as a whole.

The third and perhaps most important task in the ecological assessment of classroom behavior is the identification of regularities in teacher behaviors. Whether they are aware of it or not, teachers play critical roles in the establishment of classroom ecology especially in the awareness of cross-cultural variables in the environment (Truscott & Truscott, 2005). They generate rules for behavior that are specific to the classroom setting and deliver consequences to children in accordance with these rules.

The fourth and final step in the ecological assessment of classroom behavior involves the assessment of behavioral processes. Specifically, once regularities in both teacher and student behavior have been identified, the issue becomes one of determining just how the behaviors in which the teacher engages are used to consequence the behaviors in which students engage. Through an ecological mapping of contingencies common to classroom settings, it becomes possible to draw comparisons between behaviors that teachers would like to encourage in students and behaviors that they actually do encourage through their interactions.

Ecological assessment can be time-consuming and complex, but it is often a rewarding process for truly under-standing the behavior of children. The present summary draws heavily on the work of Kounin (1970), Gump (1975), Martens et al. (1999), and Reynolds, Gutkin, Elliott, and Witt (1984). Readers interested in cross-cultural aspects of ecological assessment are referred to Truscott and Truscott (2005).

## REFERENCES

Gump, P. V. (1975). Ecological psychology and children. In M. Hetherington (Ed.), *Review of child development research* (Vol. 5). Chicago: University of Chicago Press.

Kounin, J. S. (1970). *Discipline and group management in classrooms.* New York: Holt, Rinehart & Winston.

Martens, B., Witt, J., Daly, E., & Vollmer, T. (1999). Behavior analysis: Theory and practice in educational settings. In C. R. Reynolds & T. B. Gutkin (Eds.), *The handbook of school psychology* (3rd ed., pp. 638–663). New York: Wiley.

Reynolds, C. R., Gutkin, T. B., Elliott, S. N., & Witt, J. C. (1984). *School psychology: Essentials of theory and practice.* New York: Wiley.

Truscott, S. D., & Truscott, D. M. (2005). Challenges in urban and rural education. In C. L. Frisby & C. R. Reynolds (Eds.), *Handbook of multicultural school psychology* (pp. 357–391). New York: Wiley.

Wahler, R. G. (1975). Some structural aspects of deviant child behavior. *Journal of Applied Behavior Analysis, 8,* 27–42.

JOSEPH C. WITT
*Louisiana State University*

**APPLIED BEHAVIOR ANALYSIS**
**CLINICAL INTERVIEW**

# ECOLOGICAL EDUCATION FOR CHILDREN WITH DISABILITIES

Ecology refers, generally, to the study of the relationship between an organism and its environment. Although the roots of ecology as a field of study are found in early anthropology, the application of ecological theories, models, and principles in special education is relatively new. The first attempt to examine the interaction of environmental effects and certain persons with disabilities, and to specify related treatment approaches, is found in the works of Heinz Werner, Alfred A. Strauss, Lora Lehtinen, and William M. Cruickshank. These researchers of the 1940s, 1950s, and 1960s studied children with brain injuries and adults and the effects that various environmental stimuli had on their learning and overall behavior. An important concept derived from their research was the idea of the "stimulus-reduced" environment, first prescribed for classically brain-injured adults and children, then extended to certain "exogenous" mentally retarded children, and finally to children with learning disabilities. Although this work began in the 1940s, these researchers, and those who built on their pioneering efforts, did not refer formally to their efforts as ecological in nature. The term ecology itself, derived primarily from the biological sciences, surfaced as an educational variable with studies of emotionally disturbed children in the late 1960s and early 1970s.

The most notable contributions to the field include the work of Hobbs (1966) with Project Re-Ed and the University of Michigan studies in child variance (Feagans, 1972). Project Re-Ed recognized that many of the socialization problems experienced by so-called emotionally disturbed children did not have a locus within the child. Rather, problems existed in the interaction between the labeled child and the important social institutions in which he or she acted. Since there was a bad fit between child and environment (i.e., home, family, school, community), it was necessary to remove the child temporarily from this failure situation, not just to work with the child, but also to change contributing factors in the environment. While specially trained teachers aided the student, social services personnel and mental health consultants worked with the significant others in the child's world before re-merging the two again. Segregation was to be as brief as possible; normalization was always the goal.

The Michigan work, accomplished within the university's Institute for Mental Retardation and Related Disorders, reviewed, integrated, and synthesized the research, theories, and conceptual models bearing on childhood emotional disturbance. The group then developed and implemented various dissemination and training activities based on their synthesis of differing approaches to emotional disturbance. Though ecological theory was only one of six major approaches studied, the Michigan efforts helped in large part to enhance the role of ecological theory in special education.

Broadly, the ecological approach to the study and treatment of emotionally disturbed and other children with disabilities attempts to break down traditional views of disabilities as something found exclusively in the involved child. The disturbance is not intrinsic per se, but a description of the interaction of a particular child with a particular environment. The search is for the source of the mismatch in the ecosystem. The study of the child occurs not in the sterility of the psychological laboratory, but in the naturalistic, real-world, holistic settings in which the child's problems occur. This is not to deny that emotional disturbance, or mental retardation, or learning disabilities are not real, or that problems in learning or adjustment that certain children experience may not have contributing neurological or biochemical substrata. The ecological focus in special education tries to show that looking only at internal factors cannot give the whole picture, and that treatment approaches based on simplified, historical, etiological views can limit the success parents and professionals might have with handicapped learners.

Since a purely medical, psychological, or multicultural explanation alone is not sought when students with disabilities are viewed through ecological theory, a multidisciplinary team approach to diagnosis, classification, education, and treatment emerges. Special education ecologists look not only at how the child acts on his or her environment, but how the environment in its broadest sense acts on the child. Rather than overemphasize causal factors, proponents of the ecological approach seek to find or establish a state of equilibrium between child and surroundings. Specific coping skills may be taught to bring about a greater match between the child's behavior and the expectations placed on him or her by the physical and social environment. Rather than just attempting to change, or cure, what is purportedly going on within the child, the ecological special educator seeks to study the cultural relativity of the child's behavior, and adaptation (or synomorphy) between child and environment. The focus is on the reciprocity of behavior and reaction. Algozzine, Schmid, and Mercer (1981) ask: Is the disturbance merely in the eye of the beholder? Is the child really disturbed, or just disturbing?

The ecological approach to special education goes by many names. It has been termed environmental psychology, architectural psychology, ecological psychology, sociophysical technology, person-environment relations, man-environment studies, and environmental design cybernetics (Preiser & Taylor, 1983). Ecological principles have been used to examine not only brain-injured and socially/emotionally maladjusted students, but also children and youths with other conditions. Some of these studies found, for example, that the mere proximity of toys led to greater interaction and gradual expansion of the recreation setting for severely/profoundly disabled individuals (Wehman, 1978). Other writers (Marsh & Price, 1980) looked into the interaction of environmental variables such as flexibility of school settings and information reception or reading disabilities and academic achievement, in secondary-age learning-disabled youth. Sarason and Doris (1979) coined the phrase "iatrogenic educable mental retardation" in describing the school-related disabilities found in learners from lower socioeconomic status backgrounds. Autistic, brain-injured, and normal children have been shown to demonstrate differential social responses to the density of the class or group setting in which they are placed (Hutt & Viazey, 1966). Even classroom lighting amounts and types have been examined to determine any possible effects they may have on student learning and behavior (Fletcher, 1983). As Zentall (1983) notes, professionals place regular and special education students in learning environments for about 1,100 hours per year, without any empirical basis for the design of that environment—a design that, to a large extent, can be modified or controlled.

Though special and regular educators have shown cognizance of the environmental needs of certain physically and sensorily disabled children (e.g., preferential seating for the hard of hearing, plant modifications for children with physical disabilities, magnifiers and enlarged materials for partially sighted students), they still have not totally embraced the prosthetic environments described by behavioral engineers such as Ogden Lindsley (1964). Ecologists in the field would claim that special educators should continue to move away from the former child-focus approach, and more toward a pedagogy in which they test, observe, and teach in the real-world settings where skills must ultimately be generalized and successfully demonstrated if they are to say that learning truly has occurred (Hutchins & Renzaglia, 1983). Ecologically valid assessment has moved forward in recent years due to the increase of cultural competency expectations for teachers and researchers in special education (Frisby & Reynolds, 2005).

## REFERENCES

Algozzine, B., Schmid, R., & Mercer, C. D. (1981). *Childhood behavior disorders: Applied research and educational practice.* Rockville, MD: Aspen.

Feagans, L. (1972). Ecological theory as a model for constructing a theory of emotional disturbance. In W. C. Rhodes & M. L. Tracy (Eds.), *A study in child variance* (Vol. 1). Ann Arbor: University of Michigan.

Fletcher, D. (1983). Effects of classroom lighting on the behavior of exceptional children. *Exceptional Education Quarterly, 4*(2), 75–89.

Frisby, C. L., & Reynolds, C. R. (2005). *The handbook of multicultural school psychology.* New York: Wiley.

Hobbs, N. L. (1966). Helping disturbed children: Psychological and ecological strategies. *American Psychologist, 21,* 1105–1115.

Hutchins, M. P., & Renzaglia, A. (1983). Environmental considerations for severely handicapped individuals: The needs and the questions. *Exceptional Education Quarterly, 4*(2), 67–71.

Hutt, C., & Viazey, J. M. (1966). Differential effects of group density on social behavior. *Nature, 209,* 1371–1372.

Lindsley, O. R. (1964). Direct measurement and prosthesis of retarded behavior. *Journal of Education, 147,* 62–81.

Marsh, G. E., & Price, B. J. (1980). *Methods for teaching the mildly handicapped.* St. Louis, MO: Mosby.

Preiser, W. F. E., & Taylor, A. (1983). The habitability framework: Linking human behavior and physical environment in special education. *Exceptional Education Quarterly, 4*(2), 1–15.

Sarason, S. B., & Doris, J. (1979). *Educational handicaps, public policy and social history.* New York: Free Press.

Wehman, P. (1978). Effects of different environmental conditions on leisure time activity of the severely and profoundly handicapped. *Journal of Special Education, 12*(2), 183–193.

Zentall, S. S. (1983). Learning environments: A review of physical and temporal factors. *Exceptional Education Quarterly, 4*(2), 90–115.

JOHN D. WILSON
*Elwyn Institutes*

**ECOLOGICAL ASSESSMENT**

# EDGERTON, ROBERT B. (1931– )

Robert Edgerton was introduced to the study of mental retardation at the Pacific State Hospital, California, after completing his PhD in anthropology (1960) from the University of California, Los Angeles (UCLA). He has taught at UCLA since that time in the departments of psychiatry and anthropology, becoming professor in 1972 and an administrator of socio-behavioral studies in the Mental Retardation Research Center in 1970.

Edgerton provided major contributions to the study of mental retardation primarily through his intensive and atypical methods of research. As a strong advocate of participant/observation and the qualitative approach to gathering scientific data, he conducted research using anthropological perspectives and methodologies.

At a time when deinstitutionalization is in practice, the qualitative results of Edgerton's research have been useful for social policy evaluation. He has provided insights into the everyday lives of mentally retarded persons that directly affect the design of community residential policies and criteria for reinstitutionalization. Author of over 75 books, articles, and monographs, Edgerton's principal publications include *The Cloak of Competence, Mental Retardation,* and *Environments and Behavior: The Adaptation of Mentally Retarded Persons.* His work has been featured in Schalock and Siperstein's (1996) publication, *Quality of Life,* dealing with the conceptualization and measurement of quality of life for persons with mental retardation and developmental disabilities.

## REFERENCES

Edgerton, R. B. (1967). *The cloak of competence.* Berkeley and Los Angeles: University of California Press.

Edgerton, R. B. (1979). *Mental retardation.* Cambridge, MA: Harvard University Press.

Kernan, K., Begab, M., & Edgerton, R. B. (Eds.). (1983). *Environments and behavior: The adaptation of mentally retarded persons.* Baltimore: University Park Press.

Schalock, R. L., & Siperstein, G. N. (Eds.). (1996). *Quality of life: Vol. 1. Conceptualization and measurement.* Washington, DC: American Association on Mental Retardation.

ELAINE FLETCHER-JANZEN
*University of Colorado at Colorado Springs*
First edition

TAMARA J. MARTIN
*The University of Texas of the Permian Basin*
Second edition

# EDUCABILITY

In its broadest sense, educability refers to the likelihood of a child with cognitive disabilities benefiting from and progressing in a course of education. As such, it is appropriate to refer to the educability of a blind child or a hearing child. However, the concept is most closely related to mental retardation and has become part of the classificatory nomenclature in that area. In fact, the concept of educability can be viewed as the driving force behind the development and growth of psychometrics.

In 1904 Alfred Binet was charged with developing a process by which children unlikely to pass a standard curriculum could be identified and placed in alternative settings or excluded altogether. Working from a viewpoint that normal children achieved certain developmental stages at predictable rates, Binet and his associate Theodore Simon developed an instrument for evaluating a child's mental age. This allowed for projections of the child's functioning in school and for more heterogeneous groupings.

While the concept of mental retardation had long been accepted as a separate entity, Binet's scale had the unexpected side effect of demonstrating that the differences were on a quantitative continuum rather than being qualitatively distinct. A new group of individuals who fell between the normal and the retarded emerged. MacMillan (1977) points out that such individuals were unable to be identified prior to intelligence testing, because they were generally able-bodied, socially competent, and normal looking. Only when placed in academic situations were their learning difficulties brought to the attention of school authorities.

Just as this group of individuals is identified only in relation to school performance, it is this same sphere that causes the greatest obstacles to them, creating what the President's Committee on Mental Retardation termed the "six-hour retarded child." This is the child who is considered retarded only during that period of the day that he or she is in school, and who is indistinguishable from others for the remaining time. By extension, many of these individuals are "cured" simply by leaving school and entering the work force.

The definition of educable mentally retarded varies from state to state. Sedlak and Sedlak (1985) present a listing of criteria that serves to demonstrate the diversity to be found in such a classification. They list some common traits that set this group apart from so-called normal learners. These include reduced learning potential, attentional and memory deficits, decreased ability to profit from incidental learning, and atypical motivational characteristics. In addition, these individuals often have marked language difficulties and decreased personal/social skills. Lambert, Wilcox, and Gleason (1974), Sedlak and Sedlak (1985), and the American Association on Mental Retardation (2006) provide more in-depth analyses of the issues related to assessment, programming, and expectations for these children.

## REFERENCES

American Association on Mental Retardation. (2005). *AAMR home page*. Retrieved January 31, 2006, from http://www.aamr.org/

Grossman, H. J. (1973). *Manual on terminology and classification in mental retardation*. Washington, DC: American Association on Mental Deficiency.

Lambert, N. M., Wilcox, M. R., & Gleason, W. P. (1974). *The educationally retarded child: Comprehensive assessment and planning for slow learners and the educable mentally retarded*. New York: Grune & Stratton.

MacMillan, D. C. (1977). *Mental retardation in school and society*. Boston: Little, Brown.

Sedlak, R. A., & Sedlak, D. M. (1985). *Teaching the educable mentally retarded*. Albany: State University of New York Press.

DENNIS M. FLANAGAN
*Montgomery County*
*Intermediate Unit,*
*Norristown, Pennsylvania*

**AAMR, AMERICAN ASSOCIATION ON MENTAL RETARDATION**
**MENTAL RETARDATION**
**SIX-HOUR RETARDED CHILD**

# EDUCABLE MENTALLY RETARDED

See MENTAL RETARDATION.

# EDUCATEUR

The educateur, sometimes referred to as the psychoeducateur, is a trained generalist whose primary concern goes beyond that of the traditional teacher's interest in student learning to include a focus on the personality and emotional development of the child (Morse & Smith, 1980). The role of the educateur dates to the years immediately following World War II, when the presence of large numbers of displaced emotionally disturbed children (victims of the psychological traumas of war) were identified in France and Scotland (Daly, 1985). Inadequate numbers of qualified mental health workers to meet the many needs of these children led to the development of a new profession, that of the educateur, a professional trained in the skills of teaching, social work, psychology, and recreation.

In the mid 1950s in Canada, Guindon (1973) adapted the European educateur model for use with delinquent and emotionally disabled children and youths. Guindon's psychoeducateur intervention had an ecological orientation, emphasizing the significance of change in the child's environment and using interventions associated with other perspectives.

Drawing from a combination of psychodynamic and

developmental approaches, educateur treatment seeks to restructure completely all activities and relationships in the child's environment. To accomplish this, the child is placed in a residential setting for an average period of 18 months. Here, the educateur initially works to provide a highly structured environment with maximum external control. Then external controls are gradually reduced with concomitant increase in flexibility and individual expression for the child.

Linton (1971) described the educateur working in these specialized facilities as being trained to effect positive changes by focusing specifically on the interaction between child and environment and on the natural support systems such as family and community. Thus the educateur functions as a child advocate and environmental change agent to reduce discord and restore harmony in a manner that ultimately permits complete withdrawal of external intervention. The educateur's goal is to help the child acquire problem-solving skills and behavioral repertoires for successfully meeting both known and unfamiliar situations (Goocher, 1975).

Project Re-ED (Hobbs, 1982) is considered by some individuals to represent an Americanized version of the educateur model with the term teacher-counselor replacing educateur. For those individuals interested in acquiring educateur skills, Daly (1985) reports that at least four American colleges or universities (Ohio State University, Southern Connecticut State College, Western Michigan University, and the University of Virginia) provide training programs using the term educateur. The training in these programs includes recreation, special education, and behavioral sciences as well as an internship in a child service agency.

**REFERENCES**

Daly, P. M. (1985). The educateur: An atypical childcare worker. *Behavioral Disorders, 11,* 35–41.

Goocher, B. E. (1975). Behavioral applications of an educateur model in child care. *Child Care Quarterly, 4,* 84–92.

Guindon, J. (1973). The reeducation process. *International Journal of Mental Health, 2*(1), 15–26, 27–32.

Hobbs, N. (1982). *The troubled and troubling child.* San Francisco: Jossey-Bass.

Linton, T. E. (1971). The education model: A theoretical model: A theoretical monograph. *Journal of Special Education, 5,* 155–190.

Morse, W., & Smith, J. (1980). *Understanding child variance.* Reston, VA: Council for Exceptional Children.

KATHY L. RUHL
*Pennsylvania State University*

**PROJECT RE-ED**

# EDUCATIONAL AND PSYCHOLOGICAL MEASUREMENT

*Educational and Psychological Measurement* is a bimonthly journal devoted to the development and application of measures of individual differences. Articles published in the journal are divided into sections.

The first section consists of articles reporting the results of research investigations into problems in the measurement of individual differences in education and psychology. Articles include investigations on known or new statistical and psychometric procedures, the psychometric characteristics of tests, descriptions of testing programs, and the use of tests and measurements in education, industry, and government.

The second section is devoted to validity studies on new or existing tests for measuring individual differences. This section is published at least twice a year, in the summer and winter issues. It is an excellent source for consumers or researchers wishing to obtain current validity information on new or newly revised tests.

A third section is devoted to computer studies, with reports on the use(s) of already existing or new computer programs. These programs may be used for carrying out computations in statistical analyses when assessing the measurement of individual differences.

The journal also publishes occasional book reviews. Correspondence should be submitted to: Bruce Thompson, *EPM* Editor, Department of Educational Psychology, Texas A&M University, College Station, TX 77843-4225. Copies of the various journal guidelines and editorials are available on the Internet at http://acs.tamu.edu/~bbt6147/.

GWYNETH M. BOODOO
*Texas A&M University*
First edition

BRUCE THOMPSON
*Texas A&M University*
Second edition

# EDUCATIONAL DIAGNOSTICIAN

An educational diagnostician is an individual who often functions as a member of the multidisciplinary team that determines whether a child is eligible for special education programs. The educational diagnostician differs from the school psychologist both in preparation and function. Generally, the educational diagnostician is a certified or licensed regular or special education teacher with three or more years of experience in the classroom. Graduate training, typically a two-semester master of education program, is focused on content and techniques concerned with diagnosis and remediation of learning problems. The school psychologist is generally not a certified or licensed teacher but has graduate or advanced graduate training of two or more years, the focus of which is on the content and techniques related to assessment of intellectual and behavioral functioning of children and training in psychological interventions including both direct and indirect service delivery. While most states offer certification for school psychologists, fewer states actually offer formal certification, licensure, or endorsement for educational diagnosticians.

The role of the educational diagnostician has been influenced by the Education for All Handicapped Children Act of 1975 (PL 94-142), its follow-up legislation (IDEIA) and state legislation and/or regulations. The school psychologist performed some of the functions of educational diagnosis prior to the recent development of the position of educational diagnostician. The terms educational diagnostician and educational specialist are often used interchangeably.

Federal and state requirements for assessment of current levels of educational performance, the prohibition of a single test score in determining eligibility, and the requirement that eligibility for special education be made by a multidisciplinary team have increased the demand for educational diagnosticians in most states. Eligibility for special education generally requires team consideration of educational, social, psychological, and medical information.

McLeod (1983) suggests the purpose of educational diagnosis is to answer a generic question about how the child may be helped to learn basic school skills effectively. Specific questions, while differing from child to child, generally include further questioning about how the child learns, why he or she is failing, and what can be done about it. Determination of learning style—visual or aural—is seen as a basic need in the diagnostic process. Rote learning versus learning through insight should also be specified.

Hargrove and Poteet (1984) specify assessment, diagnostic, and prescriptive activities as the components of educational evaluations. In conducting the evaluation, the diagnostician uses the three basic skills of looking, listening, and questioning. Tools and techniques used by the diagnostician include rating scales, interviews, observations, tests, and clinical judgment.

In most school districts using educational diagnosticians, their primary role relates to the evaluation of students referred for special education programs or services, though in most states they are prohibited from working with emotionally disturbed children, a task more suited to the school psychologist. The educational diagnostician can perform a valuable function in working with other students who may be experiencing learning problems but who would not be considered in need of special education.

## REFERENCES

Hargrove, L. J., & Poteet, J. A. (1984). *Assessment in special education.* Englewood Cliffs, NJ: Prentice Hall.

McLeod, J. (1983). The art and science of educational diagnosis. *Exceptional Child, 30,* 57–66.

PHILIP R. JONES
*Virginia Polytechnic Institute
and State University*

**MULTIDISCIPLINARY TEAMS
SCHOOL PSYCHOLOGY**

## EDUCATIONALLY DISADVANTAGED

According to the Office of Elementary and Secondary Education, educationally deprived children are children whose educational attainment is below the level that is appropriate for children their age. These children are often referred to as educationally disadvantaged. A cause for this scholastic retardation in depressed areas is attributed to the attitudes and behavior of school personnel (Passow, 1967). These children often come from culturally deprived homes that fail to equip the children to fit into and adapt well to the school environment (Passow, 1967). Daniels (1967) adds that the disadvantaged have become disabled because of social or environmental conditions in their ability to learn and to acquire skills and abilities for coping with the problems of earning a living and enjoying a satisfying life. He accepts the estimate that the disadvantaged constitute 25 percent of the school population, and in larger cities 30 to 40 percent.

Title I of the Elementary and Secondary Education Act was designed to overcome the debilitating burdens placed on educationally disadvantaged students by certain school personnel and culturally deprived families. Title I was one in a series of legislative efforts aimed at addressing the needs of the culturally disadvantaged. Some of the others were the Civil Rights Act of 1964, the Economic Opportunity Act of 1964, the Vocational Act of 1963, and the National Defense Act (revised in 1965). Additional related legislation aimed at reducing discrimination policies toward the educationally disadvantaged and other specific targeted populations were Title IX of the Education Amendments of 1972 (PL 92-318), the Education for All Handicapped Children Act (PL 94-142), the Rehabilitation Act of 1973 (PL 93-112), and the Individuals with Disabilities Education Act (IDEA).

Chapter 1 of PL 97-35 addresses the issue of financial assistance to meet the educational needs of disadvantaged children. This legislation replaced Title I of the Elementary and Secondary Act of 1965. Chapter 1 continues to be the main legislation addressing the educational needs of deprived children. The act will fund local education agency school programs to meet the needs of educationally deprived children. According to PL 97-35:

> Such programs and projects may include the acquisition of equipment and instructional materials, employment of special instructional and counseling and guidance personnel, employment and training of teacher aides, payments to teachers in amounts in excess of regular salary schedules (as a bonus for service in schools serving project areas), the training of teachers, the construction, where necessary, of school facilities, other expenditures authorized under Title I. . . . (p. 1701)

The law in this area has undergone a major change with the passage, in 2001, of the No Child Left Behind Act, which shifted focus of federal assistance from educationally disadvantaged and low-income students to "underperforming" schools without regard to the socioeconomic status of the students who attend them. For a more complete discussion of the new law, see the entry on No Child Left Behind, elsewhere in this encyclopedia.

Passow's (1967) assessment of the underlying causes for educational deprivation and cultural deprivation still appear to be valid, even though much federal legislation has been written to address this American educational need. Passow has stated that educationally disadvantaged children's problems stem from poverty, unemployment, segregation, discrimination, and lack of equal opportunity in housing and employment. In addition, he suggests that discontinuities with the majority culture, rising out of difference in life style, child rearing practices, and skills for urban living; and inadequate educational attainment of those skills essential in a technical society are also problematic. Promising practices, he states, fall into nine categories: in-service education and recruitment, reading, summer programs, community-school aspects, guidance activities, early admissions programs, team teaching programs, special placement classes, and job-retraining programs. The challenge for schools in developing promising practices is to keep in mind the question, How can the school educate inner-city children out of their subcultures into society's mainstream while preserving and developing their individuality and diversity, as well as the positive elements of their cultures?

The current literature suggests that schools can increase their effectiveness by changing their focus from considering the culturally disadvantaged as disadvantaged to considering them as culturally different. This shift in focus permits one to accept the fact that the culturally different may continue having disadvantages, but they also have benefits for society. Programs that include emphasis on the benefits to society by the culturally different are basically encompassed in the concept of multicultural education.

Rodriguez (1983) defines multicultural education as education that values cultural pluralism. Multicultural education recognizes that cultural diversity is a valuable resource and should be extended into American society. Schools should not melt away cultural differences or merely tolerate cultural pluralism. Each cultural unit lives as part of an interrelated whole. According to Bennett (1986), the goal of multicultural education is to change the total educational environment so that it will develop competencies in multiple cultures and provide members of all cultural groups with equal educational opportunity. Equity is at the heart of multicultural education.

It appears, therefore, that effective programming for the educationally disadvantaged can be enhanced if the needs of the disadvantaged are perceived in an educational milieu that also recognizes the benefits to society of the students' culture.

### REFERENCES

Bennett, C. I. (1986). *Comprehensive multicultural education: Theory and practice* (p. 53). Boston: Allyn & Bacon.

Daniels, W. G. (1967). Some essential ingredients in educational programs for the socially disadvantaged. In J. Hellmuth (Ed.), *Disadvantaged child. Vol. 1: Special child* (pp. 202–221). Seattle, WA: Seguin School.

Passow, H. A. (1967). Education of the culturally deprived child. In J. Hellmuth (Ed.), *Disadvantaged child. Vol. 1: Special child* (pp. 171–180). Seattle, WA: Seguin School.

Rodriguez, F. (1983). *Education in a multicultural society.* Lanham, MD: University Press of America.

STAN A. KARCZ
*University of Wisconsin at Stout*

**CULTURAL BIAS IN TESTING**
**PLURALISM, CULTURAL**

## EDUCATIONAL PRODUCTS INFORMATION EXCHANGE

Established in 1967 and chartered by the New York Board of Regents, the Educational Products Information Exchange (EPIE) is devoted to helping educators effectively select and use instructional materials. Its members are primarily educational practitioners in local school districts.

The EPIE is a source of information, advocacy, and training concerning instructional materials. The organization has emphasized the need for consumers and producers to examine products with respect to the congruence of instructional design, intrinsic quality dimensions, practicality, and user effects. A central feature of this advocacy is the systematic application of "learner verification and revision," which involves testing to ensure that a product does what its producer claims and what teachers expect it to do. The EPIE's product evaluation procedures are based on a sophisticated analysis, a user review system, and a comprehensive list of criteria.

In the mid-1990s, EPIE produced the landmark report, "Creating Learning Communities: A Guide to the Networking of Schools, Homes, and Communities." The report was the result of two years of research funded by the MacArthur Foundation, and web-published by the Consortium for School Networking (COSN) and the U.S. Department of Education.

As a result, since 1995, EPIE's work has focused on developing a web-based means for schools and families to provide in-home access to web-based "whole curriculum" learning. In 1995 EPIE cofounded LINCT Coalition (Learning and Information Networking for Communities via Technology, www.linct.org). LINCT is an informal coalition of socially concerned nonprofit organizations, local community groups, schools, churches, families, and cooperating businesses.

The EPIE Institute publishes a newsletter, "Epiegram," which reviews research findings derived from product development and evaluation studies and from practitioners' uses of products. The EPIE Institute may be contacted at 475 Riverside Drive, New York, New York 10027, or at www.epie.org.

JUDY SMITH-DAVIS
*Counterpoint Communications Company*

JESSI K. WHEATLEY
*Falcon School District 49, Colorado Springs, Colorado*
Third edition

# EDUCATIONAL RESOURCES INFORMATION CENTER

The Educational Resources Information Center (ERIC) is a national information system that provides access to the literature of education. Operating since 1965 and funded by the National Institute of Education, the ERIC system consists of a coordinating staff in Washington, DC, and 16 clearinghouses located at universities or professional organizations, each specializing in a major area in the field of education. The clearinghouse responsible for selecting, acquiring, cataloguing, abstracting, and indexing documents related to handicapped and gifted children is located at the Council for Exceptional Children (CEC) in Reston, Virginia.

The 16 clearinghouse prepare abstracts of relevant documents for two monthly ERIC publications. *Current Index to Journals in Education* (*CIJE*), a guide to current periodical literature in education, covers approximately 780 major educational and education-related journals; *Resources in Education* (*RIE*), a guide to other current literature in education, covers research findings, project and technical reports, speeches, unpublished manuscripts, and books. The clearinghouses also prepare interpretive summaries and annotated bibliographies on high-interest topics. The ERIC Clearinghouse on Handicapped and Gifted Children prepares a quarterly publication, *Exceptional Child Education Resources* (*ECER*), that includes indexes and abstracts of material included in both *RIE* and *CIJE*. The *RIE* and *CIJE* can be searched manually using author, subject, and institution indexes; they are also available for online computer searching through major commercial database brokerage systems. The ERIC system also produces a thesaurus of descriptors used to index documents. Documents indexed and abstracted in *RIE* are available from the ERIC Document Reproduction Service, except when noted, in both microfiche and paper copy, or in microfiche only. The ERIC microfiche collections are maintained at numerous university libraries across the country. ERIC is available for online search through the Internet.

LINDA J. STEVENS
*University of Minnesota*

## COUNCIL FOR EXCEPTIONAL CHILDREN

# EDUCATIONAL TESTING SERVICE

Educational Testing Service (ETS) is a nonprofit corporation established in 1947. It was originally intended to carry out the College Entrance Examination Board (CEEB) testing program. The ETS also was involved in assisting the testing functions of the Carnegie Corporation and the American Council on Education. In addition to providing contract services to these, and now many other agencies (ETS develops and is responsible for carrying out the Law School Admissions Test, Graduate Record Examination, and numerous other programs), ETS has a world-renowned research and development staff.

The largest percentage of ETS's activity is devoted to developing, administering, scoring, and reporting services for the Scholastic Aptitude Test (SAT). The SAT is administered regularly at more than 5,000 testing centers to more than 1 million college applicants each year. The use of ETS-administered admissions testing programs periodically stirs great controversy, mostly centering around charges of unfairness to certain classes of individuals.

In all of its testing programs, ETS regularly makes accommodations for individuals with disabilities. Not only are readers or recorded tests provided for the blind and for the dyslexic, but prostheses and special administrative procedures for orthopedically disabled individuals are provided as well; such special arrangements must be requested far in advance of the intended testing date.

ETS has become heavily involved in competency testing and examinations for licensure and certification of professions.

ETS has pioneered educational measurement research and analysis, innovative product development, and original policy studies to advance learning worldwide. ETS has a PATHWISE® series which includes professional development workshops, mentor training, support materials, advanced courses for experienced teachers, online instruction, and professional development programs for school leaders. These include a School Leadership Series for principals, superintendents, and other school leaders.

ETS also provides licensure programs in most states. These programs include the Praxis Series: Professional Assessments for Beginning Teachers, and the National Board for Professional Teaching Standards® assessments for accomplished teaching practice.

In addition, ETS offers products and services in support of nonnative speakers of English. The Test of English as a Foreign Language Program provides a complement of assessments and other information to assist in the evaluation, admission, placement, and education of nonnative speakers of English.

CECIL R. REYNOLDS
*Texas A&M University*

JESSI K. WHEATLEY
*Falcon School District 49,
    Colorado Springs, Colorado*
Third edition

# EDUCATION AND TRAINING IN MENTAL RETARDATION AND DEVELOPMENTAL DISABILITIES

*Education and Training in Mental Retardation and Developmental Disabilities* is the quarterly journal published by the Division on Mental Retardation and Developmental Disabilities, a division of The Council for Exceptional Children. Content focuses on the education and welfare of people with mental retardation/developmental disabilities through data-based and expository articles as well as critical reviews of the literature. The editorial policy statement places major emphasis on identification and assessment, educational programming, characteristics, training of instructional personnel, habilitation, prevention, community understanding, and legislation. Editorial offices are located at Special Education Program, P.O. Box 872011, Arizona State University, Tempe, AZ 85287-2011.

PHILIP R. JONES
*Virginia Polytechnic Institute
    and State University*

JESSI K. WHEATLEY
*Falcon School District 49,
    Colorado Springs, Colorado*
Third edition

# EDUCATION AND TREATMENT OF CHILDREN

*Education and Treatment of Children* (*ETC*) is a refereed, scholarly journal published quarterly by The Roscoe Ledger in cooperation with California University of Pennsylvania and West Virginia University. The journal's goal is to disseminate reliable information related to educational and treatment services for children and youths. Manuscripts accepted for publication are judged on their relevance to a variety of child care professionals for improving the effectiveness of teaching and training techniques.

*ETC* utilizes a broad base of educators, researchers, clinical practitioners, and graduate students in the editorial review process, representing most geographic areas of the United States and portions of Canada.

Since its initial publication in 1976, *ETC* has published manuscripts describing a wide variety of experimental studies as well as nonexperimental procedures and/or services and programs for exceptional and normal children and youths. A considerable portion of each issue is devoted to reviews of books and other published materials in the areas of education and treatment of children and youths. The content of the journal is informative and practical for practitioner and researcher alike and should prove useful in improving treatment practices.

JULIA A. HICKMAN
*Bastrop Mental Health
    Association*

JESSI K. WHEATLEY
*Falcon School District 49,
    Colorado Springs, Colorado*
Third edition

# EDUCATION FOR ALL HANDICAPPED CHILDREN ACT OF 1975 (PL 94-142)

See INDIVIDUALS WITH DISABILITIES EDUCATION IMPROVEMENT ACT OF 2004 (IDEIA).

# EDUCATION FOR "OTHER HEALTH IMPAIRED" CHILDREN

"Other Health Impaired" children include those pupils whose health problems severely affect their learning. Federal law designates this group as children with severe orthopedic impairments, illnesses of a chronic or acute nature that require a prolonged convalescence or which limit that child's vitality and strength, congenital anomalies (e.g., spina bifida and clubfoot), other physical causes (e.g., amputation and cerebral palsy), and other health problems including, but not limited to, hemophilia, asthma, ADHD, severe anemia, and diabetes. This category constitutes about 5 percent of children classified as disabled. Unfortunately, the terminology used for children suffering other health impairments does not indicate any commonality in student need, as the categorization is based on recognizable differences in condition and not on necessary educational interventions (Reynolds & Birch, 1982).

Other health impairments may be the result of congenital defects or adventitious (acquired) disabilities. The tremendous heterogeneity associated with the term requires attention to the one obvious common factor of such children, a physical condition that interferes with normal functioning. This limits the child's opportunity to participate fully in learning activities by affecting the body's supply of strength and energy or the removal of wastes, reducing mobility, and creating severe problems in growth and development (Grice, 2002; Kneedler, 1984).

Although the continuum of degree may range from mild to severe, educational principles for other health impaired children include:

1. Placement and education within the mainstream of the public school to the maximum capability of the child. In addition, for those children requiring a special class, school, or home/hospital instruction, directing efforts to return them as soon as possible to regular education (Heron & Harris, 1982).

2. Architectural modifications including the removal of all architectural barriers for full school integration and the modification of classroom structure and environment to allow optimal mobility and exploration.

3. Parent and family education is assumed by the school to provide for coordination of effort, resources, and services.

4. Trained teachers and paraprofessionals who will assist other health impaired children within the school setting.

5. Coordination and utilization of all necessary support and resource personnel by school districts serving such children include transportation modifications, physical and occupational therapy, adaptive physical education, and vocational education and counseling (Gearheart & Weishahn, 1980).

## REFERENCES

Gearheart, B. R., & Weishahn, M. W. (1980). *The handicapped child in the regular classroom* (2nd ed.). St. Louis, MO: Mosby.

Grice, K. (2002). *Eligibility under IDEA for other health impaired children.* Retrieved January 31, 2006, from http://www.incinfc.log.unc.edu/pubs/electronicver

Heron, T. E., & Harris, K. C. (1982). *The educational consultant: Helping professionals, parents, and mainstreamed students.* Boston: Allyn & Bacon.

Kneedler, R. D., Hallahan, D. P., & Kauffman, J. M. (1984). *Special education for today.* Englewood Cliffs, NJ: Prentice Hall.

Reynolds, M. C., & Birch, J. W. (1982). *Teaching exceptional children in all America's schools.* Reston, VA: Council for Exceptional Children.

RONALD S. LENKOWSKY
*Hunter College, City University of New York*

CATEGORICAL EDUCATION
CEREBRAL PALSY
EDUCATION FOR THE TERMINALLY ILL
OTHER HEALTH IMPAIRED
SPINA BIFIDA

# EDUCATION FOR THE TERMINALLY ILL

The teacher confronted by the crisis of a terminally ill child is faced with a complex and difficult situation. The role of the educator requires interaction with the life-threatened child and that child's family, peers, and classmates. Medical and technological advances have increased the life expectancy of terminally ill children and allowed many to return to school during periods of remission or control of their illness (Desy-Spinetta & Spinetta, 1983). To be helped and comforted by a return to the familiar atmosphere of school, the dying child requires the active support and assistance of school personnel (Eklof, 1984).

There are several stages of instruction to be observed in the education of terminally ill children. The initial phase should begin with the instruction and counseling of those who will teach them. It is necessary for educators to face, express, and deal with their own feelings toward death and dying before they can effectively identify and meet the emotional needs and presenting problems of such children. Denial, avoidance, fear, and helplessness are attitudes commonly encountered in unprepared teachers that directly affect the quality of the terminally ill child's experiences in school (Cairns, 1980). Instructional modules devoted to teacher self-awareness and the reality of facing and coping with death and dying are recommended for inclusion in teacher preparation programs (Sirvis, 1981).

As terminally ill children often choose a caring adult other than a parent with whom to communicate and express their feelings, the second stage in teacher preparation must be familiarization and understanding of the psychological stages encountered by the terminally ill and the "language of feelings" employed by such children. Professionals must be aware of the different ways children may select to communicate those feelings in order to be helpful and supportive (Kubler-Ross, 1983).

The second phase in a comprehensive education program for the terminally ill must address the needs and fears of the peers and classmates of the dying child. Wass and Corr (1982) stress the need for curriculum units on death and terminal illness to prepare teachers to instruct on such topics, while Jeffrey and Lansdown (1982) also recommend the inclusion of curriculum units on death and dying for both regular and special education class pupils.

The final phase in educating the terminally ill child offers directed strategies for the teacher. These include: (1) the maintenance of regular classroom routines for such children and the continued application of rules, limits, and reasonable goal-setting (Noore, 1981); (2) the use by teachers of such methods as life space interviews, adjunctive therapy, expressive writing, bibliotherapy (literature), role playing, magic circle discussions, art therapy, and play therapy to cope with the child's presenting problems (Ainsa, 1981); (3) the preparation by teachers to deal effectively with behaviors that may range from withdrawal to defiance while helping friends and classmates grieve and recover on the death of the child; (4) the maintenance by teachers of a primary role and the fulfillment of teaching responsibilities while emphasizing views in the classroom that stress maintaining meaning in the life of the terminally ill child (Stuecher, 1980). Most terminally ill children continue to receive educational services until they are too ill to benefit from them and may receive in-home teaching services as Other Health Impaired through special education.

There are many online resources for teachers, parents and caregivers on terminal illness. In addition, online resources for children with terminal illnesses are plentiful and can be accessed at http://www.musckids.com, http://www.patient.co.uk/showdoc, http://www.webmd.com/hw/raising_a_family.

**REFERENCES**

Ainsa, T. (1981). Teaching the terminally ill child. *Education, 101,* 397–401.

Cairns, N. (1980). The dying child in the classroom. *Essence: Issues in the Study of Aging, Dying, and Death, 4,* 25–32.

Desy-Spinetta, P., & Spinetta, J. J. (1983). The child with cancer returns to school: Preparing the teacher. In J. E. Schowalter, P. R. Patterson, M. Tallmer, A. H. Kutscher, S. V. Gullo, & D. Peretz (Eds.), *The child and death.* New York: Columbia University Press.

Eklof, M. (1984). The terminally ill child: How peers, parents and teachers can help. *PTA Today, 10,* 8–9.

Jeffrey, P., & Lansdown, R. (1982). The role of the special school in the care of the dying child. *Developmental Medicine & Child Neurology, 24,* 693–696.

Kubler-Ross, E. (1983). *On children and death.* New York: Macmillan.

Noore, N. (1981). The damaged child. *Journal for Special Educators, 17,* 376–380.

Sirvis, B. (1981). Death and dying: An instructional module for special educators. *Dissertation Abstracts International,* Order no. 76-21039, *39,* 164 pp.

Wass, H., & Corr, C. A. (1982). *Helping children cope with death: Guidelines and resources.* New York: Hemisphere.

RONALD S. LENKOWSKY
*Hunter College, City University
of New York*

FAMILY COUNSELING
FAMILY RESPONSE TO A CHILD WITH DISABILITIES
PHYSICAL DISABILITIES

# EDUCATION OF CHILDREN WITH BLINDNESS/VISUAL DISABILITIES

Educationally significant, noncorrectable vision impairments are prevalent in approximately 12.2 students in 1,000 (National Information Center for Children and Youth with Disabilities [NICCYD], 2006). Educators use one of two basic classifications in identifying students who are visually impaired: blind and visually impaired/low vision. Those who are blind may have no light perception or may have some light perception without projection. The low-vision learner is considered severely impaired (even with corrective assistance such as glasses), but is able to read print (often in modified form).

According to Kirk and Gallagher (1986), research on the impact of visual impairments indicates that, for the vast majority of students, (1) intellectual abilities are not markedly affected; (2) the perception of other senses is not substantially different from that of seeing persons; (3) language development is affected only in those areas where the meanings of words are dependent on visual concepts; and (4) self-esteem and self-confidence are not distorted except when a peer group has negatively influenced the individual's attitude.

The influence of recent social and educational movements to serve disabled citizens in less restrictive settings has realized a particular impact on the education of visually impaired students. Prior to 1960, approximately 80 percent of visually impaired learners were prepared in residential schools; currently over 70 percent of visually impaired learners are served in local educational programs. The integration of visually impaired students into regular school environments such as the innovative local programming promoted by Barraga (1983) focuses on adaptations in the presentation of learning experiences, modifications in instructional materials, and refinements in the learning environment.

Depending on the nature and severity of the visual impairment, Reynolds and Birch (1982) have identified the continuum of services that should be available to appropriately serve the blind or low-vision student placed in local school programs. The range of services and other resources includes specialized instruction directed to the unique learning needs and style of the visually impaired. This instruction may be offered by consultants, itinerant teachers, resource teachers, or specially assisted regular classroom teachers or teacher aides. Particularly important in the development of effective programming for this population is the substitution of auditory or tactual learning programs to compensate for the loss of visual capabilities (NICCYD, 2006).

The range of services also includes instruction in orientation and mobility and the availability of readily accessible programs and facilities. To ensure the maximum possible classroom integration, modifications in facility structure, classroom arrangement, and lighting may be necessary. In addition, specialized materials and technologies such as braille, advanced reading machines (e.g., Kurzweil Reader, Optacon), recorded information, and large print documents and magnifiers are offered, along with comprehensive early intervention programming for infants and young children and a strong, ongoing program of career preparation and placement.

## REFERENCES

Barraga, N. (1983). *Visual handicaps and learning* (Rev. ed.). Austin, TX: Exceptional Resources.

Kirk, S. A., & Gallagher, J. J. (1986). *Educating exceptional children* (5th ed.). Boston: Houghton Mifflin.

National Information Center for Children and Youth with Disabilities (NICCYD). (2006). *Visual impairments fact sheet.* Retrieved January 31, 2006, from http://www.nichcy.org/pubs/factshe/fs13txt.htm

Reynolds, M. C., & Birch, J. W. (1982). *Teaching exceptional children in all America's schools* (Rev. ed.). Reston, VA: Council for Exceptional Children.

GEORGE JAMES HAGERTY
*Stonehill College*

**VISUAL IMPAIRMENT**

# EDUCATION WEEK

*Education Week* is a weekly newspaper published 42 times during the typical academic year. It is published by Editorial Projects in Education Inc., a Washington, DC based corporation. *Education Week* carries news, comment, and editorials of interest and concern to professional educators and researchers in the field. The paper monitors budgetary concerns and federal policy. Special education news is regularly included, as are position papers on topics of special interest such as learning disabilities diagnosis and mainstreaming. Each year in January *Education Week* issues a new edition of Quality Counts examining a central issue in education. Each edition also includes state report cards and extensive data on state education policy. Available both in print and on the web, Quality Counts has become an essential resource for educators, policymakers, and researchers at all levels. Letters to the editor and commentary on current events in education and previously published news items, features, or commentaries are accepted. Classified ads and listings of job openings are also included.

CECIL R. REYNOLDS
*Texas A&M University*

JESSI K. WHEATLEY
*Falcon School District 49,*
*Colorado Springs, Colorado*

# EEG ABNORMALITIES

The electroencephalogram (EEG) is a graphic representation of the electrical activity of the brain that is generated in the cortex by the flow of synaptic currents through the extracellular space. Electrical changes in the brain that manifest in EEG abnormalities represent the heart of the epileptic attack (Bennett & Ho, 1997; Camfield & Camfield, 1999; Kandel, Schwartz, & Jessell, 1991). When an epileptic seizure occurs, large populations of neurons are activitated synchronously in regions of the cortex. During the evaluation of a patient, it is not uncommon to find an abnormal EEG when there is no overt evidence of a seizure disorder. The criteria for determining the presence of a seizure disorder in an individual with an abnormal EEG are rarely stated explicitly. Hill (1957) has reported that a high percentage of schizophrenic patients show paroxysmal abnormalities in their EEGs (e.g., synchronous spikes, spike and wave complexes, and slow wave bursts). The relationship between an abnormal EEG and behavioral disturbances in nonepileptic individuals is more difficult to define. It also has been demonstrated that commonly used drugs can often cause EEG changes that can mimic seizure activity (Fink, 1963; Ulett, Heusler, & Word, 1965). Some of these changes are described in Table 1.

Defining the limits of normality in an EEG presents a major problem with which clinicians and investigators have struggled for years. There is no doubt that spikes, spike-wave discharges, focal slowing with phase reversal, and paroxysmal activity during wakefulness are always abnormal; however, there are many instances and EEG patterns that do not contain any of the above but still may be considered abnormal. In patients who drink alcohol heavily

Table 1 Effect of commonly used drugs on the EEG[a]

| Drug type | Effect on basic frequencies | EEG changes synchronization | New waves | Persistence after drug discontinued |
|---|---|---|---|---|
| Phenothiazine | Beta slowing (occasional) | Increased | High voltage sharp | 6–10 weeks |
| Tricyclics | Increased beta | Increased | Sharp | Unknown |
| Barbiturates | Increased beta; slowing | Increased in low doses; decreased in high doses | Spindles | 3–6 weeks |
| Meprobamate | Increased beta | Increased | Spindles | 3–6 weeks |
| Benzodiazepines | Increased beta | Increased | Fast, sharp | 3–6 weeks |

[a]All of these drugs except barbiturates tend to increase preexisting dysrhythmias. Withdrawal from high levels of barbiturates and meprobamate can induce increased slowing, synchronization, and paroxysmal activity, and may result in seizures.

or who have received tranquilizers or other medications, EEG abnormalities may be seen and represent the effect of these drugs or withdrawal from them. EEG abnormalities seen in some psychopathic individuals with a history of aggressive behavior may be due to brain damage. Positive electroencephalographic abnormalities and brain damage thus may be a result and not the cause of emotional disturbance. Even with these possibilities there remains impressive literature correlating EEG abnormalities with certain psychiatric symptomatology (e.g., Dodrill, 1981; Hartlage & Hartlage, 1997).

In a large study of unselected, nonepileptic individuals, it was possible to differentiate those with abnormal EEGs from those with normal EEGs on the basis of their symptoms (Tucker, Detre, Harrow, & Glaser, 1965). Symptoms classically associated with schizophrenia were significantly more common in psychiatric patients with abnormal EEGs; they included impaired associations, flattened affect, religiosity, persecutory and somatic delusions, auditory hallucinations, impaired personal habits, and destructive-assaultive behavior. The group with abnormal EEGs also exhibited symptoms normally associated with neurological diseases such as time disorientation, perseveration, recent memory difficulties, and headaches. Neurotic and depressed individuals had approximately the same incidence of abnormal EEGs as the general population (18 percent). (Also see reviews by Bennett & Ho, 1997; Hartlage & Hartlage, 1997; and Murphy & Heller, 1994.)

Research by Wilkus and Dodrill (1976) demonstrated that increasing involvement of the brain with epileptiform discharges (epilepticlike EEG abnormalities) is related to decreased cognitive performance. Furthermore, the decreased performances associated with this condition are conspicuously widespread and involve many different kinds of functions. The EEGs of epileptics have been studied with respect to abnormalities in rhythm frequency. Generally, decreased abilities were associated with slower rhythm frequencies. Dodrill and Wilkins (1976) studied the perfor-

mance of a large group of epileptic individuals on a broad range of tests and found that performance was not substantially decreased until the dominant posterior rhythm frequency dropped below 8 Hz, when performance decreased precipitously. Although decreased abilities were seen across a wide range of skills, those requiring simultaneous attention and complex mental manipulations showed the greatest losses. However, the social and emotional consequences of epilepsy are the most serious consequences of this disorder (Camfield & Camfield, 1999; Murphy & Heller, 1994).

## REFERENCES

Bennett, T., & Ho, M. (1997). The neuropsychology of pediatric epilepsy and antiepileptic drugs. In C. R. Reynolds & E. Fletcher-Janzen (Eds.), *Handbook of clinical child neuropsychology* (2nd ed., pp. 517–538). New York: Plenum.

Camfield, P. R., & Camfield, C. S. (1999). Pediatric epilepsy: An overview. In K. F. Swaiman & S. Ashwal (Eds.), *Pediatric neurology* (pp. 629–633). St. Louis, MO: Mosby.

Dodrill, C. B. (1981). Neuropsychology of epilepsy. In S. B. Filskov & T. J. Boll (Eds.), *Handbook of clinical neuropsychology* (pp. 366–395). New York: Wiley.

Dodrill, C. B., & Wilkus, R. J. (1976). Neuropsychological correlates of the electroencephalogram in epileptics: II. The waking posterior rhythm and its interaction with epileptiform activity. *Epilepsia, 17,* 101–109.

Fink, M. (1963). Quantitative EEG in human psychopharmacology: Drug patterns. In G. H. Glaser (Ed.), *EEG and behavior* (pp. 143–169). New York: Basic Books.

Hartlage, P. L., & Hartlage, L. C. (1997). The neuropsychology of epilepsy: Overview and psychosocial aspects. In C. R. Reynolds & E. Fletcher-Janzen (Eds.), *Handbook of clinical child neuropsychology* (2nd ed., pp. 506–516). New York: Plenum.

Hill, D. (1957). Electroencephalogram in schizophrenia. In R. Richter (Ed.), *Schizophrenia: Somatic aspects* (pp. 30–72). London: Pergamon.

Kandel, E., Schwartz, J., & Jessell, T. (1991). *Principles of neural science* (3rd ed.). New York: Elsevier.

Murphy, S., & Heller, W. (1994). Seizure disorder: Psychological issues. In R. Olson, L. Mullins, J. Gillman, & J. Chaney (Eds.), *The sourcebook of pediatric psychology* (pp. 185–198). Boston: Longwood.

Tucker, G. J., Detre, T., Harrow, M., & Glaser, G. H. (1965). Behavior and symptoms of psychiatric patients and the electroencephalogram. *Archives of General Psychiatry, 12,* 278–292.

Ulett, G. A., Heusler, A. F., & Word, T. J. (1965). The effect of psychotropic drugs on the EEG of the chronic psychotic patient. In W. P. Wilson (Ed.), *Applications of electroencephalography in psychiatry: A symposium* (pp. 23–36). Durham, NC: Duke University Press.

Wilkus, R. J., & Dodrill, C. B. (1976). Neuropsychological correlates of the electroencephalogram in epileptics. I. Topographic distribution and average rate of epileptiform activity. *Epilepsia, 17,* 89–100.

RICHARD A. BERG
*West Virginia University*
*Medical Center, Charleston*
*Division*

**EPILEPSY**
**NEUROPSYCHOLOGY**

**EEOC**

See EQUAL EMPLOYMENT OPPORTUNITY COMMISSION.

## EFFECTIVENESS OF SPECIAL EDUCATION

The work of Jean-Marc-Gaspard Itard with Victor, the "wild boy of Aveyron," usually marks the beginning of modern special education (Itard, 1806/1962). Although innovative and comprehensive, the education program developed by Itard produced only modest improvement in Victor's performance. The enduring perception was that the Itard experiment "failed" (e.g., Kirk & Johnson, 1951) but, in reality, the modest gains were substantial and become more meaningful when emphasis shifts from results to methods (Gaynor, 1973).

Questions about the efficacy of special education remain: Is special education special? Unequivocal answers have been difficult to attain and this has resulted in a cyclical nature for special education that oscillates between optimism and pessimism (Sarason & Doris, 1979). Answers to questions about efficacy are typically sought in the research literature, but difficulties arise when individual study findings do not agree. The disagreement makes it necessary to combine findings to produce "usable knowledge" (Lindblom & Cohen, 1979) that provides a basis for decision-making about efficacy.

Special education has historically assumed a goal of correcting or reversing the altered learning functions of students. Beginning with Itard, special education has focused on enhancing cognitive *processes* so special education students may then be able to learn in the same way as general education students. Consequently, process training has long been a primary form of special education (see Mann, 1979). Although intuitively appealing, does research support the theoretical assumption that training processes enhance learning ability?

A large body of empirical research has investigated the efficacy of process training but difficulties arise in deciding "what the research says" as illustrated in the case of psycholinguistic training, a prominent form of process training during the 1960s and 1970s. Psycholinguistic training was developed by Samuel A. Kirk and embodied in the *Illinois Test of Psycholinguistic Abilities* (ITPA). The model was based on the assumption that psycholinguistic ability is comprised of discrete components and that these components can be improved with training. By the mid 1970s, empirical research summaries revealed very different interpretations.

A review of 39 studies offered by Hammill and Larsen (1974) concluded that, "the idea that psycholinguistic constructs, as measured by the ITPA, can, in fact, be trained by existing techniques remains nonvalidated" (p. 11). In response, Minskoff (1975) offered a more positive evaluation and concluded that psycholinguistic deficits can be remediated. The Minskoff review was immediately challenged by Newcomer, Larsen, and Hammill (1975) who concluded that, "the reported literature raises doubts regarding the efficacy of presently available Kirk-Osgood psycholinguistic training programs" (p. 147). The divergent interpretations made it increasingly difficult to determine "what the research says" about the efficacy of psycholinguistic training.

Several years later, Lund, Foster, and McCall-Perez (1978) reevaluated the original 39 studies and concluded that, "It is, therefore, not logical to conclude either that all studies in psycholinguistic training are effective or that all studies in psycholinguistic training are not effective" (p. 319). Hammill and Larsen (1978) contested the Lund et al. analysis and concluded that, "the cumulative results . . . failed to demonstrate that psycholinguistic training has value" (p. 413). Although polemics abounded, a primary question remained unanswered: What is really known about the efficacy of psycholinguistic training?

The difficulty is that traditional means for combining research findings does not eliminate potential bias in evaluating outcomes. To exclude the subjectivity associated with traditional methods of reviewing research findings (see Cooper & Rosenthal, 1980), quantitative methods, usually termed "meta-analysis" (Glass, 1976), have become an accepted means of combining empirical findings. Meta-analysis is the application of statistical procedures to collections of empirical findings from individual studies for the purpose of integrating, synthesizing, and making sense of them (Glass, McGaw, & Smith, 1981).

As a research methodology, meta-analysis uses rigorous and systematic procedures that permit quantification and standardization of individual study findings with the "effect size" (ES) statistic (Kavale, 2001). An ES is most often interpreted as a $z$-score indicating level of improvement on an outcome assessment for students initially at the 50th percentile. To gain greater insight, an ES may also be interpreted with the "binomial effect size display" (BESD; Rosenthal & Rubin, 1982), which addresses the question: What is the percentage increase in the number of successful responses when using a new instructional practice? Based on converting an ES to $r$, the BESD for the use of intervention (ES = 1.6, for example) would show an increase in success rate from 25 to 75 percent. The 50-percentage-point spread between treatment (75 percent) and comparison (25 percent) success rate shows that the use of intervention Z possesses not only statistical significance, but also *practical* significance. Another ES interpretation is based on notions of statistical power where Cohen (1988) offered "rules of thumb" for classifying ES as small (.20), medium (.50), or large (.80).

To accumulate findings about the effectiveness of psycholinguistic training in a more objective manner, Kavale (1981) conducted a meta-analysis on 34 studies that yielded an average ES of .39. In a statistical sense, an ES shows outcomes in standard deviation (SD) units that can be interpreted in terms overlapping distributions (treatment versus control). The ES of .39 indicates that the average treated subject would gain 15 percentile ranks on the ITPA and would be better off than 65 percent of control (no treatment) subjects. The BESD ($r = .19$) for psycholinguistic training shows a success rate increase from 40 percent to 60 percent. Using Cohen's (1988) rules of thumb, the ES approaches a "medium" level. The 15 percentile rank gain, 20 percent increase in success rater, and almost medium statistical power level suggest modest efficacy for psycholinguistic training.

The modest efficacy does not represent an unequivocal endorsement of psycholinguistic training, however, and suggests the need for further analysis to determine where psycholinguistic training may be more or less effective. When ES data were aggregated by ITPA subtest, five of nine ITPA subtests revealed "small," albeit positive, effects. Such a modest level of response suggests that training would not be warranted in these five cases. For four subtests (Auditory and Visual Association, Verbal and Manual Expression), however, training improves performance from 15 to 24 percentile ranks and makes the average trained subject better off than approximately 63 to 74 percent of untrained subjects.

The findings regarding the Associative and Expressive constructs appear to belie the conclusion of Hammill and Larsen (1974) that, "neither the ITPA subtests nor their theoretical constructs are particularly ameliorative" (p. 12). The meta-analytic findings should *not*, however, be interpreted as approval for psycholinguistic training. In the case of Auditory Association, for example, there are difficulties in defining the skill: What is Auditory Association? Additionally, it is important to determine whether improvement in Auditory Association provides enhanced functioning in other than that discrete ability. In contrast, the case for Expressive constructs, particularly Verbal Expression, presents a different scenario because it represents the tangible process of productive language behavior whose improvement is critical for school success. In fact, the Verbal Expression ES (.63) exceeds what would be expected from 6 months of general education language instruction (ES = .50). Thus, the Kavale (1981) meta-analysis showed where psycholinguistic training might be effective and might be initiated when deemed an appropriate part of an intervention program.

Mann (1979) suggested that, "process training is, in fact, one of the oldest forms of education and that, despite periodic discontinuities in its practice, it has continued unabated into our own day" (p. 537). Table 1 reveals that popular forms of process training demonstrate limited efficacy. (The reported ES were obtained from the meta-analyses listed in Appendix A and represent either the ES reported in a single meta-analysis investigating a particular intervention or a weighted mean ES from meta-analyses investigating the same intervention.) For example, perceptual-motor training, the embodiment of 1960s special education, had practically no effect on improving educational performance. In fact, perceptual-motor training has a small effect on improving perceptual-motor functioning (ES = .17). The popular programs developed during the 1960s revealed very modest effectiveness (see Table 2). For example, the BESD reveals that the Kephart program produces only a slight increase in success rate (6 percent).

The limited efficacy of process training may be related to difficulties in attempting to ameliorate unobservable (hypothetical) constructs. The outcomes of training (products) are the only observable component while the means by which those products were achieved (process) are not observable. Although these difficulties are evident for constructs like

Table 1 Effectiveness of process training

| Method | Mean effect size | Percentile rank equivalent | Power rating |
|---|---|---|---|
| Irlen Lenses | −.02 | 49 | Negative |
| Perceptual-Motor Training | .08 | 53 | Negligible |
| Diet Modification (Feingold) | .12 | 55 | Small |
| Modality-Matched Instruction | .14 | 56 | Small |
| Social Skills Training | .36 | 64 | Small |
| Psycholinguistic Training | .39 | 65 | Small–Medium |

Table 2  Average effect size for perceptual-motor training programs

| Training program | Mean effect size | Percentile equivalent | Power rating |
|---|---|---|---|
| Kephart | .06 | 52 | Small |
| Frostig | .10 | 54 | Small |
| Cratty | .11 | 54 | Small |
| Getman | .12 | 55 | Small |
| Barsch | .16 | 56 | Small |
| Delacato | .16 | 56 | Small |

perception, the same problems can be identified for, as an example, social skills training where the actual skills represent products that are presumed related to the hypothetical construct of social competence. The limited efficacy of social skills training is found across special education populations. Forness and Kavale (1996) found an ES of .21 for students with LD, while Quinn, Kavale, Mather, Rutherford, and Forness (1999) found an ES of .20 for students with EBD. Thus, regardless of special education designation, social skill deficits appear difficult to remediate.

Although attacks on process training have been vigorous (e.g., Mann, 1971), its historical, clinical, and philosophical foundation creates a resistance to accepting negative evidence (e.g., Hallahan & Cruickskank, 1973) because, "the tension between belief and reality provides a continuing sense of justification for process training" (Kavale & Forness, 1999, p. 35). The failure to change beliefs about efficacy was found for modality-matched instruction (ES = .14), which has received a number of previous negative evaluations (e.g., Arter & Jenkins, 1979; Larrivee, 1981; Tarver & Dawson, 1978). Nevertheless, teachers maintain a strong belief that students learn best when instruction is modified to match individual modality patterns (Kavale & Reese, 1991). But when difficulties in assessing modality preferences (ES = .51, indicating only 2 out of 3 correct preference decisions) are considered in addition to the modest 6 percentile rank gain, modality-matched instruction does not appear warranted. Thus the empirical evidence demonstrating the limited efficacy of process training suggests that it should not be a major focus in program planning.

The long dominant tradition of process training in special education reflected a pathology model; academic problems were regarded as a "disease" and interventions were aimed at "curing" the disease (i.e., removing the pathology; Kauffman & Hallahan, 1974). By about 1975, the realization that process training was not producing desired outcomes shifted attention to an "instructional imbalance" model where school failure was viewed as the result of a mismatch between instructional methods and student developmental level (Hagin, 1973). The "effective schools" research (see Bickel & Bickel, 1986) was a major influence that stressed, for example, the importance of teachers believing that *all* students can achieve, that basic skill instruction should be

emphasized, and that clear instructional objectives should be used to monitor student performance.

At the same time, a "learning process" model emerged that viewed teaching within a "process-product" paradigm where variables that depict what occurs during teaching are correlated with products (i.e., student outcomes; Needels & Gage, 1991). Research revealed the importance of a number of principles, for example, encouraging student's active engagement in learning, exploring innovative approaches to grouping and organizing classroom instruction, and making learning meaningful by keeping it enjoyable, interesting, student centered, and goal oriented (see Brophy & Good, 1986). These principles became "best practice" and were interpreted for special education (e.g., Christenson, Ysseldyke, & Thurlow, 1989; Reith & Evertson, 1988; Reynolds, Wang, & Walberg, 1992).

Research investigating the teaching-learning process has identified a number of effective instructional practices. Table 3 shows a sample of effective instructional practices and reveals that substantial positive influence on learning are possible by modifying the way instruction is delivered.

The use of effective instructional practices moves special education toward the general education teaching-learning

Table 3  Effective instructional practices

| Practice | Mean effect size | Power rating | Binomial effect size display (success rate increase:) | |
|---|---|---|---|---|
| | | | From (%) | To (%) |
| Mnemonic Instruction | 1.62 | Very large | 18 | 82 |
| Self-Monitoring | 1.36 | Very large | 22 | 78 |
| Reinforcement | 1.17 | Very large | 25 | 75 |
| Self-Questioning | 1.16 | Very large | 25 | 75 |
| Drill & Practice | .99 | Large | 28 | 72 |
| Strategy Instruction | .98 | Large | 28 | 72 |
| Feedback | .97 | Large | 28 | 72 |
| Direct Instruction | .93 | Large | 29 | 71 |
| Applied Behavior Analysis | .93 | Large | 29 | 71 |
| Visual Displays | .90 | Large | 29 | 71 |
| Computer-Assisted Instruction | .87 | Large | 30 | 70 |
| Repeated Reading | .76 | Large | 32 | 68 |
| Error Correction | .72 | Medium large | 33 | 67 |
| Formative Evaluation | .70 | Medium large | 33 | 67 |
| Peer Mediation | .64 | Medium | 35 | 65 |
| Diagnostic-Prescriptive Teaching | .64 | Medium | 35 | 65 |
| Peer Tutoring | .62 | Medium | 35 | 65 |
| Positive Class Morale | .60 | Medium | 36 | 64 |
| Grouping | .43 | Small medium | 40 | 60 |
| Increased Time | .38 | Small medium | 41 | 59 |

model and away from a reliance on "special" interventions (e.g., process training). For example, mnemonic instruction (MI) is a strategy that transforms difficult-to-remember facts into a more memorable form through recoding, relating, and retrieving information (Mastropieri & Scruggs, 1991). A student receiving MI would be better off than 95 percent of students not receiving MI and show a 45 percentile rank gain on an outcome measure. The BESD shows a 64 percent increase in success rate, which indicates substantial practical significance. Compare the success rate of MI to, for example, perceptual-motor training (ES = .08) where the modest 4 percent increase in success rate indicates a negligible statistical effect and almost no practical significance.

The ultimate purpose of implementing effective instruction is to enhance academic performance. Achievement outcomes are shown in Table 4 and indicate the potential for substantial gains across subject areas. All achievement domains show "large" ES with gains ranging from 29 to 41 percentile ranks on academic achievement measures. The BESD reveals a success rate increase from 27 to 73 percent indicating an average 46 percent improvement in the number of students showing a positive response to instruction.

The example of reading comprehension demonstrates how meta-analysis can be useful for judging the magnitude of "real" effects. Two meta-analyses contributed almost all ES measurements and produced ESs of 1.13 and .98, a modest three percentile rank difference in outcomes (87 versus 84). When specific methods for improving reading comprehension are compared, the two meta-analyses revealed similar findings. The largest effects (ES = 1.60 and 1.33) were found for metacognitive techniques (e.g., self-questioning, self-monitoring). Text-enhancement procedures (e.g., advanced organizers, mnemonics) produced

ES of 1.09 and .92. The least powerful (but nevertheless effective) techniques involved skill-training procedures (e.g., vocabulary, repeated reading) with ES of .79 and .62. The meta-analytic evidence suggests that, on average, the "real" effect of reading comprehension instruction is 1.04, a level comparable to 1 year's worth of reading comprehension instruction in general education (ES = 1.00). Thus, methods adapted for the purposes of special education produced the same effect as 1 year of general education instruction, but did so in approximately 20 hours. Clearly, special education students can significantly improve their ability to better understand what they read.

A hallmark of special education is the provision for related services to be provided when deemed appropriate in augmenting the instruction program. Table 5 shows a sample of adjunct activities and most demonstrate, at least, "medium" ES. On average (ES = .65), related services produce a 24 percentile rank gain on an outcome assessment with the BESD (r = .30), showing a 20 percent increase in success rate (45 to 65 percent). Thus, related services appear to be useful supplements to the instructional program.

Placement has often been viewed as having a positive influence on student performance (see Kavale & Forness, 2000). The ES magnitude (.12) negates such a view and indicates that the success rate associated with placement increases only 6 percent, from 47 to 53 percent (BESD). Although the ES (.12) favors placement in general education, the actual advantage is small and is found only for students with MR (IQ < 75) and "slow learners" (IQ 75–90). In contrast, for students with LD or EBD, placement in special classes appears more advantageous (ES = .29). The average students with LD or EBD placed in a special class

Table 4  Effective special education instruction

| Subject area | Mean effect size | Percentile rank equivalent | Binomial effect size display (success rate increase:) | |
|---|---|---|---|---|
| | | | From (%) | To (%) |
| Handwriting | 1.32 | 91 | 22 | 78 |
| Oral Reading | 1.31 | 90 | 22 | 78 |
| Language | 1.27 | 90 | 23 | 77 |
| Reading Comprehension | 1.04 | 85 | 27 | 73 |
| Word Recognition | .98 | 84 | 28 | 72 |
| Narrative Writing | .97 | 83 | 28 | 72 |
| Math | .96 | 83 | 28 | 72 |
| Spelling | .87 | 81 | 30 | 70 |
| Vocabulary | .85 | 80 | 30 | 70 |
| Problem-Solving | .82 | 79 | 31 | 69 |

Table 5  Effective special education related services and activities

| Service | Mean effect size | Power rating | Binomial effect size display (success rate increase:) | |
|---|---|---|---|---|
| | | | From (%) | To (%) |
| Memory Training | 1.12 | Very large | 25 | 75 |
| Prereferral | 1.10 | Very large | 26 | 74 |
| Cognitive Behavior Modification | .74 | Large | 32 | 68 |
| Psychotherapy | .71 | Medium large | 33 | 67 |
| Stimulant Medication | .62 | Medium | 35 | 65 |
| Counseling | .60 | Medium | 35 | 65 |
| Consultation | .55 | Medium | 36 | 64 |
| Rational-Emotive Therapy | .50 | Medium | 38 | 62 |
| Attribution Training | .43 | Small medium | 39 | 61 |
| Placement | .12 | Small | 47 | 53 |

would be better off than 61 percent of those who remained in a general education class. Nevertheless, ES associated with placement are "small" suggesting that "what" (i.e., nature of the instruction) is a more important influence on student outcomes than "where" (i.e., placement). Efforts aimed at preventing the need for special education appear to be effective. Prereferral activities produce significant positive efforts (ES = 1.12) and appear successful in about 78 out of 100 cases. Prereferral "works" because it is predicated on modification of *instructional* activities, and its 48 percent success rate means that almost half of students given preferential activities will *not* need to enter special education.

Drug treatment is often an integral part of the treatment regimen for special education students. Stimulant medication (usually Ritalin) is the most popular and produces significant positive changes in behavior, averaging 23 percentile ranks on behavior ratings and checklists. The ES (.62) was obtained primarily from a meta-analysis done in 1982 (ES = .58) and a replication completed in 1997 (ES = .64). The consistency of the ES found (i.e., .58 and .64) provides confirmation for the positive influence of stimulant medication. The use of stimulant medication has long been criticized and more natural and unobtrusive treatments have been sought. One such alternative, popularized during the 1970s, was the Feingold diet designed to eliminate all foods containing artificial substances from the diet. The ES (.12) obtained for the Feingold diet (see Table 1) clearly indicates that it has limited influence on modifying behavior. A comparison of the two treatments shows stimulant medication to be greater than five times more effective than the Feingold diet; the debate about efficacy appears unequivocal.

Special education has demonstrated increased efficacy that may be attributable to a change in instructional emphasis. Until about 25 years ago, special education emphasized its "special" nature by developing singular and different methods not found in general education. The goal was to enhance hypothetical constructs (e.g., "processes") that were presumed to be the cause of learning deficits. Basic skill instruction was a secondary consideration until processes were remediated and learning became more efficient. When intervention activities emphasize, for example, process training and basic skill instruction is subordinate, the nature of special education can be conceptualized as *SPECIAL education,* use of unique and exclusive "special" interventions. The limited efficacy of *SPECIAL education* (see Table 1) suggest that process deficits are difficult to "fix" and such a focus in intervention activities produces little benefit.

The recognition that "special" interventions did not produce desired outcomes moved special education to emphasize "education" in an effort to enhance academic outcomes. When intervention activities emphasize alternative instructional "education" techniques, the nature of special education can be conceptualized as *special EDUCATION.* Such instructional techniques usually originate in general education and are adapted to assist students with disabilities in acquiring and assimilating new knowledge; *special EDUCATION* demonstrates significant success (see Table 2) and produces improved *achievement* outcomes (see Table 3).

The difference between the two forms of special education are seen in the mega ES (mean of means) for "special" (.15) versus "education" (.89) techniques. The comparison reveals *special EDUCATION* to be six times more effective than *SPECIAL education;* it produces achievement outcomes (mega ES = 1.04) that exceed 1 year's worth of general education instruction (ES = 1.00). On average, *SPECIAL education* provides only a 6 percent advantage, meaning that the group receiving "special" interventions exceeds only about 56 percent of the group not receiving such interventions; a modest level of improvement slightly above chance (50 percent). Additionally, across meta-analyses investigating *SPECIAL education,* about 25 percent of the calculated ES were negative indicating that in one out of four cases the student *not* receiving the "special" intervention performed better. Clearly, there is little reason to include *SPECIAL education* in most intervention programs.

In contrast, the methods associated with *special EDUCATION* provide an efficacious foundation for designing an instructional program. The use of effective techniques is likely to move the average student in special education from the 50th to the 81st percentile. The 31-percentile-rank gain is better than 5 times the gain found with the use of "special" interventions, and indicates students are better off than 81 percent of those not receiving *special EDUCATION.* For example, Direct Instruction (DI), a behaviorally oriented teaching procedure based on an explicit step-by-step strategy (ES = .93) is 6½ times more effective than the intuitively appealing modality-matched instruction that attempts to enhance learning by capitalizing on learning style differences (ES = .14). Students in special education taught with DI would be better off than 87 percent of students not receiving DI and would gain over 11 months credit on an achievement measure compared to about 1 month for modality-matched instruction. With its grounding in effective instructional methodology, *special EDUCATION* can sometimes be up to 20 times more effective than *SPECIAL education.*

The meta-analyses summarized provide insight into the indications and contra-indications of special education interventions (Lipsey & Wilson, 2001). The interventions associated with *special EDUCATION* may be considered a form of "evidenced-based practice" (EBP; Odom, Brantlinger, Gersten, Horner, Thompson, & Harris, 2005) where intervention decisions are based on empirical findings demonstrating that the actions produce efficacious and beneficial outcomes. The use of EBP promotes *instructional validity* where changes can be attributed to the specific activities and can be used to produce similar results with other students (generalization).

Because students in special education, by definition, possess unique learning needs, instructional decisions are critical in the design of *individualized* programs. The complexities surrounding the instructional decision making introduces a degree of "uncertainty" (i.e., the program may not work; Glass, 1979). Besides uncertainty, there is also the possibility of "risk" (i.e., negative outcomes) that can be described in meta-analysis by the standard deviation (SD), a measure of dispersion around the mean ES, representing an index of variability. Taken together, the ES and SD provide a theoretical expectation about intervention efficacy (i.e., ES ± SD). For example, psycholinguistic training (.39 ± .54) spans a theoretical range (–.15 to .93) from negative ES to "large" ES; the difficulty is the inability to predict the outcome (i.e., ES) for a particular student. The mega ES for *SPECIAL education* (.15) is associated with a larger mega SD (.48) making "special" interventions actually more variable than effective (.15 ± .48). The theoretical range for *SPECIAL education* (–.33 to .63), although possibly producing "medium" effects, also includes significant risk (i.e., the possibility of a negative ES indicating that those *not* receiving the intervention perform better). In contrast, *special EDUCATION* (.89 ± .87) reveals itself to be more effective than variable and, although the theoretical range shows that it may not "work" in some cases (ES = .02), there also exists the possibility of being almost twice as effective (ES = 1.76).

Although the use of *special EDUCATION* can reduce risk (i.e., no negative ES), the special education teaching-learning process remains a capricious enterprise (i.e., variable, unpredictable, and indeterminate). To create more certainty, instructional decisions should not be prescriptive (i.e., do A in circumstance X or Y, and do B in circumstance Z) but rather based on an assortment of effective options (i.e., practices with large ES). This means that teachers are central characters in the special education decision-making process who must replace dogmatic beliefs with rational choices about "what works." Instructional decisions thus include elements of science (theoretical and empirical knowledge) and art (interpretation necessary to initiate action; see Gage, 1978). The teacher's goal is to narrow the gap between the state of the art (what has been demonstrated to be possible) and the state of practice (current ways of providing instruction). Consequently, the actions of

> special education practitioners will need to go beyond the scientific basis of their work . . . and must be mediated through the teacher's own creative rendering of best practice . . . because quality education for special education students will always be based on the artful application of science. (Kavale & Forness, 1999, p. 93)

## REFERENCES

Arter, J. A., & Jenkins, J. R. (1977). Examining the benefits and prevalence of modality considerations in special education. *Journal of Special Education, 11*, 281–298.

Bickel, W. E., & Bickel, D. D. (1986). Effective schools, classrooms, and instruction: Implications for special education. *Exceptional Children, 52*, 489–500.

Brophy, J., & Good, T. (1986). Teacher behavior and student achievement. In M. C. Wittrock (Ed.), *Handbook of research on teaching* (Vol. 3, pp. 328–375). New York: Macmillan.

Christenson, S. L., Ysseldyke, J. E., & Thurlow, M. L. (1989). Critical instructional factors for students with mild handicaps: An integrative review. *Remedial and Special Education, 10*, 21–31.

Cohen, J. (1988). *Statistical power analysis for the behavioral sciences* (2nd ed.). Hillsdale, NJ: Erlbaum.

Cooper, H., & Hedges, L. V. (Eds.). (1994). *Handbook of research synthesis*. New York: Sage.

Cooper, H. M., & Rosenthal, R. (1980). Statistical versus traditional procedures for summarizing research findings. *Psychological Bulletin, 87*, 442–449.

Forness, S. R., & Kavale, K. A. (1996). Treating social skill deficits in children with learning disabilities: A meta-analysis of the research. *Learning Disability Quarterly, 19*, 2–13.

Gage, N. L. (1978). *The scientific basis of the art of teaching.* New York: Teachers College Press.

Gaynor, J. F. (1973). The "failure" of J. M. G. Itard. *Journal of Special Education, 7*, 439–445.

Glass, G. V. (1976). Primary, secondary, and meta-analysis of research. *Educational Researcher, 5*, 3–8.

Glass, G. V. (1979). Policy for the unpredictable (uncertainty research and policy). *Educational Researcher, 8*, 12–14.

Glass, G. V., McGaw, B., & Smith, M. L. (1981). *Meta-analysis in social research.* Beverly Hills, CA: Sage.

Hammill, D. D., & Larsen, S. C. (1974). The effectiveness of psycholinguistic training. *Exceptional Children, 41*, 5–14.

Hammill, D. D., & Larsen, S. C. (1978). The effectiveness of psycholinguistic training: A reaffirmation of position. *Exceptional Children, 44*, 402–414.

Hedges, L. V., & Olkin, I. (1985). *Statistical methods for meta-analysis.* San Diego, CA: Academic Press.

Itard, J. M. G. (1962). *The wild boy of Areyron.* (G. Humphrey & M. Humphrey, trans.). New York: Appleton-Century-Crafts. (Original work published 1806)

Kavale, K. A. (1981). Functions of the Illinois Test of Psycholinguistic Abilities (ITPA): Are they trainable? *Exceptional Children, 47*, 496–510.

Kavale, K. A. (1984). Potential advantages of the meta-analysis technique for research in special education. *Journal of Special Education, 18*, 61–72.

Kavale, K. A. (2001a). Meta-analysis: A primer. *Exceptionality, 9*, 177–183.

Kavale, K. A. (2001b). Decision making in special education: The function of meta-analysis. *Exceptionality, 9*, 245–268.

Kavale, K. A., & Forness, S. R. (1999). *Efficacy of special education and related services.* Washington, DC: American Association on Mental Retardation.

Kavale, K. A., & Forness, S. R. (2000). History, rhetoric, and reality: Analysis of the inclusion debate. *Remedial and Special Education, 21*, 279–296.

Kavale, K. A., & Reese, J. H. (1991). Teacher beliefs and perceptions about learning disabilities: A survey of Iowa practitioners. *Learning Disability Quarterly, 14,* 141–160.

Kirk, R. E. (1996). Practical significance: A concept whose time has come. *Educational and Psychological Measurement, 36,* 746–759.

Larrivee, B. (1981). Modality preference as a model for differentiating beginning reading instruction: A review of the issues. *Learning Disability Quarterly, 4,* 180–188.

Lindblom, C. E., & Cohen, D. K. (1979). *Usable knowledge: Social science and social problem solving.* New Haven, CT: Yale University Press.

Lipsey, M. W., & Wilson, D. B. (2001). *Practical meta-analysis* (Vol. 49). Thousand Oaks, CA: Sage.

Lund, K. A., Foster, G. E., & McCall-Perez, G. C. (1978). The effectiveness of psycholinguistic training: A reevaluation. *Exceptional Children, 44,* 310–319.

Mann, L. (1971). Psychometric phrenology and the new faculty psychology: The case against ability assessment and training. *Journal of Special Education, 5,* 3–14.

Mann, L. (1979). *On the trail of process: A historical perspective on cognitive processes and their training.* New York: Grune & Stratton.

Mastropieri, M. A., & Scruggs, T. E. (1991). *Teaching students ways to remember: Strategies for learning mnemonically.* Cambridge, MA: Brookline Books.

McGraw, K. O., & Wong, S. P. (1992). A common language effect size. *Psychological Bulletin, 111,* 361–365.

Minskoff, E. (1975). Research on psycholinguistic training: Critique and guidelines. *Exceptional Children, 42,* 136–144.

Needels, M. C., & Gage, N. L. (1991). Essence and accident in process-product research on teaching. In H. C. Waxman & H. J. Walberg (Eds.), *Effective teaching: Current research* (pp. 3–31). Berkeley, CA: McCuthan.

Newcomer, P., Larsen, S., & Hammill, D. (1975). A response. *Exceptional Children, 42,* 144–148.

Odom, S. L., Brantlinger, E., Gersten, R., Horner, R. H., Thompson, B., & Harris, K. R. (2005). Research in special education: Scientific methods and evidence-based practices. *Exceptional Children, 71,* 137–148.

Quinn, M. M., Kavale, K. A., Mathur, S., Rutherford, R. B., & Forness, S. R. (1999). A meta-analysis of social skill interventions for students with emotional or behavioral disorders. *Journal of Emotional and Behavioral Disorders, 1,* 54–64.

Reith, H. J., & Evertson, C. (1988). Variables related to the effective instruction of difficult-to-teach children. *Focus on Exceptional Children, 20,* 1–8.

Reynolds, M. C., Wang, M. C., & Walberg, H. J. (1992). The knowledge bases for special and general education. *Remedial and Special Education, 13,* 6–10, 33.

Rosenthal, R., & Rubin, D. B. (1982). A simple, general purpose display of magnitude of experimental effect. *Journal of Educational Psychology, 74,* 166–169.

Sarason, S. B., & Doris, J. (1979). *Educational handicap, public policy, and social history.* New York: Cambridge University Press.

Tarver, S. G., & Dawson, M. M. (1978). Modality preference and the teaching of reading: A review. *Journal of Learning Disabilities, 11,* 5–17.

U.S. Department of Education. (1999). Assistance to states for the education of children with disabilities program and the early intervention program for infants and toddlers with disabilities: Final regulations. *Federal Register, 64*(48), CFR Parts 300 and 303.

## APPENDIX A

Reported Effect Size were obtained from the following sources:

Adams, G. L., & Englemann, S. (1996). *Research on Direct Instruction: 25 years beyond DISTAR.* Seattle, WA: Educational Achievement Systems.

Ang, R. P., & Hughes, J. N. (2002). Differential benefits of skills training with antisocial youth based on group composition: A meta-analytic investigation. *School Psychology Review, 31,* 164–186.

Arnold, K. S., Myette, B. M., & Casto, G. (1986). Relationships of language intervention efficacy to certain subject characteristics in mentally retarded preschool children: A meta-analysis. *Education and Training of the Mentally Retarded, 21,* 108–116.

Beelman, A., Pfingsten, U., & Losel, F. (1994). Effects of training social competence in children: A metaanalysis of recent evaluation studies. *Journal of Clinical Psychology, 23,* 260–271.

Borman, G. D., Hewes, G. M., Overman, L. T., & Brown, S. (2002). *Comprehensive school reform and student achievement: A meta-analysis* (Report No. 59). Baltimore: Center for Research on Education of Students Paced At-Risk, Johns Hopkins University.

Browder, D. M., & Xin, Y. P. (1998). A meta-analysis and review of sight word research and its implications for teaching functional reading to individuals with moderate and severe disabilities. *Journal of Special Education, 32,* 130–153.

Burns, M. K. (2004). Empirical analysis of drill ratio research: Refining the instructional level for drill tasks. *Remedial and Special Education, 25,* 167–173.

Burns, M. K., & Symington, T. (2002). A meta-analysis of prereferral intervention teams: Student and systemic outcomes. *Journal of School Psychology, 40,* 437–447.

Carlberg, C., & Kavale, K. (1980). The efficacy of special versus regular class placement for exceptional children: A meta-analysis. *Journal of Special Education, 14,* 296–309.

Casto, G., & Mastropieri, M. A. (1986). The efficacy of early intervention programs: A meta-analysis. *Exceptional Children, 52,* 417–424.

Conners, F. A. (1992). Reading instruction for students with moderate mental retardation: Review and analysis of research. *American Journal on Mental Retardation, 96,* 577–597.

Cook, S. B., Scruggs, T. E., Mastropieri, M. A., & Casto, G. C. (1985–86). Handicapped students as tutors. *Journal of Special Education, 19,* 483–492.

Crenshaw, T. M., Kavale, K. A., Forness, S. R., & Reeve, R. E. (1999). Attention deficit hyperactivity disorder and the efficacy of stimulant medication: A meta-analysis. In T. E. Scruggs & M. A. Mastropieri (Eds.), *Advances in learning and behavioral disabilities* (Vol. 13, pp. 135–165). Stamford, CT: JAI Press.

de Castro, B., Veerman, J. W., Koops, W., Bosch, J. D., & Monshouwer, H. J. (2002). Hostile attribution of intent and aggressive behavior: A meta-analysis. *Child Development, 73,* 916–934.

Didden, R., Duker, P. C., & Karzilius, H. (1997). Meta-analytic study on treatment effectiveness for problem behaviors with individuals who have mental retardation. *American Journal on Mental Retardation, 101,* 387–399.

Dunn, R., Griggs, S. A., Olson, J., Beasley, A., & Gorman, B. S. (1995). A meta-analytic validation of the Dunn and Dunn model of learning style preferences. *Journal of Educational Research, 88,* 353–362.

Durlak, J. A., Fuhrman, J., & Lampman, C. (1991). Effectiveness of cognitive-behavior therapy for maladapting children: A meta-analysis. *Psychological Bulletin, 110,* 204–214.

Elbaum, B., Vaughn, S., Hughes, M., Moody, S. W., & Schumm, J. S. (2000). How reading outcomes of students with disabilities are related to instructional grouping formats: A meta-analytic review. In R. Gersten, E. Schiller, & S. Vaughn (Eds.), *Contemporary special education research* (pp. 105–135). Mahwah, NJ: Erlbaum.

Engles, G. I., Garnefski, N., & Diekstra, R. F. W. (1993). Efficacy of rational emotive therapy: A quantitative analysis. *Journal of Consulting and Clinical Psychology, 61,* 1083–1090.

Forness, S. R. (2001). Special education and related services: What have we learned from meta-analysis? *Exceptionality, 9,* 185–198.

Forness, S. R., & Kavale, K. A. (1993). Strategies to improve basic learning and memory deficits in mental retardation: A meta-analysis of experimental studies. *Education and Training in Mental Retardation, 28,* 99–110.

Forness, S. R., & Kavale, K. A. (1996). Treating social skill deficits in children with learning disabilities: A meta-analysis of the research. *Learning Disability Quarterly, 19,* 1–13.

Forness, S. R., Kavale, K. A., Blum, I. M., & Lloyd, J. W. (1997). Mega-analysis of meta-analysis: What works in special education and related services. *Teaching Exceptional Children, 29*(6), 4–9.

Fuchs, L. S., & Fuchs, D. (1986). Effects of systematic evaluation. A meta-analysis. *Exceptional Children, 53,* 199–208.

Gersten, R., & Baker, S. (2001). Teaching expressive writing to students with learning disabilities: A meta-analysis. *Elementary School Journal, 101,* 251–272.

Glass, G. V., & Smith, M. L. (1979). Meta-analysis of research on class size and achievement. *Educational Evaluation and Policy Analysis, 1,* 2–16.

Gonzalez, J. E., Nelson, J. R., Gutkin, T. B., Saunders, A., Galloway, A., & Shwery, G. S. (2004). Rational emotive therapy with children and adolescents: A meta-analysis. *Journal of Emotional and Behavioral Disorders, 12,* 222–235.

Gresham, F. M. (1998). Social skills training: Should we raze, remodel, or rebuild? *Behavioral Disorders, 24,* 19–25.

Gresham, F. M., Sugai, G., & Horner, R. H. (2001). Interpreting outcomes of social skills training for students with high-incidence disabilities. *Exceptional Children, 67,* 331–344.

Hedges, L. V., & Stock, W. A. (1983). The effects of class size: An examination of rival hypotheses. *American Educational Research Journal, 20,* 63–85.

Hillocks, G. (1984). What works in teaching composition: A meta-analysis of experimental treatment studies. *American Journal of Education, 93,* 133–170.

Horn, W. F., & Packard, T. (1985). Early identification of learning problems: A meta-analysis. *Journal of Educational Psychology, 77,* 597–607.

Innocenti, M. S., & White, K. R. (1993). Are more intensive early intervention programs more effective? A review of the literature. *Exceptionality, 4,* 31–50.

Joseph, L. M., & Scery, M. E. (2004). Where is the phonics? A review of the literature on the use of phonetic analysis with students with mental retardation. *Remedial and Special Education, 25,* 88–94.

Kavale, K. (1981a). Function of the Illinois Test of Psycholinguistic Abilities (ITPA). Are they trainable? *Exceptional Children, 47,* 496–510.

Kavale, K. (1982a). The efficacy of stimulant drug treatment for hyperactivity: A meta-analysis. *Journal of Learning Disabilities, 15,* 280–289.

Kavale, K. (1982c). Psycholinguistic training programs: Are there differential treatment effects? *The Exceptional Child, 29,* 21–30.

Kavale, K. A. (1984). A meta-analytic evaluation of the Frostig test and training program. *The Exceptional Child, 31,* 134–141.

Kavale, K. A. (1990). Variances and verities in learning disability interventions. In T. E. Scruggs & B. Y. L. Wong (Eds.), *Intervention research in learning disabilities* (pp. 3–33). New York: Springer-Verlag.

Kavale, K. A., & Dobbins, D. A. (1993). The equivocal nature of special education interventions. *Early Child Development and Care, 86,* 23–37.

Kavale, K. A., & Forness, S. R. (1983). Hyperactivity and diet treatment: A meta-analysis of the Feingold hypothesis. *Journal of Learning Disabilities, 16,* 324–330.

Kavale, K. A., & Forness, S. R. (1987). Substance over style: Assessing the efficacy of modality testing and teaching. *Exceptional Children, 54,* 228–239.

Kavale, K. A., & Forness, S. R. (2000). Policy decisions in special education: The role of analysis. In R. Gersten, E. Schiller, & S. Vaughn (Eds.), *Contemporary special education research* (pp. 281–326). Mahwah, NJ: Erlbaum.

Kavale, K. A., & Glass, G. V. (1982). The efficacy of special education interventions and practices: A compendium of meta-analysis findings. *Focus on Exceptional Children, 15*(4), 1–14.

Kavale, K. A., & Glass, G. V. (1984). Meta-analysis and policy decisions in special education. In B. K. Keogh (Ed.), *Advances in special education* (Vol. IV, pp. 195–247), Greenwich, CT: JAI.

Kavale, K. A., Mathur, S. R., Forness, R., Rutherford, R. B., & Quinn, M. M. (1997). Effectiveness of social skills training for students with behavior disorders: A meta-analysis. In T. E. Scruggs & M. A. Mastropieri (Eds.), *Advances in learning and behavioral disabilities* (pp. 1–28). New York: Elsevier.

Kavale, K. A., & Mattson, P. D. (1983). "One jumped off the balance beam": Meta-analysis of perceptual-motor training. *Journal of Learning Disabilities, 16,* 165–173.

Kroesbergen, E. H., & VanLuit, J. E. H. (2003). Mathematics interventions for children with special educational needs: A meta-analysis. *Remedial and Special Education, 24,* 97–114.

Lapadat, J. C. (1991). Pragmatic language skills of students with language and/or learning disabilities: A quantitative synthesis. *Journal of Learning Disabilities, 24,* 147–158.

Lipsey, M. W., & Wilson, D. B. (1993). The efficacy of psychological, educational, and behavioral treatment. *American Psychologist, 48,* 1181–1209.

Mastropieri, M. A., Bakken, J. P., & Scruggs, T. E. (1991). Mathematics instruction for individuals with mental retardation: A perspective and research synthesis. *Education and Training in Mental Retardation, 26,* 115–129.

Mastropieri, M. A., & Scruggs, T. E. (1985–86). Early intervention for socially withdrawn children. *Journal of Special Education, 19,* 429–441.

Mastropieri, M. A., Scruggs, T. E., & Casto, G. (1985). Early intervention for behaviorally disordered children: An integrative review. *Behavior Disorders Monograph, 11,* 27–35.

Mastropieri, M. A., Scruggs, T. E., & Casto, G. (1985–86). Early intervention for behaviorally disordered children: An integrative review [Monograph]. In R. B. Rutherford, Jr. (Ed.), *Monographs in behavior disorders* (pp. 27–35). Tempe, AZ: Council for Children with Behavior Disorders.

Mathur, S. R., Kavale, K. A., Quinn, M. M., Forness, S. R., & Rutherford, R. B. (1998). Social skills interventions with students with emotional and behavioral problems: A quantitative synthesis of single-subject research. *Behavioral Disorders, 23,* 193–201.

Niemiec, R., & Walberg, H. J. (1987). Comparative effects of computer-assisted instruction: A synthesis of reviews. *Journal of Educational Computing Research, 3,* 19–37.

Nye, C., Foster, S. H., & Seaman, D. (1987). Effectiveness of language intervention with the language/learning disabled. *Journal of Speech and Hearing Disorders, 52,* 348–357.

Quinn, M. M., Kavale, K. A., Mathur, S., Rutherford, R. B., & Forness, S. R. (1999). A meta-analysis of social skill interventions for students with emotional or behavioral disorders. *Journal of Emotional and Behavioral Disorders, 7,* 54–64.

Robinson, T. R., Smith, S. W., Miller, M. D., & Brownell, M. T. (1999). Cognitive behavior modification of hyperactivity-impulsivity and aggression: A meta-analysis of school-based studies. *Journal of Educational Psychology, 91,* 195–203.

Schmidt, M., Weinstein, T., Niemic, R., & Walberg, H. J. (1985–86). Computer-assisted instruction with exceptional children. *Journal of Special Education, 19,* 494–501.

Schumm, J. S., Moody, S. W., & Vaughn, S. (2000). Grouping for reading instruction: Does one size fit all? *Journal of Learning Disabilities, 33,* 477–488.

Scotti, J. R., Evans, I. M., Meyer, L. H., & Walker, P. (1991). A meta-analysis of intervention research with problem behavior: Treatment validity and standards of practice. *American Journal on Mental Retardation, 96,* 233–256.

Scruggs, T. E., Mastropieri, M. A., Cook, S., & Escobar, C. (1986). Early intervention for children with conduct disorders: A quantitative synthesis of single-subject research. *Behavioral Disorders, 11,* 260–271.

Scruggs, T. E., Mastropieri, M. A., Forness, S. R., & Kavale, K. A. (1988). Early language intervention: A quantitative synthesis of single-subject research. *Journal of Special Education, 22,* 259–283.

Shonkoff, J. P., & Hauser-Cram, P. (1987). Early intervention for disabled infants and their families: A quantitative analysis. *Pediatrics, 80,* 650–658.

Skiba, R. J., & Casey, A. (1985). Interventions for behaviorally disordered students: A quantitative review and methodological critique. *Behavioral Disorders, 10,* 239–252.

Smith, M. L., & Glass, G. V. (1980). Meta-analysis of research on class size and related estimators. *American Educational Research Journal, 17,* 419–433.

Smith, M. S., Glass, G. V., & Miller, T. I. (1980). *The benefits of psychotherapy.* Baltimore: Johns Hopkins University Press.

Soto, G., Toro-Zambrana, W., & Belfiore, P. J. (1994). Comparison of two instructional strategies on social skills acquisition and generalization among individuals with moderate and severe mental retardation working in a vocational setting: A meta-analytical review. *Education and Training in Mental Retardation and Developmental Disabilities, 29,* 307–320.

Swanson, H. L. (1999a). *Interventions for students with learning disabilities: A meta-analysis of treatment outcomes.* New York: Guilford.

Swanson, H. L. (1999b). Reading research for students with LD: A meta-analysis of intervention outcomes. *Journal of Learning Disabilities, 32,* 504–532.

Swanson, H. L. (2001). Research on interventions for adolescents with learning disabilities: A meta-analysis of outcomes related to higher-order processing. *Elementary School Journal, 101,* 331–348.

Swanson, H. L., Carson, C., & Sachsee-Lee, C. M. (1996). A selective synthesis of intervention research for students with learning disabilities. *School Psychology Review, 25,* 370–391.

Swanson, H. L., & Hoskyn, M. (1998). Experimental intervention research on students with learning disabilities: A meta-analysis of treatment outcomes. *Review of Educational Research, 68,* 277–321.

Swanson, H. L., & Hoskyn, M. (2000). Intervention research for students with learning disabilities: A comprehensive meta-analysis of group design studies. In T. E. Scruggs & M. A. Mastropieri (Eds.), *Advances in learning and behavioral disabilities* (Vol. 14, pp. 1–153). Stamford, CT: JAI Press.

Swanson, H. L., O'Shaughnessy, T. E., McMahon, C. M., Hoskyn, M., & Sachsee-Lee, C. M. (1998). A selective synthesis of single subject design intervention research on students with learning disabilities. In T. E. Scruggs & M. A. Mastropieri (Eds.), *Advances in learning and behavioral disabilities* (Vol. 12, pp. 79–126). Greenwich, CT: JAI Press.

Therrien, W. J. (2004). Fluency and comprehension gains as a result of repeated readings: A meta-analysis. *Remedial and Special Education, 25,* 252–261.

Thurber, S., & Walker, C. E. (1983). Medication and hyperactivity: A meta-analysis. *Journal of General Psychology, 108,* 79–86.

VanIjzendoorn, M. H., & Bus, A. G. (1994). Meta-analytic confirmation of the nonword reading deficit in developmental dyslexia. *Reading Research Quarterly, 29,* 267–275.

Vaughn, S., Gersten, R., & Chard, D. J. (2000). The underlying message in LD intervention research: Findings from research syntheses. *Exceptional Children, 67,* 99–114.

Walberg, H. J. (1984). Improving the productivity of America's schools. *Educational Leadership, 41,* 19–30.

Wang, M. C., & Baker, E. T. (1985–86). Mainstreaming programs: Design features and effects. *Journal of Special Education, 19,* 503–521.

Waxman, H. C., Wang, M. C., Anderson, K. A., & Walberg, H. J. (1985). Adaptive education and student outcomes: A quantitative synthesis. *Journal of Educational Research, 78,* 228–236.

Weisz, J. R., Weiss, B., Han, S. S., Granger, D. A., & Morton, T. (1995). Effects of psychotherapy with children and adolescents revisited: A meta-analysis of treatment outcome studies. *Psychological Bulletin, 117,* 450–468.

White, K. R. (1985–86). Efficacy of early interventions. *Journal of Special Education, 19,* 401–16.

White, W. A. T. (1988). A meta-analysis of the effects of direct instruction in special education. *Education and Treatment of Children, 11,* 364–374.

Whiteley, B. E., & Frieze, I. H. (1985). Children's causal attributions for success and failure in achievement settings: A meta-analysis. *Journal of Educational Psychology, 77,* 608–616.

Wilson, S. J., Lipsey, M. W., & Derzon, J. (2003). The effects on aggressive behavior: A meta-analysis. *Journal of Consulting and Clinical Psychology, 71,* 136–149.

Xin, Y. P., & Jitendra, A. K. (1999). The effects of instruction in solving mathematical word problems for students with learning problems: A meta-analysis. *Journal of Special Education, 32,* 207–225.

KENNETH A. KAVALE
*Regent University*

RESPONSE TO INTERVENTION
INDIVIDUALS WITH DISABILITIES EDUCATION
IMPROVEMENT ACT OF 2004 (IDEIA)

## EGBERT, ROBERT L. (1923–2001)

Robert L. Egbert obtained his BS and MS degrees from Utah State University, later earning his doctorate at Cornell University, Ithaca, New York. He was a full professor at the Center for Curriculum and Instruction of the University of Nebraska, Lincoln for 28 years and the college's dean from 1971–1982. He was a member of the boards of directors of the High/Scope Educational Research Foundation and American Association of Colleges for Teacher Education, and a director of the National Commission for Excellence in Teacher Education.

Used both regionally and nationally, his articles and reports have focused on improvement and change in teacher education (Egbert, 1971, 1974, 1985b). In 1985, he directed the preparation of the report, "A Call for Change in Teacher Education," and in February 1991, his paper presenting a history of project Head Start and the four phases of the Follow Through Program between 1967 and 1991 was featured in a conference sponsored by the U.S. Office of Educational Research and Improvement. As a leading expert in the field of education, he addressed the 1985 annual meeting of the American Association of Colleges for Teacher Education, delivering the Charles W. Hunt Lecture, "A Time for Beginnings."

A lifelong educator and a specialist in early childhood education, Egbert officially retired in 1999, but remained active in the college until shortly before his death, never ceasing to be a strong advocate for the teaching profession.

### REFERENCES

Egbert, R. L. (1971). Follow through. *National Elementary Principal, 51,* 104–109.

Egbert, R. L. (1974). Improving teacher education through the use of research information. *Journal of Teacher Education, 35*(4), 9–11.

Egbert, R. L. (1985a). *A call for change in teacher education.* National Commission for Excellence in Teacher Education.

Egbert, R. L. (1985b). The practice of preservice teacher education. *Journal of Teacher Education, 36,* 16–22.

Packard, S. (Ed.). (1985). *The leading edge: Innovation and change in professional education* (Report No. 0-89333-045-0). Alexandria, VA: AACTE.

Ramp, E. A., & Pederson, C. S. (Eds.). (1992). *Follow through: Program and policy issues* (EDD Publication No. 300-87-0114). Washington, DC: U.S. Government Printing Office.

ROBERTA C. STOKES
*Texas A&M University*
First edition

TAMARA J. MARTIN
*The University of Texas of the
Permian Basin*
Second edition

JESSI K. WHEATLEY
*Falcon School District 49,
Colorado Springs, Colorado*
Third edition

## EISENSON, JON (1907–2001)

Jon Eisenson received his BSS from the College of the City of New York in 1928. He earned both his MA in 1930 and his PhD in clinical psychology in 1935 from Columbia University. In his early years as a psychologist, he believed that understanding the nature of language, its relationship to thinking and learning, and how it is used and abused by humans was important to understanding the behavior of persons with or without disabilities.

His major fields of interest included language and the brain, aphasia, stuttering, dyslexia, and communication. Eisenson served as the assistant chief clinical psychologist in the United States War Department in 1944 and 1945 during World War II. For many years, his primary interests were the effects of brain damage on language behavior and developing techniques for recovery and reading problems, both congenital and acquired.

Eisenson's principal publications included *Aphasia in Children,* which addressed the problems of severely linguistically impaired children with aphasia, and *Communicative Disorders in Children,* written for professionals who wish to improve the communicative abilities of children with impairments severe enough to interfere with normal communication. Additional writings include *Adult Aphasia,* dealing with aphasia acquired as a result of disease or accident, *Reading for Meaning,* a psycholinguistic approach to the teaching of reading, *Is My Child's Speech Normal,* and *How To Speak American English.*

Eisenson was a fellow and past president of the American Speech and Hearing Association and the American Speech and Hearing Foundation.

Eisenson authored numerous articles and books, and was an experienced teacher and guest lecturer. In addition to his many professional pursuits, he wrote poetry for children and adults.

**REFERENCES**

Eisenson, J. (1984). *Adult aphasia* (2nd ed.). Englewood Cliffs, NJ: Prentice Hall.

Eisenson, J. (1984). *Language and speech disorders in children.* Elmsford, NY: Pergamon.

Eisenson, J. (1985). *My special zoo.* Tulsa, OK: Modern Education.

Eisenson, J. (1998). *Reading for meaning* (Rev. ed.). PRO-ED.

Eisenson, J., & Ogilvie, M. (1983). *Communication disorders* (5th ed.). New York: Macmillan.

TAMARA J. MARTIN
*The University of Texas of the
Permian Basin*

JESSI K. WHEATLEY
*Falcon School District 49,
Colorado Springs, Colorado*
Third edition

# ELABORATED v. RESTRICTED VERBAL CODES

The expressions "elaborated" and "restricted" code were introduced by the British sociologist Basil Bernstein in 1974 and were defined:

on a linguistic level, in terms of the probability predicting for any one speaker which syntactic elements will be used to organize meaning. In the case of an elaborated code, the speaker will select from a relatively extensive range of alternatives and therefore the probability of predicting the pattern of organizing elements is considerably reduced. In the case of a restricted code, the number of these alternatives is often severely limited and the probability of predicting the pattern is greatly increased. (pp. 76–77)

Bernstein hypothesized that these different codes were functions of different social structures. Comparisons of groups of middle-class and working-class children showed significant differences for grammatical and lexical features. Middle-class children used a significantly higher proportion of subordinations, complex verbal stems, the passive voice, uncommon adjectives, adverbs and conjunctions, and the pronoun I.

In later publications, Bernstein refined and extended his theory. A code was then said to be "a regulative principle controlling speech realizations in diverse social contexts" (Bernstein, 1974, p. 12). "Elaborated codes give access to universalistic orders of meaning, which are less context bound, whereas restricted codes give access to particularistic orders of meaning, which are far more context bound, that is, tied to a particular context" (p. 197).

The four contexts Bernstein cites are the regulative, instructional, imaginative, and interpersonal. In each of these contexts, speech variants can be observed that are characteristically elaborated or restricted (codes cannot be observed because they belong to the deep structure of communication). The variants are elaborated if they appear to be selected from a wide range of syntactic alternatives that can be used in various contexts (universality); they are restricted if they are chosen from a much more limited, therefore more predictable, number of possibilities. The distinction between speech variants and codes is important because elaborated speech variants can appear in elaborated and restricted codes, as can restricted variants. What distinguishes the codes is the relative frequency of the two types of variants in both codes.

As social roles are first learned in the family, the way socialization occurs is of crucial importance for the development of one or the other coding activity. Bernstein distinguished two kinds of families. Person-oriented families, in which the child learns to play his or her part among the other members of the family, are more likely to endow a child with an elaborated code. The child growing up in a positional family, in which roles are preestablished, is less likely to learn to adapt his or her language to that of interlocutors and, as a consequence, is more likely to build up a restricted code.

Bernstein insists that a restricted code is not in itself inferior to an elaborated code. The main problem for working-class children belonging to families that seem to be predominantly of the positional type is that their restricted code will constitute a severe handicap when they go to school. "For the schools are predicated on elaborated code and its system of social relationships. Although an elaborated code does not entail any specific value system, the value system of the middle class penetrates the texture of the very learning context itself" (Bernstein, 1974, p. 186).

Bernstein was criticized, on the one hand, for the vagueness of his definitions and the crudeness of the linguistic distinctions he operated with, and on the other hand, for having given scientific support to the theory of linguistic deprivation (Labov, 1970) and eventually to compensatory education programs (Bereiter & Engelmann, 1966). The latter criticism does not seem to be justified, as it ignores the evolution in Bernstein's ideas after 1962.

## REFERENCES

Bereiter, G., & Engelmann, S. (1966). *Teaching disadvantaged children in the pre-school.* Englewood Cliffs, NJ: Prentice Hall.

Bernstein, B. (1974). *Class, codes and control* (Vol. 1). London: Routledge & Kegan Paul.

Dittmar, N. (1973). *Sociolinguistics. A critical survey of theory and application.* London: Arnold.

Labov, W. (1970). The logic of non-standard English. In J. Alatis (Ed.), *Report of the 20th Annual Round Table Meeting on Linguistics and Language Studies.* Washington, DC: Georgetown University Press.

S. De Vriendt
*Vrije Universiteit Brussels,
Brussels, Belgium*

**EXPRESSIVE LANGUAGE DISORDERS
LANGUAGE DELAYS
LANGUAGE DISORERS**

# ELAVIL

Elavil is the trade name for the generic tricyclic antidepressant amitriptyline. Elavil and other tricyclic antidepressants (TCA) usually are prescribed for endogenous depressions. These are affective disorders that present with vegetative disturbance (i.e., psychomotor slowing, poor appetite/weight loss, loss of sexual interest) and usually cannot be ascribed to a situational cause. Persons with endogenous depression often have positive familial histories for an affective disorder.

Therapeutically, TCAs are intended to reduce symptom intensity, increase mood elevation and physical activity, reestablish appetite and sleep patterns, and, in general, facilitate activity levels that will promote social adjustment (Blum, 1984). Such effects are assumed to be a result of TCA's blocking brain amine re-uptake, thus making more of the various catecholamines available at their specific receptor sites (Seiden & Dykstra, 1977).

Elavil differs from other TCAs in that it tends to produce greater sedation and a greater degree of anticholinergic side effects: visual blurring, urinary retention, constipation, concentration difficulties (Katzung, 1982). The TCAs are not often used in the treatment of children, because children appear to be more at risk for cardiovascular side effects and seizure-facilitating side effects of high doses (Blum, 1984). However, in titrated doses, TCAs have been used to treat enuresis and severe obsessive-compulsive disorders in children (Detre & Jarecki, 1971). In the 1990s, widespread use of TCAs was curtailed in favor of the SSRIs, selective serotonin reuptake inhibitors, such as Prozac. It is not recommended for children under 12 years (Fletcher-Janzen & Williams, 2005).

## REFERENCES

Blum, K. (1984). *Handbook of abusable drugs.* New York: Gardner Press.

Detre, T. P., & Jarecki, G. H. (1971). *Modern psychiatric treatment.* Philadelphia: Lippincott.

Fletcher-Janzen, E., & Williams, J. (2005). Medications and the special education student. In E. Fletcher-Janzen & C. R. Reynolds (Eds.), *Special education almanac* (pp. 405–480). New York: Wiley.

Katzung, B. G. (1982). *Basic and clinical pharmacology.* Los Altos, CA: Lange Medical.

Seiden, L. S., & Dykstra, L. A. (1977). *Psychopharmacology: A biochemical and behavioral approach.* New York: Van Nostrand Reinhold.

Robert F. Sawicki
*Lake Erie Institute of
Rehabilitation*

**DOPAMINE
HALDOL
TRANQUILIZERS**

# ELECTIVE MUTISM

Elective mutism (now commonly referred to as selective mutism) is a disorder of infancy, childhood, and adolescence that consists of a child's consistent failure to speak in certain social situations, in which there is an expectation for speaking, despite speaking in other situations (*Diagnostic and Statistical Manual of Mental Disorders,* fourth edition, text revision [*DSM-IV-TR*], American Psychiatric Association, 2002). The Classification of Mental and Behaviour Disorder: Clinical Description and Diagnostic Guidelines (ICD-10; World Health Organization, 1992) defines elective mutism as a condition characterized by a marked, emotionally determined selectivity in speaking, such that the child demonstrates a language competence in some situations but fails to speak in other (definable) situations.

The disorder usually is associated with marked personality features involving social anxiety, withdrawal, sensitivity, or resistance. Onset usually occurs during the preschool years, before age 5. Characteristics associated with elective mutism include shyness, anxiety, fear of social embarrassment, social isolation, withdrawal, dependency upon parents, negative controlling personality, oppositional behavior, Enuresis, Encopresis, depression, separation anxiety, and language dysfunction (Black & Uhde, 1995; Dummit, Klein, Tancer, Asche, & Martin, 1996; Schum, 2002; Tatem & DelCampo, 1995).

Elective mutism occurs in less than 1 percent of the population (Ford et al., 1998; Powell & Dalley, 1995; Tatem & DelCampo, 1995). This prevalence rate is the same for the school age as well as the general population. Elective mutism occurs more often in females than males, with sex ratio estimates ranging from 1.6:1 to 2:1 (Anstendig, 1998; Tatem & DelCampo, 1995).

Etiology of elective mutism is largely unknown. Theories about what causes elective mutism have focused on individual or family dynamics, anxiety, overprotection, developmental language and speech disorders, Mild Mental Retardation, immigration, hospitalization or trauma before age 3, and extreme shyness or anxiety disorders (Ford, Sladeczek, Carlson, & Kratochwill, 1998; Joseph, 1999; Tatem & DelCampo, 1995).

A diagnosis of selective mutism (elective mutism) must include the absence of speech that interferes with educational or occupational achievement or with social communication, that lasts at least 1 month (not limited to the first month of school), is not due to a lack of knowledge of or comfort with the spoken language required in the social situation, is not better accounted for by a communication disorder, and does not occur exclusively during the course of a Pervasive Developmental Disorder, Schizophrenia, or other Psychotic Disorder (*DSM-IV-TR*, American Psychiatric Association, 2002).

Guidelines exist for a two-part assessment of elective mutism (Dow, Sonies, Scheib, Moss, & Leonard, 1995). A parental interview should occur first. It should provide a description of the child's symptom history, whether the child is verbally and nonverbally inhibited, the child's academic and medical history, family history, and an informal evaluation of speech and language ability. A child interview should be made, using nonverbal means (e.g., observation, play therapy) to allow for direct observation of the severity and nature of the child's mutism. During this interview the child can respond to questions by using puppets, pantomime, or writing, if he or she is old enough. In addition, physical examination is necessary to rule out any medical problems. Auditory testing as well as a speech and language evaluation should be completed to ensure that the elective mutism is not due to hearing or receptive and/or expressive language difficulties. Finally, standardized psychological nonverbal tests should be used to acquire an understanding of the child's cognitive abilities.

Elective mutism often is highly resistant to treatment (Kehle, Madaus, Baratta, & Bray, 1998). Effective treatments of elective mutism may occur through several modalities, including family systems therapy, behavioral interventions, psychopharmacological interventions, and individual psychotherapy (Anstendig, 1998).

The family treatment approach views elective mutism as a result of inadequate familial relationships characterized by heightened dependence and ambivalence coupled with an excessive need to control. Families with electively mute children are characterized by intense attachments, interdependency, fear and distrust of the outside world, fear and distrust of strangers, language and cultural assimilation difficulties, marital disharmony, and withholding of speech by one or more of the parents in the home. The child's mutism is a way to keep family secrets and withhold involvement with his/her outside environment (Anstendig, 1998). Interventions are designed to help the problematic dynamics of the family by modifying the communication and interaction patterns within the family unit.

Behavioral treatment approaches views elective mutism as a learned response in which the refusal to speak is a method for manipulating the environment. The behavioral approach also views the child's silence as functional in an environment that helps to create and maintain this way of interacting. Behavioral approaches include contingency management, positive reinforcement, shaping, stimulus fading, escape-avoidance, self-modeling techniques, labeling and functional language, and social-psychological functions of reward. Interventions begin with an in-depth analysis of the nonverbal behavior, including an ecological analysis to examine cues in the environment that help him/her unlearn this way of operating (Anstendig, 1998). Multimethod interventions, where a combination of techniques serves to address different aspects of the child's mutism, work best (Anstendig, 1998; Watson & Kramer, 1992). The main goal of behavioral interventions is to extinguish all reinforcement for the child's mutism (Dow et al., 1995).

Psychopharmacological treatments view elective mutism as a variant of an anxiety disorder (i.e., a social phobia; Anstendig, 1998). The main intervention is the use of medication (fluoxetine [Prozac], phenelzine, fluvoxamine) alone or in combination with other interventions. Psychopharmacological treatments are effective in eliminating the disorder. However, whether psychopharmacological treatments can be generalized to all children with elective mutism or only those who are electively mute and anxiety disordered is unclear (Anstendig, 1998).

Psychodynamic methods view elective mutism as a symptom of a severe underlying intrapsychic conflict related to psychotic spectrum disorders or part of another specific disorder of childhood (e.g., stranger anxiety, selective attention,

Dissociative Identity Disorder; Anstendig, 1998). Consistent with psychodynamic approaches to therapy, verbal interactions, art, or play typically are used.

Various school interventions may be helpful, including involving the child with peers in various activities, promoting more spontaneity in behavior, and watching for opportunities to reinforce small improvements (Schum, 2002).

If not treated, elective mutism will likely go away as the child gets older because it becomes increasingly more difficult to function without speaking. Children usually become more comfortable in their surroundings and begin to realize that they must speak in order to get what they want. However, the longer elective mutism persists, the more resistant it becomes to intervention (Kehle et al., 1998). Also, some individuals with a history of elective mutism continue to experience social anxiety later in life (Bergman et al., 2002). After elective mutism is treated, expressive language delays may become obvious because a child did not speak during critical periods of language development. Thus, language intervention may be needed.

## REFERENCES

American Psychiatric Association. (2000). *Diagnostic and statistical manual of mental health disorders* (4th ed., text revision). Washington, DC: Author.

Anstendig, K. (1998). Selective mutism: A review of the treatment literature by modality from 1980–1996. *Psychotherapy, 35*(3), 381–391.

Bergman, L. R., Piacentini, J., & McCracken, J. T. (2002). Prevalence and description of selective mutism in a school-based sample. *Journal of the American Academy of Child and Adolescent Psychiatry, 41*(8), 938–946.

Black, B., & Uhde, T. W. (1995). Psychiatric characteristics of children with selective mutism: A pilot study. *Journal of the American Academy of Child and Adolescent Psychiatry, 34*(7), 847–857.

Dow, S. P., Sonies, B. C., Scheib, D., Moss, S. E., & Leonard, H. L. (1995). Practical guidelines for the assessment and treatment of selective mutism. *Journal of the American Academy of Child and Adolescent Psychiatry, 34*(7), 836–846.

Dummit, E. S., III., Klein, R. G., Tancer, N. K., Asche, B., & Martin, J. (1996). Flouxetine treatment of children with selective mutism: An open trial. *Journal of the American Academy of Child and Adolescent Psychiatry, 35*(5), 15–21.

Ford, M. A., Sladeczek, I. E., Carlson, J., & Kratochwill, T. R. (1998). Selective mutism: Phenomenological characteristics. *School Psychology Quarterly, 13*(3), 192–227.

Joseph, P. R. (1999). Selective mutism: The child who doesn't speak. *Pediatrics, 104,* 308.

Kehle, T. J., Madaus, M. R., Baratta, V. S., & Bray, M. A. (1998). Augmented self-modeling as a treatment for children with selective mutism. *Journal of School Psychology, 36*(3), 247–260.

Powell, S., & Dalley, M. (1995). When to intervene in selective mutism: The multimodal treatment case of persistent selective mutism. *Psychology in the Schools, 32,* 114–123.

Schum, R. L. (2002). Selective mutism: An integrated treatment approach. *ASHA Leader, 7,* 4–6.

Sheridan, S. M., Kratochwill, T. R., & Ramirez, S. Z. (1995). Assessment and treatment of selective mutism: Recommendations and a case study. *Special Services in the Schools, 10*(1), 55–78.

Tatem, D. W., & DelCampo, R. L. (1995). Selective mutism in children: A structure family therapy approach to treatment. *Contemporary Family Therapy, 17*(2), 177–194.

Watson, S. T., & Kramer, J. J. (1992). Multimethod behavioral treatment of long-term selective mutism. *Psychology in the Schools, 29,* 359–366.

World Health Organization (WHO). (1992). *Classification of mental and behaviour disorder: Clinical description and diagnostic guidelines (ICD-10).* Geneva: Author.

KATRINA RAIA
*University of Florida*

## LANGUAGE DISORDERS

# ELECTROENCEPHALOGRAPH

An electroencephalograph is a machine that is used to measure the electrical activity of the brain. Fluctuations in brain electrical activity are recorded by electrodes attached to the scalp. The placement of the electrodes has been standardized for clinical use and is accepted internationally (Jasper, 1958). The potentials of the brain are shown on paper in a record called an electroencephalogram (EEG). The amplitude of the brain's electrical activity is small; it is measured in microvolts (millionths of a volt) and must be amplified by the electroencephalograph. The fluctuations in voltage that appear on the EEG have a fairly rhythmic character. The wavelike patterns that are produced will vary with the brain region being recorded as well as with the age and state of alertness of the patient.

The primary information in the EEG is its frequency, which varies from 0.5 to 60 Hz (cycles per second). Attempts have been made to provide rough categories for the classification of frequency. The characteristic pattern for adults in the waking state is dominated by the so-called alpha frequencies, a roughly sinusoidal shape pattern ranging from 8 to 12.5 Hz. Current usage usually identifies five frequency bands that are used in both clinical practice and research, particularly sleep research: delta, 0.5–4 Hz; theta, 4–8 Hz; alpha, 8–13 Hz; beta 1, 13–20 Hz; and beta 2, 20–40 Hz (Greenfield & Sternbach, 1972).

As a general rule, it is possible to predict what sort of brain wave pattern an individual will produce in the absence of brain damage. Variations from expected patterns can constitute a basis for postulating impaired brain functioning. Lewinsohn (1973) notes that the major pathologic changes include waves that are too fast, too slow, or too flat, with all of these conditions being either focal or diffuse.

A major limitation of the EEG is that normal-appearing

records may be obtained in the presence of clear-cut evidence of severe organic brain disease (Chusid, 1976). Additionally, about 15 to 20 percent of the normal population produce abnormal EEG recordings (Mayo Clinic, 1976). Diagnostically, EEGs have been found to be about 60 percent accurate (Filskov & Goldstein, 1974). EEGs have proven most useful in the diagnosis of seizure disorders (Camfield & Camfield, 1999).

## REFERENCES

Camfield, P. R., & Camfield, C. S. (1999). Pediatric epilepsy: An overview. In K. F. Swaiman & S. Ashwal (Eds.), *Pediatric neurology* (pp. 629–633). St. Louis, MO: Mosby.

Chusid, J. G. (1976). *Correlative neuroanatomy and functional neurology.* Los Altos, CA: Lange Medical Publications.

Filskov, S. B., & Goldstein, S. G. (1974). Diagnostic validity of the Halstead-Reitan Neuropsychological Battery. *Journal of Consulting & Clinical Psychology, 42,* 382–388.

Greenfield, N. S., & Sternbach, R. A. (1972). *Handbook of psychophysiology.* New York: Holt, Rinehart & Winston.

Jasper, H. H. (1958). The ten twenty electrode system of the International Federation. *Electroencephalography & Clinical Neurophysiology, 10,* 371–375.

Lewinsohn, P. M. (1973). *Psychological assessment of patients with brain injury.* Washington, DC: Division of Research, Department of Health, Education and Welfare.

Mayo Clinic. (1976). *Clinical examinations in neurology.* Philadelphia: Saunders.

RICHARD A. BERG
*West Virginia University
Medical Center, Charleston
Division*

ABSENCE SEIZURES
EEG ABNORMALITIES
EPILEPSY
GRAND MAL SEIZURES

## ELECTROENCEPHALOGRAPHY (EEG) BIOFEEDBACK

Electroencephalography (EEG) biofeedback is a learning strategy that enables individuals to alter brain wave activity and theoretically then alter behavior or emotions (see Biofeedback). EEG biofeedback is a painless, noninvasive procedure typically measuring six electrical signals in the brain: alpha, beta, theta, delta, SMR, and high beta. Researchers have demonstrated that individuals with certain conditions, including those related to psychiatric illness, typically exhibit atypical patterns of electrical activity in the brain often measured as ratio differences between certain brain waves at certain parts of the brain (e.g., theta/beta ratio in the right pre-frontal cortex). EEG biofeedback has become particularly popular for the evaluation and treatment

of Attention Deficit-Hyperactivity Disorder (ADHD) despite absence of strong scientific support. Electrophysiological measures were among the first to be used to study brain processes among children with ADHD. These measures have been used both in research to describe and quantify the neurophysiology of ADHD and also in the clinical assessment, diagnosis, and treatment. Early EEG studies found that children with ADHD exhibited abnormalities such as excess slow-wave activity and eleptiform spike and wave activity. These findings were interpreted as indicating abnormal brain processes among children with ADHD, specifically a maturational delay marked by underarousal. Proponents of the condition promise success rates of 90 percent absent well-accepted, supportive scientific literature. Proponents of this treatment suggest that the treatment represents a learning process and results are seen gradually over time. Proponents of EEG biofeedback promise success rates of 90 percent in treating ADHD and other conditions absent well-accepted, supportive scientific literature. Twenty to 40 sessions are recommended for most conditions at a rate of 2 or more sessions per week.

SAM GOLDSTEIN
*University of Utah*

## ELECTRONIC TRAVEL AIDS

Blind persons who travel independently rely on essentially three kinds of travel aids: long canes, dog guides, and electronic travel aids. Electronic travel aids serve as guidance devices that extend the range of perception of the environment beyond the fingertip, tip of the long cane, or handle of the dog guide's harness. These sensory aids enable the blind person to determine the approximate elevation, dimensions, azimuth, and possibly surface texture of objects detected within the range that the ultrasonic or electromagnetic waves penetrate. Information put out as auditory sounds or tactile vibrations permits the user to decide whether to avoid direct contact with the source of the signal, make contact with it, or simply use it as a reference point for orientation and navigation purposes.

Of the four most commonly used electronic travel aids, three are considered secondary aids that complement and enrich information received from the long cane or dog guide. The Russell Pathsounder is a small battery-operated unit that can be mounted on the user's chest. The unit emits ultrasonic waves that penetrate the area in front of the unit to a distance of 6 ft. If the invisible waves hit an object and produce an echo picked up by the receiver in the unit, then an auditory and/or vibrating signal is triggered. The chest unit vibrates until the object appears in the inner protection zone less than inches from the traveler's chest. Once within that zone, the vibrator in the back of the neck strap is activated to signal the closer proximity. The auditory warning signal is a buzzing sound that switches to a high-pitched beep when objects enter the inner protection zone. The Pathsounder can supplement the long cane by protecting the upper body. Wheelchair users also find the device helpful (Farmer, 1980).

The Sonicguide developed in New Zealand is another secondary aid that provides protection for the vulnerable area between the knees and the head. The unit emits pulses of ultrasonic waves from a source mounted in eyeglass frames. The pitch of the sound represents distance from an object within a 20-ft range; the stereophonic effect reveals location to the left or right of the head direction; and the sound quality or timbre suggests characteristics of the surface texture (Mellor, 1981).

The Mowat Sensor is a small hand-held sonar device that can be used to detect landmarks, openings, and specific objects like bus stop signs or water fountains. The Mowat Sensor has two ranges of operation extending to 13 ft. When an object appears within range, the entire unit vibrates at a rate related to the distance of the object (Farmer, 1980).

The LASER (light amplification by stimulated emission of radiation) cane is considered both a primary and secondary aid. It is an adaptation of the long cane with three built-in laser sources that send out beams of infra red light in three directions. The beams are only 1 in. wide at 10 ft from the source to permit rather precise location of objects. The upward beam detects objects in line with the head, the forward beam locates objects in the direct line of travel, and the downward beam picks up drop-offs such as curbs or stairs (Farmer, 1980). For a more detailed discussion of mobility aids in general and electronic travel aids in particular, see Farmer's chapter on mobility devices in Welsh and Blasch (1980) and Yen (2006).

**REFERENCES**

Farmer, L. (1980). Mobility devices. In R. Welsh & B. Blasch (Eds.), *Foundations of orientation and mobility.* New York: American Foundation for the Blind.

Mellor, C. M. (1981). *Aids for the 80's: What they are and what they do.* New York: American Foundation for the Blind.

Yen, Duen Hsi. (2006). *Electronic travel aids for the blind.* Retrieved March 8, 2006, from http://www.noogenesis.com

MARJORIE E. WARD
*The Ohio State University*

**MOBILITY INSTRUCTION**
**VISION TRAINING**

# ELEMENTARY AND SECONDARY EDUCATION ACT

The Elementary and Secondary Education Act of 1965 (ESEA; PL 89-10) included the first major program of fed-

eral assistance to local school districts (Eidenberg & Morey, 1969). Title I of ESEA, amended and renamed Chapter 1 of the Education Consolidation and Improvement Act (ECIA) in 1981, provided federal grants through states to school districts based on the number of children from families in poverty. The grants were to provide compensatory education services to educationally deprived children. Children were determined to be eligible for services based not on family income but on local determination, within federal guidelines, that they were educationally disadvantaged.

Also included in this statute is the authorization for the Chapter 1 state agency program for handicapped children in state-operated or state-supported schools. Grants are made to the states to provide supplementary educational services based on the number of handicapped children in such programs. This authority predated the Education for All Handicapped Children Act (PL 94-142) and was aimed primarily at children in institutional settings. Children served in Chapter 1 state agency programs were subject to all the requirements of IDEA. For purposes of federal reimbursement, however, a child with disabilities could be counted in either the Chapter 1 state agency grant (250,000 children in December 1984) or in the IDEA state grant (4.1 million children in December 1984), but not both.

In 2001, the Federal government passed the No Child Left Behind Act (NCLB), which significantly amends the ESEA to implement many of the educational reforms proposed by President George W. Bush. Although the relevant statutory provisions in the U.S. Code (a compilation of all federal statutes currently in force) are still technically referred to as the ESEA, the statute has been changed substantially as a result of NCLB. For a full discussion of these changes, please see the entry entitled "No Child Left Behind Act" in this encyclopedia.

**REFERENCES**

Eidenberg, E., & Morey, R. (1969). *An act of congress.* New York: Norton.

Rehab Group. (1979). *Assessment of educational programs in state-supported and state-operated agencies.* Falls Church, VA: Author.

Riddle, W. (1985). *Elementary and Secondary Education Act: A condensed history of the original law and major amendments.* Washington, DC: Congressional Research Service.

JAMES R. RICCIUTI
*United States Office of
Management and Budget*
Second edition

KIMBERLY F. APPLEQUIST
*University of Colorado at
Colorado Springs*
Third edition

## THE ELEPHANT MAN

Renowned in both late Victorian England during his lifetime and contemporarily more by his "professional name," the "Elephant Man," than his real one, Joseph Carey Merrick has been fascinating to both professionals and the public for over 100 years. First brought to recent attention by Ashley Montagu (1972) in his biography, *The Elephant Man: A Study in Human Dignity,* Merrick has been the subject of at least one other biography (Howell & Ford, 1980), a successful play and subsequent movie, and numerous professional and popular articles. Howell and Ford's book not only contains a detailed biography, but many photographs and drawings, contemporary accounts, and Merrick's autobiography, which serve as the sources for this entry.

Merrick may well as an adult have been the "ugliest man in the world," as he was frequently called. Born normal to lower-class parents in Leicester, England in 1860, Merrick began to develop deformities in the head, limbs, and back such that regular employment became impossible, although he held several jobs for a short time in early adulthood. His mother died when he was young, and his father virtually abandoned him when he remarried. Unable otherwise to make a living, Merrick allowed himself for many years to be exhibited as a sideshow freak as the "Elephant Man." When a London physician, Frederick Treves, saw him in Whitechapel, he left Merrick one of his cards. When the show was closed in England as an affront to human decency, Merrick and a manager went to Belgium, where the manager abandoned him when the show was again pursued by police. Merrick, with money gained by pawning some possessions, made his way back to London. This time, he was pursued and jeered by curious crowds. Finally, he ended up at London Hospital where Treves worked. After some difficulty. Treves arranged for a room to be furnished in the hospital, where Merrick spent most of the rest of his life.

Treves at first thought Merrick was retarded, but found that he was intelligent, and perhaps surprising given his years of mistreatment, sensitive, friendly, and sociable. Indeed, he became a society celebrity, and was visited by many notables, including the Prince and Princess of Wales and the Duke of Cambridge in 1887. Visitors frequently brought small gifts, which Merrick treasured. His head was so large that he could only sleep with his head between his knees. Unfortunately, his condition became progressively more serious and debilitating. He was found dead in his room, lying flat on his bed, on April 11, 1890. Treves suggested that he had tried to rest more like normal people and had lain down. Pressure from the weight of his head suffocated him. The *London Times* published an announcement of his death.

How ugly was he? Perhaps his own words serve best:

> The measurement around my head is 36 inches, there is a large substance of flesh at the back as large as a breakfast cup, the other part in a manner of speaking is like hills and valleys, all lumped together, while the face is such a sight that no one could describe it. The right hand is almost the size and shape of an Elephant's fore-leg, measuring 12 inches round the wrist and 5 inches round one of the fingers; the other hand and arm is no larger than that of a girl 10 years of age, although it is well proportioned. My feet and legs are covered with thick lumpy skin, also my body, like that of an Elephant, and almost the same colour, in fact, no one would believe until they saw it, that such a thing could exist. (Howell & Ford, 1980, p. 168)

What caused his deformities? He thought that he knew. Again in his words:

> The deformity which I am now exhibiting was caused by my mother being frightened by an Elephant; my mother was going along the street when a procession of animals were passing by, there was a terrible crush of people to see them, and unfortunately she was pushed under which frightened her very much; this occurring during a time of pregnancy was the cause of my deformity. (Howell & Ford, 1980, p. 168)

But, however popular such explanations were at the time, he was, of course, wrong. Treves had viewed the disorder as being congenital, but neither he nor anyone else at the time could suggest a specific disorder. However, as early as 1909, a diagnosis of neurofibromatosis was suggested. Now known to be a single-gene dominant disorder, it is a likely candidate since many of the symptoms fit with Merrick's condition and it frequently arises through spontaneous mutation. The most characteristic manifestation is neurofibromas, masses of tumors comprised of densely packed nerve and fibrous tissue. Common also are patches of darkened skin, termed café au lait spots. Recently, however, alternatives have been suggested, most notably Proteus syndrome. Proteus is characterized by "macrocephaly, hyperostosis of the skull; hypertrophy of long bones; and thickened skin and subcutaneous tissues, particularly of the hands and feet, including plantar hyperplasia, lipomas, and other unspecified subcutaneous masses" (Tibbles & Cohen, 1986, p. 683). Over a hundred years after his death, Joseph Merrick indeed remains a subject of fascination.

### REFERENCES

Howell, M., & Ford, P. (1980). *The true history of the elephant man.* London: Allison & Busby.

Montagu, A. (1972). *The elephant man: A study in human dignity.* New York: Outerbridge & Dienstfrey.

Tibbles, J. A., & Cohen, M. M., Jr. (1986). The Proteus syndrome: The Elephant Man diagnosed. *British Medical Journal (Clinical Research Edition), 293,* 683–685.

ROBERT T. BROWN
*University of North Carolina at Wilmington*

## ELLIS, NORMAN R. (1924–    )

Norman R. Ellis, born in Springville, Alabama, September 14, 1924, is known for his theoretical work on mental retardation, for research on memory and learning by persons with mental retardation, and for editing major works on mental retardation. He is a major proponent of the difference or deficit theory, which proposes that people with mental retardation have mental processes that are in some ways qualitatively different from those of persons with normal intelligence. From this model, it follows that the goal of research should be to discover and study those processes that predict differences in intellectual ability. In the area of research, Ellis is credited with formulating the stimulus trace deficit theory, which states that short-term memory deficits of subjects who are mentally retarded are due to rapid deterioration of stimulus traces in the brain. He also proposed a three-stage model of memory: primary memory, secondary memory, and tertiary memory (Borkowski, Peck, & Damberg, 1983; Determan, 1983). Ellis is editor of major works on mental retardation, including two editions of the *Handbook in Mental Deficiency* (1963, 1979) and 13 volumes of *International Review of Research in Mental Retardation* (1966–1986). He is the author of nearly 100 scholarly articles, including "Further Evidence for Cognitive Inertia of Persons with Mental Retardation," a study examining postpractice interference effects in naming colors of Stroop words (Ellis & Dulaney, 1991), and "Automatized Responding and Cognitive Inertia in Individuals with Mental Retardation," research providing some support for age-related inherent structural differences leading to greater rigidity in older adults (Dulaney & Ellis, 1994).

Ellis received his BA degree in 1951 from Howard College, an MA in general experimental psychology from the University of Alabama in 1952, and a PhD from Louisiana State University in 1956 in general experimental psychology. He is professor of psychology and director of the doctoral training program in mental retardation and developmental disabilities, University of Alabama. He previously held positions at George Peabody College, Louisiana State University, and State Colony and Training School, Pineville, Louisiana.

Ellis is a fellow of the American Association on Mental Retardation and American Psychological Association. He received the American Association on Mental Retardation

Award for Outstanding Research in 1972 and the Edgar A. Doll Award for Outstanding Research from the American Psychological Association in 1986. He has received numerous awards from the University of Alabama. He is listed in the twelfth edition of *American Men and Women in Science.*

### REFERENCES

Borkowski, J. G., Peck, V. A., & Damberg, P. R. (1983). Attention, memory, and cognition. In J. L. Matson & J. A. Mulick (Eds.), *Handbook of mental retardation* (pp. 479–497). New York: Pergamon.

Determan, K. D. (1983). Some trends in research design. In J. L. Matson & J. A. Mulick (Eds.), *Handbook of mental retardation* (pp. 527–539). New York: Pergamon.

Dulaney, C. L., & Ellis, N. R. (1994). Automatized responding and cognitive inertia in individuals with mental retardation. *American Journal on Mental Retardation, 99*(1), 8–18.

Ellis, N. R., & Dulaney, C. L. (1991). Further evidence for cognitive inertia of persons with mental retardation. *American Journal on Mental Retardation, 95*(6), 13–21.

ELEANOR BOYD WRIGHT
*University of North Carolina at Wilmington*

## ELWYN INSTITUTES

Elwyn Institutes was founded in 1852. It is located on a 400-acre campus near Media, Pennsylvania. It is a comprehensive service facility, and it provides day and residential programs for children and adults who are learning disabled, developmentally delayed, retarded, deaf/blind, neurologically disabled, brain damaged, visually impaired, physically disabled, deaf, hard of hearing, or multidisabled and deaf.

Elwyn Institutes' continuum of services features rehabilitation programs that coordinate residential and community living arrangements with special education, vocational training, and sequential programs that lead to independence in the community. Students in residence live in modern living accommodations on campus and in apartments within the local communities.

Elwyn Institutes maintains programs in Philadelphia; Wilmington, Delaware; Fountain Valley, California; and Israel. Management and administrative supervision is provided at the American Institute for Mental Studies, also known as the Vineland Training School, in Vineland, New Jersey.

Elwyn Institutes' educational programs are offered to students with day and residential accommodations from preschool years through to 21 years. These programs provide a wide range of educational services, including comprehensive evaluations, preschool programs, daycare facilities, and elementary and secondary levels of education and training. Ancillary services include audiological evaluations, speech and language therapy, mobility training, occupational therapy, psychiatric and psychological services, and medical and dental care.

Elwyn Institutes is located at 111 Elwyn Road, Elwyn, PA 19063.

## REFERENCE

Sargent, J. K. (1982). *The directory for exceptional children* (9th ed.). Boston: Porter Sargent.

PAUL C. RICHARDSON
*Elwyn Institutes*

## EMBEDDED FIGURES TEST

The Embedded Figures Test (EFT; Witkin, 1950) is an individually administered test designed to measure field dependence-independence. Field-independent individuals are able to locate the previously viewed geometric figure within the larger figure more quickly than field-dependent individuals. It consists of 16 simple straight line figures to be traced within a larger, more complex figure. This test is designed for individuals 12:0 and older, while the Children's EFT is for ages 5:0 through 11:0, and the Preschool EFT is for ages 3:0 through 5:0. A group test is also available. A shorter form was developed during a factor analysis study that eliminates the two most difficult items and reduces the administration time (Mumma, 1993). The EFT was designed to measure field dependence-independence.

The EFT consists of 24 complex figure cards, 8 sample figure cards, and a stylus used to trace the embedded figures. Twelve cards are administered during the test. Standard scores are developed after an average disembedding time is determined by dividing the total search time by 12. During administration, the item to be disembedded is presented beside the larger figure. The simple figure is presented to the right of the complex figure for right handed individuals and to the left of the complex figure for left handed subjects.

Reliability studies show both internal consistency and test-retest stability. The EFT correlates well with other measures of field dependence-independence.

## REFERENCES

Buros, O. K. (Ed.). (1965). *The sixth mental measurements yearbook.* Lincoln, NE: Buros Institute of Mental Measurements.

Mumma, G. H. (1993). The Embedded Figures Test: Internal structure and development of a short form. *Personality & Individual Differences, 15,* 221–224.

Witkin, H. A. (1950). Individual differences in ease of perception of embedded figures. *Journal of Personality, 19,* 1–15.

RON DUMONT
*Fairleigh Dickinson University*

JOHN O. WILLIS
*Rivier College*

## EMOTIONAL DISORDERS

The greatest amount of progress on behalf of the emotionally disturbed (ED) occurred in the twentieth century. Assessment instruments, residential schools for the emotionally disturbed, special classes in public schools, child guidance clinics, juvenile courts and legal statutes specifically written for delinquent and abused children, and hundreds of texts dealing with the etiology, diagnosis, and treatment of children were all products of the twentieth century.

By the 1960s and 1970s, dramatic progress had been made on behalf of children and youth. Behavior modification techniques became a popular treatment method and ecological approaches to treatment of the disturbed child were developed. Public Law 94-142 mandated an appropriate education for all children. Efforts were made to deinstitutionalize children and to mainstream them in the public schools. By the late 1970s and early 1980s, a family systems approach to treatment of the disturbed child came into vogue. Today efforts are being made to educate the emotionally disturbed child in the classroom and to supplement education with a therapeutic treatment program.

The problems in defining normal functioning in children make it difficult to classify abnormalities. This is particularly the case in emotional disturbance, where behavioral rather than academic criteria are primarily employed. Stemming from the realities of providing educational remediation, however, Bower (1969) spearheaded efforts to conceptualize emotional disturbances in children. He provided a practical definition consisting of the following five characteristics: (1) learning problems are not explained by intellectual, sensory, or health factors; (2) there are difficulties in initiating and maintaining interpersonal relationships; (3) behavioral or emotional reactions are not appropriate to circumstances; (4) there is pervasive unhappiness or depression; and (5) there is the development of physical symptoms or fears related to school or personal problems. Any one or more of these five characteristics occurring to a marked extent over a long period of time are sufficient for diagnosis. Bower's criteria were adopted verbatim in PL 94-142. Public Law 94-142 additionally labeled schizophrenic and autistic children as seriously emotionally disturbed and differentiated socially maladjusted from emotionally disturbed children. Autistic children were dropped from the emotionally disturbed category and placed in the health-impaired category in 1981, and later received their own category.

Despite its official sanction as a category of childhood exceptionality, the label emotional disturbance has evoked considerable debate in the literature. It has been reported that the differentiation of emotional and behavioral disorders in children is difficult to make (Boyle & Jones, 1985), and that the distinction between primary and secondary emotional disturbance in learning disabilities is similarly confused (Chandler & Jones, 1983). Inadequacies in definition may have resulted in the underdetection and underserving of emotionally disturbed children (Long & McQueen, 1984). Although Bower (1981) has openly discussed the nebulous nature of basing a classification category on disturbances in emotion, he has continued to advocate the application of the revised term emotionally handicapped and his original diagnostic criteria.

Incidence rates of emotional disturbances, or the number of newly diagnosed cases at any point in time, are practically nonexistent because of the difficulties in accurately defining the onset and duration of childhood psychiatric disorders. Estimates of prevalence, or the number of existing cases at any point in time, however, are available and are based on data collected from educational and psychiatric perspectives.

A number of individual difference variables have been identified as significant correlates of childhood emotional disturbance. Sex is a particularly important factor. Males are more likely than females to be identified throughout the school years, with more males receiving the psychiatric diagnosis of conduct disorder and more females receiving the psychiatric diagnoses of specific emotional disorders, especially during adolescence (Offord, 1983). Racial and family characteristics have also been implicated. Blacks are more likely than whites to be identified, and identification varies inversely with parent education level as well as family socioeconomic status (Zill, 1985). The importance of family variables is supported by the strong association between childhood psychiatric diagnoses in general and broken homes, marital discord, and parental deviance (Offord, 1983).

The etiology of mild to moderate emotional disturbances may not always be precise, but two major causative factors seem to predominate. These include socioenvironmental factors and biological factors. Genetic factors are important, but from the information to date, only the more severe forms of psychopathology seem to result from a genetic predisposition. This will be discussed in the section on seriously emotionally disturbed children.

## Etiology

In the last quarter of the twentieth century, marked changes occurred in the family as we knew it. Single-parent families, blended families ("his and her children" in second mar-

riages), parents working outside the home, "latchkey" children, apartment living, and family mobility all contributed to socioenvironmental factors as one of the major etiologies of emotional disturbances in children. Parental deprivation or distortions in parent-child relationships as a result of parental psychopathology are all too common. Many children are seriously neglected, and/or emotionally, physically, and even sexually abused by a parent or surrogate parent. Chronic neglect of a pervasive nature can and does affect the child's emotional and personal development. Physically and sexually abused children often exhibit depression or emotional agitation, poor self-image, cognitive deficits, and difficulties interrelating with peers (Willis, 1985).

Children and youth reared in extreme poverty are at higher risk for developing personality disorders and delinquent behavior. These disadvantaged children often exhibit cognitive delays. Thus, early school performance may be deficient, which may further accentuate a negative self-image.

In the biological realm, children with chronic health or other physical disorders may create added stress within the family. The exceptional child may be overprotected or rejected. In addition, the parent(s) may feel ambivalent toward the child. Any or all of these reactions can lead to maladaptive parental behaviors that can then create problems for the child and family.

A child's temperament may also determine, to an extent, a predilection toward emotional problems, especially if the child's temperament does not match parental and other environmental expectations. Ten temperament characteristics are described by Thomas, Chess, and Birch (1968): activity level, approach-withdrawal, rhythmicity, adaptability, mood, threshold, intensity, distractibility, persistence, and attention span. A difficult child is characterized by being slow to adapt to change, withdrawing from new stimuli, exhibiting a negative mood, manifesting biological irregularity, and demonstrating a high level of expressiveness. The difficult child is more likely to develop behavior disorders because his or her ability to interact with the environment and others is not always easy and nonstressful. This child may be at greater risk for abuse merely because he or she is, by nature, difficult. Children who present with neurological dysfunction or brain damage as the result of prematurity, pre- or post-natal infections, complications during pregnancy, and head trauma owed to accidents or injuries, may present with a diagnosis of emotional disturbance.

## Classification of ED

Bower's (1969) definition of emotional disturbance provides a set of criteria for labeling and differentiating a group of children who may respond to educational remediation. From a psychiatric perspective, however, the label emotional disturbance encompasses a wide range of childhood psychopathology. A number of different psychiatric disorders are included; they are the product of disparate etiologies and respond differentially to the treatment strategies that are available. Once a child receives the categorical label of emotionally disturbed, it is important to provide a more specific psychiatric diagnosis to facilitate effective treatment.

A brief discussion of some of the major childhood psychiatric syndromes included under the emotional disturbance label follows. The reader is referred to texts on childhood psychopathology or exceptionality by Achenbach (1982), Brown and Reynolds (1986), and Steinhauer and Rae-Grant (1983), and to the fourth edition of the *Diagnostic and Statistical Manual of Mental Disorders* of the American Psychiatric Association (*DSM-IV;* 1994) for more specific and comprehensive information.

Childhood depression has been recognized as a viable diagnosis in recent years. Estimates of prevalence vary according to diagnostic criteria, but one study placed the prevalence rate of depression at just over 5 percent for elementary school-aged children (Leftowitz & Tesiny, 1985). The rising incidence of suicide in children and adolescents is undoubtedly linked to increasing rates of childhood depression. With pervasive unhappiness or depression included as one of the diagnostic criteria for emotional disturbance, it is clear that childhood depression or depressive affect related to other psychological problems will appear frequently in groups of emotionally disturbed children.

Childhood depression differs from adult depression along a number of lines. The major presenting complaints in children are extreme sadness and accompanying withdrawal. Masked versions, in which the presenting complaints involve acting out behaviors, are not uncommon. Vegetative symptoms do not occur as frequently in children as they do in adults. However, both acute and chronic depression in children have been reported. The withdrawn, uncommunicative child is definitely a candidate for this diagnosis. Rapid, unexplained increases in acting out behaviors also necessitate consideration of an underlying depressive reaction.

A number of childhood psychiatric problems are linked directly to anxiety disorders. Anxiety may be the primary symptom or reactions to anxiety may produce somatic complaints and/or behavioral changes.

Phobias occur when anxiety and its somatic or behavioral concomitants are displayed in the presence of a feared object or situation. School phobia is a specific phobic reaction resulting from fears about school experiences, about separation from parents, or a combination of both. Panic disorder and generalized anxiety reactions refer to more global anxiety responses that are not linked to specific aspects of the environment yet may reflect underlying emotional conflict. In posttraumatic stress disorder, symptoms based on both anxiety and depression occur following a traumatic event that a child reexperiences repeatedly on a psychological level. With the incidence of child abuse increasing, the latter diagnosis is appearing more frequently in populations of emotionally disturbed children.

Other childhood disorders such as psychosomatic disorders may be seen in the special education child. Psychosomatic disorders are any physical conditions that can be initiated, exacerbated, or prolonged by psychosocial factors (Schaefer, Millman, & Levine, 1979).

The notion that health-related problems are caused by the interaction of biological, social, and psychological factors constitutes the cornerstone of psychosomatic disorders. Indeed, psychosomatic dysfunction is one of the major causes of school absence. For example, the child who presents with asthma, gastrointestinal disorders such as ulcers, diarrhea, vomiting, or abdominal pain, migraine headaches or hypertension, skin disorders such as dermatitis, and even hysterical symptoms may manifest an exaggeration of symptoms secondary to emotional stress. The stress may result from environmental demands, learning problems, or parent-child problems. Basically, physical symptoms that are rooted in or exacerbated by emotional conflict are the primary presenting complaints in psychosomatic disorders. Preexisting physiological vulnerability, such as ulcers or asthma, can be worsened by emotional stresses within the individual or family.

Children who have a history of multiple or prolonged hospitalization, or a history of chronic illness, may also present with emotional disturbance secondary to the trauma of medical surgeries or procedures. The effects of hospitalization and physical illness on the developing child can be understood best by reading Willis, Elliot, and Jay (1982) and Olson et al. (1994).

Personality disorders are characterized by maladaptive and inflexible patterns of behaviors, thoughts, and emotions that affect an individual's functioning across situations and time. The symptoms of personality disorders are ego syntonic, meaning that they are not viewed by the individual as problematic. They are diagnosed more frequently in adults than in children because rapid developmental changes in children complicate predictions regarding stability of functioning. Childhood precursors of personality disorders have been applied as specific diagnoses in childhood populations.

Based on symptom clusters, personality disorders and their childhood precursors have been grouped into three categories (Steinhauer & Berman, 1983). The first group is defined by emotional constriction, rigidity, aloofness, and the inability to maintain interpersonal relationships. Schizoid disorders of childhood and adolescence are included in this category, as well as schizoid, paranoid, and schizotypal personality disorders. The second group is defined by dramatic, emotional, self-centered, and unstable behaviors. Identity disorders of childhood and adolescence and conduct disorders are the childhood precursors within this category. Histrionic, narcissistic, and antisocial personality disorders are also included. Intrapsychic struggles between anxiety and defenses against anxiety characterize the third group. Avoidant disorder and oppositional disorder are diagnoses applied to children manifesting these characteristics. Avoidant, dependent, compulsive, and passive-aggressive are labels used to describe fully developed personality disorders based on these intrapsychic struggles.

Children who present with a behavior disorder are often seen in the school setting. This population differs from children who present with social maladjustment when the following criteria are present: the presence of guilt or anxiety; a specific etiology; and responsiveness to treatment. Often these children experience enormous frustration, intrapsychic conflicts, poor self-esteem, feelings of failure, and high anxiety levels. They may act out their frustrations in an aggressive way (Group for the Advancement of Psychiatry, 1966); as opposed to socially maladjusted children, they frequently feel remorse for their aggressive acts.

Immature behaviors displayed in the school setting (thumb sucking, crying, whining, negativism, baby talk) are often seen in children under stress and are indicative of some underlying, perhaps transient, problem occurring at home or elsewhere in the child's environment. Some children who have been overprotected by their parents may be bright, but immature in their social and environmental behavior. The withdrawn child does not interact with peers, is often viewed as a loner, is overly shy, and may be deficient in social skills. The immature or withdrawn child requires intervention but does not necessarily require individual treatment.

## Treatment

Since there is no cookbook method of treating all disorders with which a child might present, the mental health professional treating an emotionally disturbed child must consider a number of factors when planning treatment strategies. It is not within the scope of this section to advocate one therapeutic orientation over another. Rather, an overview of psychodynamic therapy, behavior therapy, family and group therapy, and parent consultation will be presented.

Psychodynamic therapy deals with the underlying psychological causes creating a child's disturbance rather than overt symptoms. Feelings, fantasies, and fears are played out by the child in play therapy. The therapist may make dynamic interpretations of the child's verbal or nonverbal communication. It is hoped that the interpretations will make the child aware of unconscious thoughts and feelings that perpetuate his or her overt symptoms and that change in behavior may result from this therapeutic and educational style of interaction. In behavior therapy, the notion is that all behavior is learned and that some children learn maladaptive ways of interacting or relating or do not learn appropriate behaviors and social skills. The behavior therapist focuses on symptoms rather than causes, and seeks to actively manipulate the unacceptable behavior. This is an excellent technique to use when children present with discrete symptoms or present with a paucity of verbal insight skills. Relaxation training, a specific behavioral technique,

might be used to aid children who are experiencing stress and other tension-related disorders.

Group psychotherapy is especially helpful for children experiencing peer or social interaction problems, since in group therapy usually two or more children are seen by a therapist. The orientation of the group can be behavioral, psychodynamic, or supportive, but the goal of the therapist is usually to increase the child's awareness and control of his or her emotions.

The decision to treat a child in the context of family therapy is made when the therapist perceives the family as maintaining and perpetuating the child's problem. The therapists attempts to identify and modify maladaptive family patterns that perpetuate the child's problems (Jay, Waters, & Willis, 1986). Parent consultation is also used to teach parents means of modifying behavior at home, to offer advice on child rearing, to explain a child's behavior, and to give support. A more detailed account of treatment methods used with children can be found in Jay et al. (1986), Olson et al. (1994), and Ollendick (1998).

## REFERENCES

Achenbach, T. M. (1982). *Developmental psychopathology.* New York: Wiley.

American Psychiatric Association. (1994). *Diagnostic and statistical manual of mental disorders* (4th ed.). Washington, DC: Author.

Bower, E. M. (1969). *Early identification of emotionally handicapped children in school* (2nd ed.). Springfield, IL: Thomas.

Bower, E. M. (1981). *Early identification of emotionally handicapped children in school* (3rd ed.). Springfield, IL: Thomas.

Boyle, M. H., & Jones, S. C. (1985). Selecting measures of emotional and behavioral disorders of childhood for use in general populations. *Journal of Child Psychology & Psychiatry, 26,* 137–159.

Brown, R. T., & Reynolds, C. R. (1986). *Psychological perspectives on childhood exceptionality.* New York: Wiley.

Chandler, H. N., & Jones, K. (1983). Learning disabled or emotionally disturbed: Does it make any difference? *Journal of Learning Disabilities, 16,* 432–434.

Gould, M. S., Wunsch-Hitzig, R., & Dohrenwend, B. (1981). Estimating the prevalence of childhood psychopathology. *Journal of the American Academy of Child Psychiatry, 20,* 462–476.

Group for the Advancement of Psychiatry. (1966). *Psychopathological disorders in childhood: Theoretical considerations and a proposed classification* (Vol. 6, Report No. 2). New York: Author.

Jay, S., Waters, D. B., & Willis, D. J. (1986). The emotionally exceptional. In R. T. Brown & C. R. Reynolds (Eds.), *Psychological perspectives on childhood exceptionality.* New York: Wiley.

Leftowitz, M. M., & Tesiny, E. P. (1985). Depression in children: Prevalence and correlates. *Journal of Consulting & Clinical Psychology, 53,* 647–656.

Long, K. A., & McQueen, D. V. (1984). Detection and treatment of emotionally disturbed children in schools: Problems and theoretical perspectives. *Journal of Clinical Psychology, 40,* 378–390.

Offord, D. R. (1983). Classification and epidemiology in child psychiatry: Status and unresolved problems. In P. D. Steinhauer & Q. Rae-Grant (Eds.), *Psychological problems of the child in the family* (2nd ed.). New York: Basic Books.

Ollendick, T. (1998). Children and adolescents: Clinical formulation and treatment. In A Bellack & M. Hersen (Eds.), *Comprehensive clinical psychology* (Vol. 5). New York: Elsevier.

Olson, R., Mullins, L., Gillman, J., & Chaney, S. (1994). *The sourcebook of pediatric psychology*. Boston: Longwood.

Schaefer, C. E., Millman, H. L., & Levine, G. (1979). *Therapies for psychosomatic disorders in children*. San Francisco: Jossey-Bass.

Steinhauer, P. D., & Berman, G. (1983). Anxiety, neurotic, and personality disorders in children. In P. D. Steinhauer & Q. Rae-Grant (Eds.), *Psychological problems of the child in the family* (2nd ed., pp. 230–257). New York: Basic Books.

Steinhauer, P. D., & Rae-Grant, Q. (Eds.). (1983). *Psychological problems of the child in the family* (2nd ed.). New York: Basic Books.

Thomas, A., Chess, S., & Birch, H. G. (1968). *Temperament and behavior disorders in children*. New York: New York University Press.

Willis, D. J. (1985). *Psychological investigation of physical and sexual abuse of children*. Presidential address. Los Angeles: American Psychological Association.

Willis, D. J., Elliot, C., & Jay, S. (1982). Psychological effects of physical illness and its concomitants. In P. Magrab (Ed.), *Handbook for the practice of pediatric psychology*. New York: Wiley.

Wright, L., Schaefer, A. B., & Solomons, G. (1979). *Encyclopedia of pediatric psychology*. Baltimore: University Park Press.

Zill, N. (1985). *The school-age handicapped*. Prepared by Child Trends, incorporated under Department of Education contract number 300-83-0198. Washington, DC: U.S. Department of Education.

DIANE J. WILLIS
E. WAYNE HOLDEN
*University of Oklahoma Health Sciences Center*

**CHILDHOOD PSYCHOSIS**
**CHILDHOOD SCHIZOPHRENIA**
**CONDUCT DISORDER**
**PSYCHONEUROTIC DISORDERS**
**SERIOUSLY EMOTIONALLY DISTURBED**

## EMOTIONAL LABILITY

Emotional lability refers to rapidly shifting or unstable emotions (American Psychiatric Association, 1994). It is a psychiatric term that developed from attempts to classify the qualitative aspects of inappropriate emotional functioning in clinical cases. Lability has been most frequently applied in descriptions of serious emotional disturbance where rapid changes in emotional status are readily apparent. Unstable emotions are also characteristic of less severe psychopathologies and can be used to describe normal children's functioning during periods of stress or crisis. Sustained emotional lability, however, is considered to be pathological and results from a number of different causative factors. The primary etiological agents in children are fragile central nervous system functioning and frustration in meeting environmental demands (Swanson & Willis, 1979).

Some familiarity with the psychiatric terminology used to describe emotion (Kaplan, Freedman, & Saddock, 1980) is needed to clearly understand the role of lability in the description of a child's functioning. Mood refers to sustained internal sensations that are stable and influence all aspects of an individual's functioning. Affect, on the other hand, is the immediate expression of emotion that is attached to specific environmental events. Affect can vary from situation to situation, while mood is pervasive emotional tone occurring across situations. The outward manifestations of affect are the basis for describing emotional responding. Lability refers to changes in affect that are repetitious and abrupt; both negative and positive affect may be displayed. Emotional responding is intense and typically does not fit environmental demands. Lability can be contrasted with other terms used to describe affective expression. Restricted affect is characterized by a reduction in the range and intensity of responding; blunted affect refers to a severe reduction in the intensity of responding; and flat affect is the complete absence of emotional responding.

Children receiving special education services who are classified emotionally disturbed are at greatest risk for displaying emotional lability. Unstable emotions are a primary diagnostic feature in a number of childhood psychiatric conditions included under the emotional disturbance label. Other categories of childhood exceptionality, however, are not exempt from rapidly shifting or unstable emotions. Labile affect is frequently displayed secondary to cognitive disturbance in learning-disabled and mentally retarded children. Emotional lability may also be present in children with sensory or physical disabilities owed to frustrations with meeting environmental demands. Even gifted children can display emotional lability when they are not appropriately challenged in the classroom setting. It is clear that emotional lability can be applied to all categories of childhood exceptionality and not restricted to children who have been diagnosed with a psychiatric condition.

**REFERENCES**

American Psychiatric Association. (1994). *Diagnostic and statistical manual of mental disorders* (4th ed.). Washington, DC: Author.

Kaplan, H. I., & Freedman, A. M., & Saddock, B. J. (1980). *Comprehensive textbook of psychiatry / III*. Baltimore: Williams & Wilkins.

Swanson, B. M., & Willis, D. J. (1979). *Understanding exceptional children and youth.* Chicago: Rand McNally.

E. Wayne Holden
Diane J. Willis
*University of Oklahoma Health
Sciences Center*

## ACTING OUT
## EMOTIONAL DISORDERS
## SERIOUSLY EMOTIONALLY DISTURBED

## EMPIRICALLY SUPPORTED TREATMENT

Empirically supported treatments (ESTs) are psychological interventions that have been tested in research studies and have exceeded certain levels of research support. The term "empirically supported treatments" (also sometimes referred to as "empirically validated treatments") is most closely associated with efforts initiated by the American Psychological Association (APA) during the 1990s to identify effective psychological treatments. These efforts were in part a response to the evidence-based medicine movement (see entry for Evidence-Based Practice) and were based on the premises that (a) client care can be enhanced by empirical knowledge, (b) it is difficult for clinicians to keep up with new research relevant to their practice, (c) if clinicians do not keep up with new research their knowledge will deteriorate after their training, and (d) clinicians will benefit from summaries of evidence provided by expert reviews and guidelines on how to apply this evidence to clinical practice (Chambless & Ollendick, 2001). The purpose of the APA's Task Force on the Promotion and Dissemination of Psychological Procedures (referred to here as the Task Force) was to maintain a current list of effective practices for distribution to practitioners and training programs in clinical psychology.

The criteria for ESTs developed by the Task Force consist of three levels of empirical support (Chambless et al., 1998): Well-established treatments, probably efficacious treatments, and experimental treatments. Well-established treatments are supported by at least two randomized clinical trials demonstrating superiority to a pill or placebo condition or another treatment or equivalence to another well-established treatment. Alternatively, these treatments could have been supported by a large series of single-case design studies comparing the intervention to another treatment. Additional requirements for well-established treatments include that the treatments must be clearly described in treatment manuals, the characteristics of the treated samples must be clearly defined, and the efficacy of the treatments have to have been established by at least two different teams of investigators. Probably efficacious treatments are treatments that have been supported by at least one randomized clinical trial or by single-case design

studies, but do not meet all criteria for well-established treatments (e.g., the treatment has only been studied by one group of investigators). Finally, the Task Force defined treatments not meeting either level of support as experimental treatments.

The original APA Task Force published two lists of ESTs (Chambless et al., 1998; Task Force, 1995) and led to the establishment of a second APA task force focused on child clinical psychology and to other efforts to define ESTs. In 2001, Chambless and Ollendick published a summary of these efforts, combining them into a single list of ESTs, spanning the adult and child literatures, including interventions for geriatric populations and children being seen in medical settings. Efforts to identify new ESTs are ongoing, including a special issue of the *Journal of Clinical Child and Adolescent Psychology* (Silverman & Hinshaw, 1995) published in 1995 with a list of treatments for children. Other similar ongoing efforts include the Evidence-Based Intervention Workgroup in school psychology (see Kratochwill & Shernoff, 2003) and the Department of Education's What Works Clearinghouse, listing effective practices in all areas of education (2005).

These efforts to identify ESTs have not been without controversy. One of the concerns most commonly raised by opponents of this movement is that ESTs will not work in clinical care settings because the samples they were tested on are not representative of typical clients (e.g., Westen, Novotny, & Thompson-Brenner, 2004). While some evidence exists to counter this argument (see Chambless & Ollendick, 2001, for a summary of this evidence), these concerns have led to a call for increased research to test these treatments outside of research settings with typical clinical settings, practitioners, and clients (e.g., the National Advisory Mental Health Council Workgroup on Child and Adolescent Mental Health Intervention Development and Deployment, 2001).

## REFERENCES

Chambless, D. L., Baker, M. J., Baucom, D. H., Beutler, L. E., Calhoun, K. S., Crits-Christoph, P., et al. (1998). Update on empirically validated therapies II. *The Clinical Psychologist, 51,* 3–16.

Chambless, D. L., & Ollendick, T. H. (2001). Empirically supported psychological interventions: Controversies and evidence. *Annual Reviews of Psychology, 52,* 685–716.

Kratochwill, T. R., & Shernoff, E. S. (2003). Evidence-based practice: Promoting evidence-based interventions in school psychology. *School Psychology Quarterly, 18,* 389–408.

The National Advisory Mental Health Council Workgroup on Child and Adolescent Mental Health Intervention Development and Deployment. (2001). *Blueprint for Change: Research on Child and Adolescent Mental Health.* Washington, DC.

Silverman, W. K., & Hinshaw, S. P. (1995). Empirically supported psychosocial interventions for children: An overview. *Journal of Clinical Child and Adolescent Psychology, 34,* 11–24.

Task Force on Promotion and Dissemination of Psychological Procedures. (1995). Training in and dissemination of empirically-validated psychological treatments: Report and recommendations. *The Clinical Psychologist, 48,* 3–23.

Westen, D., Novotny, C. M., & Thompson-Brenner, H. (2004). The empirical status of empirically supported therapies: Assumptions, findings, and reporting in controlled trials. *Psychological Bulletin, 130,* 631–663.

U.S. Department of Education's Institute of Education Sciences. (2005). *What works clearinghouse.* Retrieved September 4, 2005, from http://www.whatworks.ed.gov/

AMANDA JENSEN DOSS
TIA BILLY
*Texas A&M University*

**EFFECTIVENESS OF SPECIAL EDUCATION**
**EVIDENCE-BASED PRACTICE**
**INTERVENTION**
**INTERVENTION IN SCHOOL AND CLINIC**

## ENCEPHALITIS, MYCOPLASMA PNEUMONIAE

Mycoplasma pneumoniae encephalitis is a bacterial infection that mimics a virus; that is, the bacterias lack a cell wall and receptor sites for common antibiotics. Mycoplasmas are transmitted via the respiratory route and are the smallest free-living parasites known to exist (Clyde, 1997). This type of pneumonia occurs more often in the winter months and is often accompanied by bulbous myringitis (eardrum inflammation) and otitis media (ear infections). The infection is more commonly found in school-age children and adolescents. Neurologic complications are rare: 1–7 percent of pneumoniae cases (Johnson, 1998), but the condition has been associated with a variety of serious problems, including lethargy, altered consciousness, agitation, psychotic behavior, seizures, aphasia, paresthesis, cranial nerve palsies, and cerebellar ataxia (Thomas, Collins, Robb, & Robinson, 1993). It has also been found in patients diagnosed with meningitis and Guillain-Barre syndrome.

The pathogenesis of mycoplasma infection is not known; however, researchers have hypothesized that the condition is due to one of three causes. The most likely explanation is that the infection results from an autoimmune response in which free-floating antibodies in the brain react with complimentary mycoplasma antibodies. Other explanations include a direct insult of the central nervous system (CNS) by bacteria crossing the blood-brain barrier and bacteria releasing a neurotoxin that damages the CNS (Thomas et al., 1993); however, few cases have been found in which bacteria has been isolated in the CNS, and the release of neurotoxins has only been shown in animals.

Characteristics may include the following:

1. The bacterial infection mimics a virus and occurs more commonly in school-age children and adolescents than adults.
2. Eardrum inflammation and ear infections are common.
3. Neurologic symptoms include lethargy, agitation, seizures, and altered consciousness.
4. Prognosis is generally good, but in some cases sequelae persist such as optic atrophy, intellectual deterioration, and spastic quadriplegia.

Although respiratory infection typically precedes neurological symptoms, in some cases there is no known antecedent respiratory illness or infection. Mycoplasma pneumoniae infection, however, should be considered a possibility in all cases of acute encephalitis. The diagnosis is typically made through serologic tests that detect the antibodies (i.e., IgG and IgM). Lumbar puncture, magnetic resonance imaging, and computerized tomography scanning have all been used, but these tests are often inconclusive. Although increased levels of protein concentrations and lymphocytes are often found, bacteria in the CSF is not typically found.

The most effective treatment is that of an antibiotic, such as erythromycin and tetracycline. Penicillin and cephalosporin are not effective despite their frequent use. These antibiotics are helpful in treating bacterial infections, but there is no evidence that there is any impact on the neurologic sequelae. Further, there is no evidence that corticosteroids are effective with this infection and its aftermath (Thomas et al., 1993). Fortunately, prognosis is generally good. There are very few cases of death caused by mycoplasma pneumoniae infections; however, the seriousness of certain sequelae means that these children need to be evaluated carefully for problems such as intellectual deterioration, short-term memory impairment, seizures, optic atrophy, and movement disorders (e.g., spastic quadriplegia).

Treatment depends on the severity and the nature of the impact. For example, in cases of physical impairment, services from physical and occupational therapists are often warranted. These children may qualify for special education services under Other Health Impairment or even Section 504. In most cases, certain classroom accommodations will be needed. When cognitive impact is severe, school-age children may even warrant services for students with Intellectual Disabilities and Specific Learning Disabilities. When emotional and behavioral needs become so great as to interfere with learning and social progress, special education services for students with Emotional Disturbance may be needed. Given the impact that eardrum inflammation and ear infection can have on hearing, audiologists and speech and language pathologists should be consulted so that the child can be properly evaluated for services. Furthermore, school psychological services should be obtained to ensure that the student's educational and emotional needs are properly assessed (e.g., pre- and postencephalitis functioning and educational needs) and that interventions are appropriately designed and implemented. Children with mycoplasma pneumoniae encephalitis should also be offered counseling services to help them cope with the sudden onset of this illness (and its sequelae) and the fears and uncertainty about the future. It is critical that parents be involved in the assessment and intervention process to ensure that the child with mycoplasma pneumoniae encephalitis has the benefit of state-of-the-art services.

## REFERENCES

Clyde, W. A. (1997). Mycoplasmal diseases. In W. M. Scheld, R. J. Whitley, & D. T. Durack (Eds.), *Infections of the central nervous system* (2nd ed.). New York: Lippincott Raven.

Johnson, R. T. (1998). *Viral infections of the nervous system.* New York: Lippincott Raven.

Thomas, N., Collins, J., Robb, S., & Robinson, R. (1993). Mycoplasma pneumoniae infection and neurological disease. *Archives of Disease in Childhood, 69,* 573–576.

Loni Kuhn
Elaine Clark
*University of Utah*

# ENCEPHALITIS, POSTHERPETIC

Postherpetic encephalitis, or herpes simplex encephalitis (HSVE), is caused by the herpes simplex virus-1 (HSV-1) and is characterized by inflammation of the parenchyma and the surrounding meninges. The herpes simplex virus has a predilection for certain areas of the brain, specifically, the frontotemporal region. HSVE accounts for 10 percent of all cases of encephalitis and is one of the most common types of fatal sporadic encephalitis (Clifton, 1991). This type of encephalitis is uncommon: It occurs annually in an estimated 1 in 250,000 individuals but is more prevalent in children than in adults. It is not entirely clear how the virus gains access to the brain, but some researchers question olfactory and orbital routes.

Symptoms of HSVE include alterations in mental status (e.g., loss of consciousness, confusion, and memory loss), headache, fever, lethargy, nausea and vomiting, generalized and focal seizures, and hemiparesis. Neurologic impairment can be permanent, including impairment in sensorimotor, language (e.g., dysnomia), intellectual skills, and behavioral functions.

Characteristics may include the following:

1. HSVE is caused by the herpes simplex virus-1 and affects more children than adults.
2. Herpes simplex viruses have a predilection to the frontotemporal region of the brain and are charac-terized by inflammation of the parenchyma and the surrounding meninges.
3. Rapid onset of symptoms is common and can include alterations in mental status, headache, vomiting, fever, lethargy, seizures, and hemiparesis.
4. Mortality rates are as high as 70 percent if untreated, but drug therapies such as Acyclovir help.
5. Sensorimotor, intellectual, language, and behavioral changes are common.

HSVE is diagnosed by a number of methods, including electroencephalograms (EEGs), computed tomography (CT), tissue biopsies, and cerebral spinal fluid (CSF) evaluation. Brain biopsies have been shown to be the most reliable diagnostic tools, but examining CSF for lymphocytes, antibodies, and red blood cells has also been shown to be the most practical (Ratho, Sethi, & Singh, 1999). EEG and neuroimaging have been useful in identifying areas of the brain impacted by the virus, and they predict sequelae from the infection.

If untreated, HSVE can result in death—in some cases in 70 percent of all individuals infected (Clifton, 1991). The antiviral drug Acyclovir has been successful in reducing mortality rates (in some studies to 28 percent) and morbidity. In addition to Acyclovir, corticosteroids are occasionally given to reduce intracranial pressure. Concern has been expressed about a potential negative interaction among steroid use, the antiviral agent, and the virus itself; however, recent research in rats has failed to show an increase in herpes simplex replication using the two treatments (Blessing, Blessing, & Wesselingh, 2000).

The prognosis is improved with early diagnosis and treatment, but problems can persist long after the acute phase of illness. Educators need to be aware of potential long-term neurologic impairments caused by HSVE. This includes problems with memory and cognition, motor and language problems, and aggression, to name a few. Special education is likely to be needed, so children who have had HSVE need to be evaluated for special education—as well as regular education—needs. Speech and language therapists, as well as occupational and physical therapists, may play an important role in the child's ability to achieve.

Future research is needed to better explain the pathogenesis of the infection, in particular, where the virus is more likely to gain access. This may provide critical information for finding ways to prevent the encephalitis and facilitate early diagnosis and treatment.

## REFERENCES

Blessing, K. A., Blessing, W. W., & Wesselingh, S. L. (2000). Herpes simplex replication and dissemination is not increased by corticosteroid treatment in a rat model of focal herpes encephalitis. *Journal of Neurovirology, 6*(1), 25–32.

Clifton, E. R. (1991). Herpes simplex encephalitis: An overview. *Journal of Mississippi State Medical Association, 32*(12), 437–440.

Ratho, R. K., Sethi, S., & Singh, S. (1999). Role of serology in the diagnosis of herpes simplex encephalitis. *Indian Journal of Pathological Microbiology, 42*(3), 333–337.

Loni Kuhn
Elaine Clark
*University of Utah*

## ENCEPHALITIS, POSTINFECTIOUS MEASLES

Postinfectious measles encephalitis is an autoimmune response characterized by inflammation and demyelination that is triggered by the measles virus. The measles virus is transmitted through respiratory droplets and is thought to have impacted civilizations as early as 4000 B.C. A young Danish physician, Peter L. Panum, however, is credited with much of the information that is now known about measles, including the highly contagious nature of the disease. Panum was sent to the Faroe Islands in the mid-1800s to assist with a large-scale measles outbreak and discovered that measles have an incubation period of about 14 days (Griffin, Ward, & Esolen, 1994). In most cases, individuals begin to show signs of improvement about five days after the measles rash appears. It is not clear how the measles virus triggers the autoimmune reaction that causes encephalomyelitis. However, when this occurs there is considerable neurologic involvement, and prior to the introduction of the measles vaccine, it was the most common cause of neurological disability. Encephalitis-associated symptoms include fever, headache, seizures, and coma. It has been estimated that 50 percent of individuals who contract postinfectious measles encephalitis develop seizures and nearly 100 percent show impaired consciousness during the episode (Scheld, Whitley, & Durack, 1997). Other neurologic-related sequelae include intellectual deterioration, hemiparesis, paraplegia, and ataxia (Scheld et al., 1997).

Characteristics can include:

1. An autoimmune response characterized by demyelinization and inflammation
2. Triggered by the measles virus, and affecting 1 per 1,000 measles cases
3. Commonly diagnosed following neurological complications from rashes
4. Mortality rate of approximately 25 percent
5. Neurologic sequelae including intellectual decline, hemiparesis/plegia, and ataxia

Because the measles vaccine is commonly administered in North America and Europe, measles infections are fairly infrequent. In other areas of the world, measles epidemics occur often, as does the corresponding encephalitis. Encephalitis occurs in 1 of every 1,000 cases of measles and is more commonly found among young people and the elderly (Griffin et al., 1994). There does not appear to be a sex difference as males and females are equally affected.

Most often, the diagnosis of postinfectious encephalitis is made based on clinical signs and symptoms of neurological complication (i.e., following the measles rash). In some cases, the disease is found in the urine, blood, and cerebral spinal fluid (CSF), and especially in increased levels of mononuclear cells and protein (Johnson, 1998). But these are not consistent findings, so follow-up is needed even in cases where there is no evidence of the disease in the blood or urine and the lumbar puncture is clean. Other methods to follow up on the disease include use of electro-encephalograms (EEGs) and magnetic resonance imaging (MRI). In cases of postinfectious measles encephalitis, the EEG commonly displays diffuse, symmetric slowing, and the MRI often shows demyelination in the cerebellum and brain stem.

The prognosis for individuals who contract postinfectious measles encephalitis is often poor: Approximately 25 percent die from the disease. There are no antiviral drug treatments to treat postinfectious measles encephalitis. Although the administration of immunoglobulins following exposure has been shown to alter the course some, conflicting evidence has been found, and the overall consensus seems to be that corticosteroid treatments are not very helpful in alleviating the disease. Clearly, the most effective treatment is prevention through vaccines. In countries where the vaccine is widely used, the disease is essentially nonexistent.

For those who survive, special education services may be necessary. This includes services under the category of Other Health Impairment, Intellectual Disabilities, and Specific Learning Disabilities. Given the complexity and severity of symptoms following the contraction of the disease, regardless of special education eligibility, children will likely need some accommodations in the classroom and ancillary services such as occupational and physical therapies. Psychological services are likely to be critical to evaluate the neuropsychological consequence of the disease and determine necessary services. Home-school collaborations are likely to be necessary to ensure that the child is receiving appropriate services and making the expected progress educationally and socially. Depending on the severity of the disability caused from the disease, vocational testing and services may also be called for; therefore, children need to be evaluated early to reduce frustration and provide them with the best education possible.

### REFERENCES

Griffin, D., Ward, B., & Esolen, L. (1994). Pathogenesis of measles virus infection: An hypothesis for altered immune responses. *Journal of Infectious Diseases, 170*(Suppl. 1), 24–31.

Johnson, R. T. (1998). *Viral infections of the nervous system.* New York: Lippincott Raven.

Scheld, M., Whitley, R., & Durack, D. (1997). *Infections of the central nervous system.* New York: Lippencott Raven.

LONI KUHN
ELAINE CLARK
*University of Utah*

## ENCOPRESIS

Encopresis involves the repeated passage of feces into inappropriate places (e.g., clothing or the floor), whether involuntarily or intentional. It is differentiated into either primary or secondary subtypes: the primary subtype indicates that the individual has never established fecal continence, whereas the secondary subtype indicates the disturbance developed after a period of established continence. Encopresis may stem from psychological reasons such as anxiety about defecating in a public place, a more generalized anxiety, or oppositional behavior or may be caused by physiologically induced dehydration related to hypothyroidism, a febrile illness, or a side effect of medications. Secondary encopresis may begin following a stressful event, such as the birth of a sibling, the beginning of school, or separation from a parent due to divorce or death.

Encopresis cannot be diagnosed prior to the age of 4, and there must be at least one event per month for at least three months. It is estimated that 1 percent of 5-year-olds have encopresis, and the disorder is five to six times more prevalent in males. Referrals for encopresis account for approximately 3 percent of pediatric outpatient referrals (Abrahamin & Lloyd-Still, 1984) and 5 percent of referrals to psychiatric clinics. A history of constipation, developmental delays in other areas, attention-deficit/hyperactivity disorder, or coercive or premature bowel training increases the risk for developing encopresis (Maxmen & Ward, 1995). Frequency of encopresis decreases with age, with a spontaneous remission rate of about 28 percent per year (Schaefer, 1979). Encopresis can persist intermittently for years but rarely becomes a chronic condition.

In addition to the primary and secondary distinctions of encopresis, three major categories of encopresis exist (Howe & Walker, 1992). The most common is retentive encopresis, which accounts for 80–95 percent of all encopretic cases (Christopherson & Rapoff, 1983). Retentive encopresis occurs when a child becomes constipated and liquid fecal mater leaks around the fecal obstruction and soils undergarments. The second type of encopresis includes chronic diarrhea and irritable bowel syndrome, most commonly associated with stress and anxiety. The third and least common form of encopresis is manipulative, intentional soiling, most commonly associated with oppositional defiance or conduct disorders.

Characteristics often include:

1. Repeated passage of feces into inappropriate places whether involuntarily or intentionally.
2. Primary encopresis: At least one such event per month for at least 3 months.
3. Secondary encopresis: One full year of being continent prior to current episode of encopresis.
4. Chronological age is at least 4 years (or equivalent developmental level).
5. The behavior is not exclusively due to direct physiological effects of a substance (e.g., laxatives) or a general medical condition except constipation.
6. Code as either with constipation and overflow incontinence or without constipation and overflow incontinence.
7. Treatment usually includes both medical and behavioral interventions.

Treatment of encopresis usually includes both medical and behavioral interventions (Mash & Barkley, 1996). It is believed that a multifaceted approach that treats a wide range of systems (organic, behavioral, cognitive, and environmental) will achieve the most efficacious results. To avoid the retention-leakage cycle, a combination of enemas, laxatives, stool softeners, or increased dietary fiber are used to evacuate the colon. In rare cases surgical extraction of the fecal material may be required. Children are then scheduled to have regular sessions on the toilet for the purpose of muscle retraining. They are given the responsibility of cleaning both themselves and any soiled clothing or surrounding areas after bowel movements. Rewards for appropriate toileting behavior and establishing a regular time for bowel movements (usually immediately after a meal) are also helpful for treating encopresis. Shaping and fading, behavioral modification techniques, are often used to increase stimulus control as a child transitions from a diaper to the toilet (Smith, Smith, & Lee, 2000). Parents are encouraged to keep a matter-of-fact approach in helping their children in order to avoid inadvertently reinforcing attention-seeking behaviors.

The child with encopresis often feels ashamed and embarrassed, which can lead to avoidance of school and other social situations. The amount of impairment is a direct function of the effect on the child's self-esteem, social ostracism by peers at school and in the community, and rejection by the caregiver. Special education accommodations may be made if the encopresis falls under the handicapping condition of Other Health Impairment. Support and planning by the school personnel may assist the child and parent in creating a plan to decrease school absenteeism and peer isolation. Due to the nature of the disorder, children with involuntary encopresis often experience psychological problems stemming from the encopresis, rather than causing encopresis. Children with deliberate soiling behaviors may receive rewards (i.e., parental attention, school absence, etc.) that inadvertently reinforce the soiling and smearing behaviors. When incontinence is deliberate, features of oppositional defiant disorder or conduct disorder may also be present.

The frequency of encopresis decreases with age, with a spontaneous remission rate of 28 percent per year (Schaefer, 1979). Therefore, the initial prognosis for encopresis is good. However, the psychological impact may reach farther because the child faces the social isolation and stigmatism already created within his or her peer group. School-based interventions may decrease peer isolation and increase the child's feelings of mastery of bowel control while in social situations. School personnel may provide discrete scheduled toileting times during the school day, enhance effective toileting strategies by providing rewards for reduction of soiling, and providing a place for cleaning of clothes and self if a soiling incident occurs. The school psychologist or counselor can facilitate increased communication between school, medical personnel, and the school, encouraging consistent intervention strategies. Encopresis can persist intermittently for years, but it rarely is a chronic condition. Intervention at the school level is critical for continued social and academic success for the child experiencing encopresis.

The need for future research is evident, primarily because available studies addressing encopresis are based on case studies. Valid experimental designs to evaluate treatment effectiveness, such as random assignment of cases to experimental and control groups or to alternate treatment groups, reversal designs (ABAB), and multiple baseline design studies are needed (Schaefer, 1979) in order to rule out spontaneous remission or extraneous effects on bowel control. There is also a need for further study in identifying differential treatment for continuous versus discontinuous encopresis and for longitudinal investigations of the natural history of encopresis (Schaefer, 1979).

### REFERENCES

Abrahamin, R., & Lloyd-Still, J. D. (1984). Chronic constipation in childhood: A longitudinal study of 186 patients. *Journal of Pediatric Gastroenterology and Nutrition, 3,* 460–467.

Christopherson, E. R., & Rapoff, M. A. (1983). Toileting problems in children. In C. E. Walker & M. C. Roberts (Eds.), *Handbook of clinical child psychology* (pp. 593–615). New York: Wiley.

Howe, A. C., & Walker, C. E. (1992). Behavioral management of toilet training, enuresis, and encopresis. *Pediatric Clinics of North America, 39,* 413–432.

Mash, E. J., & Barkley, R. A. (1996). *Child psychopathology.* New York: Guilford.

Maxmen, J., & Ward, N. (1995). *Essential psychopathology and its treatment* (2nd ed.). New York: W. W. Norton.

Schaefer, C. E. (1979). *Childhood encopresis and enuresis.* New York: Van Nostrand Reinhold.

Smith, L., Smith, P., & Lee, K. (2000). Behavioral treatment of urinary incontinence and encopresis in children with learning disabilities: Transfer of stimulus control. *Developmental Medicine and Child Neurology, 42,* 276–279.

LESLIE COYLE FRANKLIN
BRIAN JOHNSON
*University of Northern Colorado*

## ENDOCRINE DISORDERS

The endocrine system consists of the pituitary, thyroid, parathyroid, adrenal, pancreas, gonads, and placenta. The general function of the endocrine system is to control growth and reproduction and to maintain chemical homeostasis in the body.

Disorders associated with the endocrine system may result from partial or total insensitivity of tissue to endogenous hormones, hypersecretion of hormones, or hyposecretion of hormones. Endocrine disorders may have a variety of etiologies including chromosomal abnormalities, prenatal deficiencies, maternal hormonal deficiencies during gestation, and a variety of environmental variables (e.g., toxins, traumatic brain injury, brain tumors, and viruses).

Endocrine disorders also vary in prevalence and in the age at which symptoms appear. Commonly, endocrine disorders in children are detected because a child's development is premature or delayed (Sandberg & Barrik, 1995). Relatively common endocrine disorders of childhood include Turner syndrome, Klinefelter syndrome, congenital adrenal hyperplasia, hyperthyroidism, diabetes mellitus, and obesity. Rarer forms of the disorders may include hypothyroidism, which rarely appears as a birth defect, and multiple endocrine neoplasia Type 2 (MEN 2), which involves an overactivity and enlargement of the endocrine glands.

Characteristics may include the following:

1. Effects of the disorders can be direct (i.e., alteration of physical state), indirect (i.e., secondary effects based on social consequences of atypical physical or hormonal development), or a combination of both direct and indirect effects.

2. Endocrine dysfunction can have direct and indirect effects on physical, sexual, behavioral, and emotional development depending on the glands involved.

3. Cognitive, motor, and speech delays are common in hypothyroidism and Klinefelter syndrome but may appear in other disorders if appropriate treatment is not provided.

4. Behavioral, emotional, and social problems are common with many endocrine disorders and may result from the following:

   a. Hormonal imbalances

   b. Early or delayed development of secondary sexual characteristics leading to age-inappropriate sexual behavior

   c. Feelings of isolation or rejection because of physical abnormalities

5. The severity of symptoms varies widely across disorders. Some endocrine disorders such as congenital adrenal hyperplasia can be fatal. Other disorders such as diabetes are chronic conditions in which symptoms can be maintained with few functional impairments. There are also disorders such as benign tumors of the parathyroid gland in which individuals may not have noticeable symptoms. These patients may initially report feeling normal and then report improved sleep and concentration following surgical removal of the benign tumor.

Medical treatment for the hormonal imbalance is the standard defense against endocrine disorders. Hormone replacement therapy is widely used for disorders of hyposecretion or tissue insensitivity such as Turner's syndrome or hypopituitary syndromes. Estrogen replacement therapy is used to supplement the underproductive gonads of females with Turner syndrome. In hypopituitary syndromes, growth-hormone replacement therapy is used to stimulate growth. For disorders involving hypersecretion of endocrine glands, medical treatment seeks to reduce hormone levels through the use of natural or synthetic hormones (e.g., gonadatropin-releasing hormone for overactive pituitary glands).

The psychoeducational sequelae of endocrine disorders vary as widely as do the etiology and symptoms. Disorders associated with under- or overactive pituitary glands are typically not associated with cognitive deficits. At the other extreme, global deficits in cognitive functioning can result from endocrine disorders such as hypothyroid disorders. Furthermore, domain-specific deficits may also be associated with endocrine problems. For example, chromosomal disorders such as Klinefelter syndrome and Turner syndrome are associated with average intelligence but with specific deficits in reading and visual-spatial processing respectively.

The psychological sequelae of endocrine disorders are also important to consider in managing these conditions. Behavioral and emotional problems may result from hormonal imbalances, reactions to treatments, or reactions to looking and feeling different from peers. Future research should focus on the direct and indirect effects of the various disorders on academic and social development. The effects on school performance and behavior of the intrusive or chronic medical procedures associated with these disorders should also be evaluated.

## REFERENCE

Sandberg, D. E., & Barrick, C. (1995). Endocrine disorders in childhood: A selective survey of intellectual and educational sequelae. *School Psychology Review, 24*(2), 146–170.

LATHA V. SOORYA
*Binghamton University and
The Institute for Child
Development*

## ENDORPHINS

Endorphin is a term proposed by Goldstein (1976) to apply to all endogenous peptides that exhibit pharmacological properties like morphine. Since the first report by Hughes in 1975 of the isolation of a morphinelike substance in brain tissue, there has been much research and speculation as to the biological function of these peptides. Many of the first studies concentrated on locating and identifying the compounds. In addition to brain tissue, endorphins have also been found in the pituitary gland and gastrointestinal tract (Cooper, Bloom, & Roth, 1982). Within the brain, endorphins have been located in a number of areas. In particular, high concentrations have been found in areas involved in pain perception, memory, and arousal of emotions (Synder, 1977).

Considerable effort has also been made to understand the physiological and behavioral effects of the endorphins. Injection of endorphins produces many of the same physiological effects of morphine such as analgesia, hypothermia, nausea, vomiting, muscular rigidity, and severe akinesia (Cooper et al., 1982).

It has been theorized (and it is a widely held view) that the endogenous opiate system is relatively inactive during normal conditions and exerts an effect only under specific environmental or physiological circumstances (Amir, Brown, & Amit, 1980). However, determining the behavioral effects of the endorphins and the conditions under which they do exert an effect has been a controversial endeavor. The number of whole animal effects that have been attributed to the endorphinergic system has grown considerably in the last few decades, but still remains open to much more comprehensive analysis. In addition to pain perception, proposed physiological properties that may be regulated by endorphins include blood pressure, body temperature, respiration, eating and drinking, sexual activity, and memory (Cooper et al., 1982). There have also been reports suggesting that disruption of this system may be involved in some mental disorders, but the evidence for this is even more equivocal than for other roles (McGeer, Eccles, & McGeer, 1978).

Akil (1977) has hypothesized that the endorphins evolved from primitive systems involved with pain and stress modulation and later become important in drives, emotions, and mood states, and in interfacing sensory and hormonal mechanisms. Preliminary studies do suggest that the role of the endorphins is multiple and involves much more than dulling the sensation of pain. It is likely that the endorphins are involved in analgesia, metabolism, affective states, and the processing of sensory information, though at present it is too early to draw any conclusions.

## REFERENCES

Akil, H. (1977). Opiates: Biological mechanisms. In J. D. Barchas, P. A. Berger, R. D. Ciaranello, & G. R. Elliot (Eds.), *Psychopharmacology: From theory to practice.* New York: Oxford University Press.

Amir, S., Brown, Z. W., & Amit, Z. (1980). The role of endorphins in stress: Evidence and speculations. *Neuroscience & Biobehavioral Reviews, 4,* 77–86.

Cooper, J. R., Bloom, F. E., & Roth, R. H. (1982). *The biochemical basis of neuropharmacology.* New York: Oxford University Press.

Goldstein, A. (1976). Opioid peptides (endorphins) in pituitary and brain. *Science, 193,* 1081–1086.

Hughes, J. (1975). Isolation of an endogenous compound from the brain with pharmacological properties similar to morphine. *Brain Research, 88,* 295–308.

McGeer, P. L., Eccles, J. C., & McGeer, E. G. (1978). *Molecular neurobiology of the mammalian brain.* New York: Plenum.

Synder, S. H. (1977, March). Opiate receptors and internal opiates. *Scientific American,* pp. 44–56.

POLLY E. SANDERSON
*Research Triangle Institute*

METABOLIC DISORDERS
STRESS AND INDIVIDUALS WITH DISABILITIES

## ENGLEMANN, SIEGFRIED E. (1931–    )

Siegfried E. Englemann obtained his BA in education at the University of Illinois in 1955. He was a research associate at the University of Illinois from 1964 to 1966; from 1966 to 1977 he was a senior educational specialist at the University of Illinois. From 1970 to 1974 he was associate professor at the University of Oregon. Since 1974 he has been a professor of special education at the University of Oregon.

Englemann's major area of study is working with disadvantaged children in the classroom setting. Englemann and Bereiter (1966) believe that the "how" of educating disadvantaged children is as important as the "what," and that to fail in developing more effective teaching methods is perhaps to fail completely in equalizing the educational attainment of children from differing cultural backgrounds. Englemann and Bereiter (1966) also feel that direct instruction is a thoroughly feasible and highly effective way of teaching needed academic skills to the young. The most important side effect of the direct teaching is the development of self-conscious pride and confidence in one's own ability to learn and think. The American Psychological Association presented Englemann with the Fred Keller Award of Excellence in 1994.

Some of Englemann's major works include *Teaching: A Basic Course in Applied Psychology, Teaching I: Classroom Management,* and *Teaching II: Cognitive Learning and Instruction.* He also contributed chapters to many books and has written over 80 articles, including "Observations on the Use of Direct Instruction with Young, Disadvantaged Children," "Teaching Formal Operations to Preschool Children," and many others.

## REFERENCES

Becker, W. C., Englemann, S. E., & Thomas, D. R. (1969). *Teaching: A basic course in applied psychology.* Chicago: Science Research Associates.

Englemann, S. E. (1969). *Preventing failure in the primary grades.* Chicago: Science Research Associates.

Englemann, S. E., & Bereiter, C. (1966). Observations on the use of direct instructions with young, disadvantaged children. *Journal of School Psychology, 4*(3), 55–62.

ELIZABETH JONES
*Texas A&M University*

## ENGLAND, SPECIAL EDUCATION IN

Special education in England and Wales is heavily influenced by the Warnock Report (Department of Education and Science, 1978). The Report formulated a framework for the special educational needs system that largely was established in a 1981 Act and that continues to underpin special needs education in England. This framework has five significant elements: (1) children's special educational needs were defined in very general terms as difficulty in learning; (2) a large minority of children (one in six at any one time) was deemed to have these needs and many of these would be maintained in mainstream schools; (3) special educational needs were to be assessed on an individual basis by teachers, educational psychologists, doctors, and other professionals; (4) the assessment would lead to the local education authorities making provisions to meet the needs; and (5) provision could be made equally well in mainstream as in special settings.

Children are identified as having special educational needs on the basis of difficulties they experience in school rather than simply on the basis of any impairments or medical conditions that they experience (Department for Education and Skills, 2001a). In 1994, the Code of Practice on the Identification and Assessment of Special Educational Needs was developed (Department for Education, 1994) and revised in 2001. This Code provides guidance for schools and local education authorities on the stage-based approach to conceptualizing special needs in mainstream schools. Schools are legally bound to provide services for children who have been placed on their special needs register. During the early stages of implementing the Code of Practice, this service is provided from within the school. However, if the child's needs require external support, the local education authority is legally obliged to provide them. Finally, if the needs are severe, then a Statement of Special Educational Need is prepared. This legal process is designed to help ensure that a child has a full and comprehensive assessment of his or her needs. Parents have the right to see all copies of reports and the right to appeal decisions. All children being educated in special schools have this Statement.

Approximately 18 percent of children in primary schools and 15 percent in secondary schools (National Statistics, 2003a) are identified as having special educational needs. In 2004 the average percentage of pupils ages 0–19 who are placed in special schools and other segregated settings is 0.82 percent (101,612 pupils; Rustemier & Vaughan, 2005). Since the nature of services is determined at the local level, this figure varies enormously between local education authorities, from 0.06 percent in a local education authority in London to 1.46 percent in a local education authority in the north of England (Rustemier & Vaughan, 2005). Local education authorities determine how many special school places to fund and which students to place in them. Private providers are being used increasingly for a small minority of children. However, figures relating to special school placement are misleading as many students are placed in specialist units or resource rooms within mainstream schools. In addition, approximately 32,000 students (0.34 percent) excluded from school for disciplinary reasons are in pupil referral units (National Statistics, 2003a, 2003b).

In October 1997, the government announced its support for inclusive education (Department for Education and Employment, 1997) by endorsing the Salamanca Statement on Special Needs Education (United Nations Educational, Scientific and Cultural Organization, 1994). This move was unusual because the language of inclusion was relatively new in England in that English governments usually do not align themselves with international declarations in education or look elsewhere for models on which to develop policy (Dyson, 2005). In 1998, a Programme of Action was produced with the goal to identify practical ways to make inclusive education a reality (Department for Education and Employment, 1998). In the following year, as part of a major revision of the curriculum in 1999, statutory guidance on inclusion was issued by the agency responsible for overseeing the national curriculum (Department for Educa-

tion and Employment and Qualifications and Assessment Authority, 1999).

In 2001, legislation was passed to protect pupils against discrimination on the grounds of their disability. The Special Educational Needs and Disability Act also gave parents of children with special educational needs stronger rights to choose a mainstream placement. At about the same time, the national schools inspectorate, the Office for Standards in Education, issued guidance on how to inspect the inclusiveness of schools (Office for Standards in Education, 2000) and the government issued guidelines to local education authorities on how best to fund inclusive provision (Department for Education and Skills, 2001b) and to schools on how to interpret the new legislation (Department for Education and Skills, 2001c). In 2004, a second Programme of Action was produced that promised to give new impetus to the inclusion agenda (Department for Education and Skills, 2004).

The emergence of parental choice has had a considerable impact on special needs provision. The education reforms of the 1980s and 1990s, focusing on the 1988 Education Reform Act, removed the power of local education authorities to place children in local schools and gave parents the right (with certain restrictions) to choose a school for their child. There often is a contest between parents, who want to secure additional resources by having children's needs recognized and others (e.g., local education authorities) that must manage the budgets out of which resources to meet those needs must be found. The sometimes-bitter disputes that arise around the formal statements of the needs of individual children pose a major challenge to the English special education system (Audit Commission, 2002a). The new programme of action (Department for Education and Skills, 2004) has strengthened and formalized procedures, such as independent tribunals where parents can appeal against local education authority decisions (Department for Education, 1994) and determine the placement of their children (Department for Education and Skills, 2001b).

Special needs education has been aligned more closely with the mainstream standards agenda, as the title of the new programme of action reveals: Removing Barriers to Achievement (Department for Education and Skills, 2004). This new strategy attempts to promote personalized learning for all children and innovative education that responds to the diverse needs of individual children, thus reducing reliance on separate special educational needs structures and processes. Removing Barriers to Achievement builds on the current reform of children's services outlined in *Every Child Matters* (Department for Education and Skills, 2004). The development of integrated services involving education, health, social care, and juvenile justice is part of the government's commitment to reducing child poverty, investing in early years education, and delivering lasting benefits to children with special educational needs and their families.

## REFERENCES

Audit Commission. (2002). *Policy focus paper: Statutory assessment and statements of special educational needs.* London: Author.

Department for Education. (1994). *Code of practice on the identification and assessment of special educational needs.* London: Author.

Department for Education and Employment. (1997). *Excellence for all children: Meeting special educational needs.* London: The Stationery Office.

Department for Education and Employment. (1998). *Meeting special educational needs: A programme of action.* London: Department for Education and Employment. Retrieved April 6, 2004, from http://www.teachernet.gov.uk/_doc/5915/Action_Programme _Full.doc

Department for Education and Employment and Qualifications and Assessment Authority (Qualifications and Assessment Authority). (1999). *The National Curriculum: Handbook for primary / secondary teachers in England.* London: Author.

Department for Education and Science. (1978). *Special educational needs: Report of the Committee of Enquiry into the Education of Handicapped Children and Young People (The Warnock Report).* London: Her Majesty's Stationery Office.

Department for Education and Skills. (2001a). *Special educational needs code of practice.* London: Author.

Department for Education and Skills. (2001b). *The distribution of resources to support inclusion.* London: Author.

Department for Education and Skills. (2001c). *Inclusive schooling: Children with special educational needs.* London: Author.

Department for Education and Skills. (2004). *Removing barriers to achievement: The government's strategy for special educational needs.* London: Author. Retrieved April 10, 2004, from http://www.teachernet.gov.uk/wholeschool/sen/senstrategy/

Dyson, A. (2005). Philosophy, politics and economics? The story of inclusive education in England. In D. Mitchell (Ed.), *Contextualising inclusive education.* London: Routledge.

National Statistics. (2003a). *Statistics of education: Special educational needs in England: January 2003.* London: The Stationery Office. Retrieved April 10, 2004, from http://www.dfes.gov .uk/rsgateway/DB/SBU/b000429/specialneeds.pdf

National Statistics. (2003b). *Statistics of education: Schools in England.* London: The Stationery Office. Retrieved April 19, 2004, from http://www.dfes.gov.uk/rsgateway/DB/VOL/v000417/schools _volume_2003.pdf

Office for Standards in Education. (2000). *Evaluating educational inclusion.* London: Author.

Rustemier, S., & Vaughan, M. (2005). *Segregation trends—Local education authorities in England 2002–2004. Placement of pupils with statements in special schools and other segregated settings.* Bristol: Centre for Studies on Inclusive Education.

United Nations Educational, Scientific and Cultural Organization. (1994). *Salamanca statement and framework for action on special needs education.* Paris: Author.

SUSIE MILES
ALAN DYSON
PETER FARRELL
*University of Manchester*

**BELGIUM, SPECIAL EDUCATION**
**DENMARK, SPECIAL EDUCATION**
**FRANCE, SPECIAL EDUCATION**

## ENGLISH AS A SECOND LANGUAGE (ESL) AND SPECIAL EDUCATION

See SECOND LANGUAGE LEARNERS IN SPECIAL EDUCATION.

## ENGRAMS

Psychologists have long questioned how information is stored and subsequently retrieved from the brain. As early as 1900, Müller and Pilzecker argued that memory involves an unobservable physical change in the central nervous system that becomes relatively permanent as a result of repeated presentation of information. In keeping with this notion, most neurobiological theories of memory have hypothesized the existence of a memory trace or engram. Generally, this term is used to denote the relatively permanent structural or biochemical change in the brain consistent with the long-term storage of information (Hillgard & Bower, 1975). Information in short-term memory, on the other hand, appears to be less stable and is inaccessible unless converted into the enduring long-term store.

Retrieval of the memory trace is seen to be based on a reactivation of the same physical structure or biochemical conditions that were responsible for the initial storage or encoding process (Bloch & Laroche, 1984). This reactivation process seems to be triggered by stimuli that are the same or similar to the original stimulus event. From this point of view, both storage and retrieval are based on similar "neuronal circuits."

## REFERENCES

Bloch, V., & Laroche, S. (1984). Facts and hypotheses related to the search for the engram. In G. Lynch, J. L. McGaugh, & N. M. Weinberger (Eds.), *Neurobiology of learning and memory* (pp. 249–260). New York: Guilford.

Hillgard, E. R., & Bower, G. H. (1975). *Theories of learning.* Englewood Cliffs, NJ: Prentice Hall.

Müller, G. E., & Pilzecker, A. (1900). Experimentelle beitrage zur lehre von gedachtniss. *Zeitschrift fur Psychologie, 1,* 1–300.

JEFFREY W. GRAY
*Ball State University*

RAYMOND S. DEAN
*Ball State University*
*Indiana University School of Medicine*

**MEMORY DISORDERS**

# ENRICHMENT

Enrichment is a term that is frequently used to denote one form or approach to differentiating instruction for gifted youth. It is also often used to denote supplementary curriculum for youth at any level of ability. When the term refers to a form of instruction for gifted youth, it may be defined, by contrast, with terms such as acceleration, individualization, or grouping. These terms may, however, relate chiefly to administrative arrangements, just as enrichment may relate to an approach that administratively refers to provision for the gifted by the regular teacher in a typical heterogeneous classroom. Administrative acceleration may simply refer to a gifted child's early admission to school, grade skipping in the elementary school, or early admission to college. Individualization may refer to the administrative arrangement of continuous progress in an ungraded school. Finally, grouping may refer to the gathering of all mathematically talented youth into a single "honors" mathematics class in seventh grade. While these administrative approaches may stem in part from concern with the nature or needs of gifted youth, they tend to acquire a functional autonomy that makes them independent alternatives or options, regardless of gifted youths' specific needs.

Masse and Gagne (1983) argued that proper definitions of the term *enrichment* and the associated terms, *acceleration, individualization,* and *grouping,* must grow out of consideration of the special and unique characteristics of the gifted and their correlated special needs. They noted, however, that lists of characteristics of gifted (and talented) youths can be extensive and even contradictory. From their own review of research on characteristics of the gifted they concluded that there are four basic and pervasive characteristics: (1) rapid learning; (2) ease in learning complex material; (3) diversity of interests; and (4) depth of specific interests. Renzulli's (1979) three-ring conception of giftedness would probably be similar in stressing the components of ability (rapid learning, complex learning, and task commitment) and depth of interest, but Renzulli's third component, creative ability, is probably not reflected in Masse and Gagne's concept. However, in his enrichment triad instructional model, Renzulli (1977) proposed a Type I enrichment that provides gifted youths with an opportunity for exploratory learning in areas of varied interests. Such activity might meet the need generated by the characteristic of "varied interests" noted by Masse and Gagne. Type II enrichment in the triad model refers to group instructional activities to teach thinking and feeling processes, while Type III refers to enrichment through opportunities to investigate real problems. Type III activities tie in with depth of specific interest, which Masse and Gagne identified as a primary characteristic of gifted students.

Stanley (1979) proposed four types of enrichment. The first is busywork, or simply more of the same type of work done by all students. A second type is irrelevant academic enrichment, which is supplementary instruction that pays no attention to the special talents or characteristics of gifted youth. The third type is cultural enrichment, which ignores the student's talents or abilities but offers curriculum in the arts and foreign languages. The fourth type, relevant enrichment, provides special instruction directly related to gifted youths' special talents or characteristics (e.g., an enriched mathematics course for mathematically talented youths). In contrast to these four types of enrichment, Stanley proposed that acceleration is always vertical, moving a gifted youth to higher levels. In contrast to his use of the term of vertical to refer to acceleration, the term horizontal is often used to refer to enrichment. Stanley characterized it as a process of teaching more content but at the same level of difficulty or complexity.

Tannenbaum (1983) argued that enrichment for the gifted always requires a curriculum that is differentiated from the regular curriculum in that it is designed to meet the special needs of gifted youths. Tannenbaum (1983) went on to propose an enrichment matrix that can be used to design a curriculum for the gifted. The matrix calls for five types of content adjustment: (1) expansion of basic skills; (2) teaching core content in less time; (3) broadening the knowledge base; (4) teaching content related to the teacher's special expertise; and (5) out-of-school mentoring experiences. The matrix also attends to teaching higher-level thinking skills (Baer, 1988) and social-affective modification. These modifications can be applied to all curricular areas.

The term enrichment is best used to refer to curriculum experiences that are supplements to or replacements for the regular curriculum. Enrichment for the gifted should be designed to meet their specific needs and their capacity to learn more complex material. The term acceleration refers to instruction or learning at an earlier age than normal and at a faster pace. Administrative acceleration should be used to meet the needs of gifted youths for instruction at a level that matches their readiness or achievement levels and their need to learn rapidly or at a faster pace.

The ideal educational program for gifted youths offers a combination of enriched curriculum and accelerated instruction. That is, these students are allowed to move into higher and appropriate levels of the regular school curriculum, to be taught at a pace that matches their capacity to learn, and to experience an enriched or augmented curriculum that meets their need for extended and more complex learning.

## REFERENCES

Baer, J. (1988). Let's not handicap gifted thinkers. *Educational Leadership, 45*(7), 66–72.

Masse, P., & Gagne, F. (1983). Observations on enrichment and acceleration. In B. M. Shore, F. Gagne, S. Larivee, R. H. Tali, & R. E. Tremblay (Eds.), *Face to face with giftedness* (pp. 395–413). New York: Trillium.

Renzulli, J. S. (1977). *The enrichment triad model: A guide for developing defensible programs for the gifted and talented.* Mansfield Center, CT: Creative Learning Press.

Renzulli, J. S. (1979). *What makes giftedness?* Los Angeles: National State Leadership Training Institute for the Gifted/Talented.

Stanley, J. C. (1979). Identifying and nurturing the intellectually gifted. In W. C. George, S. J. Cohn, & J. C. Stanley (Eds.), *Educating the gifted, acceleration and enrichment* (pp. 172–180). Baltimore: Johns Hopkins University Press.

Tannenbaum, A. J. (1983). *Gifted children, psychological and educational perspectives.* New York: Macmillan.

JOHN FELDHUSEN
*Purdue University*
First edition

JOHN BAER
*Rider University*
Third edition

**CREATIVITY**
**CREATIVITY TESTS**

# ENRICHMENT TRIAD MODEL

The Enrichment Triad Model is a teaching-learning model developed by J. S. Renzulli (1977) specifically for teaching gifted children. Renzulli's model is designed to be used with students who have three interacting clusters of traits—creativity, high ability, and task commitment. Identified students with these traits take part in a program based on three interrelated categories of enrichment that are depicted in Figure 1. These categories include (1) Type I, general exploratory activities; (2) Type II, group training activities; and (3) Type III, individual and small group investigations of real problems. The first two categories (Types I and II) are considered appropriate for all learners, whereas the third category (Type III) consists of advanced-level experiences that gifted students pursue on a self-selected basis.

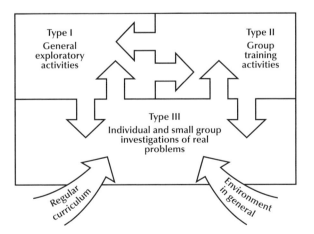

**Figure 1** The enrichment triad module

*Source:* From *The Enrichment Triad Model* by J. S. Renzulli. Copyright 1977 by Creative Learning Press. Reprinted by permission.

Type I enrichment consists of general exploratory experiences that are designed to expose students to a variety of topics or areas of study that are not ordinarily covered in the regular curriculum. This type of enrichment is provided through a variety of activities such as interest or learning centers, audio-visual materials, field trips, guest speakers, or teacher demonstrations.

In Type II enrichment, the teacher uses special methods, materials, and instructional techniques that are specifically designed to develop higher-level thinking processes, research skills, and processes related to personal and social development. These are exercises that will help students deal more effectively with content and solve problems in a variety of areas and new situations.

Type III enrichment activities are individual and small group investigations, and these are the major focus of this model. These activities are considered especially appropriate for gifted students. Students are encouraged to gather new data, use the authentic methods of researchers in particular fields of knowledge, and share the results of their work with appropriate audiences. According to Renzulli (1977), when students have superior potential for performance in particular areas of sincere interest, they "must be allowed the opportunity to pursue topics therein to unlimited levels of inquiry" (p. 17). To develop his model, Renzulli investigated the characteristics of eminent adults (Roe, 1952), studied Ward's (1961) ideas for inquiry, and adopted Bruner's (1960) and Torrance's (1965) conclusions that young children are able to engage in critical and creative investigations.

The Enrichment Triad Model has been popular in many schools because it is very inclusive. All students may participate in Type I and Type II activities, and students who have the ability and interest can design their own Type III investigations for in-depth explorations of topics of special interest. These individual and small-group research projects are often carried out during school time that has been freed up through compacting requirements of the regular curriculum.

## REFERENCES

Bruner, J. S. (1960). *The process of education.* Cambridge, MA: Harvard University Press.

Renzulli, J. S. (1977). *The Enrichment Triad Model.* Wethersfield, CT: Creative Learning Press.

Roe, A. (1952). *The making of a scientist.* New York: Dodd&Mead.

Torrance, E. P. (1965). *Gifted children in the classroom.* New York: Macmillan.

Ward, V. S. (1961). *Educating the gifted: An axiomatic approach.* Columbus, OH: Merrill.

JUNE SCOBEE
*University of Houston, Clear Lake*
First edition

JOHN BAER
*Rider University*
Third edition

CREATIVITY
CREATIVITY, THEORIES OF

# ENURESIS

Enuresis may be broadly defined as the repeated involuntary voiding of urine that occurs beyond the age at which bladder control is expected and for which there is no organic or urologic explanation. According to the American Psychiatric Association (1994), diagnostic criteria include at least two events per month for children between the ages of 5 and 6, or at least one monthly episode for older children. However, many (e.g., Campbell, 1970; Doleys, 1977; Eufemia, Wesolowski, Trice, & Tseng, 1984) note that children as young as 3 years old may be considered enuretic.

Childhood enuresis is classified as either nocturnal (occurring during sleep) or diurnal (occurring during waking hours). Distinctions have also been made between primary enuresis (child has always been enuretic) and secondary enuresis (child loses previously acquired control). According to Sorotzkin (1984), the view that secondary enuresis is related to higher levels of psychological stress or organic etiology is not based on empirical evidence. Furthermore, the lack of prognostic value of distinguishing primary and secondary enuresis also attests to not making such a distinction.

Reported prevalence estimates vary greatly. In a review of literature, Siegel (1983) reports that there are more than 3 million enuretic children in America. He also states that approximately 20 percent of all children are nocturnal enuretics at age 5, with half of these children remaining enuretic at age 10. The American Academy of Family Physicians (AAFP; 2006) reports that between 5 and 7 million children experience enuresis. Most researchers report that enuresis is about twice as prevalent among males than females.

Enuresis has been studied from a variety of theoretical perspectives. Although there are many variants of the psychoanalytic orientation, all share the assumption that enuresis is merely the symptomatic expression of intrapsychic problems. For example, enuresis has been variously viewed as an expression of repressed sexual drives, an act of displaced aggression against parents, a masochistic expulsion of destructive energy, a functional equivalent of a fetish, and a desire for regression that frequently occurs with the birth of a sibling or separation (Mountjoy, Ruben, & Bradford, 1984; Sorotzkin, 1984). Siegel (1983) concludes that empirical evidence does not support the view of enuresis as a symptom of underlying psychological disturbance.

A number of biological factors have been studied in relation to enuresis. The maturational lag hypothesis, for example, posits that neurological immaturity is responsible for primary enuresis; this perspective has been seriously questioned, however, since nearly all 5-year-old nocturnal enuretics have occasional dry nights, indicating maturation has occurred (Sorotzkin, 1984). Other biological variables that have been implicated include genetic factors, infections, atypical sleep patterns, and small functional bladder capacities (Sorotzkin, 1984). Of these factors, diminished functional bladder capacity is most supported by research although even that support is equivocal.

From a behavioral perspective, enuresis is essentially viewed as the failure to appropriately respond to both physiological and environmental cues for urination. Current behavioral theories consider both classical and operant factors.

Although a diverse array of treatments for enuresis have been reported (e.g., drug therapy, psychotherapy, hypnotherapy, fluid restrictive diets, elimination diets, and surgery), behavioral approaches have unquestionably received the most empirical attention. Among the many behavioral treatments, the most frequently employed are urine alarm procedures, retention control training, and treatment packages that incorporate multiple components.

The urine alarm procedure involves the use of an apparatus by which an alarm is activated at the onset of urination. While the device was originally developed for (and most often used for) treating nocturnal enuresis, it has been adapted and used to treat diurnal enuresis as well. There is some disagreement regarding whether the procedure represents classical conditioning (i.e., after repeated pairings of the bell, which causes the child to awaken and inhibit urination and heed full bladder cues, distention of the bladder eventually acquires discriminative stimulus properties) or operant conditioning (i.e., the bell is an aversive stimulus that is avoided by inhibiting urination and awakening). Empirical evidence attests to the efficacy of the procedure. Doleys (1985) reports that typical data indicate a 75 percent success rate, with relapse rates of 40 percent; reapplication of the procedure is typically successful with 60 to 70 percent of those who initially relapse. Procedural variations such as gradually requiring the child to drink large quantities prior to bedtime and using an intermittent schedule of alarm presentation have yielded higher success rates and/or lower relapse rates (Doleys, 1977).

Retention-control training is a procedure in which the child is required to refrain from urinating for progressively longer periods of time. It is based on the premise that such training increases functional bladder capacity (i.e., the volume at which evacuating contractions occur). Although some evidence exists to support the procedure, it has not proven universally successful (Doleys, 1977; Siegel, 1983).

A multicomponent treatment for nocturnal enuresis is the dry-bed training procedure of Azrin, Sneed, and Foxx (1974). Among the features of this intensive program are the use of a urine alarm, increased intake of liquids, retention control training, practice in toileting, positive reinforcement for appropriate urination, hourly awakenings, and verbal reprimands and positive practice overcorrection for accidents. The dry-pants training program (Azrin & Foxx, 1974) is directed at diurnal enuresis and is procedurally similar to the dry-bed program. The total program is regarded as highly successful; however, program modifications such as eliminating the alarm should be made with caution (Eufemia et al., 1984; Siegel, 1983; Sorotzkin, 1984).

## REFERENCES

American Academy of Family Physicians (AAFP). (2006). *Enuresis (bed wetting)*. Retrieved June 10, 2006, from http://www.family doctor.org/366.xml

American Psychiatric Association. (1994). *Diagnostic and statistical manual of mental disorders* (4th ed.). Washington, DC: Author.

Azrin, N. H., & Foxx, R. M. (1974). *Toilet training in less than a day*. New York: Simon & Schuster.

Azrin, N. H., Sneed, T. J., & Foxx, R. M. (1974). Dry-bed training: Rapid elimination of childhood enuresis. *Behavior Research and Therapy, 12,* 147–156.

Campbell, M. F. (1970). Neuromuscular neuropathy. In M. F. Campbell & T. H. Harrison (Eds.), *Urology* (Vol. 2, pp. 1935–1948). Philadelphia: Saunders.

Doleys, D. M. (1977). Behavioral treatment of nocturnal enuresis in children: A review of the recent literature. *Psychological Bulletin, 84,* 30–54.

Doleys, D. M. (1985). Bell and pad conditioning. In A. S. Bellack & M. Hersen (Eds.), *Dictionary of behavior therapy techniques* (pp. 46–48). New York: Pergamon.

Eufemia, R. L., Wesolowski, M. D., Trice, A. D., & Tseng, M. S. (1984). The long and short term effects of dry bed training. *Education and Treatment of Children, 7,* 61–66.

Mountjoy, P. T., Ruben, D. H., & Bradford, T. S. (1984). Recent technological advances in the treatment of enuresis: Theory and research. *Behavior Modification, 8,* 291–315.

Siegel, L. J. (1983). Psychosomatic and psychophysiological disorders. In R. J. Morris & T. R. Kratochwill (Eds.), *The practice of child therapy* (pp. 253–286). New York: Pergamon.

Sorotzkin, B. (1984). Nocturnal enuresis: Current perspectives. *Clinical Psychology Review, 4,* 293–315.

JAMES P. KROUSE
*Clarion University of Pennsylvania*

APPLIED BEHAVIOR ANALYSIS
ENCOPRESIS

# EPICANTHIC FOLD

The epicanthic fold, also known as epicanthus, refers to the vertical fold of skin from the upper eyelid covering the lacrimal caruncle at the inner canthus of the eye (the point where the upper and lower eyelids meet). The expression of epicanthus may be extreme, covering the entire canthus, or mild. It is a normal feature in some ethnic groups, such as those of Asian descent. Epicanthus also is commonly seen in infants under approximately 3 years (Waldrop & Halverson, 1971).

In persons for whom there is no evidence of ethnic etiology, the presence of epicanthus may represent a congenital anomaly. Epicanthus is a physical anomaly that typically is observed in persons with Down's syndrome, for example (*Blakiston's,* 1979). Epicanthus also is one of several minor physical anomalies that has been associated with learning and behavior problems in children (Rosenberg & Weller, 1973; Waldrop & Halverson, 1971).

## REFERENCES

*Blakiston's Gould medical dictionary* (4th ed.). (1979). New York: McGraw-Hill.

Rosenberg, J. B., & Weller, G. M. (1973). Minor physical anomalies and academic performance in young school children. *Developmental Medicine & Child Neurology, 15,* 131–135.

Waldrop, M. F., & Halverson, C. F. (1971). Minor physical anomalies and hyperactive behavior in young children. In J. Hellmuth (Ed.), *The exceptional infant* (Vol. 2, pp. 343–380). New York: Brunner/Mazel.

CATHY F. TELZROW
*Kent State University*

DYSMORPHIC FEATURES
MINOR PHYSICAL ANOMALIES

# EPIDEMIOLOGY

Epidemiology is reviewed within two models: medical and psychological. Epidemiology is the study of specific medical disorders within communities to measure risk of attack and to uncover etiological clues and modes of spread. Reid (1960) defines epidemiological inquiry as "the study of the distribution of diseases in time and space, and of the factors that influence this distribution."

While elucidating etiology is a prime concern, collected data are used in planning services and devising treatment modes (Graham, 1979). Basic data include (1) identification of a particular disorder in a defined population, (2) incidence rates, (3) prevalence rates, and (4) dynamic patterns of occurrence over time. In addition to identifying disease syndromes and origins, epidemiology serves to test the reliability of concepts derived solely from clinical studies, thus avoiding assumptions based on relationships that may be merely correlational rather than causative. Correlational data do not permit inferences of causality.

Epidemiology employed to study psychological disorders uncovers common underlying factors in nonmedical problems. The premise of both models remains unchanged: to complete the clinical picture (Morris, 1964). Neither model is used solely to collect information but to use data to further effective treatment and services for disordered populations.

One basic difference between medical and psychological epidemiology is that the former has definitive criteria for judging physical normalcy while the latter, focusing primarily on behavior, is left with a range of altering, social criteria that are difficult to quantify. Another difference between the models concerns the search for etiology that may or may not be relevant to nonmedical surveys, depending on the conceptual perspective of the researcher (e.g., psychoanalytic, behavioral systems theory). Nevertheless, a profitable psychological inquiry employs quantitative cut-off points, if defined arbitrarily, to identify deviations from the norm (Rutter et al., 1970). Epidemiologists who take behavior as the starting point define disorders according to social criteria, itemize behaviors, count behaviors empirically, and factor analyze data to examine the amount of variance explained by particular behavior dimensions for different populations (Rutter, 1977).

Methodological problems in the psychological approach include (1) whether the population is represented in sampling; (2) questionnaire reliability; (3) whether nonresponders represent an atypical group; and (4) whether observed behavior is related to events and people in a subject's life. Psychological epidemiology is the vehicle for a number of comprehensive studies along a wide range of topics: child abuse (Baldwin & Oliver, 1975; Light, 1973); specific reading retardation in relation to deviant behavior (Rutter & Yule, 1973); disorders of middle childhood (Pringle et al., 1966; Rutter et al., 1970); adolescent turmoil (Rutter et al., 1976); autism (Folstein & Rutter, 1977); and a host of others (see especially Ollendick, 1998).

## REFERENCES

Baldwin, J. A., & Oliver, J. E. (1975). Epidemiology and family characteristics of severely abused children. *British Journal of Preventive & Social Medicine, 29,* 205–221.

Folstein, S., & Rutter, M. (1977). Generic influences and infantile autism. *Nature, 265,* 726–728.

Graham, P. (1979). Epidemiological studies. In H. C. Quay & J. S. Werry (Eds.), *Psychopathological disorders of childhood.* New York: Wiley.

Light, R. J. (1973). Abused and neglected children in America: A study of alternative policies. *Harvard Educational Review, 43,* 556.

Morris, J. N. (1964). *Uses of epidemiology.* Baltimore: Williams & Wilkins.

Ollendick, T. (Ed.). (1998). *Children and adolescents: Clinical formulation and treatment.* In A. Bellack & M. Hersen (Eds.), *Comprehensive clinical psychology* (Vol. 5). New York: Elsevier.

Pringle, M. L. K., Butler, N. R., & Davie, R. (1966). *11,000 seven-year-olds.* London: Longmans.

Reid, D. D. (1960). *Epidemiological methods in the study of mental disorders.* Geneva, Switzerland: World Health Organization.

Rutter, M. (1977). Surveys to answer questions. In P. J. Graham (Ed.), *Epidemiological approaches in child psychiatry.* New York: Academic.

Rutter, M., Graham, P., Chadwick, O., & Yule, W. (1976). Adolescent turmoil: Fact or fiction. *Journal of Child Psychology & Psychiatry, 17,* 35–56.

Rutter, M., Tizard, J., & Whitmore, K. (Eds.). (1970). *Education, health and behavior.* London: Longmans.

Rutter, M., & Yule, W. (1973). Specific reading retardation. In L. Mann & D. Sabatino (Eds.), *The first review of special education.* Philadelphia: JSE.

C. MILDRED TASHMAN
*College of St. Rose*

**DIAGNOSIS IN SPECIAL EDUCATION**
**ETIOLOGY**
**RESEARCH IN SPECIAL EDUCATION**

## EPILEPSY

See SEIZURE DISORDERS.

## EPILEPSY FOUNDATION OF AMERICA

The Epilepsy Foundation of America (EFA) is a nonprofit, voluntary health organization devoted to epilepsy care, treatment, research, and education. The national foundation, together with its numerous local chapters, provides information on a wide variety of issues related to epilepsy, including low-cost anticonvulsant medication, legal rights, and employment. The foundation provides a discount drug pharmacy service for its members.

Numerous excellent publications relevant to the school-age child with epilepsy are available from the foundation. These include pamphlets such as "What Everybody Should Know About Epilepsy," "Epilepsy: The Teacher's Role," and "Epilepsy School Alert." School Alert is one of two major annual educational programs sponsored by the foundation. In operation since 1972, the School Alert program was developed in conjunction with the Department of School Nurses and the National Education Association; it is designed for EFA chapter use with schools in the local chapter vicinity. Some state departments of education have officially endorsed the School Alert program.

The address for the Epilepsy Foundation of America is 4351 Garden City Drive, Landover, MD 20785 information is available online at www.efa.org.

## REFERENCES

*Epilepsy school alert.* (1974). Washington, DC: Epilepsy Foundation of America.

Foster, J. C., Szoke, C. O., Kapisovsky, P. M., & Kriger, L. S. (1979). *Guidance, counseling, and support services for high school students with physical disabilities.* Cambridge, MA: Technical Education Research Centers.

CATHY F. TELZROW
*Kent State University*

# EPINEPHRINE

Epinephrine is one of the naturally occurring catecholamines (together with norepinephrine and dopamine). Its action sites are mainly in the sympathetic nervous system (Katzung, 1982). Leavitt (1982) suggests wider involvement of epinephrine in automatic processes owing to its presence in the hypothalamus. The gross actions of epinephrine are to relax bronchial muscles, constrict bronchial vasculature, and increase cardiac output, thus increasing overall oxygenation. Secondary central nervous system effects may occur through the overall increase in blood pressure and oxygen availability (McEvoy, 1984). Thus, the overall action of epinephrine is that of a mild stimulant. Because of its action as a bronchodilator, one of the chief uses of epinephrine is in providing symptomatic relief for sufferers of asthma and chronic obstructive pulmonary diseases and allergic reactions (MedlinePlus, 2006).

Side effects of epinephrine overdosage or sensitivity are similar to those of other stimulants (i.e., fear, anxiety, tenseness, restlessness, sleeplessness, or excitability; Blum, 1984). More serious reactions appear similar to amphetamine toxicity and include psychomotor agitation, assaultiveness, disorientation, impaired memory, panic, hallucinations, and homicidal or suicidal ideation/tendencies (McEvoy, 1984). Toxicity is more likely to occur among persons who are hypertensive or hyperthyroid (McEvoy, 1984).

## REFERENCES

Blum, K. (1984). *Handbook of abusable drugs.* New York: Gardner Press.

Katzung, B. G. (1982). *Basic and clinical pharmacology.* Los Altos, CA: Lange Medical.

Leavitt, F. (1982). *Drugs and behavior.* New York: Wiley.

McEvoy, G. K. (1984). *American hospital formulary service: Drug information 84.* Bethesda, MD: American Society of Hospital Pharmacists.

MedlinePlus. (2006). *Epinephrine injection.* Retrieved February 6, 2006, from http://www.nlm.nih.gov/medlineplus/druginfo/

ROBERT F. SAWICKI
*Lake Erie Institute of
Rehabilitation*

CATECHOLAMINES
DOPAMINE

# EQUAL EDUCATIONAL OPPORTUNITY

In its earliest form, equal educational opportunity referred to a belief that education would "close no entrance to the poorest, the weakest, the humblest. Say to ambition everywhere, the field is clear, the contest fair; come, and win your share if you can!" (Woodard & Watson, 1963). A number of judicial decisions have affirmed this basic premise that underlies equal educational opportunity (e.g., *Brown* v. *Board of Education,* 1954, 1955; *Lau* v. *Nichols,* 1974; *Regents of California* v. *Bakke,* 1978).

While there is general agreement on what constitutes equal educational opportunity, there is some uncertainty as to whether this implies equal access to education, the process of education, or the outcomes of education (Hyman & Schaaf, 1981). In the case of disabled learners, the concept of equal opportunity has focused on equal access and equity in the process of education.

The first equal opportunity decision involving disabled students (*PARC* v. *Commonwealth of Pennsylvania,* 1971) resulted in an order providing that the state of Pennsylvania could not postpone or deny disabled children access to a publicly supported education. In addition, those school districts that provided education to preschool children were required to provide such education for disabled children. A similar case in the District of Columbia (*Mills* v. *Board of Education,* 1972) resulted in a similar judicial order, with the court indicating that if sufficient funds are not available to finance all of the services and programs that are needed and desirable in the system, then the available funds must be expended equitably in such a manner *that* no child is entirely excluded from a publicly supported education consistent with his or her needs and ability to benefit therefrom.

Apart from protections afforded by the judiciary, attorney generals in a number of states interpreted state laws, regulations, and administrative guidelines to include the public education of disabled children and youths (e.g., Arkansas, 1973; Wisconsin, 1973).

With the passage of PL 94-142, the Education of All Handicapped Children Act, the federal government extended the concept of equal educational opportunity to include the process by which education is delivered. These rights are reaffirmed in the Individuals with Disabilities Education Act and in the Americans with Disabilities Act. Not only was access to education required, but it was to he provided, to the extent possible, with nondisabled students in regular education classrooms. Moreover, disabled students were to receive specially designed instruction to meet their unique needs, as well as the related services (e.g., audiology, psychological services) required for disabled students to benefit from special education.

## REFERENCES

Hyman, J. B., & Schaaf, J. M. (1981). *Educational equity: Conceptual problems and prospects for theory.* Washington, DC: National Institute of Education.

U.S. Department of Education. (1985). *Seventh annual report to Congress on the implementation of the Education of the Handicapped Act.* Washington, DC: Author.

Woodard, C. V., & Watson, T. (1963). *Agrarian rebel.* New York: Oxford University Press.

PATRICIA ANN ARRAMSON
*Hudson Public Schools, Hudson, Wisconsin*
Second edition

KIMBERLEY APPLEQUIST
*University of Colorado at Colorado Springs*
Third edition

**AMERICANS WITH DISABILITIES ACT**
**BROWN v. BOARD OF EDUCATION**
**INDIVIDUALS WITH DISABILITIES EDUCATION**
  **IMPROVEMENT ACT OF 2004 (IDEIA)**
**MAINSTREAMING**
**MILLS v. BOARD OF EDUCATION**
**PENNSYLVANIA ASSOCIATION FOR RETARDED CITIZENS**
  **v. PENNSYLVANIA**

# EQUAL EMPLOYMENT OPPORTUNITY COMMISSION

The purpose of the Equal Employment Opportunity Commission (EEOC) is to eliminate discrimination based on race, ethnicity, religion, national origin, and age in hiring, promoting, firing, wages, testing, training, apprenticeship, and all other conditions of employment. The commission also promotes voluntary action programs by employers, unions, and community organizations to make equal employment opportunity an actuality. The EEOC also is responsible for all compliance and enforcement activities relating to equal employment among federal employees and applicants, including discrimination on the basis of disability.

The EEOC was created under Title VII of the Civil Rights Act of 1964. Title VII was amended by the Equal Employment Opportunity Act of 1972 and the Pregnancy Discrimination Act of 1978. In 1990, the EEOC's authority was expanded to include enforcement of claims of discrimination on the basis of disability status under Title I of the Americans with Disabilities Act, which prohibits private employers, state and local governments, employment agencies, and labor unions from discriminating against individuals with disabilities in employment matters. The commission consists of five commissioners appointed by the president with advice and consent of the Senate to 5-year terms. The president designates a commissioner as chairperson and appoints a counsel general. The work of the commission has been credited with widespread banning of various forms of discrimination against a variety of groups. Reorganization Plan One of 1978 transferred to the EEOC Section 501 of the Rehabilitation Act of 1973, which pertains to employment discrimination against individuals with disabilities in the federal government.

The EEOC has field offices that receive written complaints against public or private employers, labor organizations, joint labor-management, and apprenticeship programs for charges of job discrimination or age discrimination. Charges of Title VII violations in private industry or state or local government must be filed with the commission within 180 days of the alleged violation. The commission has the authority to bring suit in federal district court if a negotiated settlement cannot be found. The commission encourages settlements prior to determination by the agency through fact-finding conferences and informal methods of conciliation, conference, and persuasion.

The EEOC has issued several guidelines on employment policies and practices, the most comprehensive of which are the Guidelines on Discrimination Because of Sex (April 5, 1972) and the Guidelines on Employee Selection Procedures (August 1, 1970). The commission is also a major publisher of employment data on minorities and women. For further information, contact the EEOC's National Contact Center at U.S. Equal Employment Opportunity Commission, P.O. Box 7033, Lawrence, KS, 66044.

## REFERENCES

Darby, M. (1983). Equal employment opportunity commission. In D. R. Whitman (Ed.), *Government agencies.* Westport, CT: Greenwood.

Equal Employment Opportunity Commission (EEOC). (1983). 17th annual report. *American statistics index* (Suppl. 10). Washington, DC: U.S. Government Printing Office.

DANIEL R. PAULSON
*University of Wisconsin at Stout*
Second edition

KIMBERLY F. APPLEQUIST
*University of Colorado at Colorado Springs*
Third edition

**AMERICANS WITH DISABILITIES ACT**
**CIVIL RIGHTS OF INDIVIDUALS WITH DISABILITIES**
**EQUAL EDUCATION OPPORTUNITY**

# EQUAL PROTECTION

Equal protection is a term often applied to the need for due process in the differential treatment of any persons in society. In special education, equal protection applies to placement proceedings or any other action that might result in differential treatment of a child. The term is derived from the Fourteenth Amendment to the U.S. Constitution.

The Fourteenth Amendment equal protection clause provides, in a simple, straightforward statement, the far-reaching assertion that "no state shall . . . deny to any person within its jurisdiction the equal protection of the laws." The court system has interpreted this statement in numerous cases and generally holds that it does not require that all persons be treated equally under all laws at all times. According to Overcast and Sales (1982), the essence of the constitutional guarantee provided by the equal protection clause of the Fourteenth Amendment is that any classifications made in a rule or a law must be reasonable and not of an arbitrary nature. In determining the reasonableness of a classification, the courts normally look to see whether (1) the classification itself is a reasonable one, (2) the classification furthers an appropriate or legitimate government purpose, and, (3) the classification's subgroups, or classes, are treated equally (Overcast & Sales, 1982; Sales et al., 1999).

Whenever the classification affects a fundamental right or is related to suspect criteria (e.g., is statistically related to membership in a protected class such as race or handicap), the judiciary also will examine two additional criteria. The court wishes to determine in these circumstances, which circumstances are always extant in special education, whether the classification is necessary to promote some compelling state interest, and whether the classification represents the least burdensome alternative available or that can be designed. Suspect criteria that have been identified by the courts include race, religion, national origin, alien status, legitimacy, poverty, and sex. Discrimination related to these categories takes place almost daily in the schools, however, it must be based on a valid distinction among the groups.

The courts have held that they have the right to intervene in the actions of schools and others when any basic constitutional safeguard is violated, including the equal protection clause (e.g., *Epperson* v. *Arkansas,* 1968; *Ingraham* v. *Wright,* 1977). The equal protection clause has been used to protect students' right to an education on a number of occasions; this clause may be (and certainly has been) interpreted as granting the right to equal educational opportunity. School systems cannot discriminate among groups of people when providing an education unless there is a substantial and legitimate purpose for the discrimination (Bersoff, 1982). Prior to the passage of PL 94-142, the Education for All Handicapped Children Act of 1975, advocates fighting for the right of individuals with disabilities to attend public schools, from which they were frequently excluded, relied heavily on the equal protection clause of the Fourteenth Amendment in winning their cases. The equal protection clause also has been invoked in favor of children classified as disabled who have argued they are not disabled and claimed that by placing them in special education programs, they have been denied equal protection through exclusion from access to regular education with normal children (Bersoff, 1982; Reschly & Bersoff, 1999).

## REFERENCES

Bersoff, D. N. (1982). The legal regulation of school psychology. In C. R. Reynolds & T. B. Gutkin (Eds.), *The handbook of school psychology.* New York: Wiley.

Overcast, T. D., & Sales, B. D. (1982). The legal rights of students in the elementary and secondary public schools. In C. R. Reynolds & T. B. Gutkin (Eds.), *The handbook of school psychology.* New York: Wiley.

Reschly, D., & Bersoff, D. (1999). Law and school psychology. In C. R. Reynolds & T. B. Gutkin (Eds.), *The handbook of school psychology* (3rd ed.). New York: Wiley.

Sales, B. D., Krauss, D., Sacken, D., & Overcast, T. (1999). The legal rights of students. In C. R. Reynolds & T. B. Gutkin (Eds.), *The handbook of school psychology* (3rd ed.). New York: Wiley.

CECIL R. REYNOLDS
*Texas A&M University*

**LARRY P.
MARSHALL v. GEORGIA
MATTY T. v. HOLLADAY**

# EQUINE THERAPY

Equine therapy refers to prescribed medical treatment that uses horsemanship to alleviate an extensive array of physical, psychological, cognitive, and social disabilities. Brought to the United States from Europe, it has grown steadily in this country in popularity and credibility since 1970. Its effectiveness depends on the integration of services provided by a physician who prescribes treatment, a physical therapist who designs the therapeutic regimen, and an instructor who implements the program.

Kuprian (1981) distinguishes between hippotherapy, in which the horse's symmetrical rhythms are transferred to the rider's body passively, and riding therapy, in which the rider engages in active exercise (relaxation, stretching, strengthening). Still more advanced is vaulting, in which gymnastics are introduced (Kroger, 1981), and riding as sport, in which an individual competes against others, having accomplished a sufficient degree of fitness and skill (Heipertz, 1981). To the extent possible, grooming, tacking, and general horsemanship are added to each of these.

Among the benefits accredited to equine therapy by its proponents, riding skill notwithstanding, are improved physical mobility, stability, muscle tone, coordination, and balance; sensory integration; cognitive training and retraining; academic performance; emotional stability (self-esteem, accountability, diminished aggression); communication facility; and the ability to relate to others and function within a group (Brooke, 1976; Mason, 1980; Minner, Lawton, & Rusk, 1983; Stanford & Hawn, 1982). The fact that riding offers so many advantages to individuals of varying capacities is attributable, according to Rosenthal (1975), to its ability to satisfy the need inherent in all people for controlled risk activity. It is not recommended for all disabilities, however. Epilepsy characterized by seizures, for example, is considered too risky, as are bone and joint anomalies.

Additional information may be obtained from the North American Riding for the Handicapped Association (NARHA), P.O. Box 33150, Denver, Colorado, 80233. 1-800-369 RIDE or online at NARHA@NARHA.org.

## REFERENCES

Brooke, G. A. G. (1976). What riding offers the mentally handicapped. *Voice, 26*(2), 12–13.

Heipertz, W. (1981). Riding therapy for orthopaedic cases. In W. Heipertz (Ed.), *Therapeutic riding: Medicine, education, sports* (translated by M. Takeuchi; pp. 55–66). Canada: National Printers.

Kroger, A. (1981). Vaulting as an educational aid in schools for behaviorally disturbed children. In W. Heipertz (Ed.), *Therapeutic riding: Medicine, education, sports* (translated by M. Takeuchi; pp. 40–54). Canada: National Printers.

Kuprian, W. (1981). Hippotherapy and riding therapy as physiotherapeutic treatment methods. In W. Heipertz (Ed.), *Therapeutic riding: Medicine, education, sports* (translated by M. Takeuchi; pp. 14–39). Canada: National Printers.

Mason, H. (1980). A ride to health. *Special Education in Canada, 54*(4), 28–29.

Minner, S., Lawton, S., & Rusk, P. (1983). Equine therapy for handicapped students. *Pointer, 27*(4), 41–43.

Rosenthal, S. R. (1975). Risk exercise and the physically handicapped. *Rehabilitation Literature, 36*(5), 144–149.

Stanford, E., & Hawn, P. (1982). *Equestrian therapy in the treatment of traumatic head injury patients.* Paper presented at the Fourth International Congress on Therapeutic Riding, Malvern, PA.

Susan Shandelmier
*Eastern Pennsylvania Special
Education Regional Resources
Center*

**OCCUPATIONAL THERAPY
PHYSICAL THERAPY**

# ERRORLESS LEARNING

Errorless and near-errorless learning describes a method of instruction designed specifically to prevent the production of errors and to develop appropriate stimulus control (i.e., correct responding in the presence of the discriminative stimulus). Specifically, systematic antecedent (i.e., instructional prompts), response, and consequence manipulations (i.e., differential reinforcement) are arranged to increase the likelihood that correct or desired responding will occur in the presence of the desired antecedent conditions and not occur when those antecedent conditions are not present.

Errorless learning is based on three premises. First, environmental stimuli occasion or establish the opportunity for specific responses. Second, to achieve errorless learning, differential reinforcement, or delivering reinforcement for target behaviors in the presence of target (discriminative) stimuli versus in their absence and withholding reinforcement in the presence of target stimuli when undesired behavior occurs, is necessary. Differential reinforcement ensures control over target responding will be governed by discriminative stimuli rather than irrelevant stimuli. Last, error production limits the possibility to present positive reinforcement for the target behavior and the establishment of desired stimulus control (i.e., correct responding in the presence of the discriminative stimulus). Further, practicing errors may expose the learner to repeated failure and frustration. Instead, providing carefully sequenced stimulus examples and scaffolded antecedent instruction increases the learner's access to positive reinforcement and learning success.

Errorless learning methods are dependent on the use of either stimulus prompts or response prompts. The use of prompts increases the likelihood that a target behavior will occur and reinforcement be delivered, in the presence of the desired antecedent stimulus. Prompts can take many forms, including (1) verbal cues, (2) physical prompts, or (3) visual cues, and can be of full or partial intensity and intrusiveness.

Errorless learning approaches can be categorized as stimulus shaping and fading procedures and response prompting procedures. Stimulus shaping and fading is the process of providing sequentially fewer prompts that emphasize the relevant features of discriminative stimuli and nondiscriminative stimuli, until accurate responding occurs in the presence of discriminative stimuli themselves. For example, emphasizing the long tail of the letter /h/ with a different color, length, or width initially may help a student correctly identify the letter. Prompts may be removed gradually as the student continues to identify the letter /h/ correctly. Additionally, minimally different nonexamples from the letter /h/, such as /n/, may be presented. The short tail length of letter /n/ may initially be emphasized and gradually minimized, as the learner continues to accurately discriminate the letter /h/ from /n/.

Response prompting is a process of providing prompts that increases the probability that the target behavior will occur. Four types of response prompting procedures exist (1) increasing assistance (least-to-most prompts), (2) graduated guidance, (3) time delay (constant and progressive), and (4) decreasing assistance (most-to-least prompts). Increasing assistance procedures Increasing assistance procedures involve presenting a discriminative stimulus and providing the least intrusive prompt possible to ensure correct responding. If the target behavior does not occur, a more intrusive prompt is provided in the next instructional trial. This process of providing successively more intrusive prompts will continue, until the target behavior is performed.

Graduated guidance is most useful for teaching chained behaviors or complex skills (e.g., hand-washing, physical education skill), and refers to a procedure in which a discriminative stimulus is presented and full assistive prompts are immediately provided. As the learner independently engages in the target behavior, the pressure and intrusiveness of assistance is reduced (e.g., holding an arm versus touching it). However, if the learner begins to engage in an incorrect behavior, assistance is immediately reinstated. A teacher may eventually "shadow" the learner or follow the learner's movements closely without touching him or her, as they gain independence.

Time delay is a procedure in which a delay is imposed between the presentation of the discriminative stimulus and a prompt. A progressive time delay occurs when the time delay between the presentation of a discriminative stimulus and a prompt is initially brief. On successive trials, the time delay will increase until the target behavior is performed before the prompt is presented. A constant time delay is similar to a progressive time delay, except the delay is always the same length of time.

Decreasing assistance involves providing the most intrusive prompt after a discriminative stimulus is presented. As the learner engages in the target behavior, the intrusiveness of the prompt is systematically and gradually reduced, until the learner engages in the target behavior without a prompt.

## Research

Studies demonstrating the effectiveness of errorless learning strategies span multiple areas of behavioral research and practice. Haupt, Van Kirk, and Terraciano (1975) used two prompting methods to teach math facts. Both methods involved presenting the learner with math facts with the answers clearly visible. Gradually, the answers were covered up and eventually the learner correctly answered the math facts without the answers being visible.

MacDuff, Krantz, and McClannahan (1993) found that graduated guidance procedures were effective in teaching participants with autism to engage in picture activity schedules. The participants were also able to correctly perform novel activity schedules. In another example, Lamm and Greer (1988) implemented a least-to-most prompting procedure to encourage swallowing behavior in 3 infants with gastronomy tubes. The procedure was successful in evoking swallowing behavior for all 3 infants and the feeding tubes were removed for 2 of the infants (the other tube remained due to unrelated health problems).

Errorless learning has been effectively used to teach a variety of behaviors such as dressing skills (Engelman, Altus, Mosier, & Mathews, 2003), grocery shopping skills (Morse & Schuster, 2000), and teaching an individual to identify his or her name (Malott, Whaley, & Malott, 1997). Stimulus shaping and fading and response prompting procedures continue to be popular instructional methods, assisting individuals to acquire new behaviors.

## Guidelines for Practice

A multitude of errorless learning prompting procedures have been used to teach new skills. Some experts suggest that time-delay procedures may be the most efficient response prompting strategies. Others state that both progressive time delay and decreasing assistance strategies are superior to increasing assistance strategies (Billingsley & Romer, 1983). Le Grice and Blampied (1997) suggest that increasing assistance strategies are not only effective but are less intrusive and require less teacher effort. In general, a substantial body of research evidence supports the use of a variety of errorless learning strategies to improve teaching outcomes in different contexts and with different populations.

When selecting prompts, a few guidelines will be helpful. Prompts should be selected that emphasize the relevant features that are desired to control responding. For example, when teaching "zebra," stripes would be one stimulus feature to emphasize. Consideration should be given to how prompts are presented, which prompts will be easiest to fade, and which stimulus conditions promote generalization. For example, verbal prompts may be difficult to fade or minimize and a prompt always presented by the same person may promote stipulated responding. Last, to avoid overstipulated responding, instructional prompts should be faded and removed as quickly as possible when correct responding is observed.

Complex or chained behaviors are more difficult to teach than discrete behaviors (requiring one response). When teaching complex behaviors, the chain of behaviors should be broken down (task analyzed) into discrete components so that each discrete behavior is shaped and gradually linked to other behaviors in the chain. The goal is to provide positive reinforcement contingent upon occurrences of larger "chunks" of linked behaviors.

## Case Examples

### Example 1

"Monica" is a 4-year-old who knows her colors but is learning to identify the word *red*. Her teacher has an index card with the word red printed on it with a piece of red fabric attached. Her teacher uses decreasing assistance by first presenting the index card and says "What word is this?" Immediately her teacher says, "Say red," and positively reinforces Monica's response. Next, her teacher presents the index card and question without the verbal prompt until Monica reliably and accurately responds. Monica's teacher then removes the red fabric and presents the index card and question by itself. After correct responding without the red fabric, Monica's teacher presents the word in different fonts and on different paper, to ensure Monica can identify the word red when it is presented in other ways.

### Example 2

"Joseph" is learning to use a spoon. Joseph's father, Dan, uses the graduated guidance technique to teach him this skill. First, Dan holds and guides Joseph's hand and wrist while he spoons preferred food to his lips. Next, Dan decreases the pressure used to hold Joseph's hand and wrist while using his spoon. Dan then stops holding Joseph's hand and wrist and moves to touching Joseph's arm lightly while using the spoon, later his shoulder, and then does not touch Joseph at all, unless he misses or performs a step incorrectly.

### Example 3

"Miguel" is learning addition facts. His teacher uses a progressive time-delay procedure and asks Miguel to answer math fact questions. Miguel's teacher provides the answer to the math fact questions after waiting a second, when Miguel does not respond. After Miguel responds correctly within a second, his teacher begins to wait 3 seconds until providing the answer, then waits 9 seconds, 30 seconds, and finally does not provide the answer for any of the math facts, as Miguel reliably answers them all correctly.

### REFERENCES

Billingsley, F. F. & Romer, L. T. (1983). Response prompting and the transfer of stimulus control: Methods, research, and a conceptual framework. *Journal of the Association for Persons with Severe Handicaps, 8,* 3–12.

Engelman, K. K., Altus, D. E., Mosier, M. C., & Mathews, R. M. (2003). Brief training to promote the use of less intrusive prompts by nursing assistants in a dementia care unit. *Journal of Applied Behavior Analysis, 36,* 129–132.

Haupt, E. J., Van Kirk, M. J., & Terraciano, T. (1975). An inexpensive fading procedure to decrease errors and increase retention of number facts. In E. Ramp & G. Semb (Eds.), *Behavior analysis: Areas for research and application.* Upper Saddle River, NJ: Prentice Hall.

Lamm, N., & Greer, R. D. (1988). Induction and maintenance of swallowing responses in infants with dysphagia. *Journal of Applied Behavior Analysis, 21,* 143–156.

Le Grice, B. & Blampied, N. M. (1997). Learning to use video recorders and personal computers with increasing assistance prompting. *Journal of Developmental and Physical Disabilities, 9,* 17–29.

Long, E. S., Miltenberger, R. G., Ellingson, S. A., & Ott, S. M. (1999). Augmenting simplified habit reversal in the treatment of oral-digital habits exhibited by individuals with mental retardation. *Journal of Applied Behavior Analysis, 32,* 353–365.

MacDuff, G. S., Krantz, P. J., & McClannahan, L. E. (1993). Teaching children with autism to use photographic activity schedules: Maintenance and generalization of complex response chains. *Journal of Applied Behavior Analysis, 26,* 89–97.

Malott, R. W., Whaley, D. C., & Malott, M. E. (1997). *Elementary principles of behavior.* Upper Saddle River, NJ: Prentice Hall.

Morse, T. E. & Schuster, J. W. (2000). Teaching elementary students with moderate disabilities how to shop for groceries. *Exceptional Children, 66,* 273–288.

SARAH FAIRBANKS
GEORGE SUGAI
*University of Connecticut*

**DIRECT INSTRUCTION TEACHING STRATEGIES**

# ERTL INDEX

The problem of cultural bias in traditional measures of intelligence led to the development of alternative assessment strategies. One rather exotic strategy is the use of the Neural Efficiency Analyzer (NEA). Introduced by Ertl (1968), this instrument was purported to measure the reaction time of brain waves to 100 randomly presented flashes of light. Ertl argued that in contrast to traditional methods of intellectual assessment, the score obtained from the Neural Efficiency Analyzer (Ertl Index) was free of cultural influences and thus was appropriate for use with any ethnic group regardless of age.

The Ertl Index consists of the average time from the onset of the stimulus light to the appropriate brain wave change. Based on this average evoked potential, an estimate of the subject's performance on a more traditional measure of cognitive functioning (e.g., Wechsler Intelligence Scale for Children) is also calculated. In support of this proposed relationship between the Ertl Index and intellectual functioning, Ertl (1968) presented data suggesting a concomitant decrease in the neural efficiency score upon ingestion of chemicals known to impede cognitive functioning (e.g., alcohol). Moreover, Ertl found that when these chemicals were removed, the neural efficiency scores returned to normal limits.

Clinically, Ertl proposed that the Ertl Index would serve as a screening measure for cognitive difficulties. He argued that special educational placement based on culturally free measures such as the Ertl Index would eliminate the educational misclassification of culturally deprived children. Moreover, Ertl proposed that the Ertl Index "should permanently dispel the myth of racial inequality in the United States" (Tracy, 1972, p. 90). In support of this argument, Ertl (Tracy, 1972) presented data suggesting that there were no significant differences between the brain wave activities (Ertl Index) of blacks and whites.

While the Neural Efficiency Analyzer appeared to be an innovative attempt to minimize the cultural bias in intelligence testing, empirical evidence does not support the use of this measure on a clinical basis. Indeed, Evans, Martin, and Hatchette (1976) showed that the Ertl Index did not discriminate between children with learning problems and normal controls. Similarly, it was found that the Ertl Index did not significantly predict college grade point averages (Sturgis, Lemke, & Johnson, 1977). A review of more than a dozen major texts in assessment, psychophysiology, and learning disabilities published in the 1990s failed to produce a reference to this method, and it appears to have faded from any serious consideration at this point.

## REFERENCES

Ertl, J. (1968). *Evoked potential and human intelligence.* Final Report, USOE, Project No. 6-1454.

Evans, J. R., Martin, D., & Hatchette, R. (1976). Neural Efficiency Analyzer scores of reading disabled, normally reading and academically superior children. *Perceptual & Motor Skills, 43,* 1248–1250.

Sturgis, R., Lemke, E. A., & Johnson, J. J. (1977). A validity study of the Neural Efficiency Analyzer in relation to selected measures of intelligence. *Perceptual & Motor Skills, 45,* 475–478.

Tracy, W. (1972). Goodbye IQ, hello EI (Ertl Index). *Phi Delta Kappan, 54,* 89–94.

JEFFREY W. GRAY
*Ball State University*

RAYMOND S. DEAN
*Ball State University*
*Indiana University School of*
*Medicine*

INTELLIGENCE
INTELLIGENCE TESTING
NEURAL EFFICIENCY ANALYZER

## ESQUIROL, JEAN E. (1722–1840)

Jean E. Esquirol, a French psychiatrist, studied under Philippe Pinel in Paris, and succeeded him as resident physician at the Salpetriere. His exposure of inhumane practices in French institutions for the mentally ill contributed greatly to the development of properly run hospitals in France. Esquirol identified and described the main forms of mental illness, and in 1838 published *Des Maladies Mentales,* the first scientific treatment of the subject.

## REFERENCE

Esquirol, J. E. (1838). *Des maladies mentales.* Paris: Bailliere.

PAUL IRVINE
*Katonah, New York*

## ESTONIA, SPECIAL EDUCATION IN

In Estonia, teaching children with special educational needs started in the 19th century. Due to the initiative of doctors and churchmen, charitable institutions for children with behavior problems, Mental Retardation, deafness, and blindness were established in 1845. The first special school for deaf children was founded in 1866. The ideas of special education were well received and encouraged, given the country's high literacy rates (at that time, 91 percent could read and 78 percent could write). A parliamentary republic was formed following Estonia's independence in 1918. Between 1920 and 1939, a restricted system of special educational services developed. State schools for children who were deaf, blind, and mildly to moderately mentally retarded were founded. Hugo Valma greatly influenced the ideology and development of special education. He published books and articles on educating children with Mental Retardation. In 1928, speech therapy developed as a specialization. In 1939, the Baltic countries were assigned to the Soviet sphere of influence and remained in isolation until 1991. During this period of Soviet influence, a system of special educational service was founded for children starting from age 3. A national curriculum for special schools was developed. However, education was available only for children with slight mental disabilities; children with moderate, severe, and profound mental disabilities were sent to nursing homes and were regarded as non-teachable. During the 1970s, special nursery schools were established. During the 1980s, speech therapists began serving children with reading and writing problems and with slight speech problems in mainstream schools.

From 1991, when the Republic of Estonia was restored, all discriminatory restrictions have been removed and all children have a right to education suitable for their abilities. In 1995, the Disability Policy of the Republic of Estonia was adopted on the basis of the United Nations rules of equal opportunities. Terminology has been changed; labeling has been removed.

Children with special needs, ages 3 to 7, may study in special nursery schools (*erilasteaed*), mainstream nursery schools in integration groups (*sobitusrühm*), or groups for children with special needs (*erirühm*). While the number of special nursery schools has decreased (e.g., in 1995, there were 7 special nursery schools and now there are 3), the number of special groups has increased. Special groups are available for children with physical disabilities, sensory disabilities (deafness and hearing impairment; blindness and visual impairment), multiple disabilities, speech impairment and specific developmental disorders, and Mental Retardation (moderate, severe, and profound learning disabilities). In integration groups, children with special education needs (physical, speech, sensory, mental disabilities, psychiatric disorders, and specific developmental disorders) study together with their nondisabled peers. Groups are established by county or city administrations.

At ages 7 through 20, children with special needs may study in mainstream schools, in special classes of mainstream schools, receive various forms of support, or study in special schools, depending on a student's needs. The number of special needs students is increasing due, in part, to teachers becoming more skilled at identifying special needs children and new ways to think about special needs children. At the same time, the number of students in general education is decreasing.

Special needs children are recommended to a suitable school, group, class, or curriculum following a decision by a counseling committee composed of five members: special education teacher, speech therapist, psychologist, social worker, and a representative of the county administration or of the city administration. The parents decide whether the child attends a special school or a mainstream school. The number of special schools, about 46, has been consistent during the last 2 decades. Special needs children increasingly are being place in mainstream schools of which there are 603. Some special nursery and basic schools recently have been reorganized into regional counseling centers.

Special schools and classes are available for students with physical disabilities, speech impairments, sensory or learning disabilities, mental disorders, and behavior problems. Sanatorium schools are available for students with health disorders. Special needs children may study in vocational schools that offer a small group instruction for a special group together with individual instruction for special needs children who are studying in a mainstream or special group. Opportunity classes (*tasandusklass*) exist for children with learning difficulties, supplementary learning classes (*abiklass*) for children with slight learning disabilities, coping classes (*toimetulekuklass*) for children with moderate learning disabilities, and nursing classes (*hooldusklass*) for children with severe and profound learning disabilities. The following support systems are available in mainstreams schools: individual curricula; remedial groups that provide learning support for students with learning difficulties, speech therapy, long day groups, and home study (with the possibility to attend lessons of music,

arts, handicraft, and physical education); and boarding school facilities for children who have social problems.

Education requirements are determined by a national curriculum for nursery schools, basic schools, and upper-secondary schools. The simplified national curricula for basic schools (supplementary learning curriculum; students with a slight learning disability) and the national curriculum for students with moderate and severe learning disabilities determine the requirements of basic education of special needs children. A special national curriculum is being developed for students with profound learning disabilities. For special needs children, an individual curriculum may be specified based on the child's abilities. When evaluating special needs children, a differentiated evaluation allows knowledge and skills to be evaluated according to the student's individual characteristics. In conducting final examinations for graduation from basic school, the characteristics of the special needs child and the aims specified in the curriculum are considered. A final examination may not be conducted when the curriculum was simplified as a result of a student's moderate or severe learning difficulties.

Regular class teachers, special education teachers, and speech therapists teach special needs children. As a rule, teachers working in special or nursery schools or in special groups or classes must have advanced education, including special education or an education program that required 320 hours of in-service training in special education. Since 1968, the University of Tartu has prepared special education teachers. Earlier, special education teachers and speech therapists studied the same curriculum. However, after a curriculum reform in 1991, students specialize either in special education or speech therapy. Starting from 1997, special education teacher-counselors (who work mainly in mainstream nursery and basic schools) are educated in the University of Tallinn. Both universities provide in-service courses in special education.

School psychologists, social workers, and social pedagogues also provide services for special needs children. School psychologists are involved in the assessment and counseling of children. During the last few years, their responsibilities for implementing individual instruction have grown. Specialists working with special needs children in nursery and basic schools are employed by county and city governments. In towns, there are speech therapists in most nursery schools and mainstream schools and school psychologists in the majority of mainstream schools. In special schools and institutions for special groups, additional speech therapists and/or special teachers may be employed. A few schools have hired social workers. They serve several schools in towns and in rural areas. The number of special education teachers, speech therapists, and school psychologists who work in rural areas is insufficient.

Although some services for special needs children have been provided for decades, contemporary theoretical approaches together with policies promulgated by the European Union are profoundly impacting special education in Estonia. The state is obliged to have a clear education policy; to permit amendments, supplements, and adaptations of curricula depending on a student's needs; and to ensure the quality of study materials, in-service teacher training, and the existence of support teachers. Not all of these obligations are met. Obstacles arise due to the country's small size, limited financial and professional resources, and lack of regulations pertaining to the implementation of legislation in some areas. Considerable work is occurring in implementing laws and regulations and educating teachers, parents, politicians, and others who work with special needs children.

## REFERENCES

*Laws and Acts*

Alushariduse raamõppekava kinnitamine [National Curriculum for Nursery Schools], Riigi Teataja I 1999, 80, 737. Retrieved September 30, 2005, from https://www.riigiteataja.ee/ert/act.jsp?id=77809

Eesti Vabariigi Haridusseadus [Republic of Estonia Law on Education], Riigi Teataja I 2004, 75, 524. Retrieved July 30, 2005, from https://www.riigiteataja.ee/ert/act.jsp?id=816786

Individuaalse õppekava järgi õppimise kord [Regulation of Learning According to Individual Learning Curriculum], Riigi Teataja L 2004, 155, 2329. Retrieved July 30, 2005, from https://www.riigiteataja.ee/ert/act.jsp?id=824971

Koolieelse lasteasutuse seadus [Law On Pre-School Child Institutions], Riigi Teataja I, 2004, 41, 276. Retrieved July 30, 2005, from https://www.riigiteataja.ee/ert/act.jsp?id=754369

Kutseõppeasutuse seadus [Vocational Educational Institutions Act], Riigi Teataja I 2005, 31, 229. Retrieved July 30, 2005, from https://www.riigiteataja.ee/ert/act.jsp?id=908863

Kutseseadus [Professions Act], Riigi Teataja I 2003, 83, 559. Retrieved July 30, 2005, from https://www.riigiteataja.ee/ert/act.jsp?id=690522

Lasteaed-algkooli, algkooli, põhikooli ning gümnaasiumi eripedagoogide ja koolipsühholoogide miinimumkoosseis [Staff Minimum for special education teachers and school psychologists in Nursery-primary school, primary school, basic school, and upper secondary school], Riigi Teataja L 2003, 4, 39. Retrieved July 30, 2005, from https://www.riigiteataja.ee/ert/act.jsp?id=238473

Pedagoogide kvalifikatsiooninõuded [Standards of Qualification for Teachers], Riigi Teataja I 2005, 6, 42. Retrieved July 30, 2005, from https://www.riigiteataja.ee/ert/act.jsp?id=839432

Põhikooli ja gümnaasiumi riiklik õppekava [National Curriculum for Basic Schools and Upper Secondary Schools], Riigi Teataja I 2004, 67, 468. Retrieved July 30, 2005, from https://www.riigiteataja.ee/ert/act.jsp?id=802290

Põhikooli- ja gümnaasiumiseadus [Basic School and Upper Secondary School Act], Riigi Teataja I 2004, 56, 404. Retrieved July 30, 2005, from https://www.riigiteataja.ee/ert/act.jsp?id=784125

Põhikooli lihtsustatud riikliku õppekava (abiõppe õppekava) kinnitamine [Simplified National Curriculum for basic schools (supplementary learning curriculum)], Riigi Teataja L 2004, 106, 1705. Retrieved July 30, 2005, from https://www.riigiteataja.ee/ert/act.jsp?id=792367

Toimetuleku riikliku õppekava kinnitamine [National Curriculum for Students with Moderate and Severe Learning Disabilities], Riigi Teataja L 2004, 106, 1705. Retrieved July 30, 2005, from https://www.riigiteataja.ee/ert/act.jsp?id=790670

*Literature*

The Information Database on Education Systems in Europe. The Education System in Estonia. (2003/2004). Retrieved July 30, 2005, from http://www.eurydice.org/Eurybase/Application/frameset.asp?country=EE&language=EN

Kõrgesaar, J. (2002). *Sissejuhatus hariduslike erivajaduste k"sitlusse (Introduction into the field of special needs)*. Tartu: Tartu Šlikooli Kirjastus.

Kõrgesaar, J., & Veskiväli, E. (1987). *Eripedagoogika Eestis (Special Education in Etsonia)*. Tartu: Tartu Ülikooli Kirjastus.

Padrik, M. (2002). Ver"nderungen der Behindertenp"dagogik in einer ver"nderten Gesellschaft: das Beispiel Estland. In *Reader Internationale Woche* (pp. 73–83). Universität Bremen.

Statistical Office of Estonia (2005). Statistical database. Retrieved July 20, 2005, from http://pub.stat.ee/px-web.2001/dialog/statfileri.asp

MARIKA PADRIK
EVE KIKAS
*University of Tartu*

## INTERNATIONAL ETHICS AND SPECIAL EDUCATION

## ETHICS

In its broadest sense, ethics is that branch of philosophy concerned with the study of how people ought to act towards each other. To state this point in the traditional manner, we would say that ethics is interested in "what ought to be" rather than simply "what is, has been, and will be" (Sidgwick, 1902, p. 22). Within the educational, medical, and mental health professions that most often work with special education populations, ethics is more often discussed in terms of ethical principles and the formal ethical codes of the various professions, which provide standards and guidelines by which professionals can guide their practice. Though it is true that ethics is concerned with telling the difference between "right and wrong," the more important, and much more difficult, ethical distinctions which the special education professions must make involve decision-making when all the alternatives are either good or bad (Steininger, Newell, & Garcia, 1984). Such situations are true ethical dilemmas, in that a reasonable case can be made for choosing each alternative, yet the ethical principles underlying each choice are in conflict. And usually, one choice precludes the other.

Special education professionals include special education

teachers, counselors, social workers, psychologists, and re-searchers, and they work in a variety of settings that range from working with special needs children in mainstream classrooms, self-contained classrooms, residential settings, rehabilitation hospitals, homes of chronically ill children, and juvenile justice educational settings, among others. While the demands and organizational structures of the settings within which special education services are offered vary tremendously, the ethical principles and standards by which professionals guide their practices are very similar. Originating in and published by the various professional organizations, all the ethical codes embody the fundamental ethical principles of autonomy, justice, fidelity, nonmaleficence (the duty to do no harm), and beneficence (the duty to do good) identified by Kitchener (1984), who built upon the work of earlier ethicists Beauchamp and Childress (1983) and Drane (1982).

The various ethical codes, including those of the American School Counselors Association (1992), the American Counseling Association (1995), the National Education Association (1985), the American Psychological Association (1992), the National Association of Social Workers (1993), and others, are periodically revised to reflect changes in social values and priorities, as well as evolving legal rulings and statutory requirements. All professionals have a responsibility to be knowledgeable about the ethical codes of their particular profession, as those codes represent the profession's expectations of its members. In certain cases, these codes mandate or prohibit specific behaviors, and in less clear-cut situations they provide direction for further thought and consideration.

Considering the complexity of professional practice today, it is not possible for any ethical code to address every conceivable difficulty a professional might find themselves in, and thus the codes cannot be all-inclusive. When the codes are insufficient for reasoning through the conflicting interests that make up complex ethical questions, the professional should turn next to the ethical principles for guidance.

Several excellent models of ethical reasoning have been published, notably those of Kitchener (1984) and Welfel (1998), both of which stress the need for continued attention to and discussion with colleagues of the ethical dimensions of one's practice even in the absence of specific problems or decisions to be made. Such diligence increases sensitivity to the ethical aspects of all actions, thus improving the ethical reasoning skills needed when ethical dilemmas do arise.

There are many competing and conflicting interests in the field of education, and even more so in special education, many of which revolve around questions of

1. the best educational choices for the special needs child,
2. allocation of resources,
3. respect for parental rights, and, not least,

4. the difficulties involved in making professional decisions within a bureaucratic and politicized organizational structure whose priorities are frequently very different from those working directly with the child.

For the professional, the primary ethical responsibility lies in identifying and providing the most appropriate services for the client, which in this case is the special needs child. When competing interests prevent, or seek to prevent, those services, it is the professional's ethical responsibility to advocate for the interests of the client, even if such advocacy is unsuccessful. In addition, there are several clear ethical mandates for special education professionals, including knowing the ethical standards embraced by the profession and establishing and maintaining professional levels of competence, which requires acceptable levels of knowledge, skill, and diligence (Welfel, 1998).

There are also certain ethical issues that are practically endemic to special education. Two of the most frequent are issues of informed consent, and confidentiality. Parents of special education children have a right to information about their child, their educational and cognitive status, and the plans and interventions being considered for them. The children themselves also have a right to as much of such information as they can understand, and it is the professional's responsibility to explain to both children and parents in understandable, jargon-free language so that parents understand about their child's evaluation, results, and education, and so that consent is fully informed. Confidentiality requires that the student's privacy be respected, and therefore that the child's information and records be kept confidential from everyone not directly involved in their case. In school systems, where information is routinely shared and where counselors frequently have no place to store confidential material, confidentiality is a very difficult issue.

Finally, professionals are mainly obligated to choose educational interventions and alternatives that will do no harm, either physically, mentally, or emotionally, to the special needs child, and that are the best choices for enhancing the child's development.

## REFERENCES

American Counseling Association (ACA). (1995). *Code of ethics and standards of practice.* Alexandria, VA: Author.

American Psychological Association (APA). (1992). *Ethical principles of psychologists and code of conduct.* Washington, DC: Author.

American School Counselors Association (ASCA). (1992). *Ethical standards for school counselors.* Alexandria, VA: American Counseling Association.

Beauchamp, T. L., & Childress, J. F. (1983). *Principles of biomedical ethics* (2nd ed.). Oxford, England: Oxford University Press.

Drane, J. F. (1982). Ethics and psychotherapy: A philosophical perspective. In M. Rosenbaum (Ed.), *Ethics and values in psychotherapy*. New York: Free Press.

Kitchener, K. (1984). Intuition, critical evaluation and ethical principles: The foundation for ethical decisions in counseling psychology. *The Counseling Psychologist, 12,* 43–55.

National Association of Social Workers (NASW). (1993). *Code of ethics*. Silver Spring, MD: Author.

National Education Association. (1985). *NEA Handbook: 1985–86.* Washington, DC: Author.

Sidgwick, H. (1902). *Philosophy: Its scope and relations.* New York: Macmillan.

Steininger, M., Newell, J. D., & Garcia, L. T. (1984). *Ethical issues in psychology.* Boston: Wadsworth.

Welfel, E. R. (1998). *Ethics in counseling and psychotherapy: Standards, research, and emerging issues.* Pacific Grove, CA: Brooks/Cole.

KAY KETZENBERGER
*The University of Texas of the Permian Basin*

# ETHICS, INTERNATIONAL, AND SPECIAL EDUCATION

Codes of ethics are found in numerous professional fields and are designed to protect the public by prescribing and proscribing behaviors professionals are expected to exhibit. Issues such as what constitutes professional practice, training, and licensure are intertwined with ethics. Ethics codes typically contain principles and standards that reflect both unenforceable general virtues (e.g., beneficence, fidelity) and specific, enforceable behaviors (e.g., research participant protection; Nagy, 1999). In most countries mature professional associations develop their own codes. Nevertheless, virtues and standards addressed in these codes often overlap across nations.

The need for codes of ethics is increasing due, in part, to growing skepticism of professionals, the growth of professionalism, and growing practice of professionals to transcend country and cultural boundaries because of business and technological changes.

International ethics codes allow for uniformity of appropriate professional behavior and highlight common threads that bridge multiple professions and countries. They can offer a shared meaning across cultures. For example, standards of care differ depending on one's country, yet an international code could solidify accepted standards. International codes also would facilitate international research by defining human participant protections that transcend cultures. Finally, they can help standardize acceptable training requirements that can be incorporated internationally.

The following provides information about the status of ethics codes regionally and internationally that may impact special education. Various professions are committed to work in special education, including educators, social workers, counselors, and those from medicine. Psychology has had an abiding interest in special education. Codes that emanate from psychology are discussed in the following paragraphs. They generally are well developed and often are on the cutting edge of ethics code development.

In 1995 the European Federation of Professional Psychologists Associations endorsed a Meta-Code of Ethics in the first attempt to present global unifying principles for psychological organizations and psychologists. This brief document addresses four main principles: respect for a person's rights and dignity, competence, responsibility, and integrity. Gauthier (2002) extended this work for individual psychologists by proposing the Universal Declaration of Ethical Principles for Psychologists. Its purpose is to promote professional unity within the profession internationally by including ethical practices regardless of country or culture. It is not intended to replace existing codes but it is predicted that a number of its elements will be included when countries revise their codes.

Ethics guidelines that extend across countries yet retain some cultural influences are needed. The International School Psychology Association devised an ethics code that covers professional responsibilities, confidentiality, professional growth and limitations, relationships, assessment, and research. It was developed following a review of ethics codes from psychological associations that are members of the International Union of Psychological Sciences.

Leach and Harbin (1997) compared psychological codes from 23 countries and found significant overlap among some codes (e.g., Australia, South Africa), and differences among others. As expected, there was considerable overlap with principles. However, the standards addressed in the codes tended to differ. Differences were noted based on topic area (e.g., testing and assessment) and unique features of countries' codes were also noted (e.g., prohibiting torture, policy statements; Leach, Glosoff, & Overmier, 2001).

Informed consent and confidentiality comprise legal and professional standards that often transcend countries. Both are important to special education. Parents and guardians have rights to receive and understand information generated by professionals who work with their children. Additionally, maintaining confidentiality of information pertinent to their family reflects a basic right to privacy and may be important to effective treatment (Ketzenberger, 2001). Informed consent and confidentiality are considered cornerstones of ethical behavior and are found in practically all ethics codes.

Psychologists and others working in special education often use testing and other assessment procedures. Test use is universal. However, some countries use them broadly and wisely while others focus on specific areas (e.g., assessing

Mental Retardation; Hu & Oakland, 1991; Leach & Oakland, 2005) and use them with little professional regard.

A number of organizations have developed test-related standards (e.g., International Test Commission, 2000; Joint Commission on Testing Practices, 2005; National Council on Measurement in Education, 1995), while others address theoretical and specialized areas of test development and use (e.g., Standards for Educational and Psychological Testing, American Educational Research Association, American Psychological Association, and National Council on Measurement in Education, 1999). The International Test Commission (ITC; www.intestcom. org) developed guidelines for adapting tests, including those that impact ethics (Oakland, 2005). The ITC recently developed guidelines for computer-based and Internet-delivered testing (Coyne & Bartram, 2004). It too has an ethics component.

Thus, as international professional boundaries continue to diminish, the need for ethics codes that transcend national boundaries becomes paramount. Although ethics codes always will reflect cultural differences and individual professional nuances, principles and standards exist with which all professions committed to working with special needs children probably can agree. As codes continue to develop they are likely to include principles and standards advanced by international organizations. Thus, over time, codes are likely to increasingly reflect universal issues.

## REFERENCES

American Educational Research Association, American Psychological Association, and National Council on Measurement in Education. (1999). *Standards for educational and psychological testing.* Washington, DC: American Educational Research Association.

Coyne, I., & Bartram, D. (2004). *International test commission computer-based and Internet delivered testing guidelines.* Draft March 5, 2002. Paper presented to the Council of the International Test Commission, Beijing, and The People's Republic of China.

Gauthier, J. (2002). *Toward a universal declaration of ethical principles for psychologists: A progress report.* Paper presented at the International Congress of Applied Psychology. Singapore.

Hu, S., & Oakland, T. (1991). Global and regional perspectives on testing children and youth: An international survey. *International Journal of Psychology 26*(3), 329–344.

International Test Commission. (2000). *International guidelines for test use.* Liverpool, England: Author.

Joint Commission on Testing Practices. (2005). *Code of fair testing practices in education.* Washington, DC: American Psychological Association.

Ketzenberger, K. (2001). Ethics. In C. R. Reynolds & E. Fletcher-Janzen (Eds.), *Encyclopedia of special education* (2nd ed., pp. 703–704). New York: Wiley.

Leach, M. M., Glosoff, H., & Overmier, J. B. (2001). *International ethics codes: A follow-up study of previously unmatched standards and principles.* In J. B. Overmier & J. A. Overmier (Eds.), Psychology: CD-Rom; IUPsyS Global Resource.

Leach, M. M., & Harbin, J. J. (1997). Psychological ethics codes: A comparison of twenty-four countries. *International Journal of Psychology, 32,* 181–192.

Leach, M. M., & Oakland, T. (2005). *Ethics standards impacting test development and use: A review of 31 ethics codes impacting practices in 35 countries.* Manuscript submitted for publication.

Nagy, T. M. (1999). *Ethics in plain English: An illustrative casebook for psychologists.* Washington, DC: American Psychological Association.

National Council on Measurement in Education. (1995). *Code of professional responsibilities in educational measurement.* Washington, DC: Author.

Oakland, T. (2005). Selected ethical issues relevant to test adaptations. In R. Hambleton, C. Spielberger, & P. Meranda, (Eds.), *Adapting educational and psychological tests for cross-cultural assessment.* Mahwah, NJ: Erlbaum.

Hambleton, R., Spielberger, C., & Meranda, P. (Eds.). (2005). *Adapting educational and psychological tests for cross-cultural assessment.* Mahwah, NJ: Erlbaum.

MARK M. LEACH
*University of Southern Mississippi*

**INTERNATIONAL TEST USE IN SPECIAL EDUCATION
INTERNATIONAL SCHOOL PSYCHOLOGY ASSOCIATION**

## ETIOLOGY

Etiology is the study of causes of diseases and impairments. When considering those with disabilities, however, one must consider not only the specific cause, if known, but the affected individual's developmental history and exposure to intervention. Increasingly, technology is not only leading to increasing knowledge about the origins of various disorders, but also to increasing ability to ameliorate some of the conditions. Only in the most severe cases is the relationship between cause and outcome one-to-one. Research is also leading to reconsideration of some presumed origins of disorders and the extent to which various factors may underlie these origins. In particular, findings from behavior genetics research is leading to changed views of both normal and abnormal development.

This research is having impact not only in the professional literature, but in the popular press as well. Consider the query on the April 1998 *Life* magazine cover, "Were you BORN that way? Personality, temperament even life choices. New studies show that it's mostly in your genes." Well, perhaps, but the new studies actually suggest that genetic factors play varying roles in influencing human traits. The first page of the article itself hardly qualifies the cover:

Table 1  Source of handicapping conditions

| Source | Example or effect |
|---|---|
| *Genetic* | |
| Chromosomal | |
| Autosomal trisomies | Down syndrome |
| Autosomal deletions and additions | Cri du chat |
| Sex-chromosome aneuploidies | Klinefelter, Turner, XXY syndromes |
| Constriction or weakness | Fragile X syndrome |
| Single-gene | |
| Dominant | Neurofibromatosis, tuberous sclerosis |
| Recessive | Inborn errors of metabolism (e.g., PKU, galactosemia, Tay Sachs) |
| Sex-linked | Lesch-Nyhan syndrome |
| QTL | Mild mental retardation, predisposition toward variety of impairments |
| HIV | Mental retardation, variety of other impairments, progressive deterioration |
| *Prenatal teratogens* | |
| Radiation | Growth failure, major malformations |
| Maternal infections | |
| TORCH complex (toxoplasmosis, rubella, cytomegalovirus, herpes) | Growth retardation, visual and auditory impairments, mental retardation |
| Syphilis | Mental retardation, meningitis |
| Drugs and hormones | |
| Thalidomide | Limb, digit, external ear malformations |
| Alcohol | Fetal alcohol syndrome |
| Androgens | Masculinization of females |
| Antitumor agents | Major growth and central nervous system defects |
| Anticoagulants | Growth retardation, visual and auditory impairments |
| Anticonvulsants | Fetal hydantoin syndrome |

Table 1 (*continued*)

| Source | Example or effect |
|---|---|
| *Perinatal factors* | |
| Maternal infection | |
| Herpes | Same as TORCH complex |
| Prematurity | Cerebral palsy, mental retardation |
| Low birth weight | Growth retardation, mental retardation, cerebral palsy |
| Asphyxia | Cerebral palsy, variety of other impairments |
| *Postnatal chemical or traumatic factors* | |
| Infection | |
| Encephalitis | Mental retardation |
| Toxins | |
| Lead | Mental retardation, epilepsy, sensory impairments |
| Accidents and child abuse, including shaken baby syndrome | Brain damage (specific) leading to variety of impairments |
| *Learning* | |
| Conditioning (Pavlovian) | Phobias |
| Operant conditioning | Negative self-concept, avoidant disorders, conduct disorders |
| Observational learning | Phobias, articulation disorders |

However, research also is increasingly documenting the importance of both prenatal factors as causes of handicapping conditions and interactions between risk factors for handicapping conditions with other developmental factors.

Regardless of advances, however, the specific cause of most handicapping conditions still cannot be conclusively identified. This entry overviews various sources of handicapping conditions and developmental considerations, many of which are described in other individual entries. It also overlaps with a variety of others, particularly Early Experience and Critical Periods. A summary of the sources is in Table 1.

## Genetically Based Disorders

A variety of specific disorders have a specific chromosomal or single-gene basis. In the case of some disorders, family history and other methods support an OGOD (one gene, one disorder) basis, in which a single gene is both necessary and sufficient for the development of a disorder. Even in such disorders, however, intervention may significantly reduce their adverse impact, PKU being perhaps the best known example. Thus, owing to interaction among genes, and among genes and the pre- and postnatal environment,

"It's not just brown eyes. Your inheritance could also include insomnia, obesity, and optimism. Yet scientists are saying that genes are not—quite—destiny" (Colt, 1998, p. 39). Not many years ago, such statements would have been almost inconceivable. After all, prevailing thought was that adult personality was largely determined by early experience, particularly before 5–6 years of age and particularly with the parents (see Early Experience and Critical Periods in this encyclopedia). Increasingly, research is indeed questioning the role of postnatal social experience in general, and that of parents in particular, in development of personality.

individuals' phenotypes (their actual appearances) often do not reflect their genotypes or genetic makeup (e.g., Kopp, 1983; Plomin & McClearn, 1993; Vogel & Motulsky, 1979). Many other disorders, as well as normal traits on which humans vary continuously (e.g., height, weight), have genetic predispositions that owe to the interaction among multiple genes, no one of which is either necessary or sufficient. These traits and disorders were formerly called polygenic, but that term, which implied a large number of genes each of unmeasurably small effect size, has been replaced. The new term, quantitative trait loci (QTL), implies that some potentially identifiable number of genes of varying effect size operate additively and interchangeably (Plomin, Owen, & McGuffin, 1994).

### Chromosomal Abnormalities

Normal humans have 23 pairs of chromosomes in their body cells—22 pairs of similar autosomes and one pair of sex chromosomes. Females have two relatively long X, whereas males have one X and one shorter Y, sex chromosomes. In the development of germ cells (meiosis), each pair normally splits such that each germ cell has 23 chromosomes. However, occasionally one chromosome does not split (nondisjunction), resulting in a double dose or absence of that chromosome, or a chromosome breaks and becomes partly attached to another (translocation). These, and other processes, can lead to chromosomal abnormalities.

Most such abnormalities lead to spontaneous abortion, but the incidence in live births is about 1 in 200. Involving large numbers of genes, these abnormalities have broad and typical physical and behavioral effects. They tend to produce general intellective deficiency, minor in some syndromes but severe in others.

Autosomal trisomies involve an extra autosomal chromosome; affected individuals have 47 chromosomes. Down's syndrome (trisomy 21) is the most common, but at least five others have been described. Virtually all increase in incidence with maternal age and result in growth failure and mental retardation.

Autosomal partial deletions and additions are low-incidence disorders that, except for 18 p–, which shows highly variable effects, generally result in severe mental retardation. The best known is 5 p–, cri du chat, so named because affected infants' cries sound like a cat's meows.

Sex chromosome aneuplodies involve an added or missing sex chromosome. Klinefelter (XXY) and XYY syndromes affect only males; Turner syndrome (XO) affects only females. Intelligence of affected individuals averages about 90, but this is highly variable.

### Single-Gene Effects

Except for sex-linked recessive traits, individuals inherit a gene for each single-gene trait from each parent. Different forms (alleles) of a given gene can lead to different manifestations of a trait. Individuals are said to be homozygotic or heterozygotic for a given trait if they have inherited two similar or two different alleles, respectively. Single-gene traits follow Mendelian principles of inheritance: a dominant trait will be expressed if the individual has inherited at least one dominant gene for the trait, whereas a recessive trait will be expressed only if the individual inherits the recessive gene from both parents. An exception is sex-linked recessive traits, the genes for which are carried on the sex chromosomes. Such traits may be expressed if the recessive gene is inherited from one parent and no counterpart gene is inherited from the other parent to suppress its effects. In part because the Y-chromosome is shorter than the X and therefore carries fewer genes, such sex-linked traits appear much more commonly in males; these traits are transmitted by their mothers, who are carriers. Both X-linked dominant and X-linked recessive traits may appear. Other patterns of inheritance such as codominance and partial dominance complicate the notion of simple dominance-recessiveness relations, as do the phenomena of penetrance, pleiotropy, and variable expressivity (e.g., Plomin & McClearn, 1993; Thompson & Thompson, 1980).

Dominant, recessive, and sex-linked single-gene disorders now number in the thousands (e.g., McKusick & Francomano, 1994), and new ones are discovered regularly. They lead to a variety of essentially OGOD conditions—over 100 are linked to mental retardation, 100 to hearing impairment, and 15 to spinocerebellar ataxia. A number are also invariably fatal in infancy. With the exception of sex-linked disorders, they occur in equal frequency in males and females. Because of their number and variety, only a few can be described.

Approximately 4,500 dominant single-gene disorders have been identified (McKusick & Francomano, 1994). If one parent is heterozygotic for the gene and manifests the disorder, offspring have a 50 percent chance of developing it. But about 50 percent of all cases arise from spontaneous mutation and thus have no family history. Obviously, individuals with the mutated gene can transmit the disorder to their children. Dominant disorders mainly involve structural abnormalities. Achondroplasia, for example, is a form of short-limb dwarfism. Many dominant disorders have highly variable expressivity, in which the manifestation is great in some individuals but hardly noticeable in others. Some disorders may appear to skip a generation when the effects are so minimal as to be essentially unseen (Thompson & Thompson, 1980). Further, dominant disorders, as well as many recessive ones, manifest pleiotropy, multiple effects of a single gene. An example is neurofibromatosis, a relatively high-incidence condition (approximate incidence: 1/3,000), which involves a variety of structural abnormalities. Its effects range from hardly noticeable to obvious deformities, with some risk of mental retardation and other developmental disabilities (e.g., Batshaw, 1997). Until recently, the most famous example of neurofibromatosis appeared to be Joseph Merrick, the Elephant Man (e.g., Howell & Ford, 1980), but he now appears likely to have had Proteus syndrome (see Elephant Man entry in this encyclopedia).

A child has a 25 percent chance of inheriting a recessive single-gene defect if both parents are heterozygotic (carriers) for the defect. Recessive single-gene defects may result in a variety of conditions, including sensory impairment, ataxia, and mental retardation.

In a large number of cases a defective gene results in impaired metabolism that in turn leads to the accumulation of some unmetabolized substance, which may be toxic. Among the more common and better understood of such inborn errors of metabolism or metabolic disorders are phenylketonuria, galactosemia, and Tay-Sachs disease. Some disorders can be detected through amniocentesis, and a few can be treated through dietary intervention.

A variety of single-gene-based defects that appear more commonly in males than females are sex-linked, frequently called X-linked. Among these are several forms of sensory impairments, the best known of which is red-green color-blindness. Lesch-Nyhan syndrome, which appears virtually solely in males, is an X-linked inborn error of metabolism that results in deterioration of motor coordination, mental retardation, and self-destructive behavior.

Beginning around 1980, improved test procedures enabled reliable identification of fragile chromosomal sites, where constriction or weakness occurs. Shortly thereafter, Fragile X was described, which now appears to be second only to Down's syndrome as a genetically-based cause of mental retardation. Although originally termed a chromosomally-based disorder, Fragile X has recently been linked to a single gene on the X chromosome, and thus is more accurately described as sex-linked. It is unusual in that it affects females as well as males, although with a lower incidence and less severity, and has highly variable expressivity.

Higher incidence in males than females and familial patterns of incidence suggest that some types of attention deficit disorders and learning disabilities may have X-linked predisposition.

## Quantitative Trait Loci (QTL)

As stated above, QTL traits are those influenced by a number of genes. Virtually all quantitatively-varying human traits which have been studied have identifiable QTL bases (e.g., Plomin et al., 1994). Phenotypically, these traits are the outcome of the interaction among the genes themselves and among the genes and the developmental environment. Coming largely from adoption studies and concordance studies with monozygotic and dizygotic twins, identified traits include: general intelligence as well as verbal and spatial abilities (Plomin & DeFries, 1998); the "Big 5" personality traits (extraversion, neuroticism, conscientiousness, agreeableness, and openness) and temperament (Bouchard, 1990);

and disorders such as mild mental retardation, alcoholism, criminality, schizophrenia, autism, major depression, reading disability, neural tube defects, and idiopathic seizure disorders. Particularly strong predisposition is indicated for autism. Interestingly, QTL predisposition towards diagnosed alcoholism, once thought to be fairly large, appears to be relatively small and occurs only in males; greater genetic influence is shown on amount of alcohol consumed (e.g., Plomin et al., 1994).

### Other presumed genetic disorders

Many low-incidence disorders have presumed genetic bases, owing to their patterns of inheritance, predominance in one gender, or concordance, although the exact basis has not been established. Autism and schizophrenia have already been mentioned. An interesting and tragic example is Rett syndrome, a neurodevelopmental disorder that occurs only in females and is associated with apparently initial normal development followed by developmental arrest and deterioration (e.g., Brown & Hoadley, 1999).

### Prenatal Influences

Prenatal development is generally divided into three periods: germinal or ovum (weeks 0–2), embryonic (weeks 3–8), and fetal (weeks 9–birth). Major developments in each period are germinal—the ovum (fertilized egg) becomes implanted on the uterine wall and differentiates into placental and embryonic tissue; embryonic—characterized by differentiation of all major organs and systems and external body features; and fetal—characterized by rapid growth and further differentiation of internal and external systems and features.

Although the embryo/fetus is generally well protected from environmental insult, a variety of chemicals, called teratogens, can cross the placenta and cause malformations (see Table 1). Teratogens have their major adverse impact during critical periods, times of most rapid tissue differentiations. There are less severe effects during sensitive periods. As shown in Figure 1, systems have individual but overlapping critical periods, mainly around the time of the embryonic periods, and sensitive periods that extend into the fetal period. Sensitive periods for central nervous system, eyes, and external genitalia extend well after birth, so these systems are unusually sensitive to later teratogenic influence. During the early germinal period, teratogens generally either have no effects or are lethal, although they may cause certain major malformations (Moore, 1982).

Radiation, maternal infections, and a number of drugs have serious teratogenic impact (see Table 1). Maternal infections in general are a concern because the symptoms may be mild or absent in the pregnant woman, but have severe adverse effects on the embryo/fetus. Of major concern now is the growing number of cases, perhaps over 20,000, of pe-

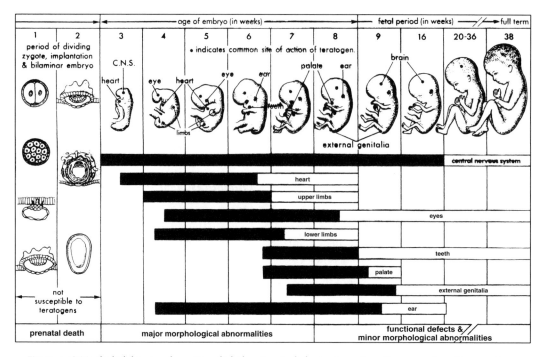

Figure 1  Critical (dark bars) and sensitive (light bars) periods for teratogenic action on various tissue systems
*Source:* From Moore (1982).

diatric HIV, transmitted through the mother. Affected children show a variety of CNS damage, including progressive encephalopathy, atrophy of the cortex, and an assortment of other conditions (Belfer, Krener, & Miller, 1987). Resulting neuropsychological, psychological, and social impairments include mental retardation, seizures, learning disabilities, motor coordination, language delays, and emotional and attentional disturbances (e.g., Armstrong, Seidel, & Swales, 1993). Recently, folic acid deficiency during pregnancy has been recognized as such a common cause of neural tube defects (e.g., spina bifida) that supplements are now being routinely supplied (Liptak, 1997).

Of the many teratogenic drugs (see Carta et al., 1994, for a review), the one of major concern is alcohol. Fetal alcohol syndrome is now, with Down's and Fragile X syndromes, one of the three most common specific causes of mental retardation in the Western world, having an incidence of perhaps 1 in 1,000 births. Complicating outcomes for affected children is the likelihood that their mothers may be abusing multiple substances and live in poverty conditions. Interestingly, the predicted onslaught of "crack babies," essentially unteachable, aggressive children, into our schools has fortunately not materialized. Prenatal cocaine has adverse effects, but to a lesser extent than originally thought—and publicized in the popular media (see Day & Richardson, 1993, for a summary of the controversy).

Effects shown are of severe manifestations and are highly variable; in many cases exposed infants will be asymptomatic. The action of teratogens can be summarized as follows (Brown, 1986).

1. No agent is 100 percent teratogenic; influence is affected by both maternal and embryonic factors.

2. Teratogens act in specific ways and have specific effects, but some have multiple effects and different teratogens may have similar effects (e.g., TORCH complex).

3. Organ systems have individual but largely overlapping critical and sensitive periods.

4. Major effects of teratogens are death, malformations, growth retardation, and functional deficits.

5. Adverse effects are dose dependent, increasing in frequency and severity with increased degree and duration of exposure to a teratogen.

6. Some agents that have major teratogenic influence on the embryo may have little adverse effect or even positive effect on the mother. TORCH complex is an example of the former, and thalidomide and dilantin are examples of the latter.

## Perinatal Influences

No single definition of the perinatal period has been universally accepted; Freeman (1985a) defines the period as a few hours or days before birth, whenever in gestation that occurs, to a few hours or days after delivery. Since herpes is almost always transmitted to the newborn as it passes through the birth canal, it is, strictly speaking, a perinatal influence, although it is classified as a member of the TORCH complex.

Major perinatal events are prematurity and low birth weight (LBW): "Premature birth, whether defined as either low birth weight (LBW) or as birth prior to term gestation [prematurity], remains the major contributing factor to neonatal morbidity and mortality" (Barden, 1983, p. 139). In the United States alone, each year some 350,000 LBW (<2,500 gm) infants are born, comprising about 8.5 percent of all births (Bernbaum & Batshaw, 1997). Known correlates include amniotic fluid/membrane infection, substance abuse, young or old mother, poor prenatal care, African-American mother, and maternal illness, but the specific cause in most cases is unknown. Physical characteristics of affected infants are presence of body hair, reddish skin color, and absence of skin folds. Behavioral characteristics include breathing difficulties, low motor tonus, absence of normal newborn reflexes, inability to maintain body temperature, high-pitched and irritating cries, and hyperreactivity to stimulation. Importantly, the behavioral characteristics may interfere with normal parent-child interactions and set the stage for future problems. Major complications of both conditions owe largely to asphyxia, which may result in hypoxic ischemic encephalopathy (HIE), intraventricular hemorrhage (IVH), and other conditions which themselves result in brain damage. Retinopathy of prematurity is another problem. Although most premature/LBW infants with birthweights above 1,500 gm show normal development, incidence of mental retardation, cerebral palsy, visual and hearing impairments, and seizure disorders are increasingly likely outcomes with lower birth weights (Bernbaum & Batshaw, 1997).

Increases in knowledge about the effects of prematurity and LBW along with advances in treatment options have dramatically improved prognosis for premature/LBW infants and decreased mortality and morbidity. For example, survival rate for 1,500–2,500 gm and 1,000–1,500 gm infants has increased from 50 percent and 30 percent in 1960 to over 90 percent in the 1990s. Of surviving infants in 1950, over 90 percent of those with birthweights less than 1,500 showed serious later neurodevelopmental problems; in 1980, that figure had dropped to less than 20 percent. With extremely low birth weight infants, however, severe disability is still a likely outcome (Bernbaum & Batshaw, 1997).

## Postnatal Chemical and Physical Effects

Birth is clearly a landmark, associated with adaptation to an external environment and self-breathing and feeding. But many developmental processes begun prenatally continue, including development of the central nervous system and vulnerability to insult.

Brain damage can, of course, lead to virtually all impairments, with type and degree a function of the area damaged, the extent of damage, and the age at which the damage occurred. Infections, high fever, malnutrition, and certain toxins can cause diffuse damage to major areas of the brain, whereas physical insult can result in focal lesions, damage to more limited areas. A major issue is the effect of age at time of injury on recovery from brain damage. The Kennard principle that recovery is easier the earlier the brain damage is no longer accepted. Relations appear to be complicated, involving, in addition to age and type of damage, the individual's prior experience.

Infants are at particular risk for infection, and diseases such as meningitis may result in seizures and brain damage that can lead to later mental retardation, cerebral palsy, epilepsy, or specific learning disabilities (Thompson & O'Quinn, 1979).

Because of their effects on developing central nervous system tissue, certain toxins pose considerable risk for children. Of particular concern is lead poisoning, which in severe doses can produce devastating brain damage in children, resulting in severe mental retardation, sensory impairment, and seizures. In lesser doses it may produce lowered intelligence, behavioral problems, and specific learning difficulties. The effects are dose dependent, and apparently no level of blood lead is safe (e.g., Needleman, 1993).

Malnutrition in infancy, particularly when severe enough to lead to marasmus or kwaskiorkhor, is a potential cause of diffuse brain damage and resulting mental retardation. Of particular concern is severe malnutrition occurring early in infancy or lasting more than 4 months; this may result in later retardation regardless of the adequacy of subsequent diet (Cravioto & Delicardie, 1970). Early effective treatment of malnutrition leads to "catch-up growth," lessening long-term consequences (Brann & Schwartz, 1983). However, even later sufficient dietary treatment may in some cases largely overcome the effects of early malnutrition, while later malnutrition can also lead to brain injury (Brown & Pollitt, 1996). Effects of less severe but chronic malnutrition manifest themselves less in terms of gross brain damage than in behavioral deficits, such as low energy, inattentiveness, and poor motor control, that interfere with normal education. Of importance is the extent to which other environmental factors can ameliorate or exacerbate the effects of malnutrition. As Brown and Pollitt (1996) emphasize, the traditional "main effects," or one-to-one, model developmental influences is oversimplified in the face of evidence for interactional processes.

Failure to thrive resulting from either parental neglect or infant-based impairments may have long-term consequences.

Accidents, particularly automobile accidents, are a common cause of specific brain damage in children. Child abuse is increasingly seen as another important factor.

## Role of Learning

Learning plays such a ubiquitous role in the development of normal human behavior that its role in causing or exacerbating impaired behavior is sometimes overlooked in discussing etiology. Learning processes can result in direct impairments or the indirect exacerbation of other impairments. For example, phobias can be acquired through Pavlovian (classical or respondent) conditioning, in which an initially neutral stimulus such as a dentist is paired with pain, or through observational learning (imitation), in which a child observes a parent's severe fear of dentists.

Operant conditioning, or learning by consequences such as reinforcement and punishment, has an important influence on the way in which children with impairments react to those impairments and to themselves. If, for example, a retarded child's attempt to solve problems meets with failure (and perhaps ridicule as well), then the child may develop fear of failure and a poor self-concept. Through respondent conditioning, the child may become highly anxious in subsequent problem-solving settings. Anxiety, in turn, can lead to avoiding problem settings and increasing dependency on others, further reducing the child's own competence. Zigler (1967) has described the negative role that a number of such learned motivational-emotional factors can have on children with mental retardation. Research indicates that these factors adversely affect children with other impairments as well (Brown & Reynolds, 1986).

If a child's responses have no contingent impact on the environment and the child has no control over what happens, then learned helplessness may result, leading to an expectation of failure and apathy.

Reinforcement, particularly negative reinforcement of inappropriate emotional behaviors in boys by their parents, has been shown to be an important initial step in Patterson's (e.g., Patterson, Reid, & Dishion, 1992) coercion model of antisocial behavior. When a parent objects to a boy's behavior and the boy argues or throws a tantrum, the parent may back off, positively reinforcing the boy's inappropriate behavior. When the parent backs off, the boy stops his inappropriate behavior which negatively reinforces the parent's backing off. In this way, a maladaptive behavioral cycle may result.

## Developmental Considerations

### Temperament

Children's own characteristics influence their development and the way in which others behave toward them. In reports from the landmark New York Longitudinal Study, Thomas, Chess, Birch, and their colleagues (e.g., Chess & Thomas, 1984) have documented the importance of temperament as a factor in children's development. Temperament is a relatively stable personality variable that affects such responses as adaptation to new situations and persistence. Children whose temperamental style is described as difficult are more likely to manifest behavior disorders than are other children.

Summaries of various approaches to temperament

(Kagan, 1994; Strelau, 1998) further support the role of temperament as an important developmental factor. Temperament interacts with other developmental factors and may predispose children either to be abused or to develop conduct disorders.

### Poverty

Poverty contributes to impairments both directly and indirectly and may be self-perpetuating. A number of factors that may lead to or exacerbate impairments are higher in low SES groups. These include poor prenatal care; obstetric and perinatal complications, especially prematurity and low birth weight; malnutrition; abusive parents; restricted verbal codes; and inadequate caretaking.

Birch and Gussow (1970) propose that a cycle of poverty acts to transmit poverty across generations. Risk factors associated with low-SES-based factors lead children to be more likely to suffer school failure. School failure leads to unemployment and underemployment which, in turn, maintain poverty conditions and thus perpetuate the cycle into another generation.

Inadequate caretaking behavior occurs in poorly trained parents, particularly under the stress of large families and low SES conditions. Such parents may be able to cope with a normal infant but be stretched beyond their limits in dealing with infants with pre- or perinatal complications. Such infants may, because of their behavioral characteristics, evoke inadequate and even abusive parenting behavior, exacerbating already present impairments and inducing them in infants who under more appropriate conditions would develop normally.

### Interactions

The inadequacy of simple main-effects models has been apparent in several places in this entry. Development in general is characterized as being multi-causal and interactional.

1. Interactions between infants and caretakers are crucial in the development of some impairments. Indeed, in a now classic review, Sameroff and Chandler (1975) found little evidence for a "continuum of reproductive casualty." Instead, the way in which caretakers could or could not adequately cope with their infants determined later impairments, resulting in what they termed a "continuum of caretaking casualty." Interactions between characteristics of infants and characteristics of caretakers are important factors in development.

2. Depression is now seen to occur much more frequently in children than had been thought only a few years ago. Although a genetic predisposition for depression

exists, its actual manifestation depends on interactions among a number of internal (biological, cognitive, and socioemotional) factors and external parental and broader contextual factors. The complexity of the developmental process is described admirably by Cicchetti and Toth (1998).

3. Evidence exists for both genetic and prenatal bases of schizophrenia. However, whether or not an individual actually develops schizophrenia or some other serious behavior disorder depends on factors in the developmental environment. If parents provide a disturbed family environment, children predisposed to develop schizophrenia are more likely actually to manifest the disorder. The Finnish Adoption Study (e.g., Tienari et al., 1994) has compared adopted children of biological mothers who had schizophrenia with adopted children of biological parents without schizophrenia. Of adopted children whose biological mothers had schizophrenia, only those raised in psychologically-disturbed family settings were more likely to develop a serious disorder than those with no family history of schizophrenia. When raised by well-functioning parents, adopted children from both groups showed equivalent and low rates of serious disorders.

4. Environmental factors associated with poverty interact with biological risk factors to exacerbate developmental problems in children (as described in the entry for Social Class and Biological Factors). On the other hand, whether or not at-risk children, through prematurity or poverty, develop serious problems or school failure depends partly on their developmental environment. If raised under inadequate conditions, they are likely to show adverse consequences, but if provided with appropriate interventions, they may develop normally or at least more normally.

## Prevention of Impairments

Applications of present knowledge and techniques could significantly reduce incidence and severity of impairments (Brown, 1986). Some methods are (1) wider use of genetic screening and counseling; (2) more adequate prenatal care for at-risk pregnant women; (3) training in parenting skills for prospective parents; (4) wider dissemination of information materials, and training on birth control to reduce family size in at-risk groups and early pregnancy in adolescents (school-based clinics should be considered); and (5) provision of adequate postnatal nutrition, medical care, and psychological stimulation for at-risk infants. Prevention, although expensive, is both less costly and more humane than remediation.

Additionally, adequacy of therapy has obvious impact on the development of children with conditions that may lead to impairments. The more serious the condition, the more extreme and unusual will be the necessary treatment, resulting in a "continuum of therapeutic environment" (Brown, 1986). In some cases, treatment will be required that simply does not exist in the natural environment. Thus PKU is treated with a synthetic diet and newborns with perinatal complications or birth injuries are placed in increasingly sophisticated neonatal intensive care units.

Intervention through the broad-based Infant Health and Development Program significantly increased the number of premature, low-birthweight infants scoring in the normal range in cognitive, social, health, and growth measures at 3 years of age relative to nontreated controls (e.g., Bradley et al., 1994).

Although its effectiveness has frequently been questioned (e.g., Herrnstein & Murray, 1994), early intervention with children from poverty environments may under appropriate conditions have significant and long-term effects. The Abecedarian Project (e.g., Campbell & Ramey, 1995) began an intensive intervention program with poverty-level infants and carried through early childhood. In adolescence, the subjects have maintained significantly higher levels of cognitive and social skills and particularly school performance over matched controls. Of particular importance, both school retention and assignment to special education are lower in the experimental children. To be effective, however, such programs must (1) begin early, preferably in infancy, and be maintained over a long period of time; (2) be intensive; (3) provide structured experiences directly rather than be mediated through the parents; (4) provide broad interdisciplinary assistance, including health and social services, individual therapy where needed, parent services and training, and optimal educational programs; (5) adjust to the varying needs of individual children; and (6) provide social and other support after the formal program has ended (e.g., Ramey & Ramey, 1998).

## REFERENCES

Abuelo, D. N. (1983). Genetic disorders. In J. L. Matson & J. A. Mulick (Eds.), *Handbook of mental retardation* (pp. 105–20). New York: Pergamon.

Armstrong, F. D., Seidel, J. F., & Swales, T. P. (1993). Pediatric HIV infection: A neuropsychological and educational challenge. *Journal of Learning Disabilities, 26,* 92–103.

Avery, G. (1985). Effects of social, cultural and economic factors on brain development. In J. H. Freeman (Ed.), *Prenatal and perinatal factors associated with brain-disorders* (Publication No. 85-1149, pp. 163–176). Bethesda, MD: National Institutes of Health.

Barden, T. P. (1983). Obstetric management of prematurity. Part 2. Premature labor. In A. A. Fanaroff & R. J. Martin (Eds.), *Behrman's neonatal-perinatal medicine* (3rd ed., pp. 139–149). St. Louis, MO: Mosby.

Batshaw, M. L. (Ed.). (1997). *Children with disabilities* (4th ed.). Baltimore: Brookes.

Behrman, R. E. (1983). The field of neonatal-perinatal medicine. In A. A. Fanaroff & R. J. Martin (Eds.), *Behrman's neonatal-perinatal medicine* (3rd ed., pp. 1–3). St. Louis, MO: Mosby.

Belfer, M. L., Krener, P. K., & Miller, F. B. (1987). AIDS in children and adolescents. *Journal of the American Academy of Child and Adolescent Psychiatry, 27,* 147–151.

Bernbaum, J. C., & Batshaw, M. L. (1997). Born too soon, born too small. In M. L. Batshaw (Ed.), *Children with disabilities* (4th ed., pp. 115–139). Baltimore: Brookes.

Birch, H. G., & Gussow, J. D. (1970). *Disadvantaged children: Health, nutrition, and school failure.* New York: Grune & Stratton.

Bradley, R. H., Whiteside, L., Mundfrom, D. J., Casey, P. H., Kelleher, K. J., & Pope, S. K. (1994). Contributions of early intervention and early caregiving experiences to resilience in low birthweight, premature children living in poverty. *Journal of Clinical Child Psychology, 21,* 425–434.

Brann, A. W., Jr., & Schwartz, J. F. (1983). Central nervous system disturbances. In A. A. Fanaroff & R. J. Martin (Eds.), *Behrman's neonatal-perinatal medicine* (3rd ed., pp. 347–403). St. Louis, MO: Mosby.

Brown, J. L., & Pollitt, E. (1996). Malnutrition, poverty, and intellectual development. *Scientific American, 274*(2), 38–43.

Brown, R. T. (1986). Etiology and development of exceptionality. In R. T. Brown & C. R. Reynolds (Eds.), *Psychological perspectives on childhood exceptionality: A handbook* (pp. 181–229). New York: Wiley.

Brown, R. T., & Hoadley, S. L. (1999). Rett syndrome. In S. Goldstein & C. R. Reynolds (Eds.), *Handbook of neurodevelopmental and genetic disorders in children.* New York: Guilford.

Brown, R. T., & Reynolds, C. R. (Eds.). (1986). *Psychological perspectives on childhood exceptionality: A handbook.* New York: Wiley.

Campbell, F. A., & Ramey, C. T. (1995). The effectiveness of early intervention on intellectual and academic achievement: A follow-up study of children from low-income families. *Child Development, 65,* 684–698.

Carta, J. J., Sideridis, G., Rinkel, P., Guimaraes, S., Greenwood, C., Baggett, K., Peterson, P., Atwater, J., McEvoy, M., & McConnell, S. (1994). Behavioral outcomes of young children prenatally exposed to illicit drugs: Review and analysis of experimental literature. *Topics in Early Childhood Special Education, 14,* 184–216.

Chess, S., & Thomas, A. (1984). *Origins and evolution of behavior disorders.* New York: Brunner/Mazel.

Cicchetti, D., & Toth, S. L. (1998). The development of depression in children and adolescents. *American Psychologist, 53,* 221–241.

Colt, G. H. (1998, April). Were you BORN that way? *Life,* 39–50.

Cravioto, J., & Delicardie, E. (1970). Mental performance in school-age children. *American Journal of Diseases in Children, 120,* 404–410.

Day, L., & Richardson, G. A. (1993). Cocaine use and crack babies: Science, the media, and miscommunication. *Neurotoxicology and Teratology, 15,* 293–294.

Freeman, J. M. (1985a). Introduction. In J. M. Freeman (Ed.), *Prenatal and perinatal factors associated with brain disorders* (Publication No. 85-1149, pp. 1–11). Bethesda, MD: National Institutes of Health.

Freeman, J. M. (1985b). Summary. In J. M. Freeman (Ed.), *Prenatal and perinatal factors associated with brain disorders* (Publication No. 85-1149, pp. 13–32). Bethesda, MD: National Institutes of Health.

Herrnstein, R. J. & Murray, C. (1994). *The bell curve.* New York: Free Press.

Howell, M., & Ford, P. (1980). *The true history of the Elephant Man.* New York: Penguin.

Kagan, J. (1994). *Galen's prophecy: Temperament in human nature.* New York: Basic Books.

Kopp, C. B. (1983). Risk factors in development. In P. H. Bertenthal, M. M. Haith, & J. J. Campos (Eds.), *Handbook of developmental psychology* (4th ed., Vol. 2, pp. 1081–1188). New York: Wiley.

Liptak, G. S. (1997). Neural tube defects. In M. L. Batshaw (Ed.), *Children with disabilities* (4th ed., pp. 529–552). Baltimore: Brookes.

McKusick, V. A., & Francomano, C. A. (1994). *Mendelian inheritance in man: A catalog of human genes and genetic disorders* (11th ed.). Baltimore: Johns Hopkins University.

Moore, K. L. (1982). *The developing human* (3rd ed.). Philadelphia: Saunders.

Pasamanick, B., & Knoblock, H. (1966). Retrospective studies on the epidemiology of reproductive casualty: Old and new. *Merrill-Palmer Quarterly, 12,* 1–26.

Patterson, G. R., Reid, J. B., & Dishion, T. J. (1992). *Antisocial boys.* Eugene, OR: Castalia.

Plomin, R., & DeFries, J. C. (1998, May). The genetics of cognitive abilities and disabilities. *Scientific American, 278,* 62–69.

Plomin, R., & McClearn, G. E. (Eds.). (1993). *Nature, nurture, & psychology.* Washington, DC: American Psychological Association.

Plomin, R., Owen, M. J., & McGuffin, P. (1994). The genetic basis of complex human behaviors. *Science, 264,* 1733–1739.

Ramey, C. T., & Ramey, S. L. (1998). Early intervention and early experience. *American Psychologist, 53,* 109–120.

Sameroff, A. J., & Chandler, M. J. (1975). Reproductive risk and the continuum of caretaking casualty. In F. D. Horowitz, M. Hetherington, S. Scarr-Salapatek, & G. Siegel (Eds.), *Review of child development research* (Vol. 4, pp. 187–244). Chicago: University of Chicago Press.

Strelau, J. (1998). *Temperament: A psychological perspective.* New York: Plenum.

Thompson, J. S., & Thompson, M. W. (1980). *Genetics in medicine* (3rd ed.). Philadelphia: Saunders.

Thompson, R. J., & O'Quinn, A. N. (1979). *Developmental disabilities.* New York: Oxford University Press.

Tienari, P., Wynne, L. C., Moring, J., Lahti, I., Naarala, M., Sorri, A., Wahlberg, K.-E., Saarento, O., Seitamaa, M., Kaleva, M., & Lasky, K. (1994). The Finnish adoptive family study of schizophrenia: Implications for family research. *British Journal of Psychiatry, 164*(Suppl. 23), 20–26.

Vogel, F., & Motulsky, A. G. (1979). *Human genetics.* Berlin: Springer-Verlag.

Wilson, J. Q., & Herrnstein, R. J. (1985). *Crime and human nature.* New York: Simon & Schuster.

Zigler, E. (1967). Familial mental retardation: A continuing dilemma. *Science, 155,* 292–298.

ROBERT T. BROWN
*University of North Carolina at Wilmington*

AUTISM
BRAIN DAMAGE
CAFE AU LAIT SPOTS
CHILD ABUSE
CONDITIONING
INBORN ERRORS OF METABOLISM
LEAD POISONING
LEARNED HELPLESSNESS
LOW BIRTH WEIGHT INFANTS
MALNUTRITION
PREMATURITY
SEIZURE DISORDERS
SPINA BIFIDA
TEMPERAMENT
TORCH COMPLEX

## EUGENICS

The term eugenics refers to attempts to improve the hereditary characteristics of man. The idea of improving the human stock arose from the observation of the great diversity of human characteristics and abilities and the tendency for characteristics to run in families. Thus the human population might be improved by breeding from the best stock, as is commonly done with considerable success in plants and animals. This idea was expressed by the Greek poet Theognis as early as the sixth century BC, and various eugenics plans for the ideal state were included in the writings of Plato.

Although eugenics is an ancient idea, it gained intellectual credibility with the general acceptance of the Darwinian theory of evolution and the idea that man is a product of an evolutionary process that continues in the present and will extend into the future. The term eugenics was coined in 1883 by Francis Galton, who was greatly influenced by the work of his cousin, Charles Darwin. Galton's eugenics proposals centered around providing scholarships and other inducements for superior young people to marry and raise large families, as well as assistance to those of low ability in limiting family size.

The modern history of eugenics can be divided into two contrasting periods (Haller, 1984). In the first part of the twentieth century, prior to World War II, there was widespread acceptance of the hereditary basis for human differences among scientists and the general public alike. The eugenics movement flourished, and in the United States was influential in the establishment of restrictive immigration and the passage of sterilization laws in a number of states. The second period, following the war, was characterized by the opposite trend. There was virtual consensus among behavioral scientists that the earlier conceptions were mistaken and there was a strong taboo inhibiting research and publication concerning the hereditary basis of human behavior. Eugenics became a bad word, and the term fell into disuse.

This massive swing of the pendulum appears to be purely ideological; it was not based on surprising new findings of any kind. No doubt the events of World War II, including the Holocaust and other excesses of the Nazis, created widespread revulsion toward attempts to change human populations. The civil rights movement and attempts to improve the lot of the disadvantaged probably also contributed to a new respect for human rights that seemed incompatible with many of the eugenics proposals of the earlier period.

Some eugenics proposals have been modest in scope and entirely voluntary. Muller (1965) proposed that sperm from outstanding males be stored and made available to women who voluntarily choose to conceive a child with it. Although such sperm banks are in existence, they have not yet gained the popularity that Muller invisioned. Shockley (1972) proposed that a bonus amounting to $1,000 for each IQ point below 100 be offered for voluntary sterilization to nonpayers of income tax. It is interesting to note that both Muller and Shockley are winners of the Nobel Prize and that both used their prestige to urge public acceptance of the eugenics idea, but the climate was turning in the opposite direction.

It seems clear that a properly administered eugenics program could achieve considerable success over a period of time, but it is instructive to note that no such program has been properly administered for a long enough time to demonstrate success on even a small scale. To have any effect on the course of human evolution, a eugenics program would have to alter the relative fertility of substantial segments of the world population over a long period of time. The human population is now so large and so disorganized politically that it is difficult to imagine how any of the past eugenics proposals could have a significant impact. Human reproductive patterns appear to be governed by forces that are still beyond human control.

Homo sapiens evolved from a common ancestor with modern apes over a period of about a million years. Although little is known about the details of this process, the early humanoids probably lived dangerously as hunters and gatherers in small isolated groups dispersed over a wide area. There must have been extremely strong selection for intelligence, language usage, and cooperativeness, since evolution of these traits was rapid. It seems likely that favorable cultural adaptations were selected along with favorable genetic traits, so that human culture evolved along with human biology.

For the past 10,000 years, humans have lived as farmers in fixed abodes. Osborn (1968) has reviewed studies of the fertility of agrarian primitive peoples performed before they were subjected to modern influences. These studies show that the more successful farmers tended to have larger families than the less successful, and that their offspring tended to have a better chance for survival. Statistics from the past century also tend to show that those more successful in terms of education and income tended to have more surviving children than did the less successful. Thus, during most of its history, humankind appears to have had a eugenic reproductive pattern. This is undoubtedly the basic cause of the current level of human achievement.

A dysgenic reproductive pattern has emerged worldwide. In the United States, for example, education and family income are now negatively related to births. Van Court and Bean (1985) have shown a significant negative correlation between vocabulary test score and number of children in a large and representative sample of American adults. In the past, differences in survival contributed significantly to differential fertility, but infant mortality has declined to the point that it is no longer a significant factor. Differential birth rates are now the only source of reproductive advantage.

On a larger scale, the most successful national populations are growing at less than half the rate of the less successful. The industrial democracies (such as Canada, Denmark, France, Germany, Japan, the United Kingdom, and the United States) had between 60 and 72 births per 1,000 women aged 15 to 49 in 1973, while virtually all less developed nations had in excess of 100 births per 1,000 women. A number (such as Algeria, Kenya, Mexico, and Nicaragua) had more than 200 births per 1,000 women. In aggregate, the less developed regions are increasing in population at 2.3 percent per year, while the developed regions are increasing at 0.9 percent per year.

These trends appear to be beyond rational control. Osborn (1968) attributed them to advances in birth-control technology, which provides effective methods that require information, foresight, planning, and money. Thus the most successful have been the first to take advantage of the enhanced ability to control reproduction. Osborn optimistically predicted that this effect is likely to be temporary, and that favorable birth differentials will return when the new technology has been completely assimilated and everyone has the number of children they desire and can support.

In fact, the future of human heredity is exceptionally difficult to forecast at this time because of the rapid advances that are being made in genetics and biology that will likely result in new technologies of reproduction. Already we have

in vitro fertilization, which could be used to separate genetic selection from childbearing and child rearing. Perhaps the future will bring the ability to clone humans and to alter the human genetic code. With these possibilities on the horizon, and others that cannot be foreseen, the present may not be the opportune time to undertake the politically awesome task of reversing the current dysgenic reproductive trends.

## REFERENCES

Bajema, C. J. (1976). *Eugenics then and now.* Stroudsburg, PA: Dowden, Hutchinson, & Ross.

Haller, M. H. (1984). *Eugenics.* New Brunswick, NJ: Rutgers University Press.

Muller, H. J. (1965). Means and aims in human genetic betterment. In T. M. Sonneborn (Ed.), *The control of human heredity and evolution.* New York: Macmillan.

Osborn, F. (1968). *The future of human heredity.* New York: Weybright & Talley.

Shockley, W. (1972). Dysgenics, geneticity, raceology: A challenge to the intellectual responsibility of educators. *Phi Delta Kappan, 53,* 297–312.

Van Court, M., & Bean, F. D. (1985). Intelligence and fertility in the United States: 1912–1982. *Intelligence, 9,* 23–32.

ROBERT C. NICHOLS
DIANE JARVIS
*State University of New York at Buffalo*

GENETIC COUNSELING
GENETIC FACTORS IN BEHAVIOR

# EUSTIS, DOROTHY HARRISON (1886–1946)

Dorothy Harrison Eustis introduced the use of guide dogs for the blind in the United States. Born in Philadelphia, Eustis established an experimental breeding kennel for dogs at her estate in Switzerland. With her husband, George Morris Eustis, and Elliott S. (Jack) Humphrey, an American horse breeder and trainer, she began a program of experimental breeding of dogs for police and army duty. She was also aware that trained guide dogs had been used successfully by the blind in Germany.

Convinced that guide dogs could make the difference between independent and dependent living for the blind, she wrote an article, "The Seeing Eye," for *The Saturday Evening Post,* urging the use of dogs as guides for the blind. The resulting deluge of mail from blind Americans led to the establishment, in 1929, of the United States' first guide-dog training school, in Nashville, Tennessee. Seventeen men and women and their dogs were trained the first year, after which the school was moved to Morristown, New Jersey, where it continues to the present day.

## REFERENCES

Eustis, D. H. (1927, November 5). The seeing eye. *The Saturday Evening Post,* 43–46.

Putnam, P. B. (1979). *Love in the lead.* New York: Dutton.

PAUL IRVINE
*Katonah, New York*

# EVALUATION

See CURRICULUM-BASED ASSESSMENT; EVIDENCE-BASED PRACTICE; RESPONSE TO INTERVENTION.

# EVENT RECORDING

Event recording is a direct observation method that is used in a systematic fashion to determine the frequency of a targeted behavior. Event recording is most suitable for the measurement of discrete behaviors (Wolery, Bailey, & Sugai, 1988). A discrete behavior is a behavior that has a distinguishable beginning and end and that is typically equivalent in duration (Sulzer-Azaroff & Mayer, 1991). Examples of discrete behaviors include correct verbal responding, hand raising, hitting, and the number of questions a student asked during an instructional period.

As with any systematic direct observation system, the first step is to operationally define the target behavior. An operational definition is a written statement that precisely defines the behavior you wish to measure in terms that are observable, measurable, and replicable (Fletcher-Janzen & De Pry, 2003). Next, the observer should define the observation period, including recording the start and stop times. Finally, the data collector will carefully observe the person of concern. When he or she observes a behavior that matches the operational definition, a tally mark will be recorded on the data collection sheet. At the end of the observation period, the total number of tally marks will be added and graphed as the frequency of the behavior for that observation session. In some cases, the teacher or researcher might be interested in the rate of the targeted behavior. The rate of behavior can be calculated by dividing the frequency of the behavior over the total time of the observation period. For example, 60 behaviors over a 30-minute observation period would yield a rate of 2 behaviors per minute.

One of the many benefits of event recording is ease of use. Teachers and researchers typically tally the number of behaviors on a data collection sheet. However, other methods, such as mechanical counters, moving paper clips from one pile to another, using computer software that is loaded on a laptop or a handheld device, and using a pocket calculator to count the occurrences of a behavior, are equally as effective and can increase the efficiency of this data collection method (Alberto & Troutman, 2006). As with all direct observation systems, collecting interobserver reliability data is critical. The formula for calculating interobserver reliability for event recording is taking the smaller number and dividing by the larger then multiplying by 100. This formula will give you the percent of agreement between the primary observer and an independent observer.

## REFERENCES

Alberto, P. A., & Troutman, A. C. (2006). *Applied behavior analysis for teachers* (7th ed.). Upper Saddle River, NJ: Prentice Hall.

Fletcher-Janzen, E., & De Pry, R. L. (2003). *Teaching social competence and character: An IEP planner with goals, objectives, and interventions.* Longmont, CO: Sopris West Educational Services.

Sulzer-Azaroff, B., & Mayer, G. R. (1991). *Behavior analysis for lasting change.* Fort Worth, TX: Harcourt Brace.

Wolery, M., Bailey, D., Jr., & Sugai, G. (1988). *Effective teaching: Principles and procedures of applied behavior analysis with exceptional students.* Boston: Allyn & Bacon.

RANDALL L. DE PRY
*University of Colorado at Colorado Springs*

## BEHAVIORAL ASSESSMENT

# EVIDENCE-BASED PRACTICE

Evidence-based practice (EBP) is a term broadly used in many health care and education fields to refer to practice that is informed by the findings and conclusions of research. The origins of the term are most often attributed to the evidence-based medicine movement, which formally begin in 1981 when a group of clinical epidemiologists published a series of articles in the *Canadian Medical Association Journal* to guide clinicians on how to read journal articles (Guyatt, 2002). This series spawned a similar series in the *Journal of the American Medical Association* between 1993 and 2000, resulting in the *Users' Guides to the Medical Literature: A Manual for Evidence-Based Clinical Practice* (Guyatt & Rennie, 2002), a definitive text on the principles and processes of EBP. While this text was developed to specifically apply to evidence-based medicine, its guidelines can be applied to EPB in other fields.

According to Guyatt et al. (2002), EBP "acknowledges that intuition [and] unsystematic clinical experience . . . are insufficient grounds for clinical decision making; and it stresses the examination of evidence from clinical research" (p. 4). At the same time, one fundamental principle of EBP is that research evidence alone, without consideration of the individual situation, is never enough to make a clinical decision. Guyatt et al. assert that decisions must also include consideration of risks and benefits, inconvenience, costs, and patient values. Other factors to be considered when integrating research into practice include the similarity between the practice population and the participants of the research (e.g., the most well-tested intervention in the research literature for a particular problem might have only been tested with 12-year-olds, whereas a practitioner might be working with a 6-year-old) and the fit between the setting characteristics and the research recommendations (e.g., research might suggest that an intervention should be administered in the home, but the practice setting does not have the resources to do so). EBP requires practitioners to use their clinical training and decision-making skills to determine how best to apply research results to individual cases.

The second fundamental principle of EBP is that there is a hierarchy of evidence to guide decision making (Guyatt et al., 2002). For example, results from a study that tests a behavioral intervention in several different schools should be given more weight than the results of a study testing that intervention in a single classroom, which in turn would be given more weight than a case study testing that intervention with a single child. Factors to be considered when determining the relative utility of different forms of evidence include the type of study design (e.g., a randomized study comparing an intervention group with a control group provides stronger evidence than a single case study), the quality of the study design (e.g., a study involving random assignment of participants to groups likely provides stronger evidence than a study comparing self-selected groups), the quality of the study measurement (e.g., a study that demonstrates effects of an intervention on child mental health, family functioning, and academic outcomes provides stronger evidence than a study only demonstrating effects on child mental health alone), and the size of the evidence base (e.g., an intervention that has been tested in several studies has more evidence supporting its use than an intervention only tested in a single study).

Cournoyer and Powers (2002) have posited that EBP also dictates that "every client system, over time, should be individually evaluated to determine the extent to which the predicted results have been attained as a direct consequence of the practitioners' actions" (p. 15). In other words, EBP involves a scientific approach not only to making clinical decisions, but also to monitoring the consequences of those decisions.

The Empirically Supported Treatments (ESTs; e.g., Chambliss & Ollendick, 2001; see entry for Empirically Supported Treatment) movement in clinical psychology

and other efforts to list specific EBPs (e.g., The Evidence-Based Intervention Workgroup in school psychology; e.g., Kratochwill & Shernoff, 2003) represent a form of EBP. However, EBPs are not necessarily limited to interventions on these types of lists, as these lists often only include treatments that have particular kinds and levels of evidence supporting their use and typically do not list treatments that fall below these evidence thresholds or that have different types of evidence for their support. By contrast, EBP, while placing preferential weight to more rigorously tested research conclusions, involves consideration of the full range of available evidence.

## REFERENCES

Chambliss, D. L., & Ollendick, T. H. (2001). Empirically supported psychological interventions: Controversies and evidence. *Annual Review of Psychology, 52,* 685–716.

Cournoyer, B. R., & Powers, G. T. (2002). Evidence-based social work: The quiet revolution continues. In A. R. Roberts & G. Green (Eds.), *The social work desk references* (pp. 798–806). New York: Oxford University Press.

Guyatt, C. (2002). Preface. In G. Guyatt & D. Rennie (Eds.), *Users' guide to the medical literature: A manual for evidence-based clinical practice* (pp. 3–12). Chicago: American Medical Association.

Guyatt, G., & Rennie, D. (Eds.). (2002). *Users' guide to the medical literature: A manual for evidence-based clinical practice.* Chicago: American Medical Association.

Guyatt, C., Haynes, B., Jaeschke, R., Cook, D., Greenhalgh, T., Meade, M., et al. (2002). Introduction: The philosophy of evidence-based medicine. In G. Guyatt & D. Rennie (Eds.), *Users' guide to the medical literature: A manual for evidence-based clinical practice* (pp. 3–12). Chicago: American Medical Association.

Kratochwill, T. R. & Shernoff, E. S. (2003). Evidence-based practice: Promoting evidence-based interventions in school psychology. *School Psychology Quarterly, 18,* 389–408.

AMANDA JENSEN DOSS
*Texas A&M University*

## EMPIRICALLY SUPPORTED TREATMENT
## INTERVENTION IN SCHOOL AND CLINIC
## RESPONSE TO INTERVENTION

## EXCEPTIONAL CHILDREN

*Exceptional Children* is the official scholarly journal of the Council for Exceptional Children (CEC), and has been published continuously since 1934. The quarterly journal will solicit and publish the following types of articles: scholarly data-based research papers in the field of special education, papers that will have a broad base of interest among practitioners in special education, major research projects that are of specific interest, papers that integrate previously published research into a set of conclusions, and illustration of the applications of research to educational practice.

THOMAS E. ALLEN
*Gallaudet College*
First edition

TAMARA J. MARTIN
*The University of Texas of the
Permian Basin*
Second edition

## EXHIBITIONISM

Exhibitionism is the repeated exposure of the genitals to unwitting strangers to produce sexual excitement without attempts at further sexual activity (American Psychiatric Association, 1982). Convicted exhibitionists are almost exclusively male. Approximately one-third of all sex offenders are arrested for exhibitionism, making it the most common sexual crime in the United States (Rosenhan & Seligman, 1984).

Viewed from a psychoanalytical perspective, exhibitionism is considered a symptom of a more fundamental problem such as a defense against a fear of castration or a fixation at the phallic stage of development. Behavioral views are in stark contrast with this position. Although there are numerous behavioral approaches, all place emphasis directly on the exhibitionistic behavior and the variables that promote or maintain it (Wilson & O'Leary, 1980). Behaviorally based treatments have received the most empirical scrutiny.

One of the earliest behavioral treatments of an exhibitionist was reported by Bond and Hutchison (1960). The systematic desensitization program used, however, proved only partially successful. Quirk (1974), reporting on a follow-up of the person treated by Bond and Hutchison, used a biofeedback desensitization method. For 1 year following treatment, there were no instances of exhibitionism. A single instance then occurred, at which time a reapplication of the treatment proved successful at a 2-year follow-up. Maletzky (1977) also found some individuals benefited from posttreatment "booster sessions" in an assisted covert sensitization treatment that used aversive imagery and noxious odors.

Hayes, Brownell, and Barlow (1978) found a self-administered covert sensitization technique in which realistic aversive scenes (e.g., being arrested) were used was effective. There is evidence that techniques that are effective with persons voluntarily seeking treatment are equally effective with persons who are treated involuntarily (Maletzky, 1980).

### REFERENCES

American Psychiatric Association. (1982). *Desk reference to the diagnostic criteria from diagnostic and statistical manual of mental disorders* (3rd ed.). Washington, DC: Author.

Bond, I. K., & Hutchison, H. C. (1960). Application of reciprocal inhibition therapy to exhibitionism. *Canadian Medical Association Journal, 83,* 23–25.

Hayes, S. C., Brownell, K. D., & Barlow, D. H. (1978). The use of self-administered covert sensitization in the treatment of exhibitionism and sadism. *Behavior Therapy, 9,* 283–289.

Maletzky, B. M. (1977). "Booster" sessions in aversion therapy: The permanency of treatment. *Behavior Therapy, 8,* 460–463.

Maletzky, B. M. (1980). Self-referred versus court-referred sexually deviant patients: Success with assisted covert sensitization. *Behavior Therapy, 11,* 306–314.

Quirk, D. A. (1974). A follow-up on the Bond-Hutchison case of systematic desensitization with an exhibitionist. *Behavior Therapy, 5,* 428–431.

Rosenhan, D. L., & Seligman, M. E. P. (1984). *Abnormal psychology.* New York: Norton.

Wilson, G. T., & O'Leary, K. D. (1980). *Principles of behavior therapy.* Englewood Cliffs, NJ: Prentice Hall.

JAMES P. KROUSE
*Clarion University of
Pennsylvania*

## EXPECTANCY AGE

Expectancy age refers to a method used to compare performance on an intelligence or scholastic aptitude measure with performance on an achievement measure. The practice most likely had its origins in the accomplishment ratio proposed by Raymond Franzen in 1920. Franzen advocated dividing a pupil's subject age, obtained from an achievement test, by his or her mental age, obtained from an intelligence test (Formula 1):

$$100 = \left(\frac{\text{Subject age}}{\text{Mental age}}\right) = \text{Subject ratio}$$

Formula 1 was applied to each subject matter domain measured by a particular achievement test. Separate ratios were computed for reading, mathematics, and other subjects for which achievement test results were available. Subject ratios above 100 denoted performance greater than expected for the pupil's mental age, while subject ratios below 100 signified performance lower than expected for the pupil's mental age. The average of a pupil's subject ratios was termed the accomplishment quotient, an overall index of achievement in relation to mental age. A number of serious technical flaws resulted in the abandonment of the use of ratios in relating achievement to intellectual ability or capacity.

Present-day test developers and users, like their 1920 counterparts, continue to search for meaningful ways to relate intelligence and achievement test results. Government intervention in establishing procedures for identifying children with severe learning disabilities in connection with PL 94-142 has undoubtedly served to intensify pressures placed on test users. The proliferation of several discrepancy formulas that use age equivalents or grade equivalents has resulted in further confusion and inappropriate practices (Reynolds, 1981). For example, the use of a mental age, obtained either directly from an intelligence test or indirectly when only an IQ is available, to establish an expectancy age has sometimes occurred from solving for MA in Formula 2:

$$MA = \frac{(CA)(IQ)}{100}$$

Age equivalents in various achievement domains (e.g., reading, mathematics, spelling) are then compared one by one with the expectancy age to identify discrepancies between intelligence and achievement. Such practices are technically indefensible for the following reasons.

Age equivalents constitute a scale of unequal units. The difference in performance between an age equivalent of 6-0 and 7-0 is, for example, much greater than the difference in performance between an age equivalent of 14-0 and 15-0 for both the intelligence and the various achievement domains. In fact, an age equivalent must be extrapolated after about age 16 for most traits because there is little real growth beyond this age. Both the unequal units of the age equivalent scale and their artificial extension, or extrapolation, render them unsuitable for any sort of statistical manipulation. Thus the simple arithmetic operation of subtraction needed to search for discrepancies between ability and achievement is untenable.

Further difficulties with age equivalents result from their unequal variability, both at successive age levels within one subject matter domain as well as among different subject matter domains. The variability of age equivalents in arithmetic computation, for example, will be considerably smaller at a particular age level than that for reading comprehension. For this reason, there is no technically sound method to interpret discrepancies at different age levels within a single subject matter domain or across subject matter domains.

An added difficulty occurs when an attempt is made to compare age equivalents from tests having dissimilar norm groups. If the norming sample for an intelligence test differs from that for an achievement test, then observed discrepancies between age equivalents on the two measures may merely represent systematic differences between the two norm groups.

One other difficulty that must be mentioned in connection with such comparisons is the correlation between intelligence and achievement in various subject matter domains. Because the relationship between intelligence and reading comprehension, for example, differs from that for intelligence and arithmetic computation, the magnitude of observed discrepancies cannot be accepted at face value without taking into account the phenomenon known as regression to the mean. Interpretation of differences is thus difficult because the correlation between each intelligence-achievement pairing differs both within a single age level as well as across age levels. For these reasons, the practice of using an expectancy age as a benchmark for undertaking achievement test comparisons to identify pupils with suspected learning disabilities or atypical ability-achievement relationships cannot be recommended on technical or logical grounds.

### REFERENCES

Franzen, R. (1920, November). The accomplishment quotient. *Teachers College Record,* 114–120.

Otis, A. S. (1925). *Statistical method in educational measurement.* New York: Harcourt Brace Jovanovich.

Reynolds, C. (1981). The fallacy of "two years below grade level for age" as a diagnostic criterion for reading disorders. *Journal of School Psychology, 19*(4), 350–358.

GARY J. ROBERTSON
*American Guidance Service*

GRADE EQUIVALENTS
LEARNING DISABILITIES, SEVERE DISCREPANCY ANALYSIS IN

## EXPRESSIVE LANGUAGE DISORDERS

See LANGUAGE DISORDERS.

## EXPRESSIVE VOCABULARY TEST

The Expressive Vocabulary Test (EVT; Williams, 1997) is an individually administered measure of expressive vocabulary and word retrieval. Younger children are required to label pictures or body parts presented, while older examinees are required to provide a synonym for the word and picture provided. The labeling items (1–38) are designed for younger examinees because labeling is one of the first stages of expressive language development. The synonym task was chosen for older subjects because it allows sampling of a variety of vocabulary and because of the labeling task's early ceiling effect. Both labeling and synonym items are presented with pictures. The examinee responds to each item with a one-word answer. The presentation easel includes colorful pictures that are balanced for gender and ethnic representation. The record form indicates both the correct and the most frequently given incorrect answers, which facilitates the scoring process. The record form also indicates to the examiner which responses require further prompting. A computer scoring program called AS-SIST is also available. The program provides graphs of repeated testing results and suggests vocabulary-building exercises. A variety of scores are reported, including standard scores (M = 100, SD = 15), percentile ranks, and age equivalents.

The EVT was conormed with the Peabody Picture Vocabulary Test III (PPVT-III), a receptive vocabulary measure, on a population of 2,725 examinees ages 2 years 6 months to 90+ years. The sample was representative of the 1994 U.S. Census with respect to gender, race/ethnicity, region, and socioeconomic status. Because the EVT and the PPVT-III were conormed, scores from these measures are directly comparable.

The EVT reliability analyses indicate a high degree of internal consistency. Median split-half reliability is .91, while the median internal alpha reliability is .95. Test-retest reliability coefficients derived from four studies of different-aged samples ranged from .77 to .90. Concurrent validation studies found EVT scores more correlated with the Verbal than the Performance scale on the Wechsler Intelligence Scale for Children–Third Edition. The EVT was also correlated with the Oral Expression Scale and Written Language Scales (OWLS). The EVT was not more highly correlated with crystallized than with fluid intelligence on the Kaufman Adolescent and Adult Intelligence Test (KAIT), a finding opposite of what was expected.

## REFERENCES

Carlson, J. F. (2001). Expressive Vocabulary Test. *Journal of Psychoeducational Assessment, 19,* 100–105.

Gray, S., Plante, E., & Vance, R. (1999). The diagnostic accuracy of four vocabulary tests administered to preschool-age children. *Language, Speech, & Hearing Services in Schools, 30,* 196–206.

Plake, B. S., & Impara, J. C. (Eds.). (2001). *The fourteenth mental measurements yearbook.* Lincoln, NE: Buros Institute of Mental Measurements.

Smith, T., Smith, B. L., & Eichler, J. B. (2002). Validity of the Comprehensive Receptive and Expressive Vocabulary Test in assessment of children with speech and learning problems. *Psychology in the Schools, 39,* 613–619.

Ukrainetz, T. A., & Blomquist, C. (2002). The criterion validity of four vocabulary tests compared with a language sample. *Child Language and Teaching Therapy, 18,* 59–78.

Williams, K. T. (1997). *Expressive Vocabulary Test manual.* Circle Pines, MN: American Guidance Service.

RON DUMONT
*Fairleigh Dickinson University*

JOHN O. WILLIS
*Rivier College*

## EXTENDED SCHOOL YEAR FOR CHILDREN WITH DISABILITIES

Following the passage of the Education for All Handicapped Children Act of 1975, and between 1977 and 1981, 46 cases were filed in state and federal courts to contest the unwillingness of local educational agencies to provide special education for a period beyond the traditional school year (Marvell, Galfo, & Rockwell, 1981). The issue in those cases was whether a state or local policy of refusing to consider or provide education beyond the regular school year (usually 180 days) for children with disabilities violated mandates under Part B of the Education of the Handicapped Act (EHA).

In the leading case, *Battle* v. *Pennsylvania* (1980), the federal Third Circuit Court of Appeals held that Pennsylvania's inflexible application of a 180-day maximum school year prevented the proper formulation of appropriate educational goals and was, therefore, incompatible with the EHA's emphasis on the individual. Most of the courts that have considered limitations on the length of the school year, as applied to children with disabilities, have invalidated them for essentially the same reasons stated in the *Battle* decision.

The court decisions have provided some general guidelines, but controversial areas remain relative to the provision of extended-year services to children with disabilities. One major issue relates to determining which children with disabilities are eligible for extended-year services. Generally, the individual plaintiffs or class of plaintiffs involved in those lawsuits consisted of children with severe disabilities, a term that generally is not confined to a separate and specific category but indicates a degree of disability that necessitates intensified services. Courts have made it clear that determination of whether a child will receive a program in excess of the traditional school year must be made on an individual basis. To prevail, an individual must demonstrate that such a program is required for a particular child to benefit from the education provided during the preceding school year, in accordance with the interpretation of "free appropriate public education" set forth by the U.S. Supreme Court in *Board of Education* v. *Rowley* (1982).

Courts generally have accepted the argument advanced in the *Battle* case that children with severe disabilities, as compared with children without disabilities, have greater difficulty in acquiring and transferring skills, are more likely to lose a greater number of skills over time (or regress), and take a longer time to recoup those skills. There is disagreement, however, as to whether a continuous program of education, without extended breaks, would lessen the likelihood of regression in certain children with severe disabilities. In accordance with the *Rowley* decision, courts have stressed the importance of the individualized education program (IEP) process mandated by the Individuals with Disabilities Education Act (IDEA) in educational decision making regarding extended-year services (e.g., *Crawford* v. *Pittman,* 1983).

Another major area of controversy concerns the cost of extended-year services. Courts have rejected arguments by school officials that limited fiscal resources justify limitations on the services that may be provided for children with disabilities. Since *Mills* v. *Board of Education* (1972), courts have almost uniformly held that lack of funds may not limit the availability of appropriate educational services for children with disabilities more severely than for children without disabilities (Sales et al., 1999).

### REFERENCES

Marvell, T., Galfo, A., & Rockwell, J. (1981). *Student litigation: A compilation and analysis of civil cases involving students, 1977–1981.* Williamsburg, VA: National Center for State Courts.

Sales, B., Krauss, D., Sacken, D., & Overcast, T. (1999). The legal rights of students. In C. R. Reynolds & T. B. Gutkin (Eds.), *The handbook of school psychology* (3rd ed., pp. 1113–1145). New York: Wiley.

SHIRLEY A. JONES
*Virginia Polytechnic Institute
and State University*
First edition

KIMBERLY F. APPLEQUIST
*University of Colorado at
Colorado Springs*
Third edition

## EXTINCTION

Extinction, also termed planned ignoring, is a behavior reductive procedure that occurs when a behavior that has been previously reinforced is no longer reinforced in order to reduce or eliminate the occurrence of that behavior (Sulzer-Azaroff & Mayer, 1986). Extinction has been used to effectively reduce a wide variety of inappropriate behaviors, usually those that are maintained by social attention (Spiegler, 1983).

The reductive effect on behavior is best demonstrated when extinction is effectively implemented as follows:

1. All sources of reinforcement to the behavior are identified and withheld.
2. Reinforcement of an alternative desirable behavior occurs along with extinction of the undesirable behavior.
3. Extinction is applied consistently following the emission of the response in question.
4. Extinction conditions are maintained for a sufficient period of trials until reduction in behavior is complete.

There are further considerations in the use of extinction. Extinction is a gradual behavior-reduction technique and does not work immediately. In addition, an immediate increase in the rate and intensity of the response under extinction conditions may occur temporarily before reduction in response. Extinction conditions of one behavior may initially induce aggression in other behaviors. Finally, behaviors reduced under extinction may be situation-specific and may not generalize to other conditions. Although extinction is an effective behavior-reduction technique, because of its limitations (considerations), it should not be used for the immediate reduction of severely abusive behaviors.

### REFERENCES

Spiegler, M. D. (1983). *Contemporary behavioral therapy.* Palo Alto, CA: Mayfield.

Sulzer-Azaroff, B., & Mayer, G. R. (1986). *Achieving educational excellence using behavioral strategies.* New York: Holt, Rinehart, & Winston.

RHONDA HENNIS
LOUIS J. LANUNZIATA
*University of North Carolina at
Wilmington*

**AVERSIVE CONTROL**
**AVERSIVE STIMULUS**
**BEHAVIOR MODIFICATION**
**PUNISHMENT**

## EYE-HAND COORDINATION

Eye-hand coordination refers to the ability of an individual to direct fine motor activities of the hand in response to directive input and feedback provided by the visual system. Eye-hand coordination is a subskill of the larger concept of visual-motor coordination. The latter concept refers to the role of vision in directing and controlling voluntary movements of the body.

A deficiency in eye-hand coordination can arise from many sources, including deficiency in visual perception, acuity, figure-ground distortion, and discrimination. Similarly, underdeveloped muscles of the hand or damage in the lower sensory-neural pathways can affect the outcome of eye-hand coordination efforts. However, excluding obvious visual defects and/or disturbance in the lower neural or musculature systems, eye-hand coordination difficulty is most likely traceable to disruption within the cerebellum.

The cerebellum is a small mass attached to the brain stem near the (dorsal, inferior) base of the cerebrum. According to Gaddes (1985), the cerebellum collects sensory inputs not only from haptic sensitivity (touch) but also from the perception of visual stimuli. The structure is apparently capable of rapid activity following relatively limited input. The cerebellum apparently "acts as a filter to smooth and coordinate muscular activity" (Gaddes, 1985, p. 53). Moreover, dysfunction in the mid-cerebellum may produce generalized motor clumsiness. If the clumsiness is manifested in a visual-motor disability, the result is a decrement in manual dexterity (apraxia). Perceptual activities, writing, and other fine motor activities are generally affected. Although such conditions do disrupt the development of school progress, Gaddes (1985) maintains that little empirical evidence specifically relates dysfunction of the cerebellum to the special education classification of learning disabilities. Exceptions to this view, however, have been offered (Ayres, 1972; Valk, 1974).

As noted, eye-hand coordination has generally been studied under the more comprehensive topic of visual- (or visuomotor) motor deficiency. Several academic and behavioral deficits have been associated with this problem, including speech and language problems as well as problems in reading, arithmetic, spelling, and handwriting. Additionally, elements of emotional disorders have been associated with visual-motor difficulties. These disorders appear to stem largely from the negative attitudes developed toward academics.

The importance of eye-hand coordination is apparent. However, central issues pertaining to assessment and training remain a source of empirical controversy. Informal assessment often proceeds from the observation of daily skills thought to be dependent on eye-hand coordination ability. Activities that might be used for informal diagnosis (and perhaps training) include tracing, scissor use, lacing, design copying, and other similar tasks (Lerner, 1981). More formal assessment might be approached through laboratory-derived procedures (e.g., use of the rotary pursuit) or published tests (e.g., the Developmental Test of Visual-Motor Integration [Beery, 1982]). It should be noted that reviews of the formal tests associated with eye-hand coordination

generally reveal a lack of evidence of appropriate development, reliability, and validity (Salvia & Ysseldyke, 1985).

A number of authors have argued strongly the importance of visual-motor activities as a basis for academic deficiency and as a trainable (remediable) skill. Among the more forceful proponents of this theory was Getman (1965), who emphasized the importance of visual training, a developmental model that employed the training of a visuomotor learning schema. In Getman's view failures in visuomotor activities, of which eye-hand coordination is an element, can result in behavioral, cognitive, and academic failure. Despite Getman's and other theorists' models, the efficiency of visuo-training approaches remains controversial.

### REFERENCES

Ayres, A. J. (1972). *Sensory integration and learning disorders.* Los Angeles: Western Psychological Services.

Beery, K. E. (1982). *Revised administration, scoring and teaching manual for the Developmental Test of Visual-Motor Integration.* Cleveland, OH: Modern Curriculum Press.

Gaddes, W. H. (1985). *Learning disabilities and brain function: A neuropsychological approach* (2nd ed.). New York: Springer-Verlag.

Getman, G. N. (1965). The visuomotor complex in the acquisition of learning skills. In J. Hellmuth (Ed.), *Learning disorders* (Vol. 1). Seattle, WA: Special Child Publications.

Hallahan, D. P., & Cruickshank, W. (1973). *Psychoeducational foundations of learning disabilities.* Englewood Cliffs, NJ: Prentice Hall.

Lerner, J. (1981). *Learning disabilities: Theories, diagnosis and teaching strategies* (3rd ed.). Boston: Houghton Mifflin.

Salvia, J., & Ysseldyke, J. E. (1985). *Assessment in special and remedial education* (3rd ed.). Boston: Houghton Mifflin.

Valk, J. (1974). Neuroradiology and learning disabilities. *Tydschrift Voor Orthopedogogiek, 11,* 303–323.

TED L. MILLER
*University of Tennessee*

**VISUAL-MOTOR AND VISUAL-PERCEPTUAL PROBLEMS**
**VISUAL PERCEPTION AND DISCRIMINATION**

# EYSENCK, HANS J. (1916–1997)

Eysenck was born and educated in Berlin, Germany, openly opposing Hitler and his requirement of Nazi party membership for university admission, and moving to England in the late 1930s in protest. He received his BA in 1938 and PhD in Psychology in 1949 from the University of London. In 1946 Eysenck became senior research psychologist at Maudsley Hospital, a year later becoming head of the psychology department, founded by him within the Institute of Psychiatry at that hospital. For over 30 years he was professor of psychology at the University of London and director of the psychology unit at Maudsley Hospital. Hans J. Eysenck died on September 4, 1997 at the age of 81.

Eysenck has been described as one of the most influential, provocative, and controversial psychologists of his generation. He was a persistent critic of psychoanalysis, psychotherapy, and projective assessment, and a moving force in the establishment of clinical psychology and behavior therapy. As a behaviorist, he advocated scientific methods of personality assessment and denied the theory of the subconscious, denouncing Freud as a charlatan in the process. Eysenck applied research methods traditionally used in the study of intelligence to the study of personality, utilizing factor analysis and discriminant function analysis to identify major factors. He attempted to develop hypotheses linking those factors to widely accepted psychological and physiological concepts. This approach to the treatment of scientific data was a general theme throughout his research.

Eysenck was a pioneer in defining the structure of personality, attracting students and collaborators from around the world with his analysis of the layers of personality. *Dimensions of Personality* (1947) and *The Structure of Human Personality* (1970) provide explanations of his theory of personality, identifying the measurable areas as intelligence, neurosis, psychosis, extroversion, and introversion, all later components of psychological tests. In the behaviorist tradition, Eysenck was unconcerned about aspects of personality that could not be measured, claiming that what was not measurable did not exist. His belief in interventions based on unlearning the maladaptive behaviors that had been learned, drew criticism that he was merely treating symptoms of mental disorders, not the disease itself. He argued, however, that the symptoms are the disorder.

The most heated controversy of his career was prompted by Eysenck's publication of an article in *The Harvard Education Review* (1969), arguing that the difference between scores of Blacks and Whites on intelligence tests was due to genetic as well as environmental factors. At the height of this controversy, he was attacked by students calling him a racist and fascist while attempting to deliver a lecture, and was accompanied by a bodyguard to ensure his safety.

Generating further criticism, Eysenck's book, *Smoking,*

*Health and Personality,* was published in 1965. In it he described the "cancer-prone" type personality, one characterized by feelings of hopelessness, helplessness, and depression, unable to express emotions and reacting inappropriately to stress. He argued that smoking itself does not cause cancer, and that both smoking and cancer are merely symptoms of the same personality disorder, one most likely of genetic origin.

During his career, Eysenck published some 80 books and 1,600 journal articles dealing with a vast array of subjects. In *Decline and Fall of the Freudian Empire* (1985), he proposed that Freud was "a genius, not of science, but of propaganda," and despite his rationalism, in his later work he concluded that powerful evidence exists to support extra-sensory perception and found a significant correlation between personality and the position of the planets. His self-help books such as *Check Your Own IQ* sold in the millions, and he founded two journals, *Behavior Research and Therapy* and *Personality and Individual Differences*. In 1990 he published his autobiography, *Rebel With a Cause*.

## REFERENCES

Eysenck, H. J. (1947). *Dimensions of personality*. London: Routledge & Kegan Paul.

Eysenck, H. J. (1965). *Smoking, health and personality*. London: Weidenfeld & Nicolson.

Eysenck, H. J. (1966). *Check your own IQ*. Harmondsworth, England: Penguin.

Eysenck, H. J. (1970). *The structure of human personality* (Rev. ed.). London: Methuen.

Eysenck, H. J. (1985). *Decline and fall of the Freudian empire*. Harmondsworth, England: Penguin.

Eysenck, H. J. (1990). *Rebel with a cause: The autobiography of H. J. Eysenck*. London: Allen.

ELAINE FLETCHER-JANZEN
*University of Colorado at
Colorado Springs*
First edition

TAMARA J. MARTIN
*The University of Texas of the
Permian Basin*
Second edition

# F

## FACILITATED COMMUNICATION

Facilitated communication (FC) is among the most controversial techniques in special education in particular, and in education and psychology in general. In FC, a trained person, called a "facilitator," supports the hand, wrist, or arm of a communication-impaired individual, most commonly one with autism or another developmental disability. The individual is thus allegedly enabled to use a finger to point to or press the keys of a typewriter, computer keyboard, or alphabet facsimile (Kirkel, 1995). Supporters (e.g., Biklen, 1997) allege that this method allows the impaired individual to communicate by typing letters, words, sentences, and numbers (Jacobson, Mulick, & Schwartz, 1995).

FC first emerged in the 1970s in Australia. Rosemary Crossley initiated use of the technique while working with physically disabled persons (Prior & Cummins, 1992). Douglas Biklen, who observed Crossley's methods during a trip to Australia, introduced FC to the United States in 1989. Biklen extended use of the therapy to include those afflicted with cerebral palsy, autism, and Down syndrome (Kerrin et al., 1998).

Biklen's results using FC were purportedly successful. As Jacobson et al. (1995, p. 753) state, ". . . previously nonverbal students were typing, with facilitation, words, sentences, and paragraphs of remarkable clarity and intellect." Reports of FC's successes and Biklen (e.g., 1993) and his Syracuse University group's workshops, publications, and conferences led to widespread adoption of, and support for, the new technique. The media, combined with hopeful parents and teachers, aroused further excitement about FC's possibilities (Rimland, 1991).

With all of the support for FC, attention began to turn to exactly what the students were typing. Biklen (1993) stated that autistic individuals reported through their facilitators that they are of normal intelligence and social competence. However, not all facilitated messages reported such happy news. Some children and adolescents using FC apparently claimed that they had been physically and sexually abused for many years, although unable to report it (Zirkel, 1995). Outrage began to spread as criminal charges were filed against parents who were forcibly separated from their children. In one case, "Michael" supposedly alleged through FC that his father was sexually abusing him (Zirkel, 1995). Michael's father was criminally charged and Michael sent to live in a foster home. In an attempt to confirm Michael's alleged claim of abuse, two different facilitators working with Michael reported that he claimed to have been abused. However, prior to working with Michael, both facilitators had been informed of his previous claims. Importantly, the details of the reported abuse varied drastically between the facilitators (Zirkel, 1995). Michael's father was later cleared of all criminal charges, and he pressed charges against the facilitation agency.

The outrage caused by the claims of abuse and the skepticism of many scientists led to scientific investigations of FC. Questions were raised concerning the sophistication of the untaught skills that many disabled persons displayed. Those who had never been taught to read, write, spell, or add were seemingly able to produce complex and correctly spelled sentences, solve difficult math problems, and compose sensitive poetry. Describing use of FC with two boys diagnosed as autistic and severely mentally retarded, Donnellan, Sabin, and Majure (1992, p. 70) stated, "Neither young man had been given any formal training in reading, writing, or spelling, nor had either one shown any obvious interest in these skills. Yet, in the first . . . sessions of facilitated communication . . . both were able to produce meaningful complex sentences." Professionals began to question whether the students or the facilitators were really the ones communicating (Prior & Cummins, 1992; Silliman, 1992; Thompson, 1994).

Skepticism of FC developed as quickly as had initial support. The results of numerous experiments suggested that FC was, in terms of actually enabling those with disabilities to communicate, a hoax. Well-controlled, double blind studies of FC demonstrated consistently that messages were coming not from the students, but from their facilitators. On trials where both the student and the facilitator had correct information, the facilitated message was correct, but on those trials on which only the student had correct information, the message was incorrect (Thompson, 1993). In other studies, researchers used screens to separate the student's and the facilitator's visual fields, showed them both a series of pictures, and asked the student to type what s/he saw. When student and facilitator saw the same picture, the facilitated answer was correct, but when the pictures were different, the answer corresponded to what the facilitator, not the student, had seen. Further, observations of students and facilitators consistently indicated that although the facilitators consistently looked at the keyboard, the students generally did not and had no home base, as do skilled typists. Without either looking at the board or having such a base, accurate typing is virtually impossible. Individuals with impairments using various methods of adapted communication always look at the instrument through which they are communicating. Much of this evidence may be seen in the videotape, *Prisoners of Silence* (Palfreman, 1993).

Virtually all well-controlled research indicated that the facilitators were themselves, although wholly without awareness, producing the messages (Jacobson, Mulick, & Schwartz, 1995). As several authors have suggested, this unconscious motor movement is similar to what occurs in dowsing, automatic writing, and Ouija. As an example of one study that supports this hypothesis, Burgess et al. (1998) showed a Biklen FC training videotape to 40 undergraduate students. They then asked the students to facilitate the communication of "Jackie," a confederate, who was described as disabled and unable to speak, but who was really a normal individual. Students were given different information about "Jackie" before the facilitation session. Eighty-nine percent of the answers that "Jackie" gave to questions about herself during the FC session corresponded to information provided to the particular student.

With all of the evidence against FC, however, Biklen and the Syracuse University group still support the technique, as reflected in a recent book (Biklen & Cardinal, 1997) and website (http://suedweb.syr.edu/thefci/). In addition, Vermont, Washington, and Indiana have facilitated communication coalitions where FC is still taught and implemented (http://www.bloomington.in.us). Perhaps Biklen and others are correct in claiming that FC is effective in some cases, but they need to provide stronger and more consistent evidence than they have to date. Unfortunately, the best conclusion at this time appears to be that, in spite of its hopes and bandwagon support, FC, as have so many other methods, appears to be wholly ineffective in enabling those with severe disabilities to communicate at all, let alone normally.

## REFERENCES

Biklen, D. P. (1993). *Communication unbound: How FC is challenging traditional views of autism and ability / disability.* New York: Teachers College Press.

Biklen, D., & Cardinal, D. N. (Eds.). (1997). *Contested words, contested science: Unraveling the facilitated communication controversy.* New York: Teachers College Press.

Burgess, C. A., Kirsch, I., Shane, H., Niederauer, K. L., Graham, S. M., & Bacon, A. (1998). Facilitated communication as an ideomotor response. *Psychological Science, 9,* 71–74.

Cramer, S., & Cramer, V. (1993, May). Laura. *Yankee, 57*(5), 78–83.

Donnellan, A. M., Sabin, L. A., & Majure, L. A. (1992). Facilitated communication: Beyond the quandary to the questions. *Topics in Language Disorders, 12,* 69–82.

Jacobson, J. W., Mulick, J. A., & Schwartz, A. A. (1995). A history of facilitated communication: Science, pseudoscience, and antiscience. *American Psychologist, 50,* 750–765.

Kerrin, R. G., Murdock, J. Y., Sharpton, W. R., & Jones, N. (1998). Who's doing the pointing? Investigating facilitated communication in a classroom setting with students with autism. *Focus on Autism and Other Developmental Disabilities, 13,* 73–75.

Mulick, J. A., Jacobson, J. W., & Kobe, F. H. (1993). Anguished silence and helping hands: Autism and facilitated communication. *Skeptical Inquirer, 17,* 270–287.

Palfreman, J. (1993, October 19). *Prisoners of silence.* Frontline, Public Broadcasting Service.

Prior, M., & Cummins, R. (1992). Questions about facilitated communication and autism. *Journal of Autism and Developmental Disorders, 22,* 331–336.

Rimland, B. (1991). Facilitated communication: Problems, puzzles and paradoxes: Six challenges for researchers. *Autism Research Review International, 5*(2), 3.

Silliman, E. R. (1992). Three perspectives of facilitated communication: Unexpected literacy, clever Hans, or enigma? *Topics in Language Disorders, 12*(4), 60–68.

Thompson, T. (1994). Reign of error: Facilitated communication. *American Journal on Mental Retardation, 98,* 670–673.

Zirkel, P. A. (1995). Facilitated communication of child abuse. *Phi Delta Kappan, 76,* 815–818.

LAUREN WEBSTER
ROBERT T. BROWN
*University of North Carolina at Wilmington*

**ASPERGER SYNDROME**
**AUTISM**

# FACTOR ANALYSIS

Factor analysis is a term encompassing several distinct statistical techniques all intended to investigate the relationships among a set of variables. The primary purposes include (a) reducing a large set of variables to a smaller set that reproduces most of the properties of the initial set; and (b) verifying (or not) theoretically proposed relationships among a set of variables. A key concept in factor analysis is termed latent structure or latent factor. A latent factor is not directly observable, but inferred from the interrelationships among observed (also termed manifest) variables. One or more latent factors may be inferred from observed variables' relationships to each other, and any single observed variable may be related to one, some, or all latent factors.

Factor analysis has a long history in psychology, beginning with Charles Spearman's investigations in the early 1900s (Spearman, 1904) concerned with the measurement of intelligence. Indeed, most efforts to construct a theory of intelligence included concomitant developments in factor analysis over the next century. Parallel developments in biology and the physical sciences focused on data reduction under a method later termed principal components. This method was also termed dimensional reduction, and it created observed variables that were linear combinations of the original set. Again, the goal was fewer of the new principal component variables than the number of variables in the original set.

A major distinction between principal components analysis and the evolving factor analysis procedures due to Spearman, Cyril Burt, Karl Pearson, Karl Holzinger and others (Harman, 1967) was the concept of measurement error. Principal components, followed from physical sciences in which measurement error was generally assumed to be near zero, while psychometric models of measurement developed with the concept of measurement error central to its theory. Measurement error remains the single most important aspect of factor analysis that differentiates it from physical science models of data.

Factor analysis initially focused on the Pearson correlation matrix for a set of variables. By necessity, various ad hoc procedures were developed to permit computations within the capabilities of paper and pencil or adding machines of the time. As solutions were generated the issues of a best solution and of the most interpretable solution arose. The concept of simple structure, coined by Thurstone, was formulated by attempting to find a solution in which variables related mainly (or entirely) to one factor. This led to an interactive process in which observed variables, usually test scores, were changed in the test development so as to create near-simple structure or variables deleted to create it. The method of principal axes was developed by Hotelling by the 1930s and, with refinements, remains the primary method of analysis under the term exploratory factor analysis (EFA).

By the 1960s, the availability of computers permitted analysis of factor analysis models that previously had been too tedious for hand or adding machine computations. New developments in interpretation of factor analysis solutions were created to "rotate" the solutions toward simple(r) structure. Two general approaches evolved: orthogonal rotation and oblique rotation. Orthogonal rotation effectively reoriented the factor solution within its space assuming all factors were uncorrelated with all others. Conceptually, this was equivalent to starting with a spatial orientation such as a room of a house with one corner of walls and floor the origin and rotating the walls and floor while leaving alone the variables relationship to each other and to each factor. The intent was to align as closely as possible each factor to a subset of variables most closely associated with it while keeping each factor uncorrelated with any others. Oblique rotation permitted the factors to become correlated along with aligning each factor most closely with a subset of variables. Varimax rotation is the method most commonly used for orthogonal rotation, and methods such as oblimin and promax are commonly used for oblique rotations.

In the 1960s and 1970s, Swedish statistician Karl Jöreskog (1969, 1973) developed procedures for analyzing pre-determined models for data. A major part of that development, termed linear structural relations, or LISREL, and later revised as structural equation modeling (SEM), was the specification of a factor structure for a set of observed variables. This procedure allowed testing of the adequacy of fit of the data to the theorized factor structure, and this has been termed confirmatory factor analysis or CFA. CFA permits an overall model test using a chi square statistic and various derivative standardized measures somewhat similar to squared multiple correlation-type indices. The most commonly used include the comparative fit index (CFI), normed fit index (NFI), adjusted goodness-of-fit index (AGFI), and root mean square error of approximation (RMSEA). General heuristic rules for acceptably good fit tend to require the fit indices to be above .90 or .95 and the RMSEA to be below .08. CFA can be conducted using various computer programs commercially available and many now include graphical drawing programs that do not require writing mathematical equations. Their proper use, however, should include consultation with an expert on CFA as there are many potential pitfalls in the estimation process.

EFA and CFA were intended to be complementary processes in that EFA explores the potential structure of a set of variables or test items, while CFA was intended to test a hypothesis concerning a specific factor model for the variables. There has been much blurring of the procedures in recent years, however, and unsatisfactory fit of CFA models now generally leads to a mixed use of EFA and CFA procedures. How adequate these are has yet to be determined.

## REFERENCES

Harman, H. H. (1967). *Modern factor analysis*. Chicago: University of Chicago Press.

Jöreskog, K. G. (1969). A general approach to confirmatory maximum likelihood factor analysis. *Psychometrika, 34,* 183–202.

Jöreskog, K. G. (1973). A general method for estimating a linear structural equation system. In A. S. Goldberger & O. D. Duncan (Eds.), *Structural equation models in the social sciences* (pp. 85–112). New York: Academic Press.

Spearman, C. (1904). General intelligence, objectively determined and measured. *Applied Journal of Psychology, 14,* 201–293.

VICTOR L. WILLSON
*Texas A&M University*

**DISCRIMINANT ANALYSIS**
**MULTIPLE REGRESSION**
**RESEARCH IN SPECIAL EDUCATION**

# FAILURE TO THRIVE

Failure to thrive (FTT) is defined as the failure of an infant or child to acquire height and weight normal for their ages as a result of inadequate calorie intake (Iwaniec, 2004). Failure to thrive has a long standing history with its origins dating specifically to Kasper Hauser syndrome and marasmus (Racicot, 2000). Failure to thrive originally was classified as having organic and nonorganic origins. However, these classifications have been replaced by broader classifications that incorporate medical and psychosocial factors. Although prevalence rates for FTT vary because of different criteria used for diagnosis, it accounts for 1 percent to 5 percent of all pediatric hospitalization and usually is seen in children three and under (Iwaniec, 2004; Racicot, 2000).

Although well-accepted indices or universal diagnostic criteria to diagnose FTT in children have not been established, the presence of height and weight growth trajectories below the 3rd to 5th percentiles in children, based on the National Center for Health Statistics norms (Marino, Weinman, & Soudelier, 2001; Phelps, 1991), often are used as the criterion for FTT. Consequences of FTT include growth deficits, decreased immunologic resistance, diminished physical activity, cognitive deficits, emotional and behavioral problems, and learning difficulties (Black, 1995; Iwaniec, 2004; Phelps, 1991).

Etiology of FTT focuses on medical and non-medical issues and may be due to a combination of conditions. Medical factors include gastrointestinal, endocrine or genetic disorders, as well as illness (Black, 1995; Iwaniec, 2004). Nonmedical factors include family issues, psychological variables, and degree of social support. The home environments of infants with FTT often differ from those of normal growing infants (Casey, Bradley, & Wortham, 1984). Large family size, poor marital relationships, and lack of economic security may lead to severe stress levels in adults and inadequate attention to the nutritional needs of children (Alderette & DeGraffenried, 1986; Phelps, 1991). Substance abuse, maternal depression, infant temperament, and lack of social support also may contribute to FTT (Racicot, 2000). Mothers of children with FTT often have had negative childhoods characterized by inadequate nurturing, stress, and abuse and, therefore, develop poor parenting skills (Steward & Garvin, 1997). Children with FTT often display difficult temperaments including lethargy, hypervigilance, irritability, apathy, and poor feeding ability, which often results in deficient interactions with caregivers (Black, 1995; Steward & Garvin, 1997). Unsuitable relationships between the mother and child may be conditions that contribute to FTT.

Various treatments are available for children who display FTT. Food supplementation programs (e.g., Special Supplemental Food Program for Women, Infants, and Children) are an attempt at preventing nutritional problems (Black, 1995). Other interventions include parenting classes, home visits, and individual and family counseling. These are family-focused and concentrate on the relationship between the child and the caregiver (Black, 1995; Phelps, 1991; Racicot, 2000). Failure to thrive may have long-lasting effects for children even after their condition improves. They may show delays academically and socially and need intervention to combat their delays.

## REFERENCES

Alderette, P., & DeGraffenried, D. F. (1986). Nonorganic failure-to-thrive syndrome and the family system. *Social Work, 31*(3), 207–211.

Black, M. M. (1995). Failure to thrive: Strategies for evaluation and intervention. *School Psychology Review, 24*(2), 171–185.

Casey, P. H., Bradley, R., & Wortham, B. (1984). Social and nonsocial home environments of infants with nonorganic failure-to-thrive. *Pediatrics, 73,* 348–353.

Iwaniec, D. (2004). *Children who fail to thrive: A practice guide.* England: Wiley.

Marino, R., Weinman, M. L., & Soudelier, K. (2001). Social work intervention and failure to thrive in infants and children. *Health & Social Work, 26*(2), 90–97.

Phelps, L. (1991). Non-organic failure-to-thrive: Origins. *School Psychology Review, 20*(3), 417–427.

Racicot, L. C. (2000). *Lexis, my little fairy princess: Literature review and case report on non-organic failure to thrive (NOFTT).* (ERIC Document Reproduction Service No. ED481101)

Steward, D. K., & Garvin, B. J. (1997). Nonorganic failure to thrive: A theoretical approach. *Journal of Pediatric Nursing, 12*(6), 342–347.

KATRINA RAIA
*University of Florida*

## DEPRIVATION, BIONEURAL RESULTS OF DEVELOPMENTAL DELAY MALNUTRITION

## FALSE POSITIVE AND FALSE NEGATIVE

The term false positive, developed in the vocabulary of medicine, is often confusing when used in other circles. In medicine, a condition is reported as positive when the condition is present. When the condition is reported as negative it is in the normal or average range. Therefore, a false positive refers to a judgment about the presence of an exceptional attribute that is actually in the average range or a score or judgment that incorrectly indicates a diagnosis (or a classification) of an individual who has been diagnosed as brain injured when in fact he or she is only exhibiting reasonably normal developmental delays. A false negative, the opposite of a false positive, results when an individual is determined to be average when in fact the individual is exceptional. For example, occasionally a child with cerebral palsy (who by medical diagnosis and by definition is brain injured) will reproduce, almost perfectly, drawings of geometric figures from a test for brain injury. By the results of the drawing test, the individual is a false negative. Whereas a negative interpretation of a clinical test indicates that nothing unusual has been found, a positive interpretation indicates exceptionality or pathology.

Further confusion may result when terms used in personnel selection are mixed with clinical terminology. In personnel selection, false rejections corresponds to false positives in clinical terminology. In the language of personnel specialists, a false rejection is an individual who has a score on a selection instrument that is below the cutoff (e.g., too exceptional to be successful on the job) but who is eventually successful on the job. False acceptances are those individuals who have scores on the selection tests above the cutoff but who are failures on the job. Even though nonnumerical conditions may influence the cutoff score, or various conditions may determine success on the job, such individuals are known as false negatives.

One of the most crucial factors in determining the number of false negative and false positive decisions is the cutoff score (which may be multiple scores on many parts of an assessment) used to indicate the presence (positive) or absence (negative) of pathology or whatever exceptional attribute is being evaluated. Personnel using a suicide prediction scale would be inclined to use a cutoff score that would deliberately decrease the number of persons who would be considered to be in the normal range (i.e., false negative) so that adequate protection could be put in place. Where incorrectly diagnosing pathology has dire implications but the condition itself is mild, a cutoff score would be set to underdiagnose, that is, to increase the number of false negatives and reduce the number of false positives.

Figure 1 gives an illustration of the concept of false negative and false positive as it has been used in the diagnosis of learning disabilities (Reynolds, 1984). Four cells are illustrated: students who are learning disabled and are so diagnosed are true positives; students who are learning disabled but are diagnosed as normal are false negatives; students who are not in fact learning disabled are false positives; students who are not learning disabled and are not diagnosed as learning disabled are true negatives. Frequently, in deciding on a diagnosis, assessment results are interpreted in a way to minimize either false negatives or false positives. In special education, learning disability diagnosis is best structured to minimize false negatives (Reynolds, 1984) while the diagnosis of mental retardation is best designed to minimize false positives.

Authors and publishers of tests and other predictive devices should provide an indication of the predictive confidence associated with each score. For many predictions, locally developed tables will be better than national data. Such tables should be developed, if they are not provided, to indicate the efficiency of various cutoff scores. Data should be provided about the percentage of correct classifications, especially for scores close to the cutoff, and about the expected percentage of false positive and false negative classifications for each group being considered. Prediction is often improved when more than one score is used, as in a formula derived from multiple regression. Data of various kinds and types usually produce better predictive information than scores from similar instruments.

## REFERENCE

Reynolds, C. R. (1984). Critical measurements issues in learning disabilities. *Journal of Special Education, 18,* 451–476.

JOSEPH L. FRENCH
*Pennsylvania State University*

## LEARNING DISABILITIES, SEVERE DISCREPANCY ANALYSIS IN RESEARCH IN SPECIAL EDUCATION

## FAMILIAL DYSAUTONOMIA

Familial dysautonomia was first identified as a syndrome by Riley and his associates in 1949; it was termed Riley-Day syndrome (Riley, Day, Greeley, & Langford, 1949). The symptomatology, which is extensive, results from involvement of the central (CNS) and peripheral nervous systems (PNS) and impacts on other developing systems of the body. Primarily found in Jews of eastern European extraction, dysautonomia is transmitted genetically, with the mode of inheritance believed to be autosomal recessive. The disorder is prominently marked by the individual's insensitivity to pain, absence of lacrimation, and absence of taste buds, in addition to many functional incapacities from birth (Brown, 2003). Dysautonomia is rarely diagnosed during the neo-

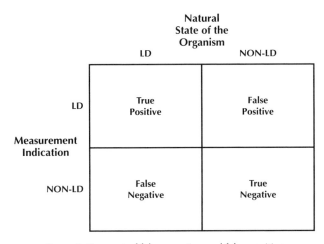

Figure 1  Concept of false negative and false positive

natal period (Perlman, Benady, & Sassi, 1979), although early identification is important to its management and to provision of appropriate treatment and educational services. The disorder is progressive, with those involved rarely living beyond the fourth decade of life. Exceptions have been noted, however, and because improvement can occur, an optimistic attitude may enhance the emotional relationship between family members (Meijer & Hovne, 1981).

Neonatal functioning, when identified, may be marked by unusual posture and limb movements as well as difficulties in swallowing (Perlman et al., 1979). The latter may be associated with other oropharyngeal deficits, may interfere with subsequent normative speech development, and may require the assistance of speech therapy. With regard to problems of swallowing, early identification and the provision of a feeding program would greatly assist the young child, as feeding problems have also been found in a large percentage of this population (Ganz, Levine, Axelrod, & Kahanovitz, 1983). As an adult, the dysautonomic may be dysarthric, resulting from involvement of the CNS. The presence of altered posture and limb movements may further interfere with the integration of more complex motor patterns, and delayed developmental milestones may also be noted (Ganz et al., 1983).

Orthopedic problems, including scoliosis and kyphosis, may also develop, thus requiring the use of adaptive aids for positioning and, in severe cases, to aid in locomotion. Physical therapy input would probably be indicated by this time, as might occupational therapy to assist the individual in maintaining range of motion. If the disorder progresses to the point where hospitalization becomes necessary, as much contact as possible should be maintained with the child or adolescent's educational placement and home setting by the hospital. "Hospitalization is indeed a disrupting and threatening experience even for the older, more experienced adult patient . . . and the younger child with more limited coping skills . . . is at particular psychological risk" (Barowsky, 1978, p. 48). Decreased vitality, resulting from compromised vital functions that may occur with severe scoliosis and kyphosis, as well as with cardiovascular and pulmonary problems associated with dysautonomia, may dictate adjustment of the individual's activity levels and routines. Additionally, the presence of ataxia (difficulties with balance and maintaining position in space) presents problems of both coordination and safety to the dysautonomic individual.

Dysautonomia is generally not marked by a decrease in IQ, therefore individuals can benefit from full inclusion. They may also take an active role in the treatment and educational process and thus feel more in control of the disorder that has altered their lives. The maintenance of maximal functional ability can best be attained by the active involvement of dysautonomics on their own behalf, rather than through their passive compliance, often ascribed to the old medical model of treatment. Thus, individuals with familial dysautonomia require specialized educational, medical, and

psychological treatment through their lifespans: the absence of any of these components represents a marked deficit in the management process.

## REFERENCES

Barowsky, E. I. (1978). Young children's perceptions and reactions to hospitalization. In E. Gellert (Ed.), *Psychosocial aspects of pediatric care*. New York: Grune & Stratton.

Brown, R. T. (2003). Familial dysautonomia. In E. Fletcher-Janzen & C. R. Reynolds (Eds.), *Childhood disorders diagnostic desk reference* (pp. 222–223). New York: Wiley.

Ganz, S. B., Levine, D. D., Axelrod, F. B., & Kahanovitz, N. (1983). Physical therapy management of familial dysautonomia. *Physical Therapy, 63*(7), 1121–1124.

Meijer, A., & Hovne, R. (1981). Child psychiatric problems in "autonomous dysfunction." *Child Psychiatry & Human Development, 12*(2), 96–105.

Perlman, M., Benady, S., & Sassi, E. (1979). Neonatal diagnosis of familial dysautonomia. *Pediatrics, 63*(2), 238–241.

Riley, C. M., Day, R. L., Greeley, D. M., & Langford, W. S. (1949). Central autonomic dysfunction with defective lacrimation. I. Report of five cases. *Pediatrics, 3,* 468–478.

ELLIS I. BAROWSKY
*Hunter College, City University of New York*

## CENTRAL NERVOUS SYSTEM ORTHOPEDIC IMPAIRMENTS

## FAMILIAL RETARDATION

The term familial is used in the field of retardation as a synonym for cultural-familial retardation and also to refer to retardation associated with known heredity disorders. Discussions about whether retardation is inherited or owed to inappropriate environmental stimulation are a part of the debate on the basis of intelligence—the nature-nurture or heredity-environment controversy—that dates back to the 1930s. That debate is unresolved, but it is now abundantly clear that some medical disorders associated with mental retardation are transmitted genetically, whereas the etiology of others is uncertain (Westling, 1986).

Numerous studies have found evidence suggesting hereditability in the cultural-familial group with mild, or educable, retardation. Reed and Reed (1965) provided extensive data on the issue. Of their 289 probands (initial cases), there were 55 who had the diagnosis of "cultural-familial, probably genetic" and had no other medical diagnosis associated with retardation. All of the 55 probands had at least one retarded primary family member, and retardation was found across two or three generations. The Reeds estimated that when both parents have cultural-familial retardation, the probability of retardation in a child born to them is about

40 percent, in contrast to a probability of about 1 percent if neither parent is retarded. The Reeds estimated that retardation incidence could be reduced by one-third to one-half if retarded couples chose not to have children. Analysis of the results of over 40 studies (excluding the challenged British studies) of identical and fraternal twins and other family relationships strongly suggests that hereditary factors are associated with intelligence, so the existence of a polygenic factor in cultural-familial retardation is credible. Consensus now seems to be that a polygenic pattern in combination with adverse environmental factors best explains retardation in the cultural-familial group.

Diagnosis of genetically based medical syndromes is more probable in cases where the degree of mental impairment is severe. Among the genetically determined disorders with which mental retardation is associated are metabolic disorders such as phenylketonuria (PKU) and chromosomal anomalies such as cri du chat (5p monosomy). Genetic defect may be inherited from the parents, or it may be due to a mutation caused by viruses, certain chemicals, or radiation. Mutant genes may be dominant or recessive, and inheritance thereafter follows normal Mendelian laws.

Since about 1950, a large number of chromosomal anomalies, many associated with retardation, have been described in the literature. The most common of these is Down syndrome, which has an incidence of about 1 in 700 births. It occurs most often in births to mothers over 35 years old. About 95 percent of the cases are due to mutations; most of the others are inherited from a parent who is a carrier of the gene. Males with Down syndrome do not reproduce, but the rare females who have children will pass on the affected gene to all offspring. Most people with Down syndrome have trisomy 21, meaning that they have three rather than two chromosomes at location 21. Translocations involve location of part or all of a chromosome in the wrong place and include D/G translocations involving chromosomes 13–15 with 21 and G/G translocations involving 21/22. The rare mosaic Down cases result from trisomy that begins after cells have begun to multiply; incidence of mosaicism is about 1 in 3,000 births overall, but about 1 in 10 if the mother shows a mosaic karyotype (a diagrammatic representation of form, size, and attachments of chromosomes). The retardation may be at any level, but IQ averages reported from surveys are around 35 to 50 for persons of school age or above. However, early reports on small numbers of children participating in two intensive early educational programs indicated that many of those children with Down syndrome scored at or above the mild retardation level on language or intelligence tests when tested after the preschool program or in primary grades (Hayden & Haring, 1976; Rynders & Horrobin, 1975). In cases of moderate or worse levels of mental retardation, about 82 percent have known causes but only 55 percent of mild cases have a known etiology. Familial retardation continues to be considered of unknown causes (Gillberg, 1995).

Nearly all abnormalities of amino acid metabolism are potential causes for mental retardation, but the likelihood of retardation varies greatly (Lee, 1980). The best known cause is phenylketonuria (PKU), which has an incidence of between 1 in 5,000 and 1 in 20,000 in different countries. Fortunately, a simple blood screening test in the first week of life alerts physicians to the possibility of PKU and further diagnostic tests are easily made. Modification of diet beginning in infancy can prevent the extremely deleterious effects of PKU. However, women with hyperphenylalaniemia (silent PKU) are more likely than others to produce retarded children. Since inheritance follows the usual Mendelian laws for recessive genes, babies born to treated adults with PKU are at high risk for PKU or carrier status (Guthrie, 1972).

Other rare genetic metabolic disorders associated with retardation include histidinemia, hereditary fructose intolerance, Wilson disease (hepatolenticular degeneration), galactosemia, maple syrup urine disease, Hartnup syndrome, Hurler disease (lipochondrodystrophy or gargoylism), and several of the amaurotic familial idiocy group, including infantile Tay-Sachs disease. Adults who are carriers of some of these disorders (e.g., Tay-Sachs) can be identified and may choose not to have children. Early death is associated with some metabolic disorders, but for some others medical treatments may prevent the severe disability associated with the disorder (Grossman, 1983; Lee, 1980).

Approximately one-third of the cases of hypothyroidism (cretinism) are of the nonendemic familial type, which is hereditary. Untreated cretins have retardation, short stature, and other physical signs. Hypothyroidism is readily diagnosed in infancy and most cases respond readily to medical treatment. Among other rare inherited conditions associated with retardation are cri du chat, Patou, Edwards, Lesch-Nyhan, Hunter, Duchenne, Williams, and Lawrence-Moon-Biedl syndromes, and tuberous sclerosis, congenital ectodermoses, neurofibromatosis, and trigeminal cerebral angiomatosis. Retardation is also found with greater than expected frequency in the genetic disorders of Turner and Klinefelter syndromes, but the majority of those victims are not retarded (Feingold, 1980; Grossman, 1983; Sciorra, 1980).

In summary, heredity is clearly a factor in some disorders with retardation as a concomitant condition. However, those are the minority of retardation cases, usually associated with severe retardation, and found primarily in cases of chromosomal defects and endocrine dysfunction. In other disorders, genes are indicated, but the mechanism is unclear. It is probable that there is a hereditary component in cultural-familial retardation, but the mechanism and amount of genetic contribution is uncertain.

## REFERENCES

Feingold, M. (1980). Delineation of human genetic syndromes with mental retardation. In M. M. McCormack (Ed.), *Prevention of mental retardation and other developmental disabilities.* New York: Marcel Dekker.

Gillberg, C. (1995). *Clinical child neuropsychiatry.* Cambridge: Cambridge University Press.

Grossman, H. J. (Ed.). (1983). *Classification in mental retardation.* Washington, DC: American Association on Mental Deficiency.

Guthrie, R. (1972). Mass screening for genetic disease. *Hospital Practice, 7,* 93–100.

Hayden, A. H., & Haring, N. G. (1976). Programs for Down's syndrome children at the University of Washington. In T. D. Tjossem (Ed.), *Intervention strategies for high risk infants and young children.* Baltimore: University Park Press.

Lee, M-L. (1980). Aminoacidopathy and mental retardation. In M. M. McCormack (Ed.), *Prevention of mental retardation and other developmental disabilities.* New York: Marcel Dekker.

Reed, E. W., & Reed, S. C. (1965). *Mental retardation: A family study.* Philadelphia: Saunders.

Rynders, J. E., & Horrobin, J. M. (1975). Project EDGE: The University of Minnesota's communication simulation program for Down's syndrome infants. In B. Friedlander, G. Sterritt, & G. Kirk (Eds.), *Exceptional infant: Assessment and intervention* (Vol. 3). New York: Brunner/Mazel.

Sciorra, L. J. (1980). Chromosomal basis for developmental disability and mental retardation. In M. M. McCormack (Ed.), *Prevention of mental retardation and other developmental disabilities.* New York: Marcel Dekker.

Westling, D. L. (1986). *Introduction to mental retardation.* Englewood Cliffs, NJ: Prentice Hall.

SUE ALLEN WARREN
*Boston University*

CONGENITAL DISORDERS
CRETINISM
CRI DU CHAT SYNDROME
DOWN SYNDROME
PHENYLKETONURIA
TAY-SACHS DISEASE

# FAMILIES OF CULTURALLY/LINGUISTICALLY DIVERSE STUDENTS IN SPECIAL EDUCATION

See CULTURALLY/LINGUISTICALLY DIVERSE STUDENTS IN SPECIAL EDUCATION, FAMILIES OF.

# FAMILY COUNSELING

Family counseling is an interactive process that aims to assist families in regaining a balance comfortable to all members (Mash, 2005; Perez, 1979). Family counseling is a therapeutic technique for exploring and alleviating the current interlocking emotional problems within a family system by helping family members to change dysfunctional transaction patterns together (Goldenberg & Goldenberg, 1985).

Family counseling is usually indicated when the family's ability to perform becomes inadequate. Unlike individual counseling, which focuses on the person's intrapsychic difficulties, family counseling emphasizes the relationships that transpire during therapeutic settings (Goldenberg & Goldenberg, 1983). Family counseling evolved from an extension of psychoanalytic treatment to coverage of a full range of emotional problems. The field includes work with families, the introduction of general systems theory, the evolution of child guidance and marital counseling, and an increased interest in new clinical techniques such as group therapy. It grew out of a need to expand traditional therapy from a linear approach to a multifactor systematic view of individuals and their families (Frank, 1984).

Goals of family counseling include (1) increasing each member's tolerance for each member's uniqueness; (2) increasing each member's tolerance for frustration when loss, conflict, and disappointment are encountered; (3) increasing the motivation of each member to support, encourage, and enhance each other member; and (4) increasing congruent perceptions of family members (Perez, 1979).

Families of children in special education require family counseling frequently simply because of the multiplicity of crises with which they are faced. Black (1982) indicates that the treatment of children with disabilities and their families is as complex and diverse as are the disorders from which they suffer. The communication problems indigenous to handicapping conditions (sensory, affective, or cognitive) cause enormous problems of communication within the family. These problems can be mitigated through the use of family therapy. A frame of reference must be retained, however, in that the presence of a child with disabilities does not presume family problems.

Through the use of family counseling, parents and other family members may alter their behavior patterns to produce positive changes in the behaviors of their children (Kozloff, 1979).

**REFERENCES**

Black, D. (1982). Handicap and family therapy. In A. Bentovin, G. Barnes, & A. Cooklin (Eds.), *Family therapy* (Vol. 2). New York: Grune & Stratton.

Frank, C. (1984). Contextual family therapy. *American Journal of Family Therapy, 12*(1), 3–12.

Goldenberg, I., & Goldenberg, H. (1983). Historical roots of contemporary family therapy. In B. B. Solman & G. Stricker (Eds.), *Handbook of family and marital therapy.* New York: Plenum.

Goldenberg, I., & Goldenberg, H. (1985). *Family therapy: An overview.* Monterey, CA: Brooks/Cole.

Kozloff, M. A. (1979). *A program for families of children with learning and behavior problems.* New York: Wiley.

Mash, E. J. (1998). Treatment of child and family disturbance. In E. J. Mash & R. A. Barkley (Eds.), *Treatment of childhood disorders* (pp. 3–50). New York: Guilford.

Perez, J. (1979). *Family counseling: Theory and practice.* New York: Van Nostrand.

ANNE M. BAUER
*University of Cincinnati*

**COUNSELING INDIVIDUALS WITH DISABILITIES**
**FAMILY RESPONSE TO A CHILD WITH DISABILITIES**
**FAMILY THERAPY**

# FAMILY EDUCATIONAL RIGHTS AND PRIVACY ACT

The Family Educational Rights and Privacy Act (FERPA), also known as the Buckley Amendment, is a 1974 amendment to the Elementary and Secondary Education Act of 1965 (ESEA; Jacob-Timm & Hartshorne, 1995). The purpose of FERPA is to ensure that parents and eligible students have access to the education records of the student, to give parents and eligible students (students who are at least 18 years old or are attending school beyond the level of high school) the right to challenge the accuracy of the content of the education records of the student at a hearing, and to limit disclosures of the student's education records to others for unauthorized purposes (Rosenfield, 1989). FERPA applies to public schools and state and local educational agencies (SEAs and LEAs) that receive federal funding (National Center for Educational Statistics [NCES], 1997). Federal funds are not made available to public schools, SEAs, or LEAs that are not in compliance with the record-keeping procedures outlined in FERPA (Jacob-Timm & Hartshorne, 1995).

Prior to the enactment of FERPA, numerous anomalies existed in the schools' record-keeping policies and procedures. First, many schools had exercised the authority of denying parents access to their child's educational records, while allowing many third parties, such as government agents and prospective employers, unlimited access to the education records. Second, certain types of information tended to accrete in the student's education records, and the information was not always based on fact or used for educational purposes. Third, the right of access to a student's education records varied from state to state and was often based on common case law and/or local policy. Fourth, parents were often denied the opportunity to challenge the accuracy of the content of their child's education records, and the parents' requests and the schools' denials went unrecorded (Rosenfield, 1989).

To address the preceding irregularities or anomalies in schools' record-keeping policies and procedures, the U.S. Congress passed FERPA, sponsored by U.S. Senator James Buckley, in 1974. However, it would take an additional 12 years before the final version of the FERPA regulations were promulgated due to restructuring in the U.S. President's cabinet (specifically, establishment of the Department of Education, transferring of the FERPA regulations from what was once known as the Department of Health, Education, and Welfare and is now known as the Department of Health and Human Services to the Department of Education; and codifying the regulations in the Code of Federal Regulations). The final version of the FERPA regulations were published in 1988, although they have been revised several times since then, with the most recent revision effective in 2005.

The 1988 final version of the FERPA regulations were more simplified and clearer than the initial regulations issued in 1976. The 1988 final version of FERPA also reduced some of the regulatory burden placed on colleges and universities (American Association of Collegiate Registrars and Admissions Officers [AACRAO], 1995).

Since 1988, various acts and other amendments have modified FERPA. The Crime Awareness and Campus Security Act amended FERPA in 1990. This act led to modifications in the FERPA disclosure rules. In 1992, the Higher Education amendments also led to modifications in the FERPA provisions. The amendments excluded certain law enforcement records of institutes of higher education from being categorized as student education records. In 1995, modifications were made in the exclusion of certain law enforcement records as well (AACRAO, 1995). The Improving America's Schools Act in 1994 also had a major impact on the FERPA regulations. The Improving America's Schools Act essentially tightened privacy assurances for students and their families.

With the passage of the Improving America's Schools Act of 1994, a critical piece of legislation for the schools, several key components in FERPA were amended. First, parents or eligible students are now given the right to review the education records of the student maintained by the SEAs. Second, a stiff penalty is imposed on third parties who release through inappropriate means personally identifiable information from the student's education records. Third parties who release information in the student's education records through inappropriate means are not allowed to have access to education records for the next five years. Third, information on the disciplinary actions against students may now be shared with other education institutions without prior consent from a parent or eligible student. Fourth, schools may release education records of the student in order to be in compliance with certain law enforcement judicial orders or subpoenas without notifying parents or eligible students. The Improving America's Schools Act of 1994 plus the other acts and amendments enacted since

1988 are not only attempts to tighten privacy assurances for students and their families but also to extend protection to the public (NCES, 1997).

Under FERPA, parents and eligible students have four basic rights. These four basic rights include: (1) the right to examine the education records of the student; (2) the right to consent to disclosure of personally identifiable information in the education records of the student; (3) the right to challenge the content of the education records of the student at a hearing; and (4) the right to know their rights under FERPA (Rosenfield, 1989).

Parents and eligible students must be informed of their rights under FERPA, how they can act on these rights, and where they can view a copy of the school district's policies and procedures with regard to their rights. Schools must provide parents and eligible students with an annual notice informing them of their rights to examine, review, and request changes in the student's school records (34 C.F.R. § 99.7). In addition, schools must provide parents and eligible students with a written copy of the district's policies and procedures for inspection and amendment of the education records of the student, a list of the type of school records held, and location of these records upon request (34 C.F.R. § 99.6).

Another right granted under FERPA is the right of access to school records by parents and eligible students. A parent is defined as "a parent of a student and includes a natural parent, guardian, or individual acting as a parent in the absence of a parent or guardian" (34 C.F.R. § 99.3). Parental separation, divorce, or custody does not affect parents' rights to inspect and review their child's school records. Both parents have equal access to their child's records unless a court order, state statute, or legally binding document states otherwise (34 C.F.R. § 99.4). In the absence of notification, school personnel may assume that the noncustodial parent has the right to examine his or her child's school records (see *Fay* v. *South Colonie Central School District,* 1986). An eligible student, on the other hand, is defined as "a student who has reached 18 years of age or is attending an institution of postsecondary education" (34 C.F.R. § 99.3). When a student turns 18 years old, the rights of the parents are transferred to the student (34 C.F.R. § 99.5). However, parents retain their rights of access to the student's records as long as the student is claimed as a dependent for federal tax purposes (34 C.F.R. § 99.32). Specifically, the law requires that an educational agency or institution comply with a parent or eligible student's request for access to education records within 45 days of the formal request (34 C.F.R. § 99.10). The educational agency or institution must provide explanations and interpretations of the records upon request to ensure that parents or eligible students understand the content of the records (34 C.F.R. § 99.10). The educational agency or institution must also provide parents or eligible students with a copy of the records if failure to do so would prevent parents or eligible students from exercising their

rights to inspect and review the records (34 C.F.R. § 99.11). The educational agency or institution may charge a fee for the copies unless the fee would prevent parents or eligible students from exercising their rights to inspect and review the records. However, the educational agency or institution may not charge an administrative fee for searching for and retrieving education records (34 C.F.R. § 99.11). Eligible students also have the right to have their medical or psychological treatment records reviewed by appropriate professionals on their behalf. In addition, the educational agency or institution is forbidden to destroy education records once an active request has been made to inspect and review them (34 C.F.R. § 99.10–99.11).

The right to inspect and review education records is limited in a number of different areas at the postsecondary level (see AACRAO, 1995; Rosenfield, 1989) as well as the elementary and secondary levels (Rosenfield, 1989). There are also certain limitations to access that are inherent in the law's definition of what constitutes an education record (Hickman, 1987). Education records are defined as "records that are (1) directly related to a student; and (2) maintained by an educational agency or institution or by a person acting for such an agency or institution" (34 C.F.R. § 99.3). Education records may come in a variety of record forms including handwritten, print, computer media, video- or audiotape, film, microfilm, and microfiche. Education records may include the results of a student's psychological evaluation or individualized education program (IEP), a videotape of a student's classroom behavior, or an audiotape of a student's oral reading performance in the classroom (Hartshorne & Boomer, 1993). Records collected or used, but not originating in the school district, are also considered to be education records, such as juvenile court or social service agency reports that the schools maintain in their files. Therefore, it is the use of the record rather than its source of origin that defines an education record under FERPA (Hartshorne & Boomer, 1993).

However, there are a number of different records which are maintained by the schools that are expressly excluded from the definition of education records under FERPA. Law enforcement records of school-based law enforcement units that are kept apart from the education records of the student and maintained solely for law enforcement purposes are excluded (34 C.F.R. § 99.3). School employee records are also excluded, although records of students who are employed as a result of their status as students are not exempted. Certain medical and psychological records of students who are 18 or older and/or are attending postsecondary institutions are exempted if the records made or maintained by a physician, psychiatrist, psychologist, or related professional are made, maintained, or used only in connection with the provision of treatment for the student and disclosed only to individuals providing that treatment (34 C.F.R. § 99.3). However, if the medical or psychological records are made, maintained, or used in the student's treatment, and that treatment consists of remedial education or instructional programming, then the records are not excluded (Jacob-Timm & Hartshorne, 1995). Directory information records are another category of records which are not considered to be education records under the FERPA definition. Directory information records are records that include personal information about students such as their name, address, telephone number, major field of study, degrees and awards received, and activities and sports participation. Schools are allowed to release this information about students without the consent of parents or eligible students as long as public notice of the categories of information to be disclosed has been given and a reasonable amount of time has been allowed for parents or eligible students to object to the disclosure (34 C.F.R. § 99.37). Prior to disclosure, however, a school official should check to see if the parents or eligible student have requested that the information be withheld. Disclosure of what appears to be common, ordinary information may in actuality be harmful to the student and may be an invasion of privacy. For example, if a student attended a special school for youth with severe emotional problems, then the disclosure of the name of the student's previous school in the directory of information would be considered an invasion of privacy (Hartshorne & Boomer, 1993). The last category of education records not subject to FERPA regulations is sole possession records. Sole possession records are "records that are kept in the sole possession of the maker, are used only as a personal memory aid, and are not accessible or revealed to any other person except a substitute for the maker of the record" (34 C.F.R. § 99.3). Teachers, counselors, and other school personnel's private notes about students (e.g., observations in the classroom) that are not revealed to another individual except a substitute are considered to be sole possession records. Once teachers, counselors, or other school personnel reveal their private notes to another individual, then their notes are no longer sole possession records. Under these circumstances, the notes become part of the student's education record (Hummel, Talbutt, & Alexander, 1985).

Another area of concern in record keeping is the parents' or eligible student's access to test protocols. Psychological and educational test protocols are not private notes but are considered to be part of a student's education records (*John K.* v. *Board of Education from School District 65, Cook County,* 1987). For school psychologists, the parental access requirements of FERPA appear to conflict with the profession's obligation to maintain test security and observe the copyright laws of tests and test protocols (Jacob-Timm & Hartshorne, 1995). Numerous sources are available that discuss the impact of the FERPA regulations on the functioning of certain school personnel, such as school psychologists (see Bersoff & Hofer, 1990; Jacob-Timm & Hartshorne, 1995).

Even though private notes are sole possession records, not education records as defined by FERPA, private notes may still be subpoenaed in a court of law. Definitive case law is limited with regard to private notes, thus, confusion surrounds the permissible nature or scope of private notes of school personnel under FERPA (Jacob-Timm & Hartshorne, 1995). Therefore, school personnel must exercise extreme caution and good judgment in the creation and maintenance of these notes.

If upon review of education records as defined by FERPA, the parents or eligible student find the information in the records to be inaccurate or misleading, or to violate the privacy or other rights of the student, then the parents or eligible student have the right to challenge the content of the records and request changes or corrections be made in the records (34 C.F.R. § 99.20[a]). These requests should be made in writing according to the agency's annual notice of procedures for exercising rights to amend records. Schools must respond within a reasonable amount of time, which is not clearly defined in the law, to the parents' or eligible student's request (34 C.F.R. § 99.20[b]). The school, based on its own assessment of the accuracy of the records, may agree with the parents or eligible student and amend the record, or may disagree, advise the parents or eligible student of the denial of their request, and inform the parents or eligible student of their right to a hearing (34 C.F.R. § 99.20[c]). If a hearing is conducted, any party, including an official of the educational agency or institution, who does not have a direct interest in the outcome of the hearing, may conduct the hearing (34 C.F.R. § 99.22[c]). The parents or eligible student are afforded the opportunity in a hearing to present evidence relevant to the issues raised and may be assisted or represented by individuals of their own choosing at their own expense, including an attorney (34 C.F.R. § 99.22[d]). Once the evidence has been presented, the educational agency or institution makes a decision on amending the record (34 C.F.R. § 99.22[e]). The educational agency or institution must present its findings related to its decision in writing. If the educational agency or institution agrees with the parents or eligible student that the education record is inaccurate, misleading, or in some way violates the student's rights, then the education record is amended and written notification is given to the individuals initiating the request. On the other hand, if the educational agency or institution disagrees with the parents of the eligible student, the agency or institution informs the parents or eligible student of their decision in writing and allows the parents or eligible student to add a written statement to the education record explaining their objection to the content in the record (34 C.F.R. § 99.20–99.22). This written statement must be maintained as long as the record is maintained and is subject to the same guidelines if disclosed to a third party (Hickman, 1987).

A court right granted to parents and eligible students under FERPA is the right to confidentiality of records, or the right to consent to disclosure of personally identifiable information in the education records of the student to a third party. Personally identifiable information includes the student's name, family members' names, student personal identification numbers, personal characteristics of the student that would easily lead to the identification of the student, and other information that would make the student's identity known (34 C.F.R. § 99.3). Disclosures of personally identifiable information are prohibited without informed consent of the parents or eligible student unless specifically authorized by the act. When the educational agency or institution releases information from the student's record at the request of the parents or eligible student, the educational agency or institution must obtain a signed written consent from the parents or eligible student. The written consent form must specify the records to be disclosed, state the purpose of the disclosure, and identify the third party to whom the disclosure is to be made (34 C.F.R. § 99.30). A copy of the information disclosed to a third party must be provided to the parents or eligible student upon their request.

As mentioned previously, there are certain disclosures authorized under FERPA that do not require informed consent from the parents or eligible student. Generally, school officials within an agency, including teachers, who have a "legitimate educational interest," may review a student's education records if needed to assist them in fulfilling their professional responsibilities. An educational agency or a school district must specify the criteria for determining school officials within an agency or school district who have a "legitimate educational interest" in their annual policies and procedures. The law is unclear, however, as to what constitutes a legitimate educational interest and which school personnel do or do not meet the criteria of a school official (NCES, 1997). School officials from another school may have access to a student's education records without the parents' or eligible student's informed consent once notification by the parents or eligible student of a transfer to the other school has been received (34 C.F.R. § 99.34). In addition, information from a student's records may be released to certain government officials to conduct audits or to review records for compliance with federal regulations or to comply with state laws (34 C.F.R. § 99.35).

Schools may also disclose information from a student's education records without informed consent from the parents or eligible student in response to a subpoena or court order. School officials must make a reasonable effort, however, to contact the parents prior to complying with the subpoena or court order, unless the subpoena is issued to enforce a law and specifies not to notify the parents. In emergency situations or crisis situations, information in a student's education records may be released without consent to protect the health or safety of the student or others (34 C.F.R. § 99.36). Organizations conducting appropriate research studies for or on behalf of the school may have access to information in a student's records, as long as the personally identifiable information on the student and student's family is destroyed when it is no longer needed (Rosenfield, 1989).

However, if research is not conducted on behalf of the school, informed consent is needed for the release of personally identifiable information from the education records of the student. For example, if a school or school district decides it is in the public's interest to participate in policy evaluations or research studies and student records are to be released for these purposes, then the school or school district must obtain prior consent from the parents and eligible students before records are released (NCES, 1997). Testing organizations may also receive information if anonymous. The education records of the student may be released to certain accrediting organizations as well. Parents of a dependent student who attends a postsecondary institution may also have access to the student's education records without the consent of the student.

In general, an educational agency or institution must maintain a record that is kept with the student's education record indicating each request for record access and each disclosure of information from the student's education record. However, the requests and disclosures of parents, eligible students, and school officials who have a legitimate educational interest are exempted from this provision. The record of access must include the name of the individual who is seeking information about the student, the date access was given, and the purpose of access (Hartshorne & Boomer, 1993). The record of access must be maintained until the school or agency destroys the student's education record. Third parties who receive education records of the student must also receive a written explanation of the restrictions on the re-release of personally identifiable information from the student's records (NCES, 1997). An important recent change to the law under the Uniting and Strengthening America by Providing Appropriate Tools Required to Intercept and Obstruct Terrorism Act of 2001 (USA PATRIOT Act) states that no written request is required when access to a student's record is granted by court order in connection with an investigation under that act.

The Family Policy Compliance Office in the U.S. Department of Education handles complaints filed about alleged violations of FERPA. Complaints filed by parents or eligible students must be submitted to the Family Policy Compliance Office in writing. Once received, the office notifies each complainant and the educational agency or institution against which the violation has been alleged in writing about the complaint. The educational agency or institution is then given an opportunity to submit a written response (34 C.F.R. § 99.63).

The Family Policy Compliance Office conducts investigations based on alleged violations of FERPA and provides each complainant and educational agency or institution with written statements regarding the findings of their investigation. If an educational agency or institution is found to be out of compliance, then the Family Policy Compliance Office provides specific steps for an agency or institution to follow to remedy the situation. If an educational agency or institution does not voluntarily comply within a specified period of time, the matter is referred to a review board for a hearing (34 C.F.R. § 99.63).

Hearing panels designated by the chairman of the review board conduct the hearings (34 C.F.R. § 99.65). In a hearing, the hearing panel affords each party the opportunity to present their case. The hearing panel then prepares an initial written decision. Copies of the initial decision are submitted to each party as well as to the Secretary of the Department of Education. The Secretary of the Department of Education has the right to modify or reverse the hearing panel's decision. If no action is taken by the Secretary, then the initial decision of the hearing panel stands and becomes the final decision of the Secretary (34 C.F.R. § 99.67). If the Secretary finds the educational agency or institution out of compliance and it is evident that voluntary compliance cannot be secured, then federal funding is terminated until the educational agency or institution comes into compliance (34 C.F.R. § 99.64).

Portions of the FERPA regulations were incorporated into the Education for All Handicapped Children Act of 1975 (PL 94-142; Hickman, 1987), now known as the Individuals with Disabilities Education Act or IDEA. IDEA is the major special education law in the United States. Under the act, parents are guaranteed certain procedural safeguards. One of the procedural safeguards guaranteed to parents is the opportunity for parents to examine all relevant records of their child with respect to the identification, evaluation, placement, and provision of a free appropriate public education (FAPE). With the passage of the 1997 amendments to IDEA, a change or modification has been made in this procedural safeguard. Parents are now given the opportunity to examine all, not just relevant, records of their child with respect to the identification, evaluation, placement, and provision of FAPE (National Association of State Directors of Special Education [NASDSE], 1997).

The Family Educational Rights and Privacy Act is one of the nation's strongest privacy protection laws. Since its passage in 1974, Congress has strengthened the privacy safeguards of the education records of students, as well as refined and clarified family rights and agency responsibilities to protect those rights. Educational agencies and institutions must have a written policy consistent with the FERPA regulations. School personnel should be familiar with and comply with the FERPA provisions. Under FERPA, parents and eligible students have the right to review, confirm the accuracy, and limit the disclosure of the education records of students. FERPA has made major strides in eliminating the anomalies existing in the U.S. schools' record-keeping policies and procedures.

## REFERENCES

American Association of Collegiate Registrars and Admissions Officers (AACRAO). (1995). *Implementation of the Family Educational Rights and Privacy Act of 1974 as amended—revised edition* (Report No. ISBN-0-929851-26-9). Annapolis Junction, MD: AACRAO Distribution Center. (ERIC Document Reproduction Service No. ED 384 333)

Bersoff, D. N., & Hofer, P. T. (1990). The legal regulation of school psychology. In T. B. Gutkin & C. R. Reynolds (Eds.), *The handbook of school psychology* (2nd ed., pp. 939–961). New York: Wiley.

Family Educational Rights and Privacy Act of 1974, 34 C.F.R. § Part 99 (2005).

*Fay* v. *South Colonie Central School District,* 802 F.2d.21 (2nd Cir. 1986).

Hartshorne, T., & Boomer, L. (1993). Privacy of school records: What every special education teacher should know. *Teaching Exceptional Children, 25*(4), 32–35.

Hickman, J. A. (1987). Buckley Amendment. In C. R. Reynolds & L. Mann (Eds.), *Encyclopedia of special education* (pp. 256–258). New York: Wiley.

Hummel, D. L., Talbutt, L. C., & Alexander, M. D. (1985). *Law and ethics in counseling.* New York: Van Nostrand-Reinhold.

Jacob-Timm, S., & Hartshorne, T. (1995). *Ethics and law for school psychologists.* Brandon, VT: Clinical Psychology Publishing.

*John K.* v. *Board of Education for School District 65, Cook County,* 504 N.E. 2d. 797 (Ill. App. 1 Dist. 1987).

National Association of State Directors of Special Education (NASDSE). (1997). *Comparison of key issues: Current law & 1997 IDEA amendments.* Washington, DC: National Association of State Directors of Special Education.

National Center for Education Statistics (NCES). (1997). Protecting the privacy of student education records—revised. (Report No. NCES-97-859). Washington, DC: Council of Chief School Officers. (ERIC Document Reproduction Service No. ED 405 643)

Rosenfield, S. (1989). *EHA and FERPA confidentiality.* Washington, DC: EDLAW.

PATRICIA A. LOWE
*University of Kansas*

CECIL R. REYNOLDS
*Texas A&M University*
Second edition

KIMBERLY F. APPLEQUIST
*University of Colorado at
Colorado Springs*
Third edition

## BUCKLEY AMENDMENT
## INDIVIDUALS WITH DISABILITIES EDUCATION IMPROVEMENT ACT OF 2004 (IDEIA)

## FAMILY POLICY COMPLIANCE OFFICE

The Family Policy Compliance Office (FPCO) is an office of the U.S. Department of Education whose mission is to meet the needs of learners of all ages by effectively implementing legislation that seeks to ensure student and parental rights in education: the Family Educational Rights and Privacy Act (FERPA) and the Protection of Pupil Rights Amendment (PPRA).

Parents and eligible students who need assistance and/or wish to file a complaint under FERPA or PPRA should do so in writing to the FPCO at:

Family Policy Compliance Office
U.S. Department of Education
400 Maryland Avenue, SW
Washington, D.C. 20202-5920

STAFF

# FAMILY RESPONSE TO A CHILD WITH DISABILITIES

Youngsters with disabilities have the potential to substantially alter the dynamics of family life (Knoblock, 1983). Changes in the family structure typically start with the parents' reactions to the exceptional child. Initially there is the impact of a child on parental adjustment; then there is the combined influence of the child and the resulting parental reactions on other siblings in the family.

Parents are often slow to recognize that their child is not developing normally. Typically, someone outside of the family unit (e.g., pediatrician, teacher, psychologist, etc.) will make the initial diagnosis (Cartwright, Cartwright, & Ward, 1985). Once the parents acknowledge that a problem exists, they may be initially comforted in knowing that a more severe disorder is not present. For example, a husband and wife may be relieved that their child is learning disabled but not mentally retarded. They may also be initially consoled in the belief that the problem can be cured relatively quickly. Unfortunately, many disability conditions cannot be corrected. Others may require years of education or therapy before the child is no longer affected by the disorder. The parents' recognition that the problem will not go away easily may trigger a crisis reaction. This reaction has been described by Luterman (1979) with reference to deaf youngsters and Kubler-Ross (1969) with reference to the terminally ill.

A state of shock is typically the first reaction of parents to learning that their child has a disability. This period often lasts from a couple of hours to a few days and is characterized by a calm detachment from the actual problem. Parents eventually become aware that a real problem exists. Their emotional reaction at this time is heightened. Typical emotional reactions include inadequacy when faced with the demands of raising a child with special needs, confusion in light of the vast amount of new and highly technical information offered by professionals about the disorder, anger that the child does not conform to the parents' expectations, and guilt that the parents could have avoided or prevented the disability.

As a defense against these strong emotions, many parents begin to deny the existence of a problem. This denial may take the form of seeking professional opinions that are overly optimistic, or becoming angry with professionals who present a modest prognosis for the child's development. When parents begin to accept that the child does have a handicap, they may discuss their child's problem with both professionals and casual acquaintances. Parents in this phase offer realistic statements regarding the prognosis for the child's overcoming the disorder. Acknowledgment clears the way for the final stage, in which the parents actually adapt to the demands of having a disabled child.

Parents eventually become committed to providing the experiences and opportunities necessary to maximize the child's potential. The acknowledgment and constructive action phases are likely to recur throughout the child's development. Each time a new stage is reached (e.g., adolescence, adult independence, etc.), the parents will again have to acknowledge the problem and initiate an appropriate course of action.

Parental reaction to the child with disabilities may have an equally strong influence on siblings in the family (Wolfensberger, 1967). As parents progress through the preceding stages, their relationship with other children in the family is likely to change. In general, the more time parents spend in constructive action, the more favorable the influence of siblings. Parents who actively support the development of their child are likely to provide the siblings with numerous opportunities to observe and model positive attitudes and behaviors. Siblings able to benefit from these experiences are likely to develop a positive relationship with their exceptional brother or sister. Further, these experiences may result in the siblings' developing problem-solving skills that enhance their own adjustment.

Conversely, parents who fail to reach the stage of constructive action are likely to have an adverse influence on their other children. A parent's denial, for example, may involve the youngster in the sibling's social activities. This, of course, may cause the sibling to resent his or her brother or sister with disabilities. Recognition of the problem without constructive action may cause a parent to have unrealistic expectations for the child's siblings. The nondisabled child's exceptional performance may be expected to offset the guilt and disappointment resulting from the child's limited performance.

The care and attention required by many children with disabilities may substantially diminish the time available for nondisabled family members. When a parent spends an excessive amount of time with a youngster with disabilities, it may deprive the other children of opportunities and experiences important for their own growth and development.

In conclusion, parents of children with disabilities are likely to experience a crisis reaction. This reaction begins with the initial shock and ends in acknowledgment of the disability and constructive action. The parents' ability to move quickly through the stages of the crisis reaction to the point of constructive action will, to a large extent, determine the overall adjustment of the family.

## REFERENCES

Cartwright, G. P., Cartwright, C. A., & Ward, M. E. (1985). *Educating special learners* (2nd ed.). Belmont, CA: Wadsworth.

Knoblock, P. (1983). *Teaching emotionally disturbed children.* Boston: Houghton Mifflin.

Kubler-Ross, E. (1969). *On death and dying.* New York: Macmillan.

Luterman, D. (1979). *Counseling parents of hearing impaired children.* Boston: Little, Brown.

Wolfensberger, W. (1967). Counseling the parents of the retarded. In A. A. Baumeister (Ed.), *Mental retardation: Appraisal, education and rehabilitation.* Chicago: Aldine.

PATRICK J. SCHLOSS
*Pennsylvania State University*

## PARENTAL COUNSELING
## PARENT EDUCATION

## FAMILY SERVICE AMERICA

Founded in 1911 as the Family Welfare Association of America, and then the Family Service Association of America, the current name is Family Service America. The association is a federation of 280 local agencies located in over 1,000 communities. The local agencies provide a variety of services designed to resolve problems of family living, including family counseling, family life education, and family advocacy services dealing with parent-child, marital, and mental health problems. The association assists member agencies in developing and providing effective family services. In 1998, FSA was renamed the Alliance for Children and Families Inc. (ACF) and formed Ways to Work Inc. The Alliance, formed by the 1998 merger of Family Service America and the National Association of Homes and Services for Children, helps member agency leaders successfully meet today's and tomorrow's challenges by drawing upon its more than 90 years of leadership in the human services community. The ACF provides services to nonprofit child and family services and economic empowerment organizations. Motivated by a vision of a healthy society and strong communities, they work to strengthen America's nonprofit sector and through advocacy assure the sector's continued independence.

Strong family life is promoted through contact with the media, government, business, and industry. The ACF compiles statistics, conducts research, sponsors competitions, and bestows awards. Publications include books, the journal *Families in Society: The Journal of Contemporary Human Services,* and a directory of member agencies. Public information activities include the production and dissemination of manuals, pamphlets, brochures, and public service releases. Biennial meetings are held in odd-numbered years. The ACF maintains a library with primary holdings in social work, family life, psychology and nonprofit agency management. A placement service is also available. ACF offices are located at 11700 W. Lake Park Drive, Milwaukee, WI 53224, and the organization may be contacted by telephone at (414) 359-1040.

PHILIP R. JONES
*Virginia Polytechnic Institute*
*and State University*
First edition

MARIE ALMOND
*The University of Texas of the*
*Permian Basin*
Second edition

JESSI K. WHEATLEY
*Falcon School District 49,*
*Colorado Springs, Colorado*
Third edition

## FAMILY THERAPY

Family therapy offers a distinctive theoretical approach for working with human problems, with the focus on the individual and their relationships with others, especially within the family structure. This interpersonal and systemic perspective challenged and revolutionized the etiology and treatment of psychological difficulties, and created advances in the way we view human functioning.

Prior to family therapy, methods of helping individuals focused on the individual, and sought to help the person resolve personal or intrapsychic conflicts. Thus, most therapists would treat the individual, and refuse to see the client's spouse or family members. Family therapy, however, believes that problems and solutions lie in the patterns and connections among people, that people exist in a context of mutual influence and interaction, and thus the individual must be considered part of a larger system, such as the family.

The theoretical foundations for family therapy began in the 1920s and came from diverse areas. First, research exploring the dynamics of small groups found similarities with family functioning, in that the individual exists as part of a social structure, and group membership defines various roles and interactions. Second, the child guidance movement discovered that families often played a part in the successful treatment of childhood difficulties. Third, social work, with their tradition of community service, provided additional support that the family is an important focus of intervention. Finally, research investigating family functioning and schizophrenia observed dramatic differences in the patient's behavior when family members were present, and concluded that families were a major influencing factor in mental disorders. All of these different sources suggested families play an important part in life and development, and an interpersonal approach to solving problems is the most appropriate model from which to provide treatment.

It was not until the 1950s that family therapy as a practice was initiated by a number of individuals from a wide range of professions including social work, psychiatry, and psychology. They included John Bell at Clark University, Murray Bowen at the Menninger Clinic and later at NIMH, Nathan Ackerman in New York, and Don Jackson and Jay Haley in Palo Alto. Others making significant contributions to the development of family therapy were Lyman Wynne, Theodore Lidz, Virginia Satir, Carl Whitaker, Ivan Boszormenyi-Nagy, Christian Midelfort, Robert MacGregor, and Salvador Minuchin.

Presently, family therapy practitioners are represented by several national organizations, with The American Association for Marriage and Family Therapy being the most prominent at over 23,000 members. The association is located in Washington, DC, and has primary responsibility for the certification and endorsement of training programs and individual practitioners.

Family therapy and the systemic principles on which it is founded continue to be utilized today in mental health centers, community agencies, and educational settings. Family therapy represents a challenging and beneficial method of intervention for many personal difficulties.

### REFERENCES

Becvar, D. S., & Becvar, R. J. (1996). *Family therapy: A systemic integration* (3rd ed.). Boston: Allyn & Bacon.

Gladding, S. T. (1998). *Family therapy: History, theory, and practice* (2nd ed.). Upper Saddle River, NJ: Prentice Hall.

Goldenberg, I., & Goldenberg, H. (1991). *Family therapy: An overview* (3rd ed.). Belmont, CA: Brooks/Cole.

Nichols, M. P., & Schwartz, R. C. (1998). *Family therapy: Concepts and methods* (4th ed.). Boston: Allyn & Bacon.

LINDA M. MONTGOMERY
*The University of Texas of the Permian Basin*

**PARENTAL COUNSELING**

## FARRELL, ELIZABETH E. (1870–1932)

Elizabeth E. Farrell, who began her teaching career in an ungraded rural school in upstate New York, accepted a position as an elementary teacher in New York City in 1900. Observing that some children were unable to make satisfactory progress in the elementary classes, Farrell, using her experience in the rural school in which she had taught all grades, formed an ungraded class for these children, the first special class in the public schools of New York City. In 1906 a Department of Ungraded Classes was formed with Farrell as director, a position she held until her death.

Farrell designed the nation's first training program for special class teachers in 1911 at the Maxwell Training School in New York City, and she taught the first university courses for special class teachers at the University of Pennsylvania in 1912. Largely through her efforts, a program to prepare special class teachers was established at the Oswego (New York) Normal School in 1916.

Farrell originated and edited *Ungraded,* the journal of the Ungraded Class Teachers' Association. She was a founder of the Association of Consulting Psychologists. In 1922 she was one of 12 special educators who founded the International Council for Exceptional Children, and she served as its first president.

### REFERENCE

Warner, M. L. (1944). Founders of the International Council for Exceptional Children. *Journal of Exceptional Children, 10,* 217–223.

PAUL IRVINE
*Katonah, New York*

## FEARS

See PHOBIAS AND FEARS.

## FEBRILE CONVULSIONS

Febrile convulsions are seizures associated with fevers or high body temperature in childhood and are a form of acute symptomatic seizures (Sinnar, 1999). Single or multiple generalized seizures in infancy or early childhood may be associated only with fever in about 4 percent of the population. Typically, febrile convulsions occur soon after the onset of a fever-producing illness not directly affecting the central nervous system. Usually the seizure occurs 3 to 6 hours after the onset of the fever (Livingston, 1972), although such seizures can be seen during the second or third day of an illness (Lennox-Buchtal, 1973). When the seizure begins, body temperature is usually at its peak at 39 to 40 degrees C. Acute upper respiratory infection, tonsillitis, otitis media, and bronchial pneumonia are some common causes of febrile convulsions. The seizure is usually generalized and of short duration, although some may last as long as 20 minutes or more (Spreen, Tupper, Risser, Tuokko, & Edgell, 1984). The movements seen with these convulsions are bilateral but may show unilateral elements. Males have been found to be more susceptible to febrile seizures than females. Most investigators feel that there is an inherited susceptibility to seizure above a certain threshold of body temperature with autosomal dominant transmission (Brazier & Coceani, 1978; Sinnar, 1999).

Typically, this form of seizure activity is benign. Initially, it is difficult to separate these benign febrile convulsions from seizures caused by brain damage owed to unrecognized meningitis or congenital brain defects. The signs of a benign prognosis include (1) onset of the convulsions between the ages of 6 months and 4 years; (2) a normal EEG within a week after the seizure; (3) the absence of clinical signs of brain damage; and (4) the lack of atypical features or excessive duration of the attack. The chances of additional febrile seizures are about one in two if the first episode occurs before the age of 14 months, and much lower if the first attack occurs after 33 months of age. Few children have attacks later in life; however, it is not always possible to predict whether subsequent febrile or nonfebrile seizures will follow (Goldensohn, Glaser, & Goldberg, 1984).

Children who have a single febrile seizure have an excellent prognosis, as there appears to be little, if any, lasting neurological or mental deficit (National Institutes of Health, 1980; Sinnar, 1999). For those children who have a febrile convulsion in conjunction with a febrile seizure, preexisting central nervous system abnormalities, or a fever-inducing illness involving the central nervous system resulting in a convulsive episode, the prognosis is much less positive (Spreen et al., 1984).

**REFERENCES**

Brazier, M. A. B., & Coceani, F. (Eds.). (1978). *Brain dysfunction in infantile febrile convulsions.* International Brain Research Organization Monograph Series. New York: Raven.

Goldensohn, E. S., Glaser, G. H., & Goldberg, M. A. (1984). Epilepsy. In L. P. Rowland (Ed.), *Merritt's textbook of neurology* (7th ed.) (pp. 629–650). Philadelphia: Lea & Febiger.

Lennox-Buchtal, M. (1973). Febrile convulsions: A reappraisal. *Electroencephalography & Clinical Neurophysiology, 32*(Suppl. 1).

Livingston, S. (1972). Epilepsy in infancy, childhood, and adolescence. In B. Wolman (Ed.), *Manual of child psychopathology* (pp. 45–69). New York: McGraw-Hill.

National Institutes of Health. (1980). Febrile seizures. A consensus of their significance, evaluation, and treatment. *Pediatrics, 66,* 1009–1030.

Sinnar, S. (1999). Febrile seizures. In K. F. Swaiman & S. Ashwal (Eds.), *Pediatric Neurology* (pp. 676–691). St. Louis, MO: Mosby.

Spreen, O., Tupper, D., Risser, A., Tuokko, H., & Edgell, D. (1984). *Human developmental neuropsychology.* New York: Oxford University Press.

RICHARD A. BERG
*West Virginia University
Medical Center*

## SEIZURE DISORDERS

# FEDERAL REGISTER

The *Federal Register (FR)* is a uniform system for publishing all executive orders and proclamations, proposed and final rules, regulations, and notices of agencies authorized by Congress or the president, certain documents required to be published by an act of Congress, and other documents deemed by the director of the *FR* to be of sufficient interest. It does not contain rules of Congress or of the courts. As such, it serves as formal notice to the public of legally significant actions and is typically the first place of public appearance of these documents (Cohen & Berring, 1984).

Since the *FR* publishes notices promulgated by federal agencies such as the U.S. Department of Education, it is an important source for regulations pertaining to special education. Regulations promulgated under the Education for All Handicapped Children Act (PL 94-142), for example, were first published here. Also, the *FR* is the primary source for the announcement of grant and contract competitions administered by special education programs. Guidelines and priorities for the spending of federal special education monies are contained therein as well.

The *FR* was established by the Federal Register Act of 1935 and is considered prima facie evidence of the filing and text of the original documents. It is issued each federal working day.

**REFERENCE**

Cohen, M. L., & Herring, R. C. (1984). *Finding the law.* St. Paul, MN: West.

DOUGLAS L. FRIEDMAN
*Fordham University*
Second edition

KIMBERLY F. APPLEQUIST
*University of Colorado at
Colorado Springs*
Third edition

# FEEBLE-MINDED

Feeble-minded is the historical term applied to individuals of borderline or mild mental retardation. The term was used as early as the sixteenth century. The Swiss physician Aurealus Theophastus Bombastus von Hahenheim, better known as Paracelsus (1493–1541), used the term feeble-minded to describe individuals who act as "healthy animals."

J. Langdon Down (1826–1896) categorized distinct types of feeble-mindedness. Accidental feeble-mindedness resulted from trauma, inadequate prenatal care, prolonged delivery, inflammatory disease, or the unwise use of medication. Developmental feeble-mindedness resulted from disturbed mothers, parents inebriated at the time of conception, overexcitement during infancy through early childhood, or pressure from school at the time of second dentification or puberty. Although his patients were from poverty-stricken, urban neighborhoods, Down did not conceive of environmental factors as influencing development.

Edouard Seguin (1812–1880) offered yet another classification scheme: idiocy, or moderately to profoundly retarded; imbecility, or mildly retarded with defects in social development; backward or feeble-minded (enfant arriere); and simpleness or superficial retardation evidenced by the slowing down of development. The feeble-minded child was described by Seguin as a child who is retarded in development, and who has low muscle tone, uncoordinated use of the hands, and limited comprehension but no sensory deficits. Unlike Down, Seguin was sensitive to the fact that environmental factors and neglect could have a negative impact on development. Owing to the work of Samuel Gridley Howe (1801–1876) in the mid 1800s, it became more widely recognized that a percentage of feeble-minded children were the result of impoverished environments.

In the late 1800s, three broad categories of intellectual functioning appeared: idiot (severely and profoundly retarded); imbecile (moderately retarded); and feeble-minded (mildly retarded). With the introduction of standardized tests of intelligence in the United States, the Committee on Classification of Feeble-Minded of the American Association for the Study of the Feeble-Minded (now the American Association on Mental Retardation) in 1910 issued a definition that set reasonable parameters on who could be classified as feeble-minded:

> The term feeble-minded is used generically to include all degrees of mental defect due to arrested or imperfect development as a result of which the person so affected is incapable of competing on equal terms with his normal fellows or managing himself or his affairs with ordinary prudence. The tripartite classification of mental retardation included: idiots (those so deeply defective that their mental development does not exceed that of a normal child of about 2 years); imbeciles (those whose mental development is higher than that of an idiot but does not exceed that of a normal child of about 7 years); and moron (those whose mental development is above that of an imbecile but does not exceed that of a child of about 12 years). (p. 61)

In the 1930s feeble-mindedness was defined as retarded intelligence with social incompetence. During the 1940s the term mentally deficient replaced feeble-minded as a generic label. The term is no longer applied in clinical or educational practice.

## REFERENCES

Committee on Classification of Feeble-minded. (1910). *Journal of Psycho-Asthenics, 15,* 61–67.

Kanner, L. (1967). Historical review of mental retardation (1800–1965). *American Journal of Mental Deficiency, 72,* 165–189.

Scheerenberger, R. C. (1983). *A history of mental retardation.* Baltimore: Brookes.

Seguin, E. (1971). *Idiocy and its treatment by the physiological method.* New York: Kelly.

Sloan, W., & Stevens, H. (1976). *A century of concern: A history of the American Association on Mental Deficiency 1876–1976.* Washington, DC: American Association on Mental Deficiency.

CAROLE REITER GOTHELF
*Hunter College, City University of New York*

**IDIOT**
**MENTAL RETARDATION**

# FEINGOLD DIET

One of the most widely acclaimed (particularly in the popular press) yet least empirically supported treatment modes for hyperactive children is the Feingold diet (Feingold, 1975, 1976). Specifically, Feingold (1975, 1976) has insisted that children with learning and behavioral disturbances have a natural toxic reaction to artificial food colors, flavorings, preservatives, and other substances that are added to foods to enhance their shelf life. The Feingold diet purports to be an additive-free dietary regimen that attempts to eliminate artificial flavorings, colorings, and even several nutritional fruits and vegetables containing salicylates. While the use of the Feingold diet has been frequently advocated in the therapeutic treatment of hyperactivity, learning disabilities, and other behavioral disorders, Feingold (1975) has claimed his additive-free diet to be effective in treating other handicapping conditions, including mental retardation, autism, and conduct disorders.

Feingold's unempirically substantiated claims have suggested that nearly 50 percent of hyperactive children in his clinical population have displayed marked improvements, and that in the majority of cases, the children have had a complete remission of symptoms as a result of the additive-free dietary regimen (Feingold, 1975, 1976). According to the Feingold group, these improvements have been demonstrated in both the social and cognitive domains. Feingold has even claimed striking academic improvements as a function of the additive-free diet, despite the fact that academic achievement has been an area little influenced by therapeutic efforts with this population (Barkley & Cunningham, 1978). Further, Feingold has insisted that the younger the child, the more expedient and pervasive the improvement that may be observed. For example, according to Feingold (1975), the efficacy of the additive-free diet in infants and toddlers may be documented in as little as 24 hours to one week. Feingold has noted that in adolescents, where improvement is predicted to be least successful, notable effects often take as long as several months to be seen.

The intense debate resulting from Feingold's claims has spawned a number of empirical studies supported by the federal government. A consensus of these studies (Conners, 1980; Spring & Sandoval, 1976) did not support Feingold's claims, and criticized Feingold's earlier work on the basis of its marginal research methodology, including poor placebo controls. Although Conners (1980) has accused Feingold of making "gross overstatements" (p. 109) regarding his diet, Conners does concede that a small number of hyperactive children (less than 5 percent) do respond favorably to the diet. Nonetheless, it is still unclear whether it is the Feingold diet that is responsible for the observed improvements in this small percentage of children or the regimen associated with the laborious preparations surrounding this special diet. For example, one research group (Harley & Matthews, 1980) has attributed any success of the Feingold diet to a placebo effect. They claim altered aspects of family dynamics often result from special procedures and efforts in implementing the Feingold diet. Others have attributed its effects to the familiar Hawthorne effect. A careful review and meta-analysis of purported support for the Feingold diet by Kavale and Furness (1999) conclude there is little support for the Feingold hypothesis. Further, it must be cautioned that many practitioners have recognized that several of the foods Feingold has recommended for elimination from children's diets contain important nutrients necessary for their growth and development. Consequently, there has been concern in the pediatric community that the Feingold diet may not fulfill the nutritional needs of children treated with this approach.

Despite the frequent failures to corroborate Feingold's (1975, 1976) original claims (Conners, 1980; Kavale & Furness, 1999) the Feingold diet continues to have loyal followers. Many parents have even formed a national association, frequently contacting food manufacturers to provide additive-free food products. Perhaps contributing to its widespread acceptance is the fact that the Feingold diet is commensurate with society's penchant for dieting, health food fads, and natural foods. Further, the Feingold diet offers an alternative to psychotropic medication, which many parents perceive as risky and having side effects, although this has not been verified in the research literature (Ross & Ross, 1982). Citing the etiology and treatment of hyperactivity as an allergic reaction to food may be more palatable to parents than neurological or psychogenic hypotheses, but it is almost certainly less valid.

## REFERENCES

Barkley, R. A., & Cunningham, C. E. (1978). Do stimulant drugs improve the academic performance of hyperactive children? A review of outcome studies. *Clinical Pediatrics, 17,* 85–92.

Conners, C. K. (1980). *Food additives and hyperactive children.* New York: Plenum.

Feingold, B. F. (1975). *Why your child is hyperactive.* New York: Random House.

Feingold, B. F. (1976). Hyperkinesis and learning disabilities linked to the ingestion of artificial food colors and flavors. *Journal of Learning Disabilities, 9,* 551–559.

Harley, J. P., & Matthews, C. G. (1980). Food additives and hyperactivity in children. In R. M. Knights & D. J. Bakker (Eds.), *Treatment of hyperactive and learning disordered children.* Baltimore: University Park Press.

Kavale, K., & Furness, S. A. (1999). Effectiveness of special education. In C. R. Reynolds & T. B. Gutkin (Eds.), *Handbook of school psychology* (3rd ed.). New York: Wiley.

Ross, D. M., & Ross, S. A. (1982). *Hyperactivity: Current issues, research and theory* (2nd ed.). New York: Wiley-Interscience.

EMILY G. SUTTER
*University of Houston, Clear Lake*

RONALD T. BROWN
*Emory University School of Medicine*

**ATTENTION-DEFICIT/HYPERACTIVITY DISORDER**
**HYPERKINESIS**
**IMPULSE CONTROL**

# FELDHUSEN, JOHN F. (1926–    )

*Excellence in Educating Gifted and Talented Learners,* the title of a 1998 book with six chapters written by John Feldhusen and edited by Joyce Van Tassel-Baska, is also the definitive theme of the work that has evolved from Feldhusen's first publications on comparisons of mental performance among children of low, average, and high intelligence to his present studies on giftedness. Feldhusen, born in Waukesha, Wisconsin, received his BA in 1949, his MS in 1955, and his PhD in 1958 from the University of

John F. Feldhusen

Wisconsin, Madison. An interim period as counselor and teacher provided practical background for his early studies on such diverse topics as programmed instruction, testing and measurement, delinquency, and classroom behavior. His contributions to the field of educational psychology culminated in his presidency of Division 15 of the American Psychological Association in 1975.

Feldhusen has exhibited a continuing concern for instruction in creative thinking and problem solving. His primary interest in using research theory and evaluation to guide program and curriculum development in gifted education became the impetus for advocacy of professional training for teachers of the gifted, numerous cooperative efforts with public school personnel, and in-service training throughout Indiana. It also has resulted in a steady stream of publications and teacher-targeted presentations and workshops throughout the United States. Feldhusen became chairman of the Educational Psychology and Research Section of Purdue University in 1977 and Director of the Purdue Gifted Education Resource Institute in 1978. He is also an active promoter of graduate programs in gifted education.

Feldhusen is committed to the concept that gifted and talented youths are individuals who need special services not only to achieve as highly as possible, but also to experience self-fulfillment as human beings. Thus he believes that identification of the gifted must focus on finding those who need services, rather than on labeling youths, and on guiding development of individualized programs. Feldhusen's contributions to gifted education have been recognized by his 1981 election to the presidency of the National Association for Gifted Children. He was awarded the status of distinguished scholar in that organization in 1983, and was appointed editor of the association's journal, *Gifted Child Quarterly,* in 1984. In 1991 he was named a Distinguished Professor at Purdue University, and in 2002 he was awarded the Mensa Lifetime Achievement Award.

## REFERENCE

Van Tassel-Baska, J. (Ed.). (1998). *Excellence in educating gifted and talented learners.* Denver, CO: Love.

PATRICIA A. HAENSLY
*Texas A&M University*
First edition

TAMARA J. MARTIN
*The University of Texas of the
Permian Basin*
Second edition

## FENICHEL, CARL (1905–1975)

Carl Fenichel was founder and director of the League School for Seriously Disturbed Children in Brooklyn, New York. At the school, Fenichel provided one of the early demonstrations that it is feasible to educate severely emotionally disturbed children in a day program when the parents are given intensive training in appropriate home management and care.

Educated at the City College of New York, the New School for Social Research, and Yeshiva University, where he earned the doctorate in education, Fenichel began his professional career as a teacher and psychologist. During his years at the League School, he served as professor of education at Teachers College, Columbia University, and as a lecturer at the Downstate Medical College in Brooklyn. Fenichel's pioneering League School, which he founded in 1953, served as a model for many of the first day programs for severely emotionally disabled children in the United States.

PAUL IRVINE
*Katonah, New York*

## FERAL CHILDREN

From Peter in 1724 to Victor in 1799, Kasper Hauser in 1828, and Amala and Kamala—the "Wolf Children"—in 1920, feral children have fascinated philosophers, physicians, anthropologists, educators, and psychologists. Many have looked to them for answers to questions about the nature of man, the permanence of early experience, the efficacy of education in overcoming early deprivation, and, perhaps most basically, what each of us owes to heredity and what we owe to environment. Feral children have spent various, usually unknown, amounts of their childhood living in wild or at least uncivilized conditions.

For convenience, feral children may be divided into two basic groups: (1) those who have grown up in open "wild" settings such as jungles or forests, and (2) those who have grown up under extreme environmental and social deprivation. Victor and Kasper Hauser are examples of the two groups respectively. In addition, a subgroup of "wild" children has supposedly been raised by animals. Amala and Kamala, the wolf girls of Midnapore, are but two examples. Such so-called wolf children continue to fascinate the public at large.

The antiquity of interest in using conditions of early rearing to learn of man's nature is indicated by King Psammitichus's experiment, as reported by Herodotus. To determine what language was the most ancient, the king ordered that two infants be nursed by goats and separated from all contact with humans. Supposedly the first word they said was Phrygian for bread, and the Egyptians yielded to the primacy of the Phrygians. Ireland (1898) indicated that similar experiments were conducted by Emperor Frederick II and James IV of Scotland. Interest in feral children peaked in the eighteenth century with scientific uncertainty about who are and are not humans (the word orangutan comes from Malaysian for wild man). There were attempts to discriminate between Descartes' endowment of humans with innate ideas and Locke's empiricist concept of the human mind as a blank slate. Feral children were studied as models of Rousseau's noble savage (Lane, 1986; Shattuck, 1980).

Craft's (1979) claim of "some 50 documented cases of animal-reared children . . . " (p. 139) notwithstanding, no fully documented examples of children reared by wolves, bears, gazelles, baboons, or any nonhumans, exist. Singh's claim that Amala and Kamala were reared by wolves was accepted by Zingg and the famous pediatrician-psychologist Arnold Gesell (1942), but the claim was convincingly disputed by Ogburn and Bose. Ogburn later detailed how a particular feral child falsely became converted into the "Wolf Boy of Agra," even though the child had not been with wild animals at all. Although Maclean (1977) claims evidence to support Amala and Kamala's wolf rearing, this is dubious and not subject to verification. We have no more hard evidence on the general subject than did Ireland (1898), who concluded that the notion of wolf children belonged with nursery myths.

Similar controversy exists over other questions asked about feral children. Arguments still rage over whether, as Pinel felt about Victor, all such children were retarded to begin with and thus abandoned (Dennis, 1951), or whether, as Itard felt about Victor, they had initially been essentially normal and behaved primitively because of severe deprivation (Lane, 1976, 1986), or whether they had become autistic because of uncaring mothers (Bettelheim, 1959).

Unfortunately, we probably will never have clear answers to any of the questions asked of feral children. Their stories have the shortcomings of all retrospective case histories—lack of complete information, potentially biased observers, the lack of repeatability and control, the impossibility of knowing how the children would have behaved if raised under normal conditions, and the virtual impossibility of empirical verification of events in the children's lives before their discovery. As one example, Dennis (1951) has pointed out that many of the children apparently did not disappear from their families until they were several years of age. How, then, can the supposed permanence of their primitive characteristics be attributed to their normal early experience? As another example, we do not know whether Genie, a contemporary deprived child, would have developed normal language under normal conditions. Given the limits of the data, the problem of direction of causality seems unsolvable. Attributing all behavioral deficits to these children's unnatural rearing environment is a clear case of illogical *post hoc ergo propter hoc* (after this, because of this) reasoning. Thus cases of feral children are almost inevitably open to alternative interpretations.

We do know from reports of numerous modern cases that considerable intellective, motor, social-emotional, and even language development can occur in formerly severely deprived, abused or neglected, and institutionalized children (Clarke & Clarke, 1976). Early deprivation, if not extremely prolonged, can be overcome, particularly with special and intensive intervention. Early adverse learning experiences are not irreversible, a message of considerable optimism to those in special education. Candland (1993) has sensitively portrayed the lives of many feral children and their relationships not only to the questions listed at the beginning of this entry but also to other interesting cases of humans and nonhumans.

## REFERENCES

Bettelheim, B. (1959). Feral children and autistic children. *American Journal of Sociology, 64*, 455–467.

Candland, D. K. (1993). *Feral children and clever animals.* New York: Oxford University Press.

Clarke, A. M., & Clarke, A. D. B. (Eds.). (1976). *Early experience: Myth and evidence.* New York: Free Press.

Craft, M. (1979). The neurocytology of damaging environmental factors. In M. Craft (Ed.), *Tredgold's mental retardation* (12th ed., pp. 137–143). (Bailliere-Tindall.) Saunders.

Dennis, W. (1951). A further analysis of reports of wild children. *Child Development, 22*, 153–159.

Gesell, A. L. (1942). *Wolf child and human child.* New York: Harper.

Ireland, W. W. (1898). *Mental affections of children, idiocy, imbecility, and insanity.* London: J. & A. Churchill.

Lane, H. (1976). *The wild boy of Aveyron.* Cambridge, MA: Harvard University Press.

Lane, H. (1986). The wild boy of Aveyron and Itard. *History of Psychology, 18*, 3–16.

Maclean, C. (1977). *The wolf children.* New York: Hill & Wang.

Shattuck, R. (1980). *The forbidden experiment.* New York: Farrar Straus Giroux.

ROBERT T. BROWN
*University of North Carolina at Wilmington*

**EARLY EXPERIENCE AND CRITICAL PERIODS**
**GENIE**
**ITARD, JEAN M. G.**
**KASPAR HAUSER SYNDROME**
**WILD BOY OF AVEYRON**

**Walter E. Fernald**

## FERNALD, GRACE MAXWELL (1879–1950)

Grace Maxwell Fernald received her PhD in psychology from the University of Chicago in 1907. In 1911 she became head of the psychology department and laboratory at the State Normal School at Los Angeles. The remainder of her career was spent at the Normal School and the University of California at Los Angeles.

Fernald's lasting contribution to the field of education is her method for teaching disabled readers, a method that uses not only visual and auditory approaches, but kinesthetic and tactile cues as well. In 1921, UCLA's Clinic School, later renamed the Fernald School, was founded by Grace Fernald.

### REFERENCES

Fernald, G. (1943). *Remedial techniques in basic school subjects.* New York: McGraw-Hill.

Sullivan, E. B., Dorcus, R. V., Allen, R. M., Bennet, M., & Koontz, L. K. (1950). Grace Maxwell Fernald. *Psychological Review, 57,* 319–321.

PAUL IRVINE
*Katonah, New York*

**Grace Maxwell Fernald**

## FERNALD, WALTER E. (1859–1924)

Walter E. Fernald received his medical degree from the Medical School of Maine, served as assistant physician at the State Hospital in Minnesota, and then became the first resident superintendent of the Massachusetts School for the Feeble-Minded (later renamed the Walter E. Fernald State School). A leader in the movement for humane treatment of mentally retarded persons, he developed an educational plan that provided a 24-hour-a-day program for each child. He devised a system for diagnosing and classifying mentally retarded people on the basis of total development rather than test results alone. Under his leadership, the Massachusetts school became an international center for the training of workers in the field of mental retardation. Fernald was also influential in the development of federal and state legislation relating to mental retardation (Wallace, 1924).

### REFERENCE

Wallace, G. L. (1924). In memoriam Walter E. Fernald. *American Journal of Mental Deficiency, 30,* 16–23.

PAUL IRVINE
*Katonah, New York*

## FERNALD METHOD

Multisensory remedial reading methods, commonly used in remedial and special education, are based on the premise that some children learn best when material is presented in several modalities. Typically, kinesthetic and tactile stimulation are used along with visual and auditory modalities. The multisensory programs that feature tracing, hearing, writing, and seeing are often referred to as VAKT (visual-auditory-kinesthetic-tactile; Hallahan, Kauffman, & Lloyd, 1985).

One of the most widely known and used multisensory

approaches to teaching handicapped children to read is the Fernald method (Gearheart, 1985). The rationale for the Fernald Word Learning Approach, which is usually known as the VAKT approach, was described by Fernald in 1943; it is based on the belief that if a child learns to use all senses, the child will make use of these experiences in learning to read. If one modality is weak, the others will help to convey the information. In practice, the VAKT approach is not confined to reading, but includes spelling and writing instruction. In essence, it is a language experience and whole-word approach (Kirk & Chalfant, 1984).

Fernald believed that overcoming the emotional problems failing students have with reading would be easier if their reading material were of interest to them. Therefore, stories are written down as suggested by the students, with as much help from the teacher as needed, and then read. Also, a student selects words that he or she wishes to learn and works on them, repeatedly feeling, spacing, seeing, saying, and hearing a word until it can be written from memory. Words that have been mastered are kept in a file so that a student may refer back to them as needed. Fernald was opposed to having the student sound out words; she emphasized the reading and writing of words as a whole. Although the Fernald approach has strong advocates who can provide case studies documenting its successful use, research evidence does not reveal that it has been particularly successful (Myers, 1978).

### REFERENCES

Fernald, G. (1943). *Remedial techniques in basic school subjects.* New York: McGraw-Hill.

Gearheart, B. R. (1985). *Learning disabilities.* St. Louis, MO: Times Mirror/Mosby.

Hallahan, D. P., Kauffman, J. M., & Lloyd, J. W. (1985). *Introduction to learning disabilities.* Englewood Cliffs, NJ: Prentice Hall.

Kirk, S., & Chalfant, J. C. (1984). *Academic and developmental learning disabilities.* Denver: Love.

Myers, C. A. (1978). Reviewing the literature on Fernald's technique of remedial reading. *Reading Teacher, 31,* 614–619.

JOSEPH M. RUSSO
*Hunter College, City University of New York*

## HEGGE, KIRK & KIRK APPROACH
## ORTON-GILLINGHAM METHOD

## FETAL ALCOHOL SYNDROME

Fetal alcohol syndrome (FAS) is a complex of physical anomalies and neurobehavioral deficits that may severely affect the children of heavy-drinking mothers. More widespread than Down's syndrome and Fragile X syndrome, FAS is the leading type of mental retardation in the Western world (Abel & Sokol, 1987; Cde Baca, 2003). FAS is certainly the most prevalent environmental and preventable type of mental retardation. In 1987, Abel and Sokol estimated that as much as 11 percent of the annual cost of mental retardation in the United States might be devoted to FAS cases, and that the annual cost of treatment of all FAS-related effects was $321 million. Prenatal exposure to alcohol has a range of effects, with less serious sequelae termed fetal alcohol effects (FAE) or alcohol-related neurodevelopmental disorder (ARND; Batshaw & Conlon, 1997). FAS is associated with three major effects, known as "the triad of the FAS" (Rosett & Weiner, 1984, p. 43): (1) growth retardation of prenatal origin, (2) characteristic facial anomalies, and (3) central nervous system dysfunction. First described in 1973 (Jones, Smith, Ulleland, & Streissguth; Jones & Smith), FAS has since been the subject of over 2,000 scientific reports (Streissguth et al., 1991). Follow-up studies, described below, confirm that alcohol is a teratogen that produces lifelong impairments.

### Diagnostic Criteria and Common Characteristics

The Fetal Alcohol Study Group of the Research Society on Alcoholism (Rosett, 1980) established minimal criteria for diagnosis of FAS, based largely on Clarren and Smith's (1978) summary of 245 cases. FAS should be diagnosed only when all three criteria are met:

1. Prenatal and/or postnatal growth retardation (below 10th percentile for body weight, length, and/or head circumference, when corrected for gestational age). However, although growth retardation has been viewed as the most common characteristic of FAS, some suggest that it may not be a primary feature and perhaps not a defining characteristic (Carmichael Olson & Burgess, 1997).

2. Central nervous system dysfunction (neurological abnormality, developmental delay, or mental impairment < 10th percentile).

3. Characteristic facies (at least two of the following three facial dysmorphologies: (1) Microcephaly [head circumference < 3rd percentile]; (2) Microphthalmia and/or short palpebral fissures; (3) Poorly developed philtrum, thin upper lip, and flattening of the maxillary area). See figure 1.

In addition to these three diagnostic criteria, a history of drinking during pregnancy should be present for confident diagnosis, since no individual feature is specific to prenatal exposure to alcohol (Sokol et al., 1986). However, Streissguth, Sampson, Barr, Clarren, & Martin (1986, p.

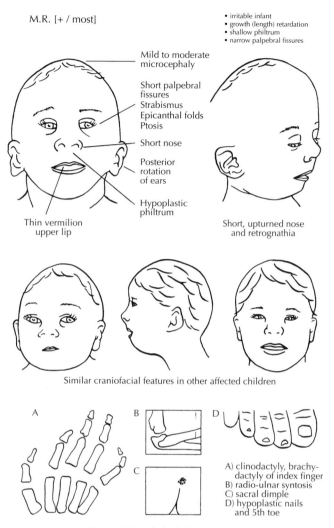

M.R. [+ / most]

• irritable infant
• growth (length) retardation
• shallow philtrum
• narrow palpebral fissures

Mild to moderate microcephaly

Short palpebral fissures
Strabismus
Epicanthal folds
Ptosis

Short nose

Posterior rotation of ears

Hypoplastic philtrum

Thin vermilion upper lip

Short, upturned nose and retrognathia

Similar craniofacial features in other affected children

A) clinodactyly, brachy-
      dactyly of index finger
B) radio-ulnar syntosis
C) sacral dimple
D) hypoplastic nails
      and 5th toe

Figure 1  Fetal alcohol syndrome

64) have suggested that "... FAS and alcohol teratogenicity are reciprocal terms. . . . [I]dentifying a child with all the features of FAS strongly suggests that the child was affected by alcohol *in utero*." Of importance, they also stated (p. 64) that although alcohol teratogenicity may cause a "milder" FAS or FAE phenotype, such milder phenotypes should not be inferred to result necessarily from alcohol: "[O]ther environmental or genetic problems could produce similar manifestations. . . . When examining the individual patient, the examiner cannot be sure that alcohol produced a 'possible' fetal alcohol effect, even when a maternal history is positive for alcohol." An important attributional implication is that women who have occasionally consumed small amounts of alcohol during pregnancy and have slightly deformed infants should not be made to feel guilt or that alcohol caused the deformities. Women should certainly take precautions during their pregnancy, but do not have control over everything that may affect their babies (Rosett & Weiner, 1984).

Although low birthweight is associated with other ma-

ternal factors (several of which, including smoking, malnutrition, and drug abuse, are also associated with alcohol abuse), two lines of evidence suggest that alcohol induces prenatal growth retardation: (1) The other maternal factors are rarely associated with other defining features of FAS (Rosett & Weiner, 1984), and (2) Offspring of pregnant animals given alcohol show both growth retardation and virtually all other physical and neurobehavioral features of FAS (e.g., Abel, 1984; Riley & Barron, 1989).

As West (1986b, p. vi) has observed, "Central nervous system dysfunction is the most devastating and one of the more consistently observed clinical abnormalities in surviving offspring of mothers known to have consumed large amounts of alcohol during pregnancy." Mental retardation or subnormality is the most common CNS indicator associated with FAS (see Streissguth, 1986, for a detailed review). Average IQ of affected children is about 65–75, but variability is high (Mattson & Riley, 1998). Children with the most severe morphology and growth indicators have the most severe intellectual and other CNS deficits. Affected infants and children may also show failure to thrive, poor sucking, retarded speech and motor development, fine-motor dysfunction, repetitive self-stimulating behaviors such as head rolling or head banging, auditory deficits, and seizures. Symptoms of attention-deficit/hyperactivity disorder (ADHD) are common and associated with school problems. Seizures occur in about 20 percent of cases, but are not considered characteristic of FAS. Prenatal alcohol has a variety of adverse effects on the developing CNS (see Abel, 1984 and West, 1986a for reviews). Underdiagnosis, even recently thought to be a problem (Little, Snell, Rosenfeld, Gilstrap, & Gant, 1990), is now unlikely, owing to increased knowledge of FAS (Abel & Hannigan, 1995).

## Historical Background

Although a number of authors have claimed to find ancient reference to damaging effects of maternal alcohol consumption, Abel (1984) suggested that those claims rest on erroneous secondary sources or mistranslations. Abel (1984) does report suggestions of adverse effects of maternal drinking in 17th century England and that several writers observed, during the "gin epidemic" in the early 18th century, that children of mothers who drank heavily were small, sickly, and mentally slow. Further, a number of 19th century reports linked stillbirth, infant mortality, and mental retardation to maternal drinking during pregnancy.

But studies in the 20th century failed to find a link between maternal drinking and adverse effects on offspring. Elderton and Pearson (1910) reported no relationship between parental drinking and intelligence or appearance of children, and suggested that children of alcoholics might have problems because parents and children shared "defective germ plasm" or because the parents provided a poor home environment. Although their claim was much criticized, it was later supported by Haggard and Jellinek (1942), who denied that prenatal alcohol produced malformations. Thus, however inaccurate from our perspective, Montagu's (1965, p. 114) conclusion was apparently well-founded at the time: "Unexpectedly, alcohol in the form of beverages, even in immoderate amounts, has no apparent effect on a child before birth. . . . (I)t now can be stated categorically . . . that no matter how great the amount of alcohol taken by the mother—or the father, for that matter—neither the germ cells nor the development of the child will be affected." The timing of Montagu's publication has a certain irony, appearing at about the time Lemoine, Harousseau, Borteryu, and Menuet began their study of the offspring of 127 alcoholic parents. In 1968, they reported that several of the children had such characteristic anomalies that maternal alcoholism could be inferred from them. The abnormalities were in the three areas now associated with FAS: growth retardation, low intelligence, and facial anomalies. Their paper, published in French with an English abstract, had little impact (Abel, 1984; Rosett & Weiner, 1984), and was unknown to Jones and Smith and their colleagues at the time of their initial reports in 1973 (Abel, 1984). Those reports brought the effects of maternal alcohol to international attention, in part by providing a name, fetal alcohol syndrome, that "dramatically refocused interest on an important perinatal risk" (Sokol et al., 1986, p. 88).

## Incidence and Risk Factors

Although estimates vary widely across study and country, worldwide incidence of FAS is estimated as approximately 1.02 per 1,000 live births. However, most cases are in the United States, where incidence is estimated to be 1.9 per 1,000 births (Abel & Hannigan, 1995). The varying estimates may reflect sampling error and use of different diagnostic criteria as well as actual national/regional differences. As would be expected, incidence varies most with degree of prenatal maternal drinking. Full-blown FAS appears to be associated only with heavy maternal drinking; no cases have been reported among moderate drinkers (Abel & Sokol, 1987). FAS may occur in 30–50 percent, and FAE in 50–70 percent, of offspring of truly alcoholic women who consume eight or more drinks daily (Little et al., 1990). Some studies report incidence as high as 80 percent in low SES samples (Bingol et al., 1987).

Incidence of human newborns with some features of FAS also increases with amount of prenatal maternal alcohol consumption (Streissguth, Landesman-Dwyer, Martin, & Smith, 1980). Degree of physical growth retardation is also dose-related (Abel, 1984). A dose-response curve is found in virtually all animal studies: Number and severity of offspring anomalies increases with amount of prenatal exposure to alcohol (see Abel, 1984, for a summary). Well-controlled animal studies have confirmed that the damage

is from prenatal alcohol and not secondary to some other effect (Abel, 1984; Streissguth et al., 1980).

Some effects of prenatal alcohol appear to occur only above a certain threshold level of exposure (Ernhart, Sokol, Ager, Morrow-Tlucak, & Martier, 1989; Streissguth, 1986). For example, Ernhart et al. (1989) reported that women who drank small amounts of alcohol early in pregnancy had children with no incidence of FAS-related neonatal physical anomalies above that of a control group. However, teratogens typically have neurobehavioral effects at levels below those at which physical defects are shown (Abel, 1989). Indeed, Mattson and Riley (1998) report that groups of FAS children and alcohol-exposed children who had no characteristic physical features of FAS showed significant and largely similar deficits in IQs relative to normal children.

Importantly, FAS is seen much more commonly in offspring from lower socioeconomic status (SES) mothers (Abel, 1984; Abel & Hannigan, 1995; Bingol et al., 1987). A variety of possible reasons exist for this relationship, including the fact that alcoholism is inversely related to SES status. Even when alcohol intake was equated, however, Bingol et al. (1987) found that incidence of FAS and FAE was 71 percent in offspring of heavy-drinking low SES mothers and only 4.6 percent in offspring of heavy-drinking middle to upper SES mothers. SES was confounded with ethnicity, complicating interpretation, but Abel and Hannigan argue persuasively that SES is the major factor. Binge drinking, certain ethnic factors, smoking, and undernutrition also contribute to the manifestation of FAS in offspring of drinking mothers (Abel & Hannigan, 1995).

Both human and nonhuman research suggests that some of the variability in incidence of FAS/FAE stems from genetic factors. Clinical reports indicate that dizygotic (fraternal) twins of alcoholic mothers show differential development and performance (Streissguth, 1986). Maternal factors are implicated in research by Chernoff (1977, 1980): Pregnant mice from two different strains given comparable doses of alcohol had different blood-alcohol levels, and the strain with higher levels had offspring with higher incidence of anomalies.

## FAS Effects from Childhood to Adulthood

FAS has effects, although in somewhat modified form, that last into adulthood. According to longitudinal studies (e.g., Streissguth, 1986; Streissguth et al., 1991; Streissguth, Clarren, & Jones, 1985), FAS/FAE adolescents and adults were about two standard deviations below the mean in height and head circumference, although variability was high; little overall catch-up growth had occurred. The characteristic low weight of FAS/FAE children had largely disappeared, although weight/height ratios were even more variable than other measures.

The facial dysmorphologies characteristic of FAS children became less distinctive with age. Although some features, such as short palpebral fissure length, remained, growth in a number of facial areas reduced the extent of the overall abnormal appearance.

The average IQ of the 61 FAS/FAE adolescents and adults reported by Streissguth et al. (1991) was 68, just into the mild retardation level. The FAS mean was 66 and the FAE was 73. Variability was again high, with IQ ranging from 20 to 105; no FAS individual's IQ was above the low 90s. Those with the most severe growth retardation and facial dysmorphologies in childhood continued to have the lowest later IQ scores. Only 6 percent of the 61 were in regular classes and not receiving special help; 28 percent were in self-contained special education classes, 15 percent were neither in school nor working, and 9 percent were in sheltered workshops. Although academic deficits were broad, arithmetic deficits were particularly large. Academic performance had not improved since childhood.

Children and adolescents with FAS/FAE show a number of additional behavioral deficits and excesses that present serious educational and other challenges (Carmichael Olson, & Burgess, 1997; Mattson & Riley, 1998; Steinhausen & Spohr, 1998). Among the more common features are hyperactivity, inattention, impaired learning (but not impaired memory of verbal material), a wide variety of receptive and expressive language problems, and fine motor coordination. Of particular concern are reports of temper tantrums in younger affected children and serious conduct disorders in older ones. Not surprisingly, FAS children have difficulty conforming to social norms.

In Streissguth et al. (1991), even FAS/FAE adolescents and adults who were not mentally retarded showed poor socialization scores and an unusually high level of maladaptive behaviors, including poor concentration and attention, sullenness, impulsivity, lying, and cheating. However, their family environments were highly unstable, making difficult the determination as to whether these effects owed to prenatal alcohol exposure, postnatal environment, or an interaction between difficult infants and inadequate parenting. Only 9 percent were still living with both parents; the mothers of 66 percent had died, many from alcohol-related causes.

Of particular concern for those in special education are the wide variety of behavioral sequelae, their varying degree, and the extent to which some may not be related to physical characteristics of FAS individuals. The suggestion that early stimulation may reduce the extent of some effects indicates the need for early and continued intervention (Phelps, 1995).

## Prevention

Although 100 percent preventable theoretically, FAS may prove resistant to reduction efforts in practice (Cde Baca, 2003). Alcohol abuse is notably resistant to treatment, and relapse rates 12 months after treatment are as high as 75

percent (Tucker, Vuchinich, & Harris, 1985). Thus, education programs on the adverse effects of prenatal alcohol may lower alcohol consumption of moderately drinking women during pregnancy, but are unlikely to affect alcohol-abusing or alcoholic women, whose infants are most at risk. Although a variety of general approaches are available (Cox, 1987; Milkman & Sederer, 1990), treatment/prevention programs targeted specifically at women (Kilbey & Asghar, 1992; National Institute on Alcohol Abuse and Alcoholism, 1987; Streissguth & LaDue, 1987) may be necessary if we wish to decrease the incidence of this tragic condition.

For more information, contact the National Organization on Fetal Alcohol Syndrome at http://www.nofas.org/.

### REFERENCES

Abel, E. L. (1984). *Fetal alcohol syndrome and fetal alcohol effects.* New York: Plenum.

Abel, E. L. (1989). *Behavioral teratogenesis and behavioral mutagenesis.* New York: Plenum.

Abel, E. L., & Hannigan, J. H. (1995). Maternal risk factors in fetal alcohol syndrome: provocative and permissive influences. *Neurotoxicology and Teratology, 17,* 445–462.

Abel, E. L., & Sokol, R. J. (1987). Incidence of fetal alcohol syndrome and economic impact of FAS-related anomalies. *Drug and Alcohol Dependence, 19,* 51–70.

Batshaw, M. L., & Conlon, C. J. (1997). Substance abuse: A preventable threat to development. In M. L. Batshaw (Ed.), *Children with disabilities* (4th ed., pp. 143–162). Baltimore: Brookes.

Bingol, N., Schuster, C., Fuchs, M., Iosub, S., Turner, G., Stone, R. K., & Gromisch, D. S. (1987). The influence of socioeconomic factors on the occurrence of fetal alcohol syndrome. *Advances in Alcohol and Substance Abuse, 6*(4), 105–118.

Carmichael Olson, H., & Burgess, D. M. (1997). Early intervention for children prenatally exposed to alcohol and other drugs. In M. J. Guralnick (Ed.), *The effectiveness of early intervention* (pp. 109–145). Baltimore: Brookes.

Cde Baca, C. (2003). Fetal alcohol syndrome. In E. Fletcher-Janzen & C. R. Reynolds (Eds.), *Childhood disorders diagnostic desk reference* (pp. 233–238). New York: Wiley.

Chernoff, G. F. (1977). The fetal alcohol syndrome in mice: An animal model. *Teratology, 15,* 223–230.

Chernoff, G. F. (1980). The fetal alcohol syndrome in mice: Maternal variables. *Teratology, 22,* 71–75.

Clarren, S. K., & Smith, D. W. (1978). The fetal alcohol syndrome. *New England Journal of Medicine, 298,* 1063–1067.

Cox, W. M. (Ed.). (1987). *Treatment and prevention of alcohol problems.* New York: Academic.

Elderton, E. M., & Pearson, K. (1910). A first study of the effect influence of parental alcoholism on the physique and ability of the offspring. *Eugenics Laboratory Memoir, 10,* 1–46. (As described in Abel, 1984).

Ernhart, C. B., Sokol, R. J., Ager, J. W., Morrow-Tlucak, M., & Martier, S. (1989). Alcohol-related birth defects: Assessing the risk. In D. E. Hutchings (Ed.), *Prenatal abuse of licit and il-*

*licit drugs* (pp. 159–172). *Annals of the New York Academy of Sciences, 592.*

Haggard, H. W., & Jellinek, E. M. (1942). *Alcohol explored.* Garden City, NJ: Doubleday.

Jones, K. L., & Smith, D. W. (1973). Recognition of fetal alcohol syndrome in early infancy. *Lancet, 2,* 999–1001.

Jones, K. L., Smith, D. W., Ulleland, C. N., & Streissguth, A. P. (1973). Pattern of malformation in offspring of chronic alcoholic mothers. *Lancet, 1,* 1267–1271.

Kilbey, M. M., & Asghar, K. (Eds.). (1992). *Methodological issues in epidemiological, prevention, and treatment research on drug-exposed women and their children.* Research monograph 117. Rockville, MD: National Institute on Drug Abuse.

Lemoine, P., Harousseau, H., Borteryu, J. P., & Menuet, J. C. (1968). Les enfants de parents alcooliques: Anomalies observees a propos de 127 cas. *Ouest Medical 21,* 476–482. (As described in Abel, 1984).

Little, B. B., Snell, L. M., Rosenfeld, C. R., Gilstrap, L. C. III, & Gant, N. F. (1990). Failure to recognize fetal alcohol syndrome in newborn infants. *American Journal of Diseases in Children, 144,* 1142–1146.

Mattson, S. N., & Riley, E. P. (1998). A review of the neurobehavioral deficits in children with fetal alcohol syndrome or prenatal exposure to alcohol. *Alcoholism: Clinical and Experimental Research, 22,* 279–294.

Milkman, H. B., & Sederer, H. B. (Eds.). (1990). *Treatment choices for alcoholism and substance abuse.* New York: Lexington.

Montagu, A. (1965). *Life before birth.* New York: Signet.

National Institute on Alcohol Abuse and Alcoholism. (1987). *Program strategies for preventing fetal alcohol syndrome and alcohol-related birth defects.* Rockville, MD: Author.

Phelps, L. (1995). Psychoeducational outcomes of fetal alcohol syndrome. *School Psychology Review, 24,* 200–212.

Riley, E. P., & Barron, S. (1989). The behavioral and neuroanatomical effects of prenatal alcohol exposure in animals. In D. E. Hutchings (Ed.), *Prenatal abuse of licit and illicit drugs* (pp. 173–177). *Annals of the New York Academy of Sciences, 592.*

Rosett, H. L. (1980). A clinical perspective of the fetal alcohol syndrome. *Alcoholism: Clinical and Experimental Research, 4,* 119–122.

Rosett, H. L., & Weiner, L. (1984). *Alcohol and the fetus.* New York: Oxford University Press.

Sokol, R. J., Ager, J., Martier, S., Debanne, S., Ernhart, C., Kuzma, J., & Miller, S. I. (1986). Significant determinants of susceptibility to alcohol teratogenicity. In H. M. Wisniewski & D. A. Snider (Eds.), *Mental retardation: Research, education, and technology transfer* (pp. 87–100). *Annals of the New York Academy of Sciences, 477.*

Streissguth, A. P. (1986). The behavioral teratology of alcohol: Performance, behavioral, and intellectual deficits in prenatally exposed children. In J. R. West (Ed.), *Alcohol and brain development* (pp. 3–44). New York: Oxford University Press.

Streissguth, A. P., Aase, J. M., Clarren, S. K., Randels, S. P., LaDue, R. A., & Smith, D. F. (1991). Fetal alcohol syndrome in adolescents and adults. *Journal of the American Medical Association, 265,* 1961–1967.

Streissguth, A. P., Clarren, S. K., & Jones, K. L. (1985). Natural history of fetal alcohol syndrome: A 10-year follow-up of eleven children. *Lancet, 2,* 85–91.

Streissguth, A. P., Landesman-Dwyer, S., Martin, J. C., & Smith, D. W. (1980). Teratogenic effects of alcohol in humans and laboratory animals. *Science, 209,* 353–361.

Streissguth, A. P., Sampson, P. D., Barr, H. M., Clarren, S. K., & Martin, D. C. (1986). Studying alcohol teratogenesis from the perspective of the fetal alcohol syndrome: Methodological and statistical issues. In H. M. Wisniewski & D. A. Snider (Eds.), *Mental retardation: Research, education, and technology transfer* (pp. 63–86). *Annals of the New York Academy of Sciences, 477.*

Tucker, J. A., Vuchinich, R. E., & Harris, C. V. (1985). Determinants of substance abuse relapse. In M. Galizio & S. A. Maisto (Eds.), *Determinants of substance abuse* (pp. 383–421). New York: Plenum.

West, J. R. (Ed.). (1986a). *Alcohol and brain development.* New York: Oxford University Press.

West, J. R. (1986b). Preface. In J. R. West (Ed.), *Alcohol and brain development.* New York: Oxford University Press.

ROBERT T. BROWN
JENNIFER L. CONDON
*University of North Carolina at Wilmington*

**ATTENTION-DEFICIT/HYPERACTIVITY DISORDER
FETAL HYDANTOIN SYNDROME
TERATOGEN**

# FETAL HYDANTOIN SYNDROME

The anticonvulsant agent phenytoin (Dilantin) has teratogenic effects. Uncertainty whether negative effects in infants and children was caused by medication or seizures themselves has been eliminated, owing in part to successful animal models (e.g., Adams, Vorhees, & Middaugh, 1990). Children of epileptic mothers who took phenytoin during pregnancy may show a complex of anomalies, known as fetal hydantoin syndrome (FHS) or fetal Dilantin syndrome, that include (1) mild to moderate growth deficiency, microcephaly (with associated mental deficiency); (2) cleft lip and palate, wide anterior fontanel, depressed nasal bridge, and other facies; (3) limb abnormalities, including hypoplasia of nails and terminal digits, a digitalized thumb, and dislocation of the hip; and (4) a variety of other abnormalities (Jones, 1997; Moore & Brown, 2003). Risk of damage to infants exposed prenatally to hydantoin is relatively low; exposed infants are estimated to have about a 10 percent chance of developing the syndrome and approximately a 33 percent chance of showing some effects (Jones, 1997). The fetal genotype is an important influence on susceptibility to prenatal hydantoin

(Jones, 1997), and rodent models additionally indicate a dose-response relationship (Adams et al., 1990).

The biggest concern for infants diagnosed with the syndrome is the degree of mental deficiency. Although effects are generally mild relative to some other teratogens, IQs of children with the full syndrome is 71 (Jones, 1997). The infants also show a failure to thrive in the early months of life for unknown reasons.

Many other anticonvulsant medications, including carbamazepine (Tegretol), valproic acid (Depakene), primidone (Mysoline), and phenobarbitol also appear to have similar teratogenic effects, and prenatal exposure to multiple medications appears to increase risk to the fetus (Jones, 1997). Women with seizure disorders who are at risk for pregnancy should be tested to determine if medication can be suspended if they have been seizure free for two years or at least maintained on as low a dose as possible. The conflict between potentially adverse effects of seizures on mother and fetus and of medication on the fetus may be difficult to resolve. For more information, contact the National Organization for Rare Disorders, Inc. (http://www.rarediseases.org).

## REFERENCES

Adams, J., Vorhees, C. V., & Middaugh, L. D. (1990). Developmental neurotoxicity of anticonvulsants: Human and animal evidence on phenytoin. *Neurotoxicology and Teratology, 12,* 203–214.

Graham, E. M., & Morgan, M. A. (1997). Growth before birth. In M. L. Batshaw (Ed.), *Children with disabilities* (4th ed., pp. 53–69). Baltimore: Brookes.

Jones, K. L. (1997). *Smith's recognizable patterns of human malformation* (5th ed.). Philadelphia: W. B. Saunders.

Moore, M., & Brown, R. T. (2003). Fetal hydantoin syndrome. In E. Fletcher-Janzen & C. R. Reynolds (Eds.), *Childhood disorders diagnostic desk reference* (pp. 238–239). New York: Wiley.

ROBERT T. BROWN
JENNIFER L. CONDON
*University of North Carolina at Wilmington*

**DILANTIN**
**FETAL ALCOHOL SYNDROME**

## FEWELL, REBECCA R. (1936–    )

Rebecca R. Fewell received her BA in sociology from Agnes Scott College, Georgia, in 1958. She then went on to receive her MA in 1969 and her doctorate in special education in 1972 from George Peabody College, Tennessee. On graduation she joined the Peabody faculty and remained there until 1979. While at Peabody, Fewell directed projects and a diagnostic training center for deaf-blind and disabled children.

**Rebecca R. Fewell**

Additionally, she was chairman of the special education department and was the elected faculty representative to the Peabody College Council on Student Policy.

Fewell's areas of interest have included the following programs: Program for Children with Down's Syndrome and Other Developmental Delays; the Supporting Extended Family Members program, a program for fathers, siblings, and grandparents of handicapped children; the Computer-Assisted Program Project for using resources at the University of Washington to serve children in rural areas throughout the United States; a research program comparing a direct instructional model to a cognitive mediated learning model for preschool intervention; and the Infant Health and Development Program for Premature Infants. Her other research involves the development of affective behavior and play skills in disabled and nondisabled children.

Fewell has served on the editorial boards of five journals and as senior editor of *Topics in Early Childhood Special Education*. Additionally, she has published over 75 articles, several books, and two tests, the Developmental Activities Screening Inventory and the Peabody Developmental Motor Scales and Activity Cards. Her recent work includes publication of a multivolume series dealing with early childhood special education, which included such topics as instructional models, mainstreaming, obtaining family information, and controversies associated with early intervention (Deutscher & Fewell, 2005; Fewell, 1991; Fewell & Neisworth, 1990).

## REFERENCES

Deutscher, B., & Fewell, R. R. (2005). Early predictors of attention-deficit/hyperactivity disorder and school difficulties in low birth weight, premature children. *Topics in Early Childhood Education, 25,* 445–453.

Fewell, R. R., & Langley, B. (1984). *Developmental activities screening inventory.* Austin, TX: PRO-ED.

Fewell, R. R., & Neisworth, J. T. (1990–1992). *Topics in early childhood special education* (Vols. 10–11). Austin, TX: PRO-ED.

Fewell, R., & Vadasy, P. F. (Eds.). (1986). *Families of handicapped children: Needs and supports across the lifespan.* Austin, TX: PRO-ED.

Folio, R., & Fewell, R. R. (1983). *Peabody developmental motor scales and activity cards.* MA: Teaching Resources.

Garwood, S. G., & Fewell, R. R. (1983). *Educating handicapped infants.* Rockville, MD: Aspen.

ROBERTA C. STOKES
*Texas A&M University*
First edition

TAMARA J. MARTIN
*The University of Texas of the Permian Basin*
Second edition

# FIELD DEPENDENCE–INDEPENDENCE

The concepts field dependence (FD) and independence (FI) were introduced into psychology and education by H. A. Witkin. He identified FD and FI as two distinct cognitive polarities that developed out of the theory of psychological differentiation. They were the terms used to accommodate broad patterns of psychological functioning associated with individual differences.

Witkin's research began with investigations of individual differences in the perception of the "upright" in the rod and frame, body adjustment, rotating room, and embedded figures tests. In each of these tests, subjects differed in the extent to which they used the external visual field or the body itself for locating the upright in space. The rod and frame test was used in early FD–FI research. Seated in darkness, the subject looks at a rod suspended in a frame. The rod and frame are independent of one another. The subject has the examiner adjust the rod to a perceived vertical position. How the subject rotates the rod in relation to the frame indicates field dependence or independence. At one extreme, when perception of the upright is dominated by the previous field (frame), this is designated field dependence. When the person sees the items as distinct from the surrounding field, this is designated field independence. The Embedded Figures Test (Witkin et al., 1977) is used more frequently and especially with younger children because of its simplicity. In this test, subjects are asked to locate a simple figure in a complex background. Witkin used this test to determine FD–FI in children between 3 and 9 years of age. However, there is a scarcity of current research available.

Many of the concepts derived from FD–FI styles are useful to special education. These are applicable to such issues as how children think, perceive, solve problems, and learn to relate to others. Field dependence-independence has been applied to the education of various groups, including the mentally retarded, gifted, physically disabled, and emotionally disturbed.

**REFERENCE**

Witkin, H. A., Moore, C. A., Goodenough, D. R., & Cox, P. W. (1977). Field dependent and independent cognitive styles. *Review of Educational Research, 47,* 1–64.

STEVEN GUMERMAN
*Temple University*

## VISUAL-MOTOR AND VISUAL-PERCEPTUAL PROBLEMS
## VISUAL PERCEPTION AND DISCRIMINATION

# FILIAL THERAPY, SPECIAL EDUCATION AND

Filial therapy was developed in the 1960s by Bernard Gurney and Michael Andronico (Andronico & Gurney, 1967). It is a "psychotherapeutic technique utilizing parents as therapeutic agents for their own children" (Hornsby & Applebaum, 1978). Primarily intended for emotionally disturbed children and their parents in outpatient school settings, filial therapy has been adapted to residential settings with borderline mentally retarded and autistic children (Hornsby & Applebaum, 1978; White, Hornsby, & Gordon, 1972). This approach is considered integrative; it empowers the parents as therapists and enlists them as agents of change. Instead of the child being taken away from the family to be helped, the message is clear that the parents are a necessary and integral part of the process. Filial therapy is a method of treatment that can be used as a preventive or remedial approach to help parents become more effective in their parenting skills.

Although filial therapy has been used in the schools (Andronico & Gurney, 1967) to lighten the work loads of school psychologists, current usage is mainly in residential facilities where psychological therapy is the central treatment focus. A typical filial therapy session has a multiimpact format. After the family has undergone initial evaluation, designed to determine the internal dynamics of the family members, the filial sessions begin. The parent who is considered to be the most distant from the child is used as the "primary therapist." It is this parent who will work with the child in the therapy playroom. The psychologist supplies this patient with a "bug" (a hearing device placed in the ear) and retires with the other parent to an observation room. The psychologist gives suggestions and directions to the parent engaging in play with the child, and uses the other parent as a co-observer and resource. After the play session is over, the family and therapist process feelings, observations, and thoughts regarding the relationship and communication patterns between the primary therapist and the child. In addition, there is an emphasis on overall reactions to the filial therapy process. As sessions progress, the bug is removed and therapy focuses on generalizing what has been learned by the parent and child to the home setting. Ultimately, the goals of filial therapy are to enhance and improve family relations, communications, and behavior management and to increase motivation of the parents to succeed and be responsible for changes in the family system.

Filial therapy has not gained widespread recognition in the schools. However, parent training programs such as Parent Effectiveness Training (PET; Gordon, 1970), Systematic Training for Effective Parenting (STEP; Dinkmeyer & McKay, 1976), and Children: The Challenge (Dreikurs & Soltz, 1964), all use essentially the same principles of parents assuming cotherapeutic management of the child with the school. In other words, schools have recognized the importance of offering parental guidance. The resurrection of filial therapy in a residential setting perhaps reflects the reintegration of the emotionally disturbed child back into the public sector and the necessity for change to be supported by the family system.

Special education personnel may use the principles of filial therapy in one of three ways: (1) as a continuation of filial therapy with emotionally disturbed children re-entering the public schools from residential or outpatient treatment; (2) where academic and behavioral deficits require support from the home environment; and (3) as a preventive measure in classes with behaviorally disturbed children. Modifications will certainly have to be made in the school setting. For example, the bug could be replaced by the teacher modeling appropriate academic or behavioral instruction in front of the parent or the parent and child engaging in academic or behavioral instruction with the educator observing and making suggestions. The benefits of filial therapy to the special educator include enhanced rapport with the child and parents, emphasizing a cooperative and holistic effort; reinforcement of appropriate learning from home, thereby assisting the child in generalization and transfer of training; and improved communication and interaction among family members.

## REFERENCES

Andronico, M. P., & Gurney, B. (1967). The potential application of filial therapy to the school situation. *Journal of School Psychology, 6,* 7–12.

Dinkmeyer, D., & McKay, G. (1976). *Systematic training for effective parenting.* Circle Pines, MN: American Guidance Service.

Dreikurs, R., & Soltz, V. (1964). *Children: The challenge.* New York: Duell, Slone, & Pearce.

Gordon, T. (1970). *Parent effectiveness training.* New York: Wyden.

Hornsby, L. G., & Applebaum, A. S. (1978). Parents as primary therapists: Filial therapy. In N. L. E. Arnold (Ed.), *Helping parents help their children.* New York: Brunner/Mazel.

White, J. H., Hornsby, L. G., & Gordon, R. (1972). Treating infantile autism with parent therapists. *International Journal of Child Psychotherapy, 1,* 83–95.

DAVID FLETCHER-JANZEN
*Colorado Springs, Colorado*

# FINGERSPELLING

The American manual alphabet consists of 26 distinct hand configurations that represent the letters of the alphabet. Fingerspelling is the rapid execution of a series of these configurations to communicate words visually. As such, it is more a representation of written language than of spoken language because it excludes the phonological alterations and prosodic aspects of speech. Fingerspelling skills include the hand configurations, the characteristic positioning of the hand in a fixed central location, and the set of possible transition movements from one configuration to the next (Padden & LeMaster, 1985).

Dactylology (the study or use of the manual alphabet) has attributed the origin of fingerspelling to medieval monks who used it to communicate without breaking their vows of silence. A Spanish Benedictine monk, Pedro Ponce de Leon, is thought to have been the first person to use fingerspelling to instruct the deaf. His work was built on by another Spaniard, Juan Martin Pablo Bonet, who in 1620 published the first book on educating the deaf. This book included a diagram of a manual alphabet that is remarkably similar to the one used in the United States today. It is believed that this alphabet was later brought to France and used to improve the alphabet of Abbé Charles de l'Epée, founder of the first French public school for the deaf in the eighteenth century. It was de l'Epée's methods and alphabet that were later imported to the United States by Laurent Clerc and Thomas Hopkins Gallaudet. This alphabet, further modified and evolved, has become the American manual alphabet.

There are numerous manual alphabets in use in different countries around the world. The American manual alphabet, however, with only two exceptions (t and d), was adopted by the Fourth Congress of the World Federation of the Deaf in 1963 as the international hand alphabet. This was in part because English and French (which uses a very similar system) are the official languages of the federation, and in part because the American alphabet was already in use in many countries (Carmel, 1975; Schein, 1984).

Fingerspelling is generally used as an adjunct to sign language, especially to render proper nouns, technological terms for which no signs exist, and slang. To the uninitiated, fingerspelling seems an indistinguishable part of sign language. There are, however, several differences between signing and fingerspelling. Signs usually use one or two distinct hand configurations, while in fingerspelling there are as many configurations as there are letters in the word. Fingerspelling is done in a much smaller space than signing, with the hand remaining in a nearly fixed position as only the configuration changes. Palm orientation in fingerspelling is restricted almost exclusively to a palm out position, in contrast to signing, in which there is no such restriction. Another important difference is that while signing evolved as a means of communication in the deaf community, fingerspelling originated as an instructional tool (Padden & LeMaster, 1985).

Although fingerspelling is used primarily as a supplement to sign language, a method of manual communication exists that relies exclusively on the use of fingerspelling. This is known as the Rochester Method, after the Rochester School for the Deaf where the superintendent of the school, Zenas Westervelt, initiated its use in 1878. The method gradually fell into disuse after Westervelt's death in 1912, and though proponents of it still exist, it is seldom used today, not even in the school for which it was named (Schein, 1984).

American deaf people are noted for more frequent use, and more rapid execution, of fingerspelling than other sign communities throughout the world (Padden & LeMaster, 1985). This may in part be responsible for the phenomenon known as loan signs. These are signs that originated as fingerspelled words, but in which the number of hand configurations has been reduced to two. In addition, other features such as palm orientation and movement have been added so that a phonologically well-formed sign is produced (Battison, 1978). Lessons in fingerspelling can be obtained free on the Internet at http://www.asl.ms/.

### REFERENCES

Battison, R. (1978). *Lexical borrowing in ASL.* Silver Spring, MD: Linstock.

Carmel, S. J. (1975). *International hand alphabet charts.* Rockville, MD: Studio Printing.

Padden, C. A., & LeMaster, B. (1985). An alphabet on hand: The acquisition of fingerspelling in deaf children. *Sign Language Studies, 47,* 161–172.

Schein, J. D. (1984). *Speaking the language of sign.* New York: Doubleday.

PEG EAGNEY
*School for the Deaf, New York,
New York*

AMERICAN SIGN LANGUAGE
DEAF EDUCATION

## FINLAND, SPECIAL EDUCATION IN

The first act for public education in Finland dates from the middle of the nineteenth century. The first schools for children with disabilities started at that time, beginning with special provision for the deaf and blind. Compulsory education was enacted in 1921. After that, every community had to organize primary education and every municipality with more than 10,000 inhabitants had to arrange education for persons with mental retardation. There has been a strong emphasis in welfare of students in compulsory education. The schooling itself, medical care, school transportation, and hot meals are free for all pupils.

However, the equality of educational opportunities for all children was not ensured until the Comprehensive School Act of 1970 (CSA). Since then, the nine-year comprehensive school has been compulsory for all children except the severely mentally retarded, who have eleven-year compulsory schooling beginning at age six.

Special education in Finland's current comprehensive system is complementary to the mainstream education by nature, meeting the diverse needs of an entire age group and helping to fulfill the demand for organizing education to match the student's age and developmental stage.

Currently, roughly 94,000 pupils of comprehensive school age receive some kind of special education, which is close to 16 percent of the age group. For most of the pupils with special needs, the comprehensive schooling is arranged with the help of part-time special education, which may be given to any comprehensive school pupil without administratively transferring the student to special education. The proportion of this kind of special educational provision has grown rapidly from the late 60s and has been around 80 percent of all special education pupils over the past twenty years.

Part-time special education is concentrated in the early years of primary level comprehensive schooling, and is therefore remedial (speech disorders and specific reading and writing difficulties) and preventative by nature. At the secondary level (stages 7–9), the clinic-type part-time education mostly deals with academic learning difficulties (for example, difficulties in foreign languages and mathematics) and with behavioral problems (see Figure 1). In most cases, the pupils have this clinic-type special education only one or two hours per week and not necessarily throughout the whole school year.

Full-time special education exists in special classes in comprehensive schools or in separate special schools. The proportion of independent and segregated special schools has decreased and they are often located as a functional part of a bigger comprehensive school complex. According to the statistics (year 1994–1995), 12.2 percent (11,000 pupils) were enrolled at special schools, and 6.6 percent of students were enrolled in integrated special classes in comprehensive schools. The most important forms of full-time special

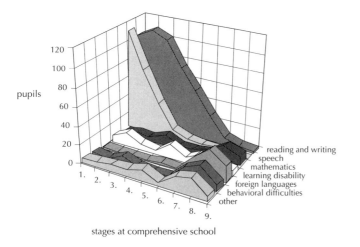

Figure 1 Delivery of part-time special education services and forms of special needs at the stages of 9 years comprehensive schooling
*Source:* Kuusela, Hautamški, & Jahnukainen (1996).

education are special provisions for slow learners (so-called adjusted education), for children with emotional and behavioral disorders, and for children with disabilities.

Although the mainstreaming and integration at the level of physical environment has been progressive, the individual integration of disabled pupils to full-time mainstream teaching groups is still moving slowly. Less than 1 percent of special education students are studying full-time in integrated general education groups. The most progress has been made with vision-impaired students, who are mainly educated in integrated mainstream groups.

The dropout rate in comprehensive schooling is quite low. A little more than 100 pupils of whole age groups (less than 0.3 percent) leave school every year without completing their compulsory studies. The dropout problem is more serious in later education and with the former students of special education, especially vocational education. According to different investigations, the admission or acceptance to further studies is not a problem. However, former students of special classes, especially former pupils of classes for emotionally and behaviorally disordered students, are at the highest risk to interrupt their studies at the vocational level. Although since 1988 the state has guaranteed that every young person with special education needs will have a place in further studies, more efforts have been put towards building transition programs for students with special needs.

Special teacher education is given in four universities, in Jyvškylš, Joensuu, Helsinki, and Vaasa, the Swedish-speaking department of special education. There are two ways to become qualified as a special education teacher. However, both are based on Master's level degrees as well as the other teacher diplomas in Finland. The traditional way is to take primary school teacher qualification and an MEd degree (160 study weeks) in education. After that, teachers take a one-year specialization course (40 study weeks) to get a special education teacher diploma. It is also

possible to earn an MEd degree in education with special education as a major subject and to qualify to teach only special education.

The New Comprehensive Education Act was enacted August 1, 1998. The most important change is the demand of individualized education plans for pupils with special needs. The new law gives more power to municipalities for arranging the best possible education for all children. Thus, the role of special educator is reformed to more consultative and collaborative work with other school personnel as well as with other professionals.

The preparation for this kind of work is one of the key topics in the Quality of Special Education Project funded by the National Board of Education. Also, regular school teachers at primary or secondary schools, as well as teachers at schools for further education, will need more education for teaching students with special needs and, in particular, for working as a team member in IEP and ITP processes. This could be the next step in building inclusive schooling in Finland.

**REFERENCES**

Kivinen, O., & Kivirauma, J. (1989). Special education as a part of the school system and as a classification system: The case of Finland in the twentieth century. *Skandinavian Journal of Educational Research, 33,* 67–78.

Kivirauma, J. (1991). The Finnish model of special education: A mixture of integration and segregation. *Skandinavian Journal of Educational Research, 35,* 193–200.

Kuusela, J., Hautamški, J., & Jahnukainen, M. (1996). Mitš, milloin ja kenelle? Erityisopetuksen virrat ja oppilaat. [What, where and to whom? The flow of students in special education]. In H. Blom, R. Laukkanen, A. Lindstrom, U. Saresma, & P. Virtanen (Eds.), *Erityisopetuksen tila* [The current state of special education]. Helsinki: National Board of Education.

Laukkanen, R., & Lindstršm, A. (Eds.). (1996). *A comprehensive evaluation of special education in Finland.* Helsinki: National Board of Education.

Tuunainen, K. (1994). Country briefing: Special education in Finland. *European Journal of Special Needs Education, 9,* 189–198.

MARKKU JAHNUKAINEN
*University of Helsinki*

# FITZGERALD KEY

The Fitzgerald key is used to teach deaf children to generate correct language structures. Developed by Elizabeth Fitzgerald, a deaf teacher, the key was originally described in 1926 in Fitzgerald's book, *Straight Language for the Deaf.* For the next 40 years it was widely used throughout the United States and Canada in schools and programs for the deaf (Moores, 1978; Myers & Hammill, 1976).

The key provides the deaf child with a visual guide for structuring sentences, thus helping to compensate for the lack of hearing. Fitzgerald (1976) recommended that it be used for all subjects and at all age levels. To facilitate its use she suggested that the key be painted in washable yellow paint across the top of the most prominent blackboard in the classroom.

The key consists of ordered (left-to-right) headings (key words) and six symbols that constitute a sentence pattern. Key words are used to classify new vocabulary. Nouns, for example, are classified under the keywords what and who; adjectives under the key words how many, what kind, what color. Symbols are used to classify parts of speech for which there are no associated key words. For example, the symbol for verb is =; for pronoun –. Fitzgerald was careful to point out that each of the six written symbols should always be verbally paired with the name of the part of speech it represents. The teacher may also pair the symbol with its written name. Fitzgerald believed that the use of symbols helps children at beginning levels of instruction to sense the difference between parts of speech more easily than terms such as verb, participle, etc.; however, she recommended that their use be dropped as soon as possible. The following example shows how words are combined into a sentence pattern using key words and symbols:

| Who: | | How many: | What color: | Whom: | Where: |
|------|--|-----------|-------------|-------|--------|
| What: | | | | What | |
| | = | | | | |
| George brought | a | | blue | car | to school |

Initially, students are taught to combine words into simple phrases under appropriate key words (Moores, 1978). Instruction emphasizes the use of correct word order. Gradually, the complexity of the phrases is increased until students are able to work with the complete key to formulate sentences.

In 1947 Pugh (1955) published *Steps in Language Development for the Deaf,* a book of carefully sequenced language lessons using the key and based on the principles of instruction set forth by Fitzgerald. Although Pugh slightly modified Fitzgerald's approach, her book complemented Fitzgerald's so well that both books are traditionally used together (Myers & Hammill, 1976).

The Fitzgerald key also has been recommended as an instructional program for learning-disabled students with either severe auditory or visual modality problems (Myers & Hammill, 1976). The extent of its use with this population and the degree of success achieved in remediating learning disabilities has not been documented.

### REFERENCES

Fitzgerald, E. (1976). *Straight language for the deaf.* Washington, DC: Alexander Graham Bell Association for the Deaf.

Moores, D. F. (1978). *Educating the deaf: Psychology, principles, and practices.* Boston: Houghton Mifflin.

Myers, P. I., & Hammill, D. D. (1976). *Methods for learning disorders* (2nd ed.). New York: Wiley.

Pugh, B. L. (1955). *Steps in language development for the deaf.* Washington, DC: Volta Bureau.

MARIANNE PRICE
*Montgomery County
Intermediate Unit,
Norristown, Pennsylvania*

DEAF EDUCATION
LANGUAGE DISORDERS

## FOCUS ON AUTISM AND OTHER DEVELOPMENTAL DISABILITIES

In 1988, PRO-ED, Inc. bought the quarterly newsletter, *Focus on Autistic Behavior,* from Aspen Press. In 1996, the publication was upgraded to a 64 page-per-issue quarterly journal to respond to multidisciplinary matters related to autism as well as to other types of developmental disabilities. The journal was retitled *Focus on Autism and Other Developmental Disabilities.* This journal covers practical elements of management, treatment, planning, and education of interest to practitioners, researchers, higher education personnel, parents, and other persons concerned with understanding and improving practices and conditions affecting persons with autism and other developmental disorders. Included are articles on a variety of topics, including assessment, vocational training, curricula, educational strategies, treatments, integration methods, and parent/family involvement.

JUDITH K. VORESS
*PRO-ED, Inc.*

## FÖLLING DISEASE

See PHENYLKETONURIA.

## FOLLOW THROUGH

Follow Through was initiated through an amendment to the Economic Opportunity Act. Project Head Start had begun as an early intervention program for children from low-income families under this legislation (Rhine, 1981). Early reports on small groups of Head Start children had shown an average increase in IQ of about 10 points after a year of preschool, but the first major evaluation of Head Start showed initial gains dissipating soon after the children entered elementary school. Follow Through was intended to provide continued support when children were in the elementary grades to help preserve and enhance any gains made in preschool (Haywood, 1982).

Follow Through was plagued by insufficient funds and by conflicting interpretations of data gathered in evaluation studies of planned variations of different educational models. One of the largest studies, by Stebbins and colleagues in 1977 (Hodges & Cooper, 1981), used as primary measures of effectiveness the Metropolitan Achievement Test (MAT), the (Raven) Progressive Matrices, Coopersmith's Self-Esteem Inventory, and the Intellectual Achievement Responsibility Scale. Stebbins reported much variability in scores from site to site, but little significant difference among models. Models emphasizing basic skills facilitated learning of basic skills and yielded higher self-concept scores than other models. If models did not emphasize basic skills, they were not enhanced. No program model was superior to others in increasing cognitive conceptual skills. In general, where there were large effects, they were related to specific program goals (Hodges & Cooper, 1981). Careful consideration of the measures used by Stebbins suggests that high variability of test scores across settings should not have been surprising because of the tests used (only the MAT has unusually well-demonstrated reliability and validity). Other problems in determining the efficacy of Follow Through related to the difficulty of using a true experimental design, confounding variables, and sample loss.

Probably the safest statement to make about the Follow Through planned variation experiment is that with structured approaches such as applied behavior analysis or direct instruction models, scholastic achievement is facilitated, but clearly there is still much to be learned about compensatory programs and their effects.

### REFERENCES

Haywood, H. C. (1982). Compensatory education. *Peabody Journal of Education, 59,* 272–300.

Hodges, W., & Cooper, M. (1981). Head Start and Follow Through: Influences on intellectual development. *Journal of Special Education, 15,* 221–238.

Rhine, W. R. (1981). Follow Through: Perspectives and possibilities. In W. R. Rhine (Ed.), *Making schools more effective.* New York: Academic.

SUE ALLEN WARREN
*Boston University*

**ABECEDARIAN PROJECT**
**HEAD START**

## FOOD ADDITIVES

In the 1970s and 1980s, one particularly fashionable explanation in the etiology of a number of learning disorders was proposed by Feingold et al. (Feingold, German, Brahm, & Slimmers, 1973). They contended that naturally occurring salicylates in fruits, vegetables, and other foods, artificial food colorings, and preservatives could produce a toxic reaction of cerebral irritability that could result in hyperactivity and other learning disorders in genetically predisposed children. This hypothesis has been subsequently revised by Feingold (1975a, 1976) to mitigate the importance of naturally occurring salicylates and to emphasize the role of two antioxidant preservatives, BHA (butylated hydroxyanisole) and BHT (butylated hydroxytoluene; Feingold & Feingold, 1979). It is important to note that there has been a significant distinction made between food additives' allergic effect, which does occur for a small percentage of hyperactive children (Conners, 1980), and the toxic effect of these additives, which Feingold and Feingold (1979) have more recently hypothesized to explain the origins of learning disorders.

There has been some evidence posited (Brenner, 1979) to suggest that those children who appear to be affected by food additives differ biochemically from children who are not affected. Evidence that low concentrations of food dye (frequently referred to as Red Dye No. 3) used in a number of confections prevent brain cells from ingesting dopamine, a substance having significant effects on motor activity, provide this biochemical hypothesis with further impetus. In fact, in one seminal piece of research, Lafferman and Silbergeld (1979) concluded that the food dyes' blocking of dopamine is consistent with the notion that the dye could induce hyperactivity in some children.

Although some research has tentatively supported the mechanism of the toxic effect of certain food dyes for particular children, Feingold (1975a) has made a plethora of unsupported statements attesting to the efficacy of his additive-free therapeutic diet. In fact, Feingold (1975a) has even suggested that nearly half of his clinical practice evidenced complete remission of symptoms as a function of a diet that was additive-free. Despite the fact that these claims were not based on empirical data and were refuted later by other investigators (National Advisory Committee on Hyperkinesis and Food Additives, 1980), the claims from Feingold (1975b) still continued at high pitch; he contended that eliminating food additives would decrease motor incoordination and increase academic achievement for hyperactive children (Feingold, 1975b).

Feingold's claims resulted in a proliferation of reports by the popular press attesting to the potential link of food additives to hyperactivity (Ross & Ross, 1982). Further, there were also reports of behavioral improvements ascribed to additive-free diets (Ross & Ross, 1982). Understandably, the food industry perceived these claims as a direct threat and thus organized with the Food and Drug Administration committees to review the evidence pertaining to Feingold's claims. The committees concluded that there was no empirical evidence linking food additives to behavioral or learning dysfunctions in children. The committees further recommended (Ross & Ross, 1982) that carefully controlled empirical studies be conducted to test any validity of food additives in causing hyperactivity or other learning disorders in children.

Subsequently, a series of methodologically sophisticated studies were funded by the federal government. In them Feingold's hypotheses regarding food additives were put to careful tests. The results of these studies, which were reviewed by the National Advisory Committee on Hyperkinesis and Food Additives (1980), have generally "refuted the claim that artificial food colorings, artificial flavorings, and salicylates produce hyperactivity and/or learning disability." Based on their findings, the National Advisory Committee also recommended that further funding efforts in this area cease.

## REFERENCES

Brenner, A. (1979). Trace mineral levels in hyperactive children responding to the Feingold diet. *Journal of Pediatrics, 94,* 944–945.

Conners, C. K. (1980). *Food additives and hyperactive children.* New York: Plenum.

Feingold, B. F. (1975a). *Why your child is hyperactive.* New York: Random House.

Feingold, B. F. (1975b). Hyperkinesis and learning disabilities linked to artificial food flavors and colors. *American Journal of Nursing, 75,* 797–803.

Feingold, B. F. (1976). Hyperkinesis and learning disabilities linked to the ingestion of artificial food colors and flavors. *Journal of Learning Disabilities, 9,* 551–559.

Feingold, H., & Feingold, B. F. (1979). *The Feingold cookbook for hyperactive children and others with problems associated with food additives and salicylates.* New York: Random House.

Feingold, B. F., German, D. F., Brahm, R. M., & Slimmers, E. (1973). *Adverse reaction to food additives.* Paper presented to the annual meeting of the American Medical Association, New York.

Lafferman, J. A., & Silbergeld, E. K. (1979). Erythrosin B inhibits dopamine transport in rat caudate synaptosomes. *Science, 205,* 410–412.

National Advisory Committee on Hyperkinesis and Food Additives. (1980). New York: Nutrition Foundation.

Ross, D. M., & Ross, S. A. (1982). *Hyperactivity: Current issues, research and theory* (2nd ed.). New York: Wiley-Interscience.

EMILY G. SUTTER
*University of Houston, Clear Lake*

RONALD T. BROWN
*Emory University School of Medicine*

ATTENTION-DEFICIT/HYPERACTIVITY DISORDER
FEINGOLD DIET
DOPAMINE

## FORNESS, STEVEN R. (1939–    )

Steve Forness began his college education at the U.S. Naval Academy but received his BA in English in 1963 and his MA in educational psychology in 1964 from the University of Northern Colorado at Greeley. After two years of teaching high school English, he completed his EdD in special education at UCLA in 1968. He has remained at UCLA for his entire career and is currently a professor in the Department of Psychiatry and Biobehavioral Sciences. Forness also holds the position of principal of the UCLA Neuropsychiatric Hospital (NPH) inpatient school and is chief educational psychologist in the child outpatient department. From 1985 to 1992, he was also director of the UAP Interdisciplinary Mental Retardation and Developmental Disabilities Program. His research has been in four main areas: (1) direct classroom observation of children at risk in the primary grades; (2) comorbidity of learning disabilities in children with various psychiatric diagnoses; (3) classroom aspects of psychopharmacologic medications; and (4) special education identification of children in Head Start. In addition to being coauthor of eight textbooks on special education and learning disabilities, he has published more than 200 journal articles and book chapters on school learning and behavior problems.

Winner of CEC's 1992 Wallin Award for outstanding professional and research contributions, Dr. Forness is also a fellow of the American Association on Mental Retardation and of the International Academy for Research on Learning

**Steven R. Forness**

Disabilities. In 1976, he was a Fulbright Scholar assigned to the Ministry of Education in Portugal. He has been national president of the Council for Children with Behavioral Disorders, a member of the *DSM-IV* Committee on Learning Disorders, coauthor of the *Practice Parameters on Learning and Language Disorders* for the American Academy of Child and Adolescent Psychiatry, and author of the education paper for the 1998 NIH Consensus Development Conference on ADHD. Forness also received the Midwest Symposium on Leadership in Behavior Disorders Outstanding Service Award, CCBD Leadership Award, AAMR (Region II) Education Award, and TED/Merrill Teacher Educator of the Year Award.

**REFERENCES**

Hewett, F. M., & Forness, S. R. (1984). *Education of exceptional learners* (3rd ed.). Newton, MA: Allyn & Bacon.

Kavale, K. A., & Forness, S. R. (1985). *The science of learning disabilities*. San Diego: Singular.

Kavale, K. A., & Forness, S. R. (1995). *The nature of learning disabilities: Critical elements of diagnosis and classification*. Hillsdale, NJ: Erlbaum.

Kavale, K. A., & Forness, S. R. (1998). *Efficacy of special education and related services*. Washington, DC: American Association on Mental Retardation.

STAFF

# FORREST v. AMBACH

Muriel Forrest, a school psychologist with the Edgemont Union Free School District in Winchester, New York, was dismissed with only a five-day notice in May 1979. The district dismissed Forrest ostensibly because her work was unsatisfactory and she had refused to follow orders directing her to change. The dismissal was appealed to the Commissioner of Education for the State of New York (*In re Forrest*, 1980). Forrest based that appeal on three points. First was her contention that she had acquired tenure status. As a four-fifths-time employee, the district argued no, while Forrest argued yes on the basis of being included in the collective bargaining agreement (tenure status would mandate a formal hearing prior to dismissal). The second point (the crux of system procedure/professional standard interaction) involved the district's order that Forrest shorten reports, delete technical language, and refrain from making recommendations to parents prior to referrals being made to the Committee on the Handicapped. Forrest's position was that these requirements forced her to perform in a manner that violated her professional organization's ethical standards and state and federal law. The third issue was the district's refusal to permit her to present a paper at a professional conference, infringing, therefore, on a constitutionally protected right.

In April 1980, Commissioner Ambach dismissed the appeal on the basis that Forrest had failed to demonstrate that the speech in question is constitutionally protected and that her exercise of her rights was a substantial or motivating factor in the respondent board's decision to terminate her services. Ambach went on to say that

> the Education Law provides that an appeal to the Commissioner of Education may be brought by any party considering himself aggrieved, [and that] the person asserting the claims must demonstrate that he or she is injured in some way by that action. Even if respondents were neglecting their statutory duties regarding handicapped children, an issue I do not here decide, petitioner failed to show how such neglect caused harm to her. Petitioner is not an aggrieved party within the meaning of Section 310 and her claim regarding respondents' performance of statutory duties which do not concern her are dismissed. (p. 5)

With that ruling in hand, Forrest sought judgment in the court to invalidate Ambach's decision (*Forrest* v. *Ambach*, 1981). Appearing as *amici curiae* were the National Association of School Psychologists, American Psychological Association, New York State Psychological Association, and the Westchester County Psychological Association. Justice Kahn rendered his decision late in 1980. In finding in part for Forrest, the court ordered that Commissioner Ambach review and reconsider the dismissal of Forrest from her position as a school psychologist. The court addressed two issues in the written opinion. First, whether Forrest was a tenured employee and therefore not subject to dismissal without a due process hearing, and second,

> whether the Commissioner was correct in declining to consider petitioner's specific allegations concerning the reason for her dismissal by holding that she lacked standing to challenge respondents' alleged neglect of their statutory duties regarding handicapped children. (p. 920)

With regard to the first question, the court upheld the commissioner's ruling that Forrest had not gained tenured status. However, the court went on to quickly add that the commissioner should have provided a forum for a review of the allegation made by Forrest. Forrest claimed that she was injured (loss of job) by the board's (district's) alleged misconduct. Justice Kahn identifies this as the "hub of her claim" and the commissioner's decision not to review whether the district was neglecting its statutory duties "resulted in a failure to have her grievance aired." Therefore, the opinion identifies the commissioner's determination as "a 'Catch 22' and is arbitrary and capricious in that there is not a rational basis therefore" (p. 920).

While a school board is in the position of an employer, those professionals employed by a school board do have a level of professional competence and standards which must be recognized and respected, not only for the profession itself, but for the purpose of rendering the best service to the school board and ultimately to the students they service. *The ethical standards of any professional employed by a school board cannot be cavalierly dismissed as irrelevant to the employer-employee relationship, and may indeed become quite relevant in certain circumstances* (emphasis added). If, in fact, petitioner was dismissed solely due to her own professional standards as a psychologist, then her dismissal by said school board would be arbitrary, capricious and unconstitutional. (p. 920)

Justice Kahn affirms the special education legislation and regulation and the explicit requirement of equal educational opportunity with a relevant reminder that "a school board should not be permitted to, in any way, impede the noble goals of such a law" (p. 920). Subsequent to the court's decision and directives, Ambach reheard Forrest's appeal and once again ruled in favor of the school district. Forrest appealed the decision to the state supreme court, and then the appellate division, losing each time. New York's highest court, the Court of Appeals, declined to review the case. The decision of Forrest accentuates the importance of professional standards and serves to underline the real and potential conflict that exists between such standards and system policy and procedure. In that sense, the decision provides an important foundation for establishing legal precedent in similar situations.

### REFERENCES

*Forrest* v. *Ambach,* 436 N.Y.S. 2d 119, 107 Misc. 2d 920 (Sup. Ct. 1981).

*In re Forrest.* New York Education Department No. 10237 (April 2, 1980).

DAVID P. PRASSE
*University of Wisconsin*

### ETHICS
### NATIONAL ASSOCIATION OF SCHOOL PSYCHOLOGISTS

## FOSTER HOMES FOR CHILDREN WITH DISABILITIES

Foster homes for children with disabilities and adults have been used for many years (Sanderson & Crawley, 1982). With the advent of deinstitutionalization in the 1970s, alternatives to housing had to be considered. Although group homes were predicted to be the primary providers for this population, Roos (1978) affirmed that adoption or foster care would be the preferred residential placement. Willer

and Intagliata (1982) compared group home and foster home placements on clients' achievement of self-care skills, adaptive behavior, community living skills, social skills, and community access. Interestingly, few differences were found across the two residential settings. Nevertheless, the authors concluded that family-care homes provided more opportunities to develop age-appropriate personal and interpersonal behaviors, while group homes provided more opportunities to develop community and independent living skills. Two major implications were made from these results. First, placement of persons with disabilities into community residential facilities must be based on the individual needs of the client. Second, "group-home staff members could benefit from training in behavior-management techniques, whereas family-care providers could benefit from training in how to encourage residents to develop and utilize more independent community living skills" (Willer & Intagliata, 1982, p. 594). Although cost-effectiveness data were not examined, the authors concluded that the cost for foster care was significantly lower than for group-home placement.

Despite the issues of best placement, children and adults with disabilities continue to be placed in foster homes. Many questions arise when considering these placements. What kinds of children are being placed in foster homes? What kinds of families take foster children with disabilities? What are the needs of families with foster children with disabilities?

It is estimated that over 500,000 children in the United States live in foster homes (CASA, 1995; Olsen, 1982). Foster homes have served a variety of children with developmental, emotional, physical, and medical problems. Traditionally, abused and neglected children have been in foster care. Many of these children are severely emotionally disturbed. Programs across the country have been developed to place severely mistreated children into safe and secure home environments. For example, the Intensive Treatment Homes (ITH) Project in Sacramento used a complete team approach for placing abused and neglected children into foster care (Harling & Harines, 1980). Less than half of the 43 children served in the first year of the project were able to return to their natural parents. One child was institutionalized, 2 were adopted, 11 were being considered for adoption, and the remaining 10 were referred for long-term foster care placement.

Foster homes for children with retardation and motor delays have been a constructive alternative to residential placement. For example, in a report by Taylor (1980), two case studies were presented from a foster parent's perspective. The achievements made by each of Taylor's foster children were remarkable. To meet the needs of foster parents such as these, Arizona developed a curriculum for foster parents of children with retardation (Drydyk, Mendeville, & Bender, 1980). The curriculum, Foster Parenting a Retarded Child, is available for purchase from the Child Welfare League of America, 67 Irving Place, New York, NY 10003.

Medically fragile children also have been placed in foster homes (CASA, 1995). Often it is a nurse who will take a foster child with medical needs such as tracheotomy care, tube feeding, sterile dressing, and physical therapy. In many cases, these children would remain hospitalized indefinitely because of the biological parents' inability to provide care. Additionally, it was estimated that in 1983 the cost of foster care for these children was $1,000 per month, while the average cost of a month's hospitalization was $10,500 (Whitworth, Foster, & Davis, 1983).

What kinds of families take foster children with disabilities into their homes? Demographically, foster parents are often of low to middle socioeconomic status, have little or no education, are married, and have children of their own (Carbino, 1980; CASA, 1995; Enos, 1982; Hampson & Tavormina, 1980). The motives of foster parents vary from love of children, desire to help, and interest in children's well being to wanting a child to nurture or wanting a playmate for another child (Hampson & Tavormina, 1980). Many experience disruptive family patterns when a child is placed within their home; often children with disabilities will be moved from one foster home to another (CASA, 1995).

The specific needs of foster parents vary depending on the child's disability, the family support system, and the coping abilities of the foster parents. Because of the reported emotional strain on families, it is critical that foster parents be provided with intensive orientation, training, and counseling sessions. Enos (1982) reports that foster parents leave foster care programs because of the unexpected demands of foster children, low payments, and interference with their own family's well being. Barsh, Moore, and Hamerlynck (1983) point out that foster parents of children with disabilities have similar problems to those of the biological parents such as finding babysitters, transporting the child to clinics, and managing disruptive behavior. Furthermore, Edelstein (1981) reports that many foster parents go through a period of grieving when children are returned to their biological parents. It is clear that foster parents need to be aware of the problems inherent in foster parenting and to feel safe in discussing their feelings with professionals or other foster families (Foster, 1984). Training families in first aid, behavior management, therapeutic techniques, and crisis intervention may better prepare families for the care of a child with a disability. Foster homes provide an invaluable service to children with disabilities. Professionals serving children with disabilities need to recognize the needs of foster parents in order to enhance the services provided to them and their foster children.

## REFERENCES

Barsh, E. T., Moore, J. A., & Hamerlynck, L. A. (1983). The foster extended family: A support network for handicapped foster children. *Child Welfare, 62,* 349–359.

Carbino, R. (1980). *Foster parenting, an updated review of the literature.* New York: Child Welfare League of America.

CASA. (1995). *Why children are in foster care.* Retrieved February 8, 2006, from http://www.casanet.org/library/foster-care/why.htm

Drydyk, J., Mendeville, B., & Bender, L. (1980). Foster parenting a retarded child. *Children Today, 9,* 10, 24–26.

Edelstein, S. (1981). When foster children leave: Helping foster parents grieve. *Child Welfare, 60,* 467–473.

Enos, S. L. (1982). More people to love you: Foster parents look at foster care. *Journal of Human Services Abstracts, 49,* 19.

Foster, P. H. (1984). Medical foster care: An ethnography. (Doctoral dissertation, University of Florida).

Hampson, R. B., & Tavormina, J. B. (1980). Feedback from the experts: A study of foster mothers. *Social Work, 25,* 108–112.

Harling, P. R., & Harines, J. K. (1980). Specialized foster homes for severely mistreated children. *Children Today, 9,* 16–18.

Olsen, J. (1982). Predicting the permanency status of children in foster care. *Social Work Research & Abstracts, 18,* 9–19.

Roos, S. (1978). The future residential services for the mentally retarded in the United States: A Delphi study. *Mental Retardation, 16,* 355–356.

Sanderson, H. W., & Crawley, M. (1982). Characteristics of successful family-care parents. *American Journal of Mental Deficiency, 86,* 519–525.

Taylor, S. W. (1980). Foster care: A foster mother's perspective. *Exceptional Parent, 10,* L4–L8.

Whitworth, J. M., Foster, P. H., & Davis, A. B. (1983). *Medical foster care for abused and neglected children of dysfunctional families.* Washington, DC: U.S. Department of Health and Human Services. Federal Grant #90-CA-0932.

Willer, B., & Intagliata, J. (1982). Comparison of family-care and group homes as alternative to institutions. *American Journal of Mental Deficiency, 86,* 588–595.

VIVIAN I. CORREA
*University of Florida*

ADOPTEES
FAMILY COUNSELING

# FOUNDATION FOR CHILDREN WITH LEARNING DISABILITIES

The Foundation for Children with Learning Disabilities (FCLD) is a charitable foundation incorporated in the state of New York and holding tax exempt status with the Internal Revenue Service. The FCLD is located at 99 Park Avenue, New York, NY 10016. It was founded in 1977 by Carrie Rozelle, who remains the president of the organization. The FCLD publishes *Their World,* an annual devoted to developing public awareness of learning disabilities. An annual benefit and other activities are carried out each year to raise funds to support the goals of FCLD.

In 1985 FCLD launched two major efforts aimed at service as well as public relations for the learning disabled. The FCLD has a grant program for public libraries to develop live programs for parents, teachers, learning disabled children, and the public about learning differences. A second grant program has been designed and implemented to educate both the public and the judiciary about the potential link between learning disabilities and delinquency. The organization is devoted to developing public awareness of the problems associated with learning disabilities and to providing general educational services to the public on the topic. The FCLD does not provide direct services to children with learning disabilities.

CECIL R. REYNOLDS
*Texas A&M University*

## THEIR WORLD

## FOUNTAIN VALLEY TEACHER SUPPORT SYSTEM IN MATHEMATICS

The 1967–1968 mathematics program teacher's guide for the Fountain Valley School District, California, included the following mathematics content: numbers and numerals, geometry, measurement, applications, statistics and probability, sets, functions and graphs, logic, and problem solving. The teacher's guide also listed manipulative aids, audio-visual materials, and demonstration materials for use with elementary school-age students.

The outstanding feature of the Fountain Valley program is the mainstreaming of 60 educable mentally handicapped (EMH) and 30 educationally handicapped (EH) students into regular classes. The goal of the project was to determine whether they could be effectively educated in those settings. Effective education was defined as improvement in mathematics, reading, peer and teacher acceptance, and self-concept. The students were provided with individually prescribed programs of instruction that were based on daily assessment and prescription by a resource teacher. The resource teacher worked with regular classroom teachers to coordinate pupils' programs of instruction with regular classroom activities. Regular classroom teachers attempted to help students with disabilities feel that they were valuable class members. Information available includes descriptions of scope, personnel, organization, services, instructional equipment and materials, budget, parent-community involvement, and evaluation.

Pre- and posttest assessments were administered to evaluate project objectives that were concerned with pupils' growth in academic achievement, acceptance by regular classroom teachers and students, and self-concept. Data indicated that EMR and EH students progressed an average of 12 months in mathematics and 9 to 11 months in reading. No difference was apparent in teachers' overall perception of handicapped versus nonhandicapped students as measured by Osgood's Semantic Differential. Also reported was the fact that the majority of students reached criterion levels of self-concept measures.

### REFERENCES

Flint, D. (1971). *Supplement to district mathematics guide.* Fountain Valley, CA: Fountain Valley School District.

Zweig, R. L. (1972). *Fountain Valley teacher support system in mathematics.* Huntington Beach, CA: Author.

FREDERICKA K. REISMAN
*Drexel University*

## ARITHMETIC REMEDIATION

## FOURTEENTH AMENDMENT RIGHTS

See EQUAL PROTECTION.

## FOXX, RICHARD M. (1944–    )

Richard M. Foxx received his BA from the University of California, Riverside in 1967, his MA from California State University, Fullerton in 1970, and his PhD from Southern Illinois University in 1971. His major fields of interest include mental retardation, autism, and emotionally disturbed adolescents. He is considered a leading authority on the treatment of severe forms of maladaptive behavior.

His current interests include the development of nonintrusive methods of behavioral reduction and the study

**Richard M. Foxx**

of the generalization of social skills, staff training, and the interface between environmental design and applied behavior analysis.

Foxx's work includes numerous books, scientific articles, and training films on the use of behavioral principles to treat individuals with mental retardation and autism. Among his most significant publications are *Increasing the Behavior of Retarded and Autistic Persons* (1982b), *Decreasing Behaviors of Persons with Severe Retardation and Autism* (1982a), *Toilet Training for the Retarded* (1980), and *Thinking It Through: Teaching a Problem-Solving Strategy for Community Living* (1989). As a featured speaker at the 1987 annual Conference of the Association for the Severely Handicapped, he presented the paper *Teaching a Generalized Language Strategy,* later published in book form (1990). Foxx is a fellow of the American Psychological Association and American Association on Mental Retardation and is the recipient of numerous awards and honors.

**REFERENCES**

Foxx, R. M. (1980). *Toilet training for the retarded* [Videocassette]. Champaign, IL: Research.

Foxx, R. M. (1982a). *Decreasing behaviors of persons with severe retardation and autism.* Champaign, IL: Research.

Foxx, R. M. (1982b). *Increasing the behavior of retarded and autistic persons.* Champaign, IL: Research.

Foxx, R. M. (1990). *Teaching a generalized language strategy.* Anna, IL: Anna Mental Health and Development Center.

Foxx, R. M., & Bittle, R. G. (1989). *Thinking it through: Teaching a problem-solving strategy for community living.* Champaign, IL: Research.

TAMARA J. MARTIN
*The University of Texas of the
Permian Basin*

# FRAGILE X SYNDROME

Little known until the 1980s, fragile X [fra(X)] is a chromosomal abnormality that is now seen to be the most common heritable cause, and second only to Down syndrome as a genetically-based cause, of mental retardation. (Down syndrome, generally arising through nondisjunction of chromosome pair 21 during meiosis, is genetic but not inherited.) Based in a weak or fragile site on the X chromosome, fra(X) is sex-linked and thus expressed more frequently in males. It is the only one of the more than 50 X-linked disorders associated with mental retardation that occurs frequently (e.g., Brown et al., 1986) and it is largely responsible for the higher prevalence of mental retardation in males than females. Although estimates vary across studies, incidence is about 1 in 1,500 in males and 1 in 2,000 in females (Fryns, 1990). Fragile X may account for over 5 percent of retarded

males and about 0.3 percent of retarded females (Jones, 1997). Of males with mental retardation serious enough to require extensive support, 6–14 percent have fra(X), as do 3–6 percent of individuals with autism (Batshaw, 1997). Individuals with mental retardation of unknown cause are now routinely screened for fra(X).

## History

From the beginning of the twentieth century, researchers noted a considerable excess of males, frequently about 25 percent, with mental retardation. Martin and Bell in 1943 and others thereafter described families in which mental retardation was inherited in an X-linked pattern. Although Lubs first described the fragile X site in 1969, his description drew little interest until Sutherland (1977) reported that some fragile sites were expressed only if lymphocytes were grown in a culture medium that lacked folic acid. The discovery of folic-acid sensitivity of fra(X) and some other fragile sites led to more accurate diagnosis, which in turn led to the discovery of the high incidence of fra(X) and an exponential growth of interest generally in X-linked mental retardation (Fryns, 1990; Sutherland & Hecht, 1985). Retesting has indicated a fra(X) basis for the retardation in the family studied by Martin and Bell.

## Genetics of fra(X)

Fra(X) is unusual genetically in several ways. In typical X-linked disorders, a carrier female who has no characteristics of the disorder passes the defective gene on average to half of her children. Of those children who inherit the defective gene, males will express any effects, whereas females will be unaffected but carriers. In fra(X), however, the situation is more complicated. Heterozygotic (carrier) females, who have one normal X chromosome and one with the fragile site, may manifest some fra(X) characteristics, including impaired intelligence and specific learning disabilities. About 20 percent of males who inherit the fragile site show no apparent physical or psychological effects and no evidence of fragility. They do, however, pass the X chromosome on to their daughters who may have affected sons (Brown, 1990). As a further complication, repeated cytogenetic testing fails to reveal the fragile site in more than 50 percent of unaffected carrier females.

Research in the 1990s clarified the basis and inheritance patterns of fra(X) and its precursors. The description that follows is closely modeled after Batshaw's (1997) exposition. Initially, the specific defective gene, the FMR1 (fragile X mental retardation gene) was found in all males who expressed the fra(X) syndrome. The defective gene was later found to interfere with a particular protein apparently important in brain development. Fragile sites themselves were found to be abnormal expansions of perseverations or repetitions commonly seen in three nucleotide base pairs of the genetic code. The expansion of the triplet repeat is likely to increase over generations. The fragile X site (FRAXA) normally contains some 6–50 repeats of the cytosine-guanine-guanine (CGG) triplet base pair sequence. Asymptomatic transmitting males and carrier females have 50–90 and 50–200 CGG repeats, respectively; do not show a fragile X site; and are said to have a premutation. Such premutations are relatively common, occurring in about 1 in 500 males and 1 in 250 females. Males and females who have the full mutation of 200–3,000 CGG fragile X repeats have observable fragile X sites and show various symptoms. All males and 50 percent of females will show mental retardation.

The increased expansion of CGG repeats over successive generations leads to increased fra(X) symptomatology over the same generations. Premutations of more than 100 CGG repeats almost always expand into full mutation range in the next generation. Transmitting males usually have less than 100 CGG repeats, so their daughters will tend also to have premutations and be asymptomatic. Since these daughters will likely have CGG repeats expanded into the 90–200 range, their male and female children who inherit the fra(X) site are likely to have CGG repeats of over 1,000. That, of course, is in the full mutation range, and those children will display fra(X) symptoms. As Batshaw (1997, p. 379) observed, "Thus, transmitting males tend to have grandchildren manifesting fragile X syndrome, a very unusual pattern for an X-linked disorder!"

## Characteristics of Affected Males

About two thirds of affected adult males show a "clinical triad": (1) moderate to severe mental retardation; (2) characteristic craniofacial features, including large forehead, protruding chin, and elongated ears; and (3) large testes (macroorchidism; Curfs, Wiegers, & Fryns, 1990; Fryns, 1990; Sutherland & Hecht, 1985). However, affected individuals show such a variety of characteristics that diagnosis can firmly be based only on cytogenetic analysis. Females and prepubertal males are even more variable. Although most males show an "overgrowth syndrome" from birth, with head size, fontanel, and body measurements exceeding the 97th percentile, macroorchidism and craniofacial features are much less distinct in prepubertal boys (Curfs et al., 1990). The following summary of characteristics of affected individuals is based on information in Batshaw (1997); Bregman, Dykens, Watson, Ort, and Leckman (1987); Brown et al. (1986); Curfs et al. (1990); Dykens and Leckman (1990); Fryns (1990); and Hagerman (1990).

### Physical Features

In addition to the characteristic craniofacial features, macroorchidism, and overgrowth described above, males with fra(X) may show a variety of other features, such as hyperextensible joints, high arched palate, mitral valve prolapse (a form of heart murmur), flat feet, and low muscle tonus. Female carriers, particularly those with subnormal intelligence, may also show facial features, including high broad forehead and long face, and hyperextensibility.

### Cognitive Features

Approximately 95 percent of affected males have mental retardation, but the degree of retardation varies from mild to profound, with a small percent of cases in the low normal range of intelligence. Males frequently show a decline in intelligence quotient, but not absolute intelligence, with age. Affected males have particular difficulty with sequential processing and short-term memory for information presented serially, performing poorly on tasks requiring recall of series of items or imitation of a series of motor movements. This deficit in sequential processing differentiates fra(X) individuals from those with other forms of mental retardation (Zigler & Hodapp, 1991). Affected males perform relatively well on tasks requiring simultaneous processing and integration, such as block design. Auditory memory and reception is poor.

### Language

About 95 percent of affected males show some form of communication disorder. Language development in general is delayed beyond their mental retardation. Additionally, specific problems such as perseverations, repetitions, echolalia, cluttered speech, and dysfluencies are often shown, some of which may stem from general deficits in sequential processing. Word-finding problems and irrelevant associations are exacerbated by anxiety.

### Behavioral Characteristics

About 75 percent of affected individuals show serious behavior problems, including hyperactivity and attention deficits, stereotyped self-stimulatory behaviors, and aggression. About 60 percent show autistic features and 20 percent have seizures. The combination of features leads many to be diagnosed with pervasive developmental disorder (Batshaw, 1997). Many affected individuals are also socially withdrawn, show gaze aversion, and engage in self-injurious behavior, particularly self-biting.

## Characteristics of Affected Females

About 70 percent of carrier females show no clear physical, cognitive, or behavioral problems. The remaining 30 percent show a variety of symptoms, which manifest less severely than in males. About 10 percent show mild mental retardation, 20 percent have learning disabilities, 30 percent have communication problems, and 30 percent have emotional disturbances. Frequent learning disabilities include problems in visual-spatial skills, executive function, and simultaneous processing. Language problems, similar to males, include cluttered and perseverative speech. Some evidence suggests that, unlike males, intelligence quotient of affected carrier females increases with age.

## Treatment

Folic acid has often been used in attempts to reduce symptoms associated with fra(X). Double-blind studies (e.g., Brown et al., 1986; Hagerman, 1990) indicate that such treatment does not affect scores on intelligence tests but may reduce hyperactivity and increase attention span. However, questions exist as to whether folic acid treatment is as effective as traditional treatment for ADHD with stimulant medication (Hagerman, 1990).

Advances in the field of molecular biology are examining a molecular or protein treatment that might be available in coming years (McHugh, 2003).

## Some Implications

Psychological approaches are of importance in dealing with fra(X) for at least two reasons (Curfs et al., 1990): (1) The diffuse and variable physical effects of fra(X) in children place additional significance on the role of psychological assessment in identifying potentially fra(X) children for cytogenetic analysis; and (2) cognitive characteristics of those with fra(X) have important implications for treatment and educational programs. Owing to the variety and variation in problems exhibited by those with fra(X), a team approach is recommended for treatment (Hagerman, 1990). Further, the clear distinction between characteristics of those with fra(X) and those with Down's syndrome indicates heterogeneity among groups with organic retardation, which may have theoretical implications (Burack, Hodapp, & Zigler, 1988; Dykens & Leckman, 1990; Zigler & Hodapp, 1991). Fra(X) can be identified antenatally with a special test (Brown et al., 1986), but the incomplete penetrance in males, phenotypic effects in a significant number of carrier females, and difficulty of diagnosis in unaffected females all complicate genetic counseling.

Numerous websites are available for additional information on fragile X. One useful site is http://www.ncbi.nlm.nih.gov/entrez/dispomim.cgi?id=309550.

### REFERENCES

Batshaw, M. L. (1997). Fragile X syndrome. In M. L. Batshaw (Ed.), *Children with disabilities* (4th ed., pp. 377–388). Baltimore: Brookes.

Bregman, J. D., Dykens, E., Watson, M., Ort, S. I., & Leckman, J. F. (1987). Fragile-X syndrome: Variability of phenotypic expression. *Journal of the American Academy of Child and Adolescent Psychiatry, 26,* 463–471.

Brown, W. T. (1990). Invited editorial: The fragile X: Progress toward solving the puzzle. *American Journal of Human Genetics, 47,* 175–180.

Brown, W. T., Jenkins, E. C., Krawczun, M. S., Wisniewski, K., Rudelli, R., Cohen, I. R., Fisch, G., Wolf-Schein, E., Miezejeski, C., & Dobkin, C. (1986). The fragile X syndrome. In H. M. Wisniewski & D. A. Snider (Eds.), *Mental retardation: Research, education, and technology transfer* (pp. 129–149). *Annals of the New York Academy of Sciences, 477.*

Burack, J. A., Hodapp, R. M., & Zigler, E. (1988). Issues in the classification of mental retardation: Differentiating among organic etiologies. *Journal of Child Psychology and Psychiatry, 29,* 765–779.

Curfs, L. M. G., Wiegers, A. M., & Fryns, J. P. (1990). Fragile-X syndrome: A review. *Brain Dysfunction, 3,* 1–8.

Davies, K. E. (Ed.). (1990). *The fragile X syndrome.* Oxford, UK: Oxford University Press.

Dykens, E., & Leckman, J. (1990). Developmental issues in fragile X syndrome. In R. M. Hodapp, J. A. Burack, & E. Zigler (Eds.), *Issues in the developmental approach to mental retardation* (pp. 226–245). Cambridge, UK: Cambridge University Press.

Fryns, J. P. (1990). X-linked mental retardation and the fragile X syndrome: A clinical approach. In K. E. Davies (Ed.), *The fragile X syndrome* (pp. 1–39). Oxford, UK: Oxford University Press.

Hagerman, R. (1990). Behaviour and treatment of the fragile X syndrome. In K. E. Davies (Ed.), *The fragile X syndrome* (pp. 66–75). Oxford, UK: Oxford University Press.

Jones, K. L. (1997). *Smith's recognizable patterns of human malformation* (5th ed.). Philadelphia: W. B. Saunders.

Lubs, H. A. (1969). A marker X chromosome. *American Journal of Human Genetics, 21,* 231–244.

Martin, J. P., & Bell, J. (1943). A pedigree of mental defect showing sex-linkage. *Journal of Neurology, Neurosurgery, and Psychiatry, 6,* 154–157.

McHugh, S. (2003). Fragile X syndrome. In E. Fletcher-Janzen & C. R. Reynolds (Eds.), *Childhood disorders diagnostic desk reference* (pp. 245–246). New York: Wiley.

Sutherland, G. R. (1977). Fragile sites on human chromosomes: Demonstration of their dependence on the type of tissue culture medium. *Science, 197,* 265–266.

Sutherland, G. R., & Hecht, F. (1985). *Fragile sites on human chromosomes.* New York: Oxford University Press.

Zigler, E., & Hodapp, R. M. (1991). Behavioral functioning in individuals with mental retardation. *Annual Review of Psychology, 42,* 29–50.

ROBERT T. BROWN
ELAINE M. STRINGER
*University of North Carolina at Wilmington*

AUTISM
CHROMOSOMES, HUMAN ANOMALIES, AND CYTOGENETIC ABNORMALITIES
CONGENITAL DISORDERS
DOWN SYNDROME
MENTAL RETARDATION

Selma Horowitz Fraiberg

## FRAIBERG, SELMA HOROWITZ (1918–1981)

Selma Horowitz Fraiberg received her BA in 1940 and MSW in 1945 from Wayne State University. She was a professor of child psychoanalysis at the University of Michigan, Ann Arbor.

As a social worker, Fraiberg advocated using appropriately trained social workers to work with children. Realizing that most caseworkers are trained to help adults, Fraiberg noted that resources are usually not available for a child with problems to be seen by any professional other than a caseworker. Fraiberg saw the difficulty in determining where casework ends and other professions begin when addressing children's problems. She contended that a child with problems affects the lifestyle of an entire family, and that, she believed, is a casework problem that is difficult to resolve without the involvement of a caseworker. She stressed that the effective caseworker must have appropriate training.

Fraiberg's 1977 book, *Every Child's Birthright: In Defense of Mothering,* was written to publicize the practical aspects of research on the rearing of children. Much of the research studied the development of children from the Depression and the two world wars who grew up without their parents and frequently without other family as well. Her belief is that the survival of humankind depends at least as much on the nurturing care and love given to a child in infancy and childhood as it does on preventing war and surviving natural disasters. Another of Fraiberg's interests, how blind children develop and form bonding attachments when they cannot see their parents, was the basis of *Insights from the Blind: Comparative Studies of Blind and Sighted Infants* (1977). *The Magic Years* (1969) was another important work by Fraiberg. Among her honors, Fraiberg was elected to *Who's Who of American Women* (1975), and *Who's Who in World Jewry: A Biographical Dictionary of Outstanding Jews* (1972). A native of Detroit, Michigan, Selma Horowitz Fraiberg died on December 19, 1981 in San Francisco, California.

### REFERENCES

Fraiberg, S. H. (1969). *The magic years: Understanding and handling the problems of early childhood.* New York: Scribner's Sons.

Fraiberg, S. H. (1977). *Every child's birthright: In defense of mothering.* New York: Basic Books.

Fraiberg, S. H., & Fraiberg, L. (1977). *Insights from the blind: Comparative studies of blind and sighted infants.* New York: Basic Books.

Karpman, I. J. Carmín. (Ed.). (1972). *Who's who in world Jewry: A biographical dictionary of outstanding Jews.* New York: Pitman.

*Who's who of American women, ninth edition.* (1975). Wilmette, IL: Marquis Who's Who.

E. VALERIE HEWITT
*Texas A&M University*
First edition

TAMARA J. MARTIN
*The University of Texas of the Permian Basin*
Second edition

## FRANCE, SPECIAL EDUCATION IN

During the eighteenth century, special education in France had various pioneers, including Valentin Haüÿ, who established the first institute for children who were blind, and l'Abbé de l'Epée, who invented a sign language for children who were deaf and mute. Vincent Itard, perhaps the best known, was headmaster of the Institute for Deaf and Mute Children and one of the first French pedagogues to study and educate children with mental retardation. His story was depicted in the movie *The Wild Child* and in the book *Wild Boy of Aveyron.*

In 1909, French law established the first special classes and schools for children with mental retardation. The famous French psychologist Alfred Binet was requested by the Ministry of Public Instruction (now named the Ministry of Education) to develop a test of intelligence, which was later disseminated worldwide.

In 1945, at the end of World War II, 174 special classes in public schools served children with physical, sensory, or mental disabilities. The majority of children with disabilities were serviced in private institutions under the control of the Ministry of Health. During the 1950s and 1960, the Ministry of Education developed special classes and schools and defined various disability categories.

During the 1970s, primary and secondary prevention programs were established using one of two models. In the first, prevention teams consisting of one school psychologist and two specialized teachers worked in psycho-pedagogic aid groups to help children who were able to follow regular programs in a regular classroom but who might develop future learning or behavior problems if not helped. Younger children (last year of pre-elementary school and first and second grade) were especially targeted. A second model integrated classes for students with moderate learning difficulties.

In 1975, the French Parliament passed the Orientation Law in Favour of Individuals with Disabilities (L. 75-534), which obligated France to work to prevent and, when needed, diagnose handicaps and to provide healing, education, vocational guidance, and professional training for children and adults with disabilities. This law also initiated the school inclusion policy since it recommended their education occur in regular classes and schools without regard for their disabilities. This policy of school inclusion subsequently was promoted and developed through a wide range of regulations issued mainly from the Ministry of Education in partnership with the Ministry of Health and Social Affairs and, for some, the Ministry of Justice. In 1990, the term *Groupe d'Aide Psycho-Pédagogique* [Psycho Pedagogic Support Group] changed to *Réseau d'Aides Spécialisées aux Elèves en Difficulté* [Specialized Support Network for Students with Difficulties]. Prevention remained one of its important tasks.

There are 12 million students in public and private schools from ages 2 (pre-elementary school/kindergarten) through 18 (senior high school). Fifty thousand children are enrolled in special classes in both public and private schools. Due to the policy of inclusion promoted since 1990, the number of students in special classes has decreased. Fifty thousand special needs students receive an individual inclusion program in regular classrooms. The "Handiscol" program (*handiscol* is the general term to qualify a project aiming to facilitate the schooling of handicapped children) recommends children with physical and/or sensory disabilities (blind or deaf) to receive specific material (including computer education). They may be helped by an *auxiliaire de vie scolaire* [school life assistant], a person paid either by the local education authority and/or the family to provide material support to the child within the classroom. The child also may receive services from *Service d'Education Spéciale et de Soins à Domicile* [Special Education Service and Remediation at Home].

One hundred fifteen thousand children diagnosed with one or more of the following eight disorders receive their education in special schools: mental retardation, multi-handicaps (usually severe mental retardation together with a motor disability), behavior, emotional and/or personality difficulties, motor disabilities, blind or visually impaired, deaf or hearing impaired, blind and deaf, or psychiatric affections. Twelve thousand children, 50 percent for less than one school year, receive services in classrooms integrated in general hospitals and Health Houses. Seven thousand children are in homes for children with social and family

problems (about 50 percent for a short period before joining their own family or a surrogate family appointed by a judge for children). Four thousand five hundred children are in special classes for students who have been expelled from regular classes for disruptive behaviour or who have dropped out before the end of compulsory education (grade 10 or age 16). Usually they stay about four months in these classes before joining a regular school (70 percent) or a special school. The Ministry of Justice may provide various educational services to children and youths "at risk" or already condemned for criminal offences at *Centres d'Action Educative* [Educational Action Centres]. In some cases, the youth may stay in his/her family under the control of a specialized educator appointed by the judge for children. Three thousand children are in jail. Closed Educational Centres (Programmatic and Orientation Law on Justice: L.09/10/2002) provide an alternative to jail in which condemned youths receive a special reinforced educational and pedagogical program.

A large number of children with moderate learning and/or behavior-emotional difficulties who receive services from a Specialized Support Network program are not included in the above statistics. These pupils follow a regular school program in a regular class and receive additional educational and psychological services, sometimes within the classroom and most often outside of the classroom. Although they are not eligible for special education (i.e., their case is not studied by the Local Commission for Special Education), the Specialized Support Network staff, including school psychologists and special teachers who help them, are special education personnel.

Professionals who serve students with special needs are employed by the French Ministries of Education, Health and Social Affairs, and Justice. Each is discussed below. The French Ministry of Education employs about 30,000 teachers who work in schools, mainly with primary school students (ages 6 to 10). Another 6,000 general and technical educators are employed by the Ministries of Health and Social Affairs, and Justice and work in special schools and structures depending on these ministries. Teachers hold the *Certificat d'Aptitude Professionnelle pour les Aides Spécialisées, les Enseignements Adaptés et la Scolarisation des Elèves en Situation de Handicap* [Professional Degree for Specialized Support, Adapted Teaching and Schooling of Students with Disabilities] and work in schools that provide specialized services to students diagnosed with one of the aforementioned eight disabilities, depending on their specialty. Local education authorities employ *auxiliaires de vie scolaire* [school life-assistants]. They support children with special needs within the classroom and outside and provide a broader level of support when several special needs children are being served.

The Ministry of Education also employs physicians, school nurses, school psychologists and vocational counselors-psychologists to work in a coordinated fashion to contribution to programs designed to prevent disabilities, diagnosis, orientation and decision making, integrate special needs students in regular schools, and develop individual and group programs designed to meet children's needs.

The professional degree of special school principal is prepared at the National Centre for Study and Training in Special Education and delivered by the Ministry of Education. The role of these principals is similar to those in regular schools. Inspectors for special education have administrative responsibilities locally for implementing policies applicable to special needs students and to supervise regular teachers in a given area. Inspectors are given an eight-week program in special education.

The Ministry of Health and Social Affairs employs technical specialized educators (who have a twofold competence in special education and in a professional or technical area and who work with children and adults with special needs in educational and professional settings), specialized educators (who work in various settings in the social or medical-educational fields, at time to support students when they work in Special Education and Remediation at Home or Integrated Pedagogical Units), principals of medical and social cares schools (trained at the National School for Public Health to get a specific professional degree), and inspectors of Health and Social Affairs (who control public and private medico-educational and socio-educational structures).

The Department for the Judiciary Protection of Children and Youth within the Ministry of Justice employs specialized educators (who play a central role in the support, follow-up, and social inclusions of these children who are either in jail, open structures, or with their families) and technical teachers (who work in various settings to facilitate professional preparation for future social and professional inclusion) to provide services to young delinquents.

Policies from the Ministries of Education and Health and Social Affairs guide the referral, diagnosis and decision-making practices for children and youth who may be eligible for services provided by special classes or special schools, the *Commission Départementale de l'Education Spéciale* [Local Commission for Special Education] is responsible for diagnosing and placing children with special needs. The commission is composed of administrators from the Ministries of Education, and Health and Social Affairs, teachers, social workers, and school physicians. One or several technical teams consisting of school psychologists, psychiatrists, social workers and others as needed are attached at the commission. Children proposed for therapy in a Child Guidance Centre need not be referred by the commission. The diagnostic and decision-making process considers information from four reports: a pedagogical evaluation of student's achievement and behavior written by the teacher; a psychological evaluation of cognitive capacities and personality written by the school psychologist who has observed and examined the child; a social evaluation that describes the family's social background, including relation-

ships within the family, educational competencies written by the social worker; and a medical evaluation written by the physician. The child's family is invited to the commission's meeting to present its information and to accept or reject the commission's proposal.

The Local Commission for Special Education decides the financial provisions (e.g., whether special education grants or scholarships will be used to fund needed services), if needed, and may offer other programs that provide social and financial advantages to persons with disabilities. The Local Commission also may recommend ways to transport the student as well as accommodations when taking exams (e.g., use of a calculator, more time). If the Local Commission decides a child needs specific educational support or to be separated from his/her family temporarily, the work of a *Procureur de la République* [District Attorney] is needed as well as a social enquiry that includes an evaluation of the child's situation. This issue is referred to a children's court in which a judge decides the case's outcome. During this process, families may solicit help from the Social Help to Children Service in order to resolve the issues before the case reaches the judge.

Local handiscol coordination groups are intended to improve cooperation between regular schools, medical, and social services. These groups are in charge of the observation, follow-up evaluations of special needs students, and those suffering from chronic diseases. As in many countries, changes in the law are impacting services for children with special needs. Three important laws recently passed by the French Parliament are summarized below. Their impact on special education is expected to be significant.

The School Orientation Law[1] attempts to combat social inequity and school failure and to offer more opportunities for success. Among the law's 14 tracks, one that is of major concern for school psychologists and special education teachers is the *Contrat Individuel pour la Réussite Educative* [Individual Contract for Educational Success]. Currently, the Specialized Support Network team and the school psychologist can be required by a school to help children with learning difficulties or other problems that prevent him/her from deriving benefits from schooling. In the new law, the role expected from professionals who currently work to help children with special educational needs has not been clarified.

The Law for Equal Opportunity, Participation, and Citizenship of Handicapped Persons,[2] an implementation of the Orientation Law of 1975, requires all local education authorities, including overseas regions, to create a House of Handicapped Persons with responsibilities to receive, inform, accompany, and advise handicapped persons and their families; to organize multidisciplinary teams to assess competencies and needs of the persons referred and to propose an individual program of schooling and professional development; to create a Commission for the Rights and the Autonomy of Handicapped Persons; and to provide follow-up evaluations and reviews of each handicapped person.

The recently passed Social Cohesion Law[3] focuses on employment and lodging. Chapter II of this law addresses issues of students with difficulties. Programs designed to promote educational success of children and youth (from pre-elementary school through the end of secondary school) are to be implemented by municipalities with financial assistance from the federal government. These programs are to be targeted at children and youth living in culturally and socio-economically deprived areas. The law recommends the creation of 750 teams to implement these programs. This law is innovative in its cooperative relationships among agencies that do not have a history of working together. Finally, a fiscal law that establishes the national budget for 2006 will clarify which programs within the Ministry of Education are to be directed toward children with special needs both inside and outside of schools.

**NOTES**

[1]L.2005-380.Loi d'orientation pour l'avenir de l'école 2005.04.23
[2]L.2005-102. Loi d'orientation pur l'égalité des droits et des chances, la participation et la citoyenneté des personnes handicapées .2005.02.11.
[3]L.2005-32.Loi de programmation pour la cohésion sociale .2005.01.18.

**REFERENCES**

Guillemard, J. C., & Guillemard, S. (1997). *Manuel pratique de psychologie en milieu educatif (Practical Handbook of Psychology in Educational Settings).* Paris: Masson.

Organisation de l'Adaptation et de l'Intégration Scolaire (Organization of Adaptation and School Inclusion). (2002, May). *Official Bulletin of the French Ministry of Education n°19.*

Website of the French School Psychologists' Association (AFPS): www.afps.info

Website of the French Ministry of Education: www.education .gouv.fr

Website of the CNEFEI (Centre National d'Etudes et de Formation pour l'Enfance Inadaptée/National Centre for Study and Training in Special Education): www.cnefei.fr

Text of laws mentioned in this paper may be found on the website of the Journal Officiel de la Republique francaise [Official Journal of the French Republic]: www.journal-officiel.gouv.fr

J. C. GUILLEMARD
*Dourdan, France*

**ENGLAND, SPECIAL EDUCATION IN**
*See* INTERNATIONAL SCHOOL PSYCHOLOGY ASSOCIATION

# FREE APPROPRIATE PUBLIC EDUCATION

One of the major provisions incorporated in the Education for All Handicapped Children Act (PL 94-142) and reinforced in its reauthorization, the Individuals with Disabilities Education Act, is the requirement that all handicapped children and youths, ages 3 through 21, be afforded a free and appropriate public education (FAPE). Initial federal statutory requirements were that services be provided to all children ages 3 through 5 and youths ages 18 through 21 apply to all states and U.S. territories except where state law or court order expressly prohibits the provision of FAPE to children or youths within these age ranges. The U.S. Congress then passed legislation (PL 99-457) to extend federally supported services to handicapped infants and toddlers from birth through 2 years of age.

The definition of a free and appropriate public education comprises three discrete, yet interrelated, provisions:

1. *Free.* Essentially this component of the FAPE mandate requires that special education and related services be provided at no cost to the parent or guardian.

2. *Appropriate.* This component of the FAPE principle requires that all special education and related services (a) be specifically tailored to the student's unique needs and capabilities (as established during the evaluation process); (b) conform to the content of the student's individualized education program (IEP); and (c) be provided in the least restrictive environment (LRE).

3. *Public Education.* The public education requirement mandates that all local, intermediate, or state agencies that directly or indirectly provide special education or related services must provide for FAPE. In meeting the FAPE requirements, public agencies (e.g., local school districts) may contract with private day or residential facilities to appropriately address the unique educational needs of a handicapped child or youth. Although the provision of FAPE does not fully apply to those handicapped children who, by parental discretion, are enrolled in private or parochial schools, these students must (by federal statute and regulation) be afforded genuine opportunities to participate in special education activities supported under Education for All Handicapped Children Act and IDEA funding.

Turnbull, Leonard, and Turnbull (1982) indicate that the provisions contained in the federal free and appropriate public education requirements have their foundations in several prominent civil rights court cases. These judicial decisions include *PARC* v. *Commonwealth of Pennsylvania, Mills* v. *D.C. Board of Education, Wyatt* v. *Stickney, New York State Association for Retarded Citizens* v. *Rockefeller, Diana* v. *State Board of Education,* and *Larry P.* v. *Riles.*

In establishing the concept of free and appropriate public education, the U.S. Congress (1983) statutorily defined FAPE as:

Special education and related services which (A) have been provided at public expense, under public supervision and direction, and without charge, (B) meet the standards of the State educational agency, (C) include an appropriate preschool, elementary, or secondary school education in the State involved, and (D) are provided in conformity with the individualized education program required under section 614(a)(5).

This definition of FAPE has been maintained unchanged in the most recent reauthorization of the IDEA, the Individuals with Disabilities Education Improvement Act of 2004.

In expanding on the legislative and judicial foundations supporting the provision of FAPE, Turnbull et al. (1982) specify six major principles for the administration of special education: implementation of the zero reject concept, development of nondiscriminatory evaluation models, preparation of IEPs, maintenance of the full continuum of least restrictive placement options, administration of compliant due process systems, and the assurance of full parent participation in all programming decisions.

**REFERENCES**

Turnbull, A., Leonard, J. L., & Turnbull, H. R. (1982). *Educating handicapped children: Judicial and legislative influences.* Washington, DC: American Association of Colleges for Teacher Education.

U.S. Congress. (1983). The Education of the Handicapped Amendments of 1983 (Public Law 98-199). Washington, DC: U.S. Government Printing Office.

GEORGE JAMES HAGERTY
*Stonehill College*
Second edition

KIMBERLY F. APPLEQUIST
*University of Colorado at
Colorado Springs*
Third edition

**INDIVIDUALIZED EDUCATION PLAN
INDIVIDUALS WITH DISABILITIES EDUCATION
  IMPROVEMENT ACT OF 2004 (IDEIA)
LEAST RESTRICTIVE ENVIRONMENT**

# FREEDOM FROM DISTRACTIBILITY

Numerous factor-analytic studies of the Wechsler Intelligence Scales revealed freedom from distractibility as an additional, smaller factor that underlies test performance, separate from the two larger factors that reflect the Verbal and Performance constructs that underlie all of Wechsler's scales. The first two factors that correspond to Verbal IQ and Performance IQ are typically labeled verbal comprehension and perceptual organization; each is robust in its makeup

and generally invariant in its subtest composition. The third, or distractibility factor, usually consisted of the arithmetic, digit span, and coding/digit symbol subtests, although some distractibility factors are composed only of the first two of these subtests (Kaufman & Lichtenberger, 1999). Indeed, the Wechsler Intelligence Scale for Children–Third Edition (WISC-III) included four factor indexes in addition to the IQs, one of which is composed of the arithmetic and digit span subtests and is labeled *freedom from distractibility*. Coding was not aligned with this factor, but instead joined a new speeded subtest (symbol search) to form the fourth factor index, processing speed. Similarly, arithmetic and digit span (plus a new subtest, letter-number sequencing) formed a distractibility-like factor index on the Wechsler Adult Intelligence Scale–Third Edition (WAIS-III). However, in a departure from tradition, the WAIS-III uses the name working memory for that factor index.

The freedom from distractibility factor was first reported by Cohen (1952), who used a comparative factor analysis (considered a powerful exploratory technique at that time) to examine the performance of a group of psychiatric patients on the Wechsler-Bellevue. Expressing concern that the rationales for intelligence tests were intuitively developed and lacked needed experimental testing, Cohen found and labeled Factor A (verbal), Factor B (nonverbal organization) and Factor C (freedom from distractibility). The last factor was found to include substantial loadings by the subtests that required alert, undistracted attention for good performance. He followed up this original work with a similar factor analysis of the Wechsler Adult Intelligence Scale (WAIS; Cohen, 1957). In this factor analysis he labeled Factor C as memory. In the Wechsler Intelligence Scale for Children (WISC) factor analysis, Cohen (1959) reverted to his original interpretation of Factor C as freedom from distractibility. Baumeister and Bartlett (1962a, 1962b) identified a third WISC factor that bore a close resemblance to the distractibility factor in their studies of groups of institutionalized and noninstitutionalized retarded individuals; they labeled that factor Stimulus Trace, referring to a hypothetical physiological basis for the construct involving disruption in the amplitude and duration of the stimulus trace.

Although the exact meaning of the so-called freedom from distractibility factor (or memory or stimulus trace factor) remains to be discovered, it has sometimes been identified as the capacity to resist distraction (Wechsler, 1958) and is sometimes referred to as the anxiety triad (Lutey, 1977), although Lutey stressed that the factor may be primarily a measure of number ability. Bannatyne (1974) interpreted the factor as measure of sequential ability. Kaufman (1979, 1990, 1994) suggests that the factor may reflect a variety of cognitive faculties in addition to number facility, such as sequential processing and short-term memory, rather than just the behavioral attributes of distractibility or anxiety. Horn (1989) considers the factor to be primarily a memory dimension, which he labels short-term apprehension and retrieval, one of about eight aspects of intelligence that define his fluid-crystallized (*Gf-Gc*) theory. Wielkiewicz (1990) emphasizes that the distractibility factor may be thought of as a measure of executive processing.

The distractibility factor can play a key role in some individual test interpretations, but caution is advised against using it indiscriminately. For the WISC-R, the composition of the freedom from distractibility factor has been found to vary somewhat from one age group to another; for example, in Kaufman's (1975) study of standardization data, coding did not load meaningfully on the factor at ages 6–7, but did at ages 8–16. Also, a significant WISC-R freedom from distractibility factor has been found in studies of various racial groups (Gutkin & Reynolds, 1981) and socioeconomic groups (Carlson, Reynolds, & Gutkin, 1983), but these findings are not universal. Sandoval (1982), among others, reported that a distractibility factor emerged for Whites but not for groups of African American and Mexican American children. Furthermore, the factor is occasionally not isolated in factor-analysis studies (e.g., Reschly, 1978); the factor is cognitively complex (Stewart & Moely, 1983); and, when compared with the larger factors of verbal comprehension (information, similarities, vocabulary, and comprehension) and perceptual organization (picture completion, picture arrangement, block design, object assembly, and mazes), the third factor clearly accounts for a smaller percentage of variance.

For the WAIS-R, likewise, the distractibility factor varies in composition from age to age (Parker, 1983) and from clinical group to clinical group (Leckliter, Matarazzo, & Silverstein, 1986), sometimes does not emerge in factor-analysis studies (Kaufman, 1990), and accounts for a relatively small amount of variance (Leckliter et al., 1986).

The variability in the subtest composition of the distractibility factor that characterizes the plethora of WISC-R and WAIS-R studies is no longer a pertinent issue for the current editions of Wechsler's scales. The WISC-III, as noted, has a two-subtest distractibility factor that is a formal scale, yields standard scores with mean = 100 and standard deviation = 15, and has been validated (Wechsler, 1991) and cross-validated with large, representative samples in the United States (Roid, Prifitera, & Weiss, 1993) and Canada (Roid & Worrall, 1997); it has also been validated for children with handicapping conditions such as mental retardation and learning disabilities (Konold, Kush, & Canivez, 1997). Its composition is not in question; furthermore, the fact that Symbol Search consistently loads with Coding on a fourth factor (processing speed) virtually eliminates the question of whether or not coding would join arithmetic and digit span or split off. For the WAIS-III, the addition of letter-number sequencing and the renaming of the factor as a measure of working memory has made the issue of the composition or nature of the adult distractibility factor a moot point; future research will undoubtedly focus on the constructs underlying the working memory index. And, finally, the preschool

Wechsler Scale, the WPPSI-R, yields only two interpretable factors, resembling the global verbal and performance IQ scales, and no freedom from distractibility factor at all (Stone, Gridley, & Gyurke, 1991; Wechsler, 1989).

The latter finding for the WPPSI-R is of extreme interest regarding the interpretation of the distractibility factor. Children within the WPPSI-R's age range (3 to 7 years) are by nature distractible. If a third factor does not emerge for the WPPSI-R just as it did not emerge for its predecessor, the WPPSI for ages 4 to 6 years (Hollenbeck & Kaufman, 1973) then how can one justify labeling this dimension in terms of the distractibility behavior? That contention does not mean that poor attention and concentration, or distractible, anxious behavior, will not lower children's scores on oral arithmetic, memory, and highly-speeded tasks. Any experienced clinician knows that such behaviors do indeed lower test scores, and those specific types of tasks are the most vulnerable to inattentive and distractible behaviors. However, freedom from distractibility itself cannot lead to high scores on those tasks, and has sometimes been shown not to correlate with objective measures of attention (Riccio, Cohen, Hall, & Ross, 1997). Furthermore, many other reasons, some of them cognitive deficiencies, can also lead to depressed scores on the so-called distractibility factor.

Because the WPPSI-R does not yield a distractibility factor, the WAIS-III yields a working memory index instead of a distractibility score, and the WISC-III includes a simple, well-validated, two-subtest freedom from distractibility index, the composition, or even the existence, of a distractibility factor is of limited current interest. Of greater value are research studies devoted to the score profiles of clinical populations to determine whether they have a strength or weakness on the distractibility factor. It has long been known that low scores on the WISC-R distractibility factor tend to characterize the test performance of groups of reading-disabled and learning-disabled children (Kaufman, 1979; Rugel, 1974). In addition, studies of learning disabled adolescents, learning disabled college students, and dyslexic adults also reveal a relative weakness on the distractibility factor (Kaufman, 1990, Table 13.12), although these studies often interpret the dimension as sequential ability from Bannatyne's (1974) perspective.

Kaufman (1994, pp. 212–213), summarizing the results of numerous WISC-R studies, also identified deficits on the distractibility factor for a diversity of populations such as children with attention-deficit/hyperactivity disorder (ADHD), unilateral lesions to either cerebral hemisphere, leukemia (following cranial irradiation treatment), epilepsy, autism, language disorders, schizophrenia, and Duchenne muscular dystrophy. A summary of WISC-III studies, reported in the WISC-III manual (Wechsler, 1991) or a special volume devoted to the WISC-III (Bracken & McCallum, 1993), indicates depressed performance on the distractibility factor for children with learning disabilities, reading disorders, dyslexia, ADHD, hearing impairment, and severe language impairment (Kaufman, 1994, Table 5.1). In contrast, the following samples scored about as well on the distractibility factor as on other WISC-III indexes: gifted, mentally retarded, and severely emotionally disturbed (Kaufman, 1994, Table 5.1).

However, a group weakness on the distractibility factor does not mean that all, or even most, members of that group display a low distractibility profile, a finding that has been shown over and over in research studies (e.g., Joschko & Rourke, 1985). The clinician's goal, therefore, is to interpret the meaning of the distractibility factor for each individual assessed, a goal that is entirely consistent with the notion that the distractibility factor can be interpreted from such a variety of cognitive and behavioral perspectives.

The first question is, When should the freedom from distractibility factor be interpreted? And the second question is, What does the factor mean for the specific individual? For the WISC-R and WAIS-R, Kaufman (1979, 1990) advised adhering to the Wechsler Verbal-Performance dichotomy under ordinary circumstances, and to only interpret the distractibility factor when it seemed to reflect a clear and unitary ability, for example, the person scored about equally well or poorly on its component subtests, and the overall distractibility score differed significantly from at least one of the larger factor scores. For the WISC-III, Kaufman (1994) recommends a more specific set of guidelines for when to interpret the distractibility factor, but the intent is still to determine whether it is a discrete, unitary ability: (a) scaled scores on arithmetic and digit span must not differ by more than 3 points, and (b) the freedom from distractibility index must differ significantly from the verbal comprehension and/or perceptual organization index. Kaufman and Lichtenberger (1999) offer similar guidelines for interpreting the WAIS-III working memory index.

If an examiner determines that an interpretation of the distractibility (or working memory) factor is warranted, the matter of how to interpret the factor still remains. To automatically ascribe an explanation of distractibility to a child who scores low on arithmetic and digit span would be absurd if the child had concentrated on each task and attended closely to each item processed. A hypothesis of distractibility or anxiety should be substantiated by test behavior indicating an attention deficit or failure to concentrate. In addition to behavioral observation, other subtest scores, the nature of wrong responses, and conditions outside the testing situation must also be considered in a comprehensive and individualized interpretation (Kaufman, 1994; Kaufman & Lichtenberger, 1999). When sequencing ability is believed to be the difficulty (or the strength), the scaled score on the picture arrangement subtest should be examined for corroboration. Also, the examiner should look closely at background and referral information, noting any sequencing deficiency such as failure to follow directions. On the other hand, finger counting or writing and an inability to solve arithmetic problems during the time allowed,

along with a low achievement in math, all point to a difficulty with numerical symbols as a probable explanation for a low distractibility index. Individuals who experience more difficulty with reversing digits in digit span (which requires mental number manipulation) than they do repeating the digits forward also may have a number problem. By contrast, a high score on the distractibility index coupled with evidence of very good math achievement suggest an interpretation of strength in number ability.

Lutey (1977) and Kaufman (1979, 1990, 1994) both warn against a simplistic interpretation of the distractibility factor, stressing that the factor can yield valuable information if it is considered in a larger context that features the more global perspective of the entire test performance, the test behavior, and the personal history of the individual. Information yielded by interpreting the distractibility factor provides insight into the cognitive and behavioral functioning of clinical groups, and it offers potentially useful information about an individual's strengths and weaknesses (Kaufman, 1994); differential diagnosis based on the distractibility factor, however, is often not supported by research data (e.g., Anastopolous, Spisto, & Maher, 1994). Nonetheless, the distractibility factor is invariably lower for exceptional than normal samples, impelling Kaufman (1994) to state that the distractibility factor is like a land mine that explodes on a diversity of abnormal populations but leaves most normal populations unscathed (p. 213).

The Freedom from Distractibility factor was retained up to the fourth edition of the WISC for historical continuity. However, during revision the label no longer fit with current neuropsychological research and it was omitted from the fourth edition (Longman, 2005).

## REFERENCES

Anastopolous, A. D., Spisto, M. A., & Maher, M. C. (1994). The WISC-III freedom from distractibility factor: Its utility in identifying children with attention deficit hyperactivity disorder. *Psychological Assessment, 6,* 368–371.

Bannatyne, A. (1974). Diagnosis: A note on recategorization of the WISC scaled scores. *Journal of Learning Disabilities, 7,* 212–274.

Baumeister, A. A., & Bartlett, C. J. (1962a). A comparison of the factor-structure of normals and retardates the WISC. *American Journal of Mental Deficiency, 66,* 641–646.

Baumeister, A. A., & Bartlett, C. J. (1962b). Further factorial investigation of WISC performance of mental defectives. *American Journal of Mental Deficiency, 67,* 257–261.

Bracken, B. A., & McCallum, R. S. (Eds.). (1993). Journal of Psychoeducational Assessment monograph series. *Advances in psychoeducational assessment: Wechsler Intelligence Scale for Children–Third Edition.* Germantown, TN: Psychoeducational Corporation.

Carlson, L., Reynolds, C. R., & Gutkin, T. B. (1983). Consistency of the factorial validity of the WISC-R for upper and lower SES groups. *Journal of School Psychology, 21,* 319–326.

Cohen, J. (1952). Factors underlying the Wechsler-Bellevue performance of three neuropsychiatric groups. *Journal of Abnormal and Social Psychology, 47,* 359–365.

Cohen, J. (1959). The factorial structure of the WISC at ages 7–6, 10–6, and 13–6. *Journal of Consulting Psychology, 23,* 285–299.

Gutkin, T. B., & Reynolds, C. R. (1981). Factorial similarity of the WISC-R for White and Black children from the standardization sample. *Journal of Educational Psychology, 73,* 227–231.

Hollenbeck, G. P., & Kaufman, A. S. (1973). Factor analysis of the Wechsler Preschool and Primary Scale of Intelligence (WPPSI). *Journal of Clinical Psychology, 29,* 41–45.

Horn, J. L. (1989). Cognitive diversity: A framework of learning. In P. L. Ackerman, R. J. Sternberg, & R. Glaser (Eds.), *Learning and individual differences* (pp. 61–116). New York: Freeman.

Joschko, M., & Rourke, B. P. (1985). Neuropsychological subtypes of learning-disabled children who exhibit the ACID pattern on the WISC. In B. P. Rourke (Ed.), *Neuropsychology of learning disabilities: Essentials of subtype analysis* (pp. 65–68). New York: Guilford.

Kaufman, A. S. (1975). Factor analysis of the WISC-R at 11 age levels between 6 1/2 and 16 1/2 years. *Journal of Consulting and Clinical Psychology, 43,* 135–147.

Kaufman, A. S. (1979). *Intelligent testing with the WISC-R.* New York: Wiley.

Kaufman, A. S. (1990). *Assessing adolescent and adult intelligence.* Boston: Allyn & Bacon.

Kaufman, A. S. (1994). *Intelligent testing with the WISC-III.* New York: Wiley.

Kaufman, A. S., & Lichtenberger, E. O. (1999). *Essentials of WAIS-III assessment.* New York: Wiley.

Konold, T. R., Kush, J. C., & Canivez, G. L. (1997). Factor replication of the WISC-III in three independent samples of children receiving special education. *Journal of Psychoeducational Assessment, 15,* 123–137.

Leckliter, I. N., Matarazzo, J. D., & Silverstein, A. B. (1986). A literature review of factor analytic studies of the WAIS-R. *Journal of Clinical Psychology, 42,* 332–342.

Longman, R. S. (2005). Tables to compare WISC-IV index scores against overall means. In A. Prifitera, D. H. Sakalofske and L. Weiss (Eds.), *WISC-IV clinical use and interpretation* (pp. 66–100). Burlington, MA: Elsevier.

Lutey, C. (1977). *Individual intelligence testing: A manual and sourcebook* (2nd ed.). Greeley, CO: Lutey.

Parker, K. (1983). Factor analysis of the WAIS-R at nine age levels between 16 and 74 years. *Journal of Consulting and Clinical Psychology, 51,* 302–308.

Reschly, D. J. (1978). WISC-R factor structures among Anglos, Blacks, Chicanos, and Native-American Papagos. *Journal of Consulting and Clinical Psychology, 46,* 417–422.

Riccio, C. A., Cohen, M. J., Hall, J., & Ross, C. M. (1997). The third and fourth factors of the WISC-III: What they don't measure. *Journal of Psychoeducational Assessment, 15,* 27–39.

Roid, G. H., Prifitera, A., & Weiss, L. G. (1993). Replication of the WISC-III factor structure in an independent sample. In B. A. Bracken & R. S. McCallum (Eds.), *Journal of Psychoeducational Assessment* monograph series. *Advances in psychoeducational assessment: Wechsler Intelligence Scale for Children–Third Edition* (pp. 6–21). Germantown, TN: Psychoeducational Corporation.

Roid, G. H., & Worrall, W. (1997). Replication of the Wechsler Intelligence Scale for Children–Third edition four-factor model in the Canadian normative sample. *Psychological Assessment, 9,* 512–515.

Rugel, R. P. (1974). WISC subtest scores of disabled readers: A review with respect to Bannatyne's recategorization. *Journal of Learning Disabilities, 7,* 48–55.

Sandoval, J. (1982). The WISC-R factoral validity for minority groups and Spearman's hypothesis. *Journal of School Psychology, 20,* 198–204.

Stewart, K. J., & Moely, B. E. (1983). The WISC-R third factor: What does it mean? *Journal of Consulting and Clinical Psychology, 51,* 940–41.

Stone, B. J., Gridley, B. E., & Gyurke, J. S. (1991). Confirmatory factor analysis of the WPPSI-R at the extreme end of the age range. *Journal of Psychoeducational Assessment, 8,* 263–270.

Wechsler, D. (1958). *The measurement and appraisal of adult intelligence* (4th ed.). Baltimore: Williams and Wilkins.

Wechsler, D. (1989). *Manual for the Wechsler Preschool and Primary Scale of Intelligence–Revised (WPPSI-R).* San Antonio, TX: Psychological Corporation.

Wechsler, D. (1991). *Manual for the Wechsler Intelligence Scale for Children–Third Edition (WISC-III).* San Antonio, TX: Psychological Corporation.

Wielkiewicz, R. M. (1990). Interpreting low scores on the WISC-R third factor: It's more than distractibility. *Psychological Assessment, 2,* 91–97.

ALAN S. KAUFMAN
*Yale University School of
Medicine*

JAMES C. KAUFMAN
*California State University, San
Bernardino*

FACTOR ANALYSIS
PROFILE VARIABILITY
WECHSLER ADULT INTELLIGENCE SCALE–THIRD EDITION
WECHSLER INTELLIGENCE SCALE FOR CHILDREN–
  FOURTH EDITION

# FREEMAN SHELDON SYNDROME

Freeman Sheldon syndrome, also known as Whistling Face syndrome, is a rare inherited condition that includes a very small mouth, mask-like face, joint contractures, and hypoplasia of the nasal cartilage. Crossed eyes, drooping eyelids, and development of scoliosis may also be encountered. Intelligence is usually normal, although some patients have been mentally retarded. Usually inherited in an autosomal dominant pattern, there are also sporadic cases and others with an autosomal recessive pattern of inheritance. There is no laboratory test to confirm the disorder. There is considerable overlap of symptoms with Schwartz-Janpel syndrome (Fletcher-Janzen, 2003).

The small mouth causes difficulties with speech, oral hygiene, and dental care. Contractures of the fingers complicate fine motor function. Orthopedic and plastic surgery can improve appearance and function but a potentially fatal reaction (malignant hyperthermia) to certain inhaled anesthetic agents necessitates careful preoperative planning with a knowledgeable anesthesiologist. There are several voluntary health agencies focusing on children with craniofacial abnormalities which offer additional information for families and professionals. Two such resources are Children's Craniofacial Association (P.O. Box 280297, Dallas, Texas 75228, (800)535-3643) and About-Face International (99 Crowns Lane, 4th Floor, Toronto, Ontario, Canada M5R 3P4, (800)665-3223).

Edward Livingston French

**REFERENCES**

Fletcher-Janzen, E. (2003). Freeman-Sheldon Syndrome. In E. Fletcher-Janzen & C. R. Reynolds (Eds.), *Childhood disorders diagnostic desk reference* (p. 247). New York: Wiley.

Freeman, E. A., & Sheldon, J. H. (1938). Craniocarpotarsal dystrophy: An undescribed congenital malformation. *Archives of Diseases of Childhood, 13,* 277–280.

Jones, K. L. (1997). Freeman-Sheldon Syndrome. *Smith's recognizable patterns of human malformation* (5th ed., pp. 214–15). New York: W. B. Saunders.

PATRICIA L. HARTLAGE
*Medical College of Georgia*

vereux Schools in *Special Education Programs within the United States* describes the principles of residential therapy on which the Devereux program is based. He served as president of both the Clinical Biochemistry and Behavioral Institute and the Division of School Psychologists of the American Psychological Association, and he was a trustee of the National Association of Private Psychiatric Hospitals.

**REFERENCES**

French, E. L. (1968). The Devereux Schools. In M. V. Jones (Ed.), *Special education programs within the United States.* Springfield, IL: Thomas.

French, E. L., & Scott, J. C. (1967). *How you can help your retarded child: A manual for parents.* New York: Lippincott.

PAUL IRVINE
*Katonah, New York*

## FRENCH, EDWARD LIVINGSTON (1916–1969)

Edward Livingston French began his professional career as a teacher at Chestnut Hill Academy in Philadelphia. Following three years of military service in World War II, he served as chief psychologist at the Training School at Vineland, New Jersey, where he was associated with Edgar A. Doll. In 1949 both French and Doll joined the Devereux Schools in Pennsylvania, French as director of psychology education. French became a member of the board of trustees of the Devereux Foundation in 1954. Three years later he was made director of the foundation; in 1960 he became president and director.

French received his PhD in clinical psychology from the University of Pennsylvania in 1950. He co-authored *How You Can Help Your Retarded Child.* His chapter on the De-

## FRENCH, JOSEPH L. (1928–    )

Joseph L. French earned his BS (1949) and MS (1950) degrees from Illinois State University at Normal and his EdD (1957) in educational psychology and measurements from the University of Nebraska. He held faculty positions at Illinois State University at Normal, the University of Nebraska at Lincoln, University of Missouri at Columbia, and Penn State University (1964–1997). He is best known for his work with gifted children and those with physical disabilities. His *Pictorial Test of Intelligence* (French, 1964a), designed for use with children with cerebral palsy, has been translated to German, Italian, Korean, and Spanish, and an English variation has been used in Britain. He has authored several

Joseph L. French

chapters on testing exceptional children and on intellectual assessment.

French has also edited books on the gifted which have been widely used in graduate school classes across the United States and abroad. In 1959, he edited *Educating the Gifted,* a collection of articles on identifying and providing education and services for the gifted and creative. He has authored five chapters and numerous articles about the education of gifted children, including one article dealing with gifted high school dropouts that was read by Senator Jacob Javitts into the *Congressional Record.* In addition, French has had a long-standing interest in intelligence and its assessment (French & Murphy, 1985; Stavrou & French, 1992), and on issues in school psychology (French, 1984, 1985).

French's externally funded research focused on the transition of Head Start alumni through the primary grades, characteristics of high school dropouts of high ability, the effect of test item arrangement on physically measured stress in young children, and the reactions of high school students to televised teachers. He was an active member of the Council for Exceptional Children (CEC) and the American Psychological Association (APA). He served as president of the Association for the Gifted in 1969, was a member of the CEC Research Committee from 1966 to 1969, and was on its Board of Governors from 1969 to 1972. His contributions to APA included serving as president of the Division of School Psychology (1976–1977), on the Council of Representatives (1984–1991), the Committee on Accreditation (1982–1985), and membership on several joint APA-National Association of School Psychologists committees.

French's numerous honors include the Certificate of Merit from The Association for the Gifted (1971), a Certificate of Recognition from the United States Office of Education (1976), a Paul Witty Fellowship (1979), the Distinguished Service Award from the APA Division of School Psycholo-

gists (1985), and the Award for Distinguished Contributions to the Science and Profession of Psychology from the Pennsylvania Psychological Association (1996). In 1998 he was named the Distinguished Alumnus of Illinois State University at Normal.

French is currently Professor Emeritus at Pennsylvania State University, and continues to be professionally active.

## REFERENCES

French, J. L. (1964a). *The Pictorial Test of Intelligence.* Boston: Houghton Mifflin.

French, L. (Ed.). (1964b). *Educating the gifted* (Rev. ed.). New York: Holt, Rinehart, & Winston.

French, J. L. (1984). On the conception, birth, and early development of school psychology, with special reference to Pennsylvania. *American Psychologist, 39,* 976–987.

French, J. L. (1985). An essay on becoming a school psychologist when school psychology was becoming. *Journal of School Psychology, 23,* 1–12.

French, J. L., & Murphy, J. (1985). Intelligence, its assessment and its role in the comprehensive evaluation. In J. R. Bergan (Ed.), *School psychology in contemporary society.* Columbus, OH: Merrill.

Stavrou, E., & French, J. F. (1992). The K-ABC and cognitive processing styles in autistic children. *Journal of School Psychology, 30,* 259–267.

ANN E. LUPKOWSKI
*Texas A&M University*
First edition

TAMARA J. MARTIN
*The University of Texas of the Permian Basin*
Second edition

## FREUD, ANNA (1895–1982)

Anna Freud was the youngest of Sigmund Freud's six children. She was educated at the Cottage Lyceum, and although an excellent student, left without a degree in 1912. Her father was her mentor in psychoanalytic theory and practice. Following the Nazi takeover of Austria, the family moved to London in 1938. Anna and her father remained professionally active and influential after their emigration. She was her father's devoted companion and associate until his death in 1939.

Anna Freud's many professional contributions resulted from her interest in applying psychoanalytic theory to the study of child development and in formulating and conducting psychotherapy appropriate to the special needs of young patients. Her work stimulated others, including

Erik Erikson, whose study of psychoanalysis she encouraged. Her theoretical contributions included elaborating and extending her father's concept of ego defense mechanisms, particularly displacement and identification. She wrote prolifically, producing more than 100 articles and many important books, including *Introduction to the Technique of Child Analysis* (1927), *Psychoanalysis for Teachers and Parents* (1931), *The Ego and the Mechanisms of Defense* (1936), and *Psychoanalytic Treatment of Children* (1946). She also edited the 24-volume edition of her father's works (1953–1956).

Her interest in promoting child psychoanalysis led her to found in 1947 a clinic and a serial publication, both of which are still active. The Hampstead Child-Therapy Course and Clinic in London treats children and trains psychoanalytic child therapists; *The Psychoanalytic Study of the Child* is a scholarly forum for theoreticians and practitioners.

Anna Freud received the highest professional recognition of her contemporaries in 1970 when she was named the most outstanding living child psychoanalyst. Other distinctions include awards, medals, and honorary degrees from Clark, Yale, Columbia, and Harvard universities, and an honorary MD in 1972 from the University of Vienna.

Because of Anna Freud's modest and private nature, frustratingly little is known about her personal and professional development (Jackson, 1982). However, a memorial section of Volume 39 of *The Psychoanalytic Study of the Child* (1984) includes five papers discussing her contributions to the fields of law, developmental psychology, politics, and training in child analysis.

### REFERENCE

Jackson, D. J. (1982). Psychology of the scientist: XLVI. Anna Freud. *Psychological Reports, 50,* 1191–1198.

PAULINE F. APPLEFIELD
*University of North Carolina at Wilmington*

## FREUD, SIGMUND (1856–1939)

Sigmund Freud, the founder of psychoanalysis, entered medical practice as a neurologist in Vienna in 1886. Psychoanalysis, developed out of Freud's clinical practice, revolutionized not only psychiatric treatment but man's view of himself. Freud introduced the concept of the unconscious mind and its influence on behavior. Free association and dream interpretation were developed as techniques for reaching the unconscious. Freud demonstrated the role of mental conflict in human development and identified the motivating forces of sexuality and aggression. He also identified the existence and importance of infantile sexuality, and

the influence of childhood development on adult behavior. After the annexation of Austria by Nazi Germany in 1938, Freud moved to London, where he resided until his death the following year.

### REFERENCES

Freud, S. (1933). *New introductory lectures on psycho-analysis.* New York: Norton.

Freud, S. (1970). *An outline of psychoanalysis.* New York: Norton.

Jones, E. (1953–1957). *The life and work of Sigmund Freud* (3 vols.). New York: Basic Books.

PAUL IRVINE
*Katonah, New York*

## FRIEDREICH'S ATAXIA

Friedreich's ataxia (FA) applies to a varied group of problems whose major symptoms usually appear in the late childhood or early adolescent years. The condition is generally transmitted along family lines through Mendelian inheritance as an autosomal recessive trait, though some cases of dominant mode transmission have been recognized. At the core of the disorder is progressive dysfunction of the spinal cord and cerebellum. Cardiac muscle fiber degeneration may also be present.

The early signs of FA are an increasing disturbance of normal gait followed by progressive loss of muscular coordination in the upper extremities and trunk. Skeletal anomalies such as club foot, hammer toes, and highly arched feet, along with scoliosis, may be present. Cardiac failure, enlargement of the heart (or arrhythmias), nystagmus of the eyes, optical nerve atrophy, tremors, dysarthria, and feeding disorders may be noted. Loss of sensation, especially in the feet, is common in this disorder, and the risk of development of seizure disorders is high. The diagnosis of FA is completely reliant on these clinical manifestations. Lab findings are generally of little assistance in diagnosis, except for cases where electrocardiogram changes indicating myocarditis are observed. Most individuals with FA become wheelchair-bound and eventually bedridden. There is no known cure for this disorder, with death from myocardial failure in childhood, adolescence, or early adulthood the usual result.

Friedreich's ataxia has been separated diagnostically from other similar disorders such as ataxia-telangiectasia, Roussy-Levy syndrome, and Bassen-Kornzweig syndrome.

### REFERENCES

Batshaw, M. L., & Perret, Y. M. (1981). *Children with handicaps: A medical primer.* Baltimore: Brookes.

Bleck, E. E., & Nagel, D. A. (1982). *Physically handicapped children: A medical atlas for teachers.* New York: Grune & Stratton.

Vaughan, V. C., McKay, R. J., & Behrman, R. E. (1979). *Nelson textbook of pediatrics.* Philadelphia: Saunders.

JOHN D. WILSON
*Elwyn Institutes*

**GAIT DISTURBANCES**
**GENETIC COUNSELING**

## FROSTIG, MARIANNE (1906–1985)

Born in Vienna, Austria, Marianne Frostig received a degree as a children's social worker from the College of Social Welfare, Vienna, Austria, in 1926. Several years later, she and her neuropsychiatrist husband worked in a psychiatric hospital in Poland before he accepted a position in the United States. When the Nazis invaded Poland, they killed everyone in the hospital. In the United States, Frostig earned the first BA ever issued by the New School for Social Research (1948). She received her MA (1940) from Claremont Graduate School and her PhD (1955) from the University of Southern California. She became ill and died while on a lecture tour in Germany.

Believing that every person is a unique individual who needs to be assessed and treated as such, Frostig was interested in finding the most appropriate education/treatment for each child. She thought that education should be adjusted to meet the needs of all children, especially those who, for various reasons, find learning difficult. To Frostig, a problem child is a child whose needs are not being met. *Education for Dignity* was intended to be a practical guide for the regular classroom teacher to meet those needs.

The Marianne Frostig Developmental Test of Visual Perception was the first test to segregate different visual abilities. Prior to this, all visual problems were grouped together. Frostig retired as director of the Marianne Frostig Center for Educational Therapy in 1972.

Marianne Frostig (right)

Frostig received the *Los Angeles Times* Woman of the Year Award and the Golden Key Award of the International Association for Children with Learning Disabilities. She has been included in *Who's Who of American Women, American Men and Women of Science,* and the *Dictionary of International Biography.*

### REFERENCES

Frostig, M. (1976). *Education for dignity.* New York: Grune & Stratton.

Frostig, M., Lefever, D. W., & Whittlesey, J. R. B. (1964). *The Marianne Frostig Developmental Test of Visual Perception* (3rd ed.). Palo Alto, CA: Consulting Psychologists.

E. VALERIE HEWITT
*Texas A&M University*

## FROSTIG REMEDIAL PROGRAM

The Frostig Program of Visual Perception, developed in 1964, is designed to train children who have visual problems in perceptual and motor skills. Using a series of workbooks and worksheets, the program focuses on five areas. First, eye motor coordination, which involves drawing lines in carefully prescribed boundaries. Second, figure-ground, in which the child finds hidden figures in distracting and overlapping backgrounds. Third, perceptual constancy; here the child learns to recognize that an object remains the same even if its shape or color changes. Fourth, position in space; in this part of the program the child discovers that figures and objects remain the same although they may occupy different positions. Often, the child is provided with a model, then given several other models and is asked to select the shape or design that is exactly like the original. The fifth area is spatial relationships; at this point the child develops skills in perceiving positional relationships between objects or points of reference such as the arrangement of material or figures on a printed page (Bannatyne, 1971; Hallahan & Kaufman, 1976).

The assumption underlying the Frostig program is that brain damage in children results in neurological disabilities giving rise to visual perceptual problems. This assumption, based on the seminal works of Goldstein, Strauss, Werner, and Cruickshank, concludes that manifestations of brain dysfunctions, usually perceptual problems, can occur even if no specific damage to the brain can be found (Hallahan & Kaufman, 1976). The Frostig program is one of several commercially developed training programs to aid learning-disabled children who exhibit perceptual deficiencies (Frostig & Maslow, 1973).

In conjunction with this program, the Frostig Developmental Test of Visual Perception was designed. This test purports to measure the five functions of visual perception and provides a means to compare children's performance with norms for their ages. The assumption on which the test is based, that visual perception is a critical element in school learning, has been questioned. Moreover, the effectiveness of the test and the Frostig training has not been documented. While the test itself provides an adequate measure of global perception of young children, its ability to assess specific areas of perceptual difficulty has not been shown. Mann (1978) cautions that a low score on the test should not be construed as a signal to begin a perceptual training program. In addition, he states that the test and its related training program has "stimulated wide and often injudicious programming for learning-disabled children" (p. 1276). Critics also have claimed that Frostig's names for traits are simply conjecture and the test and program both represent a psychometric era that has passed (Mitchell, 1985).

## REFERENCES

Bannatyne, A. (1971). *Language, reading and learning disabilities.* Springfield, IL: Thomas.

Frostig, M., & Maslow, P. (1973). *Learning problems in the classroom.* New York: Grune & Stratton.

Hallahan, D., & Kaufman, J. (1976). *Introduction to learning disabilities.* Englewood Cliffs, NJ: Prentice Hall.

Mann, L. (1978). Review of the Marianne Frostig developmental test of visual perception. In O. K. Buros (Ed.), *Mental measurements yearbook.* Highland Park, NJ: Gryphon.

Mitchell, J. V. (1985). *Ninth mental measurements yearbook.* Highland Park, NJ: Gryphon.

FORREST E. KEESBURY
*Lycoming College*

## DEVELOPMENTAL TEST OF VISUAL PERCEPTION–SECOND EDITION
## MOVIGENICS
## VISUAL-MOTOR AND VISUAL-PERCEPTUAL PROBLEMS
## VISUAL PERCEPTION AND DISCRIMINATION

## FUNCTIONAL ANALYSIS

Functional analysis is a term that describes a procedure involving the experimental manipulation of contextual variables which have been hypothesized to predict and/or maintain persistent problem behavior. Typically, these hypotheses are derived from indirect and/or direct functional assessments. Using functional analysis, teachers and researchers systematically identify functional relationships between environmental events (i.e., antecedents and consequences) and chronic or persistent problem behavior (Fowler & Schnacker, 1994; O'Neill et al., 1997). Alberto and Troutman (2006) write that the goal of a functional

analysis "is to examine the effect of each variable's presence, absence, heightening, or lessening" (p. 192). For example, the researcher might manipulate a number of conditions to verify the hypothesis that was derived from the functional assessment (e.g., alone condition, demand condition, attention condition, play condition). Upon demonstration of a functional relationship, interventions are developed and incorporated into a comprehensive behavior support plan for the person of concern (Mace, 1994; O'Neill et al., 1997; Wacker, Berg, Asmus, Harding, & Cooper, 1998).

Miltenberger (1998) outlines three features that need to be in place when conducting a functional analysis: (1) objective measurement of the problem behavior under experimental conditions, (2) demonstration of a change in the problem behavior following the systematic manipulation of antecedent and/or consequent events, and (3) systematic replication of the above process. Two different experimental designs are used to establish a functional relationship between environmental events and the problem behavior, these include the ABAB withdrawal design (e.g., no attention and attention phases or hard tasks and easy tasks phases) and the multi-element design (e.g., alone, demand, tangible, and attention conditions; Alberto & Troutman, 2006; O'Neill et al., 1997; Wolery, Bailey, & Sugai, 1988).

## REFERENCES

Alberto, P. A., & Troutman, A. C. (2006). *Applied behavior analysis for teachers* (7th ed.). Upper Saddle River, NJ: Prentice Hall.

Fowler, R. C., & Schnacker, L. E. (1994). The changing character of behavioral assessment and treatment: An historical introduction and review of functional analysis research. *Diagnostique, 19,* 79–102.

Mace, F. C. (1994). The significance and future of functional analysis methodologies. *The Journal of Applied Behavior Analysis, 27,* 385–392.

Miltenberger, R. G. (1998). Methods for assessing antecedent influences on challenging behaviors. In J. K. Luiselli & M. J. Cameron (Eds.), *Antecedent control: Innovative approaches to behavioral support* (pp. 47–65). Baltimore: Paul H. Brooks.

O'Neill, R. E., Horner, R. H., Albin, R. W., Sprague, J. R., Storey, K., & Newton, J. S. (1997). *Functional assessment and program development for problem behavior: A practical handbook* (2nd ed.). Pacific Grove, CA: Brooks/Cole.

Wacker, D. P., Berg, W. K., Asmus, J. M., Harding, J. K., & Cooper, L. J. (1998). Experimental analysis of antecedent influences on challenging behaviors. In J. K. Luiselli & M. J. Cameron (Eds.), *Antecedent control: Innovative approaches to behavioral support* (pp. 67–86). Baltimore: Paul H. Brooks.

Wolery, M., Bailey, D., Jr., & Sugai, G. (1988). *Effective teaching: Principles and procedures of applied behavior analysis with exceptional students.* Boston: Allyn & Bacon.

RANDALL L. DE PRY
*University of Colorado at*
*Colorado Springs*

**BEHAVIORAL ASSESSMENT**
**FUNCTIONAL ASSESSMENT**

## FUNCTIONAL ASSESSMENT

Functional assessment (FA) is a term that describes a process for gathering information about the factors that predict and/or maintain chronic or persistent problem behavior. Data from functional assessments are used to develop and implement comprehensive behavior support plans, including data of any setting events, immediate antecedents, and consequent events that are hypothesized to maintain the problem behavior. The behavior support plan delineates environmental modifications, curricular adaptations, and instructional strategies for teaching replacement responses that serve the same function of the problem behavior, but are more socially acceptable given the individual's home, school, and work environments. These modifications and strategies are increasingly being applied as part of a systemic change model of proactive school-wide discipline and are often referred to as positive behavioral supports (PBS; Sugai, Horner, Dunlap, Hieneman, Lewis, Nelson et al., 2000).

Historically, educators have created behavioral interventions that were based on the topography of the problem behavior, that is, how the behavior is performed. For example, students who destroy workbooks, tear up assignments, and carve holes in their desks are all damaging school property. Typically, each student receives consequences that are designed to reduce the problem behavior, such as a time-out, in-school suspension, or a response cost procedure. While many topographically-based interventions are effective in the short term, they do not teach the student positive alternative responses and may fail to generalize to other persons or places (Lewis, Scott, & Sugai, 1994; Wolery, Bailey, & Sugai, 1988). However, a closer examination of the students' behaviors using functional assessment techniques might reveal that the first student engages in the problem behavior because she is late for school and misses her breakfast several times per week, the second student engages in the problem behavior because he has learned to escape or avoid difficult academic tasks by tearing up his assignments, and the third student engages in the problem behavior because she has learned that damaging school property is an effective way of getting peer attention. By understanding the underlying purpose or function of the problem behavior, educators can collaboratively create behavior support plans that are based on functional assessment data and more effective than standard behavior reduction techniques that are topographically based.

O'Neill, Horner, Albin, Sprague, Storey, and Newton (1997) suggest that problem behavior is maintained by getting or obtaining events that are desirable and/or escaping and avoiding events that are undesirable. Examples of desirable conditions include socially mediated conditions such as getting or obtaining attention, access to desired items, access to tangibles, and behaviors that allow a person to get or obtain sensory stimulation (e.g., visual or tactile stimulation). Examples of undesirable conditions include escaping or avoiding socially mediated events such as attention, difficult or non-preferred activities, teacher requests or demands, and behaviors that allow a person to escape or avoid internal stimulation (e.g., pain, voices, hunger).

O'Neill et al. (1997) conclude that all functional assessments should include the following features: (a) an operational definition of the problem behavior; (b) an identification of any events, persons, times, or situations that predict when the problem behavior occurs and when the problem behavior does not occur; (c) identification of the consequences that maintain the problem behavior; (d) summary or hypothesis statements that include any setting events, predictors, and maintaining consequences; and (e) direct observation data that supports the summary statements. A comprehensive functional assessment includes both indirect and direct methods for gathering information about the contextual features of the problem behavior. Indirect methods involve persons who are familiar with the student (e.g., teacher, parent, caregiver, paraprofessional) and incorporate interviews, behavioral rating scales, and questionnaires. Direct observation methods incorporate the use of systematic direct observation techniques that are conducted in environments where the problem behavior occurs and other environments when feasible. Data from indirect and direct functional assessment procedures are used to develop behavior support plans.

Indirect functional assessments that are summarized below include the *Functional Assessment Interview* (O'Neill et al., 1997), the *Student-Directed Functional Assessment Interview* (O'Neill et al., 1997), the *Student-Assisted Functional Assessment Interview* (Kern, Dunlap, Clarke, & Childs, 1994), the *Motivation Assessment Scale* (Durand & Crimmins, 1988), and the *Problem Behavior Questionnaire* (Lewis et al., 1994). Direct functional assessment instruments that are summarized below include *A-B-C Assessment* (Bijou, Peterson, & Ault, 1968), and the *Functional Assessment Observation Form* (O'Neill et al., 1997).

The *Functional Assessment Interview* (O'Neill et al., 1997) is a structured interview that includes the following categories: (a) operational definitions of the behaviors of concern; (b) questions related to setting events that predict or set up the problem behaviors; (c) questions related to antecedents that predict when the behaviors are likely and not likely to occur; (d) questions related to consequences that maintain the problem behavior; (e) a description of the efficiency of the problem behavior; (f) descriptions of alternative behaviors that the person already knows; (g) questions related to the communicative abilities of the person; (h) questions related to known ways of supporting the person; (i) descriptions of what the person finds reinforcing; and (j) descriptions of programs that have been tried in the past and the effect that these interventions have had on the person's behavior. According to the authors, the *Functional Assessment Interview* can take up to 90 minutes to complete. Upon completion of the interview, summary statements are collaboratively created that describe any setting events, antecedents, the problem behavior, and maintaining consequences that were notable from the interview.

*Student-Directed Functional Assessment Interview* (O'Neill et al., 1997) is an interview that is designed to be given by a person who has a positive relationship with the student. The interview takes up to 40 minutes to complete and includes student-generated responses regarding (1) any behaviors of concern; (2) completion of a schedule analysis where the student indicates the times and places where problem behaviors are least likely and most likely to occur; and (3) the creation of summary statements that diagram what was learned during the interview and possible interventions.

*Student-Assisted Functional Assessment Interview* (Kern et al., 1994) is comprised of four sections and takes up to 30 minutes to complete. Section I consists of 12 closed-ended questions regarding potential functions of the student's problem behavior. Each question allows the student to respond using one of three options (e.g., "always," "sometimes," and "never"). Section II consists of seven open-ended questions that solicit information about when and where the target behavior is likely to occur. Section III lists academic subject areas and asks the student to rate how much he/she likes each subject using a Likert type scale. Section IV consists of 22 questions that ask what the student likes and dislikes about selected subjects in school.

*Motivation Assessment Scale* (Durand & Crimmins, 1988) is a 16-question rating scale that is designed to provide data on four functions (motivations) of problem behavior (e.g., attention, escape, tangibles, and self-stimulation). The instrument has four questions for each of the targeted functions. Upon completion of the *Motivation Assessment Scale,* the educator sums the responses and calculates the mean score and relative ranking for each category.

The *Problem Behavior Questionnaire* (Lewis et al., 1994) is an instrument that includes 15 questions that are correlated with five potential maintaining variables and a series of open-ended questions that allow the respondent to provide data on how often the behavior occurs, where the behavior occurs, relationship of the problem behavior to an academic skills deficit, and the like. The maintaining variables assessed in the *Problem Behavior Questionnaire* include: (1) access to peer attention, (2) access to teacher attention, (3) escape or avoidance of peer attention, (4) escape or avoidance of teacher attention, and (5) setting events.

*A-B-C Assessment* (Bijou et al., 1968) is a direct observation procedure that involves the descriptive analysis of environmental events that are recorded anecdotally over a speci-

fied period of time. Direct observation data is collected and recorded on the antecedent-behavior-consequence relations that occur over multiple observation periods (Blakeslee, Sugai, & Gruba, 1994). From this data, educators are able to identify antecedent events that precede problem behavior and consequence events that occur in response to the problem behavior. Data collected over time can provide the behavior support team with important information about possible functional relationships between the environment and the student's problem behavior (Wolery et al., 1988). Guidelines for using *A-B-C Assessment* include: (a) only recording the targeted students observable behavior (avoid interpretation), (b) recording what happened before the targeted student's behavior (antecedents), (c) recording what happened after the targeted student's behavior (consequences), and (d) conducting multiple observations before developing summary statements (Alberto & Troutman, 1999; Cooper, Heron, & Heward, 1987).

*Functional Assessment Observation Form* (FAO; O'Neill et al., 1997) is a direct observation instrument that is used to collect data across settings and over time. O'Neill et al. write that "the FAO documents the predictor events and consequences associated with instances of problem behavior. The form is organized around problem behavior events. An event is different from a single occurrence of a problem behavior. An event includes all the problem behavior in an incident that begins with a problem behavior and ends only after 3 minutes of no problem behavior" (p. 37). The FAO form allows the observer to indicate which problem behaviors (events) were observed, any predictors or immediate antecedents that were observed, and the perceived function the behavior served for the individual. Additional sections are available for indicating the actual consequences the person received and any observer comments that may add to understanding the problem behavior.

The inclusion of functional assessment requirements in the 1997 reauthorization of the Individuals with Disabilities Education Act (IDEA) provides a unique opportunity for all educators to improve current policies, programs, and practices for children and youth with chronic or persistent problem behavior. In particular, IDEA now requires that the FA is used to gather information on the function or purpose of the problem behavior and develop a plan of behavior support for students who engage in chronic or persistent problem behavior and may need a change of placement. IDEA mandates that the FA results in the use of positive behavior interventions and supports which help the student directly and address the problem behavior (Quinn, Osher, Warger, Hanley, Bader, & Hoffman, 2000). Tilly et al. (1998) indicate that this requirement provides the team with useful information, including why the student engages in persistent problem behavior, when the student is least and most likely to engage in the behavior, and summary statements that guide the team as it collaboratively develops strategies that can be used to teach the student more appropriate responses as part of their comprehensive plan of behavior support (Sugai & Horner, 1994). In addition, the use of a student-directed functional assessment and student-directed behavior support planning process allows students to participate in their assessment and planning process which promotes self-determination and participatory decision making (Martin, Marshall, & De Pry, 2005).

## REFERENCES

Alberto, P. A., & Troutman, A. C. (1999). *Applied behavior analysis for teachers* (5th ed.). Upper Saddle River, NJ: Merrill.

Bijou, S. W., Peterson, R. F., & Ault, M. H. (1968). A method to integrate descriptive and experimental field studies at the level of data and empirical concepts. *Journal of Applied Behavior Analysis, 1,* 175–191.

Blakeslee, T., Sugai, G., & Gruba, J. (1994). A review of functional assessment use in data-based intervention studies. *Journal of Behavioral Education, 4,* 397–413.

Cooper, J. O., Heron, T. E., & Heward, W. L. (1987). *Applied behavior analysis.* New York: Macmillan.

Durand, V. M., & Crimmins, D. (1988). Identifying variables maintaining self-injurious behavior. *Journal of Autism and Developmental Disorders, 18,* 99–117.

Lewis, T. J., Scott, T. M., & Sugai, G. (1994). The problem behavior questionnaire: A teacher-based instrument to develop functional hypotheses of problem behavior in general education settings. *Diagnostique, 19,* 103–115.

Kern, L., Dunlap, G., Clarke, S., & Childs, K. E. (1994). Student-assisted functional assessment interview. *Diagnostique, 19,* 29–39.

Martin, J. E., Marshall, L. H., & De Pry, R. L. (2005). Participatory decision-making: Innovative practices that increase student self-determination. In R. W. Flexer, T. J. Simmons, P. Luft, & R. Baer (Eds.), *Transition planning for secondary students with disabilities* (2nd ed., pp. 246–275). Columbus: Merrill.

O'Neill, R. E., Horner, R. H., Albin, R. W., Sprague, J. R., Storey, K., & Newton, J. S. (1997). *Functional assessment and program development for problem behavior: A practical handbook* (2nd ed.). Pacific Grove, CA: Brooks/Cole.

Quinn, M. M., Osher, D., Warger, C. L., Hanley, T. V., Bader, B. D., & Hoffman, C. C. (2000). *Teaching and working with children who have emotional and behavioral challenges.* Longmont, CO: Sopris West Educational Services.

Sugai, G., & Horner, R. (1994). Including students with severe behavior problems in general education settings: Assumptions, challenges, and solutions. In J. Marr, G. Sugai, & G. Tindal (Eds.), *The Oregon Conference Monograph* (pp. 102–120). Eugene: University of Oregon.

Sugai, G., Horner, R. H., Dunlap, G., Hieneman, M., Lewis, T. J., Nelson, C. M., et al. (2000). Applying positive behavior support and functional behavioral assessment in schools. *Journal of Positive Behavior Interventions, 2,* 131–143.

Tilly, W. D., III, Kovaleski, J., Dunlap, G., Knoster, T. P., Bambara, L., & Kincaid, D. (1998). *Functional behavioral assessment: Policy development in light of emerging research and practice.* Alexandria, VA: National Association of State Directors of Special Education.

Wolery, M., Bailey, D., Jr., & Sugai, G. (1988). *Effective teaching: Principles and procedures of applied behavior analysis with exceptional students.* Boston: Allyn & Bacon.

RANDALL L. DE PRY
*University of Colorado at
Colorado Springs*

**APPLIED BEHAVIOR ANALYSIS**
**BEHAVIORAL ASSESSMENT**
**FUNCTIONAL ANALYSIS**

## FUNCTIONAL CENTERS HYPOTHESIS

The functional centers hypothesis, the Soviet view of learning disorders expounded by and associated primarily with Vygotsky and Luria, was further investigated and supported by other researchers in the Soviet Union (Holowinsky, 1976). It is based on Pavlovian psychology and on the dialectical-materialistic interpretation of human behavior: behavior, that is, on the elementary and higher levels, the product of phylogenetic, ontogenetic, and sociohistorical influences.

Central to the understanding of the hypothesis is the notion that an individual's mental functions (i.e., attention, memory, perception, thinking) are not only adaptive and acquired, but also are localized in and mediated by areas of cerebral cortex centers. Speech problems, language disorders, learning dysfunctions, and other handicaps are related to such centers but have psychoneurological etiologies. However, the functions "as complex functional systems with dynamic levels of localization in the brain" (Luria, 1980) are differentially related to various areas of the brain that are themselves highly differentiated in their structure. Mental functions are not, therefore, totally localized in particular/isolated areas of the brain (e.g., neuron, cortex), but operate as systems of functional combination centers. Localization in the Lurian brain for higher cortical function is dynamic, not static (Reynolds, 1981).

Mental functions appear in the developmental process first in elementary form as a result of natural development (determined by environmental stimulation). They then are changed primarily because of cultural development and self-regulated stimulation by the individual into a higher form (Vygotsky, 1978). Vygotsky considered voluntary control, conscious realization, social origins and nature, and mediation by psychological tools as characteristics of higher mental functioning (Wertsch, 1985). The development of speech is crucial because it provides new tools and signs that on mastery will clarify the operations of mental functioning to the individual.

Society plays a preeminent role in human development and functioning. In fact, higher mental functions (e.g., abstract thought, voluntary action) are formed during everyday activities. In a social context, they enable individuals to use a high level of organization, find new ways of regulating behavior, and establish new functional systems (Luria, 1978). Thus human beings can develop extracerebral connections and have the capacity to form numerous new functional systems and new functional centers in the cerebral cortex.

As a function is "a complex and plastic system performing a particular adaptive task and composed of a highly differentiated group of interchangeable elements" (Luria, 1980, p. 24), damage to any part of the cortical area can lead to a disintegration of the functional system. However, such a disturbance is likely to differ depending on the factors and on the role each part of the brain plays in the organization of the system during different stages of functional development (early or late).

In treating the learning disabled and mentally handicapped, the practitioner operates on the premise that a mental function may be performed by one of several intercenter connections in the functional centers. If one such connection is damaged—the damage or loss is not permanent—another system or cortical function can be trained to compensate for the deficit and take over the lost function. Thus restoring the disturbed or disorganized function is merely reorganizing that function and forming a new functional system.

## REFERENCES

Holowinsky, I. Z. (1976). Functional centers hypothesis: The Soviet view of learning dysfunctions. In L. Mann & D. A. Sabatino (Eds.), *The third review of special education* (pp. 53–69). New York: Grune & Stratton.

Luria, A. R. (1978). L. S. Vygotsky and the problem of functional localization. In M. Cole (Ed.), *The selected writings of A. R. Luria* (pp. 273–281). White Plains, NY: Sharpe.

Luria, A. R. (1980). *Higher cortical functions in man* (2nd ed.) (B. Haigh, Trans.). New York: Basic Books. (Original work published 1962)

Reynolds, C. R. (1981). The neuropsychological basis of intelligence. In G. W. Hynd & J. E. Obrzut (Eds.), *Neuropsychological assessment and the school-aged child: Issues and procedures.* New York: Grune & Stratton.

Vygotsky, L. S. (1978). *Mind in society: The development of higher mental processes.* Cambridge, MA: Harvard University Press.

Wertsch, J. V. (1985). *Vygotsky and the social formation of mind.* Cambridge, MA: Harvard University Press.

HAGOP S. PAMBOOKIAN
*Elizabeth City, North Carolina*

**LURIA, A. R.**
**THEORY OF ACTIVITY**
**ZONE OF PROXIMAL DEVELOPMENT**

# FUNCTIONAL COMMUNICATION TRAINING

Functional Communication Training (FCT) is an intervention approach in which individuals with problem behavior are taught specific communicative responses that undermine the necessity for future displays of their problem behavior. In illustration, consider a young girl who tantrums to get her mother's attention. The child would be taught specific communicative phrases (e.g., "Look what I drew!") as an alternative way of securing her mother's attention. When Mom responds to these communicative attempts, tantrums decrease. Functional Communication Training highlights an important paradox relevant to effective intervention for problem behavior, namely, that the best time to treat problem behavior is when it is not occurring. Thus, the teaching of communication skills occurs at a time when the child is calm and not displaying problem behavior. Because FCT is proactive in nature (i.e., focused on prevention), emphasizes an educational (i.e., skill-building) approach to behavior difficulties, and is designed to enhance an individual's quality of life, it is a prime example of what has come to be known in the literature as Positive Behavior Support (Carr et al., 2002). Since FCT was first introduced into the scientific literature (Carr & Durand, 1985), there have been more than 100 studies published demonstrating its efficacy and effectiveness as a method for reducing or eliminating problem behavior.

## Background

The conceptual origins of FCT are ancient. Writing in 348 BC, the Greek philosopher, Plato, noted that problem behavior, such as that of a young child crying and screaming, could be viewed as a primitive form of communication. Caregivers attempt to quell the behavior by trying to guess what the child wants: ". . . if the child is quiet when something is offered it, she (the caregiver) thinks she has found the right thing, but the wrong if it cries and screams" (Plato, c. 348 BC/1960, p. 174). The French philosopher, Rousseau, went one step further than Plato and suggested that teaching children to communicate verbally might ameliorate their problem behavior: "When children begin to speak, they cry less . . . as soon as they can say with words . . . why would they say it with cries?" (Rousseau, 1762/1979, p. 77).

More recently, psycholinguists have demonstrated that children communicate long before they can speak (Bates, Camaioni, & Volterra, 1975). Protoimperatives, that is, nonverbal prelinguistic communicative forms are an effective means by which young children influence adults. Importantly, some child psychologists (Bell & Ainsworth, 1972; Brownlee & Bakeman, 1981) have suggested that protoimperatives may take the form of crying and aggression and can serve as a primitive form of communication. Taken together, the literature in philosophy, psycholinguistics, and child psychology suggests the usefulness of viewing problem behavior as a primitive form of communication that might be remediated by teaching the child more sophisticated forms of communication.

## Variables Influencing the Effectiveness of FCT

### Functional equivalence

What communicative responses should be taught to maximize the likelihood of reducing problem behavior? The answer to this question is the sine qua non of effective use of FCT. Specifically, the communicative response taught should be *functionally equivalent* to the problem behavior that it is intended to replace (Carr, 1988). In lay language, both the communicative act and the problem behavior should serve the same purpose (i.e., have the same function) for the individual. Problem behavior can have many functions and these can be identified through a process known as functional assessment. Functional assessment involves systematically observing and/or manipulating the antecedents and consequences for problem behavior and noting which sets of these variables produce orderly changes in the level of the behavior. From such assessments, many variables (functions) have been identified. These include getting attention from others, escaping/avoiding aversive situations, terminating unwanted social interactions, enhancing access to tangible items (e.g., food, toys) or events (e.g., favorite activities), and generating desired sensory stimulation (Carr, 1994).

Functional assessment information is then used to select appropriate communicative alternatives to problem behavior. In illustration, a young boy might be found to become intermittently aggressive when his teacher asks him to do difficult math problems, but not any other task. The aggressive behavior causes the teacher to withdraw the math demands. This assessment information suggests that aggressive behavior might function to help the boy to escape from an aversive situation (i.e., having to do math). In this case, the boy would be taught to request assistance (i.e., "I can't do these problems. Please help me."). The communicative phrase has the same function as the problem behavior—both help the child to reduce the aversiveness associated with mathematics tasks. In other words, the two responses are functionally equivalent. If a communicative phrase were taught that had a different function, for example, attention seeking (e.g., the boy was taught to say, "Look at all my nice math work"), the two responses would not be equivalent and data suggest that aggressive behavior would likely persist (Carr & Durand, 1985). Functional equivalence is necessary for FCT to be effective.

### Efficiency

Functional equivalence is a necessary but insufficient condition for FCT to succeed. It is also necessary for the com-

municative response to be more *efficient* than the problem behavior it is intended to replace. The replacement response should require less effort, provide a richer schedule of reinforcement, and pay off (i.e., be reinforced) more rapidly than the problem behavior (Horner & Day, 1991). Consider the earlier example of the boy who was taught to say, "I can't do these problems" in response to a math assignment. Suppose the boy had severe articulation difficulties due to cerebral palsy. It might require substantial physical effort on his part to utter the sentence. Also, if others could not understand him, then they might respond to his request rarely if at all (i.e., thin schedule of reinforcement). Finally, it might take others some time to ascertain what he was trying to communicate as they repeatedly asked him to clarify what he was trying to say. Therefore, there would be a considerable delay of reinforcement. In this situation, the communicative response is far less efficient than the problem behavior, and the problem behavior would likely persist. On the other hand, if a different, more efficient communicative response were taught (e.g., the use of a communication device to produce the sentence), then problem behavior would likely decrease.

### Multicomponent intervention

In complex, natural settings such as the home, school, community, and workplace, problem behavior is typically under the control of multiple variables and serves multiple functions. Therefore, no single intervention, including FCT, is likely to be effective. Instead, best practice, based on available research evidence, strongly suggests the desirability and necessity of combining FCT with other interventions to produce a multicomponent package. Thus, if a child's problem behavior is motivated by escape from certain tasks, FCT may be combined with opportunities for the child to choose among a variety of similar tasks, some of which may be preferred (choice-making). If a child has trouble waiting for reinforcement after appropriately communicating, FCT may be combined with procedures that help the child bridge the time gap between the appropriate behavior and the reinforcing consequences (building tolerance for delay of reinforcement). If a child finds a specific task highly aversive, the teacher or parent may combine FCT with procedures that embed the aversive tasks among a variety of preferred tasks (embedding/interspersal/behavior momentum). If it appears that the child is continuing to receive reinforcement for problem behavior after FCT has been introduced, then FCT may be combined with procedures that ensure that such reinforcement is no longer forthcoming (extinction).

By combining FCT with the procedures just described plus many others that have been identified in the research literature, meaningful reductions in problem behavior can often be produced, even in complex natural settings (Carr & Carlson, 1993; Carr, Levin et al., 1999; Carr, Smith, Giacin, Whelan, & Pancari, 2003; Kemp & Carr, 1995).

## Generalization and Maintenance

There is good evidence that the positive effects of FCT can transfer from the original training situation to new situations in which training has not occurred (generalization). There is also good evidence that once FCT effects have been established, they can be quite durable over time (maintenance).

With respect to generalization, Durand and Carr (1991) demonstrated that, after several teachers had successfully implemented FCT across a number of tasks and settings (a strategy known as multiple exemplar training), increases in appropriate communication as well as dramatic reductions in problem behavior were observed across new tasks, environments, and teachers. One explanation for this successful transfer of effects was that the students used their communication skills to recruit relevant reinforcers from new teachers in new situations, thereby undermining the necessity for displaying problem behavior to acquire these reinforcers in the new situations.

With respect to maintenance, Durand and Carr (1991, 1992) demonstrated that reductions in problem behavior following FCT were durable and could be maintained for 18 to 24 months after introduction of the procedure. In a six-year study that used a multicomponent intervention emphasizing FCT, Carr et al. (1999) demonstrated that the procedure could produce substantial reductions in problem behavior lasting up to 2.5 years and engendered improvements in quality of life (enhanced community integration) for the participants involved. Maintenance effects likely result from the fact that, once an individual has acquired an effective communicative repertoire to meet his/her needs (i.e., access relevant reinforcers), the continued necessity for problem behavior is undermined, and, therefore, the behavior remains infrequent over time.

## Generality

Evidence exists that FCT has considerable generality with respect to behavioral topographies, behavioral functions, communicative forms, chronological age, applicable venues, and type of population (Carr, Horner et al., 1999; Doss & Reichle, 1989; Dyer, 1993). Clinically significant behavioral topographies that have been successfully treated include aggression, self-injury, property destruction, tantrums, self-stimulation, and noncompliance/disruptive behavior. Major functions addressed include attention, task avoidance, social avoidance, and tangible/activity seeking. Further, although the communicative form most commonly taught has been verbal in nature (speech), FCT has also been used successfully when the form taught involved sign language, picture cards, gestures, and microswitches. Importantly, the procedure has been applied to individuals ranging in age from preschool to middle age. In addition, applicable venues have included home, school, community, and the workplace. Finally, many populations have benefited from FCT, namely, individuals exhibiting a variety of types of mental retardation, Autism Spectrum Disorders (ASD), and Emotional and Behavioral Disorders (EBD).

## Limitations

Given that the use of FCT is predicated on the assumption that problem behavior has a social-communicative function, the procedure is likely inappropriate when it is suspected that the behavior is being controlled primarily by biochemical and/or neurological factors such as those involving genetics, brain dysfunction, or hormonal processes (Schroeder, Oster-Granite, & Thompson, 2002). While it is important to be aware of this potential limitation, it is equally important not to routinely assume that difficult problem behavior that has been unresponsive to prior behavioral/psychoeducational intervention is biologically based and will therefore not respond to FCT, particularly when FCT is embedded in a multicomponent intervention.

## Available Resources

The multifactorial nature of problem behavior and its treatment through FCT pose considerable assessment and intervention challenges. However, manuals are available to help the teacher, parent, and service provider to implement FCT in an organized, systematic, and effective manner (Carr et al., 1994; Durand, 1990). These resources, as well as the numerous references previously cited, help ensure the continued viability of this widely used strategy for dealing with serious problem behavior.

### REFERENCES

Bates, E., Camaioni, L., & Volterra, V. (1975). The acquisition of performatives prior to speech. *Merrill-Palmer Quarterly, 21,* 205–226.

Bell, S. M., & Ainsworth, M. D. S. (1972). Infant crying and maternal responsiveness. *Child Development, 43,* 1171–1190.

Brownlee, J. R., & Bakeman, R. (1981). Hitting in toddler-peer interaction. *Child Development, 52,* 1076–1079.

Carr, E. G. (1988). Functional equivalence as a mechanism of response generalization. In R. Horner, R. L. Koegel, & G. Dunlap (Eds.), *Generalization and maintenance: Life-style changes in applied settings* (pp. 194–219). Baltimore: Paul H. Brookes.

Carr, E. G. (1994). Emerging themes in the functional analysis of problem behavior. *Journal of Applied Behavior Analysis, 27,* 393–399.

Carr, E. G., & Carlson, J. I. (1993). Reduction of severe behavior problems in the community using a multicomponent treatment approach. *Journal of Applied Behavior Analysis, 26,* 157–172.

Carr, E. G., Dunlap, G., Horner, R. H., Koegel, R. L., Turnbull, A. P., Sailor, W., Anderson, J., Albin, R. W., Koegel, L. K., & Fox, L. (2002). Positive behavior support: Evolution of an applied science. *Journal of Positive Behavior Interventions, 4,* 4–16, 20.

Carr, E. G., & Durand, V. M. (1985). Reducing behavior problems through functional communication training. *Journal of Applied Behavior Analysis, 18,* 111–126.

Carr, E. G., Horner, R. H., Turnbull, A. P., Marquis, J. G., Magito McLaughlin, D., McAtee, M. L., Smith, C. E., Anderson Ryan, K., Ruef, M. B., & Doolabh, A. (1999). *Positive behavior support for people with developmental disabilities: A research synthesis.* Washington, DC: American Association on Mental Retardation.

Carr, E. G., Levin, L., McConnachie, G., Carlson, J. I., Kemp, D. C., & Smith, C. E. (1994). *Communication-based intervention for problem behavior: A user's guide for producing positive change.* Baltimore: Paul H. Brookes.

Carr, E. G., Levin, L., McConnachie, G., Carlson, J. I., Kemp, D. C., Smith, C. E., & Magito McLaughlin, D. (1999). Comprehensive multisituational intervention for problem behavior in the community: Long-term maintenance and social validation. *Journal of Positive Behavior Interventions, 1,* 5–25.

Carr, E. G., & Smith, C. E., Giacin, T. A., Whelan, B. M., & Pancari, J. (2003). Menstrual discomfort as a biological setting event for severe problem behavior: Assessment and intervention. *American Journal on Mental Retardation, 108,* 117–133.

Doss, S., & Reichle, J. (1989). Establishing communicative alternatives to the emission of socially motivated excess behavior: A review. *Journal of the Association for Persons with Severe Handicaps, 14,* 101–112.

Durand, V. M. (1990). *Functional communication training: An intervention program for severe behavior problems.* New York: Guilford.

Durand, V. M., & Carr, E. G. (1991). Functional communication training to reduce challenging behavior: Maintenance and application in new settings. *Journal of Applied Behavior Analysis, 24,* 251–264.

Durand, V. M., & Carr, E. G. (1992). An analysis of maintenance following functional communication training. *Journal of Applied Behavior Analysis, 25,* 777–794.

Dyer, K. (1993). Functional communication training: Review and future directions. *The Behavior Therapist, 16*(1), 18–21.

Horner, R. H., & Day, H. M. (1991). The effects of response efficiency on functionally equivalent competing behavior. *Journal of Applied Behavior Analysis, 24,* 719–732.

Kemp, D. C., & Carr, E. G. (1995). Reduction of severe problem behavior in community employment using an hypothesis-driven multicomponent intervention approach. *Journal of the Association for Persons with Severe Handicaps, 20,* 229–247.

Plato. (1960). *The laws* (A. E. Taylor, Trans.). London: J. M. Dent. (Original work published circa 348 BC)

Rousseau, J. J. (1979). *Emile.* (A. Bloom, Trans.). New York: Basic Books. (Original work published 1762)

Schroeder, S. R., Oster-Granite, M. L., & Thompson, T. (2002). (Eds.). *Self-injurious behavior: Gene-brain-behavior relationships.* Washington, DC: American Psychological Association.

EDWARD G. CARR
*State University of New York at Stony Brook*

BEHAVIORAL ASSESSMENT
POSITIVE BEHAVIORAL SUPPORT

# FUNCTIONAL DOMAINS

Educators, psychologists, and other health professionals will often assess and describe a child's performance in a number of areas, called functional domains, in addition to describing the child's overall performance and development in a global fashion. Theoretically, an assessment of the child's strengths and weaknesses in the various domains gives a snapshot of the child's functional status or the child's performance and ability to do things most other children do. Functional status is closely related to the concept of health status in the health field (Starfield, 1974; Stein & Jessop, 1984) and to the concept of social competence in the early childhood field (Zigler & Trickett, 1978).

Although typologies for the number and name of the functional domains vary, they generally are divided into four major areas: physical, cognitive, social, and emotional. Sometimes, the social and emotional areas are considered together and called psychological or mental health. The key to assessments in all functional domains is that behavior should be seen in a developmental context or framework so that the dynamic qualities of a child's development are considered (Walker, Richmond, & Buka, 1984).

Examples of behaviors or constructs that might be assessed under each functional domain are the physical (height and weight, activities of daily living); cognitive (intelligence, learning style); social (peer relationships, leadership skills); and emotional (self-concept, depression).

Because the measurements of these domains have been shown to be distinct, it is strongly recommended that researchers and practitioners do not try to combine the individual functional domain measures into an overall index or measure score (Eisen, Donald, Ware, & Brook, 1980). Instead, a profile approach to the child's performance and functioning in terms of his or her strengths and liabilities in the various functional areas is preferred (Starfield, 1974). Assessments of a child's performance in various functional domain areas are much easier to translate directly into educational and other service programs for the individual child than more generic global index scores. This profile or multidimensional approach is recommended for both individual and group or population descriptions.

## REFERENCES

Eisen, M., Donald, C. A., Ware, J. E., & Brook, R. H. (1980). *Conceptualization and measurement of health for children in the health insurance study.* Santa Monica, CA: Rand.

Starfield, B. (1974). Measurement of outcome: A proposed scheme. *Millbank Memorial Fund Quarterly, 52,* 39–50.

Stein, R. E. K., & Jessop, D. J. (1984). Assessing the functional status of children. In D. K. Walker & J. B. Richmond (Eds.), *Monitoring child health in the United States.* Cambridge, MA: Harvard University Press.

Walker, D. K., Richmond, J. B., & Buka, S. L. (1984). Summary and recommendations for next steps. In D. K. Walker & J. B. Richmond (Eds.), *Monitoring child health in the United States.* Cambridge, MA: Harvard University Press.

Zigler, E. F., & Trickett, D. K. (1978). IQ, social competence and evaluation of early childhood intervention programs. *American Psychologist, 33,* 789–798.

DEBORAH KLEIN WALKER
*Harvard University*

ADAPTIVE BEHAVIOR
INTELLIGENCE
MENTAL STATUS EXAMS

# FUNCTIONAL EQUIVALENCE

Functional equivalence has been defined and used in a variety of ways in fields such as psychology and general and special education (Sidman, 1994). This entry will discuss the term as it has been used in relation to problem behaviors of students with disabilities (Horner & Billingsley, 1988).

The term is typically used in reference to situations in which students are exhibiting problem behaviors, including aggression toward others, self-injurious behavior (e.g., head-hitting), destruction of materials, and other disruptive behaviors (e.g., talking out in the classroom). Over the last several decades, a variety of successful approaches has been developed for intervening in such situations (Scotti & Meyer, 1999). One such approach involves teaching and/or prompting a student to engage in a desired appropriate behavior that is *functionally equivalent* to the problem behavior (Carr, 1988). This means that the appropriate behavior allows the student to access the same outcomes that are reinforcing and maintaining the problem behaviors. Another way to say this is that both the problem and appropriate behaviors can serve the same *function* for the student with regard to accessing the desired outcome (e.g., to get social attention or to escape from an undesired task or activity). From a more technical perspective, one can say that both the problem and appropriate behaviors become part of the same *response class* (Horner & Day, 1990). A response class is a group of behaviors which may differ in how they are performed, but result in the same outcome (e.g., a student can either tantrum or raise their hand to recruit social attention from an adult).

This approach for reducing or eliminating problem behaviors by teaching and/or prompting functionally equivalent behaviors has been referred to by a variety of terms, including functional equivalence training (Horner et al., 1990), differential reinforcement of communication (DRC; Wacker & Steege, 1993), and most frequently, functional communication training (FCT; Carr & Durand, 1985; Durand, 1990). Other terms that have been used in the literature include teaching *alternative* or *replacement* behaviors. The FCT process involves two main steps. First, a functional behavioral assessment (FBA) must be carried out to determine the variables that are (a) triggering and (b) reinforcing and maintaining the problem behaviors (O'Neill et al., 1997). Second, a functionally equivalent appropriate behavior is taught to the student that s/he can use to obtain the same reinforcing outcomes as the problem behavior. (Note: If the desired alternative response is already in the student's repertoire the process becomes more a matter of prompting the student about when and where to exhibit the behavior, versus teaching an entirely new response.) The goal is for the desired alternative response to become functionally equivalent to the problem behavior, and thereby successfully compete with and replace it.

A brief example will illustrate this approach. Horner, Sprague, O'Brien, and Heathfield (1990) reported a study involving David, a 14-year-old student with physical disabilities who had been labeled as having moderate mental retardation. David did not use speech, and his physical limitations made manual signing difficult. He used a Canon Communicator device to type out messages to communicate his wants and needs. However, he often had difficulty manipulating the keys on the device. During difficult task activities he would often become agitated and begin yelling, hitting or kicking, and tipping over tables and chairs. The teaching staff, working with the researchers, decided to program David's Communicator so that touching a single button would produce the message "Help please." David was taught to use this highly efficient response when he was engaged in difficult tasks for which he required assistance. The data reported demonstrated that he quickly learned to use the desired response to request help, and as a result his aggressive and disruptive behavior very rarely occurred.

Much of the research on and application of FCT has involved teaching social communicative responses as alternatives to problem behaviors, as illustrated in the example described above. This research has demonstrated that appropriate communicative behaviors (e.g., speech, sign language) can successfully compete with and serve as *functionally equivalent* alternatives to problem behaviors (Carr et al., 1994; Halle, Bambara, & Reichle, 2005). This approach to reducing or eliminating problem behaviors has been a main component of an overall approach referred to as *positive behavioral support* (PBS; Bambara, Dunlap, & Schwartz, 2004).

## REFERENCES

Bambara, L. M., Dunlap, G., & Schwartz, I. (Eds.). (2004). *Positive behavior support: Critical articles on improving practice for individuals with severe disabilities.* Austin, TX: PRO-ED.

Carr, E. G. (1988). Functional equivalence as a mechanism of response generalization. In R. H. Horner, G. Dunlap, & R. L. Koegel (Eds.), *Generalization and maintenance: Life-style changes in applied settings* (pp. 221–241). Baltimore: Paul H. Brookes.

Carr, E. G., & Durand, V. M. (1985). Reducing behavior problems through functional communication training. *Journal of Applied Behavior Analysis, 18,* 111–126.

Carr, E. G., Levin, L., McConnachie, G., Carlson, J. I., Kemp, D. C., & Smith, C. E. (1994). *Communication-based intervention for problem behavior: A user's guide for producing positive change.* Baltimore: Paul H. Brookes.

Durand, V. M. (1990). *Functional communication training: An intervention program for severe behavior problems.* New York: Guilford.

Halle, J. W., Bambara, L. M., & Reichle, J. (2005). Teaching alternative skills. In L. M. Bambara & L. Kern (Eds.), *Individualized supports for students with problem behaviors: Designing positive behavior plans* (pp. 237–274). New York: Guilford.

Horner, R. H., & Billingsley, F. F. (1988). The effect of competing behavior on the generalization and maintenance of adaptive behavior in applied settings. In R. H. Horner, G. Dunlap, and R. L. Koegel (Eds.), *Generalization and maintenance: Life-style changes in applied settings* (pp. 197–220). Baltimore: Paul H. Brookes.

Horner, R. H., & Day, H. M. (1990). The effects of response efficiency on functionally equivalent competing behaviors. *Journal of Applied Behavior Analysis, 24,* 719–732.

Horner, R. H., Sprague, J. R., O'Brien, M., & Heathfield, L. T. (1990). The role of response efficiency in the reduction of problem behaviors through functional equivalence training: A case study. *Journal of the Association for Persons with Severe Handicaps, 15,* 91–97.

O'Neill, R. E., Horner, R. H., Albin, R. W., Storey, K., Sprague, J. R., & Newton, J. S. (1997). *Functional assessment and program development for problem behavior: A practical handbook* (2nd ed.). Belmont, CA: Wadsworth.

Scotti, J. R., & Meyer, L. (Eds.). (1999). *Behavioral intervention: Principles, models, and practices.* Baltimore: Paul H. Brookes.

Sidman, M. (1994). *Equivalence relations: A research story.* Boston: Author's Cooperative.

Wacker, D. P., & Steege, M. W. (1993). Providing outclinic services: Evaluating treatment and social validity. In R. Van Houten & S. Axelrod (Eds.), *Behavior analysis and treatment* (pp. 297–319). New York: Plenum.

ROBERT O'NEILL
*University of Utah*

**BEHAVIORAL ASSESSMENT**
**POSITIVE BEHAVIORAL SUPPORT**

# FUNCTIONAL INSTRUCTION

Functional instruction refers to the use of activities that involve skills of immediate usefulness to students as well as the employment of teaching materials that use real rather than simulated materials (Wehman, Renzaglia, & Bates, 1985). For example, a student could be taught to increase fine motor skills by assembling vocational products from local industry rather than by placing pegs in a board or stringing beads. Or a student could be required to place one cup at each place setting as opposed to placing one chip on each colored circle in an effort to teach one-to-one correspondence.

There are several reasons to support the use of functional instruction techniques, especially when considering the needs of students with severe disabilities (Brown, Nietupski, & Hamre-Nietupski, 1976). First, the use of artificial materials and settings may fail to prepare students for the skills they will need to perform practical tasks in natural settings. One cannot make any inferences about the ability of students with severe disabilities to generalize skills taught in simulated settings or with artificial materials to natural environments where these skills will be needed. Second, the actions required to do artificial tasks or materials may have little or no relation to the actions required in natural settings. For instance, labeling of plastic fruit and placing it in a small plastic shopping cart to be wheeled around the classroom may not prepare students for locating, selecting, bagging, and purchasing fruit in a local supermarket. Third, since the focus of education for students with severe disabilities is on preparing them to function in heterogeneous adult environments, instruction should occur in community-based (natural) settings. It is only through instruction in such nonartificial settings that students will learn to attend to and respond to the myriad of activities of individuals without disabilities in such settings. In addition, instruction in community sites will enable students to discriminate among a variety of novel stimuli found in natural environments (e.g., different types of soap dispensers in public restrooms).

The proliferation of nonfunctional activities in classrooms can be traced to several possible origins (Wehman et al., 1985). First, the large amount of commercial material that has appeared on the market has significantly influenced the teachings of pupils with severe disabilities. These commercially made materials are not always directly related to materials and activities that will be required by students in natural environments. Second, some educators believe that traditional nonfunctional activities (e.g., pegs in boards, stacking rings on post) are necessary for the student's readiness for more complex activities. Such a philosophy perpetuates the acquisition of isolated skills that have little correlation with skills needed in natural settings in adulthood. Unlike their nondisabled peers, individuals with severe disabilities may not generalize skills taught in nonfunctional readiness activities to those needed in natural environments. Only with direct instruction of functional skills using nonartificial materials will students with severe disabilities be able to exhibit competence in nonschool or postschool settings.

The use of functional materials and instruction involves the examination of individual needs in current and future environments. An ecological inventory (Brown et al., 1979) or ecological analysis (Wehman et al., 1985) can be conducted to determine individual student needs. By looking at aspects of the student's current environments (e.g., home, school, vocational site) and his or her future environments (e.g., group home, community recreation facility, vocational site), one can determine which skills will enable that student to function independently. By further breaking down current and future environments into subenvironments (e.g., group home: bathroom, living room, bedroom) and determining what activities are necessary in those subenvironments, one can determine the types of functional materials to be used during instruction. Careful consultation with parents or guardians as well as staff at future residential sites is also needed to ensure the functionality of skills targeted for instruction during the school years.

## REFERENCES

Brown, L., Branston-McClean, M. B., Baumgart, D., Vincent, L., Falvey, M., & Schroeder, J. (1979). Using the characteristics of current and subsequent least restrictive environments in the development of curricular content for severely handicapped students. *AAESPH Review, 4,* 407–424.

Brown, L., Nietupski, J., & Hamre-Nietupski, S. (1976). Criterion of ultimate functioning. In M. A. Thomas (Ed.), *Hey, don't forget about me!* Reston, VA: Council for Exceptional Children.

Wehman, P., Renzaglia, A., & Bates, P. (1985). *Functional living skills for moderately and severely handicapped individuals.* Austin, TX: PRO-ED.

CORNELIA LIVELY
*University of Illinois, Urbana-Champaign*

## ECOLOGICAL EDUCATION FOR CHILDREN WITH DISABILITIES
## TRANSFER OF TRAINING

## FUNCTIONAL MRI

Functional MRI (fMRI) is a well-established neuroimaging technique that uses the same equipment as conventional MRI. Functional MRI relies on detecting small changes in the signals used to produce magnetic resonance images that are associated with neuronal activity in the brain. It produces unique and valuable information for applications in both basic and clinical neuroscience. Functional MRI is safe, non-evasive and repeatable in adults and children and thus has widespread potential uses. Functional MRI is a technique for determining which parts of the brain are activated by different types of physical sensation or activity such as sight, sound or tactile response. It is achieved by setting up an advanced MRI scanner in a special way so that increased blood flow to the activated areas of the brain show up on fMRI scans (Gore, 2003).

Functional MRI detects the blood oxygen level–dependent (BOLD) changes in the MRI signal that arises when changes in neuronal activity occur following a change in brain states such as may be produced by a stimulus or task. One of the underlying premises of many current uses of functional imaging is that various behaviors and brain functions rely on the recruitment and coordinated interaction of components of "large scale" brain systems that are spatially distinct, distributed and yet connected in functional networks (Gore, 2003).

Functional MRI has found applications in both clinical and more basic neuroscience. Appropriate experiments may now be designed to address specific hypotheses regarding the nature of distributed systems responsible for various functional responses. For clinical applications, simple mapping of critical sensory and motor functions can be readily performed by subjects lying in the bore of a magnet where they perform simple tasks or experience sensory stimuli in blocks. This is the primary approach for evaluation of the brains of patients prior to neurosurgery or radiation therapy. Standard protocols have been developed at many sites that permit efficient mapping of auditory, visual, motor and language areas to inform surgeons of the positions of critical functional areas. Functional MRI data can readily be integrated with image guided neurosurgical procedures (Schlosser, Aoyagi, Fulbright, Gore, & McCarthy, 1998).

Functional MRI has several limitations. The use of fast imaging reduces the spatial resolution to a few millimeters, somewhat worse than conventional MRI. The BOLD effect is small and thus the sensitivity is limited so that fMRI experiments require multiple samplings of brain responses. Temporal resolution is poor and the reliability is reduced when there is significant subject motion or physiologically related variations (Gore, 2003).

## REFERENCES

Gore, J. C. (2003). Principles and practice of functional MRI of the human brain. *Journal of Clinical Investigation, 112,* 4–9.

Schlosser, M., Aoyagi, N., Fulbright, R. K., Gore, J. C., & McCarthy, G. (1998). Functional MRI studies of auditory comprehension. *Human Brain Mapping, 6,* 1–13.

RICHARD RIDER
*University of Utah*

**BIOFEEDBACK**
**DIFFUSION TENSOR IMAGING**
**MAGNETIC RESONANCE IMAGING**
**SPECT**

# FUNCTIONAL SKILLS TRAINING

Functional skills are generally considered to be those skills and competencies that are necessary for everyday living. These competencies are also referred to by many as "survival skills." The skills could be relatively simple for many people, such as counting change from a basic purchase, reading the sign for a restroom in an unfamiliar location, or realizing when to walk across an unfamiliar intersection. They could also be more complicated and involve the balancing of a checkbook, the completion of an application for employment, or comparative shopping. Many students are able to acquire these types of skills either within their normal environment, through incidental learning, or through general instruction within a formal classroom setting. The exceptional child, however, may not be able to acquire these competencies through incidental learning in his or her environment, and may not be able to generalize and transfer classroom learning to everyday situations out of the formal learning situation. Thus, the exceptional child may lose the opportunity to learn the very skills necessary for existence within our society.

Techniques for instruction of functional skills within the special education classroom will vary with the degree of impairment of the students involved. The techniques would include teaching of the "3 R's," generally referred to as the basics of academic instruction. Additionally, the social skills that are usually acquired by nonhandicapped students through environmental influences may require specific instruction by the special education teacher. Essentially, the teacher must decide whether to remediate deficits in academic subject areas or to concentrate on instruction in areas that could enable the student to function in as independent a manner as possible considering the limits of his or her abilities.

In functional reading, the sight-word approach is generally used to give a reading vocabulary. Teachers should consider the purpose of the instruction before selecting a method of instruction. In many cases, the level of literacy should be the level necessary for personal protection and information. Reading for protection requires minimal competence in reading itself, and must be practical for the survival of the individual (Palloway, Payne, Patton, & Payne, 1985). The sight vocabulary must include words such as restroom, men, women, danger, exit, walk, do not enter, and poison. For most special education students, vocational application of sight word skills would be a reasonable expectation. These skills would include those required to obtain and hold employment, to pass a driver's test, to complete a job application, and to order from a menu.

Functional skills training in mathematics should include those skills needed to provide a foundation for competence in vocational areas and daily living. Instruction should provide an understanding of measurement (both in carpentry and cooking), ordering, checking, paying bills, time, budgeting, purchasing, and making change. Mathematics is used much more in daily life than is realized by individuals who are able to assimilate knowledge without formal instruction. Consider the complexities involved in calculating a grocery bill, including taxes, without the ability to perform multiplication procedures, much less percent calculations. It is highly recommended that the use of a hand-held calculator be included in all programs of mathematics for special education students. Estimation should be included also so that the individual will be able to recognize correct and incorrect calculations. Counting of change is an extremely important aspect of functional mathematics skills for the disabled. Remediation of deficits is not appropriate for the disabled as a rule. Functional skills should be considered in mathematics prior to instruction in the more traditional mathematics operations. A project for developing survival skills for nondisabled students is discussed by Frey-Mason (1985). This technique could easily be adapted for the special education population.

Training in functional skills in written language should emphasize legibility. A student should be instructed in signing his or her name, completing an employment application, taking an order, writing a personal check, and executing basic personal correspondence. The signature should be accomplished in cursive style; however, all other writing can be in either cursive or manuscript, whichever is more legible. A student will be able to write only what he or she is able to read in most cases; therefore, the amount of written language will depend to a great extent on reading skills. The use of computers is encouraged for the disabled in writing tasks. Lerner (1985) provides an overview of methods and theories of written language for the special child.

Frequently, the individual with disabilities will require specific training in social skills. These should include specific instruction in developing appropriate peer relationships, classroom behaviors, and relationships with adults. While many children are able to learn these skills from their environment, specific techniques should be considered for the special education child to enable him or her to function in a socially acceptable manner.

## REFERENCES

Frey-Mason, P. (1985). Teaching basic mathematics and survival skills. *Mathematics Teacher, 78,* 669–671.

Lerner, J. (1985). *Learning disabilities: Theories, diagnosis, and teaching strategies* (4th ed.). Boston: Houghton Mifflin.

Palloway, E. A., Payne, J. S., Patton, J. R., & Payne, R. A. (1985). *Strategies for teaching retarded and special needs learners* (3rd ed.). Columbus, OH: Merrill.

JAMES H. MILLER
JOHN F. CAWLEY
*University of New Orleans*

FUNCTIONAL DOMAINS
FUNCTIONAL VOCABULARY

## FUNCTIONAL VISION

Functional vision is associated with the name of Natalie Barraga, a pioneer figure in emphasizing the importance of helping children with severe visual limitations to use their residual visual abilities as effectively as possible (Barraga, 1964, 1970, 1976, 1980). Functional vision, as defined by Barraga (1976, p. 15) denotes "how a person uses whatever vision he may have." Vision is functional if a child is able to utilize visual information to plan and carry out a task (Topor, 2006).

The federal regulations for IDEA have defined visual disabilities for school purposes so that the consideration of functional vision is primary. As defined in that law, "Visually handicapped means a visual impairment which, even with correction, adversely affects a child's educational performance." Thus the concept of functional vision is one that emphasizes what the visually impaired child can do, rather than a particular type of physical visual limitation.

A functional vision assessment of children with visual problems attempts to determine how well a visually handicapped student is able to use the visual abilities and skills he or she possesses (Livingston, 1986). It usually involves the use of informal checklists that professionals working with the visually handicapped (e.g., teachers of visually impaired students, low-vision specialists, optometrists, orientation and mobility specialists) are asked to complete as per their particular observations. These assessments can be affected or influenced by the child's visual acuity, visual field, control of eye movements, lighting, color, contrast, the age of onset of the low vision, intelligence, and etiology of the low vision.

The California Ad Hoc Committee on Assessment (Roessing, 1982) developed a comprehensive criterion-referenced checklist for functional vision assessment. This covered the skills required for activities of daily living within a school setting, mobility, and academics. Barraga (1983) developed the Program to Develop Efficiency in Visual Functioning, which provided an observational checklist and a diagnostic assessment procedure (DAP) for the developmental assessment of a wide range of visual skills. She also provided lesson plans to develop visual efficiencies.

The Low Vision Online website (LVO; 2006) cites seven areas of functional vision, based on Barraga's research, that should be assessed: (1) Awareness and attention to objects; (2) control of eye movements—tracking; (3) control of eye movements—scanning; (4) discrimination of objects; (5) discrimination of details to identify actions and match objects; (6) discrimination of details in picture; and (7) identification and perception of patterns, numbers, and words.

Children with multiple disabilities require specialized assessment, therefore a number of functional vision assessment devices have been created to meet their needs. Among them is Langley's (1980) Functional Vision Inventory for the Multiply and Severely Handicapped.

### REFERENCES

Barraga, N. C. (1964). *Increased visual behavior in low vision children.* New York: American Foundation for the Blind.

Barraga, N. C. (1970). *Teacher's guide for development of visual learning abilities and utilization of low vision.* Louisville, KY: American Printing House for the Blind.

Barraga, N. C. (1976). *Visual handicaps and learning: A developmental approach.* Belmont, CA: Wadsworth.

Barraga, N. C. (1980). *Source book on low vision.* Louisville, KY: American Printing House for the Blind.

Barraga, N. C. (1983). *Visual handicaps and learning.* Austin, TX: Exceptional Resources.

Langley, M. B. (1980). *Functional vision inventory for the multiply and severely handicapped.* Chicago: Stoelting.

Livingston, R. (1986). Visual impairments. In N. G. Haring & L. McCormick (Eds.), *Exceptional children and youth* (4th ed., pp. 398–429). Columbus, OH: Merrill.

Low Vision Online. (2006). *Low vision assessment.* Retrieved February 8, 2006, from http://www.lowvisiononline.unimelb.edu.au

Roessing, L. J. (1982). Functional vision: Criterion-referenced checklists. In S. S. Mangold (Ed.), *A teacher's guide to the special educational needs of blind and visually handicapped children.* New York: American Foundation for the Blind.

Topor, I. (2006). *Fact sheet functional vision assessment.* Retrieved February 8, 2006, from http://www.cde.state.co.us

JANET S. BRAND
*Hunter College, City University
of New York*

INDIVIDUALS WITH DISABILITIES EDUCATION
IMPROVEMENT ACT OF 2004 (IDEIA)
VISUAL IMPAIRMENT

## FUNCTIONAL VOCABULARY

The development of functional reading vocabularies acquired significance as a result of the realization that the acquisition of functional academic skills was the upper limit of academic achievement for persons with moderate to severe retardation (Gearheart & Litton, 1975). Prior to the time of that realization (late 1950s and 1960s) many curricula for retarded individuals, although watered down, were not designed for functionality.

The content of an appropriate functional vocabulary (whether reading or speaking) is determined by analyzing the current and expected environmental demands for the student. Factors that influence the content include the age of the student, the degree of mobility independence the student has, the expected adult environment (e.g., sheltered workshop, competitive employment, custodial care), and the student's likes and dislikes. According to Musselwhite and St. Louis (1982), functional vocabulary content for severely disabled persons should be based on client preferences and should be in the here and now rather than the future or past directed. They should also be words that occur with frequency. Many writers (Baroff, 1974; Holland, 1975; Lichtman, 1974; Schilit & Caldwell, 1980; Snell, 1983) have attempted to develop core functional lexicons or lists of sources for such lexicons. However, most researchers (including the mentioned writers) would agree that for a vocabulary to be truly functional, it must be based on an individual's experience and not on assumed common experience.

Bricker (1983) states that vocabulary instruction for children with moderate and severe retardation must involve the primary caregiver (usually a parent). Instruction must involve association with an object, the client's use of the object, and word recognition in context. Guess, Sailor, and Baer (1978) provide support and extension for Bricker's statement. Functional words must be used consistently and frequently by all persons in the child's environment if they are to be learned (Musselwhite & St. Louis, 1982). According to Guess et al. (1978) and Bricker (1983), it is important to teach a child words that allow him or her to gain a degree of control over the environment, as these words are likely to lead to reinforcing consequences.

The content of a functional reading vocabulary for an individual is likely to change considerably over time. For elementary school-aged children, the content is usually aimed at warning signs and survival (e.g., danger, stop, men, women), whereas at the secondary and adult level, the content will include words associated with work, travel, and money management (Baroff, 1974; Drew et al., 1984). Sources for functional reading vocabularies include newspapers, street signs, price tags, job applications, recipes, telephone directories, and bank forms. Schilit and Caldwell (1980) produced a list of the 100 most essential career/vocational words, but Brown and Perlmutter (1971) contend that such lists are ineffective since they often do not match the experiences of individual clients.

Although most persons with mental retardation are severely limited with regard to reading, a number of researchers have been able to demonstrate that instruction based on a whole word/task analysis approach is effective (Brown et al., 1974; Sidman & Cresson, 1973). Any functional reading vocabulary should be taught in context. Snell (1983) offers an example of a pedestrian skills program during which students would take walks and read walk, don't walk, and stop signs. Brown et al. (1974) suggest a similar approach.

## REFERENCES

Baroff, G. A. (1974). *Mental retardation: Nature, cause and management.* New York: Holsted.

Bricker, D. (1983). Early communication: Development and training. In M. E. Snell (Ed.), *Systematic instruction of the moderately and severely handicapped* (pp. 269–288). Columbus, OH: Merrill.

Brown, L., Huppler, B., Pierce, F., York, R., & Sontag, E. (1974). Teaching trainable level students to read unconjugated action verbs. *Journal of Special Education, 8,* 51–56.

Brown, L., & Perlmutter, L. (1971). Teaching functional reading to trainable level retarded students. *Education & Training of the Mentally Retarded, 6,* 74–84.

Drew, C. J., Logan, D. R., & Hardman, M. L. (1984). *Mental retardation: A life cycle approach.* St. Louis, MO: Times Mirror/Mosby.

Guess, D., Sailor, W., & Baer, D. (1978). Children with limited language. In R. L. Schiefelbusch (Ed.), *Language intervention strategies* (pp. 101–143). Baltimore: University Park Press.

Holland, A. (1975). Language therapy for children: Some thoughts on context and content. *Journal of Hearing Disorders, 40,* 514–523.

Lichtman, M. (1974). The development and validation of R/EAL: An instrument to assess functional literacy. *Journal of Reading Behavior, 6,* 167–182.

Musselwhite, C. R., & St. Louis, K. W. (1982). *Communication programming for the severely handicapped: Vocal and nonvocal strategies.* San Diego, CA: College-Hill.

Schilit, J., & Caldwell, M. L. (1980). A word list of essential career/vocational words for mentally retarded students. *Education & Training of the Mentally Retarded, 15*(2), 113–117.

Sidman, M. (1971). Reading and audio visual equivalencies. *Journal of Speech & Hearing Research, 14,* 5–13.

Sidman, M., & Cresson, O. (1973). Reading and cross modal transfer of stimulus equivalencies in severe retardation. *American Journal of Mental Deficiency, 77,* 515–523.

Snell, M. E. (1983). Functional reading. In M. E. Snell (Ed.), *Systematic instruction of the moderately and severely handicapped* (pp. 445–487). Columbus, OH: Merrill.

JAMES K. MCAFEE
*Pennsylvania State University*

**AAMR, AMERICAN ASSOCIATION ON MENTAL RETARDATION**
**MENTAL RETARDATION**
**FUNCTIONAL COMMUNICATION TRAINING**
**FUNCTIONAL DOMAINS**
**FUNCTIONAL INSTRUCTION**
**FUNCTIONAL SKILLS TRAINING**
**FUNCTIONAL VISION**

# FUTURE PROBLEM SOLVING PROGRAM

In an effort to develop an effective model to teach critical and creative thinking, problem solving, and decision-making skills to elementary, middle, and high school students, the Future Problem Solving Program (FPSP) was formulated. According to James Alvino, FPSP is a nonprofit educational program that trains teams of youngsters, grades K–12, in a six-step creative problem-solving process to tackle global and community problems (Alvino, 1993). FPSP seeks to stimulate critical and creative thinking skills in students, while encouraging these students to develop a vision for the future.

The FPSP's six-step problem solving model consists of the following components: (1) identify challenges; (2) select an underlying problem; (3) produce solution ideas; (4) generate and select criteria; (5) apply criteria to solution ideas; and (6) develop an action plan. Students conduct research on selected topics and are coached in the use of the problem-solving model to address the specified area of need.

The FPSP promotes observance of standards for curriculum and instruction, language arts, social studies, science, the arts, math, geography, civics, technology, life skills, and behavioral studies. The program's use of research and investigation of topics deemed relevant to the student affords opportunities for students to gain skills necessary to achieve and exceed educational standards.

## REFERENCES

Alvino, J. (1993). Future problem solving in the year 2000—Challenges and opportunities for business. *Business Horizons, 36*(6), 16–22.

FLOYD HENDERSON
*Texas A&M University*

## CREATIVE PROBLEM SOLVING
## CREATIVITY

# G

## GAIT DISTURBANCES

Walking depends on the integration of sensory-motor-vestibular brain systems, as well as the functional strength and range of motion of the component body parts (Stolov & Clowers, 1981). Normal walking is developmentally linked to the orderly sequential integration of postural reflexes into automated smooth, adaptive responses that permit movement forward, backward, and up and down stairs by approximately 3 years of age. Clinical experience with children with impaired gaits suggests there may be as many gait disturbances as there are muscles and joints within the body.

Any skeletal or joint injury defect or disease that limits the normal range of joint motion produces a lack of fluidity in walking, or limping gait, because of necessary compensatory movements to maintain balance. Examples may be seen in children with arthritis, arthrogryposis, achondroplastic dwarfism, and fractures. The shortening of one leg produces a characteristic pelvic tilt that can contribute to scoliosis or spinal curvature in a growing child. Pain or foot deformities can also produce a limping gait.

Cerebellar gait or ataxia is a wide-based gait with irregular steps and unsteadiness, with staggering on turning; it is characteristic of children who lack balance. Young children or those with developmental delay often walk with an ataxic-like gait, with arms elevated to assist with balance.

In hemiplegic gait, the child with spastic hemiplegia leans to the afflicted side and swings the affected leg out to the side and in a semicircle (circumduction). The antigravity muscles of upper extremities are often held fixed in flexor patterns.

In scissors gait, the legs are adducted and internally rotated so that with each step the child tends to trip over the opposite foot. Toe walking increases the balance difficulty. Steps are short, jerky, and slow, with many extraneous movements of the upper extremities to facilitate balance. This is the typical pattern for the child with spastic paraplegia or mild quadriplegic cerebral palsy.

Staggering or drunken gait is seen in persons with alcohol intoxication. It may also be observed in children with brain tumor, drug poisoning, or other central nervous system impairment.

Steppage gait is characterized by lifting the knees high to flop the foot down; foot drop is evident. Some children with initial stage muscular atrophy walk in this manner. Children with Duchenne muscular dystrophy show a gait somewhat similar to the steppage gait in initial stages. As their heel cords tighten these children walk more on their toes and often fall. To maintain their tenuous balance they lean back in lordosis. As weakness progresses, these children find it increasingly difficult to come to an erect position after a fall. They use their hands to "walk up their legs" to push themselves into an erect position and achieve balance. This process is the Gower's sign. These children are vulnerable in a regular school setting because a slight touch may disturb their precarious balance and weakness prevents their using their arms to catch themselves when falling; hence, serious head injuries and fractures can result.

The gait patterns of children with involuntary movement disorders are highly variable (Davis, 2003). Some individuals with athetoid and choreiform movements, which are severe and extensive, walk with a fair degree of speed and safety while their windmill involuntary movements occur. Others with less involuntary movement may have severe concomitant balance problems that require supportive safety devices.

Specific description, diagnosis, and medical intervention relative to gait disturbances usually occurs as a result of consultation among the pediatrician, orthopedist, and neurologist. Assistive devices such as braces, corsets, splints, canes, crutches, and wheelchairs require individualized fitting and training to provide the most effective locomotion compatible with health and safety. Readjustments in the nature and use of these devices must be adapted to changes owed to growth and disease status. Clinical experience suggests that many severely disabled children who learn crutch walking for short distances find the energy required for long distances dictates wheelchair mobility to conserve energy. Mobility evaluation, including transfer and self-care status, has been found to be essential in vocational planning for young adults with gait disturbances to help them achieve more realistic vocational goals. The orthotist (brace maker) and physical and occupational therapists may implement specific exercise and training for cane and crutch walking and assist in the selection and use of wheelchairs.

## REFERENCES

Banus, B. S., Kent, C., Norton, Y., Sudiennick, D., & Becker, M. (1979). *The developmental therapist* (2nd ed.). Thorofare, NJ: Slack.

Barr, M. L. (1979). *The human nervous system: An anatomic viewpoint* (3rd ed.). New York: Harper & Row.

Chusid, J. G. (1978). *Correlative neuroanatomy and functional neurology* (16th ed.). Los Angeles: Lang Medical.

Davis, A. (2003). Gait disturbances. In E. Fletcher-Janzen & C. R. Reynolds (Eds.), *Childhood disorders diagnostic desk reference* (pp. 251–252). New York: Wiley.

Stolov, W. C., & Clowers, M. R. (Eds.). (1981). *Handbook of severe disability* (stock #017-090-00054-2). Washington, DC: U.S. Government Printing Office.

RACHAEL J. STEVENSON
*Bedford, Ohio*

ATAXIA
MUSCULAR DYSTROPHY
PHYSICAL ANOMALIES

## GALACTOSEMIA

Galactosemia, first described in 1908, is an inborn error of galactose metabolism resulting in an accumulation of galactose in the blood, tissue, and urine. Three types of galactosemia are known, each due to a specific enzyme deficit. Classic galactosemia (the primary emphasis of this review) is the most prevalent and most severe form. It occurs in approximately 1/70,000 births and is attributed to a marked deficiency of galactose-1-phosphate uridyl transferase. Galactosemia is caused by an autosomal recessive gene, and heterozygotes for the trait exhibit reduced enzyme activity (VHGI, 1999). Galactokinase deficiency, less severe, occurs in 1/155,000 births and leads to the development of cataracts. A rare form, with no clear clinical abnormalities, is attributed to a deficit of EDP-glucose-4-epimerase (Hug, 1979). The overall incidence of variant forms of galactosemia is approximately 1/16,000 (Desposito & Cho, 1996).

Symptoms of classic galactosemia begin within two weeks after birth and may include jaundice, vomiting, hypoglycemia, lethargy, hepatosplenomegaly, cataracts, and failure to thrive (Brown & Sessoms, 2003; Desposito & Cho, 1996; VHGI, 1999). Without treatment, the disorder is usually lethal, and many affected infants die during the first few weeks of life. Failure to thrive, liver failure, and sepsis are associated with additional abnormalities, such as Fanconi syndrome and cerebral edema, and may be fatal if untreated (Desposito & Cho, 1996; Holton & Leonard, 1994). Biochemical changes owing to galactosemia have even been reported in the liver of a second trimester fetus, suggesting the development of the disorder in utero (Allen, Gillett, Holton, King, & Pettit, 1980). The potential prenatal origin may account for the lack of relationship between either the age at which treatment begins or the severity of the neonatal disorder and the long-term outcome (Holton & Leonard, 1994). Other clinical manifestations include cataracts, liver damage, ataxia, seizures, cerebral palsy, proteinuria, and aminoaciduria (Desposito & Cho, 1996). Continued ingestion of galactose may lead to mental retardation, malnourishment, progressive failure, and death (Hug, 1979). Even among treated children, mental retardation and learning disabilities are common (VHGI, 1999).

Diagnosis is determined by severity of the symptoms, previous diagnosis of galactosemia in siblings or parents, amniocentesis, and neonatal screening. The prevalent screening technique is a blood analysis for elevated galactose followed by a test for deficient enzyme activity. Given the disastrous consequences of late diagnosis, one should not be surprised that as of June 1997, only three states (Louisiana, Pennsylvania, and Washington) did not routinely practice neonatal screening for galactosemia (Herndon, 1998). Although the tests are extremely accurate, especially for classic galactosemia, turnaround time for the results is about four to five days (Cornell Medical Center, 1999). Some infants may die before the results of the screening test are returned because of susceptibility to E coli septicemia (Desposito & Cho, 1996).

Treatment consists of elimination of galactose and lactose from the diet as early as possible (Brown & Sessoms, 2003). Since galactose is mainly formed by digestion of disaccharide lactose found in milk (milk sugar), a formula made from cow's milk is replaced with a meat-based or soybean formula. On dietary intervention, most physical symptoms subside. The infant gains weight; vomiting, diarrhea, and liver anomalies disappear; and cataracts regress, although any brain damage is permanent. Since the monosaccharide galactose does not occur in free forms in food, certain carbohydrates, lipids, and proteins that eventually metabolize to galactose must also be eliminated. A balanced galactose-free diet should be maintained throughout life (Desposito & Cho, 1996). The diet does not in any way cure the disorder, but reduces its effects on the developing person. Galactosemic women should adhere to the diet when they become pregnant to reduce levels of circulating toxins and resulting damage to the unborn fetus. Although affected women bear children, the frequency of ovarian failure is high (Desposito & Cho, 1996). Mothers of galactosemic children should also adhere to the diet during subsequent pregnancies to lessen symptoms present at birth (American Liver Foundation, 1995).

Even early dietary intervention may only partially reduce the degree and severity of cognitive damage. IQs cluster in the below normal to low-normal range, although variability is high (Desposito & Cho, 1996; Staff, 1982). Normal IQ has been reported in some cases where treatment was started before ten days of age (Desposito & Cho, 1996). Other specific difficulties may interfere with the education of treated galactosemic children. About 50 percent of treated children are developmentally delayed, and learning difficulties increase with age. These effects are apparently due to progressive neurological disease or brain damage sustained at an earlier age that becomes more apparent with age (Holton & Leonard, 1994). Additionally, galactosemic children may show growth retardation; visual-perceptual, speech, motor function, balance, and language difficulties; short attention spans; and difficulty with spatial and mathematical relationships. They generally present no significant behavior problems except for occasional apathy and withdrawal that in some severe cases is shown as a personality disorder characterized by timidity and lack of drive (Holton & Leonard, 1994). According to Roth and Lampe (1995), "[G]alactosemia has humbled us. It has evaded all attempts to categorize and systematize it, consistently becoming more, rather than less, complicated." In other words, "[W]e still have much to learn" (Holton & Leonard, 1994). Those in special education should be aware of the many and varied problems that treated galactosemic children may have.

## REFERENCES

Allen, J. T., Gillett, M., Holton, J. B., King, G. S., & Pettit, B. R. (1980). Evidence of galactosemia in utero. *Lancet, 2*, 603.

American Liver Foundation. (1995). *Galactosemia.* Retrieved January 20, 1999, from http://www.gastro.com/liverpg/galactos .htm

Brown, R. T., & Sessoms, A. (2003). Galactosemia. In E. Fletcher-Janzen & C. R. Reynolds (Eds.), *Childhood disorders diagnostic desk reference* (pp. 252–253). New York: Wiley.

Cornell Medical Center. (1999). Galactosemia screen. *Manual of Laboratory X-Ray and Special Procedures.* The New York Hospital. Retrieved January 20, 1999, from http://infonet.med .cornell.edu/lab/tests/G_Galactosemia_Screen.htm

Desposito, F., & Cho, S. (1996). Newborn screening fact sheets. *Pediatrics, 28*, 473–501.

Herndon, Ken. (1998). Newborn screening programs. *Galactosemia resources and information.* Retrieved January 20, 1999, from http://www.miele-herndon.com/galactosemia/galactosemia .htm

Holton, J. B., & Leonard, J. V. (1994). Clouds still gathering over galactosemia. *Lancet, 344*, 1242–1243.

Roth, K. S., & Lampe, J. B. (1995). Literature reviews: The gene—A multipurpose tool. *Clinical Pediatrics, 34*, 567.

Staff. (1982). Clouds over galactosemia. *Lancet, 2*, 1379–1380.

VHGI. (1999). *Vermont newborn screening program: Galactosemia online.* Retrieved January 20, 1999, from http://www.vtmednet .org/~m145037/vhgi_mem/nbsman/galacto.htm

DEBORAH E. BARBOUR
ROBERT T. BROWN
*University of North Carolina at Wilmington*

BIOCHEMICAL IRREGULARITIES
CONGENITAL DISORDERS
INBORN ERRORS OF METABOLISM

## GALLAGHER, JAMES J. (1926– )

James J. Gallagher earned his BS in psychology from the University of Pittsburgh and went on to obtain the MS and PhD in child and clinical psychology from Pennsylvania State University. During his distinguished career, Gallagher was director of the Frank Porter Graham Child Development Center and Kenan Professor of Education at the University of North Carolina, Chapel Hill. His work has primarily focused on disabled and gifted children, including actively formulating public policies dealing with their special needs (Gallagher, 1984).

In the area of public policy implementation, he served as Associate Commissioner of Education (1967–1970), was the first chief of the Bureau of Education for the Handicapped of the U.S. Office of Education, and chaired the Social Policy Committee for Research in Child Development (1977–1978). As chair of the North Carolina Competency Test Commission, he emphasized the importance of the role of competency testing in remediation (Gallagher, 1979).

Gallagher's (1972a) conception of the Special Education Contract, an agreement between the school and the exceptional child's family detailing the educational plan and its objectives, was instrumental in the development of the individualized education plan (IEP), a tool widely accepted by educators today. His early work in the areas of special and regular education addressed systemic problems such as cost and staffing, frequently emphasizing the need for a "true educational system," one with supporting systems developed using educational technology (Gallagher, 1972b).

As a leader in the field of gifted and talented education, he served as President of the Council for Exceptional Children (1966), the Association for the Gifted (1970), and the

James J. Gallagher

World Council for Gifted and Talented Children (1981–1985). Gallagher's prolific body of work includes *Blending Middle School Philosophy and the Education of Gifted Students* (1997), *The Million Dollar Question: Unmet Service Needs for Young Children with Disabilities* (Gallagher, 1997), *The Study of Federal Policy Implementation* (Gallagher, 1998), and *Educating Exceptional Children* (Kirk, Gallagher, & Anastasiow, 1996).

## REFERENCES

Coleman, M. R., Gallagher, J. J., & Howard, J. (1997). *Blending middle school philosophy and the education of gifted students: Five case studies.* Washington, DC: National Association for Gifted Children.

Gallagher, J. (1972a). The special education contract for mildly handicapped children. *Exceptional Children, 38,* 527–535.

Gallagher, J. (1972b). *The search for the educational system that doesn't exist.* Arlington, VA: Council for Exceptional Children.

Gallagher, J. (1979). Minimum competency: The setting of educational standards. *Educational Evaluation & Policy Analysis, 1,* 62–67.

Gallagher, J. (1984). The evolution of special education concepts. In B. Blatt & R. J. Morris (Eds.), *Perspectives in special education.* Glenview, IL: Scott, Foresman.

Gallagher, J. (1985). *Teaching the gifted child* (3rd ed.). Boston: Allyn & Bacon.

Gallagher, J. (1997). *The million dollar question: Unmet service needs for young children with disabilities.* Washington, DC: U.S. Department of Education.

Gallagher, J. (1998). *The study of federal policy implementation: Infants / toddlers with disabilities and their families: A synthesis of results.* Chapel Hill: University of North Carolina.

Kirk, S., Gallagher, J., & Anastasiow, N. J. (1996). *Educating exceptional children* (8th ed.). Boston: Houghton Mifflin.

ANN E. LUPKOWSKI
*Texas A&M University*
First edition

TAMARA J. MARTIN
*The University of Texas of the Permian Basin*
Second edition

## GALLAUDET, EDWARD M. (1837–1917)

Edward Miner Gallaudet, the originator of higher education for the deaf, was the youngest son of Thomas Hopkins Gallaudet, founder of the first school for the deaf in the United States. While teaching in his father's school, Gallaudet was chosen to organize a new school for the deaf in Washington, DC, the Columbia Institution, which came into existence in 1857 with Gallaudet as superintendent. Believing that deaf students should have the same opportunity as hearing students to receive a higher education, Gallaudet obtained legislation, approved by President Lincoln, giving the Columbia Institution the power to grant college degrees. A higher education department was created, and in 1894 it was named Gallaudet College, in honor of Edward Gallaudet's father.

An early eclectic in the education of the deaf, Gallaudet advocated a system of instruction that combined the language of signs with speech and speech reading. He was primarily responsible for the adoption of oral teaching methods by the state residential schools for the deaf in the United States.

## REFERENCE

Boatner, M. T. (1959). *Voice of the deaf: A biography of Edward Miner Gallaudet.* Washington, DC: Public Affairs Press.

PAUL IRVINE
*Katonah, New York*

## DEAF
## GALLAUDET COLLEGE

## GALLAUDET, THOMAS HOPKINS (1787–1851)

Thomas Hopkins Gallaudet established the first school for the deaf in the United States in Hartford, Connecticut, in 1817, using methods that he had learned when visiting the *Institution Nationale des Sourds Muets* in Paris, and assisted by a teacher from that school, Laurent Clerc. Gallaudet served as principal of the Hartford school, later named the American School for the Deaf, until 1830, and continued on its board of directors for the rest of his life.

Gallaudet married one of his first students at the school. His oldest son, Thomas, became a minister to the deaf. His youngest son, Edward, established a school for the deaf in Washington, DC, the advanced department of which became Gallaudet College, named in honor of Thomas Hopkins Gallaudet.

## REFERENCES

DeGerring, E. B. (1964). *Gallaudet, friend of the deaf.* New York: McKay.

Lane, H. (1984). *When the mind hears.* New York: Random House.

PAUL IRVINE
*Katonah, New York*

# GALLAUDET COLLEGE

Gallaudet College, in Washington, DC, is the only liberal arts college for the deaf in the world. The college was formed in 1864 as a department of the Columbia Institution for the Deaf, now the Kendall School for the Deaf, by Amos Kendall, who had been postmaster general under President Andrew Jackson, and Edward Miner Gallaudet, superintendent of the Columbia Institution. The two men obtained the necessary federal legislation, which was signed by President Lincoln, to establish this national college for the deaf. In 1894 the college department became Gallaudet College, named in honor of Edward Miner Gallaudet's father, Thomas Hopkins Gallaudet, who established the first school for the deaf in the United States.

In addition to a distinguished record of success in the education of its students, Gallaudet College has provided much of the leadership in the education of the deaf in the United States. Its teacher-training program has provided both deaf and hearing teachers of the deaf. Many of the leaders in the field during the past century have been products of the Gallaudet College program.

## REFERENCES

Boatner, M. T. (1959). *Voice of the deaf: A biography of Edward Miner Gallaudet.* Washington, DC: Public Affairs.

Gallaudet, E. M. (1983). *History of the College for the Deaf, 1857–1907.* Washington, DC: Gallaudet College Press.

PAUL IRVINE
*Katonah, New York*

## DEAF

# GALTON, FRANCIS (1822–1911)

Sir Francis Galton, born in England in 1822, came from an intellectual family; his mother, Violetta Darwin, was the aunt of Charles Darwin, and his grandfather, Samuel Galton, was a fellow of the Royal Society. The youngest of a family of nine, he was brought up in a large house near Birmingham, where his father ran a bank. Galton was a precocious child. From material in Pearson's biography, Terman (1917) estimated Galton's childhood IQ at 200. He was the author of over 300 publications, including 17 books covering a broad range of topics.

Galton pioneered the development of psychological testing and the formulation of the major genetic principle of segregation of inherited characteristics. He is perhaps best known for his work on the genetic basis of individual differences in intelligence as discussed in his book, *Hereditary Genius* (1869). He was an early proponent of eugenics, a term coined by him.

In his research on the relationship of the characteristics of parents and offspring, Galton discovered the phenomenon of regression toward the mean and developed the concept of correlation, a term first used by him. Galton's measure of correlation was later given mathematical refinement by Karl Pearson, who later wrote a biography of Galton (Pearson, 1914). A more recent biography was prepared by Forrest (1974).

## REFERENCES

Forest, D. W. (1974). *Francis Galton: The life and work of a Victorian genius.* New York: Toplinger.

Galton, F. (1869). *Hereditary genius: An inquiry into its laws and consequences.* London: Macmillan.

Galton, F. (1908). *Memories of my life.* London: Methuen.

Pearson, K. (1914). *The life, letters and labours of Francis Galton.* Cambridge, England: Cambridge University Press.

Terman, L. M. (1917). The intelligence quotient of Francis Galton in childhood. *American Journal of Psychology, 28,* 209.

ROBERT C. NICHOLS
DIANE JARVIS
*State University of New York at Buffalo*

# GAMMA-AMINOBUTYRIC ACID

Gamma-aminobutyric acid (GABA) is a major inhibitory neurotransmitter in the central nervous system. Specific functions of the brain depend on adequate levels of neurotransmitters in the areas that control such functions. This knowledge has stimulated a search for drugs that can augment or reduce the supply of particular neurotransmitters. A deficiency of GABA has been associated with several diseases, including schizophrenia and epilepsy (Hammond & Wilder, 1985; Swaiman, 1999).

## REFERENCES

Hammond, E. J., & Wilder, B. J. (1985). Gamma-vinyl GABA: A new antiepileptic drug. *Clinical Neuropharmacology, 8*(1), 1–12.

Swaiman, K. F. (1999). Movement disorders and disorders of the basal ganglia. In K. F. Swaiman & S. Ashwal (Eds.), *Pediatric neurology* (pp. 801–831). St. Louis, MO: Mosby.

BARBARA S. SPEER
*Shaker Heights City School District, Shaker Heights, Ohio*

# GARGOYLISM

See HURLER SYNDROME.

# GARRETT, EMMA (1846–1893)

Emma Garrett, seeking a way to demonstrate the effectiveness of the oral method of teaching the deaf, obtained a grant that enabled her, with her sister Mary, to establish the Pennsylvania Home for the Training in Speech of Deaf Children Before They Are of School Age, also known as the Bala Home. Located in Philadelphia, the home began operation in 1891. Emma Garrett was superintendent, and both sisters served as teachers. The Bala Home was widely influential as an example of the effectiveness of the oral method of teaching the deaf and of the efficacy of early intervention. Following Emma Garrett's death in 1893, her sister became superintendent of the Bala Home and carried on the work that the two of them had begun.

## REFERENCE

Fay, E. A. (1893). *Histories of American schools for the deaf, 1817–1893* (Vol. 3). Washington, DC: Volta Bureau.

PAUL IRVINE
*Katonah, New York*

# GARRETT, MARY SMITH (1839–1925)

Mary Smith Garrett, with her sister Emma, in 1891 founded in Philadelphia the Pennsylvania Home for the Training in Speech of Deaf Children Before They Are of School Age, also known as the Bala Home. Mary Garrett succeeded her sister as superintendent after Emma died in 1893. She continued in this position for the remainder of her life.

Mary Garrett was a leading advocate of the oral method of teaching the deaf and helped to develop a curriculum based on this approach. Her system of teaching oral communication was based on early intervention, with speech training beginning as early as 2 years of age. Through the efforts of Mary and her sister, Pennsylvania became the first state to appropriate funds for preschool speech and language training for deaf children.

Mary Garrett was instrumental in the enactment of legislation establishing a juvenile court and probation system for Pennsylvania. She was also a leader in the National Congress of Mothers, the forerunner of the National Congress of Parents and Teachers, where she promoted such social reforms as child labor laws and juvenile court legislation.

## REFERENCE

Fay, E. A. (1893). *Histories of American schools for the deaf, 1817–1893* (Vol. 3). Washington, DC: Volta Bureau.

PAUL IRVINE
*Katonah, New York*

# GARRISON, S. OLIN (1853–1900)

S. Olin Garrison, minister and educator, founded in New Jersey in 1887 the school for retarded children that later became the Training School at Vineland. The school featured a cottage system of small, homelike facilities, a strong educational program, and a research department that published some of the nation's most influential works on mental retardation. Garrison served as superintendent of the Training School until his death in 1900. He was also responsible for the establishment by New Jersey of the State Home for Girls and of a school for epileptic children.

## REFERENCE

McCaffrey, K. R. (1965). *Founders of the Training School at Vineland, New Jersey: S. Olin Garrison, Alexander Johnson, Edward R. Johnstone.* Unpublished doctoral dissertation. Teachers College, Columbia University, New York.

PAUL IRVINE
*Katonah, New York*

# GATES-MACGINITIE READING TEST

The Gates-MacGinitie Reading Test (GMRT), developed by Walter H. MacGinitie, Ruth K. MacGinitie, Katherine Maria, and Lois G. Dreyer, is a formal assessment of balanced reading skills across grade levels. These levels encompass Pre-Reading, Beginning Reading, Level 1, and Level 2. Skills tested include phonemic awareness, decoding skills, phonological awareness, vocabulary, comprehension, word knowledge, and fluency.

Materials required are student test booklets or answer sheets, teacher directions for administering the test, and the manual for scoring and interpretation, which is optional. These tests are also machine scorable.

This instrument is designed to be given to a group of children. The various subtests are timed. The instrument is a multiple-choice test for all grade levels. It is a thorough assessment of reading skills and can be used by the teacher to assess areas of strength or weakness, for both individual students and an entire class. Raw scores are translated into percentile rankings, stanine scores, grade equivalency scores, extended scale scores, and normal curve equivalency scores.

Internal consistency along with means and standard deviations for total scores and subscales for each level of the GMRT are evident for both spring and fall administration. These are quite satisfactory and fall in the upper .80s and .90s for grades 1 to 12 (Swerdlik, 1992). Validity data support the intercorrelations among subtests. Validity data also provide evidence that the GMRT is a powerful test for assessing reading achievement at the lower and upper levels.

The bulk of the validity evidence relates to providing data that support substantial relationships between the GMRT and other instruments that are assumed to measure the same constructs of reading vocabulary and comprehension. These tests include general achievement screening batteries such as the Iowa Test of Basic Skills (ITBS), Tests of Achievement and Proficiency (TAP), the Comprehensive Tests of Basic Skills (CTBS), California Achievement Test (CAT), Metropolitan Achievement Test (MAT), the Survey of Basic Skills (SBS), the Verbal and Mathematics sections of the Preliminary Scholastic Aptitude Test (PSAT) and the Scholastic Aptitude Test (SAT), and the English, Math, Social Science, Natural Science, and Composite sections of the American College Test Program (ACT; Swerdlik, 1992). Reviews of the fourth edition of this test are pending for the *Sixteenth Mental Measurements Yearbook.*

### REFERENCES

Dumont, R., & Willis, J. (2006). *A sampling of reading tests.* Retrieved from http://alpha.fdu.edu/psychology/a_sampling_of _reading_tests.htm

Swerdlik, M. (1992). Review of the Gates-MacGinitie Reading Tests, third edition. In J. Kramer & J. Conoley (Eds.), *The mental measurements yearbook* (Vol. 12, pp. 352–353). Lincoln: University of Nebraska.

RON DUMONT
*Fairleigh Dickinson University*

JOHN O. WILLIS
*Rivier College*

## GAZE AVERSION

Eye contact, the study of facial characteristics during human intercourse, has been a topic that has always captivated inquiry. Why do we maintain eye contact during social interaction? What is there in facial cues that provide others social clues and what do these clues address? Are there normal patterns of gaze aversion?

The answer to the last question is a definite yes. It is neither socially correct nor communicatively enriching to look continuously at another person's face. Researchers (Beattie, 1979) have advanced a hypothesis that gaze aversion is a technique that reduces distractibility and permits thinking and speech planning. Ehrlichman (1981) advanced this hypothesis, which his data supported, as a statement of cognitive interference. Simply, the hypothesis postulates that people look away more often during periods of speech hesitancy than during periods of fluency. Gaze aversion is used while thinking and planning the next speech pattern.

Coss (1979) believed that the dimensions of gaze in psychotic children were different in several respects. He ran three studies. The first examined 10 nonpsychotic and 10 psychotic children during presentations of five models comprising a blank model and models with one through four concentric discoid elements separated by the same interpupillary distance as human eyes. The second experiment examined 15 psychotic children using models presenting two concentric discoid elements in vertical, diagonal, and horizontal orientations. The third experiment examined 10 nonpsychotic and 10 psychotic children using five models comprising two schematic facing eyes as represented by concentric discoid elements. The psychotic children looked longer at the models than did the nonpsychotic children. However, these groups did not differ for the model with two concentric discoid elements. Both groups, particularly the psychotic children, looked less at the model presenting two concentric discoid elements than at the models presenting other arrangements of concentric discoid elements in the first experiment. Similarly, in the third experiment, both groups looked less at the model with two concentric discoid elements than at models with staring and averted irises. In sum, nonpsychotic children and psychotic children did not differ appreciably in their gaze under varying conditions.

Currently, there is no data to support the long-standing belief that gaze aversion occurs with greater duration or more frequency among emotionally disturbed than among normal children. Scheman and Lockhard (1979) generated data from 573 children suggesting that gaze or stare is developmentally determined. Children under 18 months of age rarely establish eye contact. Children 18 months to 5 years do not avert their gaze. From 5 to 9 years, behavioral patterns specific to the youth are well established. This study took place in a suburban shopping center where the children were unprotected by parents' wishes when confronted by gazes from strange adults. This work lends strong support to the communication theory of gaze aversion. That, in turn, suggests that gaze aversion is not solely a function of development, conditions, difficulty of task (Doherty-Sneddon, Bonner, Longbotham, & Doyle, 2002) or emotional problems, but is a device that provides and protects concentration and is instrumental in speech production. Therefore, children with fluency difficulties (e.g., stutters), may have increased gaze aversion, a contention that is also supported in the research literature.

## REFERENCES

Beattie, G. W. (1979). Planning units in spontaneous speech: Some evidence from hesitation in speech and speaker gaze direction in conversation. *Linguistics, 17,* 61–78.

Coss, R. G. (1979). Perceptual determinants of gaze aversion by normal and psychotic children: The role of two facing eyes. *Behavior, 3–4,* 228–253.

Doherty-Sneddon, G., Bonner, B. L., Longbotham, S., & Doyle, C. (2002). Development of gaze aversion as disengagement from visual information. *Developmental Psychology, 38,* 3, 438–445.

Ehrlichman, H. (1981). From gaze aversion to eye movement suppression: An investigation of the cognitive interference explanation of gaze patterns during conversation. *British Journal of Social Psychology, 20,* 233–241.

Scheman, J. D., & Lockhard, J. S. (1979). Development of gaze aversion in children. *Child Development, 50,* 594–596.

DAVID A. SABATINO
*West Virginia College of
Graduate Studies*

## CHILDHOOD PSYCHOSIS
## CHILDHOOD SCHIZOPHRENIA

## GEARHEART, BILL R. (1918–2001)

Bill R. Gearheart earned his BA in math and physics from Friends University in Wichita, Kansas, in 1949. He received his MEd in school administration from Wichita State University in 1955 and his PhD in educational psychology and special education from the University of Northern Colorado in 1963. In the early part of his career in public education, Gearheart filled the roles of teacher, elementary principal, director of special services, and assistant superintendent.

**Bill R. Gearheart**

In 1966 he moved on to the university level and eventually became full professor. During his tenure at the University of Northern Colorado, Gearheart spent 6 years as director of the Navajo Education Project. Gearheart took early retirement and served as professor emeritus of special education at the University of Northern Colorado.

Gearheart's academic interests included preparation of regular classroom teachers to work with mildly disabled students, administration of special education, and professional writing in special education. He was most prolific in this last area, and wrote numerous college texts on special education. One major text, *Learning Disabilities: Educational Strategies* is currently in its fifth edition (Gearheart & Gearheart, 1989), and another text, *The Exceptional Student in the Regular Classroom* (formerly *The Handicapped Child in the Regular Classroom*) is in its sixth edition (Gearheart, Weishahn, & Gearheart, 1996).

Gearheart was a specialist in organizing educational programs for handicapped children and was involved in legislation relating to children with disabilities. He was an active special education advocate at the national level. From 1967 to 1970, he served on the U.S. Office of Education panel involved in awarding federal grants in special education; for two of those years he served as chairperson. He spent 5 years as a field adviser to the Bureau of Education for the Handicapped, evaluating applications for research funds. Gearheart also was a member of different federal site visit teams, visiting numerous major universities that offer the doctorate in special education. At the state level, Gearheart was involved with special education projects for various state departments of education. In addition, he assisted numerous local education agencies in planning and programming various special education services.

Involved in special education for over 25 years, Gearheart's major contributions to the field were twofold. First, he wrote a dozen texts in special education (three in foreign translations). His development of practitioner-oriented texts made his work familiar to many special educators and regular classroom educators. Second, he was involved in the preparation of special educators at the doctoral level. His training contributions are seen in former students who now reside in more than half of the states and several foreign countries. A unique contribution to the field was Gearheart's directorship of the Navajo Education Project, initiating special education programming in Board of Indian Affairs schools of the Navajo reservation. Gearheart taught courses at the University of Northern Colorado and conducted workshops on professional writing. His work in the field of special education continued with the publication of *Exceptional Individuals: An Introduction* (1992).

## REFERENCES

Gearheart, B. R., & Gearheart, C. J. (1989). *Learning disabilities: Educational strategies* (5th ed.). Columbus, OH: Merrill.

Gearheart, B. R., Mullen, R. C., & Gearheart, C. J. (1992). *Exceptional individuals: An introduction*. Pacific Grove, CA: Brooks/Cole.

Gearheart, B. R., Weishahn, M. W., & Gearheart, C. J. (1996). *The exceptional student in the regular classroom* (6th ed.). Englewood Cliffs, NJ: Merrill.

KATHRYN A. SULLIVAN
*Branson School Online*
First edition

TAMARA J. MARTIN
*The University of Texas of the
Permian Basin*
Second edition

# GENERAL APTITUDE TEST BATTERY

The General Aptitude Test Battery (GATB) was developed by the U.S. Employment Services as a means of assisting clients (and those at state employment offices) in identifying possible successful occupation areas. The battery is composed of 12 separately timed and scored tests that measure nine aptitudes for individuals age 13 through adulthood. Scores are then used to point out areas of client strengths and weaknesses. There are two forms. The following nine vocational aptitudes are measured:

1. Intelligence—the general learning ability of the client;

2. Verbal aptitude—the ability to understand words and their relationships;

3. Numerical aptitude—the ability to perform arithmetic quickly and accurately;

4. Spatial aptitude—the ability to think visually of geometric forms and to recognize relationships resulting from the movement of objects in space;

5. Form perception—the ability to perceive pertinent details and make visual discriminations;

6. Clerical perception—the ability to discriminate similarities and differences in verbal material;

7. Motor coordination—the ability to coordinate eyes and hands rapidly and accurately;

8. Finger dexterity—the ability to move and manipulate small objects with the fingers rapidly and accurately; and

9. Manual dexterity—the ability to move the hands skillfully in placing and turning motions.

In the manual for the GATB (1967), scores on the various subtests are correlated with occupations, and tentative cutoff scores are provided for each occupational area. The test was validated to predict performance in over 400 professional, semi-, and unskilled occupations (Buros, 1978). A Spanish version of the GATB is available, as is a nonreading measure of the same aptitudes. There is also a special edition for deaf persons. The GATB takes approximately two hours to complete. To administer the GATB, one must obtain certification by attending a workshop that teaches administration and interpretation of the GATB. State employment offices present these workshops.

## REFERENCES

United States Employment Services (USES). (1967). *Manual for the USES General Aptitude Test Battery*. Minneapolis: Intran.

USES General Aptitude Test Battery. (1978). In O. K. Buros (Ed.), *The eighth mental measurements yearbook* (Vol. II, pp. 675–680). Highland Park, NJ: Gryphon.

RONALD V. SCHMELZER
*Eastern Kentucky University*
First edition

ELIZABETH O. LICHTENBERGER
*The Salk Institute*
Second edition

# GENERALIZABILITY THEORY

Generalizability theory was developed by Cronbach and his associates (Cronbach, Gleser, Nanda, & Rajaratnam, 1972) to evaluate the generalizability of results obtained when measurement is carried out for assessing, for example, differences among students. The theory is primarily concerned with identifying and estimating the variances associated with the effects present in the design used to collect the evaluation data. Variances are estimated within an analysis of variance (ANOVA) framework. These estimated variances are then used to describe the relative contribution of each effect to the observed variance and to compute measurement error variance and, if desired, generalizability coefficients for each factor of interest.

Two types of studies are conducted using generalizability theory: G(generalizability)-studies and D(decision)-studies. A G-study is carried out when developing a measurement procedure for use in a D-study later on. Thus, a G-study is designed to encompass the "universe of admissible observations" (Cronbach et al., 1972, p. 20); for instance, a universe including all the variables (factors) under which observations could be collected in subsequent D-studies. A D-study draws observations from the "universe of generalization" (i.e., the universe to which we wish to generalize the results in a specific situation). The universe of generalization is then a subset of, or the same as, the universe of admissible operations. The results of a G-study are used to design D-studies. In many instances, however, a G- and D-study may be conducted using the same data set; for instance, the data are used both for making decisions and for improving the design of future D-studies so that the universe of admissible observations is the same as the universe of generalization.

Suppose a 20-item test is administered for diagnostic purposes to a sample of 30 referred students. To investigate the generalizability of the test for differentiating among the students, a G-study is conducted by first identifying the effects present in the linear ANOVA model associated with the design of the study. These effects are student, item, and student × item interaction, including random error. Next, using the ANOVA technique, the mean squares associated with each effect are obtained, and variances are estimated for each using a procedure such as that proposed by Cornfield and Tukey (1956). For the example above, the variances are estimated as follows: students—.0610 (22.13 percent), items—.0700 (25.82 percent), interaction—.1401 (51.68 percent).

Next, a D-study is carried out using the results of the G-study. First the estimated variances are examined. They show that approximately the same proportion of variation in the design is shown by the students and the items, while twice as much is attributable to the differences between students' responses to items and random error. The measurement error associated with differences among students is .0701/20 = .0025, since differences among students are shown in their differing responses to the same items. Divide by 20, since it is assumed that students are differentiated on the basis of their performance over all 20 items. A generalizability coefficient, $p^2$, analogous to a reliability coefficient, is estimated as

$$p^2 = \frac{\text{student variance}}{\text{student variance and error variance}}$$

$$= \frac{.0610}{.0610 + .0035}$$

$$= .8971$$

In summary, from a generalizability analysis we estimate variance associated with each factor in the design, measurement error, and a generalizability coefficient associated with the factor of interest. The practitioner or researcher wishing to conduct generalizability analysis should read Brennan (1983), Fyans (1983), and Shavelson and Webb (1981).

### REFERENCES

Brennan, R. L. (1983). *Elements of generalizability theory.* Iowa City, IA: American College Testing Program.

Cornfield, J., & Tukey, J. W. (1956). Average values of mean squares in factorials. *Annals of Mathematical Statistics, 27,* 907–949.

Cronbach, L. J., Gleser, G. C., Nanda, H., & Rajaratnam, N. (1972). *The dependability of behavioral measurements: Theory of generalizability for scores and profiles.* New York: Wiley.

Fyans, L. J. (Ed.). (1983). *Generalizability theory: Inferences and practical applications.* San Francisco: Jossey-Bass.

Shavelson, R. J., & Webb, N. M. (1981). Generalizability theory: 1973–1980. *British Journal of Mathematical & Statistical Psychology, 34,* 133–166.

GWYNETH M. BOODOO
*Texas A&M University*

**RESEARCH IN SPECIAL EDUCATION**

# GENERALIZATION

Generalization is the demonstration of a behavior in circumstances other than those in which it was trained. The term is also used to refer to the occurrence of a behavior similar to, but different than, the learned behavior under the same circumstances as during training (Rutherford & Nelson, 1988; Scruggs & Mastropieri, 1984). These two types of generalization are referred to as stimulus generalization and response generalization. Stimulus generalization, the type most commonly studied by special education researchers, may be said to have occurred when a learner demonstrates a skill or behavior in different surroundings, at different times, or with different people. For example, a student who is trained to insert the correct amount of change into a soda machine at school and subsequently performs the same skill at a recreation center is said to have generalized the response. Response generalization refers to the spread of effects to other related behaviors and is exemplified by a student opening a large can after having successfully learned to open a small can.

Generalization is necessary to the development of a wide repertoire of behavior. It was once assumed that generalization occurred automatically with the learning of a behavior, but this principle has not proven true, especially for handicapped learners (Stokes & Baer, 1977). If generalization is to occur, it must be a component of the actual training process (Baer, Wolf, & Risley, 1968).

There is a greater probability of success in training for generalization if several factors are addressed.

1. *Initial Training.* The behavior to be generalized should be firmly established in the learner's repertoire. Time between initial acquisition and training for generalization should be short. If conditions during training are tightly controlled, generalization may take more time than if initial training is "loose" (i.e., stimuli and responses are not narrowly defined).

2. *Stimulus Variables.* The stimulus variables to be changed (time, number, setting) should be manipulated systematically during training. There is little agreement whether this should be accomplished one

variable at a time or all at one time. However, the more similarities between stimuli in the initial learning environment and those in the generalization environment, the easier the process for the learner (Stokes & Baer, 1977).

3. *Other Persons.* To the extent possible, significant others in the learner's environment should be included in the training. If they understand the purpose and method, they will be able to reinforce the learner whenever and wherever the behavior occurs.

4. *Reinforcers.* Artificial reinforcers should be faded as soon as possible and replaced by those reinforcers found in the environment in which behavior is most likely to occur. Likewise, regardless of the schedule of reinforcement used for training, an intermittent schedule should be in place before generalization is attempted. Intermittent reinforcement will more closely resemble schedules found in the natural environment.

5. *Criteria for Completion.* Criteria for successful generalization should be established. The number of exemplars required to assure generalization will vary, but training should continue until some spontaneous generalization is observed in nontraining environments (Stokes & Baer, 1977).

Success in training for generalization has varied and researchers differ in their opinions regarding its efficacy (Scruggs & Mastropieri, 1984). Some propose that failure to train for generalization is due to a lack of educational technology; others contend that inherent deficiencies in the intellectual functioning of persons with disabilities make generalization difficult. The former analysis implies that new and better training techniques are needed and that the problem is a teaching one. The latter implies a learning problem and that attempts to train for generalization should be replaced by more effort spent training desired behaviors in the environments in which they are required (Scruggs & Mastropieri, 1984). The failure of generalization has been a major drawback in the application of strictly behavioral methods to learning (Martens & Witt, 1988).

## REFERENCES

Baer, D. M., Wolf, M. M., & Risley, T. R. (1968). Some current dimensions of applied behavior analysis. *Journal of Applied Behavior Analysis, 1,* 91–97.

Martens, B., & Witt, J. (1988). On the ecological validity of behavior modification. In J. Witt, S. Elliott, & F. Graham (Eds.), *Handbook of behavior therapy in education* (pp. 325–339). New York: Plenum.

Rutherford, R., & Nelson, C. (1988). Generalization and maintenance of treatment effects. In J. Witt, S. Elliott, & F. Graham (Eds.), *Handbook of behavior therapy in education* (pp. 277–324). New York: Plenum.

Scruggs, T. E., & Mastropieri, M. A. (1984). Issues in generalization: Implications for special education. *Psychology in the Schools, 21,* 397–403.

Stokes, T. F., & Baer, D. M. (1977). An implicit technology of generalization. *Journal of Applied Behavior Analysis, 10,* 349–367.

SARA PANKASKIE
PAUL T. SINDELAR
*Florida State University*

TRANSFER OF TRAINING

## GENERIC SPECIAL EDUCATION

Generic special education is a cross-categorical orientation to training teachers and delivering special education services to children with mild to moderate disabilities. This approach came about as a result of a variety of educational movements in special education. In the 1960s, there was growing dissatisfaction among educators with the use of traditional medical-model categories to identify disabled pupils. This concern was due, in part, to increased recognition of the heterogeneity of learner characteristics within a specific handicap classification and to reports that many pupils have similar educational needs despite differences in their handicapping conditions (Hewett & Forness, 1984).

Legal requirements to educate children with disabilities in the least restrictive educational environment according to an individualized educational plan (IEP) further eroded the historical categorical boundaries to instruction. According to IDEA, selection of instructional services for individuals with disabilities is based on pupils' educational needs as determined by a committee of educators and parents who develop the IEP. After analyzing pupils' levels of performance, the appropriate educational placement is prescribed. A variety of instructional options have been developed to meet pupils' individual needs, including placement in regular classes, the use of consulting and itinerant special education teachers, resource and self-contained special education classes, special day schools, residential centers, hospital schools, and homebound instruction (Deno, 1973; Reynolds & Birch, 1982). The specific nature of instructional services, including decisions concerning curricula and teaching strategies, should be determined by the individual needs and instructional characteristics of the pupil; they should not be arbitrarily prescribed on the basis of the child's handicapping condition.

Concern for individualization is evident throughout the entire continuum of services provided by schools and agencies. From infant stimulation to vocational preparation programs that emphasize the transition from school to work, pupils who require special education services receive them based on their individual needs rather than on their categorical label. Within this context of individualization of instruction, generic special education focuses on identifying and meeting the learning needs and characteristics of specific pupils regardless of disability category. For example, owing to similarities in performance characteristics, many learning-disabled, mildly retarded, and emotionally disturbed youngsters may be effectively served in the same classroom with the same curricula.

As special education instructional services evolved from a rigid categorical approach to a functional orientation, so did teacher training programs change. With the support of federal funds in the early 1970s, several institutions of higher education initiated cross-categorical special education teacher training programs (Brady, Conroy, & Langford, 1984). These programs exhibited a variety of characteristics differentiating them from the traditional categorical orientation to teacher education. For example, each program's name described the role or function of the teacher rather than a particular handicapping condition (e.g., diagnostic-prescriptive teacher, consulting teacher). The programs were primarily developed at the master's degree level for already certified teachers, and although students were trained noncategorically, their certification remained categorical. Later, teacher training programs emphasized greater interaction with regular education, offered programs at both bachelor's and master's levels, and were located in states that began initiating noncategorical certification, primarily by collapsing certain categories into a general one. These training programs tended to collapse categorical course offerings to meet the challenge of noncategorical certification.

Associated with these movements in service delivery and teacher training has been a trend for state education agencies to develop noncategorical teacher certification in special education, growing from only 12 states in 1979 to 34 states and the District of Columbia in 1983 (Idol-Maestas, Lloyd, & Lilly, 1981). Nearly all states now provide some form of generic certification. Names of these new certificates range from descriptions of pupils (e.g., learning disabled, mildly handicapped) to descriptions of programs (e.g., resource room specialist, diagnostic prescriptive teacher) to nonspecific terms such as generic special educator.

## REFERENCES

Brady, M. P., Conroy, M., & Langford, C. A. (1984). Current issues and practices affecting the development of noncategorical programs for students and teachers. *Teacher Education & Special Education, 7*(1), 20–26.

Deno, E. N. (Ed.). (1973). *Instructional alternatives for exceptional children.* Arlington, VA: Council for Exceptional Children.

Hewett, F. M., & Forness, S. R. (1984). *Education of exceptional learners* (3rd ed.). Boston: Allyn & Bacon.

Idol-Maestas, L., Lloyd, S., & Lilly, M. (1981). A noncategorical approach to direct service and teacher education. *Exceptional Children, 48*(3), 213–220.

Reynolds, M., & Birch, J. W. (1982). *Teaching exceptional children in all America's schools* (2nd ed.). Reston, VA: Council for Exceptional Children.

CAROL ANDERSON
DOUGLAS J. PALMER
LINDA H. PARRISH
*Texas A&M University*

**HOLISTIC APPROACH AND LEARNING DISABILITIES HUMANISM AND SPECIAL EDUCATION**

# GENETIC COUNSELING

There have been many advances in the management of hereditary disorders in the past 35 years (e.g., plastic surgery, dietary manipulation, prenatal diagnosis, and most recently, gene therapy). Genetic counseling provides the vehicle for the transmission of relevant information needed by the client to make an informed decision about the treatment and prevention of hereditary disorders.

The first American genetic counseling center on record was the Eugenic Records Office in Cold Spring Harbor, New York, founded by Dr. Charles B. Davenport in 1915. Genetic counseling fell out of favor in the 1930s as the role of environment in human behavior became better understood. During the next 20 years, the study of genetics was predominantly an academic pursuit. Informal counseling was done by academicians who were primarily involved in basic genetic research rather than clinical medicine.

By the 1960s, great strides had been made in understanding human genetics. The new information gave counselors a broader and more scientific basis for telling families about the recurrence, risks, and inheritance patterns of an increasing number of diseases. The development of genetic tests based on blood and cell samples introduced the field of prospective counseling and helped shift counseling from primarily nonmedical settings to medical screening programs in hospitals and universities. Today, there are approximately 800 centers and satellite facilities specializing in genetics in the United States. Both the National Foundation—March of Dimes, 1275 Mamaroneck Avenue, White Plains, New York 10605, and the National Society of Genetic Counselors, 401 N. Michigan Avenue, Chicago, Illinois 60611, can direct those in need of counseling to an appropriate source.

Until recently, a professional providing genetic counseling was typically a physician with an interest in genetics, or a PhD geneticist with an interest in medicine. In the past 20 years, postdoctoral fellowship positions have prepared physicians and PhD geneticists in the full range of clinical genetics. In addition, genetic counselors with MS degrees emerged in response to a substantial increase in the number of individuals seeking genetic counseling and screening. The varied training and backgrounds of genetic counselors, and recognition by the American Society of Human Genetics for the need to certify counselors, led to the creation of a board certification process. Since 1981, hundreds of professionals have been certified by the American Board of Medical Genetics.

A good counselor needs a sound grasp of genetic principles, a wide knowledge of the scientific literature on diseases of possible genetic origin, and much empathy, tact, and good sense. The counselor may be in the role of information giver, facilitator of the counselee's decision process, psychotherapist, or moral advisor.

Genetic counseling usually begins with an individual wanting to know whether a disease suspected of being genetic will recur in close relatives. The traditional role of the counselor is to estimate $P$, the probability of recurrence, and when asked, to assist the client in deciding what is the appropriate action. In all cases, the decision must be left to the family. Clients may want to know whether they should have another baby. Others may want to know about the risk for affected children's children, or for the children of unaffected brothers and sisters. Prenatal diagnosis using cytogenetic or biochemical analyses of fetal cells, amniotic fluid, or mother's blood can now provide clear answers to questions concerning genetic disorders. In certain populations in which a severe genetic disorder is unusually high, such as Tay-Sachs disease, screening programs have been organized to detect and counsel heterozygotes (President's Commission for the Study of Ethical Problems in Medicine and Biomedical and Behavioral Research, 1983).

The National Society of Genetic Counselors provide an excellent set of resources for those interested in practice guidelines, tools for obtaining family histories, genetic discrimination resources, and sources for scholarly journals. The website for the organization can be found at http://www.nsgc.org/.

**REFERENCES**

Nora, J. J., & Fraser, F. C. (1981). *Medical genetics: Principles and practice* (2nd ed.). Philadelphia: Lea & Febiger.

President's Commission for the Study of Ethical Problems in Medicine and Biomedical and Behavioral Research. (1983). *Screening and counseling for genetic conditions*. Washington, DC: U.S. Government Printing Office.

KENNETH A. ZYCH
*Walter Reed Army Medical Center*

GENETIC FACTORS IN BEHAVIOR
TAY-SACHS SYNDROME
SEE ALSO: SPECIFIC SYNDROMES

## GENETIC FACTORS IN BEHAVIOR

Little is known about the genetics of human behavior, either normal or abnormal, and it is unlikely that there are specific genes for behavior or any other phenotypic trait. Behavior genetics is more complex than the study of genetic influences on physical traits because it is hard to define behavioral traits reliably, to assess them validly, and to control situational influences. Nonhuman species offer advantages of convenience and control for genetic research, but the lack of precise analogs between human and animal behavior, especially pathological behavior, limits the value of animal research for human behavior genetics.

However, a number of human pathological genes have more or less specific effects on behavior. The child with phenylketonuria (PKU) is likely to be hyperactive and irritable, have outbursts of temper, abnormal postural attitudes, and agitated behavior; about 10 percent of those affected show psychotic behavior. Characteristic behavioral changes often precede the choreic movements in Huntington's chorea. Congenital cretinism, which may be recessively inherited, produces effects on personality. Perhaps the most striking example of a gene-induced behavioral defect is the bizarre tendency for self-mutilation in Lesch-Nyhan syndrome.

Chromosomal aberrations also have effects on behavior. Children with Down syndrome are thought to be happier and more responsive to their environment than other children of comparable IQ; they often display musical ability. Girls with Turner syndrome rate high on verbal IQ tests but below average on performance measures; they seem to have a deficit in perceptual organization. The XYY karyotype is alleged to show a predisposition to criminality and aggressive behavior; however, a causal link between an excess or deficiency of chromosomal material and a behavior phenotype is obscure.

There is more information about the genetics of abnormal behavior than about how normal behavior is encoded in the gene loci. Schizophrenia, with incidence in the 1 percent range, has been studied in families, and 2 to 5 percent of the parents and 6 to 10 percent of the siblings are affected. If a propositus and parent are both affected, the risk for the siblings is higher. Concordance is much greater for monozygotic than for dizygotic twin pairs. Children of schizophrenic parents raised by their natural parents and those raised by adoptive parents show the same incidence of schizophrenia. This finding seems to establish a role for heredity in schizophrenia. However, questions of genetic heterogeneity, the role of environmental stress, and the nature of the biochemical abnormalities associated with schizophrenia remain to be answered. At present, it does not seem reasonable to suspect a single gene-determined basic defect.

The affective disorders are somewhat similar to schizophrenia in terms of population incidence and frequency within families. It has been suggested that bipolar disease is an x-linked dominant disease, but so simple a hypothesis seems implausible on the basis of current evidence. Biochemical evidence of a single-gene basis for either the bipolar or the unipolar type is still lacking.

Developmental aphasia appears to be caused by the inability of the aphasic child to process auditory stimuli presented at a normal rate. This ability does develop eventually, but at a later age than average, and it is suspected to be an autosomal dominant trait (Thompson & Thompson, 1980). The evidence favoring the familial nature of dyslexia is compelling, but the factors that account for the aggregation of cases remain unclear. Some types of dyslexia seem to be influenced by the genes and it is speculated that dyslexia is an autosomal dominant condition with some degree of sex limitation (males are affected far more frequently).

A number of disorders that are considered behavioral, such as the pervasive developmental disorders and conduct disorders, have genetic links that are almost certainly polygenetic and cannot be linked to a single gene (Gillberg, 1995). This has made studying the genetic basis of complex human behavior at the single gene level quite complex. It is difficult to predict precise behavioral outcomes or patterns for children, even with extensive data on parents.

By the application of biometrical genetics and twin studies, evidence for heritability has been found for infant behavior and temperament, introversion-extroversion, and neuroticism. Empirical evidence on sibling resemblance in intelligence published since 1915 in the United States and Europe, including more than 27,000 sibling pairs, showed that genetic factors are the major source of individual differences in intelligence (Paul, 1980).

## REFERENCES

Gillberg, C. (1995). *Clinical child neuropsychiatry.* Cambridge: Cambridge University Press.

Paul, S. M. (1980). Sibling resemblance in mental ability: A review. *Behavior Genetics, 10*(3), 277–290.

Thompson, J. S., & Thompson, M. W. (1980). *Genetics in medicine* (3rd ed.). Philadelphia: Saunders.

KENNETH A. ZYCH
*Walter Reed Army Medical
Center*

**AUTISM**
**CONDUCT DISORDERS**
**CRETINISM**
**EMOTIONAL DISORDERS**
**FRAGILE X**
**GENETIC COUNSELING**
**HUNTINGTON'S CHOREA**
**LESCH-NYHAN SYNDROME**

# GENETIC MAPPING

Developing new and better tools to make gene hunts faster, cheaper, and practical for any scientist was a primary goal of the Human Genome Project (HGP). One of these tools is genetic mapping, the first step in isolating a gene. Genetic mapping—also called linkage mapping—can offer firm evidence that a disease transmitted from parent to child is linked to one or more genes. It also provides clues about which chromosome contains the gene and precisely where it lies on that chromosome.

Genetic maps have been used successfully to find the single gene responsible for relatively rare inherited disorders, like cystic fibrosis and muscular dystrophy. Maps have also become useful in guiding scientists to the many genes that are believed to interact to bring about more common disorders, such as asthma, heart disease, diabetes, cancer, and psychiatric conditions.

To produce a genetic map, researchers collect blood or tissue samples from family members where a certain disease or trait is prevalent. Using various laboratory techniques, the scientists isolate DNA from these samples and examine it for the unique patterns of bases seen only in family members who have the disease or trait. These characteristic molecular patterns are referred to as polymorphisms, or markers.

Before researchers identify the gene responsible for the disease or trait, DNA markers can tell them roughly where the gene is on the chromosome. This is possible because of a genetic process known as recombination. As eggs or sperm develop within a person's body, the 23 pairs of chromosomes within those cells exchange—or recombine—genetic material. If a particular gene is close to a DNA marker, the gene and marker will likely stay together during the recombination process, and be passed on together from parent to child. So, if each family member with a particular disease or trait also inherits a particular DNA marker, chances are high that the gene responsible for the disease lies near that marker.

The more DNA markers there are on a genetic map, the more likely it is that one will be closely linked to a disease gene, and the easier it will be for researchers to zero in on that gene. One of the first major achievements of the HGP was to develop dense maps of markers spaced evenly across the entire collection of human DNA.

Genetic markers themselves usually consist of DNA that does not contain a gene; however, they can tell a researcher the identity of the person a DNA sample came from. This makes markers extremely valuable for tracking inheritance of traits through generations of a family; markers have also proven useful in criminal investigations and other forensic applications.

Although there are several different types of genetic markers, the type most used on genetic maps today is known as a microsatellite map. However, maps of even higher resolution are being constructed using single-nucleotide polymorphisms, or SNPs (pronounced "snips"). Both types of markers are easy to use with automated laboratory equipment, so researchers can rapidly map a disease or trait in a large number of family members.

The development of high-resolution, easy-to-use genetic maps, coupled with the HGP's successful sequencing and physical mapping of the entire human genome, has revolutionized genetics research. The improved quality of genetic data has reduced the time required to identify a gene from a period of years to, in many cases, a matter of months or even weeks. Genetic mapping data generated by the HGP's laboratories is freely accessible to scientists through databases maintained by the National Institutes of Health and the National Library of Medicine's National Center for Biotechnology Information (NCBI; ncbi.nih.gov). The information in this entry was provided by the public domain web site for the National Human Genome Research Institute of the National Institute of Health and can be reached online at http://www.genome.gov.

STAFF

# GENETIC AND RARE DISEASES INFORMATION CENTER

The Genetic and Rare Diseases Information Center (GARD) was created in 2002 by the National Human Genome Research Institute (NHGRI) and the Office of Rare Diseases (ORD)—two agencies at the National Institutes of Health (NIH)—to help people find useful information about genetic and rare diseases. GARD provides immediate, virtually round-the-clock access to experienced information specialists who can furnish current and accurate information, in both English and Spanish, about genetic and rare diseases.

So far, GARD has responded to over 12,000 inquiries on rare and genetic diseases. Requests come not only from patients and their families, but also from physicians, nurses, and other health care professionals. GARD also has proved useful to genetic counselors, occupational and physical therapists, social workers, and teachers who work with people with a genetic or rare disease. Even scientists who are studying a genetic or rare disease and who need information for their research have contacted GARD, as have people who are taking part in a clinical study.

Community leaders looking to help people find resources for those with genetic or rare diseases and advocacy groups who want up-to-date disease information for their members have contacted GARD. And members of the media who are writing stories about genetic or rare diseases have found the information GARD has on hand useful, accurate, and complete. GARD has information on:

- What is known about a genetic or rare disease
- What research studies are being conducted
- What genetic testing and genetic services are available
- Which advocacy groups to contact for a specific genetic or rare disease
- What has been written recently about a genetic or rare disease in medical journals

STAFF

GENETIC MAPPING
HUMAN GENOME PROJECT

# GENETIC TESTING

Genetic tests can be done to confirm a suspected diagnosis, to predict the possibility of future illness, to detect the presence of a carrier state in unaffected individuals (whose children may be at risk), and to predict response to therapy. Genetic tests may be carried out in the prenatal arena, either through preimplantation genetic diagnosis (where the diagnosis is made of an individual embryo before implantation), chorionic villus sampling (CVS), or amniocentesis. Most newborns in industrialized countries are tested at birth for a few genetic disorders that require immediate treatment. Genetic tests may be carried out on children (to confirm a diagnosis, but generally not to predict adult-onset disorders unless an intervention in childhood is essential). Genetic tests may be carried out on adults for all of these indications.

About 900 genetic tests are now offered by diagnostic laboratories (see www.genetests.org for a wealth of information on the specifics). Some genetic tests look at whether the number of chromosomes is correct and whether there is any evidence of a chromosome rearrangement or other abnormality. This kind of test, for instance, would detect Down syndrome (an extra chromosome 21). Most genetic problems are more subtle than this, so tests able to detect them must look at the actual DNA sequence of a particular gene. To detect a carrier of Huntington's disease, for instance, the test must discover a particular expanded repeated sequence of a gene on chromosome 4. If this repeat of CAGCAGCAG is very long, there is a high likelihood of the future onset of illness. For many genes, however, there are multiple different ways that the gene can be misspelled; in that situation, an effective test may need to detect many possible misspellings (usually referred to as mutations). A standard test for cystic fibrosis, for instance, looks for 32 different mutations in the so-called CFTR gene, but will still miss rare ones. Other types of genetic tests do not look at DNA at all, but look at RNA (the messenger that is transcribed from the gene), or at the actual protein product of the gene. Carrier detection for Tay-Sachs disease, for instance, actually measures the enzyme activity of the protein product.

### What Kinds of Tests Are Available Now for Predicting Disease Susceptibility?

The number of tests is growing, but most of these are currently applied only in families where there is a strong history of the disorder. For instance, BRCA1 and BRCA2 testing are only offered to individuals with a strong family history of breast and ovarian cancer. Similar situations exist for diseases such as colon cancer or Huntington's disease. But in the next few years, it is expected that a much longer list of susceptibility tests will become available, and may be offered to anyone interested in the information, regardless of family history.

Pharmacogenomics are tests that predict response to therapy. Some such tests are already available, such as a test for estrogen receptors in a breast tumor sample to see whether the drug Herceptin will be effective. A much larger array of tests that predict drug responsiveness for cancer, heart disease, asthma, and other disorders is under development, and some will reach the market soon.

It is likely that the major genetic factors involved in susceptibility to common diseases like diabetes, heart disease, Alzheimer's disease, cancer, and mental illness will be uncovered in the course of the next 5 to 7 years. For many of these conditions, altering diet, lifestyle, or medical surveillance could be beneficial for high-risk individuals. That will open the door to wider availability of genetic tests to identify individual predispositions to future illness, potentially for virtually anyone. If applied properly, this could usher in a new era of individualized preventive medicine that could have considerable health benefits. It will be important to remember, however, that most of these tests will not be "yes or no" but rather will predict relative risk. For this paradigm to succeed, it will also be essential that predictive genetic information is used to benefit individuals, rather than to injure them by discriminatory misuse.

This article was reproduced from public domain resources January 24, 2003, written by Francis S. Collins, MD, PhD, Director of the National Human Genome Research Institute at http://www.genome.gov/10506784.

STAFF

## GENETIC TRANSMISSIONS

Genetics, the scientific study of heredity, is the phenomenon wherein biological traits appear to be transmitted from one familial generation to the next. Gregor Mendel, the nineteenth-century Austrian monk, did the seminal studies leading to the founding of the field of genetics. The history of human genetics since that time has included the development of cytogenetics, biochemical genetics, molecular genetics, immunogenetics, population genetics, applied genetics, and clinical genetics. The science of genetics has shown that inherited traits result from the transmission of the parents' genes to their offspring. Genes interact with one another and with their environment to produce distinctive characteristics or phenotypes. Therefore, offspring tend to exhibit phenotypes similar to those of their parents.

There are two types of cell division that occur within the human body. Mitosis is the process of cell division that occurs in all cells, except for the sex cells or gametes. Gametes are divided during the process of meiosis.

Critical to genetic transmission are chromosomes, which are the small, rod-shaped bodies located in the nuclei of each cell. Each normal human body cell has 23 pairs or 46 chromosomes. During mitosis, cells divide by duplicating themselves, and each daughter cell contains 46 chromosomes that are identical to the 46 chromosomes contained in the original cell. During meiosis, the gametes divide by splitting into two separate distinct cells that each contain 23 chromosomes of the original cell. During reproduction, the male and female gametes join and produce a zygote that contains 46 chromosomes. One pair of the 23 chromosomes is different in size and shape and this atypical pair is related to sex determination. In all mammals, the female has two similarly sized chromosomes, called X, while the male has one X and a smaller Y chromosome. If an ovum is fertilized by a Y-bearing sperm, the zygote will be a male, but if the ovum is fertilized by an X-bearing sperm, the zygote will be female.

The actual units of hereditary transmission are the deoxyribonucleic acid (DNA) molecules or genes residing at specific loci on the chromosome. A recent estimate has indicated there are over 30,000 structural genes per haploid set of 23 chromosomes. The different variants of genes that control a particular trait and occupy corresponding loci on the paired chromosomes are called alleles. For example, one allele, or variant, of the gene for eye color produces blue eyes, while a different allele produces brown eyes. The paternal and maternal alleles for eye color are aligned beside each other in two adjoining chromosomes of the offspring.

According to Mendel's laws, one allele dominates the other in the phenotypic expression of a heterozygous genotype (genetic constitution). Dominant alleles are represented by capital letters and recessive alleles with small letters. Whenever one or both parents are heterozygous for a trait, as often occurs, their children are not all likely to inherit the same genotype as distinguished from its physical appearance (phenotype). For example, a male inherits blue-eyed (b) alleles from both his mother and father. He is therefore homozygous for eye color (bb); both alleles are the same, the zygote is homogeneous for eye color. The boy will have blue eyes and can pass only an allele for blue eyes to his offspring. If the boy mates with a girl who has alleles only for brown eyes, she can pass only a brown-eyed (B) allele to their child. Since this child receives the blue allele (b) from one parent and the brown allele (B) from the other, the child is heterozygous for eye color (Bb). The child will have brown eyes because brown eye color is a dominant trait. Because so many different gene combinations can arise from two parents, two siblings seldom have the same genes, unless they come from the same zygote; these offspring are identical or monozygotic twins.

## REFERENCES

King, R. C., & Stansfield, W. D. (1985). *A dictionary of genetics* (3rd ed.). New York: Oxford University Press.

Nora, J. J., & Fraser, F. C. (1981). *Medical genetics: Principles and practice* (2nd ed.). Philadelphia: Lea & Febiger.

Thaddeus, K. E. (1980). *Clinical genetics and genetic counseling.* Chicago: Year Book Medical.

Thompson, J. S., & Thompson, M. W. (1980). *Genetics in medicine* (3rd ed.). Philadelphia: Saunders.

KENNETH A. ZYCH
*Walter Reed Army Medical
Center*

**CHROMOSOMES, HUMAN ANOMALIES, AND
    CYTOGENETIC ABNORMALITIES
GENETIC COUNSELING
HUMAN GENOME PROJECT
KARYOTYPE**

## GENETIC VARIATIONS

The independent assortment of chromosomes during meiosis is a major reason for the variation of the genetic constitution in different individuals. Each gamete has 8 million possible combinations of chromosomes from the 23 pairs, and each set of parents has $7 \leftrightarrow 1013$ possible chromosome combinations to offer their children. Thus, with the incomplete exception of monovular twins, every person is and will be potentially genetically unique.

While genetics is the study of biological variations, medical genetics is the study of those variations that result in, or predispose one to, disease. Genetic diseases make a considerable contribution to the burden of mortality and morbidity in childhood. Mendelian and chromosomal diseases account for about 12 to 15 percent of childhood mortality, with congenital malformations contributing an additional 25 to 30 percent. Of all individuals with IQs below 50, at least 40 percent have a chromosomal disorder (of which Down syndrome accounts for about three-quarters); 15 percent have a single-gene disease (e.g., Huntington's disease, x-linked mental retardation, Tay-Sachs disease); and 45 percent have severe developmental malformation (Porter, 1982).

Generally, three major varieties of genetic disease afflict humans: Mendelian disorders caused by a single gene, cytogenetic disorders caused by chromosomal abnormalities, and multifactorial genetic diseases. In Mendelizing or single-gene diseases, the genetic factor is relatively simple. Three distinct patterns are recognized: dominant, recessive, and x-linked, of which there are 800, 550, and 100 known conditions, respectively. The most important of the genetic disorders of early development affect metabolism (e.g., phenylketonuria [PKU], a disorder of amino acid metabolism). Untreated, PKU results in severe mental retardation, decreased attention, and lack of responsiveness to the environment. Well-known autosomal dominant diseases are Huntington's disease, deafness (dominant forms), and neurofibromatosis (Von Recklinghausen disease). Cystic fibrosis is the most prevalent autosomal recessive disorder in white children. Tay-Sachs disease, also an autosomal recessive disorder, has a high prevalence rate among Ashkenazi Jews. Hemophilia is an x-linked recessive disease in which the blood fails to clot normally. Another genetic blood disease characterized by a tendency of the red cells to become grossly abnormal in shape is sickle cell disease, which affects about 0.25 percent of American blacks.

The second category of diseases results from failure of chromosomes to develop properly (chromosomal dysgenesis) during the formation of the oocyte or spermatocyte, or during conception and germination, resulting in an irreversibly abnormal chromosome makeup in the embryo. Extra and mismatched chromosomes, as well as structural anomalies, are major forms of dysgenesis. Examples of dysgenesis are trisomy 21, 18, and 13, as well as partial trisomies, mosaicisms, monosomies, deletions, and inversions. Sex chromosomal anomalies include Turner syndrome and Klinefelter's syndrome (XXY). For the most part, the disorders in this category are not inherited, but they involve the genetic material, the chromosomes. Mental retardation and physical abnormalities are the most common consequences of chromosomal disorders.

The more common abnormal genetic conditions are multifactorial in their causation and are characterized by a complex interaction of genetic and environmental factors. The genetic effects are complex and determined by the interaction of many genes, each contributing a small effect. Cleft lip and palate, congenital dislocation of the hip, pyloric stenosis, talipes, and equinovarus are well-known examples;

perhaps the best known examples are anencephaly and meningomyelocele, known collectively as neural tube defects. Carcinogens have been found to induce some kind of chromosomal rearrangements that are associated with a variety of human cancers (Radman, Jeggo, & Wagner, 1982).

## REFERENCES

Porter, I. H. (1982). Control of hereditary disorders. *Annual Review of Public Health, 3,* 277–319.

Radman, M., Jeggo, P., & Wagner, R. (1982). Chromosomal rearrangement and carcinogenesis. *Mutation Research, 98,* 249–264.

KENNETH A. ZYCH
*Walter Reed Army Medical Center*

GENETIC COUNSELING
GENETIC FACTORS IN BEHAVIOR
GENETIC MAPPING

# GENIE

The case of Genie involves an adolescent who experienced a degree of social isolation and experiential deprivation so far unparalleled in medical literature. The case came to light in 1970, when Genie was 13½ years of age.

From the age of 20 months to 13 years, 7 months, Genie was confined to a small bedroom at the rear of the family home. There, she was physically harnessed to an infant potty seat. At night, when she was not forgotten, she was removed from the harness and put into a sleeping bag which had been modified to hold Genie's arms stationary. She was then put into a crib with wire mesh sides and a wire mesh cover.

Genie received a minimum of care and stimulation. She was fed only infant food and wore no clothing. There was no TV or radio in the home, and as there were two doors separating her bedroom from the front of the house, where the remainder of the family lived, she could hear little of any family conversations. As her bedroom was set in the back of the house, away from the street, she heard few environmental noises. Her room contained only the potty and crib—no carpet, no pictures on the walls. The room's two windows were covered up except for a few inches at top. Genie's mother, having become blind shortly after Genie's birth, was unable to care for Genie, and so it was Genie's father and brother who were her primary caretakers. Together, they committed many acts of cruelty and abuse, among which was their consistent unwillingness to talk to her and beatings inflicted on Genie for making noise.

When Genie was found, she was extremely malnourished. She weighed only 59 pounds and was only 54 inches tall.

Never having been fed solid food, she was unable to chew or bite. She could not stand erect, and could barely walk. She was incontinent for feces and urine. Having been beaten for making noise, she was silent. She knew only a few words. She was essentially unsocialized and untrained.

Genie's case caught the attention of the scientific community because of the unique opportunity it offered for studying the human potential to "catch up" as it were—to develop social, cognitive, and linguistic knowledge after the typical points in development. Particular interest in Genie's potential for linguistic development was fostered by Lenneberg's (1967) critical age hypothesis for language acquisition. Lenneberg proposed that, as is the case with many maturationally timed species-specific behaviors, there is a critical period for first language acquisition—between the ages of two and puberty, beyond which a first language could not be learned. Genie faced the task of first language acquisition at 13½. Thus, her ability to learn language directly tested Lenneberg's hypothesis.

In the 9 years she was studied, Genie showed very uneven language learning ability. Most important in this regard is the striking contrast between her acquisition of morphology and syntax on the one hand and her acquisition of semantic knowledge on the other. Genie's acquisition of vocabulary and of how to express meaningful relations through words steadily progressed and increased, whereas her utterances remained largely ungrammatical and hierarchically flat (Curtiss, 1977, 1981, 1982). Genie's case, then, supports a weak form of Lenneberg's hypothesis in that while she developed some language, she did not acquire language fully or normally. Her case also suggests that different components of language are differentially vulnerable to the age at which language acquisition is carried out. In particular, her case points to the separability of a conceptual or referential linguistic component (which involves lexical knowledge and knowledge of semantic roles, and which is resilient in its developmental potential) from a grammatical component, which involves the constraints and rules of grammar, for which the acquisition potential appears to be far more maturationally constrained.

Although most of the scientific investigation carried out with Genie concentrated on her language development, a considerable number of standardized intelligence tests and tests of Piagetian operations were also administered. Remarkably, Genie evidenced 1 year's mental growth every year past her discovery and demonstrated full operational intelligence in spatial knowledge, with less developed ability in some other areas, specifically, those relying on verbal mediation.

The cognitive profile that Genie displayed lends support to a modular view of the mind in which grammar represents a distinct faculty of mind, separate from other components of language and separate from other mental abilities. For details regarding Genie's case history and language acquisition, see Curtiss, 1977. For details regarding her nonlinguistic cognitive abilities, see Curtiss, 1979. For a discussion of Genie's case and the critical age hypothesis, see Fromkin et al., 1974. For a discussion of Genie's case in connection with theories of language learning and cognitive development, see Curtiss, 1981 and 1982. Unfortunately, relations between Genie's mother and the research team studying her soured, and some disputes among those working with her arose. Lawsuits and other disruptions followed, and as a result, not only research on Genie but contact between her and the research team was legally restricted. For an interesting story of this aspect of Genie, see Rymer, 1993.

## REFERENCES

Curtiss, S. (1977). *Genie: A psycholinguistic study of a modern-day "wild child."* New York: Academic.

Curtiss, S. (1979). Genie: Language and cognition. *UCLA Working Papers in Cognitive Linguistics, 1,* 16–62.

Curtiss, S. (1981). Dissociation between language and cognition. *Journal of Autism & Developmental Disorders, 11,* 15–30.

Curtiss, S. (1982). Developmental dissociations of language and cognition. In L. Obler & L. Menn (Eds.), *Exceptional language and linguistics.* New York: Academic.

Fromkin et al. (1974). The development of language in Genie: A case of language acquisition beyond the critical period. *Brain & Language, 1,* 81–107.

Lenneberg, E. H. (1967). *Biological foundations of language.* New York: Wiley.

Rymer, R. (1993). *Genie: An abused child's flight from silence.* New York: HarperCollins.

SUSAN CURTISS
*University of California, Los Angeles*

**EXPRESSIVE LANGUAGE DISORDERS**
**LANGUAGE DISORDERS**
**LINGUISTIC DEVIANCE**

## GENIUS

The original conception of genius was of a deity that would reside within an individual and have a profound influence on the development of his or her mental powers and spiritual growth. Recently the concept of genius has been subsumed within psychology and philosophy. Galton (1869) developed a quantitative concept of genius as an innate or inherited ability, and Lombroso (1891) conceived of genius as a manifestation of abnormal psychology—as akin to madness. Hirsch (1931) even proposed that the genius should be viewed as a separate psychological species.

Historically, the term genius has been used synonymously with the term giftedness as measured by standardized tests of intelligence. In the early stages of Terman's research, Terman equated giftedness with high IQ, and expressed the view on many occasions that from high IQ children "and no where else, our geniuses in every line are recruited" (Terman, 1924). Also, in approaching his monumental longitudinal study of gifted children, Terman (1925) used the term gifted, but he nevertheless titled the entire series of books that resulted *Genetic Studies of Genius.*

Today, researchers note the differences observed between giftedness and genius, and thus make a conceptual distinction between the two constructs (e.g., Jensen, 1996; Simonton, 2000). Also, the term "genius" is used less frequently than it was. When it is used, it often references extremely high levels of adult creativity and accomplishment. Contemporary giftedness researchers incorporate the distinction between childhood giftedness and real world genius into their theories. Renzulli (2005) distinguishes between "schoolhouse giftedness" (which is most important during the grade school years) and "creative-productive giftedness" (which is most important for high levels of adult, real world achievement). Tannenbaum (1986) notes the distinction between those who are consumers of knowledge and those who are the producers of knowledge. Gagné (2005) makes the distinction between giftedness (which can be conceptualized as childhood potential) and talent (which may be conceptualized as adulthood achievement). Contemporary giftedness researchers are interested in determining the factors that link gifted potential to adult eminence.

Research on the origins and nurturance of genius has often taken the form of studies of eminent people or very high achievers, an approach pioneered by Galton (1869). In Volume 2 of *Genetic Studies of Genius* (1926), Catherine Cox and others (including Lewis Terman) studied the early mental traits of 300 geniuses, and estimated their IQs.

The biographical method continues today, with detailed analyses of unambiguously defined geniuses who are no longer living. There has been an increasing recognition among biographical researchers as to the importance of family, schooling, hard work, and other variables in determining giftedness. Howe (1999b) provides case studies suggesting the important influence of a stimulating and intellectual background in the development of genius. Gardner's (1993) analysis of seven eminent creators demonstrates that creators put enormous amounts of time and energy into their work. Taking a more quantitative approach, Simonton (1994) has attempted to identify environmental and personal trends that have affected the quality and quantity of a large number of famous creators.

Research by Bloom (1985), however, focused on living subjects who have achieved world recognition. The research by Bloom and his predecessors agree in the finding that genius, giftedness, special talent, and high ability often appear as precocious behavior; for instance, accomplishments in youth that far exceed normal achievements. However, Howe (1999a) notes case studies of individuals who were not particularly precocious while younger, but nonetheless grew up to be highly eminent creators. The reasons why childhood and adulthood are not always linked is an ongoing topic of interest among scholars.

## REFERENCES

Bloom, B. S. (Ed.). (1985). *Developing talent in young people.* New York: Ballantine.

Cox, C. M. (1926). *Genetic studies of genius. Vol. 2: The early mental traits of three hundred geniuses.* Stanford, CA: Stanford University Press.

Gagné, F. (2005). From gifts to talents: The DMGT as a developmental model. In R. J. Sternberg & J. E. Davidson (Eds.), *Conceptions of giftedness* (2nd ed., pp. 98–120). New York: Cambridge University Press.

Galton, F. (1869). *Hereditary genius.* London: Macmillan.

Gardner, H. (1993). *Creating minds.* New York: Basic.

Hirsch, N. D. M. (1931). *Genius and creative intelligence.* Cambridge, MA: Sci-Art.

Howe, M. J. A. (1999a). Prodigies and creativity. In R. J. Sternberg (Ed.), *Handbook of creativity* (pp. 431–449). New York: Cambridge University Press.

Howe, M. J. A. (1999b). *The psychology of high abilities.* New York: New York University Press.

Jensen, A. R. (1996). Giftedness and genius: Crucial differences. In C. P. Benbow & D. Lubinski (Eds.), *Intellectual talent* (pp. 393–409). Baltimore: Johns Hopkins University Press.

Lombroso, C. (1891). *The man of genius.* London: Scott.

Renzulli, J. S. (2005). The three-ring definition of giftedness: A developmental model for promoting creative productivity. In R. J. Sternberg & J. E. Davidson (Eds.), *Conceptions of giftedness* (2nd ed., pp. 246–280). New York: Cambridge University Press.

Simonton, D. K. (1994). *Greatness.* New York: Guilford.

Simonton, D. K. (2000). Genius and giftedness: Same or different? In K. A. Heller, F. J. Monks, R. J. Sternberg, & R. F. Subotnik (Eds.), *International handbook of giftedness and talent* (pp. 111–123). Oxford, UK: Elsevier.

Tannenbaum, A. J. (1986). Giftedness: A psychosocial approach. In R. J. Sternberg & J. E. Davidson (Eds.), *Conceptions of giftedness* (pp. 21–52). New York: Cambridge University Press.

Terman, L. M. (1924). The physical and mental traits of gifted children. In G. M. Whipple (Ed.), *Report of the society's committee on the education of gifted children* (pp. 157–167). The Twenty-Third Yearbook of the National Society for the Study of Education. Bloomington, IL: Public School Publishing.

Terman, L. M. (1925). *Genetic studies of genius: Vol. 1. Mental and physical traits of a thousand gifted children.* Stanford, CA: Stanford University Press.

SCOTT BARRY KAUFMAN
*Yale University*

**GIFTED AND TALENTED CHILDREN**
**GIFTED CHILDREN**

## GEORGE, WILLIAM REUBEN (1866–1936)

William Reuben "Daddy" George was born on June 4, 1866, in the hamlet of West Dryden in central New York. As a young man, he moved to New York City, where he established a small manufacturing business. Through his church, George began working with children in one of the city's most oppressive slums. He had notable success with city gangs, forming his own "law and order" gangs, which transformed young people from lawbreakers to law enforcers. Because children from the slums were often not accepted into the summer fresh air programs for city children, George started a program that provided a camping experience in a rural setting for these needy young people. George's summer program began in 1890 on a farm at Freeville, near West Dryden, and continued until he conceived the idea of a permanent community for young people based on the structure of the U.S. government: "our glorious republic in miniature—a junior republic."

In 1895 George gave up his business to remain at Freeville at the end of the summer with a number of students to begin a year-round program. The community that they developed was based on the principles of self-support—the students worked for their food and lodging—and self-government—the students made and enforced the laws governing the community.

George's ideas attracted the attention of educators and social reformers, and of prominent men and women who provided much of the financial support for the "junior republic." There was great interest in other parts of the country as well, and George supervised the establishment of nine similar communities in other states. None of these institutions consistently followed George's principles, however, and he considered the expansion effort a failure.

At the Freeville junior republic, George developed an

William Reuben George

elaborate educational and social system based on the principles of self-government and self-support. "Nothing without labor" became the junior republic's motto. The students, or citizens, as they came to be called, attended school, worked in the various jobs that made the junior republic almost entirely self-sufficient, and ran their own government.

George's junior republic, an early demonstration of the progressive education principle of learning by doing, was a major force in the development of programs for deprived, delinquent, and troubled youths in schools and institutions in the first part of the century. George headed the junior republic until his death on April 25, 1936. It is a tribute to the power of his ideas that George's junior republic, which today enrolls 170 adolescents referred by public schools, courts, and parents, still carefully adheres to its founder's precepts of self-support and self-government.

### REFERENCES

Holl, J. M. (1971). *Juvenile reform in the progressive era: William R. George and the junior republic movement.* Ithaca, NY: Cornell University Press.

Van Dyck, H. D., & Van Dyck, R. (1983). George junior republic: Fresh start for troubled teens. *Journal of the New York State School Boards Association,* pp. 15–20.

PAUL IRVINE
*Katonah, New York*

## GEORGIA STUDIES OF CREATIVE BEHAVIOR

The Georgia Studies of Creative Behavior is a research program devoted to the study of creativity. Established at the University of Georgia in 1966 by E.P. Torrance, it continued and expanded a similar program of research and development at the University of Minnesota—the Minnesota Studies of Creative Behavior (1958–1966). The Minnesota and Georgia research program has been concerned with the identification of creative potential, developmental patterns in creative thinking abilities, predictions of adult creative achievement, future imaging, instructional models and strategies to enhance creative thinking, the presence of creativity in various population groups, teacher training, creative problem solving, and cross-cultural studies of creative behavior.

The contributions to theory and practice regarding creative behavior from the Minnesota and Georgia studies have been numerous. Significant achievements and events have included the development and refinement of a battery of creative thinking tests, the Torrance Tests of Creative Thinking (TTCT), for use from kindergarten through adulthood; a 22-year longitudinal study to assess the creative achievement of adults whose IQs and creativity had been tested in elementary school; the Incubation

Model, an instructional model to enhance creative thinking and incubation; the wide-scale application of this model into the Ginn Reading 360 and 720 series; the Ideal-Pupil Checklist and the Torrance Checklist of Creative Positives; and the founding of the Future Problem Solving Program and the International Network of Gifted Children and their Teachers.

The program of the Georgia studies was supported and directed by Torrance with the assistance of J. Pansy Torrance, numerous graduate research assistants from different countries, postdoctoral students, and visiting scholars. Torrance (1984b) observed that graduate students throughout the world have participated in the studies through their questions, suggestions, and research findings.

Headquarters for the Georgia Studies of Creative Behavior are now located at the University of Georgia. Current activities are concerned with investigating the nature of mentoring relationships; sociodrama as an instructional strategy; developing and revising the streamlined scoring procedures for the TTCT; and verbal and figural work with the Torrance Center for Creative Studies at the University of Georgia in developing the Torrance Creative Scholars Program and the Torrance Creative Scholar-Mentor Network.

The work of the Minnesota and Georgia studies has resulted in the publication of over 1,600 articles, over 40 books, monographs, instructional materials, films, filmstrips, and other creative learning materials. The collection of these materials and other references on creativity, giftedness, and future studies are contained in the library and archives of Torrance, which are housed at the University of Georgia Library and coordinated through the Torrance Center for Creative Studies.

### REFERENCES

Torrance, E. P. (1974). *Georgia studies of creative behavior: A brief summary of activities and results (1966–1974).* Unpublished paper, Department of Educational Psychology, University of Georgia, Athens.

Torrance, E. P. (1979). *Highlights: Georgia studies of creative behavior (1970–1979).* Unpublished paper, Department of Educational Psychology, University of Georgia, Athens.

Torrance, J. P. (1984a). *Over the years: Research insights of E. Paul Torrance.* Unpublished paper, Georgia Studies of Creative Behavior, Athens, GA.

Torrance, J. P. (1984b). A retrospective view of the Minnesota and Georgia Studies of Creative Behavior. In *New directions in creativity research* (pp. 65–73). Ventura, CA: National/State Leadership Training Institute on the Gifted and Talented.

MARY M. FRASIER
*University of Georgia*

## CREATIVITY
## TORRANCE CENTER FOR CREATIVE STUDIES

# GERMANY, SPECIAL EDUCATION IN

Germany provides a well-equipped system of institutions for special education of disabled children and youth. Traditional special education services were developed under the concept of segregation. Not until the 1970s did a movement for integration emerge. It slowly moves forward, against quite a resistance.

Special education in Germany for many children starts in their first years of life. Early intervention for infants who run the risk of becoming handicapped or who are handicapped takes place in the child's home. Young children should not be institutionalized, if possible. In periodical turns—for instance, once a week for one hour—the early educator leaves the responsible resource center to meet the family, provided they agree, in order to give pedagogical and therapeutic help in a playing manner. In practice, this spread method of early intervention can be stonewalled if the family's living circumstances are not suitable or if the adults refuse regular house visits. In these cases, parents can visit the resource center with their handicapped child regularly. Special early intervention can also take place in an institution. In some regions of Germany, this centralized form is still preferred to the early home intervention. The reasons for this preference are more organizational than pedagogical.

Special early intervention also reaches clinical institutions, especially sociopediatrical clinics, where handicapped children and children at risk can get medical treatment, psychological consultation, and pedagogical support.

Early educational attention often continues during kindergarten time (3 to 6 years old). The early educator can visit the child at home; however, often this educator visits the child in the ordinary kindergarten and gives support in the children's group. The other children may participate in the pedagogical and therapeutic games and exercises. This prevents the handicapped child from being seen by other students as "special" and improves the child's social integration.

In addition, however, there are also many special kindergartens, each of which specializes in one specific kind of handicap. There are working governesses, most of whom have completed an additional course in special education, with groups of, for example, only mentally handicapped infants or only hearing-impaired infants. In some parts of Germany, special kindergartens have begun to open themselves to children without disabilities in order to promote integration. In Germany, for school-aged children and youth with special educational needs, there exist two main options: separate education in special schools, or integrative education with special educational support in ordinary schools. Special educational classes in regular schools exist as well, but are rare. Segregated schooling is built on a 200-year long tradition and still is quite prevalent. In the 1995/96 school year, 391,100 pupils attended special schools; that

equals 3.94 percent of all 9,931,500 pupils of general schools in Germany (Bundesministerium, 1996). The number of integratively-educated children represents only one-tenth of all students; nevertheless, the number is slowly increasing. Exact official statistics showing the number of integrated pupils with special educational needs in Germany does not yet exist.

Since the German reunion in 1990, the Federal Republic of Germany (F.R.G.) consists of 16 Laender. In their territories, the Laender maintain the sovereignty for culture and education. Some Laender with conservative school politics keep special needs students in compulsory special schools; other Laender are promoting integration in regular schools. The Conference of the Ministers for Culture and Education in the F.R.G. (KMK) intends to avoid development in different directions. According to a recommendation given in 1972 by the KMK, 10 types of special schools exist in Germany.

(1) Schools for learning disabilities:
With about 221,000 pupils (95/96), schools for learning disabilities are the most common type of special schools, but at the same time they are especially criticized, because learning disabilities are only defined in relation to school, and because before education age they cannot actually be diagnosed. Learning deficiencies fundamentally depend on the efficiency of regular schools, which can either support slow learners adequately or not. Through administrative trials, low performance in school is reduced to an intellectual handicap, which is indicated by an IQ between 55 to 85.

(2) Schools for the mentally handicapped:
Schools for the mentally handicapped were not founded until the 1960s. These schools take pupils who are not able to follow classes in schools for learning disabilities (IQ usually under 60). Nearly 60,000 children attend these schools.

(3) Schools for speech problems:
About 32,000 pupils in Germany attend these special schools. For many of them, it is a school to pass through on their way to another (regular) school or another type of special school.

(4) Schools for behavioral disorders:
In Germany, about 21,000 students with behavioral disorders attend this type of special school, which is in several Laender called *school for (special) educational support*. This type of special school is meant to be a temporary school, like the schools for speech problems; it should educate the pupils on the learning level of regular schools and send them back to a regular school after a few years' time. However, this happens very rarely.

(5) Schools for physically handicapped students:
Schools have about 20,000 pupils who are all very different from each other in the degree of their physical handicap as well as in their learning abilities. Many children

in the schools for physically handicapped students suffer from additional disorders such as speech development, sensory organ impairment, and mental retardation.

(6 & 7) Schools for the hard of hearing and deaf:
Both types of schools together teach about 10,000 pupils, most of them hard of hearing children. In the official statistics, hearing impaired and deaf students are not separated from each other. The Institution for the Deaf and Dumb, founded in 1778 in Leipzig, is considered the oldest special school in Germany. Special schools for hard of hearing children in Germany did not originate until 1900.

(8 & 9) Schools for the visually impaired and blind:
These two types of special schools are attended only by about 4,000 pupils; only about 1,000 of them attend schools for the blind. Quite often, schools for the blind and schools for the visually impaired are situated next to one another, so single students can easily change from one school to the other according to their educational needs.

(10) Clinic schools:
For most ill young people, this is a transitory school, because they are educated there only during the time of their medical treatment in the hospital. Instruction takes place in the clinic part for children, or if necessary, at the bed or their home.

Besides these 10 special schools, there exist further specialized institutions; for instance, schools for multiple-disordered students, such as deaf-blind students.

The continuously spreading expansion of special schools in Germany was decelerated in 1973 for the first time by the German Education Council, which pled for less segregation and more integration (Deutscher Bildungsrat, 1973). Therefore, since the mid-1970s, educational pilot experiments with integrated schooling ("Integrationsklassen") in primary schools (class 1–4 or 1–6) came into being, first in West Berlin and later in other German cities. Experiments also began later in secondary schools. Integrative classes are classes in regular schools, where three to five children with different disabilities are educated together with other children (without disorders) by two teachers: one teacher for ordinary students and one special education teacher. Since the mid-1980s, integrated schooling can also take place as "single-integration," which means that one single disabled child visits the school appropriate for its residential area, and a special education teacher comes for support only a few hours a week.

Both organizational forms are regarded as successful, and there exists a great deal of literature about the subject of integration (e.g., Eberwein, 1997; Hildeschmidt & Schnell, 1998). Half of the 16 Laender have moved integrated schooling from the experimental into regular status, and have generally opened integrated schooling by law, but always with the restriction that the parents of the disabled child must apply for inclusion and that the necessary conditions for the integration can feasibly be prepared. To establish the required conditions in some cases costs a lot of money and therefore can be refused by local authorities. Then the child with disorders has to visit a special school.

All German Laender still provide a fully developed group of special schools. Even with integrated schooling, only a few special schools have become superfluous. After years of argument and discussion, the KMK passed a recommendation in 1994 which agrees to integrated schooling as well as segregated schooling (KMK, 1994). Each of the Laender can decide on its own how quickly and in which form alternatives for segregated schooling are developed.

Some Laender, so far, only admit inclusion students on *according learning target*. This means that the disabled child has to reach the same curriculum goals as the classmates without a disability do, or else the year has to be repeated. Most of the German educational administrations strictly divide education with according learning target or with a different learning target. If the learning objective differs, an individually adjusted education plan is arranged for the disabled child, with different curriculum goals than classmates have to approach. Thus a learning disabled, mentally handicapped, or multiple-handicapped child can stay in a regular class without having to fulfill the same standard as the other students. Practice shows that especially learning disabled students need individual goals only in some of the subjects, and in others are able to share the regular curriculum. Still, some Laender do not allow inclusion with individual learning objectives.

At the moment, all young people have difficulties finding a job, and for young people with special needs it is nearly impossible. Public working administration in Germany certainly provides a complex system of support, but businesses do not use it. In addition to the free market, 600 sheltered workshops offer 160,000 workplaces for disabled people. To continue integrated schooling, for some years now projects of supported employment according to the United States' example are being implemented in many cities.

## REFERENCES

Bundesministerium. (1996). Grund- und Strukturdaten 1996/97. Bonn: Bundesministerium für Bildung, Wissenschaft, Forschung und Technologie.

Deutscher Bildungsrat. (1973). Empfehlungen der Bildungskommission: Zur pädagogischen Förderung behinderter und von Behinderung bedrohter Kinder und Jugendlicher. Stuttgart: Klett.

Eberwein, H. (Ed.). (1994). Handbuch Integrationspädagogik. Kinder mit und ohne Behinderung lernen gemeinsam (4th ed.). Weinheim: Beltz.

Hildeschmidt, A., & Schnell, I. (Eds.). (1998). Integrationspädagogik. Auf dem Weg zu einer Schule für alle. Weinheim: Juventa.

KMK. (1972). Empfehlung zur Ordnung des Sonderschulwesens. Bonn: Sekretariat der Kultusministerkonferenz.

KMK. (1994). Empfehlungen zur sonderpädagogischen Förderung in den Schulen in der Bundesrepublik Deutschland. Bonn: Sekretariat der Kultusministerkonferenz.

ALFRED SANDER
*Universität des Saarlandes*

ANETTE HAUSOTTER
*Bis Beratungsstelle Fur Die Integration*

## DENMARK, SPECIAL EDUCATION IN
## FRANCE, SPECIAL EDUCATION IN

## GERSTMANN SYNDROME

The Gerstmann syndrome consists of a constellation of problems including finger agnosia, right-left orientation problems, inability to calculate or do math (acalculia), and inability to write (agraphia). When first described by Gerstmann (1940), Gerstmann syndrome was believed to be a discrete, localized neurological problem denoting damage specific to the left parietal lobe of the brain. Considerable disagreement currently exists regarding the specific nature and causes of Gerstmann syndrome. Benton (1961) argued that the syndrome was prematurely described and was based on a serendipitous combination of learning and behavior problems with a variety of causes. Others have argued over its precise nature, some holding that the underlying deficit is aphasic in nature and others arguing that Gerstmann syndrome is related to left-hemisphere neglect. The constellation of behaviors occurring in concert is rare and whether or not they represent a true syndrome is difficult to discern. At present, the syndrome is principally of historical and theoretical interest; there are few treatment implications beyond remediation of the specific symptomatology. Children with this constellation of problems would likely be seen as severely learning disabled and require extensive special education services.

### REFERENCES

Benton, A. L. (1961). The fiction of the Gerstmann syndrome. *Journal of Neurology, Neurosurgery, & Psychiatry, 28,* 339–346.

Gerstmann, J. (1940). Syndrome of finger agnosia: Disorientation for right and left, agraphia, and acalculia. *Archives of Neurology & Psychiatry, 44,* 398–408.

CECIL R. REYNOLDS
*Texas A&M University*

## ACALCULIA
## AGRAPHIA

## GESELL, ARNOLD LUCIUS (1880–1961)

Arnold Lucius Gesell was a high-school teacher and principal before entering graduate school at Clark University, where he received his doctorate in psychology in 1906. In 1911 he became assistant professor of education at Yale University, where he founded the Yale Clinic of Child Development and began the studies of child development that were to occupy him for the rest of his life. To improve his qualifications for this work, Gesell studied medicine at Yale, receiving his MD degree in 1915. Gesell made a detailed, step-by-step analysis of infant behavior, establishing that infant behavior develops in an orderly manner through stages that are alike from child to child.

Gesell became a household name in the United States, primarily because of three books that he coauthored: *Infant and Child in the Culture of Today* (1943), *The Child from Five to Ten* (1946), and *Youth: The Years from Ten to Sixteen* (1956).

In addition to his studies of normal development, Gesell made numerous investigations of deviations in development, including mental retardation, Down syndrome, cretinism, and cerebral palsy. Following his retirement from Yale in 1948, Gesell continued his work at the Gesell Institute of Child Development, which was founded in his honor in 1950.

### REFERENCES

Ames, L. B. (1961). Arnold L. Gesell: Behavior has shapes. *Science, 134,* 266–267.

Langfield, H. S., Boring, E. G., Werner, H., & Yerkes, R. M. (1952). *A history of psychology in autobiography* (Vol. 4). Worcester, MA: Clark University Press.

PAUL IRVINE
*Katonah, New York*

## GESELL DEVELOPMENTAL SCHEDULES

## GESELL DEVELOPMENTAL SCHEDULES

The Gesell Developmental Schedules were first published by Gesell and his colleagues in 1940, although updated administration and norms are reported by Gesell, Ilg, and Ames (1974) and Ames, Gillespie, Haines, and Ilg (1979). The schedules provide an empirical method of measuring the development of infants and young children from 4 weeks through 5 years of age. Items on the schedules are ordinally arranged, with behaviors typical of successive ages (e.g., 42 months, 48 months, 54 months) listed. The administration of the schedules requires direct observations of children's responses to stimulus objects such as toys and parent interviews.

Four areas of development are included in the schedules: motor, adaptive, language, and personal/social. Items include walking up and down stairs, saying words and sentences, and imitating drawing circles and crosses. Behavioral norms for ages 2½ through 5 years of age are reported in Ames et al. (1979). Interrater reliability coefficients over .95 have been found (Knobloch & Pasamanick, 1974). The scales are quite dated and no longer useful in this form.

## REFERENCES

Ames, L. B., Gillespie, B. S., Haines, J., & Ilg, F. L. (1979). *The Gesell Institute's child from one to six: Evaluating the behavior of the preschool child.* New York: Harper & Row.

Gesell, A., Ilg, F., & Ames, L. B. (1974). *Infant and child in the culture of today* (Rev. ed.). New York: Harper & Row.

Knobloch, H., & Pasamanick, B. (Eds.). (1974). *Gesell and Amatruda's developmental diagnosis* (3rd ed.). Hagerstown, MD: Harper & Row.

PATTI L. HARRISON
*University of Alabama*

**BAYLEY SCALES FOR INFANT DEVELOPMENT–SECOND EDITION**

## GESELL SCHOOL READINESS TEST

The Gesell School Readiness Test (Ilg, Ames, Haines, & Gillespie, 1978), a behavior test for children ages 5 through 10 years, determines children's readiness for school and promotions to succeeding grade levels according to developmental level. The administration of the test requires about half an hour. The test consists of an interview with the child (questions about the child's age, birthday, number of siblings, and father's occupation); paper and pencil tests (writing name, address, date, and numbers); copying of forms (e.g., circle, triangle, square); finishing of a drawing of an incomplete man; right and left orientation; the Monroe Visual Tests; and questions about what the child likes to do best at home and at school.

Behavioral norms (i.e., the typical scores for children at each year from 5 through 10 years of age) are provided for each section of the instrument. Ilg et al. (1978) provide detailed descriptions of average children at each year from 5 through 10 years of age. Ilg et al. (1978) also report several psychometric characteristics of the tests. These include a description of the standardization sample and sex and group differences.

## REFERENCE

Ilg, F. L., Ames, L. B., Haines, T., & Gillespie, C. (1978). *School readiness: Behavior tests used at the Gesell Institute* (Rev. ed.). New York: Harper & Row.

PATTI L. HARRISON
*University of Alabama*

**GESELL DEVELOPMENTAL SCHEDULES**

## GETMAN, GERALD N. (1913–1990)

A native of Larchwood, Iowa, Gerald M. Getman earned his doctor of optometry degree from Northern Illinois College of Optometry (NICO) in 1937. He was subsequently awarded an honorary doctor of ocular sciences degree in 1957 from NICO as well as the honorary doctor of sciences degree in 1986 from the State University of New York College of Optometry. Getman conducted most of his work in Minnesota, Pennsylvania, and California, spending three years as director of research and child development (1967–1970) at the Pathway School in Norristown, Pennsylvania, and ten years in education and research in California, first as a member of the faculty at Southern California College of Optometry and subsequently (1978–1985) as part of a group practice in developmental optometry in Newport Beach specializing in children's learning disabilities. He served as a consultant on visually related learning problems to numerous public and private schools and taught special courses and seminars on children's learning problems as a visiting member of the faculties at Ohio State University, Yale University, Temple University, the University of Chicago, and institutions of higher learning in Australia and The Netherlands. Prior to his death in April 1990, Getman had moved to the Washington area where he continued to lecture and consult.

Getman's principal contributions to special education have been equally divided between developmental/behavioral optometry and education. He is widely considered as the father of developmental optometry, with his concept of vision development strongly influenced by his pioneering work with Arnold Gesell on the visual development of infants and children. Their joint research, conducted from 1944 to 1950 at the Yale Clinic of Child Development, contributed to the vision care of children that now enjoys widespread availability from optometrists (Getman, Gesell, Ilg, Bullis, & Ilg, 1949). Getman also had a significant influence on educational procedures used to guide children with learning problems. In order to best prepare children for an increasingly technological and abstract culture, he advo-

Gerald N. Getman

cated a parental role in planning their learning programs. In establishing these programs, he viewed clinical labels as ambiguous and useless, creating confusion instead of understanding (Getman, 1976).

Getman authored more than 300 professional papers as well as the book *How to Develop Your Child's Intelligence* (1962), which has become important internationally to both teachers and parents. His numerous publications include *Smart in Everything . . . Except School* and *Developmental Optometry* (both 1992). He is the recipient of the Pioneer Award of the National Association for Children with Learning Disabilities, the Special Award of Distinction of the International Federation of Learning Disabilities, and the Apollo Award, the highest commendation given by the American Optometric Association. Getman has also been recognized in *Who's Who in the Midwest*.

## REFERENCES

Getman, G. N. (1962). *How to develop your child's intelligence.* Luverne, MN: Getman.

Getman, G. N. (1976). *Teaching children with learning disabilities: Personal perspectives.* Columbus, OH: Merrill.

Getman, G. N. (1992a). *Developmental optometry: The optometric appraisal of vision development and visual performance.* Santa Ana, CA: Optometric Extension Program.

Getman, G. N. (1992b). *Smart in everything . . . Except school.* Santa Ana, CA: VisionExtension.

Getman, G. N., Gesell, A., Ilg, F., Bullis, G., & Ilg, V. (1949). *Vision, its development in infant and child.* New York: Hoeber.

E. Valerie Hewitt
*Texas A&M University*
First edition

Tamara J. Martin
*The University of Texas of the
Permian Basin*
Second edition

# *g* FACTOR THEORY

Charles Spearman (1863–1945) proposed a general intellectual ability, *g*, to account for the fact that all mental abilities are to some degree positively intercorrelated (Spearman, 1904, 1927). Spearman considered *g* to be a hereditary general mental energy that is manifest most strongly in tasks involving "the education of relations and correlates" (i.e., inductive and deductive reasoning) and "abstractness."

Spearman developed the statistical method of factor analysis by which it is possible to determine the *g* loading of a test, or the proportion of variation in the test score that is shared with all other tests in the analysis. This led to Spearman's two-factor theory of mental ability, in which the variation of each measured ability is divided into two parts: a part owed to *g* and a part specific to the particular test. The two-factor theory was later expanded to admit the possibility of group factors, representing groups of tests that share variation in addition to their general and specific variation.

More recent studies confirmed Spearman's observation that nearly all mental abilities are positively correlated. It has proved to be virtually impossible to devise a test that appears to involve mental ability that is not positively correlated with all other such tests when administered to a representative sample of people. Factor analysis of such positively correlating tests can always be made to yield a large general factor representing the variation that the tests share in common as indicated by their positive correlations. In such analyses, the tests with the highest *g* loadings tend to involve comprehension and abstract reasoning across a broad range of content. The greater the degree of mental manipulation of the input elements of the test items, the higher the general factor loading tends to be.

The observations that led Spearman to develop the theory of *g* are now well established; however, rival conceptualizations of the same observations have gained wide acceptance among psychologists. Thurstone (1938) extended Spearman's method of factor analysis to accommodate correlated factors and adopted the criterion of simple structure to determine the best set of multiple factors to represent the abilities contained in the tests being analyzed. The name primary mental abilities, which Thurstone attached to these factors, focused attention on the multiple differential abilities. The general factor, although still present, was hidden in the correlations among the primary factors. Following Thurstone, the number of known ability factors steadily increased. They have been organized into a model of the structure of intellect by Guilford (1967).

There is now general agreement that there are a number of distinct factors of mental ability that are substantially correlated with each other and that the correlation among the distinct factors represents a large general factor. The disagreement centers on which is most important, the multiple distinct factors or the single underlying general factor, *g*.

Jensen (1979, 1985) interpreted *g* as the basic biological factor of intelligence and attempted to relate it to general speed of mental processing. He pointed out that *g*, more than any other factor of ability, corresponds to the commonsense notion of intelligence, that it is most predictive of success in academic and occupational situations demanding mental ability. Today, users of intelligence tests have options as to how they measure *g*, if at all. The Wechsler Intelligence Scale for Children, Fourth Edition, for example, allows the examiner to calculate purer measures of *g*, such as the GAI index as opposed to the full scale index that includes processing speed and working memory (Prifitera, Weiss, Saklofske, & Rolfhus, 2005).

On the other hand, Dettermann (1982) suggested that

*g* may simply be an artifact of the difficulty of obtaining independent measures of the specific components of human ability. He pointed out that any complex system will have interrelated parts, which will tend to produce a general factor of functioning. Attending to the general factor, however, will not help in understanding the components of the system, which must be studied if one is to gain insight into the nature of intelligence.

## REFERENCES

Dettermann, D. K. (1982). Does '*g*' exist? *Intelligence, 6,* 99–108.

Guilford, J. P. (1967). *The nature of human intelligence.* New York: McGraw-Hill.

Jensen, A. R. (1979). *g*: Outmoded theory of unconquered frontier? *Creative Science & Technology, 2,* 16–29.

Jensen, A. R. (1985). The nature of the black-white difference on various psychometric tests: Spearman's hypothesis. *Behavioral & Brain Sciences, 8,* 193–219.

Prifitera, A., Weiss, L., Saklofske, D. H., & Rolfhus, E. (2005). The WISC-IV in the clinical assessment context. In A. Prifitera, D. H. Saklofske, & L. Weiss (Eds.), *WISC-IV clinical use and interpretation* (pp. 3–32). Burlington, MA: Elsevier.

Spearman, C. (1904). General intelligence, objectively determined and measured. *American Journal of Psychology, 27,* 229–239.

Spearman, C. (1927). *The abilities of man.* New York: Macmillan.

Thurstone, L. L. (1938). Primary mental abilities. *Psychometric Monographs, 1.*

ROBERT C. NICHOLS
DIANE JARVIS
*State University of New York at Buffalo*

CULTURE FAIR TEST
INTELLIGENCE TESTING
SPEARMAN'S HYPOTHESIS

# GIFTED AND LEARNING DISABILITIES

The incidence rate of a child to have both giftedness and a learning disability has not yet been adequately determined, although estimates range from less than 1 percent to as high as 10 percent (Karnes, Shaunessy, & Bisland, 2004). This discrepancy is due to a lack of common definitions as well as differences between state policies in program delivery for gifted children with or without learning disabilities. In a review of state policies for 2001, only 27 states mandated full or partial gifted programs, 9 required an individualized program, and only 4 required identification of gifted children to be conducted in the same manner as identifying children with learning disabilities (Shaunessy, 2003).

Some researchers and parents argue that giftedness is underidentified in children with learning disabilities because these children are able to compensate enough to function in the average range of academic ability. Part of this discrepancy is due to the generic term of "gifted," which may refer to global giftedness, or may refer to areas of giftedness such as cognitive, creative/artistic, leadership, or specific academic fields. Complicating this are the definitions and terms associated with learning disabilities, including the federal definition, state interpretation of federal definition, and ancillary terms (e.g., perceptual disabilities, dyslexia, minimal brain dysfunction). In 1993, Toll developed a conceptual classification of gifted and learning disabled children that continues to be used. The subtle gifted/learning disabled have been identified as gifted, and also have learning problems that begin to widen the gap between ability and performance. The hidden gifted/learning disabled are those children who may have both giftedness and learning disabilities, but neither is clearly seen. For example, a child with superior cognitive ability and a reading disability may be functioning in the average range, and thus would not be identified as either gifted or having a learning disability. A third group are students who have been identified as learning disabled and are being served as learning disabled; however, giftedness is shunted aside or ignored as the focus is on the learning disability.

Research would suggest that the best practices in assessment for gifted and for learning disabilities are the same. Careful multidimensional assessment of children is essential, whether looking for giftedness or learning disabilities. Identification of strengths and weaknesses is crucial, along with a careful analysis of discrepancies in scores. Information gathering from multiple sources, including teachers and family, is also important. In every situation, the assessment should consider if giftedness or learning disability includes each other.

## REFERENCES

Fetzer, E. (2000). The gifted/learning disabled child. *Gifted Child Today Magazine, 23*(4), 44–50.

Karnes, F. A., Shaunessy, E., & Bisland, A. (2004). Gifted students with disabilities: Are we finding them? *Gifted Child Today Magazine, 27*(4), 16–22.

Shaunessy, E. (2003). State policies regarding gifted education. *Gifted Child Today, 26*(3), 16–21.

Toll, M. F. (1993). Learning-disabled and gifted: A kaleidoscope of needs. *Gifted Child Today, 16*(1), 34–35.

CONSTANCE J. FOURNIER
*Texas A&M University*

ACCELERATION OF GIFTED CHILDREN
GIFTED AND TALENTED CHILDREN
GIFTED AND TALENTED, COUNSELING THE

# GIFTED AND TALENTED CHILDREN

Gifted and talented are terms that have many definitions that are influenced by theory, research, and political considerations. From a historical perspective, gifted referred to those who were in the highest 1 percent of those taking cognitive ability tests. In many states' definitions of gifted, the assumption is that giftedness is an ability that is formed and finished, rather than a trait that needs developing (Stephens & Karnes, 2000). These narrow views of giftedness have been changing. The concept of talent, which refers to above-average abilities that may be exceptional if nurtured, has entered the conversation. This concept is becoming more widely accepted, because talent can encompass academic abilities, which are traditionally associated with giftedness, as well as athletic, artistic, and other areas. Currently, the terms gifted and talented are interrelated and are often interchangeable in the literature.

Renzulli (2002) has proposed a definition of giftedness that includes three elements: above-average ability, creativity, and task commitment. These elements interact with the child's personality and the environment. Above-average ability refers to both general ability as well as specific abilities. Creativity refers to the ability to generate novel ideas. Task commitment refers to the energy and perseverance the child brings to a specific task or performance. The child needs support and challenge to bring out the best of the giftedness. This framework can apply to the concept of talent as well.

A key issue in the discussion of giftedness and talent is identification. While there may be opportunities to identify children with academic giftedness/talent, other forms of giftedness/talents may be less likely to be identified, particularly if there are no avenues for children to demonstrate abilities. This remains a dilemma in the educational system. Once a child is identified as gifted or talented, most experts agree that enrichment and acceleration can be helpful. Enrichment refers to extending the learning to include higher-level thinking, combining subject matter or skills, and including the child's interests. Acceleration allows learners to move faster in content or skill areas, often being placed with older peers who are at similar levels of ability.

## REFERENCES

Renzulli, J. S. (2002). Emerging conceptions of giftedness: Building a bridge to the new century. *Exceptionality, 10*(2), 67–75.

Smith, D. D. (2004). *Introduction to special education* (pp. 226–246). Boston: Pearson.

Stephens, K., & Karnes, F. (2000). State definitions for the gifted and talented revisited. *Exceptional Children, 66,* 219–238.

CONSTANCE J. FOURNIER
*Texas A&M University*

# GIFTED AND TALENTED, COUNSELING THE

For many years, research related to counseling the gifted populations was relatively scarce, because of prevailing beliefs that those who were gifted were also well adjusted (Keitel, Kopala, & Schroder, 2003; Martin, 2005). Currently, more attention has been seen in this area. Several areas that can be important for counseling children who are gifted have been identified.

One area is self-concept. The child who is labeled gifted may have issues integrating this into a more holistic concept of self. For instance, adults around the child may be focused on the giftedness, at the cost of the child feeling different and alienated from peers. Helping children who are gifted explore all aspects of themselves and feel good about themselves in general is important to overall adjustment.

Social skills development is another area that may require counseling. While many children who are gifted have good social skills, others may need support. For example, children who are gifted may have a difficult time understanding why peers can't see the world the way they do, and may respond with frustration, irritation, or sarcasm. This in turn affects relationships. Helping take another's point of view and having skills in how to deal with social situations that can be uncomfortable can be useful for the gifted child.

Traits often associated with giftedness, such as perfectionism or obsessive thinking, can be a focus of counseling (Lupart, Pyryt, Watson, & Pierce, 2005). The degree to which these conditions interfere with learning and social relationships will dictate the need for counseling.

Additional co-occurrence of mental health problems can occur with children who are gifted. Research suggests that children who are gifted may also have any of the mental health disorders seen in childhood (e.g., Flint, 2001; Little, 2002; Pfeiffer, 2001). Asperger syndrome, a form of autism, has recently come under examination, as some children with this syndrome may also have skills and/or talents that are highly developed and in some cases fall into the gifted range. These children may need counseling and intervention targeted toward symptom clusters, particularly in social interactions, stereotypical behaviors, and interference with social, academic, or occupational areas of functioning (Henderson, 2001).

Family issues can be a focus for counseling, especially

in terms of understanding reasonable expectations for the child who is gifted, as well as siblings who may be more typical. For example, how is the family handling the all "A" report card from the child who is gifted and put forth minimal effort, compared with the "A, B, & C" report card from a sibling who has put forth great effort? In particular, helping families adjust to typical and atypical developmental expectations can be helpful. As another example, the child who is gifted academically may be more typical in emotional development. The child's well-developed vocabulary and reasoning ability may mask emotional needs. Other issues that bring typical families to counseling, such as dealing with loss or behavioral problems, can also be a focus for families with children who are gifted.

Career counseling is important for the adolescent who is gifted. Often, while the child who is gifted can do well academically, there may be issues in deciding on career choices. Some children who are gifted move from interest to interest, making decisions about career choices challenging. Other children who are gifted focus in one area of interest, which may constrict career choices. Having the ability to explore career choices can be helpful, especially in terms of college choices and exploring which interests may be related to career and which interests may lead to important leisure choices.

There is no clear evidence that children who are gifted respond differently to empirically supported interventions for particular mental health support (e.g., career counseling or family psychoeducational counseling) or for specific disorder intervention (e.g., for depression or ADHD) when compared with more typical peers. This suggests that at this time, using empirically supported interventions associated with the presenting (or determined) issue is likely to be a reasonable course of action. There is no one specific theoretical approach or intervention type that appears to be best for counseling with children who are gifted and their families. In general, the counselor needs to be competent in the theoretical approach and interventions used. Further, the counselor must be sensitive to how well family and child expectations meet therapist expectations (Bourdeau & Thomas, 2003). In particular, the counselor may have to assist the family with a gifted child in negotiating the insurance system in order to be able to receive counseling (Anderson, 2001). Finally, the counselor must continue to monitor research to provide the best possible empirically supported interventions to meet the mental health needs of children who are gifted and their families.

## REFERENCES

Anderson, C. E. (2001). The role of managed mental health care in counseling gifted children and families. *Roeper Review, 24*(1), 26–32.

Bourdeau, B., & Thomas, V. (2003). Counseling gifted clients and their families: Comparing clients' and counselors' perspectives. *Journal of Secondary Gifted, 12*(2), 114–126.

Flint, L. (2001). Attention-Deficit/Hyperactivity Disorder; gifted children. *Teaching Exceptional Children, 33*(4), 62–70.

Henderson, L. M. (2001). Asperger's syndrome in gifted individuals. *Gifted Child Today Magazine, 24*(3), 28–36.

Jackson, C. M., & Snow, B. M. (2004). *In the eyes of the beholder: Critical issues for diversity in gifted education* (pp. 191–202). Waco, TX: Prufrock.

Keitel, M. A., Kopala, M., & Schroder, M. A. (2003). Counseling gifted and creative students: Issues and interventions. In J. Houtz (Ed.), *The educational psychology of creativity*. Cresskill, NJ: Hampton.

Little, C. (2002). Depression and the gifted child. *Understanding Our Gifted, 14*(3), 12–14.

Lupart, J. L., Pyryt, M. C., Watson, S. L., & Pierce, K. (2005). Gifted education and counseling in Canada. *International Journal for the Advancement of Counseling, 27*(2), 173–190.

Martin, L. R. (2005). Counseling the gifted and talented: Editorial and introduction. *International Journal for the Advancement of Counseling, 27*(2), 169–172.

Pfeiffer, S. I. (2001). Professional psychology and the gifted: Emerging practice opportunities. *Professional Psychology: Research and Practice, 32*(2), 175–180.

CONSTANCE J. FOURNIER
*Texas A&M University*

**GIFTED AND TALENTED, UNDERACHIEVEMENT OF THE
GIFTED CHILDREN
GIFTED CHILDREN AND READING
SIDIS, WILLIAM JAMES**

## GIFTED AND TALENTED, UNDERACHIEVEMENT OF THE

Underachievement is a discrepancy between ability and demonstrated performance, with performance considerably lower than ability. The child who is gifted may have many causal factors that contribute to underachievement. One set of factors may be in an overall biased attitude toward gifted children. Other children noticing differences or showing envy may influence the gifted child to not show his or her ability in order to fit in with peers. Another bias may be in the school and external support systems, which may act in a belief system that there is no need to provide support and services to help the child reach potential. Both of these biases can contribute to underachievement, where the child does not or cannot develop abilities.

Another key factor in underachievement is motivation.

Motivation, which can be described as the inner drive of enthusiasm and direction applied to behavior, can be negatively influenced by frustration and lack of success. The gifted child can be frustrated by curriculum that is unchallenging, a pace that is too slow, repetition of mastered material, too few opportunities to explore areas of interest, and emphasis on lower level thinking skills. In addition, the gifted child can feel support through identification with others who are functioning in a similar range (McCoach & Siegle, 2003). Without support and challenge, gifted children can lose their enthusiasm and drive. Without motivation, the child may not put forth the effort needed to acquire new skills and knowledge.

Underachievement can also occur but not be noticed if the gifted/talented child is not identified, or if the focus on a child with a co-occurring learning disability is solely on the disability. Three key elements in avoiding underachievement in children who have giftedness/talent include identification of ability, challenge and support of ability, and coordinated support of the child at school and at home.

**REFERENCES**

Ablard, K. E. (2002). Achievement goals and implicit theories of intelligence among academically talented students. *Journal for the Education of the Gifted, 25*(3), 15–32.

Gross, M. U. M. (2000). Exceptionally and profoundly gifted students: An underserved population. *Understanding Our Gifted, 12*(2), 2–9.

McCoach, D. B., & Siegle, D. (2003). Factors that differentiate underachieving gifted students from high-achieving gifted students. *Gifted Child Quarterly, 47*(2), 144–154.

Reis, S. M., & McCoach, D. B. (2002). Underachievement in the gifted and talented students with special needs. *Exceptionality, 10*(2), 113–125.

Smith, D. D. (2004). *Introduction to special education* (pp. 226–246). Boston: Pearson.

CONSTANCE J. FOURNIER
*Texas A&M University*

**GIFTED AND LEARNING DISABILITIES**
**GIFTED AND TALENTED CHILDREN**
**GIFTED AND TALENTED, COUNSELING THE**

# GIFTED CHILD QUARTERLY

*Gifted Child Quarterly* is a major publication in the field of the education of gifted children. It is published by the National Association for Gifted Children, 1707 L St. NW, Ste. 550, Washington, DC 20036-4201. The quarterly was first published in 1958 with an emphasis toward educational researchers, administrators, teachers, and parents of gifted children. The journal publishes manuscripts that offer new or creative insights about giftedness and talent development in the context of the school, the home, and the wider society. The journal also publishes quantitative or qualitative research studies as well as manuscripts that explore policy and policy implications. It is a refereed publication with a panel of 30 reviewers and an editor elected by the association board. All members of the association receive the quarterly as part of their membership privileges.

JOHN F. FELDHUSEN
*Purdue University*
First edition

MARIE ALMOND
*The University of Texas of the Permian Basin*
Second edition

# GIFTED CHILDREN

The major pioneer of the scientific study of gifted children in the United States was Lewis Terman, whose research on intellectually gifted students refuted popular myths regarding the physical and social inferiority of highly able children and showed that gifted youths were largely neglected in school (Terman, 1925).

The research of Terman (1925), Hollingworth (1942), Cox (1926), Witty (1930), and others promoted the establishment of prototype programs for the gifted such as Cleveland's Major Work Program (Barbe, 1957), and special schools for talented students such as the Bronx High School of Science (Galasso & Simon, 1981). Federal support, however, was limited and gifted programming was limited to centers of interest within the major cities.

In 1957 the advent of Sputnik generated national concern regarding the quality of science education in the United States and a concomitant focus on gifted youth. This spurred a second wave of programs for the gifted, this time concentrating on students with specific academic ability, particularly in the sciences and mathematics. The National Education Association commenced its Project on the Academically Talented and issued a series of publications on educating children talented in a range of specific curriculum areas (Bish, 1975).

In 1972 the Marland Report (Marland, 1972) broadened concepts of giftedness still further by defining the gifted as those who possessed outstanding abilities or potential in the areas of general intellectual capacity, specific academic aptitude, creative or productive thinking, leadership ability, visual or performing arts, and psychomotor ability.

The Marland Report also established criteria for differentiated programming for the gifted arising out of the broader definition. Appropriate curriculum for the gifted was defined as (1) based on higher level cognitive concepts and processes; (2) involving instructional strategies that accommodate differentiated learning styles; and (3) accommodating a variety of special grouping arrangements.

The establishment of the Federal Office for the Gifted in 1974 and the appropriation of funding for the establishment of gifted programs led to the strengthening of state support agencies, the establishment of national networks, and increased cross-fertilization of ideas among states and centers of interest in gifted education. The passage of PL 95-561 in 1978 provided for the escalation of funding for gifted education at the federal level. In 1981, however, the Office of Gifted and Talented was eliminated along with many other federal programs.

The early 1980s saw a proliferation of research studies on the effectiveness of gifted programming in the United States. Richert (1982) surveyed methods used to identify gifted and talented youths and found great diversity in procedures. Gallagher, Weiss, Oglesby, and Thomas (1983) surveyed teachers and parents of the gifted to determine which program models are most frequently used and preferred; resource rooms were most common at the elementary level and special classes at the secondary level.

Definitions of giftedness determine program design and curriculum development. Tannenbaum (1983) offers one of the most promising of new definitions of giftedness in children. He states "giftedness . . . denotes their potential for becoming critically acclaimed performers or exemplary producers of ideas in spheres of activity that enhance the moral, physical, emotional, social, intellectual, or aesthetic life of humanity" (p. 86). He goes on to suggest five basic factors related to giftedness. They are (1) general intelligence, (2) special talents, aptitudes or ability, (3) nonintellective factors such as dedication and ego strength, (4) environmental conditions that are stimulating or supportive, and (5) chance factors. Feldhusen (1986) has added to that definition by suggesting that the gifted need a self concept that recognizes and accepts their unusual potential for high-level achievement. Feldhusen suggests that giftedness in a child or adolescent consists of psychological and physical predispositions for superior learning and performance in the formative years and high-level achievement or performance in adulthood.

## REFERENCES

Barbe, W. B. (1957). What happens to graduates of special classes for the gifted? *Ohio State University Educational Research Bulletin, 36,* 13–16.

Bish, C. E. (1975). The academically talented project, gateway to the present. *Gifted Child Quarterly, 19*(4), 271, 282–289.

Cox, C. M. (1926). *Genetic studies of genius: Vol. 2. The early mental traits of 300 geniuses.* Stanford, CA: Stanford University Press.

Feldhusen, J. F. (1986). A conception of giftedness. In R. J. Sternberg & J. E. Davidson (Eds.), *Conceptions of giftedness.* New York: Cambridge University Press.

Galasso, V. G., & Simon, M. (1981). Model program for developing creativity in science at the Bronx High School of Science. In I. S. Sato (Ed.), *Secondary programs for the gifted / talented* (pp. 55–57). Los Angeles: National/State Leadership Training Institute on the Gifted and Talented.

Gallagher, J. J., Weiss, P., Oglesby, K., & Thomas, T. (1983). *The status of gifted, talented education: United States surveys of needs, practices and policies.* Los Angeles: National/State Leadership Training Institute on the Gifted and Talented.

Hollingworth, L. S. (1942). *Children above 180 IQ.* New York: World Book.

Marland, S. (1972). *Education of the gifted and talented.* Report to the Subcommittee on Education, Committee on Labor and Public Welfare. Washington, DC: U.S. Senate.

Richert, E. S. (1982). *National Report on Identification.* Sewell, NJ: Educational Improvement Centre-South.

Tannenbaum, A. J. (1983). *Gifted children, psychological and educational perspectives.* New York: Macmillan.

Terman, L. M. (1925). *Genetic studies of genius: Vol. 1. Mental and physical traits of a thousand gifted children.* Stanford, CA: Stanford University Press.

Witty, P. A. (1930). *A study of 100 gifted children.* Lawrence, KS: Bureau of School Service and Research.

JOHN F. FELDHUSEN
*Purdue University*

## GENIUS
## GIFTED AND TALENTED CHILDREN

## GIFTED CHILDREN AND READING

Four basic reading goals have been offered, in one form or another, for gifted and talented pupils: (1) mechanical skills, (2) appreciation, (3) knowledge of the devices of composition and literature, and (4) evaluation and the application of written material (Barbe, 1961; Cushenbery & Howell, 1974; Endres, Lamb, & Lazarus, 1969). Dole and Adams (1983) have suggested that reading programs for the gifted are similar to programs for other students, but in gifted programs there is more stress on evaluation, analysis, research skills, rhetorical techniques, and independence.

Textual analysis, the use of genre examples, and the teaching of social-cultural-historical context are central in teaching rhetoric to students who are gifted and talented (Rindfleisch, 1981). Vida (1979) and Brown (1982) have stressed the instructional importance of well-selected examples of literary genres and nonfiction sources. The appreciation of good writing appears to be based on exposure to good writing and opportunities to react to this writing. McCormick and Swassing (1982) have highlighted access to libraries and resource materials in their consideration of reading programs for the gifted and talented pupil. Further, the modeling of appreciation by significant others, teachers, and parents would seem also to facilitate students' appreciation of good writing.

Critical reading is the evaluation of writing content. Critical reading involves the evaluation of sources: what is known versus what is assumed or stated without support. Critical reading involves the analysis of the cogency of texts. Boothby (1980) has emphasized the differentiation of connotation and denotation. Miller (1982) has recommended that critical reading for the gifted stress propaganda devices, analogy, and the use of euphemism. Criscuolo (1985) offers suggestions about reading techniques that can teach and reinforce critical reading skills: (1) evaluating the accuracy of written information, (2) discriminating between fact and opinion, and (3) drawing conclusions from unfinished passages. Critical reading includes the evaluation and weighing of evidence, as well as the examination of the structure of written argument or presentation.

Creative reading involves interaction with text, problem solving, and the application of the content of text. In creative reading, a gifted and talented pupil ought to blend what is learned with previous knowledge. A basic goal of creative reading is a pupil's innovative application of knowledge by the creative reader's ability to recognize holes in information, construct new associations, and in turn form new ideas. Torrance and Meyers (1970) have suggested that one instructional step toward creative reading is the setting of reading goals for gifted and talented pupils: (1) the resolution of an ambiguous statement or situation, (2) the presentation of a problem to be solved, or (3) the finding of missing information or a concept that is critical in an argument or explanation.

## REFERENCES

Barbe, W. (1961). Reading aspects. In L. Fliegler (Ed.), *Curriculum planning for the gifted*. Englewood Cliffs, NJ: Prentice Hall.

Boothby, P. (1980). Creative and critical reading for the gifted. *Reading Teacher, 33,* 674–676.

Brown, J. E. (1982). Supplementary materials for academically gifted English students. *Journal for the Education of the Gifted, 5,* 67–73.

Criscuolo, N. P. (1985). Helping gifted children become critical readers. *Creative and Adult Quarterly, 9,* 174–176.

Cushenbery, D., & Howell, H. (1974). *Reading and the gifted: A guide for teachers.* Springfield, IL: Thomas.

Dole, J. A., & Adams, P. J. (1983). Reading curriculum for gifted readers: A survey. *Gifted Child Quarterly, 27,* 64–72.

Endres, M., Lamb, P., & Lazarus, A. (1969). Selected objectives in the English language arts. *Elementary English, 46,* 418–430.

McCormick, S., & Swassing, R. H. (1982). Reading instruction for the gifted: A survey of programs. *Journal for the Education of the Gifted, 5,* 34–43.

Miller, M. S. (1982). Using the newspaper with the gifted. *Gifted Child Quarterly, 23,* 47–49.

Rindfleisch, N. (1981). In support of writing. In D. B. Cole & R. H. Cornell (Eds.), *Respecting the pupil: Essays on teaching able students.* Exeter, NH: Phillips Exeter Press.

Torrance, E. P., & Meyers, R. E. (1970). *Creative learning and teaching.* New York: Harper & Row.

Vida, L. (1979). Children's literature for the gifted elementary school child. *Roeper Review, 1,* 22–24.

CINDI FLORES
*California State University, San Bernardino*

## GIFTED AND TALENTED, UNDERACHIEVEMENT OF THE

# GIFTED EDUCATION RESOURCE INSTITUTE

The Gifted Education Resource Institute (GERI) was founded in 1974 to help develop the gifts of talented people of all ages, through research and through the training of educators and other professionals—working closely with the local school systems, and through services for gifted people and their families. GERI in the Department of Educational Studies at Purdue University provides graduate programs in gifted education and a certification program for K–12 educators. GERI also offers intern opportunities for teaching with their GERI Summer Camps and Super Saturdays, a 9-week program for gifted students based on the three-stage enrichment model of Dr. Feldhusen, the director of GERI. GERI Summer Camps and Super Saturdays have been ongoing for over 25 years. Eight other faculty members besides Dr. Feldhusen and about 15 graduate students also work with GERI.

MICHAEL T. LUCAS
*California State University, San Bernardino*

## CREATIVITY, THEORIES OF
## GIFTED CHILDREN AND READING

# GIFTED INTERNATIONAL

*Gifted International* is a journal published by the World Council for Gifted and Talented Children. The founding and current editor is Dr. Dorothy Sisk of the University of South Florida. The journal publishes theory, research on, and discussions of problems and practices in gifted education from around the world. In the first issue Sisk stated the following specific aims of the journal:

1. Provide a forum for the exchange of research, identification procedures, curriculum, and good educational practices for the gifted and talented.

2. Generate cooperative sharing of gifted and talented practices and resources.

3. Stimulate cross-cultural research and provide opportunities for dissemination of findings.

The secretary of the World Council is Sisk; subscription orders for *Gifted International* should be addressed to her at the College of Education, University of South Florida, Tampa, Florida.

JOHN F. FELDHUSEN
*Purdue University*

# GIFTEDNESS, CULTURAL AND LINGUISTIC DIVERSITY IN

See CULTURALLY/LINGUISTICALLY DIVERSE GIFTED STUDENTS.

# GIFTED RATING SCALES

The Gifted Rating Scales (GRS; Pfeiffer & Jarosewich, 2003) provide a standardized method of identifying children for gifted and talented programs based on teacher observations. The scales also allow for identification of relative strengths and specific areas of giftedness. The GRS are based on federal and state guidelines regarding the definition of giftedness.

Preschool and kindergarten teachers complete the GRS-P form for children between the ages of 4:0 and 6:11. The GRS-P contains five domains: intellectual, academic readiness, motivation, creativity, and artistic talent. Convergent validity studies have been conducted with the Wechsler Preschool and Primary Scale of Intelligence–Third Edition (WPPSI-III).

The school-age GRS-S form is used to evaluate children between the ages of 6:0 to 13:11 who are in grades 1 through 8. The GRS-S includes six domains: intellectual, academic, motivation, creativity, leadership, and artistic talent. Validity studies have been conducted with the Wechsler Intelligence Scale for Children–Third Edition (WISC-III) and the Wechsler Individual Achievement Test–Second Edition (WIAT-II).

## REFERENCES

Jarosewich, T., Pfeiffer, S. I., & Morris, J. (2002). Identifying gifted students using teacher rating scales: A review of existing instruments. *Journal of Psychoeducational Assessment, 20,* 322–336.

Pfeiffer, S. I., & Jarosewich, T. (2003). *The Gifted Rating Scales.* San Antonio, TX: Psychological Corporation.

RON DUMONT
*Fairleigh Dickinson University*

JOHN O. WILLIS
*Rivier College*

# GILLIAM AUTISM RATING SCALE

The Gilliam Autism Rating Scale (GARS; Gilliam, 2001) is an individually administered measure used to identify individuals ages 3 through 22 who manifest the severe behavioral problems characteristic of autism. The scale contains 42 items that are rated on the presence and frequency of certain behaviors. These items comprise three of the four subscales including Stereotyped Behaviors, Communication, and Social Interaction. The fourth subscale, Developmental Disturbances, provides 14 additional items that allow parents or caregivers to report information about the individual's development during the first 3 years of life. The four subscales are summed to produce an Autism Quotient (AQ), which indicates the likelihood that an individual has this disorder. Administration time usually takes between 5 to 10 minutes; the measure should be completed by an individual who has had direct, sustained contact with the child or young adult (e.g., parents, teachers). The record form provides the rater with instructions and contains a score summary section, a profile of scores, and an AQ interpretation guide.

This measure was normed on a sample of 1,092 individuals between 2 and 28 years of age. The sample was representative of the 1997 U.S. census data with respect to race and geographic region. There were a significantly larger percentage of males in the sample compared with females, since it has been consistently reported in research that males are three to four times more likely to be diagnosed with autism than females. The GARS yields percentile ranks and standard scores (with a mean of 10 and a standard deviation of 3) for the subtests and a percentile rank and quotient score (with a mean of 100 and a standard deviation of 15) derived from the sum of the subscale scores.

The internal consistency of the items on the GARS was determined to be .96 for the total test (all 56 items) and .88 or higher for the subtests. The GARS has also demonstrated strong interrater reliability, with correlation coefficients averaging better than .80. Test-retest reliability of the Stereotyped Behaviors subscale, Communication subscale, Social Interaction subscale, and Autism Quotient range from .81 to .88 for a 2-week interval. Since the measure is new, extensive studies of validity have not yet been completed. Studies have demonstrated that the GARS can be used to differentiate individuals with autism from other diagnostic groups, and evidence of concurrent validity has been established with strong positive correlations between scores on this instrument and scores on relevant subtests of the Autism Screening Instrument for Educational Planning (Krug, Arick, & Almond, 1993). However, there has also been some criticism that children with *DSM-IV* diagnoses of autism will be classified less frequently when using the criteria specified by the GARS (South et al., 2002).

## REFERENCES

Gilliam, J. E. (2001). *Gilliam Autism Rating Scale: Examiner's manual.* Austin, TX: PRO-ED.

Impara, J. C., & Plake, B. S. (Eds.). (1998). *The thirteenth mental measurements yearbook.* Lincoln, NE: Buros Institute of Mental Measurements.

Krug, D. A., Arick, J. R., & Almond, P. J. (1993). *Autism Screening Instrument for Educational Planning* (2nd ed.). Austin, TX: PRO-ED.

South, M., Williams, B. J., McMahon, W. M., Owley, T., Filipek, P. A., Shernoff, E., Corsello, C., Lainhart, J. E., Landa, R., & Ozonoff, S. (2002). Utility of the Gilliam Autism Rating Scale in research and clinical populations. *Journal of Autism and Developmental Disorders, 32,* 593–599.

RON DUMONT
*Fairleigh Dickinson University*

JOHN O. WILLIS
*Rivier College*

# GILLINGHAM-STILLMAN: ALPHABETIC APPROACH

Anna Gillingham and Bessie Stillman derived their remedial training for children with specific disabilities in reading, spelling, and penmanship from the work of Dr. Samuel T. Orton. Orton was a neurologist who spent his career studying and treating children and adults with specific difficulties in reading, writing, and spelling. Both Gillingham and Stillman were teachers at the Ethical Culture Schools in New York City. Gillingham left the schools to become a research fellow under Orton at the Neurological Institute at Columbia-Presbyterian Medical Center, New York. She worked closely with Orton and then Stillman to devise and refine their teaching approach for children with specific language disabilities.

The Gillingham-Stillman approach was remedial, designed for children from third through sixth grades who had normal intelligence, normal sensory acuity, a tendency for letter or word reversals, and an inability to acquire reading and spelling skills by ordinary methods, for instance, "sight word methods even when these are reinforced by functional, incidental, intrinsic, or analytic phonics, or by tracing procedures" (Gillingham & Stillman, 1960, p. 17).

The technique was based on the close association of visual, auditory, and kinesthetic elements forming what has been called the language triangle. The following is the description of phonogram presentation from the manual by Gillingham and Stillman (1960):

Each new phonogram is taught by the following processes, which are referred to as associations and involve the associations between visual (V), auditory (A), and kinesthetic (K) records on the brain. Association I. This association consists of two parts—association of the visual symbol with the name of the letter, and association of the visual symbol with the sound of the letter: also the association of the feel of the child's speech organs in producing the name or sound of the letter as he hears himself say it. Association I is V-A and A-K. Part b. is the basis for oral reading.

Part a. The card is exposed and the name of the letter is spoken by the teacher and repeated by the pupil.

Part b. As soon as the name has been really mastered, the sound is made by the teacher and repeated by the pupil.

Association II. The teacher makes the sound represented by the letter (or phonogram), the face of the card not being seen by the pupil, and says "Tell me the name of the letter that has this sound." Sound to name is A-A, and is essentially oral spelling.

Association III. The letter is carefully made by the teacher and its form, orientation, etc., explained. It is then traced by the pupil, then copied, written from memory, and finally written again with eyes averted while the teacher watches closely. This association is V-K and K-V. . . . Now, the teacher makes the sound, saying "Write the letter that has this sound." This association is A-K, and is the basis of written spelling. (p. 40)

Although the initial, primary focus was a direct approach to phonetic decoding via multiple sensory pathways, this was an integrated, total language approach. Each unit is established through hearing, speaking, seeing, and writing it. The visual, auditory, and kinesthetic patterns reinforce each other. It is a systematic, sequential approach, proceeding from the simple to the more complex in the orderly progression of language development. Such a concept originated in the works of Maria Montessori, Grace Fernald, and Samuel Orton. Currently, popular offshoots of the Gillingham-Stillman approach are Enfield and Greene's Project READ, the Slingerland method, Spalding's Writing Road to Reading, the Herman method, and Traub's Recipe for Reading. This method is the basis for most current remediation programs with dyslexic children.

## REFERENCES

Gillingham, A., & Stillman, B. (1960, 1970). *Remedial training for children with specific disability in reading, spelling and penmanship* (7th ed.). Cambridge, MA: Educators Publishing Service.

Orton, S. T. (1937). *Reading, writing and speech problems in children.* New York: Norton.

SYLVIA O. RICHARDSON
*University of South Florida*

**READING DISORDERS**
**READING REMEDIATION**

## GLAUCOMA

See VISUALLY IMPAIRED.

## GLIAL CELLS

In addition to the neuron, there are a variety of brain cells that function in a supportive role. These are the glial or neuroglial cells (Brodal, 1981). The glial cells are 5 to 10 times more numerous than neurons. The name is derived from the Greek derivative *glia,* which means glue. Originally, the glial cells were thought to function only as supportive tissue for the intricate neuronal matrix of the brain. While glial cells do play an important supportive role, it is now known that glial cells may play an even more dynamic, interactive, and regulatory role in brain function. For example, it is now known that many glial cells surround synaptic areas in an apparent network to restrict the escape of and specify the direction of neurotransmitter release between neurons. Glial cells may also play a nutritive role, providing a pathway from the vascular system to individual nerve cells (Rosenzweig & Leiman, 1982). Similarly, glial cells may assist in directing or redirecting blood flow, especially to active cerebral regions (Bloom, Lazerson, & Hofstadter, 1985). Glial cells also participate in regulating neuronal growth and direction of neuronal interaction (Cotman & McGaugh, 1980).

There are several types of glial cells, the most common being the astrocyte (Latin *astra,* meaning star). Another common glial cell is the oligodendrocyte (Greek *oligo,* meaning few), which is considerably smaller than the astrocyte, with fewer processes and appendages. The third major glial cell type is the microglial, which, as its name implies, is very small. The microglial cells function in phagocytosis of neuronal debris.

Abnormal proliferation of glial cells is the basis of many types of cerebral tumors (astrocytomas). Also, the breakdown of glial cells (e.g., the axonal myelin sheath produced by the oligodendroglia) is the basis of certain degenerative brain disorders (e.g., multiple sclerosis).

Some anatomic findings in the brain of dyslexic individuals have demonstrated significant abnormalities in not only neuronal microstructure, but also glial cell development (Duffy & Geschwind, 1985; Galaburda & Kemper, 1979). These and similar findings suggest that glial cell abnormalities may play an important role in the expression of certain neurobehavioral disorders.

## REFERENCES

Bloom, F. E., Lazerson, A., & Hofstadter, L. (1985). *Brain, mind, and behavior.* New York: Freeman.

Brodal, A. (1981). *Neurological anatomy* (3rd ed.). New York: Oxford University Press.

Cotman, C. W., & McGaugh, J. L. (1980). *Behavioral neuroscience.* New York: Academic.

Duffy, F. H., & Geschwind, N. (1985). *Dyslexia: A neuroscientific approach to clinical evaluation.* Boston: Little, Brown.

Galaburda, A. M., & Kemper, T. L. (1979). Cytoarchitectonic abnormalities in developmental dyslexia: A case study. *Annals of Neurology, 6,* 94–100.

Rosenzweig, M. R., & Leiman, A. L. (1982). *Physiological psychology.* Lexington, MA: Heath.

ERIN D. BIGLER
*Brigham Young University*

**CENTRAL NERVOUS SYSTEM**
**DENDRITES**
**MULTIPLE SCLEROSIS**

## GOALS, ANNUAL

See ANNUAL GOALS.

## GOALS, USE OF

Educational goals serve three important functions: (1) to structure teaching and curriculum development, (2) to guide learners by helping them recognize errors and discriminate among responses, and (3) to structure the evaluation process (Bloom, Hastings, & Madaus, 1971).

The use of goals in special education was mandated in 1975 by the Education for All Handicapped Children Act (PL 94-142) and has continued under its successor legislation, the Individuals with Disabilities Education Act (IDEA). Incorporation of educational goals into PL 94-142 and the IDEA was prompted by congressional concern for accountability, not by a desire to facilitate the educational purposes cited previously (Fuchs & Deno, 1982). In its fact finding for PL 94-142, Congress found that the special education needs of children with disabilities were not being met fully and that the goal specification component of the law would ensure that schools would be accountable for the quality of the programs they provide to such pupils (Turnbull & Turnbull, 1978).

Given this legal mandate, the writing of goals has become standard special education practice; that is, teachers routinely write goals on students' individual educational programs (IEPs). Additionally, as mandated by PL 94-142 and subsequently IDEA, teachers are required to monitor their students' progress toward those goals. This typically translates into informal evaluations of student goal mastery approximately two to three times each year (Fuchs & Fuchs, 1984).

Despite the widespread use of goals and periodic evaluation of goal mastery in special education, research is scant on the effects of goal use among students with disabilities. Moreover, even within the regular education literature, where empirical support for the general effectiveness of goals is provided, only limited information is available concerning specific dimensions of effective goal-writing procedures, and most studies have been conducted with adults (Fuchs, 1986).

Therefore, there is no meaningful database concerning the general effectiveness of goals for students with disabilities or the nature of specific dimensions of effective goals. Not surprisingly, it remains unclear whether special education teachers employ goals for instructional planning (Tymitz, 1981) or systematic progress monitoring (Fuchs & Fuchs, 1984) once they have fulfilled the legal requirement of completing goals on IEPs.

## REFERENCES

Bloom, B. S., Hastings, J. T., & Madaus, G. F. (1971). *Handbook on formative and summative evaluation of student learning.* New York: McGraw-Hill.

Fuchs, L. S. (1986). *Use of goals with handicapped learners.* Unpublished paper, Vanderbilt University, Nashville, TN.

Fuchs, L. S., & Deno, S. L. (1982). *Developing goals and objectives for educational programs.* Washington, DC: American Association of Colleges for Teacher Education.

Fuchs, L. S., & Fuchs, D. (1984). Criterion-referenced assessment without measurement: How accurate for special education? *Remedial & Special Education, 5*(4), 29–32.

Turnbull, H. R., & Turnbull, A. P. (1978). *Free appropriate public education: Law and implementation.* Denver, CO: Love.

Tymitz, B. L. (1981). Teacher performance on IEP instructional planning tasks. *Exceptional Children, 48,* 258–260.

LYNN S. FUCHS
DOUGLAS FUCHS
*Peabody College, Vanderbilt University*
Second edition

KIMBERLY F. APPLEQUIST
*University of Colorado at Colorado Springs*
Third edition

INDIVIDUAL EDUCATION PLAN
INDIVIDUALS WITH DISABILITIES EDUCATION
    IMPROVEMENT ACT OF 2004 (IDEIA)
TEACHER EFFECTIVENESS

Henry H. Goddard

# GODDARD, HENRY H. (1866–1957)

Henry Herbert Goddard received his PhD in psychology at Clark University. He taught at the Pennsylvania State Teachers College at West Chester before becoming director of research at The Training School at Vineland, New Jersey, in 1906. Specializing in the study of atypical children, his work at the Training School was a major influence on the education of children and adults with mental retardation in the United States. He established the first psychological laboratory devoted to the study of the mentally retarded, and developed and tested educational methods for their instruction. He translated and adapted the Binet-Simon Intelligence Scale and inaugurated its use in the United States. He also participated in the development of the group tests used to classify the men in the U.S. armed forces in World War I. Goddard conducted a classic study of mental retardation as an inherited trait, reported in 1912 in *The Kallikak Family: A Study in the Heredity of Feeblemindedness.*

In 1918 Goddard was appointed director of the State Bureau of Juvenile Research in Ohio. From 1922 until his retirement in 1938, he was professor of abnormal and clinical psychology at Ohio State University.

## REFERENCE

Goddard, H. H. (1912). *The Kallikak family: A study in the heredity of feeblemindedness.* New York: Macmillan.

PAUL IRVINE
*Katonah, New York*

# GOLD, MARC (1931–1982)

Vocational training, job placement, and respect for the moderately, severely, and profoundly mentally disabled was a vision Marc Gold forged into a reality. His interests during his teaching of the mentally retarded in Los Angeles led him to pursue a doctoral degree in experimental child psychology and special education. In 1969 he joined the University of Illinois faculty as a research professor and began working at the Institute for Child Behavior and Development.

Gold's strong philosophy of respect for persons with mental retardation acted as the foundation for all of his efforts. Gold (1980) believed that (1) the mentally handicapped are served best by training them in marketable skills; (2) individuals identified as mentally handicapped respond to learning best in a situation based on respect of their worth and capabilities; (3) given the appropriate training, the mentally retarded have the capability to demonstrate competence; (4) when a lack of learning occurs, it should first be interpreted as a result of inappropriate or insufficient teaching strategies rather than the individual's inability to learn; (5) intellectual testing is limiting to the mentally retarded; (6) the labeling of people as mentally retarded is unfair and counterproductive; and (7) trainers should never assume that they are approaching the maximum potential of their learner.

Extolling this philosophy, Gold developed Try Another Way, a systematic training program for individuals who find it difficult to learn (1980). The strategies employed were physical prompts, modeling, manipulation of the learner's hands, and short specific phrases like, "Try another way." Task completion was met with silence as Gold believed no news is good news. The Try Another Way system is based on task analysis. Components of task analysis include method (the way the task is performed), content (the amount of steps the method is divided into), and process (the way the task is taught). Process is subdivided into format (the presentation of the material), feedback (cues so the learner knows what is wanted), procedure (description of the proposed training plan), criterion (the predetermined point when learning takes place), and data collection (the charting of steps accomplished and still to be mastered).

Gold's research (1972, 1973, 1974, 1976, 1980) consistently supports task analysis as a learning strategy with the autistic, deaf/blind, and multihandicapped for tasks such as self-help, mobility, and vocational and social skills.

In addition to the development of the Try Another Way system, Gold created an organization that disseminated information regarding the program, was the president of the Workshop Division of the Illinois Rehabilitation Association, was a member of the Executive Board of the American Association for the Education of the Severely/Profoundly Handicapped, was vice president of the Vocational Rehabilitation Division of the American Association on Mental Deficiency, and was consulting editor or member of the editorial board of *The American Journal of Mental Deficiency, Mental Retardation,* and *Education and Treatment of Children.*

## REFERENCES

Gold, M. W. (1972). Stimulus factors in skill training of retarded adolescents on a complex assembly task: Acquisition, transfer, and retention. *American Journal of Mental Deficiency, 76,* 517–526.

Gold, M. W. (1973). Factors affecting production by the retarded: Base rate. *Mental Retardation, 11*(6), 41–45.

Gold, M. W. (1974). Redundant cue removal in skill training for the mildly and moderately retarded. *Education & Training of the Mentally Retarded, 9,* 5–8.

Gold, M. W. (1976). Task analysis of a complex assembly task by the retarded blind. *Exceptional Children, 4,* 78–84.

Gold, M. W. (1980). *Did I say that?* Champaign, IL: Research.

Gold, M. W., & Barclay, C. R. (1973a). The learning of difficult visual discriminations by the moderately and severely retarded. *Mental Retardation, 11*(2), 9–11.

Gold, M. W., & Barclay, C. R. (1973b). The effects of verbal labels on the acquisition and retention of a complex assembly task. *Training School Bulletin, 70*(1), 38–42.

SHARI A. BEVINS
*Texas A&M University*

# GOLDEN, CHARLES J. (1949–    )

Charles J. Golden received his BA from Pomona College in 1971 and his PhD in clinical psychology from the University of Hawaii in 1975. He completed an internship in clinical psychology at Hawaii State Hospital and established a neuropsychology laboratory at the University of South Dakota (1975–1978) and later at the University of Nebraska Medical Center. He is currently a professor of psychology at Nova Southeastern University in Fort Lauderdale, Florida. His strongest interests are in the areas of psychological assessment, with a major emphasis on clinical neuropsychology.

He is best known for his work in the development of a standardized, American version of Luria's *methode clinique,* a neuropsychological investigation of individual cases known as the Luria-Nebraska Neuropsychological Battery. This battery attempts to integrate the qualitative approach to psychological assessment advocated by Luria with the quantitative, standardized approaches to assessment that have long characterized western psychology. It also tries to provide a broad evaluation of neuropsychological skill in a general battery applicable to a wide range of patients, administered in diverse settings with a minimum of equipment. The children's version of the battery addresses special education with the assessment of learning deficit suspected of having a neurological base.

Golden is also known for his study of the neurological basis of psychiatric disorders. His work includes an integration of test results from neurological procedures such as computerized tomography and regional cerebral blood flow with psychological and behavioral test results. As a result of this work, a subgroup of psychiatric patients with organic dysfunction that can be hypothesized to be the cause of their disorder has been found.

Golden's major publications include *Clinical Interpretation of Objective Psychological Tests, Interpretation of the Halstead-Reitan Neuropsychological Battery: A Casebook Approach, Diagnosis and Rehabilitation in Clinical Neuropsychology, Item Interpretation of the Luria-Nebraska Neuropsychological Battery,* and *Interpretation of the Luria-Nebraska Neuropsychological Battery.*

## REFERENCES

Golden, C. J. (1979). *Clinical interpretation of objective psychological tests.* New York: Grune & Stratton.

Golden, C. J. (1981). *Diagnosis and rehabilitation in clinical neuropsychology.* Springfield, IL: Thomas.

Golden, C. J., Hammeke, T. A., Purisch, A. D., Berg, R. A., Moses, J. A., Jr., Newlin, D. B., Wilkening, G. N., & Puente, A. E. (1982). *Item interpretation of the Luria-Nebraska Neuropsychological Battery.* Lincoln: University of Nebraska Press.

Golden, C. J., Osmon, D., Moses, J. A., Jr., & Berg, R. A. (1980). *Interpretation of the Halstead-Reitan Neuropsychological Battery: A casebook approach.* New York: Grune & Stratton.

Moses, J. A., Jr., Golden, C. J., Ariel, R., & Gustavson, J. L. (1983, 1984). *Interpretation of the Luria-Nebraska Neuropsychological Battery* (Vols. 1 & 2). New York: Grune & Stratton.

STAFF

## GOLDENHAR SYNDROME

Goldenhar syndrome (GS) is a relatively recently enumerated syndrome that is somewhat more common among children with diagnoses of autism than in the general population. The diagnosis of GS is made in the presence of a pattern of 3 physical anomalies: ocular abnormalities that include the epibulbar dermoid; auricular abnormalities including microtia, periauricular tags and similar abnormalities of the ear; and vertebral abnormalities.

Cases are sporadic and the cause of GS is unknown but anticipated at this time to be due to a teratogen (Gillberg, 1995). Hearing loss of varying degrees is common, and callosal agenesis has also been reported. An increased prevalence of mental retardation, especially in the mild range, occurs, and there is increased incidence of autism and autistic-like behavior, although the latter tends to improve with age, especially after puberty. GS occurs in boys and girls with about equal frequency. There is no cure and treatment is entirely symptomatic. Special education is typically required but may be associated with one or more of the symptoms noted above. GS has highly variable expressivity and test-

ing is necessary to establish which of the behavioral and mental symptoms are present and to what degree. Outcome is related directly to the degree of hearing loss, the level of intellectual impairment, and the number and severity of any autistic symptoms.

## REFERENCE

Gillberg, C. (1995). *Clinical child neuropsychiatry.* Cambridge: Cambridge University Press.

CECIL R. REYNOLDS
*Texas A&M University*

## GOLDMAN-FRISTOE TEST OF ARTICULATION 2

The Goldman-Fristoe Test of Articulation 2 is a systematic measure of articulation of consonant sounds for children and young adults. The second edition of the Goldman-Fristoe Test of Articulation gives updated norms and expanded features, and it remains accurate and easy to administer. The test provides information about a child's articulation ability by sampling both spontaneous and imitative sound production. Examinees respond to picture plates and verbal cues from the examiner with single-word answers that demonstrate common speech sounds. Additional sections provide further measures of speech production. The test is used to measure articulation of consonant sounds, determine types of misarticulation, and compare individual performance to national, gender-differentiated norms.

New items have been added to sample more speech sounds—39 consonant sounds and clusters can now be tested with the Goldman-Fristoe 2. Some objectionable or culturally inappropriate items (e.g., gun, Christmas tree) have been removed. All artwork has been redrawn and reviewed for cultural bias and fairness. The age range for the Goldman-Fristoe 2 has been expanded to include ages 2 through 21. Age-based standard scores include separate normative information for females and males. Normative tables are based on a national sample of 2,350 examinees stratified to match the most recent U.S. Census data on gender, race/ethnicity, region, and SES as determined by mother's education level.

- User-friendly color-coding for recording initial-medial-final sounds
- Multiple testing of speech sounds within a word or plate for efficient test administration
- Broad sampling of the consonant sounds and clusters used in Standard American English
- Opportunity to sample both spontaneous and imitated production of speech sounds

Sounds-in-Words uses colorful, entertaining pictures to prompt responses that sample the major speech sounds in the initial, medial, and final positions. Suggested cues have been added for the examiner to help elicit spontaneous responses by the examinee. Additional sections provide a fuller sampling of the examinee's ability to produce speech sounds and to reproduce sounds when modeled by the examiner.

Three sections sample a wide range of articulation skills:

1. Sounds-in-Words Section uses pictures to elicit articulation of the major speech sounds when the examinee is prompted by a visual and/or verbal cue.

2. Sounds-in-Sentences Section assesses spontaneous sound production used in connected speech. The examinee is asked to retell a short story based on a picture cue. Target speech sounds are sampled within the context of simple sentences.

3. Stimulability Section measures the examinee's ability to correctly produce a previously misarticulated sound when asked to watch and listen to the examiner's production of the sound. The examinee repeats the word or phrase modeled by the examiner.

STAFF

## GOLDMAN-FRISTOE-WOODCOCK TEST OF AUDITORY DISCRIMINATION

The Goldman-Fristoe-Woodcock Test of Auditory Discrimination is designed to measure a child's ability to hear speech sounds. It is an individually administered test of the ability to discriminate speech sounds against two different backgrounds—quiet and noise.

The Goldman-Fristoe-Woodcock Test of Auditory Discrimination is specifically designed to assess young children. Geared to children's vocabulary levels and limited attention spans, the test moves rapidly as responses are made by pointing to appealing pictures of familiar objects. Writing and speaking are not required. The test can also be used successfully with adults.

Three parts—Training Procedure, Quiet Subtest, and Noise Subtest—provide practice in word-picture associations and provide two measures of speech-sound discrimination for maximum precision. Separate norms are provided for each subtest from ages 3 years, 8 months to 70 years and over. In addition, the examiner may use the error analysis matrix in the response form to explore the specific types of errors made on the subtests.

STAFF

## GOLDMAN-FRISTOE TEST OF ARTICULATION–2

## GOLDSTEIN, MAX A. (1870–1941)

Max A. Goldstein, an otolaryngologist, originated the acoustic method of teaching the deaf. The major significance of this method was that it used the student's residual hearing, an avenue largely neglected by educators of the deaf at the time. Goldstein employed amplification to train the student to use any remaining sound perception to understand spoken language and to guide his or her own voice in the production of speech. In 1914 Goldstein founded the Central Institute for the Deaf in St. Louis, where he demonstrated his methods and where he established the first two-year training program for teachers of the deaf and began the first nursery school for deaf children.

Goldstein was founder and editor of *The Laryngoscope,* a journal devoted to disorders of the ear, nose, and throat. To promote closer cooperation between teachers of the deaf and physicians, and to standardize teaching methods used in schools for the deaf, Goldstein established the professional society that later became the National Forum on Deafness and Speech Pathology. Goldstein served as president of the American Otological Society, the American Laryngological, Rhinological, and Otological Society, and the organization that was the forerunner of the American Speech and Hearing Association.

### REFERENCES

Goldstein, M. A. (1939). *The acoustic method.* St. Louis, MO: Laryngoscope Press.

In memoriam: Dr. Max A. Goldstein, 1870–1941. (1941). *Laryngoscope, 51,* 726–731.

PAUL IRVINE<br>*Katonah, New York*

## GOODENOUGH, FLORENCE LAURA (1886–1959)

Florence Laura Goodenough obtained the PhD degree in psychology under Lewis M. Terman at Stanford University after a number of years of experience as a teacher in the public schools and at the Training School at Vineland, New Jersey. Goodenough is well known for her Draw-A-Man Test, published in 1926, and the Minnesota Preschool Scale. As a researcher and an authority on research methodology, she was an innovator, applying a variety of research techniques to diverse research questions. Her *Experimental Child Study,* written with John E. Anderson, evaluated the pros and cons of numerous research methodologies. Goodenough served as president of the school psychology division of the American Psychological Association.

## REFERENCES

Goodenough, F. L. (1926). *Measurement of intelligence by drawings.* Yonkers, NY: World Book.

Goodenough, F. L., & Anderson, J. E. (1982). *Experimental child study.* Darby, PA: Arden Library.

PAUL IRVINE
*Katonah, New York*

## GOTTLIEB, JAY (1942–　　)

Jay Gottlieb received his PhD from Yeshiva University in New York in 1972, and is a professor in the Department of Educational Psychology at New York University as well as a researcher in the field of education. His work has included investigations dealing with the social acceptance of children with mental retardation (Goodman, Gottlieb, & Harrison, 1972), social skills training for handicapped children (Gottlieb, 1984), the impact of instructional group size in resource rooms and speech services (Gottlieb & Alter, 1997), and mainstreaming (Gottlieb, 1981; Kaufman, Gottlieb, Agard, & Kukic, 1975).

In much of his research, Gottlieb has focused on issues that relate to enhancement of the learning experience to provide the maximum benefit for students with learning problems. His studies of children with mental retardation have indicated that these youngsters tend to be easily swayed by their intellectually brighter peers, yet often fail to develop close relationships with them. In some instances, this failure prevents them from learning what is valued by others (Goodman et al., 1972). Also, he has shown that children with disabilities do not progress more rapidly in their schoolwork when taught in segregated classrooms (Kaufman et al., 1975), and that, while they tend to play alone, few differences exist between the play habits of those with learning disabilities and children who do not have learning problems (Levy & Gottlieb, 1984).

More recently, Gottlieb has focused on the area of school placement of children with disabilities, finding an overrepresentation of students of color referred for special education. He also found that referral is frequently based primarily on academic achievement, misbehavior, and speech and language problems in the absence of standardized educational criteria. Based on his findings, Gottlieb (1994) strongly advocates the development of prereferral instructional activities as a way of maintaining students in general education classes, as well as criteria for determining the success of such activities. He also stresses the necessity of improved teacher training in behavior analysis. Furthermore, he believes that once a child is placed in special education, that individual rarely, if ever, leaves that placement.

## REFERENCES

Goodman, H., Gottlieb, J., & Harrison, R. H. (1972). Social acceptance of EMR's integrated into a nongraded elementary school. *American Journal of Mental Deficiency, 76,* 412–417.

Gottlieb, J. (1981). Mainstreaming: Fulfilling the promise? *American Journal of Mental Deficiency, 86,* 115–124.

Gottlieb, J. (1984). *Social skills research integration: Final report.* New York: New York University.

Gottlieb, J. (1994). Special education in urban America: It's not justifiable for many. *Journal of Special Education, 27,* 453–465.

Gottlieb, J., & Alter, M. (1997). *An evaluation study of the impact of modifying instructional group sizes in resource rooms and related service groups in New York City.* New York: New York University.

Kaufman, J. J., Gottlieb, J., Agard, J. A., & Kukic, M. B. (1975). Mainstreaming: Toward an explication of the construct. *Focus On Exceptional Children, 7,* 6–17.

Levy, L., & Gottlieb, J. (1984). Learning disabled and non-learning disabled children at play. *Remedial and Special Education, 5,* 43–50.

E. VALERIE HEWITT
*Texas A&M University*
First edition

TAMARA J. MARTIN
*The University of Texas of the Permian Basin*
Second edition

## GOWAN, JOHN C. (1912–1986)

John C. Gowan earned his BA at Harvard University and his EdM and EdD at the University of California at Los Angeles. During his distinguished career in education, Gowan's interest focused on the areas of psychic science, guidance, and creativity, particularly as related to gifted learners (Gowan, 1980). Prior to his death in 1986, he was a professor at California State University, Northridge, for over 25 years.

Gowan is known for his work in the area of guidance for gifted children (Gowan, Demos, & Kokaska, 1980). He emphasized special problems such as the disparity between social and intellectual development sometimes associated with these children and examined the influence of right-hemisphere imagery on creativity (Gowan, Khatena, & Torrance, 1981). Gowan also noted the importance of using developmental stage theory to enhance creativity in gifted children, and his theories on the subject were explored in his book *Trance, Art, and Creativity* (1987), a psychological analysis of the relationship between the individual ego and the numinous element.

Among his contributions, Gowan served as president of

the Association for the Gifted (1971–1972), president of the National Association for Gifted Children (1974–1975), and editor of *Gifted Child Quarterly* (1974–1979). Additionally, he was a Fulbright lecturer at the University of Singapore (1962–1963) and a visiting lecturer at the University of Hawaii (1965, 1967), Southern Connecticut State College (1969), and the University of Canterbury (1970) and Massey University (1975), both in New Zealand. A compilation of his work related to gifted children was published in the 1971 book, *Educating the Ablest*.

## REFERENCES

Gowan, J. C. (1971). *Educating the ablest: A book of readings on the education of gifted children*. Itasca, IL: Peacock.

Gowan, J. C. (1980). The use of developmental stage theory in helping gifted children become creative. *Gifted Child Quarterly, 24*, 22–28.

Gowan, J. C. (1987). *Trance, art, and creativity: A psychological analysis of the relationship between the individual ego and the numinous element in three modes—prototaxic, parataxic, and syntaxic*. Buffalo, NY: Creative Education.

Gowan, J. C., Demos, G. D., & Kokaska, C. J. (1980). *The guidance of exceptional children: A book of readings* (2nd ed.). New York: Longman.

Gowan, J. C., Khatena, J., & Torrance, E. P. (Eds.). (1981). *Creativity: Its educational implications* (Rev. ed.). Dubuque, IA: Kendall-Hunt.

ANN E. LUPKOWSKI
*Texas A&M University*
First edition

TAMARA J. MARTIN
*The University of Texas of the Permian Basin*
Second edition

## GRADE EQUIVALENTS

Grade equivalents (GEs) represent a popular, though much abused and often misinterpreted, score system for achievement tests. A GE is a representation of an average level of performance of all children at a specific grade level. For example, if, on a test of reading, the average number of questions correct (the mean raw score) for children in the third month of fourth grade (typically written as 4.3) is 40, then a raw score of 40 is assigned a GE of 4.3. If the average number correct for children in the second month of fifth grade is 43, then all scores of 43 are henceforth assigned a GE of 5.2, and so forth.

Grade equivalents have numerous problems of interpretation and use, so much so that the 1985 *Standards for Educational and Psychological Testing* asks test publishers to take special care in explaining the calculation, interpretation, and appropriate uses of GEs for any particular test. Many users assume that GEs have the characteristics of standardized or scaled scores when, in fact, they do not. Often GEs are treated as being on an interval scale of measurement when they are only on an ordinal scale; that is, GEs allow the ranking of individuals according to their performance but do not tell us anything about the distance between each pair of individuals. This problem can be illustrated as follows. If the mean score for beginning fourth graders (grade 4.0) on a reading test is 37, then any person earning a score of 37 on the test is assigned a GE score of 4.0. If the mean raw score of a fifth grader (grade 5.0) is 38, then a score of 38 would receive a GE of 5.0. A raw score of 37 could represent a GE of 4.0, 38 could be 5.0, 39 could be 5.1, 40 could be 5.3, and 41, 6.0. Thus, differences of one raw score point can cause dramatic differences in the GE received. The differences will be highly inconsistent across grades with regard to magnitude of the difference in grade equivalents produced by constant changes in raw scores.

Table 1 illustrates the problems of using GEs to evaluate a child's academic standing relative to his or her peers. Frequently, in both research and clinical practice, children of normal intellectual capacity are diagnosed as learning disabled through the use of grade equivalents such as "two years below grade level for age" on a test of academic attainment. The use of this criterion for diagnosing learning disabilities or other academic disorders is clearly inappropriate (Reynolds, 1981, 1984). As seen in Table 1, a child with a GE score in reading 2 years below the appropriate grade placement for age may or may not have a reading problem. At some ages this is within the average range, whereas at others a severe reading problem may be indicated.

Grade equivalents tend to become standards of performance as well, which they clearly are not. Contrary to popular belief, GE scores on a test do not indicate what level of reading text a child should be using. Grade equivalent scores on tests do not have a one-to-one correspondence with reading series placement or the various formulas for determining readability levels.

Grade equivalents are also inappropriate for use in any sort of discrepancy analysis of an individual's test performance and for use in many statistical procedures for the following reasons (Reynolds, 1981):

1. The growth curve between age and achievement in basic academic subjects flattens out at upper grade levels. This can be seen in the table, where there is very little change in standard score values corresponding to 2 years below grade level for age after about grade 7 or 8. In fact, GEs have almost no meaning at this level since reading instruction typically stops by high school. This difficulty in interpreting GEs beyond about grade 10 or 11 is apparent in an analogy with age equivalents (Thorndike & Hagen, 1977).

Table 1 Standard scores and percentile ranks corresponding to performance "two years below grade level for age" on three major reading tests

| Grade placement | Two years below placement | Wide Range Achievement Test | | Woodcock Reading Mastery Test[a] | | Standard Diagnostic Reading Test[a] | |
|---|---|---|---|---|---|---|---|
| | | SS[b] | %R[c] | SS | %R | S | %R |
| 2.5 | K.5 | 72 | 1 | — | | — | |
| 3.5 | 1.5 | 69 | 2 | 64 | 1 | 64 | 1 |
| 4.5 | 2.5 | 73 | 4 | 77 | 6 | 64 | 1 |
| 5.5 | 3.5 | 84 | 14 | 85 | 16 | 77 | 6 |
| 6.5 | 4.5 | 88 | 21 | 91 | 27 | 91 | 27 |
| 7.5 | 5.5 | 86 | 18 | 94 | 34 | 92 | 30 |
| 8.5 | 6.5 | 87 | 19 | 94 | 34 | 93 | 32 |
| 9.5 | 7.5 | 90 | 25 | 96 | 39 | 95 | 37 |
| 10.5 | 8.5 | 85 | 16 | 95 | 37 | 95 | 37 |
| 11.5 | 9.5 | 85 | 16 | 95 | 37 | 92 | 30 |

*Source:* Adapted from Reynolds (1981).

[a]Total test.

[b]All standard scores in this table have been converted for ease of comparison to a common scale having a mean of 100 and an SD of 15.

[c]Percentile rank.

Height can be expressed in age equivalents just as reading can be expressed as GEs. It might be helpful to describe a tall first grader as having the height of an 8½-year-old, but what happens to the 5 ft, 10 in. 14-year-old female? At no age does the mean height of females equal 5 ft, 10 in. Since the average reading level in the population changes very little after junior high school, GEs at these ages become virtually nonsensical, with large fluctuations resulting from a raw score difference of two or three points on a 100-item test.

2. Grade equivalents assume the rate of learning is constant throughout the school year and that there is no gain or loss during summer vacation.

3. Grade equivalents involve an excess of extrapolation, especially at the upper and lower ends of the scale. However, since tests are not administered during every month of the school year, scores between the testing intervals (often a full year) must be interpolated on the assumption of constant growth rates. Interpolation between sometimes extrapolated values on an assumption of constant growth rates is a somewhat ludicrous activity.

4. Different academic subjects are acquired at different rates and the variation in performance varies across content areas so that "two years below grade level for age" may be a much more serious deficiency in math than in reading comprehension.

5. Grade equivalents exaggerate small differences in performance among individuals and for a single individual across tests. Some test authors even provide a caution on record forms that standard scores only, and not grade equivalents, should be used for comparisons.

Standard scores are a superior alternative to the use of GEs. The principal advantage of standardized or scaled scores with children lies in the comparability of score interpretation across age. By standard scores is meant scores scaled to a constant mean and standard deviation (SD), such as the Wechsler Deviation IQ, and not to ratio IQ types of scales employed by the early Binet and the Slosson Intelligence Test, which give the false appearance of being scaled scores. Ratio IQs or other types of quotients have many of the same problems as grade equivalents and should be avoided for many of the same reasons. Standard scores of the deviation IQ type have the same percentile rank across age since they are based not only on the mean but the variability in scores about the mean at each age level. For example, a score that falls two-thirds of a standard deviation below the mean has a percentile rank of 25 at every age. A score falling two-thirds of a grade level below the average grade level has a different percentile rank at every age.

Standard scores are more accurate and precise. When constructing tables for the conversion of raw scores into standard scores, interpolation of scores to arrive at an exact score point is usually not necessary. The opposite is true of GEs. Typically, extrapolation is not necessary for scores within three SDs of the mean, which accounts for more than 99 percent of all scores encountered. Scaled scores can be set to any desired mean and standard deviation, with the fancy of the test author frequently the sole determining factor. Fortunately, a few scales can account for the vast majority of standardized tests in psychology and education.

Nevertheless, GEs remain popular as a score reporting system in special education. This popularity seems owed to the many misconceptions surrounding their use rather than any true understanding of children's academic attainment or how better to instruct them.

## REFERENCES

Reynolds, C. R. (1981). The fallacy of "two years below grade level for age" as a diagnostic criterion for reading disorders. *Journal of School Psychology, 19,* 350–358.

Reynolds, C. R. (1984). Critical measurement issues in learning disabilities. *Journal of Special Education, 18,* 451–476.

Thorndike, R. L., & Hagen, E. P. (1977). *Measurement and evaluation in psychology and education.* New York: Wiley.

CECIL R. REYNOLDS
*Texas A&M University*

## DIAGNOSIS IN SPECIAL EDUCATION
## LEARNING DISABILITIES, SEVERE DISCREPANCY ANALYSIS IN

# GRADE RETENTION

Retention, the holding back of a child due to poor academic achievement or social immaturity, has been a very controversial topic in the past decade. Schools and researchers are unclear as to whether retention engenders positive effects both academically and socioemotionally in children. The Center for Policy Research in Education (1990) reported that by the 9th grade, approximately 50 percent of all U.S. school students have been retained. According to the National Association of School Psychologists (NASP; 1991), retention negatively impacts achievement and social-emotional adjustment in children. Though much of the research focuses on the academic effect retention precipitates, a growing number of researchers have begun to examine the effects on the socioemotional development of a child. Academic achievement is crucial for a child's success in school, especially in the primary grades. However, children's socioemotional development is equally important in contributing to a child's overall wellness. Although many children are retained every year, most studies have found it to be ineffective in achievement and adjustment for children. Some studies have agreed that grade retention could be effective if other alternatives have been tried and failed (McCoy & Reynolds, 1999).

Originally, the goal of grade retention was to improve school performance by allowing more time for students to develop adequate academic skills (Reynolds, 1992). By the 1930s, researched evidenced the negative effect of reten-

tion (Ayer, 1933; Kline, 1933). Goodlad (1954) summarized the research on retention and found that retention did not decrease the variation in student achievement levels and had no positive effect on educational gain.

McCoy and Reynolds (1999) investigated the effects of retention on school achievement, perceived school competence, and delinquency. The sample was composed of low-income, minority children who had been retained at least once by the age of 14. They found that the strongest predictors of grade retention were early achievement, parental involvement, gender (boys were more likely), and number of school moves. Grade retention was found to be associated with lower mathematics and reading achievement, but not perceived school competence and delinquency, by the age of 14.

Jimerson (1997) found similar results when studying the characteristics of children retained in early elementary school and the effects of retention on achievement and adjustment. He found those more likely to be retained were boys with significantly poorer adjustment. He also found higher parental IQ and involvement with the school in nonretained children. The retained children did show a temporary advantage in math, but this quickly disappeared when new material was presented to both groups. Furthermore, the retained group of children showed lower emotional health in the sixth grade.

Research does not support grade retention as an intervention for children with behavior problems. On the contrary, research has shown anxiety, inattentiveness, and disruptive behaviors are not only long lasting, but they also worsen exponentially after retention (Jimerson, 1997; Pagani, Tremblay, Vitaro, Boulerice, & McDuff, 2001). Grade retention has been shown to more greatly affect children's behavior problems when retention occurred in primary school years compared to those retained at a later time (Pagani et al., 2001). If retention has detrimental effects on a child's adjustment, then those children who were retained due to their adjustment will be affected on a greater scale.

While many researchers focus their studies on the negative effects immediately following retention, there have been studies which look at longer-term consequences. Jimerson (1999) found that children who were retained are more likely to drop out of high school by the age of 19 than the low-achieving promoted peers. Those retained students who do graduate from high school are much less likely to go to college or engage in any other type of postsecondary education. Even when socioeconomic status was accounted for, nonretained students were twice as likely to enroll in postsecondary education than those students retained at least once between kindergarten and eighth grades. Those retained during middle school were even less likely to go to college (Fine & Davis, 2003). Children who have been retained also are more likely to be involved in substance abuse, have deviant behaviors, receive public assistance, and end up in prison than those who have not been retained (Jimerson, 1999).

Two main theories explain how children's socioemotional development may be worsened by retention. Gottfredson, Fink, and Graham (1994) suggested that social bonds are created in school formed by relationships with peers. These social bonds prevent children from engaging in self-gratifying, impulsive acts, such as disruptive behavior. As a child is retained, the social bonds formed with peers are broken and the impulsive acts that were being controlled are now being displayed.

Pagani et al. (2001) suggested that retention increases a child's rejection sensitivity, defined as the disposition to misconstrue, expect, and overreact to social rejection. Children experience rejection and feelings of humiliation when they have been retained (Shepard, 1997). Children's feelings of rejection seem to predispose them to situations that trigger similar feelings and, in turn, they misperceive other's interactions with them. This may lead to overreacting to situations with inappropriate, aggressive behavior (Pagani et al., 2001). Other theorists have suggested that problem behaviors are due to poor self-control, and therefore grade retention would have no affect on these behaviors (Gottfredson et al., 1994). Also, self-control may worsen after grade retention due to broken social bonds with peers who had previously kept them socially accountable.

Grade retention has been shown to have many adverse effects on different children. Most research points to the detrimental effects of retention, with few positive outcomes. Keeping a child back so they have an academic advantage or so they can mature may seem like a good idea in theory. However, research has shown that there is no academic or socioemotional advantage after retention. Future research needs to examine more individualized groups. For example, different ethnicities may react differently to grade retention. Most researchers would agree that grade retention is far from the answer to helping children succeed. Others would argue that premature promotion when a child is not academically prepared is also far from perfect. The fact is that retention is detrimental to a child's socioemotional and academic development, and other interventions need to be researched. Extensive research on the effects of retention and promotion will guide future educational interventions to find a way to help children overcome academic disparities.

## REFERENCES

Ayer, F. C. (1933). *Progress of pupils in the state of Texas 1932–33.* Austin: Texas State Teachers Association.

Center for Policy Research in Education. (1990). *Repeating grades in school: Current practice and research evidence.* Washington, DC: Author.

Fine, J. G., & Davis, J. M. (2003). Grade retention and enrollment in postsecondary education. *Journal of School Psychology, 41,* 401–411.

Goodlad, J. (1954). Some effects of promotion and non-promotion upon the social and personal adjustment of children. *Journal of Experimental Education, 22,* 301–328.

Gottfredson, D. C., Fink, C. M., & Graham, N. (1994). Grade retention and problem behavior. *American Educational Research Journal, 31,* 761–784.

Jimerson, S. (1997). A prospective, longitudinal study of the correlates and consequences of early grade retention. *Journal of School Psychology, 35,* 3–25.

Jimerson, S. (1999). On the failure of failure: Examining the association between early grade retention and education and employment outcomes during late adolescence. *Journal of School Psychology, 37,* 243–272.

Kline, E. (1933). Significant changes in the curve of elimination since 1900. *Journal of Educational Research, 26,* 608–616.

McCoy, A. R., & Reynolds, A. J. (1999). Grade retention and school performance: An extended investigation. *Journal of School Psychology, 37,* 273–298.

National Association of School Psychologists (NASP). (1991). *Student grade retention: A resource manual for parents and educators.* Silver Spring, MD: Author.

Pagani, L., Tremblay, R. E., Vitaro, F., Boulerice, B., & McDuff, P. (2001). Effects of grade retention on academic performance and behavioral development. *Development and Psychopathology, 13,* 297–315.

Reynolds, A. J. (1992). Grade retention and school adjustment: An explanatory analysis. *Educational Evaluation and Policy Analysis, 14*(2), 101–121.

Shepard, L. A. (1997). Children not ready to learn? The invalidity of school readiness testing. *Psychology in the Schools, 34,* 85–97.

CLARISSA I. GARCIA
*Texas A&M University*

**NO CHILD LEFT BEHIND ACT**
**RESPONSE TO INTERVENTION**
**READING DISORDERS**


## GRAND MAL SEIZURES

See SEIZURE DISORDERS.


## GRANULOMATOUS DISEASE, CHRONIC

An inherited disease of white blood cell bacteria-killing function, chronic granulomatous disease (CGD) results in chronic infections and granuloma formation in skin, lymphatic tissues, respiratory and gastrointestinal tracts, and bones. White blood cells ingest bacteria normally but cannot kill them because of the cell's inability to generate hydrogen peroxide. Some bacteria, like pneumococci and streptococci, produce their own hydrogen peroxide and are normally disposed of by CGC white cells, while many other bacteria, including staphylococci, which do not produce hydrogen peroxide, cannot be killed.

Early in life, eczema-like rashes, enlarged lymph nodes,

and perirectal abscesses may be initial signs. Respiratory infections are the most common symptom, and there is gradual enlargement of the liver and spleen. Infections in the central nervous system and the anemia of chronic disease may have cognitive sequelae.

Prophylactic antibiotic treatment, usually with sulfa methoxazole/trimethaprim, has greatly improved life expectancy and steroids are used to shrink granulomas obstructing the airways or gastrointestinal tract. Bone marrow transplant and interferon gamma treatments have been used with success in some patients.

Information for families and professionals is available from the Chronic Granulomatous Disease Association, Inc., 2616 Monterey Rd., San Marino, CA 91108, or at www.pacific.net.net/amhurley.

**REFERENCES**

Malech, H. L., & Gallin, J. I. (1987). Neutrophils in human diseases. *New England Journal of Medicine, 317,* 687–694.

Stiehm, E. R. (1989). *Immunological disorders infants and children.* Philadelphia: W. B. Saunders.

PATRICIA L. HARTLAGE
*Medical College of Georgia*

# GRAPHESTHESIA

Graphesthesia is a medical term used to define an individual's ability to identify numbers or figures written on the skin (Hensyl, 1982). For many years, tests of graphesthesia have been a part of the clinical neurological examination to determine the intactness and integration of sensory neural systems related to sensations from within the body, at a distance from the body, and outside the body.

Chusid (1986) reports that sensation may be divided into three types: superficial, concerned with touch, pain, temperature, and two-point discrimination; deep, concerned with muscle and joint position (proprioception), deep muscle pain, and vibration sense (pallesthesia); and combined, concerned with both superficial and deep sensory mechanisms involved in stereognosis (recognition and naming of familiar unseen objects placed in the hand) and topognosis (the ability to localize cutaneous skin stimuli). Stereognosis and topognosis probably depend on the integrity of neural mechanisms within the cortex and are discriminatory in nature. The lower level mechanisms, such as touch, pain and temperature, seem more protective in nature.

Whether the form identification in graphesthesia is accomplished by identifying numbers traced on the fingertips (Reitan, 1979) or motor form replication (Ayres, 1980), there appears to be a developmental factor in responses favoring greater reliability in 8 to 11 year olds than in 5 to 6 year olds. Evaluations of graphesthesia are most useful and reliable when given as part of a battery of sensory, motor vestibular tests of sensory integrative function. These tests usually are given by therapists, psychologists, or neurologists with special training. It has been suggested (Ayres, 1980) that clusters of low scores on somatosensory tests (including graphesthesia) may be associated with a child's having difficulty with motor planning nonhabitual movement (apraxia). Children who have apraxia have severe problems learning fine motor skill tasks such as dressing and writing. A clear definition of the individual child's difficulty can lead to developmentally appropriate classroom responses and therapeutic intervention provided by related services such as occupational and speech therapy.

**REFERENCES**

Ayres, A. J. (1980). *Southern California Sensory Integration Tests examiner's manual* (Rev. ed.). Los Angeles: Western Psychological Services.

Ayres, A. J. (1981). *Sensory integration and the child.* Los Angeles: Western Psychological Services.

Chusid, J. G. (1986). *Correlative neuroanatomy and functional neurology* (16th ed.). Los Angeles: Lange.

Hensyl, W. R. (Ed.). (1982). *Stedman's medical dictionary.* Baltimore: Williams & Wilkins.

Reitan, R. M. (1979). *Manual for administration of neuropsychological test batteries for adults and children.* Tucson, AZ: Reitan Neuropsychology Laboratories.

RACHAEL J. STEVENSON
*Bedford, Ohio*

**HALSTEAD-REITAN NEUROPSYCHOLOGICAL TEST BATTERY**
**LURIA-NEBRASKA NEUROPSYCHOLOGICAL BATTERY: CHILDREN'S REVISION**
**NEUROPSYCHOLOGY**

# GRAPHIC ORGANIZERS

Lerner (2000, p. 207) defines graphic organizers (GOs) as "visual representations of concepts, knowledge, or information that incorporate both text and pictures. They make it easier for a person to understand the information by allowing the mind 'to see' complex relationships." GOs are advance organizers that are used to support student learning in reading, mathematics, and in other academic areas from primary level classes to adult education programs. GOs are widely used in general education classrooms and in many special education programs as well.

Examples of GOs are flow diagrams, Venn diagrams, tree diagrams, semantic maps, and matrices. The uses of GOs range from helping students to comprehend and remember information from textbooks at the elementary and secondary level, to utilizing text information in writing essays at the postsecondary level, to learning technical vocabulary in the area of elementary mathematics. Many publishers now include GOs as adjuncts to textbooks.

Graphic organizers are linked to schema theory, in which new learning is seen as building upon the learner's preexisting knowledge (Dye, 2000). The learner is seen as needing to create a new schema or to utilize an existing schema in order to learn new material. The advance organizer was introduced to help students to learn and retain verbal content containing unfamiliar but significant subject matter (Ausubel, 1960). Because the advance organizer is primarily a written statement, some researchers believed that graphic displays would benefit students to a greater degree than asking a student who was having trouble comprehending a passage to read a statement and relate it to the original passage (Robinson, 1998).

Research points to the efficacy of GOs as aids in learning academic content (Jitendra & DiPipi, 2002; Moore & Readence, 1984). A number of research studies have focused on learning and retaining information from text (Robinson & Kiewra, 1995). Some researchers have focused specifically on using GOs in reading and comprehending mathematics texts (Braselton & Decker, 1994; Monroe, 1997).

While much of the research on the use of graphic organizers points to positive results, Robinson (1998) warns that definitive results regarding the design and use of GOs are difficult to ascertain due to research designs that were flawed and often looked at the wrong dependent variables. Robinson recommends that further research under specific research designs be conducted to determine exactly how GOs should be constructed for use in the classroom setting and how they can most effectively be utilized in teaching students. Dunston (1992) critiqued the research examining the use of GOs in improving reading comprehension and concluded that the research had equivocal results regarding important information that would assist teachers in the classroom. The results did not indicate the type of GO to use or when and with whom they should be used (Dunston). The need for further research is indicated.

A growing body of research in the use of GOs with special needs learners demonstrates the successful use in special education classes and in inclusive classes in general education that serve students with special learning needs. Research regarding the use of GOs has shown promising results in teaching students with learning disabilities to solve mathematics word problems. In one study, the researchers studied a small group of students with learning disabilities who were taught a word problem–solving strategy using graphic representation of the problems. The students' scores on word problem–solving probe sets improved after learning the schema-based strategy and applying it to their assigned problems (Jitendra & Hoff, 1996).

Weisberg and Balaithy (1990) studied the use of GOs in teaching disabled readers to identify levels of importance of ideas in expository text, to identify main idea statements, and to summarize text. Griffin, Simmons, and Kameenui (1991) found positive results using GOs to improve comprehension and recall of science content by students with learning disabilities, although the results did not reach statistical significance.

Ellis and Lenz (1990), in their discussion of techniques for mediating content-area learning, critiqued a wide variety of research studies that examined the use of GOs as instructional supplements. Students with disorders of learning appeared to perform at a higher level when using GOs.

## REFERENCES

Ausubel, D. P. (1960). The use of advance organizers in the learning and retention of meaningful verbal material. *Journal of Educational Psychology, 51,* 267–272.

Braselton, S., & Decker, B. C. (1994). Using graphic organizers to improve the reading of mathematics. *Reading Teacher, 48,* 276–281.

Dunston, P. J. (1992). A critique of graphic organizer research. *Reading Research and Instruction, 31,* 57–65.

Dye, G. A. (2000). Graphic organizers to the rescue: Helping students link—and remember—information. *Teaching Exceptional Children, 32,* 72–76.

Ellis, E. S., & Lenz, B. K. (Eds.). (1990). *Teaching adolescents with learning disabilities: Strategies and methods* (2nd ed.). Denver, CO: Love.

Griffin, C. C., Simmons, D. C., & Kameenui, E. J. (1991). Investigating the effectiveness of graphic organizer instruction on the comprehension and recall of science content by students with learning disabilities. *Reading, Writing, and Learning Disabilities, 7,* 355–376.

Griffin, C. C., & Tulbert, B. L. (1995). The effect of graphic organizers on students' comprehension and recall of expository text: A review of the research and implications for practice. *Reading and Writing Quarterly: Overcoming Learning Difficulties, 11,* 73–79.

Jitendra, A. K., & DiPipi, C. M. (2002). An exploratory study of schema-based word-problem-solving instruction for middle school students with learning disabilities: An emphasis on conceptual and procedural understanding. *Journal of Special Education, 36,* 23–38.

Jitendra, A. K., & Hoff, K. (1996). The effects of schema-based instruction on mathematical word problem solving performance of students with learning disabilities. *Journal of Learning Disabilities, 29,* 422–431.

Lerner, J. (2000). *Learning disabilities: Theories, diagnosis, and teaching strategies.* Boston: Houghton-Mifflin.

Monroe, E. E. (1997). *Using graphic organizers to teach vocabulary: How does research inform mathematics instruction?* (ERIC Document Reproduction Service No. 120132)

Moore, D. W., & Readence, J. E. (1984). A quantitative and qualitative review of graphic organizer research. *Journal of Educational Research, 78*(1), 11–17.

Robinson, D. H. (1998). Graphic organizers as aides to text learning. *Reading Research and Instruction, 37,* 85–105.

Robinson, D. H., & Kiewra, K. A. (1995). Visual argument: Graphic organizers are superior to outlines in improving learning from text. *Journal of Educational Psychology, 87,* 455–467.

Weisberg, R., & Balaithy, E. (1990). Development of disabled readers' metacomprehension ability through summarization training using expository text: Results of three studies. *Journal of Reading, Writing, and Learning Disabilities, 6,* 117–136.

JOSEPH R. TAYLOR
*Fresno Pacific University*

**ADVANCED ORGANIZERS**

# GRAY ORAL READING TESTS–FOURTH EDITION

The Gray Oral Reading Tests–Fourth Edition (GORT-4) developed by J. Lee Weiderholt and Brian R. Bryant, provide an objective measure of growth in oral reading. Five scores give information on a student's oral reading skills in terms of the following factors:

*Rate*—the amount of time taken by a student to read a story

*Accuracy*—the student's ability to pronounce each word in the story correctly

*Fluency*—the student's Rate and Accuracy Scores combined

*Comprehension*—the appropriateness of the student's responses to questions about the content of each story read

*Overall Reading Ability*—a combination of a student's Fluency (i.e., Rate and Accuracy) and Comprehension Scores

The test consists of two parallel forms, each containing 14 sequenced reading passages with five comprehension questions following each passage. For each reading passage, raw scores are calculated for Accuracy and Rate by calculating the number of words read correctly and the length of time it takes the student to read the passage. Between 0 and 5 points are provided for each Accuracy and Rate score, depending on how quickly and accurately the student reads the passage. Those points are then summed to obtain a Fluency score. A Comprehension score is calculated by summing the number of comprehension items (between 0 and 5) answered correctly for each passage. Raw scores for all four subtests (Accuracy, Rate, Fluency, Comprehension) are then used to compute standard scores, percentile ranks, and age and grade equivalents for the subtests. The sum of the Fluency and Comprehension standard scores are converted to percentile ranks and an Overall Reading Quo-

tient. Error analysis can be completed by recording incorrect words students substitute for words in the passage and categorizing them according to the type of error, including Meaning Similarity, Function Similarity, Graphic/Phonemic Similarity, Multiple Sources, and Self-Correction. A checklist is also provided for an overall analysis of the student's reading behavior, including additions, deletions, prosody, and attitude toward reading. Fluency and Comprehension scores are calculated for each passage read.

The GORT-4 was normed on a sample of 1,677 students aged 6 through 18. The normative sample was stratified to correspond to key demographic variables including race, gender, ethnicity, and geographic region. Race in the manual was divided into white (85 percent), black (12 percent), and other (3 percent). Educational attainment of parents included less than a Bachelor's degree (72 percent), Bachelor's degree (21 percent), and Master's, professional, or doctoral degree (7 percent) categories. The disability status of the sample include the following categories: no disability (92 percent), Learning Disability (2 percent), Speech-Language Disorder (<1 percent), Attention-Deficit Disorder (2 percent), other disability (2 percent).

The reliabilities of GORT-4 are high, with average internal consistency reliabilities being .90 or above. The validity is extensive and includes studies that illustrate that GORT-4 may be used with confidence to measure change in oral reading over time. Throughout the validity section of the manual, the authors reference studies correlating earlier versions of the GORT. The authors are assuming that the content of the GORT-4 is similar enough to that of earlier versions to allow such comparisons. No evidence is provided to support this assumption, however.

**REFERENCE**

Plake, B. S., Impara, J. C., & Spies, R. A. (Eds.). (2003). *The fifteenth mental measurements yearbook.* Lincoln, NE: Buros Institute of Mental Measurements.

RON DUMONT
*Fairleigh Dickinson University*

JOHN O. WILLIS
*Rivier College*

# GRIEVING PROCESS

It has been recognized for some time that parents of children with disabilities often experience intense traumatic reactions to the diagnosis of their children. Further, these initial feelings are not the only ones that parents experience. It appears that parents go through a continual process of emotional fluctuation in the process of coming to terms with having an exceptional child (Searl, 1978). The intensity or degree of the disabilities does not seem to affect directly the appearance of these feelings. These reactions seem to occur regardless of when the parents become aware of the handicapping condition or how intense the condition is. For example, parents who have been informed that their expected child will be disabled early enough into a pregnancy to make numerous physical and financial preparations still have intense emotional reactions to the child's condition at the time of the child's birth. These reactions continue during the child's maturation (Roos, 1977). These feelings have often been likened to the mourning process experienced at the death of a loved one. Hence the reactions and the subsequent process of coming to terms with a person with disabilities within the family has been labeled the grieving process. Several authors have taken Kubler-Ross's developmental stage model of reaction to dying and have applied it to the loss associated with parenting a child with disabilities (ARCH, 2002).

It has been suggested that parents go through a series of stages. Early work focused on stages of awareness, recognition, search for a cause, and acceptance (Rosen, 1955). Since that time, the literature has focused on psychological concerns, including guilt, denial, ambivalence, depression, anger, and acceptance. Studies of parental reaction often use vastly different terminology. Further, in these studies parents often report differing information concerning the onset, duration, and intensity of a specific feeling. Although the terminology is contradictory, there appear to be common experiences that parents of handicapped children report (Blacher, 1984). These stages are of varied intensity and duration, but seem to appear with predicted regularity. Further, these feelings are experienced throughout the parents' lives. Olshansky (1962) termed this experience "chronic sorrow," referring to the permanent and ongoing grieving that parents of children with disabilities experience. Olshansky holds this is a natural and understandable process. Further, it is in the best interests of parents to work through these feelings at their own pace. Services should be provided to assist parents in managing and living with the disabled child.

Professionals can play a role in helping parents adjust to the added pressures a person with disabilities places on a family (Schleifer, 1971). The thrust of these professional efforts has been to secure appropriate services from the public sector, thus generally ignoring the emotional state of the parents. However, a more complete approach to meeting the needs of parents with exceptional children has received considerable attention for many years. Many professionals have proposed that the grieving process can be an effective tool for understanding parental behavior and a powerful tool for counseling parents to understand and deal with their feelings (Blacher, 1984).

Some have found fault with this approach because of its inability to match all case studies and the misconception that parents resolve the grieving process. Allen and Affleck (1985) have proposed that because of such weaknesses, the grieving process should be disregarded. In place of the grieving process, they have proposed providing coping strategies to parents to help them better deal with the challenges of raising an exceptional individual. The emphasis is placed on problem resolution and emotional regulation. Coping strategies focus the parent on adjustment, which the stage approach to grieving processes often does not do.

Professionals need to be aware that the grieving process may adversely affect their relationship and interactions with parents of children with disabilities. At least three considerations must be understood. First, parents may be experiencing a variety of emotional states at a given time. Single interactions may not be representative of the parents' levels of cooperation or enthusiasm, but rather a stage in grieving (e.g., anger or guilt). Second, interaction with specific agency representatives may cause emotional responses that are not expected by the professionals involved. This may not mean that a parent's total life is focused in that direction, but that current interactions are bringing out certain feelings. Third, parents may spend a prolonged amount of time in one stage or another. A parent may appear to be angry or sad during dealings with a professional. This does not mean that the parent will always remain in this emotional stage; the parent eventually may move on to other feelings in the process. Those who deal with parents must realize that not only do emotions affect interactions, but varied behaviors are normal and to be expected (Searl, 1978).

The implications of the grieving process to those who deal with the parents of children with disabilities may be summarized as follows. First, parents often experience deep and intense feelings that may require counseling. Second, these feelings may continue for long periods of time. Third, feelings change at differing rates and/or varied sequences, necessitating flexibility in interpersonal dealings. Fourth, the grieving process is experienced by parents in an individual manner, necessitating interactions with parents to reflect an individual approach.

## REFERENCES

Allen, D. A., & Affleck, G. (1985). Are we stereotyping parents? A postscript to Blacher. *Mental Retardation, 23,* 200–202.

ARCH. (2002). National Resource Center for Respite and Crisis Care Center. *Factsheet Number 21, Families and the grieving process.* Retrieved February 10, 2006, from http://www.archrespite.org/archfs21.htm

Blacher, J. (1984). Sequential stages of parental adjustment to the birth of a child with handicaps: Fact or artifact? *Mental Retardation, 22,* 55–58.

Olshansky, S. (1962). Chronic sorrow: A response to having a mentally defective child. *Social Casework, 43,* 190–194.

Roos, P. (1977). Parents of mentally retarded people. *International Journal of Mental Health, 6,* 96–119.

Rosen, L. (1955). Selected aspects in the development of the mother's understanding of her mentally retarded child. *American Journal of Mental Deficiency, 59,* 522.

Schleifer, M. (1971). Let us all stop blaming the parents. *Exceptional Parent, 1,* 3–5.

Searl, S. (1978). Stages of parent reaction. *Exceptional Parent, 8,* 27–29.

ALAN HILTON
*Seattle University*

## FAMILY COUNSELING
## FAMILY RESPONSE TO A CHILD WITH DISABILITIES

## GROHT, MILDRED A. (1890–1971)

Mildred A. Groht, a prominent educator of the deaf and developer of one of the major methods of teaching language to deaf children, was a graduate of Swarthmore College, with an honorary doctorate from Gallaudet College. She began her career as a teacher at the New York School for the Deaf and later taught at the Maryland School for the Deaf. In 1926 she joined the faculty of the Lexington School for the Deaf in New York City, where she served as principal until her retirement in 1958.

A talented teacher, she proposed and developed the influential natural language method of teaching language to the deaf. Based on the premise that deaf children can best acquire language through activities that are a natural part of a child's life, Groht's method uses a variety of activities. The teacher consistently creates situations that provide the students with language experiences and continually talks to the children and encourages them to respond with speech. Such practice in real-life situations was seen as more effective than the traditional grammatical or analytical approach, with its emphasis on language analysis and drill. The use of natural methods has increased markedly, and most programs today use a mixture of natural and analytical approaches.

Groht described the natural method in her book *Natural Language for Deaf Children.* In its foreword, Clarence D. O'Connor, then superintendent of the Lexington School for the Deaf, called Groht, "one of America's most distinguished teachers of the deaf, particularly in the field of communication arts." He went on to say:

> She has increasingly expounded the philosophy that deaf children can acquire fluent use of English comparable to that of the hearing through what has come to be known as the 'natural' method, and through her own skillful teaching of deaf children and guiding of teachers she has demonstrated that this can be done without question. Through her writings, her demonstrations, and her lecture courses, and now through the chapters of this excellent book, she has very generously passed on to her coworkers the benefits of her rich experience in this specialized field.

Active in the Alexander Graham Bell Association for the Deaf, Groht served on the association's auxiliary board for a number of years and was named to its honorary board in 1965. She died in Ossining, New York, on December 11, 1971.

### REFERENCE

Groht, M. A. (1958). *Natural language for deaf children.* Washington, DC: Alexander Graham Bell Association for the Deaf.

PAUL IRVINE
*Katonah, New York*

**Mildred A. Groht**

## GROSENICK, JUDITH K. (1942–    )

Judith K. Grosenick obtained her BS in 1964 in elementary education from the University of Wisconsin at Oshkosh (formerly Wisconsin State College), and later earned her MS in 1966 in special education and PhD in 1968 in emotional disturbance from the University of Kansas at Lawrence. She was a professor in the Department of Education and Director of Educational Studies at the University of Oregon, Eugene.

Originally an elementary school teacher, Grosenick encountered more difficulties in the classroom than she had expected or been trained to handle. Attempting to find solutions to these problems subsequently led to her increased involvement in the field of behavior disorders and special education (Grosenick, 1981). She is perhaps best known for

**Judith K. Grosenick**

her development of in-service training programs for teachers of children with behavior disorders, but is also recognized for her work in teacher and leadership personnel preparation as well as knowledge-building and dissemination.

Grosenick's extensive data-gathering and analysis in the area of district-level programs for behavior-disordered children has influenced issues and practices in the profession nationwide (Grosenick & Huntze, 1983). Her work with the National Needs Analysis Program in Behavior Disorders has resulted in the development of an evaluation instrument used to assess instructional programs for children with serious emotional disturbance. Nine categories are addressed using this method, including program philosophy, student needs and identification, instructional methods and curriculum, program design and operation, and evaluation. Information regarding the development of instruction is provided as well, outlining several necessary steps ranging from identification of a well-conceptualized program to field testing, revising, and determining the validity of the instrument (Grosenick, 1990, 1991).

Although Grosenick's primary focus is special education, she is also concerned with the integration of special and regular education in public schools as well as teacher education programs. *Educational and Social Issues,* her most recent book, was published in 1996 and coauthored by Daniel W. Close. Dr. Grosenick is currently professor emerita at the University of Oregon.

**REFERENCES**

Grosenick, J. K. (1981). Public school and mental health services to severely behavior disordered students. *Behavioral Disorders, 6,* 183–190.

Grosenick, J. K. (1990). A conceptual scheme for describing and evaluating programs in behavioral disorders. *Behavioral Disorders, 16,* 66–74.

Grosenick, J. K. (1991). Public school services for behaviorally disordered students: Program practices in the 80s. *Behavioral Disorders, 16,* 87–96.

Grosenick, J. K., & Close, D. W. (1996). *Educational and social issues.* Dubuque, IA: Kendall-Hunt.

Grosenick, J. K., & Huntze, S. L. (1983). *National needs analysis in behavior disorders: More questions than answers: Review and analysis of programs for behaviorally disordered children and youth.* Columbia: University of Missouri.

Grosenick, J. K., & McCarney, S. L. (1984). Preparation of teacher education in behavior disorders. *Teacher Education & Special Education, 7,* 100–106.

E. VALERIE HEWITT
*Texas A&M University*
First edition

TAMARA J. MARTIN
*The University of Texas of the
Permian Basin*
Second edition

# GROSSMAN, HERBERT (1934–    )

Herbert Grossman obtained his doctorate in clinical psychology from Columbia University in 1967. Formerly a member of the faculty in the special education department at San Jose State University, Grossman specializes in clinical child psychology and therapy.

His extensive work in the field of education and teacher preparation addresses a variety of topics, including gender inequities in education (Grossman & Grossman, 1994), diversity of students in special education (Grossman, 1995c), behavior management in classrooms (Grossman, 1990), teaching Hispanic-American students (Grossman, 1995b), and discrimination in special education (Grossman, 1998b). Promoting parity of educational opportunity for all students has been the prevailing theme of his writing and research. He has examined gender differences in school experiences and the origins of this disparity, particularly as this factor affects outcomes of education for male and female students. Providing procedures for educators to approach these issues, he focuses primarily on individual emotional reactions, methods of communication and learning, moral development, and interpersonal relationships (Grossman & Grossman, 1994).

Grossman's (1995d) important writing in the area of teacher preparation has promoted recognition of the diversity (i.e., socioeconomic, gender, communication, and so on) of individuals in today's schools, advocating effective, unbiased assessment and instructional methods to reduce these disparities, thus providing all youngsters the same opportunities for learning. His survey of some 500 professionals and parents in various regions of the United States and other countries posed questions related to cultural and contextual factors seen as critical to the formulation of recommendations for improving the academic achievement of Hispanic students (Grossman, 1995b).

During his distinguished career, Grossman has served as coordinator of the Bilingual/Cross Cultural Special Education Program at California State University, and he was the Director of Project Hope in Peru from 1978 to 1980. A prolific writer and researcher, he continues his significant work in the field of education, including *Special Education in a Diverse Society* (1995c), *Ending Discrimination in Special Education* (1998b), *Achieving Educational Equality* (1998a), and *Classroom Behavior Management for Diverse and Inclusive Schools* (2004).

## REFERENCES

Grossman, H. (1990). *Instructor's manual to accompany trouble-free teaching: Solutions to behavior problems in the classroom.* Mountain View, CA: Mayfield.

Grossman, H. (1995a). *Classroom behavior management in a diverse society* (2nd ed.). Mountain View, CA: Mayfield.

Grossman, H. (1995b). *Educating Hispanic students: Implications for instruction, classroom management, counseling, and assessment* (2nd ed.). Springfield, IL: Thomas.

Grossman, H. (1995c). *Special education in a diverse society.* Boston: Allyn & Bacon.

Grossman, H. (1995d). *Teaching in a diverse society.* Needham Heights, MA: Allyn & Bacon.

Grossman, H. (1998a). *Achieving educational equality: Assuring all students an equal opportunity in school.* Springfield, IL: Thomas.

Grossman, H. (1998b). *Ending discrimination in special education.* Springfield, IL: Thomas.

Grossman, H. (2004). *Classroom behavior management for diverse and inclusive schools* (3rd ed.). Toronto: Rowman-Littlefield.

Grossman, H., & Grossman, S. H. (1994). *Gender issues in education.* Boston: Allyn & Bacon.

ROBERTA C. STOKES
*Texas A&M University*
First edition

TAMARA J. MARTIN
*The University of Texas of the Permian Basin*
Second edition

JESSI K. WHEATLEY
*Falcon School District 49, Colorado Springs, Colorado*
Third edition

# GROUP HOMES

The group home design is one model of alternate living environments designed to promote independent living for disabled individuals in our society. As an alternative to large institutions, group homes provide a residential environment within a community that allows disabled individuals to function as independently as possible while protecting their civil rights (Youngblood & Bensberg, 1983).

Historically, the developmentally disadvantaged in our society were placed in large institutions housing vast numbers of disabled individuals. In 1969 Kugel and Wolfensberger reported that in the United States, 200,000 persons lived in over 150 public institutions for the retarded. An additional 20,000 resided in private institutions, with tens of thousands awaiting admittance to institutions for the mentally ill. For the most part, these institutions have been shown to be understaffed, overcrowded, and poorly managed. Violation of the rights of individuals with disabilities came into serious question (e.g., *Wyatt* v. *Stickney*, 1972). As a direct result of this, and in keeping with the civil rights movement that was raging in the late 1960s, a large deinstitutionalization movement began.

The current philosophy is one of normalization, which maintains that developmentally disabled persons have the same legal and civil rights as any other citizen as guaranteed under the Fourteenth Amendment of the U.S. Constitution. Because most alternative living arrangements involve some departure from culturally normative practices, special attention to implementation of normalization and use of the "least restrictive environment" concept must underlie all such arrangements (Accreditation Council for Services for Mentally Retarded and Other Developmentally Disabled Persons, 1984).

To qualify for federal assistance, group homes must be established according to specific guidelines set forth by the Federal Agency of the Administration of Developmental Disabilities (WAC 275.36.010). According to these guidelines, a group home is defined as a residential facility in the form of a single dwelling, series of apartments, or other sound structures that allow for a pleasant and healthful environment for human life and welfare. This structure may be owned, leased, or be part of a larger facility serving other disabled individuals.

A group home is designed to serve a maximum of 20 mentally or physically disabled individuals who participate in various jobs, sheltered workshops, daycare centers, activity centers, educational facilities, or other community-based programs that are designed for their training, rehabilitation, and/or general well-being. These facilities must be located within reasonable proximity to those community resources that are necessary adjuncts to a training, education, or rehabilitation program. The living quarters should provide a homelike atmosphere and the residents should participate in the care of the facility and of themselves.

There are two major types of group home facilities. Both are designed to house 8 to 10 individuals. The first is a transitional group home. As the name implies, this home is designed to house adults (18 or older) with the goal that the disabled person will move on to more independent living quarters (e.g., an apartment) once he or she has mastered important independent living skills. For individuals who exhibit less potential for being capable of independent living, long-term group homes are provided. These more permanent residences offer less restrictive environments than institutions, but not as independent an environment as transitional group homes. There are provisions even with long-term group homes that individuals be allowed to develop to their maximum potential. Thus, there are instances when individuals in long-term group homes have developed independent living skills to the extent that they can enter a transitional group home or can move directly into an independent living setting. Certain other groups of disabled individuals (e.g., deaf-blind) are also afforded chances for group home living. These facilities differ only in that they generally provide additional services to the transitional or long-term group home.

Group home facilities provide a wide range of services from legal assistance to sex education/family planning. The facilities, depending on states' funding patterns, are staffed by individuals ranging from house parents to supervisory professional staff members. Pros and cons of various staffing patterns are discussed by Youngblood and Bensberg (1983).

Establishing alternative living facilities (i.e., group homes) has not been always met with wholesale support, particularly by residents of communities where these residences are to be located. In keeping with the normalization principles and in accordance with state and federal guidelines for their establishment, group homes are to allow disabled individuals to experience community living to the maximum extent possible. Often residents of the community are concerned that their property values will fall because of group homes (Conroy & Bradley, 1985), or that a disabled resident might be dangerous. Researchers in the Pennhurst study found that resident attitudes following actual establishment of a group home were more positive than were attitudes toward the proposal of the same facility. The more negative attitudes were also directed toward group homes for the more severely disabled or mentally ill.

Research regarding the effects of group home living versus institutional living has been overwhelmingly positive. For example, the Pennhurst study (Conroy & Bradley, 1985) investigated whether disabled individuals ordered released from an institution following a court ruling and placed in alternative living environments, including group homes, were better off than a matched group of their peers who remained in the institution. Factors such as adaptive behavior, satisfaction with living arrangements, costs, and family and neighbor attitudes were examined. The study concluded: "the people deinstitutionalized under the Pennhurst court order *are* better off in *every* way measured . . . the results are not mixed" (pp. 322–323).

Just as residential services for the developmentally disabled today have met Wolfensberger's 1969 predictions, Willer (1981) has proposed that the concept of normalization and alternative living arrangements will again change in the future, out of necessity. He predicts "quality of life" concepts with emphasis on the individual will replace the group homes of today. Group homes as we know them, according to Willer, will be reserved for only the more severely disabled.

**REFERENCES**

Accreditation Council for Services for Mentally Retarded and Other Developmentally Disabled Persons. (1984). *Standards for services for developmentally disabled individuals.* Washington, DC.

Conroy, J. W., & Bradley, V. J. (1985). *The Pennhurst longitudinal study: A report of five years of research and analysis.* Philadelphia: Temple University, Developmental Disabilities Center. Boston: Human Services Research Institute.

Kugel, R. B., & Wolfensberger, W. (1969). *Changing patterns in residential services for the mentally retarded.* Washington, DC: President's Committee on Mental Retardation.

Willer, B. (1981). The future of residential services for mentally retarded persons. *Forum, 1*(4), 8–10.

*Wyatt* v. *Stickney.* 325F. Supp 781 (1972).

Youngblood, G. S., & Bensberg, G. J. (1983). *Planning and operating group homes for the handicapped.* Lubbock, TX: Research and Training Center in Mental Retardation.

JULIA A. HICKMAN
*Bastrop Mental Health
Association*

**ADAPTIVE BEHAVIOR
DEINSTITUTIONALIZATION
EDGERTON, ROBERT B.
LEAST RESTRICTIVE ENVIRONMENT**

# GROUP THERAPY

Group therapy is a general term that refers to any of the various types of therapeutic groups that share the broad purpose of increasing people's knowledge of themselves and others and giving people the skills necessary to enhance their personal competence. According to this general definition, group counseling, encounter groups, human relation groups, and skill-oriented groups are all types of group therapy. There are as many theoretical orientations to group therapy as there are to individual therapy. These include existentialism-humanism, gestalt, psychoanalytic, behavioral, rational-emotive therapy, reality therapy, transactional analysis, and others (Corey & Corey, 1977). The several types of group therapies plus the various theoretical orientations that may characterize group therapy make it difficult to make meaningful statements that generalize to the various types and models.

However, some generalizations do apply to most models of group therapy. First, participants can obtain honest feedback from others about how they appear to others. Thus, participants are provided with an opportunity to explore their style of relating to others and to learn more effective interpersonal skills. This feedback occurs in a group climate characterized by mutual caring and trust. Feedback from several persons, especially persons similar to a group participant, is often more powerful than a therapist's feedback in individual therapy.

Second, the group setting offers support for new behaviors and encourages experimentation. This norm of experimentation combined with the norms of feedback and support create a low-risk setting for participants to practice new behaviors such as showing compassion, intimacy, assertion, or disclosure of weaknesses.

Third, the sharing of experiences allows members to learn about themselves through the experiences of others, to experience emotional closeness, and to empathize with the problems of others. Participants learn that their problems and perceived inadequacies are not unique; they also learn new ways to cope with those problems. Some group therapists select group participants in a way that maximizes the opportunity for learning better ways of dealing with problems. For example, a group designed to help lonely children make friends would include some children who are at least moderately competent in friendship-making skills.

Fourth, group cohesiveness is necessary for a successful group. A cohesive group is characterized by mutual trust and respect and high levels of cooperation, support, encouragement, caring, productive problem solving, and the open expression of conflict. The group therapist directs much of his or her energies and skills to creating cohesive groups in which individuals experience the acceptance that is a necessary precondition for lowering defenses and risking new behaviors.

There are three major types of group therapy used in school settings: skill-oriented groups, personal growth groups, and specific focus therapy groups. The use of all three in schools is justified by the recognition that emotional and behavioral adjustment is important to a child's educational performance. Social-emotional problems like depression, loneliness, or anxiety affect school learning and adjustment.

Skill-oriented group therapy is the most widely accepted type of group therapy in school settings as it focuses on teaching specific adaptive skills such as communication, problem-solving, or social skills. An example of a skill-oriented therapy program is the structured learning therapy model developed and popularized by Goldstein (1981). In this model children with deficient social skills are taught skills through a procedure that employs instruction, modeling, behavior rehearsal, and feedback. Children in the group discuss each skill (e.g., expressing anger, offering help, disagreeing with another), citing their own examples of each skill. The skills are broken into component steps, and members practice the skills in role playing. They receive feedback from the group on their performance. Another example of a skill-oriented group is a communication skill group for adolescents. Members practice such skills as listening and perception-checking in the group setting and discuss how these skills apply outside the group.

In the personal growth group, the group setting provides the emotional support and encouragement necessary for the type of self-exploration that leads to a change in attitudes and behaviors. In schools, members of the group might share a common problem or situation such as having parents who are recently divorced. The group provides members with a place where they can express their feelings regarding their situations and discover that other people experience similar problems and feelings. These groups attempt to help members integrate their thinking and feelings and to experience greater self-acceptance. They are often directed to the normal person who is experiencing unusual stress or who wishes to become more self-actualized.

The specific focus therapy group attempts to correct an emotional or behavioral problem. An example is a group for highly anxious children. Children might share anxiety-producing situations and their reactions to those situations. They learn that different children are afraid of different situations, test the reality of their fears, and learn from other children how to cope with their anxieties. The group therapist might teach children how to use specific anxiety-management techniques such as relaxation, self-talk, or problem solving.

### REFERENCES

Corey, G., & Corey, M. S. (1977). *Groups: Process and practice.* Belmont, CA: Wadsworth.

Goldstein, A. P. (1981). *Psychological skill training: The structured learning technique.* New York: Pergamon.

JAN N. HUGHES
*Texas A&M University*

**FAMILY COUNSELING**
**PSYCHOTHERAPY**


# GUADALUPE v. TEMPE ELEMENTARY SCHOOL DISTRICT

See DIANA v. STATE BOARD OF EDUCATION.

# GUGGENBÜHL, JOHANN J. (1816–1863)

Johann J. Guggenbühl, a Swiss physician, was the originator of institutional care for the mentally retarded. Following an extensive study of cretinism, Guggenbühl established a hospital and school for mentally retarded children, the Abendberg, in the mountains of Switzerland. There he instituted for his students a program that combined healthful living, good diet, and medicine with an educational program that emphasized cognitive, sensory, and physical training. Guggenbühl found that his students, especially those who entered his school at an early age, showed improvement in both physical and mental development. Guggenbühl publicized his results widely, and institutions similar to his were established in many of the countries of Europe and in the United States.

Guggenbühl was much in demand and was often away from the Abendberg for extended periods, during which time the institution was poorly administered. This situation caused problems that, in conjunction with the high expectations that Guggenbühl had fostered, led to the closing of the Abendberg and the departure in disgrace of its founder. Nevertheless, Guggenbühl's contribution was monumental. He originated institutional care for the mentally retarded, demonstrated that young mentally retarded people could be helped to develop both physically and mentally, and developed a system of care and education that served as a model throughout the western world.

**REFERENCE**

Kanner, L. (1964). *A history of the care and study of the mentally retarded.* Springfield, IL: Thomas.

PAUL IRVINE
*Katonah, New York*

# GUIDE TO THE ASSESSMENT OF TEST SESSION BEHAVIOR

The Guide to the Assessment of Test Session Behavior for the WISC-III and the WIAT (GATSB; Glutting & Oakland, 1993) is a 29-item behavior rating scale used to evaluate the test behavior of children aged 6 years, 0 months through 16 years, 11 months. Although the scale was conormed with the Wechsler Intelligence Scale for Children–Third Edition (WISC III) and the Wechsler Independent Achievement Test (WIAT), it can be used with all individually administered cognitive tests. The GATSB allows the examiner to evaluate whether a child's behavior during testing differs substantially from behavior displayed by same age and sex peers and whether this behavioral difference affects the quality of the scores. The examiner completes the ratings immediately after the testing session. The instrument is brief, requiring less than 5 minutes to complete and score (Oakland, Glutting, & Watkins, 2005).

The GATSB assesses three broad behaviors known to influence test performance: avoidance, inattentiveness, and uncooperative mood. Children's behaviors are rated on items using a three-point scale (i.e., 0, 1, or 2) in reference to *doesn't apply, somewhat applies,* or *usually applies.* Raw scores are summed and converted to standard $T$-scores for each of the three scales and for a total score, which is a combination of the three.

The GATSB was standardized on 969 children who were representative of 1988 U.S. Census data according to age, race, ethnicity, gender, and parent education. The children's intellectual abilities and achievement levels matched the general population (Glutting & Oakland, 1993). Internal reliability estimates are high, ranging between .84 and .88 for the three scales and are .92 for the total score. Several studies have supported the construct and criterion-related validity of the GATSB. Coefficients of factorial congruence were sufficiently high to conclude that the three scales were comparable for children who differed in race/ethnicity, gender, and socioeconomic status (Konold, Glutting, Oakland, & O'Donnell, 1995). Children who exhibited higher levels of inattentiveness, avoidance, and uncooperative behaviors when taking tests also tended to exhibit lower WISC-III scores (Glutting, Oakland, & Konold, 1994). Also, children with Attention-Deficit/Hyperactivity Disorder could be distinguished from matched controls on the three test behavior domains (Glutting, Robins, & de Lancey, 1997). Although normed on the WISC-III standardization sample, GATSB scores can accurately assess behavior during testing with the Woodcock-Johnson Psychoeducational Battery–Revised and the Wide Range Assessment of Memory and Learning (Daleiden, Drabman, & Benton, 2002).

The GATSB is a valid and reliable standardized measure of test performance. The GATSB may assist in understanding test session behaviors on measures including the Clinical Evaluation of Language Functions–Third Edition, Differential Abilities Scale, Kaufman Assessment Battery for Children, Stanford-Binet Intelligence Scale: Fifth Edition, and Woodcock-Johnson Tests of Cognitive Abilities (Oakland et al., 2005). Use of the GATSB may be valuable for determining whether a student's test-taking behaviors are atypical and if the quality of his or her scores may be affected.

**REFERENCES**

Daleiden, E., Drabman, R. S., & Benton, J. (2002). The Guide to the Assessment of Test Session Behavior: Validity in relation to cognitive testing and parent-reported behavior problems in a clinical sample. *Journal of Clinical Child Psychology, 31,* 263–271.

Glutting, J., & Oakland, T. (1993). *Guide to the Assessment of Test Session Behavior for the WISC III and WIAT: Manual.* San Antonio, TX: Psychological Corporation.

Glutting, J., Oakland, T., & Konold, T. R. (1994). Criterion related bias with the Guide to the Assessment of Test-Session Behavior for the WISC III and WIAT: Possible race/ethnicity, gender, and SES effects. *Journal of School Psychology, 32,* 355–369.

Glutting, J. J., Robins, P. M., & de Lancey, E. (1997). Discriminant validity of test observations for children with attention deficit/hyperactivity. *Journal of School Psychology, 35,* 391–401.

Konold, T. R., Glutting, J. J., Oakland, T., & O'Donnell, L. (1995). Congruence of test-behavior dimensions among child groups that vary in gender, race-ethnicity, and SES. *Journal of Psychoeducational Assessment, 13,* 111–119.

Oakland, T., Glutting, J., & Watkins, M. W. (2005). Assessment of test behaviors with the WISC-IV. In A. Profitera, D. H. Saklofske, & L. G. Weiss (Eds.), *WISC-IV clinical use and interpretation: Scientist practitioner perspectives* (pp. 435–463). San Diego, CA: Elsevier.

JEFFREY DITTERLINE
*University of Florida*

## INTELLIGENT TESTING

**REFERENCES**

Guilford, J. P. (1942). *Fundamental statistics in psychology and education.* New York: McGraw-Hill.

Guilford, J. P. (1967). *The nature of human intelligence.* New York: McGraw-Hill.

Guilford, J. P. (1980). *Intelligence education is intelligent education.* Tokyo: International Society for Intelligence Education.

Guilford, J. P. (1988). Some changes in the structure-of-intellect model. *Educational & Psychological Measurement, 48,* 1–4.

Guilford, J. P., Anastasi, A., English, H., & Freeman, G. (1948). *Fields of psychology.* New York: Van Nostrand.

Primmer, H. (1995). *Kreativitatsforschung und Joy Paul Guilford.* Munchen: Akademischer Verlag.

TAMARA J. MARTIN
*The University of Texas of the
Permian Basin*

## CONVERGENT AND DIVERGENT THINKING
## STRUCTURE OF INTELLECT

## GUILFORD, J. P. (1897–1987)

A native Nebraskan, J. P. Guilford obtained his degree in psychology at the University of Nebraska and later did graduate work at Cornell University. While attending Nebraska, his association with Winifred Hyde led to an interest in psychological testing, with Karl Dallenbach and Kurt Koffka, both of whom he met at Cornell, strongly influencing his later work. Guilford died in 1987.

Guilford spent most of his academic career at the University of Southern California. In addition to writing what some consider classic texts in psychological measurement (e.g., Guilford, 1942, 1967), he is best known for his extensive work in factor analysis, the method used to develop his structure of intellect (SOI) model (Guilford, 1967, 1988). Guilford's model of intelligence postulates some 120 distinct human abilities that contribute to overall intellectual ability and was later revised to contain five content properties, including visual, auditory, symbolic, semantic, and behavioral. In the field of special education, his SOI model, particularly the concepts of convergent and divergent thought, was used to develop programs to foster creativity and improve learning of gifted and creative children.

In 1983, Guilford received the Gold Medal Award of the American Psychological Association. His numerous publications include *The Nature of Human Intelligence* (1967), *Intelligence Education is Intelligent Education* (1980), and *Fundamental Statistics in Psychology and Education* (1942). A compilation of his work in scholarly journals was published in German (Primmer, 1995).

## GUILLAIN-BARRÉ SYNDROME

Guillian-Barré syndrome (GBS) is one of many autoimmune neuropathies that progress to paralysis and involve inflammation of the peripheral nervous system (Willison, 2005). With the virtual elimination of poliomyelitis, GBS is the leading cause of neuromuscular paralysis following infection or immunization in children (DiMario, 2005). GBS includes acute inflammatory demyelinating polyradiculoneuropathy (AIDP), acute motor axonal neuropathy (AMAN), acute motor and sensory axonal neuropathy (AMSAN), Miller Fisher syndrome (MFS), and acute pandysautonomia (Finsterer, 2005). Across age groups, GBS occurs in 1.5 per 100,000, with a lifetime likelihood that an individual will acquire the disorder of approximately 1 in 1,000 (Hahn, 1998; Willison, 2005). In most cases, GBS is associated with destruction of the myelin sheath of peripheral nerves; however, in some cases there are additional variants (DiMario, 2005).

Onset of GBS is rapid and acute, generally occurring within 2 weeks after some other illness or immunization. Symptoms include weakness of limbs, absent tendon stretch reflexes, limb and back pain, and facial weakness (Bradshaw & Jones, 1992). Onset is rapid and progressive. Diagnostic testing includes evaluation of levels of protein in the cerebral spinal fluid. Following onset, there is symptom manifestation for about 1 month or more. This is followed by varying residual symptoms during what is called the recovery phase (Hartung, Kieseier, & Kiefer, 2001). Secondary deterioration may occur at later times. This pattern of manifestation is particular to GBS. It is believed that the effects in children may be somewhat milder (i.e., better recovery) than with adults (Bradshaw & Jones, 1992).

The optimal treatment window is very short; as a result, in roughly 20 percent of cases, there is total paralysis requiring mechanical ventilation. The current treatment of choice involves whole plasma exchange of intravenous immunoglobulin therapy; this minimizes the severity of syndrome manifestation (e.g., Hughes, Jewitt, & Swan, 2004). Recent studies suggest that introduction of intravenous immunoglobulin therapy decreased the time required to regain motor function (Korinthenberg, Schessl, Kirschner, & Mönting, 2005; see DiMario, 2005, for review). Notably, this intravenous treatment is not without risks (i.e., allergic reactions, headache, infection), and the risks and benefits need to be weighed carefully (DiMario, 2005).

Multiple advances have been made in what is known about GBS (Willison, 2005); however, further advances are needed to improve the outcomes of those affected. Additional information and support can be obtained from the Guillain-Barré Syndrome Foundation, P.O. Box 262, Wynnewood, PA 19096, or on the web site: www.guillain-barre.com

## REFERENCES

Bradshaw, D. J., & Jones, H. R. (1992). Guillain-Barré syndrome children: Clinical course, electrodiagnosis, and prognosis. *Muscle and Nerve, 15,* 500–506.

DiMario, Jr., F. J. (2005). Intravenous immunoglobulin in the treatment of childhood Guillain-Barré syndrome: A randomized trial. *Pediatrics, 116,* 226–228.

Finsterer, J. (2005). Treatment of immune-mediated, dysimmune neuropathies. *Acta Neurologica Scandinavica, 112,* 115–125.

Hahn, A. F. (1998). Guillain-Barré syndrome. *Lancet, 352,* 635–641.

Hartung, H. P., Kieseier, B. C., & Kiefer, R. (2001). Progress in Guillain-Barré syndrome. *Current Opinion in Neurology, 14,* 597–604.

Hughes, R. A., Jewitt, K. M., & Swan, A. V. (2004). Cochrane systematic reviews of treatments for peripheral nerve disorders. *Journal of Peripheral Nervous System, 9,* 127–129.

Korinthenberg, R., Schessl, J., Kirschner, J., & Mönting, J. S. (2005). Intravenously administered immunoglobulin in the treatment of childhood Guillain-Barré syndrome: A randomized trial. *Pediatrics, 116,* 8–14.

Willison, H. J. (2005). The immunobiology of Guillain-Barré syndromes. *Journal of the Peripheral Nervous System, 10,* 94–112.

CYNTHIA A. RICCIO
*Texas A&M University*

**CENTRAL NERVOUS SYSTEM**
**OTHER HEALTH IMPAIRED**
**PHYSICAL DISABILITIES**

# H

## HABILITATION OF INDIVIDUALS WITH DISABILITIES

Habilitation is the process of using various professional services to help persons with disabilities maximize their vocational, mental, physical, and social abilities (Rosen, Clark, & Kivitz, 1977). Whereas the term rehabilitation connotes restoration of abilities, habilitation refers to the development of abilities that never existed. The term usually refers to programming for those with developmental disabilities such as cerebral palsy, mental retardation, epilepsy, autism, or sensory impairment.

Present-day habilitation programs have evolved from decades of legislation and litigation addressing the rights and needs of the developmentally disabled. Three major pieces of legislation promoted early habilitation efforts: the Rehabilitation Act Amendments of 1973 (PL 93-112), the Education for all Handicapped Children Act of 1975 (PL 94-142), and the Education Amendments of 1976 (PL 94-482), efforts which continue to be supported by the Individuals with Disabilities Education Act (IDEA) reauthorizations and the Americans with Disabilities Act (ADA).

Sections 503 and 504 of the Rehabilitation Act mandate affirmative action for all employment openings, prohibit discrimination of individuals with disabilities in hiring, training, advancement, and retention practices, and require that all programs be accessible to persons with disabilities. Compliance is necessary to retain federal funding.

Habilitation programs for students with disabilities vary, but are similar in format to those described by Miller and Schloss (1982). Current programs focus not only on vocation, but also on academic, social, leisure, and interpersonal skills. Teaching procedures include identification of the handicap, assessment of skills, program design based on needs, interests, and skills of the individual, instruction, and behavior management and evaluation. Career education includes career awareness and exploration, development of vocational prerequisites, and preparation training. Goals of these training programs vary with the individual's skills and abilities.

### REFERENCES

Goldberg, R. T. (1984). The human sciences and clinical methods: An historical perspective (Special issue). *Rehabilitation Literature, 45*, 340–344.

Kokaska, C. J., & Brolin, D. E. (1985). *Career education for handicapped individuals* (2nd ed.). Columbus, OH: Merrill.

Miller, S. R., & Schloss, P. J. (1982). *Career-vocational education for handicapped youth*. Rockville, MD: Aspen.

Rosen, M., Clark, G. R., & Kivitz, M. S. (1977). *Habilitation of the handicapped: New dimensions in programs for the developmentally disabled*. Baltimore: University Park.

Trieschmann, R. B. (1984). Vocational rehabilitation: A psychological perspective (Special issue). *Rehabilitation Literature, 45*, 345–348.

CHRISTINE A. ESPIN
*University of Minnesota*

REHABILITATION
VOCATIONAL EDUCATION

## HABITUATION

Habituation is a decline in response to a stimulus that is presented repeatedly but that signals the onset of no other stimulus. For example, a loud noise may evoke a startle response at first but little response after its twentieth repetition. A new cuckoo clock may awaken people on the hour for the first few nights but not on later nights.

Because habituation is generally perceived as a relatively simple example of learning, it has been a popular focus for study by investigators interested in the physiology of learning. For example, the gill-withdrawal response of the sea slug *Aplysia* habituates after a tactile stimulus is repeated many times. The habituation can be traced to a single, identifiable synapse at which the pre-synaptic end bulb shrinks and releases less than normal amounts of its synaptic transmitter (Castellucci & Kandel, 1974).

Habituation may be taken as the opposite of distractibility. Someone who fails to habituate to a repeated stimulus will continue to be distracted by it. Biological factors that impair habituation also increase distractibility. Examples include damage to the frontal lobes of the cerebral cortex and a deficit of the synaptic transmitter acetylcholine (Carlton & Markiewicz, 1971). Infant rats fail to habituate before age 25 days (Feigley, Parsons, Hamilton, & Spear, 1972). This failure is attributed to the immaturity of certain areas of the brain, including the frontal cortex, prior to that age. High distractibility and slow habituation also characterize many children with an immature nervous system, including most of those who suffer from attention deficit disorder. Slow habituation also is associated with other behaviors that indicate a lack of inhibition such as impulsiveness, unresponsiveness to the threat of punishment, and failure to extinguish an unreinforced response.

Some investigators have used rate of habituation as a diagnostic technique to identify infants or young children who may have been exposed to factors that impair brain maturation. One study examined the rate of habituation by newborns as a function of alcohol use by their mothers during pregnancy (Streissguth, Barr, & Martin, 1983). Habituation was slightly but significantly slower among infants whose mothers drank alcohol during pregnancy, even if they drank a mean of less than one ounce of alcohol per day.

## REFERENCES

Carlton, P. L., & Markiewicz, B. (1971). Behavioral effects of atropine and scopolamine. In E. Furchtgott (Ed.), *Pharmacological and biophysical agents and behavior* (pp. 345–373). New York: Academic.

Castellucci, V. F., & Kandel, E. R. (1974). A quantal analysis of the synaptic depression underlying habituation of the gill-withdrawal reflex in *Aplysia. Proceedings of the National Academy of Sciences, U.S.A., 71,* 5004–5008.

Feigley, D. A., Parsons, P. J., Hamilton, L. W., & Spear, N. E. (1972). Development of habituation to novel environments in the rat. *Journal of Comparative & Physiological Psychology, 79,* 443–452.

Streissguth, A. P., Barr, H. M., & Martin, D. C. (1983). Maternal alcohol use and neonatal habituation assessed with the Brazelton scale. *Child Development, 54,* 1109–1118.

JAMES W. KALAT
*North Carolina State University*

**ATTENTION-DEFICIT/HYPERACTIVITY DISORDER
BEHAVIOR MODIFICATION
DISTRACTIBILITY**

## HALDERMAN v. PENNHURST STATE SCHOOL AND HOSPITAL (1977)

The *Halderman* case was filed as a class-action suit by a resident, T. L. Halderman, of the Pennhurst State School and Hospital (operated by the Commonwealth of Pennsylvania), the Pennsylvania Association of Retarded Citizens, and the United States of America against the Pennhurst State School and Hospital. The residents made a variety of claims that centered around the lack of rehabilitative and educational efforts at Pennhurst. The plaintiffs argued that

custodial care was insufficient for involuntary placement in the Pennhurst institution since the plaintiffs were mentally retarded and not considered dangerous.

In deciding the case, the federal judge for the Eastern District of Pennsylvania, R. J. Broderick, made three rulings that have been of major importance in modifying special education services to the institutionalized retarded. Broderick ruled that mentally retarded residents of state institutions have constitutional rights to minimally adequate habilitation services, to freedom from harm, and to the receipt of habilitation services in a nondiscriminatory manner. Broderick went on to rule in the *Halderman* case specifically that the resident's rights at Pennhurst had been violated because of failure to provide even minimally adequate habilitative services. In making his rulings, Broderick rejected the argument that improvements at Pennhurst were being made gradually and should be allowed to proceed at an incremental pace, that state law restricted the programs that could be offered, and that funding levels prevented minimally adequate habilitation programs.

Broderick wrote a lengthy decision that reviews assessment practices, programming, and management in institutional settings. All were directed at the provision of habilitative services and special education. For example, Broderick noted that although speech, hearing, and psychological evaluations had been completed on nearly all residents at approximately 3-year intervals, vocational assessments or evaluations of self-care skills were rarely conducted. Broderick saw a need for more extensive evaluations, stating that "Proper habilitation cannot be provided to retarded persons unless those responsible for providing such programs are aware of the individual's needs" (*Halderman* v. *Pennhurst,* 1977, p. 1305). Broderick required the development of individual educational plans for the institutionalized retarded that would include (1) long- and short-term goals, (2) specification of the conditions under which the individual might achieve these goals, and (3) specification of the criteria to evaluate the individual's mastery of these goals.

Broderick placed many restrictions on the use of punishment, drugs, and physical restraints. He particularly ruled that lack of sufficient staff did not allow the use of otherwise inappropriate methods of control. Physical constraints, for example, could not be used just because insufficient staff were available to supervise self-injurious residents.

Broderick made strong statements indicating favorable sentiments toward the principles of normalization as applied to the severely and profoundly retarded as well. Since the court found that the environment at Pennhurst was not conducive to normalization, Broderick ruled that the residents were to be moved to community-based living facilities as part of the injunctive relief. He noted that each community facility would be required to provide minimally adequate habilitative services. Broderick's extensive rulings regarding the provisions of habilitative services, including detailed multidisciplinary assessment and movement toward normalization, have had significant impact on the deinstitutionalization of all but the most severely and profoundly mentally retarded. The rulings have greatly impacted the lives of those remaining in institutions such as Pennhurst, and many of these provisions were later incorporated into the Developmental Disabilities Assistance and Bill of Rights Act.

CECIL R. REYNOLDS
*Texas A&M University*
Second edition

KIMBERLY F. APPLEQUIST
*University of Colorado at
Colorado Springs*
Third edition

## DEVELOPMENTAL DISABILITIES ASSISTANCE AND BILL OF RIGHTS ACT
## NORMALIZATION
## WOLFENSBERGER, WOLF

## HALDOL

Haldol (haloperidol) is considered a major tranquilizer. Unlike thorazine, which is a phenothiazine, haldol is of the drug class butyrophenone, which tends to have a greater neuroleptic effect than phenothiazine (Bassuk & Schoonover, 1977). Haldol is similar in effect to the piperazine subgroup (e.g., Stelazine) of phenothiazines. Like similar antipsychotic drugs, haldol appears to block dopamine receptors in the brain. In contrast to chlorpromazine, haldol tends to produce less sedation, less decrease in blood pressure, and less change in temperature perception (McEvoy, 1984). Haldol is used primarily for symptomatic management of psychotic conditions. Haldol also appears to have more specific effects on aggression and agitated behavior (Konopasek, 2003). Thus, it tends to be used with psychotic individuals who also show assaultive behavior, with combative adolescents, and with hyperactive brain-impaired children (Bassuk & Schoonover, 1977). Haldol also has been used as an adjunct with manic-depressive patients in the manic phase during the initiation of lithium treatment (Jefferson, Greist, & Ackerman, 1983). Although haldol was once the most popular of the neuroleptic drugs for the treatment of psychotic processes (such as schizophrenia) due to its low side-effect profile, other drugs with even fewer side effects, such as Risperidone, have gained popularity.

As may be expected from its actions, haldol produces anticholinergic side effects (i.e., dry mouth, blurred vision, urinary retention). Side effects (McEvoy, 1984) to haloperidol treatment usually develop during the initial days of treatment; they are similar to the side effects encoun-

tered during treatment with phenothiazines (parkinsonian symptoms: drowsiness or lethargy, drooling; neuromuscular reactions: motor restlessness, dystonic reactions, tardive dyskinesia; mental confusion, headache, dizziness, depression, and anxiety may also be seen). Haldol also lowers the seizure threshold, thus otherwise-controlled seizures may recur. Abrupt withdrawal in a pediatric patient, especially after relatively high doses have been used, may produce a syndrome of involuntary movements reminiscent of tardive dyskinesia in adults (Bassuk & Schoonover, 1977; Konopasek, 2003). These problems are often managed with antihistamines or with cogentin.

## REFERENCES

Bassuk, E. L., & Schoonover, S. C. (1977). *The practitioner's guide to psychoactive drugs.* New York: Plenum.

Jefferson, J. W., Greist, J. H., & Ackerman, D. L. (1983). *Lithium encyclopedia for clinical practice.* Washington, DC: American Psychiatric Press.

Konopasek, D. (2003). *Medication fact sheets.* Longmont, CO: Sopris.

McEvoy, G. K. (1984). *American hospital formulary service: Drug information 84.* Bethesda, MD: American Society of Hospital Pharmacists.

ROBERT F. SAWICKI
*Lake Erie Institute of
Rehabilitation*

## DOPAMINE

## HALL, FRANK H. (1843–1911)

Frank Haven Hall, inventor of the braille typewriter, was a school superintendent prior to becoming superintendent of the Illinois Institution for the Education of the Blind in 1890. In 1892 Hall introduced the braillewriter, a braille typewriter that quickly replaced the laborious writing device then in use—a slate and hand-held stylus—and greatly speeded up the writing of braille. Hall then adapted his machine to print multiple copies. With its speed and efficiency, Hall's machine revolutionized book-making for the blind and made feasible the mass production of braille materials.

Hall's experience at the Illinois institution convinced him that blind students should have the opportunity of participating fully in the activities of sighted individuals. He persuaded the school authorities of Chicago, who were considering the establishment of a boarding school for blind students, to establish day classes instead. As a result, the first public school day class for blind students was initiated in Chicago in 1900, with one of Hall's teachers as supervisor. The last decade of Hall's life was spent as superintendent of the Farmers' Institute of Illinois, where he effectively promoted the cause of agricultural education.

## REFERENCE

Hendrickson, W. B. (1956). The three lives of Frank H. Hall. *Journal of the Illinois State Historical Society, 44,* 271–293.

PAUL IRVINE
*Katonah, New York*

## HALL, G. STANLEY (1844–1924)

G. Stanley Hall established one of the first psychology laboratories in the United States, at Johns Hopkins University. Later, as the first president of Clark University, he instituted the first child psychology laboratory in the nation. A former student of Wilhelm Wundt in Leipzig, Hall was influential in introducing European theories and methods of psychology into the United States. He carried out pioneering studies of childhood, adolescence, senescence, human genetics, and the psychology of religion. Among Hall's students were many of the next generation of leaders in psychology and education, including John Dewey, James McKeen Cattell, Henry H. Goddard, and Lewis Terman. Hall published nearly 500 articles and books and founded four psychological journals. He was a leading figure in the formation of the American Psychological Association and was its first president.

## REFERENCES

Hall, G. S. (1923). *Life and confessions of a psychologist.* New York: Appleton.

Watson, R. I. (1968). *The great psychologists.* New York: Lippincott.

PAUL IRVINE
*Katonah, New York*

## HALLAHAN, DANIEL P. (1944–      )

Daniel P. Hallahan received his BA in psychology from the University of Michigan in 1967 and his PhD in education and psychology from the University of Michigan in 1971. His major fields of interest include learning disabilities, attention problems, cognitive behavior modification, and applied behavior analysis. His earliest work was in information processing. He suggested that many learning-disabled children exhibit strategy deficits when they attempt academic tasks (Hallahan, 1975). His recent research has focused on an educational intervention that will counteract such strategy deficiencies.

**Daniel P. Hallahan**

Hallahan is currently a professor and department chair in the Curry School of Education at the University of Virginia in Charlottesville. He has directed several leadership training projects sponsored by the U.S. Department of Education's Office of Special Education Programs and currently is the co-principal investigator of the federally-funded Center of Minority Research in Special Education. This was designed to enhance the capacity of faculty at minority institutions of higher education to conduct research on minority issues in special education. Hallahan has served in various capacities for the Division for Learning Disabilities of the Council for Exceptional Children and was publications chair from 1994 to 1997. He was the 1998–1999 president of the organization.

Hallahan is known for having popularized the notion of noncategorical education for the mildly handicapped and also for his research into the use of self-monitoring for children with attention problems. His research is in the area of cognitive interventions, methods of making learning-disabled students independent learners, and policy and ethical issues in special education.

Currently, Hallahan is concerned that the field of special education has lost its instructional momentum. Hallahan is a strong proponent of intensive instruction for students with learning disabilities. He believes that the differences in students with learning disabilities must be recognized, not ignored. An effective way to diminish these differences is through intensive instruction (Hallahan & Ward, 1998).

Hallahan's principal publications include the *Handbook of Special Education* (Hallahan & Kauffman, 1981), *Introduction to Learning Disabilities* (Hallahan, Kauffman, & Lloyd, 1996), and *Exceptional Learners: Introduction to Special Education* (Hallahan & Kauffman, 1997). He has written other books as well as numerous articles concerning special education. He was awarded the Council for Exceptional Children Research Award in 2000.

## REFERENCES

Hallahan, D. P. (1975). Comparative research studies on the psychological characteristics of learning disabled children. In W. M. Cruickshank & D. P. Hallahan (Eds.), *Perceptual and learning disabilities in children, Vol. 1: Psychoeducational practices* (pp. 29–60). Syracuse, NY: Syracuse University Press.

Hallahan, D. P., & Kauffman, J. M. (Eds.). (1981). *Handbook of special education.* Englewood Cliffs, NJ: Prentice Hall.

Hallahan, D. P., & Kaufmann, J. M. (1997). *Exceptional learners: Introduction to special education* (4th ed.). Englewood Cliffs, NJ: Prentice Hall.

Hallahan, D. P., Kaufmann, J. M., & Lloyd, J. W. (1996). *Introduction to learning disabilities* (3rd ed.). Englewood Cliffs, NJ: Prentice Hall.

Hallahan, D. P., & Ward, V. S. (1998, March). *We need more intensive instruction.* Paper presented at the Virginia Council for Learning Disabilities Conference, Charlottesville, VA.

Rebecca Bailey
*Texas A&M University*
First edition

Marie Almond
*The University of Texas of the
Permian Basin*
Second edition

## HALLERMANN-STREIFF SYNDROME

Hallermann-Streiff syndrome is a rare inherited disorder affecting an equal number of males and females. More than 150 cases have been reported in the medical literature, and no known cause has been found other than most likely a new spontaneous genetic mutation. Hallermann-Streiff syndrome is typically diagnosed shortly after birth and usually by the identification of small eyes. Characteristic facial features, premature development of teeth, or deficiency of hair on the face and on the head may also help to confirm the presence of this disorder. Other features become more apparent as the child begins to age (David, Finlon, Genecov, & Argenta, 1999).

Most typically, infants with this disorder are characterized by distinctive craniofacial abnormalities, including an abnormally small head that is usually wide with a prominent forehead; small, underdeveloped lower jaw; small mouth; and a long, narrow nose. In addition, abnormalities of the eyes, malformations of the teeth, and dwarfism (with arms and legs proportional to the body length) also occur. Abnormal widening and delayed hardening of the fibrous joints of the skull and delayed closure of the soft spot may also be evident in infants.

Craniofacial abnormalities may include underdeveloped cheekbones, small nostrils, and underdeveloped cartilage within the nose. Some cases may also include small mouth, an unusually high palate, and an abnormally large or small tongue. The presence of these abnormalities may result in narrow air passages, making it difficult for the infant to swallow, feed, and even breathe. In addition, infants may also experience recurrent respiratory infections, leading to pneumonia, obstruction of the lungs, snoring, and sleep apnea (David et al., 1999).

Ninety percent of infants born with Hallermann-Streiff syndrome experience cataracts and may experience varying degrees of vision loss and even blindness. Some infants may have small eyes, crossed eyes, rapid involuntary eye movements, and bluish discoloration of the whites of the eyes. Frequently, infants with Hallermann-Streiff syndrome experience skin and hair abnormalities, including atrophy of the skin on the scalp and in the middle of the face. The skin is usually thin and taut and may even have patches that lack any coloring. Shortly after birth, the hair commonly becomes very thin, sparse, and brittle (Cohen, 1991).

In approximately 36 percent of the cases, infants with Hallermann-Streiff syndrome are born prematurely and have low birth weight. Most of these children will continue to experience a deficiency in growth, resulting in a very short stature with arms and legs proportional to the body trunk. Some less common characteristics include hyperactivity, excessive sleepiness during the day, loss of consciousness associated with muscle contractions (generalized tonic-clonic seizures), and jerky movements combined with slow, writhing movements (Cohen, 1991).

Dental abnormalities that may be present include but are not limited to early development of teeth (sometimes prior to birth or shortly thereafter), severe tooth decay, extra teeth, and an underdeveloped hard outer layer.

Other disorders that are similar to Hallermann-Streiff syndrome and useful for differential diagnosis are Hutchinson-Gilford syndrome, Wiedemann Rautenstrauch syndrome, and Seckel syndrome. All of these disorders share but are not limited to symptoms of stunted growth and small facial features.

Some characteristics of this syndrome may include:

1. Small head
2. Small eyes
3. Wide forehead in comparison to the small head
4. Small underdeveloped lower jaw
5. Malformation of teeth
6. Beak-like nose
7. Dwarfism (with arms and legs proportional to the body length)
8. Cataract that may result in vision loss in varying degrees
9. Skin and hair abnormalities

Due to the complexity of this disorder, a multidisciplinary team is necessary in order to treat children with this disorder in a comprehensive manner. Pediatricians, surgeons, ophthalmologists, dental specialists, and mental health professionals are some of the professionals necessary for a comprehensive intervention. Other support services that may be beneficial to affected children may include special education services, physical therapy, and social and vocational specialists. Early intervention is crucial.

## REFERENCES

Cohen, M. M. (1991). Hallermann-Streiff syndrome: A review. *Journal of Medical Genetics, 41,* 488–489.

David, L. R., Finlon, M., Genecov, M., & Argenta, L. C. (1999). Hallermann-Streiff syndrome: Experience with 15 patients and review of the literature. *Journal of Craniofacial Surgery, 10*(2), 160–168.

LISA FASNACHT-HILL
*Children's Hospital, Los Angeles*

## HALLUCINATIONS

Hallucinations are sensory events that are without any input from the surrounding environment (Barlow & Durand, 2005). Hallucinatory events may occur in any sensory modality, including visual, auditory, olfactory gustatory, and tactile.

Hallucinations are most often associated with the psychotic mental disorder of schizophrenia, but can occur in extreme cases of depression (Comer, 2004), or medical conditions like dementia, brain tumors, Cushing's syndrome, or Substance-Induced Psychotic Disorder (American Psychiatric Association, 1994). Substance abuse disorders can produce episodes of hallucinations when, for example, too much amphetamines are taken by an individual (Mack, Franklin, & Frances, 2003). Amphetamine use stimulates the nervous system by enhancing activity of norepinephrine and dopamine, making them more available throughout the brain, which can lead to hallucinations and even paranoid delusions.

Concerning schizophrenia, hallucinations are regarded as one of four major characteristic symptoms (i.e., criterion A) associated with the disorder. The other characteristic symptoms are delusions, disorganized speech, grossly disorganized or catatonic behavior, and negative symptoms (i.e., affective flattening, alogia, or avolition). Auditory hallucinations are by far the most common type of hallucination in individuals with schizophrenia (American Psychiatric Association, 1994), and are included as one of the top ten "first-rank" symptoms of schizophrenia (Andersen & Flaum, 1991; Ho, Black, & Andreasen, 2003). Auditory hallucinations usually involve separate/distinct "voices" in the head that are often pejorative, threatening, or can be multiple voices carrying on "conversations" with each other or providing "commentaries" about the individual's thoughts and behaviors. If these types of auditory hallucinations are present, then criterion A of the diagnosis of schizophrenia is satisfied and does not require any more characteristic symptoms in the criteria A list to be present (criteria B, C, D, E, and F still must be considered before making a full diagnosis). The American Psychiatric Association (1994) does not consider hallucinations that occur while falling asleep (hypnogogic) or while waking up (hypnopompic) as indicators of schizophrenia because they are within the range of normal experience. Humming in the head, or isolated occasions where one hears their name called (especially if it lacks the quality of coming from "outside" the head), are also not considered to be associated with schizophrenia. Interestingly, people tend to experience hallucinations more frequently when they are unoccupied or restricted from sensory input, such as in solitary confinement (Margo, Hemsley, & Slade, 1981).

In addition to being considered one of the major characteristic symptoms, hallucinations are also referred to as one of the "positive symptoms," along with delusions, disorganized speech (i.e., frequent derailment or incoherence), and grossly disorganized or catatonic behavior, because of the observed (or reported) excess or distortion of normal functions (Barlow & Durand, 2005). Negative symptoms are regarded as those in which a dimunition or loss of normal functions has occurred, such as is the case with symptoms like flattening of affect or loss of personal volition (American Psychiatric Association, 1994). As mentioned, hallucinations are included in the top ten first rank symptoms list that psychiatry uses for diagnosing schizophrenia, a diagnostic list that is meant to strike an optimal balance between efficient classification and comprehensive description of the disorder (Andersen & Flaum, 1991).

There has been an increased interest in using brain-imaging techniques to try and localize activity when hallucinations occur. Specifically, single photon emission computed topography (SPECT) is used to study cerebral blood flow in schizophrenic patients when they are having auditory hallucinations and when they are not (cf. Silbersweig et al., 1995). A study by Hoffman, Rapaport, Mazure, & Quinlan, 1999) found that the active part of the brain during hallucinations was Broca's area, which is usually associated with speech production. Researchers expected that Wernicke's area would be most active because it involves language comprehension or understanding the speech of others. This finding supports a growing theory that people who are hallucinating are not hearing the voices of others, but are in fact listening to their own thoughts, but can not recognize the difference; this also suggests that deficits in language processing are at work as well.

## REFERENCES

American Psychiatric Association. (1994). *Diagnostic and statistical manual of mental disorders* (4th ed.). Washington, DC: Author.

Andreasen, N. C., & Flaum, M. (1991). Schizophrenia: The characteristic symptoms. *Schizophrenia Bulletin, 17,* 27–49.

Barlow, D. H., & Durand, V. M. (2005). *Abnormal psychology: An integrative approach* (4th ed.). Belmont, CA: Wadsworth.

Comer, R. J. (2004). *Abnormal psychology* (5th ed.). New York: Worth.

Ho, B-C., Black, D. W., & Andreasen, N. C. (2003). Schizophrenia and other psychotic disorders. In R. E. Hales & S. C. Yudofsky (Eds.), *Textbook of clinical psychiatry* (4th ed., pp. 379–438). Washington, DC: American Psychiatric Publishing.

Hoffman, R. E., Rapaport, J., Mazure, C. M., & Quinlan, D. M. (1999). Selective speech perception alterations in schizophrenic patients reporting hallucinated "voices." *American Journal of Psychiatry, 156,* 393–399.

Mack, A. H., Franklin, J. E., & Frances, R. J. (2003). Substance use disorders. In R. E. Hales & S. C. Yudofsky (Eds.), *Textbook of clinical psychiatry* (4th ed., pp. 309–377). Washington, DC: American Psychiatric Press.

Margo, A., Hemsley, D. R., & Slade, P. D. (1981). The effects of varying auditory input on schizophrenic hallucinations. *British Journal of Psychiatry, 139,* 122–127.

Silbersweig, D. A., Stern, E., Frith, C., Cahill, C., Holmes, A., Grootoonk, S., et al. (1995). A functional neuroanatomy of hallucinations in schizophrenia. *Nature, 378,* 176–179.

ROLLEN C. FOWLER
*Eugene 4J School District,*
*Eugene, Oregon*

CHILDHOOD PSYCHOSIS
CHILDHOOD SCHIZOPHRENIA
DELUSIONS

## HALLUCINOGENS

Blum (1984) describes three classes of hallucinogenic drugs: adrenergic compounds (e.g., mescaline, adrenaline); indole types (e.g., lysergic acid diethylamide [LSD]); and anticholinergic hallucinogens (e.g., scopolamine, atropine). An additional hallucinogen, which has been sold as everything from cocaine to LSD, is phencyclidine (PCP), which was originally marketed as an animal anesthetic. For a complete review of hallucinogenic agents, see Blum (1984).

In reviewing the personality characteristics of the users of hallucinogenic drugs, several trends have been noted. LSD users tend to be more introverted and artistic (McGothlin, Cohen, & McGothlin, 1966). Comparisons of personality test findings suggest that persons using hallucinogens are more socially distant, interpersonally suspicious, dominant, anxious, creative, and accident-prone (Kleckner, 1968). These trends have been replicated in additional studies (Pittel et al., 1970, cited in Leavitt, 1982), suggesting a contributory role for childhood chaos and above average stress in substance abuse.

The following are examples of characteristic hallucinogenic actions (Blum, 1984).

1. *Adrenergic Types.* Examples of this class are peyote, mescaline analogs (e.g., DOM/STP 2,5-dimethoxy-4-methylamphetamine), epinephrine, and amphetamines. Characteristically, these drugs increase pulse rate, raise blood pressure, and act as a stimulant. Peyote tends to produce colored visual hallucinations as well as hallucinatory experiences. Sensations of depersonalization, ego distortion, and loss of time perception also have been described. The period of intoxication lasts from 4 to 16 hours, with aftereffects (e.g., delusions) occurring, in some cases for several months after intoxication.

2. *Indole Types.* LSD-25 is the major example of drugs of this class; however, mushrooms containing psilocybin and the substance DMT (N-dimethyltryptamine) also are included. The major effects of LSD are related to its action on the central nervous system. Responses may be grouped into autonomic symptoms and perceptual symptoms. Autonomic effects include pupillary dilation, rise in blood pressure, and increase in pulse. Perceptual changes include distortions in which objects appear to lose their boundaries, colors are amplified, and new hues are formed. Sensory experiences also seem to merge (synesthesia: e.g., sounds may be perceived as having associated hues). Emotional responsiveness to such experiences and the range of sensory experience appear to be enhanced. LSD intoxication can become frightening since many of the distortions appear related to intrapersonal issues and situational ambience. The degree of perceptual discontinuity itself can produce panic, which in turn is amplified. The immediate effects of intoxication may last up to 48 hours, with usual periods being between 6 and 18 hours.

Of particular concern is the fact that an LSD experience may recur spontaneously (flashback) even 2 years after the last ingestion. Competing theories for the cause of such flashbacks include intense psychologic reliving and fatty storage of LSD, which creates a flashback on subsequent release of residual LSD. Attempting to calm and reassure an individual who is LSD intoxicated and experiencing a panic reaction is reported to be the most effective intervention. The focus of the technique is to reassure the individual that what is being experienced is a distortion that will stop and that he or she is not alone.

3. *Anticholinergic Types.* Examples include plants from which either atropine, or atropine-type alkaloids, or scopolamine may be derived (e.g., belladonna, henbane, mandrake, and datura species). Of particular concern is that the dosage necessary to produce intoxication with these substances is close to dosage that produces toxicity and sometimes poisoning. Along with expected anticholinergic

effects, these drugs also may produce a toxic psychosis, lethargy, loss of attention, memory inefficiency for recent events, and delirium. Occasionally these drugs are added to other hallucinogens to increase their effect.

4. *Phencyclidine (PCP)*. This substance has become increasingly available and abused owing to the ease of its creation. Besides PCP itself, there are many variations of the PCP formula that also produce hallucinogenic drugs. Effects generated by PCP appear to be related to dose and the chronicity of use. Initially, small doses produce a state similar to alcohol inebriation; larger doses produce analgesia (pain insensitivity) and disorientation; extremely large doses may produce unconsciousness and convulsions. Chronic usage of PCP has been followed by recurrent psychotic episodes, depression, and confusional syndromes. Chronic users, even during periods when the drug is not ingested, are reported to experience memory inefficiency, visual disturbance, disorientation, and communication difficulties. Of particular concern are outbursts of violence and general belligerent, assaultive, and antisocial behavior demonstrated by some intoxicated users. Unlike the visionary experience produced by other hallucinogenic drugs, PCP users experience body image distortions, frank thought disorganization, interpersonal negativism, and aggressiveness. Treatment during the intoxicated episode is symptomatic with a focus on hyperactivity and safety maintenance. Many abusers do not recall much of the intoxicated period, therefore PCP offers nothing in the way of existential experience. For the most part the cost of the inebriation far outweighs its benefit.

**REFERENCES**

Blum, K. (1984). *The handbook of abusable drugs.* New York: Gardner.

Kleckner, J. (1968). Personality differences between psychedelic drug users and non-users. *Psychology, 5,* 66–71.

Leavitt, F. (1982). *Drugs and behavior.* New York: Wiley.

McGothlin, W., Cohen, S., & McGothlin, M. (1966). Personality and attitude changes in volunteer subjects following repeated administration of LSD. *Excerpta Medica International Continuing Reports, 129,* 425–434.

ROBERT F. SAWICKI
*Lake Erie Institute of
Rehabilitation*

DRUG ABUSE
SUBSTANCE ABUSE

# HALSTEAD-REITAN NEUROPSYCHOLOGICAL BATTERY

The Halstead-Reitan Neuropsychological Battery was developed as a comprehensive neuropsychological test battery and is made up of three separate test batteries: the Halstead Neuropsychological Test Battery for Adults (ages 15 and older), the Halstead Neuropsychological Test Battery for Children (ages 9 through 14), and the Reitan-Indiana Neuropsychological Test Battery for Children. All three tests use the same approach to assess the brain-behavior relationship. The core part of the adult battery is composed of:

- *Category Test (CT):* Subject is visually presented with seven sets of slides and must press one of four levers in response to each slide. Subject had previously been informed that there was some single principle which underlies each set of slides. Examinees are to figure out what that principle is. This test is related to abstraction and reasoning abilities, particularly concept formation.

- *Tactual Performance Test (TPT):* The TPT employs a version of the Seguin-Goddard Form Board, a flat wooden puzzle board into which differently shaped blocks can be placed. Without using vision the subject must place the blocks in the board using the dominant, nondominant, and both hands. This test provides a variety of measures, particularly manual dexterity, spatial memory, and tactile discrimination.

- *Seashore Rhythm Test (RT):* Derived from a subtest in the Seashore Measures of Musical Talent, the Rhythm Test requires subjects to discriminate between 30 pairs of rhythmic beats as either different or the same. Classified as a measure of nonverbal auditory discrimination, the RT is particularly sensitive to the subject's ability to attend and concentrate, skills frequently impaired in individuals with brain damage.

- *Speech-sounds Perception Test (SSPT):* A set of 60 nonsense words based on the vowel sound 'ee' are played by a tape recorder. The subject must choose which sound is heard from four printed alternatives. The test is a measure of attention, verbal auditory discrimination, and auditory-visual integration.

- *Finger Tapping Test (FTT):* Also called Finger Oscillation Test (FOT): Subjects are given multiple 10-second trials on a manual tapping device using the index finger of the dominant and nondominant hand. The test is a measure of motor speed and manual dexterity.

Other recommended tests for this battery are

- *Trail Making (TM):* The Trail Making test has two forms, Trails A and Trails B. For Trails-A, subjects must connect 25 numbered circles in numeric order. The circles are distributed in a random fashion across a page. The test measures a variety of functions including motor speed, visual scanning, and visual-motor integration. For Trails-B, subjects must perform a task similar to Trails-A, but the circles contain either numbers or letters. The subjects must connect the circles in alternating order between numbers and letters, that is, 1-A-2-B, and so on. In addition to motor speed, visual scanning, and visual-motor integration, this test requires attention and cognitive flexibility.

- *Reitan-Indiana Aphasia Screening Test:* This is a diverse collection of 32 items that require the examinee to demonstrate abilities such as naming, reading, writing, spelling, arithmetic, identifying body parts, and identifying and copying shapes.

- *Reitan-Klove Sensory Perceptual Examination:* Similar to many neurological approaches to sensory-perceptual evaluation, this exam employs both unilateral and bilateral simultaneous stimulation across tactile, visual, and auditory channels; finger localization upon tactile stimulation, finger-tip number writing, and the tactile recognition of shapes.

- *Strength of Grip Test (SOGT):* The SOGT employs a standard hand dynamometer to measure the strength of both dominant and nondominant hands.

- *Lateral Dominance Examination:* Right versus left preferences are measured for tasks involving hands, arms, legs, feet, and eyes.

Many of these tests were simplified to create the Halstead Neuropsychological Test Battery for Children. Even more modifications were made to the adult tests in addition to the development of new tests to create the Reitan-Indiana Neuropsychological Test Battery for Children.

The original norms of the Halstead tests were not representative of the patients who undergo testing (Halstead, 1947). However, new norms have been established that take both gender and education into account and allow for conversion to *T*-scores. Lezak (1995, p. 493) argues that this test's administration procedures are particularly discomforting and distressing to individuals with brain injuries or among the elderly. She argues that it should only be given under special circumstances.

All three batteries have been shown to be effective in discriminating between those with brain damage and those without (84–98 percent accuracy). Reitan (1986) claimed that the test scores could be used to determine the nature and size of the lesion, although this idea is not supported by everyone.

## REFERENCES

Halstead, W. C. (1947). *Brain and intelligence.* Chicago: University of Chicago Press.

Mitchell, J. V., Jr. (Ed.). (1985). *The ninth mental measurements yearbook.* Lincoln, NE: Buros Institute of Mental Measurements.

Reitan, R. M. (1986). Theoretical and methodological bases of the Halstead-Reitan Neuropsychological Test Battery. In I. Grant & K. M. Adams (Eds.), *Neuropsychological assessment of neuropsychiatric disorders.* New York: Oxford University Press.

Reitan, R. M., & Wolfson, D. (1993). *The Halstead-Reitan Neuropsychological Test Battery: Theory and clinical interpretation.* Tucson, AZ: Neuropsychology Press.

Reitan, R. M., & Wolfson, D. (2001). The Halstead-Reitan Neuropsychological Test Battery: Research findings and clinical application. In A. S. Kaufman & N. L. Kaufman (Eds.), *Specific learning disabilities and difficulties in children and adolescents: Psychological assessment and evaluation* (pp. 309–346). New York: Cambridge University Press.

RON DUMONT
*Fairleigh Dickinson University*

JOHN O. WILLIS
*Rivier College*

## HAMMILL, DONALD (1934–    )

Donald Hammill received his BS degree in speech education in 1956, his MA in secondary education in 1961, and an EdD in psychology/special education in 1963. From 1963 to 1965, he was an assistant research professor of logopedics at Wichita State University. He served as a full professor of special education at Temple University in Philadelphia from 1965–1972.

Hammill's interests include language development, learning disabilities, remedial education, and assessment methods. He has authored numerous tests, including the *Tests of Language Development,* the *Detroit Tests of Learning Aptitude,* the *Test of Written Language,* the *Comprehensive Test of Nonverbal Intelligence,* and the *Hammill Mutability Achievement Test.*

In the 1970s Hammill demonstrated that disorder processing or ability models for learning disabilities were of questionable value to educators. This evidence was partly responsible for the 1977 guidelines for the implementation of PL 94-142, which minimized the use of ability tests. In addition, it opened the door for the increased use of behavioral or skill models for evaluation and classification.

Hammill currently is president of PRO-ED Publishing Company in Austin, Texas.

## REFERENCES

Hammill, D. D., & Larsen, S. C. (1974). The effectiveness of psycholinguistic training. *Exceptional Children, 41,* 5–15.

Hammill, D. D. (1990). On defining learning disabilities. *Journal of Learning Disabilities, 23,* 74–84.

Hammill, D. D. (1993). A brief look at the learning disabilities movement in the United States. *Journal of Learning Disabilities, 26,* 295–310.

Hammill, D. D., & Bartel, N. R. (1995). *Teaching students with learning and behavior problems* (6th ed.). Austin, TX: PRO-ED.

STAFF

## HANDEDNESS AND EXCEPTIONALITY

Handedness, though seemingly a phenomenon in its own right, is actually one component of a more general pattern of lateralization. Lateralization refers to the fact that most people tend to favor one side of their body over the other. A minority of individuals demonstrate inconsistent or weak lateralization, meaning they have a mixed pattern of hand dominance, foot dominance, eye dominance, or cerebral hemisphere dominance.

Research has documented that the left side of the brain controls the right side of the body, and vice versa, for basic sensory and motor activity, and that the left side of the brain is generally more efficient than the right side at processing language. These two facts, considered along with estimates that right-handers constitute approximately 90 percent of all humans, indicate that the most common pattern of lateralization includes both right-handedness and left hemisphere cerebral dominance for language. Left-handers, who are more apt to use both hemispheres of the brain for language than right-handers, might then be thought of as having weak or "deviant" lateralization. It is this deviant lateralization, of which handedness is but one component, rather than handedness per se, that has been linked to exceptionalities throughout the literature.

Deviant or weak lateralization may be inherited (Annett, 1964) or it may be caused by injury to the brain (Corballis & Beale, 1983). Whatever the etiology, deviation from the usual pattern of right-handedness and left hemisphere language representation can be manifested in a number of ways. On the positive side, weakly lateralized left-handers tend to be overrepresented among highly gifted and creative individuals. Leonardo da Vinci, Harpo Marx, and Charlie Chaplin are examples. On the negative side, left-handers may be particularly susceptible to a myriad of pathological conditions. Throughout the ages, left-handers have been overrepresented among schizophrenics, epileptics, and various types of criminals (Corballis & Beale).

Investigations have revealed a higher incidence of left-handedness in special education populations. Fein, Waterhouse, Lucci, Snyder, and Humes (1984) found 18 percent of a sample of school-age autistic children were left-handed. This figure is consistent with previous studies of autistic children, and is comparable to Satz's (1973) estimate of 83 percent right-handedness in retarded and epileptic populations. Those findings represent an approximate doubling of the left-handedness consistently found in normal populations. Other studies have found markedly greater frequencies of immune disease, migraine, and learning disabilities among left-handers (Geschwind & Behan, 1982).

Two other pathological conditions that have been linked to the deviant lateralization associated with left-handedness are dyslexia, a form of reading disability, and stuttering. The concept of dyslexia, first formulated about 100 years ago, has been surrounded by a great deal of controversy. Disagreement as to whether the disorder actually exists, its nature, and how it should be diagnosed and treated abound. A distinction can be drawn between developmental dyslexia, which implies a developmental or maturational anomaly, and acquired dyslexia, which implies brain damage.

Orton (1928) proposed a unique theory for developmental dyslexia based on his own clinical experience with children suffering from reading and writing problems. Orton believed that reversals of letters and words occurred because the brains of dyslexic children lack cerebral dominance. He argued that the dominant hemisphere recorded events in the correct orientation (e.g., CAT), while the nondominant hemisphere recorded them in the reverse orientation (e.g., TAC). If a child failed to learn to suppress the activity of the nondominant hemisphere, the reversed word would intrude, creating left-right confusion. While Orton's theory generated much research, it soon became apparent that there was no evidence that mirror images of stimuli are projected to the nondominant hemisphere. As such, Orton's theory gradually lost favor.

Within the last 35 years, much progress has been made in understanding the neuropsychological processes involved in developmental dyslexia. Research has shown that dyslexics as a group are deficient in a wide variety of skills necessary for the development of adequate reading ability. Dyslexic children comprise a heterogeneous population that can be subdivided into groups, each with a distinct neurological deficit or cluster of deficits, which are related to dysfunction of left, right, or both cerebral hemispheres; and they may also be related to handedness. One subgroup of developmental dyslexia involves difficulty in integrating written symbols with their sounds, with resulting disability in developing phonic word analysis or decoding, skills often associated with a disordered function of the left cerebral hemisphere. Another subgroup manifests weaknesses in visual perception and memory for letters and whole-word configurations, resulting in problems with developing a sight vocabulary. The difficulties of this latter group have been associated with the impaired visuospatial functioning of the right side of the brain. A third subgroup demonstrates the difficulties of both of the other subgroups, suggesting dysfunction in both hemispheres (Hynd & Cohen, 1983).

It was also Orton (1937) who originated the dominance theory of stuttering. Stuttering was thought to be caused by a disruption of fine control of articulation resulting from lack of cerebral dominance. The more skilled and meticulous investigators became, however, the more frequently they failed to discover any neurological differences between stutterers and nonstutterers.

Some investigators, however, suggest a return to the dominance theory, as convincing evidence continues to surface suggesting stutterers often exhibit deviant lateralization association with left-handedness. For example, Jones (1966) reported that four left-handers with a family history of left-handedness and bilateral speech representation experienced cessation of stuttering following surgical ablation of a portion of one hemisphere. Other neurosurgical reports have described epileptic stutterers as regaining fluent speech following surgery to either the right or left hemisphere to relieve epilepsy. Studies of stutterers and nonstutterers on dichotic listening tasks have reported a significantly greater number of stutterers than nonstutterers show a left ear advantage, implying right hemisphere language involvement (Corballis & Beale, 1983).

Despite the fact that it is still widely believed that stuttering is related to left-handedness, and in particular that it is caused by forcing a natural left-hander to write with the right hand, there is no evidence to show that changed handedness has any influence on cerebral representation of speech control. Moreover, it is difficult to separate left- or changed-handedness from the more general condition of weak or deviant lateralization (Dean & Reynolds, 1997).

Both dyslexia and stuttering occur more frequently among males than females. Since both of these conditions have been linked to weak or deviant lateralization, it seems contradictory that evidence suggests that generally females have weaker lateralization than males, both with respect to left hemispheric representation of language and right hemispheric representation of spatial functions (Corballis & Beale, 1983). This contradiction may be attributed to several different factors. First, males tend to be more susceptible to pathological influences at birth resulting in injury-induced deviant lateralization (Annett, 1964). Second, weaker female lateralization is specific to adults, as boys tend to lag behind girls in the development of lateralization (Bakker, Teunissen, & Bosch, 1976). The development of lateralization may be complete earlier in girls than in boys since girls generally reach puberty before boys. Dyslexia and stuttering typically develop well before puberty, when lateralization may be more highly developed in girls than in boys. Third, a factor more closely associated with males than females may actually trigger these two conditions. Geschwind and Behan (1982) believe that the male hormone, testosterone, slows development of the brain's left side, allowing the right hemisphere to assume some typically left-brain functions. The end result can be left-handedness or simply weaker or deviant cerebral lateralization.

Overall, there is convincing evidence that weak or deviant lateralization, of which handedness is one important component, is linked to various exceptionalities. While deviant lateralization should not be taken as a sufficient cause of learning disabilities, dyslexia, stuttering, or any of the other pathological conditions herein mentioned, it cannot be overlooked that those who manifest weak cerebral dominance are more apt to develop one of these afflictions than those who manifest strong lateralization. Deviant lateralization is most likely a comorbid symptom, however, and not the fundamental cause of these problems (Dean & Reynolds, 1997).

Some interesting resources about handedness can be found online at the Handedness Research Institute at http://www.handedness.org.

## REFERENCES

Annett, M. (1964). A model of the inheritance of handedness and cerebral dominance. *Nature, 204,* 59–60.

Bakker, D. J., Teunissen, J., & Bosch, J. (1976). Development of laterality-reading patterns. In R. M. Knights & D. J. Bakker (Eds.), *The neuropsychology of learning disorders* (pp. 207–220). Baltimore: University Park Press.

Corballis, M. C., & Beale, I. L. (1983). *The ambivalent mind.* Chicago: Nelson-Hall.

Dean, R. S., & Reynolds, C. R. (1997). Cognitive processing and self-report of lateral preference. *Neuropsychology Review, 7,* 127–142.

Fein, D., Waterhouse, D., Lucci, D., Snyder, D., & Humes, M. (1984, February). *Cognitive functions in left and right-handed autistic children.* Presentation at the annual meeting of the International Neuropsychological Society, Houston, TX.

Geschwind, N., & Behan, P. (1982). Left-handedness: Association with immune disease, migraine, and developmental learning disorder. *Proceedings of the National Academy of Science, U.S.A., 79,* 5097–5100.

Hynd, G. W., & Cohen, M. (1983). *Dyslexia: Neuropsychological theory, research, and clinical differentiation.* New York: Grune & Stratton.

Jones, R. K. (1966). Observations on stammering after localized cerebral injury. *Journal of Neurology, Neurosurgery, & Psychiatry, 29,* 192–195.

Orton, S. T. (1928). Specific reading disability-strephosymbolia. *Journal of the American Medical Association, 90,* 105–109.

Orton, S. T. (1937). *Reading, writing, and speech problems in children.* New York: Norton.

Satz, P. (1973). Left-handedness and early brain insult: An explanation. *Neuropsychologia, 11,* 115–117.

GALE A. HARR
*Maple Heights City Schools,
Maple Heights, Ohio*

**DYSLEXIA**
**LEFT BRAIN/RIGHT BRAIN**
**STUTTERING**

# HANDICAPISM

Handicapism is a term created by Biklen and Bogdan (1976) to identify both an evolving social movement and a set of behaviors toward those with disabilities. It has been defined by its authors as "a theory and set of practices that promote unequal and unjust treatment of people because of apparent or assumed physical or mental disability" (p. 9). Handicapism is evident in our personal lives, social policy, cultural norms, and institutional practices (Biklen & Bogdan). Like racism and sexism, handicapism is evident in the language often used to describe disabled individuals. Such language tends to be discriminatory and serves to devalue the capabilities of the person (Heward & Orlansky, 1984; Mullins, 1979).

Common words and phrases that devalue rather than enhance a disabled person's characteristics include, "had a fit," "a basket case," and "ree tard." Handicapist phrases such as "he's a moron," handicapist humor such as "what did the twit say," and handicapist behavior, for instance, avoiding contact with a disabled person, are examples of handicapism in our personal lives. People with physical disabilities are often confronted with inaccessible entrances to buildings, bathrooms that do not accommodate wheelchairs, and public transportation systems that are difficult to use. Handicapism is also evident in the limited employment opportunities that prevail for the disabled, in media reporting that often transforms the severely disabled into objects rather than people, and in the attitudes of helping professions that often overlook the disabled person's need for privacy and human dignity.

Handicapism can be corrected. Major steps in eliminating it are (1) learning to identify and correct handicapist statements (Biklen & Bogdan, 1976); (2) providing persons with disabilities opportunities to participate in activities that make them part of the mainstream of society (Mullins, 1979); (3) demanding equal access to all facilities for all people (Biklen & Bogdan); and (4) recognizing that persons with disabilities deserve the same rights and services as those who are nondisabled. The term is rapidly becoming archaic and has appeared in texts and journals with decreasing frequency since the mid-1980s.

## REFERENCES

Biklen, D., & Bogdan, R. (1976, October). Handicapism in America. *WIN*, 9–13.

Heward, W., & Orlansky, M. D. (1984). *Exceptional children* (2nd ed., p. 7). Columbus, OH: Merrill.

Mullins, J. B. (1979). Making language work to eliminate handicapism. *Education Unlimited*, June, 20–24.

MARSHA H. LUPI
*Hunter College, City University
of New York*

CIVIL RIGHTS OF INDIVIDUALS WITH DISABILITIES
INDIVIDUALS WITH DISABILITIES EDUCATION
IMPROVEMENT ACT OF 2004 (IDEIA)

# HANDICAPPED, DEFINITION OF

See CHILD WITH A DISABILITY, DEFINITION OF.

# HANDICAPPED CHILDREN, SOCIAL MAINSTREAMING OF

Mainstreaming was a special education procedure designed to ensure that special students were serviced in the least restrictive environment in accordance with IDEA. Traditionally, a student who demonstrated academic proficiency in the special education class may qualify for regular classroom placement. Throughout this transition, academic performance was closely monitored but the affective domain may be ignored. Commonly, disregard for the affective development of the special education student socially segregated the student entering the regular classroom (Cartwright, Cartwright, & Ward, 1995; Gresham, 1982; Ray, 1985; Sabortine, 1985).

Efforts to study empirically the social skill level of special education students have been fraught with methodological difficulties. The three most common methods for evaluating social ability have been teacher ratings, sociometric ratings, and direct observation (Gresham, 1982). These measures rest on the perceptions of peers and may not mirror actual social interactions among students (Gresham, 1982; Ray, 1985). Other measurement concerns include situation-specificity (e.g., playground to reading group), poor standardization, and vulnerability to events that precede the observation (Gresham, 1982).

In any case, a plethora of social skills training strategies have emerged to train social skills to exceptional students. Traditionally, social skills training has involved instrumental and classical learning techniques as well as modeling (Gresham, 1982). The concern over social mainstreaming also contributed to interest in cooperative learning strategies (Cartwright et al., 1995; Johnson & Johnson, 1986) and reverse mainstreaming (nondisabled students in special education classrooms, espoused by Jenkins, Speltz, and Odom [1985]). Inclusion practices that presume total immersion in general education made 'social mainstreaming' obsolete.

## REFERENCES

Bruininks, V. L. (1978). Actual and perceived peer status of learning disabled students in mainstreamed programs. *Remedial & Special Education, 12*, 51–58.

Cartwright, P., Cartwright, C., & Ward, M. (1995). *Educating special learners*. New York: Wadsworth.

Gresham, G. M. (1982). Misguided mainstreaming: The case for social skills training with handicapped children. *Exceptional Children, 48*(5), 422–431.

Jenkins, J. R., Speltz, M. L., & Odom, S. L. (1985). Integrating normal and handicapped preschoolers: Effects on child development and social interaction. *Exceptional Children, 52,* 7–17.

Johnson, D. W., & Johnson, R. T. (1986). Mainstreaming and cooperative learning strategies. *Exceptional Children, 52,* 553–561.

Ray, B. M. (1985). Measuring the social position of the mainstreamed handicapped child. *Exceptional Children, 52,* 57–62.

Sabortine, S. J. (1985). Social mainstreaming of handicapped students: Facing an unpleasant reality. *Remedial & Special Education, 6*(2), 12–16.

HARRISON C. STANTON
*Texas A&M University*

INCLUSION
INDIVIDUALS WITH DISABILITIES EDUCATION
  IMPROVEMENT ACT OF 2004 (IDEIA)
SOCIAL SKILLS INSTRUCTION

# HANDICAPPED CHILDREN'S EARLY EDUCATION ASSISTANCE ACT (PUBLIC LAW 90-538)

The Handicapped Children's Early Education Program (HCEEP) began in 1968 with the passage of the Handicapped Children's Early Education Assistance Act (PL 90-538). The major goals of the program were to design experimental approaches to meet the special needs of young children with disabilities; to develop programs to facilitate the intellectual, mental, social, physical, and language development of children; to acquaint the community with the problems and potential of young children with disabilities; to coordinate with the local school system in the community being served; and to encourage parental participation in the development of programs. The program originally was composed of one of its five current components—demonstration projects.

## Demonstration Projects

To accomplish HCEEP's goals, the Act authorized grants and contracts to public and private agencies and organizations for the establishment of experimental preschool and early education demonstration projects. The chosen projects showed promise of developing comprehensive and innovative approaches for meeting the special needs of children with disabilities from birth to 8 years of age. These projects were expected to serve as models providing highly visible examples of successful practices, and encouraging others to initiate and/or improve services to young children with disabilities. In this respect, HCEEP was viewed not as a direct service mechanism, but as an indirect mechanism for expanding and improving the quality of services.

Geographical dispersion of demonstration projects was extremely important for a program that relied on increasing services by example. Therefore, major efforts were made to establish demonstration projects in as many states as possible. An evaluation of the demonstrations, conducted when the first cohort had reached its third year of funding, indicated that the demonstrations were only beginning to pay off. To avoid losing the ground gained, and to assist the demonstrations in communicating the results of their efforts, it was decided to make outreach funds available. An additional component was added to HCEEP—the Outreach Component.

## Outreach Projects

The Outreach Component, developed in 1972, had two goals: to stimulate and increase high quality services to preschool children with disabilities, birth through 8 years, and to stimulate replication of innovative models developed in the demonstration projects. Successful demonstration projects were expected to apply for outreach funds at the end of 3 years. To be even eligible for consideration, a demonstration project had to obtain funds from other sources to continue providing direct services to children and their families. Recently, projects not funded previously as early childhood demonstration projects have been allowed to compete for outreach funds.

## State Plan Grants

The third component of HCEEP had its roots prior to 1976. Aware of the need for state planning to consider the needs of young children with disabilities, HCEEP had made technical assistance available to states that desired to improve or expand services to the early childhood age range. The expectation was that federal funds would be available in the immediate future to help implement these states' plans. When such funds did become available in 1976 through the State Implementation Grant (SIG) initiative, states applying were awarded grants on a competitive basis. The goal of SIG was to assist state education agencies in building a capacity to plan for the initiation and expansion of early intervention services. To some degree, this planning process was expected to be enhanced simply by creating financial resources for an early childhood planning position within each state.

Public law 98-199 carried this initiative further with the creation of the current State Plan Grant Component. The state plan grant is intended to enable each state and territory to plan, develop, or implement a comprehensive service delivery system for special education and related services to children with disabilities from birth to 5 years of age. States may apply for a grant to support planning, to support development, or to support implementation activities depending on their assessment of appropriateness and readiness. At least 30 percent of the HCEEP appropriation must be used for this component in recognition of the need for state commitments to serving these children.

## Research Institutes

In 1977, the fourth component of HCEEP was initiated. In cooperation with the Research Projects Branch of the Office of Special Education Programs, HCEEP funded four research institutes to carry out longitudinal research. Topics of research included social, emotional, physical, cognitive, and behavioral aspects of the child; theories and methods of intervention; parent-child interaction; and assessment techniques.

The institutes were seen as investments in the future, paying off not only in terms of the immediate research results, but in terms of the training of future special education researchers and service providers. A second generation of institutes was funded in 1982 to investigate problems concerning services for autistic-like children, cost and efficacy data for early childhood interventions, and programming for parental involvement. In addition, another institute was funded in 1985 to focus on evaluating the impact of various methods of early intervention for children with disabilities as a whole and in various subgroups.

## Technical Assistance

In 1971, the Technical Assistance Development System (TADS) was funded to assist demonstration projects. From 1977 to 1982, two technical assistance systems, TADS and WESTAR, were operating in order to provide geographical coverage for the large number of demonstration projects and SIGs. When the number of demonstrations decreased in 1982, the need for technical assistance also was reduced and TADS again became the sole designated external provider of technical assistance to demonstration projects. A new technical assistance effort, the State Technical Assistance Resource Team (START), was funded in 1985 to provide assistance to the state plan grant projects.

JAMES BUTTON
*United States Department of*
*Education*
Second edition

KIMBERLY F. APPLEQUIST
*University of Colorado at*
*Colorado Springs*
Third edition

# HANDICAPPING CONDITIONS, HIGH INCIDENCE

See HIGH-INCIDENCE DISABILITIES.

# HAND TEST

The Hand Test (Wagner, 1983) is a brief, performance-based measure of psychopathology and personality used with children and adults. It is a projective measure that is easy to administer; training in the use of projective measures such as the Hand Test is needed in order to understand and interpret the results obtained. The test consists of nine line drawings of hands in ambiguous positions; the child or adult is asked to tell the examiner what the hand might be doing. There is also a blank card; the same direction is given for the blank card. There are 15 quantitative scores and seven summary scores that are generated from the responses of the child or adult for the 10 cards. Adequate reliability and empirical support have been found for the Interpersonal, Environmental, Maladjustive, Withdrawal, Acting Out Score (AOS), and Pathological summary scores as well as the Aggression variable (e.g., Clemence, Hilsenroth, Sivic, & Rasch, 1999; Smith, Blais, Vangala, & Masek, 2005). Of these, the Pathology, AOS, and Aggression scores have proved most useful in discriminating between clinical and typical groups of children. Additional evidence of psychometric properties of the Hand Test has been summarized (e.g., Carter & Moran, 1991; Clemence, Hilsenroth, Sivic, Rasch, & Waehler, 1998; Clemence et al., 1999).

Smith et al. (2005) examined the usefulness of the Hand Test with children who have medical issues as compared to children with psychiatric disorders. They found that the children with psychiatric problems consistently obtained higher scores on the Aggression, Withdrawal, and Pathological scales than the children with medical problems. This supports the use of these scales in the identification of childhood psychopathology and emotional disturbance. Further, they found that the Hand Test added to what was gained from parent and self-report and facilitated (i.e., added to the incremental validity) differentiation of the two groups.

## REFERENCES

Carter, D. E., & Moran, J. J. (1991). Interscorer reliability for the Hand Test administered to children. *Perceptual and Motor Skills, 72*, 759–765.

Clemence, A. J., Hilsenroth, M. J., Sivic, H. J., & Rasch, M. (1999). Hand Test AGG and AOS variables: Relation with teacher rating of aggressiveness. *Journal of Personality Assessment, 73*, 334–344.

Clemence, A. J., Hilsenroth, M. J., Sivic, H. J., Rasch, M., & Waehler, C. A. (1998). Use of the Hand Test in the classification of psychiatric inpatient adolescents. *Journal of Personality Assessment, 71,* 228–241.

Smith, S. R., Blais, M. A., Vangala, M., & Masek, B. J. (2005). Exploring the Hand Test with medically ill children and adolescents. *Journal of Personality Assessment, 85,* 82–91.

Wagner, E. E. (1983). *The Hand Test manual* (Rev. ed.). Los Angeles: Western Psychological Services.

CYNTHIA A. RICCIO
*Texas A&M University*

PERSONALITY ASSESSMENT
THEMATIC APPERCEPTION TEST

# HANDWRITING

See DYSGRAPHIA.

# HAPPY PUPPET SYNDROME

See ANGELMAN SYNDROME.

# HARD OF HEARING

See DEAF.

# HARING, NORRIS G. (1923–    )

Norris G. Haring obtained a BA from Kearney State Teachers College (Nebraska) in 1948. He went on to the University of Nebraska, receiving an MA in 1950 and an EdD from Syracuse University in 1956. He is presently professor of education (special education) and director of the Washington Research Organization in the College of Education at the University of Washington.

Haring's major field of interest lies in dealing with exceptional children in the classroom environment. Haring's philosophy about exceptional children is that they should have the benefit of experiences with their nonexceptional peers whenever possible because they will eventually be required to achieve a satisfactory adjustment within a predominantly normal society (Haring, Stern, & Cruickshank, 1958).

Haring's major research has dealt with the behavior management of children with learning disabilities and behavioral disorders in the classroom. His textbook on this subject, *Educating Emotionally Disturbed Children* (Haring & Phillips, 1962), is now considered a classic.

Subsequent research concentrated on the development and refinement of the learning environment and the ecology that promotes adaptive social behavior. This research resulted from work with the emotionally disturbed and behaviorally disordered and investigations of classroom performance measurement and data-based decisions in terms of instructional procedures, methodology, and curriculum. The application of behavioral principles in special education guided his research for nearly 10 years. His book *Exceptional Teaching* (White & Haring, 1980) concentrates on the application of precision teaching strategies in regular and self-contained classrooms. Haring is known for the research and development of behaviorally validated stages of learning in a learning hierarchy.

Haring was the director of the Experimental Education Unit at the University of Washington for 12 years. During that period he became interested in the application of modern behavior technology to the education of the severely handicapped. Haring worked with national leaders in the field to develop the Association for Persons with Severe Handicaps (TASH), and served as founding president of that organization. He directed the Washington Research Organization in a series of studies designed to investigate ways to promote generalization with severely handicapped students and the application of research information to facilitate their transition to vocational success and adult life. Haring remains professionally active and continues to be associated with the University of Washington.

**REFERENCES**

Haring, K. A., Lovett, D. L., & Haring, N. G. (1992). *Integrated lifecycle services for persons with disabilities: A theoretical and empirical perspective.* New York: Springer-Verlag.

Haring, N. G. (1987). *Assessing and managing behavior disabilities.* Seattle: University of Washington Press.

Haring, N. G. (1994). *Exceptional children and youth: An introduction to special education.* Paramus: Prentice Hall.

Haring, N. G., & Liberty, K. A. (1990). Matching strategies with performance in facilitating generalization. *Focus on Exceptional Children, 22,* 1–16.

Haring, N. G., & Phillips, E. L. (1962). *Educating emotionally disturbed children.* New York: McGraw-Hill.

Haring, N. G., & Romer, L. T. (1995). *Welcoming students who are deaf-blind into typical classrooms: Facilitating school participation, learning, and friendships.* Baltimore: Brookes.

Haring, N. G., Stern, G., & Cruickshank, W. M. (1958). *Attitudes of educators toward exceptional children.* Syracuse, NY: Syracuse University Press.

Haring, N. G., & Whelan, R. J. (1965). Experimental methods in education and management of emotionally disturbed children. In N. J. Long, W. C. Morse, & R. G. Newman (Eds.), *Conflict in the classroom: The education of emotionally disturbed children.* Belmont, CA: Wadsworth.

Romer, L. T., & Haring, N. G. (1994). The social participation of students with deaf-blindness in educational settings. *Education & Training in Mental Retardation, 29,* 134–144.

Romer, L. T., White, J., & Haring, N. G. (1996). The effect of peer mediated social competency training on the type and frequency of social contacts with students with deaf-blindness. *Education & Training in Mental Retardation, 31,* 324–338.

White, O. R., & Haring, N. G. (1980). *Exceptional teaching* (2nd ed.). Columbus, OH: Merrill.

ELIZABETH JONES
*Texas A&M University*
First edition

MARIE ALMOND
*The University of Texas of the
Permian Basin*
Second edition

## HARVARD EDUCATIONAL REVIEW

The *Harvard Educational Review* was first published in 1931 under the name of *Harvard Teachers Record* by the offices of the Harvard Graduate Schools of Education. The present name was taken in 1937. This journal consists of opinions and research related to the field of education. Articles are read blind, then selected, edited, and published by an editorial board of graduate students from various Harvard schools. The selection process of the editorial board involves the distribution of letters to the faculty requesting nominations from the student body and the posting of information on bulletin boards at Harvard schools asking the students to apply for consideration. Students are then selected according to their ability and by their diversity of interests. The board of 20 students is balanced among men and women and minorities, each of whom receives a small stipend. There is one chairperson who receives a slightly larger stipend. This position changes yearly.

Sixty-seven volumes have now been published and there are an estimated 10,000 in circulation annually. Each journal, published quarterly, contains on the average three manuscripts equaling 500 to 550 pages a year.

TERESA K. RICE
*Texas A&M University*

## HAÜY, VALENTIN (1745–1822)

Valentin Haüy, a French pioneer in the education of the blind, developed a system of raised letters with which he taught blind students to read and write, providing one of the earliest demonstrations that it is possible for a blind person to be educated. It was one of Haüy's students, Louis Braille, who later developed the system in use today, replacing Haüy's raised letters with a system of dots.

In 1784, with support from a philanthropic society, Haüy established in Paris the first school for the blind that admitted both blind and sighted children and educated them together. The great success of Haüy's school led to the rapid development of similar schools throughout Europe.

### REFERENCE

Ross, I. (1951). *Journey into light.* New York: Appleton-Century-Crofts.

PAUL IRVINE
*Katonah, New York*

## HAVIGHURST, ROBERT J. (1900–1991)

Robert J. Havighurst was born in De Pere, Wisconsin; graduated from Ohio Wesleyan University; and received his doctorate from The Ohio State University in 1924. Although trained as a chemist and physicist, he ultimately became interested in the broader aspects of general education. He was a professor of education and psychology at the University of Chicago for over forty years: he retired in 1983 but continued to teach and conduct research until 1990. Before joining the University of Chicago faculty in 1941, he had taught at Miami University, the University of Wisconsin, and The Ohio State University. Robert Havighurst died in 1991 at the age of 90.

In 1943, Havighurst introduced his theory of developmental tasks, which he continued to develop throughout his career (Havighurst, 1979). Described as skills, knowledge, functions, or attitudes normally acquired by an individual during a specific period of life, he believed in the existence of "teachable moments," meaning those periods when a person is most able and receptive to learning new skills. According to the theory, if a task is not learned at the appropriate time, it is much more difficult to learn later.

Havighurst found that adolescents prefer the approval of the larger community to that of the peer group (Havighurst, 1970). If the larger society does not reward the adolescent meaningfully, the child will usually fail to become socialized. Havighurst believed that the larger society, especially the school system, must learn to provide important reinforcement to adolescents, especially minority or disadvantaged youths.

Havighurst was an early advocate of integrated public schools, believing they were crucial in creating opportunities for poor children. He proposed that children's performance in school depends not upon the socioeconomic status of the child or the child's family, but rather upon the socioeconomic status and character of the school itself. He also focused on the sociological aspects of old age and retirement, identifying and discussing the need for retirees to develop new roles as they aged and new ways of obtaining satisfaction once those previously achieved through work were no longer available.

Havighurst was a student of social and economic conditions in Germany and was Director of the Rockefeller Foundation's European Rehabilitation Program. In the late 1950s, he was codirector of the Brazilian government's effort to prepare a national system of elementary and secondary schools.

## REFERENCES

Havighurst, R. J. (1970). Minority subcultures and the law of effect. *American Psychologist, 25,* 313–322.

Havighurst, R. J. (1979). *Developmental tasks and education* (4th ed.). New York: Longman.

E. Valerie Hewitt
*Texas A&M University*
First edition

Tamara J. Martin
*The University of Texas of the
    Permian Basin*
Second edition

## HAWTHORNE EFFECT

The origins of the Hawthorne Effect can be traced to a collection of studies (Roethlisberger & Dickson, 1939) conducted between 1927 and 1932 at the Hawthorne plant of the Western Electric Company. Researchers designed these studies to determine the factors that may lead to more efficient production in the workplace. Variables such as lighting, social interaction, length of the workday, and break time were systematically manipulated. Regardless of how the working conditions were manipulated, researchers noted that productivity steadily increased, suggesting that the special and personal attention given to the workers accounted for improved productivity (Mahoney & Baker, 2002). This unexpected beneficial result has since been labeled the Hawthorne Effect.

The result of these studies substantially affected research practices. Researchers questioned whether positive changes in behavior during controlled studies were the result of the independent variable or the participants' knowledge that they were in an experiment. This concern is especially salient in laboratory experiments in which participants, in novel and artificial settings, are fully aware of their participation. As a result, the use of naturalistic field research methods increased as an alternative to the laboratory research (Adair, 1984). However, unless the participants and experimental observers are unaware of the experimentation, the Hawthorne Effect also may be noticed in naturalistic settings (Mason & Bramble, 1997).

Several critics have challenged the implications of the Hawthorne studies. For example, Mason and Bramble (1997) noted that if novel treatments result in beneficial outcomes, one would expect new, innovative interventions in education to show greater effects than has been the case thus far. Further, the results of a meta-analysis of 86 studies in educational research employing controls for the Hawthorne Effect failed to support the existence of an overall Hawthorne Effect (Adair, Sharpe, & Huynh, 1989). Considerable disagreement exists as to the description and definition of the Hawthorne Effect (Adair, 1984).

Despite these concerns and the absence of clear evidence supporting the existence of the Hawthorne Effect, it continues to influence research methodologies. Researchers continue to employ techniques to control for the Hawthorne Effect by having a control group receive the same level of attention in a similar unfamiliar setting, yet without receiving the intervention.

## REFERENCES

Adair, J. G. (1984). The Hawthorne Effect: A reconsideration of the methodological artifact. *Journal of Applied Psychology, 69*(2), 334–345.

Adair, J. G., Sharpe, D., & Huynh, C.-L. (1989). Hawthorne control procedures in educational experiments: A reconsideration of their use and effectiveness. *Review of Educational Research, 59*(2), 215–228.

Mahoney, K. T., & Baker, D. B. (2002). Elton Mayo and Carl Rogers: A tale of two techniques. *Journal of Vocational Behavior, 60,* 437–450.

Mason, E. J., & Bramble, W. J. (1997). *Research in education and the behavioral sciences: Concepts and methods.* Chicago: Brown & Benchmark.

Raywid, M. A. (1979). In praise of the Hawthorne Effect: Perspectives from the profs. *Journal of Teacher Education, 30*(3), 64.

Roethlisberger, F., & Dickson, W. (1939). *Management and the worker.* Cambridge, MA: Harvard.

Eric Rossen
*University of Florida*

## RESEARCH IN SPECIAL EDUCATION

## HAYDEN, ALICE HAZEL (1909–1994)

Alice Hazel Hayden received her MS degree in chemistry from Oregon State University at the age of 19, and later received her PhD from Purdue University. She began teaching at the University of Washington in 1946, and was eventually awarded Professor Emeritus in education from that institution. She stayed at the University of Washington for 33 years, retiring in 1979. Alice Hayden died in 1994, at the age of 85.

Hayden was well known for her research on mental retardation in children, particularly the education of children with Down syndrome. In contrast to the prevailing views of the day, she emphasized the importance of recognizing the disability as early as possible, and strongly advocated that intervention begin in infancy for those identified with Down syndrome. In 1960, she codirected the experimental Pilot School for children with disabilities, which was the forerunner to the Experimental Education Unit at the Child Development and Mental Retardation Center at the University of Washington, where she served as associate director following her retirement.

One of her principal publications was *The Improvement of Instruction,* coedited with Norris G. Haring, a book of readings from a workshop designed to provide the classroom teacher with information about various ways of choosing instructional programs to accomplish teaching objectives and to assist teachers in arranging better classroom conditions to improve instruction. Her book *Systematic Thinking about Education,* coedited with Gerald M. Torkelson, discusses the technology of education and technology in teaching. It suggests that teachers and the school as an institution must be responsive to the world community and the advancing instruments and processes that people continue to create for a better life, in order to convey the most current techniques and advancements in education to students.

**REFERENCES**

Hayden, A. H., & Haring, N. G. (Eds.). (1972). *The improvement of instruction.* Seattle, WA: Special Child.

Hayden, A. H., & Torkelson, G. M. (Eds.). (1973). *Systematic thinking about education.* Bloomington, IN: Phi Delta Kappa Educational Foundation.

REBECCA BAILEY
*Texas A&M University*
First edition

TAMARA J. MARTIN
*The University of Texas of the
Permian Basin*
Second edition

# HAYWOOD, H. CARL (1931–    )

Carl Haywood holds AB (1956) and MA (1957) degrees from San Diego State College (now San Diego State University) and the PhD from the University of Illinois (1961) in clinical psychology, with minors in experimental psychology and education. He has served on the faculty of Peabody College of Vanderbilt University since 1962 (professor emeritus, 1994). At Peabody he was, successively, director of the mental retardation research training program, director of the Institute on Mental Retardation and Intellectual Development,

H. Carl Haywood

director of the John F. Kennedy Center for Research on Education and Human Development, director of the Office of Research Administration, Professor of Special Education, and director of the Cognitive Education Research Group. He served also as Professor of Neurology in Vanderbilt's School of Medicine until his retirement from Vanderbilt in 1994. In 1993 he established the Graduate School of Education and Psychology at Touro College in New York City, and served as its dean. This graduate school was the first to be organized entirely around cognitive development and cognitive education principles, and includes master's degree programs in education, special education, school psychology, and school administration/supervision. Haywood retired from Touro College in 2000.

Haywood's program of scholarship and research centered on intellectual and cognitive development, mental retardation, individual differences in intrinsic motivation, cognitive education, learning efficiency, psychopathology, and public policy relating to the welfare of children. As an advisor to state and federal governments, he served on the National Advisory Child Health and Human Development Council (NIH), the Governor's (Tennessee) special task forces on healthy children and on mental retardation, and as a frequent reviewer of grant applications for the National Institutes of Health and the U.S. Department of Education.

Haywood is the principal author (with P. H. Brooks and M. S. Burns) of *Bright Start: Cognitive Curriculum for Young Children,* a cognitive education program that is now used widely in the preschool education of children with special needs. He has published over 150 research reports, books, chapters, and reviews on mental retardation and cognitive development. He served as president of the American Association on Mental Deficiency (1980–81; now AAMR), as editor of the *American Journal of Mental Deficiency* (1969–79; now *AJMR*), founder and president (1988–92) of the International Association for Cognitive Education, and president (1979–80) of the American Psychological Association's division on mental retardation. Honors include the leadership and research awards of AAMD/AAMR; the distinguished service award of the International Association for Cognitive Education; the Alexander Heard Distinguished Service Professorship of Vanderbilt University; the Distinguished Alumnus Award of the College of Science, San Diego State University; and the Edgar Doll Award (for research in the field of mental retardation) of Division 33, American Psychological Association. His major works include *Brain Damage in School Age Children, Social-Cultural Aspects of Mental Retardation, Bright Start: Cognitive Curriculum for Young Children, Living Environments for Developmentally Retarded Persons, Interactive Assessment,* and *Developmental Follow-up,* as well as numerous research and integrative works on task-intrinsic motivation and its relation to learning effectiveness.

**REFERENCES**

Friedman, S., & Haywood, H. C. (Eds.). (1994). *Developmental follow-up: Concepts, domains, and methods.* San Diego: Academic.

Haywood, H. C. (Ed.). (1968). *Brain damage in school age children.* Washington, DC: Council for Exceptional Children.

Haywood, H. C. (Ed.). (1970). *Social-cultural aspects of mental retardation.* New York: Appleton-Century-Crofts.

Haywood, H. C. (1997). Interactive assessment. In R. Taylor (Ed.), *Assessment of persons with mental retardation* (pp. 103–129). San Diego: Singular Publishing Group.

Haywood, H. C., Brooks, P. H., & Burns, M. S. (1992). *Bright start: Cognitive curriculum for young children.* Watertown, MA: Charlesbridge Publishing.

Haywood, H. C., & Newbrough, J. R. (Eds.). (1981). *Living environments for developmentally retarded persons.* Baltimore: University Park Press.

Haywood, H. C., & Switzky, H. N. (1992). Ability and modifiability: What, how, and how much? In J. S. Carlson (Ed.), *Cognition and educational practice* (Vol. 1, pp. 25–85). Greenwich, CT: JAI Press.

Haywood, H. C., & Tzuriel, D. (Eds.). (1992). *Interactive assessment.* New York: Springer-Verlag.

STAFF

# HEAD INJURY

See TRAUMATIC BRAIN INJURY.

# HEAD START

Head Start began in 1965 as a federally funded 8-week summer program for over 550,000 children from low-income families. Its initiation reflected the era's optimism for the role of preschool education in fighting the effects of poverty.

It also reflected the environmentalist view of intellectual development, a belief in a critical period for human learning, the recommendations in the 1962 report of the President's Panel on Mental Retardation, and the need for a highly visible symbol of President Lyndon Johnson's war on poverty. By 1972 most programs ran the full year.

Head Start was intended to counteract negative environmental effects because of the well-known relationships between low school achievement and such factors as poverty, racial/ethnic membership, and socioeconomic status. Those factors were believed to be related to developmental and ecological variables that should be subject to modification. Early intervention was expected to eliminate the progressive decline in intellectual functioning and academic achievement that was typical of many children from poor families. Head Start emphasized local community involvement and autonomy; therefore, programs varied greatly across sites. The government encouraged parent volunteers and parent training, and published numerous training materials.

Research support for the expectation that preschool education would counteract effects of environmental disadvantages came from early reports of experimental preschool programs for poor, black children begun in 1958 by Susan Gray in Tennessee, Martin Deutsch in New York City, and David Weikart in Michigan (Lazar & Darlington, 1982). Their experimental work was theoretically anchored, carefully monitored, designed, and implemented by skilled professional educators and psychologists. However, for early Head Start programs there was not enough time for advance planning of curriculum and evaluation and limited direct supervision and monitoring of actual experiences of children. There were also too few teachers trained in early childhood education and a limited amount of in-service training for teachers and volunteers. Ironically, a program for disadvantaged children began at a disadvantage.

Head Start placed strong emphasis on medical, dental, and social services; initially, these were the most readily documented benefits. Millions of children were vaccinated, had vision and hearing tests, and received medical and dental examinations. A substantial percentage also received medical and dental treatment.

Early evaluation of sustained effects on cognitive and academic skills raised serious doubts about the program's effect on academic skills (Cicirelli, 1969). Media coverage was extremely negative. The program was modified. A Planned Variations project was devised to seek factors related to successful intervention. Training programs for Head Start personnel were greatly expanded.

Data from dozens of Head Start studies comparing group averages of Head Start graduates with averages of children without preschool programs lead to these conclusions: Head Start has positive effects on intellectual development (although in most studies average test scores are somewhat below the national average); Head Start children have fewer retentions in grade and fewer special education placements (although they still contribute disproportionately to special education and retention); some Head Start programs produce advantages in reading or arithmetic as measured by standardized tests; different curricula do not appear to produce differential effects (although such differences are found in experimental pre-school programs for high-risk children); most parents of Head Start children are highly supportive; and full-year Head Start programs are superior to short summer ones. Positive effects reported in some studies include improvement in social behavior, parent-child interactions, skills of parents, and nutrition (Haywood, 1982; Hubbell, 1983).

As evidence of program efficacy increased, criticisms from professionals decreased and public approval increased. A highly laudatory article in the national newspaper *USA Today* (Kanengiser, 1985) described Martin Deutsch's report that his group of Head Start graduates were more likely to finish high school, go to college, and hold full-time jobs than similar children who had no preschool experience. Such findings suggest that Head Start may affect motivation for education.

Edward Zigler, who was Head Start's first federal administrator, viewed Head Start's goal as the development of social competence. He commented that when one realistically examines its true effectiveness, it cannot be dismissed as a failure, but neither should so fragile an effort over one year of a child's life be viewed as the ultimate solution to poverty, illiteracy, and failures in life (Zigler, 1979). Dozens of additional studies have shown overwhelmingly that Head Start has myriad of positive effects (Cartwright, Cartwright, & Ward, 1995).

The ability of Head Start programs to serve the needs of preschoolers is currently in serious jeopardy because of attempts on the part of the Bush Administration to cut funding or eliminate programs altogether (National Head Start Association, 2006).

### REFERENCES

Cartwright, P., Cartwright, C., & Ward, M. (1995). *Educating special learners.* New York: Wadsworth.

Cicirelli, V. G. (1969). Project Head Start, a national evaluation: Summary of the study. In D. G. Hayes (Ed.), *Britannica review of American education* (Vol. 1). Chicago: Encyclopedia Britannica.

Haywood, H. C. (1982). Compensatory education. *Peabody Journal of Education, 59,* 272–300.

Hubbell, R. (1983). *A review of Head Start research since 1970.* Washington, DC: Administration for Children, Youth, and Families (Superintendent of Documents, U.S. Government Printing Office).

Kanengiser, A. (1985, October 3). Head Start really gives a head start. *USA Today,* 4D.

Lazar, I., & Darlington, R. (1982). Lasting effects of early education: A report from the consortium for longitudinal studies. *Monographs of the Society for Research in Child Development, 47* (serial nos. 2–3).

National Head Start Association (NHSA). (2006). *Special report: The Bush Administration's Fiscal Year 2007.* Retrieved February 10, 2006, from www.nsha.org

Zigler, E. (1979). Project Head Start: Success or failure? In E. Zigler & J. Valentine (Eds.), *Project Head Start: A legacy of the war on poverty.* New York: Free Press.

SUE ALLEN WARREN
JACQUELINE E. DAVIS
*Boston University*

## HEALTH IMPAIRMENTS

Public Law 94-142, IDEA, and its reauthorizations divide the classification of physical handicaps into two categories for purposes of special education: orthopedic impairments and health impairments (Bigge & Sirvis, 1986). The second category of health impairments consists of physical conditions that affect a child or youth's educational performance such as "limited strength, vitality or alertness due to chronic or acute health problems such as a heart condition, tuberculosis, rheumatic fever, nephritis, asthma, sickle cell anemia, hemophilia, epilepsy, lead poisoning, leukemia, or diabetes" (*Federal Register,* 1977, p. 42478). Such children are often diagnosed and managed medically and socially as chronically ill children. Phelps (1998) provides a review of the educational consequences of more than 95 health impairments of children, and Clay (2004) is an excellent and practical resource for special education personnel.

### REFERENCES

Bigge, J., & Sirvis, B. (1986). Physical and health impairments. In N. G. Haring & L. McCormick (Eds.), *Exceptional children and youth* (4th ed., pp. 313–354). Columbus, OH: Merrill.

Clay, D. L. (2004). *Helping school children with chronic health conditions.* New York: Guilford.

Phelps, L. (1998). *Health-related disorders in children and adolescents: A guidebook for understanding and educating.* Washington, DC: American Psychological Association.

U.S. Office of Education. (1985). *Seventh annual report to Congress on the implementation of Public Law 94-142: The Education of All Handicapped Children Act.* Washington, DC: U.S. Government Printing Office.

LESTER MANN
*Hunter College, City University
of New York*

# HEALTH MAINTENANCE PROCEDURES

Under PL 94-142 and IDEA, educators may be held responsible for monitoring specific health maintenance activities required in order for the child to attend school. Teachers may oversee students taking medication, conducting bowel and bladder maintenance procedures, and adjusting braces. In addition, monitoring of such health maintenance equipment as ventilators, cardiac monitors, reciprocal braces, and shunts may be a part of required teacher activity. Before monitoring or helping with any health maintenance activity, the teacher should have a written school district and school policy to follow, have completed first aid and cardiopulmonary resuscitation courses, have been trained by parents and a school health official, and have written, dated, and signed specific directions requesting that a procedure be carried out while the child is at school.

Whenever possible, the student should be responsible for carrying out all health maintenance activities. Medications should be taken by the student in the presence of an adult who checks the prescription bottle for name, directions for administration, and the log for last time taken. If students are incapable of carrying out the required procedure (e.g., catheterization), they should be taught the procedure as soon as possible if there is enough potential motor and intellectual skill to carry out the task.

Issues of liability should be taken into account (1) accountability for which or how much medication was taken; (2) record keeping when monitoring equipment (e.g., a log should be kept of date, time, signature, and any signs of abnormal functioning of the child or the equipment); (3) written procedures for administration of medication; and (4) written school board policy for protocols to follow in meeting routine and emergency health maintenance needs of the child (Dykes & Venn, 1983).

## REFERENCE

Dykes, M. K., & Venn, J. (1983). Using health, physical and medical data in the classroom. In J. Unbreit (Ed.), *Physical disabilities and health impairments: An introduction.* Columbus, OH: Merrill.

MARY K. DYKES
*University of Florida*

MEDICALLY FRAGILE STUDENT
MEDICAL MANAGEMENT

# HEARING IMPAIRED

See DEAF.

# HEBER, RICK F. (1932–    )

Rick Heber was born January 12, 1932. He received his BA degree from the University of Arkansas in 1953. After a year as principal of the Manitoba School for Mental Deficiency, Heber attended Michigan State University, obtaining his MA degree there in 1955. He then went on to achieve his PhD in 1957 from George Peabody College. Heber joined the faculty of the University of Wisconsin, Madison in 1959 as coordinator of the special education program.

Heber is best known for his work as principal investigator of the Milwaukee Project and the subsequent controversies surrounding the project. A major finding of the project was that the variable of maternal intelligence proved to be by far the best single predictor of the level and character of intellectual development in the offspring. Heber believed that the prevalence of mental retardation associated with the slums of American cities is not randomly distributed but is actually strikingly concentrated within individual families who can be identified on the basis of maternal intelligence (1988). Heber was a member of the faculty of the University of Wisconsin at Madison when he was indicted on charges stemming from the misuse of federal funds allocated to the project. He was subsequently convicted and served time in the federal prison in Bastrop, Texas. Previously a respected scholar in the field of mental retardation, his academic work on the Milwaukee Project has been called into serious question. It is now questionable whether the project ever actually existed as it had been described by Heber.

## REFERENCES

Heber, R. F. (1970). *Epidemiology of mental retardation.* Springfield, IL: Thomas.

Heber, R. F. (1988). Mental retardation in the slums. In G. W. Albee & J. M. Joffe (Eds.), *Prevention, powerlessness, and politics: Readings on social change.* Newbury Park, CA: Sage.

Heber, R. F., & Garber, H. (1975). The Milwaukee Project: A study of the use of family intervention to prevent cultural-familial mental retardation. In B. Z. Friedlander, G. Kirk, & G. Sterritt (Eds.), *The exceptional infant* (Vol. 3). New York: Brunner/Mazel.

CECIL R. REYNOLDS
*Texas A&M University*
First edition

MARIE ALMOND
*The University of Texas of the Permian Basin*
Second edition

MILWAUKEE PROJECT, THE

# HEELCORD OPERATION

The heelcord operation is an orthopedic surgical treatment for children with spastic cerebral palsy. It is performed to compensate for equinus, a condition in which the foot is involuntarily extended owing to contracted tendons in the heel. Palsied children with equinus often have severe gait problems (Batshaw & Perret, 1981). The operation itself involves cutting and lengthening the Achilles tendon and rotating the heel to a normal position. The operation is typically followed by 6 weeks in a cast and roughly 6 months of physical therapy.

Without surgery, treatment of this condition is often painful and unsuccessful. It involves the use of braces, splints worn at night, and regular heelcord stretching exercises. The success rate of the operation is very high. Research has shown an overall recurrence rate for patients receiving surgery of only 9 percent, although recurrence is related to age; 2 year olds, for example, have a recurrence rate of 75 percent (Lee & Bleck, 1980). Improvements in mobility improve multiple outcomes in cerebral palsy (Nagle & Campbell, 1998).

## REFERENCES

Batshaw, M. L., & Perret, Y. M. (1981). *Children with handicaps: A medical primer.* Baltimore: Brookes.

Lee, C. L., & Bleck, E. E. (1980). Surgical correction of equinus deformity in cerebral palsy. *Developmental Medicine and Child Neurology, 22,* 287–294.

Nagle, R., & Campbell, L. (1998). Cerebral palsy. In L. Phelps (Ed.), *Health-related disorders in children and adolescents.* Washington, DC: American Psychological Association.

THOMAS E. ALLEN
*Gallaudet College*

CEREBRAL PALSY

# HEGGE, KIRK, KIRK APPROACH

Hegge, Kirk, and Kirk (1936) formulated the phono-graphovocal method of remedial reading while teaching children with mild mental retardation. Emphasizing programmed learning techniques, this method incorporated sound blending and kinesthetic experiences (Kirk & Gallagher, 1983). Basic to this method was a set of remedial reading drills presented in four parts. Part I provided drills in sounding out consonants, short vowels, and vowel combinations such as *ee, ay, ow, ing, all, ight, ur,* and the final *e* marker. Drills in Part I were printed on one line from left to right, reinforcing directional patterns in reading. Early drills were simple, showing that only the initial consonant changes in words such as sat-mat-rat. More complex drills were successively introduced by changing the first and last consonant of words. After repeated drills on the consonants, the short vowels, a, e, i, o, and u, are emphasized.

In Part II words were presented using the sounds already learned in Part I. Children were taught to read hand as h-an-d instead of h-a-n-d. Through frequent review and drills (the hallmark of this method) children move from vocalizing and recognizing simple sounds to incorporating these sounds into words.

Parts III and IV were for those children who, after having been repeatedly drilled on the sound blends in Parts I and II, were beginning to read by rapidly sounding out words. Part III required children to read new words in syllables or wholes.

In Part IV of this approach children were drilled on sounds that could not be systematically presented in earlier drills. Reinforcement drills were used with children who exhibit problems in specific areas such as confusing b, d, and p or m and n (Kirk, 1940).

Kirk (1940) warned that the Hegge, Kirk, Kirk method, developed in 1936, should not be used as a general teaching method or for children in higher grade levels. Rather it was applicable to first-, second-, and third-grade students whose reading level is at least 2 years below the norm, who are trainable in sound blending, and who demonstrate the desire to learn to read. This program was of little value to those children who were accurate but slow readers because they already possessed the skills inherent in the practice drills.

## REFERENCES

Hegge, T., Kirk, S., & Kirk, W. (1936). *Remedial reading drills.* Ann Arbor, MI: Wahr.

Kirk, S. (1940). *Teaching reading to slow-learning children.* Cambridge, MA: Riverside.

Kirk, S., & Gallagher, J. (1983). *Educating exceptional children* (4th ed.). Boston: Houghton Mifflin.

FORREST KEESBURY
*Lycoming College*

ORTON-GILLINGHAM METHOD
READING DISORDERS
READING REMEDIATION

# HEINICKE, SAMUEL (1727–1790)

Samuel Heinicke, a German educator, founded the first oral school for the deaf about 1755. He established Germany's first public school for the deaf in 1778 at Leipzig. Using published accounts of the teaching of deaf children by Jacob Pereire and others, Heinicke devised a highly successful method for teaching reading, writing, speech, and speech reading to deaf students, a method that formed the basis for the later development of the oral method in Germany by Moritz Hill.

Some of Heinicke's ideas anticipated later educational practice. He taught the reading of whole words before teaching the letters. He advocated classes at the University of Leipzig for preparing teachers of the deaf, and attempted, apparently unsuccessfully, to establish with the university provision for his deaf students to participate in university activities. Heinicke's work was continued after his death by his widow, who took charge of his school, and his son-in-law, who established a school for the deaf near Berlin.

## REFERENCE

Bender, R. E. (1970). *The conquest of deafness*. Cleveland, OH: Case Western Reserve University Press.

PAUL IRVINE
*Katonah, New York*

## HELEN KELLER INTERNATIONAL

Founded in 1915, Helen Keller International assists governments and agencies in developing countries in providing services to prevent or cure eye diseases and blindness and to educate or rehabilitate the blind and visually impaired. Headquarters are in New York City and there are programs in 25 countries around the world. Subsumed under Helen Keller International are the Association for Chinese; Permanent Blind Relief War Fund; American Braille Press for War and Civilian Blind; and the American Foundation for Overseas Blind (Gruber & Cloyd, 1985).

The organization offers courses for teachers of blind children and adults as well as for field workers dealing with the rural blind. A training focus is prevention and treatment of blindness caused by malnutrition, trachoma, cataracts, and other eye diseases. Additionally, there are programs to prepare volunteers to counsel families of blind babies.

An important function of this international agency is the collection and compilation of statistics on blindness throughout the world. Publications include an annual report, a newsletter, fact sheets, technical reports, educational materials, and training information. There is one annual conference and an annual board meeting. Headquarters are at 15 West 16th Street, New York, NY 10011.

## REFERENCE

Gruber, K., & Cloyd, I. (1985). *Encyclopedia of associations* (Vol. 1, 20th ed.). Detroit, MI: Gale Research.

C. MILDRED TASHMAN
*College of St. Rose*

JESSI K. WHEATLEY
*Falcon School District 49,
Colorado Springs, Colorado*

## DEAF-BLIND

## HEMIBALLISMUS

Hemiballismus is a rare condition that is characterized by violent, flinging, involuntary movements in the extremities on one side of the body. The movements are typically more pronounced in the arm than in the leg and may be severe enough to cause bruising of the soft tissues or exhaustion. Involvement also has been reported in the muscles of the neck. Hemiballistic movements disappear during sleep.

Onset of the condition usually occurs in adulthood and often is associated with a prior cerebral vascular accident (stroke) involving the subthalamic nucleus. Tumors rarely are involved but hemiballism occasionally occurs in multiple sclerosis. In a few instances, the severity of hemiballism spontaneously subsides after several weeks. Death from exhaustion, pneumonia, or congestive heart failure within 4 to 6 weeks of onset also has been reported. Severe movement abnormalities may persist for several months or years without noticeable diminution in many of those who survive these initial weeks. Hemiballistic movements also may subside and be replaced by milder hemichoreatic movements in some instances. Fatalities are rare.

Chlorpromazine and haloperidol have been reported to substantially reduce or eliminate hemiballistic movements over a period of 3 months to more than 1 year. In some individuals, medications have been reduced gradually and ultimately eliminated with no recurrence of the condition. The prognosis has become more optimistic in recent years owing to increased use of these medications. There is also some optimism that other classes of neuroleptics may also be beneficial (e.g., Risperdal).

## REFERENCES

Berkow, R. (Ed.). (1982). *The Merck manual of diagnosis and therapy* (14th ed.). Rahway, NJ: Merck, Sharp & Dohme.

Fahn, S. (1985). Neurologic and behavioral diseases. In J. Wyngaarden & L. Smith, Jr. (Eds.), *Cecil textbooks of medicine* (17th ed., p. 2075). Philadelphia: Saunders.

Kalawanis, H. L., Moses, H., Nausieda, P. A., Berger, D., & Weiner, W. J. (1976). Treatment and prognosis of hemiballismus. *New England Journal of Medicine, 295,* 1348–1350.

Magalini, S., & Scarascia, E. (1981). *Dictionary of medical syndromes* (2nd ed., pp. 110–111). Philadelphia: Lippincott.

DANIEL D. LIPKA
*Lincoln Way Special Education
Regional Resources Center*

**CHOREA
MULTIPLE SCLEROSIS**

## HEMIPARESIS

Hemiparesis is a condition involving a neurological deficit in which one side of the body has weakness or is partially paralyzed (Hynd & Obrzut, 1981). In hemiparesis, neurological compromise is limited to the hemisphere contralateral to the weakened or partially paralyzed side of the body. The etiology of hemiparesis has been linked to unilateral strokes, transient ischemic attacks, migraines, head injuries, diabetes mellitus, tumors, infections, demyelinating conditions, and hereditary diseases (Family Practice Notebook, 2001; Lezak, 1995). The incomplete paralysis or weakness may present as limb rigidity, spasticity, or both. Weakness and spasticity are usually the main causes of limb deformities associated with hemiparesis. This condition may involve ataxia and gait disorders.

Characteristics of hemiparesis may include:

1. Weakness or paralysis on one side of the body.
2. Movement or gait disorders.
3. Poorly coordinated motor skills.
4. Limb deformity.
5. Rigidity or spasticity on the involved side of the body.
6. Excess hip and knee flexion during movement.
7. Decreased weight-bearing capabilities.
8. "Drop-foot" involving limited ankle control.
9. Asymmetrical standing postures and abnormal center of gravity.
10. Decreased walking speed.
11. Becomes fatigued easily.
12. Eyes may track toward the involved hemisphere.

Cognitive deficits in individuals with hemiparesis vary depending on which hemisphere has been compromised. For individuals with left hemiparesis, the right hemisphere is implicated, and for individuals with right hemiparesis, the left hemisphere is involved. The presence of left hemiciated with the right hemisphere (e.g., sensory testing, spatial orientation, and visuospatial construction). Right hemiparesis may involve deficits in functions usually associated with the left hemisphere (e.g., speech, object naming, writing, reading, comprehension, and tactile perception).

The degree of physical and cognitive development varies greatly in children with hemiparesis. Due to the nature of this disability, it is imperative that a transdisciplinary approach to educational and treatment programming be utilized to enhance learning and maximize independent functioning. Most children with hemiparesis would benefit from special services including occupational therapy, physical therapy, speech and language therapy, adapted physical education, and special education. Intervention goals should be designed to assist children with hemiparesis to increase their ability to perform purposeful activities and follow daily routines.

Spasticity in hemiparesis ranges from mild to moderate, which can negatively influence motor control and motor planning. In locomotor movements such as running, a child with hemiparesis may ambulate with a limp and effectively pump with only the noninvolved arm. In hemiparesis, the spastic arm is typically bent and pronated while the spastic leg is noticeably smaller than the normal one. Individuals with hemiparesis generally make two types of movement— either small steps with the paretic limb or larger steps with the nonparetic limb (Jiang, McIlroy, Black, & Maki, 1998). These two motions produce asymmetrical movements that reduce functional stability. Adaptive equipment designed to improve locomotion ability in children with hemiparesis could include therapy balls to reduce spasticity and help with relaxation; rocking on a vestibular board to reduce spasticity and to develop better equilibrium reactions; wearing a shoe lift on the nonparetic limb; and scooter boards, dumbbell kickers, and adaptive tricycles to encourage the use of both hands and both legs (Aruin, Hanke, Chaudhuri, Harvey, & Rao, 2000; Sherrill, 1993).

Coordination skills and motor planning may also be problematic for children with hemiparesis and render them unable to adapt to new settings or to generalize tasks. Due to motor planning deficits, a child with hemiparesis may have difficulty executing coordinated movement patterns or sequences. Activities that may help strengthen a child's motor planning and coordination skills are beanbag activities, obstacle courses, locomotor movements using a ladder on the floor, and motor skills kits to create specific sequential patterns for motor planning skill development (Sherrill, 1993). Due to lack of falling, when developing educational and treatment programs for children with this disorder, caution should be taken to reduce their chance of sustaining physical injury.

Children with hemiparesis often have balance problems, which can affect many areas of the child's performance not only motorically but also academically. The integration of the intersensory skills important to balance is also vital to reading and writing skills (Bailey & Wolery, 1989). In addition to balance problems, hemiparesis may result in visual perception problems. Activities to remediate visual perceptual problems include beeper or jingle balls, auditory guessing games, locomotor movements using a drumbeat, games in which the child must track using his or her eyes to follow a moving object, and exploring different ways to move body parts in a stationary position.

In addition to gross motor delays, children with hemiparesis may experience delays in the development of fine motor skills. The degree of abnormal muscle tone correlates with difficulties in the performance of fine motor tasks. Vision, head, and trunk control, upper extremity function, posture, and volitional movements all need to be carefully assessed to determine their impact on a child's fine motor development (Sherrill, 1993). Treatment programs designed to improve a child's fine motor skills must be conducted in conjunction with activities to improve muscle tone and overall movement patterns.

In the case of hemiparesis, speech and language services may be warranted, depending on which hemisphere of the brain has been damaged and the extent of the impairment. If speech services are provided, it is critical to teach functional communication skills across a variety of settings. Additionally, alternative and augmentative communication modes may need to be taught when a child has highly unintelligible speech or is nonverbal (McCormick & Schiefelbusch, 1984).

The special education teacher's role will depend on the level of cognitive involvement of the child with hemiparesis. As the severity of the cognitive disability increases, the special education teacher's involvement will typically increase. In a transdisciplinary approach, the special education teacher is usually responsible for the coordination and implementation of all services so that an optimal learning environment is provided for the child to learn new skills and to generalize these skills across different environments. In addition to being responsible for assessing and teaching cognitive skills, the special educator may also be responsible for the assessment and daily implementation of sensorimotor, play, social, communication, motor, and self-help skills. Facilitating parent-child interactions and integration issues and strategies may also be a responsibility of the special education teacher.

## REFERENCES

Aruin, A. S., Hanke, T., Chaudhuri, G., Harvey, R., & Rao, N. (2000). Compelling weightbearing in persons with hemiparesis following stroke: The effect of a lift insert and goal-directed balance exercise. *Journal of Rehabilitation Research and Development, 37*(1).

Bailey, D. B., Jr., & Wolery, M. (1989). *Assessing infants and preschoolers with handicaps.* New York: Macmillan.

Family Practice Notebook.com. (2001). *Hemiplegia: Hemiparesis.* Retrieved from http://www.fpnotebook.com/NEU60.htm

Hynd, G. W., & Obrzut, J. E. (1981). *Neuropsychological assessment and the school-age child: Issues and procedures.* Boston: Allyn & Bacon.

Jiang, N., McIlroy, W. E., Black, S. E., & Maki, B. E. (1998, August). *Control of compensatory limb movement in chronic hemiparesis.* Paper presented at the North American Congress on Biomechanics, Waterloo, Ontario, Canada.

Lezak, M. D. (1995). *Neuropsychological assessment* (3rd ed.). New York: Oxford University Press.

McCormick, L., & Schiefelbusch, R. L. (1984). *Early language intervention.* Columbus, OH: Merrill.

Sherrill, C. (1993). *Adapted physical activity, recreation and sport: Crossdisciplinary and lifespan.* Dubuque, IA: WCB Brown & Benchmark.

SHAWN POWELL
*United States Air Force Academy*

BARBARA CORRIVEAU
SHARINE WEBBER
*Laramie County School District #1, Cheyenne, Wyoming*

**HEMIPLEGIA**
**PHYSICAL ANOMALIES**

## HEMIPLEGIA

Hemiplegia, or paralysis of one side of the body, usually is the result of a cerebral vascular insult or injury (Reed, 2001). This condition generally involves rupture or closure of cerebral blood flow in part of the brain (O'Sullivan, 2001). Because some parts of the nerve cells of the brain have been damaged and cannot function, the part of the body controlled by the damaged portion of the brain cannot function (Dzurenko, 1999). For example, when the left side of the brain is involved, the child's right extremities are affected; the results of this may include paralysis, sensory loss, and aphasia that may be temporary or permanent (Young, 2000). In most cases, there will be permanent neurological deficits ranging from slight neurological problems to complete loss of function in motor, sensory, or language ability (Young). Crossed hemiplegia is characterized by muscular weakness on one side of the body. This condition is extremely rare and generally begins before the child is 18 months old (Misulis, 2000). Monoplegia refers to weakness in one limb on one side of the body (Rowland).

Pediatric strokes are the most common cause of hemiplegia in children (Gold & Cargan, 2000). The estimated annual incidence of stroke in children under the age of 14 is 2.52 per 100,000 (Gold & Cargan). Causes of strokes in children have been linked to inherited clotting disorders, congenital heart disease, and sickle cell disease (Gold & Cargan). Other causes of strokes that may lead to hemiplegia include shaking an infant, sports, and substance abuse by the mother or by a child. Hemiplegia may be caused, in some rare cases, by spinal cord damage or tumors on the spinal cord (Misulis, 2000).

In infants and children, stroke symptoms include seizures, coma, and paralysis of one side of the body (Young, 2000). Additional symptoms may involve the loss of previously acquired speech and seizures (Young). Hemiplegia is usually diagnosed by a physician using a magnetic resonance imaging (MRI) test (Young).

Course and outcome of children with hemiplegia are variable and are dependent upon a number of factors. In the case of newborns, most continue to have seizures, motor difficulty, and some cognitive impairment (Young, 2000). In most cases, children will have persistent limb weakness. Children may experience delays in language, processing, memory, attention, and cognition, depending on the side of the brain that is involved (Reed, 2001). For example, if the left hemisphere of the brain was involved, the child may experience difficulty in language and auditory processing as well as motoric impairments. Although the child may always demonstrate residual effects, positive outcomes have been linked to return of adequate blood flow to the brain (Young).

Special education services will likely be needed to assist the child with hemiplegia. Due to the varying levels of impairment that different children experience, individualized education plans need to be tailored to the child's unique needs. The child may require assistance with many different areas, including learning, academics, self-care, motoric ability, cognitive issues, and psychosocial problems (Reed, 2001). Special education services need to focus on the building of remedial strategies, the teaching of new or lost skills, and compensatory education, the teaching of different skills to accommodate for the skills lost (D'Amato, Rothlisberg, & Work, 1999). The child may benefit from compensatory and remedial strategies in the following areas: physical therapy, occupational therapy, learning interventions, and social skills training. Physical therapy may focus on the reduction of muscle atrophy and an increase in flexion and extension. Occupational therapy could focus on grasping objects and the functional use of both the affected side of the body and compensatory strategies using the unaffected side of the body. Learning interventions may include compensatory and remedial strategies in any affected areas of academics. Social skills training may need to focus on the teaching of prosocial behaviors, increasing self-confidence, and peer relationship development (Reed). Research needs to progress in the area of intervention studies for children with hemiplegia.

## REFERENCES

D'Amato, R. C., Rothlisberg, B. A., & Work, P. H. (1999). Neuropsychological assessment for intervention. In C. R. Reynolds & T. B. Gutkin (Eds.), *The handbook of school psychology*. New York: Wiley.

Dzurenko, J. (1999). Rehabilitation nursing: Educating patients toward independence. In M. G. Eisenberg, R. L. Glueckauf, & H. H. Zaretsky (Eds.), *Medical aspects of disability: A handbook for the rehabilitation professional*. New York: Springer.

Gold, A. P., & Cargan, A. L. (2000). Stroke in children. In L. P. Rowland (Ed.), *Merritt's neurology*. Philadelphia: Lippincott, Williams, & Wilkins.

Misulis, K. E. (2000). Hemiplegia and monoplegia. In W. G. Bradley, R. B. Daroff, G. M. Fenichel, & C. D. Marsden (Eds.), *Neurology in clinical practice: Practice and principles of diagnosis and management*. Woburn, MA: Butterworth-Heinemann.

O'Sullivan, S. B. (2001). Stroke. In S. B. O'Sullivan & T. J. Schmitz (Eds.), *Physical rehabilitation: Assessment and treatment*. Philadelphia: F. A. Davis.

Reed, K. L. (2001). *Quick reference to occupational therapy*. Gaithersburg, MD: Aspen.

Rowland, L. R. (1995). Head injury. In L. P. Rowland (Ed.), *Merritt's textbook of neurology*. Media, PA: William & Wilkins.

Young, R. K. (2000). Stroke in childhood. In W. G. Bradley, R. B. Daroff, G. M. Fenichel, & C. D. Marsden (Eds.), *Neurology in clinical practice: The neurological disorders*. Woburn, MA: Butterworth-Heinemann.

NICOLE R. WARNYGORA
*University of Northern Colorado*

## HEMIPARESIS

## HEMISPHERECTOMY

Hemispherectomy is a surgical procedure involving the removal of "a cerebral hemisphere, including the frontal, temporal, parietal, and occipital lobes while leaving intact parts of the thalamus and basal ganglia" (Menard, Le Normand, Rigoard, & Cohen, 2000, p. 333). A hemispherectomy may be performed as a treatment for severe seizure disorders, fatal tumors, hemiplegia, and Rasmussen encephalitis. The procedure is usually reserved as a life-saving measure or may be employed to improve the life of a child with intractable seizures resulting from unilateral brain dysfunction (de Bolle & Curtiss, 2000; Estes, 2000).

*Characteristics:* Note tht these symptoms usually result in a hemispherectomy, and some may exist following this surgical procedure.

1. Intractable epileptic seizures of an ongoing severe nature

2. Hemiplegia or hemiparesis

3. Progressive declines in cognitive functioning

4. Visual neglect contralateral to the damaged hemisphere

5. Impaired expressive and receptive language functioning

6. Delayed social communication skills

7. Delayed academic achievement

8. Increased occurrence of mental illness, specifically those involving thought disorders

In cases involving a hemispherectomy, cerebral damage from atrophy, sustained seizures, disease processes, tumors, or traumatic insults may be present. The result of such damage usually involves a reduction in cognitive functioning. This reduction in cognition may be widespread or specific, depending on the etiology, course, duration, and age of occurrence when the cerebral damage initially started (Caplan, Curtiss, Chugani, & Vinters, 1996). Additionally, seizure activity may be generalized (i.e., bilateral), or focal (i.e., unilateral). In the case of bilateral seizures, the remaining hemisphere may be damaged, which prompts questions regarding its structural integrity (Boatman et al., 1999).

Depending on the age of disease onset or injury and the age when the hemispherectomy is performed, there is evidence that the remaining cerebral hemisphere may mediate functions normally associated with the removed hemisphere (Caplan et al., 1996; de Bolle & Curtiss, 2000). Thus, the right hemisphere in children with a left hemispherectomy may mediate language functions, and the left hemisphere in children with a right hemispherectomy may mediate visual-spatial functions. The age of injury and age of the hemispherectomy procedure may be more important determinants of future cognitive functions than the severity of the injury or disease process (Bradshaw & Mattingley, 1995). It has been suggested that insults that occur during a critical period of maturation result in less opportunity for the full development of specific abilities. For example, when an insult occurs during a critical period of language development, it reduces the likelihood that a child would acquire full language skills (Menard et al., 2000).

Following a hemispherectomy, a full complement of special education services may be essential to ensure that the child has the best possible opportunity to make educational gains. These services may include speech language therapy, mobility support, occupational therapy, physical therapy, school nursing services, academic support, counseling, and case management. In addition to school-based services, frequent communication with medical care providers is necessary in order to provide the best possible educational services and to better understand the child's recovery. Seizure precautions and protocols should be established and followed because seizure disorders may persist following the hemispherectomy. General guidelines to reduce seizure activity include taking antiseizure medication as prescribed, eating three meals daily, drinking fluids, reducing or eliminating caffeine, following regular sleeping patterns, allowing rest periods, and using stress management techniques (Estes, 2000).

Parental contact should occur on a regular basis with the frequency of these contacts determined by the child's needs. Depending on the age of the child, a daily notebook between home and school may be beneficial in increasing communication. Transitional services and vocational planning with available community resources for children who have had a hemispherectomy will likely increase their ability to adapt and function as independently as possible as they mature.

### REFERENCES

Boatman, D., Freeman, J., Vining, E., Pulsifer, M., Miglioretti, D., Minahan, R., et al. (1999). Language recovery after left hemispherectomy in children with late-onset seizures. *Annals of Neurology, 46*(4).

Bradshaw, J. L., & Mattingley, J. B. (1995). *Clinical neuropsychology: Behavioral and brain science.* San Diego, CA: Academic.

Caplan, R., Curtiss, S., Chugani, H. T., & Vinters, H. V. (1996). Pediatric Rasmussen encephalitis: Social communication, language, PET, and pathology before and after hemispherectomy. *Brain and Cognition, 32,* 45–66.

de Bolle, S., & Curtiss, S. (2000). Language after hemispherectomy. *Brain and Cognition, 43,* 135–205.

Estes, R. (2000). A closer look: Seizures. *Premier Outlook, 1*(2).

Menard, A., Le Normand, M. T., Rigoard, M. T., & Cohen, H. (2000). Language development in a child with left hemispherectomy. *Brain and Cognition, 43,* 332–340.

SHAWN POWELL
*United States Air Force Academy*

CEREBRAL DOMINANCE
LEFT BRAIN/RIGHT BRAIN
NEUROPSYCHOLOGY

## HEMISPHERIC FUNCTIONS

Hemispheric functions refers to the specialization of each cerebral hemisphere of the brain for various processes. The right hemisphere usually has been associated with processing information in a simultaneous, spatial, and holistic fashion (Kinsbourne, 1997; Speery, 1974). In contrast, the left hemisphere of the brain has been shown to best process information in a sequential, temporal, and analytic mode (Kinsbourne, 1997; Speery, Gazzaniga, & Bogen, 1969).

Although hemispheric lateralization usually refers to the processing of specific information by predominantly one hemisphere, undifferentiated hemispheric preference for the processing of certain information also exists. Gordon (1974), for example, found that when melodies recorded from an electric organ were simultaneously presented, one to each ear, no hemispheric superiority was noted. Few reliable hemispheric differences were noted for lower level sensory elements such as brightness, color, pressure, sharpness, pitch, and contour (Gordon, 1970). Symmetrical processing of information does not occur on tasks that require complex cognitive processes such as categorization, integration, and abstraction. As the level of cognitive complexity increases, so does the lateralization for the task in question.

The notion of lateralization of functions within cerebral hemispheres can be dated back to the late 1800s, when Broca and Wernicke demonstrated that aphasia (or the inability to express or comprehend language) resulted from lesions to the left hemisphere. Moreover, the left hemisphere was portrayed as the dominant hemisphere by virtue of its leading role in such activities as speech and calculation, whereas the right hemisphere was seen as the minor hemisphere, serving activities associated with perception and sensation (Geschwind, 1974; Kinsbourne, 1997).

Invasive techniques that have been used to investigate brain functioning consist of electrical stimulation of the brain, hemispheric anesthetization, and split-brain research. Direct electrical stimulation of the brain was pioneered by Penfield (Penfield & Roberts, 1959) as a means of mapping areas of the brain that controlled specific functions prior to other surgical procedures. Given that the brain does not contain pain receptors, electrical stimulation was applied to various parts of the brain while the patient was fully conscious. This technique has been successful in examining areas of the brain associated with vision, hearing, olfaction, and haptic sensations.

Another invasive technique to investigate speech lateralization involved the injection of sodium amytal to the carotid artery, which is located on either the right or left side of the patient's neck. This procedure, which is commonly referred to as the Wada test (Wada & Rasmussen, 1960), quickly anesthetizes or temporarily paralyzes the hemisphere that receives the injection. The hemisphere is anesthetized for approximately 3 to 5 minutes, thereby enabling the examiner to assess which hemisphere is responsible for processing linguistic information. The last invasive technique, split-brain surgery, involves the severing of the corpus callosum, a large band of nerve fibers that permit the left and right hemispheres to communicate with one another. This procedure is primarily performed to prevent the spreading of a seizure from a focal point in one hemisphere to the other by way of the corpus callosum. By severing the corpus callosum, communication

between the hemispheres is blocked, thereby allowing the examiner to determine the hemispheric lateralization for such functions as language, visual discrimination, touch, olfaction, and motoric control (Hacaen, 1981).

Research that has resulted from the use of the preceding techniques has found that the right hemisphere plays a dominant role in processing certain information. Specifically, the right hemisphere is dominant for processing nonlinguistic information involving nonverbal reasoning, visual-spatial integration, visual-constructive abilities, haptic perception, pattern recognition, and other related tasks (Camfield, 2005; Dean, 1984). Conversely, the left hemisphere has been shown to be responsible for tasks that require speech, general language, calculation, abstract verbal reasoning, etc. (Camfield, 2005; Dean, 1984).

Noninvasive techniques for investigating hemispheric specializations have also been employed. The dichotic listening technique attempts to determine if auditory information for verbal and nonverbal information is lateralized to one hemisphere. Here, the subject is simultaneously presented with different information in each ear and is required to recall or recognize the information presented. Given that greater numbers of nerve connections cross over from ear to hemisphere, the hemisphere opposite the ear that obtains the greatest number of correct responses (ear advantage) is inferred to be the functional hemisphere for the specific information presented. For example, most normal children and adults have a right-ear advantage (left hemisphere) for linguistic information (Dean & Hua, 1982). When nonverbal auditory information such as tones are presented, a left-ear advantage (right hemisphere) is found for most normal right-handed individuals (Kimura, 1967). The dichotic listening paradigm has been successful in suggesting specific functions of each hemisphere.

Similar to the dichotic listening methodology, the split visual-field technique presents visual information to either the left or right visual half fields. It should be noted that each retina is separated into a left and right half visual field. Therefore, information presented to the two left halves of each retina is processed by the right hemisphere and, conversely, information presented to the two right halves is processed by the left hemisphere. To study the lateralization of visual stimuli, different information is simultaneously presented on a tachistoscope. As would be expected, a right visual half advantage (left hemisphere) is found for linguistic information (Marcel & Rajan, 1975) while a left visual half advantage (right hemisphere) has been noted for nonverbal spatial information (Kimura & Durnsford, 1974). One noted difficulty with this technique, however, is the attentional scanning of the stimuli that occurs once the information has been presented (Dean, 1981).

Differences in hemispheric specializations may be due, in part, to anatomical differences of the cortical hemispheres. In examining anatomical differences, it was found that the left temporal planum structure that serves language functions is larger than the right temporal planum (Geschwind & Levitsky, 1968). Similarly, the Sylvian fissure, a large lateral depression in the brain that contains the major speech area, is found to be larger for the left side of the Sylvian fissure than the right (Geschwind, 1974). In addition, the left hemisphere is noted to be approximately 5 gr heavier than the right hemisphere. Another anatomical difference is the projection of nerve fibers from the left hemisphere that cross over earlier at the base of the brain than do nerve fibers from the right hemisphere. Such structural differences between the hemispheres may partially account for cerebral lateralization of specific functions.

When gender differences are examined, subtle anatomical dissimilarities between males and females are found to exist shortly after birth. Perhaps more striking than anatomical are functional changes that exist between adult male and female brains (Kinsbourne, 1997; Kolata, 1979). As a group, males have been shown to perform better on tasks of spatial ability than females, who present superior verbal facility (Witelson, 1976). The spatial ability of males may be partially due to an earlier right hemisphere lateralization of spatial functions. Males also have been shown to have an earlier hemispheric specialization for language, while females are noted to be less consistent in lateralization for language activities (Levy, 1973). This less established hemispheric specialization for females, however, can be contrasted to their firmer lateralization for peripheral activities such as handedness (Annett, 1976) and visually guided motor activities (Dean & Reynolds, 1997). That is, while females are more bilateral for cognitive activities such as language, they have more established preference than do males for consistently using the same hand, ear, eye, etc., for related activities.

This paradoxical finding for females seems to be a function of the tenuous relationship between lateral preference patterns for peripheral activities and hemispheric specialization for language. Inferring hemispheric lateralization from lateral preference patterns from simple measures of handedness should be cautioned against. Dean (1982) has shown that lateral preference is a factorially complex variable and a function of the system (e.g., eyes, ears, hands, etc.) under study. Lateral preference patterns, then, may be more heuristically represented on a continuum from entirely left to entirely right instead of categorically as either left or right (Dean & Reynolds, 1997).

## REFERENCES

Annett, M. (1976). Hand preference and the laterality of cerebral speech. *Cortex, 11,* 305–329.

Camfield, D. (2005). Neurobiology of creativity. In C. Stough (Ed.), *Neurobiology of exceptionality* (pp. 53–72). New York: Kluwer.

Dean, R. S. (1981). Cerebral dominance and childhood learning disorders: Theoretical perspectives. *School Psychology Review, 10,* 373–380.

Dean, R. S. (1982). Assessing patterns of lateral preference. *Clinical Neuropsychology, 4,* 124–128.

Dean, R. S. (1984). Functional lateralization of the brain. *Journal of Special Education, 18,* 239–256.

Dean, R. S., & Hua, M. S. (1982). Laterality effects in cued auditory asymmetries. *Neuropsychologia, 20,* 685–690.

Dean, R. S., & Reynolds, C. R. (1997). Cognitive processing and self-report of lateral preference. *Neuropsychology Review, 7,* 127–142.

Geschwind, N. (1974). The anatomical basis of hemispheric differentiation. In S. J. Dimond & J. G. Beaumont (Eds.), *Hemisphere function in the human brain.* New York: Wiley.

Geschwind, N., & Levitsky, W. (1968). Human brain: Left-right asymmetries in temporal speech region. *Science, 161,* 186–187.

Gordon, H. W. (1970). Hemispheric asymmetries in the perception of musical chords. *Cortex, 6,* 387–398.

Gordon, H. W. (1974). Auditory specialization of the right and left hemispheres. In M. Kinsbourne & W. L. Smith (Eds.), *Hemispheric disconnection and cerebral function.* Springfield, IL: Thomas.

Hecaen, H. (1981). Apraxias. In S. B. Filskov & T. J. Boll (Eds.), *Handbook of clinical neuropsychology.* New York: Wiley.

Kimura, D. (1967). Functional asymmetry of the brain in dichotic listening. *Cortex, 3,* 163–178.

Kimura, D., & Durnsford, M. (1974). Normal studies on the function of the right hemisphere in vision. In S. J. Dimond & J. G. Beaumont (Eds.), *Hemisphere function in the human brain.* London: Elek Scientific.

Kinsbourne, M. (1997). Mechanisms and development of cerebral lateralization in children. In C. R. Reynolds & E. Fletcher-Janzen (Eds.), *Handbook of clinical child neuropsychology* (pp. 102–119). New York: Kluwer-Plenum.

Kolata, G. B. (1979). Sex hormones and brain development. *Science, 205,* 985–987.

Levy, J. (1973). Lateral specialization of the human brain: Behavioral manifestations and possible evolutionary basis. In J. A. Kriger (Ed.), *The biology of behavior.* Corvallis: Oregon State University Press.

Marcel, T., & Rajan, P. (1975). Lateral specialization of recognition of words and faces in good and poor readers. *Neuropsychologia, 13,* 489–497.

Penfield, W., & Roberts, L. (1959). *Speech and brain mechanisms.* Princeton, NJ: Princeton University Press.

Rattan, G., & Dean, R. S. (1987). Cerebral dominance. In C. R. Reynolds & L. Mann (Eds.), *Encyclopedia of special education.* New York: Wiley.

Speery, R. W. (1974). Lateral specialization in the surgically separated hemispheres. In F. O. Schmitt & F. G. Worden (Eds.), *The neurosciences: Third study program.* New York: Wiley.

Speery, R. W., Gazzaniga, M. S., & Bogen, J. H. (1969). Interhemispheric relationships: The neocortical commissures: Syndromes of hemisphere disconnection. In P. Vinken & G. W. Bruyn (Eds.), *Handbook of clinical neurology* (Vol. 4). New York: Wiley.

Wada, J. A., & Rasmussen, T. (1960). Intracarotid injection of sodium amytal for lateralization of cerebral speech dominance:

Experimental and clinical observation. *Journal of Neurosurgery,* *17,* 266–282.

Witelson, S. F. (1976). Abnormal right hemisphere specialization in developmental dyslexia. In R. M. Knights & D. F. Bakker (Eds.), *Neuropsychology of learning disorders: Theoretical approaches.* Baltimore: University Park Press.

GURMAL RATTAN
*Indiana University of*
*Pennsylvania*

RAYMOND S. DEAN
*Ball State University*
*Indiana University School of*
*Medicine*

## CEREBRAL DOMINANCE
## LEFT BRAIN/RIGHT BRAIN

## HEMOLYTIC UREMIC SYNDROME

Hemolytic uremic syndrome (HUS) is a systemic disease marked by renal failure, hemolytic anemia, thrombocytopenia (platelet deficiency), coagulation defects, and variable neurological signs (MedlinePlus, 2002). This disorder is most common in children. It frequently occurs after a gastrointestinal (enteric) infection, often one caused by a strain of specific E. coli bacteria (*Escherichia coli* O157: H7). It has also been associated with other enteric infections, including shigella and salmonella, and with some nonenteric infections (MedlinePlus, 2002; Rothenberg & Chapman, 1994).

HUS often begins with vomiting and diarrhea (which may be bloody). Within a week the patient develops weakness and irritability. Urine output decreases dramatically and may almost cease. Because red blood cells are being destroyed (a process called hemolysis), the patient rapidly becomes anemic and pale (MedlinePlus, 2002).

The incidence of HUS is 1–3 per 100,000, with the highest incidence occurring in the summer and fall. The age of onset is most common under the age of 4 years. HUS is the most common cause of acute renal failure in children (Pedlynx, 2002).

There are two forms of HUS: the typical form (idiopathic) and the atypical or sporadic form. The typical form usually affects children 3 months to 6 years of age (80 percent < 3 years) and is caused by an E. coli serotype 0157:H7 that can produce specific enterocytotoxins. The risk factors for E. coli acquisition are undercooked ground beef and contact with a person with diarrhea within 2 weeks prior to disease onset. One in 10 children who have E. coli 0157:H7 will go on to develop HUS (Pedlynx, 2002).

The atypical or sporadic form may be associated with an inherited autosomal recessive or dominant form and with scleroderma, radiation of kidneys, and essential or malignant hypertension. There is also a pregnancy or oral contraceptive association related to preeclampsia or postpartum renal failure (Pedlynx, 2002).

Characteristics of hemolytic uremic syndrome may include:

1. Gastroenteritis
   - Usually precedes illness by 5–10 days
   - Diarrhea, bloody stool, severe colitis
   - Fever, nausea, and vomiting
   - Rectal prolapse
2. Renal manifestations
   - Microscopic or gross hematuria
   - Proteinuria that can progress to the nephrotic level
   - Complications such as nephritic syndrome (edema, hypertension, azotemia, oliguria), nephrotic syndrome (edema, hypoalbuminemia, hyperlipidemia), and renal failure that can range from mild renal insufficiency to acute renal failure (ARF).
3. Hematological manifestations
   - Anemia
   - Sudden onset of pallor, irritability, lethargy, weakness
   - Hepatomegaly-hepatosplenomegaly
   - Thrombocytopenia (90 percent)
4. Complications
   - Irritability, seizures, coma
   - Colitis with melena and perforation
   - Acidosis, congestive heart failure, diabetes mellitus, fluid overload, hyperkalemia, rhabdomyolysis

Treatment usually includes transfusions of packed red cells, and platelets are given as needed. Kidney dialysis may be indicated. Medications prescribed include corticosteroids and aspirin. Plasmapheresis, also called plasma exchange (or passage of the plasma through a Protein A filter) may be performed, although its role is much less well documented than in TTP (thrombotic thrombocytopenic purpura). The blood plasma (the portion that does not contain cells, but does contain antibodies) is removed and replaced with fresh (donated) or filtered plasma to remove antibodies from the circulation (MedlinePlus, 2002). In addition, medical management of the complications such as nephritic syndrome, nephrotic syndrome, and chronic renal failure may include dialysis, kidney transplant, or both (Pedlynx, 2002).

Special education may or may not be needed for children with HUS. The course and outcome of the disease are highly variable, and individual educational needs will vary as well. Chronic renal problems and medications may well create the need for typical chronic illness counseling and supportive assistance.

Ninety percent of patients survive the acute phase with no renal impairment if aggressive management of acute renal failure (ARF) is instituted. A positive prognosis is associated with the age of the child, typical form, and summer months for diagnosis. A poor prognosis is associated with shock, significant renal involvement, neurological signs and symptoms, and atypical form. The prognosis for children with HUS includes a mortality rate of 7–10 percent and renal dysfunction of 20 percent (Pedlynx, 2002).

The known cause of HUS, E. coli in hamburger and ground meats, can be prevented by adequate cooking. Other unrecognized causes may not be preventable at this time.

## REFERENCES

MedlinePlus. (2002). *HUS*. Retrieved from http://www.nlm.nih .gov/medlineplus/ency/article/000510.htm

Pedlynx Pedbase. (2002). Retrieved April 2002, from http://www .icondata.com/health/pedbase/files/HEMOLYTI.HTM

Rothenberg, M. A., & Chapman, C. F. (1994). *Dictionary of medical terms*. New York: Barron's.

Elaine Fletcher-Janzen
*University of Colorado at
Colorado Springs*

# HEMOPHILIA A, "CLASSIC" HEMOPHILIA

Factor VIII deficiency is one of the most common forms of severe hereditary bleeding disorders. Hemophilia has been known since antiquity, as is evidenced by Talmudic scripts advising against ritual circumcision of male infants whose siblings died from bleeding caused by the procedure.

Hemophilia occurs in about 1 in 5,000 males. Eighty-five percent of these individuals have Factor VIII deficiency. The remainder have Factor IX deficiency (hemophilia B). Both disorders are transmitted in an X-linked recessive manner, with females acting as carriers of the abnormal gene. This carrier state may also cause mild clotting abnormalities.

Multiple mutations of the Factor VIII gene are associated with several clinical classifications of hemophilia. Unimpaired clotting activity requires Factor VIII levels that are 35–40 percent of normal. Severe hemophilia is characterized by less than 1 percent of normal Factor VIII levels. Moderate cases range from 1–5 percent. Mild hemophilia is over 5 percent. About 5–10 percent of patients with hemophilia A produce abnormal, nonfunctioning Factor VIII. Forty-five to 50 percent of those with severe disease have an identical genetic mutation and generate no detectable Factor VIII at all.

Characteristics of hemophilia A can include:

1. Bleeding symptoms in the newborn are uncommon. Intracranial hemorrhage is occasionally seen. Only about 30 percent of affected males have excessive bleeding with circumcision.

2. Easy bruising, bleeding into muscle (intramuscular hematoma), and bleeding into joints (hemarthrosis) usually do not begin until the child starts to crawl and walk. However, 10 percent of hemophiliacs have no symptoms during their 1st year.

3. Hemarthrosis is the defining characteristic of this disease. It may be spontaneous or posttraumatic. The ankle is the most commonly affected joint in toddlers. Hemarthroses of the elbow and knee occur more frequently in older children and adolescents. Repeated bleeds into a joint cause scarring, severe pain, erosion of cartilage at the ends of bones forming the joint and—eventually—complete fusion.

4. Life-threatening hemorrhages are the result of bleeding into the brain, upper airway, or other vital organ. Exsanguination can occur with gastrointestinal bleeds, external blood loss, or massive intramuscular hematomas.

5. Mildly affected patients may not experience spontaneous bleeding. Their most common presenting symptoms is prolonged bleeding following dental work, surgery, or moderate trauma.

Successfully treating hemophilia requires several considerations. Prevention of trauma is important, but many bleeding events are spontaneous. Early family counseling will help parents strike a suitable compromise between overprotecting their child and permitting him reasonable freedom. Hemophiliacs should avoid aspirin and nonsteroidal anti-inflammatory drugs (e.g., ibuprofen), because such drugs may aggravate bleeding tendencies. Patients should complete the hepatitis B immunization series during infancy, and they should be screened periodically for hepatitis and abnormal liver function.

Specific therapy with Factor VIII given intravenously is needed to end bleeding events. Serious or life-threatening bleeds require Factor VIII levels to be 100 percent of normal. Individuals with mild hemophilia may respond to the drug DDAVP, which causes release of Factor VIII from storage sites in this particular subset of patients.

Previously, Factor VIII infusions were given only when active bleeding was evident or suspected. Prior to the introduction of purification techniques employed for about the past 15 years, repeated Factor VIII administration was associated with a high risk for infection with transmittable viral disease (hepatitis A, B, and C and HIV). The only product available until recently was derived from pooled human plasma and was therefore not totally safe. However, a recombinant Factor VIII produced from genetically altered bacteria is now being marketed. Considerable interest exists for the prophylactic use of this material because it is free from any known viral contaminants. Prophylactic Factor

VIII therapy prevents hemarthroses and greatly reduces the incidence of crippling joint pathology in hemophiliacs.

Education of educators and other school personnel is a integral part of keeping the child safe in the school environment. Helping them to provide play and leisure activities that will not result in compromising the health of the child with Factor VIII deficiency will be important. By providing preventive education, the school counselors can work with the other students to understand the need for safety, help the student with Factor VIII adjust to the modifications, and in turn facilitate peer relationships and self-esteem issues. Should the child with Factor VIII experience bleeding in his brain, it will be important to have a comprehensive neuropsychological evaluation completed. Depending on those results, the educators will be able to develop an educational program that focuses on the child's strengths and provides ways to remediate his cognitive weaknesses.

The prognosis for newly diagnosed children with hemophilia A is generally favorable. A referral to large hemophilia comprehensive care centers is imperative for the most satisfactory outcomes. Staffed by professionals in several disciplines, these facilities employ a modern approach to factor replacement therapy (prophylactic treatment), recognize and aggressively treat initial signs of joint debilitation, and manage the complications of prolonged Factor VIII administration (hepatitis and HIV). The most realistic "cure" for this disorder is gene replacement therapy, which should become available during the lifetimes of today's patients.

For more information and parent support, please contact National Hemophilia Foundation, 116 West 32nd Street, 11th Floor, New York, NY 10001, (212) 328-3700, (800) 424-2634, e-mail: handi@hemophilia.org, home page: http://www.hemophilia.org

World Federation of Hemophilia, 1425 Rene Levesque Boulevard West, Suite 1010, Montreal, Quebec, H3G-1T7, Canada, (514) 87-5-7944, e-mail: wfh@wfh.org, home page: http://www.wth.orgn

## REFERENCES

Montgomery, R. R. (2000). Hemorrhagic and thrombotic disease. In R. E. Behrman, R. M. Kleigman, & H. B. Jenson (Eds.), *Nelson's textbook of pediatrics* (16th ed. pp. 1504–1525). Philadelphia: W. B. Saunders.

National Organization for Rare Disorders. (1999). *Factor XIII deficiency.* Retrieved from http://www.stepstn.com/cgi-win/nord.exe?proc=GetDocument&rectype=0&recnum=66

BARRY H. DAVISON
*Ennis, Texas*

JOAN W. MAYFIELD
*Baylor Pediatric Specialty Service*

# HEMOPHILIA B

Hemophilia is a sex-linked inherited disorder in which the individual lacks the necessary blood-clotting factors to stop bleeding (Harcourt Health Sciences, 2002). The condition is transmitted via the X chromosome, but it is believed that some individuals are affected by hemophilia due to mutation of the genes on that chromosome. There are two forms of hemophilia: Type A (with the blood-clotting Factor VIII missing) and Type B (with the blood-clotting Factor IV missing; Hemophilia, 2000). Hemophilia A and B are further defined by their severity and range from mild to severe.

The condition exists in all races and ethnicities. The prevalence rate for Hemophilia A is 1 in 10,000 men and for Hemophilia B it is 1 in 40,000 men (Cutler, 2001). Fifty percent of all sons of a female carrier will be affected and 50 percent of the daughters will be carriers. All daughters of affected men will be carriers, but the disease affects women very rarely (Greene, 2001a). Approximately 17,000 people with hemophilia are currently living in the United States (Mayo Clinic, 2001).

Characteristics of hemophilia B may include:

1. The symptoms vary with the degree of the deficiency of the blood-clotting factors.
2. Often diagnosed when infants begin crawling; their injuries cause internal bleeding as in their joints and muscles, which are then visible by bruises, and their injuries bleed profusely.
3. Symptoms associated with the disorder are nosebleeds; bruising; spontaneous bleeding; bleeding into joints and associated pain and swelling; gastrointestinal tract and urinary tract hemorrhage; blood in urine or stool; prolonged bleeding from cuts, tooth extraction, and surgery; and excessive bleeding following circumcision (Greene, 2001a).

Individuals with hemophilia must be under medical care to assist with the replacement of the blood-clotting factors that are administered intravenously. The reduction or prevention of bleeding is essential during treatment because such bleeding can be life-threatening. For example, immunizations should be administered subcutaneously cutan versus intramuscularly to prevent hemorrhages. The importance of dental hygiene must be explained to the individual to prevent tooth decay and possible gum infections. Aspirin and some medications used for arthritis must be avoided because they act as blood thinners. Education of the patient regarding his or her environment and how to interact with it to avoid injury is essential for his or her well being.

Swimming and walking should be preferred over contact or high-impact sports such as boxing or football (Greene, 2001b). MedicAlert tags must be worn by the child, and emergency procedures and emergency numbers must be known by all pertinent individuals in the child's environment (Hemophilia.org, 2001b). Serious consideration must be given to any bleeding in the mouth, throat, or neck, because the patient could suffocate as a result of the bleeding. Bleeding in the joints is also a concern and—if untreated—could lead to a loss in mobility (Canadian Hemophilia Society, 2001).

To help the individual cope with the impact of the bleeding disorder, the child is best served if home, school, and medical caregivers form a strong alliance. Joining support groups with other afflicted individuals can help alleviate the stress as well. Genetic counseling for family members and afflicted individuals is also recommended (Cutler, 2001). Depending on the severity of the condition, hospitalizations and longer periods might prevent the child from participating in school on a regular basis (Hemophilia.org, 2001c). Tutoring at home and possibly at school is recommended to help the child compensate for lost school time. As precautionary measures to prevent injuries, some activities might have to be limited or avoided completely. Protective gear such as helmets and padding for elbows and knees should be available. This gear is especially important for smaller children so that the danger from hard toys and sharp edges can be minimized. To prevent the possible trauma to the child of a child abuse investigation, teachers, and care-providers must be educated about the symptoms of hemophilia. These symptoms include visible and recurring bruises and can easily be mistaken for damage resulting from child abuse (Hemophilia.org, 2001).

Due to the advances of modern medicine, individuals with hemophilia can lead happy and successful lives. Without medical attention, this condition is life threatening. There is no cure for hemophilia at this time.

## REFERENCES

Canadian Hemophilia Society. (2001). *The treatment of hemophilia.* Retrieved December 12, 2001, from http://www.hemophilia .ca/en/2.1.7.html

Cutler, T. S. (2001, June 7). *Hemophilia. eMedicine Journal, 2*(6). Retrieved December 27, 2001, from http://www.emedicine.com/ emerg/topic224.html

Greene, A. R. (2001a). *Disease: Hemophilia A.* Retrieved December 29, 2001, from http://sitemaker.medseek.com/websitefiles/ drgreene/body.cfm

Greene, A. R. (2001a). *Disease: Hemophilia B.* Retrieved December 29, 2001, from http://sitemaker.medseek.com/websitefiles/ drgreene/body.cfm

Harcourt Health Sciences. (2002). Hemophilia A & B. In *Mosby's medical, nursing, & allied health dictionary* (6th ed., pp. 800–801). St. Louis, MO: Author.

Hemophilia. (2000). In *Human diseases & conditions* (Vol. 2, pp. 434–438). New York: C. Scribner & Sons.

Hemophilia.org. (2001a). *Child abuse issues.* Retrieved December 13, 2001, from http://208.254.25.93/bdi/bdi_newly9.htm

Hemophilia.org. (2001b). *Information for teachers & childcare providers.* Retrieved December 13, 2001, from http://208.254.25.93/ bdi/bdi_providers.htm

Hemophilia.org. (2001c). *Psychological issues.* Retrieved December 13, 2001, from http://208.254.25.93/bdi/bdi_newly3.htm

Mayo Clinic. (2001, September 14). *Hemophilia.* Retrieved December 27, 2001, from http://www.mayoclinic.com/findinformation/ conditioncenters/invoke.cfm

MONIKA HANNON
*Colorado Springs, Colorado*

## HEMOPHILIA C

Hemophilia is a bleeding disorder in which there is a deficiency of selected proteins in the body's blood-clotting system. "Clotting is the process by which your blood changes from a liquid to a solid state in order to stop bleeding" (Mayo Clinic, 2001). There are three main types of hemophilia in which a different clotting factor is missing or deficient. In the most common type, Hemophilia A, clotting Factor VIII is missing or deficient. In Hemophilia B, Factor IX is missing or deficient, and in Hemophilia C, Factor XI is missing or deficient. All three types can cause prolonged bleeding.

Hemophilia is an inherited sex-linked genetic defect in which a defective X chromosome is passed from a mother to her male child. Males cannot pass along the gene that causes hemophilia to their sons because the defect is located on the X chromosome, which is inherited from the mother. In extremely rare cases, a girl may be born with hemophilia, but only if a man with hemophilia has children with a female carrier whose defective X chromosome is passed to the female child. A 1998 study estimated that one of every 5,000 boys of all races born in the United States has some form of hemophilia. The National Hemophilia Foundation estimates that more than 16,000 males in America have hemophilia, whereas in females, the incidence is only 1 in 1 million (Willett, 2001).

Characteristics of hemophilia C may include:

1. Abnormal bruising and bleeding.
2. Spontaneous hemorrhages into various joints—knees, elbows, ankles, and hips.
3. Possible limitation of movement and swelling.
4. Internal bleeding.
5. Patient may also suffer from chronic arthritis, anemia, gastritis, and epistaxis (severe and chronic nosebleeds).

There is no cure for hemophilia—it is a lifelong condition. Treatment involves injecting the blood clotting factor that is missing into the patient's blood. Clotting factors can be injected on a regular preventive basis in an attempt to keep bleeding from occurring. Prior to the mid-1980s, it was more common for people with hemophilia to become infected with the HIV virus or with hepatitis because of contaminated blood products. The risk of infection through blood products has decreased, however, because of genetically engineered clotting products called recombinant factors, which are free of infection (Mayo Clinic, 2001). With regular injections, even persons with severe cases of hemophilia can lead near-normal lives.

Students with hemophilia could qualify for special education services under the category of Other Health Impairment. The student would most likely require a health plan so that school personnel are adequately prepared in emergencies. It is important that anyone who takes care of the child knows about the condition. The role of the school psychologist is to provide support for the student and his or her family in the form of counseling. The school psychologist could also provide education to the staff and other students about hemophilia in order to reduce the amount of misinformation that others may have about the disease.

Future research for hemophilia appears to be in the area of genetic therapy. There is also research being conducted into understanding the makeup of the factor VIII protein that is used during treatment.

## REFERENCES

Katz, A. (1970). *Hemophilia: A study in hope and reality.* Springfield, IL: Charles C. Thomas.

Mayo Clinic. (2001). *Hemophilia.* Retrieved November 2001, from http://www.mayoclinic.com/findinformation/diseaseand conditions

Willett, E. (2001). *Hemophilia.* Berkeley Heights, NJ: Enslow Publishers.

CHRISTINE D. CDE BACA
*University of Northern Colorado*

# HERPES SIMPLEX I AND II

Although clinically and pathologically described as early as 100 BCE, herpesvirus hominus (HVH) was not identified until the 1920s; the existence of two antigenic types was not known until the 1960s; and genital herpes was not recognized as a venereal disease until the late 1960s. In the past, infections above and below the waist have generally been attributed to oral herpes (HVH-1) and genital herpes (HVH-2), respectively. However, the site of the infection does not always point to the particular type of herpes. HVH-1 and 2 now appear in both genital and oral areas, perhaps owing to increased frequency of oral-genital sexual contact (Bahr, 1978). Oral herpes most commonly causes cold sores in infants and children; however, it may cause eye infections and lesions on the fingers as well. Genital herpes has serious effects on both affected individuals and the offspring of affected women; both types of effects are described in this entry.

Genital herpes is a highly contagious and prevalent venereal disease characterized by the appearance of pus-containing sores in the genital region. In 1994, the herpes simplex virus had infected an estimated 45 million Americans. Prevalence has quintupled among white teenagers since 1988, and one out of five Americans twelve years of age or older may be infected with the virus (Fleming et al., 1997). Genital lesions are the most common symptom of herpes in adolescents (Margo & Shaughnessy, 1998). With society's changing mores regarding sexual activity outside of marriage and increasing acceptance of oral sex, as well as increasing numbers of sexual partners, the number of people, including adolescents, with genital manifestations of both genital and oral herpes will probably remain high.

The transfer of genital herpes usually occurs through genital or oral-genital contact. Autoinoculation from infected to uninfected areas of the body commonly occurs through touching the infected area during masturbation, washing, or inspection (Himell, 1981). Inanimate objects such as toilet seats, towels, and medical equipment are generally believed not to contribute to the spread of the herpes virus (Lukas & Corey, 1977), although the virus may survive for up to 72 hours on such objects (Eastman, 1983).

## Genital Herpes in Adults

### Symptoms and Progression of the Infection

Active infection begins, on average, six days after exposure (range 2 to 20 days) and lasts approximately three weeks, with symptoms most severe between days 10 and 14. Once in the person, the virus can be reactivated with symptoms lasting 10 to 21 days. The first manifestation of the infection is generally the longest and most severe; subsequent infections are shorter and less painful. Patients experience an average of four recurrences a year (Himell, 1981). Local itching and tingling and painful urination are followed by the appearance of painful, blistered red lesions. In females, the lesions may appear on the vulva or vaginal surface, thighs, buttocks, and lower back; in males, the lesions may appear on the penis, thighs, or buttocks. The blisters may open into shallow, open ulcerated areas which eventually heal without scarring. Other occasional symptoms include enlarged lymph glands, fever, and headaches (Ross, 1997). Genital and oral herpes have been linked with carcinoma of the cervix and lip, respectively. In addition, the occurrence of spontaneous abortion during the first trimester of pregnancy is three times greater in women who have genital herpes (Naib, Nahmias, Josey, & Wheeler, 1970).

Herpes increases the risk of acquiring HIV, a virus that causes AIDS, because herpes provides a point of easy entry into the body. In people who have suppressed immune systems, outbreaks can be extremely severe and linger for a much greater amount of time (Schacker et al., 1998).

### Friendship and Family Living Concerns

Adolescents with genital herpes are frequently concerned about transmitting the disease to close friends or family members. This may be a genuine concern. However, careful and precise hygienic methods usually prevent the spread of the infection. The herpes victim should thoroughly clean bathroom facilities after using them. During periods when the disease is active or their genital sores are at the weeping stage, victims should not bathe with others in hot tubs or sit on edges of hot tubs and swimming pools.

Because of possible recurrences of infection, genital herpes victims sometimes fear that family members and friends will learn about their disease. If victims understand that direct and intimate sexual contact is the primary mode of transmission, these fears may be reduced.

People with herpes infections of the lips should not kiss anyone, particularly babies, until sores are healed, and should wash their hands well before handling a baby (Ross, 1997).

### Pharmacological Treatment

As of yet, no cure for the herpes simplex virus is available. Two types of drug intervention are currently being used for treatment. Acute therapy involves taking a drug to diminish the symptoms of an outbreak, as well as to reduce the duration of the occurrence. This type of therapy requires taking medication for a short length of time, beginning immediately with the first signs of a potential outbreak. The other alternative is suppressive therapy, which requires a daily dose of medication to help prevent reactivation of the virus.

In previous years, the medication acyclovir (Zovirax) was the only option available for treatment. Acyclovir is available by prescription only, and is offered in both oral and topical forms. It works by impeding the spread of the virus in cells without damaging normal cells (Griffith, 1996).

The U.S. Food and Drug Administration has approved two drugs for treatment of the virus. Famciclovir (Famvir) and Valacyclovir (Valtrex) are being prescribed more frequently than acyclovir. They have been proven to be more effective in absorption by the body, and require fewer daily doses for effectiveness. Famciclovir has proven to be especially useful in suppressive therapy (Diaz-Mitorna et al.,

1998). Acyclovir is still regularly prescribed for treatment of herpes infections in newborns (Margo & Shaughnessy, 1998). Treatment with any three of the antiviral medications for five days will cost $70–80 (Margo & Shaughnessy, 1998).

### Sexual Concerns

Having genital herpes does not mean that victims are always infectious; appropriate care can minimize the possibility of transmitting the disease to sexual partners. Prevention should begin with the prodrome, the tingling or itching sensation that many victims have several hours or days before sores are seen. The prodrome state may be infectious itself, and should be thought of as the beginning of the contagious period. Therefore, no oral-genital or genital sexual intercourse should occur from the start of the prodrome to the completion of the healing process as indicated by the disappearance of lesions. Condoms do not prevent the transmission of the disease during an outbreak because the virus can pass through the pores in the condom.

Incidence of cervical herpes has dramatically increased. Females are generally not aware that they have the disease until a gynecological examination has been performed. Since the cervix contains few nerve endings, the victim does not experience the discomfort usually associated with genital herpes. A vaginal discharge may occur, and this usually motivates the woman to seek medical attention. Since these victims do not experience the prodrome or discomfort, they may be unaware that they are having a recurrence. At the first signs of sores on the cervix, restriction of sexual behavior becomes necessary. Health care providers can teach women to perform pelvic self-examinations to enable them to recognize cervical lesions. Also, female victims should be aware that they can spread the virus to the cervix during outbreaks if they use tampons.

Herpes victims also should be aware that having the disease does not immunize against reinfection, as is frequently the case with other diseases. Thus a herpes victim can be reinfected by having sexual relations with a partner who is experiencing a genital herpes attack.

### Psychological Consequences

Herpes can have serious psychological consequences, especially for adolescents. Luby (1981) has noted a sequence of responses to genital herpes: (1) shock and emotional numbing; (2) search for an immediate cure; (3) development of feelings of isolation and loneliness and fear that companionship, sexual relations, and children are not in one's future; (4) anger, which can reach homicidal proportions, directed toward the person who is believed to be the transmitter of the disease (at this point fear generalizes and anxiety may result); (5) a "leper" effect, accompanied by depression, which may deepen with time and recurrences. Common feelings at this point include hopelessness, guilt, unworthiness, and self-hatred. Finally, developing herpes can make manifest any latent psychopathology.

Not all victims are emotionally affected, but for many adolescents, it can become a psychologically crippling experience. Individual counseling or membership in a herpes self-help group may be helpful. Herpes self-help groups generally work to achieve several goals, including relief from isolation and loneliness, establishment of a new social network, provision of mentors, and ventilation of rage. If depression with sleep disorder, loss of appetite, psychotic symptoms, or suicidal ideation occur, a psychiatric referral may be required (Luby, 1981). Stress of a variety of kinds appears to increase reactivation of the infection (Keller, Shiflett, Schleifer, & Bartlett, 1994).

### Suggestions for Working with Affected Students

Teachers, coaches and others who work with students who have herpes can help by being sympathetic listeners and having an understanding of the disease that enables them to dispel myths and untruths regarding herpes. Also, they can help students develop a realistic view of their situation by stressing that the disease can be medically managed and is not fatal.

Adolescents' self-esteem can be deeply affected. If this occurs, referral to the school's guidance counselor or family physician should be arranged. Suicide cannot be ruled out. The teacher or coach should not hesitate in making a referral to the guidance counselor or to a mental health professional if emotional disturbances are noted. Remind the victims that they need to isolate active lesions, not themselves.

### Effects of Congenital Herpes on Offspring

Transmission from mother to newborn is much more likely if it is the mother's first episode (Margo & Shaughnessy, 1998). Genital herpes may have devastating effects on affected newborns. Although frequently classified with other maternal infections in the STORCH complex (Syphilis, Toxiplasmosis, varicella and other infections, Rubella, Cytomegalovirus, and Herpes; e.g., Graham & Morgan, 1997), herpes generally affects newborns during birth rather than prenatally. Of affected infants, 85 percent contract the infection during birth as they pass through an infected maternal genital tract or contact the virus through ruptured fetal-maternal membranes, about 10 percent contract it later, and 5 percent earlier in utero. Risk of infection of newborns during birth is about 50 percent among women who have an active initial infection during labor and delivery, about 5–10 percent among women with recurrent symptoms or lesions present, and less than 1 percent for women with recurrent infection but asymptomatic at delivery (Graham & Morgan, 1997). Women with herpes lesions in the genital area at the time of delivery are delivered by cesarean section to reduce the likelihood of transmission to the offspring.

Symptoms of perinatal infection, which may or may not include the presence of vesicles, appear a few days after birth. The severity ranges from mild skin infection to death. Common symptoms include irritability, jaundice, and respiratory distress. If untreated, about 75 percent of affected infants will develop the disseminated infection or encephalitis with a consequent mortality rate of about 70 percent. Even with antiviral treatment, about 60 percent of infants with disseminated infections die (Graham & Morgan, 1997). Most survivors show serious sequelae such as mental retardation, epilepsy, and sensory impairments (Douglas, 1985). Infants with congenital herpes infection acquired prenatally show signs common to the STORCH complex, including growth delay, microcephaly, microphthalmia, chorioretinitis, and seizures (Douglas, 1985; Graham & Morgan, 1997).

Assistance can be found at a local chapter of HELP. If there is no local phone number, contact the National Herpes Resource Center, PO Box 100, Palo Alto, CA, 94302.

### REFERENCES

Bahr, J. (1978). Herpesvirus hominis type 2 in women and newborns. *American Journal of Maternal Child Nursing*, pp. 16–18.

Diaz-Mitorna, F., Sibbald, R. G., Shafran, S. D., Edmonton, A., Boon, R., & Saltzman, R. L. (1998). Oral Famciclovir for the suppression of recurrent genital herpes. *Journal of the American Medical Association, 280*, 861–944.

Douglas, R. G., Jr. (1985). Herpes simplex virus infections. In J. G. Wyngaarden & L. H. Smith, Jr. (Eds.), *Cecil textbook of medicine* (17th ed., pp. 1714–1717). Philadelphia: Saunders.

Fleming, D. T., McQuillan, G. M., Johnson, R. E., Nahmias, A. J., Aral, S. O., Lee, F. K., & St. Louis, M. E. (1997). Herpes simplex virus 2 in the U.S.: 1976–1994. *New England Journal of Medicine, 337*, 1106–1111.

Graham, E. M., & Morgan, M. A. (1997). Growth before birth. In M. L. Batshaw (Ed.), *Children with disabilities* (4th ed., pp. 53–69). Baltimore: Brookes.

Griffith, H. W. (1996). *Complete guide to prescription and nonprescription drugs*. Triangle Park: Putnam Berkeley.

Himell, K. (1981). Genital herpes: The need for counseling. *Journal of General Nursing*, pp. 446–447.

Keller, S. E., Shiflett, S. C., Schleifer, S. J., & Bartlett, J. A. (1994). Stress, immunity, and health. In R. Glaser & J. Kiecolt-Glaser (Eds.), *Handbook of human stress and immunity* (pp. 217–244). San Diego, CA: Academic.

Luby, E. (1981). Presentation at the National Genital Herpes Symposium. Philadelphia. *The Helper, 3*(4), 2–3.

Lukas, J., & Corey, L. (1977). Genital herpes simplex virus infection: An overview. *Nurse Practitioner, 7*, 7–10.

Margo, K. L., & Shaughnessy, A. F. (1998). Antiviral drugs in healthy children. *American Family Physician, 57*, 1073–1077.

Naib, Z., Nahmias, A., Josey, W., & Wheeler, J. (1970). Association of maternal genital herpetic-infection with spontaneous abortion. *Obstetrics & Gynecology, 35*, 260–263.

Ross, L. M. (1997). *Sexually transmitted diseases sourcebook.* Detroit, MI: Omnigraphics.

Schacker, T., Ryncarz, A. J., Goddard, J., Diem, K., Shaughnessy, M., & Corey, L. (1998). Frequent recovery of HIV-1 from genital herpes simplex virus lesions in HIV-1 infected men. *Journal of the American Medical Association, 280,* 61–66.

C. SUE LAMB
KATHERINE FALWELL
ROBERT T. BROWN
*University of North Carolina at Wilmington*

## DEPRESSION, CHILDHOOD AND ADOLESCENT

## TORCH COMPLEX

## HESS, ROBERT (1920–1993)

Robert Hess received his BA at the University of California at Berkeley in 1947 and his PhD in developmental psychology at the University of Chicago in 1950. He was the Lee L. Jacks Professor Emeritus of Child Education at Stanford University and codirector of the graduate training program in Interactive Educational Technology. Robert Hess died in 1993 at the age of 73.

Hess' major interests focused on the relationships of teachers who interact with young children's home lives, external realities, and inner lives within the atmosphere of the classroom. He believed that the future of a society rests in its ability to train or socialize the young. He held that the growth of programs in early education and the large-scale involvement of schools and the federal government represented a fundamental shift in the relative roles and potential influence of the two major socializing institutions of society, the family and the school (Hess & Bear, 1968). Thus, he saw the need for social experimentation in order to deal effectively with this shift.

Hess was best known for his work in the late 1950s and early 1960s at the University of Chicago. There he conducted a number of studies on the environmental deprivation of children in poverty, consequently helping to establish the theoretical background for Head Start and other similar government programs. Later research included a 1965 study of communication and instruction methods used by mothers with their children and a longitudinal cross-cultural study, conducted in the 1970s in Japan and the United States, on the interactions of mothers and their children. The latter was one of the first major collaborations between child development researchers in the two countries.

In later years, Hess' interests broadened to include research involving the use of computers in the classroom. Results of this work indicated a distinct gender gap in computer interest and usage among young people.

Some of his major writings include *Early Education: Current Theory, Research, and Action* (1968), *Family Worlds: A Psychosocial Approach to Family Life* (1995), and *Teachers of Young Children* (1972).

### REFERENCES

Hess, R. D., & Bear, R. M. (1968). *Early education: Current theory, research, and action.* Chicago: Aldine.

Hess, R. D., & Croft, D. J. (1972). *Teachers of young children.* Boston: Houghton Mifflin.

Hess, R. D., & Handel, G. (1995). *Family worlds: A psychosocial approach to family life.* Lanham, MD: University Press.

ELIZABETH JONES
*Texas A&M University*
First edition

TAMARA J. MARTIN
*The University of Texas of the Permian Basin*
Second edition

## HETEROPHORIA

See STRABISMUS, EFFECT ON LEARNING.

## HEWETT, FRANK M. (1927– )

Frank M. Hewett received his MA in 1958 and PhD in 1961 in clinical psychology from the University of California in Los Angeles (UCLA). He remained at UCLA as principal of the Neuropsychiatric Institute School until 1964. He then joined the faculty in the Graduate School of Education, gaining his present status of professor of education and psychiatry in 1971.

Hewett's work has mainly dealt with the emotionally disturbed population, and his contribution to the area of learning disabilities has been described as vital (Haring & Bateman, 1977, p. 47). Instead of entering the debate on the definition or etiology of learning disabilities, Hewett has sought educational strategies that allow a wider portion of public school children to learn effectively and efficiently. From a generalist orientation, he developed a sequence of educational tasks that delineate six levels of learning competence (Hewett & Taylor, 1980). These levels of learning competence are a synthesis of work on developmental stages done by Kephart, Piaget, Maslow, Freud, and others. Hewett's competence levels were operations directly related to classroom learning (Haring & Bateman, 1977). Hewett's principal publications include *Education of Exceptional*

*Learners* and *The Emotionally Disturbed Child in the Classroom: The Orchestration of Success.*

## REFERENCES

Haring, N. G., & Bateman, B. (1977). *Teaching the learning disabled child.* Englewood Cliffs, NJ: Prentice Hall.

Hewett, F. M. (1987). The ecological view of disturbed children: Shadow versus substance. *Pointer, 31,* 61–63.

Hewett, F. M. (1988). The engineered classroom re-visited. In R. B. Rutherford & C. M. Nelson (Eds.), *Bases of severe behavioral disorders in children and youth* (pp. 283–289). Boston: College-Hill Press/Little, Brown.

Hewett, F. M., & Forness, S. (1984). *Education of exceptional learners* (3rd ed.). Boston: Allyn & Bacon.

Hewett, F. M., & Taylor, F. (1980). *The emotionally disturbed child in the classroom: The orchestration of success* (2nd ed.). Boston: Allyn & Bacon.

Elaine Fletcher-Janzen
*University of Colorado at Colorado Springs*
First edition

Marie Almond
*The University of Texas of the Permian Basin*
Second edition

# HIGHER EDUCATION, MINORITY STUDENTS WITH DISABILITIES AND

College campuses are quickly becoming multiracial, multicultural, and multilingual societies (Sue, Arredondo, & McDavis, 1992). The number of students with disabilities and the number of minority students entering colleges and universities are increasing. It is natural to assume that the two groups will overlap; however, research devoted to ethnic/racial minorities with disabilities in higher education is limited. While special education in public schools continues to battle the overrepresentation of minority students in special education programs, institutions of higher education often fail to acknowledge the presence of minorities with disabilities and their needs for specialized attention. This is exhibited when disability service providers fail to recognize the need for service provision appropriate to the individual student's culture.

Disability service providers in higher education must recognize the need for multicultural awareness and prepare themselves for the pivotal role they may play in the success of minority students with disabilities. Sue and Sue (1990) indicate that preparation for this type of role involves confronting, becoming aware of, and taking actions in dealing with personal biases, stereotypes, values, and assumptions about human behavior, as well as being aware of the culturally different student's worldview, values, and assumptions about human behavior. Harry (1992) adds that it is perhaps more important for service professionals to recognize the cultural base of their own belief systems than to know the particular characteristics of any one cultural group.

Section 504 of the Rehabilitation Act of 1973 and the Americans with Disabilities Act of 1990 provide for reasonable accommodations and program access for students with disabilities in postsecondary settings. How these services are offered to the university community can be crucial in a university's ability to relate to a culturally diverse student population. For example, many minority group individuals find one-on-one counseling very formal, removed, and even intimidating (Sue et al., 1992).

Ponterotto (1991) further explains that traditional models of education are ethnocentric in that they embrace white middle-class values (e.g., individualism, competition, time linearity) as the norm toward which all cultures are expected to acculturate. Even within colleges and universities that host international student populations, this philosophy of education holds true. Some minority groups will struggle to conform to these guidelines of seemingly appropriate behavior. For example, strict adherence to a timetable for appointments, project deadlines, and classes is expected of all college students. However, this rigid timetable may go against some cultures, which may mark time by events rather than by the clock or calendar (Sue et al., 1992). Additionally, the dominant mode of U.S. schools has been referred to as the "culture of competition," to which students from more cooperatively oriented cultures must adapt (Trueba, 1989).

Disability issues can be extremely personal to any individual, but the impact of self-disclosing a disability and requesting assistance in dealing with the disability may be overwhelming to college students of a different culture. The vast majority of disability service providers in higher education expect the student with a disability to exhibit some degree of openness. They encourage the student with a disability to talk about or discuss intimate aspects of the disability. This forces the student with a disability to be the primary active participant in the discussion. Sue and Sue (1990) tell us that in some cultural groups, subtlety is a valued art. This type of verbal discussion would be considered offensive or arrogant, yet the opposite behaviors would be considered evidence of passivity and the need for the individual to learn assertiveness skills (Sue & Sue). It is essential, as Harry (1992) states, that "professionals . . . understand the tension that exists between an outsider's and an insider's view of minority people's experience: the dimensions of power/powerlessness, traditional/atraditional, cultural pride/cultural shame . . ." (p. 23).

A disability in any culture is considered different than the norm; however, disability service providers must continually be aware that there is no universal measure of normality. This notion must be accepted for all cultures. It will continue to be essential that professionals working with multicultural students with disabilities be sensitive to concepts of disability and to traditional communication patterns among different cultural groups. We must understand and respect the traditional values of these cultures while succeeding in achieving collaboration between disability service provider and student.

## REFERENCES

Harry, B. (1992). *Cultural diversity, families, and the special education system: Communication and empowerment.* New York: Teachers College Press.

Ponterotto, J. G. (1991). The nature of prejudice revisited: Implications for counseling intervention. *Journal of Counseling & Development, 70,* 216–224.

Sue, D. W., Arredondo, P., & McDavis, R. J. (1992). Multicultural counseling competencies and standards: A call to the profession. *Journal of Counseling & Development, 70,* 477–486.

Sue, D. W., & Sue, D. (1990). *Counseling the culturally different* (2nd ed.). New York: Wiley.

Trueba, H. T. (1989). *Raising silent voices: Educating linguistic minorities for the 21st century.* Cambridge, MA: Newbury House.

ANNE REBER
*Texas A&M University*

## HIGH-INCIDENCE DISABILITIES

Although often used synonymously, the terms incidence and prevalence are not equivalent and therefore interchangeable use is erroneous. Marozas, May, and Lehman (1980) note that incidence represents new cases during some specified period of time (frequently one year), while prevalence denotes the total number of individuals affected at any particular point in time. Hypothetically, a school system might find 75 previously unidentified cases of learning disabilities during a specific academic year. If 150 previously identified cases are then added, prevalence is 225. This total may then be used to specify a prevalence rate; if the school system contains 10,000 students the prevalence rate is 225/10,000, or about 2 percent.

Prevalence and incidence need not reflect the same proportions of the population. For example, if an effective preventive technique could be found to prevent the occurrence of a disabling condition (but not remediate it), the incidence rate (new cases) approaches zero. However, the prevalence rate would fall off more gradually since existing cases would continue. The terms are related but distinct. Blurring the distinction can result in the development of inaccurate statistics or the erroneous interpretation of statistics.

The expression high-incidence disability refers to an exceptionally large proportion of a particular type of ex-

ceptionality during some particular period of time relative to the incidence of other conditions. The expression high incidence is arbitrarily defined, however, as no specific numerical proportion is required. Unfortunately, the special education literature provides mention of both high-incidence and high-prevalence disability; therefore, the reader must keep this distinction in mind.

## REFERENCE

Marozas, P. S., May, D. C., & Lehman, L. C. (1980). Incidence and prevalence: Confusion in need of clarification. *Mental Retardation, 18,* 229–230.

TED L. MILLER
*University of Tennessee at
Chattanooga*

## CATEGORICAL EDUCATION

## HIGH INTEREST–LOW VOCABULARY

High interest–low vocabulary refers to reading materials that have been designed to interest older students who have low vocabularies and low reading levels. Often, adolescents who have reading levels in the lower elementary grade levels become even more frustrated if given the reading books that have been designed for their reading levels. Such reading books can insult the adolescents because they are geared for the interest level of a third grader, not a ninth grader.

Many publishers have designed materials to deal with this problem. For example, the *Corrective Reading* series (Engelmann et al., 1978) was designed for students from fourth to twelfth grade who have not developed adequate reading, decoding, and comprehension skills. The vocabulary introduced in these stories was very controlled. Only word patterns that have been taught and practiced were included in the lessons (low vocabulary). More important, however, the interest level of the stories was geared to the older reader; the topics covered did not insult the older reader by assuming his or her interests were similar to those of a third grader.

Other published materials were also designed to be used as supplements for the older, lower reader's instructional program. Mercer and Mercer (1985) present a listing of 35 such materials, with corresponding reading grade levels and approximate interest grade levels. The *Pal Paperback Kits* (Xerox Education Publications) and the *Mystery Adventure Series* (Benefic Press) are two examples. These series, however, do not present as carefully sequenced phonetic skills as a linguistic basal reader series or *Corrective Reading* series previously mentioned.

Online resources for individuals interested in these types

of books and related products abound. The Resource Room, an online resource for special educators and parents, supplies a broad analysis of high-interest–low vocabulary books and rationale for their design. The Resource Room web site can be found at http://www.resourceroom.net/comprehension/idhilocomp.asp.

## REFERENCES

Engelmann, S., Johnson, G., Hanner, S., Carnine, L., Meyers, L., Osborn, S., Haddox, P., Becker, W., Osborn, W., & Becker, J. (1978). *Corrective reading program*. Chicago, IL: Science Research.

Mercer, C. D., & Mercer, A. R. (1985). *Teaching students with learning problems* (2nd ed.). Columbus, OH: Merrill.

Thomas E. Scruggs
Margo A. Mastropieri
*Purdue University*

**READING DISORDERS**
**READING IN THE CONTENT AREAS**
**READING REMEDIATION**

# HIGHLY QUALIFIED TEACHERS

The passage of the No Child Left Behind Act (NCLB) of 2001 marked a growing, bipartisan recognition to address the challenge of raising the academic achievement for all students. At the core of NCLB are measures designed to close achievement gaps between different groups of students, offering more flexibility to states, giving parents more options, and teaching students based on what works (Office of Elementary and Secondary Education, 2005). The NCLB, signed into law on January 8, 2002 (Tuerk, 2005), has expanded the federal role in education and set requirements in place that affect every public school in America. In order to meet the standard of high academic achievement for all students, NCLB issued the mandate that every child be instructed by a teacher who meets the rigorous standards for earning a "highly qualified" classification.

NCLB is the latest revision of the 1965 Elementary and Secondary Education Act (ESEA) and is regarded as the most significant federal education policy initiative in a generation (deBettencourt, 2004). Under the law's strong accountability provisions, states must describe how they will close the achievement gap and make sure all students, including those with disabilities, achieve academically. The specific goals of the law, as spelled out in the *Federal Register* issued on March 6, 2002, are as follows:

- All students will reach high standards, at a minimum attaining proficiency or better in reading and mathematics by 2013–2014.

- By 2013–2014, all students will be proficient in reading by the end of the third grade.
- All limited English proficient students will become proficient in English.
- All students will be educated in learning environments that are safe, drug free, and conducive to learning.
- All students will graduate from high school.

To help schools and districts meet these goals, the law provides a blend of requirements, incentives, and resources. The requirements include (Paige, 2004):

- Annual testing of all students against state standards in reading and mathematics in grades 3 to 8 and in science at three times in a student's school career (including once in high school).
- "Verification" of each state's assessment system via required participation (every other year) by selected districts in the NAEP test.
- Aggregate and disaggregate analysis and reporting of student achievement results.
- A state definition and timeline for determining whether a school, district, and the state are making "adequate yearly progress" (AYP) toward the goal of 100 percent of students meeting state standards by the 2013–2014 school year.
- Support for students not meeting standards and/or for those who have special needs (e.g., homeless, limited English proficiency).
- The use of "scientifically-based" programs and strategies.
- Technical assistance, and then sanctions, for schools, districts, and the state for failure to make AYP.
- Highly qualified teachers in core academic subjects by 2005–2006.
- Highly qualified aides or paraprofessionals.

## Highly Qualified Teachers

A major objective of NCLB is to ensure high-quality teachers for all students, regardless of race, ethnicity or income, because a well-prepared teacher is vitally important to a child's education (Rosenberg, Sindelar, & Hardman, 2004). In fact, research demonstrates the clear correlation between student academic achievement and teacher quality (Sanders & Rivers, 1996). Subsequent to the full implementation of the highly qualified mandate, all school principals are required by law to send a notification to each child's parent/guardian informing them if their child's teacher does not meet the mandate. According to Sanders and Rivers, parents should never hesitate to inquire within their school and district about the qualifications of teachers instructing their children.

The purpose of NCLB is to help states and school districts ensure that all students have highly qualified teachers; that is, teachers with the subject matter knowledge and teaching skills necessary to help all children achieve high academic standards, regardless of individual learning styles or needs. The NCLB Act requires local school districts to ensure that all teachers hired to teach core academic subjects after the first day of the 2002–2003 school year are highly qualified (Paige, 2004). The requirements to be considered "highly qualified" are threefold (Office of Elementary and Secondary Education, 2005): (1) teachers should hold at least a bachelor's degree; (2) teachers should be fully licensed by the State; and (3) teachers should demonstrate competency in each core subject area in which they teach. According to NCLB, core subjects include English, reading or language arts, mathematics, science, foreign languages, civics and government, economics, arts, history and geography. NCLB also calls for all teachers of the core academic subjects (teaching in Title I programs or elsewhere) to be highly qualified by the end of school year 2005–2006 (Paige, 2004).

Current teachers do not have to return to school or take a test in every subject to demonstrate that they meet highly qualified requirements. NCLB allows states to create an alternative method (High, Objective, Uniform State Standard of Evaluation or HOUSSE) for teachers not new to the field—as determined by each state—to certify that they know the subject they teach by demonstrating content-related competencies that recognize, among other things, the experience, expertise, and professional training garnered over time in the profession (Paige, 2004).

## Highly Qualified Provisions for Special Education Teachers

NCLB does not differentiate between special educators and general educators. This is most evident within the recent reauthorization of the Individuals with Disabilities Act, known as the Individuals with Disabilities Education Improvement Act (IDEIA). IDEIA specifies the requirements for a highly qualified special education teacher in that only special education teachers who teach core academic subjects must meet highly qualified teacher requirements (Mooney, Denny, & Gunter, 2004). The professionals who do *NOT* need to meet highly qualified requirements include the following (Paige, 2004): (1) special education teachers who provide consultation to teachers of core academic subjects by adapting curricula or selecting appropriate teaching strategies/accommodations; (2) resource room teachers who do not teach core academic subjects for a grade or credit; and (3) special education teachers who team teach in a general education classroom (this also holds true whether the special education teacher gives the grade for the team-taught class). If a special education teacher is providing direct instruction in multiple subject areas at the secondary level, he or she *MUST* satisfy the highly qualified definition at the secondary

level for each of those content areas (Office of Elementary and Secondary Education, 2005). A teacher at the secondary level can demonstrate his or her qualifications if they meet one or more of the following requirements (deBettencourt, 2004): (1) a major in the subject they teach; (2) a minimum of 24 credit hours of professional development courses that are equivalent to a major in the subject; (3) passage of a state-developed test; (4) a graduate degree; (5) an advanced certification from the state; or (6) HOUSSE. HOUSSE allows current teachers to demonstrate subject matter competency and meet highly qualified teacher requirements. Proof may consist of a combination of teaching experience, professional development, and knowledge in the subject garnered over time in the profession (deBettencourt).

## Conclusion

An integral component within NCLB is that it will provide substantial funding to help states and districts recruit, train, reward, and retain effective teachers, toward ensuring that teachers of core academic subjects meet certain minimum requirements they need to become effective educators. To further the goal of having a highly qualified teacher in every classroom, traditional approaches for preparing teachers must be expanded to include preparation programs that are innovative and nontraditional and can be made available to ". . . *anyone, anytime, and anywhere*" (Paige, 2004, p. 39). States should be provided with financial assistance in the form of personnel preparation grants, which can prompt this innovation and reform. Through these efforts, the goal of providing all students with highly qualified teachers will be achieved.

**REFERENCES**

deBettencourt, L. (2004). Critical issues in training special education teachers. *Exceptionality, 12,* 193–194.

Mooney, P., Denny, R., & Gunter, P. (2004). The impact of NCLB and the reauthorization of IDEA on academic instruction of students with emotional or behavioral disorders. *Behavioral Disorders, 29,* 237–246.

Office of Elementary and Secondary Education. (2005). *Improving teacher quality state grants: Non-regulatory guidance.* U.S. Department of Education. Retrieved from www.ed.gov/programs/teacherqual/

Paige, R. (2004). *The secretary's third annual report on teacher quality.* U.S. Department of Education, Office of Postsecondary Education. Retrieved from http://www.ed.gov/about/reports/annual/teachprep/2004Title2-Report.pdf

Rosenberg, M., Sindelar, P., & Hardman, M. (2004). Preparing highly qualified teachers for students with emotional or behavioral disorders: The impact of NCLB and IDEA. *Behavioral Disorders, 29,* 266–278.

Sanders, W., & Rivers, J. (1996). *Cumulative and residual effects of teachers on future academic achievement.* Knoxville: University of Tennessee Value-Added Research and Assessment Center.

Tuerk, P. (2005). Research in the high-stakes era: Achievement, resources, and no child left behind. *Psychological Science, 16,* 419–425.

JULIE A. ARMENTROUT
*University of Colorado at Colorado Springs*

## INDIVIDUALS WITH DISABILITIES EDUCATION IMPROVEMENT ACT OF 2004 (IDEIA)
## RESPONSE TO INTERVENTION

## HIGH RISK

The phrase high risk refers to a baby at risk for the development of a disability owing to factors present prior to conception, during pregnancy, delivery, or the first three years of life. Presently, couples contemplating having a baby take a 3 to 5 percent chance of producing a high-risk child (Deppe, Sherman, & Engel, 1981). This percentage can be reduced by developing awareness of factors that can place a child at risk and taking steps to minimize their impact.

The first set of factors that place a child at risk occurs prior to conception and is hereditary in nature. Hereditary factors include the genetic history of both parents. Specifically, parents may produce a high-risk child if either has a mentally or physically disabled child in the extended family; is a known or suspected carrier of a chromosome abnormality; is black or of Jewish or Mediterranean descent. In addition, hereditary factors include previous miscarriages during the first trimester of pregnancy and a maternal age greater than 35 at the time of anticipated birth. Couples falling into any of these categories may seek genetic counseling to estimate the risk of occurrence of a genetic disorder, understand options available for dealing with the risk, decide on a course of action, and increase their knowledge of diagnosis, prognosis, and management techniques available.

The second set of factors increasing the probability of producing a high-risk child occurs during pregnancy. Specific factors include maternal malnutrition, use of alcohol or drugs, smoking, and exposure to diseases. Maternal malnutrition has been related to mental retardation, cerebral palsy, and learning disabilities. Use of alcohol during pregnancy has been linked to mental retardation, joint distortions, facial abnormalities, and congenital heart disease (Furey, 1982; Merck, 2003). Medicine purchased over the counter or by prescription may adversely influence the health of a baby. For example, disabled babies were born to women using thalidomide. Similarly, there is an increased incidence of vaginal cancer in young women whose mothers used diethylstilbestrol to prevent miscarriages. Other drugs,

such as heroin, have been linked to an increased incidence of low birth weight, intrauterine growth, retardation, and prematurity (Crain, 1984; Merck, 2003). Smoking has been associated with smaller birth weight and may be a factor in sudden infant death syndrome. Exposure to diseases such as German measles is associated with visual impairments, hearing impairments, and heart disease. Couples anticipating the birth of a child can take precautionary steps to reduce the chance of producing a high-risk baby. These steps include proper diet, use of medicines only under the supervision of a physician, limited consumption of alcohol, and no cigarette or drug use.

The third set of factors associated with the birth of high-risk babies occurs during the perinatal period. These factors include the use of an anesthesia, hemorrhage, knotting of the umbilical cord, and shock owing to loss of blood in the mother (Cartwright, Cartwright, & Ward, 1995; Merck, 2003). All of these factors may cause fetal anoxia (lack of oxygen), resulting in mental retardation, cerebral palsy, or convulsive disorders.

Finally, factors placing a child at high risk may occur from birth to 3 years of age and include physical trauma, deprivation, and severe infection. Physical traumas such as accidents may result in brain damage or a physical disability. Similarly, children who suffer nonaccidental injuries such as child abuse may be brain damaged, physically disabled, or emotionally disturbed. Deprivation includes physical neglect (e.g., inadequate levels of medical attention, food, clothing, supervision, and housing) and emotional neglect (an environment nonconducive to a child's learning and development). Severe infections such as meningitis, rheumatic fever, or encephalitis frequently result in hearing impairments, heart damage, or convulsive disorders. Many of the factors placing a child at risk from birth to three years of age can be controlled by parents or professionals. Careful supervision of young children, adequate physical and emotional care, and prompt medical attention can minimize the impact of high-risk factors during the first three years of life.

The U.S. National Library of Medicine and the National Institutes of Health provide prodigious resources concerning high-risk situations on MedlinePlus at http://www.nim.nih.gov/medlineplus/highriskpregnancy.html

### REFERENCES

Cartwright, G. P., Cartwright, C. A., & Ward, M. E. (1995). *Educating special learners.* Belmont, CA: Wadsworth.

Crain, L. S. (1984). Prenatal causes of atypical development. In M. J. Hanson (Ed.), *Atypical infant development* (pp. 27–55). Baltimore: University Park Press.

Deppe, P. R., Sherman, J. L., & Engel, S. (1981). *The high risk child: A guide for concerned parents.* New York: Macmillan.

Furey, E. M. (1982). The effects of alcohol on the fetus. *Exceptional Children, 49,* 30–34.

Merck. (2003). *Risk factors that develop during pregnancy*. Retrieved February 14, 2006, from http://www.merck.com/mmhe/sec22/ch258/ch258c.html

MAUREEN A. SMITH
*Pennsylvania State University*

GENETIC COUNSELING
HIGH-RISK REGISTRY
PREMATURITY

# HIGH-RISK REGISTRY

A high-risk registry is based on the premise that early identification of infants and young children with disabilities is critical to the success of an early intervention treatment program. The registry contains factors associated with an increased risk for the development of a handicapping condition (Feinmesser & Tell, 1974). These factors typically include birth weight of less than 1500 gr; billirubin level of less than 20 mg/100 ml of serums; exposure to or the presence of bacterial infections such as meningitis; exposure to or the presence of nonbacterial infections such as rubella or herpes; multiple apneic spells; and 5-minute Apgar scores less than 5.

The Apgar score (Apgar, 1953) is a simple measure of neonatal risk routinely obtained during the medical assessment of a newborn infant 1 and 5 minutes after delivery. The infant's heart rate, respiration, reflex irritability, muscle tone, and skin color are rated on the basis of 0, 1, or 2. For example, a heart rate between 100 and 140 beats per minute is rated a 2, while a heart rate less than 100 beats per minute is rated 1; no heartbeat is rated 0. A composite score reflects the infant's ability to adapt to the postnatal environment (Gorski, 1984). Scores under 3 at the five minute Apgar assessment predict quite certainly that neurodevelopmental impairments and learning difficulties will be present later on in life (Moster, Lie, & Markestad, 2002).

The staff at a hospital participating in a high-risk registry typically completes a card after each live birth. Information regarding birth weight, billirubin levels, the presence of bacterial or nonbacterial infections, apneic spells, and Apgar scores is provided by the obstetric staff or the attending physician. Maternal interviews provide additional information regarding exposure to bacterial or nonbacterial infections and any parental concern for the health of the baby. The presence of any one of these factors tentatively identifies an infant as at risk and warrants referral for additional evaluation at 6, 9, and 12 months of age. If during subsequent evaluation, the baby no longer displays any abnormal characteristics, and if parents express no concern, the baby's name is removed from the files. If subsequent evaluation does indicate the presence of a disability, the

parents are encouraged to pursue additional assessment, a medical evaluation, and a treatment program.

## REFERENCES

Apgar, V. (1953). A proposal for a new method of resolution of the newborn infant. *Current Researchers in Anesthesia & Analgesia, 32*, 260–267.

Feinmesser, M., & Tell, L. (1974). Evaluation of methods for detecting hearing impairment in infancy and early childhood. In G. T. Mencher (Ed.), *Early identification of hearing loss* (pp. 102–113). Pratteln, Switzerland: Thur AG Offsetdruck.

Gorski, P. A. (1984). Infants at risk. In M. J. Hanson (Ed.), *Atypical infant development* (pp. 59–75). Baltimore: University Park Press.

Moster, D., Lie, R. T., & Markestad, T. (2002). Joint association of Apgar scores and early neonatal symptoms with minor disabilities at school age. *Archives of Disease in Childhood Fetal and Neonatal Edition, 86*, 16–21.

MAUREEN A. SMITH
*Pennsylvania State University*

EARLY EXPERIENCE AND CRITICAL PERIODS
EARLY IDENTIFICATION OF CHILDREN WITH
  DISABILITIES
HIGH RISK
INFANT STIMULATION
PREMATURITY

# HIRSCHSPRUNG DISEASE

Hirschsprung disease is a congenital genetic disorder characterized by a lack of nerve cells in a segment of the bowel resulting in constipation, diarrhea, and abdominal distention. This condition was originally named for Harold Hirschsprung, a Danish physician in Copenhagen who first described the disease in 1886 (Passarge, 1993). It is also referred to as aganglionic megacolon.

Hirschsprung disease is caused by the absence of nerve cells, called ganglia, in the wall of the intestines. From the fifth to the twelfth week of pregnancy, nerve cells form in a downward manner through the alimentary tract from the mouth to the anus. These nerve cells control the squeezing and relaxation of the intestinal wall, which moves the stool through the bowel. In the baby with Hirschsprung disease, the downward migration of nerve cells is not completed, and a portion of the intestine remains aganglionic, or lacking nerve cells. The portion of intestine that is aganglionic is unable to relax and the stool is unable to pass through. This condition causes a build-up of bowel contents behind the obstruction. Most often the disease begins in the last foot or two of the bowel, called the sigmoid colon and the rectum, and always ends at the anus. The length of the aganglionic portion of the bowel varies, but rarely involves the entire bowel.

Hirschsprung disease occurs in about one out of every 5,000 live births. More males than females are affected with the disease, with a ratio as high as 4:1. When more than half of the large intestine is aganglionic, the ratio of boys to girls is lower. Parents of Hirschsprung children have an increased risk for having additional children with the disease. Diagnosis may be considered when an infant does not pass meconium, the dark sticky substance that is a newborn's first bowel movement, within 24 hours of birth. The newborn may also exhibit abdominal distention and vomiting after the first feedings. Other symptoms may include constipation or diarrhea, anemia, and growth delay. Other children may develop chronic constipation and abdominal distention, but do not become acutely ill. Enterocolitis, a severe inflammatory condition of the bowel wall, is the most life-threatening emergency in Hirschsprung disease. Diagnosis is usually made by a barium enema x-ray to identify the affected intestinal area. A biopsy, or tissue sample, may be necessary to confirm the absence of nerve cells. An anorectal manometry test may also be conducted.

Treatment may include a temporary colostomy (surgically opening the large intestine) or ileostomy (opening the lower part of the small intestine), which will later be surgically closed. Surgical removal of the diseased section of the intestine may also be necessary. For most children with Hirschsprung disease, there are no long-term complications after successful surgery. A small but significant minority of children, however, do experience persistent constipation, encopresis, or persistent enterocolitis.

## REFERENCES

McKusick, V. (1993). #142623 *Hirschsprung disease*. Online Mendelian Inheritance in Man OMIM™, developed by the National Center for Biotechnology Information (NCBI). Retrieved from http://www3.ncbi.nlm.nih.gov80.

Passarge, E. (1993). Wither polygenic inheritance: Mapping Hirschsprung disease. *Nature Genet, 4,* 325–326. PubMed ID: 8401573.

STAFF

## HISKEY-NEBRASKA TEST OF LEARNING

The Hiskey-Nebraska Test of Learning Aptitude (HNTLA) is individually administered to assess the learning aptitude of persons age 3 through 17. The test is appropriate for use with deaf and hard-of-hearing persons as well as those without sensory defects. The HNTLA is composed of 12 subtests; 3 of the 12 are administered to subjects of all ages; 5 are administered only to children under age 12; and 4 are administered only to students over age 11. Items are uniformly administered either in pantomime fashion or by verbal directions. Examinees respond to items motorically, by pointing to one of several response alternatives, drawing picture parts, or manipulating objects such as beads, colored sticks, picture cards, or wooden blocks. The type of tasks on the HNTLA range from memory for color sequences to puzzle completion, picture analogy, and spatial reasoning. The tasks administered to children ages 3 to 11 primarily involve short-term visual memory, perceptual organization, visual discrimination abilities, and freedom from distractibility. The tasks administered to older examinees primarily involve perceptual organization, visual discrimination abilities, and analogical reasoning.

An examinee's raw score is based on the median subtest performance and converted to a learning age (LA) if pantomimed directions were used or a mental age (MA) if verbal directions were used. Learning ages are based on norms for deaf children; MAs are based on norms for hearing children. By using norms tables, LAs and MAs can be converted to learning quotients and IQs respectively. The current edition of the HNTLA was normed in 1966 for hearing and deaf children. Reviewers have consistently noted the lack of more current reliability or validity for the test, but frequently acknowledge it as the best, and only appropriate, device available for the assessment of deaf children. It is a useful instrument for evaluating the intellectual functioning of children with language disorders.

## REFERENCES

Bolton, B. F. (1978). Review of the Hiskey-Nebraska Test of Learning Aptitude. In O. K. Buros (Ed.), *The eighth mental measurements yearbook* (pp. 307–308). Highland Park, NJ: Gryphon.

Mira, M., & Larson, A. D. (1986). Review of the Hiskey-Nebraska Test of Learning Aptitude. In D. J. Keyser & R. C. Sweetland (Eds.), *Test critiques* (Vol. 3, pp. 331–339). Kansas City, MO: Test Corporation of America.

Newland, T. E. (1972). Review of the Hiskey-Nebraska Test of Learning Aptitude. In O. K. Buros (Ed.), *The seventh mental measurements yearbook* (pp. 738–740). Highland Park, NJ: Gryphon.

Salvia, J., & Ysseldyke, J. E. (1985). *Assessment in special and remedial education* (3rd ed.). Boston: Houghton Mifflin.

GEORGE McCLOSKEY
*Philadelphia College of
Osteopathic Medicine*

INTELLIGENCE TESTING

## HISTORY OF SPECIAL EDUCATION

Prehistoric societies, whose survival could depend on the fitness of each member, did not protect children who were born with defects, generally allowing them to die at birth or in infancy. Some ancient peoples, believing that physical deformities and mental disorders were the result of possession by demons, rejected, punished, or killed those who were afflicted. However, there is some evidence of persons with disabilities being treated with kindness, or even revered as being possessed of supernatural powers.

The ancient Greek and Roman societies gave us the first recorded attempts at the scientific understanding and treatment of disability in children. Some physicians and scholars in these cultures began to look on such conditions as treatable, and although infanticide was common, some efforts were made to preserve the lives of children with disabilities.

In the Middle Ages, persons with disabilities were often objects of amusement, and sometimes were used for entertainment. More often, however, they were derided, imprisoned, or executed. During this period, the church began to foster humane care for people with disabilities and to provide asylums for them. The Renaissance brought a greater belief in the value of human life, and laid the groundwork for the popular revolutions that later overthrew the domination of royalty in much of Europe and in America. Interest in educating children with disabilities, then, grew out of the new humanism of the Renaissance, the belief in the worth of every individual, and the associated struggles for freedom for the common man.

## Education of Individuals with Hearing Impairments

Special education, as the scientific study and education of exceptional children, started about 1555 when a Spanish monk, Pedro Ponce de Leon (1520–1584), taught a small number of children who were deaf to read, write, speak, and to master academic subjects. Another Spaniard, Juan Pablo Bonet (1579–1629?), wrote the first book on the education of individuals who were deaf in 1620. He described his methods, probably derived from those of Ponce de Leon, and set forth a one-handed manual alphabet that provided the basis for the one used today.

In 1644 in England, John Bulwer (1614–1684) published the first book in English on the education of the deaf. This was followed in 1680 by the most significant of the early books in English, *Didasopholus; or, The Deaf and Dumb Man's Tutor,* by George Dalgarno (1628?–1687). The author made the startling assertion that people who are deaf have as much capacity for learning as those who can hear, and outlined instructional methods that came to be widely used by subsequent educators.

The first permanent school for the deaf in Great Britain was established in 1767 in Edinburgh by Thomas Braidwood (1715–1806). Braidwood's school was successful from the beginning, and in 1783 he moved it to Hackney, near London, to draw students from the larger population of the London area. Braidwood's nephew and assistant, Joseph

Watson (1765–1829), later established the first school in Great Britain for children who were poor and deaf, in the London area. Braidwood's method combined manual and oral elements, teaching his students a manual alphabet and signs as well as articulation.

In Germany, at about the same time, Samuel Heinicke (1729–1784) developed a purely oral method of instruction, emphasizing the development of lip reading and speaking skills. Heinicke's method, as further developed by Friedrich Moritz Hill (1805–1874), was the basis for the oral method that became accepted practice throughout the world.

In France, Abbé Charles Michel de L'Epée (1712–1789) and Abbé Roch Ambroise Sicard (1742–1822) were developing the modern language of signs. Based on earlier work by Jacob Pereire (1715–1790), the instructional system was characterized by use of signs and a manual alphabet for communication. The French system also emphasized training of the senses of sight and touch, a forerunner of the sensory training that became an integral part of special education in the next century.

Organized education for children who were deaf in the United States began with the training of Thomas Hopkins Gallaudet (1787–1851) by Sicard in the French method of teaching persons who were deaf. Gallaudet, who had been chosen to start America's first school for the deaf, returned to Hartford, Connecticut, well trained in Sicard's methods and accompanied by a recruit from France, Laurent Clerc (1785–1869), a teacher of the deaf who was deaf himself. In 1817, they established the first school for children who were deaf in the United States, now the American School for the Deaf. This was the first educational program for exceptional children established in the United States. The New York Institution for the Deaf opened the next year, and by 1863, 22 schools for the deaf existed in the nation. In 1867, the first oral schools for the deaf were established in the United States, the Clarke School for the Deaf in Massachusetts and the Lexington School for the Deaf in New York. Gallaudet College, the only liberal arts college for students who are deaf in the world, was established in 1864. The first day school classes for any exceptionality in the United States were established for children who were deaf in Boston in 1869. Adult education for persons who were deaf began in New York City in 1874.

The subsequent development of services for persons who were deaf in the United States was aided immeasurably by a number of prominent advocates, most notably Alexander Graham Bell (1847–1922), inventor of the telephone and tireless worker for education for the deaf, and Helen Keller (1880–1957), who, deaf and blind from early childhood, was a living example of the effectiveness of special educational methods in overcoming even the most severe disabilities.

The development of services for persons who were deaf were hindered in the United States and elsewhere by bitter disagreements between advocates of oral and manual methods of instruction, with a resulting lack of cohesive effort toward common goals. These disagreements continue to this day, with some educators advocating oral speech-language and others promoting gestural language or a combination of methods. Most educators agree that the goal is to provide an adequate means of communication for the individual, and the predominant teaching method today is total communication which incorporates various modes of communication.

## Education of Children with Visual Impairments

Education for children who were blind began in France with the work of Valentin Haüy (1745–1822), a French philanthropist who, in 1784, founded the National Institution for the Young Blind in Paris. The school admitted students who were both blind and sighted so as not to isolate students who were blind from their peers with sight. Its success led to the formation of seven similar schools in Europe during the next 15 years. The first school for children who were blind in the United States, now the Perkins School for the Blind in Watertown, Massachusetts, was begun in 1829 with Samuel Gridley Howe (1801–1876) as its first director. There followed a rapid development of residential schools, which soon began also to enroll students who were partially sighted. These residential schools provided the nation's only education services to children with visual impairments until the development of special classes in the public schools, a movement that began with the formation of a special class for children who were blind in Chicago in 1900. The first special class for children with partial sight was opened 13 years later in Boston.

Crucial to the education of students who are blind was the development of a system of reading and writing. Haüy developed a system of embossed letters to be read with the fingers and, using this system, he printed the first books for the blind. Raised letters proved to be extremely difficult to read, however, and Louis Braille (1809–1852), blind from childhood and one of Haüy's students, developed the system of reading that has become universal. Known as braille, the system uses raised dots to represent the letters of the alphabet. For many years all braille materials had to be prepared individually by hand. Two inventions by Frank H. Hall (1843–1911) greatly expanded the amount of materials in braille: a braille typewriter (1892) and a braille printing system (1893). English language braille, which developed in many variations, was standardized in 1932 with an international agreement on the code that is now called Standard English Grade Two.

## Education for Children with Mental Retardation

Education for children with mental retardation began with the attempt by a French physician, Jean Marc Gaspard Itard (1775–1838), to educate an 11-year-old boy who had been found living as a savage in the woods. Itard's efforts to educate and civilize the boy were only partially successful, apparently because the boy was mentally retarded. Itard documented his methods in a book, *The Wild Boy of Aveyron* (1801). His instructional materials and procedures formed the basis for more than a century of development in the education of those with mental retardation, most notably by Edouard Seguin (1812–1880) in France and the United States and by Maria Montessori (1870–1952) in Italy. Seguin, in his influential book, *Idiocy and Its Treatment by the Physiological Method,* published in 1866, enunciated many ideas that have persisted to the present time: education of the whole child, individualization of instruction, beginning instruction at the child's current level of functioning, and the importance of rapport between teacher and pupil. These concepts and Seguin's emphasis on sensory training were incorporated in the twentieth century into the famous Montessori method, used worldwide in the education of children both with and without disabilities. Ovide Decroly (1871–1932) in Belgium developed an effective curriculum for children with mental retardation early in the twentieth century and established schools that served as models throughout Europe. Alfred Binet (1857–1911), working in the public schools of Paris, made an immense contribution with the invention of intelligence testing, providing in 1905 the first objective instrument for selecting children for placement in special education programs.

The first instance of schooling for children with mental retardation in the United States took place in 1839 with the admission of a student who was blind and mentally retarded to the Perkins Institute for the Blind in Massachusetts. The first school designed specifically for children with mental retardation, a residential facility, was opened in 1848 in Barre, Massachusetts, by Hervey Backus Wilbur (1820–1883). Public residential facilities for children and adults with mental retardation were opened in all parts of the country during the next half century, and by 1917 all but four states were providing institutional care for individuals with mental retardation.

The first public school special class for children with mental retardation was formed in Germany in 1859, and a small number of such classes were formed in other European nations during the next several decades. In the United States the first public school special class for children with mental retardation was opened in 1896 in Providence, Rhode Island. Several cities followed suit between 1896 and 1900. During this same period "streamer classes" were set up for non-English speaking children. These special education facilities soon were a "hodgepodge bin" for nearly every sort of variant child that could not be handled with regular classrooms.

In the 1930s special education was incorporated into the secondary schools primarily in the large cities. Up until that time special education programs serving adolescents were primarily residential or housed in elementary schools. Martens (1947) cited the inclusion of exceptional students in secondary schools as a significant and gratifying indication that secondary schools were being modified to meet the needs of disabled adolescents. Special divisions in city high schools were set up for the "mentally subnormal" coming from elementary schools, and some city junior high schools offered modified programs of instruction.

In the years that followed, children with milder forms of mental retardation were educated primarily in separate classes in public schools or in residential facilities. Children with more severe mental retardation were kept at home, provided for in private programs, or were institutionalized. The normalization and deinstitutionalization movements, which began in the 1940s and continue to the present, led to an increasing number of children classified as mentally retarded being educated in the public schools. The passage of PL 94-142 in 1975 began a major shift in special educational services received by children classified as mentally retarded. More and more children classified as "educable" by the school systems were "mainstreamed" into general education and fewer were placed in separate classes and schools. Children classified as "trainable" and "severe" were educated in the public schools and no longer expected to be educated in segregated facilities.

## Education of Children with Orthopedic Disabilities and Other Health Problems

Few special educational provisions for children with orthopedic and health impairments existed prior to the twentieth century. In the United States, the first special class for orthopedically-disabled children was established in the Chicago public schools in 1899 or 1900. A class for students with lowered vitality was initiated in Providence, Rhode Island in 1908, and one for children with epilepsy was formed in Baltimore, Maryland in 1909. Special educational and related services, such as occupational and physical therapy for children with a wide variety of orthopedic and health-related problems, expanded with the passage of PL 94-142 and IDEA.

## Education of Emotionally/Behaviorally Disordered Children

References to emotionally disturbed children do not appear in the scientific literature until the nineteenth century; there is a puzzling absence of references to the subject in any literature prior to that time. The first description of childhood psychosis was published in 1838 by Jean Etienne Esquirol (1772–1840) in *Des Maladies Mentales,* a work that constituted the first scientific treatment of mental illness.

The development of school services for children with emotional disabilities is not easy to trace because of imprecision in the classification of disabilities, difficulty in diagnosis, and a tendency to place children with these types of problems in classes designed for children with other disabilities. Late in the nineteenth century, a few schools in the United States began to make formal provision for students with emotional disabilities. The New Haven, Connecticut public schools established a class in 1871 to provide for children exhibiting unmanageable behavior and the New York City public schools formed classes for unruly boys in 1874. It is noteworthy that these were the first public school special classes for exceptional students to be established in the United States.

Children with severe emotional problems began to be studied in a systematic way only in the 1930s, and even then public schools were slow to accept responsibility for educating them. But with psychiatry developing as a discipline, with individual differences a central topic in psychology, and with psychological testing increasingly useful as a diagnostic tool, schools began to assume responsibility for educating these students and for developing programs based on psychiatric diagnosis and treatment recommendations.

In 1975, ten categories of handicapped children were recognized as eligible for special education, and in 1990 PL 101-476 defined the categories of disabilities which qualify children for special education. These disabilities are mental retardation, hearing impairments (including deafness), speech or language impairments, visual impairments (including blindness), serious emotional disturbance, orthopedic impairments, autism, traumatic brain injury, other health impairments, or specific learning disabilities.

## Parent Involvement

The years since World War II have been characterized by the rapid development of services for children with disabilities in the United States, with greatly increased involvement of parents and governmental entities. Parents of children with disabilities, who had long been in the background of special education, began in the 1940s and 1950s to organize themselves to represent the needs of their children and, where necessary, to provide educational services for those children not being served by the public schools. Organizations such as the National Association of Retarded Citizens (now known as The Arc), the United Cerebral Palsy Association, and the Association for Children with Learning Disabilities (now known as the Learning Disabilities Association) have been major forces in the development of public school services for all disabled children. They have had great influence in establishing the educational rights of all children and their families, obtaining legislation relating to the rights of persons with disabilities, changing attitudes toward those with disabilities, and establishing the right of parents to participate in public school decisions about their child.

## Legislative and Governmental Action

The federal government conducted a variety of programs designed to improve educational services for children with disabilities in the years following World War II. These governmental activities included grants to the states to assist in the development of new programs for children with disabilities, funding of research and demonstration projects, funding of training of special education personnel, establishment of regional resource centers for teachers, and establishment of a network of centers for children who are deaf-blind. In 1967, the Bureau of Education for the Handicapped was established in the U.S. Office of Education to administer the training, research, and educational programs supported by the federal government throughout the nation.

The landmark legislation for children with disabilities in the United States is PL 94-142, the Education for All Handicapped Children Act, enacted by Congress in 1975. Its stated purpose is ensuring that all disabled children have available a free appropriate public education that provides special education and related services as needed to meet the student's unique needs. Public Law 94-142 required that state and local education agencies ensure that all children who are disabled be identified and evaluated; that a comprehensive, nondiscriminatory, multidisciplinary educational assessment be made; that a reassessment be made at least every 3 years; that a written individualized educational plan (IEP) be developed and maintained for each child who has been determined to be disabled; and that each child be educated in the least restrictive environment that is consistent with his or her disability. The law also granted certain rights to parents to review their child's school record, to obtain an independent evaluation of the child, to receive written notice prior to placement in special education services, and to have an impartial hearing if they wish to challenge the proposed classification or placement of their child. Compliance with the requirements of PL 94-142 has brought modest amounts of federal financial aid to the states, to be used with state and local funds to support the cost of educating disabled children. A far-reaching effect of PL 94-142 has been the virtual elimination of the exclusion of disabled children from school. As the title of the act states, the legislation provides for the education of all disabled children.

PL 94-142 was amended a number of times to increase the age of children covered under the provisions of the law and to emphasize transition services and assistive technology. A major reauthorization of PL 94-142 in 1990 changed the name of the law from Education of All Handicapped Children Act to Individuals with Disabilities Education Act, or IDEA (PL 101-476). This act increased the number of categories of disabilities to include autism and traumatic brain injury and attempted to address what were perceived to be injustices in the previous act. Amendments to IDEA in 1997 significantly changed the requirements for the IEP (Individualized Education Plan) and combined the "categorical" approach with the "functional" approach. A "child with a disability" between the ages of 3 through 9 may include a child experiencing developmental delays in one or more of the following areas: physical development,

cognitive development, communication development, social or emotional development, or adaptive development. This provision allows states to serve "at-risk" children.

A number of court decisions laid the groundwork for the enactment of PL 94-142. The decision in *Pennsylvania Association for Retarded Children* v. *Commonwealth of Pennsylvania* in 1972 established that the public schools have the responsibility to provide appropriate programs for disabled children and that a child may not be excluded from school without due process. *Mills* v. *Board of Education* in the same year established that a disabled child may not be denied an appropriate, publicly supported education, and that the school system may not use lack of funds as a reason for failing to provide the services to which a disabled child is entitled.

Section 504 of the Vocational Rehabilitation Act of 1973 (PL 93-112) serves as a statement of civil rights for the disabled, providing that no otherwise qualified disabled individual will, because of his or her disability, be denied participation in any activity or program that receives federal financial assistance. This provision established public education as a right for all disabled children, regardless of how serious the disability might be, and is also the basis for a nationwide effort to make school buildings accessible to the disabled.

The Americans with Disabilities Act (ADA) of 1990 extended the nondiscriminatory provisions of Section 504 of the Rehabilitation Act amendment in 1975 to the private sector and with its emphasis on accessibility impacts on the provision of special education. IDEA and the Rehabilitation Act deal with education and training for employment and Section 504 and ADA make sure that students with disabilities can put their education and training to use.

## Growth in Services

Special education services expanded rapidly after World War II, both in number and types of children served. New special classes and special schools dramatically increased, as did college and university preparation programs for special education personnel. Additional types of children included in the population served were children classified as trainable mentally retarded, previously served primarily in institutions or in special schools operated by parent groups, and, beginning in the 1960s, children with learning disabilities, a group that had mostly been achieving poorly in regular classes or misplaced in special classes for students with other kinds of disabilities. In addition, interest increased in providing special programs for a group of students who are not disabled but who are generally included in the definition of exceptional children: gifted and talented children. Programs for these students appeared only slowly, as they lacked strong support from most educators. Consequently, programs for the gifted and talented have not shown the rapid growth that took place in programs for students with disabilities.

Early or preschool education for children with disabilities, long provided for children who had hearing impairments or cerebral palsy and other physical disabilities, became generally available for other categories of children with disabilities in the 1970s. This development was based on research findings corroborating commonly-held beliefs that the development of young children can be changed through early educational intervention. Often initiated with federal funding, these programs provided several new emphases in special education, including organized "child-find" procedures to locate young children in need of special programming, improved multidisciplinary approaches, and parent education.

Under the provisions of PL 94-142 and Section 504 of the Vocational Rehabilitation Act, public schools are required to make appropriate educational services available to students with severe, profound, and multiple disabilities, a category that includes various degrees and combinations of mental retardation, behavior disorders, physical disabilities, and sensory disabilities. Programs for such children with severe disabilities, many of whom were previously unserved by the public schools, have become a major element of special education, and have brought with them services (such as physical therapy and occupational therapy) that had not previously been considered within the province of the schools. These programs also have necessitated the downward extension of the curriculum to include instruction in infant-level self-help skills.

Increased enrollment of students with disabilities in vocational education programs was fostered by the Vocational Education Amendments of 1976 (PL 94-482), which require each state to allocate 10 percent of its vocational funds for the education of students with disabilities. Increasingly since the enactment of these amendments, high-school students with disabilities have had a variety of occupational preparation options available to them, in both regular and special vocational education programs.

The explosion of technology that characterizes our time has directly benefited students with disabilities in some significant ways. The use of computers by children with disabilities is becoming commonplace, as it is for all students. Adaptive technology, including improved prostheses, motorized wheelchairs, and other transportation devices, has greatly increased the mobility of children with physical disabilities. Persons who are hearing impaired have benefited from vastly improved hearing aid technology, advances in surgical techniques, and increased captioning of films and television programs. Of special significance are telecommunication devices for persons who are deaf or hearing impaired, the best known being the teletypewriter and teleprinter (TTY), a device that enables the deaf to communicate by telephone, typing into the system messages that are then printed at the receiving end. Reading for persons with visual impairments is being made more effective by a number of devices. The recorded "talking book" can now be enhanced by a technique known as compressed speech, which can double the speed at which the recording is played without producing distortion in pitch or quality. The Optacon converts print into a vibrating image that can be read with the fingers. The Kurzweil Reading Machine converts print into spoken English. In the important area of mobility, the Sonicguide aids those with visual impairments by producing a sound that indicates the presence and distance of an object that lies in their path. Other technologies include translation of printed language into spoken language and braille, synthetic speech, speech-producing hand-held calculators, closed-circuit television with enlargers, optical-to-tactile and print-to-braille converters, and various portable devices. Although the cost of such devices remains high in some instances, they are enhancing the quality of services to children with disabilities in a variety of educational and community settings.

The 1970s saw the emergence of mainstreaming and least restrictive environment as dominant concepts in special education. The requirement in PL 94-142 that disabled students be educated in the least restrictive environment was a reaction to doubts about the educational and social efficacy of the existing special class model and about the willingness of the schools to give disabled students access to the regular school program. The least restrictive environment requirement has led to a significant shift in special education placements in the last decade. The shift is towards a reduction in placements in residential schools and special day schools, and increased enrollment of disabled students in special classes in regular school buildings and in regular classes, usually with assistance in the form of some type of supplementary special instruction. Placement in less restrictive environments and the provision of appropriate educational services in this context, while not without its difficulties, is serving to eliminate needless segregation of disabled students.

The debate still continues regarding the best environments in which to educate children with disabilities. IDEA creates a presumption in favor of educating students with disabilities with those who do not have disabilities to the maximum extent possible and of the school providing supplementary aids and support services. The presumption in favor of inclusion can only be set aside if the student cannot benefit from regular education. In this case the student may be placed in a less typical, more specialized, less inclusive program. IDEA also set forth the provision that schools must offer a continuum of services from more to less typical and inclusive. On the other hand, organizations such as the Learning Disabilities Association (LDA) believe that the regular classroom is not the appropriate place for many students with learning disabilities. They advocate for alternative instructional environments or teaching strategies that cannot be provided with the regular classroom. Other organizations and professionals support the LDA position, but do not advocate a return to the previous total segregation models of special education.

The history of special education reveals evolution from

initial education of specific groups in segregated settings to a movement toward total inclusion within the public schools. The restructuring of general education taking place in the 1990s (Goals 2000, etc.) and the accompanying reforms have impacted special education. These reforms are cooperative learning, cooperative/collaborative teaching, site-based management, outcomes-based education and assessment, academic standards, effective assessment tools, account-ability, and state and federal legislation.

More recent legislative developments that will continue to impact special education services in this country well into the future include the 2001 passage of the No Child Left Behind Act (NCLB), which significantly alters programs instituted under the Elementary and Secondary Education Act (ESEA), and the recent reauthorization of the IDEA in 2004. While the ESEA provided a program of federal grants to school districts based on the number of children in the district from families living in poverty, NCLB pro-vides grants to all qualifying public schools, regardless of the socioeconomic status of the children attending the schools, but imposes numerous burdens on state and local education agencies as a condition of receiving those funds, including extensive testing requirements, stringent teacher qualification standards, and a requirement that schools demonstrate adequate yearly progress toward the ultimate goal of having 100 percent of their students achieve aca-demic proficiency goals established by each state. NCLB remains controversial among parents and educators, with many decrying what is described as the punitive nature of the statute, and with special educators expressing concerns about the statute's requirement that all but those students with the most severe learning disabilities be included in each district's testing program. The 2004 reauthorization of the IDEA, while retaining many of the requirements of earlier iterations of the statute, also includes a number of changes to bring the provisions of the IDEA into compliance with NCLB, particularly in the area of establishing goals and monitoring individual student progress under individu-alized education programs (IEPs) as those requirements relate to district testing requirements. These changes have generated significant controversy, and it is anticipated that the future should hold much research to evaluate the impact of these changes on children in special education.

## REFERENCES

Bender, R. (1970). *The conquest of deafness.* Cleveland, OH: Case Western Reserve.

Blatt, B., & Morris, R. J. (1984). *Perspectives in special education: Personal orientations.* Glenview, IL: Scott, Foresman.

Despert, J. L. (1965). *The emotionally disturbed child: Then and now.* New York: Brunner.

Fancher, R. E. (1979). *Pioneers of psychology.* New York: Norton.

Fancher, R. E. (1985). *The intelligence men: Makers of the I. Q. controversy.* New York: Norton.

Gannon, J. R. (1981). *Deaf heritage: A narrative history of deaf America.* Silver Spring, MD: National Association of the Deaf.

Hatlen, P. H., Hall, A. P., & Tuttle, D. (1980). Education of the visually handicapped: An overview and update. In L. Mann & D. A. Sabatino (Eds.), *The fourth review of special education* (pp. 1–33). New York: Grune & Stratton.

Irwin, R. B. (1955). *As I saw it.* New York: American Foundation for the Blind.

Jan, J. E., Freeman, R. D., & Scott, E. P. (1977). *Visual impairment in children and adults.* New York: Grune & Stratton.

Kanner, L. (1964). *A history of the care and study of the mentally retarded.* Springfield, IL: Thomas.

Kanner, L. (1970). Emotionally disturbed children: A historical review. In L. A. Faas (Ed.), *The emotionally disturbed child: A book of readings.* Springfield, IL: Thomas.

Kirk, S. A., & Gallagher, J. J. (1983). *Educating exceptional children* (4th ed.). Boston: Houghton Mifflin.

Kirk, S. A., Gallagher, J. J., & Anastasiow, N. J. (1997). *Educating exceptional children* (8th ed.). Boston: Houghton Mifflin.

Koestler, F. A. (1976). *The unseen minority: A social history of blind-ness in the United States.* New York: McKay.

Lane, H. (1984). *When the mind hears.* New York: Random House.

Lerner, J. (1985). *Learning disabilities: Theories, diagnosis, and teaching strategies* (4th ed.). Boston: Houghton Mifflin.

Lowenfeld, B. (1976). *The changing status of the blind: From sepa-ration to integration.* Springfield, IL: Thomas.

Meyen, E. L., & Skrtic, T. M. (Eds.). (1995). *Special education and student disability: Traditional, emerging, and alternative per-spectives.* Denver: Love.

Moores, D. F. (1982). *Educating the deaf—Psychology, principles, and practices* (2nd ed.). Boston: Houghton Mifflin.

Reynolds, M. C., & Birch, J. W. (1977). *Teaching exceptional chil-dren in all America's schools.* Reston, VA: Council for Exceptional Children.

Rhodes, W. C., & Head, S. (1974). *A study of child variance.* Ann Arbor: University of Michigan.

Rosen, M., Clark, G. R., & Kivitz, M. S. (Eds.). (1976). *The history of mental retardation: Collected papers.* Baltimore: University Park Press.

Ross, I. (1951). *Journey into light: The story of the education of the blind.* New York: Appleton-Century-Crofts.

Scheerenberger, R. C. (1983). *A history of mental retardation.* Bal-timore: Brookes.

Smith, S. (1983). *Ideas of the great psychologists.* New York: Harper & Row.

Swanson, B. M., & Willis, D. J. (1979). *Understanding exceptional children and youth.* Chicago: Rand McNally.

Turnbull, A., Turnbull, R., Shank, M., & Leal, D. (1999). *Excep-tional lives: Special education in today's schools* (2nd ed.). Upper Saddle River, NJ: Merrill.

Turnbull, R., & Cilley, M. (1999). *Explanations and implications of the 1997 Amendment to IDEA.* Upper Saddle River, NJ: Mer-rill.

Wallin, J. E. W. (1955). *Education of mentally handicapped chil-dren.* New York: Harper & Row.

Watson, R. I. (1968). *The great psychologists: From Aristotle to Freud* (2nd ed.). Philadelphia: Lippincott.

Wiederholt, J. L. (1974). Historical perspectives on the education of the learning disabled. In L. Mann & D. A. Sabatino (Eds.), *The second review of special education* (pp. 103–152). Philadelphia: JSE.

Wright, E. B. (1980). *Noncategorical special education programs for the mildly handicapped in secondary schools: A review of the literature.* Unpublished manuscript.

PAUL IRVINE
*Katonah, New York*
First edition

ELEANOR BOYD WRIGHT
*University of North Carolina at Wilmington*
Second edition

KIMBERLY APPLEQUIST
*University of Colorado at Colorado Springs*
Third edition

**AMERICANS WITH DISABILITIES ACT**
**INCLUSION**
**INDIVIDUALS WITH DISABILITIES EDUCATION**
 **IMPROVEMENT ACT OF 2004 (IDEIA)**
**NO CHILD LEFT BEHIND ACT**
**POLITICS AND SPECIAL EDUCATION**

## HISTRIONIC PERSONALITY DISORDER

Hysterical personality is an obsolete term which evolved from the 18th and 19th century diagnostic label "hysteria," whose Greek root meant "wandering uterus." Used prior to 1980 to describe a personality disorder characterized by pervasive, excessive, and exaggerated emotionality, attention-seeking behavior, a focus on physical appearance as an attention-getting device, seductiveness, suggestibility, and the propensity to assume that relationships are more intimate than they really are (American Psychiatric Association, 1994), it was applied almost exclusively by male clinicians to female clients. In 1980, the third edition of the *Diagnostic and Statistical Manual of Mental Disorders* (American Psychiatric Association, 1980) replaced "hysterical" personality with the designation histrionic personality disorder, which was retained in the most recent revision of the manual (*DSM-IV*). Although the *DSM-IV* notes that some research studies have found similar prevalence rates among men and women when structured assessments are employed, actual clinical practitioners rarely use such structured assessments, and thus the diagnosis continues to be much more frequently diagnosed in women. Histrionic personality disorder is commonly diagnosed in conjunction with other personality disorders, most frequently borderline personality disorder, dependent personality disorder, or narcissistic personality disorder. Other frequent co-occurring conditions include alcohol/drug abuse, various physical complaints, depression, and anxiety.

Rather than a primary mental disorder, personality disorders are considered to be long-lasting, chronic patterns of maladaptive behaviors that represent a person's typical, customary way of responding to the everyday conditions and demands of their environment. The representative behavioral patterns of those people designated as personality-disordered cause considerable impairment in the person's interpersonal relationships, and endure over time in spite of the negative consequences such patterns characteristically provoke.

The diagnostic manual does not attempt to identify the causes of any of the diagnoses it describes. Traditionally, most attempts to specify the causes of histrionic personality disorder have committed the logical fallacy of circular reasoning, which involves using description as explanation. For example, Millon (1981) saw the histrionic personality disorder as a result of an extreme longing for attention and approval from others mixed with a fear of independence. Such a statement, however, is no more than a description of the symptoms by which the disorder is identified. It essentially says that the disorder is both characterized by, as well as caused by, craving for attention and other symptoms. Such a statement is only superficially explanatory as it offers no further clarification of the disorder.

More useful attempts to explain the etiology of this disorder have focused on problems/deficits in identity development of the young child. Mahler's (1972) views on the separation-individuation process, and Mahler, Pine, and Bergman's (1975) perspectives on the "psychological birth" of the human child describe a process wherein the child develops a strong, coherent sense of self, capable of psychological independence only in the context of a reliable, dependable relationship with a primary caretaker. Serious deficits in that primary relationship would logically result in a strong "neediness" for others' attention and approval. Kohut (1971), addressing histrionic personality disorder as a subset of narcissistic personality disorder, considers it as a disorder of the self and self/identity development.

The histrionic's typical interpersonal shallowness and extreme sensitivity to perceived criticism are almost always serious obstacles to treatment for people with this disorder. Clinicians typically find these people to be self-centered, demanding, and manipulative clients, and the therapeutic relationship is frequently difficult to establish and maintain at a level sufficient for successful psychological treatment. Masterson (1993) employs a combination of developmental and self psychological tenets, along with object relations theory, in his approach to the treatment of disorders of the self, and provides additional information for those interested in treatment strategies for this condition.

## REFERENCES

American Psychiatric Association. (1980). *Diagnostic and statistical manual of mental disorders* (3rd ed.). Washington, DC: Author.

American Psychiatric Association. (1994). *Diagnostic and statistical manual of mental disorders* (4th ed.). Washington, DC: Author.

Kohut, H. (1971). *The analysis of the self: A systematic approach to the treatment of narcissistic personality disorders.* New York: International Universities Press.

Mahler, M. (1972). On the first three subphases of the separation-individuation process. *International Journal of Psycho-Analysis, 53,* 333–338.

Mahler, M., Pine, F., & Bergman, A. (1975). *The psychological birth of the human infant.* New York: Basic Books.

Masterson, J. F. (1993). *The emerging self: A developmental, self, and object relations approach to the treatment of the closet narcissistic disorder of the self.* New York: Brunner/Mazel.

Millon, T. (1981). *Disorders of personality DSM-III: Axis II.* New York: Wiley.

KAY E. KETZENBERGER
*The University of Texas of the
Permian Basin*

# HOBBS, NICHOLAS (1915–1983)

Nicholas Hobbs began his professional career as a high school teacher, earned his PhD degree in clinical psychology from Ohio State University in 1946, and served on the faculties of Teachers College, Columbia University, Louisiana State University, and George Peabody College of Vanderbilt University. From the time of his arrival at George Peabody College in 1951 until his retirement in 1980, he held a number of positions, including chairman of the division of human development, director of the Center for the Study of Families and Children, which he created, and provost of Vanderbilt University.

Hobbs was widely known for his pioneering Project Re-ED, dedicated to "the reeducation of emotionally disturbed children." An educational approach to the treatment of emotionally disturbed children, Project Re-ED, which grew into a nationwide program, is described in Hobbs's *The Troubled and Troubling Child.*

Hobbs was appointed to a number of presidential panels and commissions and participated in the creation of the Peace Corps. He served as president of the American Psychological Association.

## REFERENCES

Hobbs, N. (1982). *The troubled and troubling child.* San Francisco: Jossey-Bass.

The legacy of Nicholas Hobbs: Research on education and human development in the public interest, Part I. (1983). *Peabody Journal of Education, 60*(3).

The legacy of Nicholas Hobbs: Research on education and human development in the public interest, Part II. (1984). *Peabody Journal of Education, 61*(3).

PAUL IRVINE
*Katonah, New York*

# HOLISTIC APPROACH AND LEARNING DISABILITIES

Holism is defined as "a theory that the universe and especially living nature is correctly seen in terms of interacting wholes . . . that are more than the mere sum of elementary particles" (*Webster's New Collegiate Dictionary,* 1979). Holism, as applied to teaching and learning, suggests an approach whereby variables are not broken down into their component parts, but are examined within the context in which they occur. This type of learning is ongoing and is not fragmented into discrete segments or skills (McNutt, 1984). In contrast, behaviorists contend that each learning task can be analyzed, segmented, and sequenced in a hierarchical order; the individual parts must be learned before the whole (the sum of the parts) can be understood. Holists believe this to be a piecemeal approach that results in learning that is irrelevant and boring (Heshusius, 1984).

Until recently the major approaches used with children who are learning disabled have been reductionist in their orientation. According to Poplin (1984a), the psychological process approach, the behaviorist approach, and the cognitive-strategies approach, all of which have been used in treating learning disabilities, share several assumptions: the learning process is divided into segments; the focus is on deficits of the individual instead of strengths; and there are right and wrong ways to process information. Holists do not agree with these assumptions and, in fact, would argue that operating in this manner hinders learning in the learning-disabled student.

> Applied to learning disabilities, holistic inquiry lends credence to the argument that processes such as memory can neither be viewed experimentally nor taught separately, and that a child's memory for academic tasks may depend more on what the child already knows and feels and her/his interests than on the function or dysfunction of any hypothetical construct. (Poplin, 1984a, p. 290)

Those advocating a holistic approach for teaching children with learning disabilities (Heshusius, 1984; Leigh, 1980; Poplin, 1984a, 1984b; Rhodes & Dudley-Marling, 1996) argue that these students need a curriculum that is rich in language and that provides frequent opportunities to engage in reading and writing. Learning-disabled students, however, often read in a slow, laborious, and disfluent manner. Rhodes and Dudley-Marling (1996) posit that disfluent readers are afraid to take risks in the process of reading and writing. These readers believe that reading and writing are done in order to practice the form of language, word recognition, spelling, and mechanics. They do not understand that the goal is to derive and communicate meaning from their reading. According to Pflaum and Bryan (1982), fluent readers use the three language systems, graphophonics, syntax, and semantics, in an interrelated way to determine meaning, while disabled readers rely mainly on graphophonics. Holists feel that learning-disabled students need to learn to treat reading and writing as language rather than as discrete sets of skills that have little meaning or relevance to the reader.

Leigh (1980) puts forth seven major principles of the whole language philosophy that provide a comprehensive description of a holistic approach to teaching:

1. Reading, writing, speaking, and listening are closely interrelated language processes rather than separate, autonomous academic skills.

2. The fundamental purpose of any language activity is to acquire, mediate, or express meaning.

3. Language, in all forms, involves an interactive process that occurs in social contexts.

4. Oral and written language are learned rather than taught.

5. Children need competence in using language for several different functions.

6. Whole-language evaluation should be based on naturalistic, observational procedures that focus on comprehension.

7. The teacher's attitudes and competencies are essential determinants of the effectiveness of a whole-language program (pp. 63–68).

A classroom for the learning disabled facilitates learning in accordance with these principles by providing a language-rich environment. The holistic classroom is a place where children have frequent opportunities to engage in reading and writing and to be exposed to demonstrations of the natural purposes and joy of written language (Dudley-Marling, 1996). School goals become the same as life goals, and children learn because the material is relevant, purposeful, and meaningful.

In holistic classrooms, teachers demonstrate a purpose for reading and writing. They write notes to students and encourage them to write notes and letters to each other. Daily schedules and lunch menus are posted in the room. Teachers write directions for assignments or class activities. Pictures of students are posted along with their biographies. Teachers and students label items in the classroom, display their writing, and read aloud to each other. Teachers and students also talk about reading, writing, and thinking. Communication is at the heart of the process by which intelligence develops (Sadler & Whimbey, 1985). When students have the opportunity to articulate their thinking and receive feedback they develop their cognitive skills. In holistic learning-disabled classrooms, students and teachers discuss books they have read or pieces they have written. Teachers share problems they have had in comprehending stories or writing papers or poems. This encourages students to think of similar situations in which they have been involved. The awareness helps them to monitor their thought processes and feel more comfortable with reading and writing processes.

A holistic classroom also provides opportunities for students to engage in reading and writing. There are reading centers that contain a variety of reading materials (e.g., books, newspapers, magazines, comics, and cookbooks). Writing centers are complete with pencils, papers, and reasons for writing. Students write journals, stories, notes, poems, plays, or recipes. Students read and write together in groups to help one another be creative or to overcome obstacles. Holistic teachers plan activities that show reading and writing is useful. For example, a cooking project includes finding recipes in books, writing grocery lists, writing and reading recipes, and talking about the experience.

The holistic classroom is a place where teaching and learning is an interactive process with the emphasis on the meaning, not the form, of language. Learning-disabled students benefit in this meaningful environment. Segmenting learning into discrete parts can discourage reluctant learners with its repetition and boredom. Holistic learning, on the other hand, motivates students because it is meaningful, purposeful, and relevant. Patel (2002) summarizes current literature and resources about the holistic approach.

**REFERENCES**

Dudley-Marling, C. C. (1996). Creating a rich language environment for written language learning. *Teaching Exceptional Children, 25,* 22–25.

Heshusius, L. (1984). Why would they and I want to do it? A phenomenological-theoretical view of special education. *Learning Disability Quarterly, 7*(4), 363–368.

Leigh, J. E. (1980). Whole-language approaches: Premises and possibilities. *Learning Disability Quarterly, 3*(4), 62–69.

McNutt, G. (1984). A holistic approach to language arts instruction in the resource room. *Learning Disability Quarterly, 7*(4), 315–320.

Patel, N. V. (2002). A holistic approach to learning and teaching interaction: Factors in the development of critical learners. *The International Journal of Educational Management, 17,* 272–284.

Pflaum, S. W., & Bryan, T. H. (1982). Oral reading research and learning disabled children. *Topics in Learning and Learning Disabilities, 1,* 33–42.

Poplin, M. S. (1984a). Summary rationalizations, apologies and farewell: What we don't know about the learning disabled. *Learning Disability Quarterly, 7*(2), 130–135.

Poplin, M. S. (1984b). Toward a holistic view of persons with learning disabilities. *Learning Disability Quarterly, 7*(4), 290–294.

Rhodes, L. K., & Dudley-Marling, C. C. (1996). *Teaching literacy to learning disabled and remedial students.* Portsmouth, NH: Heinemann Educational Books.

Sadler, W. A., Jr., & Whimbey, A. (1985, November). A holistic approach to improving thinking skills. *Phi Delta Kappan,* 199–203.

*Webster's New Collegiate Dictionary* (1979). Springfield, MA: Merriam.

Nancy J. Kaufman
*University of Wisconsin at
Stevens Point*

## ECOLOGICAL ASSESSMENT
## ECOLOGICAL EDUCATION FOR CHILDREN WITH DISABILITIES

## HOLLAND, SPECIAL EDUCATION IN

See NETHERLANDS, SPECIAL EDUCATION IN.

## HOLLINGWORTH, LETA A. S. (1886–1939)

Leta A. S. Hollingworth, psychologist, received her PhD from Teachers College, Columbia University, in 1916, after serving as a high school teacher in Nebraska and as a clinical psychologist in New York City. She was a member of the faculty of Teachers College from 1916 until her death in 1939.

Hollingworth made pioneering studies of the psychology of women, correcting prior misconceptions regarding differences in abilities between the sexes and providing the basis for her strong advocacy of professional equality between men and women. She was a leader in the establishment of standards for clinical psychologists and carried out significant investigations of both mentally retarded and gifted children.

**REFERENCES**

Gates, A. I. (Ed.). (1940). Education and the individual. *Teachers College Record, 42,* 183–264.

Hollingworth, H. L. (1943). *Leta Stetter Hollingworth.* Lincoln: University of Nebraska Press.

Hollingworth, L. (1926). *Gifted children: Their nature and nurture.* New York: Macmillan.

Paul Irvine
*Katonah, New York*

## HOLT, WINIFRED (1870–1945)

Winifred Holt founded the New York Association for the Blind in 1905. She was responsible for the creation of the committee that eventually became the National Society for the Prevention of Blindness. With a special interest in training and employment for the blind, she developed the New York Lighthouse, a workshop devoted to education, employment, and recreation for the blind. Dedicated by President William Howard Taft in 1913, the Lighthouse was so successful that Lighthouses were established in many cities in the United States, and eventually in 34 other countries.

A leader in the campaign to get blind children into the public schools, Holt helped the New York City Board of Education to establish its program for the education of blind students in classes with sighted children. She wrote two influential books, a biography of Henry Faucett, the blind English postmaster-general, and *The Light Which Cannot Fail,* which contained stories about blind men and women and a useful "handbook for the blind and their friends." In 1922 Holt married Rufus Graves Mather, a research and lecturer on art who joined her in her work for the blind.

**Winifred Holt**

## REFERENCES

Bloodgood, E. H. (1952). *First lady of the Lighthouse.* New York: The Lighthouse, New York Association for the Blind.

Holt, W. (1914). *A beacon for the blind: Being a life of Henry Faucett, the blind postmaster-general.* Boston: Houghton Mifflin.

Holt, W. (1922). *The light which cannot fail.* New York: Dutton.

PAUL IRVINE
*Katonah, New York*

## HOLTZMAN, WAYNE H., SR. (1923–    )

Wayne H. Holtzman received his BS and MS degrees from Northwestern University. In 1950, he was awarded his PhD degree in psychology and statistics from Stanford University. Since 1949, he has been a faculty member in psychology at The University of Texas at Austin. Associated with the Hogg Foundation since 1954, he is currently Professor Emeritus, Hogg Professor Emeritus in Psychology and Education, Department of Psychology. Holtzman served as Foundation President from 1970 to 1993 and as Dean of the College of Education at the University from 1964 to 1970.

From 1953 to 1954, Holtzman received a faculty research fellowship from the Social Science Research Council, and in 1962 his research in the field of inkblot perception and personality was recognized by the Helen D. Sargent Memorial Award from the Menninger Foundation. The inkblot technique, devised by Holtzman and designed to stir the imagination, focuses on the analysis of inkblots as a means of studying personality by determining individual modes of perception. This technique was ultimately revised by Holtzman, utilizing more inkblots and simplifying procedures for administration.

His numerous honorary awards and doctorates include a fellowship at the Center for Advanced Study in the Behavioral Sciences, Stanford, California (1962–1963); the title of *Professor Honorario* at the Universidad San Martin de Porres in Lima, Peru in 1979; the Doctor of Humanities degree from Southwestern University in Georgetown, Texas in 1980; the Bruno Klopfer Award for Distinguished Contributions to Personality Assessment of the Society for Personality Assessment in 1988; the Centennial Citation for International Advancement of Psychology in Education from the American Psychological Association (APA) in 1992; and a 1996 award from the APA for Distinguished International Contributions to Psychology.

Holtzman has authored over 150 articles in scientific journals, and served as editor of the *Journal of Educational Psychology* from 1966 to 1972. His books include *Holtzman Inkblot Technique; Tomorrow's Parents; Computer-Assisted Instruction, Testing, and Guidance; Placing Children in Special Education: A Strategy for Equity; Mental Health of Immigrants and Refugees;* and *School of the Future.*

## REFERENCES

Holtzman, W. H. (1961). *Holtzman inkblot technique.* New York: Psychological Corporation.

Holtzman, W. H. (1965). *Tomorrow's parents.* Austin: University of Texas Press.

Holtzman, W. H. (1970). *Computer-assisted instruction, testing, and guidance.* New York: Harper & Row.

TAMARA J. MARTIN
*The University of Texas of the
Permian Basin*

Wayne H. Holtzman, Sr.

## HOMEBOUND INSTRUCTION

Homebound instruction is defined as education for the child confined to home owing to illness, physical injury, or emotional condition, provided by an itinerant or visiting teacher. A child is eligible for a home instruction program if school attendance is made impossible by such physical or emotional conditions. The Education for All Handicapped Children Act of 1975 (PL 94-142) and the Individuals with Disabilities Education Act (IDEA) have categorized home instruction as one of the most restrictive in the available cascade of services; as a result, such placement is to be considered temporary whenever possible (Berdine & Blackhurst, 1985).

The homebound teacher is used as the provider of this instruction in those areas or school districts where such services are available. The homebound instructional component must consist of direct service to the child and regular consultation with in-school personnel, as the nature of the service will vary from helping students at home for short periods of time to maintain the pace and assignments of their classes, to providing a complete instructional program for those confined for longer periods. Authorities agree that regular liaison with school and peers to maintain contacts and social skills is vital to the student on homebound instruction, who must be brought back to school as quickly as the handicapping condition allows (Polloway, Payne, Patton, & Payne, 1985).

Some instances of the abuse of homebound instruction have been noted in urban areas with a relatively high-frequency use of such services, primarily with disruptive, delinquent, or emotionally disturbed students prohibited from school for behavioral reasons. Homebound services for the emotionally handicapped have also been overemployed with disadvantaged, black, and male students (Safer, 1982). Additional criticisms of home instruction include the danger of segregating children for prolonged periods of time, the expense to school systems, and the use of inadequately trained teachers as service providers (Haring, 1982).

New directions in special education are extending traditional homebound instruction to include home-based services for severely disabled children, deaf and blind infants and preschool children, the mentally retarded, and other high-risk infants (Cartwright, Cartwright, & Ward, 1995). These services include the use of teacher-trainers to teach parents and children, with emphasis on self-help skills, communications, and language arts, using the natural surroundings of the home environment to promote development (Kiernan, Jordan, & Saunders, 1984).

Technological advances in telecommunications and computer-linked instruction increasingly assist the homebound child and teacher until a return to a less restrictive environment is accomplished (Kirk & Gallagher, 1986).

### REFERENCES

Berdine, W. H., & Blackhurst, A. E. (1985). *An introduction to special education* (2nd ed.). Boston: Little, Brown.

Cartwright, G. P., Cartwright, C. A., & Ward, M. J. (1995). *Educating special learners* (2nd ed.). Belmont, CA: Wadsworth.

Haring, N. R. (Ed.). (1982). *Exceptional children and youth.* Columbus, OH: Merrill.

Kiernan, C., Jordan, R., & Saunders, C. (1984). *Stimulating the exceptional child: Strategies for teaching communication and behavior change to the mentally disabled.* Englewood Cliffs, NJ: Prentice Hall.

Kirk, S. A., & Gallagher, J. J. (1986). *Educating exceptional children* (5th ed.). Boston: Houghton Mifflin.

Polloway, E. A., Payne, J. S., Patton, J. R., & Payne, R. A. (1985). *Strategies for teaching retarded and special needs learners.* Columbus, OH: Merrill.

Safer, D. J. (1982). *School programs for disruptive adolescents.* Baltimore: University Park.

RONALD S. LENKOWSKY
*Hunter College, City University of New York*
Second edition

KIMBERLY APPLEQUIST
*University of Colorado at Colorado Springs*
Third edition

**CASCADE MODEL OF SPECIAL EDUCATION SERVICES
LEAST RESTRICTIVE ENVIRONMENT**

# HOMEWORK

Time spent on homework is generally related to academic achievement. This conclusion has been supported in studies conducted since the early 1900s. Keith (1982) found that homework has a higher correlation with better grades in school than any other factor except intellectual ability. Walberg (1984) found, after a review of 15 studies on graded homework, that such assignments have three times more influence on student achievement than the education, income level, or occupational status of the parents. The relative effectiveness of assigning homework versus not assigning homework results in an achievement gain of approximately .30 of a standard deviation. By grading homework, a teacher can almost triple the effectiveness of this strategy over merely assigning it for practice.

Austin (1979), after reviewing 23 experimental studies focusing on mathematical homework, concluded that the effects of homework are cumulative, more effective in enhancing computational skills than problem-solving skills, and not related to students' attitudes toward mathematics. Keith (1982) reported that if students are required to do more homework and actually do it, the potential benefits are large. Low-ability high school students doing only one to three hours of homework per week achieve the same grades as do middle-ability students doing no homework. In high-performance private schools, students are assigned at least twice as much homework as in the average public school (Coleman, Hoffer, & Kilgore, 1981).

It is not simply a question of requiring more homework to achieve higher performance. The benefits depend on how well designed, supervised, and monitored such assignments are. Keith (1982) has concluded that at some point, increased homework will probably bring smaller and smaller returns. It is probably safe to assume, however, that most students are a long way from the point of diminishing returns regarding homework. Some general rules for homework assignments are (1) require it on a regular schedule; (2) evaluate it by grades or feedback as soon as possible after the assignment; (3) make it an integral part of the in-class activities; and (4) base it on content that will be evaluated on tests.

## REFERENCES

Austin, J. D. (1979). Homework research in mathematics. *School Science & Mathematics, 79,* 115–121.

Coleman, J. S., Hoffer, T., & Kilgore, S. (1981). Cognitive outcomes in public and private schools. *Sociology of Education, 55*(23), 65–76.

Keith, T. Z. (1982). Time spent on homework and high school grades: A large sample path analysis. *Journal of Educational Psychology, 74*(2), 246–253.

Walberg, H. J. (1984). Improving the productivity of America's schools. *Educational Leadership, 41*(8), 19–27.

ROBERT A. SEDLAK
*University of Wisconsin at Stout*

ACHIEVEMENT NEED
TEACHER EFFECTIVENESS

# HONG KONG, SPECIAL EDUCATION IN

Hong Kong is a metropolis with a population of 6.8 million located at the southeastern tip of the mainland of China. It was a British colony from 1843 to 1997. On July 1, 1997, Hong Kong was returned to the People's Republic of China and became its Special Administrative Region. In the Joint Declaration with Britain, China promised that the socialist system would not be practised in Hong Kong and that Hong Kong would enjoy a high degree of autonomy for 50 years from 1997.

The educational system in Hong Kong has been modeled closely after those used in Britain, and its school system has retained many British features. In 2004, Hong Kong had about one million students enrolled in 737 kindergartens, 759 primary schools, and 519 secondary schools (Education & Manpower Bureau, 2005a).

## Development of Special Education Services

Publicly supported special education services in Hong Kong have experienced considerable advancement throughout their 40-year history. Before 1960, the Hong Kong government had little involvement in the provision of special education services. Voluntary and charitable organizations played the major roles in providing care to children with special educational needs. For example, the first school for the blind was founded by the Catholic Canossian sisters in 1863, and the first school for the deaf was founded by other missionaries in 1935. In 1959, the establishment of a special education section within the Education Department constituted a landmark in the history of special education in Hong Kong. This department assumed responsibility for the development and monitoring of special education services provided by voluntary organizations. Additionally, many special schools opened from the 1960s to 1980s. These schools accommodated students with various disabilities, including physical disabilities, mental retardation, visual and hearing impairments, speech and language impairments, and learning and behavioral difficulties.

Screening services for the early identification of children with special education needs began in the early 1970s when assessment centers were set up in the Education Department. When Hong Kong implemented 9-year free and compulsory education in 1978, special education services continued to expand. The Hong Kong government provided such services as psychological, social, and educational assessment to students with special education needs (e.g., refinement of assessment instruments and observational checklists), educational resources (e.g., hearing aids for children with hearing impairment, speech therapy for children with speech and language impairments), remedial teaching (e.g., educational placement and advice to teachers), and professional support to parents (e.g., workshops to introduce strategies to manage children with disabilities).

During the 1990s, concern for human rights and equal opportunities grew. The Hong Kong government realized the importance of integrating students with special education needs into ordinary schools (Board of Education, 1996). The White Paper on Rehabilitation–Equal Opportunities and Full Participation (Hong Kong Government, 1995) advocated for the rights of children with special education needs to receive education in ordinary schools as far as possible and as early as possible. In 1995, the Disability Discrimination Ordinance (Chapter 487) made denying admission or expelling a student because of a disability by an educational establishment unlawful. This policy paper and ordinance heralded the implementation of inclusive education. In 1997, the government launched the "Whole School Approach" to integration. Since then, students with special educational needs increasingly have been placed in ordinary schools.

There currently are two types of provisions in special education. Students with special education needs are either placed in special schools or are mainstreamed in ordinary schools. In the following are the detailed descriptions of each of these two provisions.

## Special Schools

During the 2004–2005 school year, 8,403 special-education needs students were enrolled in 66 special schools (Education and Manpower Bureau, 2005a). There are five categories of special school: visual impairment, hearing impairment, physical disability, maladjustment, and mental disability. Many schools provide residential services. As the government's main policy is to mainstream children with special educational needs, the number of special schools and the student enrollment in them has been decreasing. Students placed in special schools usually have severe disabilities that preclude them from benefiting from the curriculum in ordinary schools.

The government provides financial support to all special schools under the Code of Aid for Special Schools (Education Department, 1996). Voluntary organizations operate special schools and receive a subsidy from the government. The government also subsidizes the employment of nonteaching professionals, such as school psychologists, social workers, nurses, speech therapists, and the residential care staff of these schools. The class size of special schools ranges from 8 to 20 students, and staffing ratios range from 1 to 1.5 teachers per class, depending on the special needs of the children (Education and Manpower Bureau, 2005b). In general, the curriculum is guided by that of the ordinary schools, with adaptations made to accommodate students' special needs.

Special schools generally provide students with education until grade 9. However, there is some flexibility based on special circumstances. In 2002, the government launched the Extension of Years of Education Program in special schools. Through this program, students attend 1 or 2 more years beyond grade 9 so that they can acquire better preparation for the transition from special schools to the community.

## Inclusive Education

The overall policy of the government is to integrate students with special education needs into ordinary schools whenever possible. During the 2004–2005 school year, 711 special education classes were offered in ordinary schools. Of these, 3 were for children with visual impairment and 708 provided intensive remedial teaching programs for children with learning difficulties (Education and Manpower Bureau, 2005b). Services to these students include small-group tutorials during normal school day and after-school remedial classes. In addition, 11 resource teaching centers for students with learning difficulties were established. Students can receive tutorial services in these centers outside school hours.

Placement of students with special educational needs in special classes operated within ordinary schools constitutes a low degree of integration. In 1997, a pilot project, "Whole School Approach," was launched to realize a higher degree of integration. Students benefiting from this project include those with mild mental disabilities (i.e., IQs between 50 and 70), those with autistic disorders who display average intelligence, and those with visual impairments, hearing impairments, or physical disabilities. When placed in ordinary classrooms, special needs children receive various services, including school-based or center-based intensive remedial support in the basic subjects. Consultation is provided to their teachers and extra manpower (e.g., resources teachers) also is provided to their schools.

In 2003, a new funding model for students with special needs was piloted in an effort to further integrate students with special educational needs into ordinary schools. Under this new funding model, schools are provided with an intensive learning support grant and are requested to adopt whole-school approaches to support every student with special educational needs. This requires that a school's entire program must implement ways to accommodate students with special educational needs, including adjustments in teaching methods, curriculums, and assessment. Teaching students with special education needs becomes a joint effort of all the school personnel. The job of teaching students with special education needs no longer involves only one or two resources teachers who work with students in segregated classrooms.

During the 2004–2005 school year, 117 schools participated in the "Whole School Approach" and 170 schools participated in the new funding model. Thus, a total of 27,124 students with special education needs were studying in ordinary schools. They constituted 2.58 percent of the student population in ordinary schools.

## Difficulties and Future Directions

Despite these and other efforts made, barriers to the development of inclusive education remain. Most teachers in ordinary schools are not prepared to teach students with diverse needs. As of 2005, there has been no preservice special education training program in Hong Kong. Only two tertiary institutions (the University of Hong Kong and the Hong Kong Institute of Education) offer in-service training for special educators. Most teachers in ordinary schools have no training or experience in teaching students with special educational needs.

Tensions exist between inclusive education and elitism; Hong Kong's general education system is competitive and examination oriented. Schools are pressured to attract bright students who excel on public examinations. Students with special educational needs are burdens to schools that strive to win higher rankings in the school leagues' tables. That many ordinary schools are reluctant to implement inclusive education is understandable (Poon-McBrayer, 2004).

Hong Kong students complete many public examinations for admission to secondary schools and colleges. A school's curricula are primarily examination driven, and students with special educational needs are required to adjust to these curricula. Accommodation may be possible in lower grades when public examinations are not imminent.

However, in the face of public examinations, little accommodation can be made for students with special educational needs. They need to take the same examination as the other students. Thus, levels of achievement attained by all students are evaluated using the same assessment system without consideration of special educational needs.

Psychological and educational tests are critical to the identification of children with special educational needs. While Hong Kong has a limited number of assessment tools with local norms, the Hong Kong Wechsler Intelligence Scale for Children (Education Department, Hong Kong Government & Hong Kong Psychological Society, 1981) and Hong Kong Specific Learning Difficulties in Reading and Writing (Ho, Chan, Tsang, & Lee, 2000) are the most widely used assessment tools. However, the former has an outdated norm (established in 1981), and the latter is restricted to children under age 12.

Some schools used the 2003 new funding initiative, described previously, to buy services from third-party agencies (e.g., speech therapy, pull-out tutorials). Students with special educational needs often receive no instructional or curricula accommodation within these schools.

To develop inclusive education, Hong Kong needs to strengthen special education training for teachers, reduce competition in education, solve problems related to reliance on public examination, strengthen assessment mechanisms for identification purposes, and improve the funding model, to ensure that schools adopt genuine whole-school approaches to support students with special educational needs.

## REFERENCES

Board of Education. (1996). *Report of the sub-committee on special education.* Hong Kong: Government Printer.

Education and Manpower Bureau. (2005a). *Figures and statistics.* Retrieved August 2, 2005, from http://www.emb.gov.hk/index .aspx?nodeID=92&langno=1

Education and Manpower Bureau. (2005b). *Special education.* Retrieved August 7, 2005, http://www.emb.gov.hk/index.aspx ?nodeID=154&langno=1

Education Department. (1996). *Code of aid for special schools.* Hong Kong: Government Printer.

Education Department & Hong Kong Psychological Society. (1981). *Hong Kong Wechsler intelligence scale for children.* Hong Kong: Government Printer.

Ho, C. S. H., Chan, D. W. O., Tsang, S. M., & Lee, S. H. (2000). *The Hong Kong test of special learning difficulties in reading and writing.* Hong Kong: Hong Kong Specific Learning Difficulties Research Team, Chinese University of Hong Kong and Education Department, Hong Kong SAR Government.

Hong Kong Government. (1995). *White paper on rehabilitation: Equal opportunities and full participation: A better tomorrow for all.* Hong Kong: Government Printer.

Poon-McBrayer, K. F. (2004). To integrate or not to integrate: Systemic dilemmas in Hong Kong. *The Journal of Special Education, 37,* 249–256.

## HORSEBACK RIDING FOR STUDENTS WITH DISABILITIES

See EQUINE THERAPY.

## HORTICULTURAL THERAPY

Horticultural therapy is also known as hortitherapy, agritherapy, therapeutic horticulture, plant therapy, and hort-therapy. Horticultural therapy for disabled persons has its roots in the nineteenth century, during the rise of the large state institutions. Many of these institutions were located in rural areas and included areas for propagation of crops. Residents were trained to plant, care for plants, and harvest. The purpose of this farming was primarily economic rather than therapeutic. However, as a secondary benefit many residents were able to obtain work in agriculture and, in fact, before World War II, agriculture was one of the strongest occupational areas for the disabled.

Contemporary hortitherapy has several underpinnings. It may be a branch of occupational therapy (Burton & Watkins, 1978) used to enhance motor development. It has also been employed as a form of psychotherapy (Watson & Burlingame, 1960) to develop motivation and provide clients with a sense of responsibility for living things (Saever, 1985). Horticultural therapy has also been used as a vocational activity (Downey, 1985; Good-Hamilton, 1985; Schrader, 1979). Such training may be in a sheltered work setting or in a vocational school program for competitive employment.

There are a number of unique hortitherapy programs. Burton and Watkins (1978) described a public school program for physically disabled students in which academic concepts were taught while students were involved in plant care. The program was designed from a Piagetian point of view and was transdisciplinary, incorporating physical, occupational, and speech therapy, and classroom instruction. Saever (1985) employed agritherapy with learning-disabled students (8 to 12 years old) as a means of promoting responsibility, order, and structure, following through on plans, respect for nature, cooperative effort, and positive relationships with adults. Good-Hamilton (1985) described another public school program in which trainable mentally retarded students and learning-disabled students worked in greenhouse production to develop vocational skills (primarily work habits). More than 50 percent of the students were able to obtain employment at the conclusion of training. The American Horticultural Therapy Association provides many resources for individuals who wish to be trained in horticultural therapy, a journal for the presentation of research, and professional support. The association can be reached online at http://www.ahta.org.

**REFERENCES**

Burton, S. B., & Watkins, M. (1978). *The green scene: Horticultural experiences for the physically impaired student.* Paper presented at the 56th annual International Conference, Council for Exceptional Children, Kansas City, MO.

Downey, R. S. (1985). Teaching the disadvantaged and handicapped. *Agricultural Education Magazine, 57*(8), 5–7.

Good-Hamilton, R. (1985). Plants breed success. *Agricultural Education Magazine, 57*(8), 8–10.

Saever, M. D. (1985). Agritherapy, plants as learning partners. *Academic Therapy, 20*(4), 389–397.

Schrader, B. (1979). *Working hands and 3,000 chrysanthemums. Special report: Fresh views on employment of mentally handicapped people.* Washington, DC: President's Committee on Employment of the Handicapped.

Watson, D. P., & Burlingame, A. W. (1960). *Therapy through horticulture.* New York: Macmillan.

JAMES K. MCAFEE
*Pennsylvania State University*

**OCCUPATIONAL THERAPY**
**VOCATIONAL EDUCATION**

# HOUSE, BETTY J. (1923–    )

Betty J. House earned her BA from Oklahoma University in 1948 and her MA from Brown University in 1949. She received her PhD in 1952 from the University of Connecticut. Beginning as a research assistant at the University of Connecticut in 1954, she has remained there throughout her career and has been a professor in residence in the department of psychology since 1972. Her research interests include learning, memory, cognitive processes, intelligence, and mental retardation.

In collaboration with her husband, Dr. David Zeaman, House has conducted research in mental retardation for over 30 years. A permanent laboratory was established for their research at the Mansfield State Training School in Connecticut; the National Institute of Mental Health provided funding for their projects for over 20 years. The major accomplishment of their research has been the development and elaboration of an attention theory of retardation discrimination learning. Their model was first published in 1963. A history of their research and theory development from 1963 to 1979 can be found in Ellis' *Handbook of Mental Deficiency, Psychological Theory and Research* (1979).

House has been associate editor of the *American Journal on Mental Deficiency.* She was a consulting editor for *Child Development* from 1968 to 1981 and has been a consulting editor for the *Journal of Experimental Child Psychology.* She served as associate editor for *Psychology Bulletin* from 1982 to 1984 and became editor in 1985.

**REFERENCE**

Zeaman, D., & House, B. J. (1970). A review of attention theory. In N. R. Ellis (Ed.), *Handbook of mental deficiency, psychological theory and research* (2nd ed.). Hillsdale, NJ: Erlbaum.

KATHRYN A. SULLIVAN
*Texas A&M University*

**ZEAMAN, DAVID**
**ZEAMAN-HOUSE RESEARCH**

# HOUSE-TREE-PERSON

The House-Tree-Person (HTP), developed by J. N. Buck (1948), is a projective drawing technique used to assess personality and psychological adjustment in children and adults; the individual is asked to make freehand drawings of a house, a tree, and a person. It is considered one of the most frequently used projective instruments (Piotrowski & Zalewski, 1993; Watkins, Campbell, Nieberding, & Hallmark, 1995), most likely due to its ease of administration and students' enthusiasm for drawing. In addition, it is often viewed as a nonthreatening way to obtain clinical information and establish rapport early in the assessment process. Drawings such as the HTP are frequently used in the assessment of children who have been abused or maltreated (see Veltman & Browne, 2002), as the child is less likely to exhibit the same restraints of expression as in other formats (Groth-Marnat, 1997).

There are various administration procedures; however, the examinee is typically provided with a pencil with an eraser and three 8½ × 11 inch blank sheets of paper and then asked to draw a picture of a house, tree, and person on each sheet. The examinee is then asked to describe and elaborate on their illustrations. For example, questions such as, "Who is the person you drew?" or "What can you tell me about this house?" can be used to investigate the child's drawings. Each drawing can then be interpreted using a qualitative scoring system such as one devised by Buck (1992); Wenck (1977) also provided an illustrated handbook, with 183 sample illustrations, to facilitate the interpretation of HTP drawings. With the qualitative scoring, the clinician looks for certain characteristics in the drawings that can provide meaningful information about the psychological adjustment of the examinee (i.e., broken windows, heavily drawn tree, or person with no eyes).

Some cautions relative to HTP interpretation are needed. Any interpretation of children's drawings must take into consideration any motor production problems and motor developmental issues that could impact on their representational abilities (e.g., Thomas & Jolley, 1998). Reliability issues have been raised with regard to drawing techniques as well (e.g., Thomas & Jolley, 1998; Veltman & Browne, 2002). Although often used as a nonbiased measure that assumes cross-cultural consistency, there are some indications that, in fact, children's drawings reflect cultural differences as well as individual differences that need to be accounted for (e.g., LaVoy et al., 2001).

## REFERENCES

Buck, J. N. (1948). The H-T-P technique. *Journal of Clinical Psychology, 4*, 319–327.

Buck, J. N. (1992). *House-tree-person projective drawing technique: Manual and interpretive guide* (Rev. ed.). Los Angeles: Western Psychological Services.

Groth-Marnat, G. (1997). *Handbook of psychological assessment* (3rd ed.). New York: Wiley.

LaVoy, S. K., Pedersen, W. C., Reitz, J. M., Brauch, A. A., Luxenberg, T. M., et al. (2001). Children's drawings: A cross-cultural analysis from Japan and the United States. *School Psychology International, 22*, 53–63.

Piotrowski, C., & Zalewski, C. (1993). Training in psychodiagnostic testing in APA-approved PsyD and PhD clinical training programs. *Journal of Personality Assessment, 61*, 394–405.

Thomas, G. V., & Jolley, R. P. (1998). Drawing conclusions: A re-examination of empirical and conceptual bases for psychological evaluation of children from their drawings. *Journal of Clinical Psychology, 37*, 127–139.

Veltman, M. W. M., & Browne, K. D. (2002). The assessment of drawings from children who have been maltreated: A systematic review. *Child Abuse Review, 11*, 19–37.

Watkins, C. E., Jr., Campbell, V. L., Nieberding, R., & Hallmark, R. (1995). Contemporary practice of psychological assessment by clinical psychologists. *Professional Psychology: Research and Practice, 26*(1), 54–60.

Wenck, L. S. (1977). *House-tree-person drawings: An illustrated diagnostic handbook.* Los Angeles: Western Psychological Services.

OLGA L. RODRIGUEZ-ESCOBAR
CYNTHIA A. RICCIO
*Texas A&M University*

## DRAW-A-PERSON TEST
## KINETIC-FAMILY-DRAWING
## KINETIC-SCHOOL-DRAWING

# HOWE, SAMUEL GRIDLEY (1801–1876)

Samuel Gridley Howe, pioneer educator of the blind and the mentally retarded, was a Massachusetts physician who became superintendent of that state's first school for the blind, which opened in Howe's home in 1832. Later named the Perkins Institution and Massachusetts School for the Blind, Howe's school led in the development of programs to enable blind students to become academically competent, self-reliant, and competitively employable. Howe's most famous student was a deaf-blind child, Laura Bridgeman, and the school's success in educating her led Helen Keller's father (50 years later) to appeal to the Perkins Institution for help, with the result that Anne Sullivan became young Helen's teacher.

Howe published books for the blind, and through appeals to Congress was instrumental in the establishment of the American Printing House for the Blind in 1879. Howe accepted a blind, mentally retarded student in 1839, demonstrated that such a child could be successfully educated, and, in 1848, established an experimental program at Perkins for blind, mentally retarded students. With encouraging results in this program, Howe convinced the legislature that education of the mentally retarded should be a public responsibility, and a state school for the mentally retarded was authorized. That school, established in 1855, became the Walter E. Fernald State School.

## REFERENCES

Kanner, L. (1964). *A history of the care and study of the mentally retarded.* Springfield, IL: Thomas.

Scheerenberger, R. C. (1983). *A history of mental retardation.* Baltimore: Brookes.

Schwartz, H. (1956). *Samuel Gridley Howe, social reformer.* Cambridge, MA: Harvard University Press.

PAUL IRVINE
*Katonah, New York*

# HUMAN GENOME PROJECT

The Human Genome Project (HGP) was the international, collaborative research program whose goal was the complete mapping and understanding of all the genes of human beings. All our genes are together known as our *genome*. The HGP was the natural culmination of the history of genetics research. In 1911, Alfred Sturtevant, then an undergraduate researcher in the laboratory of Thomas Hunt Morgan, realized that he could—and had to, in order to manage his data—map the locations of the fruit fly (Drosophila melanogaster) genes whose mutations the Morgan laboratory was tracking over generations. Sturtevant's very first gene map can be likened to the Wright brothers' first flight at Kitty Hawk. In turn, the Human Genome Project can be compared to the Apollo program's bringing humans to the moon.

The hereditary material of all multicellular organisms is the famous double helix of deoxyribonucleic acid (DNA), which contains all of our genes. DNA, in turn, is made up of four chemical bases, pairs of which form the rungs of the twisted, ladder-shaped DNA molecules. All genes are made up of stretches of these four bases, arranged in different ways and in different lengths. HGP researchers have deciphered the human genome in three major ways: determining the order, or sequence, of all the bases in our genome's DNA; making maps that show the locations of genes for major sections of all our chromosomes; and producing what are called linkage maps, complex versions of the type originated in early Drosophila research, through which inherited traits (such as those for genetic disease) can be tracked over generations.

The HGP has revealed that there are probably somewhere between 30,000 and 40,000 human genes. The completed human sequence can now identify their locations. This ultimate product of the HGP has given the world a resource of detailed information about the structure, organization, and function of the complete set of human genes. This information can be thought of as the basic set of inheritable instructions for the development and function of a human being.

The International Human Genome Sequencing Consortium published the first draft of the human genome in the journal *Nature* in February 2001, with the sequence of the entire genome's three billion base pairs some 90 percent complete. A startling finding of this first draft was that the number of human genes appeared to be significantly fewer than previous estimates, which ranged from 50,000 genes to as many as 140,000. The full sequence was completed and published in April 2003.

Upon publication of the majority of the genome in February 2001, Francis Collins, the director of NHGRI, noted that the genome could be thought of in terms of a book with multiple uses: "It's a history book—a narrative of the journey of our species through time. It's a shop manual, with an incredibly detailed blueprint for building every human cell. And it's a transformative textbook of medicine, with insights that will give health care providers immense new powers to treat, prevent and cure disease" (NHGRI, 2006).

The tools created through the HGP also continue to inform efforts to characterize the entire genomes of several other organisms used extensively in biological research, such as mice, fruit flies, and flatworms. These efforts support each other, because most organisms have many similar, or homologous, genes with similar functions. Therefore, the identification of the sequence or function of a gene in a model organism, for example, the roundworm *C. elegans,* has the potential to explain a homologous gene in human beings, or in one of the other model organisms. These ambitious goals required and will continue to demand a variety of new technologies that have made it possible to relatively rapidly construct a first draft of the human genome and to continue to refine that draft. These techniques include:

- DNA Sequencing
- The Employment of Restriction Fragment-Length Polymorphisms (RFLP)

- Yeast Artificial Chromosomes (YAC)
- Bacterial Artificial Chromosomes (BAC)
- The Polymerase Chain Reaction (PCR)
- Electrophoresis

Of course, information is only as good as the ability to use it. Therefore, advanced methods for widely disseminating the information generated by the HGP to scientists, physicians, and others is necessary in order to ensure the most rapid application of research results for the benefit of humanity. Biomedical technology and research are particular beneficiaries of the HGP.

However, the momentous implications for individuals and society for possessing the detailed genetic information made possible by the HGP were recognized from the outset. Another major component of the HGP—and an ongoing component of NHGRI—is therefore devoted to the analysis of the ethical, legal, and social implications (ELSI) of our newfound genetic knowledge, and the subsequent development of policy options for public consideration. The information in this entry was provided by the public domain web site for the National Human Genome Research Institute of the National Institute of Health and can be reached online at http://www.genome.gov.

### REFERENCE

National Human Genome Research Institute (NHGRI). (2006). *All about the Human Genome Project.* Retrieved June 12, 2006, from http://www.genome.gov/10001772

STAFF

**GENETIC COUNSELING**
**GENETIC MAPPING**


## HUMANISM AND SPECIAL EDUCATION

Humanistic approaches to education draw heavily from humanistic philosophy and humanistic psychology. Examples may be found in the alternative or free schools, the most prominent of these being Summerhill, founded by A. S. Neill (1960). It was Neill's belief that children do not need teaching as much as they need love, understanding, approval, and responsible freedom. Self-direction, self-evaluation, and self-fulfillment were emphasized at his school. Another humanistic approach to education was Brown's (1971) confluent education. Believing that education of the whole person is important, he described confluent education as a philosophy and a process of teaching and learning that focuses on both the affective and the cognitive domains. Other humanistic strategies included Simon's values clarification exercises, Kohlberg's moral development activities, Ojemann's causal orientation, Glasser's classroom meetings, Palomares' magic circle, Dinkmeyer's Developing Understanding of Self and Others, Alschuler's organizational approach, Redl's life space interviewing, and Weinstein's trumpet technique. Whatever the approach or strategy, all seemed to be directed toward the goal of the fullest use of capacities by all human beings (Simpson & Gray, 1976).

Prior to 1800 little or no attention was given to the development of the capacities of individuals with disabilities. Among the earliest to provide humane treatment was Pinel. His methods, which became known as moral treatment, were elaborated on and extended by his students and admirers, the best known of whom was perhaps Itard. Not only did Itard attempt to socialize a boy found in the forests of Aveyron, France, but he also attempted to understand the mind and emotions of the child and to feel with and care for him.

The first children with disabilities to receive the attention of organized groups were probably the blind and deaf. Noteworthy here is the work of Howe, who was able to make a significant breakthrough in the education of these special children owing, in part, to his unique ability to understand their inner world. Also influential was Rush, whose emphasis on love-oriented methods of control foreshadowed current appeals for more caring relationships with children (Kauffman, 1981; Suran & Rizzo, 1979).

The positivism and humane care associated with moral treatment in the first half of the 1800s gave way to pessimism and dehumanizing institutionalization that continued into the 1900s. In works such as *Christmas in Purgatory, Exodus from Pandemonium,* and *Souls in Extremis,* Blatt (1981) revealed how society treated the mentally retarded. *In and Out of Mental Retardation* is his plea for more humane treatment. "This book took 30 years to write," he said, "and I hope it will teach someone that what we can learn from the life of Helen Keller isn't only that she was educable but that all people are educable" (p. xv). Echoing Blatt were persons such as Baum (1982), Hobbs (1974), and Long, Morse, and Newman (1980). Others calling for freedom, openness, and humanism in special education included Dennison, Grossman, Knoblock, Schultz, Heuchert, and Stampf (Kauffman, 1981).

As attitudes began to change, the rights of children were reinforced at three distinct levels: policy statements of national and international organizations such as the Bill of Rights for Children; court decisions such as *Brown* v. *Board of Education,* providing equal access to educational opportunities; and legislation enacted by Congress, the most important being the Education for All Handicapped Children Act (PL 94-142) passed in 1975 to ensure a free and appropriate public education for all special children (Suran & Rizzo, 1979). However, with regard to the legislation, Morse (1979) noted that the child too often got lost. He called for the humanization of special education with the individual student as the focus. Fischer and Rizzo (1974),

Newberger (1978), Shelton (1977), and Zeff (1977) were among those suggesting ways to humanize special education. Fischer and Rizzo offered the following suggestions in their paradigm for humanizing special education. Recognize that special children are experiencing, purposive beings; deemphasize testing and give priority to assessing how the child does what in specific circumstances; replace diagnosis with concrete recommendations; allow the child to be a co-assessor/planner (Rayder, 1978); provide students with access to their files, allowing them to have input; and shift focus from limitation to possibility, with the child participating in the direction of his or her life as much as possible.

Newberger presented a mainstreaming reintegration process, situational socialization, through which individuals with disabilities could be helped to acquire the knowledge, behaviors, and attitudes needed to interact successfully with others. Shelton focused on considerations necessary when planning a successful affective program for the learning disabled. Zeff described the implementation and outcome of a group tutorial program designed to help underachieving students.

An illustrative humanistic approach to special education was in operation at the P. K. Yonge School in Florida. There all pupils were in regular heterogeneous classroom groups. Goals were that each student develop increasingly positive perceptions of himself or herself; accept increasing responsibility for his or her behavior and learning; develop those skills and attitudes necessary for effective group living and interaction; learn to adapt to change and effect change constructively; become an effective lifelong learner; and find real meaning in life. Underlying values included sensitivity, authenticity, self-realization, involvement, creativity, pursuit of excellence, and responsibility (Brown, 1973).

Humanistic approaches to teacher education have been proposed in order to prepare humanistic teachers of special children (Bruininks, 1977; Simpson & Gray, 1976). In these programs teacher education was not centered on learning how to teach but rather on learning how to use one's self and surroundings to help students learn (Wass, Blume, Combs, & Hedges, 1974).

A teacher who devises an education for special children based on a humanistic model will be more of a resource and catalyst for children's learning than a director of activities. The classroom atmosphere will be nontraditional, affectively charged, and personal (Kauffman, 1981). Interactions between the teacher and students will be characterized by respect and acceptance, and students' needs for identity, achievement, and individual treatment will be recognized.

## REFERENCES

Baum, D. D. (Ed.). (1982). *The human side of exceptionality.* Baltimore: University Park Press.

Bernard, H. W., & Huckins, W. C. (1974). *Humanism in the classroom.* Boston: Allyn & Bacon.

Blatt, B. (1981). *In and out of mental retardation.* Baltimore: University Park Press.

Brown, G. I. (1971). *Human teaching for human learning.* New York: Viking.

Brown, J. W. (1973). *A humanistic approach to special education.* (Resource Monograph No. 8). Gainesville, FL: P. K. Yonge Laboratory School.

Bruininks, V. L. (1977). A humanistic competency-based training for teachers of learning disabled students. *Journal of Learning Disabilities, 10,* 518–526.

Fischer, C. T., & Rizzo, A. A. (1974). A paradigm for humanizing special education. *Journal of Special Education, 8,* 321–329.

Hobbs, N. (1974). *The future of children.* San Francisco: Jossey-Bass.

Kauffman, J. M. (1981). *Characteristics of children's behavior disorders* (2nd ed.). Columbus, OH: Merrill.

Long, N. J., Morse, W. C., & Newman, R. G. (1980). *Conflict in the classroom* (4th ed.). Belmont, CA: Wadsworth.

Morse, W. C. (Ed.). (1979). *Humanistic teaching for exceptional children.* Syracuse, NY: Syracuse University Press.

Neill, A. S. (1960). *Summerhill.* New York: Hart.

Newberger, D. A. (1978). Situational socialization: An affective interaction component of the mainstreaming reintegration construct. *Journal of Special Education, 12,* 113–121.

Rayder, N. F. (1978, March). *Public outcry for humane evaluation and isomorphic validity.* Paper presented at the meeting of the American Educational Research Association, Toronto, Canada.

Shelton, M. N. (1977). Affective education and the learning disabled student. *Journal of Learning Disabilities, 10,* 618–624.

Simpson, E. L., & Gray, M. A. (1976). *Humanistic education: An interpretation.* Cambridge, MA: Ballinger.

Suran, B. G., & Rizzo, J. V. (1979). *Special children: An integrative approach.* Glenview, IL: Scott, Foresman.

Wass, H., Blume, R. A., Combs, A. W., & Hedges, W. D. (1974). *Humanistic teacher education: An experiment in systematic curriculum innovation.* Fort Collins, CO: Shields.

Zeff, S. B. (1977). A humanistic approach to helping underachieving students. *Social Casework, 58,* 359–365.

GLENNELLE HALPIN
*Auburn University*

ECOLOGICAL EDUCATION FOR CHILDREN WITH
   DISABILITIES
HISTORY OF SPECIAL EDUCATION

# HUMAN RESOURCE DEVELOPMENT

Human resource development (HRD) in special education involves the implementation of approaches and interventions designed to improve the functioning of professionals and paraprofessionals in their delivery of special education services. The need for HRD in special education has been exacerbated by four historical trends and events: (1) the changing nature of special education, (2) burnout of special services providers, (3) new professional and legal requirements, and (4) the increasing demand for special education services. The changing nature of special education is evident in many ways, including the introduction of new technologies such as computers. For special services providers to keep abreast of advances, it is important that they participate in skill and knowledge development activities. Burnout and stress have been recognized as important problems for many types of employees, and a review of the literature suggests that special services providers are not exempt from burnout and high levels of job-related stress (Cherniss, 1985).

The HRD approaches and interventions may have the potential for reducing burnout and stress in special education by enriching the work experience of special services providers. The significance of HRD for special education is further underscored by changing professional and legal requirements. The advent of PL 94-142, for example, placed new demands on many special services providers such as multidisciplinary team decision making. It has been argued (Yoshida, 1980) that special services providers and others may have been ill prepared to participate in team decision making. The need for HRD in special education is evident from the increasing demand for special education services. As Sarason (1982) has noted, it is unlikely that traditional approaches to training will be able to generate the number of individuals needed to provide the requested services. Therefore, it is also important to engage various nonprofessional groups (e.g., classroom instructional aides, parents, and even students) in special education HRD.

In contrast to traditional staff development efforts, which have almost exclusively focused on technical competencies, HRD interventions can focus on a broad spectrum of areas that might be functionally related to job performance. These areas include: (1) technical competencies, (2) interpersonal competencies, (3) professional responsibilities, and (4) job satisfaction. Technical competencies refer to job-related knowledge and skills. Interpersonal competencies concern conflict resolution and assertiveness skills that are important to maintaining productive work relationships. Professional responsibilities encompass fulfilling job-related duties in a reliable and timely manner. Job satisfaction is a multidimensional concept referring to both task satisfaction and satisfaction with the organizational climate of the work setting.

Interventions intended to develop these HRD areas can be implemented within the context of several general approaches to HRD, such as in-service training, supervision, consultation, team building, job design, and professional self-management. In-service training has typically involved performance evaluations, participation in conventions and workshops, reading of professional literature, and courses at local colleges (Maher, Cook, & Kruger, 1990). Supervision that is intended to facilitate HRD might involve participatory decision making, goal setting, performance review, and feedback activities. Consultation for the purpose of HRD is voluntarily engaged in by the consultee and might involve the consultee in activities similar to those described with respect to supervision. Team-building approaches to HRD can focus on either improving the functioning of existing work teams or the development of new work teams (Woodman & Sherwood, 1980). Job design as an HRD approach focuses on changing elements of work tasks and setting work conditions so that tasks can be performed in an exemplary manner (Gilbert, 1978). A sixth approach to HRD is professional self-management (Maher, 1985). Professional self-management is characterized by self-initiated and self-sustained efforts to improve one's management of time, stress, intervention cases, interpersonal conflicts, and continuing education.

## REFERENCES

Cherniss, C. (1985). Stress, burnout, and the special services providers. *Special Services in the Schools, 2*, 45–61.

Gilbert, T. (1978). *Human competence: Engineering worthy performance.* New York: McGraw-Hill.

Maher, C. A. (1985). *Professional self-management: Techniques for special services providers.* Baltimore: Brookes.

Maher, C. A., Cook, S. A., & Kruger, L. J. (1990). A behavioral approach to human resources development in schools. In C. A. Maher & S. G. Forman (Eds.), *Providing effective educational services: Behavioral approaches.* Hillsdale, NJ: Erlbaum.

Sarason, S. B. (1982). *The culture of the school and the problem of change* (2nd ed.). Boston: Allyn & Bacon.

Woodman, R. W., & Sherwood, J. J. (1980). The role of team development in organizational effectiveness. *Psychological Bulletin, 88*, 166–186.

Yoshida, R. K. (1980). Multidisciplinary decision making in special education: Review of the issues. *School Psychology Review, 9*, 221–227.

CHARLES A. MAHER
*Rutgers University*

LOUIS J. KRUGER
*Tufts University*

MULTIDISCIPLINARY TEAMS
PERSONNEL TRAINING IN SPECIAL EDUCATION

## HUMPHREY, ELLIOTT S. (1888–1981)

Elliott S. (Jack) Humphrey, after early experiences as a jockey and a cowboy, made a career of the breeding and training of animals. He trained lions and tigers for circuses, and bred some of the dogs used by Admiral Richard E.

Elliott S. Humphrey

Byrd in his Antarctic expedition. Dorothy Eustis, who later founded The Seeing Eye, the first American organization to train dogs as guides for the blind, hired Humphrey to breed and train guide dogs for the blind. His teaching methods are credited with the immediate success of The Seeing Eye when it was established in 1928. His methods are used today by more than half a dozen other programs that train guide dogs. Faced with difficulty in finding competent instructors for The Seeing Eye, Humphrey designed and operated a school for instructors that provided not only teachers needed at The Seeing Eye but staff for other guide-dog programs as well. Humphrey published a book on the breeding of working dogs, and lectured on his specialty at Columbia University. During World War II he served as a commander in the Coast Guard, with responsibility for organizing and directing a school for dog trainers for the armed forces.

## REFERENCES

Humphrey, E. S., & Warner, L. H. (1934). *Working dogs.* Baltimore: Johns Hopkins University Press.

Putnam, P. B. (1979). *Love in the lead.* New York: Dutton.

PAUL IRVINE
*Katonah, New York*

## HUNGERFORD, RICHARD H. (1903–1974)

Richard H. Hungerford, a leader in the field of mental retardation, served from 1942 to 1953 as director of the Bureau for Children with Retarded Mental Development in the New York City public schools. Subsequently he was superintendent of the Laconia, New Hampshire, State School;

executive director of the Gulf Bend Center for Children and Youth in Victoria, Texas; executive director of Mental Health and Mental Retardation Services for the diocese of Galveston-Houston; and professor of special education at Boston University.

During the 1940s, Hungerford developed for New York City's schools a comprehensive curriculum for mentally retarded students that emphasized specific occupational preparation, training in home living skills, and activities aimed at the development of social competence. In 1943 he co-founded, with Chris J. DeProspo, *Occupational Education,* a journal for teachers of mentally retarded pupils. Hungerford's thoughtful writings, especially his beautifully written essays, such as "On Locusts," inspired both laymen and colleagues in the field of mental retardation. Hungerford served as president of the American Association on Mental Deficiency and was editor of its *American Journal of Mental Deficiency* from 1948 to 1959.

## REFERENCES

Blatt, B. (1975). Toward an understanding of people with special needs: Three teachers. In J. M. Kauffman & J. S. Payne (Eds.), *Mental retardation: Introduction and personal perspectives.* Columbus, OH: Merrill.

Hungerford, R. H. (1950). On locusts. *American Journal of Mental Deficiency, 54,* 415–418.

PAUL IRVINE
*Katonah, New York*

## HUNT, JOSEPH McVICKER (1906–1991)

Joseph McVicker Hunt was born in Scottsbluff, Nebraska, on March 19, 1906. He attended the University of Nebraska, receiving his BA degree there in 1929 and his MA in 1930. He then received his PhD degree in 1933 from Cornell University. On graduating, he became a National Research Council fellow in psychology, spending the year 1933–1934 at New York Psychiatric Institute and Columbia University and 1934–1935 at Worcester State Hospital and Clark University. After a year as visiting assistant professor of psychology at the University of Nebraska in 1935, Hunt went to Brown University as an instructor in psychology in 1936, advancing to assistant professor in 1938 and associate professor in 1944. While at Brown, Hunt became associated with Butler Hospital in Providence, Rhode Island, acting as research associate (1944–1946) and as director (1946–1951). In 1951, Hunt joined the department of psychology at the University of Illinois as professor of psychology, a position he held until gaining Professor Emeritus status in 1974. Hunt died in 1991.

Hunt is well-known for his many studies in child psychology. Aside from being professor of psychology, he was also professor of early education at the University of Illinois

**Joseph McVicker Hunt**

(1967–1974). He was chair of the White House Task Force on Early Childhood Education and was instrumental in the preparation of the report "A Bill of Rights for Children." That report recommended extending Head Start programs to very young children and promoted a follow-through program that would extend the age limits of Head Start children.

Hunt's long list of publications have dealt with problems of clinical psychology, child psychology, social casework, personality and behavior disorders, and intelligence.

## REFERENCES

Hunt, J. McV. (1950). *Measuring results in social casework: A comparison of diagnostic and functional casework concepts.* New York: Family Service Association of America.

Hunt, J. McV. (1965). *Intrinsic motivation and its role in psychological development.* Proceedings of the Nebraska Symposium on Motivation. Lincoln: University of Nebraska Press.

Hunt, J. McV. (1986). Effect of variations in quality and type of early child care on development. *New Directions for Child Development, No. 32,* 31–48.

Hunt, J. McV. (1987). Effects of differing kinds of experience in early rearing conditions. In I. C. Uzgiris & J. McV. Hunt (Eds.), *Infant performance and experience: New findings with the ordinal scales.* Urbana: University of Illinois Press.

Hunt, J. McV. (1988). Relevance to educability: Heritability or range of reaction. In S. G. Cole & R. G. Demaree (Eds.), *Applications of interactionist psychology: Essays in honor of Saul B. Sells.* Hillsdale, NJ: Erlbaum.

RAND B. EVANS
*Texas A&M University*
First edition

MARIE ALMOND
*The University of Texas of the Permian Basin*
Second edition

# HUNTER, MADELINE CHEEK (1916–1994)

Madeline Cheek Hunter developed a model for teaching and learning that has been widely disseminated in schools throughout the United States and abroad since the 1960s. Her principles of instruction, based on the premise that the teacher is a decision maker, translated psychological theory into practical language that teachers can understand and apply in the classroom (Goldberg, 1990).

Hunter viewed her model as one that increased the probability of learning by identifying decisions teachers must make, using research evidence to support those decisions, and using student data to augment or correct those decisions (Hunter, 1985). According to Hunter, every decision a teacher makes falls into one of three categories: (1) what you are going to teach, (2) what the students will do to learn it and to let you know they've learned it, and (3) what the teacher will do to facilitate and escalate that learning (Goldberg, 1990). Applied correctly, Hunter asserted that her principles of instruction are appropriate for a variety of teaching circumstances, audiences, and disciplines (Brandt, 1985).

Born in Canada, Hunter emigrated to California with her family at an early age, receiving her education (BA, MA, and PhD) at the University of California at Los Angeles. Working as a psychologist in the inner city of Los Angeles, first at Children's Hospital and later at Juvenile Hall, she found the interventions, which focused on remediation, not prevention, to be "too little, too late" (Goldberg, 1990, p. 42). Convinced that real progress could only be made through prevention, she became a school psychologist in the urban, multicultural schools of Los Angeles. In that capacity, she observed that even very dedicated and capable teachers often failed to see the connection between research and practice (Goldberg, 1990).

After 13 years in Los Angeles area public schools, in 1962 she became associated with the University of California at Los Angeles (UCLA) as principal of the University Elementary School (aka UCLA Lab School) and professor in the College of Education (Goldberg, 1990). During those years, she worked closely with John Goodlad, renowned educator and dean of the UCLA Graduate School of Education. Because Hunter was both a trained psychologist and an experienced educator, she considered herself well-versed in both theory and practice (Brandt, 1985).

During her tenure at UCLA, Hunter developed her model of instruction, which she regarded as professional decision making (Hunter, 1979). In 1967, Hunter published a series of booklets to help teachers translate theory into practice— *Motivation Theory for Teachers, Reinforcement Theory for Teachers,* and *Retention Theory for Teachers.* These programmed, or self-instructional, booklets led the educator through a series of decisions, providing both instruction and application of her model in the process. In addition to her publications, she provided professional development training for teachers and administrators throughout the United States, Asia, Russia, and Europe (Brandt, 1985).

Hunter regarded teaching as a kind of "performance be-havior like music, like dancing, like athletics, like surgery. You have to automate many behaviors so you can perform them artistically at high speed" (Goldberg, 1990, p. 42). She emphasized that the basic principles of sound teaching must underlie every lesson. Although these principles form the basis of the lesson, no lesson should look the same; the teacher should decide which elements to include in a particular lesson (Hunter, 1986). "There is absolutely nothing you should expect to see in every lesson and nothing you have to do in education—except *think*" (Goldberg, 1990, p. 43).

Over the years, she developed an entourage of educators who were practicing her model and training others to use them (Coulombe, 1994). Reflecting her belief that effective teachers are active decision makers, Hunter chose to not certify instructors nor standardize her training (Hunter, 1986). Although her principles of instruction were designed to help teachers plan and deliver instruction, in its dissemination this model was oversimplified (Hunter, 1986). This lack of standardization led to various interpretations of the "Hunter model," some of which may have been less than accurate representations of her work, sometimes becoming rigid formulas. Hunter's work is known by several different names, including a clinical theory of instruction, mastery teaching, clinical teaching, the UCLA model, and the Hunter Model (Ryan, Jackson, & Levinson, 1986).

The Hunter Model has not been without critics; debate about its pros and cons has flourished for decades, continuing into the twenty-first century (Gibboney, 1987; Johnson, 2000; Wolfe, 1998). To many, "doing the Madeline Hunter Model" meant strictly including seven elements in every lesson plan, much to Hunter's dismay (Goldberg, 1990). The oft-cited elements are (1) objectives, (2) standards, (3) anticipatory set, (4) teaching (which also includes input, modeling, and checking for understanding), (5) guided practice, (6) closure, and (7) independent practice. Hunter vehemently disavowed such practices, and was openly critical of principals who evaluated teacher performance using a checklist of these elements (Hunter, 1985).

The oversimplification of the Hunter model may lie, not in the fundamental principles of her model, but in the traditional implementation of inservice teacher education, frequently limited to a few hours (Goldberg, 1990). To successfully internalize her model of instruction, Hunter recommended about 2 years of dedicated study, with coaching as an essential component. She believed that the lack of coaching during and after inservice training of any kind is a grievous error, with the result that teachers rarely translate theory into "artistic procedures" (Hunter, 1985). Her greatest hope was that her work will help teaching become a profession, where its practitioners are decision makers who never stop learning (Goldberg, 1990).

## REFERENCES

Brandt, R. (1985). On teaching and supervising: A conversation with Madeline Hunter. *Educational Leadership, 42*(5), 61–66.

Coulombe, G. (1994). Remembering Madeline Hunter. *Educational Leadership, 67,* 337–338.

Gibboney, R. A. (1987). A critique of Madeline Hunter's teaching model from Dewey's perspective. *Educational Leadership, 44*(5), 46–50.

Goldberg, M. F. (1990). Portrait of Madeline Hunter. *Educational Leadership, 47*(5), 141–143.

Hunter, M. (1967). *Motivation theory for teachers.* El Segundo, CA: TIP Publications.

Hunter, M. (1967). *Reinforcement theory for teachers.* El Segundo, CA: TIP Publications.

Hunter, M. (1967). *Retention theory for teachers.* El Segundo, CA: TIP Publications.

Hunter, M. (1969). *Teach more—faster!* El Segundo, CA: TIP Publications.

Hunter, M. (1971). *Teach for transfer.* El Segundo, CA: TIP Publications.

Hunter, M. (1979). Teaching is decision making. *Educational Leadership, 37*(1), 62–64, 67.

Hunter, M. (1985). What's wrong with Madeline Hunter? *Educational Leadership, 42*(5), 57–60.

Hunter, M. (1986). Madeline Hunter replies: Develop collaboration; build trust. *Educational Leadership, 43*(6), 68.

Johnson, A. P. (2000). It's time for Madeline Hunter to go: A new look at lesson plan design. *Action in Teacher Education, 22*(1), 72–78.

Ryan, C. W., Jackson, B. L., & Levinson, E. M. (1986). Human relations skills training in teacher education: The link to effective practice. *Journal of Counseling & Development, 65*(2), 114–116.

Wolfe, P. (1998). Revisiting effective teaching. *Educational Leadership, 56*(3), 61–64.

ELAINE A. CHEESMAN
*University of Colorado at
Colorado Springs*

# HUNTER SYNDROME (MUCOPOLY SACCHARIDOSIS II)

Hunter syndrome (mucopoly saccharidosis II), which belongs to a general family of mucopolysaccharide disorders (including Hurler, Scheie, Hurler-Scheie, Marquio, and Sanfillipo syndromes; Brown & Trivette, 1998), is transmitted as an X-linked recessive trait that occurs primarily in males. Growth during the first 2 years is normal, with malformations occurring during years 2 to 4. There are two types of Hunter syndrome, A (severe) and B (mild). In type A, there is no clouding of corneas and death usually occurs before year 15. Concomitant mental retardation and learning levels are higher than for children with Hurler syndrome (Carter, 1978). However, behavior disorders and hyperactive and destructive behavior are often seen as a result, and the children tend to become difficult to manage as they mature. With type B, survival rates may extend to age 50, with fair intelligence possible (Wortis, 1981).

Children having Hunter syndrome will appear short in stature with stiff joints and a large abdomen (associated with enlarged organs like the spleen and liver). Children have a large head, prominent forehead, long skull, and coarse eyebrows. Thick lips, broad flat nose, and misaligned teeth are seen as the child develops. Hairiness, especially in brows and lashes, is characteristic and usually apparent by 2 to 4 years of age. Hands are clawlike, with short and stubby fingers; stiff hands and feet may present mobility and coordination problems (Lemeshaw, 1982).

Mental retardation occurs in varying degrees but because development is normal to age 2 or beyond, cognitive and verbal capabilities may be higher than in other syndromes having similar physical characteristics. Motor retardation may be more likely as the child matures. Seizures also have been noted in older children. Progressive nerve deafness and occasional vision problems are present in some Hunter syndrome children (Illingworth, 1983). Many learning-disabled like symptoms (low attention span, hyperkinesis, negative behavior) may also be displayed.

Health and behavior problems, coupled with the motoric and mental disabilities that occur later in development, may require placement in a more restricted setting than the regular classroom. Visual, speech, and hearing impairments that may occur will need to be assessed and remediated by a special education specialist. Physical and occupational therapy may also be necessary. Hunter syndrome is quite rare, occurring in about 1 per 140,000 male births (Brown & Trivette, 1998).

## REFERENCES

Brown, M. B., & Trivette, P. S. (1998). Mucopolysaccharide disorders. In L. Phelps (Eds.), *Health-related disorders in children and adolescents.* Washington, DC: American Psychological Association.

Carter, C. (Ed.). (1978). *Medical aspects of mental retardation* (2nd ed.). Springfield, IL: Thomas.

Illingworth, R. (1983). *Development of the infant and young child: Abnormal and normal* (7th ed.). New York: Churchill, Livingstone.

Lemeshaw, S. (1982). *The handbook of clinical types in mental retardation.* Boston: Houghton Mifflin.

Wortis, J. (Ed.). (1981). *Mental retardation and developmental disabilities: An annual review.* New York: Brunner/Mazel.

SALLY F. FLAGLER
*University of Oklahoma*

**HURLER SYNDROME
MENTAL RETARDATION
PHYSICAL ANOMALIES**

# HUNTINGTON'S CHOREA

Huntington's chorea, or Huntington's disease, is a degenerative condition, the progression of which is insidious. Its onset generally occurs between 25 and 50 years of age and is characterized by involuntary, irregular, jerking movements (i.e., chorea). Although the condition is often not correctly diagnosed until the onset of the chorea, Bellamy (1961) found that 29 percent of his patients manifested emotional disturbance prior to the abnormal motor movements. As the disease progresses, mental deterioration occurs and, after 10 to 20 years, ends with the death of the afflicted individual.

Huntington's chorea is rare; most prevalence studies agree that it occurs in from 4 to 7 individuals per 100,000 in the population. Although it was long thought not to occur among certain ethnic groups (e.g., Jewish families), such is not the case. However, it is apparently true that, among Japanese, the disease occurs at a much lower rate (about .4 per 100,000).

The major symptoms of the disease had been reported in earlier literature by several individuals: Charles O. Waters in 1841, Charles L. Gorman in 1848, George B. Wood in 1855, and Irving W. Lyon in 1863. Nevertheless, George S. Huntington is widely considered to deserve the use of his name in the medical nomenclature because his 1872 description of the symptoms of the disease was so accurate (DeJong, 1973).

Huntington's chorea is transmitted by a dominant autosome. That is, half of the children of a parent who carries the gene will become afflicted (Coleman, 1964). The prevalence could be reduced to zero in one generation if affected individuals would forego bearing children. Nevertheless, this solution is difficult to implement because the carrier is often unaware of the problem until after the prime reproductive years. In addition, since the disease originates as a defective gene mutation, abstinence on the part of the gene carrier from parenthood remains only a partial solution.

Unfortunately, there is no cure for Huntington's chorea. Though both drug therapy and neurosurgery have been applied successfully to alleviate the symptoms of the disease, the ultimate problem is most likely to be resolved through prevention. The precisely affected genetic structure has been mapped to 4p16.3 (Nation, Turk, & Reynolds, 1998).

The juvenile form of HC is rare and represents about 5 percent of cases of HC. Slurred speech and dysasthria are the most easily recognized symptoms in children but diagnosis is very difficult before age 20. Depression and anxiety are especially prominent in juvenile HC and seizures develop in 25 times more cases of juvenile HC (50 percent) as compared to adult HC (2 percent). Special education is typically required, but symptom management is the only form of treatment (Nation et al., 1998).

## REFERENCES

Bellamy, W. E., Jr. (1961). Huntington's chorea. *North Carolina Medical Journal, 22,* 409–412.

Coleman, J. C. (1964). *Abnormal psychology and modern life* (3rd ed.). Chicago: Scott, Foresman.

DeJong, R. N. (1973). The history of Huntington's chorea in the United States of America. In A. Barbeau, T. Chase, & G. W. Paulson (Eds.), *Advances in neurology—Huntington's chorea* (Vol. 1). New York: Raven.

Nation, P., Turk, K., & Reynolds, C. R. (1998). Huntington's disease. In L. Phelps (Ed.), *Health-selected disorders in children and adolescents* (pp. 337–42). Washington, DC: American Psychological Association.

RONALD C. EAVES
*Auburn University*
First edition

CECIL R. REYNOLDS
*Texas A&M University*
Second edition

**CHOREA
GENETIC COUNSELING**

# HURLER SYNDROME

Hurler syndrome (gargoylism; lipochondrodstrophy), a mucopolysaccharide disorder of the same family as Hunter syndrome, is an inherited metabolic disorder that can affect an individual's physical or mental development. There are two distinct forms of this disease (Stanbury, Wyngaarden, & Fredrickson, 1966). The milder form of this disorder results from an inherited sex-linked recessive gene commonly carried by the X chromosome of the twenty-third pair of chromosomes. It is more likely to be expressed in the male population. The more severe form is inherited by way of an autosomal recessive gene that may affect any one of the 22 genes inherited from either parent (Robinson & Robinson, 1965).

In its milder form, clinical indicators of Hurler syndrome may not be evident at birth, although symptoms generally begin to appear by 6 months of age. By 2 years of age, affected children may reflect retarded physical or mental growth. In its more severe form, individuals may manifest a variety of physical characteristics. Owing to a build up of mucopolysaccharides throughout the body, abnormal growths will result. Tissues in the liver, heart, lungs, and spleen are most often the areas affected. Abnormal lipid deposits may result in lesions in the gray matter of the brain. Even in its severe form, this genetic defect accounts for less than 1 percent of the severe mental retardation in children.

Physical characteristics of this disorder typically include an underdeveloped body with significant disproportion between the head and body. Limbs are short and mobility may be limited as fingers and toes are often fixed in a partial flexed position. Bone abnormalities may affect the vertebrae and result in a shortened neck and protruding belly, with possible umbilical hernia.

Individuals severely affected by Hurler disease often have an enlarged head and protruding forehead. Facial characteristics may include bushy eyebrows, a saddle-shaped nose, double chin, and enlarged tongue. The more common form of this disorder is characterized by dwarfism and corneal clouding. In this more severe form of the disorder, individuals may live only into their teens, with death resulting from heart failure or respiratory disease. In milder cases, there is an absence of corneal clouding and dwarfism, but there is a high frequency of deafness from nerve damage.

Diagnostic advances in detecting fetal abnormalities have accurately confirmed the presence of Hurler syndrome as early as 14 to 16 weeks into gestation. This diagnosis is made on the basis of finding elevated levels of the compound mucopolysaccharide in amniotic fluid (Henderson & Whiteman, 1976). A positive in vitro diagnosis of Hurler syndrome is questionable owing to the variety of related diseases. As advances are made in microtechnology, the efficacy of in vitro diagnosis will increase.

## REFERENCES

Henderson, H., & Whiteman, P. (1976). Antenatal diagnoses of Hurler's disease. *Lancet, 2,* 1024–1025.

Robinson, H. B., & Robinson, N. M. (1965). *The mentally retarded child.* New York: McGraw-Hill.

Stanbury, J. B., Wyngaarden, J. B., & Fredrickson, D. S. (Eds.). (1966). *The metabolic bases of inherited diseases* (2nd ed.). New York: McGraw-Hill.

FRANCINE TOMPKINS
*University of Cincinnati*

AMNIOCENTESIS
CHROMOSOMES, HUMAN ANOMALIES, AND
    CYTOGENETIC ABNORMALITIES
HUNTER SYNDROME

# HYDROCEPHALUS

Hydrocephalus is a condition caused by an accumulation of cerebrospinal fluid (CSF) inside the skull. Most often this condition occurs when the pathways of CSF are somehow blocked, not allowing the fluid to drain as it normally would, but it may also occur with overproduction or lack of reabsorption of CSF (Mathie & Clark, 2003). Hydrocephalus is usually a secondary outcome of another disorder. These underlying etiologies include: neural tube defects (e.g., spina bifida), aqueductal stenosis, Dandy-Walker syndrome (DWS), intraventricular hemorrhage (IVH), and complications from hypoxic-ischemic encephalopathy in premature infants (Fletcher, Dennis, & Northrup, 2000).

Congenital or early-onset hydrocephalus is diagnosed before infants reach 12 months of age. Most cases of congenital hydrocephalus are detected very early—either before, at, or shortly after birth (Fletcher et al., 2000). Babies with this condition often appear lethargic and irritable, with pupils that are sluggish. Also, because the skull sutures of infants have not completely closed, hydrocephalus at this age typically results in an abnormally large head and prominent forehead. Atrophy of the brain, mental deterioration, and convulsions are often common results of early-onset or congenital hydrocephalus. Less commonly, hydrocephalus can occur later in childhood or adulthood, usually as a result of head trauma, infections, or with dementia in adults (Fletcher et al., 2000).

The most common and effective method of treatment for hydrocephalus involves the surgical insertion of a shunt. The shunt acts as an artificial pipeline, directing the CSF around any obstructions so that it can drain away into another area, such as the abdominal cavity (Fletcher et al., 2000).

The extra intracranial pressure caused by the overaccumulation of CSF in hydrocephalus often causes other problems, damaging or impairing brain structures. Additionally, children born with the condition many times also exhibit other malformations of the brain. The corpus callosum may be deformed, the cerebellum may be displaced or partially missing, and there may be reduced brain mass overall or thinning in certain areas (Fletcher et al., 2000).

Children with hydrocephalus commonly experience a wide range of developmental and other difficulties. Specific deficiencies vary depending on the etiology and severity of each child's condition, but many trends have been noted. For example, children afflicted with hydrocephalus commonly exhibit poorly developed motor skills, below-average visual-motor abilities, and difficulty with other areas of nonverbal ability (Mathie & Clark, 2003). Once these children reach school age, a host of learning and behavior problems may arise. While not all children with hydrocephalus require special education placement, many receive services for Specific Learning Disabilities, Emotional Disturbance, Other Health Impairment, or Traumatic Brain Injury. In addition to special education placement, children with hydrocephalus may need tutoring or extra instruction to help them catch up, if they have missed school for hospital stays and medical procedures (Mathie & Clark, 2003). They also may have problems with attention, though these difficulties may be related to nonverbal skills deficiencies (Fletcher et al., 2000).

## REFERENCES

Fletcher, J. M., Dennis, M., & Northrup, H. (2000). Hydrocephalus. In K. O. Yeates, M. D. Ris, & H. G. Taylor (Eds.), *Pediatric neuropsychology* (pp. 25–46). New York: Guilford.

Mathie, H., & Clark, E. (2003). Hydrocephalus, X-linked. In E. Fletcher-Janzen & C. R. Reynolds (Eds.), *Childhood disorders diagnostic desk reference* (pp. 301–302). Hoboken, NJ: Wiley.

LISA A. LOCKWOOD
*Texas A&M University*

DANDY WALKER SYNDROME
OTHER HEALTH IMPAIRED
SPINA BIFIDA

## HYPERACTIVITY

See ATTENTION-DEFICIT/HYPERACTIVITY DISORDER.

## HYPERCALCEMIA

See INFANTILE HYPERCALCEMIA.

## HYPERKINESIS

Hyperkinesis, previously believed to be a behavioral pattern associated with neurological dysfunction, is an archaic diagnostic classification for children with a high degree of activity combined with disordered or unmanageable behavior. It is now subsumed under the classification of Attention-Deficit/Hyperactivity Disorder.

STAFF

## HYPERLEXIA

While some inconsistency in the use of the term *hyperlexia* has occurred, the predominant view is that hyperlexia refers to a developmental disorder characterized by a spontaneous and intense early interest in letters and words. According to Oberschneider, two variants of childhood hyperlexia have been proposed and supported: (1) those who demonstrate hyperlexic characteristics, while also meeting the criteria for Pervasive Developmental Delay Spectrum Disorder; and (2) those who demonstrate milder impairments of cognitive, speech/language, and social/emotional functioning while meeting the criteria for communication disorder. At present, hyperlexia is not diagnosed by itself, and, depending on the severity, occurs with other disorders such as Asperger's Disorder, autistic disorders, Pervasive Developmental Disorder, or one of the communication disorders: Mixed Receptive-Expressive Disorder or Expressive Language Disorder (Oberschneider, 2003).

Healy (1982, as cited in Sparks, 1995) noted three major symptoms in children with hyperlexia: (1) spontaneous reading of words before the age of 5; (2) impaired comprehension on both reading and listening tasks; and (3) word recognition (decoding) skills above expectations, based on other measured cognitive and linguistic abilities. Even though these children, as a group, evidence a wide range of intelligence, the majority of them present at least some degree of general intellectual limitation and many have been classified as borderline or mildly retarded (Sparks, 1995). In addition, there are social and behavioral problems that can manifest in hyperlexia. Examples of some problematic behaviors that are associated with childhood hyperlexia include infrequent initiation of social conversation, an intense need to develop or keep to routines in daily life, difficulty with transitions and ritualistic behaviors, age-appropriate development until 18 to 24 months and then regression, selective listening, or the appearance of being deaf, and specific yet unusual fears (Oberschneider, 2003).

It has been suggested that hyperlexia is associated with abnormal neurobiologic functioning and/or genetic basis because it sometimes accompanies conditions such as Prader-Willi syndrome, Tourette syndrome, Turner syndrome, and mental retardation; however, no consistent pattern of clinical neurobiological findings, laboratory findings, or prenatal, perinatal, or postnatal events have been identified so far (Oberschneider, 2003). Hyperlexia occurs more common in males, with an overall gender ratio of greater than 7:1 males:females (Aram, 1997).

Children with hyperlexia usually receive professional attention because they do not develop speech and language as expected. They rarely produce single words by age 1 and they demonstrate marked delays in the use of word combinations. However, a defining characteristic of children with hyperlexia is early reading, especially when compared to the emergence of oral language. The majority demonstrate word recognition between the ages of 2½ and 3½ years of age (Aram, 1997). Soon, they become preoccupied with reading at the expense of other age-appropriate activities. Children with hyperlexia learn to read more rapidly than controls, and scrambling word order in text disrupts their reading speed far less relative to normal readers (Nation, 1999). Most children with hyperlexia recognize words by utilizing grapheme-phoneme correspondence rules, which demonstrates good use of phonologic rules for word decoding. However, these children demonstrate the dissociation between word decoding and meaningful comprehension.

This suggests that hyperlexia is a disorder of language comprehension and that decoding is a splinter skill dissociated from meaning. Therefore, the clinician should begin with an assessment of language comprehension abilities in order to determine abilities in both meaning (semantic) and structural (syntax) domains. The assessment of comprehension abilities should be ongoing throughout treatment, and the goals of therapy should be continually modified as new behaviors and/or information is presented (Aram, 1997).

## REFERENCES

Aram, D. M. (1997). Hyperlexia: Reading without meaning in young children. *Topics in Language Disorders, 17*(3), 1–13.

Nation, K. (1999). Reading skills in hyperlexia: A developmental perspective. *Psychological Bulletin, 125,* 338–355.

Oberschneider, M. S. (2003). A case of a four-year-old boy with hyperlexia: Some considerations for diagnosis and treatment from a psychodynamic perspective. *Clinical Child Psychology and Psychiatry, 8,* 205–214.

Sparks, R. L. (1995). Phonemic awareness in hyperlexic children. *Reading & Writing: An Interdisciplinary Journal, 7,* 217–235.

ESMERELDA LÓPEZ
*Texas A&M University*

**READING DISORDERS**
**READING REMEDIATION**

# HYPEROPIA

Hyperopia is a visual disorder that results from an error of refraction. Refraction is a process by which light rays are gathered and focused onto certain portions of the retina. The hyperopic eye is too short and too weak to allow this process to take place normally (Heward & Orlansky, 1984). As a result, hyperopia develops. This impedes near vision and is commonly referred to as farsightedness.

The average, normal infant is born farsighted. As the child matures, the hyperopia decreases. This is especially true during puberty, when children who began life without the hyperopic trait will become nearsighted (Michelson, 1980). Children who are left with some farsightedness will become aware of it at different times depending on severity or occupational demands.

Hyperopia is easily treated through the prescription of glasses or contact lenses. However, if untreated, hyperopia can have significant impact on classroom performance. Since a hyperopic student will have difficulty in focusing on near objects, it may become difficult to perform certain academic functions.

## REFERENCES

Heward, W. L., & Orlansky, M. D. (1984). *Exceptional children.* Columbus, OH: Merrill.

Michelson, P. E. (1980). *Insight into eyesight.* Chicago: Nelson-Hall.

JOHN R. BEATTIE
*University of North Carolina at Charlotte*

**VISUAL ACUITY**
**VISUAL EFFICIENCY**

# HYPERTELORISM

Hypertelorism is a descriptive term designating wide orbital separation characterized by separation of the eyes. This represents a retention of the wide, primitive interorbital angle. While early studies suggested a single cause, subsequent evaluations show great variety in the clinical and radiologic appearances of the skull. The condition is distinguished from telecanthus (lateral displacement of the medical canthal tissue), where the interocular (between the eyes) distance is normal (Duke-Elder, 1963).

The retention of a wide interorbital angle is attributed to early ossification of the lesser wings of the sphenoid bone, fixing the orbits in lateral positions. An alternative hypothesis suggests the anomaly results from failure of maxillary process development with compensatory overgrowth of the frontonasal process. Further, it is important to differentiate this anomaly from physiologic variance often associated with racial groups and patients with secondary hypertelorism. Secondary forms follow disturbances in development resulting from various disorders such as frontal encephalocele and trauma. The primary, dysgenetic type may accompany a variety of congenital disorders, including craniofacial abnormalities and many chromosomal aberrations (Jones & Jakobiec, 1979).

Divergent strabismus is the most common associated ocular disorder, although other abnormalities such as microphthalmos, microcornea, and optic atrophy may occur. Mentation is generally good and most patients are described as even-tempered and gentle.

The significance of this anomaly is minimal to the educator except as a clue to other developmental defects. In general, the eye, face and brain develop concurrently; defects in one area suggest the possibility of defects in another. Only if associated with ocular or central nervous system defects would this anomaly be of particular significance.

## REFERENCES

Duke-Elder, S. (1963). *System of ophthalmology: Vol. III, Part 2, Congenital deformities.* St. Louis, MO: Mosby.

Jones, I. S., & Jakobiec, F. A. (1979). *Diseases of the orbit.* Hagerstown, MD: Harper & Row.

GEORGE R. BEAUCHAMP
*Cleveland Clinic Foundation*

# HYPERTHYROIDISM

Hyperthyroidism, also known as thyrotoxicosis, is a metabolic imbalance caused by an overproduction of thyroid hormone. The overproduction of thyroid hormone causes an overall increase in the organism's metabolic rate, which is responsible for a host of medical problems (St. Germain, 2000). Hyperthyroidism is classified as a syndrome, and diagnosis is made based on the presence of symptoms. Two medical conditions lead to the development of hyperthyroidism. In one condition, the thyroid produces too much thyroid hormone. This can occur as a result of tumors of the thyroid gland, pituitary gland, ovaries, or testes; inflammation of the thyroid; ingestion of too much iodine; and Grave's disease (in which the immune system attacks the thyroid). In the second cause, the thyroid gland becomes damaged and leaks thyroid hormone (St. Germain).

Hyperthyroidism occurs in 1:1,000 people or about 2.5 million Americans each year. Several causative conditions are more prevalent in women, including postpartum thyroiditis and Grave's disease, leading to a greater female than male incidence rate. Grave's disease accounts for about 85 percent of the cases of hyperthyroidism and is much more prevalent among women, especially age 20 to 50 years. There also appears to be an increased incidence among individuals with Down syndrome.

Some characteristics of hyperthyroidism may include:

1. Increased appetite with concurrent weight loss. Children and adolescents may be unusually tall and thin (Vaughan, McKay, & Behrman, 1979).

2. Changes in mood and thinking skills, including increased nervousness, restlessness, depression, fatigue, memory, and concentration problems that may impact school or job performance (Vaughan et al., 1979).

3. Heat intolerance and increased sweating.

4. Increased metabolism leading to muscle cramping, irregular heartbeat, chest pains, and perhaps heart attack (St. Germain, 2000).

5. Frequent bowel movements related to overactivity of the intestines (St. Germain, 2000).

6. Menstrual irregularities.

7. The development of goiters or enlargements of the thyroid gland (St. Germain, 2000).

The treatment of hyperthyroidism includes the use of medicine called beta-blockers, such as Inderol, to block the effect of too much thyroid hormone. This treatment is used to deter the effects of overproduction of thyroid on the heart and nervous system (St. Germain, 2000). Beta-blockers are usually the only intervention needed when there is a leakage and the condition tends to be temporary. In cases of overproduction, three types of treatments are available, including antithyroid drug therapy (Porpylthiouracil or Methimazole) to decrease the production of thyroid hormone; use of radioiodine, which often results in hypothyroidism that persists; and surgical removal of the thyroid gland (St. Germain). Treatment of Grave's disease tends to result in short-term remediation of the symptoms, and reoccurrence is common. In children, drug therapy lasting up to 36 months is effective for permanent remediation of symptoms in 75 percent of the children (Vaughan et al., 1979).

Hyperthyroidism occurs in children but is more prevalent among adults. If the symptoms are significant enough to interfere with a child's academic or social functioning, it will likely be labeled under Other Health Impairment according to criteria from the Individuals with Disabilities Education Act. Down syndrome children with hyperthyroidism may receive services under the Mental Disability category or Multiple Disability category. However, hyperthyroidism is a treatable disorder that should not by itself make a child eligible for special education services.

The symptoms of hyperthyroidism tend to develop slowly and are generally not painful. As a result, there may be a lag in diagnosis. The medical field may improve diagnosis so that treatment can be initiated earlier in the course of the syndrome. It is a treatable condition, but treatments may be improved in the future. For example, radioactive iodine therapy is effective, but when using this treatment, the individual must avoid being around others, especially children. In addition, radioactive iodine therapy may induce hypothyroidism, which must then be corrected by introducing natural thyroid hormone. Surgical removal of the thyroid gland also causes hypothyroidism, which must be treated.

## REFERENCES

St. Germain, D. (2000). *All about hyperthyroidism.* Retrieved from http://www.drkoop.com/dyncon/article.asp?id=5894

Vaughan, V. C., McKay, R. J., & Behrman, R. E. (1979). In W. E. Nelson (Ed.), *Nelson textbook of pediatrics* (11th ed., pp. 1164–1167). Philadelphia: W. B. Saunders.

DALENE M. MCCLOSKEY
*University of Northern Colorado*

# HYPERTONIA-RD

Hypertonia is increased tension of the muscles that can make movement difficult. It can also be defined as resistance to passive movement that is not velocity dependent (Pediatric Services, n.d.). Hypertonia usually occurs in definite patterns of flexion or extension (Pedretti & Zoltan, 1990). Difficulties are most predominant in the flexor patterns for the upper extremities and in the extensor patterns of the lower extremities.

There are two main types of hypertonia—rigidity and spasticity—but both can be present in the same individual. Specifically, spasticity is an increase in resistance to sudden passive movement that is velocity dependent. It involves an imbalance between the agonist and antagonist muscle groups. The severity of spasticity is directly related to the speed of the stretch placed on the muscle. In contrast, rigidity is increased muscle tone in both agonist and antagonist muscles simultaneously (Pedretti & Zoltan, 1990). Hypertonia is the opposite of hypotonia.

Hypertonia is commonly associated with other medical disorders such as cerebral palsy (CP), multiple sclerosis (MS), amyotrophic lateral sclerosis (ALS), spina bifida, Parkinson's disease, and head injury. Although identification of the presence of hypertonia is not difficult, determination of the actual cause is significantly more problematic. Children with hypertonia may have difficulty with both fine and gross motor movements and with motor coordination depending on the severity of the condition. Prolonged hypertonicity with spasticity can lead to shortening of the muscles and subsequent contracture and deformity, resulting in severely decreased mobility.

It is not possible to estimate the prevalence of hypertonia because it is not a specific disease, and records do not necessarily specify the frequency of particular symptoms.

Characteristics of hypertonia include: (1) Resistance to passive movement that is not dependent on the velocity of the movement; and (2) Spasticity or rigidity of muscles.

Following the identification of the presence of hypertonia, a treatment program can be developed. Although treatment will not cure the symptoms, it will aid in the prevention of future complications due to the condition. Treatment may also serve to facilitate the child's most appropriate development and teach compensatory skills. Treatment programs incorporate instruction to the child and caregivers in positioning and movement strategies. Medical and surgical interventions and drug treatments that may serve to decrease muscle tone are available.

Collaboration among parents, educators, and medical professionals is crucial to enable the most positive outcome for the child with hypertonia. Children with hypertonia are often identified at an early age through primary care medical settings. It is important for parents to be placed in contact with the local school district or state agencies that provide early intervention services for children ages 0–3 years.

Infants with hypertonia may be eligible for special education services under the provisions of Public Law 99-457 and its reauthorization in 1991 as Public Law 102-119, which mandates services for children from birth to age 3. Eligibility is dependent on associated disabilities rather than on the presence of hypertonia in and of itself. If eligible, an Individual Family Service Plan (IFSP) would be developed to identify goals and services as mandated by Part C of the Individuals with Disabilities Education Act. Preschool and elementary school children may remain eligible to receive services provided that the child falls into one of the specific eligibility classifications and meets the specific state requirements for service provision. Although a child may not be directly eligible to receive services due to the presence of hypertonia, per se, eligibility may be based on associated conditions or disorders. Specific services will be determined on an individualized basis. If educationally necessary, students with hypertonia may receive the related services of occupational, physical, and speech therapies.

The prognosis for children with hypertonia varies depending on several factors, including the root cause of the condition, the severity of the symptoms, and the provision of appropriate early interventions.

## REFERENCES

Pediatric Services. (n.d.). *Understanding the lingo*. Retrieved from http://www.pediatricservices.com

Pedretti, L. W., & Zoltan, B. (1990). *Occupational therapy: Practice skills for physical dysfunction* (3rd ed.). St. Louis, MO: Mosby.

SHELLEY L. F. PELLETIER
SUSAN SAGE
*Dysart Unified School District,*
*El Mirage, Arizona*

## CONGENITAL DISORDERS

# HYPNOSIS

While no generally accepted definition exists, hypnosis is usually considered to be an altered state of consciousness characterized by a heightened susceptibility to suggestion. As an altered state of consciousness, hypnosis is seen as a condition distinct from sleep or wakefulness, perhaps similar to deep meditation, yoga, or some other trancelike state. The heightened susceptibility characteristic relates to the observation that the hypnotized person accepts ideas more uncritically and wholeheartedly than ordinarily (American Society of Clinical Hypnosis, 1973).

Research suggests that the practice of hypnosis extends far back into the history of man. Support for such claims is found in ancient writings from many cultures, including India, Persia, China, and Egypt (Gravitz & Gerton, 1984). The modern history of hypnosis began with Franz Anton Mesmer, a Viennese physician of the late eighteenth and early nineteenth centuries. Mesmer is most famous for his theory of hypnotism as animal magnetism, a force that he believed came from within living bodies and was passed to other living bodies and objects. Mesmer's animal magnetism supposedly could be used to cure serious illnesses. His work gave rise to the term mesmerism, a synonym for hypnosis.

Mesmer's work came to the attention of James Braid, a Scottish physician of the early nineteenth century. Braid, who coined the term hypnotism, rejected Mesmer's animal magnetism theory but emphasized the importance of suggestion and concentration in hypnosis. Braid's experience led him and others to use hypnosis in the treatment of disease; during the 1800s this technique was used successfully as an anesthetic for many surgical procedures (Hilgard & Hilgard, 1975).

Since Braid's time, the use of hypnosis has gone through several periods of public and professional interest and disinterest, and has been studied by such famous scientists as Charles Darwin and Sigmund Freud. Presently, the interest in hypnosis as a medical and psychological aid is high and research into its effective use is expanding. Hypnosis is now viewed by the majority of the professional community as a respectable and useful technique for helping with medical and psychological problems.

Little agreement about the nature of hypnosis exists among the authorities in the field. Numerous competing theories have been proposed, but none seem to explain adequately the phenomenon and no theory has gained wide acceptance. Many theories fit into one of two categories, physiological and psychological. Physiological theories of hypnosis emphasize physical changes that are reported to occur during or as a result of hypnosis: alteration in metabolism, changes in the nervous system, and unusual electrical activity in the brain. Psychological theories stress the importance of psychological factors: learning, suggestion, role-playing, and modeling.

Ernest R. Hilgard, a leader in the scientific study of hypnosis, has proposed a neodissociation theory, which holds that hypnotic procedures rearrange control systems in the brain (Hilgard, 1977). Research by Hilgard and others supports this model. However, at the present time, the scientific understanding of hypnosis is at an early stage of development.

Regardless of the true nature of hypnosis, it can be used to produce some conditions in a subject that are helpful and therapeutic: relaxation, concentration, the ability to put oneself in imaginary situations, and the capacity to accept suggestions more fully. These conditions provide a basis for the application of hypnosis to the treatment of a number of medical and psychological problems.

Hypnosis has been used successfully alone or in combination with other treatment methods in dealing with the following: emotional problems, including anxiety; control of pain; surgery; psychosomatic problems; obesity and dietary problems; smoking; pediatric problems; neurological problems; rehabilitation; conditions related to obstetrics and gynecology; skin problems; sexual dysfunction; and dental procedures. Practical application of hypnosis is extensive. The American Society of Clinical Hypnosis offers extensive resources on the subject at http://www.info@asch.org.

## REFERENCES

American Society of Clinical Hypnosis–Education and Research Foundation. (1973). *A syllabus on hypnosis and a handbook of therapeutic suggestions.* Des Plains, IL: Author.

Gravitz, M. A., & Gerton, M. I. (1984). Hypnosis in the historical development of psychoanalytic psychotherapy. In W. C. Wester & A. H. Smith (Eds.), *Clinical hypnosis: A multidisciplinary approach.* Philadelphia: Lippincott.

Hilgard, E. R. (1977). *Divided consciousness.* New York: Wiley.

Hilgard, E. R., & Hilgard, J. R. (1975). *Hypnosis in the relief of pain.* Los Altos, CA: Kaufman.

ROBERT R. REILLEY
*Texas A&M University*

## PSYCHOSOCIAL ADJUSTMENT

*PSYCHOTHERAPY WITH INDIVIDUALS WITH DISABILITIES*

# HYPOACTIVITY

Hypoactivity is a condition characterized by insufficient or inadequate motor activity and the inability to focus and sustain attention on external stimuli. Myers and Hammill (1969) describe the hypoactive child as one who is lethargic and quiet, and who causes little disturbance in the classroom. These children are more difficult to recognize and identify than are their hyperactive counterparts, and their problems may escape detection.

Although hyperactive and hypoactive children are at opposite ends of an activity level continuum, both show attentional deficits that may interfere with learning. Dykman, Ackerman, Clements, and Peters (1971) discuss the child who is unable to focus attention on the written or spoken word, and who, therefore, cannot easily learn to read or spell. Most frequently, such attention deficits take the form of impulsivity and overreaction to stimuli. However, in the case of hypoactive children, inhibition, passivity, and under-reaction to stimuli are symptomatic of the deficit.

The Russian psychologist A. R. Luria (1959, 1961) has written extensively on attention deficits, and has addressed the problem of hypoactivity specifically. He refers to the syndrome of cerebral asthenia, characterized by an inability to concentrate, distractibility, and short attention span. Luria points out that this syndrome often can be expressed in two externally different but essentially similar forms. He states that nervous processes are reducible to the two basic components of excitation and inhibition, present in all individuals. The strength, concentration, equilibrium, and mobility of excitation and inhibition may be affected by brain pathology. If the pathological state of the cortical cells primarily affects the inhibitory processes, the child displays excessive impulsivity and the loss of control associated with hyperactivity. However, if the pathology is expressed in a decline of the excitatory processes, the child experiences a sharp fall of the tone of the nervous processes and enters into a state of passivity. Luria refers to such children as inhibitory types and describes them as sluggish, torpid, and slow to form new positive reactions to stimuli, much like the hypoactive, learning-disabled child.

Although the literature reflects considerable research focused on hyperactivity, there have been relatively few studies dealing with the hypoactive child. Luria (1961) investigated the role of speech as an influence on the disequilibrium between the basic nervous processes. In experiments that required sustained, focused attention, he found inhibited children failed to make correct motoric responses to stimuli. However, when these children were asked to respond verbally as well as motorically, the accuracy and frequency of their responses increased significantly. Luria concluded that the combination of verbal and motoric responses tones up the activity level of the child, and that the compensatory influence of speech serves to heighten the level of the excitatory processes.

Research by Ozolins and Anderson (1980) showed that behavioral approaches could be used successfully to influence the performance of hypoactive children. In experiments requiring sustained attention, the authors found that such children performed better when given feedback reinforcing correct answers. Knowledge of errors served only to increase already excessive levels of inhibition and reduced correct answers. Positive reinforcement made this group feel more secure and less inhibited in their responses.

**REFERENCES**

Dykman, R. A., Ackerman, P. T., Clements, S. D., & Peters, J. E. (1971). Specific learning disabilities: An attentional deficit syndrome. In H. R. Myklebust (Ed.), *Progress in learning disabilities* (Vol. 2, pp. 56–94). New York: Grune & Stratton.

Luria, A. R. (1959). Experimental study of the higher nervous activity of the abnormal child. *Journal of Mental Deficiency Research, 3,* 1–22.

Luria, A. R. (1961). *The role of speech in the regulation of normal and abnormal behavior.* New York: Liveright.

Myers, P. I., & Hammill, D. D. (1969). *Methods for learning disorders.* New York: Wiley.

Ozolins, D. A., & Anderson, R. P. (1980). Effects of feedback on the vigilance task performance of hyperactive and hypoactive children. *Perceptual and Motor Skills, 50*(2), 415–424.

Barbara S. Speer
*Shaker Heights City School
District, Shaker Heights, Ohio*

**ATTENTION-DEFICIT/HYPERACTIVITY DISORDER
ATTENTION SPAN**

# HYPOGLYCEMIA

Hypoglycemia is a physiological disorder in which a sudden rise and then rapid decrease in blood glucose level occurs within 1 to 3 hours. This abrupt drop in blood glucose sends the body into a condition of near shock that may be exacerbated by stress (Sorochan, 1981). Concomitant symptomatology may include lethargic behavior (unmotivated, fatigued, withdrawn, depressed); erratic behavior (mental confusion, unprovoked anxiety, hyperactivity, aggression); and a craving for sweets (Knapczyk, 1979). This condition of low blood glucose level marks the disorder of hypoglycemia. It is differentiated from hyperglycemia, in which the body has abnormally high blood glucose levels.

The diagnosis of hypoglycemia is made by a physician, who measures the blood glucose level at different times (e.g., before eating, immediately after eating, and a few hours after eating). Before eating, the level is low; it rises after eating and then falls after a few hours. If the rate of the drop in blood glucose level exceeds the normal range for the individual's age group, then the diagnosis of hypoglycemia is positive.

One out of 10 individuals is born with a hypersensitive pancreas (Sorochan, 1981) and is physically incapable of processing large quantities of sugar (or its various derivatives) in foods. The pancreas then produces excess insulin that results in the rapid drop of the blood glucose level. This in turn produces adverse behavior because the brain and other organs depend on an adequate supply of blood glucose for energy.

Some researchers have investigated the relationship between hypoglycemia and behavioral disorders (Knapczyk, 1979) and aggression and psychiatric symptoms (Virkkunen, 1982). Many researchers have concentrated on the area of diet, particularly the reduction of carbohydrates. One of the most effective treatments of hypoglycemia may be a well-controlled elimination diet that advocates six or more meals a day instead of three. The intention is to reduce sugar consumption as well as decrease the amount of time in which the individual is in the low blood glucose state.

Even though hypoglycemia should be diagnosed by a physician, school administrators, psychologists, and teachers also should be aware of the disorder. Consistent observation of a child's erratic behavior following eating may indicate hypoglycemia, and referral to a physician may be in order.

## REFERENCES

Knapczyk, D. R. (1979). Diet control in the management of behavior disorders. *Behavioral Disorders, 1,* 2–9.

Sclafani, A. (1982). On the role of hypoglycemia in carbohydrate appetite. *Appetite, 3,* 227–228.

Sorochan, W. D. (1981). *Promoting your health.* New York: Wiley.

Virkkunen, M. (1982). Reactive hypoglycemic tendency among habitually violent offenders: A further study by means of the glucose tolerance test. *Neuropsychobiology, 1,* 35–40.

SCOTT W. SAUTTER
*Peabody College, Vanderbilt University*

ACTING OUT
BEHAVIORAL DISORDERS
DIABETES

# HYPOTHYROIDISM

Hypothyroidism results from depletion in the concentration of thyroid hormone in the body. Thyroid hormone is released by the thyroid gland situated at the base of the neck. This important hormone is fundamental for normal metabolic rates in adults and is essential for growth and maturation in children. Depletion of thyroid hormone may occur as a result of treatment for *hyperthyroidism,* damage to the thyroid gland (i.e., primary hypothyroidism), a deficiency of iodine in the diet, or by a disorder of the pituitary gland (i.e., secondary hypothyroidism). There are three major types of hypothyroidism, and these include congenital, juvenile, and adult (Noble, Leyland, & Clark, 2000; Price & Wilson, 1997).

Congenital hypothyroidism (cretinism) is noticeable at birth and is often the result of a developmental defect (Price & Wilson, 1997). Most infants with this disorder have a defective thyroid gland or no gland at all. The infant usually has prolonged jaundice and a hoarse cry. Other noteworthy physical abnormalities include a large tongue that protrudes from the mouth and an umbilical hernia. Difficulty with feeding, excessive sleep, lethargy, and mental retardation are common (Kunz & Finkel, 1987; Price & Wilson, 1997). These infants fail to meet normal developmental milestones, and their teeth are often underdeveloped. Congenital hypothyroidism is incurable. However, immediate medical treatment at birth can circumvent mental retardation and growth failure (Beckwith & Tucker, 1988; Clayman, 1989; Dallas, 2000; Price & Wilson, 1997). Permanent intellectual deficits are typical if the condition is left untreated during the first 30 months of life (Beckwith & Tucker, 1988).

Although the age of onset differentiates juvenile from adult hypothyroidism, both types share common characteristics. Juvenile hypothyroidism becomes evident around 1 or 2 years of age, whereas adult hypothyroidism (myxedema) develops during adulthood. Juveniles and adults with hypothyroidism typically present with slowing of intellectual and motor activity, cold intolerance, decreased sweating, facial puffiness, weight gain, and fatigue (Price & Wilson, 1997). Frequently, symptoms of clinical depression are also reported (Beckwith & Tucker, 1988).

About 13 million Americans have a thyroid disorder, and more than half go undiagnosed because onset is typically gradual. Women suffer from the disorder seven times more than men, and the frequency of occurrence increases with age. Indeed, adult onset is usually seen among elderly women. The disorder remains undetected in many middle-aged women because several symptoms, including fatigue, mood swings, sleep disturbances, and depression, resemble signs of menopause (Portyansky, 1999). Hypothyroidism rarely occurs in newborns (Kunz & Finkel, 1987), affecting only about 1 in every 4,000 infants (Dallas, 2000). The disorder occurs more frequently in children with Down syndrome than in the general population. However, these children often go untreated because the two disorders share common characteristics (e.g., weight gain, poor growth, and dull affect). For this reason, physicians recommend that persons with Down syndrome be routinely screened for hypothyroidism (Noble et al., 2000).

Characteristics of hypothyroidism may include:

Congenital

1. Persistent jaundice and hoarse cry
2. Constipation, somnolence, and feeding problems
3. Short stature and coarse features
4. Protruding tongue; broad, flat nose; widely spaced eyes; and sparse hair
5. Dry skin, protuberant abdomen, and umbilical hernia
6. Hearing impairment

Juvenile and Adult

1. Fatigue and hoarseness
2. Cold intolerance and decreased sweating
3. Cool, dry skin and facial puffiness
4. Slow movements
5. Slowing of intellectual and motor activity
6. Slow relaxation of deep tendon reflexes

7. Impaired recent memory and difficulty in concentrating
8. Weight gain
9. Major depressive symptomology

Treatment for all types of hypothyroidism involves replacement therapy with the artificial thyroid hormone thyroxine (Clayman, 1989). Infants and children with hypothyroidism should take thyroid hormone as soon as possible in order to avoid irreversible damage to their nervous systems including retarded growth, delayed sexual maturity, and inhibited normal brain development (Clayman, 1989; Kunz & Finkel, 1987). Adults should feel better a few days after beginning treatment, and they should be back to normal within a few days. Biochemical tests showing either elevated (primary hypothyroidism) or lowered (secondary hypothyroidism) thyroid-stimulating hormone levels and reduced thyroxine (T4) levels make diagnosis easy (Portyansky, 1999; Price & Wilson, 1997).

The prognosis for infants who do not receive treatment is poor. Left untreated, infants will suffer irreversible brain damage and growth failure. Prognosis is good for infants who are diagnosed early, with most of the effects of hypothyroidism being reversible. Indeed, infants who are treated for hypothyroidism within the first months after birth are usually of average intelligence and grow at a normal rate.

Researchers recommend screening for congenital hypothyroidism by measuring the thyroid hormone (T4) with a blood spot test. Since the implementation of screening procedures and early childhood medical intervention, mental retardation and growth failure rarely occur (Dallas, 2000). Without early intervention, however, these children will require special education services in school and will need constant care and supervision into adulthood.

## REFERENCES

Beckwith, B. E., & Tucker, D. M. (1988). Thyroid disorders. In R. E. Tarter, D. H. Van Thiel, & K. L. Edwards (Eds.), *Medical neuropsychology: The impact of disease on behavior* (pp. 197–221). New York: Plenum Press.

Clayman, C. B. (1989). *The American Medical Association home medical encyclopedia.* New York: Random House.

Dallas, J. S. (2000). *Congenital hypothyroidism.* The Thyroid Society. Retrieved September 16, 2000, from http://www.the-thyroid-society.org/med_letter2.html

Kunz, J. R. M., & Finkel, A. J. (1987). *The American Medical Association family medical guide.* New York: Random House.

Noble, S. E., Leyland, C. A., & Clark, C. E. (2000). School based screening for hypothyroidism in Down's syndrome by dried blood spot TSH measurement. *Archives of Disease in Childhood, 82,* 27–32.

Portyansky, E. (1999). Hard-to-diagnose subclinical hypothyroidism often undertreated. *Drug Topics, 143,* 29–31.

Price, S. A., & Wilson, L. M. (1997). *Pathophysiology clinical concepts of disease processes.* St. Louis, MO: Library of Congress.

MELLISA BECKHAM
KERRY S. LASSITER
*The Citadel*

## CRETINISM

## HYPOTONIA

Hypotonia involves decreased tension of the fine muscles, making upright postures difficult to hold and independent movement difficult to produce (Pediatric Services, n.d.). It is also referred to as decreased muscle tone, flaccidity, or floppiness. Hypotonia is the opposite of hypertonia. Hypotonia is commonly associated with multiple genetic, metabolic, cerebral, spinal, or muscular disorders including muscular dystrophy, myasthenic gravis, Down syndrome, meningitis, and encephalitis. Hypotonia can also be caused by injury or trauma. Although identification of the presence of hypotonia is not difficult, determination of the actual cause of the symptom is more problematic.

Obviously, children with hypotonia are at risk for developmental delays in motor skills, poor reflexes, and limited sense of balance. Moreover, children with hypotonia are more likely to suffer from dislocations of joints, such as the hip, jaw, shoulders, and neck due to the inadequate support from the muscles to hold the joints together. Additionally, skeletal deformities are more common in children with hypotonia due to their tendency to assume abnormal positions (i.e., "W" sitting and sleeping prone in a frog-like position). Finally, other domains of functioning may be affected by hypotonia, including overall development and cognitive skill development, as the child may not be able to benefit from exploration of the environment or the child may have delayed development of language skills due to decreased muscle tone in the face and mouth.

It is difficult to estimate the actual prevalence of hypotonia, as it is not a specific disease, and records do not specify the frequency of particular symptoms.

Some characteristics of hypotonia can include:

1. Low tone, floppy, rag-doll appearance
2. Extreme flexibility, range of motion beyond normal
3. Delayed motor skills
4. Shallow breathing
5. Limited gag reflex, open mouth, protruding tongue
6. Abnormal posture (may cause skeletal deformities)
7. Unable to sustain movements (sucking, chewing, holding head up, sitting position, weight bearing)
8. Poor reflexes and balance reactions

Following identification of the presence of hypotonia, a treatment program can be developed. Although treatment will not cure the symptoms, it will aid in the prevention of future complications due to the condition. Treatment may also serve to facilitate the child's most appropriate development and teach compensatory skills. Treatment programs incorporate instruction to the child and caregivers in positioning and movement strategies. Hypotonic children may need extra stimulation through treatment programs that incorporate the use of sensory stimuli (i.e., touch, sound, sight, taste, smell, movement). Provision of general stimulation through swinging, rolling, and spinning activities may be beneficial (Trombly, 1989). Physical Therapy, Occupational Therapy, and Speech Services are often provided to facilitate skill development. Ankle-foot orthoses are sometimes used for weak ankle muscles.

Collaboration between parents, educators, and medical professionals is important to enable the most positive outcome for the child with hypotonia. Children with hypotonia will often be identified at an early age through primary care medical settings. It is important for parents to be placed in contact with the local school district or state agencies that provide early intervention services for children ages 0 to 3. Infants with hypotonia may be eligible for special education services. If eligible, an Individual Family Service Plan (IFSP) would be developed to identify goals and services. Preschool and elementary school students may continue to be eligible for Special Education services under provisions of the Individuals with Disabilities Education Act. Although a child may not be directly eligible to receive services due to the presence of hypotonia, per se, eligibility may be based on associated conditions or disorders. Specific services will be determined on an individualized basis. If educationally necessary, children may receive the related services of Occupational, Physical, and Speech Therapies.

The prognosis for children with hypotonia varies dependent on several factors, including the root cause of the condition, the severity of the symptoms, and the provision of appropriate early interventions.

**REFERENCES**

Pediatric Services (n.d.). *Understanding the lingo.* Retrieved from www.pediatricservices.com

Trombly, C. A. (1989). Neurophysiological and developmental treatment approaches. In C. Trombly (Ed.), *Occupational therapy for physical dysfunction* (3rd ed.). Baltimore: Williams & Wilkins.

SHELLEY PELLETIER
SUSAN SAGE
*Dysart Unified School District,*
*El Mirage, Arizona*

# HYPOXIA

Cerebral hypoxia refers to reduced oxygenation of brain tissue and is a leading cause of perinatal neurologic morbidity and encephalopathy in children (Hill & Volpe, 1994; Schwartz, Ahmann, Dykes, & Brann, 1993). In the absence of oxygen, cells switch to anaerobic glycolysis, which can sustain the brain for only a short time before cell death occurs (Brierley & Graham, 1976). In addition, hypoxia can initiate a cascade of toxic biochemical events that evolve over the course of hours to days, including glutamatergic excito-toxicity (Johnston, 1997).

Perinatal hypoxia is characterized by (Gross, 1990; Hill & Volpe, 1994):

1. Widespread damage to white matter, particularly in the periventricular regions and brain stem
2. Damage to the watershed regions of the cerebral cortex parasagitally
3. Focal areas of neuronal necrosis in the cerebral and cerebellar cortices, thalamus, basal ganglia, brain stem, and anterior horn cells due to concomitant ischemia or hemorrhage
4. Status marmoratus of the basal ganglia and thalamus characterized by neuronal loss, gliosis, and hyper-myelination, causing a marbled appearance of these structures
5. In the preterm infant a similar pattern of white matter and brain stem damage but parasagital cortical areas less vulnerable due to anastomoses with meningeal arteries
6. The encephalopathy that ensues from perinatal hypoxia often immediately apparent and associated with loss of consciousness, hypotonia, seizures, and brain stem findings including impairments of extraocular movements, sucking response, and respiration

Hypoxia in older children is characterized by (Brierley & Graham, 1976; Taylor, Quencer, Holzman, & Naidich, 1985):

1. Brain stem and white matter become more resistant to hypoxia with age.
2. Cerebral cortex remains vulnerable, as do the hippocampus, thalamus, cerebellum, and basal ganglia.
3. Problems with attention and memory are common.
4. Less impairment with muscle tone occurs.

Perinatal hypoxia is estimated to occur in 2–4 per 1,000 live-term births. The incidence is much higher in premature births at approximately 60 percent due to immaturity of the lungs (Schwartz et al., 1993). Hypoxia can occur at the antepartum, intrapartum, and postpartum periods.

Antepartum, the fetus is vulnerable to diseases or disorders affecting oxygen content of the mother's blood, such as cardiac arrest or hemorrhage. During the intrapartum period hypoxia may occur from abruptio placentae, uterine rupture, or traumatic delivery (Rivkin, 1997). Postpartum hypoxia can result from aspiration of meconium as well as respiratory or cardiac distress. The risk of perinatal hypoxia increases with maternal diabetes, toxemia or hypertension, delivery by cesarean section not preceded by labor, and in second twins (Gross, 1990).

In older children hypoxia can occur due to a variety of causes, including processes affecting the passage of oxygen at the alveolar level (e.g., pneumonia, asthma), inhibition of the bellows function of the chest wall (e.g., polio, spinal cord lesion), obstruction of the tracheobronchial tree (e.g., choking, hanging), and situations in which insufficient oxygen is available (e.g., drowning, high altitudes, smoke inhalation). Hypoxia can also occur secondary to ischemia, hypoglycemia, anemia, shock, cardiac disease, and histotoxic effects interfering with the cells ability to utilize oxygen (Brierley & Graham, 1976).

The newborn tends to be more resistant to the effects of hypoxia than the older child or adult. Mild perinatal hypoxia often does not result in detectable encephalopathy. The longer-term effects of moderate to severe perinatal hypoxia include mental retardation, dystonia, cerebral palsy, seizures, and death. Perinatal hypoxia has long been suspected as a causal factor in learning disabilities and ADHD. Up to 40 percent of infants with moderate hypoxia have been reported to have problems with school readiness at age 5 years (Hill & Volpe, 1994). In older children, dystonia and cerebral palsy are not as frequent, but cerebellar dysfunction may occur. Problems with attention, memory, and executive functions predominate. Impairment of visuospatial functions is also common.

Given the frequent motor involvement, physical and occupational therapy may be indicated. In addition, early evaluation and intervention to facilitate school readiness should be routinely considered. Special education services and specific cognitive rehabilitation therapy may be necessary with children of school age.

## REFERENCES

Brierley, J. B., & Graham, D. I. (1976). Hypoxia and vascular disorders of the central nervous system. In W. Blackwood & J. A. N. Corsellis (Eds.), *Greenfield's neuropathology*. Chicago: Year Book Medical.

Gross, I. (1990). Respiratory distress syndrome. In F. Oski (Ed.), *Principles and practice of pediatrics*. Philadelphia: Lippincott.

Hill, A., & Volpe, J. J. (1994). Hypoxic-ischemic cerebral injury in the newborn. In K. F. Swaiman (Ed.), *Pediatric neurology*. St. Louis, MO: Mosby.

Johnston, M. V. (1997). Hypoxic and ischemic disorders of infants and children: Lecture for the 38th meeting of Japanese Society of Child Neurology, Tokyo, Japan, July, 1996. *Brain and Development, 19*, 235–239.

Rivkin, M. J. (1997). Hypoxic-ischemic brain injury in the term newborn: Neuropathology, clinical aspects, and neuroimaging. *Clinics in Perinatology, 24*(3), 607–625.

Schwartz, J. F., Ahmann, P. A., Dykes, F. D., & Brann, A. W. (1993). Neonatal intracranial hemorrhage and hypoxia. In J. M. Pellock & E. C. Myer (Eds.), *Neurologic emergencies in infancy and childhood*. Boston: Butterworth-Heinemann.

Taylor, S. B., Quencer, R. M., Holzman, B. H., & Naidich, T. P. (1985). Central nervous system anoxic-ischemic insult in children due to near drowning. *Radiology, 156*(3), 641–646.

DAVID M. TUCKER
REBECCA VAURIO
*Austin, Texas*

## ANOXIA

# HYSTERICAL PERSONALITY

See HISTRIONIC PERSONALITY DISORDER.

# I

## IDIOT

Idiot is an archaic term used from the turn of the century through the 1950s to denote an individual with mental retardation whose measured IQ fell below 25 or 30. It represented the most severe level of Mental Retardation and was used comparatively with lesser degrees of retardation (i.e., imbecile and moron). The term acquired a pernicious quality among lay people over the years of its use and, during the 1950s, led to several revised systems of nomenclature. In America the classification system that was to become most widely adopted was published by the American Association on Mental Deficiency (now the American Association on Mental Retardation; Heber, 1959). This classification system replaced the term, idiot, with the current levels of Severe and Profound Retardation.

Originally, the terms idiocy, imbecility, and moronity represented the three levels of mental deficiency (otherwise known as amentia or feeblemindedness). These terms were considered separate from dementia, which denoted those who had acquired mental illnesses. Amentia, on the other hand, denoted "persons whose minds (had) never developed very far" (Peterson, 1925, p. 20).

The exact level of functioning of individuals designated as idiots has never been clear. However, attempts to characterize the level often focused on the use of language. In general such individuals could learn only a few simple words, but were not capable of substituting words for objects in their behavior. In addition, they were not expected to learn to wash or dress themselves and were generally cared for in institutions. Finally, the mental age of those classified as idiots did not exceed 3 years.

### REFERENCES

Heber, R. F. (1959). A manual on terminology and classification in mental retardation. *Monograph Supplement American Journal of Mental Deficiency, 64.*

Peterson, J. (1925). *Early conceptions and tests of intelligence.* Chicago: World Book.

RONALD C. EAVES
*Auburn University*

AAMR CLASSIFICATION SYSTEMS
HISTORY OF SPECIAL EDUCATION

## IDIOT SAVANT

See SAVANT SYNDROME.

## IEP

See INDIVIDUALIZED EDUCATIONAL PLAN.

## ILLINOIS TEST OF PSYCHOLINGUISTIC ABILITIES–THIRD EDITION

The Illinois Test of Psycholinguistic Abilities–Third Edition (ITPA-3; Hammill, Mather, & Roberts, 2001) measures spoken and written language. All of the subtests measure some aspect of language, including semantics, grammar, phonology, reading comprehension, word identification, and spelling. The ITPA-3 uses the following subtests to assess a children's specific linguistic ability:

*Spoken Analogies:* Examiner says a four-part analogy, with the last part missing. The child gives the missing part (e.g., "Dogs bark, cats _____").

*Spoken Vocabulary:* Examiner says a sentence or phrase that describes a noun, and the child must provide the correct word (e.g., "I am thinking of something with wheels").

*Morphological Closure:* Examiner gives an oral prompt with the last part missing and the child completes the phrase by saying the missing part (e.g., "big, bigger, _____").

*Syntactic Sentences:* Examiner says a sentence that is syntactically correct but semantically nonsensical and the child repeats the sentence (e.g., "Purple hammers are smart").

*Sound Deletion:* Examiner asks the child to delete words, syllables, and phonemes from spoken words (e.g., say "weekend" without the "end").

*Rhyming Sequences:* Examiner says strings of rhyming words that increase in length, and the child repeats them (e.g., "noon," "soon," "moon").

*Sentence Sequencing:* Child reads sentences silently and then puts them in order to form a plausible sequence (e.g., rearrange: I go to school, I get up, I get dressed).

*Written Vocabulary:* After reading an adjective the child writes a noun that is closely associated with the stimulus word (e.g., complete this: "A broken ____").

*Sight Decoding:* The child pronounces a list of printed words that contain irregular parts (e.g., "would," "laugh," "height").

*Sound Decoding:* The child reads aloud phonically regular names of make-believe animal creatures (e.g., Flant, Yang).

*Sight Spelling:* Examiner reads aloud irregular words from a list. The child is given a printed list in which the irregular part of the words and one or more phonemes are missing. The child writes in the omitted part of the words (e.g., Examiner reads "said," and the child sees s____d and fills in the missing letters).

*Sound Spelling:* The examiner reads aloud phonically regular nonsense words, and the child writes the word or the missing part.

These ITPA-3 subtests can be combined to form the following composites: General Language, Spoken Language, Written Language, Semantics, Grammar, Phonology, Comprehension, Spelling, Sight Symbol Processing, and Sound Symbol Processing.

Subtest raw scores are transformed into standard scores, percentile ranks, and age equivalents.

Normative data for a sample of 1,522 children were collected in 27 states during the years 1999 and 2000 and reflected the population characteristics of the United States for 1999. Data were stratified according to ethnicity, race, gender, disability status, geographic region, parental education, residence (rural/urban), and family income, and the results were a close match to projected percentages. In each of the 1-year age groups, the number in the samples exceeded 100 (ranging from 138 at age 12 to 239 at age 10).

Internal consistency, stability, and interscorer reliability for all subtests and composites are high (greater than .90).

## REFERENCES

Hammill, D. D., Mather, N., & Roberts, R. (2001). *The Illinois Test of Psycholinguistic Abilities–Third edition.* San Antonio, TX: Psychological Corporation.

Plake, B. S., Impara, J. C., & Spies, R. A. (Eds.). (2003). *The fifteenth mental measurements yearbook* (pp. 212–216). Lincoln, NE: Buros Institute of Mental Measurements.

RON DUMONT
*Fairleigh Dickinson University*

JOHN O. WILLIS
*Rivier College*

# IMAGERY

Imagery is the mental representation of objects, events, or concepts in some nonverbal form, a process thought to be basic to human functioning. While this representation is often assumed to be visual, such as a picture according to Klinger (1981), mental imagery includes any of the almost unceasing sensationlike experiences that are a part of our stream of consciousness and that are representative of any of our sense modalities. Although the study of mental imagery was a central part of psychology until 1920, interest by psychologists in the United States in this phenomenon did not become active until the 1960s, with the work of psychologists such as Eleanor and James Gibson, Piaget, Neisser and others. These psychologists were concerned with determining how the brain constructs and stores models through which sense can be made of the sensations that occur as the individual interacts with the environment. This latter process, labeled perception, guides the individual's actions or response to the environment. Thus the imagery constructed by an individual is central to psychological functioning and whoever can shape that imagery holds a powerful tool for controlling and altering human functioning, whether the shaper be the individual or another person (Klinger, 1981).

The facilitative effect of imagery on comprehension and recall or memory was described by early Greek scholars and experienced by Roman orators as they delivered lengthy speeches using imagery as a mnemonic tool. Recent pioneering work of Canadian psychologist Allan Paivio has provided theoretical explanations and firm empirical support for this aspect of imagery. Paivio (1971) effectively developed the case for dual coding of information by individuals. In dual coding retrieval of information is enhanced by the fact that many concrete words or concepts can be represented in both verbal and imagery systems, thus providing dual cues for recalling the information. Present investigations on imagery as an important concept in cognitive psychology are focusing on individual differences in imagery, its usefulness in problem solving and other complex human behaviors including creativity, imagery through sensory modalities other than the visual, and the possibility of affective coding of experiences.

Mental imagery appears to play a critical role in the creative processes in diverse fields, from architecture and sports (Hall, Mack, Paivio, & Housenblas, 1998), to molecular science (Shepard, 1978). The ability to process information through imagery has been used to predict and enhance creative imagination in children and adults (Khatena, 1979). In addition, directed focusing of imagery has been found to be a powerful enhancer, eliciting from the individual a holistic and directly felt bodily sense of a situation or issue (Gendlin, 1980). Perfection of various athletic or performance skills, as well as a wide variety of classroom applications, have evolved, and scripts have been developed for using such guided imagery (Roberts, 1983). Rose (1980) describes his technique for using guided fantasies in the elementary classroom to acquire new concepts, build confidence for oral reports, or handle conflicts. In special education, imagery can be used to help individuals identify negative or positive attitudes regarding a physical disability (Morgan, 1980).

Imagery has been a particularly useful tool for the psychotherapist: the patient expresses in drawings or paintings, to be interpreted clinically, information unlikely to have been offered verbally. The advantage of this type of communication is that it is given in less threatening situations, avoiding times when the patient may be withdrawn, overly aroused, or frightened (Barrios & O'Dell, 1998). In addition, imagery can be used to establish empathetic understanding, manage anxiety and stress, and even reduce pain, giving symptomatic relief to patients. Through imagery, then, humans can alter in positive ways both mental and physical functioning, their own as well as that of others.

## REFERENCES

Barrios, B. A., & O'Dell, S. L. (1998). Fears & anxieties. In E. J. Mash & R. A. Barkley (Eds.), *Treatment of childhood disorders* (pp. 249–337). New York: Guilford.

Gendlin, E. T. (1980). Imagery is more powerful with focusing: Theory and practice. In J. E. Schorr, G. E. Sobel, P. Robin, & J. A. Connella (Eds.), *Imagery. Its many dimensions and applications* (pp. 65–73). New York: Plenum.

Hall, C. R., Mack, D. E., Paivio, A., & Housenblas, H. A. (1998). Imagery use by athletes: Development of the Sport Imagery Questionnaire. *International Journal of Sport Psychology, 29*(1), 73–89.

Khatena, J. (1979). *Teaching gifted children to use creative imagination imagery.* Starkville, MI: Allan.

Klinger, E. (Ed.). (1981). *Imagery. Concepts, results and applications.* New York: Plenum.

Morgan, C. (1980). Imagery experiences of disabled persons. In J. E. Schorr, G. E. Sobel, P. Robin, & J. A. Connella (Eds.), *Imagery. Its many dimensions and applications* (pp. 232–244). New York: Plenum.

Paivio, A. (1971). *Imagery and verbal processes.* New York: Holt, Rinehart & Winston.

Roberts, N. M. (1983). Imagery: A second look: Expanding its use in the classroom. *Reading Improvement, 20*(1), 22–27.

Rose, R. (1980). Guided fantasies in elementary classrooms. In J. E. Schorr, G. E. Sobel, P. Robin, & J. A. Connella (Eds.), *Imagery. Its many dimensions and applications* (pp. 605–622). New York: Plenum.

Shepard, R. N. (1978). Externalization of mental images and the act of creation. In B. S. Randhawa & W. E. Coffman (Eds.), *Visual learning, thinking, and communication.* New York: Academic.

PATRICIA A. HAENSLY
*Texas A&M University*

**CREATIVITY**
**HYPNOSIS**

## IMPERSISTENCE

See PERSEVERATION.

## IMPULSE CONTROL

An impulse is a psychological term given to a feeling that results in an action. Research about impulse control can be found as it relates to many psychiatric disorders such as attention-deficit/hyperactivity disorder (Barkley, 2003; Pulkkinen, 1996), manic depression (McElroy, Pope, Keck, & Hudson, 1996) and so on. As used here, it refers to a trait normally measured by a test such as the Matching Familiar Figures Test. The resulting outcome of the test is an indication of whether the learner is reflective or impulsive. A reflective learner examines a stimulus slowly and takes more time to make a decision than an impulsive learner. Generally, there is some relationship between impulsive responders and high error rates. Thus, there is a need to control the response rate of the learner to cut down on errors (Kagan, Pearson, & Welch, 1966; Kendall & Wilcox, 1979).

The predominant method for the control of impulsive behavior is cognitive training (Barkley, 2003; Kendall & Finch, 1978; Kendall & Wilcox, 1979, 1980). Investigators have combined cognitive and behavioral methods. Two of the most successful strategies for the control of impulsive behavior are modeling and self-instructional training. Modeling is based on social learning theory. A learner observes a high-status adult or peer engaging in acts that are reflective and purposeful. If the tasks performed by the model are similar to the types of tasks to be performed by the learner, there is a likelihood that the reflective behavior will be modeled by the learner. As the tasks become dissimilar, the degree of transfer decreases.

Self-instructional training is based on a theory that states that voluntary control over motor behavior requires the internalization of verbal commands (Barkley, 2003; Meichenbaum & Goodman, 1971). To improve impulsive behavior by self-instruction, the learner verbalizes either aloud, in a whisper or subvocally. The practice becomes a thinking-out-loud intervention that reminds a learner to slow down, to be careful, and to follow the steps in a process.

Cognitive modeling plus self-instructional training is generally superior to cognitive modeling alone. The following five-step procedure has been used successfully to control impulsive behavior: (1) the leader models a reflective problem-solving style using overt self-instructions; (2) the learner is guided by the teacher through the same problem with verbal instructions; (3) the learner solves the problem while providing overt self-instruction; (4) the learner solves the problem while whispering; and (5) the learner solves the problem with subvocal self-instruction. This procedure appears to work well for modifying impulsive behavior on specific tasks but general classroom behavior on unrelated tasks remains unchanged.

Adding a response cost procedure to the cognitive modeling and self-instructional training enhances the training program for the control of impulsive behavior (Meichenbaum & Anarnow, 1979). In response cost, a punishment procedure is imposed for errors. The procedure is designed to discourage the child from making quick responses. Positive reinforcement is not a highly effective strategy to add to cognitive modeling and self-instructional training. The problem with using positive reinforcement in this process is that lucky guesses may be reinforced and thus maladaptive problem-solving strategies may be maintained.

Another approach to cognitive training involves the following six-step problem-solving sequence (Meichenbaum & Goodman, 1971): (1) problem definition; (2) problem approach; (3) focusing attention; (4) problem solution; (5) self-reinforcement; and (6) coping with errors. In studies following this sequence, there is a greater generalization of reflective behavior if the training deals with self-statements that are global rather than problem specific. If training focuses only on a specific problem situation, the generalization of reflective behavior is restricted. If the problem situations are broad and the strategies applicable to a wide range of behavior, generalization will be enhanced.

A final procedure for the control of impulsive behavior is the imposed delay. Students are prevented from responding for a specified number of seconds after a problem is presented. Used in isolation, learners will slow down in their responding time but errors will not change. To be effective, the strategy must be coupled with other strategies discussed previously.

## REFERENCES

Barkley, R. A. (2003). Attention-deficit hyperactivity disorder. In E. J. Mash & R. A. Barkley (Eds.), *Childhood psychopathology* (pp. 75–143). New York: Guilford.

Kagan, J., Pearson, L., & Welch, L. (1966). Modifiability of an impulsive tempo. *Journal of Educational Psychology, 57,* 359–365.

Kendall, P. C., & Finch, A. J. (1978). A cognitive-behavioral treatment for impulsivity: A group comparison study. *Journal of Consulting & Clinical Psychology, 46,* 110–118.

Kendall, P. C., & Wilcox, L. E. (1979). Self-control in children: Development of a rating scale. *Journal of Consulting & Clinical Psychology, 47,* 1020–1029.

Kendall, P. C., & Wilcox, L. E. (1980). Cognitive-behavioral treatment for impulsivity: Concrete versus conceptual training in non-self-controlled problem children. *Journal of Consulting & Clinical Psychology, 48,* 80–91.

McElroy, S. L., Pope, H. G., Keck, P. E., & Hudson, J. I. (1996). Are impulse-control disorders relaxed to bipolar disorder? *Comprehensive Psychiatry, 37*(4), 229–240.

Meichenbaum, D. H., & Anarnow, J. (1979). Cognitive-behavioral modification and metacognitive development: Implications for the classroom. In P. C. Kendall & S. D. Hollon (Eds.), *Cognitive-behavioral interventions: Theory, research, and procedures.* New York: Academic.

Meichenbaum, D. H., & Goodman, J. (1971). Training impulsive children to talk to themselves: A means of developing self-control. *Journal of Abnormal Psychology, 77,* 115–126.

Pulkkinen, L. (1996). Impulse control in children. *Journal of Forensic Psychiatry, 7*(2), 228–233.

ROBERT A. SEDLAK
*University of Wisconsin at Stout*

BEHAVIOR MODELING
BEHAVIOR MODIFICATION
SELF-MONITORING

## IMPULSIVITY-REFLECTIVITY

Impulsivity-reflectivity is a cognitive dimension defined by Kagan (1965) that describes the way children resolve uncertainty. Impulsivity-reflectivity describes the tendency to reflect on the validity of problem solving when several choices are presented. The instrument most often used to measure reflectivity and impulsivity in children is the Matching Familiar Figures Test (MFFT) which also comes in a computerized version (Hummel-Schulgar & Baer, 1996). Based on test performance, reflective children will make fewer errors and have longer response latencies than impulsive children (Kagan, 1965). The test format involves presentation of a figure such as a boat, animal, or pair of scissors with as many as eight facsimiles differing in one or more details. The subject is asked to select from the alternatives the one that exactly matches the figure. Time and response are computed. Children who score above the median on the MFFT response time and below the median on errors are called reflective. Children who score below the median on response time and above the median on errors are called impulsive (Messer, 1976). Impulsive children tend to respond quickly and make many mistakes; reflective children tend to respond more slowly and carefully and make fewer errors (Finch, 1982).

Educators and psychologists have used impulsivity and reflectivity as a way to implement programs for childhood education (Borkowski et al., 1983; Finch, 1982). This has been useful with emotionally disturbed children who display problem behavior (Finch, 1982). Finch also examined reflectivity and impulsivity in WISC-R performance in children with behavior problems. Reflective children scored significantly higher than impulsive children on verbal, performance, and full-scale IQ. Although there is no evidence that consistently links impulsivity and reflectivity to IQ scores, this does suggest that cognitive style may be related to performance on standard intelligence tests.

Sergeant et al. (1979) explored hyperactivity, impulsivity, and reflectivity and their relationship to clinical child psychology. The MFFT was used to measure hyperactivity. Although impulsivity is thought to be related to hyperactivity, their research showed that measuring hyperactivity by determining the level of impulsivity could be misleading. Impulsivity-reflectivity has been found to be related to other clinical syndromes including brain damage, epilepsy, and mental retardation (Messer, 1976). This work also indicates that impulsivity and reflectivity may be related to school performance as shown by the greater impulsivity in children with learning disabilities, reading problems, and general school failure. Messer found that reflective children will gather information more carefully and systematically than impulsive children. This same study indicated that reflectivity and impulsivity cannot accurately be measured in preschool children, since they have not yet learned to examine alternatives.

Social reasoning has also been measured in reflective and impulsive children (Peters & Bernfeld, 1983) by using the Peabody Picture Vocabulary and the MFFT. Reflective children made decisions more slowly; impulsive children made decisions more rapidly. Reflective children favored a more direct approach; impulsive children favored a more passive approach.

Kagan (1983) studied children who were given visual matching problems. The subjects with fast response times and higher error scores made more errors in reading words than subjects with long decision-making times and lower error scores. This supported the notion that primary-grade children who reflected over alternative hypotheses would be more accurate in word recognition than children who reported hypotheses impulsivity.

Reflectivity and impulsivity seem to develop with age as children typically become more reflective as they grow older (Messer, 1976). Messer reported that response times increased with age, while the amount of errors decreased. Siegelman (1969) examined the ways in which reflective and impulsive children of different ages actually deploy alternatives and scan the objects presented to them. The hypothesis was that impulsive children devote a greater amount of time to a chosen stimulus and ignore the alternatives, in contrast to the reflectives, who spent more time weighing alternatives. Results suggested that impulsive and reflective children may be using different search strategies. This indicates that the impulsive dimension may be modifiable. Kagan (1983) and Messer (1976) found that impulsivity may be modified by teaching impulsives to improve their scanning strategies. The researchers accomplished this by having children who were impulsive verbalize what they were doing.

Impulsivity and reflectivity have also been examined from a teaching perspective that has implications for classroom learning. Teachers need to be aware of individual differences among children to cope with each individual learner. Readance and Bean (1978) reported that the impulsive child has a tendency to act on his or her initial response with little reflection when solving problems. A reflective child usually delays, weighing all choices available. Reflective children are not necessarily brighter or better learners; however, the research did suggest that teachers may perceive impulsive children less favorably. Reflective students were seen as highly attentive. Impulsive boys were seen as less able to concentrate in class. This supported the notion that this particular individual difference of impulsivity and reflectivity is important for classroom learning. Evidence supports the contention that the cognitive and meta-cognitive (Palladino, Poli, Masi, & Marcheschi, 1997) dimensions of impulsivity and reflectivity are important individual differences. These dimensions will play a role in helping assess a child's ability, ultimately improving the learning process within the field of special education.

## REFERENCES

Borkowski, J. G., Peck, V. A., Reid, M. K., & Kurtz, B. E. (1983). Impulsivity and strategy transfer: Metamemory as mediator. *Child Development, 54,* 469–473.

Finch, A. J., Saylor, C. F., & Spirito, A. (1982a). Impulsive cognitive style and impulsive behavior in emotionally disturbed children. *Journal of Genetic Psychology, 141,* 293–294.

Finch, A. J., Spirito, A., & Brophy, C. J. (1982b). Reflection-impulsivity and WISC-R performance in behavior-problem children. *Journal of Genetic Psychology, 111,* 217–221.

Hummel-Schulgar, A. O., & Baer, J. S. (1996). A computer-controlled administration of the Matching Familiar Figures Test. *Behavior Research Methods, 28*(1), 93–95.

Kagan, J. (1965). *Conceptual development in children.* New York: International University Press.

Kagan, J. (1983). Reflection-impulsivity and reading ability in primary grade children. *Child Development, 54,* 609–628.

Messer, S. B. (1976). Reflection-impulsivity: A review. *Psychological Bulletin, 83,* 1026–1052.

Palladino, P., Poli, P., Masi, G., & Marcheschi, M. (1997). Impulsive-reflective cognitive style, metacognition and emotion in adolescence. *Perceptual and Motor Skills, 84*(1), 47–57.

Peters, R. D., & Bernfeld, G. A. (1983). Reflection-impulsivity and social reasoning. *Developmental Psychology, 19,* 78–81.

Readance, J. E., & Bean, T. W. (1978). Impulsivity-reflectivity and learning: An individual difference that matters. *College Student Journal, 11,* 367–371.

Sergeant, J. A., Van Velthoven, R., & Virginia, A. (1979). Hyperactivity, impulsivity and reflectivity. *Journal of Child Psychology & Psychiatry, 20,* 47–60.

Siegelman, E. (1969). Reflective and impulsive observing behavior. *Child Development, 40,* 1213–1222.

STEVEN GUMERMAN
*Temple University*

# INBORN ERRORS OF METABOLISM

Inborn errors of metabolism are classified as a group of genetic diseases and involve single-gene defects that interfere with the process of metabolism. Metabolism refers to the process in which the body breaks down food into fats, proteins, and carbohydrates. The conversion of the food into energy to maintain the life cycle of body cells is carried out by enzymes. The enzymes assist in the maintenance of homeostasis and the control of functions of blood pressure, blood sugar levels, and rate of growth. A single-gene defect may lead to a missing or malfunctioning enzyme, which if left untreated, may result in severe mental retardation or impaired bodily functions such as poor digestion. Such disorders occur in approximately 1 in 5,000 births (Batshaw & Perret, 1981).

Robinson and Robinson (1965) divided metabolic disorders into three areas: (1) ongoing faulty digestive processes identified by biochemical substances in the urine or the bloodstream; (2) storage diseases in which materials are stored because of decreased rate of metabolism or overproduction; and (3) disorders in endocrine secretions that result in anomalies in the structure of the brain and cranium or other difficulties.

Koch and Koch (1974) reported that 40 to 50 such serious diseases often are passed on by consanguineous parents. The body is constantly producing, maintaining, and recycling cells. In the metabolic process of mitosis, the cell dies and is recycled and changed into chemicals and proteins. These components are then absorbed and reused by the body. Any genetic disease that interferes with the process is called an inborn error of metabolism. For many metabolic disorders, there is no effective therapy. For some, therapy is successful only if begun immediately. When untreated, profound mental retardation, seizures, aberrant behavior, and stunted growth may accompany the metabolic abnormality. Some inborn errors of metabolism (e.g., Gaucher's) are asymptomatic and may pose little threat to a reasonably normal existence (Holland, 2003; Stanbury, Wyngaarden, & Fredrickson, 1978). However, many of these disorders have serious consequences and may be fatal if untreated. Age of onset affects severity. In several of the lipid storage diseases such as Gaucher's and Niemann-Pick disease, if the disorder is manifested during the infantile period when the brain is being myelinated, the result is a much more serious disability. Conversely, many of the hereditary metabolic disorders such as gout, hemochromatosis, or familial periodic paralysis do not become fully manifest until adulthood.

In galactosemia, a carbohydrate disorder, the infant appears normal at birth. However, because of a missing enzyme, the sugar or galactose is not used properly. It accumulates in the blood, body tissue, and urine. The injurious waste products can cause brain damage if proper dietary controls are not exercised immediately. The affected individual is unable to metabolize the galactose in milk. If milk and dairy products are withheld, the development will proceed normally (Brown & Sessoms, 2003).

Phenylketonuria (PKU) is the most well-known and successfully treated metabolic disorder. Two similar recessive genes, one from each parent, combine and produce a deficiency of the liver enzyme that normally breaks down the amino acid phenylalanine (Telford & Sawrey, 1977). The parents are carriers of the defective genes but are not themselves affected. Brain damage results from an accumulation of phenylalanine, one of the nine amino acids essential for growth. Prenatal diagnosis does not detect PKU and a child has no symptoms in infancy, hence early screening is critical. More than 90 percent of all newborns in the United States are tested for PKU (Bearn, 1979). While it is not a general test for mental retardation, it does successfully detect PKU and a few other rare inborn errors. The currently used heel stick test was developed by Dr. Robert Guthrie in 1959 (Guthrie, 1972). Phenylketonuria occurs at a rate of 1/14,000 births. Parents who have one affected child have a 25 percent chance of having another (Batshaw & Perret, 1981). In the past, this disorder led to death or severe mental retardation. Diet therapy has greatly improved prognosis. However, early treatment is not perfect. Individuals with PKU are still found to score significantly lower on IQ tests than their parents. Longitudinal studies of PKU children have found a high incidence of perceptual difficulties that interfere with academic achievement (Koch & Koch, 1974). Diet therapy can lead to malnutrition because of reduced food intake. It also is problematic to gain the full cooperation of the affected individual.

Robinson and Robinson (1965) detailed several of the storage diseases. Hurler's disease, gargoylism, results in a deformed and stunted body as well as mental retardation. Affected individuals also may exhibit visual and hearing impairments. Gaucher's, when severe, is manifested by enlarged liver, spleen, and lymph nodes. Most do not live beyond adolescence.

Some of the inherited metabolic disorders are sex linked. Hemochromatosis is more common in males because the menstrual cycle in females decreases the iron stored in the system. Hemophilia, Fabray's disease, childhood muscular dystrophy, and hyper-uricemia all occur predominantly in males.

Some metabolic disorders appear to improve as the affected individual ages (Stanbury et al., 1978). Some galactosemics gradually develop the ability to metabolize galactose (Brown & Sessoms, 2003). Individuals with adrynamia epidocis hereditaria and periodic paralysis may also cease to have attacks as they grow older.

Inborn errors of metabolism are the subject of continued intensive research. Reports of newly discovered syndromes frequently are announced. Screening still offers the best hope. The most direct method detects qualitative changes in the structure of the protein (Bearn, 1979). Mass screening for all possible single gene defects is still prohibitive financially. Therefore, with the exception of PKU, the focus is on families and at-risk populations. Amniocentesis, the use of cultured fibroblasts, and the applications stemming from the Human Genome Project will increase in the years ahead as a means of making screening programs more comprehensive. Currently, scientists apply a sophisticated battery of laboratory procedures to identify and elucidate suspected metabolic disorders.

## REFERENCES

Batshaw, M. L., & Perret, Y. M. (1981). *Children with handicaps: A medical primer*. Baltimore: Brooks.

Bearn, A. G. (1979). Inborn errors of metabolism and molecular disease. In P. Beeson, W. McDermott, & J. Wyngaarden (Eds.), *Cecil textbook of medicine* (15th ed., pp. 40–48). Philadelphia: Saunders.

Brown, R. T., & Sessoms, A. (2003). Galactosemia. In E. Fletcher-Janzen & C. R. Reynolds (Eds.), *Childhood disorders diagnostic desk reference* (pp. 252–253). New York: Wiley.

Guthrie, R. (1972). Mass screening for genetic disease. *Hospital Practice, 7*, 93.

Holland, A. (2003). Gaucher's disease. In E. Fletcher-Janzen & C. R. Reynolds (Eds.), *Childhood disorders diagnostic desk reference* (pp. 256–258). New York: Wiley.

Kelly, T. E. (1975). The role of genetic mechanisms in childhood handicaps. In R. Haslam & P. Valletutti (Eds.), *Medical problems in the classroom: The teacher's role in diagnosis and management* (pp. 113–215). Baltimore: University Park.

Koch, R., & Koch, K. (1974). *Understanding the mentally retarded child: A new approach*. New York: Random House.

Robinson, H. B., & Robinson, N. M. (1965). *The mentally retarded child: A psychological approach*. New York: McGraw-Hill.

Telford, C., & Sawrey, J. (1977). *The exceptional individual*. Englewood Cliffs, NJ: Prentice Hall.

SALLY E. PISARCHICK
*Cuyahoga Special Education
Service Center*

GALACTOSEMIA
GENETIC COUNSELING
GENETIC TRANSMISSIONS
HURLER SYNDROME

METABOLIC DISORDERS
PHENYLKETONURIA

## INCIDENCE

The term incidence refers to the estimated number of people in a given population who possess or exhibit a given characteristic at some point during their lives (Blackhurst & Berdine, 1981). Dunn (1973) believes that incidence gives the rate of occurrence of a condition while Schifani, Anderson, and Odle (1980) define incidence as the number of new cases of disabled children identified in a given period of time—usually a year. Incidence most often relates to the occurrence of some characteristic.

Incidence is often confused with prevalence but the two terms have different meanings. Prevalence refers to currently existing disabled children as opposed to those who might be considered exceptional at some point in their lives. Incidence results in a higher figure since it estimates future occurrence, where prevalence deals with a point in time figure.

Because incidence is an estimate, it is more difficult to validate or substantiate. Meyen (1978) states that state education agencies and school districts generally establish prevalence rates when conducting needs assessment surveys. He suggests that surveys and studies would be better able to establish incidence rates given the data becoming available from referral requests for service under IDEA. For general education planning purposes prevalence estimates continue to be used.

Educational planning requires an estimate of the number of children with disabilities requiring service. If program planners, for example, assume the incidence of mental retardation is 3 percent and project needed programs and services based on that figure, the result could be an overestimate of 100 percent if the actual prevalence was 1½ percent.

## REFERENCES

Blackhurst, A. E., & Berdine, W. H. (1981). (Eds.). *An introduction to special education*. Boston: Little, Brown.

Dunn, L. M. (Ed.). (1973). *Exceptional children in the schools*. New York: Holt, Rinehart, & Winston.

Meyen, E. L. (1978). *Exceptional children and youth: An introduction*. Denver, CO: Love.

Schifani, J. W., Anderson, R. M., & Odle, S. J. (Eds.). (1980). *Implementing learning in the least restrictive environment*. Baltimore: University Press.

PHILIP R. JONES
*Virginia Polytechnic Institute
and State University*

DEMOGRAPHY OF SPECIAL EDUCATION

# INCLUSION

Special education services can be offered in various settings, ranging from regular education classes to hospitals. Regular education classes and others that resemble them constitute the least restrictive settings. Hospitals and others that resemble them (e.g., residential programs, juvenile detention settings) constitute the most restrictive settings.

Inclusion refers to the placement of students who display one or more disabilities in age-appropriate general education classrooms together with needed accommodations and supports. Inclusion is based on the belief that all children are capable of learning, children with disabilities benefit from being educated with students who do not display disabilities, and inclusion promotes equal educational opportunities. Inclusion directly affects students with disabilities, their teachers, and support staff. Additionally, the impact of inclusion can be school-wide, affecting many aspects of schooling (McLeskey & Waldron, 2000).

The 1975 Education for All Handicapped Children Act (Public Law 94-142) advocated an appropriate education for all students with disabilities. The 1990 Individuals with Disabilities Education Act (IDEA) established standards for eligibility, types of services, and procedural safeguards (Murphy, 1996). Advocacy for mainstreaming, or educating students to the maximum extent appropriate with peers without disabilities (Kavale & Forness, 2000) is consistent with this legislation. Both laws promulgate placement in the least restrictive environment. The provision reflects the belief that a student should be removed from general education only when the severity of their disability requires their need for services unattainable in general education classrooms. The 2004 amendments to IDEA continued to emphasize the importance of the least restrictive environment by noting the provision of a free, appropriate public education in the least restrictive environment as a priority area for monitoring.

## Arguments in Favor of Inclusion

Those who advocate for inclusion typically emphasize one or more of the following beliefs. Some adopt philosophical value-based attitudes that parallel the ideological underpinnings of the Civil Rights movement. For them, inclusion is seen as an issue of social justice in which all forms of segregation are unacceptable, including those in education (Stainback & Stainback, 1990). The belief that ". . . the burden of proof should fall upon the shoulders of those who wish to segregate students with disabilities" (Cole, Waldron, & Majd, 2004, p. 42) is consistent with this viewpoint.

Others believe the educational and social needs of students with disabilities are not being met in self-contained classrooms. Thus, their placement in alternative settings should be explored (Kavale & Forness, 2000). Students with disabilities are thought to benefit from inclusion because the curriculum to which they are exposed is more age-appropriate, and they learn from peers who serve as suitable role models. Inclusion is thought to lead to fewer behavior problems and higher levels of self-esteem.

Still others suggest that inclusion promotes desired change in attitudes, leading to more positive views toward persons with disabilities (Burstein, Sears, Wilcoxen, Cabello, & Spagna, 2004). Students learn to appreciate differences and take pride in assisting their classmates. Over time, inclusion programs promote positive attitudes toward children with disabilities among both general and special educators.

Some research supports inclusion. For example, preschool children with disabilities who are educated with typically developing peers display more improvement than those who are educated with peers with disabilities (Odom, 2000). Students with learning disabilities in reading and math who received their instruction in inclusive school programs, compared to those who received their education in resource rooms, made comparable progress in math and more progress in reading (Waldron & McLeskey, 1998).

Advocates of inclusion indicate that principals and administrators as well as general education and special education teachers must support inclusion programs in order for them to be effective. Teachers and administrators must feel as if they own the change that is occurring in their school and it is not being imposed on them (Waldron & McLeskey, 2000).

## Arguments Against Inclusion

Those who oppose inclusion typically emphasize one or more of the following beliefs. Some dissenters believe that advocates of inclusion who base their support on philosophical and moral grounds are wishful in their thinking and instead should base their judgments on empirical evidence. Attempts to link noninclusion practices with apartheid and slavery lack evidence, are emotional in nature, and do not benefit the educational process (Mock & Kaufman, 2002). Some research confirms the belief that many students need more intense instruction and support than is provided in mainstream classrooms (Kauffman, Bantz, & McCullough, 2002).

The belief that all children can learn has been described as naïve liberalism (Raines, 1996). Raines believes the broad-scale use of inclusion is fallacious and contends that efforts by courts to support inclusion arise from a desire to emphasize the promotion of social goals consistent with the least restrictive environment rather than promoting suitable academic environments. He believes the fundamental purpose of the education system is to foster learning, not socialization (Raines, 1996).

Dissenters of inclusion point to difficulties encountered by teachers attempting to meet the needs of diverse students, especially those with moderate to severe disabilities

(Chelsey & Calaluce, 1997). Many are not prepared for these responsibilities. Some teachers utilize classroom peers to provide needed instruction even though they are untrained and ill prepared (Zigmond & Baker, 1996). In some locations, teacher contracts allow them to decide which types of disabilities and the number of students with disabilities they will accept in their classrooms.

Regular education teachers often feel unprepared and thus lack confidence in their abilities to teach students with disabilities. Some dissenters of inclusion argue against the idea that good teachers can teach all students and that general education classrooms can be successful in managing all students without some form of administrative differentiation (Kavale & Forness, 2000). Those who advocate for full inclusion may not place much importance on research evidence and instead focus on issues of compassion and caring (Kavale & Forness, 2000).

## Inclusion: National and State Trends

Students with learning disabilities constitute the majority of those receiving special education services. During the 1980s, students with learning disabilities generally were being educated in the more restrictive settings (McLeskey & Pacchiano, 1994). Later studies found an increase in placement of students with learning disabilities in general education classrooms and a 31 percent decrease in placement in separate school settings (McLeskey, Henry, & Axelrod, 1999). This increase in the number of students with learning disabilities being educated in general education classrooms may be attributed to an increase in the number of students being identified with learning disabilities (McLeskey, Hoppey, Williamson, & Rentz, 2004). During the 1990s, only 15 states educated more students in less restrictive settings while many states ended the decade educating more students in more restrictive settings.

Studies of the placement of students with Mental Retardation generally suggest a movement toward inclusive education. For example, one study conducted with 1990 data (McLeskey et al., 2004) found an increase of 27 to 43 percent being educated in general education classrooms and a decrease from 73 to 56 percent being educated in segregated settings. Furthermore, the number of students with Mental Retardation being educated in separate facilities decreased by more than half. Identification rates for this disability remained fairly stable during this period.

## Conclusions

The United States and other countries continue to struggle in their efforts to develop more effective methods to prevent disabilities and to educate those with disabilities. This theme is echoed in various entries from various countries described within this Encyclopedia. Some view inclusion as an opportunity and others view it as pathway that provides few benefits, except to those with the more mild handicapping conditions. Students with mild disabilities are more likely to be placed in inclusive classrooms than students with severe disabilities (Odom, 2000).

This discussion is brief and is not intended to provide a full discussion of inclusion. Various models of inclusion have been advanced. No one model of inclusion is necessarily best for every school district. Research and other forms of scholarship are needed to evaluate the impact of inclusion models on students with various levels and types of disabilities and disorders, their teachers, and nondisabled peers.

## REFERENCES

Burstein, N., Sears, S., Wilcoxen, A., Cabello, B., & Spagna, M. (2004). Moving toward inclusive practices. *Remedial and Special Education, 25,* 104–116.

Chelsey, G. M., & Calaluce, P. D., Jr. (1997). The deception of inclusion. *Mental Retardation, 35,* 488–490.

Cole, C. M., Waldron, N., & Majd, M. (2004). Academic progress of students across inclusive and traditional settings. *Mental Retardation, 42*(2), 136–144.

Kauffman, J. M., Bantz, J. B., & McCullough, J. M. (2002). Separate and better: A special public school class for students with emotional and behavioral disorders. *Exceptionality, 10*(3), 149–170.

Kavale, K., & Forness, S. (2000). History, rhetoric, and reality: Analysis of the inclusion debate. *Remedial and Special Education, 21*(5), 279–296.

McLeskey, J., Henry, D., & Axelrod, M. I. (1999). Inclusion of students with learning disabilities: An examination of data from reports to congress. *Exceptional Children, 66,* 55–66.

McLeskey, J., Hoppey, D., Williamson, P., & Rentz, T. (2004). Is inclusion an illusion? An examination of national and state trends toward the education of students with learning disabilities in general education classrooms. *Learning Disabilities Research & Practice, 19*(2), 109–115.

McLeskey, J., & Pacchiano, D. (1994). Mainstreaming students with learning disabilities: Are we making progress? *Exceptional Children, 60*(6), 508–517.

McLeskey, J., & Waldron, N. (2000). *Inclusive schools in action: Making differences ordinary.* Alexandria, VA: Association for Supervision and Curriculum Development.

Mock, D. R., & Kauffman, J. M. (2002). Preparing teachers for full inclusion: is it possible? *The Teacher Educator, 37*(3), 202–215.

Murphy, D. (1996). Implications of inclusion for general and special education. *The Elementary School Journal, 96*(5), 470–493.

Odom, S. L. (2000). Preschool inclusion: What we know and where we go from here. *Topics in Early Childhood Special Education, 20*(1), 20–27.

Raines, J. C. (1996). Appropriate versus least restrictive educational policies and students with disabilities. *Social Work in Education, 18*(2), 113–127.

Stainback, W., & Stainback, S. (1990). *Support networks for inclusive schooling: Interdependent integrated education.* Baltimore: Brookes.

Waldron, N., & McLeskey, J. (1998). The effects of an Inclusive School Program on students with mild and severe learning disabilities. *Exceptional Children, 64,* 395–405.

Waldron, N., & McLeskey, J. (2000). *Inclusive education in action: Making differences ordinary.* Alexandria, VA: Association for Supervision and Curriculum Development.

Zigmond, N., & Baker, J. M. (1996). Full inclusion for students with learning disabilities: Too much of a good thing? *Theory Into Practice, 35*(1), 26–34.

MARIA ARZOLA
*University of Florida*

## TEACHING: INCLUSION AND CO-TEACHING
## TEACHING AND CONSULTATION

## INCLUSION AND CO-TEACHING

See TEACHING: INCLUSION AND CO-TEACHING.

## INCORRIGIBILITY

See CONDUCT DISORDER.

## INDEPENDENT LIVING CENTERS

Independent Living Centers (ILCs) are designed to assist individuals with disabilities to achieve their maximum potential. Typically, ILCs are nonresidential, private, non-profit, consumer controlled, community-based organizations providing services and advocacy by and for persons with disabilities. Individuals living with severe disabilities were the real pioneers in the ILC movement because it afforded them options for living a more integrated life in their communities.

While the term *severe disabilities* has been defined differently by various people and agencies, it generally implies a condition in which the development of typical abilities is in some way adversely affected (Sailor & Haring, 1977; Westling & Fox, 2004). Persons with severe disabilities are often challenged by significant weaknesses in general learning abilities, personal and social skills, and frequently in areas of sensory and physical development. Individuals who experience severe disabilities commonly do not demonstrate general ability in skills necessary to maintain themselves independently. Most often these individuals require assistance and ongoing support from persons who do not experience disabilities, such as family members, friends, professionals, and care providers.

DeJong (1978) states that the ILC movement originated from two main sources, the consumers who sought to live a more fulfilling life in the able-bodied world and the efforts of rehabilitation professionals to reach disabled persons for whom a vocational goal was, until recently, unthinkable. It was not until the early 1970s that the ILC movement gained greater visibility and recognition with the creation of the Center for Independent Living (CIL) in Berkeley, California.

Professionals in the field of rehabilitation have held common beliefs that rehabilitation programs are built upon the "medical model" of service delivery, while the disability rights and ILC movement promotes a completely different approach to service delivery. Centers for independent living across the nation are working toward changing their communities rather than "fixing" the person with a disability. In the rehabilitation model, the desired outcome of service delivery is maximum physical or mental functioning, and in vocational rehabilitation the desired goal is gainful employment. Contrast these goals with the desired outcomes for ILCs that is making control over one's daily life as paramount. The term "control" does not necessarily mean having the physical or mental capacity to do everyday tasks for one's self. For some persons, complete control may not be possible, but the ILC movement continues to work toward complete consumer control wherever and whenever possible.

Certainly every community needs the rehabilitation paradigm for the provision of adequate medical-based services. Equally important, however, is that each community needs an equal amount of service and advocacy stemming from the independent living paradigm. At this time approximately 99 percent of all public dollars go into the rehabilitation paradigm while less than 1 percent goes into independent living.

The passage of the Americans with Disabilities Act of 1990 creates a vision for equal opportunity and access for all persons. This vision is shared by people involved in both the traditional rehabilitation system and the newer disability rights and ILC movement. ILCs enhance not only the lives of persons with disabilities, but also the individual communities where these Centers are located. Additionally, ILCs provide an advocacy voice on a wide range of national, state, and local issues. The nearly 500 ILCs in the United States are working to establish physical and programmatic access to housing, employment, communities, transportation, recreational facilities, as well as health and social services. The movement for independent living has been evolving for well over 4 decades. The ILC movement will continue to grow because committed individuals will seek ways to assist all persons to feel that they are valued members of their community, whether they happen to live with or without disabilities.

## REFERENCES

DeJong, G. (1978, November 17). *The movement for independent living: Origins, ideology, and implications for disability research.* Boston: Medical Rehabilitation Institute, Tufts–New England Medical Center. A paper presented at the annual meetings of the American Congress of Rehabilitation Medicine, New Orleans, Louisiana.

Sailor, W., & Haring, N. (1977). Some current directions in the education of the severely/multiply handicapped. *AAESPH Review, 2*(2), 67–86.

Westling, D., & Fox, L. (2004). *Teaching students with severe disabilities* (3rd ed.). Upper Saddle River, NJ: Pearson Education.

PETER KOPRIVA
*Fresno Pacific University*

GROUP HOMES
SELF-DETERMINATION
VOCATIONAL EDUCATION

# INDEPENDENT VARIABLE

Independent variable is a term that is used to describe the intervention or treatment that will be implemented as part of an experimental manipulation (Alberto & Troutman, 2006). Independent variables can include antecedent oriented strategies (e.g., teacher directives), consequent strategies (e.g., schedules of reinforcement), environmental modification (e.g., moving a student's desk), setting event strategies (e.g., touching base with the student following a difficult interaction), and biological strategies (e.g., methods for decreasing physical symptoms of agitation; Bailey & Burch, 2002).

The independent variable is usually implemented following a period of baseline data collection. As a rule, the independent variable is only initiated when the baseline data shows stability, such as minimal variability and/or a flat or contra-therapeutic trend (Tawney & Gast, 1984). Bailey and Burch (2002) offer several considerations for selecting and implementing an independent variable, including (a) knowing your consumer, that is being sure to select procedures with the understanding that the teacher or student is willing to use the procedure and/or considers the procedure feasible given his or her learners or context; (b) considering potential side effects, that is determining if there are any detrimental effects associated with the proposed procedure prior to implementation (e.g., use of aversives, loss of privileges, health or safety concerns); and (c) operationally defining your intervention, that is providing an observable and measurable statement that exactly defines what you plan to do as part of your intervention (see Gresham, 1996).

In conclusion, the independent variable represents the treatment or intervention that the experimenter implements to determine if he or she can demonstrate a functional relationship between the intervention and changes in the dependent variable. Gresham (1996) argues that researchers should always be mindful of treatment integrity, which is verifying that the intervention was delivered as intended. Treatment integrity can be evaluated using direct, indirect, and statistical methodologies.

## REFERENCES

Alberto, P. A., & Troutman, A. C. (2006). *Applied behavior analysis for teachers* (7th ed.). Upper Saddle River, NJ: Prentice Hall.

Bailey, J. S., & Burch, M. R. (2002). *Research methods in applied behavior analysis.* Thousand Oaks, CA: Sage.

Gresham, F. M. (1996). Treatment integrity in single-subject research. In R. D. Franklin, D. B. Allison, & B. S. Gorman (Eds.), *Design and analysis of single-case research* (pp. 93–117). Mahwah, NJ: Erlbaum.

Tawney, J. W., & Gast, D. L. (1984). *Single subject research in special education.* New York: Merrill.

RANDALL L. DE PRY
*University of Colorado at
Colorado Springs*

RESEARCH IN SPECIAL EDUCATION

# INDIA, SPECIAL EDUCATION IN

Fifty million of India's one billion people are disabled or have special needs. Information as to the number of special needs children currently receiving educational services is unavailable. In 1992, 12,590,000 children reportedly received special education services (Ministry of Human Resource Development, 1998; National Policy on Education, 1992).

All children in India who attend school have the right to education. The term *special education* denotes the education of children who deviate socially, mentally, or physically from the average to such an extent that they require major modifications of usual school practices. Students who warrant special education services include the gifted; the mentally challenged; those with communication or emotion disorders; Attention Deficit Disorders; autism; vision, hearing, or speech impairments; or those with orthopedic and neurological problems. An understanding of the status of special education in India requires some understanding of its history.

The first special school was established around 1869 when Jane Leupot started one for the blind in Benares with the support of the Church Missionary Society and Raja Kali Shankar Ghosal (Miles, 1997). Another special school was established in Amritsar in 1887 by Anne Sharpe, a missionary manager (Mani, 1988; Pandey & Advani, 1997). The first school for mentally and physically disabled children was established at Kurseong in 1918 (Pandey & Advani, 1997).

The following initiatives were taken recently at the national level. The Indian Education Commission (1964–1966) observed that, although the Indian constitution had issued specific directives on compulsory education for all, including children with disabilities, little had been done in this regard. At the time the commission made its recommendations, there were fewer than 250 special schools. The commission recognized that services for children with disabilities were extremely inadequate and recommended the adoption of two approaches, special schools and classes as well as integrated education. The commission set the following targets to be achieved by 1986: education for about 15 percent of the country's blind, deaf, and orthopedically disabled and 5 percent of its mentally retarded persons. The commission emphasized the importance of integrated education in meeting this target as it considered integrated education to be cost effective and useful in developing mutual understanding between children with and without disabilities.

In 1974, the Ministry of Welfare initiated the Integrated Education for Disabled Children program to promote the integration of students with mild to moderate disabilities into regular schools. Children were to be provided financial support for books, stationery, school uniforms, transport, special equipment, and aides. State governments were provided 50 percent financial assistance to implement this program in regular schools. However, the program met with little success. Major contributory factors for its failure were the nonavailability of trained and experienced teachers, lack of orientation among school staff on the problems of disabled children and their educational needs, and nonavailability of equipment and educational materials. By 1979–1980, only 1,881 children from 81 schools had benefited from this program (Mani, 1988). Due to the program's failure, it was revised in 1992, incorporating various recommendations of Project Integrated Education for the Disabled. Various nongovernment organizations were entitled to implement this program. Until 1990, it was implemented in only 14 states.

The Indian government's 1986 National Policy on Education (1986–1992), one that applied to all government schools, articulated a need to integrate students with disabilities and attempted to promote the following goals. Children with mild disabilities were to be educated in regular schools. Children with severe disabilities were to be in special residential schools located near their homes. Vocational education was to be initiated along with teacher training programs redesigned to prepare educators to teach disabled children. All voluntary efforts were encouraged.

Again in 1986, the National Policy on Education devoted a specific section to the education of students with disabilities. It emphasized that, whenever feasible, the education of children with motor and other mild disabilities should be provided in regular schools. This policy also stressed that children whose needs could not be met in regular schools were to be enrolled in special schools. Children in special schools were to be integrated into regular schools as soon as they acquired reasonable levels of daily living, communication, and basic academic skills. The need to restructure primary teacher training programs to prepare teachers to deal with the special difficulties of children with disabilities was emphasized (National Policy on Education, 1992).

In 1987, the Ministry of Human Resource Development, in association with UNICEF and the National Council for Educational Research and Training, undertook Project Integrated Education for the Disabled. Its goal was to strengthen the implementation of the Integrated Education for the Disabled program. Instead of confining this program to a particular institution or school, this program adopted a composite area approach to address the needs of students with special needs. Schools in a particular area were requested to share resources such as specialized equipment, instructional materials, and special education teachers. The key aspect of the project was the teacher training program. Selected teachers undertook 6 weeks intensive training in special education and were provided practical experiences in integrated and special school settings.

The project produced several positive results, including improved program planning and better management skills, thus increasing the capacity of various states to implement integration (Jangira, 1990). About 13,000 children with disabilities in eight states and two urban slums were enrolled in the program.

The 1994 District Primary Education Program emphasized in-service training of primary school teachers in such areas as early detection of disabilities, functional assessment, use of aids and appliances, and implementation of individualized education plans. This program utilized resource rooms to implement integrated education in primary schools.

The 1995 Persons with Disabilities Act marked a turning point in special education services. Although the government had made several attempts to implement integrated education programs, it lacked a firm commitment to promote integration. This largely was due to considering the provision of special education services to be a welfare issue rather than an educational issue that should be addressed by the Ministry of Education. With the passage of the 1995 Persons with Disabilities Act, the integration of students with disabilities became the legal responsibility of the Ministry of Education. The Act proposed the provision of improved educational services, medical care, vocational training and employment, and social security for all persons with disabilities. The Act further stated that, whenever possible, students with disabilities should be educated in regular school settings. The federal government's recent Five Year

Plan earmarked Rs. 1,000 million (1US dollar = Rs.43.70) for integrated education programs (Miles, 1997).

The federal government has established four national institutes of disability. These are the National Institute for the Orthopedicly Handicapped located in Calcutta and established in 1978, the National Institute for the Visually Handicapped located in Dehradun and established in 1979, the Ali Yavar Jung National Institute for the Hearing Handicapped located in Bombay and established in 1983, and the National Institute for the Mentally Handicapped located in Secunderabad and established in 1984. These institutes have played a major role in research, manpower development, documentation and information services, providing consultative services to nongovernmental organizations, and in developing service delivery models for the care and rehabilitation appropriate for local situations.

However, their manpower training efforts tended to emphasize teaching students with special needs in segregated settings. Although the educational services provided by special schools and the national institutes have contributed to some extent in meeting the needs of a large number of individuals with disabilities, current educational provisions for children with disabilities remain largely inadequate. The latest estimates indicate that over 16 million children do not have access to any form of education (Ministry of Human Resource Development, 1998).

Various conditions are needed to contribute to the success of special education in India. Specialized teachers are needed to serve as resource persons, supported by appropriate educational texts and selected aids and appliances, to prepare special materials, and to provide special instruction according to individual needs. Consultation for regular classroom teachers, school administrators, families, local health authorities, and the general public is needed on matters dealing with education of disabled children, specialized training techniques, and selection of appropriate materials. Parent education, appropriate technology, and awareness of parent attitudes toward disabilities are needed (Jayachandran, 2000). Individual educational plans should be prepared while integrating children in regular classrooms.

Evaluation also is crucial to the development and maintenance of effective special education programs and services. The aim of the evaluation process is to encourage the best possible learning conditions for exceptional children. An important step toward the achievement of this aim is the promotion of professional classroom practices. A special educator has to be specially assigned to conduct follow-up evaluations for special children.

Sensitivity to the needs of communities in rural areas, where educational facilities are poor and one-teacher schools are common, is needed. Special education is a major component of community-based rehabilitation programs and requires trained personnel for effective delivery of services. However, most services are concentrated in urban areas.

Seva-in-action, a voluntary organization, has attempted to understand the needs of people in rural areas and has developed a cost-effective, socio-culturally appropriate, comprehensive, sustainable, and holistic community-based rehabilitation program with the goal to rehabilitate all persons with disabilities in rural areas of Karnataka, South India (Nanjurdaiah, 2000).

## REFERENCES

Jangira, N. K. (1990). Desirability and feasibility of integrated education for mentally retarded children. In P. Usha Rani & P. P. Reddy (Eds.), *Mental retardation in India*. Hyderabad: Institute of Genetics.

Jayachandran, K. R. (2000, July). *Possibility of inclusive education in India based on success of integrated education in Kerala State, India*. Paper presented in the International Special Education Congress held in Manchester, England.

Mani, C. (1988). *The physically handicapped in India*. New Delhi: Ashish Publishing.

Miles, M. (1997). *Disability care and education in the 19th century India: Some dates, places and documentation*. (ERIC Document No. 408747)

Ministry of Human Resource Development. (1998). *Selected educational statistics: 1998–99*. New Delhi: Department of Education, Planning, Monitoring & Statistics Division.

Myreddi, V., & Narayan, J. (1999). Preparation of special education teachers: Present status and future trends. *Asia Pacific Disability Rehabilitation Journal, 10*(1).

Nanjundaiah, Manjula. (2000). *Shift from rehabilitation to inclusion: Implementation of Inclusive Education (IE) through rural community based rehabilitation program of Seva-in-action, India*. Paper presented in the International Special Education Congress held in Manchester, England.

National Policy on Education. (1992). Ministry of Human Resource Development, Government of India.

Pandey, R. S., & Advani, L. (1997). *Perspectives in disability and rehabilitation*. New Delhi: Vikas Publishing House Pvt. Ltd.

RUMKI GUPTA
*Indian Statistical Institute,*
*Kolkata, India*

# INDIVIDUALIZATION OF INSTRUCTION

Individualization of instruction is a method of teaching in which instruction is tailored to the unique needs of students, enabling them to advance at their own rates and to achieve their potential. Individualized instruction requires that students be placed individually within a curriculum or sequence of objectives, and that teaching methods be prescribed so as to maximize individual growth and accomplishment. Both elements—placement and prescription—are essential to the process. Schwartz and Oseroff (1975) traced the roots of individualized instruction to Harris, who in 1868, "vigerously [sic] challenged the validity of requiring all pupils to do the same amount of work and to advance at the same time" (p. 26). Nonetheless, formal recognition of its critical role in special education awaited the enactment of the Education for All Handicapped Children Act of 1975 (PL 94-142).

Public Law 94-142 and subsequent legislation, including in particular the Individuals with Disabilities Education Act (IDEA), assigned to state and local education agencies the responsibility to provide free, appropriate education to meet the unique needs of exceptional children. The act delineated guidelines for individualized placement and prescription by requiring an individual educational program (IEP) for every student with a disability. The IEP includes, among other things, statements of present levels of educational performance, annual goals, short-term objectives, and specific educational services to be provided. Ideally, then, an IEP must embody the elements of individualized instruction and in so doing "represents a formalization of the diagnostic/prescriptive approach to education" (Safer, Morrissey, Kaufman, & Lewis, 1978, p. 1).

Individualized placement within a curriculum or sequence of objectives may be accomplished through a variety of means. Many curricula include placement tests that can be used to identify the material that students have and have not mastered. However, these instruments are apparently not developed with the same rigor as standardized tests because their technical properties (reliability and validity) often fall short of established standards. Criterion-referenced tests, those that sample performance within a specified instructional domain, have stronger technical properties but may not necessarily correspond to particular curricula. Recent efforts to link performance on criterion-referenced tests to placement levels within curricula bode well for their continued use in the future. Precision teaching (PT) and data-based program modification (DBPM) define instructional levels in terms of performance within the curriculum itself and represent another useful alternative for making individualized placements.

The prescription of individualized instructional methodologies represents a more difficult problem because efforts to predict how teaching methods interact with learner characteristics have not yet proved fruitful. At the present, post hoc validation represents the most well-established approach to determining the effectiveness of instructional programs (Salvia & Sindelar, 1982). Frequent and repeated assessments of performance are evaluated against predetermined criteria to establish the adequacy of an instructional program. Here again, PT and DBPM provide methodologies for conducting such post hoc analyses.

Individualization of instruction is not synonymous and should not be confused with one-to-one instruction. The latter may or may not be individualized; the former may be accomplished with groups. Similarly, individualized in-

struction does not necessarily require that students work independently on seat-work tasks. Effective individualized instruction can occur in teacher-led groups (Stevens & Rosenshine, 1980).

## REFERENCES

Safer, D., Morrissey, A., Kaufman, J., & Lewis, L. (1978). Implementation of IEPs: New teacher roles and requisite support systems. *Focus on Exceptional Children, 10,* 1–20.

Salvia, J., & Sindelar, P. T. (1982). Aptitude testing and alternative approaches to maximizing the effects of instruction. In T. L. Miller & E. E. Davis (Eds.), *The mildly handicapped student* (pp. 221–240). New York: Grune & Stratton.

Schwartz, L., & Oseroff, A. (1975). *The clinical teacher for special education: Vol. 1. Establishing the model.* Final Report, USOE, HEW/BEH Grant No. OEG-0-71-1688 (603). Tallahassee: Florida State University.

Stevens, R., & Rosenshine, B. (1980). Advances in research on teaching. *Exceptional Education Quarterly, 2,* 1–9.

PAUL T. SINDELAR
RHONDA COLLINS
*Florida State University*
Second edition

KIMBERLY F. APPLEQUIST
*University of Colorado at
Colorado Springs*
Third edition

DATA-BASED INSTRUCTION
INDIVIDUALIZED EDUCATIONAL PLAN
PRECISION TEACHING

## INDIVIDUALIZED EDUCATIONAL PLAN

IEP is the acronym for the individualized educational plan that must now be written for each identified child with a disability prior to his or her placement in a special education program. The Education of All Handicapped Children Act of 1975 (PL 94-142) and subsequent legislation such as the Individuals with Disabilities Education Act (IDEA) required that states receiving federal funds for special education services develop and implement a written statement regarding the specific special educational services and related services each child with a disability is to receive. At a minimum, it is mandatory that each written plan include the following:

1. A statement of the child's present levels of educational performance, including:
   (i) How the child's disability affects the child's involvement and progress in the general curricu-

lum (i.e., the same curriculum as for nondisabled children); or

   (ii) For preschool children, as appropriate, how the disability affects the child's participation in appropriate activities.

2. A statement of measurable annual goals, including benchmarks or short-term institutional objectives related to:

   (i) Meeting the child's needs that result from the child's disability to enable the child to be involved in and progress in the general curriculum (i.e., the same curriculum as for nondisabled children), or for preschool children, as appropriate, to participate in appropriate activities; and

   (ii) Meeting each of the child's other educational needs that result from the child's disability.

3. A statement of special education and related services and supplementary aids and services to be provided to the child, or on behalf of the child, and a statement of the program modifications or supports for school personnel that will be provided for the child:

   (i) To advance appropriately toward attaining the annual goals;

   (ii) To be involved and progress in the general curriculum in accordance with paragraph 1, and to participate in extracurricular and other nonacademic activities; and

   (iii) To be educated with other children with disabilities and nondisabled children in the activities described in this section.

4. An explanation of the extent, if any, to which the child will not participate with nondisabled children in the regular class and in the activities described in paragraph 3.

5.  (i) A statement of any individual modifications in the administration of state or district-wide assessments of student achievement that are needed in order for the child to participate in the assessment; and

   (ii) If the IEP team determines that the child will not participate in a particular state or district-wide assessment of student achievement (or part of an assessment) a statement of:

     A. Why that assessment is not appropriate for the child; and

     B. How the child will be assessed.

6. The projected date for the beginning of services and modifications, and the anticipated frequency, location, and duration of those services and modifications.

7. A statement of:

   (i) How the child's progress toward the annual goals described in paragraph 2 will be measured; and

   (ii) How the child's parents will be regularly informed (through such means as periodic report cards), at least as often as parents are informed of their nondisabled child's progress, of:

     A. Their child's progress toward the annual goals; and

     B. The extent to which that progress is sufficient to enable to achieve the goals by the end of the year.

(34 C.F.R. § 300.347[a]). In addition, beginning at age 14 (or earlier if deemed appropriate by the IEP team), the IEP must include a statement of the transition service needs of the student, focusing on the student's course of study. Beginning at the age of 16 (or earlier, again, as deemed appropriate by the IEP team), the IEP must also include "a statement of needed transitions services for the student, including, if appropriate, a statement of the interagency responsibilities or any needed linkages" (34 C.F.R. § 300.347[b]). There are additional requirements regarding notice to the student in states where rights are transferred when the student reaches his or her majority. There are also special requirements for students with disabilities convicted of criminal offenses as adults and imprisoned in adult correctional facilities (34 C.F.R. § 300.311[b] and [c]). Proposed regulations implementing the most recent reauthorization of the IDEA, issued June 21, 2005, would make minor, primarily nonsubstantive changes to the requirements of 34 C.F.R. § 300.347 (70 Fed. Reg. 35865).

Under these guidelines, the IEP team must meet at least once a year to review and, if necessary, revise the educational program as originally outlined. It is obvious that the goals—long- or short-range—specified in the initial IEP would periodically be in need of revision for a number of reasons: the original goals may be inappropriate for the individual child, or the child may meet or make progress on many of the goals, thus requiring revision and development of new goals.

According to some authorities (e.g., Reynolds, Gutkin, Elliot, & Witt, 1984), once a year reviewing is not enough to ensure the best educational programming for a handicapped child. They do, however, acknowledge that this mandated requirement is far better than prior practices that seldom ensured the review of educational plans for handicapped students.

Although the intent of the law is commendable, the actual implementation is often less than satisfactory. One example involves the extent to which the IEP is in fact individualized for the child. It is not uncommon for educational programs to be designed specific to the child's classification (e.g., learning disabled) rather than the unique abilities of the child involved. Often individualized educational plans will simply be a reflection of the specific district or school the child attends. For example, states will frequently mandate that all children meet certain objectives within a given subject (e.g., reading). Therefore, it is not uncommon to find the short-range objectives specified for the learning-disabled child in reading to be simply a list of the reading objectives common to the district. This practice would seem in direct contradiction to the intent of the law and certainly not always in the best interests of the child with disabilities involved. Indeed, special educators have questioned the general value of these types of IEPs (Ryan & Rucher, 1991).

The law also stipulates who should be present at each IEP meeting, whether it be for the purposes of developing, reviewing, or revising a child's IEP. The educational agency is charged with ensuring that those individuals are present. According to the IDEA implementing regulations, the IEP team must include:

1. The parents of the child;
2. At least one regular education teacher of the child (if the child is, or may be, participating in the regular education environment);
3. At least one special education teacher of the child, or if appropriate, at least one special education provider of the child;
4. A representative of the public agency who—
   (i) Is qualified to provide, or supervise the provision of, specially designed instruction to meet the unique needs of children with disabilities;
   (ii) Is knowledgeable about the general curriculum; and
   (iii) Is knowledgeable about the availability of resources of the public agency;
5. An individual who can interpret the instructional implications of evaluation results, who may be a member of the team described in paragraphs (2) through (6) of this section;
6. At the discussion of the parent or the agency, other individuals who have knowledge or special expertise regarding the child, including related services personnel as appropriate; and
7. If appropriate, the child.

(34 C.F.R. §300.344). The proposed regulations issued in June of 2005 make only nonsubstantive changes to these requirements (70 Fed. Reg. 35866).

In keeping with another major intent of IDEA to protect the rights of parents of children with disabilities to fully participate in their child's education, each public agency is charged with the responsibility of exerting maximum effort in ensuring that one or both parents are present and participating (Van Reusen & Bos, 1994) at meetings where the IEP is developed, reviewed, and revised. To be in compliance with the law, the public agency serving the child with disabilities must have proof that they not only gave parents notice of the meeting, including all details, but that the meeting was arranged at a time that is mutually convenient to all involved. If the parents cannot attend the meeting, the agency must show that parent participation was elicited via other means (e.g., telephone conversations). Whether or not the parents are able to attend, they are to be given a copy of the IEP.

Various studies have been conducted investigating parental participation in IEP development and planning (e.g., Lusthaus, Lusthaus, & Gibbs, 1981; Polifka, 1981; Roit & Pfohl, 1984; Scanlon, Arick, & Phelps, 1981; Yoshida, Fenton, Kaufman, & Maxwell, 1978). Yoshida et al. (1978) found that educational personnel involved in the planning meeting expected parents to simply provide information as opposed to actively participating in the decisions as to what would constitute the plan. Interestingly, results of a parental survey conducted by Lusthaus et al. (1981) found that parents agreed that their role should be that of information giver and receiver instead of equal decision maker. This has slowly changed (Van Reusen & Bos, 1994). Roit and Pfohl (1984) indicated that printed information provided to parents regarding PL 94-142 and their rights (including their right to participate in the IEP process) was often not comprehensible to a large number of parents. More recent legislation and rulemaking has imposed stricter requirements about the notice to be provided to parents to make such notice more comprehensible to parents of children with disabilities.

Polifka (1981) reported on the results of a survey conducted as part of the Iowa Department of Public Instruction evaluation of special education services by a specific area agency. He found that parent satisfaction with the services their child received was significantly related to, among other variables, whether they were asked to help develop the IEP and whether they were invited to a meeting to review the IEP. It is impossible to determine the actual involvement these parents were allowed or whether the involvement was responsible for their satisfaction, but it does seem that active involvement should be fostered not only to ensure compliance but to promote active decision-making roles for the parents of children with disabilities.

### REFERENCES

Lusthaus, C. S., Lusthaus, E. W., & Gibbs, H. (1981). Parents' role in the decision process. *Exceptional Children, 48*(3), 256–257.

Polifka, J. C. (1981). Compliance with Public Law 94-142 and consumer satisfaction. *Exceptional Children, 48*(3), 250–253.

Reynolds, C. R., Gutkin, T. B., Elliot, S. N., & Witt, J. C. (1984). *School psychology: Essentials of theory and practice.* New York: Wiley.

Roit, M. L., & Pfohl, W. (1984). The readability of PL 94-142 parent materials: Are parents truly informed? *Exceptional Children, 50*(6), 496–506.

Ryan, L. G., & Rucher, C. N. (1991). The development and validation of a measure of special education teachers' attitudes toward the IEP. *Educational and Psychological Measurement, 51*(4), 877–882.

Scanlon, C. A., Arick, J. R., & Phelps, N. (1981). Participation in development of the IEP: Parents' perspective. *Exceptional Children, 47*(5), 373–376.

Van Reusen, A. K., & Bos, C. S. (1994). Facilitating student participation in individualized education programs through motivational strategy instruction. *Exceptional Children, 60*(5), 466–475.

Yoshida, R., Fenton, K., Kaufman, M. J., & Maxwell, J. P. (1978). Parental involvement in the special education pupil planning process: The school's perspective. *Exceptional Children, 44,* 531–533.

JULIA A. HICKMAN
*Bastrop Mental Health
Association*
Second edition

KIMBERLY F. APPLEQUIST
*University of Colorado at
Colorado Springs*
Third edition

**INDIVIDUALS WITH DISABILITIES EDUCATION
IMPROVEMENT ACT OF 2004 (IDEIA)**

# INDIVIDUALS WITH DISABILITIES EDUCATION IMPROVEMENT ACT OF 2004 (IDEIA), PL 108-446

The Individuals with Disabilities Education Act (IDEA), formerly known as the Education for All Handicapped Children Act of 1975 (EHA; PL 94-142), and most recently amended in 2004 by the Individuals with Disabilities Education Improvement Act (IDEIA; PL 108-446), represents a 30-year national commitment, beginning with EHA, to children with disabilities ("Focus on IDEA," 1997; 20 U.S.C. § 1400[c][4]; Sec. 600[c][4]). IDEA, a federal statute, is the main special education law in the United States, and when initially enacted in 1975, it represented the most sweeping statement this nation has ever made regarding the rights of children with disabilities (Haring, McCormick, & Haring, 1994). The purpose of the law, as most recently articulated by the IDEIA, is:

(1)(A) to ensure that all children with disabilities have available to them a free appropriate public education that emphasizes special education and related services designed to meet their unique needs and prepare them for further education, employment, and independent living; (B) to ensure that the rights of children with disabilities and parents of such children are protected; and (C) to assist States, localities, educational service agencies and Federal agencies to provide for the education of all children with disabilities; (2) to assist States in the implementation of a statewide, comprehensive, coordinated, multidisciplinary, interagency system of early intervention services for infants and toddlers with disabilities and their families; (3)

to ensure that educators and parents have the necessary tools to improve educational results for children with disabilities by supporting system improvement activities; coordinated research and personnel preparation; coordinated technical assistance, dissemination, and support; and technology development and media services; and, (4) to assess, and ensure the effectiveness of, efforts to educate children with disabilities. (20 U.S.C. § 1400[d]; Sec. 601[d])

Under IDEA, the state is responsible for providing for children with disabilities, whether they are attending a public or private school, the opportunity to participate in special education and related services (20 U.S.C. § 1412; Sec. 612). Denial of this opportunity by the state results in the forfeiture of federal funds (20 U.S.C. § 1416; Sec. 616).

## Historical Background

Early legislation and case law, spanning over a 20-year period, foreshadowed the enactment of the initial version of the law, EHA, in 1975 (Jacob-Timm & Hartshorne, 1995). Three landmark court cases, *Brown* v. *Board of Education of Topeka* (1954), *Pennsylvania Association for Retarded Children* v. *Commonwealth of Pennsylvania* (PARC; 1971, 1972), and *Mills* v. *Board of Education* (1972), marked a turning point in the education of children with disabilities and provided the impetus for the development and enactment of federal legislation assuring a free appropriate public education for children with disabilities. Prior to the *Brown* case, many school districts throughout the nation were operated under the "separate but equal" policy (i.e., segregated classrooms based on race) that were in actuality not equal. Many minorities (African-Americans, in the case of *Brown*) were excluded from an equal educational opportunity in public schools. This practice, according to the *Brown* ruling, was in violation of the "equal protection clause" of the 14th Amendment to the U.S. Constitution. Education, which is considered to be a property right, is protected under the equal protection clause, and in the *Brown* ruling, the property right of African-Americans to an education at the public expense was violated by the school district's racially discriminatory policies (Jacob-Timm & Hartshorne, 1995).

Following the *Brown* ruling and other successful court challenges to racial discrimination in the public schools, parents of children with disabilities began to file lawsuits on behalf of their children, alleging that the children's right to an education at the public expense was being violated under the equal protection clause. Prior to the 1970s, many schools denied children with disabilities access to a public education based on school district policies, which required a child to meet certain admission standards (e.g., possession of a certain level of adaptive living and cognitive skills). In *PARC,* parents of children with Mental Retardation brought suit against Pennsylvania because their children were denied access to a public education. In a consent decree, the parents of the children with Mental Retardation won access to the public schools for their children. Similarly, in *Mills,* the parents of children with behavioral, emotional, and learning problems brought suit on behalf of their children against the District of Columbia for denial of access to a public education. In a consent decree followed by a court order, the court ruled that the schools were required to provide each child with a disability a free and public-supported education, regardless of the degree of severity or nature of the child's disability (Jacob-Timm & Hartshorne, 1995).

In response to the successful resolution of the *PARC* and *Mills* cases, 36 additional "right-to-education" cases were filed in 27 different jurisdictions by parents on behalf of their children with disabilities (Martin, 1979). These cases served as a signal to the U.S. Congress that federal legislation was needed to ensure a full educational opportunity to all children with disabilities (Jacob-Timm & Hartshorne, 1995).

In addition to case law, early attempts were made by the U.S. Congress to address the needs of children with disabilities. Funds were made available through various education laws and amendments to develop or improve special education resources, programs, services, and personnel. Beginning as early as the 1960s with the passage of PL 87-276, Congress authorized support for the training of teachers to work with the deaf and for speech pathologists and audiologists to work with individuals with speech and hearing impairments (Abramson, 1987; Reynolds & Fletcher-Janzen, 1990). In 1965, the Elementary and Secondary Education Act (ESEA; PL 89-10), one of the first major federal programs to aid education, was enacted. One year later, Congress amended the ESEA (PL 89-750) and, with these amendments, grants were provided to states to assist in the development and improvement of programs to educate children with disabilities (Jacob-Timm & Hartshorne, 1995). Students with disabilities were also assisted when the 1968 Amendments to the Vocational Education Act (PL 90-576) were passed. With these amendments, funds were made available for students with disabilities in vocational education programs (Abramson, 1987; Reynolds & Fletcher-Janzen, 1990). The needs of young children with disabilities were addressed with the establishment of model programs under the Handicapped Children's Early Education Assistance Act (PL 90-538) in 1968 (Abramson, 1987; Reynolds & Fletcher-Janzen, 1990). In 1970, Congress repealed and replaced the 1966 amendments to the ESEA (PL 89-750; Jacob-Timm & Hartshorne, 1995). Public Law 99-230, which replaced PL 89-750, established a grant program similar to PL 89-750 to encourage states to develop special education resources and personnel (Turnbull, 1990). Federal government assistance to states for special education increased with the passage of the Education Amendments of 1974 (PL 93-380). This act also put schools on notice that federal funding for special education purposes would be contingent on the development of a state plan with the goal of providing children with disabilities a full educational opportunity (Jacob-Timm & Hartshorne, 1995).

Congress also attempted to address the needs of children with disabilities through antidiscrimination legislation (Martin, 1979). An amendment to Title VI of the Civil Rights Act of 1964 was one of the first pieces of legislation that attempted to ensure equal educational opportunities for children with disabilities. Nine years later, this amendment became part of Section 504 of the Rehabilitation Act of 1973. Section 504 is a civil rights act that prohibits discrimination against children with disabilities in schools receiving federal funds. Federal funds are not available to schools not in compliance with the act (Jacob-Timm & Hartshorne, 1995).

Through enactment of antidiscrimination legislation and education laws, passage of amendments to existing education laws, and litigation, the stage was set for the introduction of a comprehensive federal statute that would reaffirm and strengthen the educational rights of children with disabilities and increase the federal government's financial commitment to children with disabilities (Abramson, 1987; Reynolds & Fletcher-Janzen, 1990). The Education for All Handicapped Children Act was originally introduced as a Senate bill in 1972. After 3 years of extensive hearings, the U.S. Congress passed the bill in 1975 and President Gerald Ford signed the bill into law on November 29, 1975. EHA was amended in 1978 (PL 98-733), 1983 (PL 98-199), twice in 1986 (PL 99-457 and PL 99-372), in 1988 (PL 100-630), and 1990 (PL 101-476; Jacob-Timm & Hartshorne, 1995).

In 1990, President George H. W. Bush signed PL 104-476 into law. The 1990 Amendments changed the EHA's name to the Individuals with Disabilities Education Act. The law was significantly amended and reauthorized in 1997 (PL 105-17) and signed into law by President Bill Clinton. The 1997 act restructured the IDEA into four parts: Part A, General Provisions; Part B, Assistance for Education of All Children with Disabilities; Part C, Infants and Toddlers with Disabilities; and Part D, National Activities to Improve Education of Children with Disabilities (PL 105-17).

In 2002, Congress passed the cornerstone of President George W. Bush's education reform package, the controversial No Child Left Behind Act (NCLB; PL 107-110), which made significant changes to the ESEA. The intent behind the NCLB is to improve education by increasing teacher and school accountability, primarily through increased testing of all students' reading and math skills and requirements that schools demonstrate "adequate yearly progress" in their students' proficiency. Students in special education programs are not exempt from the NCLB's requirement that schools demonstrate adequate yearly progress. States and school districts are allowed to use alternate assessment standards in determining whether certain students meet proficiency requirements, but only for a maximum of 1 percent of their students, regardless of the number of students who might have serious learning disabilities or otherwise be considered children with disabilities under the IDEA. The NCLB also imposes teacher education requirements, promotes the use of evidence-based educational interventions, and provides parents with some ability to choose alternate schools if their child's local school fails to demonstrate adequate yearly progress for a specified period of time (Applequist, 2005). The law continues to generate controversy due to what one organization describes as the law's focus on "punishments rather than assistance, mandates rather than support for effective programs, [and] privatization rather than teacher-led, family oriented solutions" (National Education Association, n.d.).

When the IDEA next came before Congress for reauthorization, numerous changes were made in the statute to bring it into compliance with NCLB. The reauthorizing bill, IDEIA (PL 108-446), was enacted on December 3, 2004, by President George W. Bush. The majority of the IDEIA's provisions went into effect on July 1, 2005 (Wright, 2004); however, until regulations implementing the 2004 act have been finalized, the regulations implementing the 1997 amendments to the IDEA remain in effect to the extent that they are not inconsistent with the provisions of the IDEIA (U.S. Department of Education, n.d.).

The new legislation consists of three titles. Title I, which will be the primary focus of this article, amends and restates the IDEA, retaining the four-part structure established by the 1997 amendments. It is in Title I that the majority of changes relating to NCLB appear. Title II amends the Education Sciences Reform Act of 2002 (20 U.S.C. § 9501 et seq.), establishing a National Center for Special Education Research to sponsor research into the needs of infants, toddlers, and children with disabilities to improve their developmental, educational, and transitional results and research to improve services provided under the IDEA and support its implementation (20 U.S.C. § 9567). Title III makes miscellaneous changes to other statutory provisions, primarily in order to make them consistent with the changes to the law made by Titles I and II.

## IDEA Overview

The key provisions of IDEA include the requirement that states provide a free appropriate public education (FAPE) for all children qualified under the statute, nondiscriminatory assessment, the individualized education program (IEP), procedural safeguards, confidentiality of records, provision of education services in the least restrictive environment (LRE), and related services. State educational agencies (SEAs) are responsible for ensuring that local educational agencies (LEAs) provide FAPE to all children with disabilities. A free appropriate public education must be made available to all children with disabilities, regardless of the nature or severity of their disability, and consists of special education and related services. *Related services* are sup-

port services required to assist children with disabilities to benefit from special education. Examples of related services include psychological services, physical and occupational therapy, speech pathology, audiology, and orientation and mobility services. Related services cannot stand alone under Part B of the IDEA. Instead, such services must be attached to a special education program. In other words, a child must be eligible for special education under IDEA Part B in order to receive related services (20 U.S.C. § 1401; Sec. 602). Special education and related services must be provided to children with disabilities at no cost to the children's parents or the children (20 U.S.C. § 1401; Sec. 602).

Another key requirement of the IDEA is nondiscriminatory assessment. Testing and evaluation materials must be selected and administered so as not to be culturally or racially discriminatory. In addition, tests must be administered in the child's native language or other mode of communication, unless it is unfeasible to do so. LEAs must also ensure that standardized tests given to a child are validated for the purpose for which they are used and are administered by trained personnel in accordance with the test producer's instructions. The child must be assessed in all areas of suspected disability. The child must also be assessed with a variety of assessment tools and strategies, the instruments must be technically sound, and no single procedure must be used as the sole criterion for determining eligibility (20 U.S.C. § 1414; Sec. 614).

An IEP is required for each child with a disability who is receiving special education. Each LEA must have an IEP in place for each such child at the beginning of each school year. The child's IEP is reviewed and revised on at least an annual basis by the IEP team, and a reevaluation is conducted at least once every 3 years. The IEP team consists of the parent of the child, at least one special education teacher and one regular education teacher if the child is or may be participating in the regular education program, a representative of the LEA who is qualified to provide or supervise the provision of specially designed instruction and who is knowledgeable about the general curriculum and resources available, an individual who can interpret the instructional implications of evaluation results, other individuals at the discretion of the parent or LEA, and the child when appropriate (20 U.S.C. § 1414; Sec. 614). The IEP serves as the mechanism by which goals and objectives are established, programs are planned, and progress of the child is monitored (Abramson, 1987; Reynolds & Fletcher-Janzen, 1990).

Procedural safeguards are also included in the IDEA. Such safeguards are discussed at length in the following description of Section 615. These safeguards are intended to ensure that children with disabilities and their parents have certain rights and that these rights are protected under the law. Parents are given the opportunity to present their complaints regarding possible violations of their rights through mediation, due process hearings, and/or civil action with respect to any matter relating to the identification, evaluation, or placement of a child (20 U.S.C. § 1415; Sec. 615).

Parents' rights also extend to the educational records of their child. Educational and psychological records pertaining to the child must remain confidential except to those individuals who are directly involved in a child's education and who have a specific reason for reviewing the records (20 U.S.C. § 1417; Sec. 617). Parents have the right to examine all records, not just relevant records, with respect to the identification, evaluation, and placement of their child, and the provision of FAPE (20 U.S.C. § 1415; Sec. 615). Additional limitations and requirements regarding the confidentiality of students' records can be found in the entry for the Family Educational Rights and Privacy Act (FERPA).

Special education and related services must be provided in the LRE for children with disabilities in public or private institutions. The act requires, to the maximum extent appropriate, that children be educated together in as normal an environment as possible, and that removal from the regular education environment occurs only when education in the regular education setting with supplementary aids and services cannot be achieved satisfactorily. Therefore, the LRE for a child with a disability does not necessarily require the child to be educated entirely or in part in regular classes. Decisions about what constitutes the LRE are made on an individual basis for each child with a disability. Decisions are based on the child's needs and requirements for an educational program (20 U.S.C. § 1412; Sec. 612).

## Part A: General Provisions

Part A, General Provisions, includes the congressional findings that constitute the underpinnings of the IDEA, definitions of key terms used in the statute (e.g., "child with a disability"), and provisions establishing an Office of Special Education and Rehabilitative Services to administer the terms of the IDEA, revoking state immunity under the 11th Amendment to the U.S. Constitution for violation of the IDEA, and various other administrative provisions (relating to, e.g., promulgation of federal regulations under the IDEA; requirements that State rules, regulations, and policies be in compliance with the IDEA; and questionably named "paperwork reduction" provisions; 20 U.S.C. § 1400–1409; Sec. 601-610).

The new legislation made some changes to the congressional findings, including some adjustment to the language used to describe certain demographic changes over time and the addition of a specific reference to "improvement efforts under the Elementary and Secondary Education Act of 1965" (20 U.S.C. § 1400[c][5][C]), a reference to the changes promulgated under NCLB. It also made minor changes to the statement of the IDEA's purposes (e.g., replacing "systemic change activities" with "system improvement activities" and

adding "further education" to subsection [1][A] of the statement of purposes; see introductory portion of this article for the full text of the statement of purposes; 20 U.S.C. § 1400[d]; Sec. 601[d]).

The 2004 legislation also adds a number of new defined terms, including *core academic subjects, highly qualified* (as in, "highly qualified special education teachers"), *homeless children,* and *limited English proficiency,* that relate to provisions of ESEA/NCLB and are part of the new statute's push to make IDEA consistent with, or possibly subordinate to, NCLB (20 U.S.C. § 1401; Sec. 602). Furthermore, the new statute expands the definition of *parent* to include natural, adoptive, and foster parents, as well as guardians, and individuals acting in place of a natural or adoptive parents (e.g., grandparent, stepparent, other relative) of children who may be eligible to receive special education services under the IDEA, thus allowing for greater participation by those filling parenting roles in the processes outlined by the statute (20 U.S.C. § 1401; Sec. 602). The new statute also adds school nurse services to the list of services that make up the defined term *related services,* and makes other minor changes and additions to the defined terms list.

## Part B: Assistance for Education of All Children with Disabilities

Part B, Assistance for Education of All Children with Disabilities, contains what many would argue are the key components of the IDEA, including the formulas for calculating the maximum amounts states are eligible to receive under the act; provisions governing state and LEA eligibility for assistance under the IDEA; provisions governing evaluations, individual eligibility, IEPs, and educational placements; procedural safeguards for children and their parents; monitoring and enforcement provisions; and preschool grants. This section of the article will look at each section in Part B separately for ease of reference.

### Section 611: Authorization, Allotment, and Use of Funds

Section 611 includes information on the authorization of federal funds to the states and state requirements to receive federal funds. The federal government provides funds to the states to financially assist the states in the education of children with disabilities. Federal funds are distributed to the states based on a "child-count" formula. Under the child-count formula for fiscal years 2005 and 2006, the maximum amount that a state may receive is equal to (1) the number of children with disabilities receiving special education and related services in the State (a) aged 3 through 5 if the State is eligible for a grant under Section 619 (preschool grants), discussed in more detail elsewhere in this article, plus (b) aged 6 through 21; multiplied by (2) 40 percent of the average per pupil expenditure in public elementary and secondary schools in the United States (20 U.S.C. § 1411[a][2][A]; Sec. 611[a][2][A]).

Starting in fiscal year 2007, however, the formula will change to (1) the number of children with disabilities *in the 2004–2005 school year* receiving special education and related services in the state (a) aged 3 through 5 if the state is eligible for a grant under Section 619 (preschool grants), discussed in more detail elsewhere in this article, plus (b) aged 6 through 21; multiplied by (2) 40 percent of the average per pupil expenditure in public elementary and secondary schools in the United States; adjusted by (3) "the rate of annual change in the sum of [a] 85 percent of such State's population described in subsection (d)(3)(A)(i)(II); and [b] 15 percent of such State's population described in subsection (d)(3)(A)(i)(III)" (20 U.S.C. § 1411[a][2][B]; Sec. 611[a][2][B]). This change in the formula is troubling for two reasons. First, because it limits the child-count to the number of children with disabilities in the 2004–2005 school year, when the actual number of children with disabilities may well be much higher in subsequent fiscal years due to improved detection of children with disabilities and/or general increases in the school-age population, resulting in lower per-student distributions to the States. And second, the reference in the third part of the formula to "the population[s] described in subsection[s] (d)(3)(A)(i)(II) . . . and . . . (d)(3)(A)(i)(III)" does not make sense, because those two subsections seem to refer to the allocation of excess funds, rather than to descriptions of populations. It is to be hoped that this formula will be clarified when the final regulations are issued or corrected by a subsequent amendment to the statute itself.

Section 611 of the statute also places limits upon the amount of federal funds that can be reserved by the state for state administrative and other state-level activities, requiring other funds to be transferred to LEAs for use in administration and provision of special education and related services to children with disabilities (20 U.S.C. § 1411; Sec. 611).

## Section 612: State Eligibility

In order to receive federal funds, states are required to have a state plan in effect. The state plan must include the following key components:

1. *Free appropriate public education (FAPE).* The state must ensure that a free appropriate public education is available to all children with disabilities. However, under the 2004 legislation, a state that provides early intervention services in accordance with Part C of the IDEA (which covers infants and toddlers with disabilities) to a child who is eligible for services under Section 619 (which relates to preschool grants) is not required to provide such child with a free appropriate public education (20 U.S.C. § 1412[a][1]; Sec. 612[a][1]).

2. *Full educational opportunity goal.* The state must establish policies and procedures to ensure a full educational opportunity is available to all children with disabilities (20 U.S.C. § 1412[a][2]; Sec. 612[a][2]).

3. *Child find.* The state must identify, locate, and evaluate all children with disabilities, regardless of the severity of their disabilities. Children in private schools are included in the child find requirement, as are homeless children under the 2004 legislation. However, nothing in the statute requires classification of a child by disability as long as the child is eligible under the federal definition (20 U.S.C. § 1412[a][3]; Sec. 612[a][3]).

4. *Individualized education program (IEP).* An individualized education program or individualized family service plan (IFSP) must be developed, reviewed, and revised for each child with a disability (20 U.S.C. § 1412[a][4]; Sec. 612[a][4]).

5. *Least restrictive environment (LRE).* The state must establish procedural safeguards to ensure that children with and without disabilities are educated together to the maximum extent appropriate, and states may not use funding mechanisms that would result in placements that would violate this section (20 U.S.C. § 1412[a][5]; Sec. 612[a][5]).

6. *Procedural safeguards.* Children with disabilities and their parents must be assured the procedural safeguards required by the law, including the right to nondiscriminatory testing and evaluation (20 U.S.C. § 1412[a][6]; Sec. 612[a][6]). Procedural safeguards are explored in greater detail in the discussion of Section 615.

7. *Evaluation.* The state must ensure that children with disabilities are evaluated in accordance with the provisions of Section 614, discussed in greater detail in the following (20 U.S.C. § 1412[a][7]; Sec. 612[a][7]).

8. *Confidentiality.* The state must protect the confidentiality of any personally identifiable information, data, and records collected or maintained by the federal government, SEAs, and LEAs on students with disabilities (20 U.S.C. § 1412[a][8]; Sec. 612[a][8]).

9. *Transition from infant and toddler program to preschool program.* The state must ensure that children who will participate in the preschool programs and are currently attending infant and toddler programs will experience a smooth and effective transition to the preschool programs. LEAs are required to participate in the transition planning conferences (20 U.S.C. § 1412[a][9]; Sec. 612[a][9]).

10. *Children in private schools.* Children with disabilities who attend private schools are entitled to special education and related services. The services may

be provided on the premises of the private schools, including parochial schools to the extent consistent with the law. According to the 1997 Amendments, however, LEAs are not required to pay for the *placement* of a child with a disability if the placement was based on a unilateral parent-initiated decision (20 U.S.C. § 1412[a][10]; Sec. 612[a][10]).

11. *State educational agency responsibility.* The state must ensure that all educational programs are under the general supervision of the SEA (20 U.S.C. § 1412[a][11]; Sec. 612[a][11]).

12. *Ensuring services.* The SEA must establish interagency agreements with public agencies responsible for providing and paying for special education or related services used by children with disabilities. These agreements must be in effect. The state Medicaid agency and other public insurers' financial responsibility precedes the LEA and SEA's responsibility, but the SEA remains the payer of last resort (20 U.S.C. § 1412[a][12]; Sec. 612[a][12]).

13. *Personnel qualifications.* The state must ensure that personnel who work with children with disabilities have the highest qualified standards. In particular, under the new legislation, individuals who are employed as special education teachers must be *highly qualified* as that term is defined in Part A (which in turn is designed to conform with requirements under NCLB) in accordance with the deadlines established by NCLB. Trained and supervised paraprofessionals may assist in providing services to children with disabilities (20 U.S.C. § 1412[a][14]; Sec. 612[a][14]).

14. *Performance goals and indicators.* Under the new legislation, the state must establish goals for the performance of children with disabilities that are the same as the state's definition of *adequate yearly progress* under NCLB, address graduation and dropout rates, and are consistent (to the extent appropriate) with any other goals and standards for children adopted by the state. The state must also develop indicators to judge children's progress, including measurable annual objectives for progress under ESEA/NCLB for children with disabilities, and must report to the secretary of the Department of Education (DOE) and to the public on the state's progress, and the progress of children with disabilities in the state, toward meeting the goals established (20 U.S.C. § 1412[a][15]; Sec. 612[a][15]).

15. *Participation in assessments.* According to the new legislation, all children with disabilities must be included in all general state and district-wide assessment programs, including NCLB-required assessments, "with appropriate accommodations and alternate assessments where necessary and as indicated in their respective IEPs" (20 U.S.C. § 1412[a][16][A];

Sec. 612[a][16][A]). States are required to develop guidelines for the provision of appropriate accommodations, and such guidelines must be aligned with the state's academic achievement standards under NCLB (20 U.S.C. § 1412[a][16]; Sec. 612[a][16]).

16. *Overidentification and disproportionality.* Under the 2004 legislation, the state is required to implement policies and procedures designed to prevent inappropriate overidentification or disproportionate representation by race and ethnicity of children identified as children with disabilities (20 U.S.C. § 1412[a][24]; Sec. 612[a][24]).

17. *Prohibition on mandatory medication.* The 2004 legislation added a new provision prohibiting SEA and LEA personnel from requiring any child to obtain a prescription for a substance covered by the Controlled Substances Act as a condition of attending school, receiving an evaluation under Section 614, or receiving services under this statute, generally (20 U.S.C. § 1412[a][25]; Sec. 612[a][25]).

18. *Additional components.* Other components that must be included in the state plan are: (a) the establishment of a state advisory panel; (b) examination of suspension and expulsion rates of disabled and nondisabled children; (c) public comment prior to the adoption of new policies and procedures; (d) regulations regarding supplementation of state, local, and other federal funds; and (e) maintenance of state financial support (20 U.S.C. § 1412; Sec. 612).

### Section 613: Local Educational Agency Eligibility

Section 613 of the IDEA outlines the conditions LEAs must meet to be eligible for funding. To be eligible for funding, each LEA's plan must be consistent with the state plan. Once funding is received, LEAs are not allowed to reduce financial support for education of children with disabilities to schools by more than 50 percent of the amount of the current grant that is in excess of the amount of the grant in the previous fiscal year under the IDEA, and to the extent that the LEA reduces any such financial support it must use an amount equal to the amount of the reduction to carry out activities authorized under the ESEA/NCLB. LEAs must provide funding and serve children with disabilities who attend public charter schools in the same manner as children with disabilities who attend public schools. The new legislation also allows LEAs to allocate as much as 15 percent of the money they receive under the IDEA to develop and implement coordinated early intervening services (20 U.S.C. § 1413; Sec. 613).

The state may require LEAs to meet other conditions as well. The state may require LEAs to include disciplinary information in the records of children with disabilities and to transmit the record with the disciplinary information included in the same manner that disciplinary information is included in, and transmitted with, the student records of nondisabled children. The information transmitted may include a description of the behavior and disciplinary action taken, and any other additional information that is relevant to the safety of the child or others. When the child with a disability transfers to another school (e.g., to another elementary school), the child's most current IEP and all disciplinary action would be included in and transferred with the child's records (20 U.S.C. § 1413; Sec. 613).

### Section 614: Evaluations, Eligibility Determinations, IEPs, and Educational Placements

Section 614 of IDEA addresses the evaluation process used to determine a child's eligibility for special education and related services, the IEP developed for the child once eligibility has been determined, and the educational placement or appropriate setting for the child to receive an education. The new legislation has resulted in some changes in evaluations, reevaluations, eligibility determinations, IEPs, and placement decisions. Under the 2004 legislation, an initial evaluation of a child may be requested by a parent, and SEA, another state agency, or an LEA. The law generally requires a full and individual initial evaluation of the child to be conducted within 60 days (not 60 *school* days) of receipt of parental consent to the evaluation (although Section 615 of the statute provides procedures that can allow the evaluation to proceed in the absence of parental consent) in order to determine the educational needs of such child, before the initial provision for special education and related services is provided. The initial evaluation must be conducted with a variety of assessment tools and strategies and must use technically sound instruments. The child must be initially assessed in all areas of suspected disability. Assessments and evaluation materials used must meet certain statutory requirements, including nonbiased protections as well as the need to address the child's educational experiences and primary language. The statute also calls for parental participation in the assessment process, including incorporation of information provided by the parents (20 U.S.C. § 1414; Sec. 614).

Upon completion of the evaluation process, a determination is made as to whether a child qualifies as a child with a disability or not. A team of qualified professionals and a parent of the child make the determination about the child's eligibility and the educational needs of the child. The parent must be given a copy of the evaluation report and documentation of the determination of eligibility (20 U.S.C. § 1414; Sec. 614).

After eligibility for special education and related services has been determined, an IEP must be developed. The 2004 legislation expands upon prior requirements about what must be included in the IEP. An IEP is a written statement developed, reviewed, and revised by the IEP team for a child with a disability. It includes information regarding (a) the child's present level of academic achievement and functional performance, (b) measurable annual goals (including academic and functional goals), (c) a description of how the child's progress toward meeting the annual goals will be measured and how the parent will be informed of such progress, (d) a description of the special education and related services and supplementary aids and services to be provided to the child (based on peer-reviewed research to the extent applicable), (e) program modifications or supports for school personnel that will be provided to the child, (f) explanations of the extent of the child's nonparticipation with nondisabled children in the regular classroom, if applicable, and (g) a statement of any individual appropriate accommodations that are necessary to measure the child's academic achievement and functional performance on state and district-wide assessments. If the IEP team concludes that an alternative assessment is appropriate for the child on any such state or district-wide assessments, the IEP must also include a statement explaining why the child cannot participate in the regular assessment and why the specific alternative assessment selected is appropriate for the child. The IEP must also include transition plans for the child, beginning not later than the first IEP, to be in effect when the child turns 16 (20 U.S.C. § 1414[d][1][A]; Sec. 614[d][1][A]).

The IEP team must include, as appropriate, (a) the parent(s) of the child with the disability; (b) one (or more) of the child's regular education teachers; (c) one (or more) of the child's special education teachers or, where appropriate, special education providers; (d) a representative of the LEA who is qualified to provide or supervise the provision of specially designed instruction to meet the needs of children with disabilities, knowledgeable about the general education curriculum, and knowledgeable about the availability of resources of the LEA; (e) an individual who can interpret the evaluation results (e.g., a school psychologist), though this individual can be any of the individuals described in clauses (b) through (d) of this sentence; (f) other individuals who have knowledge or special expertise regarding the child; and (g) when appropriate, the child with the disability. The new legislation provides that a member of the IEP team may be excused from a meeting of the IEP team if the parent and LEA agree that the attendance of the team member is not necessary for the purposes of the scheduled meeting (e.g., the member's area of the child's curriculum or related services is not being modified or discussed in the meeting), or if the parents and LEA consent to the member's excusal from the meeting and the member submits written input into the development or modification of the IEP prior to the meeting (20 U.S.C. § 1414[d][1][B]; Sec. 615[d][1][B]).

The IEP, as always, must consider the child's strengths, parent concerns, and initial and most recent evaluation results, but under the new legislation, it must also consider the academic, developmental, and functional needs of the child

(20 U.S.C. § 1414[d][3]; Sec. 614[d][3]). Section 614 also addresses the behavioral needs of school children. Strategies, including positive behavioral interventions and supports to address any behavior that interferes with learning, must be considered when and where appropriate (20 U.S.C. § 1414[d][3]; Sec. 614[d][3]). A reevaluation is conducted for a child with a disability if conditions warrant a reevaluation, a child's parent or teacher requests a reevaluation, or a 3-year period has elapsed since the last evaluation. Additional testing is not required in the reevaluation process to reconfirm a child's disability. The content or components that make up a 3-year evaluation will be determined by the IEP team along with other qualified professionals with the parents' approval, and may include only existing data, such as classroom assessments and observations. More comprehensive and more frequent reevaluations may still be conducted at the parents' request. Under the new legislation, parents have the right to consent to a reevaluation. A reevaluation must now also be conducted when a child exits eligibility from IDEA (20 U.S.C. § 1414[d][4]; Sec. 614[d][4]).

In addition, the 2004 legislation establishes a pilot program permitting states to allow parents and LEAs to conduct long-term planning by offering the option of a comprehensive, multi-year IEP, not to exceed 3 years, that is designed to coincide with natural transition points for the child (e.g., from elementary school to middle school). The program must be optional for parents, and the IEP must include annual review of the child's IEP to determine the child's levels of progress and whether the child's annual goals are being met (20 U.S.C. § 1414[d][5]; Sec. 614[d][5]).

### Section 615: Procedural Safeguards

Section 615 of IDEA requires procedural safeguards to be put into place to assure the rights of children with disabilities and their parents. The procedural safeguards include:

1. The opportunity for parents to examine all of their child's records and to participate in meetings with respect to the identification, evaluation, placement, and provisions of FAPE to the child (20 U.S.C. § 1415[b][1]; Sec. 615[b][1]).

2. Protections of the child's rights when parents or guardians cannot be located. In other words, an individual is appointed to act as a surrogate parent whenever the parent or guardian is unknown. The surrogate may not be an employee of the SEA, LEA, or any other agency involved in the education or care of the child (20 U.S.C. § 1415[b][2]; Sec. 615[b][2]).

3. Written prior notice to parents when a change or refusal to make a change in the identification, evaluation, or placement of the child is anticipated by the LEA (20 U.S.C. § 1415[b][3]; Sec. 615[b][3]).

4. Written prior notice to parents provided in their native language, unless unfeasible, regarding all safeguards (20 U.S.C. § 1415[b][4]; Sec. 615[b][4]).

5. An opportunity for parents to participate in mediation in the event of disputes under the statute. Failure to participate in mediation cannot be used to delay or deny the parents' rights to a due process hearing (20 U.S.C. § 1415[b][5]; Sec. 615[b][5]).

6. An opportunity for parents to present complaints with respect to the identification, evaluation, or placement of the child or the provision of FAPE to the child. The 2004 legislation adds a new provision requiring parents to file any such complaint no later than 2 years after the parent or public agency knew or should have known about the alleged action forming the basis of the complaint (20 U.S.C. § 1415[b][6]; Sec. 615[b][6]). Earlier iterations of the IDEA contained no such statute of limitations.

7. A requirement that either party (parent or LEA), or the attorney representing either party, provide due process complaint notice to the other party (with a copy to the SEA) in connection with any complaint under the preceding paragraph. The notice must include the child's name and address and the name of the school the child is attending, a description of the problem, and a proposed resolution of the problem. This procedural safeguard has been expanded by the 2004 legislation to allow for notice by either party and to specifically include the term *due process complaint notice* (20 U.S.C. § 1415[b][7]; Sec. 615[b][7]).

8. A requirement that the SEA must develop a model form to assist parents in filing complaints (20 U.S.C. § 1415[b][8]; Sec. 615[b][8]).

As noted previously, the 2004 legislation incorporates the term *due process complaint notice,* and elsewhere provides additional requirements relating to procedures that apply to such complaints. A due process complaint notice is deemed sufficient unless the party receiving the notice notifies the hearing officer that the receiving party believes the notice has not met the requirements of Section 615(b)(7) (20 U.S.C. § 1415[c][2][A]; Sec. 615[c][2][A]). In most circumstances, LEAs have 10 days from receipt of a due process complaint notice to respond to the notice. An LEA's response must include (a) an explanation of why the agency proposed or refused to take the action that is the subject of the complaint, as appropriate, (b) a description of other options that the IEP team considered and the reasons why those options were rejected, (c) a description of each evaluation procedure, assessment, record, or report the agency used as a basis for the proposed or refused action, and (d) a description of any other factors relevant to the agency's proposal or refusal (20 U.S.C. § 1415[c][2][B][I]; Sec. 615[c][2][B][I]). The new legislation also includes procedures governing responses to notices, timing, and amended complaint notices.

The remainder of this section describes procedures parents may use to resolve disputes with LEAs and SEAs as well as placement in alternative educational settings (AES). Procedures for resolving disputes range from voluntary mediation (20 U.S.C. § 1415[e]; Sec. 615[e]) to due process hearings (20 U.S.C. § 1415[f]; Sec. 615[f]) to civil actions (20 U.S.C. § 1415[i][2]; Sec 612[i][2]). Under the 1990 amendments to IDEA, states may be sued by private citizens for violations of the law; however, parents are required, except for a few unusual circumstances, to exhaust administrative remedies (e.g., mediation, due process hearings) before pursuing civil action. If a parent wishes to appeal the result of a due process hearing, the parent may pursue civil action in a state court within 90 days of the date of the hearing officer's decision, or within such other time limitation as set by applicable state law for any such appeal (20 U.S.C. § 1415[i][2]; Sec. 615).

Parents may recover attorneys' fees if they prevail in a court action under Section 615 (Jacob-Timm & Hartshorne, 1995). Although early court decisions (e.g., *Moore* v. *District of Columbia,* 1990) suggested that parents may be able to recover attorney fees for both administration proceedings as well as litigation (Jacob-Timm & Hartshorne, 1995), changes made by the 2004 legislation suggest that any such recovery is limited only to certain services (20 U.S.C. § 1415[i][3][D]; Sec. 615[i][3][D]). Furthermore, the 2004 legislation also permits a prevailing SEA or LEA to recover attorneys' fees from parents who file a complaint or subsequent cause of action for any improper purpose, such as to harass, cause unnecessary delay, or needlessly increase the cost of litigation, and from parents' attorneys who file a complaint or subsequent cause of action that is frivolous, unreasonable, or without foundation (20 U.S.C. § 1415[i][3][B]; Sec. 615[i][3][B]).

School personnel may order a change in placement for not more than 10 school days to an interim AES, another setting, or suspension for a child with a disability who violates the school's code of student conduct, to the same extent such alternatives are applied to children without disabilities (20 U.S.C. § 1415[k][1]; Sec. 615[k][1]). Within 10 school days of any decision to change the placement of the child under this section, the LEA, the parent, and relevant members of the IEP team are required to review all relevant information in the student's file, including his or her IEP, to determine if the conduct in question was caused by, or had a direct and substantial relationship to, the child's disability, or if the conduct was a direct result of the LEA's failure to implement the IEP. If either of these is found to be the case, then the IEP is required to determine that the conduct at issue was a manifestation of the child's disability (20 U.S.C. § 1415[k][1][E]; Sec. 615[k][1][E]). If the behavior that prompted an LEA is not the result of either the child's disability or inadequate

services, the child may be disciplined under the general code of conduct in the same manner and severity as a nondisabled peer, but the child must continue to receive FAPE. However, upon any determination that the conduct was a manifestation of the child's disability, the IEP team is required to conduct a functional behavioral assessment and implement a behavioral intervention plan for the child, or, if a behavioral intervention plan was already in existence, the IEP team must review such behavioral intervention plan and modify it as necessary, and, except as described in the following, return the child to the placement from which he or she was removed, unless the parent and the LEA agree to change the placement as part of the modification of the behavioral intervention plan (20 U.S.C. § 1415[k][1][F]; Sec. 615[k][1][F]). Parents have the right to appeal any step of this process (20 U.S.C. § 1415; Sec. 615).

Notwithstanding the foregoing, school personnel are permitted to move a student to an interim AES for not more than 45 school days, even if the conduct was determined to be a manifestation of the child's disability, in cases where the child (a) carries a weapon to school or to a school function, (b) possesses, uses, or sells illegal drugs at school or a school function, or (c) inflicts serious bodily injury upon another person while at school or a school function. Under these circumstances, the child must continue to receive educational services to enable the child to continue to participate in the general education curriculum and to progress toward meeting the goals set out in the child's IEP, and should receive, as appropriate, a functional behavioral assessment and behavioral intervention services and modifications that are designed to address the behavior violation so that it does not recur (20 U.S.C. § 1415[k][1][D]; Sec. 615[k][1][D]).

A hearing officer may also order a change in placement for a child with a disability. The hearing officer may order a change in placement to an interim AES for not more than 45 school days if the hearing officer finds that keeping the child in his or her current placement is substantially likely to result in injury to the child or to others (20 U.S.C. § 1415[k][3]; Sec. 615[k][3]).

### Section 616: Monitoring, Technical Assistance, and Enforcement

The 2004 legislation has resulted in significant changes to this section of the IDEA. Section 616 now requires each state to have in place, no later than December 3, 2005, a performance plan that evaluates the state's efforts to implement the provisions of the IDEA and describes how the state will improve such implementation. The performance plan must establish measurable and rigorous targets for improvement in certain priority areas (20 U.S.C. § 1416[b]; Sec. 616[b]). The performance plan must be reviewed and approved by the secretary of the DOE (20 U.S.C. § 1416[c]; Sec. 616[c]). Based on the information provided by the state in its annual performance report, the secretary will determine if the state (a) meets the requirements of the IDEA, (b) needs assistance in implementing its requirements, (c) needs intervention in implementing its requirements, or (d) needs substantial intervention in implementing its requirements (20 U.S.C. § 1416[d]; Sec. 616[d]). If the secretary determines that a state needs assistance or intervention for 2 or 3 consecutive years, respectively, the new legislation provides certain options for the secretary to help (or force) the state to improve its performance. If the secretary determines that a state needs substantial intervention, the secretary is permitted to take stronger actions, including certain enforcement actions and the withholding of further payments to the state under the IDEA until identified problems are corrected (20 U.S.C. § 1416[e]; Sec. 616[e]). If any state does not agree with the secretary's decision with respect to the state plan, then the state may file a petition with the U.S. Court of Appeals for judicial review of the secretary's action. The judgment of the court shall be subject to review by the U.S. Supreme Court (20 U.S.C. § 1416[e][8]; Sec. 616[e][8]).

### Section 617: Administration

Section 617 addresses certain administrative components of the act. The law outlines the responsibilities of the secretary of the DOE, requires protection of the confidentiality of personally identifiable information, and authorizes the hiring of personnel to collect data for evaluation and program information purposes. The responsibilities of the secretary include promotion and dissemination of information about special education. The 2004 legislation added a new provision to Section 617 to clarify that nothing in the IDEA should be construed to authorize any officer or employee of the federal government to mandate, direct, or control a state, LEA, or school's specific instructional content, academic achievement standards and assessments, curriculum, or program of instruction. It also added a new requirement that the secretary issue certain model documents, including a model IEP form, a model individualized family service plan form, a model form of the notice of procedural safeguards required by Section 615, and a model form of prior written notice for certain actions, no later than the date the secretary issues the final regulations implementing the 2004 legislation (20 U.S.C. § 1417; Sec. 617).

### Section 618: Program Information

Under Section 618, each state is required to provide information on its program (i.e., data) to the secretary of the DOE on an annual basis. The purpose of the data collection process is to evaluate the impact of the program, the effectiveness of state efforts, and the progress made since the implementation of the act. States receiving assistance under the IDEA must provide data about a variety of subjects relevant to services provided under the statute, including information about the number of children with disabilities, by race, ethnicity, limited English proficiency status, gender, and disability category who are receiving various categories of services, such as those who are receiving FAPE, participating in regular classes, enrolled in separate classes, schools, or facilities, and so forth. Additional information is obtained on the number of children with disabilities, by race, ethnicity, and disability category who are 14–21 years of age and have stopped receiving early intervention services because of program completion or other reasons. The number of children with disabilities, by race, ethnicity, and disability category, who have been subjected to disciplinary actions or removed to an interim AES, or subjected to long-term suspensions or expulsions, is computed as well, as are the numbers of due process complaints, hearing requests, and mediations. The numbers of infants and toddlers who are at risk for substantial developmental delays and are receiving early intervention services are similarly calculated by race and ethnicity. Significant discrepancies in the data collected concerning identification and placement of children with disabilities by race as well as significant discrepancies in the suspension and expulsion rates between disabled and nondisabled children are examined, and based on these examinations, policies, practices, and procedures are reviewed and revisions are made to ensure compliance with the act. The information obtained through the data collection process is submitted on an annual basis to the U.S. Congress (20 U.S.C. § 1418; Sec. 618).

### Section 619: Preschool Grants

Preschool grants are addressed in Section 619 of the IDEA. Preschool grants are available to states to assist the states in providing special education and related services to children with disabilities aged 3 to 5, though states at their own discretion may also include 2-year-old children with disabilities who will turn 3 during the school year (20 U.S.C. § 1419[a]; Sec. 619[a]). Under the new legislation, the funding formula has changed to conform to the formula change in Part B (20 U.S.C. § 1419[c]; Sec. 619[c]). Section 619 also establishes limitations on the percentage of funds allocated under Section 619 that a state may retain for state administrative and other state-level activities (20 U.S.C. § 1419[d]; Sec. 619[d]).

### Part C: Infants and Toddlers with Disabilities

Part C of the Act, Infants and Toddlers with Disabilities, contains information about this program, including eligibility criteria, state requirements, IFSP, state application and assurances, funding issues and responsibilities, procedural safeguards, and coordination efforts among state or federal agencies. Grants are made available to states to develop statewide interagency systems for the provision of early intervention services for infants and toddlers with disabilities and their families. At-risk infants and toddlers are included in the eligibility definition. Services provided to infants and toddlers and their families must be maximally provided in natural settings. Highest qualified standards for personnel are also incorporated into Part C (20 U.S.C. §§ 1431–1444; Sec. 631–644).

## Part D: National Activities to Improve Education of Children with Disabilities

Part D, National Activities to Improve Education of Children with Disabilities, includes all other discretionary programs (i.e., state improvement grants, personnel preparation, research, technical assistance, parent training, dissemination). State improvement grants are made available to assist SEAs and their partners in reforming and improving systems for providing educational, early intervention, and transitional services to improve results for students. Grants are also made available for research and innovation and personnel preparation to improve services and results for children with disabilities (20 U.S.C. §§ 1451–1482; Sec. 651–682).

## Proposed Regulations

The Department of Education published proposed regulations to implement the 2004 legislation in the Federal Register on July 21, 2005 (70 Fed. Reg. 35,782). The proposed regulations may generate some confusion because, in addition to incorporating new provisions as required by the recent legislation, they also renumber many otherwise unchanged regulations from the last iteration of the IDEA. Where the statute has not changed due to the 2004 legislation, most of the proposed regulations remain largely consistent with existing regulations (aside from the previously noted renumbering). However, where the 2004 legislation has made changes to the IDEA, there are corresponding changes in the proposed regulations. Some of these proposed changes closely track the language of the statute, while others provide more in-depth guidelines based upon the secretary's interpretation of the new legislation.

This article was submitted to the publisher during the initial 90-day comment period on the proposed regulations, preventing the inclusion of any analysis of final regulations in the discussion of the reauthorized statute. However, it should be noted that the proposed regulations have generated a great deal of controversy among special educators, school officials, and state and local educational agencies. In particular, many of the regulatory changes designed to bring the IDEA regulations into compliance with NCLB requirements seem to be generating a great deal of concern, particularly those relating to assessment and interventions. It is anticipated that the proposed regulations will prompt a number of interested parties to submit comments to the DOE, and it is further anticipated that those comments may result in significant changes to the proposed regulations before they are finalized.

The full impact of 2004 changes to the IDEA is unknown at the present time. Additional changes to the law will continue to be made in the future, and these changes will more than likely have significant influence on children with disabilities as well as their families.

## REFERENCES

Abramson, M. (1987). Education for All Handicapped Children Act of 1975 (PL 94-142). In C. R. Reynolds & L. Mann (Eds.), *Encyclopedia of special education* (pp. 583–85). New York: Wiley.

Applequist, K. F. (2005). Special education legislation. In E. Fletcher-Janzen & C. R. Reynolds (Eds.), *Special educators' almanac*. New York: Wiley.

Focus on IDEA. (1997, July). *Span update*. Bethesda, MD: National Association of School Psychologists.

Haring, N. G., McCormick, L., & Haring, T. (1994). *Exceptional children and youth: An introduction to special education* (6th ed.). New York: Prentice Hall.

Individuals with Disabilities Act of 1997, 20 U.S.C. §§1400 et seq. (West, 1997).

Jacob-Timm, S., & Hartshorne, T. (1995). *Ethics and law for school psychologists*. Brandon, VT: Clinical Psychology Publishing.

Martin, R. (1979). *Educating handicapped children: The legal mandate*. Champaign, IL: Research Press.

*Moore* v. *District of Columbia*, 907 F.2d 165 (D.C. Cir. 1990).

National Association of State Directors of Special Education. (1997). *Comparison of key issues: Current law & 1997 IDEA Amendments*. Washington, DC: Author.

National Education Association. (n.d.). *No Child Left Behind Act / ESEA*. Retrieved September 30, 2004, from http://www.nea.org/esea/

Reynolds, C. R., & Fletcher-Janzen, E. (1990). Education For All Handicapped Children Act of 1975 (PL 94-142). In C. R. Reynolds & L. Mann (Eds.), *Concise encyclopedia of special education* (pp. 386–88). New York: Wiley.

Turnbull, H. R. (1990). *Free appropriate public education* (3rd ed.). Denver, CO: Love.

U.S. Department of Education (n.d.). *Special education and rehabilitative services: IDEA 2004 resources*. Retrieved August 1, 2005, from http://www.ed.gov/policy/speced/guid/idea/idea2004.html

Wright, P. W. D. (2004). *The Individuals with Disabilities Education Improvement Act of 2004: Overview, explanation, and comparison*. Retrieved July 27, 2005, from http://www.wrightslaw.com/

PATRICIA A. LOWE
*University of Kansas*

CECIL R. REYNOLDS
*Texas A&M University*
Second edition

KIMBERLY F. APPLEQUIST
*University of Colorado at Colorado Springs*
Third edition

## INFANT ASSESSMENT

The term infant assessment has come to represent a variety of formal and informal screening and diagnostic procedures used for the systematic collection of data. The initial purpose of assessment is to determine whether development of the infant is progressing normally.

Advances in genetics and biochemistry have made it possible to begin this assessment process prior to the birth of the infant. Information about the health of the mother and her fetus, including the identification of genetic and chromosomal disorders, can be obtained through prenatal diagnostic techniques.

The common areas of focus for the assessment of infants from birth through 2 years of age include physical and sensory attributes, cognitive and general communication abilities, and social/emotional responses and interactions.

Infant assessment begins with procedures that can be carried out quickly and inexpensively. These screening measures constitute the initial stage of the assessment process and allow for the identification of at-risk infants (i.e., individuals with known or suspected disorders or developmental delays).

For those infants considered to be at risk, the focus of assessment is expanded to include more in-depth or diagnostic procedures. The purpose for using diagnostic measures is to collect information that will help to identify and understand the nature of an impairment as it affects the development of the infant.

Screening and diagnostic information can be gathered through the combined use of direct testing (using standardized norm, criterion, or curriculum reference measures), naturalistic observations, and parent interviews. The resulting information is analyzed and used to make strategic diagnostic, placement, and intervention decisions.

Historically, the assessment of infants can be traced back to the intelligence testing movement of the nineteenth and twentieth centuries (Brooks & Weintraub, 1976). Among the first tests designed specifically for the purpose of gathering normative data on infant behavior were Gesell's Developmental Schedules and Bayley's California First Year Mental Scale.

Although many advances have been made in the development of diagnostic instruments, a lack of predictive validity for these standardized measures has continued to be the major issue in infant assessment. Research has consistently shown that it is not possible to predict the future cognitive performance of a child on the bases of infant test results (McCall, 1979).

According to Lewis and Fox (1980), the major reason for this lack of predictive validity is the nature of the tests themselves, in that the resulting scores are inaccurate indicators of a child's functioning. Lewis and Fox point out that it is not possible to validly predict future infant performance without considering the nature of parent-infant interactions and the influence these interactions can have on the future development of the child. Kagan and Moss (1962) have concluded that the predictive validity of infant assessment tests could be improved if the socioeconomic status of the parents was combined with the child's test scores.

While there is little long-range predictive validity in the assessment of normal infants, research with infants with disabilities (DuBose, 1977; Kamphaus, 2001; Meir, 1975) has provided evidence that predictive validity is greater with severely handicapped individuals. This increase appears to be related to the overall rate of development in the infant. Unlike normally developing infants, who are in a constant state of change (Honzik, 1976), infants with severe delays or deficits often exhibit very low-functioning behaviors that remain relatively stable, and thus more predictable over time (Brooks-Gunn & Lewis, 1981; Kamphaus, 2001).

It is clear that the most pervasive issue with respect to the validity of assessing infant behavior is that it may not be possible to accurately predict long-range performance based on early test results. As Sheehan and Gallagher (1984) suggest, it may be more productive for infant assessment to be used to address immediate needs of diagnoses, placement, and intervention rather than long-range predictions of a child's developmental outcome.

The assessment process should begin with the identification of the specific behaviors to be measured. Following this identification, selection of appropriate screening and diagnostic measures can be made. In-depth, diagnostic procedures must include the use of reliable and valid standardized tests (with appropriate use of adaptive equipment); multiple, systematic observations of the infant in various settings and situations; and parent interviews.

The collection and subsequent analysis of assessment data should be conducted by a multidisciplinary team, which might include a pediatrician, a psychologist, a communications specialist, and a physical therapist as well as the parents of the infant. The resulting information is used for the purpose of establishing appropriate objectives for intervention. This process of assessment also must include an evaluation of the intervention program.

## REFERENCES

Bailey, D. B., & Wolery, M. (1984). *Teaching infants and preschoolers with handicaps.* Columbus, OH: Merrill.

Brooks, J., & Weintraub, M. (1976). A history of infant intelligence testing. In M. Lewis (Ed.), *Origins of intelligence* (pp. 19–58). New York: Plenum.

Brooks-Gunn, J., & Lewis, M. (1981). Assessing young handicapped children: Issues and solutions. *Journal of the Division for Early Childhood, 2,* 84–95.

DuBose, R. F. (1977). Predictive value of infant intelligence scales with multiply handicapped children. *American Journal of Mental Deficiency, 81*(4), 388–390.

Honzik, M. (1976). Value and limitations of infant tests: An overview. In M. Lewis (Ed.), *Origins of intelligence.* New York: Plenum.

Kagan, J., & Moss, H. A. (1962). *Birth and maturity: A study in psychological development.* New York: Wiley.

Kamphaus, R. (2001). *Clinical assessment of child and adolescent intelligence* (2nd ed.). Needham Heights, MA: Pearson Education.

Lewis, M., & Fox, N. (1980). Predicting cognitive development from assessment in infancy. *Advances in Behavioral Pediatrics, 1,* 53–67.

McCall, R. B. (1979). The development of intellectual functioning in infancy and the prediction of later I.Q. In J. Osofsky (Ed.), *Handbook of infant development.* New York: Wiley.

Meir, J. H. (1975). Screening, assessment and intervention for young children at developmental risk. In N. Hobbs (Ed.), *Issues in the classification of children* (Vol. 2). San Francisco: Jossey-Bass.

Sheehan, R., & Gallagher, R. J. (1984). Assessment of infants. In M. J. Hanson (Ed.), *A typical infant development.* Baltimore: University Park Press.

FRANCINE TOMPKINS
*University of Cincinnati*

**APGAR RATING SCALE**
**DEVELOPMENTAL MILESTONES**
**INFANT STIMULATION**
**MEASUREMENT**

## INFANTILE AUTISM

See AUTISM.

## INFANTILE HYPERCALCEMIA

Infantile hypercalcemia (also called hypercalcemia, or William's syndrome) is a rare syndrome whose etiology is uncertain. It is characterized by abnormal calcium chemistry and is associated with circulatory and cardiac (particularly supravalvular aortic stenosis) defects. Many children with this syndrome have low birth weights. They may have heart murmurs, kidney problems, and gastrointestinal problems early in life. There may be reduced muscle tone and general motor difficulties (listlessness, lethargy), also noted in infants. Most children will have mild to moderate mental retardation, although some children may have normal intelligence. Some mild neurologic dysfunction has been noted (Bergsma, 1979).

Children are short in stature (and skeletal defects are often seen), with pointed chins and ears, and are often described as having elfinlike features (full cheeks, small, broad foreheads). Wide-spread and squinted eyes with epicanthal folds are typical. Teeth tend to be underdeveloped but the mouth is wide with a "cupid-bow" upper lip. No significant characteristics in upper or lower extremities are usually noted (Lemeshaw, 1982).

Affected individuals show a severe deficit of spatial cognition but have a modicum of language and face recognition (Atkinson, King, Braddick, Nores, Anker, & Braddick, 1997). Because of the varying degree of mental retardation and concomitant health and skeletal problems that may exist, a comprehensive assessment is necessary for proper placement of these children. Support medical services are usually required, and in some instances children will respond to medical treatment and surgery. Motoric problems may cause extensive immobility and may result in more restricted education placement than in a regular classroom. This decision can be made only by a complete evaluation of all the factors of this syndrome. Related services are often necessary as well.

## REFERENCES

Atkinson, J., King, J., Braddick, O., Nores, L., Anker, S., & Braddick, F. (1997). A specific deficit of dorsal stream junction in William's Syndrome. *Neuroreport, 8*(8), 1919–1922.

Bergsma, D. (1979). *Birth defects compendium* (2nd ed.). New York: National Foundation, March of Dimes.

Lemeshaw, S. (1982). *The handbook of clinical types in mental retardation.* Boston: Allyn & Bacon.

SALLY L. FLAGLER
*University of Oklahoma*

**HUNTER SYNDROME**
**HURLER SYNDROME**
**LOW BIRTH WEIGHT INFANTS**
**MENTAL RETARDATION**
**PHYSICAL ANOMALIES**

# INFANT STIMULATION

The term infant stimulation is used to represent a variety of early intervention activities (i.e., perceptual, sensorimotor, cognitive, language, and/or social/emotional) that are designed to facilitate development. The value of early intervention is based on a body of research that has demonstrated that infants, including those with disabilities, are capable of learning as a result of sustained, meaningful interactions with people and events within their environment (Osofsky, 1979).

It is believed that early experiences of the infant serve as the foundation for future growth of the individual. According to developmental theory, an infant's early sensorimotor experiences such as visually tracking and reaching for objects are precursors for later cognitive attainments such as object permanence, means-ends, and spatial relationships (Gallagher & Reid, 1981).

Since many at-risk infants (i.e., infants with known or suspected handicapping conditions) manifest deficits in perceptual or sensorimotor areas, early intervention is particularly important. Deficits that limit an infant's interaction with his or her physical and social environment often will result in delayed or deficient development (Bobath & Bobath, 1972).

There is no clear agreement about how much or what type of stimulation is most effective for facilitating development. This issue is unresolved because it is not known how to validly evaluate the effects of stimulation activities. There is general agreement, however, that the stimulation of infants does have a positive effect on immediate and future development (Alberto, Briggs, & Goldstein, 1983; Hanson & Hanline, 1984; Sheehan & Gallagher, 1983).

Over the years many programs have been developed for the purpose of stimulating the development of handicapped and at-risk infants. Detailed reviews of these programs (Bailey, Jens, & Johnson, 1983; Sheehan & Gallagher, 1983) reveal that they vary greatly in their content and effectiveness. Infant stimulation programs can be center-based (i.e., carried out by professionals in hospitals, clinics, or schools) or home-based (i.e., conducted by parents and professionals within the infant's home). There are also programs that combine center-based instruction with a home-based component.

Infant stimulation programs have been shown to be successful with low-vision infants (Leguire, Fellows, Rae, Rogers, & Bremer, 1992), with premature infants (Dieter & Emory, 1997), infants with gastric problems (de Roiste & Bushnell, 1995), and many other conditions.

Fortunately, there are general guidelines suggested for the purpose of guiding the development of programs, including the selection of intervention methods and materials, as well as program evaluation. According to these guidelines, there is a clear need for programs to use a sound theoretical framework to direct instructional content and intervention strategies. Professionals need to be clear about the purpose of instruction and to identify the population(s) most appropriate for their programs.

Activities must be meaningful and instruction should emphasize natural learning opportunities and interactions within a variety of domains (i.e., perceptual, cognitive, psycho-motor, and social/emotional). Staff must be properly trained and a program evaluation plan developed. Most important, any stimulation or early intervention program must involve the parents and family of the infant.

## REFERENCES

Alberto, P. A., Briggs, T., & Goldstein, D. (1983). Managing learning in handicapped infants. In S. G. Garwood & R. R. Fewell (Eds.), *Educating handicapped infants* (pp. 417–454). Rockville, MD: Aspen.

Bailey, D. B., Jr., Jens, K. G., & Johnson, N. (1983). Curricula for handicapped infants. In S. G. Garwood & R. R. Fewell (Eds.), *Educating handicapped infants* (pp. 387–416). Rockville, MD: Aspen.

Bobath, K., & Bobath, B. (1972). Cerebral palsy. In P. H. Pearson & C. Williams (Eds.), *Physical therapy services in the developmental disabilities.* Springfield, IL: Thomas.

Dieter, J. N. I., & Emory, K. (1997). Supplemental of stimulation of premature infants: A treatment model. *Journal of Pediatric Psychology, 22*(3), 281–295.

de Roiste, A., & Bushnell, I. W. R. (1995). The immediate gastric effects of a tactile stimulation programme on premature infants. *Journal of Reproductive & Infant Psychology, 13*(1), 57–62.

Gallagher, J., & Reid, D. K. (1981). *The learning theory of Piaget and Inhelder.* Monterey, CA: Brooks/Cole.

Hanson, M. J., & Hanline, M. F. (1984). Behavioral competencies and outcomes: The effects of disorder. In M. J. Hanson (Ed.), *A typical infant development* (pp. 109–178). Baltimore: University Park Press.

Karnes, M. B., & Teska, J. A. (1975). Children's response to intervention programs. In J. J. Gallagher (Ed.), *The application of child development research to exceptional children.* Reston, VA: Council for Exceptional Children.

Leguire, L. E., Fellows, R. R., Rogers, G. L., & Bremer, D. L. (1992). The CCH vision stimulation program for infants with low vision: Preliminary results. *Journal of Visual Impairment & Blindness, 86*(1), 33–37.

Osofsky, J. D. (Ed.). (1979). *Handbook of infant development.* New York: Wiley.

Sheehan, R., & Gallagher, R. J. (1983). Conducting evaluations of infant intervention programs. In S. Garwood & R. R. Fewell (Eds.), *Educating handicapped infants.* Rockville, MD: Aspen.

FRANCINE TOMPKINS
*University of Cincinnati*

**DEPRIVATION**
**ENRICHMENT**

**INFANT ASSESSMENT**
**LOW BIRTH WEIGHT INFANTS**

## INFORMAL READING INVENTORY

Informal reading inventory (IRI) is a generic term that refers to some type of nonstandardized technique used to assess aspects of reading performance. According to Smith and Johnson (1980), the most informal application of the diagnostic method involves having the child read selections of material silently and orally, asking comprehension questions about what has been read, and making note of the quality of reading, particularly word identification errors. Typically, the reading selections cover a range of grade or difficulty levels, from the preprimer through the eighth or ninth reader levels, as found in basal reading series. The comprehension questions based on the reading passages are usually of three types: factual or literal recall, inferential thinking, and vocabulary knowledge.

Johnson and Kress (1965) identified four purposes for administering an informal reading inventory. The IRI can be used to determine the level at which a reader can function independently, the level at which he or she can profit from instruction, the level at which the reader is frustrated by the material (Pehrsson, 1994), and the level of listening comprehension. Results of an IRI aid in determining specific strengths and weaknesses in reading, thus leading to a program of instruction or remediation. Also, the results of an IRI enable the reader to become aware of his or her own abilities and can be used as a measure of reading progress.

Betts (1946) established the earliest criteria for determining the four pedagogical levels. He determined that a child should read words in context with 99 percent accuracy and answer 90 percent of the comprehension questions correctly to be able to handle material independently. In order to profit from instruction in certain materials, the reader should recognize 95 percent of the words in context and respond correctly to comprehension questions with 75 percent accuracy. When the reader can recognize words with only 90 percent accuracy, or respond correctly to only half of the comprehension questions, then the material is too difficult and is frustrating. Finally, listening comprehension is determined by reading selections to the child with the expectation that he or she will answer 75 percent of the related questions correctly.

### REFERENCES

Betts, E. A. (1946). *Foundation of reading instruction.* New York: American Book.

Johnson, M. S., & Kress, R. A. (1965). *Informal reading inventories.* Newark, DE: International Reading Association.

Pehrsson, R. S. (1994). Challenging frustration level. *Reading and Writing Quarterly, 10*(3), 201–208.

Smith, R. J., & Johnson, D. D. (1980). *Teaching children to read* (2nd ed.). Reading, MA: Addison-Wesley.

JOHN M. EELLS
*Souderton Area School District,
Souderton, Pennsylvania*

**BASAL READERS**
**CLOZE TECHNIQUE**
**JOHNSTON INFORMAL READING INVENTORY**
**READING**

## INFORMATION PROCESSING

*Webster's Third World International Dictionary* defines a *process* as:

> The action of moving forward progressively from one point to another on the way to completion; the action of passing through continuing development from a beginning to a contemplated end; the action of continuously going along through each of a succession of acts, events, to developmental stages.

Succinctly, process may be considered a manipulation. Information processing, then, in the context of psychological study, is the manipulation of incoming stimuli, and existing or stored information, and the creation of new information by the human brain. This would include such common activities as perception, encoding, decoding, retrieval from memory, rehearsal, general reasoning ability, and a growing multitude of "new" cognitive processes. As new theories of cognitive processes occur, new names and new constructs are devised and added to the list. Implicit in theories of information processing is the assumption that each individual's behavior is determined by the information processing that occurs internally. In combination, the form, depth, and breadth of information processing is what controls behavior, overt and covert, though in all likelihood in a reciprocal relationship with the outside world.

Information processing is in the midst of a revival of study in psychology and related fields, generally under the rubric of cognitive science. During the age of behaviorism, when only clearly observable behaviors were appropriate for study, research on the internal processes of the mind continued but at a much slower pace. There were clear biases present in many journals against the publication of such work. During the 1960s a resurgence began that came to full force only in the 1980s. This resurgence was in some ways related to advances in computer technology, as analogies to computer terminology are common and provide a paradigm for how humans might analyze information. In special education, information processing has always been a major interest because of its relationship to learning and the remediation of learning disorders (Mann, 1979). Disturbances of normal information processing are believed to be at the core of the etiology of learning disabilities. The terminology of information processing has fluctuated over the years, with central processing being the most frequently used alternative term.

Since at least the early 1900s, special educators have been interested in training children in various information-processing methods as a technique for the remediation of learning disorders. Past efforts to improve academic skills through the training of processing have been notable in their failures (Glass, 1983; Mann, 1979; Myers & Hammill, 1969; Reynolds, 1981). With the revival of cognitivism has come a new wave of cognitive processes and higher order information-processing strategies to train. The effectiveness of training cognitive processes for the purpose of improving academic skills has yet to be demonstrated, and the potential of such efforts has been hotly debated (Gresham, 1986; Haywood & Switzky, 1986a, 1986b; Reynolds, 1986).

The information-processing skills of exceptional children will always be of interest to special educators. Most mentally handicapped children have some form of information processing disorder, whether it is a mild deviation from the average skill level of other same-age children or a massive disruption of higher order skills. Treating these children requires extensive knowledge of their information-processing skills.

Theories of information processing abound. The best theory on which to base generalizations about a child may vary from child to child. New theories are being formulated and old theories revised almost daily in this rapidly expanding area of research. However, we must be particularly careful in evaluating work in information processing for its application to special education. As Mann (1979) reminds us, many fads in information processing have come and gone and too many of the "new" information processing approaches are simply yesterday's failures shrouded in new jargon and repackaged for today's thinking.

Contemporary information processing models attempt to duplicate or prepare a representation of the internal flow of information in the brain. The various information-processing theories create numerous variations in number and arrangement of subsystems of processing. Information-processing models of human thinking can be represented mathematically, though most often researchers prefer to display the theory as a series of boxes connected by various arrows, much as in a flowchart with feedback loops and various checks and balances.

There are basically only three kinds of models. The first treats information processing as a linear activity, a form of processing that is serial, wherein stages of processing are linked in a straight line and the output of one stage is the input for the next stage; processing proceeds very much in a sequential step-by-step manner. Each stage must await the outcome of the preceding stage. The second primary model of processing does not need to wait for each link in the chain to be completed, but rather carries on parallel processing, doing many tasks simultaneously without awaiting output from a prior step. In parallel processing, several stages can access output from any other stage at the same time. An information processing theory with both components interlinked (serial stages and parallel stages) is a hybrid model (Kantowitz, 1984). These models tend to be more complex but may not always be more useful. They continue to be challenged by organizations such as Neural Information Processing Systems (NIPS) that study broad-based and inclusive approaches (Tesauro, Touretzky & Leen, 1995).

Information processing has progressed to the point of now being a major force in experimental psychology. It is likely to continue to occupy a significant amount of space in the leading scientific journals of psychology for some years to come. Discussions, reviews, and research related to information processing and its related theories will grow in importance in journals related to the education of exceptional children.

## REFERENCES

Glass, G. V. (1983). Effectiveness of special education. *Policy Studies Review, 2,* 65–78.

Gresham, F. (1986). On the malleability of intelligence: Unnecessary assumptions, reifications, and occlusion. *School Psychology Review, 15,* 261–263.

Haywood, H. C., & Switzky, H. N. (1986a). The malleability of intelligence: Cognitive processes as a function of polygenic-experiential interaction. *School Psychology Review, 15,* 245–255.

Haywood, H. C., & Switzky, H. N. (1986b). Transactionalism and cognitive processes: Reply to Reynolds and Gresham. *School Psychology Review, 15,* 264–267.

Kantowitz, B. H. (1984). Information processing. In R. Corsini (Ed.), *Encyclopedia of psychology* (Vol. 2). New York: Wiley-Interscience.

Mann, L. (1979). *On the trail of process.* New York: Grune & Stratton.

Myers, P., & Hamill, D. (1969). *Methods for learning disorders.* New York: Wiley.

Reynolds, C. R. (1981). Neuropsychological assessment and the habilitation of learning: Considerations in the search for the aptitude × treatment interaction. *School Psychology Review, 10,* 343–349.

Reynolds, C. R. (1986). Transactional models of intellectual development, yes. Deficit models of process remediation, no. *School Psychology Review, 15,* 256–260.

Tesauro, G., Touretzky, D., & Leen, T. (Eds.). (1995). *Advances in neural information processing systems.* Cambridge, MA: MIT Press.

CECIL R. REYNOLDS
*Texas A&M University*

PERCEPTUAL DEVELOPMENT (LAG IN)
PERCEPTUAL TRAINING
RECIPROCAL DETERMINISM
REMEDIATION, DEFICIT-CENTERED MODELS
SEQUENTIAL AND SIMULTANEOUS COGNITIVE
   PROCESSING

## INFORMED CONSENT

See CONSENT, INFORMED.

## INITIAL TEACHING ALPHABET

The Initial Teaching Alphabet, popularly known as i/t/a, was devised by Sir James Pitman of England. His work was the amalgamation of earlier work done by British advocates of the simplification of English spelling. Pitman promoted the concept of a simplified spelling of the English language requiring the addition of new symbols that augmented the alphabet from 26 characters to 44 characters. These early efforts at changing the orthography of English were known as the Augmented Roman Alphabet (Aukerman, 1971).

The 44-character Augmented Roman Alphabet was developed and publicized by the Pitman organization in 1960 under the original title Initial Teaching Medium (Aukerman, 1971). The purpose behind the development of the new orthographic system was to permit a one-letter character to represent only one English sound or phoneme. Twenty characters were added for speech sounds not represented by a single letter of the English alphabet, and no characters were provided for q and x. No distinction was made between lower-case and capital letters; capital letters were a larger type size of the lower-case form. Use of the augmented alphabet was proposed for teaching beginning reading only.

The i/t/a was used in British and American schools in the 1960s and the early 1970s. The i/t/a provided beginning readers with a true sound-symbol approach to encoding and decoding the sounds of the English language. It made phoneme-grapheme correspondence more regular and simplified spelling for beginning readers. Downing (1964) stated that i/t/a was not a method of instruction; rather, it was a teaching tool that could be used with any type of reading instruction.

Research comparing i/t/a instruction and traditional orthographic (TO) instruction was conducted in England by John Downing (1964). Longitudinal studies showed that even though various instructional methods were used, i/t/a-trained students showed significant differences in the speed with which they learned to read, their levels of comprehension, their spelling levels, and their creative writing abilities.

The i/t/a program in the United States, Early to Read, was developed by Albert Mazurkiewicz and Harold Tanyzer (1966). This program, like the British i/t/a, was divided into three phases. In Phase I, students were introduced to the i/t/a characters through the use of the language-experience approach. Phase II reinforced and extended writing, spelling, and reading skills. Phase III, which usually began during the second year of instruction, emphasized the transfer to TO. Early to Read differed from the British program in that a new reading series was written. British publishers transliterated the *Janet and John* basal series into i/t/a.

Mazurkiewicz (1967) conducted the first i/t/a research in the United States in Bethlehem, Pennsylvania. This initial study and later studies showed that pupils instructed in i/t/a continuously showed better abilities in word discrimination, word knowledge, spelling, and creative writing.

The Initial Teaching Alphabet Foundation at Hofstra University was founded to collect and disseminate information on the i/t/a. In reviewing 70 control group studies that compared i/t/a programs to TO, Block (1971) found that two-thirds of the studies indicated that i/t/a was more successful in teaching beginning reading and writing skills, that one-third showed i/t/a equally as successful as TO, and that no studies showed adverse effects of using the i/t/a approach.

Block (1971) cites the following as frequent criticisms of i/t/a: (1) children who learn i/t/a have difficulty transferring to TO; (2) i/t/a materials and training are expensive; (3) the majority of the children's environment uses TO; and (4) children in i/t/a programs experience the Hawthorne effect.

Downing (1979) reviewed the use of i/t/a with exceptional children. He reported that even though i/t/a had been successful in teaching reading disabled, mentally retarded, culturally disadvantaged, bilingual, and emotionally disturbed and socially maladjusted children to read, further research is needed. Longitudinal studies in Britain showed that the gifted benefited most from the i/t/a method (Downing, 1979).

## REFERENCES

Aukerman, R. C. (1971). *Approaches to beginning reading.* New York: Wiley.

Block, J. R. (1971). *i.t.a.—A status report—1971: The beginnings of a second decade.* Hempstead, NY: Initial Teaching Alphabet Foundation.

Downing, J. (1964). The i.t.a. (Initial Teaching Alphabet) reading experiment. *Reading Teacher, 18,* 105–109.

Downing, J. (1979). "i.t.a." in special education. *Special Education in Canada, 53,* 25–27.

Mazurkiewicz, A. J. (1967). *The Initial Teaching Alphabet in reading instruction, evaluation-demonstration project on the use of i.t.a.* Bethlehem, PA: Lehigh University.

Mazurkiewicz, A. J., & Tanyzer, H. J. (1966). *The i.t.a. handbook for writing and spelling: Early-to-read i.t.a. program.* New York: Initial Teaching Alphabet Publications.

JOYCE E. NESS
*Montgomery County
Intermediate Unit,
Norristown, Pennsylvania*

**READING DISORDERS**
**READING REMEDIATION**

# IN-SERVICE TRAINING FOR SPECIAL EDUCATION TEACHERS

In-service training for special education teachers is not clearly defined. Definitions abound (Hite, 1977; Johnson, 1980; Langone, 1983). Significant differences exist on the subjects of purpose, need, responsibility, and format. In general, however, any training of special education teachers after they have begun functioning as full professionals may be labeled in-service training. Over the past decades, the focus of in-service training for special education teachers has ranged from remedying the deficiencies in preservice training programs (i.e., undergraduate and in some cases graduate degree programs) to implementing new instructional technology.

In-service training is a way of achieving social mobility in the educational profession, not only by acquiring credentials that are necessary for more responsible positions and higher salaries, but also by gaining wider visibility in the professional world. In-service training continues to be one avenue by which an individual special education teacher's personal interest and needs can be served. In-service training can also aid the school in implementing new educational programs by helping teachers acquire understanding, skills, and attitudes essential to the roles they are to play in the new programs. In sum, the purpose of in-service training for special education teachers usually reflects one or more of the following: job or program improvement, professional growth, and personal growth (Rubin, 1971).

In the 1970s and 1980s the need for in-service training of special education teachers was intensified by social and educational forces. Foremost among the social forces affecting the schools has been the movement to secure equal educational opportunity for students with disabilities. The movement is embodied in the Education for All Handicapped Children Act of 1975 (PL 94-142). Public Law 94-142 put heavy demands on special education (and regular education) teachers and administrators—demands that they were not necessarily trained to meet. For example, many special education teachers had to learn to function as resource teachers rather than as teachers of their own special education self-contained students. Teachers trained prior to the late 1970s were ill prepared to meet the challenge of PL 94-142. Recognizing the need previously described, PL 94-142 provided for a comprehensive system of personnel development (CSPD) in each state. The CSPD is based on annual needs assessment and encompasses in-service training as well as preservice training.

Three forces within the education community have also increased the need for in-service training of special education teachers: an awareness of the limits of preservice training programs, a shift in service delivery that demands collaborative engagement in regular education classes, and an infusion of instructional technology. For decades teacher educators focused their attention on raising the standards of preservice special education teacher training programs. During this time period, in-service training was primarily viewed as a means to remedy the deficiencies in the preservice programs. In the late 1970s teacher educators began to realize that preservice training programs only prepare beginning teachers, not accomplished teachers (Howey, 1978). In addition, teacher educators also began to realize that some teaching competencies are better learned on the job, with the benefit of experience, and that other competencies cannot be learned anywhere else. For example, it is difficult to see how special education teachers can internalize complex organizational strategies or transfer principles of growth and development to instructional decisions without more substantive teaching experience than is generally provided in preservice training programs. In addition, preservice programs sustained significant problems in attending to training requirements for inclusion teaching practices. Different teaching arrangements such as co-teaching and collaboration require supplemental content and practica.

A final reason why the need for in-service training was intensified in the 1990s was the infusion of instructional technology into special education programs. Bennett and Maher (1984) identified training special education teachers for effective use of instructional technology as a critical in-service need. For example, special education teachers must learn to capitalize on the potential of instructional technology. Technology such as computer-assisted instruction can bring about more productive use of the teacher's and the student's time. Of particular importance is its capacity to provide instruction that is truly individualized for each student with disabilities.

In-service training of special education teachers does not have an established framework. The responsibility for it is not fixed. Institutions of higher education, state departments of education, and local school districts have not embraced in-service training as a basic commitment. The roles different groups play in in-service training of special education (and regular education) teachers are changing. The realignment of power in teacher education has altered or abolished traditional roles. New roles are becoming defined for some groups, for example, the state departments of education and teachers, but not for others. Higher education is particularly affected. Its role in organizing and conducting in-service training is being taken over by teachers and collaborators (Edelfelt, 1979).

Frequently used formats for in-service training of special education teachers include on-site after school workshops, release-time activities, teacher centers, and onsite college or university courses (Swenson, 1981). Among these formats, the teacher center reflects the new role played by teachers. Teacher centers are places where teachers determine their own needs, seek assistance, and develop materials or strategies to solve problems. Teacher center instructors are themselves classroom teachers, sharing their own practical, classroom-developed materials; or they are advisors—formerly classroom teachers—who view their job as stimulating, supporting, and extending a teacher's own direction of growth. Attendance at teacher center classes is voluntary, not prescribed by the school district; if indirectly required (e.g., as a way to spend release time), programs offered are based on teachers' expressions of their own training needs (Devaney & Thorn, 1975).

Collaboration as a feature of in-service training is present in some teacher centers, but it is not a distinguishing feature of them as it is of another format, the consortium of two or more educational agencies. Probably the most common type of cooperative format is a college or university and a school system working together. A variety of other cooperative approaches exist, for example, the cooperation of several school districts or several colleges and universities within the same geographic region.

With the increased attention in the 1980s and 1990s came a move to evaluate and reform in-service training. Teachers are widely known to be dissatisfied with in-service training (Johnson, 1980; Rubin, 1978). There exists little empirical evidence that in-service training has any significant effect on the behavior of special education teachers (Langone, 1983). Johnson (1980) lists the following problems with inservice training:

1. In-service education has not placed enough emphasis on improving school program or teacher performance.

2. In-service education has not addressed teachers' urgent, day-to-day needs.

3. In-service education has been required of teachers and imposed and delivered by others.

4. In-service education has violated many principles of good teaching.

5. In-service education has been fragmented, unsystematic, devoid of a conceptual framework. (pp. 29–30)

In addition, in-service training to assist in the education of culturally/linguistically diverse students is not as prevalent as it should be (Zimpher & Ashburn, 1992). Fu-

ture staff development must take into account educational reform (Little, 1993).

## REFERENCES

Bennett, R., & Maher, C. (Eds.). (1984). *Microcomputers and exceptional children.* New York: Haworth.

Devaney, K., & Thorn, L. (1975). *Exploring teachers' centers.* San Francisco: Far West Laboratory for Educational Research and Development.

Edelfelt, R. (1979, April). Inservice teacher education: A concept, an overview. *National Council of States on Inservice Education Inservice Newsletter, 15,* 4–11.

Hite, H. (1977). Inservice education: Perceptions, purposes, and practices. In H. Hite & K. Howey (Eds.), *Planning inservice teacher education: Promising alternatives* (pp. 1–20). Washington, DC: American Association of Colleges for Teacher Education.

Howey, K. (1978, March). *Inservice teacher education: A study of the perceptions of teachers, professors and parents about current and projected practice.* Paper presented at the meeting of the American Educational Research Association, Toronto. (ERIC Document Reproduction Service No. ED 152 701)

Johnson, M. (1980). *Inservice education: Priority for the '80s.* Syracuse, NY: National Council of States on Inservice Education, Syracuse University.

Langone, J. (1983). Developing effective inservice for special educators. *Journal for Special Educators, 19*(3), 33–47.

Little, J. W. (1993). Teachers' professional development in a climate of educational reform. *Educational Evaluation and Policy Analysis, 15*(2), 129–151.

Rubin, L. (1971). *Improving in-service education: Proposals and procedures for change.* Boston: Allyn & Bacon.

Rubin, L. (1978). *Perspectives on preservice and inservice education.* Syracuse, NY: National Council of States on Inservice Education, Syracuse University.

Swenson, R. (1981). The state of the art in inservice education and staff development in K-12 schools. *Journal of Research & Development in Education, 15*(1), 2–7.

Zimpher, N. L., & Ashburn, E. A. (1992). Countering parochialism in teacher candidates. In M. Dilworth (Ed.), *Diversity in teacher education* (pp. 40–62). San Francisco: Jossey-Bass.

PHILLIP J. McLAUGHLIN
*University of Georgia*

**HIGHLY QUALIFIED TEACHERS**
**TEACHER CENTERS**
**TEACHER EFFECTIVENESS**

# INSIGHT (IN THE GIFTED)

Advocates of the Gestalt school typically believe that learning takes the form of an insight, a sudden occurrence of a reorganization of the field of experience, as when one has a new idea or discovers a solution to a problem. Two authors (Koffka, 1929; Kohler, 1929) used a variety of problem situations to study the role of insight in the learning of animals. For example, Kohler studied chimpanzee behaviors associated with retrieving a banana that had been placed out of reach by the investigator. As opposed to trial-and-error behavior, the chimpanzee successfully reached the banana as if by plan. Thus, Kohler interpreted the insight involved as a seeing of relations or a putting together of events that were internally represented.

Insight has also been described in human beings by researchers such as Wertheimer (1945) and Sternberg and Davidson (1983). Wertheimer studied children's insightful solutions to geometric problems. Some children used a rote fashion to solve problems; others, however, could see the essential structure of a problem situation, and consequently used insight as their approach to learning. Sternberg and Davidson, on the other hand, developed a subtheory of intellectual giftedness based on the centrality of insight skills.

In a later work, Davidson and Sternberg (1984) proposed that insight involves not one, but three separate but related psychological processes. They referred to the products of the three operations as insights, understood in terms of three types of insight skills: (1) selective encoding, by which relevant information in a given context is sifted from irrelevant information; (2) selective combination, by which relevant information is combined in a novel and productive way; and (3) selective comparison, by which new information is related in a novel way to old information.

The authors' three-process view of insight constitutes what they believe to be a subtheory of intellectual giftedness. Whereas selective encoding involves knowing which pieces of information are relevant, selective combination involves knowing how to blend together the pieces of relevant information. Selective comparison involves relating the newly acquired information to information acquired in the past (as when one solves a problem by using an analogy). In addition, the authors reason that the three processes are not executed in simple serial order, but rather, continually interact with each other in the formation of new ideas. Thus, it is the products of these operations that they refer to as insights.

To test their subtheory, Davidson and Sternberg (1984) completed three experiments with gifted and nongifted children in grades 4, 5, and 6. Results of all three experiments support the subtheory of intellectual giftedness. It was learned that insight plays a statistically significant role in the learning of the gifted as compared with that of the nongifted.

Davidson and Sternberg (1984) suggest several benefits of their approach to understanding and assessing intellectual giftedness over alternative psychometric and information-processing approaches. First, they propose that their theoretically based approach deals with what it is that makes the gifted special. For example, they believe that what primarily distinguishes the intellectually gifted in their performance is not that they are faster, but that they are better in their insightful problem-solving skills. Second, because their measurement of insight skills has no demands on prior knowledge, their approach is appropriate for individuals with nonstandard backgrounds. Researchers are using EEG technology to investigate insight in problem-solving (Jansovec, 1997).

### REFERENCES

Davidson, J. E., & Sternberg, R. J. (1984). The role of insight in intellectual giftedness. *Gifted Child Quarterly, 28*(2), 58–64.

Jansovec, N. (1997). Differences in EEG activity between gifted and non-identified individuals: Insights into problem solving. *Gifted Child Quarterly, 41*(1), 26–32.

Koffka, K. (1929). *The growth of the mind* (2nd ed.). New York: Harcourt.

Kohler, W. (1929). *Gestalt psychology.* New York: Liveright.

Sternberg, R. J., & Davidson, J. E. (1983). Insight in the gifted. *Educational Psychologist, 18*(1), 51–57.

Wertheimer, M. (1945). *Productive thinking.* New York: Harper & Row.

JUNE SCOBEE
*University of Houston, Clear Lake*

**CULTURALLY/LINGUISTICALLY DIVERSE GIFTED STUDENTS**
**GIFTED CHILDREN**

# INSTITUTES FOR RESEARCH ON LEARNING DISABILITIES

The Institutes for Research on Learning Disabilities were created to encourage basic and applied research in order to develop and validate successful practices with learning-disabled (LD) pupils. Originally sponsored by the Bureau of Education for the Handicapped and later funded through Special Education Programs within the Department of Education, the five 6-year institutes were awarded on a contractual basis to the University of Illinois—Chicago Circle, Teachers College at Columbia University, the University of Kansas, the University of Minnesota, and the University of Virginia.

The Chicago Institute for the Study of Learning Disabilities focused on the social competence of LD children. Studies addressed LD pupils' communicative competence and reading abilities, causal attributions of success and failure, and the immediate impression the pupils make on naive observers (Bryan, Pearl, Donahue, Bryan, & Pflaum, 1983).

The Teachers College Institute at Columbia University was organized as five task forces, each of which conducted research in a specific academic skill area (Connor, 1983). One task force studied memory and study skills of LD students (Gelzheiser, 1982; Shepherd, Frank, Solar, & Gelzheiser, 1982). Two task forces investigated learning problems in the basic skills of arithmetic, reading, and spelling (Fleischner & Garnett, 1979; Fleischner, Garnett, & Preddy, 1982). The final two task forces studied reading comprehension, one from the perspective of interaction of text and reader and one from the perspective of semantics and application of schemata (Williams, 1986).

At the University of Kansas institute, research concentrated on the problems of LD adolescents. Epidemiological studies revealed the unique characteristics of LD students of high school age, and a curriculum comprised of strategy training, social skills, modified materials, and instructional procedures was investigated and developed (Schumaker, Deshler, Alley, & Warner, 1983).

The major purpose of the University of Minnesota's Institute for Research on Learning Disabilities was to study the assessment of LD children. This research incorporated two major lines of investigation. The first explored the characteristics of students referred for psychoeducational evaluation and of those found eligible for placement in school-based LD programs (Ysseldyke, Thurlow, Graden, Wesson, Algozinne, & Deno, 1983). The second line of research developed and validated repeated and direct assessment procedures for assessing students' academic progress and for formatively developing effective instructional programs (Deno, 1985).

The University of Virginia Learning Disabilities Research Institute focused its efforts on LD students with attention problems. It emphasized developing cognitive behavior modification techniques that improve children's on-task behavior and that provide children with strategies for approaching academic tasks. Studies included investigations of metacognition, information processing, self-recording of task-related behavior, and strategy training (Hallahan et al., 1983).

The work of the five Institutes for Research on Learning Disabilities began amidst considerable controversy about the nature of learning disabilities (McKinney, 1983). Nevertheless, it is generally accepted that the institutes, through the collective resources of many investigators pursuing a complex set of problems in programmatic fashion, contributed significantly to what we now know about the nature and treatment of learning disabilities (Keogh, 1983; McKinney, 1983).

## REFERENCES

Bryan, T., Pearl, R., Donahue, M., Bryan, J., & Pflaum, S. (1983). The Chicago Institute for Study of Learning Disabilities. *Exceptional Education Quarterly, 4*(1), 1–22.

Connor, F. P. (1983). Improving school instruction for learning disabled: The Teachers College Institute. *Exceptional Education Quarterly, 4*(1), 23–44.

Deno, S. L. (1985). Curriculum-based measurement: The emerging alternative. *Exceptional Children, 52,* 219–232.

Fleischner, J. E., & Garnett, K. (1979). *Arithmetic learning disabilities: A literature review* (Research Review Series 1979–1980, Vol. 4). New York: Teachers College, Columbia University, Research Institute for the Study of Learning Disabilities.

Fleischner, J. E., Garnett, K., & Preddy, D. (1982). *Mastery of basic number facts by learning disabled students: An intervention study* (Technical Report No. 17). New York: Teachers College, Columbia University, Research Institute for the Study of Learning Disabilities.

Gelzheiser, L. M. (1982). *The effects of direct instruction on learning disabled children's ability to generalize study behaviors for deliberate memory tasks.* Unpublished doctoral dissertation, Teachers College, Columbia University.

Hallahan, D. P., Hall, R. J., Ianna, S. O., Kneedler, R. D., Lloyd, J. W., Loper, A. B., & Reeve, R. E. (1983). Summary of research findings at the University of Virginia Learning Disabilities Research Institute. *Exceptional Education Quarterly, 4*(1), 95–114.

Keogh, B. K. (1983). A lesson from Gestalt psychology. *Exceptional Education Quarterly, 4*(1), 115–128.

McKinney, J. D. (1983). Contributions of the Institutes for Research on Learning Disabilities. *Exceptional Education Quarterly, 4*(1), 129–144.

Schumaker, J. B., Deshler, D. D., Alley, G. R., & Warner, M. M. (1983). Toward the development of an intervention model for the learning disabled adolescents: The University of Kansas Institute. *Exceptional Education Quarterly, 4*(1), 45–74.

Shepherd, J. J., Frank, B., Solar, R. A., & Gelzheiser, L. M. (1982). *Progress report.* New York: Teachers College, Columbia University, Research Institute for the Study of Learning Disabilities.

William, J. P. (1986). The role of phonemic analysis in reading. In J. K. Torgeson, & B. Y. L. Wong (Eds.), *Psychological and educational perspectives on learning disabilities.* Orlando, FL: Academic.

Ysseldyke, J., Thurlow, M., Graden, J., Wesson, C., Algozzine, B., & Deno, S. (1983). Generalizations from five years of research on assessment and decision making: The University of Minnesota Institute. *Exceptional Education Quarterly, 4*(1), 75–94.

DOUGLAS FUCHS
LYNN S. FUCHS
*Peabody College, Vanderbilt University*

# INSTITUTIONALIZATION

In the past, persons with disabilities (notably persons with mental retardation or mental illness) were left to fend for themselves, were shut away in rooms or houses, or worse, were placed in prisons (Wolfensberger, 1972). This often resulted in illness or death, a situation that led to the establishment of institutional residences in the nineteenth century. These facilities, called hospitals, asylums, or colonies, were constructed in rural areas with residents having little contact with community members. The original intent of such facilities was to provide a higher level of care for handicapped persons needing such care. Anywhere from 500 to 5,000 residents were maintained in each facility. The facilities often had large staffs and became communities unto themselves.

Disabled residents of institutions typically were not prepared to live and work in the community. Emphasis was placed on physical care in contrast to vocational preparation. In addition, the standard of care often was poor. Residents lived in barracks-style arrangements that were dehumanizing. Crowding was commonplace, with waking hours spent in idle activity.

Placement in a residential facility was often for life. Through the 1950s, the number of disabled persons residing in institutions increased. Then, with the advent of the deinstitutionalization movement, promoted by those who thought the physical and social environment of institutions to be detrimental, the resident institutional population declined. From 1955 to 1973, the resident population declined from 500,000 to 250,000 in spite of a 40 percent increase in the U.S. population (Telford & Sawrey, 1977). Currently, the emptying of residential institutions has slowed, with most states controlling new admissions instead of removing residents.

While many formerly institutionalized persons with disabilities can be accommodated in the community, care and treatment facilities have not kept pace with the deinstitutionalization movement. Consequently, a number of those who returned to the community have been unable to obtain needed services and have become part of the homeless contingent found in many cities. Institutions will always be required for at least some small segment of the disabled population. However, with early intervention, education, and community-based alternatives, few individuals will require intensive and lifelong care.

### REFERENCES

Arnhoff, F. N. (1975). Social consequences of policy toward mental illness. *Science, 188,* 1277–1281.

Telford, C. W., & Sawrey, J. M. (1977). *The exceptional individual* (2nd ed.). Englewood Cliffs, NJ: Prentice Hall.

Wolfensberger, W. (1972). *The principle of normalization in human services.* Downsview, CT: National Institute of Mental Retardation.

PATRICIA ANN ABRAMSON
*Hudson Public Schools, Hudson, Wisconsin*

**COMMUNITY RESIDENTIAL PROGRAMS**
**DEINSTITUTIONALIZATION**

## INSTITUTION NATIONALE DES SOURDS-MUETS

The Institution Nationale des Sourds-Muets, the first public nonpaying school for the deaf in the world, was founded in Paris in 1755 by the Abbot Charles Michel de l'Epée (1712–1789). Its name was changed in 1960 to Institut National de Jeunes Sourds (INJS; National Institute for Young Deaf). Despite its location in the heart of Paris, it has retained spacious grounds (19,300 square meters) comprising playgrounds, gardens, orchards, and vegetable gardens.

De l'Epée started to teach the deaf when he was asked to give religious instruction to two deaf twin sisters who communicated by signs. He understood that signs could express human thought as much as oral language and decided to use them for his teaching. However, probably unaware that a more elaborate sign system existed among the Paris deaf community (Moody, 1983), de l'Epée felt compelled to create additional signs. These, the methodical signs, were intended to expand the vocabulary and to adapt the existing signs so as to follow French syntax and morphology. The successor of de l'Epée was the abbot Sicard (1808), who continued to expand the methodical signs. However, their excessive development resulted in a cumbersome system unsuitable for communication. During his tenure, a trend towards greater use of natural signs gained momentum and was established as a principle by the following director, Bébian (Moores, 1978).

As early as 1805, the institute's physician, J. M. Itard (1821), introduced auditory and speech training for some pupils, and tried to teach speech to Victor, the wild child of the Aveyron (Lane, 1981). Bébian, who took charge in 1817, is probably the first protagonist of a bilingual education. He considered that the acquisition of French was facilitated when concepts were first established through signs. This official use of natural sign language allowed more and more former pupils to become teachers. Already under Sicard, however, some deaf teachers had been trained; in 1816 one of them, Laurent Clerc, accompanied Thomas Hopkins Gal-

Institut National des Jeunes Sourds (Paris)

laudet back to the United States to establish a school along the same model as the Paris institution.

During most of the nineteenth century, sign language for teaching flourished, although its use was criticized by Itard and his followers. The latter were unsuccessful in defending oralism until the 1880 Milano Congress of Educators of the Deaf, which decided that signs were inappropriate for teaching and had an adverse effect on the acquisition of spoken language. Signs were henceforth suppressed, and deaf teachers discharged.

For the rest of the nineteenth century and for more than two-thirds of the twentieth, oral education prevailed as the only official method. Signs were tolerated among pupils as a low-grade communication medium, although they were still covertly used by some teachers. Following the congresses of the World Federation of the Deaf in Paris (1971) and Washington (1975), a renewal of interest in sign language took place in France. This movement shook the strictly oralist position of the INJS and other European schools for the deaf and led several of its teachers to adopt a total communication philosophy. Today the INJS is a place where energies are expended in several directions in an attempt to revitalize deaf education. The school, which formerly was entirely residential, presently has a larger population of day pupils. Efforts are being made towards mainstreaming and some teachers have become itinerant in order to support pupils integrated into ordinary schools. Sign language teaching is organized within the institution and several teachers use it in their classrooms. Training of interpreters for the deaf has been organized. Other teachers have adopted cued speech, while some have remained exclusively oral. The venerable library contains many publications by former deaf teachers and pupils, including detailed accounts of the life of the deaf community in eighteenth- and nineteenth-century France.

The INJS deserves the title of cradle of sign language for deaf education. In its front courtyard, visitors are greeted by the statue of the Abbot de l'Epée, to whose robe clings a grateful deaf child. Many deaf people throughout the world consider de l'Epée as their spiritual father, and the INJS as the living historical landmark of his action.

**REFERENCES**

Itard, J. M. (1821). *Traité des maladies de l'oreille et de l'audition.* Paris.

Lane, H. (1981). *L'enfant sauvage de l'Aveyron.* Paris: Payot.

Moody, B. (1983). *La langue des signes.* Vincennes, France: International Visual Theatre.

Moores, D. F. (1978). *Educating the deaf: Psychology, principles and practices.* Boston: Houghton Mifflin.

Sicard, A. (1808). *Théorie des signes.* Paris: Dentu, Delalain.

OLIVIER PÉRIER
*Université Libre de Bruxelles*
*Centre Comprendre et Parler,*
*Belgium*

DEAF EDUCATION
TOTAL COMMUNICATION

## INSTRUCTIONAL MEDIA/MATERIALS CENTER

Virtually every school district, intermediate unit, and cooperative supports an instructional media/materials center as part of its overall educational effort. Originally, local instructional media centers dealt mainly with audiovisuals (films, filmstrips, multimedia kits, slide-tapes, audiotapes, videotapes, CDs, DVDs) and concentrated primarily on responding to teachers' requests for audiovisual materials and for loan and maintenance of audiovisual equipment.

The implementation of IDEA and its reauthorizations has expanded the functions of many instructional media/materials centers that today house teacher centers, professional libraries, and collections of textbooks, print materials, and adaptive devices (in addition to audiovisuals). The range of services may include circulation of new products through onsite borrowing, by mail or mobile units; information searches; in-service training; development of print and nonprint products for local use; dissemination of information on promising practices and products; assistance with the selection and adoption of new practices; and participation in school improvement programs. Some instructional media/materials centers also provide computer workshops, software development, software reviews and guides, and computer libraries.

JUDY SMITH-DAVIS
*Counterpoint Communications*
*Company*

IN-SERVICE TRAINING FOR SPECIAL EDUCATION
    TEACHERS
INSTRUCTIONAL TECHNOLOGY FOR INDIVIDUALS
    WITH DISABILITIES

## INSTRUCTIONAL TECHNOLOGY FOR INDIVIDUALS WITH DISABILITIES

Instructional technology, also known as educational technology, is a term that has been used to describe a wide range of tools or techniques developed to simplify or enhance educational efforts by either the learner or the teacher. Although commonly thought of as mechanical or electronic devices (e.g., computers and calculators) and instructional media (e.g., videotapes, DVDs, and web-based programs), certain assessment strategies (e.g., precision teaching and applied behavioral analysis procedures), and curriculum designs (e.g., specific competencies/technology design or objective-based instruction) also may be considered instructional technology. The key element in classifying something as instructional technology seems to be that the device or technique is the result of the application of a scientific principle to an educational concern.

Aside from assessment methodologies, curriculum design, and computers, all of which have broad applications across exceptionalities, there has been continued development over the past several years of technology to meet specific needs of particular handicapping conditions.

Advances in instructional technology have had, and will continue to have, significant impact on the education of individuals with disabilities by increasing efficiency of instruction, student access to information, and student ability to display knowledge. However, especially in the area of electronic and mechanical advances, with each new development there is usually a cost. Often there is disagreement among school systems, insurance companies, and public assistance agencies about who should bear the responsibility for the cost of expensive devices; this is a dilemma for which there is no simple solution but one that must be resolved if persons with disabilities are to continue to benefit from the full range of instructional technology.

The *Journal of Special Education Technology,* a quarterly publication of Utah State University, the Association for Special Education Technology, and the Technology and Media Division of the Council for Exceptional Children deal specifically with research and presentations of innovative practices in the application of instructional technology with persons with disabilities.

The Department of Educational Technology at San Diego State University provides an online *Encyclopedia of Educational Technology* at http://www.coe.sdsu.edu/eet/. This electronic encyclopedia has hundreds of articles on all aspects of educational technology. Many of the entries refer specifically to accessibility for individuals with learning problems and multiple physical disabilities. Other articles cover examples of ways to produce effective educational technology and program evaluation.

KATHY L. RUHL
*Pennsylvania State University*

COMPUTERS AND EDUCATION
COMPUTERS IN HUMAN BEHAVIOR
COMPUTER USE WITH STUDENTS WITH DISABILITIES
ELECTRONIC TRAVEL AIDS

## INTEGRATED THERAPY

The provision of specialized therapy services in the classroom and in other natural environments has been termed integrated therapy (Nietupski, Schutz, & Ockwood, 1980; Sternat et al., 1977). Integrated therapy has a number of advantages over the isolated therapy model, in which students are removed from their classroom for therapy in a segregated environment, usually a clinic or therapy room. One advantage is the potential for continuous as opposed to episodic training sessions. Therapists and classroom teaching staff are able to coordinate both training goals and procedures. Moreover, in an integrated therapy model, there are more opportunities for sharing of professional skills and information concerning students' programs.

Another important advantage of integrated therapy conditions is the potential to enhance generalization. This is particularly critical for very young students with severe disabilities who often fail to perform new skills in other than the training environment.

There are many other theoretical and practical considerations (e.g., the importance of longitudinal intervention in natural environments, the reality of limited resources and personnel) that suggest the superiority of integrated therapy conditions in most school situations, but these considerations are less important than professional commitment. The effectiveness of integrated therapy depends on the willingness of teachers and therapists to alter traditional beliefs and practices and negotiate new role functions. They must discard the notion that only a therapist can provide therapy and agree to share intervention responsibilities in natural settings.

**REFERENCES**

Nietupski, J., Scheutz, G., & Ockwood, L. (1980). The delivery of communication therapy services to severely handicapped students: A plan for change. *Journal of the Association for the Severely Handicapped, 5*(1), 13–23.

Sternat, J., Messina, R., Nietupski, J., Lyon, S., & Brown, L. (1977). Occupational and physical therapy services for severely handicapped students: Toward a naturalized public school service delivery model. In E. Sontag, J. J. Smith, & N. Certo (Eds.), *Educational programming for the severely and profoundly handicapped.* Reston, VA: Council for Exceptional Children.

LINDA MCCORMICK
*University of Hawaii, Manoa*

INCLUSION
LEAST RESTRICTIVE ENVIRONMENT
MAINSTREAMING

## INTELLECTUAL DEFICIENCY

See INTELLIGENCE; MENTAL RETARDATION.

# INTELLIGENCE

Intelligence has proven to be a difficult construct to define. From as early as 1921 (Intelligence and its measurement: A symposium, 1921) to the present (e.g., Detterman, 1994; Sternberg & Detterman, 1986; Neisser et al., 1996), psychologists have consistently failed to agree on a common conceptual definition, general theoretical approach, or assessment device. Boring's (1923, p. 35) response to the inconsistencies was his famous pronouncement that ". . . intelligence as a measurable capacity must at the start be defined as the capacity to do well in an intelligence test. Intelligence is what the tests test." Psychologists were not thrilled, perhaps not only because of the circularity of the definition but because it appeared in the *New Republic,* bringing our confusion to the attention of a wide audience. But if we consider Boring's qualifying phrase, "as a measurable capacity," the definition makes some sense, particularly given the great influence of the psychometric approach to research on intelligence.

The confusion over definition has not diminished. Indeed, a larger number and greater variety of approaches may exist now than at any other time since the outset of interest in the topic. Whether or not the number of theories of intelligence exceeds the combined memberships of the American Psychological Association and American Psychological Society is undetermined at this time. Further, as Neisser (1979, p. 185) has convincingly argued, intelligence cannot be defined in the absolute, but only in so far as an individual can be seen as resembling a prototypical imaginary "intelligent person:" "There are no definitive criteria of intelligence . . . it is a fuzzy-edged concept to which many features are relevant. Two people may both be quite intelligent and yet have very few traits in common—they resemble the prototype along different dimensions. Thus, there is no such quality as *intelligence* . . . resemblance is an external fact and not an internal essence. There can be no process-based definition of intelligence because it is not a unitary quality. It is a resemblance between two individuals, one real and the other prototypical." Neisser suggests, however, that intelligence tests are good measures of the academic intelligence subset of the larger prototype of intelligent person.

Some commonality of agreement at a fairly global level holds both among psychologists and the public at large. Consider the well-known study of implicit theories of intelligence by Sternberg, Conway, Ketron, and Bernstein (1981), who asked lay people at a supermarket, train station, and university library to describe behaviors that they would consider intelligent, academically intelligent, or everyday intelligent. Sternberg et al. (1981) then sent the entire list of behaviors to academic psychologists whose research interest was psychology and asked them to indicate how important each behavior was in characterizing intelligent, academically intelligent, or everyday intelligent people. The authors also asked a group of lay people to do essentially the same task in a laboratory setting. Factor analysis of the psychologists' ratings of intelligence revealed three factors: Verbal Intelligence ("is verbally fluent"), Problem Solving Ability ("is able to apply knowledge to problems at hand"), and Practical Intelligence ("sizes up situations well"). Factor analysis of the lay people's ratings also revealed three factors: Practical Problem-Solving Ability ("reasons logically and well"), Verbal Ability ("speaks clearly and articulately"), and Social Competence ("accepts others for what they are"). Clearly, these factors are similar for the two groups and indicate that professionals and lay people have well-developed and similar implicit theories of intelligence. Sternberg et al. (1981) suggest that problem solving, which they equated to fluid intelligence, and verbal ability, which they equated to crystallized intelligence (see the following discussion) are "integral aspects of intellectual functioning" (p. 54). Further, two elements are common to many experts' definitions of intelligence: 1) the ability to learn from experience, and 2) the capacity to adapt to one's environment.

## Theories of Intelligence

As implied previously, psychologists and educators have proposed far more theories of intelligence than can be reviewed in this entry. Summarized below are some of the more influential past and current theories. Broader and more in-depth presentations are in Detterman (1994) and Sternberg and Detterman (1986).

### Psychometric Approaches

Psychometric theories of intelligence derive from statistical analyses, particularly factor analysis, of scores on intelligence tests. Such theories could be seen as following the Boring prototype of the intelligent person, someone who does well on intelligence tests. Several strong arguments can be made in support of a single general intelligence factor, called $g$. As early as 1904, Spearman reported that scores on a variety of then-available tests all intercorrelated; that is, high scores on one test tended to be associated with high scores on others, and vice versa. The intercorrelations suggested that one intellectual factor predicted performance on the tests. He later (e.g., Spearman, 1927) conducted factor analyses, a technique he invented, on large numbers of intelligence test scores and found that scores intercorrelated, reflecting a general factor of intelligence ($g$), but that each group of tests also tapped a more specific factor ($s$).

Support for a single general intelligence has been offered in studies of reaction time. Reaction time is measured by the time it takes an individual to complete an uncomplicated task. Eysenck (1994) has provided evidence for a biological basis of the $g$ factor, and Jensen (1993) claims that the essence of $g$ relies on the speed of neural transmission. The faster an individual's neural processes, the faster their re-action time. Reaction time has been related to intelligence through its positive correlation with IQ. Others have argued against this position by claiming it does not make sense that reaction time speed and intelligence should correlate. They counter that intelligence is an engaging process that involves problem solving. Reaction time is different; it is an automatic response over which one has little control. The importance and basis of *g* remain contentious as seen in the pro and con arguments in Modgil and Modgil (1987).

Opposed to *g* theory, Thurstone (1938) proposed that intelligence was comprised of seven independent factors which he called primary mental abilities: verbal comprehension, verbal fluency, inductive reasoning, spatial visualization, number, memory, and perceptual speed. However, he found that scores on his tests of these factors, the Primary Mental Abilities Test, actually intercorrelated moderately, supporting the existence of a second-order common factor. However, Thurstone chose to emphasize the factors' separate identities.

Cattell (1971) proposed a hierarchical model of intelligence in which *g* was divided into two components, fluid intelligence and crystallized intelligence. Fluid intelligence, now referred to as *Gf*, is the ability to apply cognitions to novel problems, to acquire new information, and to induce new relationships among known information. This type of intelligence is considered abstract and culture-free. Crystallized intelligence, now referred to as *Gc*, includes skills and knowledge acquired across the lifespan that enable individuals to apply proven problem-solving skills to familiar challenges. This form of intelligence is acquired, and relies heavily on culture and experience. Under each of these two major subfactors are other more specific ones. Horn (1985) has presented new evidence for *Gf* and *Gc*, and has suggested that they are highly correlated in young children but tend to become less and less correlated as children grow and have various experiences. Eysenck's (1985) intelligence A, which includes all biological and genetically determined intelligence and is the type he and Jensen have proposed is measured through reaction time, is very similar to *Gf*, whereas intelligence B, which is any type of intelligence that is formed through the environment and experience, is similar to *Gc*.

The ultimate factor-analytic model of intelligence is Guilford's three-dimensional structure of the intellect (SOI), represented as a cube comprised of all combinations of five operations, four contents, and six products for a total of 120 factors. Guilford attempted to develop tests for these individual factors that would be independent of *g*. Little evidence supports Guilford's theory, and it has been much criticized. For example, Kline (1991) suggests that the model relies on human intuition more than scientific evidence. The SOI now appears largely of historic interest for the role it played in Guilford's resurrection of interest in the topic of creativity.

Carroll (e.g., 1993) has developed a hierarchical theory of intelligence based on factor analysis of a large sample of data sets. His model proposes over 40 primary factors in various domains (language competence, reasoning and thinking, memory and learning, visual perception, auditory reception, idea production, and cognitive speed). Analysis of the primary factors revealed seven secondary factors, many of them similar to aspects of the theories of Horn, Cattell, Eysenck, and Jensen: *Gf*, fluid intelligence; *Gc*, crystallized intelligence; *Gv*, visualization capacity; *Gs*, general cognitive speed; *Gm*, general memory; *Gr*, general retrieval capacity; and *Ga*, general auditory perception capacity. Analyses of these factors revealed, not surprisingly, Spearman's *g*. Carroll (1994, p. 62) suggests that *g* mainly loads on tasks involving "the *level of complexity* at which individuals are able to handle basic processes of induction, deduction, and comprehension."

### Beyond Psychometrics: Intelligence Broadly Conceptualized

Concerned among other things about limitations of *g*, Gardner (1983, 1993) proposed seven "multiple intelligences" (M.I.) as individual components that perform separately at differing levels. He (Gardner, 1983, p. 9) claims support for M.I. through "studies of prodigies, gifted individuals, idiots savants, normal children, normal adults, experts in different lines of work, and individuals from diverse cultures." His M.I. are: 1) linguistic intelligence, reflected in tasks such as reading or language comprehension; 2) logical-mathematical intelligence, involving calculations and logic; 3) spatial intelligence, involving transformations of objects and perception of forms; 4) musical intelligence, which supposedly develops earliest, involving such capabilities as composing or playing an instrument; 5) bodily-kinesthetic intelligence, reflected in control over the motions of one's body as well as ability to manipulate objects; 6) interpersonal intelligence, the ability to understand other individuals; and 7) intrapersonal intelligence, which relates to the ability to view oneself objectively in terms of strengths and weaknesses. Although the seven intelligences are viewed as functioning separately, they often interact to produce particular kinds of intelligent behavior.

Although generating much interest in both psychology and education, Gardner's proposal is questionable from a scientific standpoint. In the first place, he has offered no tests of his intelligences, leaving their presumed independence as well as their very existence in question. The evidence he offers is interesting, but hardly systematic or compelling, particularly since comparable evidence could be found for other presumed "intelligences." As others (e.g., Neisser et al., 1996) have pointed out, separate categories of intelligence are not all that independent; individuals who have talent in one area tend to be talented in other areas as well, relating again to the *g* factor premise. Further, also pointed out by Neisser et al. (1996), Gardner's intelligences are others' talents. Indeed, Gardner's approach conceptually resembles Taylor's (e.g., Taylor & Ellison, 1975) earlier multiple-talent model. Finally, as Hunt (1994, p. 233) has observed, Gardner attempts to incorporate far too much under the concept of intelligence: "If we make 'intelligence' coterminous with 'all the nice little abilities a human might have,' the topic will be so incoherent that it will never be understood." To be fair, Gardner (1983, p. 11) specifically stated, ". . . I want to underscore that the notion of multiple intelligences is hardly a proven scientific fact: it is, at most, an idea that has recently regained the right to be discussed seriously." That cautionary note still appears appropriate.

Also concerned about limitations of $g$ as well as believing that all good things come in threes, Sternberg (1985) has proposed a triarchic componential theory of intelligence. Intelligence is viewed as involving three types of abilities that operate on three different levels and that draw on three components of information processing. The triarchy of abilities are the analytic, creative, and practical abilities. Analytic abilities are used to evaluate and judge information to deal with problems that have only one right answer. Creative abilities are used to deal with novel problems that require thinking in a different way and that may have no one solution. Practical abilities deal with real-world problems that may have various solutions. The three levels on which the abilities operate are the internal world, the external world, and individual experience. The three information-processing components are: 1) metacomponents are executive processes which plan, monitor, and evaluate; 2) performance components implement metacomponents; and 3) knowledge-acquisition components are used for initial learning of problem solving strategies. These three components operate interdependently. Sternberg's argument against the emphasis on $g$ is that general reasoning, such as previously noted in crystallized intelligence, may be a highly-regarded aspect in some cultures, but other cultures have no use for it at all. This should not mean that they have a mental deficiency—it is simply a skill that they have never acquired.

Proponents of $g$ contend that Sternberg's theory lacks any biological basis and that his concepts are not empirically supported. Some (e.g., Eysenck, 1994) have provided evidence that originality and creativity are not aspects of cognitive ability, but traits of personality. On the other hand, a variety of evidence (Neisser et al., 1996) supports Sternberg's contention that practical intelligence is both largely independent of scores on standard intelligence tests and an important correlate of real-world problem solving.

## Aspects of Measured Intelligence

Intelligence as measured by standardized tests can be used as predictors of various criterion variables, correlated with presumptive underlying processes such as processing time, used to describe individual and group differences, and analyzed for genetic and environmental bases. The following is a brief summary of some of these findings, based on reviews by Gottfredson (1997), Humphreys (1992), and Neisser et al. (1996).

### Prediction of Scholastic Achievement

Since the time of Binet, the major purpose of intelligence tests has been to predict academic performance. As would be expected, scores on such tests do correlate with scholastic achievement as measured both by grades and standardized achievement tests. Correlations between IQs and measures of school achievement for children average about .50. At a higher educational level, SAT and scores also predict college grades, although the correlations vary considerably from one study to another. These correlations only account for about 25 percent of the total variance, indicating that a host of other factors, including personality, social, and cultural factors are also important in school performance.

### Other Correlates

Intelligence test scores correlate with years of education, occupational status, and job performance. They also correlate with socioeconomic status, but interpretation is difficult owing to the number of other correlates. The speed with which people perform a number of cognitive tasks also correlates positively with measured intelligence, and the magnitude of the correlations appears to increase with task complexity.

### Genetic and Environmental Bases

Although a topic of much research and controversy, the degree to which genetic and environmental factors contribute to intelligence remains uncertain. Many reasons are responsible for this uncertainty, including the statistical techniques and subject samples used. Further, by necessity, the more environmental factors are similar for subjects in the samples, the larger must be the contribution of genetic ones. That is, if environment differences are negligible, then any variability must owe to genetic differences. Estimates of the proportion of differences in intelligence that may be attributed to differences in genetic background range from .40 to .80, with a mean of about .50. These estimates are, however, based on studies in which subjects from very low socioeconomic levels were underrepresented. Since environmental differences are correlated with socioeconomic status, artifactually small environmental differences would necessarily exaggerate the effect of genetic differences. The proportion tends to increase with age, perhaps because as individuals develop, they increasingly select their own environments, partly to be compatible with other genetically-based traits. Of course, particular genetic conditions, such as Down's syndrome, may be responsible for individual cases of mental retardation.

Although even the highest estimates of the role of differences in genetics indicate a considerable role of environmental differences in determining differences in intelligence, determining the nature of the responsible environmental factors has been difficult. Researchers have identified numerous environmental factors as being potentially important in influencing normal variations in intelligence, including cultural, familial, social, and academic ones, but firm identification remains elusive. Doubtless, environmental factors, such as lead exposure, prenatal alcohol, prolonged malnutrition, perinatal factors (prematurity, very low birth weight) are responsible for individual cases of lowered intelligence and mental retardation, but their role in normal individual differences is small.

### Group Differences

Consistent differences exist among cultural/ethnic subgroups in measured intelligence, although the degree of difference is not as consistent. Mean IQ of Whites is the same as the standardized mean, 100, whereas that of Asian Americans is somewhat higher, about 105, and that of African Americans considerably lower, about 85. Means for Latinos and Native Americans fall in between. Many explanations, both environmental and genetic, have been offered for these differences, but all are subject to criticism. One consistent finding, however, is that group differences cannot be attributed to bias in the tests, for which no scientific evidence exists. Absence of test bias should not, however, be taken as support of a genetic interpretation. Flynn (1999), for example, has recently offered a cogent criticism of genetic interpretations of group differences. Virtually no direct evidence supports a genetic explanation, but reliable evidence of environmental factors also remains elusive. What can be said at this time is that firm claims to either position likely rest more on belief than on scientifically-supported evidence.

### The Rising IQ

"Perhaps the most striking of all environmental effects is the steady worldwide rise in intelligence test performance" (Neisser et al., 1996, p. 89). The "Flynn Effect," named after the person who first systematically reported it (e.g., Flynn, 1984, 1999), refers to the consistent and sizable increases in measured intelligence that have occurred in the United States and other western countries since at least the 1930s. The gain is approximately 0.3 IQ points each year (Flynn, 1999). Of particular interest, gains on the Ravens Progressive Matrices test, a culture-reduced and thus more g loaded test, are even higher and occur in 20 different countries (Flynn, 1999). The increases must of course be environmen-

tal, since positing genetic change over that period of time is simply untenable. Furthermore, the increases occur in the absence of any increases in achievement test scores. The reasons for the increase are unclear. Neisser et al. (1996) argue that increased test sophistication is an unlikely basis and suggest that increased cultural complexity and/or improved nutrition may play a role. But possible also is Flynn's (1987) position that the improved scores cannot reflect a comparable increase in real intelligence, or several countries would be experiencing a true cultural renaissance owing to a dramatic increase in the number of their geniuses. Flynn suggests that what has increased actually may be only a relatively narrow, for practical purposes, type of abstract problem solving.

### Some Implications

The validity of intelligence tests as predictors of school performance supports their continued use to identify children in need of special education services. The relatively low correlations between IQ and academic performance indicate that many other factors are involved. Although a hierarchical theory of intelligence with g as the highest factor is supported by much research, additional aspects of intelligence, particularly practical intelligence, appear to be important determinants of a wide range of behavior. The Flynn Effect is a clear reflection of environmental influences on measured intelligence for which theories will need to account. Formal adequate schooling, including preschools and appropriate intervention, is an important influence on intellectual development. Finally, a separation of the scientific aspects of the study of intelligence from its political implications is needed.

### REFERENCES

Carroll, J. B. (1994). Cognitive abilities: Constructing a theory from data. In D. K. Detterman (Ed.), *Current topics in human intelligence, volume 4: Theories of intelligence* (pp. 43–63). Norwood, NJ: Ablex.

Cattell, R. B. (1971). *Abilities: Their structure, growth, and action.* Boston: Houghton Mifflin.

Eysenck, H. J. (1994). A biological theory of intelligence. In D. K. Detterman (Ed.), *Current topics in human intelligence, volume 4: Theories of intelligence* (pp. 117–149). Norwood, NJ: Ablex.

Eysenck, H. J., & Eysenck, M. W. (1985). *Personality and individual differences: A nature science approach.* New York: Plenum.

Flynn, J. R. (1984). The mean IQ of Americans: Massive gains 1932 to 1978. *Psychological Bulletin, 95,* 29–51.

Flynn, J. R. (1999). Searching for justice: The discovery of IQ gains over time. *American Psychologist, 54*(1), 5–20.

Gardner, H. (1983). *Frames of mind: The theory of multiple intelligences.* New York: Basic Books.

Gardner, H. (Ed.). (1993). *Multiple intelligences: The theory in practice.* New York: Basic Books.

Gottfredson, L. S. (1997). Mainstream science on intelligence: An editorial with 52 signatories, history, and bibliography. *Intelligence, 24,* 13–23.

Guilford, J. P. (1967). *The nature of human intelligence.* New York: McGraw-Hill.

Horn, J. L. (1985). Remodeling old models of intelligence: *Gf-Gc* theory. In B. B. Wolman (Ed.), *Handbook of intelligence* (pp. 267–300). New York: Wiley.

Humphreys, L. G. (1992). Ability testing. *Psychological Science, 3,* 271–274.

Hunt, E. (1994). Theoretical models for the study of intelligence. In D. K. Detterman (Ed.), *Current topics in human intelligence volume 4: Theories of intelligence* (pp. 233–256). Norwood, NJ: Ablex.

Intelligence and its measurement: A symposium. (1921). *Journal of Educational Psychology, 12,* 123–147; 195–216; 271–275.

Jensen, A. R. (1993). Why is reaction time correlated with psychometric *g*? *Current Directions in Psychological Science, 2,* 53–56.

Kline, P. (1991). *Intelligence.* New York: Routledge.

Modgil, S., & Modgil, C. (Eds.). (1987). *Arthur Jensen: Consensus and controversy.* Falmer, England: Falmer Press.

Neisser, U. (1979). The concept of intelligence. *Intelligence, 3,* 217–227.

Neisser, U., Boodoo, G., Bouchard, T. J., Jr., Boykin, A. W., Brody, N., Ceci, S. J., Halpern, D. F., Loehlin, J. C., Perloff, R., Sternberg, R. J., & Urbina, S. (1996). Intelligence: Knowns and unknowns. *American Psychologist, 51,* 77–101.

Spearman, C. (1904). "General intelligence" objectively determined and measured. *American Journal of Psychology, 15,* 201–293.

Spearman, C. (1927). *The abilities of man: Their nature and measurement.* New York: Macmillan.

Sternberg, R. J. (1985). *Beyond IQ: A triarchic theory of human intelligence.* New York: Cambridge University Press.

Sternberg, R. J., Conway, B. E., Ketron, J. L., & Bernstein, M. (1981). People's conception of intelligence. *Journal of Personality and Social Psychology, 41,* 37–55.

Sternberg, R. J., & Detterman, D. K. (Eds.). (1986). *What is intelligence?* Norwood, NJ: Ablex.

Taylor, C. W., & Ellison, R. L. (1975). Moving toward working models in creativity: Utah creativity experiences and insights. In I. A. Taylor & J. W. Getzels (Eds.), *Perspectives in creativity* (pp. 191–223). Chicago: Aldine.

Thurstone, L. L. (1938). Primary mental abilities. *Psychometric monographs,* No. 1.

ROBERT C. NICHOLS
DIANE JARVIS
*State University of New York at Buffalo*
First edition

ROBERT T. BROWN
KATHERINE D. FALWELL
*University of North Carolina at Wilmington*
Second edition

# INTELLIGENCE: A MULTIDISCIPLINARY JOURNAL

*Intelligence,* first appearing in January 1977 and published quarterly since that time, has been edited since its inception by Douglas Detterman. David Zeaman and Robert Sternberg served as associate editors until 1984; no associate editors are currently listed. Joseph Hogan, III, served as book review editor until 1980, when James Pellegrino took the position. After 1981 book reviews were infrequent and the journal no longer lists a book review editor. *Intelligence* has a large editorial board comprised of notable scholars from different disciplines within the behavioral sciences.

When *Intelligence* was established in 1977, there were no other journals devoted exclusively to basic research in human intelligence, even though many prestigious journals were available in the field of learning. By establishing a new journal, the founder sought to "formalize the importance of the study of human intelligence and the major role it has played in the development of the behavioral sciences" (p. 2).

*Intelligence* is a scientifically oriented journal, publishing papers that make a substantial contribution to the understanding of the nature and function of intelligence. The journal is devoted to the publication of original research, but also accepts theoretical and review articles. Studies concerned with application are considered only if the work also contributes to basic knowledge. The journal is multidisciplinary in nature. Of interest to special educators are the many empirical studies published in the field of mental retardation. Other types of studies include early childhood development, measurement of individual differences, and issues in cultural test bias.

## REFERENCE

Detterman, D. K. (1977). Is *Intelligence* necessary? *Intelligence: A Multidisciplinary Journal, 1*(1), 1–3.

KATHRYN A. SULLIVAN
*Branson School Online*

# INTELLIGENCE, EMOTIONAL

"Is 'emotional intelligence' a contradiction in terms?" With that opening question, Peter Salovey and John Mayer (1989–1990) opened a modern line of research, started a hot topic in psychology, and coined a catchphrase that has made its way into the common vernacular. The subsequent fame and widespread use of the term "emotional intelligence" is due mostly to the popular bestseller of the same name by Daniel Goleman (1995). This enormous popularity, however, has come at the unfortunate cost of obscuring Salovey and Mayer's original conception of emotional intelligence and overshadowing subsequent empirical research. This resulted in the formation of two distinct concepts of emotional intelligence, each containing its own definition and approach. Caruso, Mayer, and Salovey (2002) dubbed these the mixed model and the ability model. The mixed model, the more popular of the two, merges emotional intelligence with characteristics of personality and certain skills. The ability model characterizes emotional intelligence as a class of intelligence where emotions and thinking are integrated (Caruso et al., 2002).

The idea that emotion is a significant part of our intellectual being has roots in Darwin and Freud and, more recently, in the work of Howard Gardner (1983). In Gardner's theory of multiple intelligences, two of his proposed seven intelligences involve emotions: Interpersonal intelligence (understanding other people) and Intrapersonal intelligence (understanding one's self). Robert Sternberg's theory of successful intelligence (also known as practical intelligence) is another major theory of intellect that takes into consideration the importance of emotional well-being (see Sternberg & Kaufman, 1998). The common historical view, however, is that emotions are secondary—indeed, inferior to intellect (Mayer, Salovey, & Caruso, 2004).

In 1990, Salovey and Mayer proposed a model of emotional intelligence that had three factors: appraisal and expression of emotion, regulation of emotion, and utilization of emotion. Appraisal and expression of emotion is comprised of emotion in the self (which can be both verbal and nonverbal), and emotion in others. Emotion in others consists of nonverbal perception of emotion and empathy. The second factor, regulation of emotion, is the ability to regulate emotion in the self, and the ability to regulate and alter emotions in other people. The final factor, utilizing emotional intelligence, has four aspects: flexible planning, creative thinking, redirected attention, and motivation. Flexible planning refers to the ability to produce a large number of different plans for the future, enabling the planner to better respond to opportunities. This production of many plans can result from using emotion and mood changes to one's advantage and from looking at a wide variety of possibilities. Creative thinking, the second aspect, may be more likely to occur if a person is happy and in a good mood. Redirected attention involves the idea that when strong emotions are experienced, a person's resources and attentions may be tuned to new problems. People who can use this phenomenon to their own benefit will be able to use a potentially stressful situation to focus on the most important or pressing issues involved. Motivation emotions, the final principle of emotional intelligence, refers to the art of making one's self continue to perform difficult tasks by focusing one's anxiety or tension toward the performance of that task.

Mayer and Salovey (see Mayer, 2001) compressed their theory into four branches of ability: (1) perceiving, appraising, and expressing emotions; (2) accessing and producing feelings in aid of cognition; (3) comprehending information on affect and using emotional knowledge; and (4) regulating emotions for growth and contentment (Mayer & Salovey, 1997). These branches are categorized in a certain order to show how much ability is incorporated into personality (Mayer et al., 2004). The branches create a hierarchy where the ability to regulate emotions is positioned at the top and the capacity to perceive emotion is placed at its bottom. The first branch, perception of emotion, is the degree to which one is able to distinguish emotion in other individuals, by utilizing cues from facial expression and body language. The second branch, facilitation, comes into play once emotion is recognized, which involves the integration of emotion with cognitive processes. The third branch, the understanding of emotions, is the ability to analyze emotions, to recognize the most likely path they will take over time, and to become aware of their aftereffects. The fourth branch, the management of emotion, is the ability to control emotions in order to meet an individual's set goals, having an understanding of one's self, and having societal awareness (Mayer et al., 2004).

Can emotional intelligence be measured? There are some tests of emotional intelligence that exist: The Bar-On Emotional Quotient Inventory (EQ-I; Bar-On, 1997), the Self Report Emotional Intelligence Test (SREIT; see Brackett & Mayer, 2003), and the Mayer-Salovey-Caruso Emotional Intelligence Test (MSCEIT; Brackett & Mayer, 2003). The validity of such tests has been called into question as most of these measures are self-reports and have psychometric properties that are largely unknown. However, the MSCEIT uses a consensus to score participants in place of self-reports (Mayer et al., 2004) and measures emotional intelligence based on cognitive ability (Brackett & Mayer, 2003), making it a more reliable measure than tests solely using methods of self-report.

Mayer et al. (2004) argue that emotional intelligence meets many of the current standards used to measure intelligence. Indeed, they make the assertion that emotional intelligence works through cognitions that deal directly with matters of personal, or emotional, importance. In their study, they showed that measures of emotional intelligences meet three standard criteria of a new intelligence by using the MSCEIT. The first criterion is that the test questions could be confirmed as either correct or incorrect. The second condition is that there are connections in emotional intelligence that directly relate to the ones of a standard intelligence. The third decisive factor is that when time passes, emotional intelligence continues to develop within that individual.

Emotional intelligence is still a young discipline, and much of the research and scholarship to date has been in defining exactly what are the parameters and boundaries of "emotional intelligence." While Salovey, Mayer, and colleagues define emotional intelligence in terms of how well people can understand and control their own emotions and those of others, there are several other extensions of the terms. Motivation, cognition, and morality have also been dubbed aspects of emotional intelligence (Salovey et al., 1999). Goleman (1995), in his popular book on the topic, extended the definition even further. His conception of emotional intelligence encompasses impulse control, enthusiasm, social acumen, and persistence, as well as the other variables already mentioned. In 1998, Goleman revised his model of emotional intelligence (Mayer, 2001), extending its fields to include self-awareness, self-regulation, motivation, empathy, and social skills.

Future directions in emotional intelligence research, according to Mayer et al. (2004), will likely be concentrated in the following areas: finding the correlations between emotional intelligence and more traditional types of intelligence and personality traits; assessing cultural differences and similarities in emotional intelligence (both abilities and definitions); developing more empirical measures of the construct, and determining if these measures predict an advantageous effect on academic, personal, and professional success; and using a larger range of age groups to determine how emotional intelligence develops over time.

**REFERENCES**

Bar-on, R. (1997). *EQ-I: Bar-On Emotional Quotient Inventory*. Toronto: Multi-health Systems.

Brackett, M. A., & Mayer, J. D. (2003). Convergent, discriminant, and incremental validity of competing measures of emotional intelligence. *Personality and Social Psychology Bulletin, 29*, 1147–1158.

Caruso, D. R., Mayer, J. D., & Salovey, P. (2002). Relation of an ability measure of emotional intelligence to personality. *Journal of Personality Assessment, 79*(2), 306–320.

Gardner, H. (1983). *Frames of mind: The theory of multiple intelligences*. New York: Basic Books.

Goleman, D. (1995). *Emotional intelligence*. New York: Bantam.

Mayer, J. D. (2001). A field guide to emotional intelligence. In J. Ciarrochi, J. P. Forgas, & J. D. Mayer (Eds.), *Emotional intelligence in everyday life* (pp. 3–24). Philadelphia: Psychology Press.

Mayer, J. D., Salovey, P., & Caruso, D. R. (2004). Emotional intelligence: Theory, findings, and implications. *Psychological Inquiry, 17*(3), 197–215.

Salovey, P., & Mayer, J. D. (1989–1990). Emotional intelligence. *Imagination, Cognition, and Personality, 9*(3), 185–211.

Sternberg, R. J., & Kaufman, J. C. (1998). Human abilities. *Annual Review of Psychology, 49*, 479–502.

CANDACE ANDREWS
*California State University, San Bernardino*

# INTELLIGENCE, PRACTICAL

While most people in society are aware of the existence of both "street smarts" and "book smarts," psychology, in general, has chosen to focus on the latter when it examines intelligence. Intelligence tests sometimes measure topics that have real-world implications (e.g., auditory comprehension on the Kaufman Adolescent and Adult Intelligence Test assesses understanding of a mock news broadcast; Kaufman & Kaufman, 1993), but psychometric testing of intelligence has been more focused on academic intelligence (Sternberg & Kaufman, 1996, 1998).

The history of scientific research on practical intelligence is a short one (Sternberg, 1996; Torff & Sternberg, 1998). Neisser (1976) provided a theoretical distinction between academic and everyday intelligence, and Sternberg, Conway, Ketron, and Bernstein (1981) demonstrated that both laypeople and intelligence researchers had implicit beliefs that academic and practical intelligence were separate things. Ceci and Liker (1986) and Scribner (1984) did early research on how adult subjects performed much better on tasks of mathematical reasoning when these tasks were presented in the context of a more familiar domain (e.g., filling orders in a factory), showing subjects who may not do well on traditional intelligence tests may be able to solve similar problems if they are presented in the guise of their day-to-day work.

Robert Sternberg (1984, 1988), in his triarchic theory of intelligence, proposed that there are three kinds of intelligences: Analytical intelligence, Practical intelligence, and Creative intelligence (see entry for triarchic theory of intelligence). He defines practical intelligence, being similar to "street smarts," as the ability to apply one's knowledge in a hands-on, real-world manner. One key element required for practical intelligence is tacit knowledge (Sternberg, Wagner, Williams, & Horvath, 1995; Wagner & Sternberg, 1985, 1986), that is, knowledge that is acquired without being explicitly taught. There are three features of tacit knowledge that are considered characteristic: (1) it is procedural; (2) it is related to the pursuit and achievement of valued outcomes; and (3) it is learned without assistance from other people. The third condition is one of the key distinctions between tacit and academic knowledge.

Several tacit knowledge tests have been developed and researched, including the Tacit Knowledge Inventory for Managers (TKIM; Wagner & Sternberg, 1991) and measures included on the Sternberg Triarchic Abilities Test (STAT; Sternberg, 1993) and used in studies with the College Board (Sternberg & the Rainbow Project Collaborators, 2005). These tests examine a subject's tacit knowledge by presenting scenarios specific to a particular job (e.g., business manager, military officer) and then asking questions about what actions should be taken in each situation. One typical question might be to ask subjects what they would do if a colleague asked for their advice on a project that looked terrible. Would the correct response be to give an honest assessment of the project's worth, or to give complimentary but inaccurate feedback? The subject rates each potential answer on a 1 to 7 scale, with 1 meaning that the solution is "extremely bad" and 7 meaning the solution is "extremely good."

Empirical research by Sternberg, Wagner, and others (Sternberg, 1997; Sternberg, Okagaki, & Jackson, 1990; Sternberg, Wagner, & Okagaki, 1993; Wagner & Sternberg, 1986) has found several consistent results. Tacit knowledge increases with hands-on experience; measures of tacit knowledge have repeatedly correlated at significant levels with job performance, yet show only small correlations with traditional measures of intelligence; and early results show that if one wants to teach tacit knowledge, such training should improve results on tests of practical intelligence and tacit knowledge. The behaviors obtained can differ from one culture to another (Sternberg & Kaufman, 1998; Yang & Sternberg, 1997). Practical intelligence has many important implications for education. Sternberg, Gardner, and other colleagues have combined to form a collaborative project called "Practical Intelligence for Schools" (PIFS; see Gardner, Krechevsky, Sternberg, & Okagaki, 1994). The authors defined the practically intelligent student as one who is aware of his or her individual learning styles; knows how to draw on individual strengths; understands the requirements for the variety of problems encountered across many different school subjects; and can function well interpersonally as well as academically. The authors propose a curriculum for enhancing PIFS that has three units: one that focuses on self-awareness and self-management, another that focuses on task management, and a final unit that shows students how to interact beneficially with others (Gardner et al., 1994; Sternberg et al. 1990). This curriculum resulted in improvement on a variety of measures of practical intelligence.

## REFERENCES

Ceci, S., & Liker, J. (1986). Academic and nonacademic intelligence: An experimental separation. In R. J. Sternberg & R. K. Wagner (Eds.), *Practical intelligence: Nature and origins of competence in the everyday world* (pp. 119–142). New York: Cambridge University Press.

Gardner, H., Krechevsky, M., Sternberg, R. J., & Okagaki, L. (1994). Intelligence in context: Enhancing students' practical intelligence for school. In K. McGilly (Ed.), *Classroom lessons: Integrating cognitive theory and classroom practice* (pp. 105–127). Cambridge, MA: Bradford Books.

Kaufman, A. S., & Kaufman, N. L. (1993). *Manual for the Kaufman Adolescent and Adult Intelligence Test (KAIT)*. Circle Pines, MN: American Guidance Service.

Neisser, U. (1976). General academic and artificial intelligence. In L. Resnick (Ed.), *Human intelligence: Perspectives on its theory and measurement* (pp. 135–146). Norwood, NJ: Ablex.

Scribner, S. (1984). Studying working intelligence. In B. Rogoff & J. Lave (Eds.), *Everyday cognition* (pp. 9–40). Cambridge, MA: Harvard University Press.

Sternberg, R. J. (1984). A triarchic theory of human intelligence. *Behavioral and Brain Sciences, 7,* 269–287.

Sternberg, R. J. (1988). *The triarchic mind: A new theory of human intelligence.* New York: Viking.

Sternberg, R. J. (1993). *Sternberg Triarchic Abilities Test.* Unpublished test.

Sternberg, R. J. (1996). What should we ask about intelligence? *American Scholar, 65*(2), 205–217.

Sternberg, R. J. (1997). Tacit knowledge and job success. In N. Anderson & P. Herriot (Eds.), *International handbook of selection and assessment* (pp. 201–213). New York: Wiley.

Sternberg, R. J., Conway, B. E., Ketron, J. L., & Bernstein, M. (1981). Aegnie's conception of intelligence. *Journal of Personality and Social Psychology, 41,* 37–55.

Sternberg, R. J., & Kaufman, J. C. (1996). Innovation and intelligence testing: The curious case of the dog that didn't bark. *European Journal of Psychological Assessment, 12,* 175–182.

Sternberg, R. J., & Kaufman, J. C. (1998). Human abilities. *Annual Review of Psychology, 49,* 479–502.

Sternberg, R. J., Okagaki, L., & Jackson, A. (1990). Practical intelligence for success in school. *Educational Leadership, 48,* 35–39.

Sternberg, R. J., & The Rainbow Project Collaborators. (2005). Augmenting the SAT through assessments of analytical, practical, and creative skills. In W. J. Camara & E. W. Kimmel (Eds.), *Choosing students* (pp. 159–176). Mahwah, NJ: Erlbaum.

Sternberg, R. J., Wagner, R. K., & Okagaki, L. (1993). Practical intelligence: The nature and role of tacit knowledge in work and at school. In H. Reese & J. Puckett (Eds.), *Advances in lifespan development* (pp. 205–227). Hillsdale, NJ: Erlbaum.

Sternberg, R. J., Wagner, R. K., Williams, W. M., & Horvath, J. A. (1995). Testing common sense. *American Psychologist, 50*(11), 912–927.

Torff, B., & Sternberg, R. J. (1998). Changing mind, changing world: Practical intelligence and tacit knowledge in adult learning. In R. Sternberg, C. M. Smith, & T. Pourchot (Eds.), *Adult learning and development: Perspectives from educational psychology* (pp. 109–126). Mahwah, NJ: Erlbaum.

Wagner, R. K., & Sternberg, R. J. (1985). Practical intelligence in real-world pursuits: Theory of tacit knowledge. *Journal of Personality and Social Psychology, 49,* 436–458.

Wagner, R. K., & Sternberg, R. J. (1986). Tacit knowledge and intelligence in the everyday world. In R. J. Sternberg & R. K. Wagner (Eds.), *Practical intelligence: Nature and origins of competence in the everyday world* (pp. 51–83). New York: Cambridge University Press.

Wagner, R. K., & Sternberg, R. J. (1991). *Tacit Knowledge Inventory for Managers (TKIM)*. New York: Psychological Corporation.

Yang, S-Y., & Sternberg, R. J. (1997). Taiwanese Chinese people's conceptions of intelligence. *Intelligence, 25,* 21–36.

JAMES C. KAUFMAN
*California State University, San Bernardino*

# INTELLIGENCE QUOTIENT

The intelligence quotient represents a measurement concept that was used extensively in the early days of intelligence testing but is less commonly used today. After Alfred Binet's death in 1911, Stern (1914) introduced the notion of a mental quotient, suggesting that the index of intellectual functioning derived from the Binet-Simon Scale could be expressed as the ratio of a test taker's mental age to his or her chronological age multiplied by 100 to eliminate decimals (MQ = $100 \times$ MA/CA). This MQ represented something about a person's rate of mental growth up to the time of the test. If examinees earned a mental age (MA) equivalent to chronological age (CA), their mental quotient (MQ) would be 100. An MQ of 100 represented average performance.

Working at Stanford University in California, Lewis M. Terman developed what was to become the most widely used American version of the Binet test, the Stanford-Binet. Terman (1916) incorporated Stern's notion of a mental quotient but renamed it, calling it a ratio intelligence quotient, or IQ.

The concept of the ratio intelligence quotient became increasingly popular, but it was used in a number of inappropriate ways. Its decline over the last quarter century can be attributed to a number of inherent characteristics that have been highly criticized by measurement specialists and practitioners.

Because the ratio intelligence quotient has minor differences in the magnitude of its standard deviation at various ages, a constant intelligence quotient from one age to another does not represent the same relative status. Similarly, even if the test taker's relative status remained the same from one year to another, the intelligence quotient would have to change. This suggests that intelligence quotients at different age levels are not comparable statistically (Tyler & Walsh, 1979). For example, a very bright child could obtain a higher IQ at age 12 than at age 6, even if the child's growth rate was unchanged. This difference would simply be due to the differences in the variability or standard deviations, with the variability of the IQ distribution being greater for 12 year olds than for 6 year olds.

Critics also point to the conceptual difficulty of the ratio intelligence quotient. For example, a 5 year old with a mental age of 6 and a 10 year old with a mental age of 12 would both have identical intelligence quotients of 120. However, the 6 year old is a year advanced in mental age while the 10 year old is 2 years advanced.

Another criticism of the intelligence quotient relates to its inability to describe adult intelligence (Tyler & Walsh, 1979). Critics suggest that like physical growth, adult mental growth lacks the predictable regularity characteristic of the mental development of children. Age standards lack meaning after the mid-teens, rendering mental age and therefore the intelligence quotient concept meaningless.

Owing to these criticisms of the ratio intelligence quo-tient, most major intelligence tests today yield IQs but not ratio intelligence quotients. For example, since the 1960 revision of the Stanford-Binet, the ratio intelligence quotient has been replaced by the deviation IQ. Major intelligence tests such as the Wechsler and McCarthy scales and the Kaufman Assessment Battery for Children (K-ABC) do not yield ratio intelligence quotients. However, several other intelligence tests in use today retain the concept of the ratio intelligence quotient, including the Leiter International Performance Scale, the Slosson Intelligence Test, and the Quick Test. Because of the inherent limitations of the ratio intelligence quotient, IQs yielded from these tests should be interpreted cautiously.

## REFERENCES

Stern, W. (1914). *The psychological methods of testing intelligence.* Baltimore: Warwick & York.

Terman, L. M. (1916). *The measurement of intelligence.* Boston: Houghton Mifflin.

Tyler, L. E., & Walsh, W. B. (1979). *Tests and measurements.* Englewood Cliffs, NJ: Prentice Hall.

MARK E. SWERDLIK
*Illinois State University*

DEVIATION IQ
IQ
RATIO IQ

# INTELLIGENCE TESTING, HISTORY OF

Intelligence testing, although called by many different names and used in many different forms, has been around for many centuries (Anastasi, 1982). The Chinese have been using mental tests for 3,000 years, and in the seventh and eighth centuries the Imperial Court established tests of speaking and writing and verbal and nonverbal reasoning that are similar to tasks on today's tests. The ancient Greeks, followers of Socrates, and universities in the Middle Ages, all developed methods of assessing intellectual skills.

As summarized by Kaufman (1983), the 1800s saw the beginning of the development of ideas about mental abilities and methods of measuring intelligence; these ideas formed the foundation for contemporary assessment. Not surprisingly, the scholars involved in the roots of intelligence testing were concerned with the two extremes of ability. Jean Esquirol in the early 1800s and Edouard Seguin in the mid-1800s, two French physicians, studied intelligence of mentally retarded individuals. Francis Galton, in the mid-to-late 1800s, focused on the ability of men of genius.

In the 1890s, James McKeen Cattell brought intelligence testing to the United States.

Esquirol's contributions included distinguishing between those people with very low intelligence, or the mentally retarded, and those people with emotional disturbances. He indicated that there is a hierarchy of retardation along a continuum, and coined terms like imbecile and idiot to describe different levels of mental deficiency. Although Esquirol studied several procedures, he concluded that a person's use of language is the most dependable criterion for determining intelligence, a philosophy that is apparent on many intelligence tests today.

Seguin rejected the notion that mental retardation is incurable and served as a pioneer in education for the mentally retarded. Unlike Esquirol, Seguin stressed the importance of sensory discrimination and motor control as aspects of intelligence. He developed procedures that were adopted by later developers of performance and nonverbal intelligence tests. An example is the Seguin Form board, which requires rapid placement of variously shaped blocks into their correct holes.

The English biologist Galton was primarily responsible for developing the first comprehensive individual intelligence test. As part of his research of men of genius and the heredity of intelligence, he administered tasks of sensory discrimination and sensory motor coordination in his Anthropometric Laboratory. His belief that intelligence comes to us through the senses led to the development of tasks such as weight discrimination, reaction time, strength of squeeze, and visual discrimination.

In the early 1890s, Cattell, an assistant in Galton's laboratory, established similar laboratories in the United States. During this time, Cattell used the term mental test for the first time in the psychological literature. Cattell shared Galton's view that intelligence is best measured through sensory tasks, but expanded his mentor's ideas by emphasizing that test administration must be standardized so that results are comparable from person to person and time to time.

In the early 1900s, significant advances were made in both individual and group intelligence testing (Sattler, 1982; Vane & Motta, 1984). In France, Alfred Binet, assisted by Theophile Simon and Victor Henri, rejected Galton's notions about the sensory and motor aspects of intelligence and claimed that tests of higher mental processes more effectively distinguish among the individual differences in people's intellectual abilities. This group developed numerous tests of complex intellectual functions such as memory, comprehension, imagination, and moral sentiments. The specific appointment by the French minister of public instruction to study the education of retarded children led to the development of the individually administered Binet-Simon Scale in 1905, constructed to separate mentally retarded and normal children in the Paris public schools. Two of the key aspects of Binet's approach to intelligence

testing were that he "discarded the specific test for the specific ability and took a group of tests which seemed to cover in general the chief psychological characteristics that go to make up intelligence. And, further, as the norm or standard of intelligence he took what the average child at each age could do" (Pintner & Patterson, 1925, p. 7).

The Binet-Simon Scale, including the 1911 revision that extended through adulthood, was almost immediately adapted and translated in the United States. The most successful revision was Terman's Stanford-Binet Scale in 1916. Terman carefully standardized his scale and introduced the application of the term intelligence quotient (mental age divided by chronological age multiplied by 100). The Stanford-Binet was widely adopted by individual examiners in the United States, and it is still popular today. The Binet was revised and restandardized in 1937, revised in 1960, and again restandardized in 1972. The ratio IQ, although retained in the 1937 Binet, was replaced by the deviation IQ (a standard score with a mean of 100 and standard deviation of 16) for the 1960 and 1972 Stanford-Binets. A thoroughly new version of the Binet was released in 2004.

David Wechsler, in 1939, was the first to challenge the Stanford-Binet monopoly on individual intelligence tests by publishing the Wechsler-Bellevue Scale. Wechsler, like Binet, included the concept of global intelligence in his scale, but instead of having one score, as did the Stanford-Binet, he included three scores: a verbal IQ, a performance IQ, and a full-scale IQ. Wechsler did not employ the methodology of the Stanford-Binet, which used a large number of brief and primarily verbal tasks. His scale was limited to a small number of longer tasks, half of them verbal and half nonverbal. Several versions of the Wechsler scales have been published since his Wechsler-Bellevue, and the types of tasks on later versions are virtually identical to the first scale. The main sources of Wechsler's verbal tasks were the Binet and the Army Group Examination Alpha; his performance tests came primarily from the Army Group Examination Beta and the Army Individual Performance Scale Examination.

The widespread use of group intelligence tests began, like the first Binet Scale, to meet a practical need (Anastasi, 1982). The entry of the United States into World War I in 1917 required a rapid means of classifying 1.5 million recruits for assignment into different types of training, discharge from service, and officer ability. A committee of the American Psychological Association, headed by Robert M. Yerkes, was directed to develop two group intelligence tests; these came to be known as the Army Alpha and Army Beta. The former, a verbal test modeled after the Binet, was designed for general use with literate recruits; the latter employed nonverbal items and was designed for illiterate recruits, or those recent immigrants who did not speak English well. (The Army Individual Performance Scale, mentioned previously, was given to those recruits who could not be tested validly on either the Army Alpha or Army Beta.)

The tests were released for civilian use soon after the war ended. Because of the belief that intelligence tests were better than teacher evaluations for identifying abilities, these tests became widely accepted in education (Vane & Motta, 1984). A short time after, revisions of the Army tests, as well as new group intelligence tests that used the Army tests as models, were being administered to thousands of preschool through graduate students all over the country, and to special adult groups such as employees or prisoners. The group format was attractive because it allowed the testing of many individuals simultaneously and it incorporated simple administration procedures that required little examiner training. The rapid growth of group intelligence testing resulted in the development of 37 group tests in only 5 years! (Pintner, 1923).

A new surge in group intelligence testing occurred in 1958, after the launching of Sputnik. The passage of the National Defense Education Act provided funds for states to test the abilities of schoolchildren and identify outstanding students. This testing was facilitated by the development of optical scanning for test scoring by Lindquist in 1955. Also in 1958, the National Merit Scholarship program was established to select exceptional high-school students. According to Vane and Motta (1984), another significant upturn in testing happened in the late 1970s, and this interest continues to this day.

Intelligence tests, both group and individual, are used in many different ways today. The largest users of intelligence tests are schools. Group intelligence tests are used at the preschool and kindergarten levels to distinguish children who are ready to participate in educational activities from those who need remedial preparation. At the elementary, middle, and high-school levels, group tests are used to identify exceptional students, and to aid in forming homogeneous ability groups within classrooms. Group intelligence tests are commonly used as one criterion for admission into colleges and universities. Individual intelligence tests have been administered for over half a century by well-trained clinicians for psychological, psychoeducational, and neuropsychological diagnosis. The passage of the Education of All Handicapped Children Act of 1975 (PL 94-142) and subsequent revisions resulted in the common use of individual intelligence tests as part of larger assessment batteries for the placement of children in special education programs for the mentally retarded, learning disabled, emotionally disturbed, and so forth, and for the development of individual educational programs for these children. However, the latest revision in 2004 signaled less reliance on testing and more reliance on prereferral intervention and alternate forms of assessment such as curriculum-based assessment. For adults, group and individual intelligence tests are used in a variety of settings, including business and industry, prisons, mental health centers, hospitals, and private clinical practice.

Group intelligence tests find their principal application in education, business, government, and military, in circumstances where it is feasible to obtain valid test data from many individuals at once; they are useful as well with individuals who are able to take a test by themselves without need of an examiner. In contrast, individual intelligence tests are used in clinics and special education centers, where an intensive study of individual clients is needed and a trained examiner is necessary to secure valid test results. The reasons for using group and individual tests are many and provide a basis for understanding the type of information provided by the two testing formats. A summary of these reasons, as reported by Anastasi (1982), follows.

Group tests can be administered to a large number of individuals at the same time by using booklets of printed items and forms for the examinee to indicate his or her answer. The training and experience required by the examiner is minimal, as most group tests only require the examiner to read simple instructions and accurately keep time. The minimal role of the examiner in group testing provides more uniform testing conditions than in individual testing.

Objective scoring is a key aspect of group tests. Test items are usually multiple choice, true-false, or some other type that produces responses that can be scored as correct or incorrect with no deliberation. Items on group tests can usually be scored by a clerk or a computer. In addition, group tests typically include answer sheets, separate from the test booklets that contain the items, allowing economical reuse of test booklets.

Because group tests can be administered to large groups of individuals at the same time, larger numbers of individuals can be used in the standardization programs for group tests than for individual tests. Group test norms are generally better established because they are based on standardization samples of 100,000 to 200,000 instead of the 1,000 to 4,000 used for individual tests.

On the other hand, individual intelligence tests have several characteristics that make them suitable for a variety of clinical purposes. In individual testing, the examiner has the opportunity to obtain cooperation, establish rapport, and enhance motivation of the examinee. The trained examiner in individual testing detects, reports, and uses in the interpretation of test scores the many characteristics of the examinee that may affect test performance such as anxiety, fatigue, and problem-solving style. In addition, some individuals such as emotionally disturbed and mentally retarded children and adults may perform better on individual tests than on group tests. Since most group tests require the examinee to read instructions and test items, individually administered tests, which demand little or no reading, are especially useful for learning-disabled and retarded individuals, and others who may have reading problems.

Individual intelligence tests, because they typically include short questions that require oral and open-ended responses, allow examinees to give creative and original responses to items. In individual testing, examinees are not limited to selecting one of four multiple choice answers or indicating if an item is true or false. The contents of an examinee's response on an individual intelligence test can therefore be analyzed in order to generate hypotheses about, for example, the examinee's creativity, style of thinking, cognitive development, or defense mechanisms.

Another aspect of individual intelligence testing concerns the flexibility of administration. On a group test, an examinee is required to respond to all items, or as many items as he or she can in a certain time limit. On an individual test, testing time is more effectively used because the examinee is administered only those items in the range appropriate to his or her ability level. This characteristic of individual tests helps avoid the boredom an examinee may have when working on items that are too easy or the frustration of working on items that are too difficult.

Intelligence testing has been a controversial topic since the 1960s (Kaufman, 1979). The most pressing issues that are debated within both professional and public forums concern test bias, the influence of heredity versus environment on IQ, race differences in test scores, and disproportionate placement of minority children into special education classes such as those for the retarded or gifted. These issues have been the subject of research, debate, federal guidelines, laws, and lawsuits. Just as major law cases differ on whether intelligence tests are unfair to minority children (*Larry P.* v. *Riles; PASE* decision in Chicago), so do professionals in the field of intelligence testing continue to disagree on these issues. It is likely that the future will be filled with arguments on the appropriate use of intelligence tests (Fletcher & Reschly, 2005; Kavale, Kaufman, Naglieri, & Hale, 2005) and claims that they should be banned; at the same time, it is equally certain that there will continue to be a proliferation of new and revised instruments of both the individual and group variety.

## REFERENCES

Anastasi, A. (1982). *Psychological testing* (5th ed.). New York: Macmillan.

Fletcher, J., & Reschly, D. J. (2005). Changing procedures for identifying learning disabilities: The danger of perpetually old ideas. *The School Psychologist, 59,* 1, 10–15.

Kaufman, A. S. (1979). *Intelligent testing with the WISC-R.* New York: Wiley.

Kaufman, A. S. (1983). Intelligence: Old concepts—new perspectives. In G. W. Hynd (Ed.), *The school psychologist: An introduction* (pp. 95–117). Syracuse, NY: Syracuse University Press.

Kavale, K., Kaufman, A. S., Naglieri, J. A., & Hale, J. B. (2003). Changing procedures for identifying learning disabilities: The danger of poorly supported ideas. *The School Psychologist, 59,* 1, 16–25.

Pintner, R. (1923). *Intelligence testing.* New York: Holt, Rinehart, & Winston.

Pintner, R., & Patterson, D. G. (1925). *A scale of performance.* New York: Appleton.

Sattler, J. M. (1982). *Assessment of children's intelligence and special abilities* (2nd ed.). Boston: Allyn & Bacon.

Thorndike, R. L. (1985, April). *An introduction to the revised Stanford-Binet for school psychology educators.* Paper presented at the conference of the Trainers of School Psychologists, Las Vegas, NV.

Vane, T. R., & Motta, R. W. (1984). Group intelligence tests. In G. Goldstein & M. Hersen (Eds.), *Handbook of psychological assessment* (pp. 100–116). New York: Pergamon.

ALAN S. KAUFMAN
*Yale University Medical School*

PATTI L. HARRISON
*University of Alabama*

# INTELLIGENCE
# INTELLIGENCE QUOTIENT
# INTELLIGENT TESTING
# SEE SPECIFIC TESTS

# INTELLIGENCE TESTING

The practice of formally testing skills and abilities dates back nearly 3,000 years (Wang, 1993). Moreover, individual differences in human performance have been discussed among history's greatest thinkers, including Socrates, Plato, and Darwin. Despite a history of interest in exploring human abilities, standardized and validated intelligence tests first were developed in 1905 by Binet and Simon to help predict how well children would achieve in school (French & Hale, 1990). Since then, the intelligence testing movement has gained considerable momentum as a result of the need to differentiate among individuals when providing educational services (French & Hale, 1990).

Intelligence testing is a means to observe the actual performance of individuals under standardized conditions. Its purpose is to accurately assess cognitive strengths and weaknesses. However, individual scores are samples of behavior. In addition, many other nonintellective factors influence everyday functioning and behavior. As a result, intelligence testing is used to make inferences and predictions about an individual's ability rather than serve as a direct indicator of the traits and capacities of an individual (Sattler, 1992).

Standardized measures of intelligence are used by psychologists on a daily basis. Data from intelligence tests often are used to predict school performance, especially achievement. Intelligence tests do this fairly well (Neisser et al., 1996). Approximately 25 percent of the variance associated with achievement can be attributed to intelligence. Although 75 percent of the variance in school performance can be attributed to other factors, intelligence testing remains the best single predictor of academic performance (Sattler, 1993). Further, although intelligence test scores may fluctuate due to changes in environment and quality of schooling, they are quite stable over time (Kamphaus, 2001; Neisser et al., 1996).

In addition to their predictive validity, intelligence tests provide several other benefits to students, adults, educators, and researchers. They may reveal unsuspected or unnoticed talents in children and adults that may positively impact their educational and vocational success. Similarly, tests may provide information about areas of weakness that may guide early intervention efforts. By providing a profile of strengths and weaknesses, intelligence tests may help teachers and parents develop individualized interventions to promote a child's development (Sattler, 1993).

Classroom assessments and observations provide educators and parents with information about a student's ability. However, this information is collected in relation to students in the same classroom or district. Standardized tests provide educators with an accurate method of comparing one child's performance to his or her peers nationally. In this sense, intelligence tests may be considered as a measure of an individual's ability to compete and achieve economically and socially in society. Finally, intelligence tests provide useful insight into cultural and biological differences among individuals (Sattler, 1993).

Despite the apparent benefits of intelligence testing, their use has been criticized. Some racial/ethnic groups differ in mean IQs. For example, compared to mean IQs for White/nonHispanics, those for Blacks and Hispanics are lower and those for Asian-Americans are higher (Neisser et al., 1996). Consequently, some conclude intelligence tests are culturally biased and promote racism. However, mean differences do not necessarily indicate bias. When considering intelligence tests as predictors of performance, most researchers agree intelligence tests are not biased in that they predict behaviors similarly for all groups (Neisser et al., 1996; Valdes & Figueroa, 1994). Nonetheless, critics argue that mean IQ differences lead to overrepresentation of some minority children in special education classes and the overrepresentation of White, middle- to upper-class children in gifted and talented programs.

In response to such criticisms, test developers have attempted to preserve the utility of intelligence tests through revisions that better reflect the abilities of individuals from diverse backgrounds. As a result, some nonverbal and newly revised intelligence tests claim to have smaller racial differences and therefore may be perceived as less biased.

Additional criticisms include the importance placed on scores obtained from a single test administration, the negative stigma associated with a low score, and that they assess a narrow range of intellectual abilities (Sattler, 1993). Moreover, some disagreement exists as to the nature of the construct of intelligence. For these and other reasons, intelligence testing may be disregarded among some psychologists and educators (Papanastasiou, 1999).

Although these criticisms should not be ignored, substantial empirical data support intelligence testing. Intelligence tests have considerable value in assessing processing abilities and guiding intervention design (e.g., memory deficits, processing speed deficits). The use of intelligence tests also continues to be of considerable value when assessing developmental delays, brain injury, gifted, and mental disabilities.

## REFERENCES

French, J. L., & Hale, R. L. (1990). A history of the development of psychological and educational testing. In C. R. Reynolds & R. W. Kamphaus (Eds.), *Handbook of psychological and educational assessment of children* (p. 3–28). New York: Guilford.

Kamphaus, R. W. (2001). *Clinical assessment of children's intelligence* (2nd ed.). Needham Heights, MA: Allyn & Bacon.

Neisser, U., Boodoo, G., Bouchard, T. J., Boykin, A. W., Brody, N., Ceci, S. J., et al. (1996). Intelligence: Knowns and unknowns. *American Psychologist, 51*(2), 77–101.

Papanastasiou, E. C. (1999). *Intelligence: Theories and testing.* (ERIC Document Reproduction Service No. ED441859)

Sattler, J. M. (1993). *Assessment of children: Revised and updated* (3rd ed.). San Diego: Jerome M. Sattler.

Valdes, G., & Figueroa, R. A. (1994). *Bilingualism and testing: A special case of bias.* Norwood, NJ: Ablex.

Wang, Z. M. (1993). Psychology in China: A review dedicated to Li Chen. *Annual Review of Psychology, 44,* 87–116.

ERIC ROSSEN
*University of Florida*

## INTELLIGENCE INTELLIGENT TESTING

## INTELLIGENCE, TRIARCHIC THEORY OF

The triarchic theory of intelligence extends research and practice on the subject of human intelligence. In contrast to traditional intelligence theories, particularly the general or *g* theory of intelligence (Spearman, 1946), the triarchic theory provides an expanded conception of intelligence. While similar to other efforts to broaden explanations of human abilities, such as Gardner's (1983) multiple intelligence theory, the triarchic theory of intelligence focuses on three specific components of intellectual functioning. Those three components are: (1) analytic intelligence (the ability to critique, to judge, to evaluate, to assess), (2) practical intelligence (the ability to apply, to use, to implement) and (3) creative intelligence (the ability to invent, to imagine, to predict; Sternberg, 2003b).

The Sternberg Triarchic Abilities Test (STAT) was developed to measure the three components of intellectual functioning. Researchers (Sternberg et al., 2005) have demonstrated that the STAT test has construct validity and is useful in assessing learning outcomes of teaching aimed at promoting analytic, practical, and creative abilities in the classroom. Successful intellectual functioning seems to result from a balance of each of the three components. For instance, teaching that is targeted on emphasizing each component has resulted in increased scores on traditional measures of student performance, such as the SAT (Sternberg, 2003a). In addition, Sternberg and his colleagues (Sternberg, Torff, & Grigorenko, 1998) have found that students who received instruction balancing analytic, practical, and creative abilities outperformed students who received more traditional instruction on assessments of memory and performance. Additional studies (see Sternberg et al., 2005 for a summary) suggest this type of triarchically based measure yields stronger predictive validity for college GPA than high school GPA or the SAT.

The triarchic theory of intelligence holds key epistemological implications and offers pedagogical, curriculum, and policy recommendations for teaching and instructional leadership. Because the triarchic theory of intelligence highlights experience as legitimate knowledge, the very concept that practical knowledge gained through action and the involvement of the senses is a valid component of intelligence may in fact eventually broaden our expectations of what students should know and be able to do in school, college, and in preparation for the workforce.

In addition, because schools often place a higher priority on teaching for analytic intelligence than practical and creative intelligence, the triarchic theory of intelligence enriches our understanding that a more complete education would focus on a broader approach to cultivating students' intellectual abilities. Emphasis on a wider range of intellectual abilities would help address concerns raised by creativity scholars (e.g., Csikszentmihalyi, 2003) who have criticized schooling for stifling creativity by stressing the transmission of domain knowledge (focusing on analytic abilities), instead of producing novel knowledge (creative abilities). Finally, given that past research has shown that an analytic-abilities teaching style in public schools tends to favor learning styles of Caucasian students (Sternberg et al., 2005), the STAT may hold keys for broadening equity in our school systems for students of color. To summarize, the triarchic theory of intelligence, comprised of analytic intelligence (the ability to critique, to judge, to evaluate, to assess), practical intelligence (the ability to apply, to use, to implement), and creative intelligence (the ability to invent, to imagine, to predict) offers educators an expanded way to conceptualize intelligence that embraces success for all students.

**REFERENCES**

Csikszentmihalyi, M. (2003). Key issues in creativity and development. In R. K. Sawyer, V. John-Steiner, S. Moran, R. J. Stern-

berg, O. H. Feldman, H. Gardner, J. Nakamura, & M. Csikszentmihalyi (Eds.), *Creativity and development* (pp. 149–162). New York: Oxford University Press.

Gardner, H. (1983). *Frames of mind: The theory of multiple intelligences.* New York: Basic Books.

Spearman, C. (1946). Theory of general factor. *British Journal of Psychology, 36,* 117–131.

Sternberg, R. J., Birney, D., Bridgeman, B., Cianciolo, A., Camara, W., & Drebot, M. et al. (2005). *The Rainbow project: Enhancing the SAT through assessments of analytical, practical, and creative skills* (pp. 1–76). Unpublished manuscript.

Sternberg, R. J., Torff, B., & Grigorenko, E. L. (1998). Teaching triarchically improves school achievement. *Journal of Educational Psychology, 90*(3), 374–384.

Sternberg, R. J. (2003a). Creative thinking in the classroom. *Scandinavian Journal of Educational Research, 47*(3), 325–338.

Sternberg, R. J. (2003b). What is an "expert student?" *Educational Researcher, 23*(8), 5–9.

JEN KATZ-BUONINCONTRO
*University of Oregon*

## INTELLIGENT TESTING

Intelligent testing is a philosophy or model of assessment widely espoused and best represented in the writings of Kaufman et al. (Kaufman, 1979, 1994; Kaufman & Kaufman, 1977; Kaufman & Lichtenberger, 1999; Reynolds & Clark, 1982; Reynolds & Kaufman, 1986). The intent of the intelligent testing model is to bring together empirical data, psychometrics, clinical acumen, psychological theory, and careful reasoning to build an assessment of an individual leading to the derivation of an intervention to improve the life circumstances of the subject. The promulgation of this philosophy was prompted by many factors, but particularly extremist approaches to the use of tests.

Conventional intelligence tests and even the entire concept of intelligence testing have been the focus of considerable controversy for several decades. Always the subject of scrutiny, the past two decades have witnessed intelligence tests placed on trial in the federal courts (*Larry P.,* 1979; *PASE,* 1980), state legislatures (New York's "trust-in-testing" legislation), the lay press, and open scholarly forums (Reynolds & Brown, 1984). At one extreme are issues such as those brought up by Hilliard (1984), who contends that IQ tests are inherently unacceptable measurement devices with no real utility. At the other extreme are such well-known figures as Herrnstein (1973) and Jensen (1980), who believe the immense value of intelligence tests is self-evident. While critics of testing demand a moratorium on their use with children, psychologists often are forced to adhere to rigid administrative rules that require the use of precisely obtained IQs when making placements or diagnostic decisions. No consideration is given to basic psychometric principles including measurement error (Reynolds, 1999), the influence of behavioral variables on performance, or appropriate sensitivity to the child's cultural or linguistic heritage.

A middle ground is sorely needed. Tests must be preserved, along with their rich clinical heritage and their prominent place in the neurological, psychological, and educational literature. At the same time, the proponents of tests need to be less defensive and more open to rational criticism of the current popular instruments. Knowledge of the weaknesses as well as the strengths of individually administered intelligence tests can serve the dual functions of improving examiners' ability to interpret profiles of any given instrument and enabling examiners to select pertinent supplementary tests and subtests to secure a thorough assessment of the intellectual abilities of any child, adolescent, or adult referred for evaluation. The quality of individual mental assessment is no longer simply a question answered in terms of an instrument's empirical or psychometric characteristics. High reliability and validity coefficients, a meaningful factor structure, and normative data obtained by stratified random-sampling techniques do not ensure that an intelligence test is valuable for all or even most assessment purposes. The skills and training of the psychologist engaged in using intelligence tests will certainly interact with the utility of intelligence testing beyond the level of simple actuarial prediction of academic performance. Intelligent testing provides an appropriate model.

With low-IQ children, the primary role of the intelligent tester is to use the test results to develop a means of intervention that will "beat" the prediction made by global IQs. A plethora of research during the twentieth century has amply demonstrated that very low-IQ children show concomitantly low levels of academic attainment. The clinical purpose of administering an intelligence test to a low-IQ child, then, is at least twofold: (1) to determine that the child is indeed at high risk for academic failure, and (2) to articulate a set of learning circumstances that defeat the prediction. For individuals with average or high IQs, the specific tasks of the intelligence tester may change, but the philosophy remains the same. When evaluating a learning-disabled (LD) child, for example, the task is primarily one of fulfilling the prediction made by the global IQs. Most LD children exhibit average or better general intelligence, but have a history of academic performance significantly below what would be predicted from their intelligence test performance. The intelligent tester takes on the responsibility of preventing the child from becoming an "outlier" in the prediction (i.e., he or she must design a set of environmental conditions that will cause the child to achieve and learn at the level predicted by the intelligence test).

When psychologists engage in intelligent testing, the child or adult becomes the primary focus of the evaluation and the tests fade into the background as only vehicles to understanding. The test setting becomes completely examinee oriented. Interpretation and communication of test results in the context of the individual's particular background, referral behaviors, and approach to performance on diverse tasks constitute the crux of competent evaluation. Global test scores are deemphasized; flexibility, a broad base of knowledge in psychology, and insight on the part of the psychologist are demanded. The intelligence test becomes a dynamic helping agent, not an instrument for labeling, placement in dead-end programs, or disillusionment on the part of eager, caring teachers and parents.

Intelligent testing through individualization becomes the key to accomplishment; it is antithetical to the development of computerized or depersonalized form reporting for individually administered cognitive tests such as espoused by Alcorn and Nicholson (1975) and Vitelli and Goldblatt (1979) (Reynolds, 1980a, 1980b). For intelligent testers, it is imperative to be sensitive and socially aware, and to be aware that intelligence and cognition do not constitute the total human being. The intelligence testing model is inconsistent with "checklist" approaches to the development of individual education plans (IEPs). It is a mode of true individualization and does not lend itself to mimeographed IEPs that are checked off, or to special education programs where all children are taught with the same methodology. Computer-generated reports with "individualized" recommendations are anathema to the intelligent testing philosophy.

Intelligent testing urges the use of contemporary measures of intelligence as necessary to achieve a true understanding of the individual's intellectual functioning. The approach to test interpretation under this philosophy has been likened to the approach of a psychological detective (Kaufman, 1979, 1994). It requires melding of clinical skill, mastery of psychometrics and measurement, and extensive knowledge of cognitive development and intelligence. A far more extensive treatment of this approach to test interpretation appears in the book *Intelligent Testing with the WISC-R* (Kaufman, 1979), a volume updated in 1994 by Kaufman to apply directly to the WISC-III. The philosophy is not, however, test-specific. Discussion of applications of this philosophy to preschool children may be found in Kaufman and Kaufman (1977) and Reynolds and Clark (1982).

Clinical skills with children are obviously important to the intelligent tester in building rapport and maintaining the proper ambiance during the actual testing. Although adhering to standardized procedures and obtaining valid scores are important, the child must remain the lodestar of the evaluation. Critical to the dynamic understanding of the child's performance is close, insightful observation and recordings of behavior during the testing period. Fully half of the important information gathered during the administration of an intelligence test comes from observing behavior under a set of standard conditions. Behavior at various points in the course of the assessment often will dictate the proper interpretation of test scores. Many individuals earn IQs of 100, but each in a different manner, with infinite nuances of behavior interacting directly with a person's test performance.

Knowledge and skill in psychometrics and measurement are requisite to intelligent testing (Reynolds, 1999). The clinical evaluation of test performance must be directed by careful analyses of the statistical properties of the test scores, the internal psychometric characteristics of the test, and the data regarding their relationship to external factors. As one example, difference scores have long been of inherent interest for psychologists, especially between subparts of an intelligence scale. Difference scores are unreliable, and small discrepancies between levels of performance may be best attributed to measurement error. If large enough, however, difference scores can provide valuable information regarding the choice of an appropriate remedial or therapeutic program. The psychometric characteristics of the tests in question dictate the size of the differences needed for statistical confidence in their reflecting real rather than chance fluctuations. Interpretation of subscale differences often requires integrating clinical observations of the child's behavior with data on the relationship of the test scores to other factors, and with theories of intelligence, but only after first establishing that the differences are real and not based on error.

One major limitation of most contemporary intelligence tests is their lack of foundation in theories of intelligence, whether these theories are based on research in neuropsychology, cognitive information processing, factor analysis, learning theory, or other domains. Nevertheless, many profiles obtained by children and adults on intelligence tests are interpretable from diverse theoretical perspectives, and can frequently be shown to display a close fit to one or another theoretical approach to intelligence. Theories then become useful in developing a full understanding of the individual. Competing theories of intelligence abound (Kaufman, 1994; Reynolds, 1981; Vernon, 1979; White, 1979).

Well-grounded, empirically evaluated models of intellectual functioning enable one to reach a broader understanding of the examinee and to make specific predictions regarding behavior outside of the testing situation. Predictions will not always be correct; however, the intelligent tester has an excellent chance of making sense out of the predictable individual variations in behavior, cognitive skills, and academic performance by involving the nomothetic framework provided by theory. The alternative often is to be stymied or forced to rely on trial-and-error or anecdotal, illusionary relationships when each new set of profile fluctuations is encountered. Theories, even speculative ones, are more efficient guides to developing hypotheses for understanding and treating problems than are purely clinical impressions, armchair speculations, or clinical anecdotes.

Through the elements of clinical skill, psychometric sophistication, and a broad base of knowledge of theories of individual differences emerges intelligent testing. None is sufficient, yet, when properly implemented, these elements engage in a synergistic interaction to produce the greatest possible understanding. The intelligent testing model places a series of requirements on the test but also on the tester; not every test can be used intelligently nor can everyone be an intelligent tester. The examiner's breadth of knowledge of psychometrics, differential psychology, child development, and other areas is crucial. Equally, the test must have multiple scales that are reliable, with good validity evidence, and be standardized on a sufficiently large, nationally stratified random sample. The test must offer the opportunity for good clinical observations. Without all of these characteristics, intelligent testing is unlikely to take place; when it does, however, the child is certain to benefit.

## REFERENCES

Herrnstein, R. (1973). *IQ in the meritocracy*. Boston: Little, Brown.

Hilliard, A. G. (1984). IQ testing as the emperor's new clothes: A critique of Jensen's bias in mental testing. In C. R. Reynolds & R. T. Brown (Eds.), *Perspectives on bias in mental testing*. New York: Plenum.

Jensen, A. R. (1980). *Bias in mental testing*. New York: The Free Press.

Kaufman, A. S. (1979). *Intelligent testing with the WISC-R*. New York: Wiley-Interscience.

Kaufman, A. S. (1994). *Intelligent testing with the WISC-III*. New York: Wiley.

Kaufman, A. S., & Kaufman, N. L. (1977). *Clinical evaluation of young children with the McCarthy scales*. New York: Grune & Stratton.

Kaufman, A. S., & Lichtenberger, L. (1999). Intellectual assessment. In C. R. Reynolds (Ed.), *Assessment*, Vol. 4 of M. Hersen & A. Bellack (Eds.), *Comprehensive clinical psychology*. Oxford, England: Elsevier Science.

Reynolds, C. R. (1980a). Two commercial interpretive systems for the WISC-R. *School Psychology Review, 9*, 385–386.

Reynolds, C. R. (1980b). Review of the TARDOR interpretive scoring system for the WISC-R. *Measurement & Evaluation in Guidance, 14*, 46–48.

Reynolds, C. R. (1981). The neuropsychological basis of intelligence. In G. W. Hynd & J. E. Obrzut (Eds.), *Psychoeducational assessment of the school aged child: Issues and procedures*. New York: Grune & Stratton.

Reynolds, C. R. (1999). Fundamentals of measurement and assessment in psychology. In C. R. Reynolds (Ed.), *Assessment*, Vol. 4 of M. Hersen & A. Bellack (Eds.), *Comprehensive clinical psychology*. Oxford, England: Elsevier Science.

Reynolds, C. R., & Brown, R. T. (Eds.). (1984). *Perspectives on bias in mental testing*. New York: Plenum.

Reynolds, C. R., & Clark, J. H. (1982). Cognitive assessment of the preschool child. In K. Paget & B. Bracken (Eds.), *Psychoeducational assessment of preschool and primary aged children*. New York: Grune & Stratton.

Reynolds, C. R., & Kaufman, A. S. (1986). Assessment of children's intelligence with the Wechsler scales. In B. Wolman (Ed.), *Handbook of intelligence*. New York: Wiley-Interscience.

Vernon, P. A. (1979). *Intelligence: Heredity and environment*. San Francisco: Freeman.

Vitelli, R., & Goldblatt, R. (1979). *The TARDOR interpretive scoring system for the WISC-R*. Manchester, CT: TARDOR.

White, W. (Ed.). (1979). Intelligence [Special issue]. *Journal of Research & Development in Education, 12*(1).

CECIL R. REYNOLDS
*Texas A&M University*

CULTURAL BIAS IN TESTING
INTELLIGENCE TESTING
KAUFMAN, ALAN S.
REMEDIATION, DEFICIT-CENTERED MODELS OF
SEQUENTIAL AND SIMULTANEOUS COGNITIVE
   PROCESSING

# INTERACTIVE LANGUAGE DEVELOPMENT

The notion of interactive language development has its roots in the philosophy of pragmatism and in child language pragmatics research. Pragmatics refers to the study of the social uses of language and research in the area of pragmatic language development in children. It is concerned primarily with three major focuses: (1) understanding how children learn to adapt their language to various linguistic and nonlinguistic contexts; (2) tracking development relative to the increasing repertoire of language functions; and (3) determining the role of social context in facilitating various aspects of language development (Bates, 1976; Prutting, 1982).

Interactive language development approaches rely heavily on social psychological research involving the study of adult-child interaction. Rees (1982) found a recurring theme in this literature: that pragmatic considerations have a prominent role in language acquisition "not only as a set of skills to be acquired but as motivating and explanatory factors for the acquisition of the language itself" (p. 8). Rees argues that pragmatic interactional factors assume an important role in the child's mastery of native language. Interactional factors may be seen as the source or origin of language in the child. Bruner (1975) cites the interaction between mother and infant during the first year of life, particularly in shared attention objects, people, and events of interest, as the basis of the child's capacity for reference and more broadly for meaning that eventually characterizes the human use of symbols.

Second, pragmatic interactional factors may be seen as the motivation for language learning as exemplified in the research of Halliday (1975) and Bates (1976). These researchers demonstrate how communicative functions emerge prior to the acquisition of linguistic skills. In addition to forming the basis for the development of particular linguistic structures, pragmatic interactional factors explain the development of linguistic style and code switching ability. As Rees (1982) notes, "language users typically control a range of style and code variants that are appropriate to particular listeners and particular settings, and they use these variants in establishing and maintaining social role relationships. . . . " (p. 10). Children as young as 3 or 4 years have been found to use different styles or "registers" for speaking to their parents, siblings, friends, strangers, younger and older children (Gleason, 1973; Snow & Ferguson, 1977).

As descriptions of the acquisition of pragmatic interactional abilities increased in the normal child language literature, language and communication practitioners began to develop pragmatically based assessment and intervention programs for disordered children (Prinz, 1982). Professionals involved in the treatment of language-disordered children stressed the importance of viewing communication as an interpersonal behavior that occurs in interaction with the environment. The interactional component, in which language is used to establish and maintain contact with other persons, is an integral part of many current intervention programs for language-disabled children. Specific procedures have been developed to facilitate the child's communication with the environment, including initiating and sustaining communicative interactions with others, consideration of a listener's perspective when encoding messages, and appropriate responses to listener feedback indicating a lack of understanding. Procedures for pragmatic interactional language treatment are discussed in Wilcox (1982).

## REFERENCES

Bates, E. (1976). Pragmatics and sociolinguistics in child language. In D. Morehead & A. Morehead (Eds.), *Normal and deficient child language* (pp. 247–307). Baltimore: University Park Press.

Bruner, J. (1975). The ontogenesis of speech acts. *Journal of Child Language, 2,* 1–20.

Gleason, J. (1973). Code-switching in children's language. In T. Moore (Ed.), *Cognitive development and the acquisition of language* (pp. 167–169). New York: Academic.

Halliday, M. (1975). *Learning how to mean*. London: Arnold.

Prinz, P. M. (1982). Development of pragmatics: Multi-word level. In J. V. Irwin (Ed.), *Pragmatics: The role in language development*. La Verne, CA: Fox Point and University of La Verne Press.

Prutting, C. (1982). Pragmatics as social competence. *Journal of Speech & Hearing Disorders, 47,* 123–134.

Rees, N. (1982). An overview of pragmatics or what is in the box? In J. V. Irwin (Ed.), *Pragmatics: The role in language develop-*

*ment* (pp. 15–27). La Verne, CA: Fox Point and University of La Verne Press.

Snow, C., & Ferguson, C. (1977). *Talking to children: Language input and acquisition.* Cambridge, England: Cambridge University Press.

Wilcox, M. (1982). The integration of pragmatics into language therapy. In J. V. Irwin (Ed.), *Pragmatics: The role in language development* (pp. 29–48). La Verne, CA: Fox Point and University of La Verne Press.

PHILIP M. PRINZ
*Pennsylvania State University*

COMMUNICATION DISORDERS
LANGUAGE THERAPY
PRAGMATICS AND PRAGMATIC COMMUNICATION
   DISORDERS
SOCIAL LEARNING THEORY
THEORY OF ACTIVITY

# INTERDISCIPLINARY TEAMS

Before any child receives special education services, he or she must receive an individual assessment to identify areas of educational need, determine the child's aptitude for achievement, and identify other factors that might be interfering with school performance. This individual assessment is the basis for all instructional planning. With the advent of the Education for All Handicapped Children Act of 1975 (PL 94-142) came the requirement that an interdisciplinary team (IDT), also known as a multidisciplinary team (MDT), be used to determine pupil eligibility for special education services. Public agencies assessing children suspected of having a disability must include the individuals identified by regulations as necessary for an individualized education program (IEP) team, specifically:

1. The parents of the child;
2. At least one regular education teacher of the child (if the child is, or may be, participating in the regular education environment);
3. At least one special education teacher of the child, or if appropriate, at least one special education provider of the child;
4. A representative of the public agency who—
   (i) Is qualified to provide, or supervise the provision of, specially designed instruction to meet the unique needs of children with disabilities;
   (ii) Is knowledgeable about the general curriculum; and
   (iii) Is knowledgeable about the availability of resources of the public agency;
5. An individual who can interpret the instructional implications of evaluation results, who may be a member

of the team described in paragraphs (2) through (6) of this section;
6. At the discretion of the parent or the agency, other individuals who have knowledge or special expertise regarding the child, including related services personnel as appropriate; and
7. If appropriate, the child;

(34 C.F.R. §300.344), plus "other qualified professionals, as appropriate" (34 C.F.R. §300.533). The proposed regulations issued in June of 2005 make only nonsubstantive changes to these requirements (70 Fed. Reg. 35866).

The IDT is required by the regulations to review all relevant evaluation data on the child, including:

1. Evaluations and information provided by the parents of the child;
2. Current classroom-based assessments and observations; and
3. Observations by teachers and related services providers.

(34 C.F.R. §300.533). On the basis of this information and input from the child's parents, the team identifies any additional data that may be needed to determine the child's present level of performance and needs; arranges for the administration of any tests needed; and determines whether the child is indeed eligible for special education and related services.

Since PL 94-142 and subsequently the IDEA, IDTs have become incorporated into the organizational routine of most school systems in the United States. Nevertheless, school professionals, parents, and the general public have expressed differing views regarding their value (Masters & Mori, 1986).

The IDT model is often cited as the organizational unit best suited to making evaluation and programming decisions because the different perspectives made possible by it prevent biased eligibility and placement decisions (Abelson & Woodman, 1983). However, there is no empirical evidence to support the use of teams. Ballard-Campbell and Semmel (1981) suggest forces such as litigation, parental and educator opinions, and state-level administrative practices, rather than research evidence, have been responsible for the spread of interdisciplinary practices.

Indeed, recent research findings concerning the effectiveness of the IDT model are discouraging. According to Ysseldyke (1983), the IDT model uses conceptual definitions that have not been translated into scientific or practical assessment procedures.

While IDT functioning has been widely researched, the results have been mixed; some inquiries into whether IDTs make better decisions than individuals have revealed few differences between decisions made by IDTs and those made by individual decision makers (Pfeiffer, 1982). Some researchers (Pfeiffer & Naglieri, 1983) have demonstrated that teams make more consistent and less variable decisions than do individuals. Interpretive and methodological differences between positive and negative studies make it difficult to arrive at definitive answers.

## REFERENCES

Abelson, M. A., & Woodman, R. W. (1983). Review of research on team effectiveness: Implications for teams in schools. *School Psychology Review, 12*(2), 125–138.

Ballard-Campbell, M., & Semmel, M. I. (1981). Policy research and special education issues affecting policy research and implementation. *Exceptional Education Quarterly, 2*, 59–68.

Masters, L. F., & Mori, A. A. (1986). *Teaching secondary students with mild learning and behavior problems*. Rockville, MD: Aspen.

Pfeiffer, S. I. (1982). Special education placement decisions made by teams and individuals. *Psychology in the Schools, 19*, 335–340.

Pfeiffer, S. I., & Naglieri, J. A. (1983). An investigation of multidisciplinary team decision-making. *Journal of Learning Disabilities, 15*(10), 586–590.

Ysseldyke, J. E. (1983). Current practices in making psychoeducational decisions about learning disabled students. *Journal of Learning Disabilities, 16*(4), 226–233.

JOSEPH M. RUSSO
*Hunter College, City University of New York*
Second edition

KIMBERLY F. APPLEQUIST
*University of Colorado at Colorado Springs*
Third edition

## INDIVIDUALS WITH DISABILITIES EDUCATION IMPROVEMENT ACT OF 2004 (IDEIA)

MULTIDISCIPLINARY TEAMS

## INTERMITTENT REINFORCEMENT

Reinforcement is the increase in the frequency of a response following the presentation of something pleasant (e.g., increase in homework completion following verbal praise from a parent) or the removal of something unpleasant or aversive (e.g., increase in screaming following the removal of difficult math work). A reinforcement schedule refers to how frequently a reinforcer will be delivered and there are two basic schedules of reinforcement: continuous and intermittent. Continuous reinforcement involves reinforcing the student's behavior or response each time it occurs whereas intermittent reinforcement involves reinforcing the behavior or response on some occasions but not others (Chance, 1999). In schools, the majority of student behavior is reinforced under intermittent schedules as it is typically impossible to reinforce each appropriate academic or social behavior that a student exhibits. More specifically, continuous schedules of reinforcement are best used when students are learning new behaviors or responses. In contrast, intermittent schedules are more appropriate to use when maintaining behavior over time (Kazdin, 2000).

There are four different types of intermittent schedules of reinforcement: fixed interval, variable interval, fixed ratio, and variable ratio. Interval schedules involve reinforcing behavior related to time whereas ratio schedules involve reinforcing behavior related to the frequency of responses (Alberto & Troutman, 2003). In the research literature, the name of a reinforcement schedule is often shortened (i.e., fixed interval = FI, variable interval = VI, fixed ratio = FR, and variable ratio = VR). In addition, the type of schedule is paired with a number that indicates the actual schedule of reinforcement (e.g., FR 3 = behavior will be reinforced after three responses).

A fixed interval (FI) schedule refers to the delivery of a reinforcer after a set amount of time has passed and a student has engaged in an appropriate behavior or response. For example, a student can receive a sticker each hour for engaging in no talk-outs or after every 10 minutes of being on task. A problem with FI schedules is that students can begin to predict when a reinforcer is about to be delivered based on time and thus may only engage in the appropriate behavior close to time period that he or she will be reinforced (Kazdin, 2000). In addition, there is often a drop in student performance right after the reinforcer is delivered if the student learns that a certain amount of time must pass before he or she will be able to receive a reinforcer for appropriate responding (Pryor, 1999).

In contrast to the FI schedule of reinforcement, variable interval (VI) schedules involve the delivery of a reinforcer after an average length of time rather than a set amount of time. For example, a VI schedule in a school setting is when teachers use computer signaling programs to cue themselves to provide verbal praise to students. These computer programs can be set to beep at random intervals and the average length of time can be determined by the teacher. For a VI 7-minute schedule, students will be reinforced on average every 7 minutes. Sometimes students will be reinforced after 4 or 5 minutes have passed and they are engaging in the appropriate behavior and sometimes students will receive a reinforcer after 8, 9, or 10 minutes. In general, VI schedules produce higher rates of responding compared to FI schedules (Kazdin, 2000).

A fixed ratio (FR) schedule involves the delivery of a reinforcer after a set number of correct responses or occurrences of appropriate behavior. For example, a teacher implementing an FR 5 schedule to increase completion of math problems would provide reinforcement (e.g., praise, points on a chart) after every five problems completed correctly. Similar to FI schedules of reinforcement, FR schedules may also produce a delay in responding following the delivery of the reinforcer, particularly if the ratios are large—such as requiring students to complete 40 math problems before delivering a reinforcer (Alberto & Troutman, 2003). Another characteristic of FR schedules is that students may work quickly in order to complete the number of problems or responses required to receive the reinforcer and the quality of work may suffer (Kazdin, 2000). Individuals interested in implementing this type of reinforcement schedule should focus on both quality and quantity as criteria for delivery of the reinforcer.

A variable ratio (VR) schedule of reinforcement involves delivering a reinforcer after an average number of correct responses rather than a set number of responses. That is, a different number of responses are required each time in order to receive a reinforcer. The most common example of a VR schedule is gambling: sometimes a slot machine will pay off after ten pulls and sometimes it will pay off after one pull. Typically, variable ratio schedules lead to high, stable rates of responding and are quite frequently used in educational and clinical settings (Kazdin, 2000; Lerman, Iwata, Shore, & Kahng, 1996). Another reason for the frequent use of VI schedules is that behavior is more likely to maintain once reinforcement is discontinued compared to FR or continuous schedules (Pryor, 1999).

Overall, it is important to consider which schedule of reinforcement to implement as it will greatly affect both rates of responding and the extent to which the behavior will maintain once it is no longer being reinforced. Continuous schedules of reinforcement are more appropriate during the acquisition stages of learning. In contrast, intermittent schedules of reinforcement are more appropriate after the student has learned the skill and understands the relationship between engaging in a particular behavior and receiving a reinforcer.

**REFERENCES**

Alberto, P. A., & Troutman, A. C. (2003). *Applied behavior analysis for teachers* (6th ed.). Upper Saddle River, NJ: Pearson Education.

Chance, P. (1999). *Learning and behavior.* Pacific Grove: Brooks/Cole.

Kazdin, A. E. (2000). *Behavior modification in applied settings.* Belmont: Wadsworth.

Lerman, D. C., Iwata, B. A., Shore, B. A., & Kahng, S. (1996). Responding maintained by intermittent reinforcement: Implications for the use of extinction with problem behavior in clinical settings. *Journal of Applied Behavior Analysis, 29,* 153–171.

Pryor, K. (1999). *Don't shoot the dog.* New York: Bantom Books.

LEANNE S. HAWKEN
JASON BURROW-SANCHEZ
*University of Utah*

NEGATIVE REINFORCEMENT
POSITIVE REINFORCEMENT

# THE INTERNATIONAL CENTER FOR DISABILITY RESOURCES ON THE INTERNET

The International Center for Disability Resources on the Internet (ICDRI) was founded in 1998 and is a nonprofit center based in the United States. It is an internationally recognized public policy center "organized by and for people with disabilities"; and "ICDRI seeks to increase opportunities for people with disabilities by identifying barriers to participation in society and promoting best practices and universal design for the global community." ICDRI provides disability rights education and customized programs for the public and is an active participant in public policy strategic planning and implementation for governments in the United States and abroad.

ICDRI describes the organization strengths as follows.

- ICDRI is operated by people with disabilities and benefits from the expertise of an International Advisory Board;
- ICDRI embraces a cross-disability perspective, rather than a singular focus on one type of disability, in order to include the entire community of people with disabilities;
- ICDRI is a neutral research institute that maintains independence and control over its strategic planning, business workplan, and budget;
- ICDRI is committed to be on the cutting edge of global disability law, policy, and electronic and information technology;
- ICDRI seeks to enable replication of best practices and to enable other organizations to address disability issues; and
- ICDRI operates within a framework of collaboration with local, national, and international organizations in the exchange of information and cultural perspectives. (About Us)

ICDRI's web site establishes a formal knowledge base of quality disability resources and best practices and provides education, outreach, and training. ICDRI makes this information available in an accessible format through its web site at http://www.icdri.org.

STAFF

**WEB ACCESSIBILITY**

# INTERNATIONAL CHILD NEUROLOGY ASSOCIATION

The International Child Neurology Association (ICNA) was founded in 1973, with Articles of Association approved by Royal Decree by Baudouin, King of Belgium, the following year. ICNA is a nonprofit organization composed of child neurologists and related professionals dedicated to the promotion of research in the field of child neurology and encouraging recognition of the ability and scope of those who practice within the profession. In the interest of advancing and benefiting child and infant neurological science, the association provides a forum for the exchange of scientific and professional opinions by organizing international meetings, international cooperative studies, publications, and translations as well as supporting international exchange of teachers and students in the field. The 9th International Child Neurology Congress and the 7th Asian and Oceanian Congress of Child Neurology were held in Beijing, P. R. China (September 20–25, 2002). The current president is Paolo Curatolo, University of Rome, Tor Vergata, Italy.

## REFERENCE

International Child Neurology Association. (2006). *8th International Child Neurology Congress.* Retrieved February 18, 2006, from http://dstumpf.net/icna/index.html

MARILYN P. DORNBUSH
*Atlanta, Georgia*
First edition

TAMARA J. MARTIN
*The University of Texas of the
Permian Basin*
Second edition

# INTERNATIONAL CLASSIFICATION OF DISEASES

The International Classification of Diseases (ICD) is used to classify morbidity and mortality data for statistical purposes and to index hospital records on diseases and operations for information storage and retrieval. Classifying operations for this purpose has traditionally involved structuring according to type of operative procedure, anatomic site, or a combination of these two methods. Surgical specialty serves as the primary axis for classification in the present ICD as well as in most hospitals. The way in which a classification system of diseases is applied depends on the particular data to be classified and on the final product desired. As of yet, there exists no internationally agreed on method for classifying multiple causes of death.

Although the statistical study of diseases began as early as the 1700s, the roots of the ICD are found in the work of William Farr (1807–1883), a medical statistician who produced the best classification of diseases for his time—the International List of Causes of Death. Although this classification was never universally accepted, it did lay the basis for classifying by anatomical site. In the early 1900s, Dr. Jacque Bertillon prepared the Bertillon Classification of Causes of Death. Several revisions were put forth and, in 1923, M. Michel Huber (Bertillon's successor) managed to involve other international organizations, such as the Health Organization of the League of Nations, in drafting revisions, stating that the system should be reviewed every 10 years. The Sixth Decennial Revision Conference was marked by the adoption of a system calling for international cooperation in establishing national committees on vital and health statistics to coordinate statistical activity in the United States as well as through the World Health Organization. The present ICD is in its tenth revision.

The tenth revision of the ICD is an extension of the system of causes of morbidity and mortality. Furthermore, it provides a means for developing an efficient basis for indexing diagnostic information on hospital charts so that this data may later be reviewed and studied. The ICD is divided into 17 main sections, among them: diseases caused by well-defined infective agents; endocrine, neoplasmic, metabolic, and nutritional diseases; mental diseases; complications of pregnancy and childbirth; diseases of the perinatal period; ill-defined conditions; and a classification of injuries (puncture, burn, or open wound). The last category involves a dual classification system: external cause and nature of injury. This section is designed to bear the numbers 800–999; external cause is distinguished by the prefix "E," while nature of injury is distinguished by the prefix "N." Although the broad section headings aid organization, much significance should not be placed on their inherent value, since they have never represented a consistent collection of disease conditions to serve as statistically stable and usable areas. The detailed list is comprised of 671 categories, in addition to 187 categories characterizing injuries according to the nature of the wound, and 182 categories classifying external causes of injuries. A decimal numbering system is used; thus the categories are designated by three-digit numbers. The initial two digits pinpoint important or summary groups, while the third digit sections each group into categories representing classifications of diseases according to a specific axis of specific disease entities. The three-digit categories are not numbered consecutively. Four-digit sub-categories provide additional specificity regarding etiology or manifestations of the condition. While the list of categories in the ICD provides a structure for classification, it is essential to be familiar with the diagnostic terms included within each category before the ICD can be of practical use.

MARY LEON PEERY
*Texas A&M University*

## INTERNATIONAL CLASSIFICATION OF FUNCTIONING, DISABILITY, AND HEALTH

As a new member of the World Health Organization Family of International Classifications, the International Classification of Functioning, Disability, and Health (ICF) describes how people live with their health conditions. ICF is a classification of health and health-related domains that describe body functions and structures, activities, and participation. The domains are classified from body, individual, and societal perspectives. Since an individual's functioning and disability occurs in a context, ICF also includes a list of environmental factors.

The ICF is useful to understand and measure health outcomes. It can be used in clinical settings, health services, or surveys at the individual or population level. Thus ICF complements the ICD-10, The International Statistical Classification of Diseases and Related Health Problems, and therefore is looking beyond mortality and disease.

The ICF is a multipurpose classification designed to serve various disciplines and different sectors. Its specific aims can be summarized as follows:

- to provide a scientific basis for understanding and studying health and health-related states, outcomes, and determinants;
- to establish a common language for describing health and health-related states in order to improve communication between different users, such as health care workers, researchers, policy-makers, and the public, including people with disabilities;
- to permit comparison of data across countries, health care disciplines, services, and time;
- to provide a systematic coding scheme for health information systems.

These aims are interrelated because the need for and uses of ICF require the construction of a meaningful and practical system that can be used by various consumers for health policy, quality assurance, and outcome evaluation in different cultures.

Since its publication as a trial version in 1980, ICF's predecessor, the International Classification of Impairment, Disability, and Handicap (ICIDH), has been used for various purposes, for example:

- as a statistical tool—in the collection and recording of data (e.g., in population studies and surveys, in management information systems);
- as a research tool—to measure outcomes, quality of life, or environmental factors;
- as a clinical tool—in needs assessment, matching treatments with specific conditions, vocational assessment, rehabilitation, and outcome evaluation;
- as a social policy tool—in social security planning, compensation systems, and policy design and implementation;
- as an educational tool—in curriculum design and to raise awareness and undertake social action.

ICF is inherently a health and health-related classification; therefore it is also used by sectors such as insurance, social security, labor, education, economics, social policy and general legislation development, and environmental modification. It has been accepted as one of the United Nations social classifications and is referred to in and incorporates The Standard Rules on the Equalization of Opportunities for Persons with Disabilities. Thus ICF provides an appropriate instrument for the implementation of stated international human rights mandates as well as national legislation.

ICF is useful for a broad spectrum of different applications, for example social security, evaluation in managed health care, and population surveys at local, national, and international levels. It offers a conceptual framework for information that is applicable to personal health care, including prevention, health promotion, and the improvement of participation by removing or mitigating societal hindrances and encouraging the provision of social supports and facilitators. It is also useful for the study of health care systems, in terms of both evaluation and policy formulation. Information for this entry was taken directly from the ICF webpage and this and other excellent resources can be found online at http://www.who.int/classifications/icf/en.

STAFF

## INTERNATIONAL CLASSIFICATION OF DISEASES
WORLD HEALTH ORGANIZATION

## INTERNATIONAL DYSLEXIA ASSOCIATION

The International Dyslexia Association (IDA), formally the Orton Dyslexia Society, is an international, nonprofit organization dedicated to the study and treatment of dyslexia. The IDA was established to continue the pioneering work of Dr. Samuel T. Orton, a neurologist who was one of the first to identify dyslexia and develop effective teaching approaches. Since then, the association has been a strong force in educational and scientific communities. For nearly sixty years, the IDA has been helping individuals with dyslexia, their families, teachers, physicians, and researchers to better understand dyslexia. The association believes that all individuals have the right to achieve their potential; that individual learning abilities can be strengthened; and that social, educational, and cultural barriers to language acquisition and use must be removed.

In July 1999 the following vision and purpose was developed by board members, council members, and other prominent people in the field for the future of the IDA.

The Purpose of the International Dyslexia Association is to pursue and provide the most comprehensive range of information and services that address the full scope of dyslexia and related difficulties in learning to read and write . . . In a way that creates hope, possibility and partnership . . . So that every individual has the opportunity to lead a productive and fulfilling life, and society benefits from the resource that is liberated. And our Vision and Purpose define our values . . .

### Our Core Value: Teamwork and Achieving our Best Together

We work as a team in a culture of mutual trust and respect. We communicate with each other openly and candidly. We achieve the best outcome together.

### Empowering Individuals with Dyslexia

We strive to have a meaningful impact on the lives of individuals with dyslexia, as well as their families. We work diligently to provide evidence-based information and services so people with dyslexia can advocate for themselves and achieve their best.

### Commitment and Accountability

We are committed to living our values on a daily basis and we accept personal responsibility for advancing IDA's mission and maintaining fiscal stability. We can never be complacent in the pursuit of our mission.

### Diversity

At IDA, we understand that different perspectives are necessary for informed decision making. Our actions must always reflect a commitment to inclusivity and a representation of the population at large.

### Intellectual Integrity

Intellectual integrity is the cornerstone of IDA. We value our historic roots and honor them by retaining a commitment to research and evidence-based practices. We understand that such a commitment may, at times, demand a willingness to challenge long-held beliefs.

### Leadership and Collaboration

We accept our role as a leader in promoting evidence-based practices at local, state, federal, and international levels. By exercising that leadership and by collaborating with like-minded organizations, IDA will proactively influence policies critical to the well being of people with dyslexia.

IDA provides information to approximately 30,000 people annually through international offices and/or one of the 40+ local branches. According to IDA website, more than 250,000 visitors yearly access the website. IDS conducts conferences, seminars and hosts support groups. Their international conference brings together over 200 experts in the field. IDS publishes the *Annals of Dyslexia* annually, a news letter *Perspectives* which is distributed quarterly, and fact sheets which are free to the public. IDS has an online store which sells other related publications. IDS is important in funding research and advocating for individuals with dyslexia.

Information for this entry was provided directly from the International Dyslexia Association's webpage. This Internet website is an excellent source of information for individuals interested in dyslexia and the association. The web site address is http://www.interdys.org.

RACHEL TOPLIS
*Falcon School District 49,*
*Colorado Springs, Colorado*

## INTERNATIONAL ETHICS AND SPECIAL EDUCATION

See ETHICS, INTERNATIONAL AND SPECIAL EDUCATION.

## INTERNATIONAL READING ASSOCIATION

The International Reading Association (IRA) is a nonprofit professional organization devoted to the improvement of reading instruction (IRA, 1985). Membership in IRA is open to individuals who are interested in the field of reading, including teachers, administrators, reading specialists, special educators, college-level instructors and researchers, psychologists, librarians, and parents. In addition, membership is also available to institutions and agencies that are involved with the teaching of reading or the preparation of reading teachers. The IRA endorses the study of reading as a process, promotes research into improvement of reading programs, and advocates better teacher education. The organization is also closely involved with the worldwide literacy movement and the role of reading in the general welfare of society and individuals, as promulgated in the IRA Code of Ethics (1985).

The IRA is comprised of over 1,150 councils and national affiliates in various countries around the world. Local, national, and international meetings and conventions provide an opportunity for members to come together. The four major professional journals and numerous individual volumes on reading-related topics published annually by the

IRA provide other means through which members are kept informed of current practices in reading education.

### REFERENCES

Committee on Professional Standards and Ethics. (1985). IRA Code of Ethics. *Reading Teacher, 39*(1), 56–57.

International Reading Association (IRA). (1985). Newark, DE: Author.

JOHN M. EELLS
*Souderton Area School District,*
*Souderton, Pennsylvania*

READING
READING REMEDIATION

# INTERNATIONAL SCHOOL PSYCHOLOGY ASSOCIATION

The International School Psychology Association (ISPA) emerged from efforts by Calvin Catterall and Francis Mullins to broaden the views of school psychologists within the United States to include international perspectives. They initiated the International School Psychology Committee, first within the American Psychological Association's Division of School Psychology and later within the National Association of School Psychologists.

This committee served as a vehicle through which Dr. Catterall established contacts with various school psychologists outside of the United States. This committee sponsored its first international conference in 1975. In 1979, the U.N.-sponsored International Year of the Child attracted the interests of many school psychologists internationally. Participants recognized the need for an international association that would serve ongoing interests of school psychologists internationally. ISPA's constitution and by-laws were adopted in 1982.

ISPA has four major objectives: to foster communication between psychologists in educational settings, to encourage the implementation of promising practices in school psychology, to raise the effectiveness of education, and to promote the maximum contribution of psychology to education.

Membership approximates 800 and comes from approximately 40 countries. Twenty-two national associations of school psychologists are affiliated with ISPA. ISPA sponsors yearly meetings to promote its objectives and to help stimulate the growth of school psychology in a region. ISPA also publishes a newsletter and sponsors a scholarly journal, *School Psychology International.* ISPA has approved three policy statements: an ethics code, a definition of professional practice, and a model professional preparation program. ISPA's international offices are in Copenhagen, Denmark. See Oakland (2000) as well as ISPA's web site (www.ispaweb.org) for more details.

### REFERENCES

Oakland, T. (2000). International school psychology. In T. Fagan & P. S. Wise (Eds.), *School psychology: Past, present, and future* (pp. 412–419). Washington, DC: National Association of School Psychologists.

THOMAS OAKLAND
*University of Florida*

# INTERNATIONAL TEST USE IN SPECIAL EDUCATION

Although the origins of testing occurred at least 3,000 years ago in China (Wang, 1993), current methods of test development and use can be traced directly to attempts to meet four sets of needs which grew in importance during the last 150 years: to utilize reliable and valid measures in research, to educate more students at more advanced levels, to help ensure that people with special needs were cared for properly, and to provide special services to those with more severe disorders. This article reviews the international availability and uses of tests with children and youth typically served in special education.

An international survey of test use in 44 countries, not including the United States, identified 455 tests used frequently with children and youth (Hu & Oakland, 1991; Oakland & Hu, 1991, 1992, 1994). Among these tests, 46 percent were imported for use as they were developed outside of the countries in which they were being used. Tests commonly imported for use originally were developed in the United States (22 percent), the United Kingdom (7 percent), West Germany (7 percent), France (5 percent), and Sweden (5 percent). Foreign developed tests are used more frequently than locally developed tests in 68 percent of the countries surveyed. Locally developed tests are used more frequently than foreign developed tests in only 27 percent of the reporting countries. Seven countries report no nationally developed tests.

Test use is not uniform throughout the world. Highest test use was reported by three pre-1990 socialist nations: Yugoslavia (principally Slovenia), East Germany, and Czechoslovakia. Lowest test use was reported by the least developed nations. Reliance on foreign developed tests is most common in the Middle Eastern and least developed nations.

## Types of Tests Used

Measures of intelligence (39 percent), personality (24 percent), and achievement (10 percent) appear most frequently. Tests assessing perceptual-motor abilities, vocational interests and aptitudes, school readiness, and social development are not found commonly. The 10 most frequently used tests, in rank order of frequency of use, are the Wechsler Intelligence Scales for Children, the Raven's Progressive Matrices, Bender Gestalt, Rorschach, Stanford-Binet, Wechsler Adult Intelligence Scales, Thematic Apperception Test, Differential Aptitude Test, Minnesota Multiphasic Personality Inventory, and Frostig Developmental Test of Visual Perception.

Two-thirds of the countries surveyed report a critical need for additional group and individual tests of achievement, intelligence, vocational interest and aptitudes, social development, and personality. The need for tests that assess qualities important to persons who are mentally retarded, blind, deaf, slow learners, emotionally and socially disturbed, physically impaired, and gifted were identified by almost 85 percent of the countries. Tests to assess students with learning disabilities are needed most, given an estimated 150 million worldwide.

## Psychometric Studies

Standardized tests are expected to be suitably normed and to have reliability and validity estimates (American Educational Research Association, 1985). As noted below, these important qualities often do not exist. Local norms are available on 80 percent of achievement tests, 65 percent of intelligence tests, and 58 percent of personality tests. Among measures of achievement, studies of concurrent validity are available on 71 percent, predictive validity on 43 percent, and construct validity on 48 percent. Among measures of intelligence, studies of concurrent validity are available on 63 percent, predictive validity on 56 percent, and construct validity on 54 percent. Among measures of personality, concurrent validity studies are available on 53 percent and predictive and construct validity studies on approximately 39 percent.

Reliability studies have been conducted on 50 percent to 60 percent of measures of intelligence, personality, achievement, vocational interests and aptitudes, and school readiness. Studies examining the reliability of other types of measures appear less frequently. Thus, information often is unavailable to determine the adequacy of measures commonly used with children and youth (Oakland & Hu, 1994).

## Professionals Who Use Tests

At least 16 professional groups commonly use tests with children and youth. School or educational psychologists often assume leadership for testing. Other frequently cited specialists include regular and special education teachers, clinical psychologists, and counselors (Oakland & Hu, 1991).

The educational levels of these professionals differ considerably, ranging from 2.5 years of post-secondary education for nurses to 6.5 years for physicians. The correlation

between the number of years of post-secondary education and the perceived competence of the professional groups is substantial ($r = .50, p > .001$). Thus, professions with more education are thought to be more competent in the use of tests. In addition, professionals who use individually administered tests often are educated more highly than those who use only group tests.

Levels of professional preparation differ considerably between countries. The levels are lowest among professionals working in developing third world nations, Middle Eastern, and least developed nations. These countries also tend to have fewer tests developed nationally and with national norms. The combination of these qualities (i.e., less adequately prepared professionals together with fewer and less adequate tests) severely limits efforts to deliver adequate assessment services to children and youth in these countries and to conduct needed research.

## Implication Concerning Test Use in Special Education

The availability and quality of tests used with children and youth internationally varies greatly by region and country. Resources are strongest in Western Europe and some Eastern European countries, in English-speaking countries affiliated with the United Kingdom, and Israel. Fewest resources are found in the Middle East, and Central and South America. The number of studies examining test reliability and validity clearly is deficient. Professionals commonly are required to make decisions about children and youth using measures whose psychometric qualities are unknown and whose norms were developed on children from technologically advanced countries. As a result, professional standards and professional respect are jeopardized along with the quality of services delivered to children, youth, and their families.

Efforts to promote proper test development and use internationally should address three major needs: for additional studies that examine test reliability and validity, for additional measures that have nationally representative norms, and for greater reliance on nationally developed tests.

### REFERENCES

American Educational Research Association. (1985). *Standards for educational and psychological testing*. Washington, DC: Author.

Hu, S., & Oakland, T. (1991). Global and regional perspectives on testing children and youth: An empirical study. *International Journal of Psychology, 26,* 329–344.

Oakland, T., & Hu, S. (1991). Professionals who administer tests with children and youth: An international survey. *Journal of Psychoeducational Assessment, 9*(2), 108–120.

Oakland, T., & Hu, S. (1992). The top 10 tests used with children and youth worldwide. *Bulletin of the International Test Commission, 19,* 99–120.

Oakland, T., & Hu, S. (1994). International perspectives on tests used with children and youth. *Journal of School Psychology, 31,* 501–517.

Wang, Z. M. (1993). Psychology on China: A review. *Annual Review of Psychology, 44,* 87–116.

THOMAS OAKLAND
HARRISON KANE
*University of Florida*

# INTERNATIONAL YEAR OF DISABLED PERSONS, 1981

The General Assembly of the United Nations proclaimed 1981 the International Year of Disabled Persons (Resolution 31/123, December 16, 1976). Previous initiatives had set the stage. These included the Declaration on the Rights of Mentally Retarded Persons (Resolution 2856 [xxvi], adopted on December 20, 1971) and the Declaration on the Rights of Disabled Persons (Resolution 3447 [xxx], adopted December 9, 1975).

The resolution on the International Year of Disabled Persons stressed the theme of full participation by persons with disabilities in the social, political, and economic life and development of the societies in which they live. It also promoted national and international efforts to provide disabled persons with proper assistance, training, care, and guidance, and encouraged study and research projects designed to facilitate the practical participation of disabled persons in daily life by improving such things as transport and access. One hundred and thirty-one countries took an active part in the International Year of Disabled Persons. They formed national commissions and carried out national programs, many of them focusing formally on the problem of disability for the first time.

Perhaps the greatest contribution of the International Year of Disabled Persons at the world level was the development by the United Nations of a World Plan of Action. The plan was adopted by the General Assembly at its 34th session, which concluded in December 1979. The plan set forth (on a global scale) the steps nations, non-government organizations, the United Nations, and individuals must take to continue the commitment and momentum of the International Year of Disabled Persons (Resolution A/RES/34/158, adopted January 30, 1980). Activities included measures at the national, regional, and international levels, including the organization of meetings and symposiums, the development of statistical data on disability, a review of existing legislation relating to disabled persons, the development of mass media campaigns relating to disability, and the identification of prophylaxis for disease and the prevention of disability.

On December 3, 1982, at the conclusion of its 37th ses-
sion and the end of the International Year of Disabled Persons, the United Nations' General Assembly proclaimed the United Nations Decade of Disabled Persons, 1983–1992. It also formally adopted the World Program of Action, with its stress on the prevention of disability and its effort to identify major problems facing people with disabilities throughout the world, and made recommendations of actions to be taken to respond to these problems. The majority of recommendations address strategies for prevention, rehabilitation, and equalization of opportunity. The last category includes such issues as legislation, the physical environment, income maintenance, social security, education and training, employment, recreation, culture, religion, and sports.

## REFERENCES

National Organization on Disability. (1983). *International year of disabled persons, the story of the U.S. council for IYPD.* Washington, DC: Author.

Rehabilitation International. (1981). *International statements on disability policy.* New York: Author.

United Nations. (1983). *For the benefit of the disabled, activities undertaken during the international year of disabled persons.* New York: Author.

United Nations. (1983). *U.N. decade of disabled persons, 1983–1992: World programme of action concerning disabled persons.* New York: Author.

United Nations General Assembly adopts IYPD action plan. (1980). *International Rehabilitation Review, 1,* 1.

United Nations proclaims 1983–1992 decade of disabled persons. (1982). *International Rehabilitation Review,* 4th quarter, 1.

CATHERINE HALL RIKHYE
*Hunter College, City University
of New York*

# INTERNET ACCESSIBILITY

See WEB ACCESSIBILITY.

# INTEROBSERVER AGREEMENT

Systematic direct observation of behavior has become a widely used assessment approach within school systems (Kratochwill, Sheridan, Carlson, & Lasecki, 1999). When conducted with fidelity, systematic direct observation provides a snapshot of the environment of interest. This data allows one to consider the effects of environmental contingencies, thus placing behavior within a contextual framework. Understanding a behavior in relation to the environment is one of the key components to intervention. However, the utility of systematic direct observation depends on the trustworthiness of the observation data. Assessing the reliability of observation data is a necessary prerequisite to interpreting that data and developing interventions.

## Determining the Credibility of Observation Data

One method to examine the reliability of observation data is to train two or more observers to use the same observation coding system so that the agreement between these two observers' findings can be determined. This method, called interobserver agreement, evaluates the degree of consistency in findings from different observers who rate the same behaviors. Disagreement between observers could occur for a variety of reasons. For example, if observers are not adequately trained to use the coding scheme or if the target behaviors of interest are not clearly defined, interobserver agreement may be compromised. Even when the coding system is clear and followed with integrity, there may be variability in observers' interpretations of certain behaviors. Whether observers are conscious of it or not, their personal biases or expectations may influence behavior recording.

The possibility for the miscoding of behavior highlights the need to consider interobserver agreement. Methods used to measure behavioral change are dependent upon accurate measurement of target behaviors. Consequently, researchers and practitioners must consider interobserver agreement to determine the reliability and validity of their behavioral assessments. In addition, we are in an age of accountability in our school systems, which dictates that we employ the most methodologically sound procedures we have available to ensure the credibility of our assessment data, and thus, the effectiveness of our resulting interventions. As a result, it is clear that the measurement of interobserver agreement also plays a role in day to day school procedures.

## Measures of Interobserver Agreement

Although this is by no means an exhaustive review of the various methods for calculating interobserver agreement, three popular procedures will be presented. In addition to describing each method, potential uses and limitations of each will be discussed. There are a few important similarities among these various procedures. They all share the same core concept in that each measures consistency between two or more observations of the same behavior sample. Second, all but the first method (percentage of agreement) share the same resulting coefficients in that scores of interobserver agreement range from 0 to 1, and a value as close to 1 as possible indicates greater agreement. While percentage of agreement does not result in a coefficient, it is similar in that scores range from 0 to 100 percent agreement, with scores as close to 100 percent being desirable on the part of the researcher.

### Percentage of Agreement

This is a popular procedure that compares two observers' observation data on a point-to-point basis (Salvia & Ysseldyke, 2001; Steege, Davin, & Hathaway, 2001). Percentage of interobserver agreement is calculated by dividing the number of agreements by the total number of agreements plus disagreements, and then multiplying this by 100. If there is not at least 80 percent agreement between evaluators, it is advisable to discuss differences, clarify the behavioral coding system, and repeat the training process until satisfactory agreement can be achieved. Steege and colleagues (2001) used the percentage of agreement procedure to examine the reliability of two observers' ratings after a 15-minute observation interval. Observers coded the duration of target behaviors, such as opposition, based on a 5-point Likert scale. For example, a rating of 2 indicated that the oppositional behavior occurred for 3 to 6 minutes during the 15-minute interval. If both observers coded identical ratings, it was counted as an agreement. The resulting percentage of agreement was then calculated. In this example, the ratings of two observers showed 98 percent agreement in the coding of the duration of a child's oppositional behavior.

The use of percentage of agreement persists as a popular method for reporting interobserver agreement perhaps, in part, due to its ease of calculation. However, this approach to interobserver agreement has been criticized for psychometric reasons. The primary concern is that this method is unable to take chance into account, and chance is likely to inflate agreement percentages in all cases, but especially with two coders. Thus, other approaches have been proposed to correct for the possibility that two observers' ratings may agree at times simply by chance alone.

### Cohen's Kappa

Cohen's kappa statistic (Cohen, 1960) has long been proposed as a more psychometrically sound statistic for assessing interobserver agreement. Like the simple percentage of agreement method, kappa considers the proportion of actual agreement ($P_o$), but it also accounts for the proportion of agreement that would be expected by chance alone ($P_c$). Specifically, kappa is calculated as the difference between chance agreement and actual agreement, divided by one minus chance agreement ($[P_o - P_c]/[1 - P_c]$).

Kappa is appropriate for examining interobserver agreement when the observed data is frequency or categorical data. For example, Theodore and colleagues (Theodore, Bray, & Kehle, 2004) used a partial-interval time sampling method to code the presence or absence of disruptive behavior during 15-second intervals. Interobserver agreement calculated with kappa revealed an average of .83. A value as close to 1 as possible is desirable; perfect agreement would equate to a kappa of 1, and chance agreement would equate to 0. Generally a kappa greater than .70 is considered satisfactory.

### Intraclass Coefficients (ICC)

When observation data includes continuous scores as opposed to ranks or categorical classifications, interclass coefficients are the most appropriate measure. As with kappa, high agreement is reflected by an ICC close to 1. If there is significant disagreement between two observers' data, the resulting ICC will be a low or negative correlation. It is important to note that several ICC procedures exist, and each can result in quite different results when applied to the same data. Differentiation among the various types of ICC procedures is beyond the scope of this article (see Shrout & Fleiss, 1979, for a complete review of these procedures). Instead, be aware that researchers using ICC should report which procedure was used and the reason behind the choice made.

A study by Walcott and Landau (2004) used ICC to check the reliability of a coding scheme in which observers coded 3-minute behavior samples for the presence or absence of specific expressive behaviors during consecutive 10-second intervals. The resulting scores were a frequency count of the number of behaviors exhibited by a child in each behavioral category. Intraclass correlation coefficients, using the ICC (3, 1) procedure, were calculated to measure the consistency of the two ratings while treating the observers as fixed effects (Shrout & Fleiss, 1979). Coefficients revealed satisfactory levels of consistency between observers' measurements on most categories. As with kappa, intraclass coefficients greater than .70 are generally considered satisfactory.

Several methods for determining interobserver agreement were discussed, and researchers or practitioners should consider the type of observation data being collected when choosing an appropriate method. Above all, it is crucial that we assess the credibility of direct observation data with a viable method of interobserver agreement before using it to design school-based interventions or make important educational decisions.

### REFERENCES

Cohen, J. (1960). A coefficient of agreement for nominal scales. *Educational and Psychological Measurement, 20*, 37–46.

Kratochwill, T. R., Sheridan, S. M., Carlson, J., & Lasecki, K. L. (1999). Advances in behavioral assessment. In C. R. Reynolds & T. B. Gutkin (Eds.), *The handbook of school psychology* (3rd ed., pp. 350–382). New York: Wiley.

Salvia, J., & Ysseldyke, J. E. (2001). *Assessment* (8th ed.). New York: Houghton Mifflin.

Shrout, P. E., & Fleiss, J. L. (1979). Intraclass correlations: Uses in assessing rater reliability. *Psychological Bulletin, 86*, 420–428.

Steege, M. W., Davin, T., & Hathaway, M. (2001). Reliability and accuracy of a performance-based behavioral recording procedure. *School Psychology Review, 30*, 252–261.

Theodore, L. A., Bray, M. A., & Kehle, T. J. (2004). A comparative study of group contingencies and randomized reinforcers to reduce disruptive classroom behavior. *School Psychology Quarterly, 19*, 253–271.

Walcott, C. M., & Landau, S. (2004). The relation between disinhibition and emotion regulation in boys with attention deficit hyperactivity disorder. *Journal of Clinical Child and Adolescent Psychology, 33*, 772–782.

CHRISTY M. WALCOTT
T. CHRIS RILEY-TILLMAN
*East Carolina University*

**BEHAVIORAL ASSESSMENT
POSITIVE BEHAVIORAL SUPPORT**

# INTERPRETERS FOR THE DEAF

Interpreters for the deaf are hearing individuals who listen to a spoken message and communicate it in some way to hearing-impaired people. In interpreting it is permissible to depart from the exact words of the speaker to paraphrase, define, and explain what the speaker is saying. Interpreting is differentiated from translating, which is a verbatim presentation of another person's remarks (Quigley & Paul, 1984).

Until 1964 interpreters were mainly family friends or relatives who knew sign language (Levine, 1981). In 1964 the National Registry of Interpreters for the Deaf was established to promote the recruitment and training of interpreters, to clarify their functions, to specify the competencies required for interpreting, and to maintain a list of certified interpreters.

There are various types of interpreters for the deaf: sign language interpreters, who communicate what has been said in some form of sign language or finger spelling; oral interpreters, who inaudibly repeat the speaker's message, (clearly enunciated and somewhat more slowly) to facilitate its speech reading by deaf persons (Northcott, 1984); and reverse interpreters, who convert a deaf person's sign language or difficult to understand speech into normally spoken English (Bishop, 1979). Specialized interpreters, familiar with the pertinent technical language, serve in legal, medical, psychiatric, and rehabilitative settings. Educational interpreters facilitate the mainstreaming of deaf students in schools and universities. Theatrical interpreters sign operatic performances and Broadway shows (Kanter, 1985).

The first case involving PL 94-142, the Education for all Handicapped Children Act—the precursor to IDEA—decided by the U.S. Supreme Court, was a demand for a sign language interpreter by the parents of a mainstream deaf child, Amy Rowley. The Court decided that this particular deaf child did not need an interpreter. However, in other cases, sign language interpreters have been ordered, even for elementary school students when teachers state that interpreters are needed for pupils to benefit from their classes and actively participate in them (DuBow & Geer, 1983). In 1982 the U.S. Court of Appeals mandated state vocational rehabilitation agencies to provide interpreters for deaf clients attending college.

The Vocational Rehabilitation Act of 1965 provided that interpreter services must be included as part of vocational rehabilitation services. Since then, most states have mandated that deaf individuals must be offered sign language interpreters whenever their civil rights are involved. Interpreter training programs are available throughout the United States. Many colleges offer an AA or BA degree in interpreting.

## REFERENCES

Bishop, M. (1979). *Mainstreaming.* Washington, DC: Alexander Graham Bell Association for the Deaf.

DuBow, S., & Geer, S. (1983, July). Education decisions after Rowley. *National Center for Law and the Deaf Newsletter,* pp. 1–3.

Kanter, A. (1985, Summer). *A night at the opera.* N.T.I.D. Focus, pp. 3–4.

Levine, E. (1981). *The ecology of early deafness.* New York: Columbia University Press.

Northcott, W. (1984). *Oral interpreting: Principles and practices.* Baltimore: University Park Press.

Quigley, S., & Paul, P. (1984). *Language and deafness.* San Diego, CA: College Hill Press.

ROSEMARY GAFFNEY
*Hunter College, City University
of New York*

DEAF EDUCATION
LIPREADING/SPEECHREADING

# INTERVAL RECORDING

Interval recording is a data collection method that is used when you want to measure a continuous behavior. This method is a time-based measurement system where the passage of a predetermined amount of time, not each occurrence of a behavior, is the signal for the teacher or researcher to record data (Wolery, Bailey, & Sugai, 1988). Like all time-based systems, interval recording provides a close approximation of the targeted behavior, not an exact count of each occurrence. Interval recording is suitable for behaviors such as academic engagement, playing, engaging in off-task behaviors, such as being out of an assigned seat and/or walking around the classroom, cooperative learning, and self-stimulatory behaviors, such as rocking. The two types of interval recording that are used by teachers and researchers are partial interval recording and whole interval recording.

Interval recording first requires an operational definition of the behavior of concern. An operational definition is a written statement that precisely defines the behavior you wish to measure in terms that are observable, measurable, and replicable (Fletcher-Janzen & De Pry, 2003). Next, the observer determines the length of time for each interval. Intervals are predetermined periods of time that are equivalent in length. Interval length is determined by (a) the frequency of the target behavior, (b) the context that elicits the behavior (e.g., times, place, conditions), and (c) the time demands or schedule of the teacher (Wolery, Bailey, & Sugai, 1988). Interval lengths for this method usually range from 5 to 30 seconds. As a general rule, the shorter the interval length the more accurate the data that is collected (Alberto & Troutman, 2006).

When the interval length has been determined, a data collection form should be created. The form should have the student's name, the date, the observer's name, the classroom teacher's name, information about the setting or context of the observation (to be completed at each observation session), the start and stop times, and the interval grid. Teachers who use interval recording need a signal that lets them know when to observe and record data. The signal can be visual (e.g., classroom clock, watch) or auditory (e.g., kitchen timer, countdown timer, tape player with a recorded tone).

The rules for using partial interval recording and whole interval recording are different. Partial interval recording follows the rule that you record the behavior if it occurs at any time during the interval being observed. For example, an observer is measuring "time in seat" using a 30 second partial interval recording method. The student is observed to be in her seat for 20 of the 30 seconds, but gets up to get a drink of water for the remaining 10 seconds. Because she met the operational definition for time in seat and was observed being in her seat for part of the interval, the observer would put a plus mark in the appropriate interval box (this method allows only 1 plus or minus mark per interval). The only time that the observer would put a minus mark in an interval box would be if the student did not meet the operational definition at all for the designated interval.

Whole interval recording follows the rule that the student needs to meet the operational definition for the entire 30 second interval in order for that interval to be counted as met. Using our example, the student is observed to be in her seat the entire 30 second interval, therefore a plus mark is put in the appropriate interval box. If however, the student met the definition for 25 seconds, but stood up to stretch for 5 seconds, the observer would put a minus sign in the appropriate interval box because our rule for whole interval recording requires that the student meets the operational definition for the entire 30 second interval.

Maag (1999) suggests that interval recording has two

advantages. This method provides a good estimate of the frequency or duration of the targeted behavior and it can be used to detect temporal patterns of occurrence, such as when the behavior is more likely to occur (beginning, middle, or end of the observation session). Disadvantages include the possibility of underestimating or overestimating the behavior of concern and the time demands made on the teacher or researcher for conducting the observation. This last point is especially a concern for whole interval recording (Wolery et al., 1988) given the intensity of this observation method. As with all direct observation systems, collecting interobserver reliability data is critical. The formula for calculating interobserver reliability for interval recording is taking the number of agreement intervals and dividing by the agreements plus disagreement intervals and multiplying by 100. This formula will give you the percent of agreement between the primary observer and an independent observer.

## REFERENCES

Alberto, P. A., & Troutman, A. C. (2006). *Applied behavior analysis for teachers* (7th ed.). Upper Saddle River, NJ: Prentice Hall.

Fletcher-Janzen, E., & De Pry, R. L. (2003). *Teaching social competence and character: An IEP planner with goals, objectives, and interventions.* Longmont, CO: Sopris West Educational Services.

Maag, J. W. (1999). *Behavior management: From theoretical implications to practical applications.* San Diego, CA: Singular Publishing.

Wolery, M., Bailey, D. B., Jr., & Sugai, G. M. (1988). *Effective teaching: Principles and procedures of applied behavior analysis for exceptional students.* Boston: Allyn & Bacon.

RANDALL L. DE PRY
*University of Colorado at
Colorado Springs*

BEHAVIORAL ASSESSMENT
BEHAVIOR CHARTING

## INTERVAL SCHEDULES

At home, school, and in the workplace, the quality of our interactions and performance is often judged by our sensitivity to the contingencies of reinforcement. Sometimes, for example, rapid, precise movements are required, such as when engaging in factory piecework or completing a timed math quiz in the classroom. At other times, a steady, moderate work pace is desirable, such as during individual activities in the classroom while the teacher circulates from one student to the next. It is useful for parents, teachers, and employers to take careful note of what kinds of work

patterns are desirable and to set schedules of reinforcement that are likely to influence the rate and consistency of behavior in a manner congruent with the expectations of the environment.

A schedule of reinforcement describes the conditions that must be in effect for reinforcers to be delivered (Ferster & Skinner, 1957). Interval schedules involve delivery of a reinforcer following the first response that occurs after a specified time period. During a fixed-interval (FI) schedule, the time specified after which a response is reinforced is held constant. For example, every 3 minutes, when a vibrating timer alerts a teacher, he writes the names of all students who are engaged in a reading activity on the whiteboard. At the end of 12 minutes, students whose names were written on the board may select from a bin the activities for which they have indicated a preference. Fixed-interval schedules should not be confused with fixed-time (FT) schedules, in which reinforcement is available after a specified amount of time independent of behavioral responses. In an FT schedule, it is left to chance whether desired behaviors that are being taught are occurring when the reinforcement is provided, and unless behaviors that have been taught are occurring at a very high rate, it is probable that unwanted behaviors will be reinforced.

Variable-interval (VI) schedules are similar to FI schedules, except responses are reinforced after an average amount of time. A teacher circulating throughout the classroom is unlikely to be able to reinforce all on-task behaviors every minute, but may on average get to each student who is working diligently once every 3 to 4 minutes.

Behavior is emitted in characteristic patterns depending on the schedule of reinforcement (Ferster & Skinner, 1957). Many schedules produce consistent patterns of responding across species. Human behavior under FI schedules is consistent among infants and adults with less well developed verbal skills (Lowe, Beasty, & Bentall, 1983). People with limited verbal repertoires respond and then pause briefly, engage in other behaviors, then gradually increase the rate of responses until there is a pay-off, after which the pattern repeats. Although such postreinforcement pauses are not always evident or pronounced in adults, they are common enough to merit analysis. When quizzes are given each week on Friday, students may play and work on other assignments throughout the week, study briefly on Tuesday and Wednesday, and then cram Thursday night. Unscheduled quizzes given on a VI schedule would likely produce more consistent study habits because the specific timing of the quizzes, though on average still once a week, would be unpredictable. This central difference between behavior on FI and VI schedules is prescriptive: when steady, moderate rates of behavior are desired, VI schedules are preferable.

Behavior reinforced continuously may decrease in frequency, while behavior reinforced intermittently becomes more resilient, or resistant to extinction. When praised every 3 minutes for staying in his seat, John begins testing his teacher and standing up when she is not looking. Soon other children notice and laugh, maintaining John's behavior with their attention. After recognizing this pattern, his teacher switches to a VI schedule and praises John intermittently. She offers praise on average once every 3 minutes when John is seated properly. The unpredictability of this praise schedule brings John's behavior under control.

John's teacher may do more at this point with the schedule of reinforcement to maintain the desired response. She may enlist other students' cooperation in ignoring John's behavior should he jump out of his seat. Then, to capitalize on the effect of others ignoring his behavior, she may offer praise of increased magnitude when John is seated appropriately. By adding an extinction schedule of reinforcement, John's teacher makes use of the contrast phenomenon, which is seen when two schedules are concurrently in effect and a change in one schedule produces contrasting changes in behavior under both schedules (McSweeney, 1982). Making use of contrast between behavior in the extinction schedule for being out of his seat and the intermittent reinforcement schedule for appropriate behavior fosters an increase in the desired behavior. Thus VI schedules can be used both for teaching new behaviors and for maintaining previously taught behaviors.

Investigations into the way verbal stimuli influence behavior on VI schedules have demonstrated that rules, both those provided by others and those that are self-generated, may assist or hinder learning. In one study, participants who were asked to generate their own rules describing the schedule contingency that determined reinforcement were more likely to show schedule-typical behavior than participants who were told the rules in advance (Rosenfarb, Newland, Brannon, & Howey, 1992). Horne and Lowe (1993) on the other hand, found nearly equal numbers of participants given a task to perform created rules for themselves that did not correspond to the schedule of reinforcement as participants who created functional rules. Those whose rules did not match the contingencies for earning money continued to follow the rules they had generated, in spite of failure.

Recent investigations have focused on functional combinations of instructions and modeling to promote schedule sensitivity. A preschooler who was taught to ask for preferred items but whose requests persisted when no longer reinforced developed schedule sensitivity when taught specific signals for when teacher attention was and was not available (Tiger & Hanley, 2004). Neef and colleagues (2004) found that children with Attention-Deficit/Hyperactivity Disorder developed greater schedule sensitivity when a teacher modeled choice-making than when rules for making decisions were taught in advance of an activity. The implication for those who provide care to children with special needs is that discriminative stimuli can be used to aid a child to learn behaviors that are consistent with environmental contingencies. Clearly explaining rules, asking children to

hypothesize or to generate their own statements of the rules, and modeling decision-making that follows the schedule in effect can aid children to acquire sensitivities necessary for success at home, school, and in the workplace.

During interval schedules of reinforcement, behavior occurs at a lower rate than in other schedules. One way to increase the rate of performance under an interval schedule is to require that responses occur within a specific time frame. When under a limited hold schedule (Reynolds, 1968), a person must hurry to avoid losing the opportunity to be reinforced for producing a desired behavior. Arriving at the bus stop after the bus has left means you have to wait for the next one. Handing in her homework on time means Jean gets full credit for the assignment. Using limited holds can augment rates of responding sufficiently to maintain behavior on an interval schedule.

In summary, interval schedules are easy to implement and are valuable because they promote moderate rates of performance and do not require constant monitoring by teachers or staff. FI schedules reinforce following the first response after a specified amount of time but maintain desired behavior less efficiently than VI schedules, in which a behavior is reinforced when it occurs after an average amount of specified time. Using behavioral contrast helps to maintain behaviors that have been taught on a VI schedule. Teaching individuals the rules that apply in a given schedule, asking learners to form their own rules and then reviewing these with them, and modeling choice-making in difficult situations are strategies that foster the development of behaviors that are consistent with environmental contingencies. Though interval schedules produce characteristically lower rates of responding, limited holds can be placed on behavior to help pick up the pace when this is desirable.

## REFERENCES

Ferster, C. B., & Skinner, B. F. (1957). *Schedules of reinforcement.* New York: Appleton.

Horne, P. J., & Lowe, C. F. (1993). Determinants of human performance on concurrent schedules. *Journal of the Experimental Analysis of Behavior, 59,* 29–60.

Lowe, C. F., Beasty, A., & Bentall, R. P. (1983). The role of verbal behavior in human learning: Infant performance on fixed interval schedules. *Journal of the Experimental Analysis of Behavior, 39,* 157–164.

McSweeney, F. K. (1982). Positive and negative contrast as a function of component duration for key pecking and treadle pressing. *Journal of the Experimental Analysis of Behavior, 37,* 281–293.

Neef, N. A., Marckel, J., Ferreri, S., Jung, S., Nist, L., & Armstrong, N. (2004). Effects of modeling versus instructions on sensitivity to reinforcement schedules. *Journal of Applied Behavior Analysis, 37,* 267–281.

Reynolds, G. S. (1968). *A primer of operant conditioning.* Glenview, IL: Scott, Foresman.

Rosenfarb, I. S., Newland, M. C., Brannon, S. E., & Howey, D. S. (1992). Effects of self-generated rules on the development of schedule-controlled behavior. *Journal of the Experimental Analysis of Behavior, 58,* 107–121.

Tiger, J. H., & Hanley, H. P. (2004). Developing stimulus control of preschooler mands: An analysis of schedule-correlated and contingency-specifying stimuli. *Journal of Applied Behavior Analysis, 37,* 517–521.

THOMAS G. SZABO
*Western Michigan University*

BEHAVIORAL ASSESSMENT
NEGATIVE REINFORCEMENT
POSITIVE REINFORCEMENT

# INTERVENTION

Intervention consists of all planned attempts to promote the general welfare of exceptional individuals. There are three broad types of interventions: preventive, remedial, and compensatory.

Efforts to thwart the appearance of disabilities are considered preventive. For example, phenylketonuria is an inherited condition that ultimately results in brain damage and arrested mental development. Early diagnosis and intervention via a special diet effectively prevent the otherwise predictable neurological damage and mental retardation. Though it is not invariably so, preventive interventions are most often introduced by the medical profession.

Remedial intervention is the process of overcoming a deficit by correcting or otherwise improving it directly. When a handicapped reader is taught to read at a level that is comparable to that of his or her peer group, it is called remedial intervention. Remedial interventions are generally introduced by the education profession where service delivery, in the form of individualized education programs, is developed for each child independently.

In compensatory intervention, the usual approach is to provide a child with the means to circumvent, substitute, or otherwise offset an irremediable deficit. The best known and most widely used compensatory interventions consist of teaching a child to use technological advances that at least partially obviate the need for remediation. For example, the development of close-captioned television programs effectively compensates for the inability of people who are deaf to hear the program.

Several theoretical models exist by which interventions may be classified. They include biophysical, psychological, behavioral, ecological, and sociological models. In the following sections, each model is discussed and at least one example is provided to illustrate an application of the model. The illustrations are often not pure applications but may borrow from other theoretical models.

Biophysical theorists believe that abnormalities result from physical anomalies within the organism. The causes of affective, cognitive, and motoric difficulties may be either endogenous (i.e., originating within the body) or exogenous (originating outside of the body), and generally are considered to be genetic, nutritional, neurological, or biochemical in nature.

Genetic counseling is an intervention intended to prevent hereditary disorders from occurring. Prime candidates for genetic counseling are adults who have known hereditary disorders or who find themselves in circumstances that increase the probability of bearing a child with a genetic disorder. Sickle cell anemia, hemophilia, and osteogenesis imperfecta (tarda) are just three conditions that are genetically caused and, therefore, can be prevented through genetic counseling. On the other hand, genetic counselors provide a service to older couples by informing them of the probabilities of bearing a child with a genetic abnormality such as Down syndrome.

Nutritional deficiencies can result in severe, irreversible intellectual and physical disorders. Although nutritional problems are not particularly extensive in the United States, they do exist; in many third world nations (e.g., Ethiopia) the extent of such disorders is nothing short of catastrophic. The introduction of a balanced, nutritional diet is the obvious biophysical intervention of choice.

Neurological damage incurred following accidents, low levels of oxygen in the blood, etc., also result in behavioral abnormalities. When instruction in sign language is used with victims of electrical shock or stroke in order to circumvent the resulting neurological impairment, a compensatory intervention is implemented.

Remedial interventions are also employed to overcome assumed neurological dysfunctions. For instance, cognitive interventions are those that deal with teaching the individual how to think. Such interventions primarily intend to improve perception, memory, and problem solving. Included here are approaches often referred to as process or ability training (Mann & Sabatino, 1985; Ysseldyke & Algozzine, 1984). Often, the tasks involved are neuropsychologically specific. That is, they are characterized by modality specificity (e.g., auditory, visual, or haptic) or hemisphere specificity (i.e., they are analytical, sequential, and highly language-based or global, simultaneous, and nonlanguage-based). Cognitive intervention strategies cover a wide range of topics (Hallahan, 1980). They remain among the most controversial approaches to intervention.

The core belief in the psychological intervention model is that abnormality is the result of internalized conflicts that prevent the individual from fully participating in the social and academic environment. According to the earliest view, that of Freud's psychoanalysis, these conflicts interfere with the individual's normal progression through several stages of personality development presumed to take place during childhood and adolescence.

An outgrowth of Freudian psychology, the psychodynamic

model seeks to reduce the individual's conflicts by helping him or her to better understand both behavior and the reasons for exhibiting it. Fritz Redl was one of the primary contributors to this approach, introducing such classroom techniques as the life space interview (LSI). The LSI is actually a set of interventions designed to take place immediately following crisis situations. The interventions have a temporal advantage over traditional therapy in that life events are not allowed to grow distant before the child and the teacher or therapist deal with them. Psychoeducational approaches are an outgrowth of the work of Fritz Redl and have been proposed by his students and coworkers. These interventions are deliberate attempts to adapt psychodynamic concepts to the classroom environment.

Although the behavioral intervention tradition in special education is often tied most closely to B. F. Skinner's work in instrumental (or operant) conditioning, its roots are much broader. It is true that most of the interventions known today as behavior modification do stem from Skinner's ground-breaking research in reinforcement, punishment, and extinction. However, many of the more powerful interventions being introduced to the field lately (e.g., in the writings of Kathryn Blake, Siegfried Engelman, and Douglas Carnine) come from the traditional psychological research on concept learning, verbal learning, discrimination learning, and problem solving.

Both approaches share the common characteristic that the specific techniques they employ have been well validated through a rich research history. However, they are somewhat particular in their effects. Generally, conditioning approaches powerfully affect the motivation of the individual. That is, they provide the individual with the need or desire (the motive) to act in a specific manner. They probably influence the acquisition of skills as well, but their primary effect is motivational. On the other hand, conditions that influence the various types of learning primarily affect the speed with which the individual acquires, retains, and transfers new skills. Both behavioral interventions are powerful, well-documented approaches that enjoy considerable support in the research literature.

In contrast to proponents of the biophysical and psychological models, ecological theorists consider disturbance to be the result of the dynamic interaction between the child and the environment (Rhodes & Tracy, 1974). According to the ecological intervention approach, such events as physical abuse by the parents, slothful behavior by the child, or the death of a sibling are not isolated phenomena, but are interactive in nature. That is, the individual's behavior and other environmental conditions both affect and are affected by the people and conditions within the ecosphere. Consequently, advocates of this model discuss disturbed environments, not disturbed people.

Given their views on disturbance, it follows that ecological practitioners attempt to intervene on entire ecologies or at least those aspects of the environment considered to be

disturbed. In practice, this means that virtually any existing intervention may be used within the ecological model if it is considered to be of potential benefit. For instance, the biophysical intervention of drug therapy, the psychodynamic LSI, and such behavioral techniques as positive reinforcement and extinction would not be unusual within an ecological intervention system.

Without question, the best known implementation of an ecological intervention system is that of Project Re-Ed (Hobbs, 1966). In this project, children are temporarily removed from their homes to a residential setting that focuses on education. Two teacher-counselors are responsible for eight children during the day and at night. During their relatively brief stay in the residential facility, the teacher-counselors, aided by a host of supportive personnel, "reeducate" their charges regarding the virtues of trust, competence, cognitive control, the healthy expression of feelings, etc. Prior to the reintegration of the child into the community, additional staff members prepare the home and the community for his or her return. It is the liaison teacher's task to ensure that the faculty and staff of the child's school are sufficiently aware of the child's needs so as to provide effectively for them. The psychiatric social worker engages community services (e.g., family counseling) that are expected to be needed to enhance the probability that the child's return will be successful.

Three distinct views characterize the sociological intervention model: (1) labeling theory, (2) societal rule breaking and rule following, and (3) anomie. Specific interventions that are the result of these views are difficult to identify. Rather, in labeling theory and societal rule breaking and rule following, the opposite seems true; that is, it may be the interventions themselves that lead to deviance (as it is termed by sociologists).

Labeling theorists suggest that deviance itself is sometimes the result of the painfully focused attention that the individual's behavior may receive. They contend that labels such as troublemaker and dunce are pejorative and can actually be powerful stimuli for deviant behavior. Some individuals (e.g., Lemert, 1962) further contend that the most debilitating form of deviance is that which results from a falsely applied label (i.e., instances in which significant deviance did not exist until after the application of the label). Since the label was falsely applied, there is little hope that the child will work to overcome the "deviance"; instead, it is likely that the label itself will produce rebellion and other forms of deviance where none existed before.

Unlike other perspectives, sociological theorists generally view abnormality as behavior that is significantly contrary to the rules established by society. Since normal people break rules some of the time and abnormal individuals follow established rules much or even most of the time, it is important to note the agents who enforce societal rules (e.g., police, teachers) are in the unhappy position of deciding which rule breakers to label as abnormal. Clearly, only a few rule breakers are labeled by society. Since deviance is only a vaguely defined concept, it seems certain that many injustices in the form of false positives and false negatives are committed. In particular, many believe that individuals from poor or culturally different backgrounds are especially susceptible to the application of false labels. Such logic would seem to support the notion of labeling theory.

Anomie refers to deviance that results from social changes that occur at rates too fast for society to effectively establish norms for behavior. One example might be the United States' rapid shift from an agrarian society (in which large families were an advantage) to modern U.S. society, in which the role of children remains marked by ambiguity. The frustrations one feels in attempting to deal with an inoperable vending machine or a billing error committed by a computer are minor examples of anomie.

Interventions based on sociological models are difficult to implement. Nevertheless, society has implemented a number of them in an attempt to prevent or remediate deviance. Local, state, and federal police forces are intended to both prevent and enforce societal rules that have been codified into laws. Our judicial system is intended to mete out justice to those accused of offenses. Public school programs clearly play a similar role, particularly with regard to values and mores that have not been codified as laws. Prison systems and youth detention centers assume both a punitive and a remedial intervention role where lawbreakers are concerned. Some attempts by society to intervene more effectively include an increase in mental health centers, better organized community services, crisis intervention centers, suicide help lines, normalization projects, and not least, public school inclusion programming with children who have disabilities.

## REFERENCES

Hallahan, D. (Ed.). (1980). *Teaching exceptional children to use cognitive strategies.* Rockville, MD: Aspen.

Hobbs, N. (1966). Helping disturbed children: Psychological and ecological strategies. *American Psychologist, 21,* 1105–1115.

Lemert, E. (1962). Paranoia and the dynamics of exclusion. *Sociometry, 25,* 2–20.

Mann, L., & Sabatino, D. A. (1985). *Foundations of cognitive processes in special and remedial education.* Rockville, MD: Aspen.

Rhodes, W. C., & Tracy, M. I. (Eds.). (1974). *A study of child variance: Conceptual models* (Vol. 1). Ann Arbor: University of Michigan.

Ysseldyke, J. E., & Algozzine, B. (1984). *Introduction to special education.* Boston: Houghton Mifflin.

RONALD C. EAVES
*Auburn University*

JAMES A. POTEET
*Ball State University*

BEHAVIOR MODIFICATION
CHILD PSYCHOLOGY
ECOLOGICAL ASSESSMENT

## INTERVENTION IN SCHOOL AND CLINIC

In 1988, PRO-ED, Inc. purchased the journal *Academic Therapy* from Academic Therapy Publications. In 1990, PRO-ED changed the title of the journal to *Intervention in School and Clinic;* however, the emphasis remained the same as when John Arena began *Academic Therapy* in 1965. *Intervention* is a practitioner-oriented journal designed to provide practical, research-based ideas to those who work with students with severe learning disabilities or emotional and behavioral problems for whom typical classroom instruction is not effective. The articles are easy to read, and the interventions and strategies provided can be implemented in school or special clinical settings. *Intervention* is published five times during a volume year: September, November, January, March, and May.

JUDITH K. VORESS
*PRO-ED, Inc.*

## INTERVENTIONS FOR AUTISM

Persons with autism can make considerable gains in intellectual, motor, and social development when the appropriate intervention is implemented in schools and families (Adams & Toomey, 1995; Kozloff, 1998; Lovaas, 1987; Powers, 1992; Rogers, 1996). Rogers (1996) identified two specific characteristics of interventions that are effective in lessening the debilitating effects of autism and fostering affected children's psychosocial development: (1) *Early* intervention. Children with autism appear to make the greatest gains when treatment is implemented as early as feasible, between the ages of two and four years. (2) *Intense* intervention. Programs that have at least 15 contact hours weekly and low teacher-child ratios have more successful outcomes.

### Behaviorally-Oriented Programs

Dawson and Osterling (1997) identified several elements of early interventions for autism that are present in effective treatments: (1) The content of the curriculum should emphasize five basic skills: a) to attend and follow teaching commands, b) to imitate others, c) to comprehend and use language, d) to play appropriately, and e) to engage in social interactions. (2) The learning environment should be a highly structured one that emphasizes the generalization of mastered skills to other tasks, materials, persons, and locations in a child's environment. (3) Learning environments are tailored to the child's need for routine and predictability. Both (2) and (3) are important owing to the fact that children with autism are generally highly dependent on structure. They appear to benefit greatly from stability or predictability in their environments that enables them properly to induce generalizations and to learn strategies for action. (4) A functional approach is used to modify problem behaviors. Functional analysis consists of a) identifying environmental conditions—such as antecedent events, prompts, and reinforcement contingencies—that are maintaining undesirable behaviors and/or that might be used to strengthen desirable behavior; b) planning ways to alter features of the environment in order to replace problem behaviors and accelerate desirable behaviors; c) instituting the plan and collecting formative evaluation data on effectiveness; and d) revising program plans as indicated by the data. (5) The treatment program aids in the transition from preschool to kindergarten or first grade. This transition should be a gradual process in which the child is prepared for the change and the teacher is adequately trained to accommodate the child. Many programs offer workshops for teachers and others who will be working with the child. (6) Family involvement may be an essential component of successful programs (Kozloff, 1998). Parental involvement assists in the generalization and maintenance of skills that one-on-one and group therapy sessions cannot always facilitate. Many programs provide family training workshops, which offer assistance in treating behaviors that occur in the home environment.

Empirically-supported intervention programs rely mainly on behavioral or developmental principles in treating children with autism. Behavioral approaches incorporate principles of operant conditioning: Appropriate behaviors are highly reinforced, whereas inappropriate behaviors are either ignored, leading to extinction, or mildly punished with a firm "no." At the forefront of behavioral research with autistic children, Lovaas developed the Young Autism Project at the University of California at Los Angeles (Lovaas, 1987, 1993; McEachin, Lovaas, & Smith, 1993). This method emphasizes intense 40-hour a week treatment consisting of one-on-one discrete trial training. A discrete trial involves a directive, which is presented to the child, a period of time in which the child has to attend to that directive, and a consequence (either reinforcement or an indifferent "try again"). The child is prompted until he or she is able to perform the given directive successfully and independently. Behaviors are broken down and treated by applying principles of applied behavioral analysis, such as redirecting inappropriate behavior and teaching a more appropriate alternate behavior. This treatment is usually provided by paraprofessionals such as students and employees without advanced degrees.

The Young Autism Project (Lovaas, 1987, 1993; McEachin

et al., 1993) is perhaps the best described and evaluated of the autism intervention programs. Beginning in 1970, the project worked with children who had been independently diagnosed as autistic, who were less 40 months chronological age (less than 46 months if echolalic), and whose mental age was at least 11 months at chronological age 30 months. Children were assigned to either an experimental ($n = 19$) or control ($n = 19$) group. Although assignment was nonrandom, children in the two groups were highly similar at the outset of the program. Children in the experimental group received at least 40 hours a week of one-on-one therapy, using applied behavioral analysis procedures, in their homes, schools, and communities, whereas those in the control group received only 10 hours a week of treatment. The program was in effect for at least 2 years, following a protocol that emphasized reduction of self-stimulatory and aggressive behaviors and increasing imitation, compliance with requests, use of expressive and abstract language, appropriate emotional expression, and functioning with academic skills such as reading, writing, and arithmetic. Programming for children in the experimental group was reduced to 10 hours a week for children who placed into regular first-grade classrooms.

A double-blind follow-up report when the experimental children averaged 13 years of age and the control group children averaged 10 years of age (McEachin et al., 1993) largely confirmed the dramatic differences between groups when the children averaged about 7 years of age (Lovaas, 1987). Of functional importance, 9 of the 19 experimental children (47 percent) were in regular classrooms, whereas none of the control children were. Mean IQ of the experimental children was 84.5, whereas that of the control children was 54.9. On the Vineland Adaptive Behavior Scales, experimental children had a mean composite score of 72 to the control children's 48. Similar differences appeared on all individual scales, with experimental children showing higher socialization, communication, and daily living scores, but lower maladaptive behavior scores. Although, as several commentators on the long-term follow-up report indicated, some methodological problems remain, ". . . the findings suggest that intensive early intervention could compensate for neurological anomalies in such children" (McEachin et al., 1993, p. 371).

Another effective model of intervention incorporates developmental perspectives into teaching children with autism. The developmental approach stresses the importance of recognizing the uneven developmental patterns of persons with autism. Division TEACCH (Treatment and Education of Autistic and related Communication Handicapped children), founded by Schopler and Reichler, is a particularly well-developed example of a developmentally-focused program (Bashford, Mesibov, Schopler, & Shigley, 1984). The TEACCH method emphasizes the importance of individualizing each child's program to facilitate his or her developmental level. This method also uses some behavioral therapy and special education in the treatment of persons with autism. Parents are trained and considered "cotherapists" in the treatment programs of their children. TEACCH services provide a highly structured learning environment that facilitates the autistic individual's need for predictability and routine. This model also emphasizes the importance of assisting independence at all levels of development. The Health Sciences Center program (University of Colorado) also incorporates developmental principles into the learning environment, using play as a teaching medium to facilitate progress through stages of development. Positive feedback is presented to the child to encourage appropriate social interaction and to aid in the understanding of human relationships. This program also offers parent training and family support groups.

A number of other behavioral intervention programs based on either applied behavioral analysis or developmental principles have successfully improved the functioning of persons with autism. The amount of research on behavioral programs for autistic persons has greatly expanded in the past few years, and many new, sophisticated, and efficient behavioral techniques are being implemented. Summaries of these programs and their effects are in Rogers (1996) and Dawson and Osterling (1997). Many school systems are also recognizing the importance of behavioral interventions as effective treatments for children with autism.

## Psychopharmacological Interventions

Numerous drugs have been administered to autistic children in an attempt to decrease the behavioral disturbances of autism. As reported by McDougle (1997), some drug therapies have been successful. Drugs which affect serotonin functioning, such as buspirone, fluoxetine, and lithium, as well as some drugs which affect the dopamine system, have decreased symptoms in some children. Beta-blockers, which interfere with norepinephrine functioning, have led to a reduction in aggression and self-injurious behaviors and an increase in speech and social skills in some autistic persons. Since the neurobiological component of autism is, in large part, a mystery, no drug therapies have been successful in "curing" autism.

It is important to recognize no interventions are effective in treating all children with autism. Interventions that apply behavioral or developmental principles to the treatment of autism in combination with drug therapies have led to encouraging outcomes in those with autism.

### REFERENCES

Adams, L., & Toomey, J. (1995). Naturalistic observations of children with autism: Evidence for intersubjectivity. *New Directions for Child Development, 69,* 75–89.

Bashford, A., Mesibov, R., Schopler, E., & Shigley, H. (1984). Helping autistic children through their parents: The TEACCH model.
In A. Mesibov & B. Schopler (Eds.), *The effects of autism on the family* (pp. 65–81). New York: Plenum.

Dawson, G., & Osterling, J. (1997). Early intervention in autism. In M. J. Guralnick (Ed.), *The effectiveness of early intervention* (pp. 307–324). Baltimore: Brookes.

Kozloff, M. A. (1998). *Reaching the autistic child* (Rev. ed.). Cambridge, MA: Brookline.

Lovaas, I. O. (1987). Behavioral treatment and normal educational and intellectual functioning in young autistic children. *Journal of Consulting and Clinical Psychology, 55,* 3–9.

Lovaas, I. O. (1993). The development of a treatment-research project for developmentally disabled and autistic children. *Journal of Applied Behavior Analysis, 26,* 617–630.

McDougle, C. J. (1997). Psychopharmacology. In D. J. Cohen & F. R. Volkmar (Eds.), *Handbook of autism and pervasive developmental disorder* (2nd ed., pp. 707–729). New York: Wiley.

McEachin, J., Lovaas, I. O., & Smith, T. (1993). Long term outcomes for children with autism who received early intensive behavioral treatment. *American Journal on Mental Retardation, 97,* 359–372.

Powers, M. (1992). Early interventions for children with autism. In A. Berkell (Ed.), *Autism: Identification, education, and treatment* (pp. 282–309). New York: Guilford.

Rogers, S. J. (1996). Brief report: Early intervention in autism. *Journal of Autism and Developmental Disorders, 26,* 243–246.

JENNIFER MIGHT
MARTIN KOZLOFF
*University of North Carolina at Wilmington*

## INTERVENTION PROGRAMS, EARLY

The 25-year period between 1970 and 1995 was a most remarkable time for the field of early intervention. Evolving from a collection of disparate activities and therapeutic approaches, far more coherent, highly visible, and well-established programs of early intervention supports and services for children and families have emerged. (Guralnick, 1997, p. 3)

Indeed, Guralnick and others suggest that the first generation of intervention programs has ended with the demonstration of overall effectiveness, and that now the second generation of programs must attempt the more difficult task of determining "what interventions work best, for whom, under what conditions, and toward what ends . . ." (Guralnick, 1997, p. xvi). In general, across programs and handicapping or potentially handicapping conditions, intervention is effective, producing average effects of about half or greater standard deviations (Guralnick, 1997). However, conclusions about effectiveness in many cases is qualified by the fact that many evaluation studies have serious methodological problems. Further, as would be expected, intervention is far more effective for some conditions than for others and for some domains within conditions than others.

Some programs have had effects much smaller than initially anticipated, and some conditions (neuromotor and sensory ones, for example) are likely to be relatively resistant to modification. In addition, children with the same condition may benefit to quite different degrees from intervention, depending not only on the severity of their condition, but on a variety of factors, including the presence of other risk factors, the adequacy of family and environmental support, and where appropriate, availability of follow-up services. Although some conditions may themselves be resistant to modification, adaptive technological developments are increasing dramatically the extent to which affected children may be able to function in normal settings and develop in domains other than the one in which they are disabled.

Federal legislation mandates intervention services for children with disabilities. 1986 Amendments to PL 94-142, the Education of All Handicapped Children Act of 1974, extended services to children 3 to 5 years of age, and 1997 Amendments to what had become the Individuals with Disabilities Education Act (IDEA 97, PL 105-17) further mandate services to infants and toddlers who either manifest a developmental delay or have a diagnosed condition likely to lead to a developmental delay. Although some (e.g., Ramey & Ramey, 1998) use the term "intervention program" to describe services for children at risk for developmental delay and "treatment program" to describe services for children who have a specific diagnosed condition, many (e.g., Bryant & Graham, 1993; Guralnick, 1997) use "intervention program" inclusively, as will be the case with this entry.

Intervention programs now exist for children with many potentially handicapping and handicapping conditions: (1) disadvantaged at-risk children; (2) premature and low birth weight infants; (3) infants exposed to prenatal alcohol or other substances; (4) infants with various neuromotor disorders, including cerebral palsy; (5) infants whose parents are mentally retarded; (6) infants with Down syndrome; (7) infants with autism; (8) young children with communication (speech and language) disorders; (9) young children with conduct problems; (10) children with vision or hearing impairments; and (11) maltreating parents and their children, among others. Summaries and evaluations of these programs are described in individual chapters in Guralnick (1997b). Development of programs has progressed to the point that Bryant and Graham (1993) have collected recommendations for implementing such programs.

Several sets of guiding principles have been proposed to guide intervention programs. The following list was compiled largely from those (a) developed by the Division for Early Childhood Task Force on Recommended Practices as presented in Bryant and Graham (1993b) and (b) presented in Guralnick (1997a).

1. Whatever the service delivery model, it should be the least restrictive and most natural environment for the child and family.

2. Programs should center on the needs of individual families and children, and be responsive to families' priorities.

3. Programs should not only be interdisciplinary, but should fully integrate components from each discipline.

4. Empirical results and professional and family values should guide service delivery practices.

5. Each child's and each family's services should be individualized and developmentally appropriate.

6. Intervention programs should be based in local communities.

7. Intervention programs should integrate services from a variety of agencies using a systems model.

8. Intervention programs should begin as early and be as intense as realistically possible and appropriate for the child and family. However, for some conditions, timing and intensity of treatment must be based carefully on each child's level of development since manipulations that occur too early or are too intense may have iatrogenic effects, being actually harmful.

## REFERENCES

Bryant, D. M., & Graham, M. A. (1993a). *Implementing early intervention: From research to effective practice.* New York: Guilford.

Bryant, D. M., & Graham, M. A. (1993b). Models of service delivery. In D. M. Bryant & M. A. Graham (Eds.), *Implementing early intervention: From research to effective practice* (pp. 183–215). New York: Guilford.

Guralnick, M. J. (1997a). Second-generation research in the field of intervention. In M. J. Guralnick (Ed.), *The effectiveness of early intervention* (pp. 3–20). Baltimore: Brookes.

Guralnick, M. J. (1997b). *The effectiveness of early intervention.* Baltimore: Brookes.

ROBERT T. BROWN
*University of North Carolina at Wilmington*

**ASPERGER SYNDROME**
**AUTISM**

# INTERVENTION PROGRAMS FOR AT-RISK CHILDREN

Disadvantaged children (those born into poverty conditions) are at risk for developmental delays, school failure, behavioral problems, and a variety of other conditions. These children generally score below average on standardized intelligence and achievement tests, are overrepresented in special education classes, and are likely to drop out of school. In Birch and Gussow's (1970) representation of the poverty cycle, school failure contributed directly to unemployment and underemployment, which in turn were the major perpetuators of the cycle. Such failure and resulting poverty are clearly costly to the affected individuals, their children, and society at large.

Numerous intervention programs, beginning in infancy or early childhood, have been implemented in an attempt to foster more adequate development in these children. Each focuses on prevention instead of rehabilitation, integrated provision of a variety of services through a variety of agencies, and a holistic approach that includes the families in addition to the children. Each also has a primary goal of preventing developmental delays and school failure. Thus, they are sometimes (e.g., Ramey & Ramey, 1998) described as "preventive interventions."

The effectiveness of these programs has been long and regularly questioned (e.g., Herrnstein & Murray, 1994; Jensen, 1969; Spitz, 1986), particularly in terms of attempts to raise intelligence (e.g., Brown & Campione, 1986), and indeed, the large IQ increases of children in most programs generally fade relatively quickly after the programs end. However, evidence indicates that the programs are successful in a number of other ways, including reducing school failure. Unfortunately, results are not consistent across programs, and relatively few long-term outcome studies are available (Ramey & Ramey, 1998).

## Historical Background

Most developers of intelligence tests in the United States, including Goddard and Terman, were firm believers in the concept of fixed, innate intelligence. A major opponent of this view was not a psychologist or educator, but a journalist, Walter Lippmann, who debated Terman in a series of articles and letters in the *New Republic* in the 1920s. But by the 1930s, the Iowa Group began to present evidence of considerable increases in intelligence of adopted children and others whose environments had changed. Although justifiably criticized for methodological problems, their research nonetheless supported the view that IQs are modifiable. Further, data on military inductees indicated that Whites overall had higher IQs than Blacks, and northern Blacks had higher IQs than southern Blacks, suggesting that environmental factors influenced intelligence. More detail on the early nature-nurture debate, including reprints of the Terman-Lippmann papers, is in Block and Dworkin (1976).

Beginning in the 1930s and 40s and expanding greatly in the 1950s and 60s, experimental research demonstrated dramatic effects of early experience and environment on animals' learning and problem solving. Hebb (1949) used that research as the basis for his theory that varied early experience is necessary for adequate "primary learning" that in turn was a necessary precursor to adequate later learning. Hebb proposed that primary learning was perceptual and led to the development of particular structures in the brain. In an influential book, Hunt (1961) integrated Hebb's theory with Piaget's theory of child development and suggested that human intelligence could be modified through varied early experience. The finding that varied early environmental experiences increase brain development in animals (e.g., Bennett, Diamond, Krech, & Rosenzweig, 1964) supported the views of Hebb and Hunt. In addition, a variety of research suggested that environmental factors related to socioeconomic status (SES) might have positive or negative influences on children's cognitive development. For example, Hess and Shipman (1965) reported that relatively high-SES mothers used more complex and child-oriented language styles with their children than did mothers from poverty-level backgrounds and that these differences correlated with differences in the children's performance on problem-solving tasks. Thus, research of a variety of kinds converged on the possibility that early intervention might raise IQs and school performance of at-risk children. Out of this convergence came Head Start in 1964, now including Early Head Start, and other intervention programs.

## Specific Intervention Programs

This section will review the content and evaluations of two intervention programs for disadvantaged at-risk children for which long-term follow-up evaluation is available. Many other programs, including the Chicago Child and Parent Centers, Syracuse University Family Development Research Program. Houston Parent Child Development Center, and Project CARE, have had positive effects, although the results across projects are not wholly consistent. Summaries and evaluations of these programs are in Bryant and Maxwell (1997).

### The Carolina Abecedarian Project

Abecedarian may well be the best-designed, longest duration, and most intense of the intervention programs. Some participants received intervention services from early infancy to eight years of age. Owing to its comprehensiveness, it will be described in considerable detail. As summarized in Campbell and Ramey (1995), participants were almost all African American and from poverty-level families headed by a single female who was young and poorly educated. They were predicted to be at risk for impaired cognitive development on the basis of a 13-point high-risk index that emphasized parental education and income. The project used a true $2 \times 2$ factorial experimental design, initially matching children at birth on the basis of scores on the high-risk index and then randomly assigning them to an experimental or control group. Each of those two groups was then randomly divided into two subgroups based on 48-month IQs. The two factors were: (1) Preschool intervention (experimental) vs. No preschool intervention (control); and (2) School-age intervention (E) vs. No school-age intervention (C). Thus, the study had two conditions initially (E and C) and four beginning at kindergarten (EE, EC, CE, and CC). Control children received no special services, but were assessed with the experimental children.

The preschool intervention ran five full days a week for 50 weeks a year. The program was comprehensive and dealt with four domains: language development, cognitive development, gross and fine motor skills, and social skills. It particularly emphasized language development and interaction. Teacher:child ratios ranged from 1:3 for infants to 1:6 for four-year-olds. In the summer before they entered kindergarten, E children participated in a six-week program to help them make the transition to public school class settings. Parents served on the preschool's advisory board, had the opportunity to attend social events and information meetings, and were provided with information on child health and development.

The school-age intervention program attempted to support the children's academic performance in school by involving parents in the educational process. A home/school resource teacher (HST) worked with each EE and CE child and his or her parent(s) for the first three years of school. The HST taught parents to work with their children on a home curriculum that emphasized basic math and reading skills, developed individualized home curricula for each child, consulted with each child's regular teacher, and served as an advocate for the parents and children. The HST visited each home about 15 times a year for about 30–45 minutes and made extra visits if necessary to help families deal with various crises. The school-age intervention was obviously less intense and direct than was the preschool intervention.

A follow-up evaluation of the participants at age 15 showed significant effects of preschool program on several measures. Major results are shown in Table 1. Participants in the EE and EC groups had higher scores on reading and mathematics achievement tests, fewer assignments to special education programs, and only about half as many grade retentions than did children in the CC and CE groups. Differences in measured intelligence, although small, favored the EE and EC participants. The preschool program had notably large and durable positive effects on participant's academic achievement.

### The Perry Preschool

Owing to its long-term effects and demonstrable cost-effectiveness, the Perry Preschool program may be the best known to policy makers (Bryant & Maxwell, 1997). The program, which ran from 1962 through 1965, served disadvantaged preschool children whose initial IQs were less than 90. Children were randomly assigned to a preschool that used a specially-designed High/Scope Curriculum or an untreated control group. The High/Scope Curriculum, based on Piaget's constructivist developmental theory, treated participants as active learners and focused on child-initiated learning. Participants planned and carried out their own activities, supervised and encouraged by teachers. Experiences related to broad aspects of development, including initiative, creativity, language, logic and mathematical relations, and social relations. This type of curriculum provided participants with a sense of control, which is especially important for disadvantaged children. Participants attended preschool for 2.5 hours a day, five days a week, for two years before entering school.

Follow-up evaluation indicated that the High/Scope Curriculum was successful on not only academic but also socioemotional levels. During their school years, children who attended the High/Scope preschool spent fewer than half as many years as control children (1.1 vs. 2.8) in special education programs for those with educable mental retardation and scored higher on educational achievement tests on every evaluation. Although by the age of 27, no differences in cognitive scores between the two groups remained, preschool participants had higher rate of completion of grade 12 or more, lower rates of arrest, higher income, higher rate of home ownership, and lower participation in welfare (Schweinhart & Weikart, 1993). These differences are shown in Table 2. Of particular importance are cost-effectiveness analyses that indicate that return on investment for the public was $7.16 for each dollar spent on the program. The program developers (Schweinhart & Weikart, 1993) suggest that the success of the program owes to it having empowered children, parents, and teachers.

Table 1 Summary of results of the Carolina Abecedarian Project

| Measure | Treatment condition | | | |
| --- | --- | --- | --- | --- |
| | EE | EC | CE | CC |
| Intelligence at age 15 years | 95.0 | 94.5 | 87.3 | 92.0 |
| Woodcock-Johnson reading scores | 95.0 | 92.0 | 88.8 | 87.5 |
| Woodcock-Johnson mathematics scores | 92.3 | 92.3 | 87.0 | 86.0 |
| Percentage ever retained in grade to age 15 | 31 | 30 | 52 | 56 |
| Percentage assigned to special education, K–9 | 36 | 12 | 48 | 48 |

*Note:* Data derived from figures in Campbell and Ramey (1995).

Table 2  Summary of results of the Perry Project

| | Treatment condition | |
|---|---|---|
| Measure | Preschool | Control |
| Completed grade 12 | 71% | 54% |
| Had 5 or more arrests | 7% | 35% |
| Earned at least $2,000 month | 29% | 7% |
| Owned home | 36% | 13% |
| Received welfare as an adult | 59% | 80% |

*Note:* Data from Schweinhart and Weikart (1993).

## Possible Adverse Long-Term Effects of Some Forms of Early Intervention

A strong caution about necessary effectiveness of early intervention comes from a comparison among three different types of early intervention. The same group (Schweinhart & Weikart, 1997) who conducted the Perry Preschool project also have compared the effects of three different early intervention programs. Their High/Scope Preschool Curriculum Comparison study compared the High/Scope project, described above, with a traditional nursery school, and what they termed a Direct Instruction program. Direct Instruction was the highly-structured and teacher-initiated Bereiter and Englemann program in which teachers led groups of children in 20-minute planned question and answer sessions dealing with language, mathematics, and reading. Duration of the intervention was similar to that of the Perry Preschool project.

Evaluation of the effects of the different preschools when the participants were about 23 years old revealed an interesting pattern of results. Virtually no differences in educational attainment occurred across the three programs, although participants in the High/Scope program required more compensatory education. However, adults who had participated in the Direct Instruction program showed significantly more years of identified emotional disturbance in school, reported more sources of irritation, had more felony and property crime arrests, and lower levels of community volunteer activity. Although interpretation must be qualified owing to a relatively small number of subjects and the large number of variables studied, which increases the likelihood of chance significant differences, early Direct Instruction appeared to increase certain types of antisocial behavior many years later and thus may have had iatrogenic effects. These results not only indicate that different forms of early intervention may have quite different and sometimes unexpected effects, but that early intervention programs need to be evaluated on outcomes additional to educational variables.

## Principles for Intervention Programs for At-Risk Children

Based on extensive review of intervention programs for both at-risk children and children with diagnosed disabilities, Ramey and Ramey (1998) developed a set of six general principles that apply to the development, implementation, and effects of intervention programs. The additional seventh is implied by the others, but is of sufficient importance to justify separate status.

1. *Principle of developmental timing.* Generally speaking, the earlier in development intervention begins and the longer it lasts, the more effective it is. For intervention with specific conditions, of course, the infant/child must have developed to the point where intervention will have functional impact. In many cases, however, intervention most effectively should begin in early infancy as is the case with premature, low birth weight, or at-risk children.

2. *Principle of program intensity.* Programs increase in effectiveness with increases in number of intervention hours per day and days per week, number of intervention settings, and number of intervention activities. In addition, Ramey and Ramey (1998) suggest that the greatest benefits are in children who, along with their parents, participate most regularly and actively.

3. *Principle of direct provision of learning experiences.* Whether conducted in centers or at children's homes, programs whose staff members directly provide learning experiences to participants are more effective than those which train parents to provide the experiences. A number of studies have demonstrated the relative ineffectiveness of parent-oriented home visits only in comparison with programs that combine home visits with direct provision of services. These findings are particularly important, as Ramey and Ramey (1998) indicate, given the fact that the most widely implemented intervention programs in the United States involve only infrequent home visits.

4. *Principle of program breadth and flexibility.* As would be expected, programs increase in effectiveness with increases in the range of services provided and the routes through which intervention is implemented. Thus, programs that provide transportation, health, and nutritional assistance as necessary; specific therapies; parent training; and educational programs are more effective than those providing a more restricted range of services.

5. *Principle of individual differences in program benefits.* Children respond differently to the same programs, related at least in part to their initial degree risk. Who benefits more from a given program, those initially more or less impaired, may depend on the type of initial impairment. Thus, programs for low birth weight infants are effective overall, but very low birth weight infants benefit less than do those whose birth weights are higher. On the other hand, results from the Abecedarian Project indicate that children of the lowest IQ mothers showed the greatest relative increase in performance (Ramey & Ramey, 1998). Fur-

ther, different programs may be needed for children with different risk factors.

6. *Principle of ecological dominion and environmental maintenance of development.* Effects of early intervention will likely decrease or even disappear in the absence of follow-up programming and a supportive environment. The original notion, based partly on theorizing of Hebb (1949) that early intervention would have some permanent "inoculation effect," protecting the child from the effects of an adverse environment, has proved incorrect. Since learning and adaptation to current environments are continuous processes, a child returned to a maladaptive environment is likely to adapt to it. Further, as Ramey and Ramey indicate, for a child to maintain long-term benefit from intervention, its development must continue at a normal or near normal rate throughout the developmental period. Supplemental services may well be necessary to support this development.

7 *Principle of individuation.* This principle is both so obvious and so considered in programs for handicapped children in general, each of whom after all has an IEP, that perhaps could go without statement. Its importance, however, justifies its explication. Within a category of disorder or risk factor, infants and children show wide individual differences. To be optimally effective, program contents and rates of implementation need to be adapted to the characteristics and needs of individual children and families and adjusted to the individual's level and rate of development.

## Summary and Conclusions

Intervention, if early, intense, and of long duration, can benefit at-risk children and thereby society in a number of ways. Several programs have had considerable impact scholastically, improving children's school performance, reducing retention in grade, and reducing referrals for special services or assignment to special education classes. This effect may, although the participants are as yet too young to evaluate, increase their employability and therefore help interrupt the poverty cycle (Birch & Gussow, 1970). Many programs have also significantly reduced conduct and other behavior problems.

As to why the programs haven't had a greater impact on participants' intelligence, some possible answers may be offered: (1) Few of the programs began in infancy, and recent research (e.g., Hart & Risley, 1995) suggests that the first three years of life may be particularly important in children's intellectual development; (2) Relative to the amount of time participant children spend in their home environment, none of the programs has been truly intense or of long duration. Even those programs that run for 40 hours a week for several years cannot compete with the time (128 hours a week) children spend outside of the program subject to deleteri-

ous influences of their home and social setting. Given the fact that many of these children come from single-parent homes where the mothers are themselves poorly educated and of limited coping skills, we might be surprised that the programs have effects as extensive as some have.

## REFERENCES

Bennett, E. L., Diamond, M. C., Krech, D., & Rosenzweig, M. R. (1964). Chemical and anatomical plasticity of the brain. *Science, 146,* 610–619.

Birch, H. G., & Gussow, J. D. (1970). *Disadvantaged children: Health, nutrition, and school failure.* New York: Gruen & Stratton.

Block, N. J., & Dworkin, G. (Eds.). (1976). *The IQ controversy.* New York: Pantheon.

Bryant, D. M., & Graham, M. A. (Eds.). (1993a). *Implementing early intervention: From research to effective practice.* New York: Guilford.

Bryant, D. M., & Graham, M. A. (Eds.). (1993b). Models of service delivery. In D. M. Bryant & M. A. Graham (Eds.), *Implementing early intervention: From research to effective practice* (pp. 183–215). New York: Guilford.

Bryant, D. M., & Maxwell, K. (1997). The effectiveness of early intervention for disadvantaged children. In M. J. Guralnick (Ed.), *The effectiveness of early intervention* (pp. 23–46). Baltimore: Brookes.

Campbell, F. A., & Ramey, C. T. (1995). Cognitive and school outcomes for high-risk African-American students at middle adolescence: Positive effects of early intervention. *American Educational Research Journal, 32,* 743–772.

Guralnick, M. J. (1997a). Second-generation research in the field of intervention. In M. J. Guralnick (Ed.), *The effectiveness of early intervention* (pp. 3–20). Baltimore: Brookes.

Guralnick, M. J. (Ed.). (1997b). *The effectiveness of early intervention.* Baltimore: Brookes.

Hart, B., & Risley, T. R. (1995). *Meaningful differences in the everyday experience of young American children.* Baltimore: Brookes.

Hebb, D. O. (1949). *Organization of behavior.* New York: Wiley.

Herrnstein, R. J., & Murray, C. (1994). *The bell curve: Intelligence and class structure in American life.* New York: Free Press.

Hess, R. D., & Shipman, V. C. (1965). Early experience and the socialization of cognitive modes. *Child Development, 36,* 869–886.

Hunt, J. McV. (1961). *Intelligence and experience.* New York: Ronald.

Jensen, A. R. (1969). How much can we boost IQ and scholastic achievement? *Harvard Educational Review, 39,* 1–123.

Ramey, C. T., & Ramey, S. L. (1998). Early intervention and early experience. *American Psychologist, 53,* 109–120.

Schweinhart, L. J., & Weikart, D. P. (1993). Success by empowerment: The High/Scope Perry Preschool study through age 27. *Young Children, 49*(1), 54–58.

Schweinhart, L. J., & Weikart, D. P. (1997). The High/Scope preschool curriculum comparison study through age 23. *Early Childhood Research Quarterly, 12,* 117–143.

Spitz, H. H. (1986). *The raising of intelligence: A selected history of attempts to raise retarded intelligence.* Hillsdale, NJ: Erlbaum.

ROBERT T. BROWN
ALISON SHANER
*University of North Carolina at Wilmington*

## ABECEDARIAN PROJECT, THE
## HEAD START

## INVESTMENT THEORY OF CREATIVITY

Creativity operates just like investment banking, argue Robert J. Sternberg and Todd I. Lubart, with the difference being that the currency of creativity is ideas. A creative person will "buy low" and "sell high," just like a Wall Street trader. The key is knowing when to "invest" in ideas, and when to move on and pursue other projects (Sternberg & Lubart, 1995, 1996). According to the Sternberg-Lubart theory, there are six personal resources that are required for the production of creative work: Intelligence, Knowledge, Thinking Styles, Personality, Motivation, and Environmental Context. Intelligence, Personality, Motivation and Environmental Context are commonly viewed as necessary (but not sufficient) variables in other theories of creativity (e.g., Amabile, 1996; Csikszentmihalyi, 1996; Simonton, 1994). Intelligence, Sternberg and Lubart argue, plays a part in creativity according to the triarchic theory of intelligence (Sternberg, 1984). Synthetic intelligence is involved in casting a problem in a new perspective. Analytical intelligence helps an individual decide which ideas are worth pursuing. Finally, practical intelligence is necessary for conveying an idea to a larger audience. Personality, a commonly studied variable among creative individuals (e.g., Csikszentmihalyi, 1996), is also a factor in the Sternberg-Lubart model. Creative individuals must be risk-taking and persistent, they believe, especially as the most brilliant ideas are also the ones that encounter the most resistance.

Motivation is an area that is the subject of a current, fierce debate in the field of creativity, with one side (Amabile, 1996) arguing for the importance of intrinsic motivation (e.g., enjoyment) over extrinsic motivation (e.g., rewards), and others (e.g., Eisenberger & Cameron, 1996) believing the importance of intrinsic motivation is overstated. The investment theory does not take a strong stance on this debate, impressing the importance of both intrinsic and extrinsic motivators. The final factor found in several other theories, Environmental Context, is clearly important, as some environments foster creativity, while others crush it. An individual growing up in an environment that values creativity will have an easier time producing creative works than one who does not. However, there is actually a debate over whether a "bull-market" (accepting, reinforcing) or "bear-market" (cold, traumatic) environment most leads to a creative individual. Sternberg and Lubart (1995) believe that a synthesis of the two environments is likely the answer, with creativity being encouraged and highly regarded—and yet with some obstacles to overcome.

In addition to these four factors that are common to several other theories, the authors also make a strong case for two other variables, Knowledge and Thinking Styles. Knowledge refers to both formal knowledge (i.e., if you don't know the basic laws of mathematics, you aren't going to make a creative mathematical contribution) and informal knowledge. Informal knowledge, also called "tacit" knowledge, refers to knowledge, usually procedural, that is practical, yet not taught (Torff & Sternberg, 1998). The contribution of Thinking Styles is rooted in the theory of Mental Self-Government (Sternberg, 1997), which has three primary components: Legislative, Executive, and Judicial. According to this theory, legislative thinkers prefer to create things individually, with little inherent structure. Executive thinkers prefer to follow directions and carry out orders with a great deal of structure. Judicial thinkers like to judge and evaluate things. Sternberg and Lubart argue that at least some degree of legislative thinking is required for creativity.

These six variables are all needed for buying low and selling high. "Buying low," Sternberg and Lubart (1995, 1996) say, can be defined as choosing to pursue ideas that are either unknown or unfashionable. "Selling high" is having the insight to know when to move on and pursue other ideas. This strategy does mean, however, that an element of risk is involved. The authors define two types of risk: market risk and specific risk. Market risk refers to the larger area involved, while specific risk involves the more distinct types of creative production. One reason why everyone does not "buy low" is that there are these risks, and many people are risk-averse. A strong tendency in psychology, according to Sternberg (1997), is for "fads" to dominate the field. Someone who "buys low" has to resist this temptation to research "fads," which would nearly guarantee journal publications and grants, and instead attack less popular topics, risking rejection and loss of funding.

In addition to affecting psychological research, however, risk aversion affects education as well. Sternberg and Lubart (1995, 1996) point to the phenomenon of students selecting the easiest courses to take, instead of challenging courses, because of concern over grades. This process results, the authors argue, in the students never learning to take "sensible risks." However, this skill is needed for creative production. The Investment Theory offers a number of possible strategies (also using the investment banker analogy) for creative production. One is technical analysis, which (as it applies to creativity) is studying past trends in your chosen field. This information can then be used to anticipate coming trends—and whether to challenge them or utilize them. Fundamental analysis is deciding which areas are not overexposed or overrepresented (i.e., a student assigned to write about a state in America may pick a less visible state, such as Montana, rather than New York or California). Finally, Sternberg and Lubart (1995) cover the random-walk theory which holds that the odds of predicting future trends and topics of interest is practically chance.

One variable that Sternberg and Lubart (1995) discuss is school climate and its relationship to creativity. They report that personal experience has led them to believe that students "often become less able to produce creative work as they progress through school" (p. 267). One reason for this phenomenon may be that teaching usually has an end goal, which is measured through standardized testing. These tests traditionally are more knowledge-based and do not usually give credit for creativity.

**REFERENCES**

Amabile, T. M. (1996). *Creativity in context*. Boulder, CO: Westview.

Csikszentmihalyi, M. (1996). *Creativity*. New York: HarperCollins.

Eisenberger, R., & Cameron, J. (1996). Detrimental effects of reward: Reality or myth? *American Psychologist, 51*(11), 1153–1166.

Simonton, D. K. (1994). *Greatness*. New York: Guilford.

Sternberg, R. J. (1984). Toward a triarchic theory of human intelligence. *Behavioral and Brain Sciences, 7*, 269–287.

Sternberg, R. J. (1997). Fads in psychology: What we can do. *APA Monitor, 28*(7), 19.

Sternberg, R. J. (1997). *Thinking styles*. New York: Cambridge University Press.

Sternberg, R. J., & Lubart, T. I. (1995). *Defying the crowd*. New York: Free Press.

Sternberg, R. J., & Lubart, T. I. (1996). Investing in creativity. *American Psychologist, 51*, 677–688.

Torff, B., & Sternberg, R. J. (1998). Changing mind, changing world: Practical intelligence and tacit knowledge in adult learning. In R. J. Sternberg (Series Ed.), & C. M. Smith & T. Pourchot (Vol. Eds.), *Adult learning and development: Perspectives from educational psychology* (pp. 109–126). Mahweh, NJ: Erlbaum.

JAMES C. KAUFMAN
*California State University, San Bernardino*

# IQ

In psychoeducational assessment, a difference exists between an IQ and an intelligence quotient or ratio IQ. Since the ratio IQ or intelligence quotient has decreased in use, the IQ has taken on more of a generic meaning as an index of a test taker's current level of intellectual functioning or general cognitive ability. The IQ has been found useful in understanding and predicting a number of important behaviors such as academic achievement (Sattler, 1982). In addition, diagnoses of a variety of learning disorders such as mental retardation and learning disabilities are dependent in part on determining the IQ of the student.

A test taker's composite performance on a test consisting of cognitive or intellectual tasks is represented by the IQ score. Intelligence tests can be very different from each other in item composition and consequently may yield divergent IQ estimates for the same individual. The magnitude of the IQ score and the interpretation of its meaning is dependent on the test author's theory or definition of intelligence. For example, the Wechsler Intelligence Scales yield verbal and performance IQs and a full-scale IQ. The meaning of these IQ estimates relate to Wechsler's theory of intelligence, which includes verbal and nonverbal reasoning and a heavy emphasis on language and acquired knowledge such as is tapped on the information, vocabulary, and arithmetic subtests. This theory is in contrast to Kaufman and Kaufman's (1983) definition of intelligence, which minimizes the role of language and acquired knowledge. Interpretations of IQ estimates based on Wechsler's and Kaufman and Kaufman's definitions of intelligence will certainly be different; the tests would likely yield different IQ estimates for the same individual.

Although most tests of intelligence currently in use yield IQs, they do not yield intelligence quotients representing the ratio of the test taker's mental age to his or her chronological age multiplied by 100. Rather, these intelligence tests provide tables for converting raw scores into age-corrected deviation standard scores or IQs.

David Wechsler, author of the Wechsler Intelligence Scales, proposed what he called a deviation IQ. The deviation IQ is a measure that describes how much a test taker's intellectual ability deviates from the average performance of others of the same chronological age within the standardization sample. Initially, developing a test to measure adult intelligence, Wechsler (1939) culled the standardization sample's data and constructed tables so that the person who scored at the average level for his or her age group would receive an IQ of 100. The standard deviation for all age groups was set at 15 by Wechsler. For the Wechsler Intelligence Scale for children, IQs were obtained by comparing a child's performance with the average performance of those in his or her age group. This deviation IQ is a standard score that represents how many standard deviations above or below the average the test taker's intellectual ability falls. To further aid in communicating the meaning of the IQ to nonprofessionals, IQ standard scores are often translated into a descriptive classification such as mentally deficient, a percentile rank, or an age equivalent.

The deviation IQ now represents the most common composite standard score yielded by intelligence tests, including the Wechsler scales and the Stanford-Binet. This popularity can be attributed primarily to the deviation IQ's overcoming many of the criticisms leveled at the ratio intelligence quotient. The means and standard deviations are equal across all age levels for the deviation IQ, allowing comparability for similar IQs across different ages. However, it is important for the test user to remember that deviation IQs yielded by different intelligence tests can only be compared if they have the same or similar standard deviations.

Finally, the generic terms IQ and IQ tests have often been misinterpreted by nonprofessionals and they possess a number of unfortunate negative connotations. The IQ test and the IQ have also been the subject of litigation in state and federal courts (Jensen, 1980). As a result of these negative connotations and litigation, some contemporary test developers have avoided the term IQ in labeling their composite standard scores yielded from their intelligence tests. For example, McCarthy's (1972) General Cognitive Index (GCI), Kaufman and Kaufman's (1983) Mental Processing Composite (MPC), and Reynolds and Kamphaus's (2003) Composite Intelligence Index (CIX) can be used interchangeably with the IQ.

## REFERENCES

Jensen, A. R. (1980). *Bias in mental testing.* New York: Free Press.

Kaufman, A. S., & Kaufman, N. S. (1983). *Kaufman Assessment Battery for Children.* Circle Pines, MN: American Guidance Service.

McCarthy, D. (1972). *Manual for the McCarthy scales of children's abilities.* New York: Psychological Corporation.

Reynolds, C. R., & Kamphaus, R. W. (2003). *Reynolds Intellectual Assessment Scales.* Odessa, FL: PAR.

Sattler, J. M. (1982). *Assessment of children's intelligence and special abilities.* Boston: Allyn & Bacon.

Wechsler, D. (1939). *The measurement of adult intelligence.* Baltimore: Williams & Wilkins.

MARK E. SWERDLIK
*Illinois State University*

DEVIATION IQ
INTELLIGENCE
INTELLIGENCE TESTING

## IRAN, SPECIAL EDUCATION IN

In old Iran (Persia), in particular in Zarathostrian teachings, special care for individuals with disabilities is emphasized. Persian literature and Iranian-Islamic educational philosophy also are rich in sagely counsel for people with special needs. However, before the 20th century, there was no systematic and organizational attempt to provide special education services for exceptional children.

In 1925, a German minister, E. Kristofel, founded the Institute for the Blind Students in Tabriz. At about the same time, a group of German Protestant missioners founded the Efta junior school in Tehran for students with hearing impairment. In 1929, Jabbar Baghchehbaan, an Iranian teacher, started a school for hearing impaired students in Tabriz. Subsequently, several unofficial institutions were established to serve exceptional children, including Noor-e-Aeen in Esfahan in 1929 for blind girls by English missionary Geven Gester, Esfahan Blind Boys' School in 1950 by Kristofel, Roudaki, Work and Education Association for the Blind in 1928 by the Social Services Organization in Tehran, Golbidi Hearing Impaired School in Esfahan in 1935 by Hossein Golbidi, Tabriz Exceptional Institute in 1937 by Hassan Osouli, Khazaeli Institute for Blind Adults by Mohammad Khazaeli in 1943 in Tehran, Reza Pahlavi Blind Boarding School in Tehran by the Pahlavi Foundation, Nezam Mafi Institute in 1943 by the 13th Educational District in Tehran for hearing impaired students, Nimrouz Deaf Students Institute in 1943 in Tehran by Mahmood Pakzad, Mash'had Deaf and Mute Junior School in 1947 by Parichehre Ghafforian, and Baghchehban Institute No. 2 in 1847 by Samineh Baghcheban in Tehran.

The official beginning of special education in Iran was in 1987. Laws helped open the doors of public schools to students with disabilities and mandated their absorption to the greatest degree possible into normal life. The 1990 Rehabilitation Act outlawed discrimination against exceptional children in education and mandated the elimination of all barriers that may prevent them from attending school. In 1991 the Education Department and the National Welfare Organization began to work jointly to improve special education in regular school. Colleges began training regular classroom teachers and specialists in ways to assist special needs students.

Preschool education is mandatory for all children between ages 5 and 6. This period is considered to be important and marks the beginning of the Department of Education's efforts to focus on assessing, identifying, and providing special education services for special needs students in both private and the public schools. Special education programs include those for students with learning disabilities; Mental Retardation; hearing, speech, or visual impairments; emotional disturbance; orthopedic or other physical disabilities; those with multiple handicaps; and gifted students.

All children, including those with special needs, are examined physically and mentally each year and receive psychological assessment provided by joint personnel from the departments of Health and Education.

Special education is provided for students with special needs from primary school through high school. Depending on the severity of their disability, students are placed in one of eight settings: special day schools; specialized residential facilities, including homes and hospitals; full-time residential schools; full-time special classrooms exclusive to special education students in regular schools; regular classrooms attendance with part-time special education services in a special classroom; regular classroom attendance with part-time special education services in a regular classroom with part-time help or tutoring in a resource room; full-time attendance in regular classrooms with occasional help from itinerant specialists; and full-time attendance in regular classrooms with occasional help from the regular teacher. Children with special needs receive services in 2,029 ordinary schools, 815 special schools, and 219 special classes in regular schools.

The majority of special education students able to attend public schools are assigned to regular classrooms for all or part of the day and receive instruction from regular teachers. Depending on the particular student and the degree of disability, a special resource teacher may be assigned to a classroom to provide special help, especially with students who disrupt the classroom. Resource teachers may work with special education students individually or in small groups for part of the day in resource rooms for the learning disabled. The main objectives of special education emphasize training students with skills that will facilitate their achieving independence socially and economically.

Among Iran's 18 million children, special education services are provided to 99,972. They include 60,114 who have Mental Retardation, 17,633 who have a hearing impairment, 3,615 who have a visual impairment, 7,281 who have language impairment, 6,868 who have severe learning disabilities, 3,021 preschoolers with multiple disabilities, 1,190 who have physical disability, and 250 who have serious emotional disturbance. Not all children with special needs are enrolled in school. Some students in remote areas are ignored, some families are too shy to admit they have a child with special needs, and some receive special education at home. Thus, exact numbers of those with disabilities are unobtainable.

In 1967, gifted student education began unofficially in the Hoshdar educational complex in Tehran. In 1988, responsibility for gifted educational was assumed by the Education Department, was separated from special education, and was expanded nationally. Each year students are informed of the entry competition date and conditions for gifted classes. The brightest students are selected through an extensive nationwide competitive entry examination process in two preliminary and one advanced stages that includes achievement, academic aptitude, creativity tests, and grade point averages. These students receive highly advanced scientific and technological education in 44 cities. In 2005, 5,000 boys and 5,000 girls were in classes for gifted students.

Additional opportunities for students with special needs, including the gifted, are needed, especially in rural areas. Discussions center on the best approaches to implement effective educational intervention, budgetary allocations, the training of personnel, and entry criteria.

## REFERENCES

Department of Education. (2005). *National Organization for Development of Educational Talents.* Retrieved from http://www.nodet.net/

Hajibabaei, M., & Dehghani, H. Y. (2004). *Characteristics and problems of special education in Iran.* Department of Education Publishing Co.

MONIR SALEH
*Beheshti University, Tehran, Iran*

**INTERNATIONAL SCHOOL PSYCHOLOGY ASSOCIATION**

## IRWIN, ROBERT BENJAMIN (1883–1951)

Robert Benjamin Irwin, blind from the age of five, in 1909 became superintendent of classes for the blind in the Cleveland, Ohio, public schools, one of the first school systems in the United States to educate blind children. He organized braille reading classes and, most significantly, established the first "sight-saving" classes for partially seeing students rather than group them with blind children.

Irwin became director of research and education for the newly formed American Foundation for the Blind in 1923, and served as its executive director from 1929 until his retirement in 1950. He promoted federal legislation relating to the blind, including laws authorizing the Library of Congress to manufacture and distribute "talking books" and books in braille, providing Social Security for the blind, providing income tax exemptions for the blind, and giving priority to the blind in the operation of vending stands in federal buildings. Believing that the blind should not be segregated, he opposed a movement to establish a national college for the blind.

**Robert Benjamin Irwin**

## REFERENCES

Allen, A. (1952). Robert B. Irwin—A lifetime of service. *New Outlook for the Blind, 46,* 1–3.

Irwin, R. B. (1955). *As I saw it.* New York: American Foundation for the Blind.

PAUL IRVINE
*Katonah, New York*

## ISRAEL, SPECIAL EDUCATION IN

Special education services for children with special needs have been provided in Israel since the establishment of the state in 1948. However, in 1988, the first special education law was enacted. According to this law, the purpose of special education is to advance and develop the abilities and potential of disabled children, to correct and improve their physical, mental, psychological, and behavioral performance, to convey knowledge, skills, and habits, and to adapt them to behavior acceptable to society, for the purpose of becoming part of that society and being integrated in the world of work (Meadan & Gumpel, 2002).

The law provides for special education services for individuals between the ages of 3 and 21, including teaching and systematic learning and treatment, including physiotherapy, speech therapy, occupational therapy, and other interventions as they may be defined (Israel Ministry of Education, 1988). The disabilities covered include deafness, blindness, children in hospital, mild to severe retardations, behavior disorders, cerebral palsy, learning disabilities, autism, retarded developmental and language development, and mental illness. All children with special needs in these categories are provided with all the professional and educational services required, and all costs are covered by the ministry of education and the local municipalities.

A child experiencing difficulty in school is diagnosed by a professional in the relevant area (e.g., school psychologist, child neurologist, psychiatrist, speech pathologist) and, if deemed eligible for special education services, is referred to a local committee that makes formal decisions on eligibility and placement. The committee includes a representative of the local education authority, two ministry of education superintendents, a school psychologist, a pediatrician, a social worker, and a representative of the National Special Education Parents' Organization. The committee decides where the child will be educated and gives *priority to placing the child in a recognized school that is not a special education school.* The child's parents are allowed to attend and be represented, and are entitled to read all the documents concerning their child. The psychological tests most widely used to evaluate intellectual ability are the Wechsler-III and the Kaufman K-ABC, both of which have been standardized for the Israeli population (norms for these tests are currently being developed for the Arab population). Recently, the WAIS was standardized for high school students, and Israeli norms have been developed for several specific tests for learning disabilities.

The child with special needs, a parent, or a representative of a public organization can, within 21 days, submit an appeal concerning a decision of the placement committee to a seven-member board appointed by the ministry of education. Parents are usually granted wide latitude concerning placement, and a child will seldom be placed in a special education framework against parental wishes (usually if the child presents a clear danger to self or others).

Nearly all severe problems are detected at an early age, often soon after birth, thanks to a highly developed pre- and postnatal care system in the country and to child development centers functioning in most hospitals where children diagnosed with serious developmental and physical disorders can be observed and treated. These children are later placed in special kindergartens and schools.

The special education law has undergone major revisions since 2000, partly in response to the advocacy of parents who demanded that their children with special needs receive services within regular classrooms. In 2002, the ministry of education began implementing a policy striving to include every child with special needs in regular schools whenever possible. A multi-level hearing system has been established, and a school-based statutory committee convened by the principal of the school makes decisions about children with special needs at the school level, that determines their eligibility for assistance. This committee includes the child's teacher, the school psychologist, a special education specialist, and medical and paramedical professionals relevant to the area of disability being discussed, with parents and other teachers also invited. Similar procedures are in place for kindergartens.

Local Support and Resource Centers are the organizational and operational arm of the inclusion program. These centers currently serve only mild disability categories, function in a semi-autonomous manner, and are able to allocate resources according to specific local needs. These centers are changing the very nature of service provision in Israel: special education teachers are no longer associated with specific schools, but rather with their centers. In this way, teachers and paramedical services are provided from within an itinerant consultative/collaborative framework. A major criticism against this new structure is that it has become very bureaucratic and too large a proportion of the funds allocated to children with special needs is being used to administer the new system.

In special schools, a multidisciplinary team develops an individualized education program for each special needs child at the beginning of every school year. The individualized education program includes a plan that describes the child's current performance level, the learning aims and objectives, a timetable for achieving them, the required resources, and the measuring standards.

During the 2004–2005 academic year, 17,000 students received special education services in special education settings, and about 25,000 students received special education services through Local Support and Resource Centers in preschool and general education schools. Special education does not relate to a place but rather to a range of educational, didactic, and therapeutic procedures carried out in different settings. The percentage of pupils diagnosed with special needs in separate schools in 2005 is 2.3 percent. This is a dramatic drop from a figure of about 8 percent over the last 20 years, reflecting the inclusion policy of the ministry of education.

## REFERENCES

Meadan, H., & Gumpel, T. P. (2002). Special education in Israel. *Council for Exceptional Children, 30*(5), 16–20.

Israel Ministry of Education: Special Education Law, 1988.

BERNIE STEIN
*Tel Aviv, Israel*

## INTERNATIONAL SCHOOL PSYCHOLOGY ASSOCIATION

## ITA

See INITIAL TEACHING ALPHABET.

## ITALY, SPECIAL EDUCATION IN

In 1932, Italian school regulations made its first official provision for students with disabilities. However, prior to this time, religious and institutional leaders demonstrated an awareness of special learning needs.

The field of *special pedagogy* (pedagogia speciale) evolved alongside the work of researchers such as De Santis, Montesano, and Montessori. By the late 1800s, their work focused on the learning needs of children with physical, sensory, and cognitive impairments. Such children were largely institutionalized. Research shed light on learning as influenced by environments, cognitive function, reading theory, and socioeconomic status (Cornoldi, 1990).

In the mid-19th century, Italy's unification movement came to recognize the education system as a vehicle for creating Italian citizens by galvanizing national identity. Religious, municipal, and state institutions were called upon to abandon individualized philosophical approaches and to participate instead by educating children of the elite to become leaders in the new sociopolitical identity (White, 1991).

Despite these directives, De Santis, Montesano, Montessori, and others continued their work in private institutions, pioneering special education. They developed individual education plans for the disabled, specialized in teacher training initiatives, opened the country's first orthophrenic schools (residential schools specialized in innovative instructional techniques for disabled children while providing specialized training for teachers), and brought considerable attention to the needs of students with disabilities and otherwise marginalized children. In 1907, the first elementary school specifically designed for teaching children with disabilities was opened. By 1926, Montessori's methods were the most widely recognized examples of differentiated instruction (Cornoldi, 1991).

In 1923, the Gentile Education Reform outlined provisions for children who were deaf or blind, including the first education regulations that recognized the rights of students with disabilities. Five years later, compulsory public education was extended to students who were deaf or blind provided they had no other disabilities. Students with psychological disabilities were put in special classes or in institutes for juvenile offenders (Organization for Economic Cooperation and Development, 2003).

The First Constitution of the Italian Republic in 1948 proclaimed that all citizens have equal social dignity and are equal before the law. All children between ages 6 and 14 were granted the right to a free public education. Article 34 provides persons with disabilities the right to an education and work. This provision paved the way for the eventual development of inclusionary education (McGrath, 2002).

In the late 1960s, throughout Europe and the United States, efforts were made to challenge established social order and dismantle immobile power structures. Italy was one of the countries caught in this social upheaval. The demands of trade unions helped modify social policies by calling on social services to prevent and contain marginalization. These sociopolitical changes significantly impacted the three subcultures of Italian life (Catholic, Marxist, and secular-progressive) which, in turn, had a particular impact on special education by calling for the closing of institutions whereby psychoeducational issues could be dealt with in the social realm (White, 1991). This sentiment gained sociopolitical momentum and became known as the *anti-institutional movement*, spearheaded by psychiatrist Franco Basaglia. In 1977, Law #517 provided all Italians the constitutional right to be educated, free from discrimination. This anti-institutional mandate became known as Basaglia's Law. In a similar spirit, Article 28 of Law 118 of 1971 mandates that students with disabilities are to be instructed alongside their nondisabled peers in public schools, unless their disabilities are of such gravity that they impede learning or successful inclusion (European Commission, 1995).

Law 104 of 1992, known as the Framework Law, is the principal legislative mandate for school inclusion. It extends inclusionary practice to nursery, primary, and secondary schools, universities, rehabilitation centers, and hospitals. The Framework Law outlines procedures for identifying students for entitlement to special education services. It was reinforced in 1994 with a presidential decree that called for cooperation among schools, local health units, and families to address the special needs of students with disabilities in inclusionary settings (Organization for Economic Cooperation and Development, 2003).

Today, although inclusionary education is widespread, its challenge continues to lie in the training of teachers and staff to support the continual improvement of inclusionary practice. In October 2002, a report presented by the Ministry of Education to the Parliament delineated the paucity of trained special education teachers and coherence of programming. These and other research initiatives suggest directions for further study of inclusive special education (European Commission, 1995).

## REFERENCES

Cornoldi, C. (1990). *I Disturbi dell'Apprendimento. Aspetti Psicologici e Neuropsicologici* [Learning Disabilities: Psychological and Neuropsychological Aspects]. Bologna: Il Mulino.

European Commission. (1995). *Structures of the education and initial training systems of the European Union* (2nd ed.), prepared by EURYDICE and CEDEFOP. Luxembourg: Office for official publications of the European Community.

McGrath, B. (2002). *A social context of inclusion: A three-country case study.* Unpublished doctoral dissertation, Loyola University, Chicago.

Organization for Economic Cooperation and Development. (2003). *Education at a glance.* Paris: Author.

White, S. (1991). *Progressive renaissance: America and the reconstruction of Italian education 1943–62.* New York: Garland.

JULIA COYNE
*Loyola University, Chicago*

## INTERNATIONAL SCHOOL PSYCHOLOGY ASSOCIATION

## ITARD, JEAN M. G. (1775–1838)

Jean Itard, a French physician who served on the medical staff of the famous National Institution for Deaf Mutes in Paris, is best known for his work with the wild boy of Aveyron. This child of 11 or 12 was found naked in the woods, where he had been living as a savage. He was brought to Itard for training, and Itard set out to civilize the boy, to teach him to speak and to learn. Five years of work with the boy, whom Itard named Victor, led to the conclusion that his pupil was mentally retarded. Victor learned to read and write many words and could even exchange simple written communications with others, but he never learned to speak. He became socialized to some degree; he could, for example,

dine in a restaurant with his tutor. The experiment ended unhappily when, with the onset of puberty, Victor changed from a gentle boy into a rebellious youth. Itard abandoned his work with the boy, and Victor lived in custodial care until his death at the age of about 40.

Itard's work was not in vain, however. He demonstrated that mentally retarded individuals could be trained in both cognitive and social skills and he provided essential groundwork for the development of the first educational programs for mentally retarded children by Edouard Seguin and others.

## REFERENCES

Itard, J. M. G. (1932). *The wild boy of Aveyron.* New York: Appleton-Century-Crofts.

Kanner, L. (1960). Itard, Seguin, Howe—Three pioneers in the education of retarded children. *American Journal of Mental Deficiency, 65,* 2–10.

Lane, H. (1976). *The wild boy of Aveyron.* Cambridge, MA: Harvard Press.

PAUL IRVINE
*Katonah, New York*

## ITINERANT SERVICES

Itinerant services are resource programs on wheels. This program model is most practical in areas that have limited funds for full-time services in each school or that do not have enough eligible children to warrant a full-time teacher. In addition to serving schools, itinerant services can provide instruction in the hospital or home to recuperating and chronically ill children by establishing a curriculum and offering teaching services.

Visual impairment was one of the first areas to demonstrate that itinerant instruction on a resource basis could be used in conjunction with a regular school program. Only a few decades ago, according to Reynolds and Birch (1977), it was common in many states to have blind and partially sighted students automatically referred and placed in residential schools. It has now become the prevailing practice in a great many school districts to start visually impaired children in regular school programs and to maintain them there by delivering the special instruction they need in that environment or nearby resource rooms. In many states, there are more legally blind children being educated in regular classes as a result of itinerant service programs than are being educated in special schools or classes for the blind (Deighton, 1971). Although itinerant services as a derivative of the resource room have been used primarily with visually impaired children, this program model is being employed with hearing impaired, emotionally disturbed, learning-disabled, and gifted children.

A comparative study, designed by Pepe (1973), concerned the effectiveness of itinerant services and resource room programs serving children with learning disabilities. Each group consisted of 20 students identified as learning disabled, of average ability, and 9 to 12 years of age. There was no significant difference in the treatment effect gains of students, indicating that the itinerant and resource room programs were equally effective in providing services for mildly learning-disabled children. Since there was no significant difference in gains made by students of comparable ability who were afforded less time by the special education teachers, the itinerant programs appeared to be more efficient. Similar results were obtained by Sabatino (1971).

Difficulties in operating itinerant services are described by Wiederholt, Hammill, and Brown (1978). First, teachers must carry their materials from school to school. Second, they frequently must work in the furnace room, in the lunchroom, or in the principal's or counselor's office, and may even share a room with other staff. Third, they are rarely able to provide instruction on a daily basis. Fourth, the fact that they may serve several schools makes it difficult for them to develop social and professional bonds.

An advantage of itinerant services is flexible scheduling, allowing the student's instructional program to be altered to meet changing needs. Because large numbers of young children with developing problems can be accommodated less expensively, later severe disorders may be prevented, making room for the disabled students for whom self-contained classes were originally developed. Through itinerant services, most students can receive help in their neighborhood schools; thus, the necessity of busing disabled children is reduced. Finally, in contrast to the self-contained special class program, children start the day in an integrated program with their age mates and become special for specific services. The itinerant service setting helps avoid the stigma of the special class.

## REFERENCES

Deighton, L. C. (1971). *The encyclopedia of education* (Vol. 4). New York: Macmillan.

Pepe, H. J. (1973). A comparison of the effectiveness of itinerant and resource room model programs designed to serve children with learning disabilities (Doctoral dissertation, University of Kansas, 1973). *Dissertation Abstracts, 34,* 7612A.

Reynolds, M. C., & Birch, J. W. (1977). *Teaching exceptional children in all America's schools.* Reston, VA: Council for Exceptional Children.

Sabatino, D. A. (1971). An evaluation of resource rooms for children with learning disabilities. *Journal of Learning Disabilities, 4,* 341.

Wiederholt, J. L., Hammill, D. D., & Brown, V. (1978). *The resource teacher.* Boston: Allyn & Bacon.

WARNER H. BRITTON
*Auburn University*

HOMEBOUND INSTRUCTION
ITINERANT TEACHER
RESOURCE ROOM

## ITINERANT TEACHER

An itinerant teacher has received specialized training in a particular category and provides services to homebound students, or students in hospital programs. The itinerant teacher may also travel between schools within a district, or between districts. The service rendered supplements the instruction provided by the student's classroom teacher. Although teaching is the major responsibility of itinerant teachers, they are involved in related activities such as procuring special materials, conferring with parents, assessing students, or participating in case conferences (Dejnozka & Kapel, 1982). According to Wiederholt, Hammill, and Brown (1978), itinerant teachers must also be able to manage daily details, such as scheduling and grading. In addition, they must possess considerable knowledge of many specific school-related abilities, including reading, spelling, writing, arithmetic, spoken language, and classroom behavior.

The use of itinerant teachers has developed particularly in the field of speech and hearing impairments, where only small group or individual instruction will work. In the past few years, itinerant teachers have been employed to serve learning-disabled, emotionally disturbed, and gifted students.

Disadvantages, reported by Ellis and Mathews (1982), indicate that itinerant teachers have larger caseloads than special education teachers with a self-contained classroom, which usually has an established teacher-pupil ratio prescribed by state law. The larger caseload often prevents the itinerant teacher from becoming completely familiar with the child. According to Cohen (1982), the role of the itinerant teacher has several drawbacks. For example, itinerant teachers rarely become accepted as a part of a school faculty because they are divided between schools. They are available only on a limited basis, creating problems in scheduling. Because of their itinerant schedules, these teachers are sometimes perceived to be inaccessible both by classroom teachers and parents. Itinerant teachers confess that at times their instructional roles seem dictated by schedule rather than by choice. In addition, the physical burden of transporting materials between resource rooms, the sharing of locations with other staff, and the general feeling of isolation can make itinerant teachers question their contribution to a school's program.

Advantages to employing an itinerant teacher occur when the teacher serves as an in-school consultant based on broad experience with many children exhibiting different educational and behavioral problems. More children can be served by itinerant teachers working extensively with classroom teachers through indirect services to students with mild problems. Another important advantage, according to Deighton (1971), is the effect of changing the attitude of the classroom teacher in dealing with the special student. As the classroom teacher becomes more skillful in meeting the needs of the special child, the itinerant teacher can become involved in the more severe cases that require direct services.

## REFERENCES

Cohen, J. H. (1982). *Handbook of resource room teaching.* New York: Aspen.

Deighton, L. C. (1971). *The encyclopedia of education* (Vol. 4). New York: Macmillan.

Dejnozka, E. L., & Kapel, D. E. (1982). *American educators' encyclopedia.* Westport, CT: Greenwood.

Ellis, J. R., & Mathews, G. J. (1982). *Professional role performance difficulties of first-year itinerant specialists.* Northern Illinois University, Educational Resources Information Center.

Wiederholt, J. L., & Hammill, D. D., & Brown, V. (1978). *The resource teacher.* Boston: Allyn & Bacon.

WARNER H. BRITTON
*Auburn University*

**HOMEBOUND INSTRUCTION**
**ITINERANT SERVICES**
**RESOURCE TEACHER**

# J

## JACTATIO CAPITIS

Prior to puberty, it is common for children, especially during the preschool years, to engage in rhythmic body movements and rhythmic vocalizations. Some is inconsequential beyond being annoying to adults (e.g., body rocking or incessant humming). Some will engage in more serious forms of rhythmic behavior that may include head-banging. All of such behaviors are subsumed under the term Jactatio Capitis (JC), with the additional modifier of "nocturna" in those cases where the behavior occurs only at night (Gillberg, 1995).

About 10 percent of otherwise normal children will display behavior that is consistent with JC; however, a disproportionate percentage of these children go on to develop diagnoses of disorders of attention and motor control (Gillberg, 1995). The male-to-female ratio of JC is estimated to be 3:1. It is suspected to be an inheritable disorder, but its true etiology and pathogenesis are not known. In most cases no intervention beyond reassurance of the parents and the child will be required, as the disorder is most commonly benign. There is no special treatment beyond behavioral interventions when the symptoms may be injurious to the child. Outcome is excellent in those cases that do not progress to motoric and attentional deficiencies, with most cases being entirely asymptomatic by adulthood with no intervention.

### REFERENCE

Gillberg, C. (1995). *Clinical child neuropsychiatry.* Cambridge: Cambridge University Press.

CECIL R. REYNOLDS
*Texas A&M University*

## JAPAN, SPECIAL EDUCATION IN

### Special Education within the Formal Education System

In Japan, the compulsory education system consists of 6 years of primary school education followed by 3 years of junior high school education. Children start their compulsory education at the age of 6 and finish it at 15.

School education that is provided for mentally and physically challenged children, in accordance with the type and extent of their disability and their aptitude, is called *tokushu kyoiku,* or special education. This aims to help develop children's potentials and to broaden their abilities.

Unlike the United States and some countries in Europe, Japan does not include vocational training, professional education, or the education of gifted children under the label of special education. Subsequently, in recent years, *tokushu kyoiku* has been more often referred to as *shogaiji kyoiku,* or the education of children with physical and/or intellectual disabilities. For the purpose of this paper, the author uses the English term "special education" to describe Japan's formal school education for children with physical and/or intellectual disabilities.

### System of Special Education

The special education provided for disabled children of school age is given according to the type and extent of their disability. The definition of disability includes visual and hearing impairment, intellectual development disability, physical disability, infirmity/invalidism, and emotional disturbance. Within the school education system, there are special schools, special classes offered by ordinary primary schools and junior high schools, and *tsukyu,* or resource rooms.

The special schools include schools for the visually impaired, schools for the hearing impaired, and schools for mentally and physically disabled children (including children with mental deficiency and children with a weak constitution). These schools cater to relatively seriously disabled children. Some special schools have a kindergarten and a senior high school. For those children who have difficulty commuting to school because of the severity of their impediments, teachers visit the children at their home, hospital, or other institution.

The special classes cater to children with relatively mild disabilities. The children are given special education suitable to their individual needs, considering the type and extent of their disability—mental deficiency, physical disability, weak constitution, weak sight, difficulty in hearing, speech impediment, or emotional disturbance. The law provides for ordinary senior high schools to open special classes, but in reality, none offer them.

*Tsu-kyu* literally means attending class. In the current special education system, it is a form of guidance offered in special classrooms (resource rooms) to school children with weak eyes, difficulty in hearing, a speech impediment, or emotional disturbances. These children attend classes in ordinary schools; however, in addition, they may receive a specialist's guidance appropriate to their individual needs.

Incidentally, the use of the Japanese term *seishin haku-jaku* (mental deficiency) was banned on April 1, 1999. It was replaced by *chiteki shogai* (intellectual disability). Therefore, the school or class for children with mental deficiency will be called the school or class for children with intellectual disability.

## History of Special Education

The first provisions regarding special education were made in 1872, when the modern system of formal education in Japan was inaugurated. In 1878, a school for the visually impaired and the hearing impaired came into being in Kyoto. In 1923, a legal obligation was laid on each prefecture to establish schools for the visually impaired and schools for the hearing impaired.

For children with intellectual developmental disabilities, a private school known as Takinogawa Gakuen was opened in Tokyo in 1891. During the 1920s, special classes for those with intellectual development disabilities were introduced in Tokyo and in many other parts of Japan. Classes for children who stuttered, were weak-sighted, or were hard-of-hearing were also opened one after another. In 1941, immediately before the outbreak of the Pacific War, the National Elementary School decree was instituted. Education for disabled children, in addition to the establishment of schools for the visually impaired and hearing impaired, was incorporated into the nation's school education system. However, because of the war, no progress was made in the area of special education.

## After World War II

In the aftermath of World War II, drastic educational reform was introduced. In 1947, the School Education Law was enacted based on the spirit of the new Constitution and the Fundamental Law of Education. Chapter VI, "Special Education" (Articles 77–76), presented the outline of special education. At this time, various forms of education for physically and/or mentally disabled children of school age were put together and termed special education. Thus, special education took its place legally as part of the compulsory education system for the first time in the educational history of Japan.

The law provided for the establishment of special schools, which were classified into three divisions—schools for the visually impaired (*mo gakko*), schools for the hearing impaired (*ro gakko*), and schools for physically and/or mentally disabled children (*yogo gakko*). The extent of children's handicaps was also defined by law, providing a standard teachers could use regarding special education.

Compulsory education at schools for the visually impaired and schools for the hearing impaired was introduced in 1948. However, plans for building schools for physically and/or mentally disabled children across the nation made little progress. It was not until 1979 that compulsory education was instituted at these schools. All special schools introduced compulsory education into their syllabus. The home visit system, which had already been put into practice, formally took its place as one method of instruction offered by the schools for physically and/or mentally disabled children.

Children who were expected to attend special classes were divided according to the type of disability—intellectual disability, physical disability, physical weakness, amblyopia (weak sight), impaired hearing, speech impediment, and emotional disturbance. In 1993, the system of *tsu kyu* was inaugurated, under which disabled children enrolled in ordinary schools could receive lessons in special classrooms (resource rooms).

## Numbers of Schools and Children Receiving Special Education

As of May 1996, children receiving special education accounted for 1.067 percent of all children of school age from 6 to 15 years. This percentage is low when compared with figures in the United States and other developed nations in Europe. The rate of attendance at special schools was 0.39 percent of all school-aged children.

Schools for intellectually disabled children numbered 511 with a total enrollment of 52,102. Special classes for intellectually disabled children numbered 15,511 at primary schools and 7,260 at junior high schools. These special classes were attended by 44,061 primary school pupils and 22,101 junior high school students.

There were 19,424 primary school children and 582 junior high school students who received special lessons at resource rooms under the *tsu-kyu* system. By the type of impediment, their cases were broken down into speech impediment with 83 percent, emotional disturbance with 10 percent, and impaired hearing with 6 percent.

## Curriculum

The law stipulates that special schools must offer, in principle, the same education as ordinary schools. To help improve and overcome physical and mental disabilities, special courses in such subjects as therapeutic training and exercises are provided. The objective of each lesson and the curriculum at schools for mentally disabled children are not bound by the government guidelines for teaching.

The curriculum can be organized in a flexible manner in accordance with the needs of the children.

The curriculum for special classes is organized on the basis of teaching guidelines set by the Ministry of Education. However, special curriculums can be drawn up to suit any child's individual needs.

The course of study for disabled children who receive lessons in resource rooms under the *tsu-kyu* system includes therapeutic training classes, in addition to ordinary subjects, aimed at encouraging them to improve and to overcome their disabilities.

## Standard for Class Organization

Classes at special schools for disabled children and special classes at ordinary schools are small. This is to meet the educational needs of all of the children. The maximum number of children per class is six for special schools and eight for special classes. However, a check of the 1996 statistics reveals that the average number of children per class is three at both special schools and special classes.

## Textbooks

In addition to the textbooks compiled by the Ministry of Education for the purpose of special education, the textbooks used in ordinary primary and junior high schools are also used in special schools. The textbooks made by the Ministry of Education include braille books for the visually impaired, speech and music texts for the hearing impaired, and Japanese, math, and music texts for the intellectually disabled.

In case the textbooks authorized by the Ministry of Education are unsuitable for use in special classes, books placed on the market can be used as textbooks if approved by the Board of Education.

## Home Visit System and Interaction with Other People

A survey of 970 special schools in 1998 showed that the system of home visits was practiced by 403 schools—one school for the visually impaired, 115 schools for physically disabled children, 239 schools for mentally disabled children, and 48 schools for sickly children.

Special school children sometimes have the opportunity to get together with their peers at ordinary primary and junior high schools. Children in special classes also sometimes mix with children in ordinary classes to do schoolwork or engage in other activities together. Disabled children also have opportunities to participate in events organized by neighborhood associations.

These opportunities are helpful not only in enriching the experience and social life of the disabled and building their characters, but also by increasing society's understanding of disabled children as well as special education.

## Counseling on Education and Schooling

Counseling to parents on education prior to enrollment at school is given by the Board of Education. This counseling before school age is helpful to the parents who have physically and mentally disabled children. Counselors are able to give pertinent advice on the care of disabled children in their infancy, alleviating anxiety experienced by the parents about their children's upbringings, in addition to advice on the right course of education. Whether special education should be taken is decided by local Boards of Education, with the parents' opinions always held in high regard.

## Advice about What to Do after Graduation

Most of the special school and special class children who completed their compulsory education in March 1996 went on to tertiary education—96.9 percent of the graduates from the schools for the visually impaired, 98.5 percent of those from the schools for the hearing impaired, 84.9 percent of those for mentally and physically handicapped, and 73.8 percent of those at special classes in junior high schools. Although recently the number of graduates from special schools for the intellectually disabled has been decreasing, the percentage of those who go on to the next stage of education has been increasing. The ratio was 56 percent in 1984 and it rose to 83 percent in 1996. After graduation from special schools, 43.7 percent of graduates from the schools for the visually impaired and 43.4 percent of those from the schools for the hearing impaired went on to special training courses attached to the school or university. Meanwhile, the rate of employment was 21.9 percent for graduates from the schools for the visually impaired and 35.9 percent for those from the schools for the hearing impaired.

Most graduates from the senior classes of special schools for the physically and mentally disabled entered social welfare facilities: 63 percent for the schools for the intellectually disabled, 78.9 percent for the schools for the physically disabled, and 55.5 percent for the schools for the physically weak children. The employment rates were 34.4 percent, 12.1 percent, and 16.8 percent, respectively. It has become increasingly difficult for the intellectually disabled to find employment since 1990 because of the long-term business depression in Japan.

## Teachers and Teacher Training Program

In addition to the standard teaching certification, teachers at special schools for the visually impaired, hearing impaired, and physically and/or mentally disabled are required to obtain extra certification. Instructors of acupuncture at the schools for the visually impaired have to possess an acupuncturist's license and instructors of haircutting must have a barber's license. Because of the nature of the profession, it is compulsory for teachers at special schools to undergo special vocational training on a regular basis. In special classes and resource rooms, teachers can work only if they have the standard teaching certification.

## National Expenditure for Special Education and Subsidies

The fiscal 1997 national budget showed that a total of ¥30,480 million was appropriated for special education, of which the largest ¥15.7 billion was allocated for compulsory education at schools for the visually impaired, hearing impaired, and physically and/or mentally disabled. The next largest expenditure was ¥6.07 billion for financial assistance for encouragement of special school attendance.

## Problems to Be Addressed and the Future of Special Education in Japan

Japan's special education system has long kept physically and/or mentally disabled children separated from their peers in ordinary schools. However, the trend in society today is toward the creation of equal opportunities for children, disabled or otherwise, to participate in social activities. In view of this steps are being taken in Japan to promote an educational system in which children with physical and/or mental disabilities receive the same education as children without such disabilities.

A real problem is that uniform education still prevails in some schools where the needs of the individual and the characteristics of disabilities are disregarded. Few plans, if any, of individual guidance have been implemented. Most plans scarcely reflect parental wishes, because of inadequate teacher-parent relationships. Another problem is that there are few teachers who are able to devise plans for individual guidance and carry them out.

After compulsory education is complete, most students now, instead of getting jobs, go on to a higher stage of education. This means that it will be at least three additional years before they go out into the world and become productive members of society. Consequently, the urgent need has arisen to examine educational programs during this transient period.

Furthermore, for the disabled to lead productive lives, it would be necessary to establish a regional system to support them and invite them to the open school for youth and to special classes for adult education.

### REFERENCES

Ministry of Education, Science, Sports and Culture. (1997). *To encourage zest for living: Special education in Japan.* Author.

Ministry of Education, Science, Sports and Culture. (1994). *Japanese government policies in education, science and culture.* Author.

The Japan League for the Mentally Retarded. (1996). *Rehabilitation services for people with mentally retardation in Japan.* Author.

CATHERINE HALL RIHKYE
*Hunter College, City University of New York*
First edition

MASATAKA OHTA
NAOJI SHIMIZU
*Tokyo Gakujei University*
Second edition

CHINA, SPECIAL EDUCATION IN
HONG KONG, SPECIAL EDUCATION IN

# JARGON APHASIA

Jargon aphasia refers to an expressive language deficit in which a dysphasic individual produces a profusion of unintelligible utterances. Language structure may be retained, but meaning is unclear. Intonation, rhythm, and stress patterns are normal. Speech is fluent with few if any of the hesitations or pauses characteristic of some other dysphasic speech patterns. Bizarre responses, often consisting of cliches, stock phrases, neologisms, and unusual word combination patterns are produced. Speakers seem unaware that their utterances are not meaningful, and receptive language is impaired.

Although meaningless to the listener, Eisenson (1973) feels that jargon may not be so to the speaker. Analysis of a patient's jargon speech revealed some regular sound and morpheme substitutions, confirming Eisenson's impression that some underlying meaning may exist. Eisenson considers jargon aphasia to be a transitory condition rather than a true aphasic condition.

### REFERENCE

Eisenson, J. (1973). *Adult aphasia: Assessment and treatment.* New York: Appleton-Century-Crofts.

K. SANDRA VANTA
*Cleveland Public Schools,
Cleveland, Ohio*

APHASIA
COMMUNICATION DISORDERS
DEVELOPMENTAL APHASIA
DYSPHASIA
LANGUAGE DISORDERS

# ARTHUR R. JENSEN (1923–    )

Arthur Jensen has been on the faculty of the University of California at Berkeley since 1958, and in 1994 he became professor emeritus of educational psychology. A graduate of Berkeley and Columbia University, he served his internship in clinical psychology at the University of Maryland Psychiatric Institute and was a postdoctoral research fellow at the Institute of Psychiatry at the University of London, where he studied with and was strongly influenced by Hans J. Eysenck.

Jensen turned to the study of differential psychology after a decade of research on classical problems in verbal learning. In 1969 he argued that genetic, as well as environmental and cultural, factors should be considered for understanding not only individual differences, but also social class and racial differences in intelligence and scholastic performance (Jensen, 1969). This hypothesis, that both individual and racial differences in abilities are in part a product of the evolutionary process and have a genetic basis, created a storm of protest from scientists and educators. The subject is still a sensitive one and has been explicated by Jensen in several books such as *Educability and Group Differences* (1973), *Bias in Mental Testing* (1980), and *Straight Talk about Mental Tests* (1981). The controversy has also led him to two other areas of research: the study of culture bias in psychometric tests and the investigation of the nature of g (the general intelligence factor).

Jensen presently views the g factor as (1) reflecting some property or processes of the human brain manifest in many forms of adaptive behavior in which individuals (and probably populations) differ; (2) increasing from birth to maturity and declining in old age; (3) showing physiological as well as behavioral correlates; (4) having a hereditary component; (5) being subject to natural selection in the course of human evolution; and (6) having important educational, occupational, economic, and social correlates in all industrialized societies. Jensen's theories and prolific empirical research on the nature of human mental ability are comprehensively explicated in his latest major works, *The g Factor* (Jensen, 1998), and "Thirty Years of Research on Black-White Differences in Cognitive Ability" (Rushton & Jensen, 2005).

Author of over 400 publications Jensen has been a Guggenheim fellow (1964–1965), a fellow of the Center for Advanced Study in the Behavioral Sciences (1966–1967), and a research fellow at the National Institute of Mental Health (1957–1958).

## REFERENCES

Jensen, A. R. (1969). How much can we boost IQ and scholastic achievement? *Harvard Educational Review, 39,* 1–123.

Jensen, A. R. (1973). *Educability and group differences.* New York: Harper & Row.

Jensen, A. R. (1980). *Bias in mental testing.* New York: Free Press.

Jensen, A. R. (1981). *Straight talk about mental tests.* New York: Free Press.

Jensen, A. R. (1998). *The g factor.* Westport, CT: Praeger.

Rushton, J. P., & Jensen, A. R. (2005). Thirty years of research on black-white differences in cognitive ability. *Psychology, Public Policy, and Law, 11,* 235–294.

ELAINE FLETCHER-JANZEN
*University of Colorado at
    Colorado Springs*
First edition

TAMARA J. MARTIN
*The University of Texas of the
    Permian Basin*
Second edition

**See also:** CULTURAL BIAS IN TESTS
g FACTOR THEORY

Arthur R. Jensen

# J.E.V.S.

The J.E.V.S. evaluation was developed by the Jewish Employment Vocational Service in Philadelphia, Pennsylvania, during the 1960s. It takes approximately 2 weeks to evaluate the capabilities of a client in a wide range of employment skills. The initial stages of the procedures are with simple work samples that are gradually advanced to more complex skills.

The J.E.V.S. programs measure many employment variables, including information concerning a person's vocational potential. The work samples provided enable an evaluator to assess the client's potential for competitive employment and to assess functional abilities in spatial and perceptual skills and manual dexterity. The objective areas of the J.E.V.S. program provide information concerning the client's interests, behaviors, and aptitudes in work-related situations. The program is divided into two major review areas: VIEWS (Vocational Information and Evaluation Work Samples) and VITAS (Vocational Interests, Temperaments and Aptitude Systems).

The J.E.V.S. programs evaluate two factors that are inherent in work-related situations: the specific and the global. Specific factors include discrimination skills, countering ability, eye-hand-foot coordination, finger dexterity, following diagrammatic instructions, following a model, motor coordination, manual dexterity, measuring ability, numerical ability, forms perception, clerical perception, spatial discrimination, size discrimination, and the use of hand tools. The four global factors are accuracy, following oral instructions, neatness, and organizational ability.

### REFERENCE

Vocational Research Institute. (1973). *Work sample evaluator's handbook*. Philadelphia: Jewish Employment and Vocational Services.

PAUL C. RICHARDSON
*Elwyn Institutes*

## VOCATIONAL EVALUATION

## JOB ACCOMMODATION NETWORK

The U.S. Department of Labor, Office of Disability Employment Policy, provides assistance to individuals with disabilities via the Job Accommodation Network (JAN). JAN is a tool-free information and referral service on job accommodations for people with disabilities, on the employment provisions of the Americans with Disabilities Act, and on resources for technical assistance, funding, education, and services related to the employment of people with disabilities. In addition, JAN analyzes trends and statistical data related to the technical assistance it provides. JAN can be accessed by phone or TTY at 1-800-526-7234 or 1-800-ADA-WORK (1-800-232-9675) or via its web site at http://www.dol.gov/odep/programs/job.htm and www.jan.wvu.edu.

STAFF

## JOHNSON, DORIS (1932–      )

Doris Johnson obtained her BA (1953) in speech pathology from Augustana College and went on to earn her MA (1955) in speech and language pathology and PhD (1971) in counselor education from Northwestern University. She is currently the Jo Ann and Peter Dolle Professor of Learning Disabilities at Northwestern University. Her work at Northwestern has included training learning disability specialists and extensive research at the Center for Learning Disabilities.

Johnson's primary area of interest has focused on relationships among oral language, written language, reading, and mathematics. Her work with Helmer Myklebust called attention to the significance of language disorders in learning disabilities, describing a specific disabilities model that showed that certain abilities are required for normal language development and noting that such abilities can be measured and deficits remediated (Johnson & Myklebust, 1967).

Johnson's current work includes the study of early writing development of normal and learning disabled children and the identification of co-occurring problems of adults with learning disabilities, including problems of comprehension, verbal disorders, and nonverbal learning. Her research has indicated that nonverbal disorders, including problems associated with social perception, problem solving, spatial orientation, and nonverbal communication, are often the most debilitating (Johnson, 1987, 1993, 1995; Johnson & Blalock, 1987).

Among her numerous awards, Johnson has received the Outstanding Service Award of the Association of Children with Learning Disabilities. Additionally, she has been an active member of many professional organizations, chairing the Professional Advisory Board of the Learning Disabilities Association and serving as executive director of the International Association for Research in Learning Disabilities for several years Johnson's (1967) publication with Myklebust, *Learning Disabilities: Educational Principles and Practices,* has been translated into four languages.

### REFERENCES

Johnson, D. (1987, February). Nonverbal learning disabilities. *Pediatric Annals, 16,* 133–141.

Johnson, D. (1993). Relationships between oral and written language. *School Psychology Review, 22*(4), 595–609.

Johnson, D. (1995). An overview of learning disabilities: Psychoeducational perspectives. *Journal of Child Neurology, 10*(1), 2–5.

Johnson, D. J., & Blalock, J. (Eds.). (1987). *Adults with learning disabilities: Clinical studies.* Orlando, FL: Grune-Stratton.

Johnson, D. J., & Myklebust, H. R. (1967). *Learning disabilities: Educational principles and practices.* New York: Grune Stratton.

TAMARA J. MARTIN
*The University of Texas of the Permian Basin*

## JOHNSON, G. ORVILLE (1915–    )

G. Orville Johnson was born in Cameron, Wisconsin, and attended the University of Wisconsin, Milwaukee (formerly Milwaukee State Teachers College), obtaining his BS degree in 1938. He later earned his EdM (1949) and EdD (1950) at the University of Illinois. In the years between his undergraduate and graduate studies, Johnson worked as a public school teacher in Sheboygan and Wawatosa, Wisconsin, and from 1946 to 1947 he was principal of the South Wisconsin Colony and Training School. During his distinguished career, he was associate professor of education and director of special education at the University of Denver, and also taught at the University of Syracuse, Ohio State University, and the University of South Florida at Tampa.

Johnson's research focused on the psychological characteristics of individuals with mental retardation and the effects of labeling. He proposed that the two basic classifications, behavioral and medical, are not mutually exclusive, with adequate descriptions of persons with mental retardation requiring the use of both categories.

He also advocated a behaviorally oriented, cognitive approach for teachers, counselors, and other professionals to use for management of individuals with behavior disorders. Using what he termed the coping style model, Johnson concluded that analysis of coping style was an essential element in the development of programs for these children, emphasizing removal of opportunities in the classroom to use coping styles common to children with emotional disorders and teaching more appropriate, adaptive styles (Boyd & Johnson, 1984). Johnson and Boyd (1984) also developed an assessment tool utilizing drawings of persons interacting in various settings for identification of individual coping styles.

Among his many contributions, Johnson served as associate editor of the professional publication *Exceptional Children,* and was a featured speaker at the 62nd Annual Convention of the Council for Exceptional Children (1984). His major works include *Education for the Slow Learner* (1963), *Education of Exceptional Children and Youth* (1975), and *Analysis of Coping Style: A Cognitive-Behavioral Approach to Behavior Management* (1981).

### REFERENCES

Boyd, H. F., & Johnson, G. O. (1981). *Analysis of coping style: A cognitive-behavioral approach to behavior management.* Columbus, OH: Merrill.

Boyd, H. F., & Johnson, G. O. (1984, April). *The coping style approach to understanding and dealing with behavior disorders. I. Theory and definitions.* Paper presented at the meeting of the Council for Exceptional Children, Washington, DC.

Johnson, G. O. (1963). *Education for the slow learner.* Englewood Cliffs, NJ: Prentice Hall.

Johnson, G. O., & Boyd, H. F. (1984, April). *The coping style approach to understanding and dealing with behavior disorders. II. Assessment and intervention strategies.* Paper presented at the meeting of the Council for Exceptional Children, Washington, DC.

Johnson, G. O., & Cruickshank, W. A. (1975). *Education of exceptional children and youth.* Englewood Cliffs, NJ: Prentice Hall.

ELIZABETH JONES
*Texas A&M University*
First edition

TAMARA J. MARTIN
*The University of Texas of the Permian Basin*
Second edition

## JOHNSTON INFORMAL READING INVENTORY

The Johnston Informal Reading Inventory (JIRI; Johnston, 1982) is an informal reading scale that assesses understanding of antonyms and synonyms, and silent reading comprehension skills. The test is designed for use for students in the seventh grade through adulthood. The test can be group administered or individually administered. Results of the JIRI may be used for diagnostic as well as placement purposes, according to the author.

Three types of tasks are used in the JIRI: word opposites, word synonyms, and graded narrative passages. The Word Opposites test results determine the level of the passages at which the examinee is to begin. The passages contain nine levels that progress from simple stories to more complex narratives. The examinees are asked a series of short-answer questions about the passages, which require written responses, assessing the main idea, detail, vocabulary, cause-effect, and inference. The role of the third test, Word Synonyms, is not clearly articulated by the author (Rogers, 1995).

Several problems have been noted on the JIRI. The scoring procedures lack clarity and sound empirical foundation (Rogers, 1995). The content of the JIRI is of questionable relevance to the contemporary audience, and the reliability and validity evidence is lacking altogether (Rogers, 1995; Wright, 1995). Wright (1995) notes that the JIRI is a time-efficient instrument for estimating a student's reading level; however, Rogers (1995) states that, in his opinion, other informal reading inventories made by teachers to go with their curricula may be a better choice than the JIRI.

### REFERENCES

Johnston, M. C. (1982). *Johnston Informal Reading Inventory.* Tucson, AZ: Educational Publications.

Rogers, M. R. (1995). Review of the Johnston Informal Reading Inventory. In J. C. Conoley & J. C. Impara (Eds.), *The twelfth mental measurements yearbook* (pp. 523–524). Lincoln, NE: Buros Institute of Mental Measurements.

Wright, C. R. (1995). Review of the Johnston Informal Reading Inventory. In J. C. Conoley & J. C. Impara (Eds.), *The twelfth mental measurements yearbook* (pp. 524–525). Lincoln, NE: Buros Institute of Mental Measurements.

ELIZABETH O. LICHTENBERGER
*The Salk Institute*

**READING DISORDERS**

## JOHNSTONE, EDWARD RANSOM (1870–1946)

Edward Ransom Johnstone began his career as a teacher and principal in the public schools of Cincinnati. He then served as a teacher in the Indiana School for Feeble Minded Youth, subsequently becoming principal there. In 1898 he moved to the Training School at Vineland, New Jersey, where he was employed as vice principal under the Reverend Stephen Olin Garrison, who had founded the school 10 years before. After Garrison's death in 1900, Johnstone was made superintendent. He became executive director in 1922, and director emeritus in 1944.

During Johnstone's years there, the Training School exerted tremendous influence on the education and training of mentally retarded children and adults, on the preparation of teachers of disabled children, and on educational testing. Johnstone founded a research laboratory with Henry H. Goddard as director. There numerous studies were conducted using data from the school's mentally retarded population. A summer school was conducted for teachers.

Johnstone inaugurated *The Training School Bulletin,* an influential journal in special education from its inception in 1904. Johnstone served on numerous boards and commissions and was elected to two terms as president of the American Association on Mental Deficiency.

### REFERENCES

McCaffrey, K. R. (1965). *Founders of the Training School at Vineland, New Jersey: S. Olin Garrison, Alexander Johnson, Edward R. Johnstone.* Unpublished doctoral dissertation. Teachers College, Columbia University, New York.

*The Training School Bulletin.* (1947, May). *44.*

PAUL IRVINE
*Katonah, New York*

## JOINT TECHNICAL STANDARDS FOR EDUCATIONAL AND PSYCHOLOGICAL TESTS

See STANDARDS FOR EDUCATIONAL AND PSYCHOLOGICAL TESTING.

**Reginald L. Jones**

## JONES, REGINALD L. (1931–2006)

Reginald L. Jones received his AB in psychology, cum laude, from Morehouse College in 1952 and his MA in clinical psychology from Wayne State University. He later earned his PhD in psychology, with a minor in special education, from the Ohio State University. He served as the department chair for psychology and form director of the Center for Minority Special Education at Hampton University (HU), was a Distinguished Professor of psychology and special education at that school.

Prior to his HU appointments in August 1991, he was professor of African American studies and education for 17 years at the University of California at Berkeley, and he also served as the university's faculty assistant to the Vice Chancellor. In addition, for several years he was director of Berkeley's doctoral program in special education. Other positions held by Jones include professor of psychology and special education and vice-chair of the department of psychology at Ohio State University; professor and chair of the department of education at University of California, Riverside; and professor and director of the University Testing Center, Haile Sellassie I University in Addis Abada, Ethiopia. He also taught at Miami, Fisk, and Indiana Universities, and at UCLA. For more than 25 years, Jones was a fellow of the American Psychological Association (APA).

He produced 28 instructional videotapes in psychology, written and/or presented more than 200 papers, articles, chapters, reviews, and technical reports, and edited 17 books, including *Black Psychology* (3rd ed.), *Attitudes and Attitude Change in Special Education, Psychoeducational Assessment of Minority Group Children, Black Adolescents, Black Adult Development and Aging,* and *The Handbook of Tests and Measurements for Black Populations.* From 1979 to 1983, he was the editor of *Mental Retardation,* an official journal of the American Association on Mental Retardation, and he served as an associate, advisory, or guest editor of more than a dozen other professional journals in psychology and education.

He is especially noted for his work on special education labeling, attitudes toward individuals with disabilities, and the special education of minority children. Jones was a recipient of the J. E. Wallace Wallin Award, the Council for Exceptional Children's highest honor.

Among his numerous appointments to governmental task forces and advisory committees, Jones served on President Clinton's Council of Advisors to the Education Transition Team and received various appointments by the National Academy of Sciences, Congress, and the Secretary of Health, Education, and Welfare. His service in this area led to recommendations of new and/or modified policies, programs, and practices in mental health, mental retardation, special education, and the education of African American children and youth.

Jones' many honors and awards include the Citation for Distinguished Achievement from the Ohio State University, the Distinguished Alumni Award from Wayne State University, the Education Award from the American Association on Mental Retardation, the Distinguished Psychologist and Scholarship Awards from the Association of Black Psychologists, and the Outstanding Faculty Award from the Class of 1991 African American Students of the University of California at Berkeley. He also received special recognition from the APA "... for unusual and outstanding contributions in the field of psychology," and the Berkeley Citation "for distinguished achievement and for notable service to the University," one of the highest honors bestowed by the university.

**REFERENCES**

Jones, R. L. (1984). *Attitudes and attitude change in special education: Theory and practice.* Reston, VA: Council for Exceptional Children.

Jones, R. L. (1989). *Black adolescents.* Berkeley, CA: Cobb and Henry.

Jones, R. L. (1989). *Black adult development and aging.* Berkeley, CA: Cobb and Henry.

Jones, R. L. (1991). *Black psychology* (3rd ed.). Berkeley, CA: Cobb and Henry.

TAMARA J. MARTIN
*The University of Texas of the
Permian Basin*

## JOUBERT SYNDROME

Joubert syndrome (JS) is a rare genetic disorder that is autosomal recessive, characterized by partial or complete agenesis of the cerebellar vermis (Gillberg, 1995), but without the formation of cysts and hydrocephalus common in Dandy-Walker syndrome (Greenspan, 1998). JS results in mental retardation that is typically severe or profound coupled with pronounced autistic-like behaviors, ataxia,

hypotonia, tongue protrusion, and abnormal patterns of eye movements. Exceptional cases exist with IQs reported as high as 85, but diagnoses of autism are common in the higher-IQ JS patient. Diagnosis may occur prenatally via ultrasound in some cases, but traditionally the diagnosis has been made on the basis of the clinical exam and MRI findings. Academic and psychosocial outcomes are typically quite limited due to the level of retardation and the social deficits noted. Special education services and continuous psychoeducational workups are required in all cases.

**REFERENCES**

Gillberg, C. (1995). *Clinical child neuropsychiatry.* Cambridge: Cambridge University Press.

Greenspan, S. (1998). Dandy-Walker syndrome. In L. Phelps (Ed.), *Health-related disorders of children and adolescents* (pp. 219–223). Washington, DC: American Psychological Association.

CECIL R. REYNOLDS
*Texas A&M University*

## JOURNAL FOR EDUCATION OF THE GIFTED

The *Journal for Education of the Gifted* (*JEG*) is the official journal of the Association for the Gifted (TAG), a division of the Council for Exceptional Children. Members of TAG receive *JEG* as a benefit of membership. First published in 1978, the journal currently issues quarterly publications.

*JEG* provides a forum for the analysis and communication of knowledge about the gifted and talented, as well as the exchange of ideas and diverse points of view regarding this special population. Theoretical and position papers, descriptive research, evaluation, and experimental research exemplify the types of writings published in the journal. *JEG* specifically solicits (1) original research relevant to the education of the gifted and talented; (2) theoretical and position papers; (3) descriptions of innovative programming and instructional practices based on existing or novel models of gifted education; (4) review of literature related to gifted education; (5) historical reviews; and (6) action research. Submitted writings are refereed following a blind reviewing process, and manuscript preparation follows the American Psychological Association's style manual. The current editor is Tracy L. Cross, Teachers College, Ball State University, Muncie, Indiana.

CECIL R. REYNOLDS
*Texas A&M University*
First edition

TAMARA J. MARTIN
*The University of Texas of the
Permian Basin*
Second edition

# JOURNAL OF ABNORMAL CHILD PSYCHOLOGY

The *Journal of Abnormal Child Psychology* was established in 1973 by Herbert Quay, PhD. In 1995 the journal became the official publication of the International Society for Research in Child and Adolescent Psychopathology. The journal focuses on child and adolescent psychopathology with an emphasis on empirical studies of the major childhood disorders (the disruptive behavior disorders, depression, anxiety, and pervasive developmental disorders). Research addresses the epidemiology, assessment, diagnosis, etiology, developmental course and outcome, and treatment of childhood disorders. Studies on risk and protective factors, and on the correlates of children's psychiatric disturbances, especially family and peer processes, are of interest. Treatment outcome research is also published, with an emphasis on studies that include randomized clinical trials with appropriate controls. Occasional special issues highlight a particular topic of importance in the field and conceptual articles are included from time to time. The journal is published bimonthly by Springer Netherlands.

STAFF

# JOURNAL OF APPLIED BEHAVIOR ANALYSIS

Founded in 1968, the *Journal of Applied Behavior Analysis* (*JABA*) was established to publish "reports of experimental research involving applications of the experimental analysis of behavior to problems of social importance" (*JABA*, 1998). The journal is published quarterly by the Society for the Experimental Analysis of Behavior (SEAB).

*JABA*'s first issue was published in 1968 with Montrose M. Wolf of the University of Kansas as its first editor. The journal primarily seeks to publish empirical research articles relevant to applied behavior analysis, including behavior therapy and behavior control. Innovative pilot research, replications, controlled case studies, and analogue studies are also accepted as research articles. Other categories of articles accepted for publication include technical articles contributing primarily to research methodology, data analysis, or instrumentation; discussion and review articles; book reviews; and comments from readers (*JABA*, 1998). The current editor is Patrick C. Friman, Behavioral Pediatrics and Family Services, Boys Town, Nebraska.

**REFERENCE**

*Journal of Applied Behavior Analysis.* (1998, July 10). A bit of history: Who published JEAB and JABA? Retrieved from http://envmed .rochester.edu/wwwvgl/seab/history/circulation.htm.

RAND B. EVANS
*Texas A&M University*
First edition

TAMARA J. MARTIN
*The University of Texas of the
Permian Basin*
Second edition

# JOURNAL OF AUTISM AND DEVELOPMENTAL DISORDERS

The *Journal of Autism and Developmental Disorders* was first published under the title of the *Journal of Autism and Childhood Schizophrenia*. It was born from the collaboration of Leo Kanner, regarded as the founding father of child psychiatry in the English-speaking world, and publisher V. H. Winston, the father of an autistic child. The journal was dedicated to stimulating and disseminating from diverse sources "ways to understand and alleviate the miseries of sick children." As founding editor and the discoverer of autism, Kanner convened a task force of outstanding researchers and clinicians to contribute from multidisciplinary sources. Fields such as ethology, genetics, psychotherapy, chemotherapy, behavior modification, special education, speech pathology, and neurobiology contributed. Research was conducted by investigators from the professions of medicine, psychology, neuroscience, biochemistry, physiology, and education. The unifying basis for the publication of such diverse material was the direct relevance to the understanding and remediation of autism, childhood psychoses, and related developmental disorders.

In 1974 Eric Schopler took over as editor of the journal, with Michael Rutter collaborating as European editor. Editorial policies remained the same, but there was increasing emphasis on studies demonstrating the connection between basic research and clinical application. Toward that end a "Parents Speak" column was added. It was intended to raise issues of practical concern not always accessible to current research methodologies and research issues not always clear as to their practical implications. The purpose of the column was to provide a forum for parents and researchers.

By 1979 the title of the journal was changed from the *Journal of Autism and Childhood Schizophrenia* to its current title. This change reflected primarily the growth of empirical knowledge. Initially, autism was regarded as the earliest form of childhood schizophrenia. However, increasing data suggested that autism and childhood schizophrenia were different both in onset and symptoms. Autism was usually related to early onset, before age 3, while childhood schizophrenia came with later onset and somewhat different symptoms. Moreover, the effects of development were recognized for a wide range of disorders, as was the coexistence of autism with other developmental disorders such as mental retardation. An unusual convergence of scientific knowledge and political action occurred when autism was included in the Developmental Disabilities Act of 1975. The journal's change of title and scope was intended to proclaim this infrequent marriage of science and policy.

Currently the *Journal of Autism and Developmental Disorders* publishes original articles addressing "experimental studies on the biochemical, neurological, and genetic aspects of a particular disorder; the implications of normal development for deviant processes; and interaction between disordered behavior of individuals and social or group factors. The journal also features research and case studies involving the entire spectrum of interventions (including behavioral, biological, educational, and community aspects) and advances in the diagnosis and classification of disorders" (www.ovid.com/site/catalog). The current editor is G. B. Mesibov, University of North Carolina, Chapel Hill.

ERIC SCHOPLER
*University of North Carolina at Chapel Hill*

RACHEL TOPLIS
*Falcon School District 49,
Colorado Springs, Colorado*

## JOURNAL OF CLINICAL CHILD AND ADOLESCENT PSYCHOLOGY

The *Journal of Clinical Child and Adolescent Psychology* (*JCCAP*) is the official journal of the Section on Clinical Child Psychology (Section 1), Division of Clinical Psychology (Division 12) of the American Psychological Association. It publishes original research, reviews, and articles on child advocacy and training and professional practice in clinical child psychology. Authors need not be members of the Section. Colleagues in other disciplines, students, and consumers are also encouraged to contribute. *JCCAP* is published quarterly in one volume by Lawrence Erlbaum Associates, Inc., 10 Industrial Avenue, Mahwah, NJ 07430-2262. It is edited by Wendy K Silverman, PhD, Florida International University, Miami, FL.

STAFF
RACHEL TOPLIS
*Falcon School District 49,
Colorado Springs, Colorado*

## JOURNAL OF COMMUNICATION DISORDERS

The *Journal of Communication Disorders,* first published in 1968, serves a readership of health care professionals interested in the prevention and treatment of human communication disorders. The journal contains original articles related to speech, language, and hearing disorders, and special topics issues, entitled *Clinics in Communications Dis-*

*orders,* provide information pertaining to the assessment, diagnosis, and treatment of these disorders to speech-language pathologists, audiologists, psychotherapists, otolaryngologists, and other professionals in the field. Published bimonthly, the journal is interested in publishing reports of experimental or descriptive investigations, theoretical or tutorial papers, case reports, and letters to the editor.

Originally founded by its first editor, R. W. Riever of John Jay College and Columbia University, the aim of the journal has remained the same since its inception: to publish articles on "problems related to the various disorders of communication, broadly defined." Its interests include the biological foundations of communications as well as psychopathological, psychodynamic, diagnostic, and therapeutic aspects of communication disorders.

The current editor is Luc De Nil, University of Toronto, Toronto, Ontario. The journal is now published by Elsevier Science, Inc. (*Journal of Communication Disorders,* 1998).

### REFERENCE

*Journal of Communication Disorders.* (1998, December 20). Aims and scope. Retrieved from http://elsevier.co.jp/

TERESA K. RICE
*Texas A&M University*
First edition

TAMARA J. MARTIN
*The University of Texas of the Permian Basin*
Second edition

## JOURNAL OF CONSULTING AND CLINICAL PSYCHOLOGY

The *Journal of Consulting and Clinical Psychology* was first published in 1937 by the American Psychological Association (APA) under the name *Journal of Consulting Psychology.* Its original managing editor was J. P. Symonds. The editor, appointed by the APA, is currently Annette M. La Greca, University of Miami, FL. There are nine associate editors and approximately 50 consulting editors appointed by the managing editor.

The journal publishes original contributions on such topics as the development and use of diagnostic techniques in the treatment of disordered behaviors; studies of populations of clinical interest; studies of personality and of its assessment and development related to consulting and clinical psychology; and cross-cultural and demographic studies of interest for behavioral disorders.

The journal considers manuscripts dealing with diagnosis or treatment of abnormal behavior. Manuscripts are submitted and blind-reviewed by a board of consulting editors. The journal receives approximately 400 manuscripts a year; about 25 percent of these are published.

TERESA K. RICE
*Texas A&M University*
First edition

DONNA WALLACE
*The University of Texas of the Permian Basin*
Second edition

## JOURNAL OF EMOTIONAL AND BEHAVIORAL DISORDERS

The *Journal of Emotional and Behavioral Disorders (JEBD)* is a refereed quarterly journal publishing articles on research, practice, and commentary related to children and adolescents with emotional and behavioral disorders. Established in 1993 by PRO-ED, the journal contains articles with implications for a range of disciplines, including counseling, education, early childhood care, juvenile corrections, mental health, psychiatry, psychology, public health, rehabilitation, social work, and special education. *JEBD* provides an impartial forum and draws on a wide variety of fields to further services for youngsters with emotional and behavioral problems.

JUDITH K. VORESS
*PRO-ED, Inc.*

## JOURNAL OF FLUENCY DISORDERS

The *Journal of Fluency Disorders* was begun in 1974, and is the official journal of the International Fluency Association. The journal is recognized as the only publication devoted specifically to fluency issues. It provides comprehensive coverage of clinical, experimental, and theoretical aspects of stuttering, including the latest remediation techniques. The journal also features full-length research and clinical reports; methodological, theoretical, and philosophical articles; reviews; sort communications; and more (*Journal of Fluency Disorders*, 1999). The target audience includes clinicians and researchers working in universities, hospitals, and community clinics.

### REFERENCE

*Journal of Fluency Disorders.* (1999). Aims and scope. Elsevier Science. Retrieved from http://www.elsevier.com/wps/find/homepage.cws_home

CECIL R. REYNOLDS
*Texas A&M University*
First edition

MARIE ALMOND
*The University of Texas of the Permian Basin*
Second edition

## JOURNAL OF FORENSIC NEUROPSYCHOLOGY

The *Journal of Forensic Neuropsychology (JFN)* was founded in 1998 by Jim Hom of the Neuropsychology Center of Dallas. The current editor is Bruce A. Arrigo of the University of North Carolina–Charlotte. The journal publishes articles involving legal aspects of the practice of clinical neuropsychology. It is published quarterly by the Haworth Press.

Its interest to special educators lies in its focus on head injury and litigation of head injury cases, many of which involve children and the schooling and education of brain-injured children. The journal includes original research, reviews of research, opinions, and topical presentations on matters of timely interest.

CECIL R. REYNOLDS
*Texas A&M University*

## JOURNAL OF INTELLECTUAL DISABILITY RESEARCH

The *Journal of Intellectual Disability Research* is the official journal of the International Association for the Scientific Study of Intellectual Disability and the European Association for Mental Health and Mental Retardation. It began publication as the *Journal of Mental Deficiency Research* in 1956 and was renamed in 1992. This international journal is devoted exclusively to the scientific study of intellectual disability. The journal publishes papers reporting original observations, including clinical case reports; pathological reports; biochemical investigations; genetics; and psychological, educational, and sociological studies. The results of animal experiments or studies in any discipline that may increase knowledge of the causes, prevention, or treatment of intellectual disability are also discussed. Reviews are submitted from experts from time to time on themes in which recent research has produced notable advances. All papers are reviewed by expert referees. The journal also reports the activities of special interest groups and the meetings and conferences of the International Association for the Scientific Study of Intellectual Disability.

The journal is published six times per year by Blackwell Publishing. The current editor-in-chief is A. J. Holland, Developmental Psychology Section, Cambridge, UK.

STAFF

## JOURNAL OF LEARNING DISABILITIES

The *Journal of Learning Disabilities (JLD)*, the oldest and most prestigious journal in the area of learning disabilities, contains reports of empirical research, opinion papers, and discussions of issues that are of concern to all disciplines in the field. The journal has been published consecutively since 1968. In 1986, PRO-ED purchased *JLD* from The Professional Press, a subsidiary of Capital Cities Media, Inc. *JLD* is published six times a year. All published articles are peer reviewed; consulting editors are from North America, Europe, Asia, Africa, and Australia.

JUDITH K. VORESS
*PRO-ED, Inc.*

## JOURNAL OF POSITIVE BEHAVIOR INTERVENTIONS

A journal published by PRO-ED, the *Journal of Positive Behavior Interventions (JPBI)* deals exclusively with principles of positive behavioral support in school, home, and community settings for people with challenges in behavioral adaptation. Established in 1999, *JPBI* publishes empirical research reports, commentaries, program descriptions, discussion of family supports, and coverage of timely issues. Contributors and editorial board members are leading authorities representing different disciplines involved with intervention for individuals with challenging behaviors. The journal is published quarterly.

JUDITH K. VORESS
*PRO-ED, Inc.*

## JOURNAL OF PSYCHOEDUCATIONAL ASSESSMENT

The *Journal of Psychoeducational Assessment (JPA)* was founded in 1983, and for the past 23 years has continuously published quarterly issues as well as special topic monographs on topics of interest to all assessment specialists, including psychologists, educational diagnosticians, special educators, and academic trainers. The internationally known journal originated as an outlet for the publication of research on assessment practices and procedures common to the fields of psychology and education. It provides school psychologists with current information regarding psychological and educational assessment practices, legal mandates, and instrumentation; and includes topics such as cross-cultural assessment practices, differential diagnoses, and dynamic assessment neuropsychology.

*JPA* publishes brief reports, position papers, and book and test reviews routinely addressing issues related to achievement, adaptive behavior, classroom behaviors, creativity, motor skills, intelligence, language skills, memory, and other constructs. An editorial board of some 50 members representing a wide range of expertise in assessment-related issue employs a double-blind peer review process for manuscripts submitted for publication. *JPA* is published by Sage Publications. Donald H. Saklofske of the University of Calgary, Canada, is the current editor.

MARY LEON PEERY
*Texas A&M University*
First edition

TAMARA J. MARTIN
*The University of Texas of the
    Permian Basin*
Second edition

## JOURNAL OF SCHOOL PSYCHOLOGY

The *Journal of School Psychology (JSP)* is school psychology's oldest and most prestigious journal; it first appeared in 1963. Its 58 original founders and shareholders provided the capital necessary to launch *JSP*. In its first editorial, Smith (1963) states:

> The main purpose of the *Journal of School Psychology* is to provide an outlet for research studies and articles in professional school psychology. It is a scientifically oriented journal devoted to the publication of original research reports, reviews, and articles, with the aim of fostering the expansion of school psychology as an applied science. (p. 2)

This statement of purpose has remained largely unchanged during the last 20 years, with *JSP*'s primary goal being the publication of "original articles on research and practice related to the development of school psychology as both a scientific and an applied specialty" (*JSP*, 1998). *JSP* also reviews tests and books, publishes brief reports and commentaries, and occasionally invites writers to submit manuscripts on timely topics of interest. Particular attention is given to assisting school psychologists who have not published on a regular basis.

Various persons have been instrumental to *JSP*'s growth and development. Three officers comprise a board of directors that represents the corporation. Four editors helped guide *JSP*'s growth: Donald Smith (1963–1968), Jack

Bardon (1968–1971), Beeman Phillips (1972–1981), and Thomas Oakland (1981–1986). Raymond Dean took over as editor in January of 1987, and R. Pianta of the University of Virginia, Charlottesville, is the current editor.

Nine hundred and ten persons authored or coauthored one or more articles for *JSP* during its first 20 years, and among these, 764 contributed one article, and 8 contributed 7 or more articles (Oakland, 1984). The most prolific contributors to *JSP* are actively engaged in other scholarly and professional activities. Thus, *JSP* has enabled numerous persons to contribute to the science and profession of school psychology, with articles discussing a range of topics reflecting the breadth of school psychology literature and its practice.

## REFERENCES

*Journal of School Psychology.* (1998, December 22). Aims and scope. Retrieved from http://elsevier.nl/inca/publications/store/6/9/9/699.pub.htt

Oakland, T. (1984). The *Journal of School Psychology's* first twenty years: Contributions and contributors. *Journal of School Psychology, 22,* 239–250.

Smith, D. (1963). Editor's comments: Genesis of a new *Journal of School Psychology. Journal of School Psychology, 1,* 1–4.

THOMAS OAKLAND
*University of Florida*
First edition

TAMARA J. MARTIN
*The University of Texas of the Permian Basin*
Second edition

## SCHOOL PSYCHOLOGY

# JOURNAL OF SPECIAL EDUCATION

First published in 1966, *The Journal of Special Education* (*JSE*), is internationally known as the prime research journal in the field. In 1987, PRO-ED, Inc. purchased *JSE* from Buttonwood Farms, Inc. This quarterly, multidisciplinary publication presents primary research and scholarly reviews by experts in all subspecialties of special education for individuals with disabilities ranging from mild to severe. *JSE* includes critical commentaries; intervention studies; integrative reviews of timely problems; traditional, ethnographic, and single-subject research; and articles on families, transition, technology, general/special education interface, and legislation and litigation. All published articles have undergone a rigorous peer review process.

JUDITH K. VORESS
*PRO-ED, Inc.*

# JOURNAL OF SPECIAL EDUCATION TECHNOLOGY

The *Journal of Special Education Technology* (*JSET*) is a peer-reviewed journal first published in 1985 that focuses on research and policies in the field of assistive technology. According to their website, the journal focuses on "up-to-date information and opinions about issues, research, policy, and practice related to the use of technology in the field of special education. *JSET* supports the publication of research and development activities, provides technological information and resources, and presents important information and discussion concerning important issues in the field of special education technology to scholars, teacher educators, and practitioners" (*JSET*, 2005). The journal is geared more toward K–12 assistive technology rather than higher education, but a fair number of articles in recent years have focused on issues interesting to both constituencies, such as web accessibility and universal design.

The journal is a publication of the Technology and Media (TAM) division (CEC, 2005) of the Council for Exceptional Children (CEC). The journal is published four times per year and annual subscription rates are currently $55 per year for individuals and $109 per year for institutions. Members of the TAM division of the CEC receive the publication as a member benefit. Web-based archives of the journal are located on their web site.

For more information, call 800-877-2693 or visit their web site at http://jset.unlv.edu/.

## REFERENCES

Council for Exceptional Children (CEC). (2005). *Technology and media division.* Retrieved October 10, 2005, from http://www.tamcec.org/

*Journal of Special Education Technology.* (2005). About the journal. Retrieved October 10, 2005, from http://jset.unlv.edu/shared/about.html

DAVID SWEENEY
*Texas A&M University*

# JOURNAL OF SPEECH AND HEARING DISORDERS

The *Journal of Speech and Hearing Disorders* was discontinued in 1990, but was incorporated into the *Journal of Speech, Language, and Hearing Research* in 1996. It is now published by the American Speech-Language-Hearing Association.

Each issue is divided into three major categories: "Language," "Speech," and "Hearing." Articles pertain to studies of the processes and disorders of speech, language, and hearing, and to the diagnosis and treatment of such disorders. Included are reports of original research; theoretical, tutorial, or review articles; research notes; and letters to the editor. Topics covered are screening, assessment, treatment techniques, prevention, professional issues, supervision, and administration. This journal will primarily interest researchers and professional educators, and is a refereed journal with a circulation of 73,000.

TERESA K. RICE
*Texas A&M University*
First edition

MARIE ALMOND
*The University of Texas of the*
*Permian Basin*
Second edition

## JOURNAL OF THE AMERICAN ASSOCIATION FOR THE SEVERELY HANDICAPPED

See TASH.

## JOURNAL OF VISUAL IMPAIRMENT AND BLINDNESS

The year 2006 marks the centennial of the *Journal of Visual Impairment and Blindness (JVIB)* When first published this journal was known as *Outlook for the Blind,* and later *New Outlook for the Blind.* For a century, *JVIB* has kept professionals up-to-date on all the major developments and trends of the field of visual impairment and blindness, serving as the cornerstone of the field's literature. *JVIB* is a monthly publication of research articles and discussion articles on topics of interest related to the field of visual impairment. *JVIB* provides its interdisciplinary, international subscribers with a forum for the exchange of ideas and information as well as a means of discussing controversies and issues relevant to practitioners and researchers concerned with visually impaired and blind individuals (*JVIB,* 1998).

A publication of the American Foundation for the Blind, *JVIB* contains features pertinent to all ages, which cover various aspects of visual impairment, including international news, short reports, research, innovative practice techniques, worldwide events, employment updates, and evaluation of new products and publications. A sampling of past articles finds that topics include parental concerns and involvement, educational issues of the visually impaired and blind, assessment, language development, residential schools, rehabilitation, employment, orientation, mobility, and physical fitness.

Information pertaining to the impact of technology on individuals with visual impairment is continually updated in the segment "Random Access." Another feature, entitled "Research Note," contains brief reports on cutting-edge research and relevant work from other fields. Additionally, *JVIB* presents important statistical information about blindness, and reviews fiction and nonfiction books as well as videos related to blindness (*JVIB,* 1998).

**REFERENCE**

*Journal of Visual Impairment and Blindness.* (1998, January 17). About the *Journal of Visual Impairment and Blindness.* Retrieved from http://www.afb.org/a_jbiv.html

ANNE CAMPBELL
*Purdue University*
First edition

TAMARA J. MARTIN
*The University of Texas of the*
*Permian Basin*
Second edition

RACHEL TOPLIS
*Falcon School District 49,*
*Colorado Springs, Colorado*

## JOURNALS IN EDUCATION OF INDIVIDUALS WITH DISABILITIES AND SPECIAL EDUCATION

See SPECIFIC JOURNAL.

## JUKES AND THE KALLIKAKS

In the late nineteenth and early twentieth centuries, Americans became increasingly concerned with overpopulation and unrestricted immigration. It was believed that the high birth rate of the mentally defective would have an adverse impact on the economy and social order. The eugenics movement promoted compulsory sterilization of people with undesirable traits as well as restricted immigration of unwanted races (Bajema, 1976). Research on human pedigrees provided scientific support for these efforts by showing that mental retardation and other undesirable traits tend to run in families over a number of generations. Many studies of family degeneracy were published, but the two most influential were based on the pedigrees of the Juke and the Kallikak families.

One of the most influential studies of family degeneration, *The Jukes,* written by Richard L. Dugdale as a report for the Prison Association of New York (Dugdale, 1895), was the first comprehensive study of the history of an entire family over a number of generations. By examining prison records, Dugdale discovered a family with a long history of arrest and dependence on charity. Dugdale traced 709 members of the Juke family, spanning seven generations, who were related by blood, marriage, and cohabitation.

Dugdale found that the Juke family had a high incidence of feeblemindedness, pauperism, prostitution, illegitimacy, and crime among its members. The family tended to marry its own members and produce large numbers of offspring. Dugdale calculated the cost of the Juke family in confinement and charity to be over $1 million (over $12 million in 1985).

The study concluded that crime and poverty are mainly the result of heredity, but that the environment does have some influence. Dugdale argued that crime and poverty are avoidable if the proper environmental conditions are met. He advocated a program of industrial education and personal hygiene, with imprisonment only as a last resort for the habitual criminal. Heredity was viewed as an innate force that impinged on individuals throughout their lives. In spite of Dugdale's emphasis on environmental interventions, his report of the Juke family was widely used in support of the argument that only heredity determines human behavior and consequently poverty and crime.

Although Dugdale claimed that his data-gathering methods were sound, the study has been severely criticized on methodological grounds (Gould, 1981). One problem is that feebleminded individuals were identified mainly on the basis of hearsay, rather than by testing or other standardized methods. In addition, it has been charged that the self-fulfilling prophecy may have biased the results, in that the researcher's strong expectations may have influenced his judgment of the cases.

A follow-up of the Juke family (Estrabrook, 1915) reported that the incidence of feeblemindedness, prostitution, pauperism, illegitimacy, and crime had continued at about the same rate as reported by Dugdale. This report argued against imprisoning people with criminally weak intellects, proposing instead that they receive permanent custodial care and sterilization. Sterilization was particularly advocated because the mentally impaired produced large numbers of offspring and put high demands on charity. It was claimed that the Juke family history demonstrated that criminal fathers would produce criminal offspring, making sterilization the only remedy.

The second most influential study of family degeneracy was Henry Goddard's 1912 book *The Kallikak Family: A Study of the Heredity of Feeble-Mindedness* (Goddard, 1912). Goddard's work was based on the family background of a young girl with the pseudonym of Deborah Kallikak; she was a resident at the Vineland Training School for Feeble-Minded Girls and Boys in New Jersey. Deborah's family was

traced back through six generations to Martin Kallikak. Martin first married a woman of good repute and founded a line of offspring that were upstanding citizens of normal intelligence. Martin Kallikak also had an illegitimate child with a barmaid, and this branch of the family produced large numbers of criminals, feebleminded, and charity cases. Goddard summarized the findings as follows:

> The Kallikak family presents a natural experiment in heredity. A young man of good family becomes through two different women the ancestor of two lines of descendants,—the one characterized by thoroughly good, respectable, normal citizenship, with almost no exceptions; the other being equally characterized by mental defect in every generation.... In later generations, more defect was brought in from other families through marriage....
>
> We find on the good side of the family prominent people in all walks of life and nearly all of the 496 descendants owners of land or proprietors. On the bad side we find paupers, criminals, prostitutes, drunkards, and examples of all forms of social pest with which modern society is burdened. (Goddard, 1912, p. 116)

It is interesting to note that Goddard interpreted the striking difference between the two lines of the Kallikak family as evidence for the strong influence of heredity, an interpretation uncritically accepted at the time. Later writers have pointed out, however, that this difference is actually stronger evidence for the importance of the environment, since the two lines of the family have a common ancestor, yet differed greatly in social standing (Smith, 1985).

Goddard's methodology has been subject to the same criticism as was Dugdale's study of the Jukes. He relied on untrained field workers to make diagnostic decisions about the mental abilities and personalities of family members, both living and dead. For example, the following report of a home visit was submitted by a research associate.

> The girl of twelve should have been at school, according to the law, but when one saw her face, one realized it made no difference. She was pretty, with olive complexion and dark languid eyes, but there was no mind there.... Benumbed by this display of human degeneracy, the field worker went out into the icy street. (Goddard, 1912, p. 73)

There is also uncertainty over whether Goddard's original diagnosis of Deborah's feeblemindedness was correct (Smith, 1985). Smith reviewed Goddard's diagnostic evidence and concluded that using modern standards, Deborah would not be classified as mentally retarded.

Although the studies of the Jukes and the Kallikaks are seriously flawed by present-day standards, they provided all the evidence that was needed to convince the eugenicists of the time that something must be done to stem the proliferation of mental defects. Armed with these inflammatory studies, they successfully lobbied for compulsory sterilization laws in 30 states, and helped pass the Immigration Restriction Act of 1924.

## REFERENCES

Bajema, C. J. (1976). *Eugenics then and now.* Stroudsburg, PA: Hutchinson & Ross.

Dugdale, R. L. (1895). *The Jukes: A study in crime, pauperism, disease, and heredity* (5th ed.). New York: AMS.

Estrabrook, A. H. (1915). *The Jukes in 1915.* New York: Macmillan.

Goddard, H. H. (1912). *The Kallikak family: A study in the heredity of feeble-mindedness.* New York: Macmillan.

Gould, S. J. (1981). *The mismeasure of man.* New York: Norton.

Smith, J. D. (1985). *Minds made feeble: The myth and legacy of the Kallikaks.* Rockville, MD: Aspen.

ROBERT C. NICHOLS
DIANE JARVIS
*State University of New York at Buffalo*

**EUGENICS**
**SOCIOECONOMIC STATUS**

## JUVENILE ARTHRITIS

See ARTHRITIS, JUVENILE.

## JUVENILE CEREBROMACULAR DEGENERATION

Juvenile cerebromacular degeneration (also known as juvenile neuronal ceroid lipofuscinosis) is a progressive disorder transmitted on an autosomal recessive basis. If the onset occurs between the ages of 1 and 3 years, it may be known as infantile cerebromacular degeneration or Bielschowsky syndrome. The juvenile variety occurs at 5 to 7 years of age and may also be known as Spielmeyer-Vogt disease. Both types involve a degenerative process of the gray matter of the brain and are generally classified with the lipid storage diseases, the most common of which is Tay-Sachs or amaurotic familial idiocy (Behrman & Vaughan, 1983).

Onset usually begins with visual disturbances (eventually leading to blindness; Gillberg, 1995) because of degenerative changes in the retina. These range from retinitis pigmentosa to generalized retinal atrophy, resulting in blindness, despite the fact that the pupils may remain reactive to light. The visual disturbances are followed by a progressive degeneration of cortical gray matter, which may

be detected by EEG exam long before observable behavioral changes are seen. The child may develop seizures, become hyperactive, and show a severe pattern of cognitive and motor degeneration. Speech is lost, as are most other motor functions. The later the onset of the disease, the slower it progresses. Some have survived into adolescence but there remains no cure for the disorder (Behrman & Vaughan, 1983). Treatment consists only of symptom alleviation and supportive care. Many eventually require feeding through gastrostomy tube (Kolodny, 1979). Death, with current methods of intervention, occurs between 16 and 35 years of age (Gillberg, 1995).

A blood test can detect carriers of the disease: it is strongly recommended for all those of Ashkenazic Jewish background where heterogenous carriers have been identified at the rate of about 1:30 (Bennett, 1981).

## REFERENCES

Behrman, R., & Vaughan, V. (1983). *Nelson textbook of pediatrics* (12th ed.). Philadelphia: Saunders.

Bennett, J. (1981). *Diseases, the nurse's reference library series.* Horsham, Pennsylvania: Informed Communications Book Division.

Gillberg, C. (1995). *Clinical child neuropsychiatry.* Cambridge: Cambridge University Press.

Goodman, A., & Motulsky, R. (Eds.). (1979). *Genetic disorders of Ashkenazi Jews.* New York: Raven.

Kolodny, E. H. (1979). Tay-Sachs disease. In A. Goodman & R. Motulsky (Eds.), *Genetic disorders of Ashkenazi Jews.* New York: Raven.

JOHN E. PORCELLA
*Rhinebeck Country School*

**TAY-SACHS SYNDROME**

## JUVENILE COURT SYSTEM AND INDIVIDUALS WITH DISABILITIES

The number of delinquents with disabilities being disposed of by the juvenile courts is not known, since this datum currently is not recorded by any U.S. governmental office. In a recent study, Nelson, Rutherford, and Wolford (1985) reported that the prevalence of disabilities among incarcerated youth is approximately two times that expected in a hypothetical average school. The implication of this study is that a higher number of juveniles with disabilities are being disposed of by the courts.

The juvenile courts are organized in various manners within the different states. Whatever their organizational structure, they process juvenile cases under a separate system that is based on concepts of nonculpability and re-habilitation (U.S. Department of Justice, 1983). In 1989, Illinois established the first juvenile court based on the concept that a juvenile is worth saving and is in need of treatment rather than punishment, and that the juvenile court had a mission to protect the juvenile from the stigma of criminal proceedings.

Juvenile courts differ from criminal courts in that the language used in juvenile courts is less harsh. A juvenile court accepts "petitions of delinquency" rather than criminal complaints; conducts "hearings," not trials; adjudicates "juveniles to be delinquent" rather than guilty of a crime; and orders one of a number of available dispositions rather than sentences (U.S. Department of Justice, 1983).

The number of juveniles under the age of 21 who were processed through the juvenile courts during 1980 was 1,345,200. There were approximately three times more male than female cases being disposed of by the courts (U.S. Department of Justice, 1983). In 1977, 83 percent of the under-18-year-old population was held in detention facilities prior to court disposition (including 122,503 in jails and 507,951 in other juvenile detention facilities) as suspected delinquent or status offenders (U.S. Department of Justice, 1980).

Once referred to a juvenile court, a juvenile may be located at an intake facility or a detention facility that is either secured (similar to a jail facility) or nonsecured. During the judicial process, a juvenile may experience several of the following hearings: the detention hearing; the preliminary hearing; the fitness hearing (to certify as an adult or juvenile); the hearing of motions filed; the adjudication hearing (a hearing of fact); or the disposition hearing (placement, release, and probation; U.S. Department of Justice, 1980).

A study by the U.S. Department of Justice (1980) to determine the relationship between juvenile delinquency and learning disabilities found that learning-disabled youths are disproportionately referred to the juvenile justice system and that the juvenile courts need to use procedures for identifying and referring learning-disabled youths for remediation. These findings suggest that the juvenile court could expand its available range of dispositional alternatives by incorporating the use of special education program options.

Few studies have attempted to determine the current relationship between the juvenile court and special education. Karcz (1984) found that youths in a juvenile court secure detention facility in Lake County, Illinois, who were suspected of having disabilities, or who had disabilities, were provided with screening for disabilities, referral for diagnosis, an interim special education program at the detention facility, guarantees of due process procedures, and transition services through a new special education-related service position known as the Youth Advocate Liaison (YAL). As a result of these efforts, the YAL program increased the likelihood that the average detainee with disabilities would attend school in the home school district.

## REFERENCES

Brown, E. J., Flanagan, T. J., & McLeod, M. (Eds.). (1983). *Sourcebook of criminal justice statistics, 1983.* U.S. Department of Justice, Office of Justice Programs, Bureau of Justice Statistics. Washington, DC: U.S. Government Printing Office.

Karcz, S. A. (1984). *The impact of a special education related service on selected behaviors of detained handicapped youth.* Unpublished doctoral dissertation, University of Syracuse, New York.

Karcz, S. A., Paulson, D. R., & Mayes, W. T. (1985). Abrupt transitions for youth leaving school: Models of interagency cooperation. *Techniques, 1*(6), 497–499.

Nelson, C. M., Rutherford, R. B., & Wolford, B. J. (1985). *Juvenile and adult correctional special education data.* (Corrections 1/Special Education Training [C/SET] Project). Washington, DC: U.S. Department of Education.

U.S. Department of Justice. (1980). *Juvenile justice: Before and after the onset of delinquency.* Washington, DC: U.S. Government Printing Office.

U.S. Department of Justice. (1983). *Report to the nation on crime and justice: The data.* National Criminal Justice Reference Series, NCJ-87060. Rockville, MD: Bureau of Justice Statistics.

Stan A. Karcz
*University of Wisconsin at Stout*

**CONDUCT DISORDER
JUVENILE DELINQUENCY**

# JUVENILE DELINQUENCY

Prior to the enactment of the federal Juvenile Delinquency Act in 1938, juvenile offenders violating the laws of the United States were subject to prosecution in the same manner as adults. Since the act, juvenile delinquents have been treated procedurally as juveniles (not adults) by our justice system. Juvenile delinquency is defined as the violation of the law of the United States committed by a person prior to his or her eighteenth birthday that would have been a crime if committed by an adult (Karcz, 1984). Delinquency refers to those encounters with the law where the juvenile custody (called an "arrest" for adults) is entered into the record books. Any act that could place the juvenile who committed it in jeopardy of adjudication if it were to be detected is referred to as delinquent behavior (Hopkins, 1983).

Broadly speaking, there are two categories of children and/or youth who commit a delinquent offense: status offenders and juvenile offenders. Status offenses are those subject to legal action only if committed by a juvenile.

Examples of status offenses are truancy, incorrigibility, smoking, drinking, and being beyond the control of the parent or guardian (Hopkins, 1983). This category includes minors in need of supervision (MINS), dependent minors, and neglected and abused minors. Juvenile offenders are those children and/or youth who commit index crimes. Index crimes are criminal acts that are illegal regardless of the person's age or status (e.g., shoplifting, robbery, homicide; Kauffman, 2005). A major difference between juvenile offenders and adult offenders is the importance that the juvenile places on gang membership and the tendency of the juvenile to engage in group criminal activity. Violent juvenile offenders, however, have similar characteristics to those of adult felons. Juvenile offenders and adult felons are predominately male, disproportionately black and/or Hispanic, typically disadvantaged, likely to exhibit interpersonal difficulties and behavioral problems in school, and likely to come from one-parent families with a high degree of conflict, instability, and inadequate supervision (U.S. Department of Justice, 1983).

The Office of Juvenile Justice and Delinquency Prevention (OJJDP) data indicate that juveniles had 8.6 percent of all arrests for murder (one out of every twelve arrests), one out of every nine arrests for drug abuse, and one out of every four arrests for both weapons violations and robbery. Walker, Ramsey, and Gresham (2004) write that research shows "that youths who are chronic offenders (i.e., having three or more arrests by age 12) are much more likely to be early starters in their pattern of antisocial behavior. They found that 100 percent of boys arrested before age 10 had at least three arrests before reaching age 17. They also identified 17 boys in their longitudinal sample who had committed violent acts; each of these 17 boys was found to be a chronic offender. *Thus a severe pattern of antisocial behavior that is clearly in evidence early in the schooling process, coupled with an early start in committing delinquent acts, may identify the future chronic offender*" (p. 29, emphasis added).

Prevention programs that address youth violence and juvenile delinquency fall under two broad categories: prevention at the societal and community levels and prevention at the individual and school levels (Walker, Colvin, & Ramsey, 1995). Kauffman (2005) notes that intervention efforts are typically multifaceted and focus on the reduction of risk factors, as well as proactive and preventative measures that involve the family, juvenile justice agencies, and schools and other educational agencies as part of a comprehensive system of supervision, support, and care.

## REFERENCES

Hopkins, J. R. (1983). *Adolescence: The transitional years.* New York: Academic Press.

Karcz, S. A. (1984). *The impact of a special education related service on selected behaviors of detained handicapped youth.* Unpublished doctoral dissertation, University of Syracuse, New York.

Kauffman, J. M. (2005). *Characteristics of emotional and behavioral disorders of children and youth.* Upper Saddle River, NJ: Prentice Hall-Merrill.

Office of Juvenile Justice and Delinquency Prevention (OJJDP). (2005). *FAQs on law enforcement and juvenile crime.* Retrieved October 31, 2005, from http://ojjdp.ncjrs.org/ojstatbb/crime/faqs.asp?ID=T38

Walker, H. M., Colvin, G., & Ramsey, E. (1995). *Antisocial behavior in school: Strategies and best practices.* Pacific Grove, CA: Brooks/Cole.

Walker, H. M., Ramsey, E., & Gresham, F. M. (2005). *Antisocial behavior in school: Evidence-based practices* (2nd ed.). Belmont, CA: Wadsworth/Thomson Learning.

RANDALL L. DE PRY
*University of Colorado at
 Colorado Springs*
Third edition

STAN A. KARCZ
*University of Wisconsin at Stout*
Second edition

## CRIME AND INDIVIDUALS WITH DISABILITIES

# K

## KAISER-PERMANENTE DIET

The Kaiser-Permanente (K-P) diet, frequently referred to as the Feingold diet, was proposed by Feingold (1975) for the management of learning and behavioral disorders in children. Feingold's diet essentially eliminates the chemical additives that are frequently added to foods to enhance their longevity. Rooted in the basic premise of the Kaiser-Permanente diet is the assumption that children with hyperactivity, or other learning and behavioral disorders, have a natural toxic reaction to these artificial additives. Specifically, the diet forbids artificial colors and flavorings and foods containing natural salicylates, including a number of nutritious fruits and vegetables.

Despite the vogue of the K-P diet in many households across the country, Feingold's (1976) claim that the diet would ameliorate behavioral and learning disturbances has received scant support in the research literature (Kavale & Forness, 1983). Although Conners (1980) has indicated that a small percentage of hyperactive children do respond to some type of dietary intervention, it still remains unclear whether the improvement is actually a function of the diet itself or the regimen associated with the diet. Nonetheless, despite the dubious validity of Feingold's (1975, 1976) claims, many parents are loyal followers of Feingold's diet and have formed a national association to laud its efficacy and warn the public about the harmful effects of food additives for children. Reviews (e.g., Kavale & Forness, 1999) continue to fail to find support for the K-P diet as an effective intervention.

### REFERENCES

Conners, C. K. (1980). *Food additives and hyperactive children.* New York: Plenum.

Feingold, B. F. (1975). *Why your child is hyperactive.* New York: Random House.

Feingold, B. F. (1976). Hyperkinesis and learning disabilities linked to the ingestion of artificial food colors and flavors. *Journal of Learning Disabilities, 9*(9), 551–559.

Kavale, K. A., & Forness, S. R. (1983). Hyperactivity and diet treatment: A meta-analysis of the Feingold hypothesis. *Journal of Learning Disabilities, 16*(6), 324–330.

Kavale, K., & Forness, S. (1999). Effectiveness of special education. In C. R. Reynolds & T. B. Gutkin (Eds.), *The handbook of school psychology* (3rd ed., pp. 984–1024). New York: Wiley.

EMILY G. SUTTER
*University of Houston, Clear Lake*

RONALD T. BROWN
*Emory University School of Medicine*

ADDITIVE-FREE DIETS
ATTENTION-DEFICIT/HYPERACTIVITY DISORDER
FEINGOLD DIET
IMPULSE CONTROL

## KANNER, LEO (1894–1981)

Leo Kanner, "the father of child psychiatry," was the founder of the Johns Hopkins Children's Psychiatric Clinic and the author of the widely used textbook *Child Psychiatry*. Born in Austria, he came to the United States in 1924 and was naturalized in 1930.

Associated with Johns Hopkins University from 1928 until his death, Kanner was the first to describe infantile autism, which he characterized as the innate inability of certain children to relate to other people. A prolific author who once hoped to be a poet, Kanner published more than 250 articles and books on psychiatry, psychology, pediatrics, and the history of medicine.

### REFERENCES

Kanner, L. (1964). *A history of the care and study of the mentally retarded.* Springfield, IL: Thomas.

Kanner, L. (1979). *Child psychiatry* (4th ed.). Springfield, IL: Thomas.

PAUL IRVINE
*Katonah, New York*

# KARNES, MERLE B. (1916–2005)

Merle Karnes earned her BS in 1937 at Southeast Missouri State Teachers College and her MS in 1941 and EdD in 1948 in elementary education from the University of Missouri. During her distinguished tenure at the University of Illinois, Urbana-Champaign, she pursued postdoctoral work in special education, taught in the field of education, served as coordinator of a graduate training program in gifted education, and directed research projects concerned with gifted children and those with disabilities.

Throughout her career, Karnes was particularly interested in atypical children and was especially known for her work with gifted preschool children from various socioeconomic backgrounds as well as those with and without disabilities (Karnes & Johnson, 1989, 1991; Karnes, Shwedel, & Kemp, 1985; Karnes, Shwedel, & Linnemeyer, 1982). Karnes devoted more than 20 years to the development and dissemination of models for the education of young children from low-income homes and those with disabilities. She and her staff were credited with the development of the Retrieval and Acceleration of Promising Young Handicapped and Talented (RAPYHT), an effective model for the education of young gifted/talented children funded in 1975 by the Office of Special Programs and replicated in over 20 states (Karnes, Shwedel, & Lewis, 1983).

Karnes was an active member of many organizations, serving as president of both the National Council of Administrators of Special Education and the Division of Early Childhood of the Council for Exceptional Children. Among her numerous honors, for her outstanding contributions to exceptional children, in 1973 she received the J. E. Wallin Award of the Council for Exceptional Children. Additionally, she edited the book, *The Underserved: Our Young Gifted Children* (1983), a pioneering work in the area of gifted preschool children at the time it was published. Her contributions to the field of early childhood education are continued in her current works, including *Identifying and Programming for Young Black Gifted Children* (1990), *Coordinating Assessment and Programming for Preschoolers* (1991), and *Experiencing Science: Thinking Skills and Language Lessons for the Young Child* (1990).

## REFERENCES

Karnes, M. B. (Ed.). (1983). *The underserved: Our young gifted children.* Reston, VA: Council for Exceptional Children.

Karnes, M. B., & Johnson, L. J. (1989). Training for staff, parents, and volunteers working with gifted young children, especially those with disabilities and from low-income homes. *Young Children, 44*(3), 49–56.

Karnes, M. B., & Johnson, L. J. (1990). *Identifying and programming for young Black gifted children.* Monroe, NY: Trillium.

Karnes, M. B., & Johnson, L. J. (1991). The preschool/primary gifted child. *Journal for the Education of the Gifted, 14*(3), 267–283.

Karnes, M. B., & Johnson, L. J. (1991). *Coordinating assessment and programming for preschoolers.* Tucson, AZ: Communication Skill Builders.

Karnes, M. B., & Lowmiller, C. (1990). *Experiencing science: Thinking skills and language lessons for the young child.* Tucson, AZ: Communication Skill Builders.

Karnes, M. B., Shwedel, A. M., & Kemp, P. B. (1985). Maximizing the potential of the young gifted child. *Roeper Review, 7*(4), 204–209.

Karnes, M. B., Shwedel, A. M., & Lewis, G. F. (1983). Long-term effects of early childhood programming for the gifted/talented handicapped. *Journal for the Education of the Gifted, 6*(4), 266–278.

Karnes, M. B., Shwedel, A. M., & Linnemeyer, S. A. (1982). The young gifted/talented child: Programs at the University of Illinois. *Elementary School Journal, 82*(3), 195–213.

ANN E. LUPKOWSKI
*Texas A&M University*
First edition

TAMARA J. MARTIN
*The University of Texas of the Permian Basin*
Second edition

HEATHER S. VANDYKE
*Falcon School District 49, Colorado Springs, Colorado*
Third edition

Merle B. Karnes

# KARYOTYPE

Karyotype is the chromosome set or constitution of an individual. Each species has a characteristic karyotype, not only with respect to chromosome number and morphology, but also with respect to the genes on each chromosome. Chromosomes are typically visualized in peripheral lymphocytes that have been placed in tissue culture, stimulated to divide, arrested in metaphase, and osmotically swelled. When prepared for analysis, the chromosomes of a human metaphase cell appear under the microscope as a chromosome spread. To analyze such a spread, the chromosomes are cut out from a photomicrograph and arranged in pairs in a standard classification. This process is called karyotyping.

Standardization of karyotype nomenclature has been accomplished through a series of conferences sponsored by the National Foundation-March of Dimes. The medical applications of chromosomal analysis include clinical diagnosis, linkage and mapping, polymorphism, study of malignancy, role in reproductive problems, and prenatal diagnosis. Since the advent of karyotyping and definition of the normal number of chromosomes in 1956, large numbers of chromosomal anomalies have been described. Down syndrome or trisomy 21 is the most common chromosomal abnormality associated with karyotyping. The Human Genome Project has greatly enhanced the ability to identify genetically based disorders through karyotyping.

## REFERENCES

King, R. C., & Stansfield, W. D. (1985). *A dictionary of genetics* (3rd ed.). New York: Oxford University Press.

Nora, J. J., & Fraser, F. C. (1981). *Medical genetics: Principles and practice* (2nd ed.). Philadelphia: Lea & Febiger.

Thaddeus, K. E. (1980). *Clinical genetics and genetic counseling.* Chicago: Year Book Medical.

Thompson, J. S., & Thompson, M. W. (1980). *Genetics in medicine* (3rd ed.). Philadelphia: Saunders.

KENNETH A. ZYCH
*Walter Reed Army Medical Center*

CHROMOSOMES, HUMAN ANOMALIES, AND
  CYTOGENETIC ABNORMALITIES
DOWN SYNDROME
GENETIC COUNSELING

## KASPER HAUSER SYNDROME

Children raised under highly deprived conditions are sometimes described, particularly in older literature, as Kaspar Hauser children. In 1828, when he was about 17 years of age, Kaspar Hauser appeared in rags in Nuremberg. He could write his name primitively, but was poorly coordinated and appeared retarded. Under the care of a local teacher, he learned some speech and social graces. He was able to recall that he lived alone for years in a dark room and was cared for by someone who never spoke or was seen. His story, originally written by Anselm von Feuerbach, is summarized by Shattuck (1980).

Unfortunately, as with most such cases, interpretation of Kaspar Hauser's progress is difficult because of lack of knowledge about his early environment, how he had lived prior to isolation, and whether, for example, he had previously acquired language.

Considerable development occurs in many areas after severe early deprivation, particularly when individuals are recovered in childhood. Normal language development is less likely, and prolonged deprivation cannot be completely reversed (Clarke & Clarke, 1978; Skuse, 1984). Genie, although occasionally described as a modern-day Victor (wild Boy of Aveyron), would better be described as a modern-day Kaspar Hauser since she was raised in a severely deprived environment.

## REFERENCES

Clarke, A. M., & Clarke, A. D. B. (Eds.). (1978). *Early experience: Myth and evidence.* New York: Free Press.

Shattuck, R. (1980). *The forbidden experiment: The story of the Wild Boy of Aveyron.* New York: Farrar Straus Giroux.

Skuse, D. (1984). Extreme deprivation in early childhood-II. Theoretical issues and a comparative review. *Journal of Child Psychology & Psychiatry, 25,* 543–572.

ROBERT T. BROWN
*University of North Carolina at Wilmington*

DEPRIVATION
FERAL CHILDREN
POST-INSTITUTIONALIZED CHILDREN

## KAUFFMAN, JAMES M. (1940– )

James M. Kauffman obtained his BS in 1962 in elementary education from Goshen College, his MEd in 1966 from Washburn University in Topeka, Kansas, and his EdD in special education from the University of Kansas.

Kauffman was a founding member of the International Academy for Research in Learning Disabilities. He has served as president of the Society for Learning Disabilities and Remedial Education (1980–1981) and senior editor of *Remedial and Special Education.* He is currently a member of the faculty in the department of education at the University of Virginia.

Kauffman has authored or coauthored more than 100 journal articles, book chapters, and books on topics related to special education and psychology. His major interest has been in defining emotional and behavioral disorders and developing programming for children with these disabilities (Kauffman, 1997). He and his colleague, Daniel P. Hallahan, have been proponents of noncategorical programming for individuals with mild disabilities and have collaborated in the research of attentional and strategy-oriented problems of children with disabilities, together authoring *Exceptional Learners: Introduction to Special Education* (1997). Kauffman's work has addressed problems associated with the assessment, identification, management, and placement of children with emotional and behavioral disorders; the limits of educability of these children; and teacher training using computer simulations of pupils with behavior problems (Hallahan, Kauffman, & Lloyd, 1999; Kauffman, 1995, 1997, 1998). His recent publications include *Managing Classroom Behavior* (1998) and *Characteristics of Emotional and Behavioral Disorders of Children and Youth* (1997).

## REFERENCES

Hallahan, D. P., Kauffman, J. M., & Lloyd, J. (1999). *Introduction to learning disabilities* (2nd ed.). Boston: Allyn & Bacon.

Kauffman, J. M. (1995). *Issues in educational placement: Students with emotional and behavioral disorders*. Hillsdale, NJ: Erlbaum.

Kauffman, J. M. (1997). *Characteristics of emotional and behavioral disorders of children and youth* (6th ed.). Upper Saddle River, NJ: Merrill.

Kauffman, J. M. (1998). *Managing classroom behavior: A reflective case-based approach*. Boston: Allyn & Bacon.

Kauffman, J. M., & Hallahan, D. P. (1997). *Exceptional learners: Introduction to special education* (Rev. ed.). Boston: Allyn & Bacon.

RICK GONZALES
*Texas A&M University*
First edition

TAMARA J. MARTIN
*The University of Texas of the Permian Basin*
Second edition

## KAUFMAN, ALAN S. (1944–    )

Alan S. Kaufman received his BA in natural science (honors) in 1965 from the University of Pennsylvania, where he was also a member of Phi Beta Kappa; his MA in educational psychology in 1967 from Columbia University; and his PhD in psychology (major area: measurement, research, and evaluation) in 1970, also from Columbia University. His major field of interest is assessment (psychoeducational, clinical, and neuropsychological), especially the measurement of intelligence in children and adults and its interface with the fields of school psychology, clinical psychology, psychometrics, and special education.

Kaufman has published seven books and more than 200 articles, reviews, and chapters in professional journals and books in the fields of school psychology, special education,

**Alan S. Kaufman**

clinical psychology, neuropsychology, and educational psychology. His studies and writings focus principally on the application of psychometric techniques and psychological theory, coupled with the integration of data from multiple sources, to the clinical analysis of profiles of scores on intelligence tests. More recently, he has researched aging and intelligence across the life span, studies that have produced research awards for him and his colleagues (Mensa Education and Research Foundation Award for Excellence, Mid-South Educational Research Association Outstanding Research Award). Kaufman's principal publications include *Clinical Evaluation of Young Children with the McCarthy Scales* (Kaufman & Kaufman, 1977), *Intelligent Testing with the WISC-R* (Kaufman, 1979), *Assessing Adolescent and Adult Intelligence* (Kaufman, 1990), *Intelligent Testing with the WISC-III* (Kaufman, 1994), and *Essentials of WAIS-III Assessment* (Kaufman & Lichtenberger, 1999). His books on the WISC-R and WISC-III are among the most widely cited works in school psychology and have been the standard texts on this topic in the field of children's intelligence; his 1990 text, likewise, has been influential in the clinical interpretation of intelligence tests for adolescents and adults. Kaufman was well-equipped to author these volumes. From 1968 to 1974, he was employed in several positions at The Psychological Corporation, where he was project director for development and standardization of the WISC-R and the McCarthy scales, working closely with David Wechsler and Dorothea McCarthy.

Since 1983, Kaufman has become widely known in the field of special education as a test author himself. With his wife and scholarly colleague, Nadeen L. Kaufman, he published the Kaufman Assessment Battery for Children (K-ABC; Kaufman & Kaufman, 1983), an intelligence and achievement battery for children aged 2 to 12 years. The K-ABC challenged established views of intelligence and became a diagnostic tool based on underlying neuropsychological processes in cognition; it has been translated and adapted in more than 15 countries worldwide, and is quite popular in France, Germany, and Japan. The K-ABC was followed by the Kaufman Test of Educational Achievement (K-TEA; Kaufman & Kaufman, 1985), a battery for most achievement areas, such as reading comprehension and mathematics. The K-TEA, renormed in 1996, has proved to be a popular instrument for school psychologists and special educators. In all, Kaufman and his wife have published eight tests, including the popular Kaufman Brief Intelligence Test (K-BIT; Kaufman & Kaufman, 1990) and the theory-based Kaufman Adolescent and Adult Intelligence Test (KAIT; Kaufman & Kaufman, 1993).

During his 30-year career, Kaufman has contributed to the field of special education in a pervasive and practical way. He has provided diagnostic and evaluative guidance to the practitioners who identify and teach exceptional children, and remains on the cutting edge of progress in assessment by his continued involvement in test development and book writing, his active research program, his coeditorship (since 1992) of the journal *Research in the Schools,* and his editorship (with Nadeen L. Kaufman) of the Wiley series *Essentials of Assessment.* His influence on assessment in special education has been extensive over the past three decades.

A student of the late Robert L. Thorndike, first author of the Stanford-Binet Intelligence Scale, Fourth Edition, Kaufman has continued a tradition of psychometric excellence in his work while finding appropriate means of melding psychometrics with the clinical acumen of the trained examiner. His philosophy of intelligent testing has been widely adopted in test interpretation at all levels. Kaufman is also well known as a mentor in school psychology; his former students include Bruce A. Bracken, Jack Cummings, Patti L. Harrison, Randy W. Kamphaus, R. Steven McCallum, Jack A. Naglieri, Kathleen Paget, and Cecil R. Reynolds. Kaufman received the 1997 Senior Scientist Award from APA's Division 16 (School Psychology) and is presently clinical professor of psychology at Yale University School of Medicine. In addition to collaborating with his wife, Nadeen, Kaufman enjoys collaborating in psychological research and writing with their daughter, Jennie, a PhD in clinical psychology, and son James, a forthcoming PhD in cognitive psychology under Robert Sternberg at Yale University. Kaufman has also coauthored *The Worst Baseball Pitchers of All Time* with James (Kaufman & Kaufman, 1995).

**REFERENCES**

Kaufman, A. S. (1979). *Intelligent testing with the WISC-R.* New York: Wiley.

Kaufman, A. S. (1990). *Assessing adolescent and adult intelligence.* Boston: Allyn & Bacon.

Kaufman, A. S. (1994). *Intelligent testing with the WISC-III.* New York: Wiley.

Kaufman, A. S., & Kaufman, J. C. (1995). *The worst baseball pitchers of all time* (Rev. ed.) New York: Citadel.

Kaufman, A. S., & Kaufman, N. L. (1977). *Clinical evaluation of young children with the McCarthy scales.* Boston: Allyn & Bacon.

Kaufman, A. S., & Kaufman, N. L. (1983). *Kaufman Assessment Battery for Children: Interpretive manual.* Circle Pines, MN: American Guidance Service.

Kaufman, A. S., & Kaufman, N. L. (1985). *Manual for Kaufman Test of Educational Achievement: Comprehensive Form (K-TEA).* Circle Pines, MN: American Guidance Service.

Kaufman, A. S., & Kaufman, N. L. (1990). *Manual for Kaufman Brief Intelligence Test (K-BIT).* Circle Pines, MN: American Guidance Service.

Kaufman, A. S., & Kaufman, N. L. (1993). *Manual for Kaufman Adolescent & Adult Intelligence Test (KAIT).* Circle Pines, MN: American Guidance Service.

Kaufman, A. S., & Lichtenberger, E. O. (1999). *Essentials of WAIS-III assessment.* New York: Wiley.

CECIL R. REYNOLDS
*Texas A&M University*

INTELLIGENT TESTING
KAUFMAN, NADEEN L.
KAUFMAN ADOLESCENT AND ADULT INTELLIGENCE TEST
KAUFMAN ASSESSMENT BATTERY FOR CHILDREN–II
KAUFMAN BRIEF INTELLIGENCE TEST
KAUFMAN TEST OF EDUCATIONAL ACHIEVEMENT– SECOND EDITION
McCARTHY, DOROTHEA
WECHSLER, DAVID
WECHSLER INTELLIGENCE SCALE FOR CHILDREN, FOURTH EDITION

# KAUFMAN, NADEEN L. (1945–    )

Born Nadeen Bengels in Brooklyn, New York, Nadeen L. Kaufman received her BS in education from Hofstra University in 1965. She then taught an elementary grade class of learning-disabled children prior to returning to higher education at Columbia University. Kaufman earned her MA from Columbia in educational psychology in 1972, followed by her EdM in reading and learning disabilities in 1975. She earned her EdD from Columbia University in the field of special education (specializing in neuroscience and learning disabilities) in 1978. During the period 1972 to 1978, Kaufman worked as a research consultant to the College Entrance Examination Board (1970–1972), as a field supervisor and research consultant for The Psychological Corporation (1970–1972) in the development and standardization of the McCarthy Scales and the Wechsler Intelligence Scale for Children–Revised (WISC-R), and as staff psychologist at the Rutland Center for Severely Emotionally Disturbed Children

Nadeen L. Kaufman

(1975–1977). Kaufman was an assistant professor of early childhood education at the University of Georgia. She has also held faculty positions at DePaul University, the National College of Education (NCE), California School of Professional Psychology (CSPP) in San Diego, and the University of Alabama. She has founded and directed psychoeducational clinics at NCE, CSPP, and Mesa Vista Hospital, a psychiatric facility in San Diego. From 1994 to 1997 she was professor and director of Psychoeducational Assessment Services at CSPP, and since 1997 she has been lecturer on the clinical faculty at Yale University School of Medicine.

Kaufman has made a variety of significant contributions to special education and to school psychology. In addition to numerous articles and reviews in refereed journals, mostly dealing with assessment of the handicapped and general test interpretation and application, Kaufman is coauthor of several major works in the field. With her husband and colleague, Alan S. Kaufman, she coauthored *Clinical Evaluation of Young Children with the McCarthy Scales* (Kaufman & Kaufman, 1977), and contributed numerous case reports (which she either wrote or supervised) that were published in Alan Kaufman's texts on the clinical interpretation of Wechsler's scales (Kaufman, 1979, 1990, 1994).

In 1983, Kaufman published, again with Alan Kaufman, the Kaufman Assessment Battery for Children (K-ABC; Kaufman & Kaufman, 1983), an intelligence and achievement battery for children aged 2 to 12 years that has been translated and adapted in more than 15 countries worldwide. With Bonnie Goldsmith and Alan Kaufman, she coauthored the K-SOS, Kaufman-Sequential or Simultaneous (Kaufman, Kaufman, & Goldsmith, 1984), a volume that provides guidelines and insights into the development of individualized educational programs for children based on their K-ABC profiles. In all, Kaufman has coauthored eight tests with Alan Kaufman, including the Kaufman Test of Educational Achievement (K-TEA; Kaufman & Kaufman, 1985), a popular instrument for school psychologists and special educators that measures most achievement areas,

such as reading comprehension and spelling; the commonly used two-subtest Kaufman Brief Intelligence Test (K-BIT; Kaufman & Kaufman, 1990); and the fluid-crystallized theory-based Kaufman Adolescent and Adult Intelligence Test (KAIT; Kaufman & Kaufman, 1993).

Kaufman, a past associate editor of *School Psychology Review* and current editor (with Alan S. Kaufman) of the Wiley series *Essentials of Assessment,* has a variety of honorary listings, including the *World's Who's Who of Women, Who's Who in Medicine and Healthcare,* and *Who's Who in the World.* She is a fellow of the American Psychological Association and of its Division of School Psychology. Interns and students who have been supervised and trained by Kaufman in academic institutions and the psychoeducational clinics she has directed have uniformly praised her insightful clinical skills and her warm and caring attitude toward the clients, their families, and the students themselves.

## REFERENCES

Kaufman, A. S. (1979). *Intelligent testing with the WISC-R.* New York: Wiley.

Kaufman, A. S. (1990). *Assessing adolescent and adult intelligence.* Boston: Allyn & Bacon.

Kaufman, A. S. (1994). *Intelligent testing with the WISC-III.* New York: Wiley.

Kaufman, A. S., & Kaufman, N. L. (1977). *Clinical evaluation of young children with the McCarthy scales.* Boston: Allyn & Bacon.

Kaufman, A. S., & Kaufman, N. L. (1983). *Kaufman Assessment Battery for Children: Interpretive manual.* Circle Pines, MN: American Guidance Service.

Kaufman, A. S., & Kaufman, N. L. (1985). *Manual for Kaufman Test of Educational Achievement: Comprehensive Form (K-TEA).* Circle Pines, MN: American Guidance Service.

Kaufman, A. S., & Kaufman, N. L. (1990). *Manual for Kaufman Brief Intelligence Test (K-BIT).* Circle Pines, MN: American Guidance Service.

Kaufman, A. S., & Kaufman, N. L. (1993). *Manual for Kaufman Adolescent & Adult Intelligence Test (KAIT).* Circle Pines, MN: American Guidance Service.

Kaufman, A. S., Kaufman, N. L., & Goldsmith, B. Z. (1984). *K-SOS: Kaufman sequential or simultaneous.* Circle Pines, MN: American Guidance Service.

CECIL R. REYNOLDS
*Texas A&M University*

**KAUFMAN, ALAN S.**
**KAUFMAN ADOLESCENT AND ADULT INTELLIGENCE TEST**
**KAUFMAN ASSESSMENT BATTERY FOR CHILDREN–SECOND EDITION**
**KAUFMAN BRIEF INTELLIGENCE TEST**
**KAUFMAN TEST OF EDUCATIONAL ACHIEVEMENT–SECOND EDITION**
**WECHSLER INTELLIGENCE SCALE FOR CHILDREN–FOURTH EDITION**

# KAUFMAN ADOLESCENT AND ADULT INTELLIGENCE TEST

The Kaufman Adolescent and Adult Intelligence Test (KAIT; Kaufman & Kaufman 1993) is an individually administered measure of general intellectual ability for use with persons between the ages of 11 and 85 years or over. The KAIT consists of Crystallized and Fluid Scales that yield a Composite IQ. The Crystallized Scale assesses a general store of knowledge acquired through education and sociocultural experience and includes Definitions, Auditory Comprehension, Double Meanings, and an alternate subtest—Famous Faces. The Fluid Scale, primarily a measure of problem-solving ability in novel situations, is composed of Rebus Learning, Logical Steps, Mystery Codes (Core Battery Subtests), and an alternate Memory for Block Designs subtest. The two alternate subtests are provided in the event that a Core Battery subtest is spoiled or if a measure should be substituted for other clinical reasons. In addition to the Core Battery subtests, the Expanded Battery includes memory measures that allow for interpretation of immediate and delayed recall (Rebus Delayed Recall and Auditory Delayed Recall). There is also a supplemental Mental Status subtest that is composed of 10 items assessing examinees' attention and orientation. The Core Battery takes a little over an hour to administer, while the Expanded Battery typically takes an additional half hour to complete.

Subtests' raw scores are converted to scaled scores that have a mean of 10 and a standard deviation of 3. The Fluid, Crystallized, and Composite IQ scales yield scores with a mean of 100 and a standard deviation of 15. The score for the Mental Status subtest produces raw scores that are translated into descriptive categories.

While the Cattell-Horn concept of Fluid ($Gf$) and Crystallized ($Gc$) intelligence (1966, 1967) is the predominate theory on which the KAIT is founded, the test also draws on neuropsychological and cognitive developmental models, specifically Golden's (1981) concept of planning ability as related to prefrontal lobe development and Piaget's (1972) highest stage of cognitive development, formal operations.

The test kit includes a manual, two easels, a Mystery Codes booklet, six wooden blocks, test record, and an audio-cassette tape. For ease of administration, examiner instructions are printed on the test easel pages. Most subtests provide teaching items, which give the examinee an opportunity to become familiar with the task. The start points for each subtest do not vary according to age of the examinee.

The KAIT was standardized between 1988 and 1991 on a U.S. sample of 2,000 participants from the ages of 11 to 94. The sample was representative of the 1990 U.S. census, although the western region of the United States was slightly overrepresented and the northeast was underrepresented. The sample was stratified by gender, age, geographic region, race/ethnic group, and socioeconomic status. Items were subjected to analyses of difficulty and discrimination along with Rasch item analysis. Extensive data regarding reliability and validity of the test are presented in the manual. Internal consistency is excellent for the three IQ scales (average .95). The six core subtests also have adequate split-half reliability (about .90). Test-retest reliability was ascertained utilizing a sample of 153 individuals who were retested after 6 to 99 days ($X$ = 31 days). The reliability coefficients for all three scales are good (Crystallized and Composite = .94 and Fluid = .87). Construct and concurrent validity for the KAIT is also adequate. Factor analysis supports the delineation of a crystallized factor and a fluid factor. Concurrent validity was established by comparing scores for the KAIT to established intelligence measures (WISC-R, WAIS-R, S-B: IV, and the KABC). While individual interpretation of subtests is discouraged, McGrew, Untiedt, and Flanagan (1996) found all of the subtests (except Memory for Block Designs) to be good measures of Spearman's $g$. As reported in the manual, diagnostic validity studies were carried out with a variety of clinical samples; however, Dumont and Hagberg (1994) note that mentally retarded and gifted populations were not included in the comparisons.

The KAIT is a useful measure of intelligence that can be utilized with a variety of populations. The use of Fluid and Crystallized Scales is consistent with the multiple factor theory of intelligence and allows for administration to people with diverse backgrounds. A particular strength of the test is its potential for use with the geriatric population. Furthermore, given the broad age range of the test, it could easily be substituted for the WISC-IV (for children aged 11 through 16 years 11 months) or WAIS-III. The auditory and visual nature of the subtests is also a strength and may add to examinee interest. It has been noted that "both children and adults found the test to be non-threatening and for some it was enjoyable and challenging" (Dumont & Hagberg, 1994, p. 195). However, these authors also noted that caution should be taken when using the KAIT with those possessing symptoms of dementia, or memory or reading problems. While more research is needed with specific populations (e.g., gifted and learning disabled students), the KAIT is an innovative and valid alternative to traditional intelligence tests.

## REFERENCES

Brown, D. T. (1994). Review of the Kaufman Adolescent and Adult Intelligence Test (KAIT). *Journal of School Psychology, 32,* 85–99.

Dumont, R., & Hagberg, C. (1994). Test reviews: Kaufman Adolescent and Adult Intelligence Test. *Journal of Psychoeducational Assessment, 12,* 190–196.

Dumont, R., & Whelley, P. (1995). The KAIT (Kaufman Adolescent and Adult Intelligence Test): Some thoughts from two practicing school psychologists. *Communiqué, 24,* 22–23.

Flanagan, D. P., Alfonso, V. C., & Flanagan, R. (1994). A review of the Kaufman Adolescent and Adult Intelligence Test: An advancement in cognitive assessment? *School Psychology Review, 23,* 512–525.

Golden, C. J. (1981). The Luria-Nebraska Children's Battery: Theory and formulation. In G. W. Hynd & J. E. Obrzut (Eds.), *Neuropsychological assessment and the school age child: Issues and procedures* (pp. 277–302). New York: Grune & Stratton.

Horn, J. L., & Cattell, R. B. (1966). Refinement and test of the theory of fluid and crystallized general intelligences. *Journal of Educational Psychology, 57,* 253–270.

Kaufman, A. S., & Kaufman, N. L. (1993). *Kaufman Adolescent and Adult Intelligence Test.* Circle Pines, MN: American Guidance Service.

Keith, T. Z. (1995). Review of the Kaufman Adolescent and Adult Intelligence Test. In J. C. Conoley & J. C. Impara (Eds.), *Twelfth mental measurements yearbook* (pp. 530–532). Lincoln, NE: Buros Institute of Mental Measurements.

Lassiter, K. S., Matthews, T. D., & Bell, N. L. (2002). Comparison of the General Ability Measure for Adults and the Kaufman Adolescent and Adult Intelligence Test with college students. *Psychology in the Schools, 39,* 497–506.

McGrew, K. S., Untiedt, S. A., & Flanagan, D. P. (1996). General factor and uniqueness characteristics of the Kaufman Adolescent and Adult Intelligence Test. *Journal of Psychoeducational Assessment, 14,* 208–219.

Piaget, J. (1972). Intellectual evolution from adolescence to adulthood. *Human Development, 15,* 1–12.

RON DUMONT
*Fairleigh Dickinson University*

JOHN O. WILLIS
*Rivier College*

## KAUFMAN ASSESSMENT BATTERY FOR CHILDREN–SECOND EDITION

The Kaufman Assessment Battery for Children–Second Edition (KABC-II; Kaufman & Kaufman, 2004) contains a total of 18 subtests grouped into Core or Supplemental tests. The Core subtests are those used to compute either the Fluid-Crystallized Index (FCI) or Mental Processes Index (MPI) and separate scale scores, while the Supplemental subtests provide expanded coverage of the abilities measured by the Core KABC-II subtests and allow for the computation of a Nonverbal Index (NVI). Some subtests are labeled Core at some ages and Supplementary at other ages. The battery for ages 3:0 to 3:11 consists of five (MPI) or seven (FCI) Core subtests that combine to yield the global score and five Supplemental or Out-of-Level subtests that may be administered. The battery for ages 4:0 to 5:11 includes nine (FCI) or seven (MPI) Core subtests and an additional three to nine Supplementary or Out-of-Level subtests. From ages 6:0 to 18:11 the battery includes ten (FCI) or eight (MPI) Core subtests and an additional six or seven Supplementary or Out-of-Level subtests. At all ages except 3 to 3:11, the subtests not only combine to produce the Global Index scores (FCI or MPI) but also yield up to four (Luria model) or five (CHC model) indexes. These index scores represent Sequential Processing/Short-term Memory, Simultaneous Processing/Visual Processing, Learning Ability/Long-Term Storage and Retrieval, Planning Ability/Fluid Reasoning, and Crystallized Ability. This last (Crystallized Ability) is only represented in the CHC model. Although the typical battery is given to children based on their chronological age, several subtests were also normed at overlapping age range. This overlap provides the examiner flexibility when testing children aged 3 through 7 years. In these cases, subtests appropriate for the individual's abilities are available.

The KABC-II was standardized on 3,025 children selected to be representative of noninstitutionalized, English-proficient children aged 3 years 0 months through 18 years 11 months living in the United States during the period of data collection (September 2001 through January 2003). The demographic characteristics used to obtain a stratified sample were age, sex, race/ethnicity, parental educational level, educational status for 18-year-olds, and geographic region.

In the standardization sample, there were 18 age groups: 3:0–3:5, 3:6–3:11, 4:0–4:5, 4:6–4:11, 5, 6, 7, 8, 9, 10, 11, 12, 13, 14, 15, 16, 17, and 18 years. In each 6-month age group between 3 years 0 months and 3 years 11 months, there were a total of 100 children, while from ages 4 years 0 months to 4 years 11 months and at age 18, there were 125 children. For ages 5 through 14 there were 200 children at each 1-year age group, and for ages 15 through 17 there were a total of 150 children at each 1-year age group. In each of the 18 age groups, there were approximately equal numbers of males and females. This sampling methodology was excellent.

The KABC-II, like many other standardized cognitive ability tests, uses the Deviation IQ (M = 100, SD = 15) for the five Scale Indexes (Sequential Processing/Short-term Memory, Simultaneous Processing/Visual Processing, Learning Ability/Long-Term Storage and Retrieval, Planning Ability/Fluid Reasoning, and Crystallized Ability), and the three Global Indexes (FCI, MPI, NVI) and scaled scores (M = 10, SD = 3) for the 18 individual subtests. The calculation of the KABC-II scores involves a three-step process. After each subtest is scored, raw point totals are converted to a scaled score with a range from 1 to 19. From the sums of the scaled scores for the subtests that create Scale Indexes, the examiner obtains the standard scores for the Index of the test. Finally, the standard scores obtained for the respective Scale Indexes are added and this sum is used to obtain the FCI or MPI score. Age groups are 3-month intervals for children 3 years, 0 months to 5 years, 11 months; 4-month intervals for children 6 years 0 months through 14 years 11 months; and 6-month intervals for 15 years and older.

Extensive data regarding reliability and validity of the

test are presented in the manual. Internal consistency is excellent for the index scales (average in mid- to upper .90s). The subtests also have adequate reliability, with only 4 of the 18 subtests having reliability below .80. Test-retest reliability was ascertained utilizing a sample of 205 individuals who were retested after 12 to 56 days. The reliability coefficients for all scales are good (mid-.80s to mid-.90s). Construct and concurrent validity for the KABC-II is also adequate. While individual interpretation of subtests is discouraged, the loadings on the first unrotated factor provide information about *g,* or general intelligence. The KABC-II subtests form three *g*-related clusters: The Knowledge/*Gc* subtests have the highest *g* loadings in the test. On average, the proportion of variance attributed to *g* is 56 percent for the Knowledge/*Gc* subtests, 43 percent for the Planning/*Gf* subtests, 31 percent for the Learning/*Glr* subtests, 30 percent for the Sequential/*Gsm* subtests, and 26 percent for the Simultaneous/*Gv* subtests. Subtests with the highest proportion of variance attributed to *g* are Riddles, Verbal Knowledge, and Expressive Vocabulary, all subtests of the Knowledge/*Gc* Scale Index. None of the Planning/*Gf,* Learning/*Glr* subtests, Sequential/*Gsm* subtests, or Simultaneous/*Gv* subtests are good measures of *g.* Since this test has been recently released, there were no published studies available at the time of this review.

RON DUMONT
*Fairleigh Dickinson University*

JOHN O. WILLIS
*Rivier College*

## KAUFMAN BRIEF INTELLIGENCE TEST–SECOND EDITION

The Kaufman Brief Intelligence Test–Second Edition (KBIT-2; Kaufman & Kaufman, 2004) is an individually administered test of verbal and nonverbal ability. The test is suitable to be administered to persons aged 4 through 90 and takes approximately 15 to 30 minutes to administer. The KBIT-2 consists of two scales, verbal and nonverbal. The verbal scale is composed of two parts: Verbal Knowledge and Riddles. The nonverbal scale contains the Matrices subtest. Unlike the original K-BIT, the Verbal scale on the second edition does not require the examinee to read or spell words.

Both the Vocabulary and Matrices subtests are administered using an easel. The items are in color and are designed to appeal to children. Starting points on the KBIT-2 are determined by the examinee's age. The raw scores obtained are converted to standard scores (M=100, SD = 15) for both the subtests and the resulting Composite IQ.

The KBIT-2 was conormed with the Kaufman Test of Educational Achievement, Second Edition–Brief Form for individuals aged 26 to 90. The norming sample was representative of U.S. census data with respect to race, geographic region, and socioeconomic status. Studies conducted on the KBIT-2 demonstrated high reliability and validity. The exact data from these studies were not available at the time of publication.

The KBIT-2 may be used as an intellectual screening tool and/or to assess disparity between verbal and nonverbal intelligence.

RON DUMONT
*Fairleigh Dickinson University*

JOHN O. WILLIS
*Rivier College*

## KAUFMAN FUNCTIONAL ACADEMIC SKILLS TEST

The Kaufman Functional Academic Skills Test (K-FAST; Kaufman & Kaufman, 1994) is a two-subtest measure of an individual's ability to perform typical life tasks that demand mathematical reasoning or reading comprehension. Normed for ages 15–85+, the items on the K-FAST relate to daily activities that occur outside of the traditional academic setting.

Administration time for both subtests of the K-FAST is about 15–25 minutes. The Arithmetic subtest measures reasoning and computation skills as well as mathematical concepts, using pictorial stimuli to reduce the influence of reading ability. The Reading subtest assesses the ability to recognize and understand certain rebuses, abbreviations, and phrases.

Performance on the subtests can be interpreted using age-based standard scores with a mean of 100 and standard deviation of 15, as well as percentile ranks and descriptive categories for Arithmetic, Reading, and a Functional Academic Skills Composite.

The K-FAST was normed on a representative sample of 1,424 subjects, stratified by age according to gender, geographic region, socioeconomic standing, and race/ethnic group. This sample reflected the 1988 U.S. census data. It has good reliability and validity.

The K-FAST was developed, field-tested, and standardized with the Kaufman Adolescent and Adult Intelligence Test (KAIT), the Kaufman Brief Intelligence Test (K-BIT), and the Kaufman Short Neuropsychological Assessment Procedure (K-SNAP). These four tests provide a range of cognitive assessment options.

Most adaptive behavior inventories rely on subjective information supplied by parents, teachers, guardians, and others to determine a client's ability level. However, the K-FAST directly and objectively tests adaptive functioning.

Further, the K-FAST includes many items that allow for accurate and stable measurement over a wide age range for individuals with low cognitive ability.

The K-FAST should not be interpreted as an intelligence test or used as the only measure of adaptive functioning.

## REFERENCES

Flanagan, D. P., McGrew, K. S., & Abramowitz, E. (1997). Improvement in academic screening instruments? A concurrent validity investigation of the K-FAST, MBA, and WRAT-3. *Journal of Psychoeducational Assessment, 15,* 99–112.

Impara, J. C., & Plake, B. S. (Eds.). (1998). *The thirteenth mental measurements yearbook.* Lincoln, NE: Buros Institute of Mental Measurements.

Kaufman, A. S., & Kaufman, N. L. (1994). *Kaufman Functional Academic Skills Test manual.* Circle Pines, MN: American Guidance Service.

Klimczak, N. C., Bradford, K. A., & Burright, R. G. (2000). K-FAST and WRAT-3: Are they really different? *Clinical Neuropsychologist, 14,* 135–138.

RON DUMONT
*Fairleigh Dickinson University*

JOHN O. WILLIS
*Rivier College*

# KAUFMAN SHORT NEUROPSYCHOLOGICAL ASSESSMENT PROCEDURE

The Kaufman Short Neuropsychological Assessment Procedure (K-SNAP; Kaufman & Kaufman, 1994) is a brief, individually administered test designed to assess mental functioning of individuals ages 11 to over 85 years. It assesses functioning at three differing levels of cognitive complexity.

The K-SNAP takes approximately 20 to 30 minutes to administer. The test is composed of four subtests, organized by level of complexity. The Mental Status subtest (low complexity) assesses attention and orientation; the Number Recall and Gestalt Closure subtests (medium complexity) measure simple memory and perception skills, respectively and Four-Letter Words (high complexity) assesses reasoning and planning ability. The K-SNAP yields raw scores that are converted to standard scores (M = 100, SD = 15) for the K-SNAP Composite and to scaled scores (M = 10, SD = 3) for the individual subtests. In addition, percentile ranks and descriptive categories are also available. An Impairment Index can also be calculated with the intent of providing a more objective method to determine a level of cognitive impairment and whether more comprehensive assessment is needed.

Standardization of the K-SNAP included a sample of 2,000 subjects ages 11 to 94 years, which was stratified within each age group by gender, geographic region, socioeconomic status, and race or ethnic group. U.S. Census data from 1988 was used and the sample closely approximated this data. The K-SNAP was conormed and codeveloped along with the KAIT, K-BIT, and K-FAST. It has been demonstrated that the K-SNAP has good reliability and validity.

Critiques of the K-SNAP have been positive, stating that the test is valuable as part of a more comprehensive assessment and that its standardized mental status exam is useful (Geller, 1998; Herbert, 1998). However, the K-SNAP was also described as "only moderately useful for documenting the need for comprehensive neuropsychological or intellectual evaluation because . . . it does not accurately identify those who do not need additional evaluation" (Herbert, 1998).

## REFERENCES

Geller, K. (1998). Review of Kaufman Short Neuropsychological Assessment Procedure. In J. C. Impara & B. S. Plake (Eds.), *The thirteenth mental measurements yearbook.* Lincoln, NE: Buros Institute of Mental Measurements.

Herbert, M. (1998). Review of Kaufman Short Neuropsychological Assessment Procedure. In J. C. Impara & B. S. Plake (Eds.), *The thirteenth mental measurements yearbook.* Lincoln, NE: Buros Institute of Mental Measurements.

Kaufman, A. S., & Kaufman, N. L. (1994). *Kaufman Short Neuropsychological Assessment Procedure.* Circle Pines, MN: American Guidance Service.

Kaufman, A. S., & Kaufman, N. L. (1994). *Manual for the Kaufman Short Neuropsychological Assessment Procedure.* Circle Pines, MN: American Guidance Service.

DEBRA Y. BROADBOOKS
*California School of Professional Psychology*

# KAUFMAN SURVEY OF EARLY ACADEMIC AND LANGUAGE SKILLS

The Kaufman Survey of Early Academic and Language Skills (K-SEALS; Kaufman & Kaufman, 1993) is a brief, individually-administered test which assesses young children's language, pre-academic, and articulation skills. The test was developed from and is considered an expanded form of the Cognitive/Language Profile of the Early Screening Profiles (ESP; Kaufman & Kaufman, 1990). The K-SEALS was designed for children aged 3 years 0 months to 6 years 11 months.

The K-SEALS takes about 15 to 25 minutes to administer. It consists of three subtests. The Vocabulary subtest assesses the child's receptive and expressive vocabulary. The child points to or names pictures of objects or actions and names objects from verbal descriptions of their characteristics. The Numbers, Letters, & Words subtest assesses the child's knowledge of numbers and number concepts, letters, and words. It requires the child to point to or name numbers, solve number problems, and count. The Articulation Survey subtest assesses the child's ability to clearly articulate words by pronouncing common words. The K-SEALS yields raw scores which are converted to standard scores (M = 100, SD = 15), percentile ranks, age equivalents, and descriptive categories. Interpretive scales include Language Scales (Expressive Skills Scale and Receptive Skills Scale), Early Academic Scales (Number Skills Scale and Letter & Words Skills Scale, for use with children age 5–0 to 6–11 only), and the Early Academic & Language Skills Composite.

Standardization of the K-SEALS was conducted as part of the AGS Early Screening Profiles, resulting in a K-SEALS sample of 1,000 children ages 3–0 to 6–11. The sample was selected to match variables such as age, gender, geographic region, socioeconomic level, and race or ethnic group. Data for the sample was compared to U.S. Census data from 1990; the sample was shown to closely approximate this census data. The K-SEALS has excellent reliability and validity and, in fact, has been commended for being "remarkably reliable and valid" (Ackerman, 1995).

The K-SEALS has been recommended as a screening tool or as part of a comprehensive speech-language evaluation (Ford & Turk, 1995); however, critiques have noted that it lacks differentiation among the scales and that it appears that only the overall composite is useful (Ackerman, 1995). Strengths of the test include that it correlates well with measures of intelligence and with teacher ratings of ability. Limitations include the difficulty engaging young children in tasks from a flip-easel format (Ford & Turk, 1995) and the test's apparent lack of differential diagnosis and intervention (Ackerman, 1995).

## REFERENCES

Ackerman, P. L. (1995). In J. C. Conoley & J. C. Impara (Eds.), *The twelfth mental measurements yearbook*. Lincoln, NE: Buros Institute of Mental Measurements.

Ford, L., & Turk, K. (1995). In J. C. Conoley & J. C. Impara (Eds.), *The twelfth mental measurements yearbook*. Lincoln, NE: Buros Institute of Mental Measurements.

Kaufman, A. S., & Kaufman, N. L. (1990). *Cognitive / Language Profile in the AGS Early Screening Profiles*. Circle Pines, MN: American Guidance Service.

Kaufman, A. S., & Kaufman, N. L. (1993). *Kaufman Survey of Early Academic and Language Skills*. Circle Pines, MN: American Guidance Service.

Kaufman, A. S., & Kaufman, N. L. (1994). *Manual for the Kaufman Short Neuropsychological Assessment Procedure*. Circle Pines, MN: American Guidance Service.

DEBRA Y. BROADBOOKS
*California School of
Professional Psychology*

# KAUFMAN TEST OF EDUCATIONAL ACHIEVEMENT–SECOND EDITION

The Kaufman Test of Educational Achievement–Second Edition (KTEA-II; Kaufman and Kaufman) is an individually administered battery that consists of an assessment of the key academic skills in reading, math, written language, and oral language. The KTEA-II Comprehensive Form allows for error analysis along with detailed prescriptive information for remediation planning. The KTEA-II was redesigned and expanded, and covers IDEIA, Reading First, and NCTM achievement areas.

The KTEA-2 was standardized on a nationally representative age-norm sample of 3,000 examinees aged 4:06 through 25, and a nationally representative grade-norm sample of 2,400 students in grades K through 12, who were tested at 133 sites reaching 253 communities in 39 states and the District of Columbia. Its standardization edition of the KTWA-2 Comprehensive Form consisted of two non-overlapping parallel forms, each containing the fourteen subtests of the final edition. Approximately half of the norm sample took each form. Internal consistency, alternate form, and interrater reliabilities are high to very high; validity information in the manual is extensive due to the longevity of the battery and correlations with other achievement tests. KTEA-II Comprehensive Form includes the following subtests and composites:

Reading Standard Battery
    Letter and Word Recognition
    Nonsense Word Decoding (New)
    Reading Comprehension
    Reading Composite
    Reading Supplemental Subtests
    Phonological Awareness (New)
    Rapid Automatized Naming (New)
    Fluency—Semantic and Phonological (New)
    Timed Word Recognition (New)
    Timed Nonsense Word Decoding (New)
Math Standard Battery
    Math Concepts and Applications
    Math Computation
    Math Composite
Written Language Standard Battery
    Written Expression (New)
    Spelling
    Written Language Composite
Oral Language Supplemental Subtests
    Listening Comprehension (New)
    Oral Expression (New)

The Comprehensive Form provides composite scores for Grade 1 students and older in reading, math, written language, and oral language. A Comprehensive Achievement

Composite can be computed for all examinees. Six additional subtests assess reading-related skills and give valuable diagnostic information.

Conormed with the KABC-II, the battery allows for a comparison of a student's abilities and school performance. The electronic scoring system allows for:

- A summary of student performance by composite or subtest
- Comparisons of skill areas or subtests
- Error analysis for all standard subtests
- Best practices instructional suggestions for designing individualized education plan (IEP) goals that match students' score information with remediation strategies
- Lists of math problems or reading or spelling words similar to those that were difficult for the student

The KTEA-II Brief Form includes three subtests: Reading—word recognition and reading comprehension, Math—computation and application problems, and Written Expression—written language and spelling. It was also conormed with the Kaufman Brief Intelligence Test–Second Edition (KBIT-2).

### REFERENCE

Kaufman, A. S., & Kaufman, N. L. (2004). *The Kaufman Test of Educational Achievement, Second Edition.* Circle Pines, MN: AGS Publishing.

STAFF

## KAYSER-FLEISCHER RING

This phenomenon is a visible symptom of Wilson's disease that is present in most cases of Wilson's Disease that have associated behavioral or psychiatric conditions. It should prompt a referral to an ophthalmologist when seen. It is due to a defect in liver cells that causes a disruption in the metabolism and elimination of copper from the body.

STAFF

**WILSON'S DISEASE**

## KEARNS SAYRE SYNDROME

Kearns Sayre syndrome is a relentlessly progressive multisystem disorder with childhood onset. The cardinal features are paralysis of eye muscles, pigmentary degeneration of the retina, and heart block. Other features include ataxia, hearing loss, short stature, endocrine abnormalities, and progressive decline in intellectual function. Annual reassessments of these students are needed because of their changing needs.

Deletions of sizable portions of mitochondrial DNA affect the structure and function of mitochondria, the intracellular energy factories. The cells requiring the most energy, like the brain, heart, and muscle, are most vulnerable. Collections of abnormal mitochondria are seen as ragged red fibers in muscle biopsies. Even at rest, persistent lactic acidosis is present. There is no cure for this life-limiting disorder, but cardiac pacemakers are usually indicated, and some patients have benefited from dietary supplements of coenzyme Q and carnitine.

Nearly all cases occur sporadically and it is important to recognize that there is a great deal of variability in expression in mitochondrial diseases. An apparently identical mitochondrial DNA deletion is seen in progressive external ophthalmoplegia, an adult-onset, very slowly progressive weakness of eye and limb muscles.

Kearns Sayre syndrome is a rare disease, but it has been estimated that up to 1 in 4,000 people are affected by various mitochondrial disorders. *Exceptional Parent* magazine ran a three-part series on these diseases and their management in their June, July, and August 1997 issues that was comprehensive but readable. Their address is P.O. Box 2078, Marion, Ohio, 43306-2178. Extensive information for families and professionals about these disorders is available from The United Mitochondrial Disease Foundation, P.O. Box 1151, Monroeville, Pennsylvania, 15146-1151, and at their web site: http://www.umdf.org/.

### REFERENCES

DiMauro, S., Hirano, M., Bonilla, E., & DeVivo, D. C. (1996). In B. D. Berg (Ed.), *The mitochondrial disorders in principles of child neurology.* New York: McGraw-Hill.

Moraes, C. T., DiMauro, S., Zeviani, M. et al. (1989). Mitochondrial DNA deletion in progressive external ophthalmoplegia and Kearns Sayre syndrome. *New England Journal of Medicine, 320,* 1293–1299.

PATRICIA L. HARTLAGE
*Medical College of Georgia*

## KELLER, HELEN A. (1880–1957)

Helen Adams Keller, blind, deaf, and mute from the age of 18 months, became one of the world's best known examples of victory over a severe disability. Under the direction of a dedicated and talented teacher and companion, Anne Sullivan Macy, Keller was not only educated; she also became a successful writer, lecturer, and advocate for the disabled.

She graduated cum laude from Radcliffe College in 1904 and began a long career on behalf of the disabled. She wrote, lectured on the Chatauqua circuit and in vaudeville, served on Massachusetts' State Commission for the Blind, and worked tirelessly for the American Foundation for the Blind from the time it was formed in 1923. Her lobbying for federal legislation for the blind was instrumental in the creation of federal reading services, including talking-book recordings, and the inclusion of federal grant assistance for the blind in the Social Security Act. She involved herself in numerous social causes, including women's suffrage, pacifist movements prior to both world wars, and the antinuclear movement after World War II. Most important, Keller made herself a living symbol of triumph over disability, and an inspiration to disabled people everywhere.

## REFERENCES

Brooks, V. W. (1956). *Helen Keller: Sketch for a portrait.* New York: Dutton.

Keller, H. (1904). *The story of my life.* New York: Doubleday.

Lash, J. (1980). *Helen and teacher: The story of Helen Keller and Anne Sullivan Macy.* New York: American Foundation for the Blind.

PAUL IRVINE
*Katonah, New York*

# KENNY, SISTER ELIZABETH (1886–1952)

Sister Elizabeth Kenny revolutionized the treatment of poliomyelitis and became an international heroine during the polio epidemics of the 1940s. She began working with

**Sister Elizabeth Kenny**

polio patients as a nurse in her native Australia—hence the title of "Sister," which is given to nurses in British Commonwealth countries. She developed a method of treatment that, in contrast to the prevailing procedure of immobilizing the muscles with braces or casts, involved stimulating affected muscles to enable them to regain their function. Her success attracted worldwide attention and in 1939 she was invited to the United States by a group of physicians. Her demonstration of her treatment methods to physicians in Minneapolis-St. Paul resulted in a hospital ward dedicated to the Kenny treatment. From this beginning, the world-renowned Kenny Institute was formed, and Sister Kenny's approach became the accepted method of treatment for polio.

## REFERENCE

Kenny, E. (1943). *And they shall walk: The life story of Sister Elizabeth Kenny.* New York: Dodd, Mead.

PAUL IRVINE
*Katonah, New York*

# KEOGH, BARBARA H. (1925–     )

Barbara H. Keogh received her BA in 1946 in psychology at Pomona College and her MA in 1947 in psychology from Stanford University. She later earned her PhD in 1963 in psychology at the Claremont Graduate School. Keogh is currently Professor Emeritus in the department of education at the University of California in Los Angeles.

Keogh's study has been concentrated in the areas of school psychology; psychoeducational evaluation, particularly as related to children with developmental delays; and special education. She advocates the adoption of different models of school psychology if services are to be effective for exceptional children, and proposes a broader view of psychoeducational assessment for a more productive use of school psychology. Considering the unique contributions made by school psychologists to psychoeducational evaluation (e.g., differential diagnosis, therapeutic planning), Keogh contends that assessment should focus on identification of task-relevant abilities that may be used or developed for learning success.

Keogh continues her work on issues of importance to children with disabilities and their families, recently writing on an ecocultural approach to the assessment of families of young children with developmental disabilities (Bernheimer & Keogh, 1995; Keogh & Weisner, 1993). This perspective utilizes information of the family's daily routines and living arrangements, considering both risk and protective factors in diagnosis and intervention planning. She has also raised important issues related to future research in the field of special education, suggesting a predominance of prevention and intervention as well as a coherent research program (Keogh, 1994).

Keogh has written numerous articles and books, including the five-volume series, *Advances in Special Education.*

## REFERENCES

Bernheimer, L. P., & Keogh, B. K. (1995). Weaving interventions into everyday life: An approach to family assessment. *Topics in Early Childhood Special Education, 15*(4), 415–433.

Keogh, B. K. (1971). Hyperactivity and learning disorders: Review and speculation. *Exceptional Children, 38,* 101–109.

Keogh, B. K. (1980–1986). *Advances in special education* (Vols. 1–5). Greenwich, CT: JAI.

Keogh, B. K. (1994). What the special education agenda should look like in the year 2000. *Learning Disabilities Research and Practice, 9*(2), 62–69.

Keogh, B. K., & Daley, S. (1983). Early identification: One component of comprehensive services for at risk children. *Topics in Early Childhood Special Education, 3*(3), 7–16.

Keogh, B. K., Hewett, F. M., & Becker, L. D. (1973). Research in special education. *UCLA Education, 15*(1), 4–6.

Keogh, B. K., & Weisner, T. (1993). An ecocultural perspective on risk and protective factors in children's development: Implications for learning disabilities. *Learning Disabilities Research and Practice, 8*(1), 3–10.

ELIZABETH JONES
*Texas A&M University*
First edition

TAMARA J. MARTIN
*The University of Texas of the
Permian Basin*
Second edition

## KEPHART, NEWELL C. (1911–1973)

Newell C. Kephart received his PhD from the University of Iowa in 1936. He worked as a mental hygienist at the Wayne County (Michigan) Training School and as a research analyst for the U.S. Employment Service prior to naval service in World War II. In 1946 he joined the faculty of Purdue University, where he served as professor of psychology and education and conducted the Achievement Center for Children, a research and treatment center for disabled children.

Kephart, who excelled in presenting classroom procedures in a manner readily understood and accepted by teachers, was a leading contributor to the perceptual-motor training movement of the 1960s. Following retirement from Purdue University in 1968, Kephart served until his death as director of the Glen Haven Achievement Center in Fort Collins, Colorado, a school devoted to the education of disabled children and their parents.

## REFERENCES

A special tribute. (1973). *Academic Therapy, 8,* 373–374.

Ball, T. S. (1971). *Itard, Seguin, and Kephart: Sensory education—A learning interpretation.* Columbus, OH: Merrill.

Kephart, N. C. (1971). *The slow learner in the classroom* (2nd ed.). Columbus, OH: Merrill.

PAUL IRVINE
*Katonah, New York*

## KERLIN, ISAAC NEWTON (1834–1893)

Isaac Newton Kerlin, a physician, served as superintendent of the Pennsylvania Training School for Feeble-Minded Children (now Elwyn Institute) from 1863 until his death in 1893. An excellent administrator, Kerlin made Elwyn a model that influenced the planning of institutions for the mentally retarded throughout the country. Through his efforts the Association of Medical Officers of American Institutions for Idiotic and Feeble-Minded Persons (now the American Association on Mental Retardation) was formed at Elwyn in 1876. Kerlin, as secretary of the young organization, was responsible for the extension of the membership until it included almost all American physicians interested in mental deficiency.

**Isaac Newton Kerlin**

## REFERENCES

Historical notes on institutions for the mentally defective: Elwyn Training School. (1941). *American Journal of Mental Deficiency, 45,* 341–342.

Scheerenberger, R. D. (1983). *A history of mental retardation.* Baltimore: Brookes.

PAUL IRVINE
*Katonah, New York*

## KERNICTERUS

Kernicterus is a form of neonatal brain damage that results from destruction of fetal red blood cells in utero and deposits of bilirubin in the basal ganglia (Medway & Thomas, 1998). Excess bilirubin in the blood penetrates the meningeal barrier (blood-brain barrier) and cerebral damage results. This syndrome is usually secondary to RH incompatibility and may be a result of brain lesions. However, it may also occur as a result of drugs, enzyme abnormalities of red blood cells, or liver or other blood infections (Zimmerman & Yannet, 1935). Kernicterus may also manifest athetoid and spastic paralysis in children. It is rarely seen now because it is almost always preventable (Medway & Thomas, 1998).

Physically, there is not a consistent picture of kernicterus manifestations with the exception of signs of paralysis in the upper and lower extremities. Some athetoid paralysis, weakness, or muscle rigidity may be seen. Teeth may be yellow and eyes may be hooded. Hearing loss may be present (Lemeshaw, 1982). In newborns, jaundice, poor sucking reflexes, motor delay, and reduced muscle tone may appear. Seizures may be present. Athetoid motor movements such as rigidity and posturing may be present soon after birth.

A broad range of mental retardation can occur, but in many instances it is not seen. Early feeding seems to reduce the depth of jaundice and lower complications (Illingworth, 1983). Several blood problems may occur. Depending on the severity of the athetoid condition and of the motor impairment coupled with speech dysfunction, the child may be placed in a special educational setting. While these disabilities may make proper assessment and evaluation difficult, it is important to remember that many of these children possess normal intelligence. A multidisciplinary team of evaluators will probably be necessary to accurately assess the child.

Seizures, hearing impairment, and visual and communication problems will require related services, as will motor impairments. Support services may be required to locomote and feed the child. Program placement will necessitate a cohesive effort from a variety of professionals. Settings will vary based on the degree of impairment.

## REFERENCES

Illingworth, R. (1983). *Development of the infant and young child: Abnormal and normal* (7th ed.). New York: Churchill, Livingstone.

Lemeshaw, S. (1982). *The handbook of clinical types in mental retardation.* Boston: Allyn & Bacon.

Medway, F., & Thomas, S. (1998). Jaundice (neonatal). In L. Phelps (Ed.), *Health-related disorders of children and adolescents.* Washington, DC: American Psychological Association.

Zimmerman, H., & Yannet, H. (1935). Cerebral sequelae oficterus gravis neonatorum and their relation to kernikterus. *American Journal of Diseases in Children, 49,* 418–423.

SALLY L. FLAGLER
*University of Oklahoma*

**BIRTH INJURIES**

## KETOGENIC DIET

The Ketogenic Diet is a carefully calculated diet, high in fat, low in protein, and virtually carbohydrate-free that is used for the treatment of difficult-to-control pediatric seizures. The diet was first formulated in the early 1920s at Johns Hopkins Hospital in Maryland and has proven to be very effective over the years in approximately one in three children with epilepsy. Many centers in the United States stopped using the diet to control seizures as new medications were developed. The ketogenic diet at Johns Hopkins was continued and has been refined—the materials and methodology for the diet are now on a computer disc, which helps families calculate the diet more easily.

The diet is a medical therapy and should be used only under the careful supervision of a physician and/or dietician. The diet carefully controls caloric input and requires that the child eat only what has been included in the calculations to provide 90 percent of the day's calories as fats. The diet is currently offered only to children and adolescents, although protocols are being planned for adults.

Families interested in learning more about the Ketogenic diet may contact the Charlie Foundation for Pediatric Epilepsy (1-800-367-5386) to obtain a copy of a free videotape about the diet. A book entitled *The Epilepsy Diet Treatment: An Introduction to the Ketogenic Diet* may be purchased from Demos Publications, 386 Park Avenue South, Suite 210, New York, NY 10076 (1-800-532-8663). If, after reviewing this information, a family wishes to have their child considered for the Ketogenic diet, doctors at Johns Hopkins suggest requesting the child's physician to write a letter summarizing the case. They will then decide if more information would be appropriate and will contact the family.

Correspondence should be sent to The Pediatric Epilepsy Center, Meyer 2-147, The Johns Hopkins Hospital, 600 N. Wolfe Street, Baltimore, MD 21287-7247.

Families who are using or are about to initiate the diet through other centers may wish to purchase The Ketogenic Diet computer disc, which is designed to assist dieticians planning new ketogenic diets and to help parents who wish to change their child's meal plans. It can be obtained via The Ketogenic Diet Program, c/o Epilepsy Association of Maryland, 300 East Joppa Road, Suite 1103, Towson, MD 21286-3018 (410-828-7700).

STAFF

**SEIZURE DISORDERS**

## KEYMATH-REVISED: A DIAGNOSTIC INVENTORY OF ESSENTIAL MATHEMATICS

The KeyMath-Revised (Connolly, 1988) is an untimed, individually administered diagnostic test that measures mathematical functioning. The KeyMath consists of 13 subtests examining areas such as knowledge of numbers and fractions, ability to perform operations such as addition and subtraction, and real life skills involving money and time. The subtests are classified into three major divisions: content, operations, and applications. The content area focuses on knowledge of basic mathematical concepts that are necessary to perform mathematical operations, such as numeration, rational numbers, and geometry. The mathematical operations area involves the computational processes of addition, subtraction, multiplication, and division, as well as mental computation. The applications area contains problems involving the use of mathematical processes in everyday life, such as estimation, measurement, data interpretation, time, and money.

The KeyMath-Revised is intended for students in grades K–9, and takes approximately 30 to 50 minutes to administer, depending upon the age of the child. There are two versions of this test available, forms A and B, each containing 258 items. Interpretations can be made on four diagnostic levels, which the examiner can use to identify strengths and weaknesses. These four levels include Total Test, Area, Subtest, and Domain. The information generated by the interpretations can be used for assessment for general instruction or as part of a more global assessment, pre- and post-testing, curriculum assessment, or assessment for remedial instruction.

There are two supplementary components to the Key-Math-Revised. One is a Report to Parents for the examiner to communicate the child's results to the parents. The other supplement is the KeyMath-Revised-Assist (automated system for scoring and interpreting standardized tests), which provides automatic conversion, profiling, and record management.

According to Larson and Williams (1994), the KeyMath-Revised differs from the original in several ways:

1. Instead of 14 subtests there are 13 subtests.
2. The number of total items increased from 209 in the original to 258 items.
3. In order to expand coverage of the KeyMath to include decimals and percentages, a Rational Numbers subtest was introduced.
4. Rather than two separate subtests for time and money, a single subtest covers both of these areas.
5. The Mental Computation subtest was expanded beyond mental computation chains.
6. Three new subtests were included: one to assess problem solving, one to measure the ability to estimate, and one to assess the ability to organize and interpret data.

The KeyMath was standardized in fall 1985 and spring 1986. The fall sample included 873 students in grades K–8, and the spring sample involved 925 students in grades K–9. In 1997, new norms were obtained for the KeyMath-Revised, and the newly normed version of the test is referred to as the KeyMath-Revised/Normative Update (NU; Connolly, 1997). Alternate-forms reliabilities for the KeyMath-Revised range from .53 to .80 for the subtests, from .82 to .85 for the area tests, and from .88 to .92 for the total test. For the 1997 normative update, median alternate form reliabilities were .69 for subtests, .82 for the area tests, and .92 for the total test. Split-half reliabilities for the KeyMath-Revised are shown by subtest and by grade, and although these coefficients are generally higher than the alternate-forms coefficients, the split-half reliabilities for some subtests in grades K and 1 are low (Larson & Williams, 1994). For the 1997 normative update, the median split-half reliability values were .81 for the subtests, .92 for the area tests, and .97 for the total test. There are some limitations to the validity information available about the KeyMath-Revised, and Larson and Williams (1994) report that the construct validity of the test seemingly would have been enhanced by factor analyses studies.

Larson and Williams (1994) note that a weakness of the KeyMath-Revised is the low reliability of the subtests for younger children and lower grades. This becomes a difficulty if the test is used as a basis for decision making regarding grade retention in kindergarten and first grade, although this was not one of the primary purposes of this test. Therefore, overall the KeyMath-Revised appears to be a valuable instrument when used appropriately for its intended purposes. The KeyMath is currently being revised by AGS publishing.

## REFERENCES

Connolly, A. J. (1988). *KeyMath-Revised: A Diagnostic Inventory of Essential Mathematics.* Circle Pines, MN: American Guidance Service.

Connolly, A. J. (1997). *KeyMath-Revised / Normative Update: A Diagnostic Inventory of Essential Mathematics.* Circle Pines, MN: American Guidance Service.

Larson, J. A., & Williams, J. D. (1994). KeyMath-Revised: A Diagnostic Inventory of Essential Mathematics. In D. J. Keyser & R. C. Sweetland (Eds.), *Test critiques, Volume X* (pp. 350–354). Austin, TX: PRO-ED.

SHELLEY SUNTUP
*California School of
Professional Psychology*

ACHIEVEMENT TESTS
MATHEMATICS, LEARNING DISABILITIES IN

# KEYWORD METHOD

The keyword method is one of several mnemonic (memory-enhancing) techniques used for facilitating the learning and later recall of associative information. First employed by Atkinson (1975) in teaching Russian vocabulary words to college students, the keyword method was first applied to school-age children by Pressley (1977) in the learning of Spanish vocabulary words. Since that time it has been applied in many different content domains with students of several age and ability levels (Pressley, Levin, & Delaney, 1982).

The keyword method employs what Levin (1983) has described as the 3 R's of mnemonic techniques: recoding, relating, and retrieving. For example, in learning the Italian vocabulary word *roccia* (pronounced roach-ia), which means cliff, learners are first provided with (or are asked to generate) a recorded keyword. A keyword is a word that is acoustically similar to the stimulus term, and easily pictured. In this case, *roach* would be a good keyword for *roccia*. In a second step, the keyword is related to the response term via an interactive picture or image. In the *roccia* example, a *roach* could be shown jumping off a cliff. For the final, retrieving step, the learner is asked, when given the stimulus *roccia*, to think back to the keyword *roach*, to think of the picture of the roach, recall what else was in the picture, and respond with the appropriate referent, cliff.

The keyword method has recently been used with learning disabled (Mastropieri, Scruggs, & Levin, 1985), mentally retarded (Scruggs, Mastropieri, & Levin, 1985), and gifted (Scruggs, Mastropieri, Monson, & Jorgenson, 1985) students. Results to date have suggested that the keyword may be an effective instructional strategy in special education. In addition to simple vocabulary learning instruction, several extensions have been explored in a variety of content-area domains. A combination of a keyword-pegword (rhyming system to teach numbers, e.g., one is bun, two is shoe, etc.) strategy was employed to teach the hardness levels of North American minerals according to Moh's scale. For example, to teach that pyrite is number six on the hardness scale, students were shown an interactive illustration of a pie (keyword for pyrite) on sticks (pegword for six) and taught that when asked for the hardness level of pyrite, they should think of the keyword (pie), remember the picture of the pie on sticks, and respond with the pegword equivalent, six. Since these experiments demonstrated superior performance for mnemonically instructed students, several other studies were conducted to teach multiple attributes mnemonically. These studies not only taught the hardness level of minerals, but also color and common use. For example, to teach that pyrite is six on the hardness scale, yellow in color, and used for making acid, learners were shown an interactive illustration of a yellow (color) pie (keyword for pyrite) resting on sticks (keyword for six) while acid (use) is poured on it. Additionally, similar mnemonic instruction has been adapted to the teaching of classifications in science-related content areas; in all cases, the keyword method has consistently outperformed a variety of control conditions by a wide margin.

Although the keyword method has been proven highly effective in experimental settings, the ultimate practical use of the keyword method for classroom instruction is at present unknown. Recent research by Tolfa-Veit, Scruggs, and Mastropieri (in press), however, has suggested that this technique is effective for long-term instruction of academic units, while McLoone, Zucker, Scruggs, and Mastropieri (1986) have provided evidence that learning-disabled students can be trained to transfer the strategy to independent learning. A review of keyword research efforts with exceptional populations has been provided by Mastropieri et al. (1985).

## REFERENCES

Atkinson, R. C. (1975). Mnemotechnics in second language learning. *American Psychologist, 30,* 821–828.

Levin, J. R. (1983). Pictorial strategies for school learning: Practical illustrations. In M. Pressley & J. R. Levin (Eds.), *Cognitive strategy research: Educational applications.* New York: Springer-Verlag.

Mastropieri, M. A., Scruggs, T. E., & Levin, J. R. (1985). Maximizing what exceptional students can learn: A review of research in mnemonic techniques. *Remedial and Special Education, 6,* 39–45.

McLoone, B. B., Zucker, S., Scruggs, T. E., & Mastropieri, M. A. (1986). Mnemonic strategy instruction and training with learning disabled adolescents. *Learning Disabilities Research, 2,* 45.53.

Pressley, M. (1977). Children's use of the keyword method to learn simple Spanish vocabulary words. *Journal of Educational Psychology, 72,* 575–582.

Pressley, M., Levin, J. R., & Delaney, H. D. (1982). The mnemonic keyword. *Review of Educational Research, 52,* 61–91.

Scruggs, T. E., Mastropieri, M. A., & Levin, J. R. (1985). Vocabulary acquisition of retarded students under direct and mnemonic instruction. *American Journal of Mental Deficiency, 89,* 546–551.

Scruggs, T. E., Mastropieri, M. A., Monson, J. A., & Jorgenson, C. (1985). Maximizing what gifted students can learn: Recent findings of learning strategy research. *Gifted Child Quarterly, 29,* 181–185.

Tolfa-Veit, D., Scruggs, T. E., & Mastropieri, M. A. (in press). Extended mnemonic instruction with learning disabled students. *Journal of Educational Psychology.*

THOMAS E. SCRUGGS
MARGO A. MASTROPIERI
*Purdue University*

**MEMORY DISORDERS**
**MNEMONICS**

# KHATENA, JOE (1925–    )

Born and reared in Singapore, Joe Khatena was educated in universities both in his native land and in the United States. He obtained his PhD in psychology from the University of Georgia in 1969 and went on to become a professor and the head of the department of educational psychology at Mississippi State University. Khatena has received special honors for achievements in psychology and education,

**Joe Khatena**

and has been cited in numerous listings of outstanding individuals, such as the *International Who's Who in Community Services, American Men and Women in Science, Leaders in Education,* and *Who's Who in Frontier Science and Technology.*

Khatena espouses the structure of the intellect model to explain the multidimensionality of giftedness and to support the six U.S. Office of Education (USOE) categories of giftedness, with the reservation that this model does not explain the emotional and motivational aspects so essential to higher levels of creative intellectual functioning. He emphasizes that creativity in students must be nurtured by parents and teachers, as creativity will be the characteristic that distinguishes the gifted conserver from the gifted extensor of knowledge. His contributions to gifted education have been affirmed with an USOE Office of the Gifted and Talented Certificate of Recognition (1976), presidency of the National Association for Gifted Children (1979), and the Distinguished Scholar Award of that association (1982).

Throughout Khatena's work, he has focused on the perceptual aspects of creativity and the development of measures to identify outstanding abilities in those areas, including the Khatena-Torrance Creative Perception Inventory (1976) and the Torrance-Khatena-Cunningham Thinking Creatively with Sounds and Images Measure (1980). The Khatena-Morse Multitalent Perception Inventory (1985), identifying talent in the areas of art, music, leadership, and creativity, demonstrates Khatena's emphasis on the necessity of a single measure to assess a variety of talents. His writings have also been instrumental in detailing ways of assisting children in enhancing their verbal originality and mental imagery, proposing a three-dimensional creative imagination imagery model composed of the environment, the individual, and the cosmic dimension (Khatena, 1979, 1982, 1984, 1995). Khatena continues his prolific work in the field of giftedness and creativity with his publications, *Gifted: Challenge and Response for Education* (1992) and *Guiding Creative Talent in Art* (1998).

**REFERENCES**

Khatena, J. (1979). *Teaching gifted children to use creative imagination imagery.* Starkville, MI: Allan.

Khatena, J. (1982). *Educational psychology of the gifted.* New York: Wiley.

Khatena, J. (1984). *Imagery and creative imagination.* Buffalo, NY: Bearly.

Khatena, J. (1989). Intelligence and creativity to multitalent. *Journal of Creative Behavior, 23,* 93–97.

Khatena, J. (1992). *Gifted: Challenge and response for education.* Itasca, IL: Peacock.

Khatena, J. (1995). Creative imagination and imagery. *Gifted Education International, 10,* 123–130.

Khatena, J. (1998). *Guiding creative talent in art.* Stamford, CT: Ablex.

PATRICIA A. HAENSLY
*Texas A&M University*
First edition

TAMARA J. MARTIN
*The University of Texas of the Permian Basin*
Second edition

# KICKLIGHTER, RICHARD H. (1931–    )

Richard H. Kicklighter received his PhD in 1962 from the University of Florida, with a major in student personnel services under the direction of Ted Landsman. He is a licensed psychologist and has worked in the schools and institutional and private practice with sensorially, intellectually, and emotionally impaired children and their parents. He has served as director of the Division of Standards and Assessment in the Georgia Department of Education and has worked as a consultant for the Georgia Program for Exceptional Children.

Kicklighter's primary interest has been in the areas of educational test development, statewide student assessment program administration, and coordination of school psychology service programs (Kicklighter, 1975; Kicklighter & Bailey-Richardson, 1984; Kicklighter & Holt, 1971; Kicklighter & Richmond, 1982; Richmond & Kicklighter, 1983). He is coauthor, with Bert Richmond, of the Children's Adaptive Behavior Scale (CABS), a direct assessment test of social competency, and the Children's Adaptive Behavior Report (CABR), a structured interview guide used to estimate a child's adaptive behavior. His research has also included examining the number of school psychologists necessary to provide adequate service to students, with results indicating a requirement of one psychologist for every 2,000 students.

Kicklighter's service in the fields of education and psychology has included the presidency of the Georgia Psychological Association and the Georgia Federation of the Council for Exceptional Children as well as diplomat in school psychology of the American Board of Professional Psychology. He is coeditor of *Psychological Services in the Schools* (1971), a standard textbook in the field of school psychology.

## REFERENCES

Kicklighter, R. H. (1975). *Psychological education in the elementary classroom.* Boston: Houghton Mifflin.

Kicklighter, R. H., & Bailey-Richardson, B. (1984). Psychological assessment: Tasks and time. *School Psychology Review, 13*(4), 499–502.

Kicklighter, R. H., & Holt, F. D. (Eds.) (1971). *Psychological services in the schools: Reading in preparation, organization and practice.* Iowa: William C. Brown.

Kicklighter, R. H., & Richmond, B. O. (1982). *Children's Adaptive Behavior Report (CABR): A developmental interview guide.* Atlanta, GA: Humanics.

Richmond, B. O., & Kicklighter, R. H. (1983). *Children's Adaptive Behavior Scale.* Chicago: Stoelting.

ROBERTA C. STOKES
*Texas A&M University*
First edition

TAMARA J. MARTIN
*The University of Texas of the Permian Basin*
Second edition

# KINETIC-FAMILY-DRAWING

The Kinetic-Family-Drawing (KFD), devised by Burns and Kaufman (1970, 1972), is a projective drawing technique used to assess children's psychological adjustment and family dynamics. Based on surveys of practitioners, the KFD is one of the top 10 tests used in the assessment of children and adolescents (e.g., Archer, Maruish, Imhof, & Piotrowski, 1991; Piotrowski & Zalewski, 1993). The student is provided with a blank sheet of paper (usually 8½ by 11 inches) and a pencil with an eraser. The child is then asked to make a freehand drawing of everyone in their family doing something. The basic premise is that because the drawing must depict some kind of action, the examinee will provide important information about their family relationships (Carlson, 1990). The use of drawings is presumed to enable children to put into figures thoughts or feelings that they cannot convey verbally. Once the drawing is completed, the student is asked to describe the illustration, including each person's name, relationship to the child, age, and other meaningful characteristics or data. The drawing is scored using a scoring system (e.g., Burns, 1982; Knoff & Prout, 1985; Peterson & Hardin, 1997). Features included in the qualitative interpretation include size of figures, relative placement of figures, actions, omission, and use of color, if colored markers are used. A quick scoring guide for the interpretation of KFDs also has been published (Reynolds 1978).

Interpretation of the KFD centers on the premise that the KFD is effective in identifying those individuals in the child's family who are important to the child—with limited empirical support for this premise (Veltman & Browne, 2003). Reliability and validity issues also have been raised with regard to drawing techniques as well (e.g., Thomas & Jolley, 1998; Veltman & Browne, 2003). Further, there are some indications that children's drawings reflect cultural differences that need to be accounted for in the interpretation process (e.g., LaVoy et al., 2001).

## REFERENCES

Archer, R. P., Maruish, M., Imhof, E. A., & Piotrowski, C. (1991). Psychological test usage with adolescent clients: 1990 survey findings. *Professional Psychology: Research and Practice, 22,* 247–252.

Burns, R. (1982). *Self-growth in families: Kinetic family drawings (K-F-D) research and application.* New York: Brunner/Mazel.

Burns, R. C., & Kaufman, S. F. (1970). *Kinetic family drawings (K-F-D): An introduction to understanding children through kinetic drawings.* New York: Brunner/Mazel.

Burns, R. C., & Kaufman, S. F. (1972). *Actions, styles, and symbols in kinetic family drawings (K-F-D): An interpretive manual.* New York: Brunner/Mazel.

Knoff, J. M., & Prout, H. T. (1985). *Kinetic drawing system for family and school: A handbook.* Los Angeles: Western Psychological Services.

LaVoy, S. K., Pedersen, W. C., Reitz, J. M., Brauch, A. A., Luxenberg, T. M., & Nofsinger, C. C. (2001). Children's drawings: A cross-cultural analysis from Japan and the United States. *School Psychology International, 22,* 53–63.

Peterson, L. W., & Hardin, M. (1997). *Children in distress: A guide for screening children's art.* New York: W. W. Norton.

Piotrowski, C., & Zalewski, C. (1993). Training in psychodiagnostic testing in APA-approved PsyD and PhD clinical training programs. *Journal of Personality Assessment, 61,* 394–405.

Reynolds, C. R. (1978). A quick scoring guide to the interpretation of children's kinetic family drawings (KFD). *Psychology in the Schools, 15,* 489–492.

Thomas, G. V., & Jolley, R. P. (1998). Drawing conclusions: A reexamination of empirical and conceptual bases for psychological evaluation of children from their drawings. *Journal of Clinical Psychology, 37,* 127–139.

Veltman, M. W. M., & Browne, K. D. (2003). Trained rater's evaluation of kinetic family drawings of physically abused children. *The Arts in Psychotherapy, 30,* 3–12.

OLGA L. RODRIGUEZ-ESCOBAR
*Texas A&M University*

## DRAW-A-PERSON TEST
## HOUSE-TREE-PERSON
## KINETIC-SCHOOL-DRAWING

# KINETIC-SCHOOL-DRAWING

The Kinetic-School-Drawing (KSD; Prout & Phillips, 1974) is a projective drawing technique used to assess children's psychological adjustment and school dynamics. Similar to the Kinetic-Family-Drawing (KFD; Burns & Kaufman, 1970, 1972), the student is provided with a blank sheet of paper (usually 8½ by 11 inches) and a pencil with an eraser, and then asked, "I'd like you to draw a school picture. Put yourself, your teacher, and a friend or two in the picture. Make everyone doing something. Try to draw whole people and make the best drawing you can. Remember, draw yourself, your teacher, and a friend or two, and make everyone doing something" (Knoff & Prout, 1985, p.4). As a variation of the KFD, the purpose of this projective technique is to gather information about the student's perceptions of school and their perceptions of relationships within the school setting (Kaufman & Wohl, 1992). During the inquiry phase, the student is asked to describe the illustration, including each person's name, relationship to the child, age, and other meaningful characteristics or data. The drawing can then be scored using a qualitative scoring system (e.g., Kaufman & Wohl, 1992; Knoff & Prout, 1985).

A modification of this procedure has been used to ascertain what children perceive of as a good teacher (e.g., Murphy, Delli, & Edwards, 2004). In their study, children in the second grade were asked to draw a picture of a good teacher in a classroom with a few students. Drawings were initially evaluated holistically using Kaufman and Wohl's (1992) procedure and then using key word and content analysis of information obtained during the inquiry phase. Results indicated that a majority of second graders drew the teacher larger than the students in the picture, reflecting the perception that the teacher had more power. Further, the majority of students drew classrooms with whole-group instruction. Notably, Murphy and colleagues (2004) found that there were marked differences in the drawings produced by second graders, preservice teachers, and inservice teachers.

Interpretation of the KSD centers on the premise that it is effective in identifying the child's perceptions of relations between the teacher and students in the classroom. More importantly, in clinical work, it is based on the premise that it depicts the child's relationship with his/her teacher and other students in his/her classroom. There is little empirical evidence, however, to support this supposition. Reliability and validity issues also have been raised with regard to drawing techniques, despite their continued popularity (e.g., Piotrowski & Zalewski, 1993).

## REFERENCES

Burns, R. C., & Kaufman, S. F. (1970). *Kinetic family drawings (K-F-D): An introduction to understanding children through kinetic drawings.* New York: Brunner/Mazel.

Burns, R. C., & Kaufman, S. F. (1972). *Actions, styles, and symbols in kinetic family drawings (K-F-D): An interpretive manual.* New York: Brunner/Mazel.

Kaufman, B., & Wohl, A. (1992). *Casualties of childhood.* New York: Bruner/Mazel.

Knoff, J. M., & Prout, H. T. (1985). *Kinetic drawing system for family and school: A handbook.* Los Angeles, CA: Western Psychological Services.

Murphy, P. K., Delli, L. A. M., & Edwards, M. N. (2004). The good teacher and good teaching: Comparing beliefs of second-grade students, preservice teachers, and inservice teachers. *Journal of Experimental Education, 72,* 69–92.

Piotrowski, C., & Zalewski, C. (1993). Training in psychodiagnostic testing in APA-approved PsyD and PhD clinical training programs. *Journal of Personality Assessment, 61,* 394–405.

Prout, H. T., & Phillips, P. D. (1974). A clinical note: The kinetic school drawing. *Psychology in the Schools, 11,* 303–306.

OLGA L. RODRIGUEZ-ESCOBAR
*Texas A&M University*

**DRAW-A-PERSON TEST**
**KINETIC-FAMILY-DRAWING**

# KIRK, SAMUEL A. (1904–1996)

Samuel A. Kirk, often referred to as "the Father of Learning Disabilities," received his BA in 1929 and MA in 1931 in psychology from the University of Chicago, and his PhD in 1935 in physiological and clinical psychology from the University of Michigan. His doctoral studies led him to discount biophysical identifications of disability and to recommend more behavioral descriptions that could lead to remedial planning. In 1935, he began working as the director of a teacher education program at Milwaukee State Teachers College. He joined the faculty of the University of Illinois in 1947 to develop a program in special education for undergraduates and graduates. Much of his pioneering work was done as the founding director of the Institute for Research on Exceptional Children at the University of Illinois, a position he held before and after serving as director of the Federal Office of Education's Division of Handicapped Children in 1963 and 1964. During his tenure in Washington, he contributed to early federal legislation that led to the Early Education Assistance Act of 1968 and the establishment of the Bureau for the Education of Handicapped Children. The work of this bureau eventually culminated in PL 94-142, the Education for All Handicapped Children Act of 1975. After more than 20 years at the University of Illinois, he moved to the University of Arizona at Tucson, where he continued to play an active role even after his retirement. Samuel Kirk died in 1996 at the age of 92, in Tucson, Arizona.

Kirk devoted considerable effort to developing a means of measuring specific aspects of linguistic, perceptual, and memory abilities in young children. The Illinois Test of Psycholinguistic Abilities (ITPA) appeared in an experimental version in 1961 and was revised and published in 1968 for the purpose of helping plan remediation efforts for psycholinguistic deficits. The results of the study, published in 1958 as *Early Education of the Mentally Retarded,* stimulated research on disadvantaged children and influenced the development of Head Start. Like Binet, Kirk was not obsessed with the constancy of the IQ. He believed that intelligence could be changed through educational intervention and maintained that stance throughout his career. He is credited with coining the term "learning disabilities," first in a 1962 textbook on the education of exceptional children and then in a speech he delivered in 1963, describing children who were not blind, deaf, or mentally retarded, but were still not learning in school.

Samuel Kirk published more than 200 books, monographs, and journal articles, and was the recipient of numerous awards, including the First International Award in Mental Retardation from the Joseph P. Kennedy Foundation.

**Samuel A. Kirk**

## REFERENCES

Kirk, S. A. (1958). *Early education of the mentally retarded—An experimental study.* Urbana: University of Illinois Press.

Kirk, S. A., McCarthy, J. J., & Kirk, W. D. (1968). *The Illinois Test of Psycholinguistic Abilities.* Urbana: University of Illinois Press.

Learning Disabilities Association. (1996). *LDA bids farewell to father of learning disabilities.* Retrieved from http//www.ldantl.org/newsbriefs/oct96/kirk.html

ELAINE FLETCHER-JANZEN
*University of Colorado at Colorado Springs*
First edition

DONNA WALLACE
*The University of Texas of the Permian Basin*
Second edition

# KLINEFELTER SYNDROME

Klinefelter syndrome (KS) is a chromosomal abnormality occurring in a male who has at least one extra female sex chromosome (i.e., xxy or xxxy) in contrast to the normal male genotype of xy (Reed, 1975). About two-thirds of KS patients have an xxy pattern and the remainder have an xxxy pattern (Ginther & Fullwood, 1998). The extra sex chromosome(s) has been attributed to nondisjunction during meiosis, a process that also results in Down syndrome, although the precise etiology is unknown (Hoaken, Clarke, & Breslin, 1964). This syndrome is characterized by a generally normal-appearing phenotypical male with small and nonfunctioning testes, gynecomastia (i.e., enlarged breasts), low sex drive, a high-pitched voice, eunuchoid build, obesity, scant facial hair, tallness, and deficiencies of male hormone production. The incidence is reported to vary from 0.15 to 0.3 percent of the general population or 15 to 30 in every 10,000 males (Lubs & Ruddle, 1970; Reed, 1975); however, incidence is related to maternal age directly (Ginther & Fullwood, 1998). Although it is increasingly being identified during early infancy through genetic screening, KS is typically not diagnosed until after puberty, when the testicles are noted to be abnormally small. It is medically treated with testosterone during adolescence.

Research has consistently indicated that the extra x chromosome(s) material results in proportionately higher risks for a wide variety of developmental and psychological disabilities (Haka-Ikse, Steward, & Cripps, 1979; Money, 1980; Pomeroy, 1980). It has not been established whether the increased vulnerability to disabilities is biological or environmental (Leonard & Rosenberg, 1973). However, abnormal hormones secondary to xxy have been implicated in the impaired functioning of the central nervous system (CNS) that is frequently reported in Klinefelter syndrome patients. Moreover, intellectual functioning was found to decrease with each additional x chromosome (Forssman, 1970). Most males with xxy were found to have low-average intelligence; however, there is no disproportionate severe mental retardation. Wright, Schaefer, and Solomons (1979) reviewed studies that reported on factors typically associated with learning disorders (e.g., early language delay, auditory memory, auditory discrimination). Various types of psychopathology beyond psychosexual difficulties have been reported, including severe disorders such as schizophrenia, in addition to such specific symptoms as immaturity, impulsivity, passivity, apathy, and hostility.

Wright et al. (1979) recommended that behavioral practitioners provide comprehensive evaluation of intellectual, academic, and personal-social functioning of xxy persons. They especially recommended that evaluation take place before and after hormone treatment for those first identified during adolescence. Students with KS often require special education placement and counseling, and are at high risk both academically and socially (Ginther & Fullwood, 1998). Anticipatory guidance for the child and parents is especially recommended over time regarding such issues as sterility.

## REFERENCES

Forssman, H. (1970). Mental implications of sex chromosome aberrations. *British Journal of Psychiatry, 117,* 353–363.

Ginther, D., & Fullwood, H. (1998). Klinefelter syndrome. In L. Phelps (Ed.), *Health-related disorders in children and adolescents.* Washington, DC: American Psychological Association.

Haka-Ikse, K., Steward, D. A., & Cripps, M. H. (1979). Early development of children with sex chromosome aberrations. *Pediatrics, 62,* 761–766.

Hoaken, P. C. S., Clarke, M., & Breslin, M. (1964). Psychopathology in Klinefelter's syndrome. *Psychosomatic Medicine, 26,* 207–223.

Leonard, M. F., & Rosenberg, L. (1973). Interaction of environmental and genetic factors in Klinefelter's syndrome. *Pediatrics, 52,* 118–120.

Lubs, H. A., & Ruddle, F. H. (1970). Chromosomal abnormality in the human population: Estimates of rates based on New Haven newborn study. *Science, 169,* 495–499.

Money, J. (1980). Human behavior cytogenetics: Review of psychopathology in three syndromes—47, XXY; 47, XYY; and 45, X. In S. I. Harrison & J. F. McDermott (Eds.), *New directions in childhood psychopathology* (pp. 70–84). New York: International Universities Press.

Pomeroy, J. C. (1980). Klinefelter's syndrome and schizophrenia. *British Journal of Psychiatry, 136,* 597–599.

Reed, E. W. (1975). Genetic anomalies in development. In F. D. Horowitz (Ed.), *Review of child development research* (Vol. 4, pp. 283–318). Chicago: University of Chicago Press.

Wright, L., Schaefer, A. B., & Solomons, G. (1979). *Encyclopedia of pediatric psychology.* Baltimore: University Park Press.

Joseph D. Perry
*Kent State University*

GENETIC COUNSELING
GENETIC FACTORS IN BEHAVIOR
GENETIC VARIATIONS
PHYSICAL ANOMALIES

# KNIGHT, HENRY M. (1827–1880)

Henry M. Knight, physician and educator, entered the field of mental retardation as a member of the Connecticut state legislature, when he served on a committee established to ascertain the number of mentally retarded children in that state. Following completion of a census, legislation was proposed for the construction of a school for the retarded.

Henry M. Knight

Elizabeth M. Koppitz

When the legislation failed, Knight gave up his medical practice and, in 1858, established a residential program for retarded children in his home. Through Knight's continuing campaign for public support, the legislature, in 1861, appropriated the necessary funds and Knight's school became the fifth publicly supported institution for the mentally retarded in the United States. Knight served as superintendent until shortly before his death in 1880. The institution was closed in 1917 with the opening of more modern facilities. Knight was one of the founders of the Association of Medical Officers of American Institutions for Idiotic and Feeble-Minded Persons, now the American Association on Mental Deficiency.

## REFERENCE

Brown, G. (1964). Memoir of Dr. H. M. Knight. *Association of medical officers of American institutions for idiotic and feeble-minded persons, proceedings, 1876–1886.* New York: Johnson Reprint Corporation.

PAUL IRVINE
*Katonah, New York*

## KOPPITZ, ELIZABETH M. (1919–1983)

Elizabeth M. Koppitz came to the United States from Germany in 1939. She received her PhD from Ohio State University in 1955, and worked as a psychologist in Ohio and in the public schools of New York state until her retirement in 1982. She made major contributions to the field of psychoeducational assessment of children and is best known

for the scoring system presented in the *Bender Gestalt Test for Young Children* and her studies of children's human figure drawings.

## REFERENCES

In memoriam: Elizabeth M. Koppitz. (1983). *Communique, 12,* 1–3.

Koppitz, E. M. (1964). *The Bender Gestalt Test for young children.* New York: Grune & Stratton.

Koppitz, E. M. (1968). *Psychological evaluation of children's human figure drawings.* New York: Grune & Stratton.

PAUL IRVINE
*Katonah, New York*

## KRAEPELIN, EMIL (1856–1926)

Emil Kraepelin, German psychiatrist, held teaching posts at universities in Dorpat, Heidelberg, and Munich during his long career. Best known for his classification of mental disorders, his descriptions and classifications of the symptoms of mental illness provided a common ground for psychiatric thought; they constitute the basis for the categories in use today. Kraepelin applied the methods of the psychological laboratory to the study of personality, learning, and abnormal behavior. He developed tests to evaluate sensory-motor performance and the psychological deficits of psychiatric patients. He studied the effects of alcohol and tobacco, and was the first to use scientific methods to test the effects of drugs on human behavior. He wrote extensively on the problem of crime, providing much of the basis for the

**Emil Kraepelin**

modern study of the relationship between criminality and mental illness.

**REFERENCES**

Kahn, E. (1959). The Emil Kraepelin memorial lecture. In B. Pasamanick (Ed.), *Epidemiology of mental disorders: A symposium organized by the American Psychiatric Association to commemorate the centennial of the birth of Emil Kraepelin.* Washington, DC: American Association for the Advancement of Science.

Kraepelin, E. (1962). *One hundred years of psychiatry.* New York: Citadel Press.

PAUL IRVINE
*Katonah, New York*

## KUHLMANN, FREDERICK (1876–1941)

Frederick Kuhlmann, psychologist and test developer, obtained his PhD from Clark University in Massachusetts. After holding teaching positions there and at the universities of Wisconsin, Illinois, and Minnesota, he became director of research at the Minnesota School for the Feeble-Minded in Faribault, where he specialized in the assessment and education of mentally retarded children and adults. In 1912 and 1922 Kuhlmann published revisions of the 1908 Binet-Simon Scale, which extended the range of the test down to 3 months and represented one of the earliest efforts to develop a standardized test for infants. In 1927 he and Rose Anderson published a widely used group test of intelligence, the Kuhlmann-Anderson Intelligence Tests. Kuhlmann's individually administered Tests of Mental Development appeared in 1939.

In 1921 Kuhlmann's research department at Faribault became a state office, the Bureau of Mental Examinations, which he headed until his death. Kuhlmann's articles and research reports had widespread influence on other state institutions and on the development of services for mentally retarded students in the public schools of Minnesota. In addition, Kuhlmann was responsible for much of the teaching in the training program for teachers of the mentally retarded at Faribault. Kuhlmann was an active member of the American Association on Mental Deficiency and served as its president in 1940–1941.

**REFERENCES**

Dayton, N. (1940). President Frederick Kuhlmann. *American Journal of Mental Deficiency, 45,* 3–7.

Maxfield, F. N. (1941). Fred Kuhlmann. *American Journal of Mental Deficiency, 46,* 17–18.

PAUL IRVINE
*Katonah, New York*

## KURZWEIL READING MACHINE

Developed by Raymond Kurzweil in the mid-1960s at the Massachusetts Institute of Technology, the Kurzweil Reading Machine (KRM) is a computer for blind and print-impaired individuals; it converts printed materials directly into synthesized speech. The KRM converts printed materials from a variety of sources, type sizes, and styles into synthetic, full-word, multilingual speech that is readily understandable after a short period of familiarization. The KRM also functions as a talking calculator and can serve as a full word, voice output computer terminal.

The KRM consists of two principal units: the automatic scanning system and the control panel. The scanning system automatically scans documents up to 11 × 14 inches and will read print or type from 6- to 24-point. The push-button control panel activates and directs the system (Kurzweil Computer Products). The development of the KRM offers several important advances over Braille or direct-translation reading machines. Because the output of the device is speech, it is more easily understood and requires less special training. Relatively high reading speeds (approximately 250 words per minute) are able to be attained (Goodrich et al., 1979).

Users indicate the major advantages of the KRM include providing equal access to entire print collections, immediate availability of materials, and the ability to read at their own pace, on their own schedule, with privacy and independence (Kurzweil Computer Products, 1985). Limitations pertaining to the KRM involve its cost, size, and ability to produce clear speech from poor or elaborate print. Computer scanning of text and conversion to speech has become common and is now relatively inexpensive as a result of the revolution in personal computer pricing and availability seen at present.

## REFERENCES

Dickman, I. R. (1980). *What can we do about limited vision?* New York: Public Affairs Committee.

Goodrich, G. L., Bennett, R. R., De L'aune, W. R., Lauer, H., & Mowinski, L. (1979). Kurzweil reading machine: A partial evaluation of its optical character recognition error rate. *Journal of Visual Impairment & Blindness, 3,* 389–399.

Kurzweil Computer Products. (1985). Reading Machine Department, Cambridge, MA.

McKenzie, C. (1981). Using the Kurzweil Reading Machine. *Proceedings of the Second National Seminar on Library Services for the Handicapped, National Library of Australia.* (ERIC Document Reproduction Services No. ED 221 211)

HAROLD E. HOFF, JR.
*Eastern Pennsylvania Special Education Resources Center*

**BLIND**
**ELECTRONIC TRAVEL AIDS**
**VERSABRAILLE**

# L

## LABELING

Labeling is an imprecise term referring to a series of effects, mostly negative, believed to result from formal classification of students as disabled. Hobbs (1975), in his classic work that seems as current today as when it was first published, defined classification as "the act of assigning a child or condition to a general category or to a particular position in a classification system" (p. 43). The close relationship of classification and labeling is revealed by Hobbs's (1975) definition of labeling as, "the assignment of a child to a category," which also includes, "the notion of public communication of the way a child is categorized; thus, the connotation of stigma is present" (p. 43).

The somewhat confusing definitions cited are typical of the efforts to separate the effects of classification and labeling. Labeling is the term used to refer to negative effects that are assumed to be associated with the classification of students. These negative effects are most often associated with various mild handicapping classifications, particularly the classification of mild mental retardation (MMR). Labeling effects also are assumed to exist for other classifications such as specific learning disabilities (SLD) and emotionally disturbed (ED), but the negative effects associated with these classifications have not been seen as severe.

Labeling effects depend heavily on social deviance theory (Becker, 1963). Social deviance theory was initiated to explain the effects of the formal justice system on the behavior of persons, often teenagers, who may or may not have been classified as juvenile delinquents. Social deviance theory emphasizes the effects of labels on the behavior of individuals. Formal labels are believed to exert direct influence on behavior through complex processes that, simplified, result in labels creating deviant behavior. The question of whether labels create deviant behavior or whether labels result from significant behavioral deviation is the basic issue in the voluminous professional literature on labeling effects.

One of the strongest statements claiming to show the effects of labels in creating behavior was published by Rosenthal and Jacobson (1968). This widely cited and highly influential study claimed to show the effects of communicating positive information to teachers on the intellectual development of elementary school-aged children. Rosenthal and Jacobson claimed that changes in teachers' beliefs produced by brief statements about children inserted in their educational records led to significant intellectual growth by children, presumably because of subtle changes in how those children were treated by their teachers.

Although the Rosenthal and Jacobson work was severely criticized in the professional literature, and numerous efforts to replicate the findings were unsuccessful, the notion of self-fulfilling prophecy exerted enormous influence on special education in the late 1960s and 1970s, and, to a considerable extent, into the present era. The self-fulfilling prophecy as applied to special education suggests that children and youths acquire deviant behaviors or fail to develop positive behaviors because of the special education classification.

The theme that special education classifications, particularly MMR, have significant negative effects on students was particularly prominent in a widely cited article by Dunn (1968). Dunn argued that MMR special class programs involved stigmatizing labels as well as ineffective interventions. The labeling theme, particularly regarding MMR, was developed further by a 1970 report of the President's Committee on Mental Retardation. This report coined the term six-hour retarded child. Discussions of the labeling effects in the classification/placement process also further developed the theme by Mercer (1973, 1979). Although the conclusions of Dunn, Mercer, and the concept of six-hour retarded child are widely cited, there is little or no evidence showing direct negative effects of special education labels. A continuing problem in the special education literature is the insufficient attention to empirical studies of labeling effects.

Extensive research attempting to identify effects of special education classifications or placements has been conducted. This research is very complex. Perhaps the most serious complication is the fact that labels are not randomly assigned to students (and indeed could not be due to ethical concerns). In the real world, some students are classified and placed; others are not. There are well-known, significant differences separating those who are classified and placed in special education, and therefore potentially vulnerable to labeling effects, and those who are not classified and placed. Thus, an accurate account of the effects of labels in the real world must somehow take into account the differences among students that led to the original referral and then the classification and placement decisions.

Referrals are almost always initiated because of significant learning or behavioral problems in classroom settings. Only a few students are referred, typically under

10 percent. Students who are referred receive preplacement evaluations in which a multifactored assessment is conducted. The multifactored assessment information is considered by a multidisciplinary team that may or may not recommend classification as disabled and placement in special education. Thus the students for whom some labeling effect might occur are a highly selected subsample of the general population. Possible effects of labeling, which presumably occur after formal classification and placement, are contaminated with the behavioral characteristics of students that led to their initial referral and eligibility for special education. It is impossible to separate these effects in the real world.

Research attempting to observe developmental changes in self-concept and peer acceptance before and after labeling has been conducted with mixed results. The balance of evidence would appear to suggest that labeling either improves or has no significant effect on self-concept and peer acceptance (Gottlieb, 1980; Guskin, 1978).

The research that shows negative effects of labeling typically uses methodology heavily dependent on simulation. Participants in studies are asked either to imagine their reactions to a labeling circumstance, to read a brief description of a person who has been labeled and then indicate their expectations, or to observe via videotape or film the behavior of a student who they typically have been deceived to believe is handicapped. The results of these studies, which assess the effects of labels on expectations, not on actual behavior, have been mixed. Generally, participants with little or no contact, direct or vicarious, with the person who is supposedly disabled reveal a significant expectancy effect based on the label. However, participants with more information or prolonged contact, direct or vicarious, with the allegedly disabled person show reduced and often nonexistent effects of labels on expectations. There is no simple answer to the simple question, "Do labels create expectations?" It would appear that labels do create expectations if there is little contact and limited knowledge. With knowledge and experience, even in simulated studies, the effects of labels are quite limited. Excellent reviews of the labeling and expectancy literature have been provided by MacMillan and colleagues (MacMillan, 1982; MacMillan, Jones, & Aloia, 1974). Persons wishing to draw generalizations about labeling or conduct research on labeling phenomena should consult their work.

The enormously complex labeling literature does yield at least two fairly well established generalizations. First, children and youth classified as mildly disabled do not like being labeled. Second, many persons, including professionals such as public school teachers, often misunderstand the common special education labels. These two findings provide ample reason to be cautious about the assignment of labels, to exert strong effort to avoid misclassification, to consider alternatives to the current classification system, and to deliver effective programs if labeling is deemed necessary.

Although classification of some kind is generally regarded as absolutely necessary for communication, which in turn affects all aspects of conducting research, developing services, and organizing programs for students with disabilities, there is considerable discussion today concerning alternative bases for a classification system. The current system, whereby internal attributes of students form the basis for classification, may be revised in the forseeable future in a number of ways. One possibility is to merge the current categories into a generic mild disability classification. This combination of specific learning disability, seriously emotionally disturbed, and MMR, often referred to as cross-categorical, might reduce some of the confusion and misunderstanding, particularly of MMR. Other reforms of the current classification systems, such as classifying students according to the kinds of services needed rather than according to internal attributes, have been suggested and are being attempted. However, these reforms will not eliminate all possible negative connotations, since neutral terms almost inevitably acquire negative connotations when applied to problem behaviors.

Labeling is an enormously complex phenomena about which much distortion, confusion, and misinformation have been communicated. Much work on the development of better systems of categorizing children and on noncategorical approaches to special education has been completed since passage of PL 94-142 in 1975. Despite more than 35 years of research, little has changed and no better systems have been devised. Pros and cons of the existing systems are reviewed in detail in Cartwright, Cartwright, and Ward (1995).

## REFERENCES

Becker, H. S. (1963). *Outsiders: Studies in the sociology of deviance.* Glencoe, IL: Free Press.

Cartwright, G., Cartwright, C., & Ward, M. (1995). *Educating special learners* (4th ed.). Boston: Wadsworth.

Dunn, L. (1968). Special education for the mildly retarded: Is much of it justifiable? *Exceptional Children, 35,* 5–22.

Gottlieb, J. (Ed.). (1980). *Educating mentally retarded persons in the mainstream.* Baltimore: University Park Press.

Guskin, S. L. (1978). Theoretical and empirical strategies for the study of the labeling of mentally retarded persons. In N. R. Ellis (Ed.), *International review of research in mental retardation* (Vol. 9, pp. 127–158). New York: Academic.

Hobbs, N. L. (1975). *The futures of children.* San Francisco: Jossey-Bass.

MacMillan, D. (1982). *Mental retardation in school and society* (2nd ed.). Boston: Little, Brown.

MacMillan, D., Jones, R., & Aloia, G. (1974). The mentally retarded label: A theoretical analysis and review of research. *American Journal of Mental Deficiency, 79,* 241–261.

Mercer, J. (1973). *Labeling the mentally retarded.* Berkeley: University of California Press.

Mercer, J. (1979). *System of multicultural pluralistic assessment technical manual.* New York: Psychological Corporation.

Rosenthal, R., & Jacobson, L. (1968). *Pygmalion in the classroom: Teacher expectation and pupils' intellectual development.* New York: Holt, Rinehart, & Winston.

DANIEL J. RESCHLY
*Peabody College, Vanderbilt University*

AAMR CLASSIFICATION SYSTEM
MENTAL RETARDATION
SIX-HOUR RETARDED CHILD
SYSTEMS OF CLASSIFICATION

# LAMINAR HETEROTOPIA

Laminar heterotopia are nodules in the brain formed of neurons that were supposed to migrate during gestation or infancy, but did not. They are structurally out of place in the maturing brain and form nodules or laminae. Laminar heterotopia are particularly prominent on the walls of the lateral ventricles of the brain. They are a symptom and do not form a specific syndrome in and of themselves. Outcomes depend on the underlying disorder and the size and number of the nodules.

STAFF

# LANGUAGE, ABSENCE OF

The nondevelopment of a language system in several categories of individuals does not preclude the possibility of producing separate sounds or words. For example, it is generally acknowledged that individuals with profound intellectual disabilities (with IQs below 20 and marked deficiencies in adaptive behavior) do not develop language. Past work with nonspeech language systems (Lloyd, 1976; Rondal, 1985) highlighted the possibility of equipping such individuals with gestural prosthetic communicative systems that in turn proved helpful in establishing limited functional vocal repertoires. However, one would hardly claim that such systems are truly linguistic in nature. When dealing with problems of this sort, it is useful to recall the distinction between speech and language. The absence of language does not preclude the use of speech sounds and the use of nonspeech communicative systems.

The same distinction between speech and language is relevant when dealing with nonspeech systems, such as conventional sign languages (e.g., American Sign Language), with individuals who cannot vocally communicate for reasons of organic insufficiency (either sensory or motoric). Keeping these distinctions in mind, one can propose the following dichotomy for the absence of language category.

There is an absence of language (linguistic capacity) for reasons of severe central organic insufficiency. This category encompasses etiological distinctions such as profound intellectual disabilities, childhood autism, and developmental or congenital aphasia (to be distinguished from acquired aphasia). For example, it is suggested that approximately half of children with autism are without language (Loveland, McEvoy, & Tunali, 1990; Nientimp & Cole, 1992) except for some form of simple echolalia or single-word productions (Tirosh & Canby, 1993). An interesting but unexplained cutoff point for language development in most children seems to be 5 or 6 years. If a child has not developed some primitive form of language by that age, the child appears to be unlikely to initiate language in the following years.

Conversely, there can be an absence of speech without an absence of language, for reasons of severe sensory (e.g., congenital profound deafness) or motoric (e.g., cerebral palsy) disabilities. It is well established that profoundly deaf individuals are not deprived of linguistic capacity. When properly exposed to nonspeech symbolic stimulation (e.g., sign language), they readily develop language capacities in much the same way as hearing children learn oral languages (Moores, 1978). In the same way, many individuals with severe cerebral palsy are able to express themselves symbolically and communicate with augmentative and alternative communication devices. Continued rapid technological advances can be expected in this domain.

## REFERENCES

Lloyd, L. (Ed.). (1976). *Communication assessment and intervention strategies.* Baltimore: University Park Press.

Loveland, K. A., McEvoy, R. E., & Tunali, B. (1990). Narrative story telling in autism and Down's syndrome. *British Journal of Developmental Psychology, 8,* 9–23.

Moores, D. (1978). *Educating the deaf.* Boston: Houghton Mifflin.

Nientimp, E. G., & Cole, C. L. (1992). Teaching socially valid interaction responses to students with severe disabilities in an integrated school setting. *Journal of School Psychology, 30,* 343–354.

Rondal, J. A. (1985). *Language et communication chez les handicapés mentaux. Théorie, évaluation, intervention.* Brussels: Mardaga.

Tirosh, E., & Canby, J. (1993). Autism with hyperlexia: A distinct syndrome? *American Journal of Mental Retardation, 98,* 84–92.

JEAN A. RONDAL
*University of Liege, Belgium*
First edition

ROBERT L. RHODES
*New Mexico State University*
Second edition

COMMUNICATION DISORDERS
DEAF EDUCATION
LANGUAGE DELAYS
LANGUAGE DISORDERS

# LANGUAGE ASSESSMENT

A language assessment is an evaluation of three general realms in communication competence of an individual: speech, language, and hearing (Venn, 2004). A language assessment considers communication as expressive language (conveying meaning and understanding through vocal and motor expression), receptive language (receipt and comprehension by giving meaning to input detected through the senses, typically the ears), and internal language (thinking and cognition; Venn, 2004). Developmental considerations and understanding are important in the assessment of children. Evaluation at different ages will have different manifestations of symptoms and may focus on different communication skill concerns. Assessment in the younger population can prove challenging due to the fact that although developmental stages are consistent, age of achieving milestones varies greatly. Other potential variables than can lead to erroneous results are comorbidity with other disabilities and linguistic diversity (Jitendra & Rohena-Diaz, 1996; Venn, 2004).

The process begins with a detection of potential communication concerns. At this stage, an understanding of what is considered effective communication for the child based on what is expected for a typical child with regards to variables such as gender, age, ethnicity and culture, disability, and socioeconomic status is important. A referral is then made to a qualified speech-language pathologist who assesses what area of communication (speech, language, and/or hearing) the child is experiencing difficulty and evaluates for specific attributes of the communication disorder. History provided by the family and other caregivers, which includes relevant information in the form of reports and interviews, contribute to the speech-language pathologist's determination for assessment focus. Typically, the speech-language pathologist will also dedicate time to observe the client to gather more information on the client's needs.

## Assessment Approaches

Language assessments can be conducted by one of three approaches: traditional/discrete, synergistic, or holistic assessment. The choice of approach is largely directed by the focus of the assessment and the desired format of results.

*Traditional/Discrete,* or quantitative, assessment utilizes standardized and norm-referenced instruments measuring specific linguistic components. This type of as-sessment allows for a comparison to a normative sample, assists in qualifying a child for appropriate services in the schools or local public service agencies without need for retesting, and can be time efficient. Discrete tests examine the client's language skills in fragments—specifically, phonemes, graphemes, semantics, syntax, and morphology. Such an assessment is conducted outside the context of the client's natural environment.

*Synergistic,* or qualitative, assessments are considered alternatives to traditional/discrete assessment and include methods such as *descriptive, authentic, dynamic,* and *curriculum based* (Schraeder, Quinn, Stockman, & Miller, 1999; Jitendra & Rohena-Diaz, 1996; Jitendra, Rohena-Diaz, & Nolet, 1998; Secord & Damico, 1992). This nonnormative approach arrives with what is considered a more functional and authentically relevant outcome. This approach is a pragmatic exploration because there is a consideration and sensitivity to the individual client's characteristics, such as bilingualism or having a disability. Information collected about the client includes their communication contexts. Assessment results can strengthen that facilitation of effectiveness in intervention planning.

*Holistic,* or multidimensional, assessment is a combination of traditional/discrete and dynamic. Such a comprehensive approach is ideal in that information collected allows for a direct comparison to peer performance while also tailoring to the individual child's capabilities and performance in their own natural environments (Tyler & Tolbert, 2002).

## Ethical Practice

Language assessments must be performed by a qualified (licensed or certified) speech-language pathologist who utilizes reliable and valid assessment instruments. Assessments can be conducted by either an individual speech-language pathologist or by a team of professionals (interdisciplinary collaboration). Speech-language pathologists should abide by the Code of Ethics of the American Speech-Language-Hearing Association (ASHA) in practice, which includes confidentiality, reporting, and assessment. ASHA can be contacted at 10801 Rockville Pike, Rockville, MD 20852; 800-638-8255 (voice), 301-571-0457 (fax); actioncenter@asha.org, http://www.asha.org.

**REFERENCES**

Jitendra, A. K., & Rohena-Diaz, E. (1996). Language assessment of students who are linguistically diverse: Why a discrete approach is not the answer. *School Psychology Review, 25,* 40–56.

Jitendra, A. K., Rohena-Diaz, E., & Nolet, V. (1998). A dynamic curriculum-based assessment: Planning instruction for special needs students who are linguistically diverse. *Preventing School Failure, 42,* 182–186.

Schraeder, T., Quinn, M., Stockman, I. J., & Miller, J. (1999). Authentic assessment as an approach to preschool speech-language screening. *American Journal of Speech-Language Pathology, 8,* 195–200.

Secord, W., & Damico, J. S. (1992). *Best practices in school speech-language pathology: Descriptive / nonstandardized language assessment.* New York: Psychological Corporation.

Tyler, A. A., & Tolbert, L. C. (2002). Speech-language assessment in the clinical setting. *American Journal of Speech-Language Pathology, 11,* 215–220.

Venn, J. J. (2004). *Assessing students with special needs.* Columbus, OH: Pearson Prentice Hall.

STEPHEN S. FARMER
*New Mexico State University*
Second edition

MARISSA I. MENDOZA
*Texas A&M University*
Third edition

**AMERICAN SPEECH-LANGUAGE-HEARING ASSOCIATION**
**LANGUAGE DELAYS**
**LANGUAGE DISORDERS**
**LEARNING DISABILITIES**
**SPEECH-LANGUAGE PATHOLOGIST**
**SPEECH-LANGUAGE SERVICES**

# LANGUAGE DELAYS

Language delays, language disorders, and language differences are not synonyms. *Language delays* exist when receptive and expressive language skills are slow to emerge but the skills are acquired in the same sequence that is associated with typical (normal) development (Reed, 1994). The delay is essentially the same for all features of language (e.g., semantics and syntax). Language delay may be present in one or both languages of children who are bilingual. Children with language delays learn quickly when placed in language-rich environments. There are no known neuropsychological etiological factors. The term *Specific Language Impairment* (SLI; Nelson, 1998; Paul, 1995) may be used to define children whose language skills are at the lower end of a continuum of normal variation.

By contrast, *language disorder* implies a deviation from the usual rate and sequence with which specific language skills emerge (Reed, 1994). Deviations can include differences within one aspect of language (e.g., semantics or morphology), inordinate difficulties with certain features within one aspect of language, differences in rate of acquisition among various aspects of language (e.g., relationship of semantics/syntax/pragmatics in the development of meaning) and/or age-appropriate skills in one or more aspects but

with delays in development of other dimensions of language. Because of the asynchrony in the rate of acquisition within and across various language parameters, the typical developmental sequence is disrupted. Children with language disorders need special intervention (see entry for Language Therapy). Language disorders are often associated with neuropsychological etiological factors.

*Language differences* are associated with social, academic, and employment contextual (pragmatic) bias; value bias; phonological bias; grammatical bias; and vocabulary bias that differ from Standard American English or mainstream culture communication but are appropriate to another ethnic group (e.g., African American, Asian American, Latino American; Haynes & Shulman, 1998; Shames, Wiig, & Secord, 1994).

Language delays can interfere with social and academic dimensions of the communication-learning process during early childhood. Early identification and intervention are recommended to prevent or decrease the negative effects of language delays (Nelson, 1998; Paul, 1995).

**REFERENCES**

Haynes, W. O., & Shulman, B. B. (Eds.). (1998). *Communication development: Foundations, processes, and clinical applications.* Baltimore: Williams and Wilkins.

Nelson, N. W. (1998). *Childhood language disorders in context: Infancy through adolescence* (2nd ed.). Boston: Allyn & Bacon.

Paul, R. (1995). *Language disorders from infancy through adolescence: Assessment and intervention.* St. Louis, MO: Mosby.

Reed, V. A. (1994). *An introduction to children with language disorders* (2nd ed.). New York: Merrill/Macmillan.

Shames, G. H., Wiig, E. H., & Secord, W. A. (1994). *Human communication disorders: An introduction* (4th ed.). New York: Merrill/Macmillan.

JEAN A. RONDAL
*Laboratory for Language,
Psychology, and Logopedics
University of Liege, Belgium*
First edition

STEPHEN S. FARMER
*New Mexico State University*
Second edition

**COMMUNICATION DISORDERS**
**LANGUAGE DISORDERS**
**SPEECH, ABSENCE OF**

# LANGUAGE DISORDERS

Depending on the age group studied and criteria used, language disorders affect up to 12 percent of children 3 to 21 years of age (Clegg, Hollis, Mawhood, & Rutter, 2005). Of these, an estimated 5 to 10 percent evidence difficulties of sufficient severity to warrant referral and subsequent intervention. Thus, disorders of language are among the most common disorders of higher cerebral function in children. When the problem is less severe, language problems may not be recognized until school entry. Language disorders often can be quite subtle and may manifest as a learning disorder rather than language impairment because these language problems surface in the child's difficulty in learning to read, difficulty keeping up with peers, difficulty attending to group lessons, and difficulty with organization. The prognosis for these children, based on retrospective data, is relatively guarded, with a direct relationship between prognosis and the severity of the language impairment (Clegg et al., 2005; Mawhood, Howlin, & Rutter, 2000; Stothard, Snowling, Bishop, Chipchase, & Kaplan, 1998)

Most children with language disorders do not have obvious signs of focal deficit on neurological examination, do not demonstrate electroencephalographic (EEG) abnormality, and do not exhibit identifiable lesions on computed tomography (CT) or magnetic resonance imaging (MRI) of the brain (e.g., Plante, Swisher, & Vance, 1989; Plante, Swisher, Vance, & Rapcsak, 1991). As a result, diagnosis continues to be minimally based upon speech-language and cognitive evaluation. A diagnosis of language disorder is typically made when the child demonstrates significant language deficits despite a history of normal hearing, at least low average nonverbal intelligence, and age level ability on visual/nonverbal tasks. In clinical practice, it is not uncommon for children with language disorders to be subtyped based on the extent to which both receptive and expressive language is impacted, as opposed to the presence of expressive language deficits only.

One of the more difficult tasks facing clinicians is that of differential diagnosis of language disorder as opposed to hearing impairment, global intellectual disability, and pervasive developmental disorder/autistic spectrum disorder (e.g., Mawhood et al., 2000). Further, it has been found that preschool children with language disorders frequently demonstrate behavior problems (e.g., hyperactivity, inattention, social withdrawal, immaturity, dependency); it has been suggested that these behavioral problems may be secondary to the language disorder (e.g., Linares-Orama, 2005; Riccio & Hynd, 1995).

## REFERENCES

Clegg, J., Hollis, C., Mawhood, L., & Rutter, M. (2005). Developmental language disorders—A follow-up in later adult life. Cognitive, language, and psychosocial outcomes. *Journal of Child Psychology and Psychiatry, 46,* 128–149.

Linares-Orama, N. (2005). Language-learning disorders and youth incarceration. *Journal of Communication Disorders, 38,* 311–319.

Mawhood, L., Howlin, P., & Rutter, M. (2000). Autism and developmental receptive language disorder—A comparative follow up in early adult life. I: Cognitive and language outcomes. *Journal of Child Psychology and Psychiatry, 41,* 547–559.

Plante, E., Swisher, L., & Vance, R. (1989). Anatomical correlates of normal and impaired language in a set of dizygotic twins. *Brain and Language, 37,* 643–655.

Plante, E., Swisher, L., Vance, R., & Rapcsak, S. (1991). MRI findings in boys with specific language impairment. *Brain and Language, 41,* 52–66.

Riccio, C. A., & Hynd, G. W. (1995). Developmental language disorders and Attention Deficit Hyperactivity Disorder. *Advances in Learning and Behavioral Disabilities, 9,* 1–20.

Stothard, S. E., Snowling, M. J., Bishop, D. V. M., Chipchase, B. B., & Kaplan, C. A. (1998). Language-impaired preschoolers: A follow-up into adolescence. *Journal of Speech and Language Hearing Research, 41,* 407–418.

Cynthia A. Riccio
*Texas A&M University*

LEARNING DISABILITIES
SPEECH-LANGUAGE PATHOLOGIST
SPEECH-LANGUAGE SERVICES
SPEECH THERAPY

## LANGUAGE DISORDERS, EXPRESSIVE

See LANGUAGE DISORDERS.

## LANGUAGE THERAPY

Language therapy (also referred to as language treatment) can take many forms. Six perspectives are described herein: (1) Verbal and nonverbal symbol system perspective, (2) Communication Channels perspective, (3) Language Acquisition Theory perspective, (4) Oral-Literate Discourse perspective, (5) Emic-Etic perspective, (6) Non-oral perspective.

*Verbal and Nonverbal Symbol Systems:* Language, defined as a verbal (words) and nonverbal (e.g., paralinguistics, kinesics, proxemics) symbol system, may be treated through the use of verbal symbols or nonverbal symbols. Verbal systems may be used for addressing problems in listening, speaking, reading, writing, and thinking; nonverbal systems may be used for metalanguage and pragmatic language disorders (Hulit & Howard, 1997; Lane & Molyneaux, 1992; McLaughlin, 1998; Nelson, 1998; Owens, 1996; Paul, 1995; Tiegerman-Farber, 1995).

*Communication Channels:* Language therapy may be approached through a six-channel comprehension (receptive)/production (expressive) paradigm: watching/moving, listening/speaking, reading/writing (Muma, 1978; Nelson, 1998, Tibbits, 1995).

*Language Acquisition Theories:* Three major categories of language acquisition theories are recognized: Behavioral, Innatist (Nativist, Linguistic), and Cognitive-Social Interactionist (Pragmatic; Carrow-Woolfolk, 1988; Fey, Windsor & Warren, 1995; Haynes & Shulman, 1998; Hulit & Howard, 1997; Lane & Molyneaux, 1992; McLaughlin, 1998; Owens, 1996).

The basic focus of the Behavioral theory is that language is a learned behavior resulting from antecedents and consequences of language behavior, that is learners are taught language through training and shaping by the environment. The differences between the language of a child and that of adult models constitute a disorder. Therapy uses B. F. Skinner's basic S-R-R paradigm of behavior modification to train behaviors (phonological, semantic, syntactic, and morphological) that a child does not perform.

The basic focus of the Innatist (also referred to as the Nativist or Linguistic) theory is that language is a system of abstract rules from which an individual can generate an infinite number of utterances. Noam Chomsky's suggestion that children are born with an innate language acquisition device (LAD) and his later government-binding theory of s-structures (surface) and d-structures (deep) form a foundation for this approach to therapy. Language rules are induced by a child whose own system controls the selection of rules and their internal construction; the process has universal characteristics. Differences between a child and peers are judged on developmental indexes. Language disorders are judged to be a result of a child's failure to use innate rules. Emphasis in treatment is on providing exemplars of target rules in naturalistic settings to facilitate phonological rule inhibition, and semantic, syntactic, or morphological rule induction.

The basic focus of the Cognitive-Social Interactionist (also referred to as the Pragmatic) theory is that the primary function of language is communication (i.e., the negotiation of meaning), and that its basic unit is the speech act that occurs in a context that helps to determine form. Jean Piaget, Brian McWhinney, and Jean Berko-Gleason, as well as others, have contributed to the research that has explored this theory. Language is developed through cognitive (developmental cognition, meta-abilities, and information processing; Wiig, 1989), linguistic (the rules of phonology, semantics, syntax/morphology), and social (pragmatic rules) interaction with the environment (Duchan, 1995; Duchan, Hewitt, & Sonnenmeier, 1994). Language disorders result from a breakdown in the interaction process in communication (cognitive-linguistic-social) which may be related to problems in the child's system or in the environment. Therapy is provided in naturalistic settings for developing pragmatic skills (illocutionary-intent, locutionary-surface level linguistics, and perlocutionary-comprehension by receivers). The environment is used to make target behaviors more salient.

*Oral-Literate Discourse:* Language therapy may include both oral and literate (reading and writing) forms of conversation, narration, and exposition discourse (Larson & McKinley, 1995; Merritt & Culatta, 1998; Nelson, 1998; Ripich & Creaghead, 1994; Wallach & Butler, 1994; Wallach & Miller, 1988). Treatment of discourse disorders focuses on establishing the pragmatic rules (who can communicate what, to whom, how, when, where, and why) associated with oral and written interpersonal communication-learning, understanding and producing diverse story forms, and academic communication-learning, including math language, computer language, foreign language, and employment language. The metaskills of study strategies, time management, teaching-learning styles and strategies, and contextual scripts and schemas are included in this treatment focus.

*Emic (Inside-Out)–Etic (Outside-In):* An Emic–Etic approach to language therapy, also referred to as Outside-In (client)–Inside-Out (context), includes cognitive, linguistic, and contextual dimensions of the communication-learning process (Duchan, 1995; Duchan et al., 1994; Nelson, 1998). Two tenets make up this approach: (1) a language breakdown may exist within the child and/or the context (e.g., teacher-talk, curriculum); and (2) the theory of change—first order change (of individual) and second order change (of the system). A child may experience a language-learning breakdown because of innate deficits; however, the disorder may be exacerbated because of contextual conditions (e.g., implicit, vague, or ambiguous teacher directions; complex cognitive and linguistic structures in textbooks and tests; and peer use of nonliteral language forms such as figurative language, humor, sarcasm, and teasing). It is possible to change language behavior of an individual (Inside-Out therapy) but if that person returns to a context that causes or contributes to the disorder, the individual change will not be maintained. Outside-In language therapy involves modifying the contexts in which a client functions. Emic–Etic therapy may target basic interpersonal communication skills (BICS) and/or cognitive academic language proficiency (CALP).

*Non-Oral:* Non-oral language therapy includes using symbols within a variety of augmentative/alternative communication (AAC) low-tech or high-tech systems, manual communication or sign language systems, and braille symbols (Duchan, 1995; Duchan et al., 1994; Nelson, 1998).

Language therapy is important in maximizing a person's success in social, academic, and employment situations across the life span. Treatment approaches may vary with culture, etiology, and severity of the communication disorder.

## REFERENCES

Carrow-Woolfolk, E. (1988). *Theory, assessment and intervention in language disorders: An integrative approach.* Philadelphia: Grune & Stratton.

Duchan, J. F. (1995). *Supporting language learning in everyday life.* San Diego: Singular.

Duchan, J. F., Hewitt, L. E., & Sonnenmeier, R. M. (Eds.). (1994). *Pragmatics: From theory to practice.* Englewood Cliffs, NJ: Prentice Hall.

Fey, M. E., Windsor, J., & Warren, S. F. (1995). *Language intervention: Preschool through the elementary years.* Baltimore: Brookes.

Haynes, W. O., & Shulman, B. B. (1998). *Communication development: Foundations, processes, and clinical applications.* Baltimore: Williams & Wilkins.

Hulit, L. M., & Howard, M. R. (1997). *Born to talk: An introduction to speech and language development.* Boston: Allyn & Bacon.

Lane, V. W., & Molyneaux, D. (1992). *The dynamics of communicative development.* Englewood Cliffs, NJ: Prentice Hall.

Larson, V. L., & McKinley, N. (1995). *Language disorders in older students: Preadolescents and adolescents.* Eau Claire, WI: Thinking Publications.

McLaughlin, S. (1998). *Introduction to language development.* San Diego: Singular.

Merritt, D. D., & Culatta, B. (1998). *Language intervention in the classroom.* San Diego: Singular.

Muma, J. R. (1978). *Language handbook: Concepts, assessment, intervention.* Englewood Cliffs, NJ: Prentice Hall.

Nelson, N. W. (1998). *Childhood language disorders in context: Infancy through adolescence* (2nd ed.). Boston: Allyn & Bacon.

Owens, R. E. (1996). *Language development: An introduction* (4th ed.). Boston: Allyn & Bacon.

Paul, R. (1995). *Language disorders from infancy through adolescence: Assessment and intervention.* St. Louis, MO: Mosby.

Ripich, D. N., & Creaghead, N. A. (Eds.). (1994). *School discourse problems* (2nd ed.). San Diego: Singular.

Tibbits, D. F. (Ed.). (1995). *Language intervention beyond the primary grades: For clinicians by clinicians.* Austin, TX: PRO-ED.

Tiegerman-Farber, E. (1995). *Language and communication intervention in preschool children.* Boston: Allyn & Bacon.

Wallach, G. P., & Butler, K. G. (1994). *Language learning disabilities in school-age children and adolescents: Some principles and applications* (2nd ed.). New York: Merrill/Macmillan.

Wallach, G. P., & Miller, L. (1988). *Language intervention and academic success.* Boston: College-Hill/Little, Brown.

Wiig, E. H. (1989). *Steps to language competence: Developing metalinguistic strategies.* San Antonio, TX: Psychological Corporation.

KATHERINE GARNET
*Hunter College, City University of New York*
First edition

STEPHEN S. FARMER
*New Mexico State University*
Second edition

**COMMUNICATION DISORDERS**
**LANGUAGE DELAYS**

**LANGUAGE DISORDERS**
**LEARNING DISABILITIES**

# LARGE-PRINT BOOKS

Many low-vision students learn to read using regular-sized print, with or without the use of optical aids. The print selected for low-vision students depends on factors such as the student's motivation and interest, visual acuity and fields of view, reading experience and ability, lighting, and accessibility of print (Jose, 1983).

According to Jose (1983), the advantages of large print are that it is more comfortable and easier to read; it is usually produced on nonglare paper; and it offers a less restricted field of view compared to using regular print with a magnifying lens. However, producing large-type textbooks is expensive. As a result, the number and variety of available books is limited, particularly at the high school and college level. Other disadvantages are that the pictures in these textbooks are usually missing or not as clear as the color pictures in regular print textbooks, and large-print books are large and bulky and look so different from regular print books that some students are embarrassed to use them (Barraga, 1983).

Decisions regarding print size used should be made by the visually impaired student, a teacher trained to work with visually impaired students, parents, and a low-vision team (if available). These decisions should be based on functional assessments comparing the student's performance using many different print sizes, type styles, margin widths, spaces between letters, words, and lines in respect to rate of oral and silent reading, comfort while reading, number of skipped and miscalled words, comprehension, and duration of reading before fatigue (Jose, 1983).

Heward and Orlansky (1984) advise that while size of print is an important variable in instructing low-vision students, other equally important factors to consider are the quality of the printed material, the contrast between print and page, the spacing between lines, and the illumination of the setting in which the student reads. Some low-vision students need to use a variety of media, including several different print sizes, recorded materials, and even braille (depending on the subject matter) to optimize their reading. However, special educators generally agree that a low-vision student should use the smallest print size that he or she can comfortably read (Heward & Orlansky, 1984).

## REFERENCES

Barraga, N. (1983). *Visual handicaps and learning.* Austin, TX: Exceptional Resources.

Heward, W. L., & Orlansky, M. D. (1984). *Exceptional children.* Columbus, OH: Merrill.

Jose, R. (1983). *Understanding low vision.* New York: American Foundation for the Blind.

ROSEANNE K. SILBERMAN
*Hunter College, City University
of New York*

## AMERICAN PRINTING HOUSE FOR THE BLIND
## LIBRARIES FOR THE BLIND AND INDIVIDUALS WITH PHYSICAL DISABILITIES
## LIBRARY SERVICES FOR INDIVIDUALS WITH DISABILITIES
## LOW VISION

## LARRY P.

Larry P. was one of six black children who were plaintiffs in a suit brought in 1971 against Wilson Riles, California state superintendent of public instruction. The suit charged that the IQ tests that were used in determining eligibility for placement in classes for the educable mentally retarded (EMR) were culturally biased. The lawyers for the plaintiffs based their charges of cultural bias on the fact that the average scores for blacks were lower than for whites, and that using the scores resulted in a higher percentage of black children in EMR classes than in regular classes.

As a consequence of the *Larry P.* v. *Wilson Riles* suit, the federal district court granted an injunction in 1972 that banned the use of individually administered intelligence tests for black children being considered for placement in EMR classes. This resulted in psychologists having to use alternative methods such as classroom observations, adaptive behavior assessment, and academic achievement measures to determine whether children referred for special education were intellectually retarded and, in turn, eligible for special education services.

In 1976 the case was brought to trial. The plaintiffs were represented by Public Advocates, Inc. and by *pro bono* attorneys from the San Francisco firm of Morrison and Foerster. The state was represented by a deputy attorney general from the state attorney general's office. The plaintiffs' arguments centered on the disproportion of black children in EMR classes as well as the lower average IQs earned by blacks on most standardized tests of intelligence. They contended that the tests were culturally biased because the items were drawn from white middle-class culture to which black pupils were not exposed. This contention was supported, they argued, by the fact that when the six plaintiffs were retested using the WISC-R (the same test that was used to determine their eligibility for the EMR programs, their IQs were higher because black examiners perceived racial, ethnic, or socioeconomic bias and made modifications in the administration of the test such as rewording items, accepting nonstandard responses, or extending time limits. In addition to arguments that the tests were biased against black children, the plaintiffs maintained that the

EMR classes did not cover the same subjects as did regular classes, and that the longer the children attended the EMR classes, the greater the performance gap between EMR children and their regular class peers.

The plaintiffs' legal arguments revolved around showing that blacks were overrepresented in EMR classes and that the IQ test was the sole basis for decisions regarding eligibility and placement. If the IQ was the instrument used for placement, and blacks were overrepresented in EMR classes, then, they argued, the tests had to be biased, making the special education classes suspect. Both IQ tests and special education, therefore, discriminated against black children. From a legal standpoint, the burden shifted to the state of California to show that the tests were not biased, and that even though there were more black children in special education classes, the children benefited from the special education programs.

The state's defense rested on data showing that the IQ tests were valid predictors of present and future performance, and that the tests predicted equally well for blacks and whites. Witnesses for the defense testified that the IQ test was administered only after children had a long experience of failing in regular class programs and were referred for evaluation of their eligibility for EMR classes. The state's witnesses also testified that there was a linear relationship between IQs and severity of mental retardation from the mildly (EMR) to the profoundly retarded. The state's witnesses, moreover, rebutted plaintiff testimony that there should be evidence for a biological or metabolic origin of mental retardation; mildly retarded children fall at one end of the normal distribution of intelligence just as gifted children are at the other, higher, end of the continuum. Having to explain why more black than white children were mildly retarded, the state countered with research that showed a relationship between IQs and poverty, poor nutrition, lack of cognitive stimulation, and other environmental factors.

Ultimately, the state had to contend with two factors: one related to the use of IQ tests for special education placement and the second to the benefits of special education. Plaintiffs built their charges against IQ tests on their cultural bias and the contention that they were the sole criterion for placement of certain children in EMR classes. The state showed that the tests were used to determine eligibility for special education and for a diagnosis of the extent of intellectual retardation. The numerous studies of the validity of IQ tests for distinguishing among individuals varying with respect to academic performance, and, therefore, indicative of the construct and criterion validity of IQ tests for both black and white children, were summarized by several witnesses. But the IQ test was not designed to show whether a child would benefit from or improve as a result of special education placement. A showing of a positive or remedial effect on the academic performance or on the level of intelligence of the child resulting from special education placement was necessary to satisfy the court. As the research on EMR programs had not shown this necessary positive effect, the plaintiffs argued that the IQ tests were not valid for EMR placement even though the state showed convincingly that they were valid for making inferences about current level of intellectual functioning, the only psychological inference required for a determination of mild mental retardation and eligibility for special education.

The state's effort to show that a major source of the overrepresentation was attributable more to the process by which the child was referred for psychological evaluation was not successful. Evidence regarding bias in the referral process (i.e., more black boys than black girls and more blacks than whites were referred, resulting in overrepresentation of boys over girls and black boys over white boys in EMR classes) did not convince the court that the IQ was not the primary basis for identifying a child for placement in an EMR class. Testimony that only one-fifth (approximately) of referred children were found eligible after IQ testing did not alter the court's opinion that the IQ test was the culprit.

The plaintiffs' evidence that the IQs of blacks were lower than those of whites was the evidence on which the court ultimately relied to judge that the tests were biased. Since IQs were the most frequent piece of information in the case study records of EMR children, the court concluded that the IQ test was the basis for placement in the special education program even though the state had shown that only a portion of all children with IQ scores in the EMR range were ever placed in special education classes. The overrepresentation of black children could have been tolerated if the state had been successful in demonstrating remediation of EMR children's academic deficiencies. The court, therefore, concluded that the tests were biased and the primary basis for placement in dead-end, stigmatizing special education classes.

The court handed down its opinion in 1979 and prohibited schools "from utilizing, permitting the use of, or approving the use of any standardized intelligence tests . . . or the identification of black EMR children or their placement into EMR classes, without securing prior approval of the court." Furthermore the court ruled that any tests used for special education purposes should be shown to be valid for the purposes for which they were to be used. The consequences of the *Larry P.* decision in California have been a search for alternative methods, often less reliable and valid, for determining eligibility for special education classes, as well as an attempt to select from among those who are eligible, those children who can benefit from special education.

Children who were classified as EMR in 1971, when the suit was filed, were reevaluated by order of the legislature before the trial began in 1976. The reevaluation resulted in a marked reduction in the number of children in special education, but no change in the overrepresentation of minority children in EMR classes. During the trial, the state of California adopted the California Master Plan for Special Education (almost at the same time that Congress passed PL 94-142), eliminating the category of EMR programs and substituting the category of "learning handicapped" to include mildly retarded pupils and those with learning disabilities. There was also a large amount of additional research evidence published during and after the trial on the differential validity of tests of scholastic aptitude, including individual tests of intelligence, using a variety of criterion measures including school grades and adaptive behavior assessments. These data generally have shown that aptitude tests are valid for both blacks and whites.

Have the outcomes of the *Larry P.* case improved the assessment or special education treatment of black children? We have now the burden of showing not only criterion validity, but the validity of IQ tests to identify those who will benefit from special education treatment. Aptitude and IQ tests may be excellent sources of evidence for prediction or diagnosing eligibility, but not necessarily for selecting the children who will profit most from special education. The *Larry P.* decision has not resulted in elimination of minority overrepresentation, only in fewer children being classified as mildly retarded. Some hail this outcome as a beneficial one, while others wonder what will become of children who are categorically denied special education services. Regardless of the psychological tests or procedures used, school psychologists and special education professionals are obligated to show that they are valid and reliable for diagnosing the cause of educational failure, as well as for selecting and placing those who will benefit from special education services.

Throughout this litigation, few concerns were ever raised about the fate of the six black children who were the plaintiffs in the case. Were their futures positively affected by removing them from special education during their elementary school years? Larry P. went to school out of state and was later identified for special education on the basis of his school achievement and classroom performance. By age 19, he still could not pass the test for a driver's license and was not gainfully employed. The one plaintiff who was adapting well in high school had been placed back in special education after leaving San Francisco schools at the request of his mother. If the *Larry P.* decision is to help schools to achieve a better educational outcome for mildly retarded children, educators and school psychologists may have to remain firm in their support of IQ tests as valid diagnostic procedures and turn their attention to the quality of special education interventions and strategies to tailor the specific special educational treatment to the individual needs of the children. Any educational program that separates a group of children from regular class peers can be justified only if it can be shown that there is more benefit in special education placement than in retention in a regular class.

NADINE M. LAMBERT
*University of California,
Berkeley*

CULTURAL BIAS IN TESTS
INTELLIGENCE
INTELLIGENCE TESTING

## LATENCY RECORDING

Latency recording is a direct observation method that is used to systematically measure the amount of time it takes for a student to engage in a behavior once a request has been made. In other words, "this procedure measures the length of time between the presentation of an antecedent stimulus and the initiation of the behavior" by the person of concern (Alberto & Troutman, 2006, p. 86). Like duration recording, latency recording is used to measure the temporal nature of a behavior. For example, this method can be used to measure the time between a teacher direction and when the student begins to engage in the targeted behavior (e.g., getting out instructional materials). Latency recording can also be used to measure the amount of time it takes for a student to answer a question (e.g., answering the question too quickly, or not waiting until the teacher finishes a question before answering; Cooper, Heron, & Heward, 1987). Therefore, teachers and researchers who use latency recording are interested in decreasing the time it takes to follow a request or increasing the amount of time a student considers the request before attempting to comply.

To record behavior using latency recording, you first need to operationally define the target behavior. An operational definition is a written statement that precisely defines the behavior you wish to measure in terms that are observable, measurable, and replicable (Fletcher-Janzen & De Pry, 2003). Like duration recording, a device for measuring time (a stopwatch) is used to measure the time between the teacher request and when the student begins the behavior. The teacher or observer begins the stopwatch when the request is made (antecedent stimulus) and allows the stopwatch to continue running until the student initiates the requested behavior. The data on the stopwatch is recorded on a data collection sheet and graphed for future reference. As with all direct observation systems, collecting interobserver reliability data is critical. The formula for calculating interobserver reliability for latency recording is taking the shorter number of minutes (or total seconds) and dividing by the larger number of minutes (or total seconds), then multiplying by 100. This formula produces the percent of agreement between the primary observer and an independent observer.

### REFERENCES

Alberto, P. A., & Troutman, A. C. (2006). *Applied behavior analysis for teachers* (7th ed.). Upper Saddle River, NJ: Pearson Merrill Prentice Hall.

Cooper, J. O., Heron, T. E., & Heward, W. L. (1987). *Applied behavior analysis.* New York: Macmillan.

Fletcher-Janzen, E., & De Pry, R. L. (2003). *Teaching social competence and character: An IEP planner with goals, objectives, and interventions.* Longmont, CO: Sopris West Educational Services.

RANDALL L. DE PRY
*University of Colorado at
Colorado Springs*

BEHAVIORAL ASSESSMENT
BEHAVIOR CHARTING

## LATERALITY

See CEREBRAL DOMINANCE.

## LAURENCE-MOON SYNDROME

Laurence-Moon syndrome (LMS) is an autosomal (non-sex-related chromosome), recessive genetic disorder of unknown etiology characterized by neurological, ophthalmologic, and endocrine abnormalities resulting in a deteriorating handicapping condition (Gandy, 1999). John Zachariah Laurence and Robert Moon first described this condition in 1866.

Laurence and Moon observed four members of the same family who were found to exhibit mental retardation, short stature, obesity, hypogenitalism (unusually small genitalia), and retinitis pigmentosa (narrowing of the visual fields leading to a progressive loss of vision; Nathanson, 1998). LMS is also characterized by progressive neurological involvement, including ataxia (inability to coordinate voluntary muscle movements) and spastic paraplegia (Nathanson, 1998). In the early 1920s, a French physician, George Louis Bardet, and Arthur Biedl, a professor of experimental pathology at the University of Prague, independently published descriptions of patients with a similar syndrome that also included polydactyly (having more than five fingers or toes per hand or foot). In the past, these two similar syndromes have been recognized as a single disorder and called the Laurence-Moon-Bardet-Biedl syndrome; however, they are now considered separate disorders. Although both syndromes include mental retardation, retinal abnormalities, and hypogenitalism, neurological problems are characteristic of Laurence-Moon syndrome but rarely occur in Bardet-Biedl syndrome. Polydactyly is a defining feature of Bardet-Biedl syndrome, but is not characteristic of Laurence-Moon syndrome (Morris & Morris, 1998).

The incidence of LMS is rare, with prevalence rates as low as 1 in 175,000. The age of onset is at birth, and both males and females are equally affected. A higher rate of incidence of LMS has been noted in the Arab population of Kuwait. Eighty percent of individuals with LMS have more than one family member affected as well (Castle, Roesen, & Schram, 1993). The prognosis of LMS varies with the individual; however, the natural progression of this syndrome is progressive and deteriorating, eventually resulting in blindness and loss of ability to ambulate.

Although there is no medical treatment for LMS, affected individuals of school age will require a multidisciplinary approach to effectively assess, develop, and implement appropriate educational programs and support services. Appropriate measures should be taken during evaluation to control for the visual deficits typically found in these children. Because mental retardation is characteristic of LMS, affected individuals will frequently benefit from an educational program that emphasizes functional living skills in a self-contained classroom (Nathanson, 1998), with opportunities to integrate and interact with nondisabled peers as much as possible. Students with ataxia and spastic paraplegia may require adapted physical education. Physical and occupational therapies may be necessary to develop motor skills and increase muscle tone. Severe visual impairment is also a hallmark of LMS, and affected students will require educational services for the visually impaired. Low-vision aids such as magnifiers, large print books, large print computer software, tape players, CDs, and manual and electronic Braille writers must be investigated. Transition planning will also assist the placement of LMS students in supported employment settings to help them become productive members of society. For further information regarding LMS, contact the Laurence-Moon-Bardet-Biedl Syndrome Network, 1006 Duncan Avenue, Perry, GA 31069.

### REFERENCES

Castle, J., Roesen, H. M., & Schram, A. (1993). Laurence-Moon-Bardet-Biedl syndrome and polydactyly. *Journal of Foot and Ankle Surgery, 32,* 276–279.

Morris, R. J., & Morris, Y. P. (1998). Bardet-Biedl syndrome. In L. Phelps (Ed.), *Health-related disorders in children and adolescents.* Washington, DC: American Psychological Association.

Nathanson, D. S. (1998). Laurence-Moon syndrome. In L. Phelps (Ed.), *Health-related disorders in children and adolescents.* Washington, DC: American Psychological Association.

Pediatric Database (PEDBASE): http://www.icondata.com/health/pedbase/files/LAURENCE.HTM

KIM RYAN-ARREDONDO
*Texas A&M University*

# LEAD POISONING

The health hazards associated with the use of lead have been known for over 2,000 years. Gillifan (1965) has speculated that lead poisoning may have contributed to the decline of the Roman civilization after the introduction of lead pipes for the supply of drinking water. Mental retardation, sterility, and infant mortality were frequent among influential Romans, and the unearthed bones of wealthy ancient Romans have high lead content. But the modern history of lead poisoning in children dates only from the late 1800s. Histories of the early reports and resistance of the medical community and others to recognize lead as a toxic agent in children are in studies by Needleman (1998) and Pueschel, Linakis, and Anderson (1996). That lead is toxic at some levels is now not disputed, but the extent to which low blood-lead levels (BLL) produce lasting damage is controversial, as will be described.

Although not a common element, lead is found in soil, water, and the atmosphere. It occurs more frequently than other heavy metals in the natural environment. Lead is one of the few metals that has toxic effects but seems to have no essential function in an organism. Lead can enter the body through diet, eating of lead-based paint (pica), or exposure to an environment containing a high lead content. Needleman (1980) has reported low-level lead intoxication from automobile exhaust fumes. Various other studies also implicate industrial emission as a possible source of low-level lead intoxication (Berney, 1996). Children can be exposed to toxic levels of lead in unexpected ways. In one case in rural North Carolina known to the second author of this entry, a four-year-old, whose development had been normal to that time, was admitted to hospital suffering from frequent vomiting and generalized seizures. She had an extremely high BLL. Subsequent examination indicated that she was severely retarded, functioning at an approximately 11-month level, and had major visual and auditory deficits. She had slept next to the indoor stove that the family used to heat the house by burning automobile batteries. The lead released into the air from the burning battery plates contaminated the entire house with lead and produced irreversible brain damage in the child.

In the United States, lead poisoning occurs most often in one- to five-year-old children who inhabit slum areas of large cities. However, the adverse effects of lead are a concern for children of all ages and socioeconomic backgrounds. In recent years, severe forms of encephalopathy have declined due to better social and medical care and legislation protecting homebuyers and renters against unknowingly living in a heavily leaded environment.

In children, BLL above 10μg/dl indicate overexposure and may call for nutritional intervention. However, symptoms of lead poisoning are generally not present at BLL below 20, and even at this level most cases are asymptomatic. Importantly, at BLL of 20 some children require pharmacological treatment and at BLL above 45, children must have medical intervention, which often includes chelatin therapy. Symptoms of lead encephalopathy are generally associated with BLL above 60 μg/dl. BLL below those that produce diagnosable effects have been implicated as a possible cause of subtle behavior and learning difficulties. Often, early symptoms of lead poisoning are misdiagnosed as colic in infants or reflected in attention-deficit/hyperactivity disorder in older children (Chisolm & Barltrop, 1979).

During the postnatal phase of rapid neurodevelopment, which in children extends from birth to 2 or 3 years of age, the brain is especially vulnerable to nutritional and toxic insults due to a weak blood-brain barrier. Whether such children are at a significant risk for subtle, but significant, neurobehavioral impairment has aroused much concern and is a topic of current research.

The most serious and irreversible effects of lead are seen in the nervous system. Researchers are only now better understanding the neurological changes associated with lead. Regan states that "lead exposure results in a decrease in the number of synapses and neurotransmitter receptors" (1992, p. 71). Other changes include nerve demyelination and axonal degeneration (Anderson, Pueschel, & Linakis, 1996). Initially, membrane permeability increases, with a flow of fluid into the interstitial brain spaces. This increased intracranial pressure causes lead encephalopathy, which is characterized by convulsions, mental retardation, paralysis, blindness, coma, and death (Bellinger, Stiles, & Needleman, 1992). At lower exposures, lead causes intellectual deficits that may not be reversible. The most common manifestations include hyperactivity, aggression, impulsiveness, learning disabilities, and distractibility. In the hematologic system, lead prevents the formation of hemoglobin, the absence of which causes increases in erythrocyte protoporphyrin, coproporphyrin, and delta-aminolevulinic acid, which in turn results in anemia (Beretic, 1981). Lead exposure also leads to kidney damage. However, with adequate treatment, this damage is usually reversible (Anderson et al., 1996).

The clinical manifestations of lead poisoning in children develop over a period of three to six weeks. The child becomes less playful, more irritable, and often anorexic. These symptoms may be (and often are) misinterpreted as a behavior disorder or mental retardation. Intermittent vomiting, vague abdominal pain, clumsiness, and ataxia may also be exhibited in the early stages of lead poisoning. In the final stages, vomiting becomes more persistent, apathy progresses to drowsiness and stupor, periods of hyperirritability develop, and finally, seizures and coma occur. Severe cases may result in death. In children under the age of two, the syndrome progresses rapidly, whereas in older children, recurrent and less severe episodes are more likely.

A common way of measuring blood-lead concentrations is by measuring capillary blood samples obtained by fingerstick or venous blood sampling (Linakis, Anderson, & Pueschel, 1996). The Centers for Disease Control (1991) state that evidence of elevated blood-lead concentrations obtained through fingerstick should be verified with venous samples. Chronic lead exposure is sometimes determined by measuring the lead content of teeth. Lead content in

hair samples has also been used to estimate the body's lead burden. Marlowe, Cossairt, Welch, and Errera (1984) studied the relationship between hair mineral elements and learning disabilities and found that the learning-disabled group had slightly elevated hair lead concentrations.

Controversial is the extent to which low BLL may have long-term adverse effects. The initial major evidence for such effects was in much-cited research by Needleman (e.g., 1980). However, in 1992 (e.g., Begley, 1992; Sibbison, 1992), two highly regarded researchers, Scarr and Ernhart, claimed that Needleman had made serious methodological errors in his study, and that the results could not be considered reliable. Reanalysis of Needleman's data, however, supported his original conclusions. Although arguments over the magnitude of effects of low exposure levels, methodological soundness of the research, and interpretation of results continue (e.g., Bellinger, 1995; Ernhart, 1995; Ernhart & Hebben, 1997), several recent studies appear to confirm Needleman's original position. For example, for many years, Tong and Baghurst (1996) have longitudinally studied the development of children early exposed to lead in Port Pirie, Australia. The study appears to be very well designed and conducted. When aged 11 to 13 years, as at earlier ages, the children showed deficits in IQ correlated with their lifelong BLLs. The deficit for children with BLLs of 10–20μg/dl was about three points, with effects somewhat larger in girls than boys. The obtained graded effect with BLL does not support a threshold effect or a "safe" level of lead. Further supporting conclusions of adverse effects of low-lead exposure in humans are parallel findings in experimental research with animals (e.g., Needleman, 1995). Of importance, several lines of research (e.g., Dietrich, 1996) now indicate that exposure of pregnant women to low levels of lead may have adverse effects on their offspring.

Reviews of most topics dealing with lead poisoning in childhood can be found in Pueschel, Linakis, and Anderson (1996). Information is also available from the National Lead Information Center (National Safety Council), 1019 19th St, Suite 401, Washington, DC, 20036-5105; 800-LEAD-FYI.

## REFERENCES

Anderson, A. C., Pueschel, S. M., & Linakis, J. G. (1996). Pathophysiology of lead poisoning. In S. Pueschel, J. Linakis, & A. Anderson (Eds.), *Lead poisoning in childhood* (pp. 75–96). Baltimore: Brookes.

Begley, S. (1992). Lead, lies and data tape. *Newsweek, 119*(11), 62.

Bellinger, D. C. (1995). Interpreting the literature on lead and child development: The neglected role of the "experimental system." *Neurotoxicology and Teratology, 17*, 201–212.

Bellinger, D., Stiles, K, & Needleman, H. (1992). Low-level lead exposure, intelligence and academic achievement: A long-term follow-up study. *Pediatrics, 90*, 855–861.

Beritic, T. (1984). Lead neuropathy. *CRC Critical Reviews in Toxicology, 12*(2), 149–213.

Berney, B. L. (1993). Round and round it goes: The epidemiology of childhood lead poisoning, 1950–1990. *Millbank Quarterly, 71*(1), 3–39.

Berney, B. L. (1996). Epidemiology of childhood lead. In S. Pueschel, J. Linakis, & A. Anderson (Eds.), *Lead poisoning in childhood* (pp. 15–35). Baltimore: Brookes.

Blouin, A. G., Blouin, J. H., & Kelly, T. C. (1983). Lead, trace mineral intake, and behavior of children. *Topics in Early Childhood Special Education, 3*(2), 63–71.

Centers for Disease Control (CDC). (1991). *Preventing lead poisoning in young children: A statement by the Centers for Disease Control.* Atlanta: U.S. Department of Health and Human Services, Public Health Service.

Chisolm, Jr., J. J., & Barltrop, D. (1979). Recognition and management of children with increased lead absorption. *Archives of Disease in Childhood, 54,* 249–262.

Dietrich, K. N. (1996). Low-level exposure during pregnancy and its consequences for fetal and child development. In S. Pueschel, J. Linakis, & A. Anderson (Eds.), *Lead poisoning in childhood* (pp. 117–139). Baltimore: Brookes.

Ernhart, C. B. (1995). Inconsistencies in the lead-effects literature exist and cannot be explained by "effect modification." *Neurotoxicology and Teratology, 17,* 227–234.

Ernhart, C. B., & Hebben, N. (1997). Intelligence and lead: The "known" is not known. *American Psychologist, 52,* 74.

Gillifan, S. C. (1965). Lead poisoning and the fall of Rome. *Journal of Occupational Medicine, 7,* 53–60.

Graham, P. J. (1983). Poisoning in children. In M. Rutter (Ed.), *Developmental neuropsychiatry* (pp. 52–67). New York: Guilford.

King, E. (1982). Lead poisoning. *Public Health Review, 10*(1), 49–76.

Linakis, J. G., Anderson, A. C., & Pueschel, S. M. (1996). Screening for lead poisoning. In S. Pueschel, J. Linakis, & A. Anderson (Eds.), *Lead poisoning in childhood* (pp. 59–73). Baltimore: Brookes.

Marlowe, M., Cossairt, A., Welch, K., & Errera, J. (1984). Hair mineral content as a predictor of learning disabilities. *Journal of Learning Disabilities, 17,* 418–421.

Needleman, H. (Ed). (1980). *Low-level lead exposure: The clinical implications of current research.* New York: Raven.

Needleman, H. L. (1995). Making models of real world events: The use and abuse of inference. *Neurotoxicology and Teratology, 17,* 241–242.

Needleman, H. L. (1998). Childhood lead poisoning: The promise and abandonment of primary prevention. *American Journal of Public, 88,* 1871–1878.

Pueschel, S. M., Linakis, J. G., & Anderson, A. C. (1996). Lead poisoning: A historical perspective. In S. Pueschel, J. Linakis, & A. Anderson (Eds.), *Lead poisoning in childhood* (pp. 1–13). Baltimore: Brookes.

Pueschel, S. M., Linakis, J. G., & Anderson, A. C. (Eds.). (1996). *Lead poisoning in childhood.* Baltimore: Brookes.

Regan, C. (1992). Neural cell adhesion molecules, neuronal development and lead toxicity. *Neurotoxicology, 14,* 69–74.

Sibbison, J. B. (1992). USA: Legality of misconduct inquiry challenged. *Lancet, 339,* 1102.

Tong, S., & Baghurst, P. (1996). Lifetime exposure to environmental lead and children's intelligence at 11–13 years: The Port Pirie cohort study. *British Medical Journal, 312,* 1569–1575.

KENNETH A. ZYCH
*Walter Reed Army Medical Center*
First edition

LAUREN M. WEBSTER
ROBERT T. BROWN
*University of North Carolina at Wilmington*

**BRAIN DAMAGE/INJURY**
**MENTAL RETARDATION**
**PICA**

## LEAGUE SCHOOL

The League School, now expanded and known as the League Center, was founded in 1953 by Dr. Carl Fenichel. It is a not-for-profit continuum of care serving multiply mentally disabled children and adults at four facilities in Brooklyn, New York.

When Fenichel initiated the League School, the children he served were considered uneducable. Their parents, commonly believed to be the root of the problem, often faced the necessity of abandoning their children to mental institutions, since no other options existed. Fenichel maintained that the mind-crippling disorders of severely mentally/emotionally disabled children resulted from serious learning and language deficits rather than from parental sources. In creating a day school based on this perspective, he pioneered a diagnostic, educational, and treatment program, which was daring and unpopular in the climate of the 1950s. His "reaching and teaching" model proffered the hope that intensive education and treatment would be effective if they included: (1) highly individualized programs based on comprehensive and ongoing assessment; (2) the active participation of parents in educational and treatment partnership with the school; (3) highly organized and structured training to bring order, stability, and direction to the children's disordered minds; and (4) teachers who could limit as well as accept the children.

Today the League Center's continuum of services includes a school-based home training program serving parents of severely disturbed children 18 months to 4 years of age. Both the League School Nursery and the Joan Fenichel Therapeutic Nursery provide day treatment for groups of 2 to 4 year olds. The League School is attended by more than 100 students. Since communication disorders are prevalent and contribute significantly to the students' behavior, language skills are stressed in the school program. Students with little or no language are in classes staffed by both a language and a special educator; those with some developed communication skills receive language therapy and participate in small-group conversation clinics. There are special programs in physical education, travel training, print shop, crafts, and prevocational training. A six-week summer program extends social and life skills training into a wide range of recreational activities.

The Adult Day Treatment Center serves older adolescents and adults with the goal of developing sufficient self-control and socially acceptable behavior for living independently in the community. Fenichel House is a residence for adults who require continuing supervision in order to live and work in the community. This program is small and operates in a homelike setting.

In addition to providing diagnostic, educational, and treatment programs for hundreds of New Yorkers each year, the League Center serves as a model for special day schools and treatment centers throughout the world. It also serves as a training resource for students and professionals, as a research center, and as a valuable resource for public information, leadership, and advocacy on behalf of mentally disabled and emotionally disturbed people of all ages.

KATHERINE GARNETT
*Hunter College, City University
of New York*

# LEARNED HELPLESSNESS

Learned helplessness is a concept that originated in animal behavioral experimentation in the 1960s conducted by Seligman (Seligman & Maier, 1967). Seligman's work sprouted theory that has, through the decades, been included in discussions and research relevant to depression, motivation, and trauma in humans. The learned-helplessness theory asserts that in a situation where one perceives that expected outcomes are independent of one's own effort, one can be affected with a decrease in self-esteem, a reduction in motivation, and potentially experience a depressed affect.

Abramson, Seligman, and Tasdale (1978) refined the theory in application to human psychology by incorporating attribution theory to resolve weaknesses in the original theory. Once a person comes to the conclusion that there is no contingency between their actions and outcomes, that person will attribute helplessness to a cause that is stable or unstable over time, internal or external to one's self, and global or specific in nature. In other words, it is no longer a matter of whether the person is truly without control so much as how she or he understands and perceives why she or he is not in control. In an unsolvable situation, a person may come to a conclusion of "universal helplessness" or "personal helplessness." Universal helplessness is an understanding that the failure is largely due to external forces, and that any person put in that situation is likely to fail. Personal helplessness is the internalization of the failure and attributing failure to a person's own inabilities and lack of skills. An outcome of universal helplessness or personal helplessness affects the chronicity and generality of helplessness to other domains of a person's life, affecting motivation, problem-solving skills, self-esteem, and motivation.

Learned helplessness theory has broadened in applicability in research, including research in education. Of interest is examining students and their motivation or lack of motivation to achieve. Related to this is focus on populations at higher risk, such as children with disabilities. Canino (1981) concluded that it is possible that students with a learning disability may exemplify these models of learned helplessness and attribution, such that the student's perceptions under this framework "undermine motivation, limit interest patterns, heighten negative affect (i.e., loss of self-esteem), and retard intellectual growth." Burns (2000) discussed the implications of special education labels as contributing to the outcome of learned helplessness in students with disabilities. A disability, which may be seen as internal and a stable attribution over time, may contribute to a student's perception of little or no control or ability to change situations, and thus possibly increasing depressive symptomatology. Additionally, labeling students and giving them the opportunity to accept their disability as a reason for failure leaves room for belief they could not accomplish a task even if they tried. The literature also has examined teacher and student interactions as creating a helpless response pattern and contributing to the development of learned helplessness in students with disabilities (Sutherland & Singh, 2004).

Research has consistently found inverse associations between helpless attributions and academic performance (Yee, Pierce, Ptacek, & Modzelesky, 2003). In effect, when attributions for negative outcomes or events (e.g., academic failure) are made to internal and stable causes, the result is more likely to be hopelessness and depression (Valás, 2001). Similarly, increased helplessness is associated with decreased academic effort, motivation, and success. Research suggests that negative internal attributions and resulting learned helplessness are likely to occur in children with learning difficulties (e.g., Galloway, Leo, Rogers, & Armstrong, 1995), particularly as they reach adolescence. Consistently, those children who have a history of school failure are more likely to view themselves as academically unable, and stop putting forth effort. Negative effects of failure and comparison with others have been found to result in poorer performance (Thompson & Perry, 2005). Feelings of helplessness and negative academic expectations are significantly related to overall psychological adjustment (Valás, 2001). A focus on fostering self-efficacy, locus of control, and self-determination is important in maintaining academic motivation for students experiencing academic difficulty, in order to offset potential learned helplessness (Burden & Burdett, 2005). The implications of research in the educational context relating to the learned helplessness theory have guided intervention, training, and practice formatted to include conscious efforts in behavior, such as consistency and clarification of rewards and implementation of positive interaction, both with the student and in collaboration between families and educational professionals.

## REFERENCES

Abramson, L. Y., Seligman, M. E. P., & Teasdale, J. D. (1978). Learned helplessness in humans: Critique and reformulation. *Journal of Abnormal Psychology, 87,* 49–74.

Burden, R., & Burdett, J. (2005). Factors associated with successful learning in pupils with dyslexia: A motivational analysis. *British Journal of Special Education, 32,* 100–104.

Burns, M. K. (2000). Examining Special Education: Labels through attribution theory: A potential source for learned helplessness. *Ethical Human Sciences and Services, 2,* 101–107.

Canino, F. J. (1981). Learned-helplessness theory: Implications for research in learning disabilities. *Journal of Special Education, 15,* 471–484.

Galloway, D., Leo, E. L., Rogers, C., & Armstrong, D. (1995). Motivational styles in English and mathematics among children identified as having special education needs. *British Journal of Educational Psychology, 65,* 477–487.

Seligman, M. E. P. (1975). *Helplessness: On depression, development, and death.* San Francisco: Freeman.

Seligman, M. E. P., & Maier, S. F. (1967). Failure to escape traumatic shock. *Journal of Experimental Psychology, 74,* 1–9.

Sutherland, K. S., & Singh, N. N. (2004). Learned helplessness and students with emotional or behavioral disorders: Deprivation in the classroom. *Behavioral Disorders, 29,* 169–191.

Thompson, T., & Perry, Z. (2005). Is the poor performance of self-worth protective students linked with social comparison goals? *Educational Psychology, 25,* 471–490.

Valás, H. (2001). Learned helplessness and psychological adjustment: Effects of age, gender and academic achievement. *Scandinavian Journal of Educational Research, 45,* 71–90.

Yee, P. L., Pierce, G. R., Ptacek, J. T., & Modzelesky, K. L. (2003). Learned helplessness attributional style and examination performance: Enhancement effects are not necessarily moderated by prior failure. *Anxiety, Stress, and Coping, 16,* 359–373.

MARISSA I. MENDOZA
*Texas A&M University*

**ATTRIBUTIONAL RETRAINING**
**ATTRIBUTIONS**
**DYSLEXIA**
**MOTIVATION**

# LEARNER TAXONOMIES

A *taxonomy* is a classification scheme that hierarchically orders objects or phenomena. That is, terms at the top of the taxonomy are more general, inclusive, or complex, subsuming terms at a lower level. The application of a taxonomy for education would then assume that any level of behavior is dependent on the capability of a learner to perform at the next lower level, which is, in turn, dependent on the next lower level ability, and so on. Learning taxonomies serve as the basis for what are now called higher-order thinking skills. The cognitive domain taxonomies help to create a standard around which further work can be done with the concepts of higher- and lower-order thinking.

A review of the research defines four main learning taxonomies: Bloom's Taxonomy of Objectives (Bloom, Englehart, Furst, Hill, & Krathwohl, 1956; Furst, 1981), Gagne's Taxonomy of Learning (Gagne, 1970), Merrill's Component Display Theory (Merrill, 1983), and Leith's Taxonomy of Learning (Leith, 1970, 1971).

Bloom's model includes six levels of thinking: knowledge, comprehension, application, analysis, synthesis, and evaluation. Each level not only asks more of our thinking skills but also includes the previous levels as subsets of the new level. The collection provides educators with a structure that can be used to build curriculum materials that take learners more deeply into any area of study.

Gagne identified different levels of learning for the purpose of sequencing instruction. He believed that instruction should begin with the simplest skills and proceed hierarchically to greater levels of difficulty. His taxonomy includes six levels of learning: verbal information, concrete concepts, defined concepts, rule, higher order rule, and cognitive strategy. Michael J. Striebel (1995) noted that "Instructional design theories such as Gagne's theory, take the cognitivist paradigm one logical step further by claiming that an instruction plan can generate both appropriate environmental stimuli and instructional interactions, and thereby bring about a change in cognitive structures of the learner."

An assumption of component display theory (CDT) is that different learning outcomes require different instructional conditions. Merrill developed his taxonomy of learning, over a period of years, through the analysis of school-based learning outcomes (Merrill, 1983). CDT classifies levels of content in terms of facts, concepts, procedures, and principles. Facts are arbitrary associations. Concepts are classes of objects or events. Procedures are sequences of replicable behavior. Principles are generalized explanations that relate two or more concepts and are used to predict, explain, or infer (Jonassen & Grabowski, 1993).

Leith identified 10 levels of cognitive behavior, ranging from stimulus discrimination (the perception of different sounds, shapes, and objects) to learning schemata (concepts of networks, principles, and problem situations). Other levels, increasing in complexity, include: response learning, response integration, associations, serial learning/chaining, learning set formations, concept learning, concept integration, and problem solving.

Learning taxonomies can have significant impact on the outcome of a learner. According to Jonassen and Grabowski (1993), when determining the most appropriate form of instruction or predicting how well learners will learn, the most important variable is the type of learning outcome. Learning outcomes, like learner's abilities, vary in complexity and form. It is important to understand the type of learning outcome because different types of learners possessing different learner traits will be variably able to produce different levels, and types of learning.

## REFERENCES

Bloom, B. S., Engelhart, M. D., Furst, F. J., Hill, W. H., & Krathwohl, D. R. (1956). *Taxonomy of educational objectives: Cognitive domain.* New York: McKay.

Furst, E. J. (1981). Bloom's taxonomy of educational objectives for the cognitive domain: Philosophical and educational issues. *Review of Educational Research, 51,* 441–453.

Gagne, R. M. (1970). *The conditions of learning.* New York: Holt, Rinehart, & Winston.

Jonassen, D. H., & Grabowski, B. L. (1993). *Handbook of individual differences, learning, and instruction.* Hillsdale, NJ: Erlbaum.

Leith, G. O. M. (1970). The acquisition of knowledge and mental development of students. *Journal of Educational Technology, 1,* 116–128.

Leith, G. O. M. (1971). *Working papers on instructional design and evaluation H: Analysis of objectives and tasks.* Geneva: World Health Organization.

Merrill, M. D. (1983). Component display theory. In C. Reigeluth (Ed.), *Instructional design theories and models.* Hillsdale, NJ: Erlbaum.

Striebel, M. (1995). Instructional plans and situational learning. In G. J. Anglin (Ed.), *Instructional technology: Past, present, future* (2nd ed., pp. 145–166). Englewood, CO: Libraries Unlimited.

KATHLEEN M. PHILLIPS
*University of California,
Riverside*

## LEARNING DISABILITIES

Children and adults classified as learning disabled (LD) are those individuals who are of normal intelligence but suffer mental information processing difficulties. Several definitions refer to LD as reflecting a heterogeneous group of individuals with intrinsic disorders that are manifested by specific difficulties in the acquisition and use of listening, speaking, reading, writing, reasoning, or mathematical abilities (Hammill, 1990). Most definitions assume that the learning difficulties of such individuals are:

1. *Not* due to inadequate opportunity to learn, to general intelligence, or to significant physical or emotional disorders, but to *basic* disorders in specific psychological processes (such as remembering the association between sounds and letters).

2. *Not* due to poor instruction, but to specific psychological processing problems. These problems have a neurological, constitutional, and/or biological base (e.g., Shaywitz et al., 1999).

3. *Not* manifested in all aspects of learning. Such individuals' psychological processing deficits depress only a limited aspect of academic behavior. For example, such individuals may suffer problems in reading, but not arithmetic.

Depending on the definition, the incidence of children with learning disabilities is conservatively estimated to reflect 2 percent of the public school population. It is also the largest category of children served in special education.

Because of the heterogeneity of individuals classified as LD, several subtypes have been discussed in the literature. Few of these subtypes have been considered valid because (1) the particular subtypes do not respond differently to instructional programs when compared to other subtypes, and/or (2) the skills deficient in a particular subtype are not relevant to the academic areas important in the school context.

There are two subtypes, however, with extensive research, and they are relevant to the school context: reading disabilities and mathematical disabilities. These subtypes are defined by standardized (normed referenced) and reliable measures of intelligence and achievement. The most commonly used intelligence tests are from the Wechsler measures. Common achievement tests that include measures of word recognition or identification are the Wide Range Achievement Test, Woodcock Reading Mastery Test, Kaufman Test of Educational Achievement, and the Peabody Individual Test, while common achievement tests that include arithmetic calculation include all the aforementioned tests and the Key Math Diagnostic Test. In general, individuals with IQ scores equal to or above a Full Scale IQ score of 85 and reading subtest scores equal to or below the 25th percentile and/or arithmetic subtest score equal to or below the 25th percentile capture two high-incidence disorders within LD: reading disabilities and math disabilities.

In terms of reading disabilities, Siegel (1989, 2003) argues that fundamental to evaluating reading disabilities is a focus on word recognition measures, because they capture more basic cognitive processes and responses than reading comprehension. Her research shows that difficulties in phonological processing are fundamental problems for children with reading disabilities, and this problem continues into adulthood. She also indicates that there is no evidence to suggest that development of decoding skills is a result of a specific instruction in grapheme-phoneme conversion rules.

Her work and the work of others find that there are three processes critical in analysis of reading disabilities: those related to phonological processing (ability to segment sounds), syntactical processing, and working memory (combination of transient memory and long-term memory).

In terms of math disabilities, Geary (1993, 2003) finds that children with arithmetic problems do not necessarily differ from academically normal peers in terms of the types of strategies used to solve simple arithmetic problems. Differences, however, are found in the percentage of retrieval and counting errors. Children with math disabilities have long-term memory representations of arithmetic facts that are not correct. He provides a taxonomy of three general subtypes of mathematical disability: those related to procedural errors, those related to semantic memory, and those with visual/spatial difficulties. He indicates that the ability to retrieve basic arithmetic facts from long-term memory is a defining feature of math disabilities.

*History and instructional trends.* The term *learning disabilities* was first coined in a speech by Samuel Kirk, delivered in 1963 at the Chicago Conference on Children with Perceptual Handicaps. Earlier clinical studies showed that a group of children who suffered perceptual, memory, and attention difficulties related to their poor academic performance, but who were not intellectually retarded, were not being adequately served in the educational context.

Wiederholt (1974), in reviewing the history of the LD field, indicated that its unique focus was on identifying and remediating specific psychological processing difficulties. Popular intervention approaches during the 1960s and 1970s focused on visual-motor, auditory sequencing, or visual perception training exercises. Several criticisms were directed at these particular interventions on methodological and theoretical grounds.

By the late 1970s, dissatisfaction with a processing orientation to remediation of learning disabilities, as well as the influence of federal regulations in the United States (Public Law 94-142), led to remediation programs focused on basic skills such as reading and mathematics. The focus on basic skills rather than psychological processes was referred to as *direct instruction.* The mid-1980s witnessed a shift from the more remedial-academic approach of teaching to instruction that included both basic skills and cognitive strategies (e.g., ways to better learn new information and efficiently access information from long-term memory). Children with LD were viewed as experiencing difficulty in "regulating" their learning performance. An instructional emphasis was placed on teaching students to check, plan, monitor, test, revise, and evaluate their learning during their attempts to learn or solve problems.

The early 1990s witnessed a resurgence of direct instruction intervention studies, primarily influenced by reading research that suggested that a primary focus of intervention should be directed to phonological skills. The rationale was that because a large majority of children with learning disabilities suffer problems in reading, some of these children's reading problems are exacerbated because of lack of systematic instruction in processes related to phonological awareness (the ability to hear and manipulate sounds in words and understand the sound structure of language). This view gave rise to several interventions that focused heavily on phonics instruction, and intense individual one-to-one tutoring to improve children's phonological awareness of word structures and sequences.

From the turn of the twenty-first century to the present, some interventions have been linked to assessment. A method of identifying school-aged students with LD, known as *response to intervention* (RTI), first establishes low academic performance and then determines if a disability is present. The RTI model is partially based on intervention programs that have distinguished children experiencing academic difficulty due to instructional deficits from those with disability-related deficits (Vellutino et al., 1996; Vellutino, Scanlon, & Tanzman, 1998). Federal regulations in the United States regarding the Individuals with Disabilities Education Improvement Act of 2004 (NASP, 2005) have influenced the use of RTI by supporting the concept that a child's response to scientific, research-based interventions can be used as a process for LD identification. In general, the RTI model identifies whether a student's current skill level is substantially lower than his or her instructional level (based on predetermined criteria—e.g., below the twenty-fifth percentile). Low academic performance is established using standardized, norm-referenced and/or curriculum-based measurements (Deno, 2002; Good & Kaminski, 2002). After establishing low performance, empirically based interventions are implemented to determine if a disability is present. Student progress is monitored during the intervention. When a student does not respond to high-quality intervention, the student may have a learning disability (NRCLD, 2004).

*Scientifically based treatments.* In the field of LD, the term *treatment* or *intervention* is defined as the direct manipulation (usually assigned at will by the experimenter) of variables (e.g., instruction) for the purposes of assessing learning (1) efficiency, (2) accuracy, (3) and understanding. Swanson, Hoskyn, and Lee (1999) have provided the most comprehensive analysis of the experimental intervention literature on LD to date. Interventions were analyzed at two levels: general models of instruction and components most important in instructional success.

In terms of general models, their synthesis of methodologically sound studies (those studies with well-defined control groups and clearly identified LD samples) found that positive outcomes in remediating academic behaviors (e.g., reading, writing, mathematics) were directly related to a combination of direct and strategic instructional models. These models included a graduated sequence of steps with multiple opportunities for overlearning the content and skills, cumulative review routines, mass practice, and teaching of all component skills to a level that shows mastery. The interventions involved (1) teaching a few concepts and strategies well rather than superficially, (2) teaching students to monitor their performance, (3) teaching students when and where to use the strategy in order to enhance generalization, (4) teaching strategies as an integrated part of an existing curriculum, and (5) providing teaching that includes a great deal of supervised student feedback and practice.

In terms of instructional components, Swanson (2000) found that two instructional components underlie successful instructional interventions for children with LD. One component was explicit practice, which includes activities related to distributed review and practice, repeated practice, sequenced reviews, daily feedback, and/or weekly reviews. The other component was advanced organizers, and these studies included activities (1) directing children to focus on specific material or information prior to instruction, (2) directing children about task concepts or events before beginning, and/or (3) the teacher stating objectives of instruction.

*Some issues in the field.* Fundamental problems of definition have severely affected the field of LD as a discipline. This is because considerable latitude exists among psychologists in defining LD. This latitude is influenced by social/political trends as well as nonoperational definitions of LD. The field of study is further exacerbated because the number of individuals classified with LD has increased dramatically over the last 20 years. Unfortunately, without reliable and valid definitions of LD, very little progress in terms of theoretical development will emerge.

One impediment to advances in the field is unresolved issues related to discrepancy. Traditionally, studies on children with LD have relied primarily on uncovering a significant discrepancy between achievement in a particular academic domain and general intellectual ability. The implicit assumption for using discrepancy scores is that individuals who experience reading, writing, and/or math difficulties, unaccompanied by a low IQ, are distinct in cognitive processing from slow or low achievers (e.g., Fletcher, Francis, Rourke, Shaywitz, & Shaywitz, 1992). This assumption is equivocal (e.g., Reynolds, 1981). A plethora of studies has compared children with reading disabilities (RD; i.e., children with discrepancies between IQ and reading) with nondiscrepancy-defined poor readers (i.e., children whose IQ scores are in the same low range as their reading scores) and found that these groups are more similar in processing difficulties than different (Hoskyn & Swanson, 2000; Stuebing, Fletcher, LeDoux, Lyon, Shaywitz, & Shaywitz, 2002). As a result, some researchers have suggested dropping the requirement of average intelligence in favor of a view wherein children with reading problems are best conceptualized as existing at the extreme end of a continuum from poor to good readers (Siegel, 1989; Stanovich & Siegel, 1994).

On this issue, Hoskyn and Swanson (2000) found in a synthesis of the literature that although children with RD and poor readers share some deficits in phonological processing and automaticity (naming speed), the RD group's performance was superior to poor readers on measures of syntactical knowledge, lexical knowledge, and spatial ability (see also Fuchs, Fuchs, Mathes, & Lipsy, 2000). Another important finding was that cognitive differences between the two ability groups were more obvious in the earlier grades. Perhaps more important, a meta-analysis of the intervention literature (Swanson, 2003; Swanson & Hoskyn, 1999) found that students with LD and low achievers differ in the magnitude of their responsiveness to treatment. After reviewing several intervention studies, the results show that students who have low reading scores (twenty-fifth percentile) but average IQ scores were less responsive to interventions than children whose reading and IQ scores were in the same low range (25th percentile; see also Swanson & Hoskyn, 1998, pp. 300–301).

In general, most researchers who study the processing difficulties of children with LD do not use discrepancy criteria (Swanson, 1989). The majority of researchers rely on cutoff scores on standardized measures above a certain criterion of general intelligence measures (e.g., standard score > 85) and cutoff scores below a certain criterion (e.g., standard score < 85) on primary academic domains (e.g., reading and mathematics). The experimental research shows that children with LD can be assessed and that significant gains can be made in academic performance as a function of treatment (see Vellutino, Fletcher, Snowling, & Scanlon, 2004). However, there is considerable evidence that some children with normal intelligence, when exposed to the best instructional conditions, fail to efficiently master skills in reading, mathematic, and/or writing (e.g., Fuchs & Fuchs, 1998; Torgesen, 2000). Some literature suggests that LD individuals are less responsive than generally poor readers to intervention, and that these academic problems persist into adulthood. Further, these difficulties in academic mastery reflect fundamental deficits in processing, such as phonological processing and working memory (Swanson & Siegel, 2001).

## REFERENCES

Deno, S. L. (2002). Problem solving as "Best Practice." In A. Thomas & J. Grimes (Eds.), *Best practices in school psychology* (4th ed., Vol. 1, pp. 37–56). Bethesda, MD: National Association of School Psychologists.

Fletcher, J. M., Francis, D. J., Rourke, B. P., Shaywitz, S. E., & Shaywitz, B. A. (1992). The validity of discrepancy-based definitions of reading disabilities. *Journal of Learning Disabilities, 25*, 555–561.

Fuchs, D., Fuchs, L., Mathes, P. G., & Lipsey, M. E. (2000). Reading differences between low-achieving students with and without reading disabilities: A meta-analysis. In G. Gersten, E. P. Schiller, & S. Vaughn (Eds.), *Contemporary special education research* (pp. 105–136). Mahwah, NJ: Erlbaum.

Fuchs, L. S., & Fuchs, D. (1998). Treatment validity: A unifying concept for reconceptualizing identification of learning disabilities. *Learning Disabilities Research and Practice, 13,* 204–219.

Geary, D. (1993). Mathematical disabilities: Cognitive, neuropsychological, and genetic components. *Psychological Bulletin, 114,* 345–362.

Geary, D. (2003). Learning disabilities in arithmetic: Problem solving differences and cognitive deficits In H. L. Swanson, K. M. Harris, & S. Graham (Eds.), *Handbook of learning disabilities* (pp. 199–212). New York: Guilford.

Good, R. H., & Kaminski, M. A. (Eds.). (2002). *Dynamic indicators of basic early literacy skills* (6th ed.). Eugene, OR: Institute for the Development of Education Achievement.

Hammill, D. (1990). On defining learning disabilities: An emerging consensus. *Journal of Learning Disabilities, 23,* 74–84.

Hoskyn, M., & Swanson, H. L. (2000). Cognitive processing of low achievers and children with reading disabilities: A selective review of the published literature. *School Psychology Review, 29,* 102–119.

National Association of School Psychology (NASP). *IDEA information.* Retrieved August 19, 2005, from http://www.nasponline.org/advocacy/IDEAinformation.html

National Research Center on Learning Disabilities (NRCLD). (2005). *Learning disabilities summit.* Retrieved August, 29, 2005, from http://www.nrcld.org/resources/ldsummit/fuchs4.shtml

Reynolds, C. R. (1981). The fallacy of "two years below grade level for age" as a diagnostic criterion for reading disorders. *Journal of School Psychology, 11,* 250–258.

Shaywitz, S. E., Fletcher, J. M., Holahan, J. M., Shneider, A. E., Marchione, K. E., Stuebing, K. K., Francis, D. J., & Shaywitz, B. A. (1999). Persistence of dyslexia: The Connecticut longitudinal study at adolescence. *Pediatrics, 104,* 1351–1359.

Siegel, L. S. (1989). IQ is irrelevant to the definition of learning disabilities. *Journal of Learning Disabilities, 22,* 469–478.

Siegel, L. S. (1992). An evaluation of the discrepancy definition of dyslexia. *Journal of Learning Disabilities, 25,* 618–629.

Siegel, L. S. (2003). Basic cognitive processes and reading disabilities. In H. L. Swanson, K. M. Harris, & S. Graham (Eds.), *Handbook of learning disabilities* (pp. 158–181). New York: Guilford

Stanovich, K., & Siegel, L. S. (1994). Phenotypic performance profile of children with reading disabilities: A regression-based test of the phonological-core variable-difference model. *Journal of Educational Psychology, 86,* 24–53.

Stuebing, K. K., Fletcher, J. M., LeDoux, J. M., Lyon, G. R., Shaywitz, S. E., & Shaywitz, B. A. (2002). Validity of IQ-discrepancy classifications of reading disabilities: A meta-analysis. *American Educational Research Journal, 39,* 469–518.

Swanson, H. L. (1989). Operational definitions of LD: An overview. *Learning Disability Quarterly, 14,* 242–254.

Swanson, H. L. (2000). Searching for the best model for instructing students with LD: A component and composite analysis. *Educational and Child Psychology, 17,* 101–121.

Swanson, H. L. (2003). Treatment outcomes as a function of IQ and reading level. In T. Scruggs & Mastropieri (Eds.), *Advances in learning and behavioral disabilities* (Vol. 16, pp. 205–222). New York: Elsevier.

Swanson, H. L., & Hoskyn, M. (1998). Experimental intervention research on students with learning disabilities: A meta-analysis of treatment outcomes. *Review of Educational Research, 68,* 277–321.

Swanson, H. L., & Hoskyn, M. (1999). Definition x treatment interactions for students with learning disabilities. *School Psychology Review, 28,* 644–658.

Swanson, H. L., Hoskyn, M., & Lee, C. (1999). *Interventions for students with learning disabilities: A meta-analysis of treatment outcomes.* New York: Guilford.

Swanson, H. L., & Siegel, L. S. (2001). Learning disabilities as a working memory deficit. *Issues in Education: Contributions from Educational Psychology, 7,* 1–48.

Torgesen, J. K. (2000). Individual differences in response to early interventions in reading: The lingering problem of treatment resisters. *Learning Disabilities Research and Practice, 15,* 55–64.

Vellutino, F. R., Fletcher, J. M., Snowling, M. J., & Scanlon, D. (2004). Specific reading disability (dyslexia): What have we learned in the past four decades? *Journal of Child Psychology and Psychiatry, 45,* 2–40.

Vellutino, F. R., Scanlon, D. M., Sipay, E. R., Pratt, A., Chen, R., & Denckla, M. B. (1996). Cognitive profiles of difficult-to-remediate and readily remediated poor readers: Early intervention as a vehicle for distinguishing between cognitive and experiential deficits as basic causes of specific reading disability. *Journal of Educational Psychology, 86,* 601–638.

Vellutino, F. R., Scanlon, D. M., & Tanzman, M. S. (1998). The case for early intervention in diagnosing specific reading disability. *Journal of School Psychology, 36,* 367–397.

Weiderholt, L. (1974). Historical perspective on the education of the learning disabled. In L. Mann & D. Sabatino (Eds.), *The second review of special education* (pp. 103–152). Austin, TX: PRO-ED.

H. Lee Swanson
Danielle Edelston
*University of California,
Riverside*

**LEARNING DISABILITIES, SEVERE DISCREPANCY ANALYSIS IN PRESCHOOL ASSESSMENT**

# LEARNING DISABILITIES AND CULTURALLY/LINGUISTICALLY DIVERSE STUDENTS

See CULTURALLY/LINGUISTICALLY DIVERSE STUDENTS AND LEARNING DISABILITIES.

## LEARNING DISABILITIES AND JUVENILE DELINQUENCY

Various attempts have been made to study the causal relationship between learning disabilities and juvenile delinquency, but no common agreement has been reached. Many scholars have recognized the close relationship between juvenile delinquency and learning disabilities (Keilitz & Dunivant, 1986), but research on the relationship between learning disabilities and juvenile delinquency has produced mixed results (Kirk & Gallagher, 1989). Perlmutter (1987), for example, postulated that delinquent behavior results from the learning disabled student's attempts to compensate for academic failure and frustration.

Crime statistics indicate that levels of academic achievement, school attendance, and graduation rates play an important role in the involvement of youth in the criminal justice system. Between 28 and 43 percent of incarcerated juveniles have special education needs, and many of them have learning disabilities (Fink, 1990). In addition, many other inmates suffer specific learning disabilities due to cognitive and physical difficulties (Dowling, 1991; Fink, 1991; Winters, 1993).

A possible explanation about the relationship between LD and juvenile delinquency is that because they are often harassed and denigrated by peers in a school environment they are frustration prone (Cawley, Kahn, & Tedesco, 1989). Figueria-McDonough (1986, p. 95) indicated that "in an environment where academic success is defined as an exclusive goal, inept students will acutely feel their lack of success and therefore search for alternative careers." This career may be in the area of criminal activity. Since adolescents generally want to belong to a group, some LD students may feel left out at school. This lack of acceptance by academically skilled students may encourage LD youth to join street gangs (Winters, 1997).

Learning disabilities also affect the rate of female juvenile delinquency. Hugo and Rutherford (1992) indicated that, like males, females with LD become involved in the juvenile criminal justice system early.

Some scholars note that most incarcerated LD youth receive inadequate services while they are involved in the juvenile justice system (Cook & Hill, 1990). Research also indicates that most incarcerated LD youth receive inadequate services while they are involved in the juvenile justice system (Cook & Hill, 1990). Hence, LD offenders suffer both from the lack of service delivery and inadequate placement.

Some scholars suggest that the best way to serve the special-needs population is through coordination of services between public school special education programs and correctional education programs (Coffey, 1983).

## REFERENCES

Cawley, J. F., Kahn, H., & Tedesco, A. (1989). Vocational education and students with learning disabilities. *Journal of Learning Disabilities, 22,* 630–640.

Coffey, O. D. (1983). Meeting the needs of youth from a correctional viewpoint. In S. Braatin, R. B. Rutherford, & C. D. Kardesh (Eds.), *Programming for adolescents with behavior disorders* (pp. 79–84). Reston, VA: Council for Children with Behavioral Disorders.

Cook, J. M., & Hill, G. P. (1990). Preplacement characteristics and educational status of handicapped and nonhandicapped youthful offenders. *Journal of Correctional Education, 41,* 194–198.

Dowling, W. D. (1991). Learning disabilities among incarcerated males. *Journal of Correctional Education, 42,* 180–185.

Figueria-McDonough, J. (1986). School context, gender and delinquency. *Journal of Youth and Adolescence, 15,* 79–98.

Fink, C. M. (1990). Special education students at risk: A comparative study of delinquency. In P. E. Leone (Ed.), *Understanding troubled and troubling youth* (pp. 61–81). Newbury Park, CA: Sage.

Hugo, K. E., & Rutherford, R. B. (1992). Issues in identifying educational disabilities among female juvenile offenders. *Journal of Correctional Education, 43,* 124–127.

Keilitz, I., & Dunivant, N. (1986). The relationship between learning disability and juvenile delinquency: Current state of knowledge. *Remedial and Special Education, 7,* 18–26.

Kirk, S. A., & Gallagher, J. J. (1989). *Educating exceptional children.* Boston: Houghton Mifflin.

Malmgren, K., Abbot, R. D., & Hawkins, J. D. (1999). LD and delinquency: Rethinking the "link." *Journal of Learning Disabilities, 32,* 194–200.

Perlmutter, B. (1987). Delinquency and learning disabilities: Evidence for compensatory behaviors and adaptation. *Journal of Youth and Adolescence, 16,* 89–95.

Winters, C. A. (1993). The therapeutic use of the essay in corrections. *Journal of Correctional Education, 44*(2), 58–61.

Winters, C. A. (1997). Learning disabilities, crime, delinquency, and special education placement. *Adolescence, 32,* 451–462.

XINHUA ZHENG
*University of California,
Riverside*

**CRIME AND INDIVIDUALS WITH DISABILITIES**
**JUVENILE DELINQUENCY**

## LEARNING DISABILITIES ASSOCIATION

The Learning Disabilities Association (LDA), formerly the Association for Children and Adults with Learning Disabilities, was organized as a nonprofit association in 1964 by parents of children with learning disabilities. LDA is a national volunteer organization that includes individuals with learning disabilities, their families, and professionals. Its purpose is to advance the education and general welfare of children and adults of normal or potentially normal intelligence who have learning disabilities of a perceptual, conceptual, or coordinative nature. As its mission, the association seeks to enhance the quality of life for persons with learning disabilities and their families, to allay the limiting effects, and to support efforts to determine the causes through advocacy, research, service, and cooperative efforts.

Among its goals, LDA strives to educate individuals about the nature of learning disabilities and inform them of their rights. Additionally, regular and special education are improved through organizational advocacy with the U.S. Department of Education and state departments of education; LDA also promotes education and training in learning disabilities for teachers in regular and special education. Working directly with schools, LDA assists in the planning and implementation of programs to provide early identification and improved services for individuals with learning disabilities, and maintains extensive resources at its national headquarters to aid educators in dealing with all aspects of learning disabilities.

With membership of more than 50,000 in 600 local chapters in 50 states, Washington, DC, and Puerto Rico, the Learning Disabilities Association is the largest nonprofit volunteer organization for persons with learning disabilities, advocating for over two million students of school age with learning disabilities as well as affected adults. LDA headquarters are located at 4156 Library Road, Pittsburgh, PA, 15234-1349 (LDA, 1996).

**REFERENCE**

Learning Disabilities Association (LDA). (1996). *About LDA*. Retrieved August 29, 1996, from http://www.ldanatl.org/lda/

SHIRLEY A. JONES
*Virginia Polytechnic Institute
and State University*
First edition

TAMARA J. MARTIN
*The University of Texas of the
Permian Basin*
Second edition

# LEARNING DISABILITIES MARKER VARIABLES PROJECT

Marker variables reflect the constructs that define and characterize a particular field and provide operational and conceptual organization to that field by allowing readers to assess comparability of research samples (Bell & Hertz, 1979). The purpose of the Marker Variable Project, conducted by Barbara Keogh at the University of California, Los Angeles (UCLA), was to develop and test a set of marker variables in the field of learning disabilities (Keogh, Major, Omori, Gandara, & Reid, 1980).

This UCLA Marker Variable Project sought to identify possible markers from empirical and conceptual perspectives by reviewing the learning disabilities literature to determine the descriptive variables actually used by researchers for defining and selecting subjects, and reviewing various definitions and theoretical orientations to determine which processes and/or abilities were viewed as primary components of learning disabilities. Based on this procedure, a set of marker variables was proposed and then modified by consultants at a series of conferences.

The resulting set of tentative marker variables was organized along three dimensions: (1) descriptive markers, not specific to learning disabilities research but representative of information reasonably expected in any study involving human subjects, including number of subjects, chronological age, grade level, month/year of study, geographic location, community type, race/ethnicity, source of subjects, socioeconomic status, language background, educational history, current educational status, health status, and exclusionary criteria; (2) substantive markers, particularly relevant to the study of learning-disabled children, including general ability, reading and math achievement, and behavioral and emotional adjustment; and (3) topical markers, relating to specific research areas within the learning disabilities field, including activity level, attention, auditory perception, fine motor coordination, gross motor coordination, memory, oral language, and visual perception (Keogh et al., 1980).

Many of the basic issues addressed by the Marker Variable Project continue to be relevant to the field. Learning disabilities research still suffers from inadequate description of study samples, and leaders in learning disabilities research continue to call for a richer description of subjects, the use of topical marker variables, and exploration of subtypes of learning disabilities (Torgeson & Wong, 1986).

**REFERENCES**

Bell, R. Q., & Hertz, T. W. (1979). Toward more comparability and generalizability of development research. *Child Development, 47,* 6–13.

Keogh, B. K., Major, S. M., Omori, H., Gandara, P., & Reid, H. P. (1980). Proposed markers in learning disabilities research. *Journal of Abnormal Child Psychology, 8,* 21–31.

Torgeson, J., & Wong, B. (Eds.). (1986). *Psychological and educational perspectives on learning disabilities.* Orlando, FL: Academic.

LYNN S. FUCHS
DOUGLAS FUCHS
*Peabody College, Vanderbilt
University*

# LEARNING DISABILITIES, PARADIGM SHIFT IN DETERMINATION OF

According to the definition most often used by state departments of education and stated in the Individuals with Disabilities Education Improvement Act (IDEIA) of 2004, learning disability is defined as a

> "disorder in one or more of the basic psychological processes involved in understanding or in using spoken or written language, which may manifest itself in an imperfect ability to listen, think, speak, read, write, spell or to do mathematical calculations." The Federal definition further states that learning disabilities include "such conditions as perceptual disabilities, brain injury, minimal brain dysfunction, dyslexia, and developmental aphasia." (U.S. Department of Education, 2004).

Each state is responsible for providing and regulating education in accordance with the principles established by the Constitution. The Fourteenth Amendment asserts that no state shall deprive any U.S. citizen "of life, liberty, or property without due process of the law, nor deny any person within its jurisdiction the equal protection of the laws" (Prasse, 2002). The equal protection section of the Fourteenth Amendment guarantees that all citizens will receive the same rights and benefits with respect to their government. Two landmark court cases regarding the rights of disabled citizens in public services established equal protection and due process for students qualifying for special education. The court case *PARC* v. *Commonwealth of Pennsylvania* (1972) established that educational services could not be withheld from mentally retarded children deemed uneducable on the basis that to do so violated their equal protection and due process rights. Another case, *Mills* v. *Board of Education* (1972), established that assignment of handicapped students to special classes denied them equal education rights provided to them under the Fourteenth Amendment (Prasse, 2002).

In 1975, due in large part to the *PARC* and *Mills* court decisions, federal legislation was enacted by congress in the form of the Education of All Handicapped Children Act (EAHCA). In 1990, EAHCA was amended and was retitled the Individuals with Disabilities Education Act (IDEA; Rice, 2002). IDEA was reauthorized in 1997, and again in 2004. According to the guidelines set forth by IDEA, every school must adopt a "zero reject" policy pertaining to children with disabilities, and must work to seek out children with disabilities in order to provide them with appropriate services (Prasse, 2002; Rice, 2002). IDEA also requires that children

with disabilities must receive an Individualized Education Plan (IEP) and be placed in the Least Restrictive Environment (LRE; Drasgow & Yell, 2001). An IEP is a plan based upon the student's personal learning needs, and should include goals, objectives, and a timeline for implementation. The LRE requirement of IDEA asserts that to the maximum extent possible, a child with disabilities should be educated in the general education environment (Rice, 2002). The inclusion policy involves the student attending the same school, classroom, and grade level that would otherwise be attended if he or she were not disabled.

Students receiving services under the learning disabled (LD) category comprise more than 50 percent of all students receiving special education services, making it the most prevalent category in the special education population. It is estimated that approximately 5 percent of all students in school are labeled as learning disabled (Kavale, Holdnack, & Mostert, 2005). In spite of its high prevalence, the underlying causes of learning disabilities remain largely unknown. There is some evidence to suggest that learning disabilities may be genetic. Other evidence suggests that environmental factors, ranging from inadequate learning environments to exposure to harmful substances, may be the cause of learning disabilities. There is even evidence to suggest that the brain structure of students who have reading disabilities with oral language difficulties differs from students without disabilities.

In part because the causes of LD are largely unknown, and partly as a result of IDEA regulations, there is some controversy regarding the ways in which students are classified as learning disabled. The regulations set forth by IDEA have led to a paradigm shift in the way services are delivered. System reform emphasizes a move away from the traditional approach of classification and placement, and toward a problem-solving model (Rice, 2002). The traditional process most commonly used to determine special education eligibility for a specific learning disability (SLD) in school-age students has been the IQ-achievement discrepancy model. In this traditional model of LD classification the main factor that has dominated the decision-making process has been concerned with establishing a discrepancy between a child's ability level and his or her achievement level.

Federal regulations provided criteria for determining the existence of SLD that included the existence of a severe discrepancy between achievement and intellectual ability in one or more of seven domains of academic functioning. These include: (1) oral expression; (2) listening comprehension; (3) written expression; (4) basic reading skills; (5) reading comprehension; (6) mathematics calculation; and (7) mathematics reasoning (Council for Exceptional Children, 2005). When it is determined that a child is performing at a level significantly below his or her ability, the ability-achievement discrepancy is thought to indicate that the child may have a learning disability. Diagnosis of learning disabilities through the discrepancy model has become the single most frequent activity of school psychologists, even though its use has been a source of frequent criticism.

One criticism of the discrepancy model is that it lacks treatment validity. Treatment validity is the relationship between an assessment procedure and the positive outcomes that are produced as a result. Another criticism of the discrepancy model is that the size of a discrepancy used to indicate a learning disability is, in effect, an arbitrary number chosen by each state. In California, for example, in order to qualify as learning disabled a child must have a discrepancy of one and a half standard deviations, or 22 points. The problem here is that this cutoff number will often qualify children for special education who do not need it, while disqualifying other children who really do need it (Reschly & Ysseldyke, 2002). The question arises, "does a child with a discrepancy score of 23 really have more need for special services than a child with a discrepancy score of 20?" Additionally, it has been pointed out by the National Institute of Child Health and Development (NICHD) that the discrepancy model is biased against poor readers, because it is more likely to deny them services that they need. NICHD findings show that readers with higher abilities are more likely to produce a discrepancy than readers with lower abilities, because children with both low ability and low achievement scores do not produce a significant discrepancy, effectively keeping special services away from those who may need them the most (Reschly & Ysseldyke, 2002; National Research Center on Learning Disabilities [NRCLD], 2005).

Of particular controversy in the assessment of this condition is the poor quality of procedures to establish the existence of a significant level of discrepancy between a person's ability and actual achievement. The tests for visual, auditory, and other information processes are generally considered to have questionable validity and reliability, making assessment in these areas difficult and reliant on informal techniques (Salvia & Ysseldyke, 1985). Due to ineffective procedures, the IQ-achievement discrepancy model has given school psychologists neither the ability to determine the specific educational needs of the student nor provide direction toward effective intervention strategies (Gresham & Witt, 1997). Furthermore, research shows that IQ-achievement discrepant and nondiscrepant poor readers do not differ with regard to instructional interventions needed, or even in responsiveness to such interventions. The appropriateness of the discrepancy model for determining learning disabilities has been criticized as a result.

Because the traditional model requires educators to wait until a large discrepancy is apparent, students are typically not identified for special interventions until several years after they exhibit early signs of academic difficulties. However, students identified as struggling academically are more likely to succeed in school with early academic supports. For example, students with reading problems, including students with reading disabilities, are much more likely to become proficient readers when specific instructional interventions are implemented at an early age (Baker & Smith, 2001). As a result, IDEA 2004 revisions shift away from traditional procedures adhering to the discrepancy model and, instead, move to an outcome-based orientation, thus stating several implications with regard to special education instruction and services for students classified as LD (Reschly, 2000). New requirements in the law place greater emphasis on proactive programs for students with learning disabilities, in an effort to increase academic and life-long success (Drasgow & Yell, 2001).

The history of learning disabilities has included much controversy about the procedures and criteria for determining students with LD. Most recently, response to intervention (RTI) has gained increased support as a means of determining learning disabilities in school-aged children (NRCLD, 2004). The reauthorized IDEA 2004 adds new language that allows local education agencies (LEAs) to eliminate the IQ-achievement discrepancy requirement stating that

> . . . a local education agency shall not be required to take into consideration whether a child has a severe discrepancy between achievement and intellectual ability in oral expression, listening, comprehension, written expression, basic reading skill, reading comprehension, mathematical calculation, or mathematical reasoning." Additionally, the updated law states that, "In determining whether a child has a specific learning disability, a local education agency may use a process that determines if the child responds to scientific, research-based intervention as a part of the evaluation procedures described in Section 614(a) (2) & (3)." (National Association of School Psychology, 2005)

The language used in the updated law allows for the use of the RTI model as an option to determine learning disability. Proposed as a valuable model, RTI identifies students with LD and is a preventative model for academic failure among all students (NRCLD, 2004). The RTI model identifies students' current skill and the instructional level of the classroom. When students' skills are lower than instructional level, a high-quality intervention can be implemented. Students' progress are carefully monitored on a continual basis during intervention. Based on the RTI model, when a student does not respond to high-quality instruction, the student may have a learning disability (NRCLD, 2004). Current trends include the use of curriculum-based assessment. This type of assessment utilizes curriculum-based measurement (CBM), an empirically-based systematic set of procedures designed to identify student literacy, spelling, writing, and math level. If used appropriately, CBM results in more effective instructional interventions for students (Deno, 2002).

Learning disabilities, as the category applies to students and the school environment, continue to evolve as federal and state legislature changes. The special education community is currently experiencing a paradigm shift with regard to identifying students with learning disabilities and implementing appropriate interventions to best educate these students.

## REFERENCES

Baker, S., & Smith, S. (2001). Linking school assessments to research-based practices in beginning reading: Improving programs and outcomes for students with and without disabilities. *Teacher Education and Special Education, 24*, 315–332.

Boudah, D. J., & Weiss, M. P. (2002). *Learning disabilities overview: Update 2002.* Arlington, VA: ERIC Clearinghouse on Disabilities and Gifted Education. (ERIC Document Reproduction Service No. ED462808)

Council for Exceptional Children. (2005). *Council for Exceptional Children's initial summary of selected provisions from part B proposed regulations for the Individuals with Disabilities Education Act: Learning disabilities.* Retrieved August 29, 2005, from http://www.cec.sped.org/cec_bn/pdfs/side-by-side_Learning _Disabilities.pdf

Deno, S. L. (2002). Problem solving as "Best Practice." In A. Thomas & J. Grimes (Eds.), *Best practices in school psychology* (4th ed., Vol. 1, pp. 37–56). Bethesda, MD: National Association of School Psychologists.

Drasgow, E., & Yell, M. L. (2001). Functional behavior assessment: Legal requirements and challenges. *School Psychology Review, 23*, 239–251.

Gresham, F. M., Watson, T. S., & Skinner, C. H. (2001). Functional behavioral assessment: Principles, procedures, and future directions. *School Psychology Review, 30*, 156–172.

Gresham, F. M., & Witt, J. C. (1997). Utility of intelligence tests for treatment planning, classification, and placement decisions: Recent empirical findings and future directions. *School Psychology Quarterly, 12*, 249–267.

Kavale, K. A., Holdnack, J. A., & Mostert, M. P. (2005). Responsiveness to intervention and the identification of specific learning disability: A critique and alternative proposal. *Learning Disability Quarterly, 28*, 2–16.

National Association of School Psychology. (2005). *IDEA information.* Retrieved August 19, 2005, from http://www.nasponline. org/advocacy/IDEAinformation.html

National Research Center on Learning Disabilities. (NRCLD). (2005). *Learning disabilities summit.* Retrieved August, 29, 2005, from http://www.nrcld.org/resources/ldsummit/fuchs4.shtml

National Research Center on Learning Disabilities (NRCLD). (2004). Retrieved August 19, 2005, from http://www.nrcld .org/publications/papers/mellard.shtml

Prasse, D. P. (2002). Best practices in school psychology and the law. In A. Thomas & J. Grimes (Eds.), *Best practices in school psychology* (4th ed., Vol. 1, pp. 57–76). Bethesda, MD: National Association of School Psychologists.

Reschly, D. J. (2000). The present and future status of school psychology in the United States. *School Psychology Review, 29*, 507–522.

Reschly, D. J., & Ysseldyke, J. E. (2002). Paradigm shift: The past is not the future. In A. Thomas & J. Grimes (Eds.), *Best practices in school psychology* (4th ed., Vol. 1, pp. 3–20). Bethesda, MD: National Association of School Psychologists.

Rice, S. (2002). The social construction of "disabilities": The role of law. *Educational Studies, 33*, 169–180.

Salvia, J., & Ysseldyke, J. E. (1985). *Assessment in special and remedial education* (3rd ed.). Boston: Houghton Mifflin.

U.S. Department of Education. (2004). *Laws and policy: Individuals with Disabilities Education Improvement Act of 2004 (sec. 602).* Retrieved August 29, 2005, from http://thomas.loc.gov/ egi-bin/query/z?c108:h.1350.enr:

DANIELLE EDELSTON
SAGE THORNTON
*University of California,
Riverside*

# LEARNING DISABILITIES, PROBLEMS IN DEFINITION OF

There are five reasons why educators have difficulty with identifying children with specific learning disabilities. First, many people have equated learning disabilities with any kind of learning problem. This has tended to obscure the target population. Second, there is no single observable characteristic or syndrome of behaviors that is typical of a learning-disabled child, because these children present a variety of diverse behavioral symptoms. Third, each child has his or her own unique learning pattern. The behavioral symptoms depend on the kind of disability, its severity, the child's intact abilities, and how the child tries to cope with the problem. Fourth, some of the behavioral symptoms of specific learning disabilities might also arise from visual or bearing impairments, mental retardation, emotional disturbances, social maladjustment, health problems, cultural differences, family problems, or poor instruction. Fifth, when a child is multiply handicapped and has other problems in addition to a specific learning disability, the presence of the learning disability may be overlooked because attention is drawn to the more obvious problems in health, vision, hearing, and so on. The more subtle learning disability sometimes remains undetected.

The recognition of specific learning disabilities as a type of disability is relatively recent. The term became popular in 1963 when representatives of several parent organizations dealing with brain-injured and severely disabled children met in Chicago to discuss their mutual problems and to establish a national organization. The concept and label were introduced to include a large group of children who did not fit other categories of handicapping conditions, but who did need help in acquiring school skills.

In the years since 1963, many people have tried to define learning disabilities, but no one has yet developed a definition that is acceptable to everyone. Professionals working with learning-disabled students tend to define learning disabilities from their own professional points of view. Different definitions, therefore, emphasized different aspects of learning disabilities, such as neurological damage in the central nervous system, academic failure, visual perceptual disorders, language disorders, psychological process dysfunctions, behavioral symptoms, and impaired learning efficiency.

The literature reflects over 50 items to describe learning-disabled students; Vaughn and Hodges (1973) reported 38 different definitions, and more are now evident, especially on various Web sites.

The creation of a federal definition of learning disabilities has helped reduce the number of terms and definitions in use, but this definition has serious limitations. The federal definition of learning disabilities included in IDEA reads:

> The term "children with specific learning disabilities" means those children who have a disorder in one or more of the basic psychological processes involved in understanding or in using language, spoken or written, which disorder may manifest itself in imperfect ability to listen, think, speak, read, write, spell, or do mathematical calculations. Such disorders include such conditions as perceptual handicaps, brain injury, minimal brain dysfunction, dyslexia, and developmental aphasia. Such term does not include children who have learning problems which are primarily the result of visual, hearing, or motor handicaps, of mental retardation, of emotional disturbance, or of environmental, cultural, or economic disadvantage.

Forty-eight states and the District of Columbia define learning disabilities. Two states do not define the learning-disabled population but serve them through noncategorical programs. Most states and the District of Columbia use the federal definition verbatim. An analysis of the federal definition, the modified definitions, and the "original" definitions written by states revealed five major components that might be included in a definition of learning disability. These components are (1) failure to achieve; (2) psychological process; (3) exclusionary; (4) significant discrepancy; and (5) etiological (Chalfant & Pysh, 1984).

Academic failure refers to difficulty in learning to read, write, spell, compute arithmetic, acquire receptive and expressive language, or obtain visual-motor coordination in other performance tasks. The federal definition's emphasis on academic failure has included thousands of underachieving, slow-learning, poorly motivated, conduct-disordered, culturally different students in the category of specific learning disabilities. Because these students typically fall further behind academically as they progress through school, their identification in secondary schools increases.

With 46 states including references to achievement failure in their definitions, it is easy to understand how states may fail to recognize gifted students who have a specific learning disability. Gifted students may not have academic failures, but may have a discrepancy between potential and achievement that may require either special education services or the use of special classroom strategies.

There are many factors that could contribute to task failure; this makes it important to identify all children who are failing, regardless of cause. This can be done through achievement tests, checklists, screening devices, or teacher referrals. Referrals for individual assessment should not be made, however, until classroom teachers have (1) carefully thought through the child's problems; (2) made special efforts to help the child; (3) sought advice and support from other teachers or child study teams within the building; and (4) failed to help the child.

By trying to teach children individually, teachers often are able to discover whether children are failing to learn academic skills because of poor attendance, frequent moving from school to school, bilingualism, poor instruction, cultural deprivation, or other environmental factors. Thus classroom teachers can begin the process of identification by describing task failure and identifying environmental or instructional factors that may be contributing to the child's problem.

The exclusionary component refers to the handicapping conditions, other than learning disabilities, that cause problems in learning. These include mental retardation; visual impairment; hearing impairment; social-emotional problems; physical problems; poor instruction; cultural or environmental factors; and physical problems.

The student's learning problem must be evaluated to determine whether the difficulty is due to a specific learning disability or to some other handicapping condition. To be eligible for special education services because of a learning disability, the student's primary problem must be a specific learning disability. It is necessary, therefore, to rule out or exclude all other factors that might cause a similar problem.

It is important to understand, however, that learning disabilities sometimes occur in combination with other problems. A visually impaired child, for example, might have difficulty in processing auditory or haptic information; and a hearing-impaired child might have difficulty in processing visual information. Children with multiple disabilities should receive multiple services, because the extent and kinds of services needed may be quite different for each handicapping condition.

The specific criteria for the exclusionary impairments varies from state to state. Although guidelines are rather precise about the criteria for visual and hearing impairments, mental retardation, and motor and health impairments, criteria are not clearly delineated for slow learners, social and emotional maladjustment, and cultural, environmental, and economic factors. Variation from one state to another and imprecise criteria result in inappropriate inclusion or exclusion from services for the learning disabled and further confuse the defining of the population in question.

Although the etiology of learning disabilities is included

in the definition of learning disabilities by 44 states, its role as a criterion for supporting the identification of a learning disability is minimal. Most state guidelines mention the need to review a student's developmental history and medical information as they relate to the student's daily functioning. Among the etiological factors frequently mentioned as being found among learning disabled students are:

- A history of brain injury or neurological problems
- Motor coordination problems
- Slow speech and language development
- Immature social and emotional development
- Hyperactivity or hypoactivity
- Frequent periods of illness or absenteeism from school
- Surgery at an early age
- Early symptoms such as infant or early childhood problems in feeding or sleeping, temper tantrums, frequent crying, prenatal or natal difficulties, low birth weight, or premature birth

Information or data concerning the physiological and medical status of a student is in the realm of the physician. However, educators can obtain important information through interviews with parents, reviews of developmental history, and identification of any information that might be a contributing factor to learning disabilities. Cooperation with the medical profession may link the student's classroom behavior to etiological factors that might contribute to a learning disability. This information may not help the teacher address the problems of the learning disabled, but it may help the multidisciplinary team in distinguishing which students are learning disabled (Chalfant, 1984).

One characteristic of the student with a specific learning disability is a severe discrepancy between current achievement and intellectual potential. The finding of a discrepancy between achievement and potential alone, however, does not identify a learning-disabled student, since such a discrepancy also occurs among students whose underachievement is due to frequent absences from school; frequent family relocations; negative attitudes toward school; little motivation; family problems in the home; or instructional discontinuity of any kind. Students with such problems also need help. The basic needs of these students differ from the needs of learning-disabled students. These needs can often be met within the regular classroom or through regular education alternative programs within regular education.

Five major approaches are used to determine discrepancies between achievement and potential. With informal estimates, it is possible to obtain a rough estimate of a discrepancy between a student's level of achievement and his or her intellectual potential. This can be done through observation, by using graded-level materials, or by estimating the level of listening comprehension or understanding

by asking the student to answer questions that most students of the same chronological age can answer. However, informal procedures for comparing estimated achievement with estimated potential have several disadvantages. They are subjective, arbitrary, and difficult to defend legally, and they need to be confirmed through more accurate, standardized procedures.

Grade-level discrepancy models allow the comparison of grade-level placement and achievement for the purpose of determining whether a discrepancy exists. This can be done by using a constant deviation, such as achievement of 1 or 2 years below grade placement. Although this method is easy to use, it does not take into account the number of years a student has been enrolled in school, or that a 1-year discrepancy in the eighth grade is not as significant as a 1-year discrepancy in the second grade. A second method for determining deviation from grade level is to increase the magnitude of allowed deviation as grade placement increases. Grade discrepancy models tend to overidentify students who are slow learners or borderline mentally retarded. Many of these students are functioning academically at a level appropriate to their age and intellectual ability. Also, students with high IQs are less likely to be identified as discrepant achievers.

Achievement level expectancy formulas have been used to quantify achievement expectancy level. Unfortunately, each formula emphasizes different kinds of variables, such as number of years in school, grade age, mental age, intelligence quotient, and chronological age, and includes the addition, subtraction, or division of various constant numbers. Achievement level discrepancy models identify severe cases of discrepancies, but are dependent on questionable scores from intelligence tests. These formulas fail to account for the number of years a student has attended school and rely on an arbitrary severity level. Other statistical problems are errors of measurement, norm group comparability, and regression toward the mean (Cone & Wilson, 1981). Students in the dull-normal IQ range of 80 to 90 are more likely to be identified as having a discrepancy than are students scoring 90 or above. Also, students under 8 years of age are more likely to be identified than older students (Danielson & Bauer, 1978).

With standard score discrepancy models, test scores are converted into standard scores with the same mean and standard deviation. The conversion of raw scores to standard scores allows for the comparison of scores across tests, subtests, age, and grade levels (Erickson, 1975). While standard score comparison methods answer many of the statistical criticisms associated with expectancy formulas, they do not take into account the effects of regression of IQ on achievement.

Regression models are used to determine discrepancy between achievement and potential. They take into account the phenomenon of regression toward the mean. It is assumed that regression formulas reduce overidentification of children with IQs over 100, and underidentification of children with IQs below 100 (the opposite of the case for expectancy formulas). In addition, standard score procedures, emphasizing regressive analysis, seem to be more statistically appropriate for quantifying severe discrepancies between aptitude and achievement.

Some of the major concerns about analysis follow:

1. "Regression is a precise sophisticated technique being used on tests that are gross measures of behavior" (Lerner, 1984).

2. Regression has an inherent weakness as a way to quantify discrepancy because the intelligence tests that are used have low reliability and fail to meet acceptable psychometric standards (Salvia & Ysseldyke, 1981; Shepard, 1980).

3. There are disagreements among knowledgeable statisticians and psychometrists about certain statistical derivations, concepts, and assumptions with respect to regression. It is not surprising, therefore, that many administrators, special education personnel, teachers, and parents do not understand, use, or interpret regression analysis procedures and results.

4. There is failure to account for the number of years a student has been in school.

5. Although the regression procedure makes no assumptions about the appropriateness of a given severity level, selection of an arbitrary severity level is an arbitrary decision.

6. There is lack of teacher preparation for the use of a formula.

7. There is difficulty in determining when special services should be discontinued.

Advocates for the use of regression would take issue with several of these concerns (e.g., see Reynolds, 1984). Regression is not seen as a precise, sophisticated technique, but as a quantitative reflection of what actually occurs in test data. Also, failure to account for the number of years a student has been in school should not be addressed in a formula; retention is a legitimate regular education intervention and students should not be held accountable for material to which they may not have been exposed.

The presence of a severe discrepancy between achievement and potential is not a sufficient condition for identifying a learning disability. Mellard et al. (1983) and Reynolds (1984) point out that a discrepancy yields only statistical information and must be based on more than one simple calculation by formula involving an IQ. The educational significance of any score must be considered independently of the discrepancy model.

Lerner (1984) points out that eligibility for special education services is and should be a value judgment and should not be made solely by measurement experts. There are many considerations that cannot be placed in a formula that

should be considered by administrators, psychologists, special educators, teachers, parents, and so on. The decision to determine eligibility should be made by a multidisciplinary team and be based on observation of school performance and behavior, informal assessment, responsiveness to instruction, and standardized test scores. Regression analysis is one part of the process and should be kept in perspective.

The basic factor in identifying a learning-disabled person is a disorder in one or more of the psychological processes of attention, memory, perceptual ability, thinking, or oral language. Many educators do not have a working knowledge of these psychological processes or how to assess them. It is not possible to observe psychological processes directly. Only inferences about these processes can be made from observation. At present, there is a lack of reliable and valid instruments for assessing and measuring psychological processes. There are three approaches used to determine whether there may be a disorder in one or more of the psychological processes: observing and recording behavioral symptoms; using an informal task-process checklist; and employing standardized tests (Chalfant, 1984).

A list of behavioral characteristics that are symptomatic of possible psychological process disorders is sometimes used. Such lists should be accompanied by criteria for determining a possible process disorder. Another approach is to develop categories of psychological processes believed to be most closely related to school performance. These categories either include detailed behavioral characteristics or are presented in a question format to help direct the diagnostician or teacher to the study of certain behaviors. A task process checklist can be prepared for each academic area. The academic tasks are broken down into subskills. Behaviors are listed for each subskill that might be symptomatic of a processing disability. The teacher checks on whether the student displays these symptoms while performing failed tasks. These screening procedures provide guidelines for observable behaviors that sometimes help educators to recognize students who may be learning disabled. It is necessary, however, to conduct a close evaluation through more extensive assessment procedures.

Informal task-process assessment can be used to determine the possibility of a psychological process disorder. There are five steps. First, select the academic task with which the student is having difficulty. Second, informally assess and rule out other contributing factors such as instructional, cultural, or environmental factors, sensory impairment, intellectual impairment, physical or health problems, or social-emotional maladjustment. Third, break the academic task down into its subtasks. Fourth, determine which psychological processes or developmental abilities are involved in the task. Fifth, assess the processes that are involved in each subtask through informal procedures on several tasks. In this way it is often possible to identify possible process disorders that can be confirmed by the results of standardized tests.

The results of individually administered intelligence tests are analyzed to determine whether a student is learning disabled. An individually administered intelligence test samples many different aspects of verbal and nonverbal mental functioning and provides a measure of general ability. An analysis and grouping of subtest scores can give a clearer interpretation of intraindividual cognitive strengths and weaknesses and provide a measure of general ability.

Specialized abilities tests designed to assess psychological processes are often listed. These tests are in special areas such as language functioning; auditory discrimination; auditory processing; kinesthetic processing; visual processing; and visual-motor integration. Part of the problem with many tests of specialized abilities is that they are not related to a particular academic or school-related task (with the exception of listening tests, comprehension tests, and language tests), and therefore many educators do not know how to relate the results of many specialized tests to day-to-day tasks and behavior in the classroom. For young children, greater reliance should be placed on the developmental scales supported by observation of child behavior at home and at school. Anecdotal records and rating scales also are helpful.

It is not enough to diagnose a disability in a psychological process on the basis of one or two test scores. The presence of a process disability must be validated by having the student perform tasks that require the use of the process in question. If a process disability exists, for example, a student who has difficulty in recalling and repeating what he or she has heard can be expected to have difficulty in remembering names, learning the multiplication tables by rote, or any task that requires auditory recall.

To assure a nonbiased assessment for the culturally or linguistically different student, the multidisciplinary team should include measures of adaptive behavior, criterion-referenced tests, or teacher-made tests suitable for the individual student.

Pending regulations (as of this writing) for implementing the IDEIA, propose to solve the problems of definition of learning disability by allow diagnosis on the basis of Response to Intervention (RTI).

According to Fuchs et al. (2003), RTI may be described as follows.

1. Students are provided with "generally effective" instruction by their classroom teacher
2. Their progress is monitored
3. Those who do not respond get something else, or something more, from their teacher or someone else
4. Again, their progress is monitored
5. Those who still do not respond either qualify for special education or for special education evaluation. (p. 159)

Applying the RTI method, however, is quite controversial, and is seen as premature by many, including critics of the discrepancy approach to defining learning disabilities. Reynolds (2005) noted the following issues in applying RTI to learning disability identification.

1. RTI, based on discrepancy from grade level, is simply, at its root, a special case of severe discrepancy analysis that assumes everyone is of equal ability or academic aptitude.
2. RTI creates ability tracking in essence whereby students with IQs below 90 will be greatly disproportionately identified as having a specific learning disability.
3. RTI ignores the needs of students with academic aptitude in the top 10 percent of the student population, in particular those who are able to remain on grade level in an area while excelling in most other academic areas and those who are held back academically due to their struggles within a specific academic domain, such as reading or math.
4. RTI, while clearly allowable and promoted under the recent revisions to IDEA, entirely ignores the processing disorder component of the definition of learning disability.
5. RTI is a model of diagnosis by treatment failure, which has long been proven a poor model in medicine.
6. RTI ignores the common possibility of other problems, such as emotional disturbance, ADHD, and the like, that may be responsible for the educational needs of the referred student, since it bypasses the comprehensive assessment of the student, thus promoting misdiagnosis and mistreatment.
7. RTI promotes a one-size-fits-all approach to intervention and remediation that ignores over 100 years of research on individual differences.
8. RTI assumes the regular classroom instruction provided to date has not been evidence or science based; that is, that the regular education teacher does not understand instructional methods or know how to teach effectively.

Reynolds (2005) subsequently concluded that RTI, while a very useful and praiseworthy approach to prereferral intervention, was not a promising model for diagnosis or classification. Additional problems with RTI exist as well.

RTI does not appear at this time to meet modern scientific standards of evidence as espoused by the U.S. Department of Education Institute for Education Sciences, in that studies of RTI have not included control groups, so that placebo, Hawthorne, or other effects are controlled. Following a review of the empirical literature on RTI, with special attention to its effectiveness and feasibility, Fuchs, Mock, Morgan, and Young (2003) reached the following conclusions:

On the one hand, a consensus grows that the IQ-achievement discrepancy should be abandoned as a marker of the disability. On the other hand, as we have tried to make clear, there is an absence of a validated replacement. (p. 168)

... more needs to be understood before RTI may be viewed as a valid means of identifying students with LD. (p. 157)

RTI also lacks a consistent means of determining responsiveness, and the application of different methods identifies different children, which was a common criticism of severe discrepancy criteria; that is, the method is unreliable and inconsistently applied. Fuchs, Fuchs, and Compton (2004) concluded:

alternate methods of assessing responsiveness produce different prevalence rates of reading disability and different subsets of unresponsive children. This is important because a major criticism of IQ-achievement discrepancy as a method of LD identification is the unreliability of the diagnosis. (p. 225)

As demonstrated in our analyses ... different measurement systems using different criteria [all with reference to RTI] result in identification of different groups of students. The critical question is which combination of assessment components is most accurate for identifying children who will experience serious and chronic reading problems that prevent reading for meaning in the upper grades and impair their capacity to function successfully as adults. At this point, relatively little is known to answer this question when RTI is the assessment framework. (p. 226)

For now, it appears that RTI will add to the problems of defining learning disability and will not clarify the issues.

## REFERENCES

Chalfant, J. C., & Pysh, M. V. (1984). *Teacher assistance teams* (Workshop materials). Tucson: University of Arizona.

Cone, T. E., & Wilson, L. R. (1981). Quantifying a severe discrepancy: A critical analysis. *Learning Disabilities Quarterly, 4,* 359–371.

Danielson, L. C., & Bauer, J. N. (1978). A formula-based classification of learning disabled children: An examination of the issues. *Journal of Learning Disabilities, 11,* 163–176.

Erickson, M. T. (1975). The Z-score discrepancy method for identifying reading disabled children. *Journal of Learning Disabilities, 8,* 308–312.

Fuchs, D., Fuchs, L., & Compton, D. (2004). Identifying reading disabilities by responsiveness-to-instruction: Specifying measures and criteria. *Learning Disability Quarterly, 27,* 216–227.

Fuchs, D., Mock, D., Morgan, P., & Young, C. (2003). Responsiveness to intervention: Definitions, evidence, and implications for the learning disabilities construct. *Learning Disabilities Research and Practice, 18*(3), 157–171.

Lerner, J. W. (1984). *Learning disabilities: Theories, diagnosis, and teaching strategies* (4th ed.). Boston: Houghton Mifflin.

Mellard, D., Cooley, S., Poggio, J., & Deshler, D. (1983). *A comprehensive analysis of four discrepancy methods* (Research Monograph No. 15). Lawrence: University of Kansas Institute for Research in Learning Disabilities.

Reynolds, C. R. (1984). Critical measurement issues in learning disabilities. *Journal of Special Education, 18,* 451–476.

Reynolds, C. R. (2005, August). *Considerations in RTI as a method of diagnosis of learning disabilities.* Paper presented to the Annual Institute for Psychology in the schools of the American Psychological Association, Washington, DC.

Salvia, J., & Ysseldyke, J. E. (1981). *Assessment in special and remedial education* (2nd ed.). Boston: Houghton Mifflin.

Shepard, L. (1980). An evaluation of the regression discrepancy method for identifying children with learning disabilities. *Journal of Special Education, 14,* 79–91.

Vaughan, R. W., & Hodges, L. (1973). A statistical survey into a definition of learning disabilities: A search for acceptance. *Journal of Learning Disabilities, 6,* 658–669.

JAMES C. CHALFANT
*University of Arizona*
First and Second editions

CECIL R. REYNOLDS
*Texas A&M University*
Third edition

**KIRK, SAMUEL**
**LEARNING DISABILITIES**
**LEARNING DISABILITIES, SEVERE DISCREPANCY ANALYSIS IN**
**REGRESSION (STATISTICAL)**

# LEARNING DISABILITIES, SEVERE DISCREPANCY ANALYSIS IN

For many years, the diagnosis and evaluation of learning disabilities have been the subjects of almost constant debate in the professional, scholarly, and lay literature, especially since the passage of PL 94-142. The lack of consensus regarding the definition of learning disabilities is reflected in the day-to-day implementation of PL 94-142 and its successor, IDEA; in the absence of a readily acceptable definition, many school districts experience difficulty in deciding who is eligible for services. Both under- and overidentification of learning-disabled (LD) children create significant problems. Undercounting deprives LD children of special services to which they are entitled; overcounting results in the inappropriate placement of students who are not disabled, the loss of valuable staff time, and the increased expense of operating programs (Chalfant, 1984). Overcounting thus drains resources from other programs and students; if rampant enough, it could result in the demise of LD programs altogether. Errors in LD diagnosis will never be completely eliminated, but the amount of error must be reduced as much as possible while still ensuring that as many LD children as possible receive the special services to which they are entitled.

Two broad factors seem to determine who is LD: (1) the prevailing definition of LD and (2) how that definition is applied on a day-to-day basis. The rules and regulations of implementing PL 94-142 provided a definition of learning disability for use by all states receiving federal funds for special education programs, a definition retained in IDEA. According to this definition, the diagnosis

> is made based on (1) whether a child does not achieve commensurate with his or her age and ability when provided with appropriate educational experience, and (2) whether the child has a severe discrepancy between achievement and intellectual ability in one or more of seven areas relating to communication skills and mathematical abilities.
>
> These concepts are to be interpreted on a case by case basis by the qualified evaluation team members. The team must decide that the discrepancy is not primarily the result of (1) visual, hearing, or motor handicaps; (2) mental retardation; (3) emotional disturbance; or (4) environmental, cultural, or economic disadvantage. (*Federal Register,* 1977, p. 655082)

While this definition gives states some guidance, generally the field has regarded it as vague, subjective, and resulting in diagnosis by exclusion in many cases. Operationalization of the federal definition has varied tremendously across states, resulting in great confusion and disagreement over who should be served. In fact, the probability of LD diagnosis varies by a factor of nearly five purely as a function of the child's state of residence.

Chalfant's (1984) review of state education agency (SEA) definitions across the United States identifies five major components that appear to be reasonably consistent across states. The first is failure to achieve, or, perhaps more aptly, school failure. This represents a lack of adequate levels of academic attainment in one of the principal areas of school learning. It is sometimes seen as relative to grade placement and sometimes as relative to intellectual potential for achievement. The second component, psychological process disorders, refers to disorders in one or more of the basic psychological processes that are believed to underlie school learning. Though never listed or defined in their entirety, such processes include attention and concentration, understanding and use of written and spoken language, conceptualization, and, in general, information processing of all types.

Exclusionary criteria require that the observed symptoms not be due to other factors such as sensory incapacity, mental retardation, emotional disturbance, or educational, economic, or related disadvantages. Etiology, probably the most ill-defined of all factors, typically reflects the need to evaluate a student's medical and developmental histories in order to locate factors believed to be causative of learning disability. These include history of brain injury or substan-

tive neurological problems, motor coordination problems, hyperactivity, general immaturity, delayed speech and language development, and pre- or perinatal difficulties.

The last component, severe discrepancy, is specified in the federal regulations as a child's failure to achieve commensurate with age and ability to the extent that it results in a severe discrepancy between achievement and intellectual ability in one or more of the seven areas listed in the federal regulations. It is important to note that many states seem to ignore the "and ability" component of this definition, focusing only on the mean achievement level of all children of the same age, regardless of ability. Each of these criteria should have an important role in the diagnosis of learning disabilities and each requires work in terms of definitional and operational clarity.

Although all five components are important, the psychological process component and the severe discrepancy component are the most salient. The severe discrepancy criterion seems a particularly fruitful place to begin in the endeavor to improve methods of diagnosing learning disabilities. The severe discrepancy criterion is the most widely applied across the states. Further, in spite of the fact that severe discrepancy is easily measured relative to other components of the definition of LD, methods of applying the criterion vary widely across states (Reynolds, 1984).

The Federal Work Group on Critical Measurement Issues in Learning Disabilities has recommended a procedure to determine what constitutes a severe discrepancy (Reynolds, 1984); this model seems to be the one preferred by measurement experts (e.g., Willson & Reynolds, 1984).

## Objective Determination of a Severe Discrepancy

Clinical judgment has a revered and appropriate place in all diagnostic decision making, even though it has been amply demonstrated that statistical or actuarial approaches are always as good as—and often better than—clinical judgment (Meehl, 1954; Wiggins, 1981). Nevertheless, people should hold the central role of decision making about people. Clinical judgment, however, must be guided by statistical criteria whenever possible. Most states require the demonstration of a severe discrepancy for diagnosis of LD. It is important to note, however, that determining a severe discrepancy does not constitute the diagnosis of a learning disability; it only establishes that the primary symptom of LD exists. A severe discrepancy is a necessary but insufficient condition for a diagnosis of LD.

Two conditions must be met in order to establish that a severe discrepancy exists between two test scores for a particular child. First, the simple difference between the two scores must be reliable enough to yield great confidence that the difference is real and not owed to errors of measurement. Second, the difference must be large enough to be considered unusual among non-LD children.

Formulas (such as those considered by the Bureau of

Education for the Handicapped in early proposals for the federal regulations pertaining to learning disabilities diagnosis and placement) that in any way involve the use of grade or age equivalent scores can be quickly rejected as inadequate and misleading. The reasons for this are many; in short, age and grade equivalents do not possess adequate mathematical properties for use in discrepancy analysis (Angoff, 1971; Reynolds, 1981, 1984; Thorndike & Hagen, 1977). In essence, one cannot add, subtract, multiply, or divide age or grade equivalents. In addition, grade equivalents have other problems, including ease of misinterpretation, lack of relevance to curriculum markers (though they appear directly related), and general imprecision. Only standard scores have any real potential for answering the question of severe discrepancy. The following presentations deal only in terms of standardized or scaled scores, mostly of the age-corrected deviation score genre such as those employed by the current Wechsler scales, the Kaufman Assessment Battery for Children, and the Stanford-Binet Intelligence Scale–Fourth Edition.

### Reliability of a Discrepancy

As noted, the difference between the scores on the aptitude and achievement measures should be large enough to indicate, with a high degree of confidence (i.e., $p < .05$) that the difference is not due to chance or to errors of measurement. This requires an inferential statistical test of the hypothesis that the aptitude and achievement scores for the child in question are the same. Payne and Jones (1957) first introduced such a test to interpret individual tests of intelligence. More complex methods of calculation involving the reliabilities of the respective scales and the correlation between the two measures have been proffered (Salvia & Ysseldyke, 1981), but the simple computational formula shown is the algebraic equivalent of the more complex formulas (Reynolds & Willson, 1984; Willson & Reynolds, 1984; Zimmerman & Williams, 1982). The test for the significance of the difference of two obtained scores ($X_i - Y_i$) when the scores are expressed as $z$-scores is shown in equation 1:

$$(1) \qquad z = \frac{X_i - Y_i}{\sqrt{2 - r_{xx} - r_{yy}}}$$

There is no need to be intimidated by such equations; they are easy to calculate and require no more than beginning high-school algebra. In equation 1, $X_i$ and $Y_i$ represent the child's score on an aptitude measure $X$ and achievement measure $Y$; $r_{xx}$ and $r_{yy}$ represent the respective internal consistency reliability estimates for the two scales. These reliability estimates should be based on the responses of the standardization sample of each test and should be age appropriate for the child being evaluated; these are most often reported in test manuals. The test statistic is a $z$-score that is referred to the normal curve. For a one-tailed test

with $p = .05$, the critical value of $z = 1.65$. If $z > 1.65$, one can be sufficiently confident that the difference is not due to errors inherent in the two tests. Although a one-tailed test at the .05 level is probably justifiable for evaluating children referred for the possibility of a learning disability, a two-tailed test or a higher level of confidence (e.g., $p = .01$) would provide a more conservative measure of observed differences. For a two-tailed test, the critical value of $z$ at $p = .05$ is 1.96. All other critical values can be determined from any table of values of the normal curve.

After reliability has been established, the frequency of occurrence of a difference score must be evaluated. In the following discussion it will become clear that any discrepancy meeting the recommended criteria for frequency will of necessity also have met the criteria of reliability.

### Frequency of a Discrepancy

In evaluating the frequency of a discrepancy score, one must first decide what type of discrepancy score to assess (e.g., a residualized difference between predicted and obtained achievement scores, differences between estimated true scores and residualized true scores, true difference scores). In part, this decision depends on how one interprets the PL 94-142 definition of LD.

To establish that a discrepancy is severe, one must decide which of the following two questions to address:

1. Is there a severe discrepancy between this child's score on the achievement measure and the average achievement score of all other children with the same IQ as this child?

2. Is there a severe discrepancy between this child's measured achievement level and this child's measured level of intellectual functioning?

Both of these questions involve intraindividual variations in test performance (as opposed to purely interindividual norm-referenced comparisons). While this is obvious in the case of the second question, it may not be so evident for the first, which involves an intraindividual comparison because the determination of the average achievement level of all other children with the same IQ is based on the IQ obtained by the individual child in question. Though both are clearly intraindividual difference models, the mathematical models for answering these two questions differ considerably.

The former appears to be the most pressing question for evaluating children with learning problems and is the most consistent with the intent of IDEA, because the aptitude or ability we want to define is the aptitude or ability in academic areas (Reynolds, 1984, 1985). Evaluating the second question is easier in terms of calculation; one can follow Kaufman's (1979) or Reynolds and Gutkin's (1981) recommended methodology for assessing verbal-performance IQ differences on the Wechsler scales. However, this is only the case when no directionality is implied, as in evaluating within test scatter. This is certainly not the case in the diagnosis of learning disabilities, where we are clearly interested in the case in which aptitude exceeds achievement. Thus such models as Linn's Regression Estimates of True Discrepancy Scores, promulgated by the Kansas Institute for Research in Learning Disabilities, that do not account for the regression between aptitude and achievement will be faulty (see Reynolds, 1984, for a review of this model and its problems). An adequate evaluation of the second question, when directionality is known or assumed, is not yet known.

To assess the first question requires a regression model (i.e., a mathematical model that accounts for the imperfect relationship between IQ and achievement). Once regression effects have been assessed, the frequency of occurrence of the difference between the academic performance of the child in question and all other children having the same IQ can be determined. The correct model specifies that a severe discrepancy between aptitude $(X)$ and achievement $(Y)$ exists when, assuming the two tests are scaled to a common metric,

$$(2) \qquad \hat{Y} - Y_i \geq SD_y \sqrt{1 - r_{xy}^2},$$

where $Y_i$ is the child's achievement score

$X_i$ is the child's aptitude score

$\hat{Y}$ is the mean achievement score for all children with IQ $= X_i$

$SD_y$ is the standard deviation of $Y$

$z_a$ is the point on the normal curve corresponding to the relative frequency needed to denote "severity"

$r_{xy}^2$ is the square of the correlation between the aptitude achievement measures

It is necessary to use $\hat{Y} - Y_i$ as the discrepancy score because IQ and achievement are not perfectly correlated. For example, if the IQ and achievement tests have the same mean and standard deviation $\overline{X} = 100$; SD $= 15$), and if they correlate at .60, then the average achievement score of all children with IQs of 80 is 88 and of all children with IQs of 120 is 112. Therein lies the need to compare the achievement of the child in question with the achievement of all other children with the same IQ. The term $SD_y 1 - r_{xy}^2$ is the standard deviation of the distribution $\hat{Y} - Y_i$. Since this distribution is normal, we can estimate the frequency of occurrence of any given difference $(\hat{Y} - Y_i)$ that corresponds to the point of "severity" on the normal curve. Next, one must establish a value for $z_a$, a controversial matter in itself (also see Reynolds, 1986a).

## Establishing a Value for $z_a$ in Discrepancy Models

There are no strictly empirical criteria or research methods for establishing a value for $z_a$ because we have no consensus on a definition of LD. Specifically, we do not have a definition that would allow the generation of a true and globally accepted estimate of the prevalence of the group of disorders subsumed under the term LD. To complicate this issue further, there is no consensus in the LD community regarding whether it is better to risk overidentification (in the hope that nearly all truly LD children will receive services) or to risk underidentification (in order to avoid identifying non-LD children as LD). Taking the second argument to its extreme, the proper procedure would be to identify no children as LD, since the proportion of the population exhibiting this disorder is so small (see Schmidt, 1974). Consensus regarding the relative desirability of different diagnostic errors, coupled with valid estimates of prevalence, would provide considerable guidance in establishing a recommended value of $z_a$. In the absence of such guidance, one can rely only on rational, statistical, and traditional criteria.

It has been argued that a discrepancy should occur relatively infrequently in the normal population of individuals under consideration before being considered severe. Of course, "relatively infrequently" is as open to interpretation as "severe discrepancy." Strong tradition and rational argument in psychology, particularly in the field of mental retardation, argue for a definition of severity as two standard deviations from the mean of the distribution under consideration. With regard to a diagnosis of mental retardation, a score two standard deviations below the mean of an intelligence scale is defined as a severe intellectual problem, which is one of several criteria used for diagnosis. Qualitative descriptions such as mentally or cognitively deficient or lower extreme are common designations below this point in the distribution. At the opposite end of the curve, most definitions of intellectual giftedness refer to IQs falling two or more standard deviations above the mean, with descriptions such as very superior and upper extreme being common. Such practice is widely accepted.

In inferential statistics, confidence levels of .05 in an inference or judgment that a hypothesis can be rejected are the accepted standard. The .05 number corresponds roughly to two standard errors (for a two-tailed test) of the difference being evaluated, or to two standard deviations from the mean of the distribution of the test statistic employed (e.g., $z$, $t$, $F$). There is, thus, considerable precedent in the social as well as physical sciences for using a discrepancy of two standard deviations as a criterion for severity. For a .05 level of confidence, $z = 1.96$; this is close enough to the 2.00 value to support the use of 2.00. The actual 1.96 value is used principally to avoid more fractional alpha levels that may imply an unwarranted level of precision. Thus a value of $z_a = 2.00$ is recommended for determining whether a difference score is severe, though this value needs further qualification.

Since a difference score, whether defined as $\hat{Y} - Y_i$ or as some other value, will be less than perfectly reliable, one must somehow consider this unreliability in defining a severe discrepancy. If one considers underidentification a greater risk than overidentification, then there is a reasonable solution. Otherwise, as mentioned, one would minimize total errors by not identifying any children as LD. While several methods of accounting for potential unreliability in a discrepancy score are possible, the concept of the confidence interval is both popular and applicable. Adopting the traditional .05 confidence level for a one-tailed test, the value of $z_a$ corrected for unreliability can be defined as $z_a - 1.65$ SE (i.e., $z_a$ minus the $z$ corresponding to the one-tailed .05 confidence interval times the standard error of the relevant difference score). A one-tailed value is clearly appropriate here, since we must decide in advance which side to protect; both sides cannot be protected. Under these assumptions, a discrepancy is defined as severe when, substituting 2 for $z_a$

$$(3) \qquad \hat{Y} - Y_i \geq (2SD_y \sqrt{1 - r_{xy}^2}) - 1.65SE_{\hat{Y}-Y_i}.$$

The calculation of the standard error of $Y - Y_i$ is given in Reynolds (1984). Its use is clearly optional, although it does seem advisable to account for error in the process. It is important to note here that this is not the type of measurement error assessed by equation 1. This calculation allows us to identify more children than are likely to be true LD children; on the other hand, it accounts for many possible inaccuracies in the process that might inhibit identification of a truly LD child. The other four components of the most prevalent LD definitions, as previously presented, may then be evaluated to make the final judgment regarding whether or not a child is entitled to and needs services for the learning disabled.

The procedure outlined can objectify determination of a severe discrepancy in LD diagnosis. We may think that with regard to LD diagnosis we "know one when we see one," but if there is no "severe discrepancy," chances are we are wrong, and statistical guidance is necessary to aid human judgment.

The procedure outlined provides guidance for the objective determination of severe discrepancy. A computer program by Reynolds and Stowe (1985) will perform these analyses with all tests in use. It is crucial to bear in mind, however, that mathematical manipulations cannot transform the quality of the initial data.

## Quality of the Input Data

The quality of the input or test data used is crucial in assessing a discrepancy. Tests with poor psychometric characteristics can be misleading or can fail to detect a severe discrepancy. The following standards provide guidelines for choosing tests for use in the assessment of a potentially severe discrepancy. Though one will not always be able to choose tests meeting all of these standards, the more that can be met, the better. Of course, the characteristics of the

examiner(s), that is, the person(s) gathering the data, are of equal or possibly even greater import.

Tests should meet all requirements stated for assessment devices in the rules and regulations for implementing IDEA. This is not only a requirement of law, but is consistent with good professional practice. For example, administering a test in accordance with the instructions provided by the test maker is prerequisite to interpretation of test scores. If a standardized test is not given explicitly according to the instructions provided, inestimable amounts of error are introduced and norm-referenced scores are no longer interpretable. Thus all personnel evaluating children with educational problems must be conversant with the requirements of IDEA and adhere closely to these standards.

Normative data should meet contemporary standards of practice and be provided for a sufficiently large, nationally stratified random sample of children. In practice, this standard is nearly impossible to meet in all respects. Yet it is important to approximate it as closely as possible because standardization samples are crucial to establishing levels of performance for comparison purposes. To know that an individual answers 60 out of 100 questions correctly on an achievement test and 75 out of 100 questions correctly on an intelligence test conveys very little information. On which test did this individual earn the better score? Without knowledge of how a specified referent group would perform on these tests, one cannot answer this question.

Raw scores on a test, such as the number of correct responses or percentage correct, take on meaning only when evaluated against the performance of a normative or reference group. Once the appropriate reference population has been defined, a random sample of this group is tested under as nearly identical procedures as possible with the same administration, scoring, timing rules, and so forth for all. This group is known as the standardization sample. Ebel (1972) and Angoff (1971) have discussed a number of the conditions necessary for the appropriate development and use of normative reference group data.

Standardization samples for tests whose scores are being compared must be the same or highly comparable. Under the best of all conditions, the aptitude, achievement, or other tests on which children are being compared to themselves or to others should be conormed; that is, their standardization samples should consist of precisely the same children. When this is not possible, the norms for each test should be based on comparable samplings of the same population that meet all of the requirements for normative data. Standardization of the scales should have been undertaken in the same general time period, or else equating studies should be done. Scales normed on different samples and at different times are likely not to have the same mean and standard deviation across samples, even though they may be scaled to a common metric within their respective samples. This gives the two tests the appearance of actually having the same mean and the same standard deviation across samples, even though they may be scaled to a common metric within their respective samples. This gives the two tests the appearance of actually having the same mean and the same standard deviation, even though this may not at all be true. Ample evidence demonstrates that general levels of performance on aptitude and achievement measures vary in the population across time. As just one example, the population mean level of performance on the 1949 WISC is now very close to 116 and the 1974 revision (the WISC-R) now has a mean of nearly 110, though both are scaled within their respective normative samples to a mean of 100. Use of an achievement test normed in 1984 and an intelligence test normed in 1970 would add approximately three or four points to the size of the intelligence-achievement score difference for children with achievement levels below their IQ, purely as an artifact of when the two tests were standardized. In the face of the paucity of conormed scales, using highly similar samples tested at a similar time (or with equating studies completed) is acceptable, but conorming will always be superior provided the sample meets the conditions of normative data mentioned previously.

For diagnostic purposes, individually administered tests should be used. For purely screening purposes (e.g., referral for comprehensive evaluation), group-administered tests may be appropriate, though for young children, individual screening is preferable (Reynolds & Clark, 1983). For all children, but especially for disabled children, too many uncontrolled and unnoticed factors can affect test performance in an adverse manner. The test administrator is more likely to detect these factors under the conditions of individual assessment, where close observation of the child is possible. Further, individual assessment is more conducive to the use of special adaptations and testing procedures that may be required. Finally, individual assessment allows for careful clinical observation of the child during performance of a variety of academic and intellectual tasks; this is central to the proper assessment of learning problems for children of all ages (Kaufman, 1979; Reynolds & Clark, 1983). Generally, individual assessment affords better opportunity to maximize the child's performance and provides higher quality data from which to devise interventions.

In the measurement of aptitude, an individually administered test of general intellectual ability should be used. Such a test should sample a variety of intellectual skills; it should be a good measure of what psychologists refer to as "g," the general intellectual ability that permeates performance on all cognitive tasks. If ability tests are too specific, a single strength or weakness in the child's ability spectrum may inordinately influence the overall estimation of aptitude. It is also important to assess multiple abilities in deriving a remedial or instructional plan for a disabled student and in preventing ethnic bias (Reynolds, 1982). Specific ability measures (e.g., Bender-Gestalt, Columbia Mental Maturity Scale, Peabody Picture Vocabulary Test–III) and memory tests (e.g., Test of Memory and Learning; Reynolds & Bigler,

1994) constitute a necessary complement to a good assessment, but they are inadequate for estimating the general ability level of disabled children.

Age-based standard scores should be used for all measures, and all should be scaled to a common metric. The formulas for deriving severe discrepancies require the use of, at least, interval data. Scoring systems such as age or grade equivalents, which are essentially ordinal scales, should be avoided whenever score comparisons are to be made. Such scores may be helpful for purely descriptive purposes, but they are unacceptable for comparing scores of individuals or groups except under special, infrequent circumstances. Scores that are ratios of age and/or grade equivalents such as an intelligence quotient derived from the traditional formula of (MA/CA) × 100 are also inappropriate. Grade-based standard scores are inappropriate as well. The criteria for LD given in IDEA specifically denote a discrepancy in achievement for age and ability. Age is properly considered in age-based standard scores. The scores should be age corrected at appropriate intervals. Two to six months are reasonable ranges of time in age groupings for the derivation of standard scores, but in no case should groups extend more than 6 months for children below age 6 years or more than 12 months for children above age 6 years.

Age and grade equivalents remain immensely popular despite their serious psychometric deficiencies and misleading nature. In most instances relevant to diagnosis, grade equivalents are abused, because they are assumed to have scaled score properties when in fact they represent only an ordinal scale of measurement. Grade equivalents ignore the dispersion of scores about the mean when the dispersion is constantly changing from grade to grade. Under no circumstances do grade equivalents qualify as standard scores. The calculation of a grade equivalent is quite simple. When a test is administered to a group of children, the mean raw score is calculated at each grade level and this mean raw score then is called the grade equivalent score for a raw score of that magnitude. If the mean raw score for beginning fourth graders (grade 4.0) on a reading test is 37, then any person earning a score of 37 on the test is assigned a grade equivalent score of 4.0. If the mean raw score of fifth graders (grade 5.0) is 38, then a score of 38 would receive a grade equivalent of 5.0. A raw score of 37 could represent a grade equivalent of 3.8, 38 could be 4.0, and 39 could be 5.0. Thus, differences will be inconsistent across grades with regard to magnitude of the difference in grade equivalents produced by constant changes in raw scores.

The measures employed should demonstrate a high level of reliability, which should be documented in the technical manual accompanying the test. The specific scores employed in the various discrepancy formulas should have associated internal consistency reliability estimates (where possible) of no less than .80 and preferably of .90 or higher. Coefficient alpha is the recommended procedure for estimating reliability, and should be routinely reported for each age level in the standardization sample of the test at not more than 1-year intervals. It is recognized that alpha will not be appropriate for all measures. Test authors and publishers should routinely use alpha where appropriate and provide other reliability estimates as may be appropriate to the nature of the test. When alpha is not reported, an explanation should be given. Internal consistency reliability (e.g., alpha) will almost always be the most appropriate reliability estimate for intelligence and achievement tests. Internal consistency estimates are the most appropriate of all reliability estimates for these tests because they best determine the accuracy of test scores (Nunnally, 1981).

The validity coefficient, $r_{xy}$, which represents the relationship between the measures of aptitude and achievement, should be based on an appropriate sample. This sample should consist of a large, stratified, random sample of normally functioning children. A large sample is necessary to reduce the sampling error in $r_{xy}$ to an absolute minimum, since variations in $r_{xy}$ will affect the calculation of a severe discrepancy and affect the difference score distribution the most at the extremes of the distribution, the area of greatest concern. Normally functioning children are preferred for the samples because the definition of severe discrepancy is based in part on the frequency of occurrence of the discrepancy in the normal population. When conorming of aptitude and achievement measures is conducted, this problem is simplified greatly since $r_{xy}$ can be based on the standardization sample of the two measures (which should meet the standards of normative data) without any disabled children included. Some states use validity coefficients based on estimates derived from research using disabled children. This practice is not recommended, because the IQ and achievement score distributions of disabled children are not normal; thus they restrict the range of scores and alter the correlation between IQ and achievement, making it appear artificially smaller than it is in reality.

The validity of test score interpretations should be clearly established. Though clearly stated in the rules and regulations for IDEA, this requirement should receive special emphasis, particularly with regard to Cronbach's (1971) discussion of test validation. Validation with normal samples is insufficient for application to diagnosis of handicapping conditions; validity should be demonstrated for exceptional populations (for use of equations [2] and [3], however, $r_{xy}$ should again be based on a normal sample). This requirement is an urgent one, especially in certain areas of achievement where a paucity of adequate scales exists. To determine deviations from normalcy, validation with normal samples should typically be regarded as sufficient. This requirement does not require separate normative data for each handicapping condition. The generalizability of norms and of validity data is in part a function of the question one seeks to answer with the test data, and is ultimately an empirical question (Reynolds, 1986b; Reynolds, Gutkin, Elliot, & Witt, 1984).

Special technical considerations should be addressed when one uses performance-based measures of achievement (e.g., writing skill). Some measures, such as written expression, involve special problems of reliability and validity. For example, interrater reliability of scoring on any measure calling for judgments by the examiner should be reported and should be .85 to .90 or higher. This would also hold for such tasks as the Wechsler vocabulary and comprehension measures, in which examiners are frequently called on to make fine distinctions between the levels of quality of a response. Highly speeded and primarily memory-based tasks also will pose special technical problems that must be addressed.

Bias studies on the instruments in use should be reported. Criterion-related validity should receive emphasis in this regard, but not to the exclusion of other studies of bias. Bias should be addressed with respect to appropriate demographic variables that may moderate the test's validity. At a minimum, these should include race, sex, and socioeconomic status, though not necessarily simultaneously. In the assessment and diagnosis of LD in particular, sex bias needs to be investigated, since boys outnumber girls in classes for the learning disabled by about 3.5 to 1. The procedures for evaluating bias in all aspects of a test are presented in a comprehensive form in Jensen (1980). While measures that exhibit little or no statistical bias are the measures of choice, other measures can be used with the appropriate corrections.

All of the noted points should be considered in the evaluation of test data used for determining a severe discrepancy. It bears repeating that the discrepancy formulas presented here yield results that are only as reliable as the test data used in them. Integrally related to the quality of test data are the characteristics of the examiner; the next section explores this issue.

## Who Should Be Diagnosing LD

In one sense, the question of who should be diagnosing LD in the schools has been resolved by PL 94-142 and IDEA. According to the 1977 rules and regulations implementing this law, only the multidisciplinary team is empowered to diagnose handicapping conditions of any type in the schools. It remains legitimate to ask, however, who should be doing the primary assessment of the discrepancy criterion (as well as the psychological process criterion) and interpreting these results to the team? Job titles, education, and certification requirements for any given job in the schools vary greatly from state to state. This variation is troublesome, because the quality of the personnel conducting the diagnosis or interpreting it to the team and to the parents is as important to the diagnosis of LD as the quality of the data and the objectivity of the definition.

The task of LD diagnosis is the most difficult of all psychoeducational diagnostic tasks; thus the most highly trained personnel available should be reserved for assignment to evaluating potential LD children.

Although accurate diagnosis of LD in school-aged children is considered the most difficult type of diagnosis in the schools, it is precisely the area of evaluation and diagnosis most often relegated to the least qualified, most poorly trained diagnostic personnel. Arguments and data (Bennett, 1981; Bennett & Shepherd, 1982) clearly show that the learning disabilities specialists and diagnosticians commonly assigned the task of LD diagnosis do not possess the requisite knowledge of tests and measurements to allow them to interpret test scores adequately. On a test of beginning-level measurement concepts, Bennett and Shepherd's (1982) LD specialists answered barely 50 percent of the questions correctly. A group of first-year graduate students in an introductory measurement class answered more than 70 percent of the same questions correctly. Using the best-trained staff will not solve the problems involved in diagnosis and evaluation of LD children, but it will be a step in the right direction. Who precisely this is will vary from state to state and possibly even from district to district within states; the point is that this subject desperately needs attention.

## REFERENCES

Angoff, W. H. (1971). Scales, norms, and equivalent scores. In R. L. Thorndike (Ed.), *Educational measurement* (2nd ed.). Washington, DC: American Council on Education.

Bennett, R. E. (1981). Professional competence and the assessment of exceptional children. *Journal of Special Education, 15,* 437–446.

Bennett, R. E., & Shepherd, M. J. (1982). Basic measurement proficiency of learning disability specialists. *Learning Disability Quarterly, 5,* 177–184.

Chalfant, J. C. (1984). *Identifying learning disabled students: Guidelines for decision making.* Burlington, VT: Northeast Regional Resource Center.

Cronbach, L. J. (1971). Test validation. In R. L. Thorndike (Ed.), *Educational measurement* (2nd ed.). Washington, DC: American Council on Education.

Ebel, R. (1972). *Essentials of educational measurement.* Englewood Cliffs, NJ: Prentice Hall.

*Federal Register.* (1977). Rules and regulations for implementing Public Law 94-142, 42. Washington, DC: U.S. Government Printing Office.

Jensen, A. R. (1980). *Bias in mental testing.* New York: Free Press.

Kaufman, A. S. (1979). *Intelligent testing with the WISC-R.* New York: Wiley-Interscience.

Meehl, P. E. (1954). *Clinical versus statistical prediction.* Minneapolis: University of Minnesota Press.

Nunnally, J. (1981). *Psychometric theory* (2nd ed.). New York: McGraw-Hill.

Payne, R. W., & Jones, H. G. (1957). Statistics for the investigation of individual cases. *Journal of Clinical Psychology, 13,* 155–191.

Reynolds, C. R. (1981). The fallacy of "two years below grade level for age" as a diagnostic criterion for reading disorders. *Journal of School Psychology, 19,* 350–358.

Reynolds, C. R. (1982). The problem of bias in psychological assessment. In C. R. Reynolds & T. B. Gutkin (Eds.), *The handbook of school psychology.* New York: Wiley.

Reynolds, C. R. (1984). Critical measurement issues in learning disabilities. *Journal of Special Education, 18,* 451–476.

Reynolds, C. R. (1986a). Toward objective diagnosis of learning disabilities. *Special Services in the School, 5,* 161–176.

Reynolds, C. R. (1986b). Assessment of exceptional children. In R. T. Brown & C. R. Reynolds (Eds.), *Psychological perspectives on childhood exceptionality.* New York: Wiley-Interscience.

Reynolds, C. R., & Brown, R. T. (1984). An introduction to the issues. In C. R. Reynolds & R. T. Brown (Eds.), *Perspectives on bias in mental testing.* New York: Plenum.

Reynolds, C. R., & Clark, J. H. (1983). Assessment of cognitive abilities. In K. D. Paget & B. Bracken (Eds.), *Psychological assessment of preschool children.* New York: Grune & Stratton.

Reynolds, C. R., & Gutkin, T. B. (1981). Test scatter on the WPPSI: Normative analyses on the standardization sample. *Journal of Learning Disabilities, 14,* 460–464.

Reynolds, C. R., Gutkin, T. B., Elliot, S. N., & Witt, J. C. (1984). *School psychology: Essentials of theory and practice.* New York: Wiley.

Reynolds, C. R., & Stowe, M. (1985). *Severe discrepancy analysis.* Philadelphia: TRAIN.

Reynolds, C. R., & Willson, V. L. (1984, April). *Another look at aptitude-achievement discrepancies in the evaluation of learning disabilities.* Paper presented at the annual meeting of the National Council on Measurement in Education, New Orleans.

Salvia, J., & Ysseldyke, J. (1981). *Assessment in special and remedial education* (2nd ed.). Boston: Houghton Mifflin.

Schmidt, F. L. (1974). Probability and utility assumptions underlying use of the Strong Vocational Interest Blank. *Journal of Applied Psychology, 4,* 456–464.

Thorndike, R. L., & Hagen, E. (1977). *Measurement and evaluation in education and psychology.* New York: Wiley.

Wiggins, J. S. (1981). Clinical and statistical prediction: Where are we and where do we go from here? *Clinical Psychology Review, 1,* 3–18.

Willson, V. L., & Reynolds, C. R. (1984). Another look at evaluating aptitude achievement discrepancies in the diagnosis of learning disabilities. *Journal of Special Education, 18,* 477–487.

Zimmerman, D. W., & Williams, R. H. (1982). The relative error magnitude in three measures of change. *Psychometrika, 47,* 141–147.

CECIL R. REYNOLDS
*Texas A&M University*

**DEVIATION IQ**
**GRADE EQUIVALENTS**
**INTELLIGENCE TESTING**
**LEARNING DISABILITIES**

## LEARNING DISABILITIES, PROBLEMS IN DEFINITION OF RATIO IQ

## LEARNING DISABILITY QUARTERLY

*Learning Disability Quarterly* is the official journal of the Council for Learning Disabilities. A publication generally similar to the *Journal of Learning Disabilities,* this journal is more accessible to the frontline educator and equally valuable to the academic. Special issues relating to specific topics are not uncommon.

Among recent articles are "Identifying reading disability by responsiveness-to-instruction: Specifying measures and criteria," and "State SLD identification policies and practices." The journal's goal is to enhance the education and development of people with learning disabilities.

The quarterly also seeks papers in categories such as (1) techniques in identification, assessment, remediation, and programming; (2) reviews of literature relating directly to people with learning disabilities; (3) theory and discussion of pertinent issues; (4) original research with an applied focus; and (5) practices in personnel preparation.

MARIE ALMOND
*The University of Texas of the
Permian Basin*

RACHEL TOPLIS
*Falcon School District 49,
Colorado Springs, Colorado*

## LEARNING DISABILITY SUBTYPES

The search for a classification system for learning disability subtypes has been a problem of interest to education, psychology, pediatrics, and neurology for many years. Historically, researchers focused on the theory that there was such a thing as a learning-disabled child (Fisk & Rourke, 1983). Common theories reflected the concepts of neurological deficits, perceptual deficits, and language deficits. However, the notion of a singularity of cause, characteristics, and interventions began to be replaced in the early 1960s as researchers focused more on the heterogeneity of the LD population. It has been increasingly recognized over the last 30 years that the condition known as LD definitely reflects a highly heterogeneous array of developmental disorders rather than a single entity (Obrzut, 1995).

Kavale and Forness (1995) discuss the fact that research has demonstrated a variety of differences among LD subjects, spanning a wide variety of variables, and suggest that

there is more than one form of LD. They set forth that any unitary conception of LD can explain only a limited number of LD cases. More comprehensive descriptions of LD require multiple-syndrome conceptualizations. They state that a complete rendering of LD must include not only all the associated deficits, but also the interactions between the domains and variables. Any theoretical framework must make possible a unified organizational scheme for the entire pattern of deficits in LD.

Evidence is beginning to appear that subtyping research can be helpful in reducing the variance and complexity of findings in other areas of learning disability inquiry (Speece, 2003).

Many researchers have focused attention on the identification and description of LD by examining only academic performance, especially reading (Feagans, Short, & Meltzer, 1991). The two most common types of studies on reading subtypes address (1) the validity of separating poor readers according to discrepancies between reading and IQ scores (Morris et al., 1998) and (2) the application of multivariate statistical methods, such as cluster analysis, to sort profiles of neuropsychological and education test scores (Hooper & Willis, 1989; Rourke, 1985).

Concerns arise regarding classification based on IQ discrepancies, because of difficulty demonstrating the validity of separating poor readers according to discrepancies between reading scores and IQ. Multivariate statistical methods such as clustering have fallen into disfavor due to the variations in sampling and classification methods, as well as poor assessments of reliability and validity (Morris et al., 1998; Speece, 2003).

Stanovich and Siegel (1994) assert that poor reading is predicted best by deficits in phonological awareness skills, irrespective of intelligence and how reading is assessed. However, they question whether such core deficits in phonemic awareness form patterns in distinctive ways with other linguistic and cognitive deficits or whether these patterns of deficits represent subtypes that predict level of severity, developmental course, or response to treatment.

Siegel (1992) found that reading-disabled children, whether or not their reading was significantly below the level predicted by their IQ scores, experienced significant problems in phonological processing, short-term and working memory, and syntactic awareness. On the basis of that data, she argues that there does not seem to be a need to further differentiate between individuals with dyslexia and poor readers. Both of the groups are reading disabled and have deficits in phonological processing, verbal memory, and syntactic awareness.

Wolf, Pfeil, Lotz, and Biddle (1994) suggested that children with reading disability could be subgrouped based on problems exclusively with phonological awareness skills, rapid-serial-naming abilities, or in both domains. They hypothesized that children with unitary deficits in phonological language skills would show impairment in decoding, while children with only rapid-serial-naming deficits would have problems primarily with comprehension skills.

Castles and Coltheart (1993) suggested the subtypes of reading disability should be derived exclusively from research and theory on the mechanisms underlying word recognition. In summarizing this research, Stanovich, Siegel, and Gottardo (1997) suggested that phonological dyslexia was a robust subtype, characterized by problems reading both pseudowords and real words, which was persistent across definitions and age.

Although the majority of subtyping focuses on disabilities in the area of reading, Geary (1993) asserts that there are three general subtypes in the area of mathematical disabilities: those related to procedural errors, semantic memory difficulties, and visual/spatial difficulties. He presents that instruction and ability to retrieve basic facts from long-term memory might be considered a defining feature of arithmetic disability. Children with arithmetic disabilities tend to make more errors when retrieving basic facts from long-term memory than do their nondisabled peers.

According to Forness (1990), there are two major problems in creating LD subtypes: (1) measures or variables used to subtype are unreliable, and fail to account for a significant amount of the variance, and (2) most subgroups have little predictive power to external measures. Further and most importantly, Forness has suggested that the subgrouping enterprise has not resulted in substantiated classroom applications.

### REFERENCES

Castles, A., & Coltheart, M. (1993). Varieties of developmental dyslexia. *Cognition, 47,* 149–180.

Feagans, L. V., Short, E. J., & Meltzer, L. J. (Eds.). (1991). *Subtypes of learning disabilities: Theoretical perspectives and research.* Hillsdale, NJ: Erlbaum.

Fisk, J. L., & Rourke, B. P. (1983). Neuropsychological subtyping of learning-disabled children: History, methods, implications. *Journal of Learning Disabilities, 16,* 529–531.

Forness, S. R. (1990). Subtyping in learning disabilities: An introduction to the issues. In B. Keogh & H. L. Swanson (Eds.), *Learning disabilities, theoretical and research issues* (pp. 195–200). Hillsdale, NJ: Erlbaum.

Geary, D. (1993). Mathematical disabilities: Cognitive, neuropsychological, and genetic components. *Psychological Bulletin, 114,* 345–362.

Hooper, S. R., & Willis, W. G. (1989). *Learning disability subtyping: Neuropsychological foundations, conceptual models, and issues in clinical differentiation.* New York: Springer Verlag.

Kavale, K. A., & Forness, S. R. (1995). *The nature of learning disabilities: Critical elements of diagnosis and classification.* Mahwah, NJ: Erlbaum.

Morris, R. D., Shaywitz, S. E., Shankweiler, D. P., Katz, L., Stuebing, K. K., Fletcher, J. M., Lyon, G. R., Francis, D. J., & Shaywitz, B. A. (1998). Subtypes of reading disability: Variability around a phonological core. *Journal of Educational Psychology, 90,* 347–373.

Obrzut, J. E. (1995). Dynamic versus structural processing differences characterize laterality patterns of learning disabled children. *Developmental Neuropsychology, 11,* 467–484.

Rourke, B. P. (Ed.). (1985). *Neuropsychology of learning disabilities: Advances in subtype analysis.* New York: Guilford.

Siegel, L. S. (1992). An evaluation of the discrepancy definition of dyslexia. *Journal of Learning Disabilities, 25,* 618–629.

Speece, D. L. (2003). The methods of cluster analysis and the study of learning disabilities. In H. L. Swanson, K. Harris, & S. Graham (Eds.), *Handbook of learning disabilities* (pp. 501–513). New York: Guilford.

Stanovich, K. E., & Siegel, L. S. (1994). Phenotypic performance profile of children with reading disabilities: A regression-based test of the phonological core variable-difference model. *Journal of Educational Psychology, 1,* 24–53.

Stanovich, K. E., Siegel, L. S., & Gottardo, A. (1997). Converging evidence for phonological and surface subtypes of reading disability. *Journal of Educational Psychology, 89,* 114–128.

Wolf, M., Pfeil, C., Lotz, R., & Biddle, K. (1994). Towards a more universal understanding of the developmental dyslexias: The contribution of orthographic factors. In V. W. Berninger (Ed.), *The varieties of orthographic knowledge* (Vol. 1, pp. 137–173). Dordrecht, The Netherlands: Kluwer Academic.

KATHLEEN M. PHILLIPS
*University of California,
Riverside*

## LEARNING DISABILITIES
## LEARNING DISABILITIES, PROBLEMS IN DEFINITION OF

## LEARNING DISABLED ADULT STUDENTS

Much of the thinking about learning disabilities in adulthood is an extension of what was known about learning disabilities in children (Reiff, Gerber, & Ginsberg, 1997). Adults commonly recognized with learning disabilities demonstrate deficits in one or more of these general areas: processing written material, written expression, oral expression, mathematical computation and/or comprehension, reasoning and/or memory (Hawkins, 1992; Nolting, 1991). In general, reading rate, spelling, and the mechanics of writing are the most frequently occurring deficits in adults with LD, while problems with organization, time management, and self-esteem are often evident (Vogel, 1993).

During the 1980s, a dramatic increase occurred in the numbers of students with LD who attended 2- and 4-year colleges (Bursuck, Rose, Cowen, & Yahaya, 1989). This sharp growth was attributed to (1) Section 504 regulations of PL 93-112, which include access and services for persons with learning disabilities, as well as other disabling conditions, (2) large numbers of students labeled LD in grades K–12 as a consequence of PL 94-142, and (3) greater attention paid to transition planning and programming for employment or postsecondary education (or both) by special education services, vocational rehabilitation agencies, and parents of children with learning disabilities (Rose, 1991).

Adult students with LD have presented a particular challenge to admissions personnel at institutions with competitive admissions standards in their attempt to establish nondiscriminatory admissions procedures (Leonard, 1991). Some colleges and universities have instituted a special admissions process for those who identify themselves as learning disabled. Applicants are given the opportunity to provide additional data documenting their learning disabilities, and these data become part of the decision-making process. At other institutions without a special admissions process, applicants may voluntarily submit supplementary information, and admissions personnel may review these data with a learning disabilities consultant on campus before making an admissions decision (see Leonard, 1991, for a review).

The ACT/SAT now permits students with learning disabilities to take the exam with special accommodations (i.e., extra time, reader). Many LD students are not going to have the required GPA because of the very nature of their disability (DeDecker, 1993).

Colleges and universities are playing a unique role in preparing students with learning disabilities for their transition to and success in the workplace. Most colleges and universities have responded to the needs of students with LD by developing support services ranging from minimal compliance to comprehensive programs (Gerber, Reiff, & Ginsberg, 1996).

Traditionally, services for adult students with learning disabilities have focused on relatively short-term academic goals. Now assistance and services focusing on more long-reaching effects are offered for students with learning disabilities (Gerber & Brown, 1997). Most current programs include career-related services as well as academic and counseling services. Many current support services incorporate a philosophy that respects the rights of students with learning disabilities to make decisions.

Elements of effective strategies that lead to successful adults with learning disability are believed to involve self determination, independence, self-advocacy, goal setting, career planning, and problem-solving skills. Support services are trying to give careful attention to how these elements are incorporated into the overall program model and day-to-day activities (Gerber & Brown, 1997).

## REFERENCES

Bursuck, W. D., Rose, E., Cowen, S., & Yahaya, M. A. (1989). Nationwide survey of postsecondary education services for students with learning disabilities. *Exceptional Children, 56*(3), 236–245.

DeDecker, S. (1993). *The college-bound L.D. student—let's bury the myths forever.* Paper presented at the Learning Disabilities of America Conference.

Gerber, P. J., & Brown, D. S. (1997). *Learning disabilities and employment.* Austin, TX: PRO-ED.

Gerber, P. J., Reiff, H. B., & Ginsberg, R. (1996). Reframing the learning disabilities experience. *Journal of Learning Disabilities, 29,* 98–101.

Hawkins, B. D. (1992). CCs keep pace with enrollment growth by meeting the needs of the learning-disabled. *Community College Week, 5*(3), 2–4.

Leonard, F. C. (1991). Using Wechsler data to predict success for learning disabled college students. *Learning Disabilities Research and Practice, 6,* 17–24.

Nolting, P. D. (1991). *Math and the learning disabled student.* Pompano Beach, FL: Academic Success Press.

Reiff, H. B., Gerber, P. J., & Ginsberg, R. (1997). *Exceeding expectations: Successful adults with learning disabilities.* Austin, TX: PRO-ED.

Rose, E. (1991). Project TAPE: A model of technical assistance for service providers of college students with learning disabilities. *Learning Disabilities Research and Practice, 6,* 25–33.

Vogel, S. A. (1993). A retrospective and prospective view of postsecondary education for adults with learning disabilities. In S. A. Vogel & P. B. Adelman (Eds.), *Success for college students with learning disabilities* (pp. 3–20). New York: Springer-Verlag.

XINHUA ZHENG
*University of California,
Riverside*

## LEARNING DISABILITIES

# LEARNING DISABLED COLLEGE STUDENTS

The provisions of the Rehabilitation Act of 1973, Public Law 102-569, Section 504 assure that qualified persons with disabilities may not be denied equal access, benefits, or discrimination from any federally funded program or activity. This mandate is extended by the Americans with Disabilities Act (ADA) of 1990, which also prohibits discrimination based on disability. More specifically, Title II of the ADA requires equal opportunity to benefit from state and government programs, services, or activities, including education (ADA, 2004). Unlike the Individuals with Disabilities Education Improvement Act of 2004 (IDEIA; 2004), which ensures a free and appropriate education to all kindergarten through twelfth grade students, postsecondary education students, including those with disabilities, must meet academic entrance criteria. Institutions are required to make reasonable changes to policies, practices, and procedures in the entrance process for students with disabilities to avoid discrimination. Between 1988 and 2000, 6 to 8 percent of freshmen in higher education institutions had a disability. Nearly half of college students with disabilities (63 percent at community colleges, 40 percent at universities) required remedial course work as freshmen. Their highest reported incidences of remedial tutoring in high school and expected academic accommodations in college were in mathematics, followed by English (American Council on Education, 2001; Venezia, Kirst, & Antonio, 2003).

For students in kindergarten through twelfth grade, the IDEIA (2004) provides federal standards for determining disabilities criteria, monitoring progress, and ensuring periodic reevaluation of student service needs. However, at the college level, provisions for students with disabilities are governed by the Rehabilitation Act of 1973 and the ADA, which do not specify disabilities covered or criteria for learning disabilities (U.S. Department of Justice, 2004).

Criteria are provided by the *Diagnostic and Statistical Manual of Mental Disorders* (American Psychiatric Association, 2000) and two organizations, the Association on Higher Education and Disability and the National Joint Committee on Learning Disabilities (Association on Higher Education and Disability Ad Hoc Committee on Learning Disabilities, 1997; National Joint Committee on Learning Disabilities, 1999). Among entering college students, learning disabilities initially may be documented with proof of a previous individual education plan, 504 plan, or diagnosis report. However, an additional psychoeducational evaluation often is required, to establish a disability's impact on college performance. The assessment components can focus on intellectual achievement, information processing, neuropsychological, learning styles and strategies, and mental health qualities. Learning disability diagnosis typically is dependent on establishing a significant difference between academic aptitude and achievement together with a processing deficit that impairs academic functioning.

College students may exhibit the same disabilities diagnosed in elementary or secondary school. However, the effects of a disability may become apparent upon entering college, because postsecondary education offers a more advanced range of curriculum content and more challenging achievement expectations. Learning disabilities may include reading, math, and writing. Other disabilities may include physical limitations in hearing, vision, mobility, and fine or gross motor skill deficits. Postsecondary students may also exhibit behavioral difficulties as a result of Attention-Deficit/Hyperactivity Disorder (ADHD) or serious mental illness (e.g., depression, anxiety) that impede learning.

Policies governing diagnosis and services for students vary by institution. Some institutions offer a wide range of resources, including evaluations, tutoring, study workshops, and mental health counseling centers. Others may have more limited resources and offer fewer services. Some special education placement categories (e.g., emotionally handicapped) and service models (e.g., pull-out services, self-contained) are not applicable in postsecondary institutions.

Accommodation decisions typically are made by an office providing student services. Decisions typically rely on information from both a student and a professional evaluation. The student often provides information on his or her prior diagnoses, medical history, the efficacy of previous interventions, study habits, time management techniques, coping skills particular to college adjustment, and career goal planning. Knowledge of career goals can be crucial, in that accommodations may include course substitutions that may result in limiting access to a chosen profession. Other possible accommodations include extended time on tests or assignments, notetakers, large print, taped lectures/books, reduced course loads, alternative test formats, scribe, software, spellchecker, copies of faculty lecture overheads, captioning, interpreters, extra course drops, and excused absences if related to disability (ADA Compliance Office, 2002). Accommodations may be applicable to state and national qualifying examinations (e.g., admissions test for graduate programs) as well as classroom work. Documentation of accommodation needs is provided to students by college disabilities offices. However, unlike kindergarten through twelfth grade intervention plans, college students have greater responsibility for initiating their use of resources, informing the college ADA office of their needs, reviewing the inadequacy of accommodation strategies with the personnel in the disabilities office, informing faculty of needed accommodations, and self-monitoring their own progress.

## REFERENCES

Americans with Disabilities Act Compliance Office. (2002). *Providing services and access to students and employees with disabilities in higher education: Effective and reasonable accommodations.* Gainesville: University of Florida.

American Council on Education. (2001). *College freshman with disabilities: A biennial statistical profile.* Washington, DC: Carol Henderson. Retrieved August 2, 2005, from http://www.heath.gwu.edu/PDFs/collegefreshmen.pdf

American Psychiatric Association. (2000). *Diagnostic and statistical manual of mental disorders* (4th ed.). Washington, DC: Author.

Association on Higher Education and Disability Ad Hoc Committee on Learning Disabilities. (1997). *Guidelines for documentation of learning disabilities in adolescents and adults.* Retrieved August 12, 2005, from http://www.ahead.org

National Joint Committee on Learning Disabilities. (1999). *Learning disabilities: Issues in higher education.* Retrieved August 4, 2005, from http://www.ldonline.org/njcld/higher_ed.html

U.S. Congress. *Americans with Disabilities Act of 1990.* 42 U.S.C.A. § 12101 et seq. (West 1993).

U.S. Congress. *Individuals with Disabilities Education Improvement Act of 2004.* 20 U.S.C. § 1400 et seq. Retrieved August 28, 2005, from http://www.ed.gov/policy/speced/guid/idea/idea2004.html

U.S. Congress. *Rehabilitation Act of 1973.* 29 U.S.C. § 701 et seq.

U.S. Department of Justice. (2004). *A guide to disability rights laws.* Retrieved August 6, 2005, from http://www.usdoj.gov/crt/ada/cguide.htm

Venezia, A., Kirst, M., & Antonio, A. (2003). *Betraying the college dream: How disconnected K–12 and postsecondary education systems undermine student aspirations.* Stanford, CA: Stanford Institute for Higher Education Research.

DIANA JOYCE
*University of Florida*

## LEARNING DISABLED ADULT STUDENTS

## LEARNING POTENTIAL

Strategies for the assessment of learning potential have developed as alternatives to standardized norm-referenced assessment. With this method, the student is assessed, coached on assessment tasks, then reassessed. The posttest score is a measure of the student's potential for learning. The objectives of the method are to identify how performance is affected by prior learning experiences, what the processes are by which the student learns, how modifiable the processes are, and how to develop strategies to modify them. The ultimate goal is the prescription of intervention procedures to modify these processes to enhance the efficiency of learning (Haywood, Filler, Shifman, & Chatelanat, 1975).

Although the four most prominent approaches (Budoff, 1968; Feuerstein, 1970; Haywood et al., 1975; Vygotsky, 1978) differ in varying degrees in their theoretical bases and specific techniques, they all operate on the premise that a student's true cognitive ability may be different from what it appears to be from standardized measurement. Investigators view the approach as a way of linking assessment with intervention because the psychologist knows not only what and how much a student needs, but also what instructional strategies work to improve functioning. Although the approach may hold potential as an assessment alternative, research has failed to support its predictive validity, generalizability of training, and use with a variety of populations (e.g., see review by Glutting & McDermott, 1990).

### REFERENCES

Budoff, M. (1968). Learning potential as a supplementary strategy to psychological diagnosis. In J. Hellmuth (Ed.), *Learning disorders* (Vol. 3). Seattle, WA: Special Child Publications.

Feuerstein, R. (1970). A dynamic approach to the causation, prevention, and alleviation of retarded performance. In H. C. Haywood (Ed.), *Social-cultural aspects of mental retardation.* New York: Appleton-Century-Crofts.

Glutting, J., & McDermott, P. A. (1990). Principles and problems in learning potential. In C. R. Reynolds & R. W. Kamphaus (Eds.), *Handbook of psychological and educational assessment of children* (Vol. I). New York: Guilford.

Haywood, H. C., Filler, J. W., Shifman, M. A., & Chatelanat, G. (1975). Behavioral assessment in mental retardation. In P. Mc-

Reynolds (Ed.), *Advances in psychological assessment* (Vol. 3). San Francisco: Jossey-Bass.

Vygotsky, L. S. (1978). *Mind in society: The development of higher psychological processes.* Cambridge, MA: Harvard University Press.

KATHLEEN D. PAGET
*University of South Carolina*

## LEARNING POTENTIAL ASSESSMENT DEVICE
## VYGOTSKY, LEV S.
## ZONE OF PROXIMAL DEVELOPMENT

## LEARNING POTENTIAL ASSESSMENT DEVICE

The Learning Potential Assessment Device (LPAD) is a direct teaching approach for the assessment of learning potential. The primary premise underlying the LPAD is that human beings are modifiable (Feuerstein, Feuerstein, & Gross, 1997). The LPAD is a dynamic or process approach to assessment that rests on the idea that cognitive deficiencies result from faulty adult-child mediated learning experiences and that cognitive functioning is modifiable (Lidz, 1997). This approach is different than the goal of traditional assessment, which is to detect the "hard-wired" traits of the individuals (Feuerstein et al., 1997). Designed originally for use with low-functioning adolescents, its major purposes are to determine which of a student's cognitive operations are deficient, estimate the likelihood that the student can master those operations, and design and carry out a modifiable plan.

The LPAD is not standardized in the manner of conventional tests such as the WISC-III; rather, it involves an interactive process wherein the examiner develops and tests hypotheses about the student's cognitive structures. The LPAD tasks were constructed from a model that allows a test-mediate-test technique that requires the examiner not only to observe the individual's behavior, but also to intervene and assess the behavior again to know the outcome of the intervention (Feuerstein et al., 1997). It is not designed for classification or placement purposes since only informal age comparisons can be made. Thus, it is a supplement to, rather than a substitute for, other assessment measures. Because the LPAD is a complex assessment process, extensive training before administration is necessary, even for professionals who already have training and experience in individual psychoeducational assessment.

### REFERENCES

Feuerstein, R., Feuerstein, R., & Gross, S. (1997). The Learning Potential Assessment Device. In D. P. Flanagan, J. L. Genshaft, & P. L. Harrison (Eds.), *Contemporary intellectual assessment: Theories, tests, and issues.* New York: Guilford.

Lidz, C. S. (1997). Dynamic assessment approaches. In D. P. Flanagan, J. L. Genshaft, & P. L. Harrison (Eds.), *Contemporary intellectual assessment: Theories, tests, and issues.* New York: Guilford.

KATHLEEN D. PAGET
*University of South Carolina*
First edition

ELIZABETH O. LICHTENBERGER
*The Salk Institute*
Second edition

**REMEDIATION, DEFICIT-CENTERED MODELS OF**
**THEORY OF ACTIVITY**
**ZONE OF PROXIMAL DEVELOPMENT**

# LEARNING STRATEGIES

The organized sequence of responses a person makes in a deliberate effort to learn new information or achieve the solution to a problem is called a *strategy*. It is a plan representing stages of information gathering (what information the person chooses as important) and information processing (how the gathered information is processed). Strategies are deliberate, consciously applied procedures that aid in the storage and subsequent retrieval of information. Most strategy-training studies with special children trace their research framework back to earlier research on metacognition (Flavell, 1979) and/or research on production deficiencies (Flavell, Beach, & Chinsky, 1966). In this research a distinction is made between the concepts of production and mediational deficiencies. Mediational deficiencies refer to the fact that children are unable to utilize a strategy efficiently. For example, children may not spontaneously produce a potential mediator to process task requirements, but even if they did, they would fail to use it efficiently to direct their performance. On the other hand, production deficiencies suggest that children can be taught efficient strategies that they fail to produce spontaneously and that these taught strategies would direct and improve their performance. The assumption, when applied to children with special needs, was that the more strategic information needed for effective memory performance, the more likely the task will be affected by the cognitive growth in the child.

The pioneer work in strategy development was done by Bruner, Goodnow, and Austin (1956). In their study, children were presented a series of cards that had pictures of objects that varied on the dimensional color, size, and shape. The child's task was to figure out whether each picture was or was not an example of a rule. Specifically, Bruner et al.

studied how children come to learn a conjunctive rule (red and square). They noted that children use several distinct strategies in their conceptual learning (see Table 1).

This early research laid a foundation for the notion that children's problem solving behavior is highly organized and consciously planned. Two aspects of Bruner et al.'s (1956) findings have implications for children at risk for learning failure. First, the strategies that are available to children for forming concepts vary. Second, some strategies may be more effective than others, but children might find effective strategies difficult to discover. Consequently, it cannot be assumed that all children, for example, children with learning disabilities, come equipped with the best strategies or will be able to discover the best strategies during learning activities.

*Strategies and problem solving.* Besides the work of Brunner et al. (1956), unquestionably, another major contribution to our understanding of strategies and problem-solving behavior is the research of Newell, Shaw, and Simon (1958). Their theory has taken the form of discovering proofs for theorems in symbolic logic through a complex computer program. This program, called "Logic Theorist," follows certain patterns of human processing. For example, insight to or solution of a problem is based on the logical elimination and selection of alternative hypotheses. Effective learning is not done through simple trial and error, but is determined by the extent to which behavior is governed by understanding of a rule. Furthermore, learning is accomplished by

Table 1 Conceptual learning strategies identified

*Conservative focusing:* Conservative focusing yields relevant pieces of information about a concept by a *process of elimination*. Conservative focus begins when the child accepts the first positive instance of a concept. When the concept is encountered in another instance, the child varies his or her idea of the concept by only one attribute. For example, if the first card were red and not square and an example of the concept, and the next card were green and square, the child would focus on the attribute square since red has already been established as part of the conjunctive concept.

*Focus gambling:* Focus gambling involves varying one's choices of relevant attributes (shape, color, size) to more than one value at a time.

*Simultaneous scanning:* Instead of adopting a single attribute or two attributes as a basis for elimination of irrelevant pieces of information, some children form a simple hypothesis about the solution (e.g., all red and square forms are an example of the rule). Simultaneous scanning involves generating all possible hypotheses on the basis of the first positive instance of the concept and using each following instance to eliminate untenable hypotheses.

*Successive scanning:* Successive scanning involves a trial-and-error approach (test one hypothesis at a time). The child must remember which hypothesis has been tried to avoid redundant stimulus selections.

using a sequence of operations, generating problems and remembering them in an ordered fashion.

Newell and Simon (1972) studied how a problem solver would evaluate the properties of alternative solutions in making a choice and the difficulties imposed by evaluation. They considered the chess player whose problem is to choose moves at certain points in the game that may determine the outcome of the game. The evaluation of alternatives is extremely complex because of the number of alternatives available to the player as well as the opponent. Alternatives in moves lead to a multitude of possibilities, eventually leading to a tie, loss, or win. To understand these difficulties, Newell and Simon required subjects to "think aloud" while problem solving. Their use of think-aloud protocols to understand problem solving rests on two assumptions: first, thinking aloud does not interfere with the subject's performance on the problem-solving task, and second, verbalization provides a complete record of the basic processes that are being executed.

Based on think-aloud protocols, Newell and Simon (1972) suggested that the essence of human problem solving is to be understood through a description of three major determinants: (1) space (problem space) the solver uses to represent the problem, (2) task demands, and (3) the environment in which the task takes place. The task environment describes a general class of problems to which a problem belongs (e.g., logic). Therefore, the task environment is objective and external to the subject's perceived definition of the task. The problem solver, on the other hand, defines the problem space or constraints (decisions, moves, strategies, logical relationships) incorporated into task solution. When presented with a problem, the problem solver strives to reduce the problem space. When each decision eliminates a number of available alternatives, the task becomes easier.

Newell and Simon's (1972) research has two major implications for understanding children in special education. First, what students say (based on an analysis of think-aloud protocols) verifies whether effective problem solving, via the use of strategies, is occurring. Students' verbalizations about how they problem solve allow knowledgeable observers to identify appropriate or inappropriate strategies. For example, possible strategies include generating unusual or new ideas (divergent thinking), breaking a mental set to look at a problem differently, avoiding premature judgments, clarifying the essentials of a problem, and attending to relevant facts and conditions of the problem. Second, and of more importance, Newell and Simon's research suggests that human thinking is analogous to an information-processing system. The mental components of human thinking are organized into heuristics. A heuristic is a general approach to problem solving that may or may not lead to a correct response. The heuristics include (1) a representation, understanding, or definition of the problem; (2) a means or plan for acquiring information; and (3) a means of interpreting and evaluating information for problem solution.

*Beyond heuristics.* The aforementioned heuristics provide, at best, a general constellation of the mental components involved in problem solving. Thus, an alternative regrouping of components into strategies has been done to better specify the interplay between problem solving components. Strategies that have been identified in the problem-solving literature (e.g., Hayes, 1981) include means-ends analysis, systematic use of feedback, pattern extraction, if-then logic, prioritizing strategies, and systematic trial-and-error search. The means-ends analysis or general problem solver subroutine (e.g., Newell & Simon, 1972) is assumed to assess a subject's attempt to reach a goal state by taking a sequence of steps, each of which reduces the distance to the goal. The feedback strategy represents the subject's use of new information as it becomes available during the picture arrangement process. It was assumed that when children pay attention to feedback, they can generate and test relevant hypotheses toward problem solutions (e.g., Gholson, 1980). Pattern extraction represents an interpretation of information based upon details in the picture sequences. This interpretation reflects one of two types of mediation: verbal analytic or visual spatial (Hunt, 1974). It is assumed that the type of mediation used to guide a problem-solving search reflects the amount of verbal information stored in the problem solver's memory (i.e., less verbally efficient subjects tend to use spatiovisual processing patterns, whereas more verbally efficient problem solvers rely on verbal analytic reason). The hypothetico-deductive category reflects if-then thinking, in which predictions are confirmed or disconfirmed. It is assumed that a subject generates a tentative hypothesis based on a partial understanding of the problem and then tests out his or her solution. The evaluation subroutine represents a check on the adequacy of the hypothesis. In addition, when a strategy has been evaluated as inadequate, the subject makes a transition from the previous strategy to another. This routine reflects a prioritizing and reprioritizing of strategies. The final strategy subroutine is assumed to reflect systematic problem solving that goes beyond blind trial and error (Hayes, 1981). In a blind trial-and-error search, the problem solver picks directions in problem solution, without considering whether they have already been explored. In a system trial-and-error search, it is assumed that the problem solver keeps track of the directions that have been chosen and utilizes only unexplored directions.

*Control processes.* Other strategies of application to children in special education are derived from research on memory related to control processes. Control processes in memory include a choice as to which information to scan and a choice of what and how to rehearse. Rehearsal refers to the conscious repetition of information, either subvocally or orally, to recall information (e.g., a phone number, street address) at a later time. Additional control processes involve organization (ordering, classifying, or tagging information to facilitate retrieval) and mediation (comparing new items with items already in memory). Organization strategies may include the following:

1. Chunking: grouping items so that each one brings to mind a complete series of items (e.g., grouping words into a sentence)
2. Clustering: organizing items in categories (e.g., animals, furniture)
3. Mnemonics: using idiosyncratic methods for organizing materials
4. Coding: varying the qualitative form of information (e.g., using images rather than verbal labels or substituting pictures for words)

The following may facilitate mediation:

1. Making use of preexisting associations, eliminating the necessity for new ones
2. Utilizing verbal instructions or asking the child to imagine, to aid in retrieval and organization
3. Cuing at recall by using verbal and imaginary information to facilitate mediation

## REFERENCES

Bruner, J. S., Goodnow, J., & Austin, G. (1956). *A study of thinking.* New York: Wiley.

Flavell, J. (1979). Metacognition and cognitive monitoring. *American Psychologist, 34,* 906–911.

Flavell, J., Beach, D. R., & Chinsky, J. M. (1966). Spontaneous verbal rehearsal in memory task as a function of age. *Child Development, 37,* 283–299.

Gholson, B. (1980). *The cognitive developmental basis of human learning: Studies in hypothesis testing.* New York: Academic Press.

Hayes, J. R. (1981). *The complete problem solver.* Philadelphia: Franklin Institute Press.

Hunt, E. (1974). *Quote the Raven? Nevermore!* In L. W. Gregg (Ed.), *Knowledge and cognition.* Hillsdale, NJ: Erlbaum.

Newell, A., Shaw, F., & Simon, H. (1958). Elements of theory of human problem solving. *Psychological Review, 65,* 151–166.

Newell, A., & Simon, H. (1972). *Human problem solving.* Englewood Cliffs, NJ: Prentice Hall.

H. Lee Swanson
*University of California,
Riverside*

BEHAVIOR MODELING
IMAGERY
LEARNING STYLES
MNEMONICS
TEACHING STRATEGIES

## LEARNING STYLES

Learning styles can be defined, in their simplest forms, as ways that students' personal characteristics, including their needs and preferences, stylistically affect their learning (Mann & Sabatino, 1985). However, a variety of different definitional approaches have been taken.

A learning style has been defined by Bennett (1979) as being a "preferred way of learning. It represents a cluster of personality and mental characteristics that influence how a pupil perceives, remembers, thinks, and solves problems" (Holland, 1982, p. 8). According to Hunt (1974), learning styles represent accessibility characteristics, that is, specific cognitive and motivational characteristics of the learner. Dunn (1983) says learning styles consist of "a combination of physical, psychological, emotional, and widespread elements that affect the ways individuals . . . receive, store, and use knowledge or abilities" (p. 497). Dunn believes that most people have between 6 and 14 learning-style elements that affect them strongly. It should be observed that these definitions and many others emphasize learner preferences as defining learning styles.

Learning styles actually represent subsets of cognitive styles (Mann & Sabatino, 1985). Indeed, inquiry into learning styles often encompasses study of traditional cognitive styles. Nevertheless, learning style constructs tend to be much more classroom and instruction oriented than traditional cognitive style constructs and usually are studied in and applied to instructional contexts. Another characteristic of learning styles that sets them apart from the broader category of cognitive styles is that they tend to be more oriented to environmental events. It may be said at the cost of simplification that cognitive style researchers emphasize the particular ways that individuals respond to and structure their environments, while learning style investigators are more interested in how the environment affects those individuals.

While cognitive styles are currently studied through a variety of paper and pencil methods, they originated in psychological laboratories and have a more rigorous research tradition and deeper data base support than learning styles. The latter are usually dependent on information obtained from behavior checklists, inventories, and questionnaires.

A great variety of learning styles have been identified. Many are applicable to special education (Dunn, 1983), while others are more appropriately applied to higher education (Gregoric, 1979).

Different theorists have taken different theoretical and applied approaches to the study of learning styles. Ausburn and Ausburn (1978) have emphasized the study of learning styles as cognitive styles, and vice versa. Gregoric (1979) has conceptualized learning styles on the basis of students' preferences for particular learning sources and whether students prefer to learn through concrete or abstract means. He thus has been able to distinguish among abstract-sequential, concrete-sequential, abstract-random, and concrete-random learners. Hunt (1974) has proposed a conceptual level (CL) learning style model embodying dimensions of cognitive complexity, maturity, independence, and adaptability to social environments.

Dunn and Dunn, whose work has been particularly school and classroom oriented (1975, 1977, 1979), have identified four major categories of learning-style variables: (1) environmental, (2) emotional, (3) sociological, and (4) physical.

The Dunns' environmental category involves learning style elements relating to students' preferences for learning under different conditions of light, sound, temperature, and design (the last involving preferences for studying under formal or less structured learning conditions). The Dunns' emotional category concerns students' motivation, persistence, responsibility, and need for structure. Their sociological category relates to students' preferences as to learning by themselves or with others. The physical needs category involves modality preferences in learning, which Dunn and Dunn stress heavily, and other physical needs variables they believe are important to learning.

In contrast to cognitive style remedial interventions, which often seek to assist problem and disabled students by altering or improving their learning styles, intervention efforts in learning style work are less ambitious in demanding change on the students' part. Rather than calling for methods to remediate or change unsatisfactory cognitive styles, learning styles interventionists are more likely to call for modifications in instruction and in the circumstances of learning. Fantini (1980) suggests that we are at a stage in which we should consider designing programs to fit learners rather than attempting to fit learners to standard programs. Dunn and Dunn advise that students' learning styles be matched, in a best fit manner, to teacher styles so as to optimize instruction. Kitson (1982) advises that what might appear to be learning deficits might actually be learning styles that are not being properly addressed in instruction.

In recent years, remedial teachers have been advised to modify their instruction to meet the learning style characteristics of problem readers (Carbo, 1983). Special educators have been similarly advised, for both the gifted and the disabled (Dunn, 1983; Smith, 1983). Studies have been carried out to identify the learning styles of disabled pupils; they suggest that mainstreaming approaches should use learning styles as a guide (Jones, 1980). Classroom management and instruction to learning styles also have been recommended as means of meeting the needs of gifted children (Ricca 1984).

While learning style assessments reveal distinctions between students and their learning preferences, learning style variables may not account for enough learner variances to make them major springboards for educational interven-

tion. Indeed, it is questionable as to how much learning environments can be adjusted to meet particular student needs. In special education, the individualized education plan, which does individualize instruction, conceivably could allow for more adjustment to learning styles than in regular education.

On the positive side, it is both easy and inexpensive to determine students' learning styles through a variety of paper and pencil and observational means. Insight into students' learning styles may provide useful instructional hints for teachers.

## REFERENCES

Ausburn, L. J., & Ausburn, F. B. (1978). Cognitive styles: Some information and implications for instructional design. *Educational Communications & Technology Journal, 26,* 337–354.

Bennett, C. I. (1979). Individual differences and how teachers perceive them. *Social Studies, 70,* 56–61.

Blackman, S., & Goldstein, K. M. (1982). Cognitive styles and learning disabilities. *Journal of Learning Disabilities, 15,* 106–113.

Carbo, M. (1983). Research in reading and learning style: Implications for exceptional children. *Exceptional Children, 49,* 486–493.

Dunn, R. (1983). Learning styles and its relations to exceptionality at both ends of the spectrum. *Exceptional Children, 40,* 496–506.

Dunn, R., & Dunn, K. (1975). Learning styles, teaching styles. *NASSP Bulletin, 59,* 37–49.

Dunn, R., & Dunn, K. (1977). How to diagnose learning styles. *Instructor, 87,* 123–124, 126, 128, 130, 132, 134, 136, 140, 142, 144.

Dunn, R., & Dunn, K. (1979). Learning styles, teaching styles: Should they . . . can they . . . be matched. *Educational Leadership, 36,* 238–244.

Gregoric, A. F. (1979). Learning/teaching styles: Potent forces behind them. *Educational Leadership, 36,* 234–236.

Holland, R. P. (1982). Learner characteristics and learner performance: Implications for instructional placement decision. *Journal of Special Education, 15,* 221–238.

Hunt, D. E. (1974). A conceptual level matching model for coordinating learner characteristics with educational approaches. *Interchange, 1,* 68–82.

Hunt, D. E. (1979). The B-P-E paradigm for theory, research, and practice. *Canadian Psychological Review, 16,* 185–197.

Jones, S. (1980). Mainstreaming with reference to learning styles. *Learner in the Process, 2(2),* 52–57.

Kitson, L. (1982). Learning style or learning deficit. *Academic Therapy, 17,* 317–322.

Mann, L., & Sabatino, D. A. (1985). *Foundations of cognitive processes in remedial and special education.* Rockville, MD: Aspen.

Ricca, J. (1984). Learning styles and preferred instructional strategies of gifted students. *Gifted Child Quarterly, 28,* 121–126.

Smith, C. R. (1983, April). *Matching instructional tasks to students' abilities and learning styles.* Paper presented at the annual convention of the Association for Children and Adults with Learning Disabilities, Washington, DC.

EMILY WAHLEN
LESTER MANN
*Hunter College, City University
of New York*

COGNITIVE STYLES
DYSPEDAGOGIA
TEACHER EFFECTIVENESS

# LEAST RESTRICTIVE ENVIRONMENT

## Least Restrictive Environment and Free and Appropriate Education

Two major features of the Individuals with Disabilities Education Improvement Act of 2004 (IDEIA; 2004) are in place to ensure the most appropriate education of children with disabilities. IDEIA requires that children with disabilities receive a free and appropriate public education (FAPE) in the least restrictive environment (LRE). The goal of special education services is to enable the child to be involved in and make progress in the general education curriculum. IDEIA does not require that all students be placed in general education classes. The placement that is the least restrictive environment is unique to each child, maximizing to the appropriate extent an education in a setting with students who do not have disabilities. Once the educational plan has been developed for the individualized education plan (IEP), the team determines the placement that is the least restrictive.

The overriding principle in determining the least restrictive placement for a student with a disability is that placements other than general education should be considered only when it is concluded that educational benefit, even with appropriate supplementary aids and services, cannot be achieved satisfactorily in that setting. It would be a violation of the law to place a student with a disability in a regular education classroom without the necessary aids and supports. The benefits of interacting with nondisabled peers and the potential disruption in the education of other students should also be considered.

School districts cannot make placement decisions based on disability type, availability of services, space, or cost. The placement should be at the school that is as close as possible to the student's home, minimizing transportation time. Under IDEIA, a student's placement must be reviewed on a regular basis, and must be based on the student's IEP. The participants in the IEP meeting, including the student's parent, must agree to the IEP content and make final decisions about the initial placement or any changes to a child's placement.

## Section 504 and ADA

In addition to IDEIA, Section 504 of the Rehabilitation Act of 1973 and the Americans with Disabilities Act of 1990 (ADA) protect students from discrimination on the basis of a disability and address least restrictive environment. Section 504 and the ADA define a disability as a physical or mental impairment that substantially limits a major life activity, and they may include students who are not eligible for special education under IDEIA. Section 504 requires schools to educate students with disabilities with students who are not handicapped to the maximum extent appropriate. The ADA also requires that reasonable accommodations be in place in any part of a student's special education program that may be community-based and involve job training/placement.

## Continuum of Placement Options

School districts are required to have a full continuum of placement options in place, including instruction in general education classrooms, special classes, special schools, home instruction, and instruction in hospitals and institutions. Parents are entitled to know about the range of placements available. The requirement of a continuum of alternative placements further supports the idea that placement should be determined on an individual basis, according to the needs of the child. This confirms that LRE is not synonymous with general education. The law also requires that to the maximum extent possible, children with disabilities should be educated in their neighborhood schools. An explanation of the decision to place a student in a school other than his or her neighborhood school must be provided in the IEP.

## Students with Disabilities in General Education Classrooms

*Benefits of placement in general education.* The National Association of School Psychologists (2002) identified the following benefits of including students with disabilities in general education: Peers can serve as role models; friendships are naturally developed in the student's home community; social skills are developed in the natural environment; students without disabilities learn to value diversity; additional resources in general education classrooms can benefit all students. These benefits are found in general education programs with well-trained teachers who value collaboration, provide services necessary for student success, and carefully monitor the educational outcomes of students with and without disabilities.

*Disruptive behavior.* The potential harmful effects of a placement to the child with a disability and to other students must be considered. In some cases, a student's disruptive behavior will justify a placement outside the general education classroom. The needs of children with disabilities cannot be met if behavioral problems are so disruptive in the general education classroom that their education or the education of their nondisabled peers is compromised. The district must demonstrate, however, that the full range of supplementary aids and supports has been utilized in the general education setting to minimize disruptive behavior or its effect if it is determined that this placement is not appropriate for the child with a disability.

*Teacher willingness.* Not all general education teachers welcome students with disabilities in their classrooms. However, it is a violation of law not to place a child with a disability in a general education classroom because of teacher resistance. It is the school's responsibility to ensure that general education teachers are able to address the needs of students with disabilities in their classrooms, and that the needed supports and aids are in place. Relevant staff development for general education teachers will contribute to their preparation to meet the needs of students with disabilities.

## Suspension and Expulsion

Students with disabilities are subject to long-term suspension or expulsion, but only if the misconduct has been determined not to be a manifestation of the child's disability. Under IDEIA and Section 504 of the Rehabilitation Act, children with disabilities cannot be removed from their schools for more than 10 days for misconduct without determining first if the misconduct is a manifestation of their disability. Removing a child from school for more than 10 days results in a change of placement that must be approved by the IEP team. Districts are permitted to remove children for up to 10 days without determining whether the behavior is a manifestation of the disability. A consensus must be made by a group of persons, not an individual, when determining if a behavior is related to the child's disability.

The procedural safeguards in IDEIA and Section 504 of the Rehabilitation Act require that parents be given written notice of any proposal to change placement and be informed that they have a right to a due process hearing. If the parents request a due process hearing under IDEIA, the stay-put provision applies, in which the child must remain in the current educational placement unless the district and the parents can agree on an interim placement. School districts may seek a court order to remove a child with a disability if it is determined that the child poses a danger in the current educational placement and a threat to himself or herself or to others.

## Funding and LRE

A lack of personnel or other resources does not excuse districts from their obligation to provide a free and appropriate public education to students in the least restrictive environment where the IEP can be effectively implemented. Under IDEIA, funds provided to a local education agency may be used to pay for the costs of special education and related services and supplementary aids and services provided in any setting to a child with a disability. It is permissible for these services to also benefit students without disabilities if they are also present when the services are offered.

## Court Interpretations of LRE

Court decisions have interpreted IDEIA in ways that have (1) upheld the requirement of a continuum of placements, (2) disallowed placement in restrictive settings for reasons related to cost, availability of resources, or state-of-the art methods, (3) supported to individual decisions about whether the general education classroom is considered least restrictive for particular students, (4) considered the impact of disruptive behavior on nondisabled peers in general education, (5) described tests of "educational benefit" as an indicator of FAPE for a student in a given setting, (6) supported the provision of supports and services to facilitate placement in the LRE, and (7) maintained the provision that placement changes, as part of the IEP, must be approved by the parent and school.

### REFERENCES

*Americans with Disabilities Act of 1990,* 42 U.S.C. 12101–12213 (1990).

*Individuals with Disabilities Education Act of 2004,* Pub. L. No. 108-446 (2004).

National Association of School Psychologists. (2002). *Position statement on inclusive programs for students with disabilities.* Retrieved August 25, 2005, from http://www.nasponline.org/information/pospaper_ipsd.html

*Rehabilitation Act of 1973,* 29 U.S.C. 794 (1973).

Annika White
Sharon Duffy
*University of California,
Riverside*

CASCADE MODEL OF SPECIAL EDUCATION SERVICES
INCLUSION
INDIVIDUALS WITH DISABILITIES EDUCATION
    IMPROVEMENT ACT OF 2004 (IDEIA)

## LEFT BRAIN/RIGHT BRAIN

Although we have long known that the brain contains two sides, only recently have we begun to understand the behaviors controlled by the two sides. Prior to the 1950s, it was assumed that both sides of the brain perform equal functions. However, Sperry (1913–1994) performed a series of studies which discovered that the left hemisphere is responsible for verbal information while the right hemisphere controls visual data. For summaries of this research, on which this entry is based, see Deutsch and Springer (1981), Segalowitz (1993), and Sperry (1972).

Sperry's most famous experiments, for which he won the Nobel Prize in Medicine in 1981, involved separating the two hemispheres of animals (cats and monkeys) and later humans (epileptic patients) by cutting the largest nerve tract in the brain, the corpus callosum. Originally, it was thought that the corpus callosum's main function was to hold the two sides of the brain together. However, this turned out to be grossly incorrect. During the 1960s, surgeons Bogen and Voegl carefully dissected the corpus callosum (together with the anterior and posterior commissures) in about one dozen patients with intractable epilepsy. The patients were then subjected to a series of neuropsychological tests (e.g., language). These carefully planned and ingenious studies revealed that each hemisphere controlled different types of information. Since about 90 percent of people are right handed, and since the left hemisphere controls the right part of the body (and the right hand), many neuroscientists came to the conclusion that the left hemisphere was the main or dominant hemisphere. However, Sperry believed that both hemispheres were dominant for different functions.

Sperry's research suggested that the left hemisphere was primarily responsible for the control of language, sequential thinking, and general logic, whereas the right hemisphere dealt more with visual and emotional information. More recent research indicates that Sperry was indeed correct. For example, investigators have reported that right hemisphere-damaged patients had more problems than individuals with damage to the left hemisphere on tasks involving pictorial or visual memory. In contrast, patients with strokes to the left hemisphere almost always have word-finding difficulties.

However, it is important to note that even though the two sides of the brain appear to have selective roles in behavior, the split-brain patients of Sperry and colleagues were not entirely normal. Although their seizures subsided substantially as a function of the surgery, Sperry discovered that their behavior was not integrated. For example, if words were exposed to the right hemisphere the patient was unable to identify the stimulus. He later concluded that consciousness and purposeful behavior was due to the integrated function of both the left and right brain.

### REFERENCES

Deutsch, G., & Springer, S. P. (1981). *Left brain, right brain.* New York: W. H. Freeman.

Segalowitz, S. J. (1993). *Two sides of the brain.* Englewood Cliffs, NJ: Prentice Hall.

Sperry, R. W. (1972). The great cerebral commissure. *Scientific American, 210,* 45–52.

CATHY F. TELZROW
*Kent State University*
First edition

ANTONIO E. PUENTE
*University of North Carolina at Wilmington*

KRISTA L. PUENTE
*University of North Carolina at Wilmington*
Second edition

CEREBRAL DOMINANCE
HEMISPHERIC FUNCTIONS
INFORMATION PROCESSING

## LEFT-HANDEDNESS

Left-handedness, a characteristic of fewer than 10 percent of humans, is a condition that has generated a tremendous amount of superstition. Negative properties and values have come to be associated with the left, while positive traits are associated with the right. The majority of individuals prefer using their right hands and also are more skilled with their right hands (Corballis & Beale, 1983). Our language also expresses this distinction; for example, a left-handed compliment is an insult, but a right-hand man is a trusted friend. Throughout history the left has represented darkness, evil, demons, death, the Devil, movement, the unlimited, the many, the even, the curved, and the oblong. The left also has been associated traditionally with femaleness and weakness. Since ancient times, left-handedness has implied a substandard subject (Needham, 1974).

Investigators long have been curious about the rarity of left-handedness. However, studies of historical records and artifacts have revealed enough inconsistencies in incidence to preclude any simple choice between culture or biology to explain the origin of handedness. Consequently, combinations of these various nature and nurture explanations have been invoked. Harris (1980) provides an interesting and detailed account of the various theories.

Whether accepting left-handedness as a rare reversal of the biological conditions underlying right-handedness or as a result of resistance to cultural pressure to be right-handed, many investigators have declared left-handedness to be a manifestation of pathology. The pathology theorists of the early 1900s, of whom the Italian criminologist C. Lombroso was the most influential, studied groups of lunatics and various types of criminals. They found that the incidence of left-handedness was greater in these populations and that the incidence among women almost doubled that of men. These findings lent themselves easily to prejudicial views and soon were misconstrued. At the time, it was not uncommon to find reports declaring left-handedness to be more common among blacks, savages, and the poor. These theories of pathology attempted to account for the negative properties associated with left-handedness.

With the growing awareness that the left side of the brain controls the right side of the body, and vice versa, later theorists recognized two different types of left-handedness. Evidence accumulated supporting the fact that left-handedness could result from damage to the left hemisphere of the brain or from anomalous biological or cultural conditions involving no damage to the brain. It was the former type that seemed to predominate in criminals, delinquents, and epileptics (Harris, 1980).

Today, there is no dispute that left-handedness is inherited, at least to a degree. An individual is more likely to be left-handed if one parent is left-handed, and more likely still if both parents are left-handed. However, transmission from one generation to the next is not perfect. Even if both parents are left-handed, there is only a 50 percent chance that an offspring also will be left-handed. Annett (1964) has devised a theory of handedness that explains this circumstance better than others. She suggests that most people inherit a right shift, or tendency to be right-handed, from two right-handed parents. Most will be right-handed, but a small portion may become left-handed owing to environmental influences or left-side brain damage. Right-handedness also is more marked for females than males since the latter are more susceptible to pathological influences at birth. Annett's alternative to the right shift is not a left shift, but rather a lack of the right shift. A minority of people inherit no genetic predisposition to be either left- or right-handed. Owing to various environmental or pathological influences, half will be left-handed and half will be right-handed, although a good many may be better classified as mixed-handed or ambidextrous.

Investigations have revealed a higher incidence of left-handedness in handicapped populations. Fein, Waterhouse, Lucci, Snyder, and Humes (1984) found 18 percent of a sample of school-age autistic children were left-handed. This figure is consistent with previous studies of autistic children, and is comparable to Satz's (1973) estimate of 83 percent right-handedness in retarded and epileptic populations. These findings represent an approximate doubling of the left-handedness consistently found in normal populations. Other studies have found markedly greater frequencies of immune disease, migraine, and learning disabilities among left-handers (Geschwind & Behan, 1982). While we can distinguish superstition from fact better than ever before, left-handedness continues to be an elusive phenomenon and a source of fascination and frustration. Results of research studies also may vary dramatically depending upon whether one defines handedness as either/or on a continuum (Dean & Reynolds, 1997).

## REFERENCES

Annett, M. (1964). A model of the inheritance of handedness and cerebral dominance. *Nature, 204,* 59–60.

Corballis, M. C., & Beale, I. L. (1983). *The ambivalent mind.* Chicago: Nelson-Hall.

Dean, R. S., & Reynolds, C. R. (1997). Cognitive processing and self-report of lateral preference. *Neuropsychology Review, 7,* 127–142.

Fein, D., Waterhouse, L., Lucci, D., Snyder, D., & Humes, M. (1984, February). *Cognitive functions in left and right handed autistic children.* Presentation at the Annual Meeting of the International Neuropsychological Society, Houston, Texas.

Geschwind, N., & Behan, P. (1982). Left-handedness: Association with immune disease, migraine and developmental learning disorder. *Proceedings of the National Academy of Science, USA, 79,* 5097–5100.

Harris, L. J. (1980). Left-handedness: Early theories, facts, and fancies. In J. Herron (Ed.), *Neuropsychology of left-handedness* (pp. 3–78). New York: Academic.

Needham, R. (Ed.). (1974). *Right and left: Essays on dual symbolic classification.* Chicago: University of Chicago Press.

Satz, P. (1973). Left-handedness and early brain insult: An explanation. *Neuropsychologia, 11,* 115–117.

GALE A. HARR
*Maple Heights City Schools,
Maple Heights, Ohio*

CEREBRAL DOMINANCE
HANDEDNESS AND EXCEPTIONALITY

# LEFT-HANDEDNESS, PATHOLOGICAL

An association between left-handedness and some form of abnormality has long been popular (Orton, 1937). The term pathological left-handedness (PLH) is used to refer to an involuntary switch in hand preference (from right to left) in individuals who would otherwise be right-handed. This shift is thought to result from some form of lateralized brain insult.

Research suggests that both genetic and environmental factors may contribute to the determination of hand preference (Annett, 1978; Collins, 1975; Levy & Nagylaki, 1972). Acturarial data are used as evidence in support of a genetic role. For example, the probability of two right-handed parents giving birth to a left-handed child is 0.02. When only one parent is left-handed, the probability is 0.17, but it increases to 0.46 when both parents are left-handed (Chamberlain, 1928). The unknown contribution of environmental factors, however, limits complete acceptance of a genetic hypothesis. Collins (1975), for example, postulates that cultural and environmental biases play a significant role in determining handedness.

Left-handedness is somewhat rare, occurring in approximately 10 percent of the general population. A higher incidence of left-handedness has been reported in males (Coren & Porac, 1980; Gillberg, Waldenström, & Rasmussen, 1984) and in twins (Howard & Brown, 1970). It is generally thought that these findings reflect an increased susceptibility among these populations to pre- and perinatal complications. A relationship between handedness and birth order also has been reported by Bakan (1977), who suggests that left-handedness occurs more frequently in the higher risk birth orders (first and fourth or later). Although Bakan's findings are somewhat controversial, they suggest a relationship between neurological insult and complications during pregnancy and/or birth.

A higher incidence of left-handedness has been reported to be associated with a number of conditions including mental retardation, epilepsy, dyslexia, and infantile autism. Evidence is strongest, however, for conditions with a clear neurological basis (Bishop, 1983). Attempts to assess the role of these conditions in left-handedness has resulted in a number of conflicting explanations.

Bakan (1977) maintains an extreme position and postulates that all left-handedness is pathological in origin. According to Bakan, this pathology reflects damage to the particularly vulnerable left hemisphere during the prenatal or infancy stage. This damage is thought to cause the child to favor use of the left hand.

In contrast, Satz (1972) has proposed a model of pathological left-handedness to account for a nearly twofold increase in left-handedness among brain-injured populations (mentally retarded and epileptic). This model includes two groups with distinct etiologies for left-handedness. One group is thought to be comprised of those who are natural left-handers and whose handedness is based on genetic and/or environmental factors. A second group considered in Satz's model is thought to be comprised of those who are pathologically left-handed as a result of early lateralized brain insult. It is hypothesized that early left hemisphere damage causes a shift of handedness from right to left preference.

The model further predicts that early right hemisphere damage would cause natural left-handers to become pathological right-handers (PRH). Given the lower frequency of left-handers in the population, the number of PLH will exceed the number of PRH. Moreover, since the pool of left-handers is relatively small, PLH should make up a significant portion of left-handers.

Satz's model is thought to account for a good deal of the elevated incidence of left-handedness among certain clinical populations. The model appears to be consistent with evidence that the majority of left-handers in the general population are neurologically and cognitively normal.

Although most would acknowledge that some portion of left-handedness is clearly the result of an insult to the brain, few would agree with Bakan's notion that all left-

handedness is pathological in origin. Indeed, one must use caution in applying the term pathological left-handedness since there are no proven techniques to distinguish among natural or pathological left-handers.

## REFERENCES

Annett, M. (1978). Genetic and non-genetic influences on handedness. *Behavioral Genetics, 8,* 227–249.

Bakan, P. (1977). Left handedness and birth order revisited. *Neuropsychologia, 15,* 837–839.

Bishop, D. V. M. (1983). How sinister is sinistrality? *Journal of the Royal College of Physicians of London, 17,* 161–172.

Chamberlain, H. D. (1928). The inheritance of left handedness. *Journal of Heredity, 19,* 557–559.

Collins, R. L. (1975). When left handed mice live in right handed worlds. *Science, 187,* 181–184.

Coren, S., & Porac, C. (1980). Birth factors and laterality: Effects of birth order, parental age and birth stress or four indices of lateral preference. *Behavioral Genetics, 10,* 123–138.

Gillberg, C., Waldenström, E., & Rasmussen, P. (1984). Handedness in Swedish 10-year-olds: Some background and associated factors. *Journal of Child Psychology and Psychiatry, 25*(3), 421–432.

Howard, R. G., & Brown, A. M. (1970). Twinning: A marker for biological insults. *Child Development, 41,* 519–530.

Levy, J., & Nagylaki, T. (1972). A model for the genetics of handedness. *Genetics, 72,* 117–128.

Orton, S. T. (1937). Specific reading disability-strephosymbolia. *Journal of the American Medical Association, 90,* 1095–1099.

Satz, P. (1972). Pathological left-handedness: An explanatory model. *Cortex, 8,* 121–135.

ARLENE I. RATTAN
*Ball State University*

RAYMOND S. DEAN
*Ball State University*
*Indiana University School of Medicine*

BIRTH INJURIES
BRAIN DAMAGE/INJURY
CEREBRAL DOMINANCE
LEFT-HANDEDNESS

## LEGALLY BLIND/VISUALLY IMPAIRED

Legal blindness is defined by the federal government (National Library Service, 2005) as visual acuity, as determined by competent authority, of 20/200 or less in the better eye with the aid of corrective lenses, or a visual field whose widest diameter subtends an angular distance no greater than 20 degrees.

In 2002, the United States Code (USC) was amended to include a slightly different definition. "A 'blind person' means a person whose central visual acuity does not exceed 20/200 in the better eye with correcting lenses or whose visual acuity, if better than 20/200, is accompanied by a limit to the field of vision in the better eye to such a degree that its widest diameter subtends an angle of no greater than twenty degrees. In determining whether an individual is blind, there shall be an examination by a physician skilled in diseases of the eye, or by an optometrist, whichever the individual shall select" ("Vending facility for blind in federal buildings," 2002). The effect of this slight change in wording has been that "Normal" visual acuity is defined as 20/20; that is, a person sees at 20 feet what the majority of people without a visual impairment see at 20 feet. "Normal" visual field is 140 degrees in each eye and about 180 degrees with both eyes.

An important point is that a person must be certified as legally blind by a competent authority, which is defined to include doctors of medicine or osteopathy, ophthalmologists, optometrists, registered nurses, therapists, and other qualified professionals. Visual impairment is not legally defined at the federal level, although some states have adopted definitions.

The most common definition of a visual impairment is visual acuity of 20/70 or less in the better eye with the aid of corrective lenses, or a visual field whose widest diameter subtends an angular distance no greater than 140 degrees.

For the purposes of special education, most states have adopted the federal definition of blindness. For those states that have vocational rehabilitation services, the qualifying definition is usually taken from that entity. Students who are legally blind qualify under special education services in the K–12 system (Individuals with Disabilities Education Act [IDEA]), while visually impaired students may qualify under either the special education or "504" program.

**REFERENCES**

National Library Service. (2005). *Eligibility of blind and other physically handicapped persons for loan of library materials.* Retrieved October 10, 2005, from http://www.loc.gov/nls/eligible.html

*Vending facility for blind in federal buildings,* 20USC 107e (2002).

DAVID SWEENEY
*Texas A&M University*

**BLIND**
**FUNCTIONAL VISION**

# LEGG-CALVÉ-PERTHES DISEASE

Legg-Calvé-Perthes disease, or avascular necrosis of the femoral head, involves loss of blood supply to the proximal epiphysis of the femur. This serious condition has a peak incidence between 3 and 10 years of age, affects males four to five times more than females, and affects white children 10 times more frequently than black children (Wong, 1995). The etiology is unknown (Mayo Physician Group, 1997). A defining characteristic is the disturbance of circulation to the femoral epiphysis, thereby producing an ischemic necrosis of the femoral head (Ball & Bindler, 1999). When the blood supply is diverted, the femoral head in the hip joint dies and intense inflammation and irritation develop (Wong, 1995).

Legg-Calvé-Perthes disease is usually diagnosed when the child is brought to the pediatrician and/or orthopedic surgeon because of pain and limping (Molloy & MacMahon, 1986). This pain may be caused by pathological fractures or by muscle spasms that accompany the hip irritation. Pain may also spread to other parts of the leg such as the groin, thigh, or inner knee (Herring, 1994). When the hip is moved, the pain grows more intense. Rest often relieves the discomfort.

The child with Legg-Calvé-Perthes disease can expect to have multiple x-rays over the course of treatment (Kaniklides, Lonnerholm, & Moberg, 1994). X-ray results will show a worsening condition before a gradual improvement is observed. Once a diagnosis is confirmed, the child will require careful orthopedic treatment. Legg-Calvé-Perthes disease is self-limiting, but failure to properly treat this condition may lead to significant femoral head deformity and severe degenerative arthritis (Nochimson, 1998).

The pathological events characteristic of Legg-Calvé-Perthes disease take place in four stages (Wong, 1995). Stage 1, the avascular stage, involves degenerative changes producing flattening of the upper surface of the femoral head. In stage 2, the fragmentation or revascularization stage, vascular reabsorption of the epiphysis occurs and a mottled appearance of the hip area appears on x-rays. Stage 3, the reparative stage, involves new bone formation from the periphery of the femoral head inward. In stage 4, the regenerative stage, gradual reformation of the head of the femur occurs and a spherical shape returns.

The treatment regime has changed over the past decade and now encompasses several therapies to enhance the healing process (Ball & Bindler, 1999; Nochimson, 1998; Wong, 1995). The initial therapy is rest and non-weight bearing to restore motion and reduce inflammation. Traction is often used to relieve spasms, stretch out contractures, and restore hip motion. Weight bearing should be avoided on the affected limb, so the child is also contained in a non-weight bearing device such as an abduction brace, leg casts, or harness sling. Conservative therapies are usually continued for 2–4 years. Surgical correction may speed the recovery process and allow the child to return to normal activities in 3–4 months (Wong, 1995).

Children who develop Legg-Calvé-Perthes disease before the age of 6 tend to have a better prognosis and a faster recovery (Mayo Physician Group, 1997). The later the diagnosis, the more femoral damage has occurred before treatment is implemented and the poorer the overall prognosis (Wong, 1995).

## REFERENCES

Ball, J., & Bindler, R. (1999). *Pediatric nursing: Caring for children* (2nd ed.). Stamford, CT: Appleton & Lange.

Herring, J. (1994). The treatment of Legg-Calvé-Perthes disease. *Journal of Bone and Joint Surgery, 76*(A), 448–458.

Kaniklides, C., Lonnerholm, T., & Moberg, A. (1994). Legg-Calvé-Perthes disease: Comparison of conventional radiography, MR imaging, bone scintigraphy, and arthrography. *Acta Radiology, 35,* 434–439.

Mayo Physician Group. (1997). Legg-Calvé-Perthes (LCP) condition. Retrieved February 3, 1997, from http://www.mayohealth.org/mayo/askphys/qa970201.htm

Molloy, M., & MacMahon, B. (1986). Incidence of Legg-Calvé-Perthes disease. *New England Journal of Medicine, 275,* 988–991.

Nochimson, G. (1998). *Legg-Calvé-Perthes disease.* Retrieved October 29, 1998, from http://www.emedicine.com/emerg/topic294.htm

Wong, D. (1995). *Whaley & Wong's nursing care of infants and children* (5th ed.). St. Louis, MO: Mosby-Year Book.

CATHY F. TELZROW
*Kent State University*
First edition

KARI ANDERSON
*University of North Carolina at Wilmington*
Second edition

## PHYSICAL DISABILITIES

## LEHTINEN, LAURA E. (1908–      )

In the 1940s, psychologists and educators often did not know of the existence of brain-injured children. If they did know, they did not do much research into the problems of these children. Laura E. Lehtinen was an exception. She believed that brain-injured children had disorders in perception, concept formation, and mental organization, problems that interfered with the children's learning processes. *Psychopathology and Education of the Brain-Injured Child,* originally published in 1947 and reprinted in 1989, was one of the first books to acknowledge the presence of these children, make recommendations, and reduce their symptomatic behavior disorders. The book listed the criteria for classifying the child who suffered brain damage from other than genetic causes. Lehtinen, who did not believe that brain-injured children had any limitations to their intelligence, suggested a highly structured, directive approach that was primarily kinesthetic. She put her ideas into practice as education director of the Cove School for Brain-Injured Children in Racine, Wisconsin. Her work there included devising methods to enhance reading skills of primary and elementary grade students (Dadouche, Lehtinen, & Wennberg, 1980).

Strongly influencing psychologists and educators in the 1950s, Lehtinen believed that motor learning is the necessary basis for subsequent learning. Believing that perceptual difficulties play a major role in learning disabilities, Lehtinen advocated teaching children cursive rather than manuscript writing because in the former, letters are written as units and spacing is less of a problem. Her work helped create interest in, and subsequent research into, the problems of the learning-disabled child.

## REFERENCES

Dadouche, J., Lehtinen, L., & Wennberg, J. (1980). *Phonics workbook.* Allen, TX: DLM Teaching Resources.

Strauss, A. A., & Lehtinen, L. E. (1989). *Psychopathology and the education of the brain-injured child.* Austin, TX: PRO-ED. (Original work published 1947)

E. VALERIE HEWITT
*Texas A&M University*
First edition

TAMARA J. MARTIN
*The University of Texas of the Permian Basin*
Second edition

## LEISURE-TIME ACTIVITIES

Leisure-time activities, or avocations, represent constructive use of leisure time in the pursuit of recreational activities. In addition to providing enjoyment, enhancing the development of skills, and the opportunity for meeting and interacting with individuals who share similar interests, leisure-time activities can help meet certain self-actualization and therapeutic needs.

Leisure-time activities usually involve one of two general focuses. One common focus of leisure time activities involves engagement in activities that are dissimilar to the activities that constitute an individual's vocational or educational experiences. For example, a child whose major activities involve sedentary indoor school attendance might choose outdoor activities such as hiking or horseback riding as a change of pace. The other common focus of leisure-time activities involves those activities that enhance or build on academic or vocational activities that the individual finds enjoyable. For example, a child precocious in mathematics whose schoolwork offers only limited involvement with the subject might engage in leisure-time activities such as doing mathematical puzzles or experimenting with computer simulations.

In special education, leisure-time activities can provide an especially helpful means for ameliorating personal-social and academic impairments imposed by the educationally limiting condition or conditions. The child receiving special education services, whether physically segregated from peers by special class placement or identified as being different owing to special educational problems, is at risk for developing a sense of isolation or inferiority. Counseling such a child to engage in leisure-time activities in which the educationally limiting conditions or disabilities will not be limiting may represent one approach toward ameliorating these kinds of problems. Leisure-time activities that provide the child with successful experiences can be especially helpful and can aid in the development of feelings of confidence and self-assurance that may not be facilitated in the academic sphere.

Caution may need to be used in encouraging the child with special educational problems to engage in leisure-time activities lest such activities exacerbate feelings of inability to perform. The caution necessary in such cases involves a consideration of how the child's academically limiting condition may relate to given leisure-time activities. The child with Attention-Deficit Disorder, for example, may become frustrated by leisure-time activities such as chess or table games that require extended periods of concentration over time. Similarly, the child with visual perception difficulty may experience difficulty with some craft projects or jigsaw puzzles, but find satisfaction in word games or crossword puzzles. By focusing on the child's strengths, leisure-time activities can be a source of satisfaction and sense of accomplishment rather than a source of further frustration or sense of inadequacy (Hartlage & Telzrow, 1986).

Leisure-time activities can provide supplementary skills training in academically relevant pursuits. Especially for gifted individuals, leisure-time activities can provide the opportunity for enhancing and expanding areas of academic or career interest. Building electronic systems or doing mechanical repairs may be a source of expansion for a child gifted in and interested in physics or mechanics. It can provide an out-of-school opportunity for skill enhancement and development. Even for the exceptional child with academically limiting problems, the opportunity for developing skills in the nonthreatening context of leisure-time activities can have a positive transfer to school settings. For example,

the counting in such table games as Monopoly, or the word building skills involved in Scrabble, can be encouraged as an enjoyable approach toward helping the exceptional child with counting or language difficulties.

Consideration of the child's interests, aptitudes, strengths, and weaknesses, matched with leisure-time activities either by formal matching procedures (Hartlage, 1968; Hartlage & Ells, 1983) or intuitively guided counseling, can help transform leisure-time activities into ones that can simultaneously be enjoyable, provide enhancement of existing strengths, and be a source of remediation for academic weakness and a measure of developing personal and social competence and confidence.

### REFERENCES

Hartlage, L. C. (1968). *Computer Research Avocational Guidance Test.* Phoenix, AZ: Computer Research.

Hartlage, L. C., & Ells, A. (1983). *Leisure compatibility guide.* Scottsdale, AZ: Afterwork.

Hartlage, L. C., & Telzrow, C. F. (1986). *Neuropsychological assessment and intervention with children.* Sarasota, FL: Professional Resource Exchange.

LAWRENCE C. HARTLAGE
*Evans, Georgia*

ENRICHMENT
MOTIVATION

# LEITER INTERNATIONAL PERFORMANCE SCALE–REVISED

The Leiter International Performance Scale–Revised (Leiter-R; Roid & Miller, 1997) is an individually administered nonverbal test designed to assess intellectual ability, memory, and attention functions in children and adolescents. The Leiter-R consists of two groupings of subtests: the Visualization and Reasoning (VR) battery (10 subtests), and the Attention and Memory (AM) battery (10 subtests). It also includes four social-emotional rating scales (Examiner, Parent, Self, and Teacher) that provide information from behavioral observations of the examinee. For initial screening purposes, four subtests in the VR battery can be used to measure the child's global intellectual level as part of a battery of other tests and assessments. The full VR battery (six subtests for children ages 2 to 5) can be used for identification, classification, and placement decisions. Examiners have the option of using the VR and AM batteries separately. The manual also cautions that IQ scores from the Leiter-R should never be used in isolation, and should be evaluated in the context of a wide variety of information about the child. The manual includes an extensive discussion of the interpretation of Leiter-R results and provides case studies to demonstrate the interpretation of scores.

The Leiter-R includes the following 20 subtests.

*Reasoning*

*Classification:* Examinees categorize objects or geometric designs.

*Sequencing:* Examinees identify the stimulus that comes next in a sequence.

*Repeated Patterns:* Examinees identify which of several stimuli fill in missing parts in repeated sequences of pictures or figures.

*Design Analogies:* Examinees identify geometric shapes that complete matrix analogies.

*Visualization (Spatial)*

*Matching:* Examinees match response cards to easel pictures.

*Figure–Ground:* Examinees identify designs embedded in complex backgrounds.

*Form Completion:* Examinees see randomly displayed parts of designs and must select the whole design from alternatives.

*Picture Context:* Examinees use visual-context clues to identify a part of a picture that has been removed from a larger picture.

*Paper Folding:* Examinees view an unfolded object in two dimensions and match it to a picture of the whole object.

*Figure Rotation:* Examinees identify rotated pictures of original, nonrotated objects.

*Memory*

*Immediate Recognition:* Examinees are shown five pictures for 5 seconds, and after items are removed and re-presented, they must identify the one item that is missing.

*Delayed Recognition:* Examinees, after a 20-minute delay, identify the objects presented in the Immediate Recognition subtest.

*Associated Pairs:* Examinees are shown pairs of objects for 5 to 10 seconds, and after objects are removed, students must make meaningful associations for each pair.

*Delayed Pairs:* Examinees, after a 20-minute delay, identify the items in the Associated Pairs subtest.

*Forward Memory:* Examinees remember pictured objects to which the examiner points and must repeat the sequence in which the examiner points to the objects.

*Reversed Memory:* The examiner points to pictures or figures in order, and the student must point to the same pictures in reverse order.

*Spatial Memory:* Examinees are shown increasingly complex stimulus displays, arranged in matrix format, and the examinees must then place cards in order on a blank matrix display.

*Visual Coding:* Examinees match pictures and geometric objects to numbers.

*Attention*

*Attention Sustained:* Examinees are given large numbers of stimuli and must identify those that are alike.

*Attention Divided:* Examinees divide attention between a moving display of pictures and the sorting of playing cards.

The majority of Leiter-R items require the examinee to move response cards into slots on the easel tray. Some items require arranging foam rubber shapes and pointing to responses on the easel pictures. Subtest starting points are determined by the child's age (there are three age groups for administration of the Leiter-R: 2–5, 6–10, and 11–20). The manual contains detailed scoring instructions, and for most subtests responses are scored as 0 or 1. Scoring criteria for each item are noted on the instruction page for each subtest. For some subtests, scoring requires counting the number of correct responses and the number of errors.

Raw scores on the subtests and rating scales are converted to scaled scores ($M = 10$, $SD = 3$) using tables in the manual. IQ scores are calculated from sums of subtest scaled scores and converted to IQ standard scores ($M = 100$, $SD = 15$). Composite scores can also be obtained for Fluid Reasoning, Fundamental Visualization, Spatial Visualization, Attention, and Memory. In addition, the raw scores for each subtest and IQ can be converted to growth-scale scores that express a child's abilities in a metric that can reflect growth and be useful for treatment planning and measuring change over time.

The Leiter-R Visualization and Reasoning battery was standardized between 1993 and 1995 on 1,719 typical children and adolescents, while the Attention and Memory battery was standardized on a subset of 763 of the same typical children. An additional 692 atypical children were tested to provide data for comparison studies. Data collection used a national stratification plan based on 1993 U.S. Census statistics for age, gender, and socioeconomic status. Nationally representative proportions of children who are Caucasian, Hispanic American, African American, Asian American, and Native American were included.

The manual provides internal-consistency reliability coefficients for the Visualization/Reasoning battery, the Attention/Memory battery, and the Attention/Memory Battery Special Diagnostic Scales. Fewer than half the coefficients are above .80. Reliabilities are also provided for IQ and composite scores. Most of these exceed .80. Evidence is also provided for test-retest reliability. Coefficients are high for composites and (except above age 11) low for subtests.

Evidence of content validity is based on mapping of the test to theoretical models of intelligence. Evidence of construct validity is based on completion of factor analyses showing a match between the scale and the theoretical model that guided its development. Concurrent validity between the Leiter-R (Brief and Full Scale IQ) and the Wechsler Intelligence Scale for Children (WISC-III; Performance and Full Scale IQ) on children ages 6 to 16 resulted in correlations of .85 and .86.

## REFERENCES

Athanasiou, M. S. (2000). Current nonverbal assessment instruments: A comparison of psychometric integrity and test fairness. *Journal of Psychoeducational Assessment, 18,* 211–229.

Farrell, M. M., & Phelps, L. (2000). A comparison of the Leiter-R and the Universal Nonverbal Intelligence Test (UNIT) with children classified as language impaired. *Journal of Psychoeducational Assessment, 18,* 268–274.

McCallum, S., Bracken, B., & Wasserman, J. (2000). *Essentials of nonverbal assessment.* New York: Wiley.

Plake, B. S., & Impara, J. C. (Eds.). (2001). *The fourteenth mental measurements yearbook.* Lincoln, NE: Buros Institute of Mental Measurements.

Roid, G., Nellis, L., & McLellan, M. (2003). Assessment with the Leiter International Performance Scale–Revised and the S-BIT. In R. S. McCallum (Ed.), *Handbook of nonverbal assessment* (pp. 113–140). New York: Kluwer Academic/Plenum.

Tsatsanis, K. D., Dartnall, N., & Cicchetti, D. (2003). Concurrent validity and classification accuracy of the Leiter and Leiter-R in low-functioning children with autism. *Journal of Autism & Developmental Disorders, 33,* 23–30.

RON DUMONT
*Fairleigh Dickinson University*

JOHN O. WILLIS
*Rivier College*

## LENNOX-GAUSTAUT SYNDROME

See SEIZURE DISORDERS.

## LERNER, JANET WEISS (1926–      )

A native of Milwaukee, Wisconsin, Janet Weiss Lerner received a BA in 1947 in special education at the University of Wisconsin, Milwaukee. She received her MEd in 1958 in elementary education and reading from the National College of Education, and her PhD in 1965 in education administration from New York University. She is currently

Janet Weiss Lerner

chair and professor of special education at Northeastern Illinois University.

Lerner's early experiences as an elementary school teacher, and later as an itinerant teacher of brain-injured children and a reading specialist, honed her interest in the areas of reading problems and individuals with learning disabilities. She believes that early, appropriate recognition of a child's academic problem is necessary so that the child can develop the skills needed to function well in school and later in life. Her book, *Learning Disabilities: Theories, Diagnosis, and Teaching Strategies,* 7th edition (1997) discusses learning disabilities from a variety of perspectives. She believes in being practical and in giving teachers, administrators, and other professionals ideas that they can use in their daily work with children. Lerner also believes that people must have a good grasp of theory to understand the appropriate time and place to use certain techniques and to be effective in the field of special education.

Lerner views learning disabilities as a lifelong problem affecting many areas of life. Early identification and effective teaching strategies are necessary.

## REFERENCE

Lerner, J. (1997). *Learning disabilities: Theories, diagnosis, and teaching strategies* (7th ed.). Boston: Houghton Mifflin.

E. VALERIE HEWITT
*Texas A&M University*
First edition

DONNA WALLACE
*The University of Texas of the Permian Basin*
Second edition

# LESCH-NYHAN SYNDROME

Lesch-Nyhan syndrome, a rare X-linked recessive disorder that occurs in an estimated 1 in 100,000 births (Holmes, 1992), is an inborn error of purine metabolism caused by absence of, or deficiency in, hypoxanthine-guanine phosphoribosyl transferase (HPRT). HPRT metabolizes hypoxanthine and guanine to uric acid (Anderson, Ernst, & Davis, 1992).

The disorder is characterized by behavior abnormalities, the most horrific and prevalent being aggressive, severe, and chronic self-injurious behaviors. Self-injurious behaviors (SIBs) are so persistent and potentially damaging that restraint is necessary. The onset of SIBs may occur as early as infancy or as late as teenage years. The most frequent SIBs are hand biting and lip chewing, which may lead to considerable tissue destruction and loss (e.g., Holmes, 1992; Stout & Caskey, 1989). Since pain perception is normal, affected children scream during SIBs (Nyhan, 1973) and may actually beg to be physically restrained (Schroeder, Breese, & Mueller, 1990). Lip chewing can be so self-mutilating that tooth extraction is necessary. In a particularly severe case, continual self-inflicted oral ulcerations led to removal of all of a 17-month-old infant's teeth (Rashid & Yusuf, 1997). The earlier the onset of SIBs, the worse they become over time (Anderson & Ernst, 1994). Other features include choreoathetosis and spasticity (e.g., Holmes, 1992; Stout & Caskey, 1989). New research showing that cognitive impairment is minimal questions the belief that mental retardation is a regular feature of Lesch-Nyhan syndrome. Patients have shown normal memory skills, range of emotions, concentration abilities, self-awareness, and social skills (Anderson et al., 1992).

The disease can be inherited or occur through genetic mutation. The expression of the gene is fully recessive, which makes this disease virtually exclusive to males by transmission from their mother. Females can be carriers but rarely ever exhibit the disease. A few recently reported cases in females are believed to have occurred through genetic mutation (Barabas, 1993).

Lesch-Nyhan patients appear normal at birth. The early signs of the disorder are seen when high levels of uric acid cause sand-like deposits in the infant's diaper. Affected infants show normal motor development usually until about 6 months of age, when they begin to lose any previously acquired motor skills. Arching of the back and poor head control are often indicators, and patients are unable to sit or stand without assistance. Speech is greatly limited as well. Involuntary movements are typical as muscle tone increases with maturity. Frequently the disorder is differentiated from cerebral palsy only with onset of self-mutilation. Since the disease is often misdiagnosed due to similarities to other brain disorders such as cerebral palsy, appropriate laboratory tests are needed to ensure an accurate diagnosis. These include HPRT-activity testing in tissue samples, prenatal enzyme assay, and DNA analysis through amniocentesis or chorionic villus sampling (Stout & Caskey, 1989).

A combination of metabolic abnormalities increases uric acid production and hyperuricemia, which predisposes patients to gout later in life. The neurologic abnormalities appear to be unrelated to hyperuricemia. Research suggests that self-mutilation is based on reduced dopamine-neuron function and norepinephrine turnover. Recent development of HPRT-deficient animal models, as well as research with affected humans, may lead to an understanding of the biochemical basis of self-mutilation (e.g., Schroeder et al., 1990; Stout & Caskey, 1989).

Treatment of this disorder has had only limited success. Allopurinol effectively reduces HPRT-based hyperuricemia and its various renal effects and gout, but has no effects on the neurologic abnormalities (Schroeder et al., 1990). Serotonin reuptake inhibitors have been used in attempts to correct dopamine and serotonin levels. This treatment has shown short-term improvements, but over time effectiveness significantly diminishes. Benzodiazepines are currently the most prescribed medication for behavior control, although no change in self-injury over time has been noted (Anderson & Ernst, 1994). Due to the lack of success in treatment the disorder may be an ideal candidate for gene replacement therapy (Stout & Caskey, 1989).

Behavior modification has also had limited effectiveness. The best preventative strategy has been stress reduction and protective restraint. Punishment for SIB has only resulted in an increase in the unwanted behavior. However, time-out tactics and reinforcement of non-self-injurious behavior have decreased SIBs in certain settings (Luiselli, Matson, & Singh, 1992). Undesired behaviors particularly occur when a patient is not receiving direct attention, indicating that social and environmental factors must be considered in future behavior modification treatments.

## REFERENCES

Anderson, L. T., & Ernst, M. (1994). Self-injury in Lesch-Nyhan disease. *Journal of Autism and Developmental Disorders, 24,* 67–81.

Anderson, L. T., Ernst, M., & Davis, S. V. (1992). Cognitive abilities of patients with Lesch-Nyhan disease. *Journal of Autism and Developmental Disorders, 22,* 189–203.

Barabas, G. (Ed.). (1993). Lesch-Nyhan syndrome. *Matheny Bulletin, 3*(2), 1–11.

Holmes, E. W. (1992). Other disorders of purine metabolism. In J. B. Wyngaarden, L. H. Smith, Jr., & J. C. Bennett (Eds.), *Cecil textbook of medicine* (19th ed., pp. 1115–1116). Philadelphia, PA: Saunders.

Luiselli, J. K., Matson, J. L., & Singh, N. N. (Eds.). (1992). *Self-injurious behavior.* New York: Springer-Verlag.

Nyhan, W. L. (1973). The Lesch-Nyhan syndrome. *Annual Review of Medicine, 24,* 41–60.

Rashid, N., & Yusuf, H. (1997). Oral self-mutilation by a 17-month-old child with Lesch-Nyhan syndrome. *International Journal of Pediatric Dentistry, 7*(2), 115–117.

Schroeder, S. R., Breese, G. R., & Mueller, A. B. (1990). Dopaminergic mechanisms in self-injurious behavior. In M. Wolraich & D. K. Routh (Eds.), *Advances in developmental and behavioral pediatrics* (Vol. 9, pp. 181–198). London: Kingsley.

Stout, J. T., & Caskey, C. T. (1989), Hypoxanthine phosphoribosyltransferase deficiency: The Lesch-Nyhan syndrome and gouty arthritis. In C. R. Scriver, A. L. Beaudet, W. S. Sly, & D. Valle (Eds.), *The metabolic basis of inherited disease* (6th ed., Vol. I, pp. 1007–1028). New York: McGraw-Hill.

MARSHA H. LUPI
*Hunter College, City University of New York*
First edition

KATHERINE D. FALWELL
ROBERT T. BROWN
*University of North Carolina at Wilmington*
Second edition

# GENETIC COUNSELING

# LESIONS

The term lesion refers to "an alteration, structural or functional due to a disease" (*Blakiston's,* 1979). Lesions may be acute, subacute, and chronic; these terms are not disease specific. They relate to no specific disease, syndrome, or illness but are only adjectives that describe time of onset and appearance of symptoms.

Acute lesions have a rapid sudden onset, a short course, and pronounced symptoms. The time of onset can range from minutes to a maximum of 36 to 48 hours. Examples of acute central nervous system (CNS) lesions are stroke, head injury, or seizure. Each one of these CNS disorders typically occurs suddenly and has observable behavioral symptoms and signs that indicate the need to seek further medical attention.

Subacute lesions fall between the acute and chronic stages. The signs or symptoms usually develop slowly, progressively, or intermittently and become more severe over the course of the illness. Subacute stages of an illness can range from days to a few weeks. An example of a subacute problem would be the reoccurrence of a headache, which may indicate a more severe progressing CNS problem.

Chronic lesions are those disorders that present signs or symptoms of illness or dysfunction over a longer time period than the subacute or acute stages. Chronic onset of lesions can range from a period of weeks to months or even

years. In many cases, this term has been used to describe something that is only partially treatable or that responds partially to treatment with residual dysfunction. The term does not denote progressive deterioration in any way. In fact, many children with cerebral palsy, which can be a chronic disability, improve with time because of their ability to compensate for the motor dysfunction. Other examples of chronic CNS disorders are Alzheimer's disease, characterized by progressive dementia and diffuse cerebral atrophy, or the effects of a cerebral vascular accident (e.g., a stroke; Gilroy & Meyer, 1964). Cerebral palsy and polio could also be included under a chronic stage disorder.

The terms acute, subacute, and chronic are not mutually exclusive. Each of the three stages can be observed in an individual at certain phases of an illness. Specifically, these terms refer to the initial onset or cause of a CNS lesion and the duration of the assumed outcome of such an injury.

As the observability of an injury increases, so, too, does the potential for systematic development of educational or rehabilitative efforts. Conversely, with less observability there occurs an increasing reliance on unsubstantiated relationships of brain dysfunction and behavior. Thus, with less observable types of brain damage, the decision regarding intervention strategies has often been difficult.

From an educational perspective, children who have observable brain damage owing to injury or illness pose a real challenge for the educator. National statistics estimate that 18,000 children will sustain some form of serious brain insult each year. Hence educators today are seeing a very different population entering and reentering their classrooms. While the effects of a serious insult on a youngster may be unfamiliar to educators, there are similarities in many learning theories that should be familiar to the teacher. Some of the earlier theoretical work, from a developmental perspective, has been used with observable brain-damaged children.

However, because of the diffuse and somewhat undetermined location and function of the brain damage, a teacher may be faced with a child with multiple cognitive, physical, and emotional or affective disorders. Undoubtedly, some educators will see little difference between a brain-injured child and other special needs children. There are, however, three major distinctions that must be addressed: (1) brain-injured children do not typically fit existing educational funding categories or definitions; (2) standardized tests used for placement purposes with other special needs children do not accurately predict the level of functioning for these children; and (3) program development for brain-injured children must take into account other factors such as orientation and past experiences to capitalize on the child's already learned behaviors. While the presence of brain-injured children in classrooms may be novel to educators, this special needs population will undoubtedly continue to be placed back into the mainstream of education as recovery from insult permits.

## REFERENCES

*Blakiston's pocket medical dictionary* (4th ed.). (1979). New York: McGraw-Hill.

Gilroy, J., & Meyer, J. S. (1964). *Medical neurology.* Toronto: Macmillan.

MICHAEL G. BROWN
*Central Wisconsin Center for the Developmentally Disabled*

J. TODD STEPHENS
*University of Wisconsin at Madison*

**BRAIN DAMAGE/INJURY**
**BRAIN DISORDERS**
**CENTRAL NERVOUS SYSTEM**
**LEARNING DISABILITIES**

# LEUKEMIC CHILD

Leukemia is a cancer of the white blood cells. In leukemia, normal blood elements are replaced by undifferentiated, that is, immature cells. These cells are termed blasts (Pendergrass, Chard, & Hartmann, 1985).

In chronic leukemia, there is a malignant proliferation of differentiated or mature cells. In both acute and chronic leukemia, these abnormal cells increase in number and accumulate in the victim's body. The spread can be very rapid if untreated. It will involve bone marrow, lymph nodes, kidney, liver, spleen, lungs, skin, and gonads.

Acute leukemic conditions predominate in children. Ninety-nine percent of leukemic children suffer from acute conditions, 1 percent from chronic ones. The most common acute leukemia is acute lymphoblastic leukemia (ALL; Baehner, 1978), which accounts for almost 80 percent of all childhood leukemic conditions. Acute leukemias of other types are identifiable as acute nonlymphoblastic leukemias (ANLL; Pendergrass et al., 1985).

The incidence and mortality of childhood leukemia have varied over the years, partly because of different reporting procedures and better reporting of causes of death. Reviewed by sex, 30 to 40 percent higher rates are reported for males (Cutler, Axtell, & Heise, 1967). Some studies have reported a large peak in mortality rates between the ages of two and three, but this has been found true only for white populations of European extraction (Pendergrass et al., 1985).

The treatment of childhood leukemia traditionally has been one of drug therapy. Prednisone, a steroid, has been found to be the best single drug. It is often used with other drugs to optimize treatment. Sometimes bone marrow transplants are also used; they have been found effective even in late-stage anemia. Hopeful expectations have been expressed regarding the use of bone marrow transplants with less advanced leukemic conditions.

The treatment of leukemic conditions has made major strides in recent years, with much longer survival times for leukemic children being reported (Hanson, McKay, & Miller, 1980). As a consequence, leukemia mortality rates are no longer clearly reflective of incidence and new means for establishing the latter have been developed. Data provided by the Third National Cancer Survey (Young & Miller, 1975) and by the Surveillance, Epidemiology, and End Results (SEER) Program of the National Cancer Institute (Silverberg, 1981) show a rise in the incidence for acute lymphoblastic leukemia beginning at approximately 2 years of age with a peaking during the 3- to 4-year age period. The distribution of acute nonlymphoblastic leukemias is fairly flat.

Hereditary factors have been indicated in leukemia. Three or more members of the same generation have been found to be leukemic in some studies, while in others the condition has been found to appear in some families over four generations. If one member of an identical twin pair manifests the disease, the other has about a 25 percent chance of developing the disease before the age of 40 (Pendergrass et al., 1985).

A variety of other childhood diseases or handicaps manifest higher rates of leukemia. These include immunodeficiency diseases, Fanconi's anemia, ataxia telangiectasia, and Down syndrome. This suggests that chromosomal abnormalities are related to leukemia. The role of other etiological factors (e.g., chemical exposure and radiation) are as yet unclear; however, increases in leukemia in Japanese populations exposed to atom bomb attacks made it evident that intense exposure to radiation can significantly increase the probability of eventually developing a leukemic condition.

Various stages of improvement in childhood leukemia have been described (Pendergrass et al., 1985). Complete remission is established when bone marrow, blood morphology, and physical examination all are found to be normal. An incomplete remission is one in which there are still increased numbers of blast cells to be found in the child's bone marrow, or in which there is persistent anemia, a decrease in platelet count, or abnormalities in the liver, lymph glands, or spleen. Hematologic remission is when the bone marrow is found to be normal even if leukemia persists in other parts of the body. A relapse is considered to occur when blast cells return after a complete remission was accomplished, either in the bone marrow, the central nervous system, or the testicles.

Through the use of new and more effective medical regimens, both the survival rates and remission rates of children with childhood leukemia have increased dramatically over recent decades. Remission induction rates went from a zero pretreatment level to 60 to 70 percent during the middle

1960s. By 1978 these rates had reached 90 to 95 percent for children receiving proper drug therapies. However, the length of complete remission (remission duration) without the use of therapies has not improved. Maintenance therapies must thus be anticipated even for leukemic children who are in complete remission. With maintenance therapies, significantly lengthened remission rates have been achieved.

Along with awareness of the need to continue therapies during remission has come the appreciation that there must be additional treatment to manage the side effects of continued treatment. Thus antibiotics may be given to control infection, and platelet concentrates may be given to treat overt bleeding.

The long-term prognosis for childhood leukemia is still poor. Few individuals who have childhood leukemia survive into adulthood. There are indications that they have a higher risk of manifesting cancer as adults, though there is no clear evidence to indicate that they are susceptible to other diseases.

Of considerable significance to special educators is the fact that central nervous system leukemia has been found to develop in a large percentage of children who have childhood leukemia, even in those who are in states of complete hematologic remission. Research has indicated that this is partly due to the fact that the brain has a protective mechanism that decreases the amount of drugs allowed into brain tissue. The effects of the medications used to treat childhood leukemia thus may be vitiated in respect to their effect on the central nervous system. In attempts to circumvent this problem, medication may be injected directly into the spinal fluid. This procedure has been found to reduce significantly the incidence of central nervous system leukemia and to sustain significantly longer remissions from the disease (Glidewell & Holland, 1973; Pendergrass et al., 1985).

Current medical challenges to the treatment of childhood leukemia include treating the child who fails to achieve a remission after initial therapy or who suffers relapses despite proper maintenance therapies. There are also questions as to how long to treat a child who remains in complete remission, what constitutes the minimal amount of treatment to achieve effective results, and the long-term effects of the disease and its therapies.

The psychological impact on both the child and the family of those having childhood leukemia is of major proportions. The medical management of the condition is arduous and stressful for child, family, and therapists, and often physically painful for the child. The sequelae of treatment as well as the constant knowledge of the consequences of the diseases—learned early by most children—can be overwhelming. The chronicity of the condition and of its medical management and treatment places great stress on family psyches and finances. The leukemic child's social and academic performances can be expected to suffer. The fact that the child, even when surviving into adulthood, can be expected to have lifelong problems also takes its toll. For-

tunately, the great strides forward that have been made in the disease's management encourage a positive outlook.

Children who have leukemia are entitled to special education under the provisions of IDEA. They are specifically identified as health impaired and entitled to special education under this law.

## REFERENCES

Baehner, R. L. (1978). Hematologic malignancies: Leukemia and lymphoma. In C. H. Smith (Ed.), *Blood diseases of infancy and childhood* (4th ed.). St. Louis, MO: Mosby.

Bigge, J., & Sirvis, B. (1986). Physical and health impairments. In N. G. Haring & L. McCormick (Eds.), *Exceptional children and youth* (4th ed.). Columbus, OH: Merrill.

Cutler, S. J., Axtell, L., & Heise, H. (1967). Ten thousand cases of leukemia: 1940–1962. *Journal of the National Cancer Institute, 39,* 993–1026.

Glidewell, O. J., & Holland, J. G. (1973). Clinical trials of the acute leukemia group B in acute lymphocytic leukemia in childhood. *Bibliotheca Haemetologica, 39,* 1053–1067.

Hanson, M. R., McKay, F. W., & Miller, R. W. (1980). Three-dimensional perspective of United States cancer mortality. *Lancet, 2,* 246–247.

Pendergrass, T. W., Chard, R. L., & Hartmann, J. R. (1985). Leukemia. In N. Hobbs & J. M. Perrin (Eds.), *Issues in the care of children with chronic illness.* San Francisco: Jossey-Bass.

Silverberg, E. (1981). Cancer statistics, 1981. *CA: A Cancer Journal for Clinicians, 31,* 13–28.

Young, J. L., & Miller, R. W. (1975). Incidence of malignant tumors in United States children. *Journal of Pediatrics, 86,* 254–258.

LESTER MANN
*Hunter College, City University
of New York*

CANCER, CHILDHOOD
HEALTH IMPAIRMENTS

# LEWIS, MICHAEL (1937–　　)

A native of Brooklyn, New York, Michael Lewis received his BA (1958) in sociology and his PhD (1962) in psychology from the University of Pennsylvania. He is currently University Distinguished Professor of pediatrics and psychiatry, and director of the Institute for the Study of Child Development at Robert Wood Medical School–University of Medicine and Dentistry of New Jersey. He is also a professor of psychology at Rutgers University.

His research has focused on normal and deviant emotional and intellectual development in the opening years of life, and his first book, *Children's Emotions and Moods* (1983), was devoted to normal development. His discovery of techniques to measure central nervous system functioning has provided a standard measurement system used

Michael Lewis

to predict either dysfunctional growth or normal development. He has also developed computer-based techniques for enhancing intellectual ability in children with mental retardation. His most recent work involves a study on the effect of children's environment on social adjustment and mental health, and a study of the early indications of giftedness in children (pers. comm., February 1998).

Dr. Lewis has authored a number of books, the most recent of which include the *Handbook of Emotions* and the *Handbook of Developmental Psychopathology,* as well as four monographs and over 350 articles and chapters in professional journals and scholarly texts. He is a consulting editor for the *Journal of Sex Roles* and *Psychological Inquiry,* and has served on numerous committees related to mental health and mental retardation. Lewis has been the recipient of various honors in the fields of science and psychology, and has been named a Fellow of the New York Academy of Sciences, the American Psychological Association, and the American Association for the Advancement of Science.

E. VALERIE HEWITT
*Texas A&M University*
First edition

DONNA WALLACE
*The University of Texas of the
    Permian Basin*
Second edition

## LEXINGTON SCHOOL FOR THE DEAF

The Lexington School for the Deaf was established in New York City in 1867 to provide oral education for deaf children. There were already more than a dozen schools for deaf students in the United States at that time but all used some form of sign language. The Lexington School was a pioneer in oral education and has remained a strong proponent of speech, speech reading, and aural rehabilitation.

Lexington is a world-renowned leader in the education of deaf infants, children, and adolescents in all levels of educational programs. It offers special programs for multiply handicapped deaf students, including psychiatric and psychological services. Its staff has included such outstanding educators as Mildren Groht, author of *Natural Language for Deaf Children,* Edith Buell, author of *Outline of Language for Deaf Children,* speech teachers Mary New, Eleanor Vorce, and Janet Head, and superintendents Clarence D. O'Connor and Leo Connor.

The Lexington School for the Deaf is now located in Queens, New York. In addition to educational programs, it offers a 24-hour information and referral service that provides general information and advocacy services related to hearing impairment. Auxiliary agencies of the school include the Lexington Hearing and Speech Center, the Lexington Center for Mental Health Services, and the Lexington Training Research and Educational Evaluation Service.

### REFERENCES

Moores, D. (1982). *Educating the deaf: Psychology, principles and practices.* Boston: Houghton Mifflin.

O'Connor, C. D. (1967). *Lexington School's first century of oral education of the deaf* (Volta Review Reprint 878). Washington, DC: Alexander Graham Bell Association for the Deaf.

ROSEMARY GAFFNEY
*Hunter College, City University
of New York*

## LIABILITY OF TEACHERS IN SPECIAL EDUCATION

The concern for teacher effectiveness has focused considerable attention on what happens in the special education classroom. As such, teacher performance is monitored and teachers are held accountable for their actions in the classroom. A byproduct of this is a growing wave of legal action against teachers involving teacher liability.

Teacher liability is usually defined in court as involving negligence or lack of appropriate services for the exceptional student. The result is often a malpractice suit against the teacher (Brady & Dennis, 1984). Alexander (1980) and Brady and Dennis (1984) note that malpractice liability in education usually involves negligence, intentional interference or harm, or constitutional infringement. However, if a liability suit is brought against a teacher, it will likely focus on negligence.

Teacher negligence is affirmed if the court is shown that

a teacher (1) owed a duty of care to the student, (2) did not carry out that duty, and (3) the lack of completion of that duty resulted in injury to the student (Brady & Dennis, 1984). To appropriately conduct their duties, it is commonly felt that teachers must provide proper instruction, supervision, and maintenance of equipment. If the lack of these duties results in substantial injury to a student, the teacher may be found liable (Alexander, 1980; Brady & Dennis, 1984; Connors, 1981).

Lack of proper instruction has been defined in many ways. As it pertains to teacher liability, violation of duty seems to be primarily a result of exposing students to physical risk during an instructional period. For example, student injuries in sports or laboratory settings may result in a liability suit. Thus far, the failure of a student to learn has not resulted in teacher liability.

Connors (1981) notes that proper supervision is usually defined as general supervision; for example, a teacher is responsible for being present and overseeing the activities that take place. In so doing, a teacher must be aware of the situation and the inherent risks involved and take every possible step to see that the potential risks are eliminated. If teacher presence were enough to avoid injury, lack of teacher presence often would result in a finding of liability due to negligence.

Finally, teachers must ensure that equipment used in daily activities is not defective and is in proper working order. Cases have been tried in which defective playground equipment has been the cause of an accident (*District of Columbia* v. *Washington,* 1975). In one case a defective safety guard on a chain saw caused a student to be injured (*South Ripley* v. *Peters,* 1979).

To avoid liability cases, teachers should engage in sound educational practices, consider each child's individual needs, and document the activities that have been conducted.

As more and more students are mainstreamed into the regular education classroom, the previously noted liabilities of the special education teacher are also beginning to be applied to the regular education teacher as well. In 1993, for the first time, a jury ordered a classroom teacher to pay damages to a student as a result of the teacher's refusal to implement an Individual Education Plan (IEP). The suit was filed by the parents of 16-year-old Douglas Devart (*Doe* v. *Withers,* 1993). Due to his learning disabilities, the IEP specified that his academic testing be done in an oral testing format by an LD teacher in the resource room. This modification was provided during elementary and junior high school. When Douglas was a freshman in high school, all but one of his teachers agreed to comply with this IEP requirement. This teacher, Michael Withers, refused to honor the IEP, requiring Douglas to take his exams in the same written format as all the other students. The parents alleged that Mr. Withers also refused to comply with a written directive from the high school special education coordinator, instructing him of the IEP requirement. After receipt of

the directive, Mr. Withers administered nine more written tests in history, most of which Douglas failed. The parents also alleged that Mr. Withers "insulted and belittled" their child in front of his peers.

The parents sued the teacher, the principal, the superintendent and the school board for compensatory and punitive damage under 42 U.S.C. 1983. Before the case went to the jury, the judge dismissed the complaints against the principal, the superintendent, and the school board, but allowed the complaint against the teacher to stand. The jury ordered history teacher Michael Withers to pay $5,000 in compensatory damages and $10,000 in punitive damages to Douglas Devart (Walsh, 1993).

The dispute as to whether Douglas was capable of taking his tests in the standard written format was not at issue. Withers' disagreement with the necessity of the oral testing accommodation should have been aired at the time the IEP was being established; the jury's decision clearly established that he did not have the authority to unilaterally defy the provisions of the IEP. This case represents a clear warning that regular education teachers are just as accountable as special education teachers for implementing the educational prescriptions established in a child's educational plan.

## REFERENCES

Alexander, K. (1980). *School law.* St. Paul, MN: West.

Brady, M. P., & Dennis, H. F. (1984). Integrating severely handicapped learners: Potential teacher liability in community based programs. *Remedial & Special Education, 5*(5), 29–36.

Connors, E. T. (1981). *Educational tort liability and malpractice.* Bloomington, IN: Phi Delta Kappa.

*Doe* v. *Withers,* 20 IDELR 422 (West Virginia Circuit Court, Taylor County, 1993).

Walsh, J. (1993, December). *This just in . . . Developments in special education law.* Austin, TX: Walsh, Anderson, Underwood, Schulze & Aldridge, P. C.

JOHN R. BEATTIE
*University of North Carolina at Charlotte*
First edition

DELORES J. HITTINGER
*The University of Texas of the Permian Basin*
Second edition

## DYSPEDAGOGIA

# LIBERMAN, ISABELLE YOFFE (1918–1990)

Isabelle Yoffe Liberman, educational researcher, teacher, and clinician, was a champion of the scientific study of reading during the 1970s and 1980s. Liberman proposed that because the would-be reader must connect the sequence of letters in written words to the phonemic segments they represent, reading requires an explicit awareness of the phonemic structure of words (Liberman, 1973). Working with colleagues at the University of Connecticut and Haskins Laboratories, Liberman became convinced of the enormous importance of phoneme awareness for beginning reading acquisition in the early 1970s (Liberman, 1971; Liberman, Shankweiler, Fischer, & Carter, 1974; Mattingly, 1972). Research establishing the role of phoneme awareness has been described as "the single most powerful advance in the science and pedagogy of reading" in the twentieth century (Adams et al., 1991, p. 392). Liberman proposed that reading is hard because segmentation of words into their constituent sounds doesn't come naturally to preliterate children (Liberman, 1971). The difficulty of learning to read in an alphabetic system is therefore not due to problems with visual perception or auditory perception, but to a cognitive difficulty in linking things which initially are not language—graphic symbols—to the phonetic parts of words. Thus the principle of alphabetic writing is somewhat obscure.

In the years following the groundbreaking studies of Liberman and her colleagues, research from laboratories in several countries has shown that phoneme awareness is one of the best predictors of success or failure in reading acquisition, a finding that has prompted changes in the way reading is taught and changes in the definition of dyslexia (Lyon, 1995). While emphasizing the importance of phoneme awareness, Liberman also taught that the difficulties of poor readers are not confined to awareness, but often extend more broadly across the phonological domain of language to include difficulties in word retrieval and short-term memory (Liberman, Shankweiler, & Liberman, 1989).

Born in Latvia to Russian parents, Liberman emigrated to the United States with her family at an early age, receiving her education in the United States (AB, Vassar; MA and PhD, Yale) While at Yale, she married Alvin M. Liberman, a fellow graduate student of psychology who also became a distinguished research psychologist. Isabelle Liberman decided to pursue clinical psychology after being informed that she could not expect to be hired in the same academic department as her husband.

Working at Connecticut's Children's Hospital, she became well-known as a diagnostician for children with learning disabilities. During these years, she became increasingly dissatisfied with the state of current knowledge in the field, noting that diagnosis and treatment of reading disability lacked a foundation in research and theory. Her practical experience in trying to help struggling readers inspired her search for the causes of reading problems in apparently normal children (Shankweiler, 1991).

In 1966, Liberman had the opportunity to join the faculty at the University of Connecticut in the Department of Educational Psychology. There, she directed the graduate teacher training programs in learning disabilities, and began a remarkably productive research program, shared with colleagues Donald Shankweiler and Ignatius Mattingly and her husband and colleague, Alvin Liberman. Their work, and that of their students and collaborators, helped to create a new field of cross-national and cross-language study of reading (Liberman, Liberman, Mattingly, & Shankweiler, 1980). By 2005, research had established a link between phonemic awareness and reading acquisition in numerous alphabetic languages, including (besides English) Arabic, Czech, Danish, Dutch, Finnish, German, Hebrew, Italian, Latvian, Portuguese, Russian, Serbo-Croatian, Spanish, and Turkish.

In 2000, phoneme awareness was identified by the National Reading Panel as one of the five core components for effective reading instruction (National Reading Panel, 2000). As a result, phoneme awareness was among the key elements in the No Child Left Behind Act of 2001 (2002). At this writing, phoneme awareness is included in state educational standards as an essential element of what students and their teachers must know and be able to do (Colorado Department of Education, 2000; Colorado Model Reading and Writing Standards Task Force, 1995). The research initiated by Isabelle Liberman and her colleagues continues to be applied in classrooms throughout the United States and abroad.

## REFERENCES

Adams, M. J., Allington, R. L., Chaney, J. H., Goodman, Y. M., Kapinus, B. A., McGee, L. M., Richgels, D. J., Schwartz, S. J., Shannon, P., Smitten, B., & Williams, J. P. (1991). "Beginning to read": A critique by literacy professionals and a response by Marilyn Jager Adams. *Reading Teacher, 44*(6), 370–395.

Colorado Department of Education. (2000). *Performance-based standards for Colorado teachers.* Denver: Author.

Colorado Model Reading and Writing Standards Task Force. (1995). *Colorado model content standards for reading and writing.* Denver: Colorado Department of Education.

Liberman, I. Y. (1971). Basic research in speech and lateralization of language: Some implications for reading disability. *Bulletin of the Orton Society, 21,* 72–87.

Liberman, I. Y. (1973). Segmentation of the spoken word and reading acquisition. *Bulletin of the Orton Society, 23,* 65–76.

Liberman, I. Y. (1987). Language and literacy: The obligation of the schools of education. In W. Ellis (Ed.), *Intimacy with language: A forgotten basic in teacher education* (pp. 1–9). Baltimore: Orton Dyslexia Society.

Liberman, I. Y., & Liberman, A. M. (1990). Whole language versus code emphasis: Underlying assumptions and their implications for reading instruction. *Annals of Dyslexia, 40,* 51–76.

Liberman, I. Y., Liberman, A. M., Mattingly, I. G., & Shankweiler, D. (1980). Orthography and the beginning reader. In J. F. Kavanagh & R. L. Venezky (Eds.), *Orthography, reading, and dyslexia* (pp. 137–154). Baltimore: University Park Press.

Liberman, I. Y., Shankweiler, D., Fischer, F. W., & Carter, B. (1974). Explicit syllable and phoneme segmentation in the young child. *Journal of Experimental Child Psychology, 18,* 201–212.

Liberman, I. Y., Shankweiler, D., & Liberman, A. M. (1989). The alphabetic principle and learning to read. In D. Shankweiler & I. Y. Liberman (Eds.), *Phonology and reading disability: Solving the reading puzzle* (pp. 1–33). Ann Arbor: University of Michigan Press.

Lyon, G. R. (1995). Toward a definition of dyslexia. *Annals of Dyslexia, 45,* 3–27.

Mattingly, I. G. (1972). Reading, the linguistic process, and linguistic awareness. In J. F. Kavanagh & I. G. Mattingly (Eds.), *Language by ear and by eye: The relationships between speech and reading* (pp. 133–147). Cambridge, MA: MIT Press.

National Reading Panel. (2000). *Teaching children to read: An evidence-based assessment of the scientific research literature on reading and its implications for reading instruction.* Bethesda, MD: National Reading Panel, National Institute of Child Health and Human Development.

*No Child Left Behind Act of 2001,* PL 107-110 (2002).

Shankweiler, D. (1991). The contributions of Isabelle Y. Liberman. In S. A. Brady & D. P. Shankweiler (Eds.), *Phonological processes in literacy: A tribute to Isabelle Y. Liberman* (pp. xiii–xvii). Hillsdale, NJ: Erlbaum.

ELAINE A. CHEESMAN
*University of Colorado at
Colorado Springs*

# LIBRARIES FOR THE BLIND AND INDIVIDUALS WITH PHYSICAL DISABILITIES

The National Library Service for the Blind and Physically Handicapped (of the Library of Congress) publishes books and magazines in Braille and in recorded form on disks and cassettes for readers who cannot hold, handle, or see well enough to read conventional print because of a visual or physical disability. Persons diagnosed as having a reading disability of sufficient severity to prevent their reading printed matter in a normal manner are also eligible for loan services.

Tapes and records of the over 35,000 titles in the National Library Service's collection of best-sellers, biographies, fiction, and how-to and foreign-language books and magazines can be sent free to anyone legally blind, unable to see or focus long enough to read standard print, reading disabled, or physically unable to handle books. They can also be sent free to teachers and librarians in schools with disabled pupils.

Through a nationwide network of over 160 cooperating libraries, the routine services of the National Library Service include book circulation, outreach publicity, tape duplication, equipment assignment, publications distribution, reader's advisory, reference assistance, and production of local-interest material. Subscribers to the service receive free playback equipment and the bimonthly *Talking Book Topics* or *Braille Book Review,* which list the latest books and magazines produced by the National Library Service.

In addition to the productions of the National Library Service, the American Foundation for the Blind, the American Printing House for the Blind, and Recording for the Blind also produce a wide variety of taped and recorded materials for disabled readers. While the National Library Service does not produce or distribute textbooks or curriculum materials, the American Printing House for the Blind and Recording for the Blind do.

The following equipment is loaned free of charge to eligible readers as long as Library of Congress materials are being borrowed: talking book machines (for hard and flexible discs), cassette-book machines, headphones, pillow speakers (for disabled readers who are bedridden), amplifiers (for readers with a significant hearing disability), breath switches, remote control units, solar panel battery chargers, and extension levers (for readers who have difficulty operating controls of the cassette-book machine).

The Library of Congress program that evolved into the National Library Service for the Blind and Physically Handicapped was established under President Herbert Hoover in 1931 as an effort to serve blind adults. In 1933 Congress extended the original program of providing Braille texts to include the provision of recorded materials. Congress again extended the program in 1952 to include services to blind children, in 1962 to provide musical instructional materials and scores, and again in 1966 to include individuals with physical disabilities that prevent them from reading standard print material. With over 1,000,000 subscribers, the National Library Service for the Blind and Physically Handicapped is an expanding enterprise.

## REFERENCES

Library of Congress. (1982). *An introduction to the National Service for the Blind and Physically Handicapped.* Washington, DC: Author.

Library of Congress. (1984). *Library resources for the blind and physically handicapped: A directory with FY 1983 statistics on readership, circulation, budget, staff, and collections.* Washington, DC: Author.

Library of Congress. (1984). *Volunteers who produce books.* Washington, DC: Author.

National Library Service for the Blind and Physically Handicapped. *Music services for blind and physically handicapped individuals.* Washington, DC: Author.

National Library Service for the Blind and Physically Handicapped. *Reading is for everyone.* Washington, DC: Author.

Wexler, Henrietta (1981, January/February) Books that talk. *American Education, 1*(1), 15–17.

CATHERINE HALL RIKHYE
*Hunter College, City University
of New York*

## LIBRARY SERVICES FOR INDIVIDUALS WITH DISABILITIES

# LIBRARY SERVICES FOR INDIVIDUAL WITH DISABILITIES

A free national library program of Braille and recorded materials for blind and physically disabled persons is administered by the National Library Service for the Blind and Physically Handicapped (NLS), Library of Congress. Established by an act of Congress in 1931 to serve blind adults, the program was expanded in 1952 to include children, in 1962 to provide music materials, and in 1966 to include individuals with other physical impairments that prevent the reading of standard print. The NLS program is funded annually by Congress. Regional and subregional libraries in each state receive funds from local, state, and federal sources.

With the cooperation of authors and publishers who grant permission to use copyrighted materials, NLS selects and produces full-length books and magazines in Braille and on recorded disks and cassettes. Reading materials are distributed to a cooperating network of 56 regional and more than 100 subregional libraries where they are circulated to eligible borrowers. Reading materials and playback machines are sent to borrowers and returned to libraries by postage-free mail.

Books are selected on the basis of their appeal to a wide range of interests. The national book collection currently contains more than 41,000 titles and approximately 10,000,000 copies of Braille and recorded books. Each year, approximately 2,000 press-Braille, disk, and cassette titles are mass produced for distribution through network libraries, and an additional 300 Braille titles are produced by volunteers. A limited number of titles are produced in Spanish and other languages. Registered borrowers learn of new books added to the collection through two bimonthly publications.

Seventy magazines on disk and in Braille are offered through the program. Current issues are mailed free to readers at approximately the same time the print issues appear. Persons interested in music materials may receive them directly from a collection of over 50,000 items, consisting of scores in Braille and large type; textbooks and books about music in Braille, large type, and recorded forms; and elementary instruction in voice, organ, guitar, recorder, accordian, banjo, and harmonica in recorded form.

Playback equipment is also loaned at no charge for as long as recorded materials provided by NLS and its cooperating libraries are being borrowed. Talking-book machines designed to play disk-recorded books and magazines, as well as cassette machines, are available, with such accessories as headphones and pillow speakers. Readers with limited mobility may request a remote-control unit and breath switch, while hearing-impaired readers may be eligible for an auxiliary amplifier for use with headphones.

Free correspondence courses leading to certification in Braille transcribing and proofreading are offered. Voice auditions and informal training are given to volunteer tape narrators affiliated with local recording groups. Thousands of volunteers throughout the United States produce books for libraries and individual readers, and more than 3,000 senior or retired telephone industry workers contribute their time and skills in the maintenance and repair of playback equipment.

The NLS also operates a research program directed toward improving the quality of reading materials and equipment, reducing costs, and speeding delivery of services to readers. A consumer relations staff maintains regular contact with consumer groups and individual users of the program to identify service programs and assure that users' needs are being met. Further information may be obtained from local librarians or from the National Library Service for the Blind and Physically Handicapped, Library of Congress, Washington, DC 20542.

JUDY SMITH-DAVIS
*Counterpoint Communications
Company*

## BRAILLE
## LARGE-PRINT BOOKS
## LIBRARY FOR THE BLIND AND INDIVIDUALS WITH PHYSICAL DISABILITIES

# LIBRIUM

Librium is the trade name for the generic minor tranquilizer chlordiazepoxide. It was the first benzodiazepine to be synthesized; it was marketed in 1960 (Bassuk & Schoonover, 1977). Librium is a less potent muscle relaxant than Valium, but it shares similar antianxiety properties with other benzodiazepines. Librium is recommended for short-term use to deal with psychic discomfort that accompanies unusual situational stress or crisis (Bassuk & Schoonover, 1977). As is the case with all psychotropic medications, such treatment is symptomatic and does not affect the cause of the discomfort. Additional interventions are necessary to assist the individual in crisis to reestablish equilibrium. There is no evidence to support the development of addiction to Librium; however, as with all tranquilizers, psychological dependence can develop (Blum, 1984).

As with all benzodiazepines, sensitivity or overdosage is characterized by drowsiness, fatigue, confusion, and dizziness. Geriatric patients and children are most likely to experience these adverse effects (McEvoy, 1984). A reversible dementia also has been reported among elderly patients after extended administration.

**REFERENCES**

Bassuk, E. L., & Schoonover, S. C. (1977). *The practitioner's guide to psychoactive drugs.* New York: Plenum Medical.

Blum, K. (1984). *Handbook of abusable drugs.* New York: Gardner.

McEvoy, G. K. (1984). *American hospital formulary service: Drug information, 84.* Bethesda, MD: American Society of Hospital Pharmacists.

ROBERT F. SAWICKI
*Lake Erie Institute of
Rehabilitation*

**TRANQUILIZERS**

# LICENSING AND CERTIFICATION OF SCHOOLS, CENTERS, AND FACILITIES

The licensing or certification of schools is under the purview of state governments. The federal government maintains jurisdiction only over the disbursement of federal funds and over the separation of church and state. Many of these functions have been clarified through litigation. The Supreme Court in 1971 ruled that the relationship between the public schools and private parochial schools must not entangle the state in religious affairs. To determine whether a school is religious or sectarian, the court specified a threefold test: whether the school has a secular purpose; whether the school advances or inhibits religion; and whether the school fosters excessive government entanglement with religion (*Lemon* v. *Kurtman*). The Supreme Court has also ruled that it is clearly within the rights of the states to regulate private schools. In *Purce* v. *Society of Sisters* (1925), the court ruled that

> No question is raised concerning the power of the state reasonably to regulate all schools, to inspect, to supervise, and examine them, their teachers, and their pupils, to require that all children of proper age attend some school, that teachers shall be of good moral character and patriotic disposition, that certain studies plainly essential to good citizenship be taught, and that nothing inimical to the public welfare be manifestly taught.

In *State* v. *Williams* (1960), the court ruled that the "exercise of such power must not be arbitrary and must be limited to the preservation of public safety, public health, and morals."

As a result, each state has established rules, regulations, and supervisory procedures for private and parochial schools. These are established through statutes and state education directives and through the regulation of private nonprofit and for-profit business. Each state has its own rules for the physical facilities, health, and welfare of students, the curriculum, and instructional staff of nonpublic schools.

IDEA mandates that a free appropriate public education must be made available to each disabled child by public agencies of the state. Subject to the requirements of the least restrictive environment, this could include placement in or referral to a private school or facility. The state education agency is charged with the responsibility to ensure that a disabled child placed in a private school or facility by a public agency is provided special education and related services in conformance with an individualized education program that meets all requirement of IDEA, at no cost to parents.

In a court ruling (*Wiley* v. *Scanlon*, 1983) in Pennsylvania, the commissioner of education was found to have acted properly in denying a license to Wiley House for the education of socially maladjusted and emotionally disturbed students. The court ruled that the commissioner had not denied Wiley House due process and that the private school clearly did not meet state standards. In another case (*Language Development Program of W.N.Y., Inc.* v. *Amback*, 1983) a court in New York ruled that a private school can be denied a license without violating the property rights of the owners.

DANIEL R. PAULSON
*University of Wisconsin at Stout*

**CERTIFICATION/LICENSURE ISSUES
PRIVATE SCHOOLS AND SPECIAL EDUCATION**

# LIFE EXPECTANCY AND INDIVIDUALS WITH DISABILITIES

Researchers indicate that life expectancy of individuals with disabilities is increasing (Cunningham, 1985; Dunn, 1973; Hobbs, 1983; Wilson, 1973; Zill, 1985). Factors such as an increase in total population; continued research on treatment and etiology of infant disease; better nutrition; improved housing; advanced medical and surgical knowledge; and improved prenatal and neonatal child care practices have contributed to better prognoses for premature infants and to a decrease in the number of infant deaths.

The figures found in the professional literature are frequently based on noneducational frames of reference. An individual may indeed require social or medical services and still be able to function adequately in a school setting. Children with chronic health problems that may affect vision, hearing, or speech nevertheless may function without special education services. In an address to school nurses and school personnel, Cunningham (1985) stated that many diseases that used to be lethal such as renal failure, diabetes, and inflammatory bowel disease now have a 70 to 80 percent long-term survival. He suggests that the goal of the physician and the educator must shift from survival to improving conditions of chronically ill children so that they may grow and develop in a normal fashion. In the past, such children were not expected to survive, much less attend school and engage in extracurricular and athletic activities. A range of appropriate services from hospital settings to general education classrooms must be made available.

Zill (1985) suggests that it is critical to seek new and better ways to enable individuals with disabilities to become economically productive. He indicates it could cost up to $31,000 per year to maintain an individual with disabilities in a state-run institution. Opinions regarding institutionalization have changed in recent years. Wolfensberger (1967) found that physicians influenced the choices parents made regarding institutionalization. In a study done in the 1960s, he noted that 40 percent of general practitioners, 17 percent of pediatricians, and 11 percent of obstetricians recommended immediate institutionalization for retarded children. That trend is nearly reversed today. Needed today is a range of services from hospital setting to full-time public school regular education classroom. Such services require a multidisciplinary team approach, including parents as well as medical, agency, and school personnel. A greater number of all types of trained personnel will be called for. Along with more special education teachers, a full range of ancillary personnel such as psychologists, physical, occupational, and speech therapists, and a host of other medical and educational specialists will be needed.

Children who were regularly excluded from public education present problems that may require more and varied related services: assessment, transportation, appropriate technological and educational equipment, media and materials, special classroom aids such as adaptive equipment, communication and feeding devices, and wheelchairs. Vocational education for individuals with disabilities must shift from traditional career training to a more intensive, creative K–12 approach to preparing for and matching manpower needs to individual abilities. There is also an increased demand for postsecondary school adjustment and greater assistance with the transition from school to work. There is a healthy new demand to attend to quality-of-life issues that will require that attention be given to quality programming and such things as leisure skill development.

## REFERENCES

Cunningham, R. (1985, October). *The child with chronic disease.* Paper presented at meeting of Health and Disease in the School Foundation, Cleveland, Ohio.

Dunn, L. M. (1973). An overview. In L. M. Dunn (Ed.), *Exceptional children in the schools: Special education in transition* (pp. 3–62). New York: Holt, Rinehart, & Winston.

Hobbs, N. (1983). *Chronically ill children in America: Background and recommendations.* San Francisco: Jossey-Bass.

Wilson, M. (1973). Children with crippling and health disabilities. In L. M. Dunn (Ed.), *Exceptional children in schools: Special education in transition* (pp. 467–526). New York: Holt, Rinehart, & Winston.

Zill, N. (1985, June). *How is the number of children with severe handicaps likely to change over time?* Testimony presented for the Subcommittee on Select Education of the Committee on Education and Labor, U.S. House of Representatives.

SALLY E. PISARCHICK
*Cuyahoga Special Education
Service Center*

CHRONIC ILLNESS IN CHILDREN
DEINSTITUTIONALIZATION
HANDICAPPING CONDITIONS, HIGH INCIDENCE

## LIFE SPACE INTERVIEWING

The life space interview, a form of crisis intervention for emotionally disturbed youngsters, was formulated during the 1950s by Fritz Redl. The term life space refers to events occurring within the child's immediate environment at a specific point in time. Developed in a residential milieu, it is a technique intended for use by classroom teachers and support staff for addressing children's aggressive behavior.

Redl (1966) described the life space interview as a means by which an adult helps a child to mediate an emotionally charged experience. Following a behavioral crisis, the adult and the student engage in an in-depth discussion that focuses on the student's role in the event. The life space interview is viewed as strategically important to the child's therapeutic goals, and themes discussed during the interview may resurface in formal therapy sessions. As behaviorally oriented interventions have gained popularity in schools, the life space interview, based in psychoanalytic theory, has gone into decline.

The interviewer, assessing the characteristics of the incident and student, selects one of two goals in conducting the life space interview. Redl (1966) termed the first major goal "the clinical exploitation of the life event." Here the child's awareness of personal responsibility in a given altercation is heightened. The interviewer relates the event to established and recurring behavior problems so that the groundwork for insight is developed. The second general goal is "the administration of an emotional Band-Aid," where an angry and undercontrolled child is helped to disentangle undifferentiated emotions and return to the task at hand. Once the goal is established, several techniques are available.

Redl (1966) discusses five techniques that address the clinical exploitation goal. First is the reality rub-in, where the child is helped to reconcile egocentric perceptions with objective reality. For children who possess adequate defenses but who fail to incorporate critical information into the decision-making process, the interviewer attempts to define and analyze the facts. The child is then helped to recombine factual content in a way that leads to more adaptive behavior. For more disturbed children who actively distort reality, the interviewer may provide the structure necessary for regaining contact with the real world.

The second technique is symptom estrangement. Here the child is helped to disengage from the association that equates the self with the maladaptive behavior. As part of the process, the child learns that secondary gains won through the behavior are not worth the total cost. Massaging numb value areas is the third technique discussed. Here the child is asked to relate the present behavior to long-range survival goals. For example, the juvenile may be prompted to act on a code of fairness or mutual protection. The fourth technique is new tool salesmanship. Here the goal is to teach a response that is more effective than the present maladaptive one. For example, the child might be instructed to seek counseling rather than to fight the next time angry feelings arise. The last technique involves building up resistance. Here the child is helped to break typical behavior patterns by examining the relationship between situations and behaviors. Attention is focused on how the child can exert better behavioral controls and avoid potentially troublesome settings in the future.

Five techniques are listed under the Band-Aid goal. First is draining off frustration acidity, where sympathetic communication about anger or disgust is offered. Second comes support for the management of panic, fury, and guilt. Here the child, recognized as vulnerable and egocentric, is protected from destructive negative feelings. The intermediate objective is to help put the event into perspective. The third technique is communication maintenance. Here efforts are made to prevent the deterioration of the therapeutic relationship. Fourth is the regulation of behavior and social traffic technique, which casts the interviewer in the role of a kind police officer reminding the child of rules and consequences without provoking escalation of the maladaptive behavior. Last, Redl (1966) describes umpire services, where the interviewer attempts to maintain vision and balance in a potentially loaded situation. In summary, four factors determine the choice of a technique: the goal of the intervention, the setting in which the event occurred, the individual personality of the child, and the phase of therapeutic treatment within which the child is currently engaged.

Addressing its infrequent use, Heuchert (1983) has written that the life space interview is a technique worth reviving. While acknowledging its psychodynamic heritage, Heuchert views the interview as a simple behavioral intervention that can be implemented in the classroom. The teacher knows the child, has observed the behavior, and is in a temporally close position to the event. As such, the teacher can isolate the child and prompt a retelling of the incident. The goal is to improve the child's understanding of the behavior and to develop a workable solution that will reduce future maladaptive behavior.

### REFERENCES

Heuchert, C. M. (1983). Can teachers change behavior? Try interviews. *Academic Therapy, 18*(3), 321–328.

Redl, F. (1966). *When we deal with children.* New York: Free Press.

GARY BERKOWITZ
*Temple University*

**PSYCHOANALYSIS
REDL, FRITZ**

## LIGHTNER WITMER AWARD

The Lightner Witmer Award is presented by the Division of School Psychology (Division 16) of the American Psychological Association (APA) to young scholars who have demonstrated outstanding research to the field of school psychology early in their careers. Although the recipient is not required to have a doctoral degree to be eligible for the award, they must be a fellow, member, associate, or student affiliate of Division 16; in addition, only those nominees who have earned their educational specialist or doctoral degree within the last 7 years as of September 1 of the current award year will be considered. This prestigious award is named after Lightner Witmer, who founded the world's first psychological clinic in 1896 and is considered the father of clinical psychology (McReynolds, 1997). For more information on the eligibility criteria for this award, please visit the APA web site at www.apa.org/.

### REFERENCE

McReynolds, P. (1997). *Lightner Witmer: His life and times.* Washington, DC: American Psychological Association.

OLGA L. RODRIGUEZ-ESCOBAR
*Texas A&M University*

## AMERICAN PSYCHOLOGICAL ASSOCIATION

# LIMITED ENGLISH PROFICIENCY AND SPECIAL EDUCATION

Children in need of programs supporting their acquisition of English are referred to by many acronyms: *NEP* (non-English proficient), *LEP* (limited English proficient), and *PEP* (potentially English proficient). Their language needs are established by determining the language used in the home as well as directly assessing the language dominance and language proficiency of the student. A rating is generated upon the initial language evaluation that describes the nature of the student's language. These are called Lau ratings and are the direct result of the remedies established by the courts in the *Lau* v. *Nichols* case to ensure that linguistically appropriate instruction is provided to all language minority children. *Lau A* refers to a student who is monolingual in a language other than English, *Lau B* indicates that the student is dominant in a language other than English but has some English language skills, *Lau C* refers to a student who is bilingual in English and the home language, *Lau D* describes a student who is dominant in English, and *Lau E* refers to a student who is monolingual in English. Students labeled Lau A and B are those in need of English as a Second Language (ESL) or other language support programs.

In providing services to children with disabilities who are not dominant in English, educators must first understand the differences in program options. Both bilingual and ESL programs promote the acquisition of English language skills. The difference lies in the language of instruction. Bilingual programs provide instruction in the native language (NL). They often have a strong ESL and transitional component, which allows children to move smoothly from NL to English. ESL programs provide instruction exclusively in English (Baca, 1998; Ovando & Collier, 1985). The nature of ESL programs varies. Some are pull-out programs in which the student receives instruction from an hour a day to half a day. Some school systems have devised programs that provide all day or half-a-day intensified instruction in programs called High-Intensity Language Training (HILT; Ovando & Collier, 1985). These programs are much more effective than pull-out programs in ensuring that the students acquire the English language skills they need. Content-area ESL programs are additional programs that can be very effective for special education students in the upper grades since instruction focuses less on language and more on hands-on, motivating tasks in the content areas resulting in content-area-specific English language skills.

There are different approaches and methods of teaching ESL, and special educators should be aware of the type of program used in their school. Some programs are more amenable than others in instructing special education students. The *Direct Method* is an approach in which students are immersed in English-only instruction. This approach does not rely on drill exercises but rather focuses the learning of English around special topics and materials requiring open-ended spontaneous responses. Students learn about culture and language simultaneously through experiential props focused on real-life situations. The *Audiolingual Method* incorporates an approach in which drill and repetition are used to establish language patterns. Dialogue substitutions and the memorization of grammatical patterns are intended to teach the rules of the language. This approach has been highly criticized for its inability to establish a strong communicative competence. The *Cognitive Approach* facilitates the learning of English through small-group and individualized instruction. Language is viewed as developmental and errors are acceptable. In some cases NL may be used to establish meaning and understanding. The affective aspects of motivation and self-esteem are viewed as key in acquiring a second language. *Total Physical Response* (Asher, 1977) is perhaps most useful for individuals in the early stages of second language acquisition. It is the method that has most frequently been suggested for some special education populations. The students focus on listening comprehension and then learn English by following a command or demonstrating a certain action. The depth and level of English that can be learned using this method is limited. The *Natural Approach* (Terrell & Krashen, 1983) incorporates the use of language within a context that the student can understand and is relevant to his or her experience. Understanding is key in this approach, and the teacher facilitates meaning in whatever way necessary. "Comprehensible input" and the sensitivity to affective factors in the acquisition of a second language are central to this approach. Language is accepted and treated as a developmental process, and the acquisition of English is seen as being developmentally like the acquisition of the first language. This approach has been viewed by bilingual special educators as the most viable for creating communicative competence leading to the development of literacy skills of language minority students (Yates & Ortiz, 1998).

Teachers working with ESL students with disabilities can incorporate ESL techniques in their special education classrooms or work closely with their school ESL program. If students are pulled out or receive instruction in the school's ESL program, the special education teacher needs to work closely with the ESL teacher and become informed about the approach and philosophy of the program. Some programs are more conducive to meeting the needs of special education students, and some approaches are more "special education student friendly." Of special importance is the overlap of the English language skills the student is learning in ESL and the language needed by the student to function in the special education classroom. A careful evaluation of language taught, the transitioning of those skills from one setting to the next, and the generalization of those skills to other areas is critical. Collaboration by both the special education and ESL teacher is needed to ensure that language is not fragmented and that it focuses on functional use.

If teachers are incorporating ESL techniques, they need to determine the types of approaches and methods they will use based on student needs. Training in different techniques may be necessary. In addition, educators need to be aware of aspects of second language research impacting their decisions and teaching methods. Chamot (1981), in her application of second language acquisition research to the classroom, offers these suggestions:

*The acquisition of a second language is similar to the first language; therefore, teachers should:*
- Expect errors and consider them part of the natural developmental processes.
- Respond to what the child is intending to communicate rather than the specific language used.
- Ensure that children gain meaning by providing context and action-oriented activities.
- Teach in a way that children can gain practice listening and speaking when they are ready. Do not pressure children to speak before they are ready.
- Avoid any drills and repetitive patterns. Use songs, poetry, rhymes, stories, and activities of interest to the children in teaching language.

*Social and affective factors influence the acquisition of a second language; therefore, teachers should:*
- Foster a positive environment in the classroom, especially ensuring caring attitudes between children limited in their English speaking ability and native speakers of English.
- Have the children work in small groups or conduct paired activities to lessen the anxiety and develop an atmosphere of cooperation and communication.
- Group the children and provide opportunities for language-mixed groups (ESL and native speakers of English) to interact.
- Use a variety of methods and teaching styles so that all the learning styles of the children are reflected in your instruction.
- Foster an atmosphere of understanding and acceptance of the diverse cultures (especially those represented in the class).

*The right type of input is essential in ensuring that students acquire the second language; therefore, teachers should:*
- Use and model language that is meaningful, useful, and relevant to the students.
- Use language that is slightly above the students' level of functioning, but is understandable or can be made understandable.
- Expose children to different language varieties, formal and informal, standard and nonstandard, and different styles of communicating by bringing different people into the classroom.

*Children must reach a level of language that is higher than basic communication skills; therefore, teachers should:*
- Ensure that concepts and certain subject matter knowledge has been developed in their stronger language first, if at all possible. These skills will more easily transfer into the second language.
- Use the second language when students have the concepts clearly in place and are therefore ready to attach new labels/terms to those concepts in the second language.
- Ensure that the second language is used first in less linguistically demanding subjects such as music, PE, math, and science. More linguistically demanding subject matter can be added as students become more proficient.
- When children are literate in their first language, it becomes easier to move to the learning of literacy skills in the second language. If at all possible, teach children to learn to read and decode in their stronger language.
- Be aware that children demonstrating communicative competence or the ability to communicate socially may nonetheless not have the ability to meet the linguistic challenge of an academic environment.

In a review of second language learning research and through her own studies of over 200 children acquiring English as a second language, Wong-Fillmore (1991) indicates that learner and setting characteristics play a large role in the acquisition of second language skills. Learner characteristics such as sociability and communicative need, as well as contact with speakers of English and a setting which enables interaction, are key elements in the acquisition of English. These should be especially important in determining program placement and writing individualized education plan goals and objectives for special education students in need of ESL support.

## REFERENCES

Asher, J. J. (1977). *Learning another language through actions: The complete teacher's guide.* Los Gatos, CA: Sky Oaks.

Baca, L. (1998). Bilingualism and bilingual education. In L. M. Baca & H. T. Cervantes (Eds.), *The bilingual special education interface* (pp. 26–45). Columbus, OH: Merrill.

Chamot, A. U. (1981, September). Applications of second language acquisition research to the bilingual classroom. (Issue #8). *Focus national clearinghouse for bilingual education.* Washington, DC.

Ovando, C. J., & Collier, V. P. (1985). *Bilingual and ESL classrooms: Teaching in multicultural contexts.* San Francisco, CA: MacGraw-Hill.

Terrell, T. D., & Krashen, S. D. (1983). *The natural approach: Language acquisition in the classroom.* Oxford: Pergamon.

Wong-Fillmore, L. W. (1991). Second-language learning in children: A model of language learning in social context. In E. Bialystok (Ed.), *Language processing in bilingual children* (pp. 49–69). Cambridge: Cambridge University Press.

Yates, J. R., & Ortiz, A. A. (1998). Developing individualized education programs for exceptional language minority students. In L. M. Baca & H. T. Cervantes (Eds.), *The bilingual special education interface* (pp. 188–212). Columbus, OH: Merrill.

JOZI DE LEÓN
*New Mexico State University*

# LINDAMOOD PHONEME SEQUENCING PROGRAM FOR READING, SPELLING AND SPEECH

The Lindamood Phoneme Sequencing Program for Reading, Spelling and Speech (LiPS) by Patricia C. and Phyllis D. Lindamood (1998), is a multicomponent program designed to teach phonemic awareness skills and to facilitate the application of these skills to improve reading, spelling, and speech. The LiPS program is a revision of the Auditory Discrimination in Depth program (ADD; 1975), developed by Charles H. and Patricia C. Lindamood, published originally in 1969 and revised in 1975 by Teaching Systems and Resource Corporation, Teaching Resources Division. PRO-ED, Inc. acquired the ADD program in 1994.

The LiPS program focuses on the conscious processing of sensory information that enables metacognitive phonemic awareness to develop. Research has demonstrated overwhelming evidence of the importance of phonemic awareness skills in developing literacy. The LiPS program is appropriate for use with all individuals having difficulty in reading and spelling due to an underlying weakness in phonemic awareness skills. The LiPS program is available in both Clinical and Classroom Kits, and individual materials can be purchased separately. Each kit includes a trainer's manual, research booklet, instructional video and audiotape, and various manipulative components.

Earlier editions of LiPS, formerly entitled ADD, were reviewed extensively (Kennedy & Backman, 1993; Torgesen, 1997; Truch, 1994, 1998); references for the newest edition of the program are unavailable because of the recent publication date.

## REFERENCES

Kennedy, K. M., & Backman, J. (1993). Effectiveness of the Lindamood Auditory Discrimination in Depth Program with students with learning disabilities. *Learning Disabilities Research and Practice, 8,* 253–259.

Lindamood, C. H., & Lindamood, P. C. (1975). *The ADD Program: Auditory Discrimination in Depth.* Austin, TX: PRO-ED.

Lindamood, P. C., & Lindamood, P. D. (1998). *The Lindamood Phoneme Sequencing Program for Reading, Spelling and Speech (LiPS).* Austin, TX: PRO-ED.

Torgesen, J. K. (1997). The prevention and remediation of reading disabilities: Evaluating what we know from research. *Journal of Academic Language Therapy, 1,* 11–47.

Truch, S. (1994). Stimulating basic reading processes using Auditory Discrimination in Depth. *Annals of Dyslexia, 44,* 60–80.

Truch, S. (1998). *Phonological processing, reading, and the Lindamood Phoneme Sequencing Program: A review of related research.* Austin, TX: PRO-ED.

PEGGY KIPPING
*PRO-ED, Inc.*

# LINDSLEY, OGDEN R. (1922–    )

Ogden R. Lindsley was born in Providence, Rhode Island, on August 11, 1922. He received his BA and ScM degrees from Brown University in 1948 and 1950. In 1957 he was awarded his PhD in psychology from Harvard University. Lindsley held positions as an assistant psychologist at Brown University from 1948 to 1950 and as an electrophysiologist at Harvard in 1950. He was a fellow during 1951–1952; the assistant principal investigator in psychology for the Atomic Energy Commission Project from 1952 to 1953; the director of the Behavioral Research Laboratory from 1953 to 1965; a research associate from 1956 to 1961; and an associate professor of psychology from 1961 to 1965. In 1965 Lindsley accepted a position as a professor of educational research at the University of Kansas Medical Center. Presently, he is professor emeritus in the department of educational policy and leadership at the University of Kansas at Lawrence.

One of Lindsley's major contributions to the field of special education was his development of a series of standardized procedures for the recording and management of the behavior of children identified as retarded (Lindsley, 1964). The procedures, now commonly known as precision teaching, are based on an application of the principles of operant conditioning and include (1) accurate and precise behavioral definitions, (2) clear delineation of the various stimulus, response, and consequence contingencies, and (3) close study of the behavioral processes. Lindsley (1964) felt that properly designed special education programs should be totally individualized, with all plans subject to constant scrutiny and change if necessary. His premise that "retardation is not the property of a child but of an inadequate child-environment relationship" (Lindsley, p. 79), and his subsequent work in managing environments, contributed significantly to the development of the technology of special education.

While continuing his work in the area of precision teaching, Lindsley has also devised procedures for translating technical jargon into more easily understood terminology in applied behavior analysis, studied the effects of overt responding on learning in computer-based training, and reviewed the history of free-operant conditioning laboratory research and behavioral analysis applications (Lindsley, 1991a, 1991b, 1996; Silverman, Lindsley, & Porter, 1990, 1991).

Ogden Lindsley has been awarded various honors, including the Hofeimer Research Prize by the American Psychiatric Association (1962), the Golden Plate Award by the American Academy of Achievement (1964), and the Outstanding Contributor Award by the Northern California Association for Behavior Analysis (1994).

## REFERENCES

Lindsley, O. R. (1964). Direct measurement and prosthesis of retarded behavior. *Journal of Education, 147,* 62–81.

Lindsley, O. R. (1991a). From technical jargon to plain English for application. *Journal of Applied Behavior Analysis, 24*(3), 449–458.

Lindsley, O. R. (1991b). Precision teaching's unique legacy from B. F. Skinner. *Journal of Behavioral Education, 1*(2), 253–266.

Lindsley, O. R. (1996). The four free-operant freedoms. *Behavior Analyst, 19*(2), 199–210.

Silverman, K., Lindsley, O. R., & Porter, K. L. (1990, 1991). Overt responding in computer-based training. *Current Psychology: Research and Reviews, 9*(4), 373–384.

ANDREW R. BRULLE
*Wheaton College*
First edition

TAMARA J. MARTIN
*The University of Texas of the
    Permian Basin*
Second edition

HEATHER S. VANDYKE
*Falcon School District 49,
    Colorado Springs, Colorado*
Third edition

PRECISION TEACHING


# LING METHOD

The Ling method is a systematic procedure for developing and remediating the speech of hearing-impaired children. The first book describing what has become known as the Ling method was written by Daniel Ling (1976). The method relies heavily, but not exclusively, on the optimal use of the hearing-impaired child's residual hearing. Teachers versed in the Ling method emphasize the sequential acquisition of speech skills, the use of acoustic cues, and the automatic coarticulation of sounds in syllables. The model consists of seven developmental stages on both the phonetic and phonologic levels of speech. The phonetic level is the child's capacity to produce the required sound patterns, while the phonologic level is the systematic and meaningful use of those sound patterns.

The initial steps of the Ling method are concerned with the prosodic elements of speech, which are often neglected (Cole & Paterson, 1984). Neglect of these elements results in monotonic, unnatural sounding speech. Prosodic elements in the Ling method include duration, intensity, and pitch.

Abraham and Stokes (1984) found that consistent and systematic practice with meaningful words, as advocated by the Ling method, can improve phoneme production by deaf students, and that speech drill at the syllable level, also advocated by Ling, appears to be a better way to achieve adequate levels of intelligibility for deaf pupils at the pho-

nologic level of speech development. The Ling method is designed to be taught in several brief periods throughout the day rather than in one extended formal speech period.

## REFERENCES

Abraham, S., & Stokes, R. (1984). An evaluation of methods used to teach speech to the hearing impaired using a simulation technique. *Volta Review, 86,* 325–335.

Cole, E., & Paterson, M. (1984). Assessment and treatment of phonologic disorders in the hearing impaired. In J. M. Costello (Ed.), *Speech disorders in children: Recent advances.* San Diego, CA: College Hill.

Ling, D. (1976). *Speech and the hearing-impaired child: Theory, and practice.* Washington, DC: Alexander Graham Bell Association for the Deaf.

MARY GRACE FEELY
*School for the Deaf, New York,
    New York*

DEAF
DEAF EDUCATION
SPEECH-LANGUAGE SERVICES


# LINGUISTIC DEVIANCE

The term linguistic deviance has acquired various meanings in the literature on communicative disorders. The most salient definitions include (1) a general sense in which deviance subsumes all types of linguistic disability (including delay); (2) a more restricted usage where the range of linguistic structures used is comparable to an earlier stage of normal language development, but the frequency of use of specific grammatical forms exceeds normal expectations; and (3) a significantly reduced sense, in which only specific types of structural abnormality are labeled deviant. The last definition of deviance is closest to the general sense of the term in linguistics and in the literature on communicative disorders. Deviance then would include only those utterances that would be both structurally inadmissible in the adult grammar and outside of the expected language development of normal children (Crystal, 1981). For example, if an adult monolingual speaker of English uttered "chicken a," it would be considered deviant on the basis that an adult grammar would reject this construction and that this construction is not a regular feature of normal language development in children.

It should be noted that the term linguistic deviance applies to all components of the psycholinguistic model including phonology, syntax and morphology, semantics, and pragmatics. It has been most widely used in the literature on syntactic language disabilities. Some developmental psycholinguists concerned primarily with syntactic and semantic abnormalities have emphasized the importance of various frequencies of use as a criterion for distinguishing between deviance versus delay (Leonard, 1972; Menyuk, 1964). Most definitions of language delay contain a number of criteria, including slower development of the use of certain structures as well as a reduction in terms of the overall frequency of use of structures. Consonant with the definition of deviance, most definitions of delay contain a number of criteria. Therefore, Ingram (1972) and Morehead and Ingram (1973) conclude that disorder is a function of delayed appearance of a structure, its less frequent and less creative use, and its slower acquisition time.

## REFERENCES

Crystal, D. (1981). *Clinical linguistics.* Vienna: Springer-Verlag.

Ingram, D. (1972). The acquisition of the English verbal auxiliary and copula in normal and linguistically deviant children. *Papers & Reports on Child Language Development, 4,* 79–91.

Leonard, L. B. (1972). What is deviant language? *Journal of Speech & Hearing Disorders, 37,* 427–446.

Menyuk, P. (1964). Comparison of grammar with functionally deviant and normal speech. *Journal of Speech & Hearing Research, 7,* 109–121.

Morehead, D. M., & Ingram, D. (1973). The development of base syntax in normal and linguistically deviant children. *Journal of Speech & Hearing Research, 16,* 330–352.

PHILIP M. PRINZ
*Pennsylvania State University*

**COMMUNICATION DISORDERS**

# LINGUISTIC READERS

Linguistic readers, based on the philosophy that the goal of beginning reading instruction should be the automatic recognition of major spelling patterns of the English language, are intended to be used for beginning reading instruction. They have also been used with disadvantaged children who speak nonstandard English (Center for Field Research and School Services, 1970), bilingual children (Digneo & Shaya, 1968), and children with learning disabilities (Myers & Hammill, 1976).

Following the publication of *Why Johnny Can't Read* (Flesch, 1955), in which the linguistic approach to reading was offered as a solution to the national reading problem, Bloomfield and Barnhart (1961) and Fries (1963) developed the first linguistic readers. In these readers several means were used to achieve the goals set forth for linguistic reading programs. First, the vocabulary in beginning material is controlled through phonetic regularity; that is, only one phonetic value is associated with each letter. For example, beginning materials containing words with *c*, as in *cot, cat,* and *cut,* would not contain words in which *c* has a different phonetic value, for example, *cent.* Likewise, material containing words with *i*, as in *kit, zip,* and *dig,* would not include a word like *ride.*

Second, the introduction of spelling patterns is carefully sequenced. For example, in *Let's Read* by Bloomfield and Barnhart (1961), the first 36 lessons concentrate on spelling patterns containing a consonant letter plus a vowel letter plus a consonant letter. Patterns using the vowel *a* as in *cat, fat, hat,* and *cap, lap, map* are presented first. Next, patterns using the vowel *i* as in *bit, hit, sit,* and *fib, rib, bib* are introduced. These are followed by patterns for *u, e,* and *o.*

Third, spelling patterns are introduced within the context of whole words; for example, the words *can, fan, man,* and *tan* exemplify a particular pattern. Students are guided by the teacher through a process that helps them to discover the pattern. Accompanying reading materials provide practice in applying the knowledge of spelling patterns to the pronunciation of new words and in reading words within the context of phrases and short sentences. Unlike phonics approaches, students are never directed to sound out words or to blend the sounds of individual letters into words.

Fourth, the material is designed to make minimal demands on the child in terms of reading comprehension. The vocabulary is simple. Students are not expected to learn new word meanings. Complex phrases and sentences are avoided. Fifth, oral reading is emphasized as a means of enabling the child to recognize spelling patterns. Finally, the use of pictures and context clues as aids to word recognition are discouraged.

Subsequent authors of linguistic readers modified the approach used by Bloomfield and Barnhart and Fries. Modifications have included the addition of pictures to readers, the introduction of high-frequency, irregularly spelled words such as *the,* the use of color cues, the use of controlled sentence patterns as well as word patterns, and programs that call for sounding and blending vocabulary words controlled for spelling patterns (Chall, 1967).

Chall (1967), in a review of research, concluded that the linguistic approach to teaching reading as defined by linguistic readers is more effective than the sight word approach but less effective than systematic phonics programs. The linguistic readers of the 1960s represented the first attempt to apply linguistics to the field of reading instruction, an effort that has been characterized as superficial and misguided because it was limited to a single aspect of linguistics, for example, phonology (Shuy, 1977).

## REFERENCES

Bloomfield, L., & Barnhart, C. L. (1961). *Let's read: A linguistic approach.* Detroit: Wayne State University Press.

Center for Field Research and School Services. (1970). *An evaluation of improving the teaching of English as a second language in poverty area schools.* New York: School of Education, New York University. (ERIC Document Reproduction Service No. ED 058 363)

Chall, J. (1967). *Learning to read: The great debate.* New York: McGraw-Hill.

Digneo, E. H., & Shaya, T. (Eds.). (1968). *The Miami Linguistic Reading Program, 1965–1968.* Santa Fe: New Mexico Western States Small Schools Project. (ERIC Document Reproduction Service No. ED 029 724)

Flesch, R. (1955). *Why Johnny can't read and what you can do about it.* New York: Harper & Brothers.

Fries, C. C. (1963). *Linguistics and reading.* New York: Holt, Rinehart, & Winston.

Myers, P. I., & Hammill, D. D. (1976). *Methods for learning disorders* (2nd ed.). New York: Wiley.

Shuy, R. W. (Ed.). (1977). *Linguistic theory: What can it say about reading?* Newark, DE: International Reading. (ERIC Document Reproduction Service No. ED 133 925)

MARIANNE PRICE
*Montgomery County
Intermediate Unit,
Norristown, Pennsylvania*

## LINGUISTIC DEVIANCE

## PHONOLOGY

## LIPREADING/SPEECHREADING

Lipreading is commonly defined as the art of understanding a speaker's thought by watching his or her mouth. Lipreading, or speechreading, as it is more frequently called, is the use of the visual information available in speech to facilitate its comprehension. Speechreading is a difficult skill that not all hearing-impaired persons master. Even the best speechreader cannot see everything that is said, since only about 25 percent of all speech is visible on the lips. However, a good speechreader can often identify about 75 percent of a message because speechreading improves when words, phrases, and sentences are used in context (Bishop, 1979).

The ability to speechread depends on many factors, such as visual acuity; the degree of visibility of the articulatory movement ("f" is easy to see, "h" is impossible); the speaker's rate; how well the speaker enunciates; lighting and distance; and the fact that some speech sounds cannot be discriminated from each other. Phonemes that have identical visible aspects of articulation are called homophenes (p,b,m). It has been estimated that approximately 50 percent of the words in a random sample would constitute homophenes of one or more other words (Sanders, 1982).

Training hearing-impaired students to use their residual hearing in conjunction with speechreading significantly improves their speechreading ability. Profoundly deaf individuals, however, are able to make little use of acoustic cues, and their speechreading performance remains essentially the same whether auditory cues are added or not (Sanders, 1982).

Speechreading is also included in total communication, which involves the simultaneous presentation of information through speech, speechreading, fingerspelling, signing, and other manual forms of communication. Currently, total communication is widely used in schools for deaf students throughout the United States. Recent research into speechreading has emphasized viseme grouping (a viseme is the smallest unit of visible speech); the effectiveness of the use of varying degrees of optical distortion in speechreading training; and the visual intelligibility of deaf speakers themselves (Kanter, 1985).

### REFERENCES

Bishop, M. (1979). *Mainstreaming.* Washington, DC: Alexander Graham Bell Association for the Deaf.

Kanter, A. (1985, Summer). Aiming for the best. *N.T.I.D. Focus,* 12–13.

Sanders, D. (1982). *Aural rehabilitation.* Englewood Cliffs, NJ: Prentice Hall.

ROSEMARY GAFFNEY
*Hunter College, City University
of New York*

## TOTAL COMMUNICATION

## LITERACY

Literacy is the condition or quality of being able to read and write. The term has been used in a narrow fashion (e.g., ability to sign one's name) and in some cases it has taken on much broader meaning (e.g., computer literacy or economic literacy).

Depending on how literacy is defined and measured, vastly different estimates of the literacy rate are evident. For example, Clifford (1984) reported that switching from orally administered tests to written tests decreased the number of passing grades by 50 percent in a 1964 study by the New York Board of Regents. In addition, Chall, Freeman, and Levy (1982) noted that the average (passing) reading ability on a set of eleventh-grade competency tests fell between the seventh and eighth grades. Clifford (1984), using a commonly applied criterion (i.e., adults over 25 years of age who have completed less than 5 years of school), cited the illiteracy rate as 11 percent in the United States in 1950. The National Commission on Excellence in Education (1983) reported that the illiteracy rate among 17-year-olds in the United States is approximately 13 percent. In general, illiteracy rates in various studies have ranged from 1 to 20 percent in the adult population.

The narrow views of literacy were not so much the result of carefully conceived models as they were the result of necessity. Attempts to estimate the prevalence of literacy among national populations at different times in history forced the use of restricted definitions. For instance, the most common method of estimating the literacy of the populations of Europe during the nineteenth century was the inspection of civil and church records, noting the proportion of documents on which the citizen or supplicant signed his or her name or made a mark. Clearly, the trend in conceptualizing the meaning of literacy in recent times had been toward the expansion of the term. Therefore, we now encounter advocates of computer literacy, television literacy, historical literacy, scientific literacy, civic literacy, functional literacy, technological literacy, and so on.

Literacy has been a controversial concept since its inception, which extends to the time of Socrates. Although the idea of universal literacy (schooling for all citizens) has been received positively by most people, many illustrious individuals have been opponents. For instance, neither Socrates nor Plato viewed the use of books favorably. Each considered them to result in only superficial mastery and poor retention. Modern critics have echoed those complaints and have added to the list. Specifically, the concept of the "six-hour retardate"—that is, the child who is illiterate in school but functional in the home environment—epitomizes the gap between the literacy requirements of educational institutions and adaptive traditions often found in the home and neighborhood.

With the increase in literacy has come a devaluation that did not exist when illiteracy was the rule rather than the exception. Today, illiterate individuals experience embarrassment and humiliation when their inability to read and write becomes known to others. Critics have decried the power rendered to the political-educational bureaucracies that largely control the delivery of literacy to the masses.

## REFERENCES

Chall, J. S., Freeman, A., & Levy, B. (1982). Minimum competency testing of reading: An analysis of eight tests designed for grade 11. In G. Madaus (Ed.), *The courts, validity, and minimum competency testing.* Boston: Kluwer-Nijhoff.

Clifford, G. J. (1984). Buch und lesen: Historical perspectives on literacy and schooling. *Review of Educational Research, 54,* 472–500.

National Commission on Excellence in Education. (1983). *A nation at risk: The imperative for educational reform.* Washington, DC: U.S. Government Printing Office.

RONALD C. EAVES
*Auburn University*

## LITHANE

Lithane (lithium carbonate) is used in the treatment of manic episodes of manic-depressive illness. Its use is not recommended for children under age 12. Adverse reactions may include fine hand tremor, especially during initial days of treatment. Overdose may result in drowsiness and lack of coordination at lower serum levels, with giddiness, ataxia, blurred vision, and ringing in the ears at higher levels. A brand name of Miles Pharmaceuticals, it is available as scored tablets containing 300 mg. Dosage is recommended in the range of 600 mg three times daily for treatment of acute mania, with approximately half this dosage recommended for long-term control of mania.

### REFERENCE

*Physicians' desk reference.* (1984). (pp. 1368–1369). Oradell, NJ: Medical Economics.

LAWRENCE C. HARTLAGE
*Evans, Georgia*

## LITHIUM

See LITHANE.

## LITHONATE

See LITHANE.

## LITHUANIA, SPECIAL EDUCATION IN

Lithuania, a European country located on the eastern coast of the Baltic Sea, has a population of approximately 3.45 million. In 1990, after 50 years of Soviet occupation, Lithuania regained its statehood, the roots of which date back to the 13th century. In 2004 Lithuania joined the European Union. Lithuania's first postcommunist constitution (1992) established compulsory education for all children between ages 7 and 16, thus ensuring their right to attend a publicly funded school of their choice, either state-funded, municipal, or private.

During the 2002–2003 academic year, 82 percent of 7- to 24-year-olds were enrolled in education or training and 33 percent of 19- to 24-year-olds studied in higher education institutions (Ministry of Education and Science, 2004). During the 2004/2005 school year, 563,063 students enrolled in general education. Students with special educational needs in grades 1 through 12 constituted 10.5 percent (58,837: Statistics Lithuania, 2005).

The first special schools for children who were deaf, blind, and/or mentally retarded were opened in the 1920s and early 1930s, a period of independence for Lithuania between the two World Wars. Summer courses on special pedagogy, first offered in 1938, can be considered the beginning of training special educators in Lithuania (Karvelis, 2003).

During the Soviet period after World War II, special education mainly served students with mild mental disabilities, hearing and visual impairments, speech disorders, and physical disabilities; these students were educated mostly in special (usually boarding) schools. Children with moderate, severe, and profound mental disabilities, as well as those with Down syndrome, were considered to be uneducable and remained at home with their parents or were in homes designed for their care (Aidukiene & Labiniene, 2003). The *clinical / medical model* for the organization of special education services prevailed in Lithuania and the entire former Soviet Union. This model emphasizes disability instead of ability, segregated education instead of social integration, and generalized instead of individualized educational programs.

After the restoration of Lithuania's independence in 1990, concepts guiding special education have favored integrated education for special educational needs children, including those with severe mental disabilities. Lithuania has chosen the multitrack inclusive policy that allows the choice of education in special schools or inclusion into a general educational environment.

Special needs children may be classified into one of the following 10 categories: intellectual disabilities, specific cognitive disorders, language and other communication disorders, visual impairments, hearing impairments, disorders of emotional, behavioral and social development, disorders of movement and position, chronic somatic and neurological disorders, multiple disorders, and developmental disorders.

The following laws and policy documents address the rights of special needs students and provide for their integration into society: Law on Special Education (1999), Law on Education (2003), National Education Strategy 2003–2012 (2003), Program for the Provision of Special Education Services (2004), and Law on Social Integration of the Disabled (2005).

During the 2004/2005 school year, among special needs students, 88 percent received their education in regular classes, 10.5 percent were taught at special schools or special boarding schools, and 1.5 percent in special classes at mainstream schools. Most students who were integrated into general schools had speech and communication disabilities (26,520) and specific cognitive disorders (7,190), including auditory perception, visual perception disorders, and

disorders of linguistic processes (Aidukiene & Labiniene, 2003; Ministry of Education and Science, 2004). Children with hearing impairments and mental retardation were more likely to receive their education in special schools. Efforts to integrate those with mental retardation and with hearing impairments have been somewhat successful and are ongoing. For example, since the 1990s, the number of mentally retarded children who received their services in special boarding schools has decreased about 50 percent. The plan to employ 50 sign language interpreters until 2008 in general schools also demonstrates the country's desire to promote integrated education for hearing impaired students (Program for the Provision of Special Education Services, 2004). Progress in the use of information and communication technologies in special needs education has facilitated the academic and social success of visually impaired, physically disabled, and other special needs students in general schools.

States and local authorities are required to provide medical, functional, psychological, and pedagogical support for special needs students. The National Center for Special Needs Education and Psychology is responsible for the development of a system that provides pedagogical and psychological support. The Center works in cooperation with municipal pedagogical psychological services that are responsible for the identification of a person's special needs and the recommendation of the educational environment and programs within the municipality. The responsibility for the special needs assessment, using a multiteam approach, is delegated to special education commissions, working both in the pedagogical psychological services and in schools. Assessment results are used to find the least restrictive placement that will best facilitate the children's education according to the programs assigned by special education commissions. Programs may be modified, adapted, special, or individual.

Although most of the 68 special institutions remain, the role of special schools is changing by being encouraged to assume responsibility of resource centers that address the needs of special needs children, their families, and teachers. The initiatives of nongovernmental organizations has led to the establishment of alternative institutions such as special education centers, which provide education for persons with severe, profound, and multiple disabilities. Services provided by the Early Rehabilitation Services, the Child's Development Center under the Ministry of Health, and by special preschool establishments within the educational system assist young children with developmental problems.

Since the early 1970s Siauliai University has played a leading role in preparing special education teachers. It offers bachelors, masters, and doctoral studies programs in special education. The university also publishes the journal *Special Education: Research Works,* which presents studies that have implications for the practice of special education. During the last 5 years, a master's degree program of special education has been established at Vilnius University and Vilnius Pedagogical University. Each year around 210 bachelor's level and 40 master's level special teachers graduate from these three universities. Since 1995, special needs education courses are compulsory in teachers training programs at all universities and colleges to help ensure the education of mainstreamed special needs students by qualified staff.

Strong traditions of segregated education and imperfect models for financing educational help perpetuate longstanding problems that limit the quality of special education services: Not all special needs students, especially those being educated in general schools and preschools, have equal access to qualified special educational support and special equipment. Some municipalities lack specialists who can provide good assessments. Discussion on the definition of giftedness and their identification as exceptional learners with special needs has not begun. The statistical data on some of the special needs groups (e.g., cognitive disorders) is not available. The creation of a comprehensive system of vocational training and rehabilitation, especially for students with mental retardation, also is needed. Persons with disabilities—especially mental retardation—and their families still encounter negative attitudes from society, thus creating psychosocial obstacles for true social integration. Despite these difficulties, legislative progress regarding inclusion and a growing number of special needs students successfully learning in mainstream schools reflect a united effort within Lithuania to create new opportunities for special needs students to live meaningful and successful lives.

## REFERENCES

Aidukienė, T., & Labinienė, R. (2003). Vaikų turinčių specialiųjų poreikių, ugdymo tendencijų apžvalga tarptautiniame bei Lietuvos švietimo reformos kontekste (1990–2002). In J. Ambrukaitis et al. (Eds.), *Essentials of special education. Handbook for pedagogy students* (pp. 31–49). Šiauliai: Šiauliai University Press.

Ministry of Education and Science of Republic of Lithuania. (2004). *Education in Lithuania.* Vilnius: Author.

Statistics Lithuania. (2005). *Education 2004.* Vilnius: Author.

Karvelis, V. (2003). Specialiojo ugdymo bruožai Lietuvoje (iki 1990). In J. Ambrukaitis et al. (Eds.), *Essentials of special education. Handbook for pedagogy students* (pp. 7–30). Šiauliai: Šiauliai University Press.

GRAZINA GINTILIENE
*Vilnius University, Vilnius, Lithuania*

## ESTONIA, SPECIAL EDUCATION IN

## INTERNATIONAL SCHOOL PSYCHOLOGY ASSOCIATION

## LOCUS OF CONTROL

Locus of control is a psychological construct that describes the extent to which one feels personally in control of one's life, life events, and behaviors (Rotter, 1966). The attributions that children and adolescents make about events in their lives and their behaviors are determined, to some extent, by their locus of control. If an individual has an internal locus of control, she is likely to feel personally responsible for her own behaviors and events that affect her. Thus, she will make internal attributions for her behaviors and life events, and will feel as though she has control over her successes and failures. Conversely, if an individual has an external locus of control, she is likely to feel as though others, or the environment (e.g., fate, luck), are responsible for her behaviors and events that occur in her life. She will therefore make external attributions for her behaviors and life events, and will project blame onto others when faced with adversity. She also will likely feel as though she has no control over her successes or failures, which may lead to low motivation and feelings of helplessness (e.g., "Why should I even try? Whatever I do, it doesn't matter anyway").

Clark, Olympia, Jensen, Heathfield, and Jenson (2004) note that the way in which special educational services are implemented in schools may hinder the development of an internal locus of control among students with intellectual and developmental disabilities, as such programs often include highly contingent and teacher-directed environments that may not provide students with opportunities to make their own decisions. Clark et al. express concern that these programs encourage an external locus of control among students with disabilities, and communicate to students that teachers and other caregivers do not have enough confidence in them to allow them to make their own choices. Further, these programs are likely to result in continued feelings of dependence on others. The authors provide suggestions regarding how teachers and school psychologists can increase students' feelings of autonomy and control, such as offering choices, assessing students' preferences, reinforcing independent behaviors, and developing individualized education plan (IEP) goals that specifically address independent behaviors.

A recent review of research examining the locus of control construct in students with learning disabilities demonstrated that although the literature often suggests that these students have a tendency toward an external locus of control, methodological deficiencies within the collection of empirical studies limit our confidence in this interpretation (Mamlin, Harris, & Case, 2001). Some of the common methodological weaknesses cited by Mamlin et al. include inadequate descriptions of procedures used for selecting participants, limited information regarding participants' demographic and psychological characteristics, and reliance on measures with outdated norms or inadequate psychometric properties. Thus, although it would make intuitive sense that students with learning disabilities may have a tendency toward an external locus of control due to varying degrees of academic struggles, the relationship between locus of control and learning disabilities remains unclear as a result of these methodological and measurement problems.

With regard to other applications of locus of control, research suggests that an external locus of control is associated with conduct problems among children and adolescents, as these youth tend to blame their problems on others and deny responsibility for their disruptive behaviors (Powell & Rosen, 1999; Strand & Nowicki, 1999). Such research points to the potential utility of conceptualizing the locus of control construct as a target for intervention. Finally, Huebner, Ash, and Laughlin (2001) found a mediational relationship between locus of control and school satisfaction among adolescents, in which the experience of repeated negative life events was related to an external locus of control, which then was associated with decreased school satisfaction.

In general, the literature examining the locus of control construct in children and adolescents suggests that an internal locus of control is associated with more favorable developmental outcomes, while an external locus of control is associated with more negative outcomes. Unfortunately, the extent to which we can reach conclusions regarding the relationship between locus of control and various disorders or disabilities of childhood and adolescence is limited by a general lack of current research examining these relationships with widely used, psychometrically established, and updated instruments. Given the nature and potential explanatory power of the locus of control construct, however, such relationships are likely waiting to be discovered.

## REFERENCES

Clark, E., Olympia, D. E., Jensen, J., Heathfield, L. T., & Jenson, W. R. (2004). Striving for autonomy in a contingency-governed world: Another challenge for individuals with developmental disabilities. *Psychology in the Schools, 41,* 143–153.

Huebner, E. S., Ash, C., & Laughlin, J. E. (2001). Life experiences, locus of control, and school satisfaction in adolescence. *Social Indicators Research, 55,* 167–183.

Mamlin, N., Harris, K. R., & Case, L. P. (2001). A methodological analysis of research on locus of control and learning disabilities: Rethinking a common assumption. *Journal of Special Education, 34,* 214–225.

Powell, K. M., & Rosen, L. A. (1999). Avoidance of responsibility in conduct disordered adolescents. *Personality and Individual Differences, 27,* 327–340.

Rotter, J. B. (1966). Generalized expectancies for internal versus external control of reinforcement. *Psychological Monographs, 80*(609).

Strand, K., & Nowicki, S. (1999). Receptive nonverbal processing ability and locus of control orientation in children and adolescents with conduct disorders. *Behavioral Disorders, 24,* 102–108.

JEREMY R. SULLIVAN
*University of Texas at San Antonio*

ATTRIBUTION RETRAINING
ATTRIBUTIONS
COGNITIVE BEHAVIOR THERAPY

## LOUIS-BAR SYNDROME

Louis-Bar syndrome, also known as ataxia telangiectasia (AT), is a rare, progressive, autosomal (non-sex-related chromosome) recessive genetic disorder. The hallmarks of AT are ataxia (lack of muscle control) and telangiectasia (tiny, red "spider" veins), which appear in the corners of the eyes or on the surface of the nose, ears, eyelids and inside of the elbows and knees soon after the onset of ataxia.

The earliest signs of Louis-Bar/AT include disturbances in balance, usually before the age of one year. The child's head and upper part of the body bend backwards or to one side while sitting or standing. Eventually the symptoms become so severe that by adolescence the child is confined to a wheelchair. The children also gradually develop tremors of the hands, fingers, and head. Speech becomes increasingly dysarthyric (slowed) and slurred. Affected individuals also exhibit repetitive jerky eye movements and have difficulty moving their eyes from side to side without turning their head at the same time.

The great majority of affected individuals, 80 to 90 percent, also have immunodeficiency, which results in a susceptibility to chronic infections and recurring bacterial and viral infections of the sinuses and lungs (Haugsgjerd, 1999). Persons with Louis-Bar/AT have a strong tendency to develop lymphatic malignancies such as Hodgkin and non-Hodgkin lymphomas and acute lymphoblastic leukemia (Webster, 1999). Other features of the disease may include mild diabetes mellitus, premature graying of the hair, difficulty swallowing—which causes choking and/or drooling—and slowed growth. Children with AT initially exhibit normal intelligence and regress to the mildly mentally retarded range (Gandy, 1999). Physical development includes hypogonadism (underdevelopment of the genitalia) in males and hypoplasia of the ovaries.

The prevalence of Louis-Bar/AT is 1 out of every 30,000 to 40,000 live births, and is very difficult to diagnose before the age of 4 years (Webster, 1999). The disorder affects males and females equally. There is no specific treatment for Louis-Bar/AT, and medical interventions are usually directed at specific associated problems such as infections.

Children are usually integrated in normal kindergartens or schools, but will show an increasingly complex pattern of many different disabilities and associated problems as they progress in school. Continuous adjustments to their educational program are needed as the disease progresses. Occupational and physical therapies may be helpful to maintain muscle strength and delay constriction of the limbs. Adapted physical education may also be appropriate to maintain physical activity at the child's level. As the magnitude of the motor problems intensifies and accompanying speech problems emerge, speech therapy may be helpful, as well as possible alternative communication methods such as sign language or communication boards. Children with poor vision may need corrective lenses, books with large print, magnifiers, and/or computers.

Many affected children and their families will need prolonged psychological support. The prognosis of Louis-Bar/AT creates a situation of permanent crisis, as one crisis after another develops as the disease progresses. Dermatological abnormalities such as wrinkled skin, gray hair, or dilated blood vessels on the face, ears, and neck may evoke negative reactions from other children and adults. In 1985, the parents of children with AT established their own group in the Cerebral Palsy Association. For more information, on the internet see http://www.atcp.org, or contact The Johns Hopkins Hospital, Room CMSC 1102, Baltimore, Maryland, 21287; toll-free 800-610-5691; phone 410-614-1922.

**REFERENCES**

Gandy, A. (1999). *Pediatric database* (PEDBASE). Retrieved from http://www.icondata.com/health/pedbase/files/LAURENCE.HTM

Haugsgjerd, H. (1999). *Rikshospitalet, The National Hospital University of Oslo*. Retrieved from http://www.rh.uio.no/rhdoks/rhindex.html

Webster, R. E. (1999). Louis-Bar syndrome (ataxia telangiectasia). In L. Phelps (Ed.), *Health-related disorders in children and adolescents*. Washington, DC: American Psychological Association.

KIM RYAN ARREDONDO
*Texas A&M University*

# LOVAAS, O. IVAR (1927–    )

O. Ivar Lovaas earned his BA at Luther College in 1951 and his MS and PhD in 1958 from the University of Washington, Seattle. Trained in psychoanalytic theory as well as Pavlovian and Skinnerian learning theory. Lovaas applied the formulations of behaviorism to the treatment of psychotic children. Beginning in 1961, he served as profes-

O. Ivar Lovaas

sor of psychology and staff psychologist at the Psychology Clinic, and as director of the Psychology Autism Clinic at the University of California, Los Angeles. He is currently professor emeritus at UCLA.

Lovaas is recognized as one of the principal leaders in the area of behavioral treatment and teaching of developmentally disabled children. Since 1962 he has researched and developed language, teacher, and parent training programs that have played a major role in effectively educating and treating autistic, schizophrenic, and other disabled children and youths. His early intervention program for autistic children (begun in 1970) has resulted in major and long-lasting improvements in these children. He continues his work in this area, examining intensive behavioral treatment of preschoolers with severe mental retardation and those with autistic features, finding higher mean IQ scores and more expressive speech when intensive Lovaas behavioral treatment is used (Smith, Eikeseth, Klevstrand, & Lovaas, 1997).

Lovaas (Lovaas & Buch, 1992) has noted the negative aspects associated with large mental hospitals as well as how these aspects can be used to develop alternative, community-based treatment programs. Through his efforts, group homes (or teaching homes) have been established as an alternative to institutionalization, thus allowing individuals with disabilities to lead more productive lives.

Lovaas has published and contributed over 80 journal articles, books, and related works and is a prolific speaker, presenting addresses, workshops, and lectures throughout the world. Lovaas's major published works include *The Autistic Child: Language Development Through Behavior Modification* (1986), originally published in 1977, and *Teaching Developmentally Disabled Children: The Me Book* (Lovaas et al., 1980), considered a classic in the field.

**REFERENCES**

Lovaas, O. I. (1986). *The autistic child: Language development through behavior modification.* New York: Irvington.

Lovaas, O. I., Ackerman, A., Alexander, D., Firestone, P., Perkins, J., & Young, D. (1980). *Teaching developmentally disabled children: The me book.* Baltimore: University Park Press.

Lovaas, O. I., & Buch, G. (1992). Editor's introduction. *Research in Developmental Disabilities, 13*(1), 1–7.

Smith, T., Eikeseth, S., Klevstrand, M., & Lovaas, O. I. (1997). Intensive behavioral treatment for preschoolers with severe mental retardation and pervasive developmental disorder. *American Journal on Mental Retardation, 102*(3), 230–249.

MARY LEON PEERY
*Texas A&M University*
First edition

TAMARA J. MARTIN
*The University of Texas of the
Permian Basin*
Second edition

# LOVITT, THOMAS C. (1930–    )

Thomas C. Lovitt began his professional career as a musician, earning a BA in music education from the University of Kansas in 1952. He subsequently studied at the Eastman School of Music and earned his MA in music education from the University of Kansas in 1960. From 1956 through 1961 he was a musician with the Kansas City Philharmonic, while also holding a variety of positions as a music instructor. Lovitt taught special education for several years while pursuing the EdD in special education, which was awarded by the University of Kansas in 1966.

Lovitt has been a prolific researcher in special education since receiving his doctorate, with just over 100 scholarly publications to his credit. He has worked principally in the area of learning disabilities while spending his academic career within the Experimental Education Unit of the College of Education of the University of Washington. Lovitt joined the University of Washington faculty as an assistant professor in 1966, was promoted to associate rank in 1968, awarded full professor status in 1972, and is currently professor emeritus.

Lovitt's early research focused on laboratory studies employing operant conditioning procedures to modify narrative preferences. Later, he coordinated a research classroom at the Experimental Education Unit, where he attempted to employ the principles of applied behavior analysis to the improvement of academic skill in learning-disabled youngsters. Lovitt's research interests have shifted to the public school classroom and to the development and implementation of precision teaching practices. His work in this area has demonstrated the effective use of precision-teaching instruments to enhance performance of students in both mainstream and special education settings (Stump, Lovitt, Fister, & Kemp, 1992). This research has included examining the use of innovative teaching tools such as graphic organizers, study guides, vocabulary drills, and computer-assisted instruction (Horton & Lovitt, 1994; Horton, Lovitt, & Bergerud, 1990; Horton, Lovitt, & Christensen, 1991; Stump et al., 1992).

Though most of his publishing has been in academic journals, Lovitt is perhaps best known for two of his books on children and their relationships to teachers, *In Spite of My Resistance, I've Learned from Children* (1977) and *Because of My Persistence, I've Learned from Children* (1982). Other publications include *Preventing School Dropouts* (1991), *Tactics for Teaching* (1995), and *Special Education: Common Questions, Common-Sense Answers* (1997).

**Thomas C. Lovitt**

**REFERENCES**

Horton, S. V., & Lovitt, T. C. (1994). A comparison of two methods of administering group reading inventories to diverse learners: Computer versus pencil and paper. *RASE: Remedial & Special Education, 15*(6), 378–390.

Horton, S. V., Lovitt, T. C., & Bergerud, D. (1990). The effectiveness of graphic organizers for three classifications of secondary students in content area classes. *Journal of Learning Disabilities, 23*(1), 12–22, 29.

Horton, S. V., Lovitt, T. C., & Christensen, C. C. (1991). Matching three classifications of secondary students to differential levels of study guides. *Journal of Learning Disabilities, 24*(9), 518–529.

Lovitt, T. C. (1977). *In spite of my resistance, I've learned from children.* Columbus, OH: Merrill.

Lovitt, T. C. (1982). *Because of my persistence, I've learned from children.* Columbus, OH: Merrill.

Lovitt, T. C. (1991). *Preventing school dropouts: Tactics for at risk, remedial, and mildly handicapped adolescents.* Austin, TX: PRO-ED.

Lovitt, T. C. (1995). *Tactics for teaching.* Englewood Cliffs, NJ: Merrill.

Lovitt, T. C. (1997). *Special education: Common questions, common-sense answers.* Longmont, CO: Sopris West.

Stump, C. S., Lovitt, T. C., Fister, S., & Kemp, K. (1992). Vocabulary intervention for secondary-level youth. *Learning Disability Quarterly, 15*(3), 207–222.

CECIL R. REYNOLDS
*Texas A&M University*
First edition

TAMARA J. MARTIN
*The University of Texas of the Permian Basin*
Second edition

# LOW BIRTH WEIGHT INFANTS

Low birth weight (LBW) is a term generally used to describe infants weighing less than 2,500 grams at birth. Such infants may be born at term or preterm. Advances in neonatal medicine have improved survival of smaller and smaller infants to the point that further differentiation is needed to discuss populations of LBW infants.

## Low Birth Weight

Low birth weight (LBW) infants weigh between 1,501–2,500 grams. Infants may be LBW for many reasons, including preterm birth, genetic predisposition, or growth retardation. An infant may be growth retarded at any gestation, but in general this term is used for infants greater than 37 weeks gestational age at birth. This group of neonates is often said to be intrauterine growth retarded (IUGR), implying that they have failed to achieve their full growth potential. Causes of this growth failure can be categorized as fetal, maternal, placental, and environmental (Stevenson & Sunshine, 1997). Fetal factors include chromosomal and genetic abnormalities, congenital malformations, non-chromosomal syndromes, and intrauterine infections. Maternal factors are the most common cause of IUGR, with maternal nutrition as a major factor adversely impacting fetal growth. Maternal illness, low socioeconomic status, and labor-intensive occupations also contribute to low birth weight. Abnormalities of placental function such as decreased placental size, poor implantation, and decreased placental blood flow can cause poor fetal growth. Incidence of IUGR increases with multiple gestation and may be as high as 15 to 25 percent in twins. Incidence increases significantly with triplets and quadruplets. Environmental factors are often hard to separate from maternal factors. Medications and drugs may cause fetal malformation; alcohol and substance abuse are frequently seen in conjunction with poor nutritional status and infections. Cigarette smoking is believed to negatively impact fetal growth (Stevenson & Sunshine, 1997).

Long-term effects of growth retardation include decreased terminal physical growth (small babies lead to small adults), developmental delays, decreased IQ, increased risk of cerebral palsy, and learning defects. Some studies suggest IUGR infants have an increased incidence of cardiovascular disease as adults (Stevenson & Sunshine, 1997).

## Very Low Birth Weight

Very low birth weight (VLBW) infants are preterm infants weighing between 801–1,500 grams (see Prematurity entry in this encyclopedia for causes and contributing factors for preterm birth). Approximately 42,000 VLBW infants are born each year in the United States. Survival rates are as high as 85 percent. Of survivors, 5 to 15 percent will have a form of spastic cerebral palsy and an additional 25 to 50 percent will display less handicapping but significant cognitive and school-related disorders (Graziani, 1996). Intracranial hemorrhage and periventricular leukomalicia continue to be of major concern in the development of neurological and developmental deficits. Although specific abnormalities are highly correlated to neurologic sequelae, the severity of the eventual handicap is difficult to predict.

## Extremely Low Birth Weight

In the last decade, the survival of extremely low birth weight (ELBW) infants, those weighing less than 800 grams at birth, has markedly increased. Survival rates are now over 50 percent for infants 22 to 25 weeks gestation. These infants, referred to in the literature as "micropremies," are at extremely high risk for serious physical, neurological, and developmental complications. As would be expected, the shorter the gestation period at birth, the greater the number and severity of complications. In one study, 2 percent of infants born at 23 weeks gestation survived without severe complications, whereas 21 percent born at 24 weeks and 69 percent born at 25 weeks survived without severe neurological complications. Although only 10 to 20 percent of 23 to 25 week survivors have neurodevelopmental problems, almost 60 percent have some disability, including disorders of sensory integration and learning disabilities that significantly affect their school and psychosocial functioning. Close monitoring and assessment may lead to early identification and interventions that contribute to a more positive outcome for the child and the family (Goldson, 1996).

### REFERENCES

Goldson, E. (1996). The micropremie: Infants with birthweights less than 800 grams. *Infants and Young Children, 8*(3), 1–10.

Graziani, L. J. (1996). Intracranial hemorrhage and leukomalacia in preterm infants. In A. R. Spitzer (Ed.), *Intensive care of the fetus and neonate* (pp. 696–703). St. Louis, MO: Mosby.

Stevenson, D. K., & Sunshine, P. (Eds.). (1997). *Fetal and neonatal brain injury: Mechanisms, management, and the risks of practice* (2nd ed.). Oxford, UK: Oxford University Press.

BRENDA MELVIN
*New Hanover Regional Medical Center*

**CONGENITAL DISORDERS**
**PREMATURITY**

## LOWENFELD, BERTHOLD (1901–1994)

A native of Austria, Berthold Lowenfeld began his career as a teacher of blind children in 1922. He earned his PhD in child psychology from the University of Vienna in 1927. He studied child psychology and the education of the blind in the United States in 1930–1931 as a Rockefeller research fellow. After the Nazi invasion of his homeland in 1938, he emigrated to the United States to become director of educational research for the American Foundation for the Blind in New York City. He also lectured at Columbia University and made an extensive survey for the Canadian National Institute for the Blind of all Canadian schools for the blind.

In 1949, he accepted the position of superintendent of the California School for the Blind, where he remained until 1964. From that time until his death at 93, he engaged in research and writing under the sponsorship of the U.S. Office of Education, the California State Department of Education, and the Social and Rehabilitation Service of the Department of Health and Human Services.

**Berthold Lowenfeld**

Among the honors Lowenfeld received were the 1965 Ambrose Shotwell Distinguished Service Medal for leadership and service to the blind and the Miguel Medal, the nation's highest award for service to the blind. In his lifetime, Lowenfeld wrote over 100 books and journal articles. A life-long advocate for the visually impaired, Lowenfeld died in 1994.

### REFERENCES

Lowenfeld, B. (1981). *Berthold Lowenfeld on blindness and blind people.* New York: American Foundation for the Blind.

Lowenfeld, B. (1994, May 25). *The San Francisco Chronicle.* p. C3. [Newspaper, selected stories online]. Retrieved April 30, 1998, from http://web.lexis-nexis.com/universe

E. VALERIE HEWITT
*Texas A&M University*
First edition

DONNA WALLACE
*The University of Texas of the Permian Basin*
Second edition

## LOWE SYNDROME

Lowe syndrome (LS) is an X-linked recessive disorder of unknown etiology that primarily affects males. It is also called the Oculo-Cerebro-Renal syndrome of Lowe (OCRL), reflecting the three major organ systems involved in the disorder (eyes, brain, and kidney). A rare genetic condition that causes physical and mental disabilities and medical problems, Lowe syndrome was first described in 1952 by Dr. Charles Lowe, Dr. Terrey, and Dr. MacLachlan. Prevalence estimates vary between 200–2,000 cases in the United States. Lowe syndrome has been reported in 15 females, with only 5 meeting strict diagnostic criteria (Charnas & Gahl, 1991).

The most prominent ocular symptom is congenital cataracts, and this system is mandatory for diagnosis (Lopata, 1999). Associated features include glaucoma, nystagmus (involuntary, rapid, and rhythmic eye movements), corneal keloid (an elevated, irregularly-shaped, progressively enlarging scar), and strabismus (eyes that do not track or focus together). Neurological manifestations involve both the central and peripheral nervous systems (Charnas & Gahl, 1991). These symptoms include hypotonia (less-than-normal muscle tone) and areflexia (reduced or absent deep tendon reflexes) which contribute to a tendency to develop bone fractures, scoliosis, and joint problems. Affected individuals also exhibit borderline to severe mental retardation. Seizures occur in approximately half of the cases of LS/OCRL (Charnas & Nussbaum, 1995). Renal (kidney) manifestations, also characteristic of LS, are usually seen within the first year of life. Renal Fanconi syndrome, a group of diseases caused by the dysfunction of the renal tubules, can result in episodes of vomiting, dehydration, weakness, and unexplained fever. Affected individuals with LS/OCRL often succumb to complications resulting from slow, progressive renal failure. With aggressive medical care, most of these difficulties can be avoided and life expectancy typically extends into the 20s and 30s, while some have lived into their 40s.

In 1992, the gene that causes LS was found on the Xq24-26 region of the X chromosome. In 1995, researchers discovered that the gene defect causes an enzyme deficiency, which leads to various developmental deficits, including cataracts and kidney and brain problems. Some common physical features of affected individuals include frontal bossing (rounded prominence of the frontal and parietal bones); small, deep-set eyes; elongated face caused by progressive hypotonia; and epicanthal folds (vertical fold of skin on each side of the inner eyelids; Charnas & Gahl, 1991). Cryptorchidism (undescended testicles) is estimated to occur in 15 to 40 percent of affected individuals. Peritubular fibrous tissue and azoospermia (the absence of sperm in the semen) have been alleged to reduce fertility (Lopata, 1999).

Behavioral problems are also frequently evident with LS-affected individuals, including inattentiveness, unusual obsessions or preoccupations, self-abuse, self-injury, episodic outbursts, aggression, irritability, and repetitive, nonpurposeful movements. Some parents of LS/OCRL children report that behavior difficulties often appear by age 5, worsen by age 8, and in two-thirds of the cases improve by age 14 (Lowe Syndrome Association, 1997).

There is no cure for LS/OCRL, but many of the symptoms can be treated through medication; surgery; speech, physical, and occupational therapies; and special education, often begun prior to entering school. Affected children are often provided special education services in school through the classifications of mental retardation, other health impaired, or multiply disabled. Maintenance of metabolic balance is vital and can be assisted by monitoring the physical health and activity of the child. General nutrition is also required to sustain optimal levels of critical substances. Affected children should have constant access to water in order to prevent dehydration (Charnas & Nussbaum, 1995). Behavior modification may be helpful to address behavior problems. Families of LS-affected children may need psychological support to assist with the emotional demands of caring for a child with a debilitating disease. For further information contact the Lowe Syndrome Association, 222 Lincoln Street, West Lafayette, IN, 47906 or call (765) 743-3634. The organization's email address is lsa@medhelp.org

## REFERENCES

Charnas, L. R., & Gahl, W. A. (1991). The oculocerebrorenal syndrome of Lowe. *Advances in Pediatrics, 38,* 75–107.

Charnas, L. R., & Nussbaum, R. L. (1995). The oculocerebrorenal syndrome of Lowe (Lowe syndrome). In C. R. Scriver, A. L. Beaudet, W. S. Sly, & D. Valle (Eds.), *The metabolic and molecular bases of inherited disease* (7th ed., pp. 3705–3716). New York: McGraw-Hill.

Lopata, C. (1999). Lowe syndrome. In L. Phelps (Ed.), *Health-related disorders in children and adolescents.* Washington, DC: American Psychological Association.

Lowe Syndrome Association. (1997). *Living with Lowe syndrome: A guide for families, friends, and professionals.* Retrieved from http://www.medhelp.org/lowesyndrome/

KIM RYAN ARREDONDO
*Texas A&M University*

# LOW VISION

Historically, the use of various terms related to individuals with visual impairments or those who have no sight has caused great confusion (Barraga, 1983). A committee of the World Health Organization (WHO), chaired by Colenbrander (1977), adopted a classification system of three levels of vision; low vision was identified as a term within the system. This system has allowed medical, optometric, and educational personnel to communicate with each other because the emphasis is on the functioning of the individual and not rigidly focused on exact measurement criteria (Barraga, 1983).

Definitions of low vision still vary. The WHO classification defines the level of disability in someone with severe low vision as "performs visual task at a reduced level of speed, endurance, and precision even with aid." It defines the level of disability in someone with profound low vision as "has difficulty with gross visual tasks; cannot perform most detailed visual tasks" (Colenbrander, 1977); Corn (1980) defines a person with profound low vision in a practical manner with educational implications: "one who is still severely visually impaired after correction, but who may increase visual functioning through the use of optical aids, nonoptical aids, environmental modifications, and/or techniques." Barraga (1983) further clarifies the term: "Low-vision children have limitations in distance vision but are able to see objects and materials when they are within a few inches or at a maximum of a few feet away." Regardless of the definition accepted, these children should not be referred to as "blind."

Low-vision students vary in their visual functioning; some may use their vision more efficiently than others. Some may be able to use their vision for reading, whereas others will need to use braille and other tactile materials to supplement printed materials (Barraga, 1983). A major emphasis in educational programs is to provide vision stimulation and training to low-vision students to help them develop their residual vision as effectively as possible. An excellent resource for helping such students to "learn to see" is the Program to Develop Efficiency in Visual Function developed by Barraga (1980) and the accompanying *Source Book on Low Vision.*

Many low-vision students may benefit from low-vision aids that are characterized as anything that helps people use their vision more efficiently. Optical aids are available for both distance and near vision tasks. They are prescribed by ophthalmologists or optometrists in relation to eye diagnosis, the severity of the condition, the requirements of the particular task, and the individual response of the low-vision student (Faye, 1984). Examples of optical aids are glasses for reading large print, a magnifier stand for reading small print, and a monocular telescope for looking at the blackboard (Heward & Orlansky, 1984). Nonoptical aids are used to improve environmental conditions. They include specific illumination devices such as reading lamps and flashlights; light transmission devices such as absorptive lenses, filters, and lens coatings that reduce glare and increase contrast; reflection control devices such as visors and sideshields; enhanced contrast procedures such as the use of dark colors on a light background and fluorescent strips; and linear magnification aids such as large print books (Faye, 1984). Electronic aids include opaque and transparent projection systems such as slide projectors and closed-circuit television systems (Kelleher, 1982). Regardless of the aids prescribed, the low-vision student must be given intensive follow-up training and support in learning to use them and in evaluating their usefulness in the classroom as well as in other types of indoor and outdoor environments.

Low-vision students also need to develop their auditory skills in order to avail themselves of other valuable resources for accessing knowledge such as recording devices, computers with synthesized speech output, and electronic reading machines.

## REFERENCES

Barraga, N. C. (1980). *Source book on low vision.* Louisville, KY: American Printing House for the Blind.

Barraga, N. C. (1983). *Visual handicaps and learning.* Austin, TX: Exceptional Resources.

Colenbrander, A. (1977). Dimensions of visual performance. *Archives of American Academy of Ophthalmology, 83,* 332–337.

Corn, A. (1980). *Development and assessment of an in-service training program for teachers of the visually handicapped: Optical aids in the classroom.* Unpublished doctoral dissertation, Teachers College, Columbia University, New York.

Faye, E. E. (1984). *Clinical low vision.* Boston: Little, Brown.

Heward, W. L., & Orlansky, M. D. (1984). *Exceptional children.* Columbus, OH: Merrill.

Kelleher, D. K. (1982). Orientation to low vision aids. In S. S. Mangold (Ed.), *A teachers guide to the special educational needs of blind and visually handicapped children* (pp. 45–52). New York: American Foundation for the Blind.

ROSANNE K. SILBERMAN
*Hunter College, City University
of New York*

**FUNCTIONAL VISION
VISUALLY IMPAIRED
VISUAL TRAINING**

## LOXITANE

A dibenzoxazepine compound, Loxitane represents a subclass of tricyclic antipsychotic agent used as a tranquilizer. Its use is indicated for the management of the manifestations of psychotic disorders. Side effects include rigidity (27 percent), tremor (22 percent), and drowsiness (11 percent), with less frequent incidence of confusion, dizziness, and slurred speech. Overdosage results may induce depression and unconsciousness. A brand name of Lederle Laboratories, Loxitane is supplied in capsules of 5, 10, 25, and 50 mg as an oral concentrate and in injectible units of 1 and 10 ml. Dosage levels are recommended in divided doses, two to four times a day, in initial dosage of 10 mg.

### REFERENCE

*Physicians' desk reference.* (1984). (pp. 1078–1080). Oradell, NJ: Medical Economics.

LAWRENCE C. HARTLAGE
*Evans, Georgia*

## LSD

Lysergic acid diethylamide (LSD) was initially discovered by accident by the Swiss chemist Albert Hoffman. LSD is a psychotominetic drug that elicits vivid hallucinations and intense emotions. Synesthesia, a phenomenon in which perceptions cross modalities, may occur (e.g., words are seen and colors heard). The drug is extraordinarily potent and a dosage as low as 50 mg can produce marked psychological effects. Some users report kaleidoscopic imagery that appears before their closed eyes; perceptions are reported to be richer and more intense. There is frequently a distorted perception of body parts. Spatial and temporal distortions are common. Depersonalization may result, and there is almost always a heightened suggestibility. In addition, it is common for users to report an increased awareness of the "true nature of things" and to find special significance in trivial events.

Like other psychotominetic drugs, it is clear that response to LSD is contingent on set and setting. The "bad trip" is perhaps the single most common adverse experience encountered by LSD users. The best treatment during this condition is simply companionship and support from someone who is knowledgeable about the drug and its effects. Even the worst effects typically wear off in 8 to 12 hours.

LSD is a drug that produces rapid tolerance and increasingly larger doses are required to produce an effect over the short run. However, once drug use is discontinued, tolerance rapidly abates. There is no physical dependence on the drug, and there is little evidence of long-term organic brain changes of the sort that are found with the abuse of certain other drugs. However, about 25 percent of users will experience flashbacks during which they may relive the experience of acute LSD intoxication. Flashbacks rarely occur more than a year after the last use of the drug. Some authors have argued the use of LSD may constitute a risk factor in the development of schizophrenia (Kaplan & Sadock, 1981).

## REFERENCE

Kaplan, H. I., & Sadock, D. J. (1981). *Modern synopsis of comprehensive textbooks of psychiatry* (3rd ed.). Baltimore: Williams & Wilkins.

DANNY WEDDING
*Marshall University*

## CHILDHOOD SCHIZOPHRENIA
## DRUG ABUSE

## LURIA, ALEXANDER R. (1902–1977)

Alexander Luria was a Russian neuropsychologist. He is best known for his theoretical and practical work on the behavioral consequences associated with focal brain injury. His early work integrated and expanded on the work of other Russian scientists, notably Pavlov and Vygotsky (Hatfield, 1981). Luria incorporated Vygotsky's ideas about the development of the social aspects of speech and Pavlov's neurophysiologic approach to understanding higher cortical processes (Hatfield, 1981).

Luria thought that all higher cortical functions required the concerted and coordinated working of multiple brain areas. His theory is neither a localizationist nor an equipotentialist one. Luria believed that higher cortical functions (e.g., reading) require the operation of functional systems incorporating multiple brain areas. Though specific aspects of the functional system (e.g., movement) are localizable

within the brain, the more complex, complete behavior is not localizable. Hence, focal brain damage affects a variety of specific skills because one link in the system is nonfunctional while others are intact (e.g., the brain is not equipotential or homogeneous; Luria, 1980, 1982). Luria's other contributions include methods for the assessment and treatment of aphasia using his functional systems approach to understanding cortical processes. He also is well known for his seminal work on frontal lobe functions (Pribram, 1978).

## REFERENCES

Hatfield, F. N. (1981). Analysis and remediation of aphasia in the USSR: The contribution of A. R. Luria. *Journal of Speech & Hearing Disorders, 46,* 338–347.

Luria, A. R. (1980). *Higher cortical functions in man* (2nd ed.). New York: Basic Books.

Luria, A. R. (1982). *Language and cognition.* New York: Wiley.

Pribram, K. H. (1978). In memory of Alexander Romanovitsch Luria. *Neuropsychologia, 16,* 137–139.

GRETA N. WILKENING
*Children's Hospital*

## LURIA-NEBRASKA NEUROPSYCHOLOGICAL BATTERY
## VYGOTSKY, LEV S.

## LURIA-NEBRASKA NEUROPSYCHOLOGICAL BATTERY

The Luria-Nebraska Neuropsychological Battery (Golden, Hammeke, & Purisch, 1980) is a set of tasks specifically designed for the assessment of brain-damaged individuals. Like other neuropsychological batteries (e.g., Halstead-Reitan Neuropsychological Test Battery), it was developed to provide information regarding the absence or presence of brain damage. The battery also may be used by trained neuropsychologists to assist in rehabilitation planning, to discriminate between functional and organic disorders, to suggest the localization of brain damage, and to make prognostic statements (Moses, Golden, Ariel, & Gustavson, 1983). Based on the theoretical work of A. R. Luria, the battery, though broken into "scales," is really a set of interrelated items that may be evaluated both qualitatively and quantitatively.

The adult version of the battery is composed of 269 items. It assesses motor functions, pitch and rhythm perception, tactile skills, visual perceptions, receptive and expressive language, motor writing, spelling, reading, arithmetic, memory, and intellectual processes. Intermediate memory is assessed in the adult versions. An estimate, based on demographic data, of premorbid functioning is provided. Validation studies suggest that the batteries can make relevant discriminations at acceptable levels (Golden et al., 1981; Plaisted, Gustavson, Wilkening, & Golden, 1983). There has been much controversy about the battery, however, with some authors critical of developmental methodology and content (Adams, 1980; Golden et al., 1982). The Luria-Nebraska has been translated into eleven languages.

## REFERENCES

Adams, K. M. (1980). In search of Luria's battery: A false start. *Journal of Consulting & Clinical Psychology, 48,* 511–516.

Golden, C. J., Ariel, R. N., McKay, S. E., Wilkening, G. N., Wolf, B. A., & MacInnes, W. D. (1982). The Luria-Nebraska Neuropsychological Battery: Theoretical orientation and comment. *Journal of Consulting and Clinical Psychology, 50,* 291–300.

Golden, C. J., Fishburne, F. J., Lewis, G. P., Conley, F. K., Moses, J. A., Engum, E., Wisniewski, A. M., & Berg, R. A. (1981). Cross validation of the Luria-Nebraska Neuropsychological Battery for the presence, lateralization, and localization of brain damage. *Journal of Consulting & Clinical Psychology, 49,* 491–507.

Golden, C. J., Hammeke, T. A., & Purisch, A. (1980). *The Luria-Nebraska Neuropsychological Battery.* Los Angeles: Western Psychological Services.

Moses, J. A., Golden, C. J., Ariel, R., & Gustavson, J. L. (1983). *Interpretation of the Luria-Nebraska Neuropsychological Battery* (Vol. 1). New York: Grune & Stratton.

Plaisted, J. R., Gustavson, J. L., Wilkening, G. N., & Golden, C. J. (1983). The Luria-Nebraska Neuropsychological Battery–Children's Revision: Theory and current research findings. *Journal of Clinical Child Psychology, 12,* 13–21.

GRETA N. WILKENING
*Children's Hospital*

**HALSTEAD-REITAN NEUROPSYCHOLOGICAL BATTERY
LURIA, A. R.
NEUROPSYCHOLOGY**

# LURIA-NEBRASKA NEUROPSYCHOLOGICAL BATTERY–CHILDREN'S REVISION

The Luria-Nebraska Neuropsychological Battery–Children's Revision (LNNB-C; Golden, 1987) is designed to assess the neurological functioning of children ages 8 to 12. It can be used to screen and diagnose cognitive deficits in both general and specific domains such as the lateralization and localization of brain injury. The battery takes 2 hours to administer and consists of 22 subtests: Motor Functions, Rhythm, Tactile Functions, Visual Functions, Receptive Speech, Expressive Speech, Writing, Reading, Arithmetic, Memory, Intellectual Processes, Spelling-Academic Achievement, Integrative Functions, Spatial-Based Movement, Motor Speed and Accuracy, Drawing Quality, Drawing Speed, Rhythm Perception and Production, Tactile Sensations, Receptive Language, Expressive Language, and Word and Phrase Repetition. These are formed into 11 clinical scales, 11 factor scales, and 3 summary scales. Although very similar to the adult version of the test, the children's version does not measure frontal lobe functioning.

The LNNB-C was normed on 125 Caucasian children, with 25 children at each age from 8 to 12. The test has been shown to be valid in discriminating between those with and without brain dysfunction. Reliability values have been found to range from .13 to .92 for the summary scales and from .70 to .94 for the factor scales. Reviewers have been critical of the test due to its low reliability values and disorganized presentation in the manual.

## REFERENCES

Kramer, J. J., & Conoley, J. C. (Eds.). (1992). *The eleventh mental measurements yearbook.* Lincoln, NE: Buros Institute of Mental Measurements.

Golden, C. J. (1987). *Luria-Nebraska Neuropsychological Battery: Children's Revision.* Los Angeles, CA: Western Psychological Services.

Kilpatrick, D. A., & Lewandowski, L. J. (1996). Validity of screening tests for learning disabilities: A comparison of three measures. *Journal of Psychoeducational Assessment, 14,* 41–53.

Myers, D., Sweet, J. J., & Deysach, R. (1998). Utility of the Luria-Nebraska Neuropsychological Battery: Children's Revision in the evaluation of reading disabled children. *Archives of Clinical Neuropsychology, 4,* 201–215.

Schaughency, E. A., Lahey, B. B., & Hynd, G. W. (1989). Neuropsychological test performance and the attention deficit disorders: Clinical utility of the Luria-Nebraska Neuropsychological Battery: Children's Revision. *Journal of Consulting & Clinical Psychology, 57,* 112–116.

Stephens, C. W., Clark, R. D., & Kaplan, R. D. (1990). Neuropsychological performance of emotionally disturbed students on the LNNB and LNNB-C. *Journal of School Psychology, 28,* 301–308.

RON DUMONT
*Fairleigh Dickinson University*

JOHN O. WILLIS
*Rivier College*

# M

## MA

See MENTAL AGE.

## MACMILLAN, DONALD L. (1940–    )

A former coach at Laguna Beach High School, Donald L. MacMillan has received widespread acknowledgment for his work in the field of special education generally, but in mental retardation particularly. MacMillan earned his BA degree in education in 1962 from Case Western Reserve University. He then went to the University of California, Los Angeles, (UCLA), where he earned an MA in educational psychology in 1963 followed by an EdD in exceptional children in 1967. MacMillan was graduated with honors and noted for distinction for his dissertation.

In 1968 MacMillan joined the faculty of the University of California, Riverside, where he was promoted to associate rank in 1970. He was made a professor in 1973 and began working as a research psychologist at the UCLA Pacific-Neuropsychiatric Institute the same year. At present, MacMillan is Graduate Advisor and Professor of Education at the University of California, Riverside.

MacMillan has served the field of mental retardation with distinction in a broad range of roles, including extensive consultantships (e.g., consultant to more than 10 state hospital programs, various public school districts, and federal agencies). He also has served as an editorial reviewer (e.g., as associate editor of the *American Journal of Mental Deficiency* and *Exceptional Children* and as consulting editor to the *Journal of School Psychology*), on the boards of various professional societies, and as a noted teacher and researcher. MacMillan has constantly and effectively researched affective and motivational components of mental retardation as well as related environmental and conditional determinants such as socioeconomic status, ethnicity, age, and gender (MacMillan, 1969, 1970, 1996a). MacMillan's important work involving individuals with disabilities includes his investigations of treatment for children with autism and school identification rates of mild mental retardation (Gresham & MacMillan, 1997; MacMillan, 1996b).

Donald MacMillan's awards include:

- Edgar A. Doll Award, Division 33 of American Psychological Association (1989).
- Education Award, American Association on Mental Retardation (1990).
- Humanitarian Award, Region II of American Association on Mental Retardation (1995).
- Research Award, Council for Exceptional Children (1998).
- Outstanding Research Award, Special Education Special Interest Group, American Educational Research Association (1998).

### REFERENCES

Gresham, F. M., & MacMillan, D. L. (1997). Autistic recovery? An analysis and critique of the empirical evidence on the Early Intervention Project. *Behavioral Disorders, 22*(4), 185–201.

MacMillan, D. L. (1969). Resumption of interrupted tasks by normal and educably mentally retarded subjects. *American Journal of Mental Deficiency, 73,* 657–660.

MacMillan, D. L. (1970). Reactions following interpolated failure by normal and retarded subjects. *American Journal of Mental Deficiency, 74,* 692–696.

MacMillan, D. L. (1996a). Comparison of students nominated for prereferral interventions by ethnicity and gender. *Journal of Special Education, 30*(2), 133–151.

MacMillan, D. L. (1996b). The labyrinth of IDEA: School decisions on referred students with subaverage general intelligence. *American Journal on Mental Retardation, 101*(2), 161–174.

CECIL R. REYNOLDS
*Texas A&M University*
First edition

TAMARA J. MARTIN
*The University of Texas of the Permian Basin*
Second edition

HEATHER S. VANDYKE
*Falcon School District 49, Colorado Springs, Colorado*
Third edition

Helen Keller and Anne Sullivan Macy

## MACY, ANNE SULLIVAN (1866–1936)

Anne Sullivan Macy, Helen Keller's teacher, taught the deaf, blind, and mute child from the age of 6, serving as both teacher and companion until her death in 1936. Trained at the Perkins Institution for the Blind in Boston, where she resided in the same house as Laura Bridgeman, the first deaf-blind person to be educated, the young teacher developed methods that she successfully used to teach Helen Keller to read, write, and speak, and that enabled Keller to become a well-educated and effective person. In Keller's adult years, Macy, whom Keller always addressed as "teacher," served not only as teacher and interpreter for her, but also managed her extremely busy schedule of writing, lecturing, and personal appearances for many educational and social causes.

### REFERENCES

Keller, H. (1955). *Teacher: Anne Sullivan Macy.* New York: Doubleday.

Lash, J. (1980). *Helen and Teacher: The story of Helen Keller and Anne Sullivan Macy.* New York: American Printing House for the Blind.

PAUL IRVINE
*Katonah, New York*

## MAGICAL MODEL

The magical model of exceptionality explains deviance in terms of demonic possession and other supernatural causes. Common beliefs include possession by human and animal spirits and victimization by witches and spell casters (Rosenhan & Seligman, 1984). For centuries the model competed only with the biogenic (organic) model as an explanation of exceptional behavior (Brown, 1986).

The magical model is associated frequently with witch hunts and gruesome persecutions of deviant persons. However, there have also been numerous periods in history when those following a supernatural model offered treatment to the deviant that was far more humane and at least equally effective as that offered by those using naturalistic, biological models (Erickson & Hyerstay, 1980).

Although biological, psychological, and ecological models have displaced magical models in the literature of educational professionals, some residual use of supernatural explanations occurs in the general culture. The public's attitudes toward the disabled and the disabled's attitudes toward themselves may be partially shaped by these notions of magic.

### REFERENCES

Brown, R. T. (1986). Etiology and development of exceptionality. In R. T. Brown & C. R. Reynolds (Eds.), *Psychological perspectives on childhood exceptionality: A handbook* (pp. 181–229). New York: Wiley.

Erickson, R., & Hyerstay, B. (1980). Historical perspectives on treatment of the mentally ill. In M. Gibbs, J. Lachenmeyer, & J. Sigal (Eds.), *Community psychology: Theoretical and empirical approaches* (pp. 29–74). New York: Gardner.

Rosenhan, D., & Seligman, M. (1984). *Abnormal psychology.* New York: Norton.

LEE ANDERSON JACKSON, JR.
*University of North Carolina at Wilmington*

### HISTORY OF SPECIAL EDUCATION

## MAGNESIUM

Magnesium is a light metal that represents an essential body mineral (Ensminger, Ensminger, Konlande, & Robson, 1983; Thomson, 1979). The body contains approximately 20 to 30 g of magnesium, most of which is present in the skeleton (Yudkin, 1985). Magnesium also is found in cell tissue and it represents an essential component of the body's enzyme systems (Yudkin, 1985). The recommended daily allowances of magnesium range from 50 to 70 mg for infants to approximately 300 mg for adults (Ensminger et al., 1983). Dietary sources include a wide variety of foods, including flours, nuts, and spices. The typical western diet supplies ample magnesium (Yudkin, 1985).

While magnesium deficiency is rare under normal circumstances, it may occur in alcoholics and in persons with acute diarrhea or severe kidney disease (Ensminger et al., 1983; Yudkin, 1985). Symptoms of magnesium deficiency include depression; tremors and muscular weakness; confusion and disorientation; dizziness and convulsions; and loss of appetite, nausea, and vomiting (Ensminger et al., 1983; Yudkin, 1985). The salts of magnesium (magnesium sulfate, magnesium carbonate) are used medicinally for their antacid and laxative properties (Malseed, 1983; Parish, 1977). Use in patients with impaired kidney function is contraindicated (Parish, 1977).

## REFERENCES

Ensminger, A. H., Ensminger, M. E., Konlande, J. E., & Robson, J. R. K. (1983). *Foods and nutrition encyclopedia* (Vol. 2). Clovis, CA: Pegus.

Malseed, R. (1983). *Quick reference to drug therapy and nursing considerations.* Philadelphia: Lippincott.

Parish, P. (1977). *The doctors' and patients' handbook of medicines and drugs.* New York: Knopf.

Thomson, W. A. R. (1979). *Black's medical dictionary* (32nd ed.). New York: Barnes & Noble.

Yudkin, J. (1985). *The Penguin encyclopedia of nutrition.* Middlesex, England: Penguin.

CATHY F. TELZROW
*Kent State University*

## MAGNET SCHOOLS

Magnet schools, also referred to as alternative schools, are established within a school district to allow teachers, students, and parents the right to select specific curricula and/or methods of instruction. Most magnet schools have a well-defined educational goal and provide a superior teaching environment to attract students (Carrison, 1981). These schools offer a choice not only in learning styles, but also in subject specialities designed to match students' talents and interests (Power, 1979). Although magnet schools have been in existence for years as preparation programs for gifted students (e.g., Bronx High School of Science in New York; High School of Performing Arts in New York), the emphasis since the late 1960s has been on creating alternative schools to attract students from outside the immediate neighborhood (Barr, 1982; Power, 1979). This emphasis has altered the entrance requirements for magnet schools from one of stiff competition based on auditions and academic ability to one of volunteerism based on racial quotas.

Vernon Smith, director of the Center for Options in Public Education at Indiana University, listed five ways in which alternative schools may vary from regular school programs: style of instruction, curriculum, clientele, resources, and administrative arrangement (Power, 1979).

Over the years, magnet schools have been developed around many programs. Some of these are science and math, individual guided instruction, environmental education, global education, bilingual or multicultural education, gifted and talented education, health care, marketing, college preparation, performing and visual arts, vocational and work study programs, business and management, human services, law and public administration, transportation, multiple careers for special education, back to basics, and microsociety programs where students design and operate their own democratic society (Clinchy, 1984; Doherty, 1982; Power, 1981). Magnet schools have also used business and industrial resources through special materials, instruction, and/or experiences. This involvement with industry has been called the adopt a school concept (Barr, 1982).

In the 1980s, magnet schools received much criticism in areas related to changes in the organizational and political processes within the school system (Metz, 1984). Current issues include freedom of choice, educational reform, desegregation and forced busing, and involvement of community leaders (Carrison, 1981). Many of these issues revolve around the area of quality of programming. Are these programs really superior to and different from regular programs? Are the poor really being included? Does integration really occur? Why should there be special programs that are superior to regular programs? What does that mean for the educational programs of the students who are not involved in the magnet programs (Carrison, 1981)? All of these questions will continue to be debated as the success or failure of magnet schools continues to be evaluated and public schools compete for pupils.

## REFERENCES

Barr, R. D. (1982). Magnet schools: An attractive alternative. *Principal, 61*(3), 37–40.

Carrison, M. P. (1981). Do magnet schools really work? *Principal, 60*(3), 32–35.

Clinchy, E. (1984). Yes, but what about Irving Engelman? *Phi Delta Kappan, 65*(8), 542–545.

Crawford, J., & Freeman, S. (1996). Why parents choose private schooling: Implications for public school programs and information campaigns. *ERS Spectrum, 14*(3), 9–16.

Doherty, D. (1982). Flint, Michigan: A case study in magnet schools and desegregation. *Principal, 61*(3), 41.

Metz, M. H. (1984). The life course of magnet schools organization and political influences. *Teachers College Record, 85*(3), 411–430.

Power, J. (1979). Magnet schools, are they the answer? *Today's Education, 68*(3), 68–70.

SUSANNE BLOUGH ABBOTT
*Bedford Central School District,
Mt. Kisco, New York*

## PRIVATE SCHOOLS AND SPECIAL EDUCATION

# MAGNETIC RESONANCE IMAGING

Magnetic Resonance Imaging (MRI) provides a unique view inside the human body. The level of detail that can be observed with MRI is significantly greater than with any other imaging modality. This has made MRI increasingly the method of choice for diagnosis of many types of injuries and conditions. MRI not only allows for observations of bones and organs but even the arterial system in the body.

An MRI typically consists of a very large magnet with a horizontal tube running through it from front to back. The most important component in MRI is the magnet. This magnet is so powerful that metal objects in the room such as paper clips, keys, or scissors can be pulled out of pockets or off the body without warning and fly at accelerating speeds toward the magnet. Credit cards or any other object with magnetic encoding will be erased by most MRI systems. Once attached to the magnet, these objects are often difficult to disengage. The patient lying on his or her back slides through the magnet on a special table. Once the body part to be scanned is in the exact center of the magnetic field, the scan begins. Radio wave pulses are sent from the magnet through the body. The MRI scanner can pick out a very small point inside the patient's body and essentially examine the type of tissue. The MRI system goes through the patient's body point by point, building up a two- or three-dimensional map of tissue types, and then integrates all of this information through a computer program.

The MRI applies a radio frequency (RF) pulse specific only to hydrogen. The system directs the pulse toward the area of the body under examination. The pulse causes the proteins in the area to absorb the energy required to make them spin in a different direction. This is the "resonance" part of MRI. The RF pulse forces them (only the one or two extra unmatched proteins per million) to spin at a particular frequency in a particular direction. The specific frequency of resonance is calculated on the particular tissue being imaged and the strength of the main magnetic field. MRI machines come with many different coils to apply radio frequency pulses designed for different parts of the body. These coils conform to the contour of the body part being imaged. At approximately the same time, three gradient magnets are arranged in such a manner inside the main magnet that when they are turned on and off very rapidly in a specific order they alter the main magnetic field on a very local level. This allows an examination of a very specific area of the body, and creates a view in slices. An MRI can slice any part of the body in any direction, providing a huge advantage over any other imaging modality. Additionally, the patient does not have to move for the machine to get an image from a different direction. The machine can manipulate everything within the gradient magnets. When the RF pulse is turned off, the hydrogen proteins begin to slowly return to the natural alignment within the magnetic field and release their excess stored energy. When they do this they give off a signal that the coil now picks up and sends to the computer system. The system receives mathematical data that it converts into a picture that can be put on film.

An MRI may also use an injectable contrast or dye. An MRI contrast works by altering the local magnetic field and the tissue being examined. Normal and abnormal tissue will respond differently to the slight alteration, providing different signals. These varied signals are transferred to the images, allowing visualization of many types of tissue abnormalities and disease processes.

There are no known biological hazards to humans from being exposed to magnetic fields of the strength used in MRIs. Pregnant women are often not scanned because there is a limited amount of research in the area of the biological effects on the developing fetus. MRIs are ideal to look inside the body for conditions such as multiple sclerosis, tumors, muscle injuries, and even to examine strokes in their earliest stages. The fact that MRI systems do not use ionizing radiation and that the contrast materials used have a very low incidence of side effects makes MRIs an ideal assessment tool. The machine makes quite a bit of noise and requires individuals to hold still for between 20 and 90 minutes. The procedure is still expensive and individuals with metal parts in their bodies, such as pacemakers or orthopedic hardware, cannot undergo a scan.

SAM GOLDSTEIN
*University of Utah*

**DIFFUSION TENSOR IMAGING**
**SPECT**

# MAGNETOENCEPHALOGRAPHY

Magnetoencephalography (MEG) provides a noninvasive tool to study epilepsy and brain function. When combined with structural imaging, it is referred to as Magnetic Source Imaging (MSI). MEG measures small electrical currents arising inside the neurons of the brain. These currents produce small magnetic fields. MEG generates an accurate representation of the magnetic fields produced by the neurons. MEG is somewhat similar to electroencephalography (EEG). However, the skull and tissue surrounding the brain affect magnetic fields measured by MEG much less than they affect electrical impulses measured by EEG. MEG can therefore provide greater accuracy owing to the minimal distortion of the signal. This allows for more usable and reliable localization of brain function. MEG is often used to localize the source of epileptiform brain activity, which is most likely the source of seizures. An MEG device typically appears as a large tube placed over the head but not covering the face. Patients typically lie down during this procedure. EEG electrodes are glued to the head and one is placed over the heart. Three small coils are taped to the forehead. Two other coils are attached to earplugs. A small metal coil touches all the different dots on the head to record head shape. This information goes into a computer. The coils and EEG electrodes are plugged into sensors. MEG is a completely noninvasive, nonhazardous technology for functional brain mapping, providing spatial discrimination of two millimeters and excellent temporal resolution. It localizes and characterizes the electrical activity of the central nervous system by measuring the associated magnetic fields emanating from the brain. MEG examination takes between 1 and 2½ hours. Individuals have to lie still and not move their heads.

SAM GOLDSTEIN
*University of Utah*

**ELECTROENCEPHALOGRAPH**
**ELECTROENCEPHALOGRAPHY (EEG) BIOFEEDBACK**

# MAHLER, MARGARET SCHOENBERGER (1897–1985)

A native of Sopron, Hungary, Margaret S. Mahler studied medicine and psychiatry in Germany and Austria. As a child psychiatrist, she headed a well-baby clinic in Vienna in the late 1920s and established the first psychoanalytic child guidance clinic there in the 1930s. In 1938, she emigrated to the United States. From 1941 to 1955, she taught at Columbia University's College of Physicians and Surgeons. From 1955 until her retirement in 1974, she was a clinical professor of psychiatry at the Albert Einstein College of Medicine in New York. Margaret Mahler died in 1985 at the age of 88.

Mahler was one of the earliest pioneers in the recognition and diagnosis of childhood schizophrenia. She was an early advocate of treatment programs that would include the mother, the child, and the therapist. Her research focused on what she called the "psychological birth" of the child, between infancy and age 3, during which a child moves from the experience of full psychological union with the mother to the eventual realization of separate personhood around age 3. This view of infant psychological development required the formulation of concepts about the process of separation/individuation and how it contributes to identity formation. The overall thesis was that the first three years represent a critical period in the development of a person's character. Her writings on that topic have been translated into several languages.

Mahler's honors include having received the Scroll of the New York Psychoanalytic Institute and the Frieda Fromm Reichman Award of the American Academy of Psychoanalysis.

**REFERENCES**

Bird, D. (1985, October 3). Margaret Mahler. *The New York Times,* p. 23. Retrieved April 30, 1998, from http://web.lexis-nexis.com/universe

Mahler, M. S. (1979a). *The selected papers of Margaret Mahler, M.D.: Infantile psychosis and early contributions* (Vol. 1). New York: Aronson.

Mahler, M. S. (1979b). *The selected papers of Margaret Mahler, M.D.: Separation-individuation* (Vol. 2). New York: Aronson.

E. VALERIE HEWITT
*Texas A&M University*
First edition

KAY E. KETZENBERGER
*The University of Texas of the Permian Basin*
Second edition

# MAKE-A-PICTURE STORY TEST

The Make-a-Picture Story (MAPS) Test is a variation of other projective storytelling methods used by earlier tests such as the Thematic Apperception Test (TAT) and the Children's Apperception Test (CAT). In the MAPS Test (Shneidman, 1949, 1960), the child selects figures from an array of 67 cutouts in order to make a scene against some 22 background pictures. The child then tells a story for each scene. The MAPS Test was intended to provide greater elicitation of the child's innermost feelings, needs, and desires, enhancing the projective nature of the responding (tests such as the TAT and CAT use ready-made pictures). Since every child responds to different pictures (of their creation), good studies of the reliability and validity of the technique have been nearly impossible to conduct.

The structure of the MAPS Test makes it appealing to elementary and secondary children, however, and it is used periodically in the schools in evaluating seriously emotionally disturbed children (Koppitz, 1982). The MAPS Test stories are scored the same as the TAT stories, except that the number of figures selected by the child for inclusion in the story seems to be of particular significance. There are little data to support the use of the test as other than an adjunct to other clinical methods and in developing a general understanding of a child's general mood and internal drive state. Extensive training is needed to use the MAPS Test appropriately.

## REFERENCES

Koppitz, E. M. (1982). Personality testing in the schools. In C. R. Reynolds & T. B. Gutkin (Eds.), *The handbook of school psychology*. New York: Wiley.

Shneidman, E. S. (1949). *The Make-a-Picture Story Test*. New York: Psychological Corporation.

Shneidman, E. S. (1960). The MAPS with children. In A. I. Rubin & M. R. Haworth (Eds.), *Projective techniques with children*. New York: Grune & Stratton.

CECIL R. REYNOLDS
*Texas A&M University*

## MAKER, C. JUNE (1948–      )

C. June Maker earned her BS in education in 1970 from Western Kentucky University, and her MS in special education-gifted in 1971 from Southern Illinois University. From 1971 to 1974, she worked as a regional supervisor for the Department of Exceptional Children for Illinois. In 1974 and 1975, she was an administrative intern at the Office of Gifted and Talented for the U.S. Department of Education. She then returned to school, attending the University of Virginia to earn her PhD in educational psychology in 1978.

Her major areas of work since that time have centered around curriculum and teaching strategies for the gifted (Maker, 1982; Maker & Nielson, 1995, 1996), intellect among gifted individuals with handicapping conditions (Whitmore & Maker, 1985), and identifying giftedness in children with other disabilities (Maker, 1976). Maker has attempted to direct her professional activities around the centralizing, general goal of improving the education of gifted individuals, particularly those who may have gone unrecognized, and improving education for all learners by emphasizing their strengths rather than their weaknesses. She considers her greatest contributions thus far to be (1) creating and continuing research development of the DISCOVER assessment and curriculum model, an integrated system including performance-based assessment of problem-solving strengths in multiple intellectual domains and curricula designed to nurture identified strengths in regular and special-class settings (Maker, 1992, 1993, 1994, 1996; Maker, Nielson, & Rogers, 1994); (2) continuing to be an advocate for underserved, often unrecognized gifted learners (e.g., culturally diverse individuals and individuals with disabilities or those whose first or dominant language is not English; Maker & Schiever, 1989; Maker & King, 1996) (3) and disseminating ideas and research in a practical and useful way (Maker, 1987, 1992; Maker & King, 1996).

Maker has served the profession in a variety of capacities in addition to her role as a mentor and researcher. She is presently a professor of special education at the University of Arizona, where she coordinates graduate degree concentrations in education of the gifted and is the principal investigator of the DISCOVER research and development projects. DISCOVER has been funded by the Office of Bilingual Education and Minority Languages Affairs, the Javits Gifted and Talented Education Program, and Shonto Preparatory Academy. Maker was an elected member of the Board of Directors of the National Association for Gifted Children for 19 years, and since 1975 she has held various leadership positions in the Association for the Gifted. She has served as a consultant to programs for the gifted for numerous organizations and agencies, both in the United States and abroad.

C. June Maker

## REFERENCES

Maker, C. J. (1976). Searching for giftedness and talent in children with handicaps. *School Psychology Digest, 1*, 24–37.

Maker, C. J. (1982). *Curriculum development for the gifted*. Rockville, MD: Aspen.

Maker, C. J. (1987). The gifted child. In V. Koehler (Ed.), *Educators handbook: Research into practice* (pp. 420–456). New York: Longman.

Maker, C. J. (1992). Intelligence and creativity in multiple intelligences: Identification and development. *Educating Able Learners, 12*(4), 12–19.

Maker, C. J. (Ed.). (1993). *Critical issues in gifted education. Vol. 3: Programs for gifted students in regular classrooms*. Austin, TX: PRO-ED.

Maker, C. J. (1993). Creativity, intelligence, and problem solving: A definition and design for cross-cultural research and measurement related to giftedness. *Gifted Education International, 9*(2), 68–77.

Maker, C. J. (1994). Authentic assessment of problem solving and giftedness in secondary school students. *Journal of Secondary Gifted Education, 2*(1), 19–29.

Maker, C. J. (1996). Identification of gifted minority students: A national problem, needed changes, and a promising solution. *Gifted Child Quarterly, 40*(1), 41–50.

Maker, C. J., & King, M. N. (1996). *Nurturing giftedness in young children.* Reston, VA: Council for Exceptional Children.

Maker, C. J., & Nielson, A. B. (1995). *Teaching models in education of the gifted* (2nd ed.). Austin, TX: PRO-ED.

Maker, C. J., & Nielson, A. B. (1996). *Curriculum development and teaching strategies for gifted learners* (2nd ed.). Austin, TX: PRO-ED.

Maker, C. J., Nielson, A. B., & Rogers, J. A. (1994). Giftedness, diversity and problem solving. *Teaching Exceptional Children, 27*(1), 4–19.

Maker, C. J., & Schiever, S. W. (Eds.). (1989). *Critical issues in gifted education: Vol. 2. Defensible programs for cultural and ethnic minorities.* Austin, TX: PRO-ED.

Whitmore, J. R., & Maker, C. J. (1985). *Intellectually gifted persons with specific disabilities.* Rockville, MD: Aspen.

CECIL R. REYNOLDS
*Texas A&M University*
First edition

TAMARA J. MARTIN
*The University of Texas of the Permian Basin*
Second edition

# MAINSTREAMING

Mainstreaming was the popular term used for the legal doctrine of least restrictive environment (LRE). This term and its underlying concept are the products of the civil rights movement of the 1950s and 1960s, during which time courts judged as illegal segregation on the basis of race. Segregation was said to deny some children the opportunity of an education on equal terms with others. This principle was extended to include children with disabilities in the cases of *PARC* v. *Commonwealth of Pennsylvania* (1971) and *Mills* v. *Board of Education of the District of Columbia* (1972). Educational agencies were encouraged to place students in the most normalized settings possible and discouraged from placing them in stigmatizing or segregated ones. Under the 1975 Education for All Handicapped Children Act of 1975 (PL 94-142), the 1990 Individuals with Disabilities Education Act (IDEA), and its subsequent reauthorizations, educational agencies are required to provide the least restrictive environment possible for a student's education.

Although the terms mainstreaming and least restrictive environment share historical antecedents, they are not equivalent, and careless use of them often leads to confusion about the LRE provisions of the law. The LRE doctrine mandates that, to the maximum extent possible, children with disabilities be educated with nondisabled children. Mainstreaming, in contrast, is only one of many instructional arrangements which can meet the LRE requirement; the mainstreamed student receives his or her instruction in the regular education classroom, with special education support when necessary. Such support may include direct instruction from a special education teacher, team teaching, interpreter services, education aides, curricular or instructional modification, special equipment, consultation, staff development, reduction of the ratio of students to instructional staff, and other direct or indirect services needed to implement the individual education plan.

Mainstreaming has often been interpreted to mean that students with disabilities *must* be included and instructed in regular classroom settings, which are considered to be the mainstream or normal educational environment. This is not true. In cases of severe disability, the educational agency may remove a student from regular class when instruction in that class with supplementary aids and services such as resource rooms cannot be satisfactorily accomplished. To accommodate these students, a continuum of alternative placements must be available to the extent necessary to implement the individualized education program (IEP) for each student with a disability. The alternative placements include regular classes, special classes, special schools, home instruction, and instruction in hospitals and institutions. Resource room or itinerant instruction, in which a teacher visits classes, is to be provided as a supplementary service to instruction in the regular classroom. Thus, if school personnel or others involved in evaluating and developing IEPs for students can justify a more restrictive placement than a regular classroom, that placement is acceptable, with parental consent.

The interpretation of what constitutes the least restrictive environment raged throughout the 1990s, and continues to be hotly debated. Some believe that every child, regardless of disability status, should be educated in the regular education classroom, with special supports when necessary; this approach has been termed *full inclusion*. The inclusion model, as a philosophy, seeks to merge special and general education into a unified system for meeting the educational needs of all students regardless of their abilities or disabilities. Many others involved in special education and who work with children with disabilities believe that the continuum of alternative placements discussed previously best serves the interests of the special education student.

ROLAND K. YOSHIDA
*Fordham University*
First edition

KAY E. KETZENBERGER
*The University of Texas of the Permian Basin*
Second edition

KIMBERLY F. APPLEQUIST
*University of Colorado at Colorado Springs*
Third edition

**INCLUSION**
**LEAST RESTRICTIVE ENVIRONMENT**

## MAINTENANCE

The concept of maintenance as it relates to academic school work is that a student can maintain performance with accuracy, even after task-training procedures are no longer employed. Maintenance (as suggested by Mims, 1991) is related to three other concepts: the concepts of acquisition and proficiency, which are antecedent to maintenance; and the concept of generalization, which is subsequent to maintenance.

Acquisition means that the student can do something that he or she could not do before. For example, a student is pretested on the ability to identify the 17 different ways to spell the schwa /ə/ vowel. The pretest result identifies a knowledge of only four ways to spell the schwa sound. After initial training (i.e., 30 minutes per day for 4 weeks using multisensory practice), the student knows 15 of the 17 ways. At this point the student has demonstrated by way of acquisition the initial mastery of a new skill. As the student is called on to use this newly acquired skill, and does so across time without recourse to the original task-training procedures, the student is evidencing a maintenance skill. The attainment of maintenance will probably involve the student in further appropriate practice work that can be identified as overlearning trials and distributed practice.

Overlearning trials are representative of repeated practice or overlearning work that is about half of what it was at the acquisition stage. For example, the initial learning of the 17 ways to spell the sound of schwa /ə/ required 30 minutes of appropriate practice per day for 4 weeks. We can for maintenance purposes, by way of overlearning trials, reduce the time to 15 minutes per day for 2 weeks. Distributed practice is work that is systematically distributed across a designated period of time, such as several weeks. Therefore, the concept of distributed practice as it relates to maintenance is concomitant with the practice suggested for the aspect of overlearning trials, which involve expanded practice relative to some task that the student is assigned to do.

The practical difference is that instead of designating 15 minutes of appropriate practice per day for 2 weeks, the same practice time can be scheduled two times per week for 5 weeks. A major advantage of distributed practice is that it complements long-term memory, and long-term memory likewise complements the execution of generalization. Generalizing means that a student who was previously disabled can now perform academic tasks with efficiency and do so independent of assistance. It also means that the student can randomly (or as needed) execute self-directed remedial practices. Thus the concept of generalization and its application represents independence for the learning-disabled (LD) student. When generalization occurs in reference to learning the 17 ways to spell the schwa sound /ə/, the student will spell words with the schwa sound with 96 percent accuracy across various and random settings that call for the spelling of words with that schwa sound.

What is to be stressed in reviewing the relationship of the continuum of acquisition, maintenance, and generalization is that learning evidenced through correct or corrected work will, under systematic analysis, reveal the interfacing presence of each of the previously mentioned three components. The sequential continuum of learning represented by the three concepts is identified on the following analytical outline developed by Thorpe (1981).

I. Introduction of task by the teacher
II. Acquisition of the skills that the student needs to perform the task.
   A. Instructional techniques
      1. General techniques
         a. Teach to a minimum acquisition level (usually 80 percent accuracy)
         b. Structure practice sessions
         c. Elicit maximum student response
         d. Use correction and reinforcement
         e. Present multiple activities of short duration
         f. Use distributive practices of short duration
         g. If there are multiple correct responses to a single stimulus, teach each response in isolation
         h. Teach stimuli or responses that have a similar topography in isolation
         i. Develop effective pacing of instructional material
         j. Use challenges to elicit student interest
         k. Use foolers to encourage self-reliance
      2. Group techniques
         a. Develop attention signals
         b. Use task signals to elicit unison responses
      3. Concept teaching
         a. Identify essential discriminations
         b. Present one unknown concept at a time
         c. Use examples and nonexamples
         d. Make examples representative of the concept population
         e. Move from concrete to abstract examples
         f. Irrelevant characteristics are noted and cast out
         g. Move from gross to fine differences between example and nonexamples
         h. Use descriptive language when possible

III. Maintenance
   A. Introduction
   B. Appropriate practice activities (usually about 50 percent of the practice time that was needed at acquisition)
      1. Instructional games
      2. Workbooks
      3. Worksheets
      4. Flashcards
   C. Systematic and regularly scheduled review sessions
   D. Applications of factual material
IV. Generalization
   A. Emphasize similar components
      1. Gather information about regular classroom procedures and expectations
      2. Simplify and fade the reinforcement procedures
         a. Student does not know when and/or for what he or she is being reinforced
         b. Emphasize behaviors that tend to naturally attract reinforcers
         c. Use some delay feedback procedures
      3. Work on foundational skills and their applications
         a. Emphasize prerequisites to regular classroom expectations
         b. Emphasize working at rate
         c. Emphasize the application of basis facts including using those applications creatively
      4. Work toward similar content procedures and goals
         a. Regular education materials should be introduced and used in conjunction with the special education materials
         b. Emphasize regular classroom social expectations
         c. Introduce extraneous stimuli
         d. Know the minimum level of performance in the regular classroom to which the child is going to be mainstreamed
      5. Progress from individual interactions toward group interactions
      6. Develop independent work skills
         a. Begin to fade teacher support
         b. Develop self-help techniques in the students (pp. 1–2)

Many students who have been and are associated with special education do not initially acquire and thus cannot employ generalization of study habits and skills commonly associated with the successful nondisabled student (Kavale & Forress, 1985). Thus, maintenance becomes essential. Special education students taught to employ respective concepts associated with maintenance can become independent scholars.

## REFERENCES

Kavale, K., & Forness, S. (1985). *The science of learning disabilities.* San Diego, CA: College Hill.

Mims, A. (1991). Effective instruction in homework for students with disabilities. *Teaching Exceptional Children, 24*(1), 42–44.

Thorpe, H. (1981). *A three-phase instructional strategy for teaching children who have learning difficulties.* Unpublished manuscript, University of Wisconsin, Oshkosh.

ROBERT T. NASH
*University of Wisconsin at Oshkosh*

GENERALIZATION
MASTERY LEARNING AND SPECIAL EDUCATION

# MALADAPTIVE BEHAVIOR

Maladaptive behavior is a term that can be easily misunderstood. Within a developmental psychology perspective, trajectories for normal behaviors are predictable as children mature and adapt to their environment (Mash & Barkley, 2003). Some expectations may be culturally influenced (e.g., age to sleep without parents) or context referenced (e.g., behavior in a house of worship) while others are directly related to physical growth (e.g., ability to walk). These adaptive behaviors promote the well-being of the individual and are often conceptualized in terms of domains of appropriate daily living activities. Based on definitions by the American Association of Mental Retardation (2002), adaptive behaviors include conceptual, social, and practical skills. Abilities in these domains are typically expected to increase in level of independence, complexity, and frequency. Questions on rating scales that measure adaptive behaviors will reflect skill hierarchies (e.g., can eat with a fork, can prepare own sandwich) and often use Likert scale responses (e.g., never, sometimes, almost always) that indicate the frequency of the behaviors. A person's scores are compared with those of a national sample of persons of similar age.

In contrast to adaptive behaviors, maladaptive behaviors are those that do not serve the well-being of the individual or others and are counterproductive to appropriate daily functioning skills typical of the person's age. Behaviors can be expressed in intrapunitive (e.g., self-demeaning statements, self-mutilation) or extrapunitive forms (e.g., defiance, vandalism, aggression). These behaviors may negatively impact cognitive functioning (e.g., low frustration tolerance that prohibits new learning), social functioning (e.g., poor peer relationships), and practical skills (e.g., dependence, lack of personal safety).

Although a consensus definition of maladaptive behavior does not exist, features such as severity, frequency, or coexisting behaviors can help distinguish maladaptive from more appropriate acts. Maladaptive behaviors and the resulting impairment can be conceptualized along a continuum from mild to severe. For example, an older child who sucks his or her thumb when frustrated is exhibiting a mild maladaptive self-soothing mechanism that could result in peer ridicule, whereas a child engaging in head banging when frustrated is exhibiting a severe maladaptive reaction that can incur injury. A behavior also may be considered maladaptive based on frequency, as in the case of occasional withdrawal versus selective mutism.

Some misconceptions exist. For example, maladaptive behavior is not a mental health diagnosis or special education classification. Maladaptive behaviors do not preclude coexisting, highly developed skills in other areas (e.g., strong leadership skills in a gang member), specific behaviors are not necessarily maladaptive across ages (e.g., clinging at age 2 versus age 12), and are not synonymous with pathology or serious emotional disturbance. Maladaptive behaviors may present alone (e.g., failure to bathe) or as one of many symptoms that are part of a mental health syndrome, based on the *Diagnostic and Statistical Manual of Mental Disorders* (American Psychiatric Association, 2000) criteria that represents pathology (e.g., disintegration of personal hygiene habits during a schizophrenic episode). Rather than providing exact diagnoses, maladaptive rating scales often compare the frequency behaviors occur in children, noting as well whether the behaviors are normal, at-risk, or clinically significant (i.e., consistent with clinical samples of children requiring treatment).

Risk factors for maladaptive behaviors resulting in psychopathology include genetic predispositions, poor emotional regulation or disinhibition, atypical responsiveness to rewards and punishment, dysfunctional parenting communication, insecure early parent-child attachments, history of family criminality, and low cognitive ability. Prognosis is poor when multiple social stressors exist (e.g., poverty, poor health care, addictions) or pathology is multigenerational (Evans et al., 2005; Frick, 1998; Mash & Barkley, 2003).

Analysis of serious school violence events has identified four areas that contribute to dysfunction: maladaptive behavioral patterns in the perpetrators, dysfunctional family interactions, deviant social dynamics, and perceived bullying or tolerance for mistreatment at school (Department of Justice Federal Bureau of Investigation, 1999). Preventative school initiatives to prevent bullying include supportive school environments, early identification of bullying behaviors, and social-emotional services for students (United States Secret Service, 2002).

If behaviors are sufficiently pervasive to interfere with academic functioning, a student may be eligible for services as emotionally disturbed (Individuals with Disabilities Education Improvement Act of 2004; Rehabilitative Act of 1973,

Section 504). Maladaptive behaviors also may be conceived as psychopathic (i.e., willful, predatory, without remorse), in which case a student may be considered socially maladjusted and may be excluded from special education services for emotionally disturbed in some states. Attempts to distinguish emotional disturbance and social maladjustment are difficult. Some authors recommend a thorough evaluation of the child's character pathology when investigating these two disability categories (Gacono & Hughes, 2004).

Regardless of the type of maladaptive behaviors identified, there are multiple strategies available within schools and homes to help students change these behaviors (e.g., behavioral modification, positive behavioral support, counseling therapy). The choice of intervention is based on the student's unique needs and empirical support for the chosen intervention method (Evans et al., 2005).

## REFERENCES

American Association on Mental Retardation. (2002). *Mental retardation: Definition, classification, and systems of supports* (10th ed.). Washington, DC: Author.

American Psychiatric Association. (2000). *Diagnostic and statistical manual of mental disorders* (4th ed.). Washington, DC: Author.

Department of Justice Federal Bureau of Investigation. (1999). *The school shooter: A threat assessment perspective.* Washington, DC: Author. Retrieved June 10, 2005, from http://www.fbi .gov/publications/school/school2.pdf

Evans, D. L., Foa, E. B., Gur, R. E., Hendin, H., O'Brien, C. P., Seligman, M. E., & Walsh, T. (Eds.). (2005). *Treating and preventing adolescent mental health disorders: What we know and what we don't know.* New York: Oxford Press.

Frick, P. J., (1998). *Conduct disorders and severe antisocial behavior.* New York: Plenum Press.

Gacono, C. B., & Hughes, T. L. (2004). Differentiating emotional disturbance from socially maladjustment: Assessing psychopathy in aggressive youth. *Psychology in the Schools, 41*(8), 849–860.

*Individuals with Disabilities Education Improvement Act of 2004.* 20 U.S.C. § 1400 et seq. Retrieved August 28, 2005, from http:// www.ed.gov/policy/speced/guid/idea/idea2004.html

Mash, E. J., & Barkley, R. A. (Eds.). (2003). *Child psychopathology* (2nd ed.). New York: Guilford.

*Rehabilitation Act of 1973.* 29 U.S.C. § 701 et seq.

United States Secret Service. (2002). *The final report and findings of the safe school initiative: Implications for the prevention of school attacks in the United States.* Washington, DC: Author. Retrieved June 10, 2005, from http://www.secretservice.gov/

DIANA JOYCE
*University of Florida*

## BEHAVIOR ASSESSMENT SYSTEM FOR CHILDREN–SECOND EDITION
## CONDUCT DISORDER
## DISCIPLINE

## MALE TURNER'S SYNDROME

See NOONAN'S SYNDROME.

## MALNUTRITION

Proper nutrition during infancy is essential due to rapid physical and cognitive growth during this period. Malnutrition, an inadequate supply and balance of nutrients, can result in improper physical, cognitive, and social development in young children. Malnutrition can take three forms: (1) overnutrition, which results when children consume too many calories; (2) undernutrition (also called protein-energy malnutrition), in which too few calories and nutrients are consumed; and (3) secondary malnutrition, which occurs when consumed food cannot be utilized properly due to health conditions, such as diarrhea or illness.

In developing nations, poverty may be largely responsible for malnutrition, particularly protein-energy malnutrition. Protein-energy malnutrition is responsible for over half of all deaths in children under age five in developing nations (World Health Organization, 2000). Malnourished children also are found in industrialized nations, particularly in impoverished communities. Although children in industrialized nations may not suffer from extreme malnourishment resulting from scarcity of food, they may not receive proper nutrition, which can result in cognitive deficits and problems with physical and social development (e.g., stunted growth and problems with perceptual and motor development). In the United States, many children suffer from iron deficiencies, which have been linked to lower performance on intelligence tests and slower brain wave activity than in children who are not iron deficient (Otero, Aguirre, & Porcayo, 1999).

A number of diseases are associated with malnourishment in early childhood, including marasmus and kwashiorkor. Children that are severely malnourished before one year of age may develop marasmus, a disease linked to a deficiency of calories and nutrients. Children with marasmus stop growing and the body eventually begins to waste away, which eventually may result in the child's death. Children who survive may develop wrinkled and frail appearance and may fail to attain full growth. Children who have kwashiorkor exhibit edemic bodies, particularly stomachs that fill with water, and also display skin lesions and thinning hair.

Intervention strategies for malnourished children may include psychosocial and community education programs. Children who receive psychosocial intervention programs may attain cognitive gains, as measured by standardized intelligence tests. However, despite such gains, malnourished children rarely exhibit normal cognitive abilities (Grantham-McGregor, Powell, Walker, Chang, & Fletcher,

1994). In communities in which nutritious food is not scarce, improved education about nutrition provided by health care services may result in a decreased prevalence of childhood stunted growth (Penny, Creed-Kanashiro, Robert, Narro, Caulfield, & Black, 2005).

### REFERENCES

Grantham-McGregor, S., Powell, C., Walker, S., Chang, S., & Fletcher, P. (1994). The long-term follow-up of severely malnourished children who participated in an intervention program. *Child Development, 65,* 428–439.

Otero, G. A., Aguirre, G. M. & Porcayo, R. (1999). Psychological and electroencephalographic study in school children with iron deficiency. *International Journal of Neuroscience, 99,* 113–121.

Penny, M. E., Creed-Kanashiro, H. M., Robert, R. C., Narro, M. R., Caulfield, L. E., & Black, R. E. (2005). Effectiveness of an educational intervention delivered through the health services to improve nutrition in young children: A cluster-randomized controlled trial. *Lancet, 365,* 1863–1872.

World Health Organization. (2000). Turning the tide of malnutrition: Responding to the challenge of the 21st century. Retrieved September 12, 2005, from http://www.who.int/nut/documents/nhd _brochure.pdf

ALLISON G. DEMPSEY
*University of Florida*

DEPRIVATION
EATING DISORDERS
PICA

## MANIFESTATION DETERMINATION

The requirement to conduct a manifestation determination first appeared in the reauthorization of the Individuals with Disabilities Education Act (1997) and was subsequently reauthorized through the passage of the Individuals with Disabilities Education Improvement Act (IDEIA; 2004). A manifestation determination comes into play when a student with a disability engages in behavior that is a violation of the disciplinary code of the given school that she or he attends. The manifestation determination process is conducted by the Local Education Agency (LEA), the parent, and relevant members of the Individualized Education Program (IEP) team. The group of individuals conducting the process is required to review all relevant information in the student's records. This includes the student's IEP, teacher notes and observations, and information from the parent. The team of individuals uses this information to determine if the conduct in question was caused by, or had a direct and substantial relationship to, the child's disability, or if the conduct in question was the direct result of the LEA's failure to implement the IEP (thus, a failure to provide a Free and Appropriate Public Education [FAPE]). The IEP team must conduct a functional behavior assessment (FBA) and implement a behavior intervention plan (BIP) for the child of concern if this has not already been done in the event that either of these two conditions is evident. In essence, the IEP team must answer "yes" or "no" to the question of whether the behavior of concern was a manifestation of the child's disability.

## Two Domains of Inquiry

First, the IEP team, in conducting a manifestation determination, must assess whether the student of concern understood the consequences of his or her behavior and whether or not he or she was able to control the behavior in question (e.g., Did the student understand that the behavior was a violation and did she or he have a history of being able to control the behavior under similar circumstances in the past?). The best indication of any given student's capacity in this regard is his or her prior behavior (Knoster, 2000).

Second, the IEP team must also determine whether the IEP in place at the time of the behavioral incident was appropriate and being implemented as stipulated in the IEP (e.g., was the student deriving reasonable progress from his or her IEP?). When the information being reviewed indicates that the behavioral incident was an extension of a pattern of problem behavior and poor performance, it may be concluded that the IEP and BIP had been insufficient to meet the student's needs. In this scenario, a change in the IEP and BIP may be warranted as the student was not deriving reasonable progress from the existent program. However, when a student's performance appears to be on track toward achieving the annual goals in the student's IEP and the conduct of concern represents an aberration from the student's recent level of performance, the IEP may have been appropriate (Tilly et al., 1998).

## Courses of Action

The IEP team must make relevant changes in the student's BIP and the IEP in the instance where the team determines that the behavior of concern was a manifestation of the child's disability. In such an instance, with the exception of conduct that involved weapons, drugs, or resulted in serious bodily injury, the educational placement remains unchanged unless the parent and LEA agree to a change in placement. In the event where the behavior of concern was not a manifestation of the student's disability, the LEA may proceed with the typical disciplinary procedures that they would employ with the general student body given the behavioral infraction.

## Removal to an Interim Alternative Setting

A student with a disability may be removed to an interim alternative education setting, regardless of whether the behavior of concern was a manifestation of that student's disability, if the child carries or possesses a weapon to or at school or a school function. Furthermore, the child may be removed to an interim alternative education setting if he or she knowingly possesses or uses illegal drugs or sells or solicits the sale of a controlled substance while at school, on the premises of school, or at a school function. Lastly, a child may be moved to an interim alternative education setting if she or he has inflicted serious bodily injury upon another person while at school, on school premises, or at a school function. The IDEIA (2004) defines serious bodily injury as involving (1) a substantial risk of death, (2) extreme physical pain, (3) protracted and obvious disfigurement, or (4) protracted loss or impairment of the function of a bodily member, organ, or mental faculty. Any removal to an interim alternative educational setting may last up to a maximum of 45 school days unless the parent and LEA agree to a change of placement.

## REFERENCES

*Individuals with Disabilities Education Act Amendments of 1997,* PL 105-17, 615 (K) (4) (C) (1997).

*Individuals with Disabilities Education Improvement Act Amendments of 2004,* PL 108-446, 615 (K) (4) (C) (2004).

Knoster, T. (2000). Understanding the difference and relationship between functional behavioral assessments and manifestation determinations. *Journal of Positive Behavior Interventions, 1,* 53–58.

Tilly, W. D., Knoster, T., Kovaleski, J., Bambara, L., Dunlap, G., & Kincaid, D. (1998). *Functional behavioral assessment: Policy development in light of emerging research and practice.* Alexandria, VA: National Association of State Directors of Special Education.

TIM KNOSTER
*Bloomsburg University of Pennsylvania*

FUNCTIONAL ASSESSMENT
POSITIVE BEHAVIORAL SUPPORT

# MANUAL COMMUNICATION

Human language is conceived as being primarily produced and perceived in an oral-aural mode (speaking and hearing). Yet all kinds of information are provided by nonvocal means such as facial expressions, gazes (direction, quality), hand movements, gestures, and body movements. Nonvocal communication and manual communication can have an auxiliary function, completing the information provided through the vocal channel, or be the main and often sole channel of communication.

When accompanying vocal communication, nonverbal

signs can have a semantic, syntactic, pragmatic, or dialogical function (Goldin-Meadow, 1996; Scherer, 1980). Examples for manual communication are (1) semantic function pointing at a person or an object (possibly together with gaze in the same direction); (2) pragmatic function, a hand movement by the listener expressing his or her doubt about the speaker's assertion (possibly together with facial expression, shrugging of shoulders); and (3) dialogical function, the listener lifting his or her hand or forefinger to show an intention to break in (possibly at the same time expressing the same intention through gaze and other body movements).

This kind of manual communication forms a whole with other kinds of nonvocal communication and with vocal communication, whether hand movements occur simultaneously with or between segments of vocal production.

Manual communication independent of vocal communication can be found in various small communities (e.g., that of monks), yet its best known variety is the language of the deaf. The scientific study of sign language started in the 1960s. It was initiated by the work of W. Stokoe (1960, 1978). Good introductions to these languages are Klima and Bellugi (1979) and Deuchar (1984). Like other natural languages, sign languages have their own phonology, grammar (morphology and syntax), and lexicon.

In the phonology of sign languages (first called cherology, the science of cheremes) each sign has the following features: tabula (location, the place where the sign is made); designator (the shape of the hand); signation (the movement made by the hand); and orientation (of the hand relative to the body). It has been shown that these features can in many ways be compared to the phonemes of spoken languages. Although the iconicity of part of the signs is undeniable, the above features have no meaning. On the other hand, they combine to constitute signs in the same way as phonemes of spoken languages, although they do so simultaneously instead of sequentially.

In the morphology, the categories (gender, number, tense) and the formal processes are not necessarily the same as in spoken languages (e.g., sign languages have compounds, but they have no derivation through affixation). Sign languages express a variety of distinctions such as deixis, reciprocity, number, distributional aspect, and temporal aspect (Klima & Bellugi, 1979).

In the syntax of sign languages, the order in which signs are produced is not arbitrary, i.e., sign languages have their own syntax. Sign languages also have their own lexicon. Lexical differences between sign languages or between a sign language and a spoken language are not fundamentally different from lexical differences between spoken languages (Stokoe et al., 1965).

Sign languages have existed for centuries. They are acquired as a mother tongue or learned as a second language. Since most deaf people become bilingual and bicultural (sign and spoken language; deaf and hearing culture) and sign languages are used as a medium of communication and interaction within communities, research on sign languages covers all of the domains of spoken languages: linguistics (synchrony and diachrony), psycho- and sociolinguistics, language teaching, and so on.

Although hand movements are of primary importance in sign languages, it must be stressed that signers make intensive use of other nonvocal models of expression (gaze, facial expression, movements of head, shoulders, torso, etc.). There are also systems of manual communication, generally called signed languages (e.g., signed French as opposed to the French sign language), that consist of extensions and modifications of a sign language. Most characteristic are the addition of signs for morphological categories that do not exist in the original sign language and a syntax more akin to that of the national spoken language. Signers sometimes use finger spelling, in which one hand-configuration represents one letter in the written version of the spoken language. This is done for most proper names and concepts for which there is no sign or to express a meaning more accurately than a sign allows (e.g., if a sign for poodle does not exist, the sign for dog plus the letters P, O, O, D, L, E would be used).

## REFERENCES

Deuchar, M. (1984). *British sign language*. London: Routledge & Kegan Paul.

Goldin-Meadow, S. (1996). Silence is liberating: Removing the handcuffs on grammatical expression in the manual modality. *Psychological Review, 103*(1), 34–55.

Klima, E., & Bellugi, U. (1979). *The signs of language*. Cambridge, MA: Harvard University Press.

Scherer, K. (1980). The functions of non-verbal signs in conversation. In R. St. Clair & H. Giles (Eds.), *The social and psychological contexts of language*. Hillsdale, NJ: Erlbaum.

Stokoe, W. C. (1960). *Sign language structure: An outline of the visual communication systems of the American deaf* (Studies in Linguistics, Occasional Papers, 8; reprinted 1978). Silver Spring, MD: Linstok.

Stokoe, W. C., Casterline, D. C., & Croneberg, C. G. (1965). *A dictionary of American sign language on linguistic principles*. Silver Spring, MD: Linstok.

S. DE VRIENDT
*Vrije Universiteit Brussel,
Belgium*

## AMERICAN SIGN LANGUAGE
## TOTAL COMMUNICATION

# MARASMUS

Marasmus is a form of severe malnutrition. It results from overall food deprivation from birth or early infancy. It is most common in poverty-level infants who are not breast fed. However, marasmus can occur in children of any age whose diet is grossly inadequate, especially with respect to energy intake (Kreutler, 1980).

Marasmus results in wasting of tissues and severe growth retardation. Loss of muscle mass and subcutaneous fat gives children suffering from this condition a shrunken, old appearance in the face. The rest of the body has the skin-and-bones appearance typical of starvation. Poor nutritional status lowers resistance to disease, making these children particularly vulnerable to infections such as gastroenteritis, diarrhea, and tuberculosis.

As growth rate declines, both physical stunting and mental and emotional impairment occur if nutrient deprivation continues. Marked retardation in mental development may persist in marasmic children even after physical and biochemical rehabilitation (Cravioto, 1981).

According to Kreutler (1980), when marasmus is combined with protein-energy malnutrition and kwashiorkor resulting from protein deficiency, the incidence of these severe forms of malnutrition is estimated to be from 400 to 500 million. The majority of affected persons are found in developing countries where warfare, civil strife, and drought have produced widespread famine; and cultural approaches to treatment may not be appropriate (Pelletier, 1993).

Among more affluent societies, marasmic children are usually found in extremely poor socioeconomic and emotionally deprived environments (Williams, 1985). Parents may be ignorant of food values or the importance of providing appropriate food to young infants and children. Parental neglect may also result from complex emotional or mental problems.

Among adults in developed countries, marasmus has occasionally been associated with alcoholism; it is sometimes the result of isolation or hospitalization in elderly people. Self-imposed starvation may also result from an obsession with thinness and a distorted body image as seen in anorexia nervosa (Williams, 1985).

### REFERENCES

Cravioto, J. (1981). Nutrition, stimulation, mental development and learning. *Nutrition Today, 16*(5), 4–14.

Kreutler, P. A. (1980). *Nutrition in perspective.* Englewood Cliffs, NJ: Prentice Hall.

Pelletier, J. G. (1993). Severe malnutrition: A global approach. *Children in the Tropics, 12*(1), 208–209.

Williams, S. R. (1985). *Nutrition and diet therapy* (5th ed.). St. Louis, MO: Times Mirror/Mosby.

MARYANN C. FARTHING
*University of North Carolina at Chapel Hill*

**ANOREXIA NERVOSA**
**EATING DISORDERS**
**MALNUTRITION**
**NUTRITIONAL DISORDERS**
**PICA**

## MARCH OF DIMES

The March of Dimes Foundation was founded by President Franklin D. Roosevelt in 1938 as the National Foundation for Infantile Paralysis to combat the nation's polio epidemic. Basil O'Conner, the President's former law partner, was asked to lead the organization (March of Dimes, 1985). Roosevelt, a victim of polio, recovered partial use of his legs by swimming in the warm spring waters in Georgia and exercising his leg muscles, thereby becoming a national model for polio patients. Later, he purchased the facility at Warm Springs and established the Warm Springs Foundation. Large numbers of individuals with this crippling disease came to the Warm Springs Foundation, making it necessary to build houses and roads and to provide doctors and therapists to develop various exercise programs. Indigent people who came to swim and exercise were welcomed as guests by the President, requiring the foundation to raise additional money. Roosevelt had great compassion for polio patients, many of whom were victims of the nation's economic problems and who could not receive the treatments from which he had so greatly benefited. Moreover, he felt that every city should have hospitals with iron lungs, hot-pack equipment, swimming pools, walking ramps, and lightweight braces. If everyone, Roosevelt reasoned, would give just a little bit, even a dime, a lot of money would be raised for the noble cause. Actor Eddie Cantor named the organization after suggesting that people send their dimes directly to the President at the White House (Sterling, Sterling, Ehrenberg, & National Foundation for Infantile Paralysis, 1955).

In 1953 Dr. Jonas Salk, a foundation grantee, developed a killed virus vaccine; it was declared in 1955 to be safe, potent, and effective. Before the discovery and licensing of the Sabine oral vaccine in 1962, the National Foundation, assured of its victory over polio, redirected its efforts from treatment to rehabilitation, the prevention of birth defects, and the overall improvement of the outcome of pregnancy. It changed its name to the National Foundation—March of Dimes. The present name, March of Dimes—Birth Defects Foundation, was adopted in 1979 (March of Dimes, 1985). The March of Dimes—Birth Defects Foundation is one of the 10 largest voluntary associations in America in membership and annual budget with seventy-five percent of all funds raised going to research and programs (March of Dimes, 1998). It provides research, professional education, volunteer services, and public health education. The March of Dimes maintains an Internet web site at http://modimes.org.

## REFERENCES

March of Dimes—Birth Defects Foundation. (1998). *All about the March of Dimes.* New York: Author.

Sills, S. T. (1980). *The volunteer: Means and ends in a national organization.* New York: Arno.

Sterling, D., Sterling, P., Ehrenberg, M., & National Foundation for Infantile Paralysis. (1955). *Polio pioneers: The story of the fight against polio.* New York: Doubleday.

FRANCIS T. HARRINGTON
*Radford University*

## MARFAN SYNDROME

Marfan syndrome is an autosomal dominant disorder in most cases, although it can occur as a spontaneous mutation (Gillberg, 1995). Involvement of chromosome 15 is theorized but not yet proven. The disorder is characterized by a variety of symptoms, some of which occur inconsistently with the disorder, that include primarily physical markers. Intelligence and affect are not believed to be directly affected by Marfan syndrome (Gillberg, 1995). The disorder is well known in part because Abraham Lincoln suffered from Marfan syndrome (Randall, 1990).

The primary physical hallmarks of the disorder are the elongations of the bones in particular regions of the body, primarily the arms and legs, but also including abnormally long and spindly fingers and toes. The latter is a physical characteristic known as spiderdactyly (a characteristic seen in certain other genetic disorders as well, including Klinefelter syndrome). However, there may be more severe physical problems including scoliosis, cardiac deformities, aneurysms, and even abnormal location of the lungs. Vision may be affected in some cases, and often there are dermatological problems. Children with Marfan syndrome will see an unusual number of physicians and may experience excessive absences from school. As noted, behavior and affect are not directly affected, but due to their unusual appearance, children with Marfan are subject to more emotional difficulties than the average child, especially during adolescence. Special education is not required in most cases of Marfan but may be necessary depending upon the degree of cardiac, lung, or vision impairment. Services are provided in most cases, if necessary, under the rubric of other health impaired. There is no specific treatment for Marfan syndrome beyond symptom management and possibly surgical corrections of cardiac and spinal defects.

## REFERENCES

Gillberg, C. (1995). *Clinical child neuropsychiatry.* Cambridge: Cambridge University Press.

Randall, T. (1990). Marfan gene search intensifies following identification of basic defect. *Journal of the American Medical Association, 264,* 1642–1643.

CECIL R. REYNOLDS
*Texas A&M University*

## MARLAND REPORT

The Marland Report was a response to a mandate from Congress that Commissioner of Education S. P. Marland, Jr., conduct a study to:

1. Determine the extent to which special educational assistance programs are necessary or useful to meet the needs of gifted and talented children.
2. Show which federal education assistance programs are being used to meet the needs of gifted and talented children.
3. Evaluate how existing federal educational assistance programs can more effectively be used to meet these needs.
4. Recommend new programs, if any, needed to meet these needs. (Marland, 1972, VIII)

The report identified the lack of services for gifted and talented youths as well as widespread misunderstandings about this population. Among the major findings were:

1. A conservative estimate of the gifted and talented population ranges between 1.5 and 2.5 million children.
2. Large and significant subpopulations (e.g., minorities and the disadvantaged) are not receiving services and only a small percentage of the gifted and talented population are receiving services.
3. Even where a legal administrative basis exists for providing services, funding priorities, crisis concerns, and a lack of personnel cause programs for the gifted to be impractical.
4. Identification of the gifted is hampered by apathy and even hostility among teachers, administrators, guidance counselors, and psychologists.
5. States and local communities look to the federal government for leadership in the area of education, with or without massive funding.
6. The federal role in delivery of services to the gifted and talented virtually is nonexistent.

These findings, as well as others, prompted action by the U.S. Office of Education to eliminate the widespread neglect of gifted and talented children. Activities to be initiated included:

1. Identifying a staff member in each of the regional offices of education for gifted and talented education.
2. Creating an Office for the Gifted and Talented under the jurisdiction of the Bureau of Education for the Handicapped.
3. Having the deputy commissioner for school systems complete a planning report for the commissioner on implementing a federal role in the education of the gifted and talented children by February 1, 1972.
4. Supporting two summer leadership training institutes in 1972 and additional programs in major research and development institutes to work on learning problems and opportunities among minority groups.
5. Using Title V, ESEA, and other authorizations to strengthen state education agencies' capabilities for gifted and talented education.

This report served to focus attention on gifted and talented children. The report's recommendations were important factors in developing state and national programs for the gifted and talented. Moreover, the report was of major significance in involving the federal government in the education of gifted and talented students.

### REFERENCE

Marland, S. P., Jr. (1972). *Education of the gifted and talented. Report of the Congress of the United States by the U.S. Commissioner of Education.* Washington, DC: U.S. Government Printing Office.

PHILIP E. LYON
*College of St. Rose*


## MARSHALL v. GEORGIA

*Marshall* v. *Georgia,* also known as *Georgia State Conference of Branches of NAACP* v. *Georgia,* was a class-action suit filed on behalf of African American school-age children in the state of Georgia alleging discrimination in two forms: (1) overrepresentation of African American students in the lower, and underrepresentation in the higher, achievement/ability groups within regular education, resulting in separation of African American and Anglo American students, and (2) discrimination in the evaluation and placement of African American students, resulting in overrepresentation in special education programs for the educable mentally retarded. Both claims were rejected by the trial court in a decision upheld by the Eleventh Circuit Court of Appeals.

*Marshall* was filed in June 1982 by the Georgia State Conference of NAACP and the Liberty County NAACP on behalf of 45 schoolchildren who were or who might in the future be placed in lower ability tracks within regular education or in special education programs for the educable mentally retarded. Defendants in the case were the state of Georgia and eight local school districts that were generally sparsely populated rural districts with limited economic resources. The trial in *Marshall* was held before Judge V. Avant Edenfield, District Court judge for the Southern District of Georgia, Savannah Division, from October 31 through December 20, 1983.

The allegations of discrimination for both aspects of the case were based on alleged violations in Thirteenth and Fourteenth Amendment rights, Title VI of the Civil Rights Act of 1964, and the Equal Education Opportunity Act. In addition to these provisions, the special education aspect of the case also was filed on the basis of Section 504 of the Rehabilitation Act of 1973. For reasons that are not entirely clear, the plaintiffs' attorneys did not cite the Education for All Handicapped Children Act of 1975 (EHA) as part of their legal basis, perhaps because of the issue of attorneys' fees, which, at the time of the trial, were provided under Section 504 but not under EHA. In any event, failure to file under EHA became significant.

The allegations of discrimination against African American students who were significantly overrepresented in lower ability/achievement groups and underrepresented in higher ability/achievement groups, were based on various statistical evidence and expert witness testimony claiming harm to African American students as a result of regular education tracking practices. The plaintiffs' expert witness, Martin Shapiro of Emory University, presented data, undisputed by the defendants, that the disproportionality was beyond statistical chance. Another expert witness for the plaintiffs, Robert Calfee, an educational psychologist from Stanford University, argued that the discrepancies in achievement between African American and Anglo American students were caused, at least in part, by ability/achievement grouping practices. The plaintiffs' attorneys further argued that the ability/achievement grouping disproportionality is related to past discrimination as well as to impermissible practices leading to separation of African American and Anglo American students.

The plaintiffs argued for imposition of some random assignment plan in which heterogeneous groups of African American and Anglo American students would be constituted through any method that resulted in classroom proportions reflecting general population percentages. The plaintiffs' expert witness Calfee acknowledged that heterogeneous grouping might harm gifted students and that some grouping by ability or achievement within randomly constituted classrooms would still be necessary.

Curiously, the plaintiffs did not dispute overrepresentation of African American students in other educational programs designed for remedial or compensatory purposes.

Specifically, African American students were known to be significantly overrepresented in the federally funded Chapter 1 program (under the Elementary and Secondary Education Act) and a state-funded compensatory education program. This overrepresentation, similar in pattern and degree to disproportionality in regular education groups, was apparently acceptable to the plaintiffs, an obvious inconsistency in their case.

The defendants' arguments justifying use of ability/achievement grouping were accepted by the court. The court noted with favor that a combination of methods was used to constitute the groups, that membership in the groups was based on actual performance in the basal curriculum, and that instruction was then based on students' actual performance levels; assignment to ability/achievement groups was flexible, with assignments reconsidered periodically and changes made based on the performance of students. Defendant districts were able to present data indicating that grouping varied by subject matter and that significant numbers of student assignments were changed based on periodic reviews. The court cited the defendants' expert witness Barbara Learner as arguing persuasively for the use of practices that provide instruction at the student's level. Learner's interpretation of the effective schools literature, and her warning that court intrusion in local district practices in the case of ability/achievement grouping would be a "tragic mistake," were also cited favorably by Edenfield.

The court rejected all claims of the plaintiffs concerning discrimination in the development of ability/achievement groups. The court noted that the remedial instruction provided through the ability/achievement grouping was a positive feature of these practices and the evidence presented indicated these practices benefited, not harmed, African American children. The court concluded this aspect of the case with the observation that, the fact is that students have different levels of ability which must be accommodated.

The special education aspect of the Marshall case involved circumstances similar to those in previous placement bias litigation trials, *Larry P.* v. *Riles* and *PASE* v. *Hannon*. The fundamental issue was overrepresentation of African American students in the classification of educable mental retardation (EMR). These students were placed, most often, in self-contained EMR special classes. The plaintiffs also alleged, unlike in previous cases, that African American students were suffering discrimination not just because of overrepresentation in EMR, but also because of underrepresentation in programs for the learning disabled (LD). The plaintiffs' expert witness, Martin Shapiro, presented extensive analyses of data indicating that the disproportionality of African American students in EMR and LD programs could not be attributed to statistical chance. Shapiro's finding was about the only result on which the plaintiffs and defendants agreed.

The plaintiffs and the defendants had explanations, sharply differing, for the overrepresentation. The defendants' explanation for the overrepresentation was the association of poverty with mental retardation, a finding reported throughout the 20th century for various groups in western Europe and North America (Reschly, 1986). In contrast, the plaintiffs attributed the overrepresentation to discrimination in the development and implementation of special education referral, classification, and placement procedures. Unlike previous litigation in this area, the plaintiffs did not focus on alleged biases in intelligence tests per se, but emphasized a variety of other assessment procedures and regulations that they claimed were carried out improperly by state and local defendants.

The alleged improper and inappropriate practices established and implemented by state and local defendants were assumed by the plaintiffs to differentially harm African American students. Significantly, the plaintiffs presented no evidence that any of these practices were found more frequently with African American than Anglo American students, or that revisions in requirements advocated by the plaintiffs would have any differential impact on Anglo American or African American students. The trial and appellate court verdicts were based at least in part on the fact that the plaintiffs failed to show any evidence of differential impact. In other words, even if the court agreed that the plaintiffs' remedies constituted more appropriate practices, these revised practices may have had little or nothing to do with overrepresentation.

The plaintiffs alleged five areas of improper or inappropriate practices carried out by state and local defendants. The first had to do with the IQ guidelines stated in Georgia regulations and their interpretation and application by local defendants. The Georgia IQ guidelines suggested that significantly subaverage general intellectual functioning had to be 2 or more standard deviations below the mean. However, some degree of flexibility was common with local defendants and approved by state department officials. The plaintiffs argued for a rigid cutoff score of 70, suggesting that any student with an IQ score of 70 or above was misclassified. They presented several cases in which the full-scale IQ scores of African American students in EMR programs was 70 or slightly above. The second issue had to do with the assessment of adaptive behavior, particularly whether a standardized scale must be used in assessing adaptive behavior. The plaintiffs argued for the mandatory use of a standardized scale with a specific, stringent cutoff score.

The third issue also dealt with adaptive behavior, specifically the setting in which adaptive behavior had to be assessed in order to meet state and professional association guidelines. The plaintiffs argued that adaptive behavior assessment should be focused, if not exclusively, at least primarily, on out-of-school adaptive behavior. Further, the plaintiffs' expert witness suggested that for a student to have an adaptive behavior deficit, he or she needed to be performing poorly in all environments. Finally, the plaintiffs argued that various local districts were failing to properly document compliance with all aspects of due process regulations and that there were instances in which triennial reevaluations were not conducted in a timely fashion. As noted earlier, the plaintiffs failed to show that any of the five areas of improper or inappropriate practices occurred more frequently with African American EMR students. Thus, in the view of the court, discrimination was impossible to infer.

The defendants' case was based on explaining overrepresentation owing to the effects of poverty and the use of various professional standards and guidelines. In particular, the American Association on Mental Deficiency manual (AAMD; Grossman, 1983), *Classification in Mental Retardation,* as well as the National Academy of Sciences report on special educational overrepresentation (Heller, Holtzman, & Messick, 1982) were relied on heavily by the defendants' expert witnesses, Daniel J. Reschly of Iowa State University and Richard Kicklighter of the Georgia State Department of Education. The defendants' expert witnesses argued that standards for professional practices have always supported viewing results of measures of general intelligence as a range rather than a specific point, and that rigid, inflexible application of numerical guidelines were inappropriate in view of imperfect measurement processes. Specific paragraphs from the AAMD manual were cited as further justification for a flexible IQ guideline.

The question of adaptive behavior assessment was addressed extensively by the defendants' expert witnesses, who noted that none of the available adaptive behavior scales were based on a national standardization sample.

Furthermore, adaptive behavior assessment was known to be less precise than intellectual assessment, and authoritative sources such as the AAMD classification manual suggested the application of clinical judgment in estimations of adaptive behavior. Clearly, the AAMD manual did not support the application of specific, rigidly applied cutoff scores.

A crucial issue in the case, cited in both the trial and appellate court decisions, was the most appropriate setting for assessing adaptive behavior for school-age children. The plaintiffs argued for exclusive reliance on out-of-school adaptive behavior. The defendants' experts, particularly Reschly, suggested consideration of both settings, but argued that performance in the school setting is probably more important for purposes of classification of children for the EMR program, which is, of course, an educational program. Although the court did not attempt extensive analysis of the setting issue, both the trial and appellate courts cited Reschly's recommendation for reliance on in-school adaptive behavior information for determining deficits in adaptive behavior.

Finally, the state and local defendants had little choice but to acknowledge violations in proper documentation of due process, performing reevaluations within 3 years for all students, and numerous other regulatory requirements. Local defendants generally cited limitations in resources and the availability of trained personnel as the reasons for these violations. They also noted, with considerable justification, that the violations were nearly always technical, but not substantive.

The court's analysis of the issues noted the plaintiffs' suggested remedies: (1) state and local defendants were to develop and implement rigid cutoff scores for IQ and adaptive behavior; (2) prereferral interventions were to be required prior to referral of students for possible special education classification and placement; (3) adaptive behavior was to be assessed outside of school with an appropriate standardized inventory; (4) the state was to monitor ethnic and racial data by district and cite districts for any misclassifications identified during monitoring activities; (5) all African American children in EMR programs in which African American children were overrepresented (which would have included nearly every district in the state of Georgia) were to be reevaluated within a short time span using the new state regulations as specified; (6) state and local education agencies were to provide transition programs for any students found to be ineligible under the new rules; and (7) the court was to impose a monitor, independent of the defendants, to ensure compliance with the court-imposed remedies and to report on a timely basis to the court concerning implementation of those remedies.

The court rejected all of the plaintiffs' claims concerning discrimination. In addition, all of the plaintiffs' remedies were rejected, including those related to assessment of adaptive behavior, classification criteria for general intellectual functioning and adaptive behavior, mandatory prereferral strategies, and mandatory reevaluation of all African American children. The court's basis for rejecting these claims cited various professional association guidelines, particularly the AAMD. The court explicitly endorsed the AAMD: "the court believes the practices as defined and endorsed by the AAMD evidence best professional practices in this regard" (p. 146).

The trial court, as well as the appellate court, was highly critical of the plaintiffs because they failed to provide specific evidence on differential treatment of Anglo American and African American students. Clearly, overrepresentation as such was not sufficient. The trial court stated pointedly, "The court is somewhat perplexed by plaintiffs' claims in this area. Perhaps the confusion is best explained by failure of proof on the part of plaintiffs" (p. 103). Both the trial and the appellate court argued that evidence of discrimination against African American students must be presented in order to show that various allegations and remedies presented by the plaintiffs had merit. In the absence of specific evidence, the claims could only be regarded as without proof or foundation.

The trial court did find state and local defendants liable

for regulatory violations, but noted that no discrimination was found or implied concerning these findings. State defendants were then ordered to develop a remedial plan whereby local district compliance with various state and federal regulations could be ensured in the future.

The *Marshall* trial and appeals court decisions established certain clear-cut guidelines concerning allegations of discrimination as well as the development and implementation of programs for the educable mentally retarded. Overrepresentation as such clearly was insufficient to prove discrimination. Overrepresentation had to be accompanied by evidence of discrimination, which both courts suggested needed to be based on comparisons of African American and Anglo American students with retardation. Furthermore, professional association guidelines such as those of the AAMD (Grossman, 1983), and authoritative sources such as the National Academy of Sciences report (Heller, Holtzman, & Messick, 1982), were accorded considerable deference by the courts.

*Marshall* may well be a landmark decision similar to *Larry P.* in its potential impact on classification and placement of students with retardation. Both decisions have been based on lengthy trials and upheld by appeals courts. However, the *Marshall* and *Larry P.* courts reached very different conclusions on similar issues. Future developments are therefore impossible to anticipate.

## REFERENCES

Grossman, H. J. (Ed.). (1983). *Classification in mental retardation.* Washington, DC: American Association on Mental Deficiency.

Heller, K., Holtzman, W., & Messick, S. (Eds.). (1982). *Placing children in special education: A strategy for equity.* Washington, DC: National Academy of Sciences.

Reschly, D. J. (1986). Economic and cultural factors in childhood exceptionality. In R. T. Brown & C. R. Reynolds (Eds.), *Psychological perspectives on childhood exceptionality: A handbook* (pp. 423–466). New York: Wiley-Interscience.

DANIEL J. RESCHLY
*Iowa State University*

**DIANA v. STATE BOARD OF EDUCATION**
**LARRY P.**
**NONDISCRIMINATORY ASSESSMENT**
**RACIAL DISCRIMINATION IN SPECIAL EDUCATION**

## MASTERY LEARNING AND SPECIAL EDUCATION

"Mastery learning is an optimistic theory about teaching and learning that asserts that any teacher can help virtually all students to learn excellently, swiftly and self confidently" (Bloom, cited in Block, 1984, p. 68). Bloom, Hastings and Medaus (1971) believe that both exceptional and nonexceptional learners can benefit from instruction if it is systematic, if the task is broken down into small steps, if goals are clearly stated, students are given sufficient time to achieve mastery, and there is some criterion of what constitutes mastery. From a mastery learning perspective, management of learning requires three basic stages (Block, 1984). The first is the orientation stage, where the teacher clearly states what outcomes are expected from the learner. Grading policy and the standards for mastery are explained, and the learner is oriented to the strategies he or she will be using to master the material.

The second teaching stage is where the instructor uses various approaches for teaching the content. Initially, the whole class is taught the material in a sequence and formatively tested. Subsequently, the students are grouped according to their levels of learning. Corrective procedures are used for those who have not attained a predetermined level and enrichment is provided for those who have. In the third stage, grading stage, which occurs after correctives and enrichment, each student is individually evaluated for mastery. "A"s are given to students who have reached a predetermined level and "I"s are awarded to students who score below this standard. Steps are taken to help students replace their *I*'s with *A*'s.

Bloom and his followers (Block & Anderson, 1975) assert that native intelligence matters in learning when instruction is the same for all students. But when instruction is matched to the learners' present level functioning, and other provisions for individualization are made, all students can learn what they are taught. Teachers using mastery learning procedures should find close to 80 percent of their students attain mastery levels that were previously attained by 20 percent (Guskey, 1981).

Mastery learning procedures are used successfully in special education programs throughout the United States (Glass, Christiansen, & Christiansen, 1982; Grossman, 1985; Mandell & Gold, 1984; Morsink, 1984). Implicit in PL 94-142 is the mandate that teachers plan educational programs according to the principles of mastery learning. The law requires that each student's individualized educational plan (IEP) includes current levels of performance, annual goals, short-term objectives, evaluation procedures, criteria, and schedules for measuring objectives. Teachers, when preparing IEPs, break the course content into small units, sequence the units hierarchically, and build their objectives around these units. Traditionally, regular classroom instruction has been directed to the group of learners as a whole. Students with mild to moderate learning disabilities are often unable to learn at the same pace as the other students. Exceptional education provides programs for learners with disabilities so they can achieve success in school. One of the primary methods used in special education programs to reach that goal is mastery learning, or modification of it.

Some materials used in special education classes are based on the principles of mastery learning. DISTAR (Englemann & Bruner, 1969), a reading program for elementary-aged students, breaks reading down into its smallest units, sequences those units in hierarchical order, and teaches each unit to mastery. There are programs that teach thinking skills (Black & Black, 1984) as well as programs that teach social skills (Goldstein, Sprafkin, Gershaw, & Klein, 1980) that have been developed with mastery learning in mind. The advantages of mastery learning are consistent with the goals of special education programming. More students accomplish designated objectives and earn higher grades. This, in turn, leads to a positive effect on student self-concept and a heightened interest in subjects where success is achieved (Block & Anderson, 1975).

## REFERENCES

Black, S., & Black, H. (1984). *Building thinking skills.* Pacific Grove, CA: Midwest.

Block, J. H. (1984). Making school learning activities more play like: Slow and mastery learning. *Elementary School Journal, 85*(1), 65–75.

Block, J. H., & Anderson, L. (1975). *Mastery learning in classroom instruction.* New York: Macmillan.

Bloom, B. S., Hastings, J., & Medaus, G. (1971). *Handbook on formative and summative evaluation of student learning.* New York: McGraw-Hill.

Englemann, S., & Bruner, E. C. (1969). *DISTAR reading I and II.* Chicago: Science Research.

Glass, R. M., Christiansen, J., & Christiansen, J. L. (1982). *Teaching exceptional students in the regular classroom.* Boston: Little, Brown.

Goldstein, A. P., Sprafkin, R. P., Gershaw, N. J., & Klein, P. (1980). *Skill streaming the adolescent: A structured learning approach to teaching prosocial skills.* Champaign, IL: Research Press.

Grossman, A. S. (1985, January). Mastery learning and peer tutoring in a special program. *Mathematics Teacher,* 24–27.

Guskey, L. (1981). Individualizing instruction in the mainstream classroom: A mastery learning approach. In C. V. Morsink (Ed.), *Teaching special needs students in regular classrooms.* Boston: Little, Brown.

Mandell, C. J., & Gold, V. (1984). *Teaching handicapped students.* New York: West.

Morsink, C. V. (1984). *Teaching special needs students in regular classrooms.* Boston: Little, Brown.

NANCY J. KAUFMAN
*University of Wisconsin at Stevens Point*

**DATA-BASED INSTRUCTION**
**TEACHING STRATEGIES**

# MASTURBATION, COMPULSIVE

Masturbation, or genital stimulation and gratification by oneself, is a common form of sexual behavior that occurs in almost all males and in the majority of females (Taylor, 1970). Young children may handle their genitals, but purposeful masturbation often begins when sexual drives become intense during and after puberty.

Normal adolescence is characterized by a series of developmental phases, which include accommodating the sex drive. These phases are often "long, delayed, and distorted toward passivity" among mentally retarded children (Bernstein, 1985). Such children may engage in masturbation to relieve sexual tension, or simply because it feels good. Gordon (1973) suggested that masturbation is a normal sexual expression no matter how frequently or at what age it occurs, and that all sexual behavior involving the genitals should occur only in private. Motivation for frequent public masturbation, which might be called compulsive masturbation, may be boredom or the lack of anything else interesting to do. In other cases, it may be an attention-getting device.

A recommended approach to the situation is to communicate to the masturbating person that the behavior is not socially acceptable in public (Withers & Gaskell, 1998). Such an approach gives the person exhibiting the behavior the option to continue in private, and attention-getting behavior is not reinforced. Parents of physically disabled children and adolescents should have education and training on this subject, so they will be able to guide their children appropriately (Hardoff & Milbul, 1997).

## REFERENCES

Bernstein, N. R. (1985). Sexuality in mentally retarded adolescents. *Medical Aspects of Human Sexuality, 19,* 50–61.

Gordon, S. (1973). A response to Warren Johnson (on sex education of the retarded). In F. DeLaCruz & G. D. LaBeck (Eds.), *Human sexuality and the mentally retarded.* New York: Brunner/Mazel.

Hardoff, D., & Milbul, J. (1997). Education program on sexuality and disability for parents of physically handicapped adolescents. *International Journal of Adolescent Medicine & Health, 9*(3), 173–180.

Taylor, D. L. (1970). *Human sexual development: Perspectives in sex education.* Philadelphia: Davis.

Withers, P. S., & Gaskell, S. L. (1998). A cognitive-behavioral intervention to address inappropriate masturbation in a boy with mild learning disabilities. *British Journal of Learning Disabilities, 26*(2), 58–61.

P. ALLEN GRAY, JR.
*University of North Carolina at Wilmington*

**SELF-STIMULATION**

# MATERNAL SERUM ALPHA-FETOPROTEIN SCREENING

Maternal Serum Alpha-Fetoprotein Screening is a diagnostic blood test performed on pregnant women between the fourteenth and eighteenth weeks of gestation. It determines the presence of alpha-fetoprotein (AFP), a normal protein produced by the fetus that enters the maternal circulatory system early in pregnancy (Jensen & Bobak, 1985).

Elevated levels of maternal AFP have been associated with fetal neural tube defects, the most frequently encountered central nervous system malformations. These defects include anencephaly, encephalocele, and spina bifida (Harrison, Golbus, & Filly, 1984). Anencephaly is the failure of the cerebrum and cerebellum to develop. Encephalocele is the protrusion of the brain through a congenital gap in the skull. Spina bifida is the failure of the lower portion of the spinal column to close, allowing spinal membrane to protrude (Thomas, 1985). Elevated levels indicate the need for the further tests of sonography and amniocentesis to confirm the defect.

## REFERENCES

Harrison, M. R., Golbus, M. S., & Filly, R. A. (1984). *The unborn patient, prenatal diagnosis and treatment.* Orlando, FL: Grune & Stratton.

Jensen, M. D., & Bobak, I. M. (1985). *Maternity and gynecologic care, the nurse and the family* (3rd ed.). St. Louis, MO: Mosby.

Thomas, C. L. (Ed.). (1985). *Taber's cyclopedic medical dictionary* (15th ed.). Philadelphia: Davis.

ELIZABETH R. BAUERSCHMIDT
*University of North Carolina at Wilmington*

**AMNIOCENTESIS**
**GENETIC COUNSELING**
**SPINA BIFIDA**

# MATHEMATICS, LEARNING DISABILITIES IN

Learning disabilities in mathematics manifest themselves in at least three different groupings. One of these groups is characterized by an overall deficiency in mathematics such that progress is slow and labored, but steady. A second group displays deficiencies in specific mathematics topics such as fractions, or within a subtopic such as division. A third group is characterized by comprehensive disorders of thinking, reasoning, and problem solving such that performance in both concepts and skills in mathematics is distorted and illogical.

Any discussion of learning disabilities in mathematics must be undertaken with the understanding that the focus is on learning problems and not just classroom failure. Classroom failure may be the result of inappropriate placement; the selection of courses of study that are too difficult; a mismatch between learner needs and teacher practices; or motivational, attitudinal, or behavioral problems that influence performance. Learning disabilities should be attributed to characteristics that are intrinsic to the individual and be of such a quality that progress in ordinary settings is discrepant and below the rate at which nonlearning disabled students progress. These intrinsic characteristics may influence performance in mathematics directly or indirectly. An example of indirect influence would exist with a child who has a reading disability that interferes with mathematics performance. It is not the mathematics per se that is the primary problem. It is just that the child cannot efficiently and effectively interpret the mathematics in order to complete written assignments such as tests, daily work, and homework.

It is important to distinguish between the terms *learning* and *achievement* when describing learning disabilities in mathematics. Achievement is that condition in which a child is assessed or taught at a given point in time. That is, the test is given, the number correct are tallied, and some form of score or rank (e.g., grade equivalent) is assigned; or, the lesson is taught, the child either understands or fails to understand, and the teacher proceeds to a new lesson.

Learning, by contrast, is that condition in which a baseline is obtained and the amount of time and number of repetitions or variations in instructional practices that are needed to assist the child to attain the expected standard are determined. The more important consideration is a reduction in the amount of time or repetitions it takes a child to perform to criterion. This may be realized by modifying the instructional procedures or by training the child to be a more efficient learner. The latter may be accomplished by strategy training, metacognitive approaches, or by instruction and practice in learning to learn.

Mathematics is a comprehensive subject in which emphasis must be given to the development of concepts and principles, accuracy and ease in computation, and the use of concepts and principles and computational proficiency to solve problems and make decisions. The great majority of research and programming in mathematics learning disabilities has focused on arithmetical computation. Within this area, the emphasis has been on whole numbers, where efforts have been further subordinated to addition and subtraction. In spite of the fact that teachers have indicated that division is the primary topic with which learning-disabled students have difficulty (McLeod & Armstrong, 1982), there is a paucity of research and instructional development on this topic. By contrast, the literature is replete with work in addition and subtraction (Thornton & Toohey, 1985). The stress on addition and subtraction is understandable when one considers that these are the two computational skills with which children have their initial difficulties. It has yet to be determined whether the early emergence of learning disabilities in addition and subtraction is due to learner deficiencies in concepts and principles, a more cognitive view, or learner deficiencies in attentional factors or memory capabilities, a more behavioral view. Nor has it been fully determined that children who are successful in their introduction to addition and subtraction are the same learning-disabled children who are successful with multiplication and division.

Appraisal in mathematics needs to be comprehensive. There needs to be some reasonable representation of the full range of content at various developmental levels. At the very least, this should include appraisal of concepts and skills, computation, and problem solving across the topics of numbers, fractions, geometry, and measurement. The use of a single topic measure suggests that a "g" factor is operating and that performance in one topic of mathematics is sufficient to predict performance in another topic, or that the appraisal is conducted from an interest only perspective where one topic is of primary interest to the examiner. The single topic procedure limits the search for patterns of strengths and weaknesses, but enables one to delve more fully into one area of concern. If the Key-Math Diagnostic Arithmetic Test–Revised (Connolly, Nachtman, & Prichett, 1988) is contrasted with other tests, one would note that Key Math covers more topics but does not cover any single topic to the degree that others cover computation. Given these variations, appraisal specialists need to make informed decisions as to the components of their approach.

Instruction and curriculum are interwoven in programs designed to meet the needs of persons having learning disabilities in mathematics. Curriculum choices determine content, the level of the content, and the sequence or sequences in which the content will be presented. With few exceptions (Cawley et al., 1974, 1976) special education has not directed any significant attention to the development of curriculum for mathematics. Two factors tend to influence curriculum choices. One of these is the use of the regular class curriculum, which is largely determined by the textbook in use. The second factor stresses the remedial orientation of computation in whole numbers. This second factor leaves little variation in curriculum.

Instructional choices determine the method by which the content will be presented. It is possible to separate the approaches to instruction into two categories, although it is important to note that more than two categories could be designated and that there is overlap among them. One category of approaches stresses concepts, principles, information processing, and analysis across the topics of mathematics. Another category stresses high rates of correct responses and the habituation of response behavior across a fewer number of mathematics topics, frequently whole number computation and word problem solving.

The first category is influenced by developmentalists such as Piaget (Copeland, 1970; Kamii, 1985; Voyat, 1982) and selected information-processing perspectives (Cawley, 1985; Cherkes-Julkowski, 1985). The second category is influenced by data-based instruction specialists (Blankenship, 1985; Smith & Lovitt, 1976) and direct instructional tacticians (Silbert, Carnine, & Stein, 1981). The orientation selected by teachers is often a function of their training, the amount of preparation required to implement a particular program, their own personal knowledge of mathematics, and the needs of the children. The field is not faced with an either/or conflict. Each approach has its merits, its limitations, and its benefits for children with learning disabilities in mathematics.

An area of concern that has recently been raised by the National Council of Teachers of Mathematics is the content validity of standardized tests of mathematics (Parmar, Frazita, & Cawley, 1996) for special education students. Performance in mathematics requires considerable knowledge, competence in prerequisite skills such as language and reading, and the use of a variety of cognitive acts. Proper programming and assessment for the learning disabled requires an approach as comprehensive as the subject itself.

## REFERENCES

Blankenship, C. S. (1985). A behavioral view of mathematical learning problems. In J. Cawley (Ed.), *Cognitive strategies and mathematics for the learning disabled* (pp. 49–74). Rockville, MD: Aspen.

Cawley, J. F. (1985). Thinking. In J. Cawley (Ed.), *Cognitive strategies and mathematics for the learning disabled* (pp. 139–162). Rockville, MD: Aspen.

Cawley, J. F., Fitzmaurice, A. M., Goodstein, H. A., Lepore, A., Sedlak, R., & Althaus, V. (1974, 1976). *Project MATH*. Tulsa, OK: Educational Progress Corporation.

Cherkes-Julkowski, M. (1985). Information processing: A cognitive view. In J. Cawley (Ed.), *Cognitive strategies and mathematics for the learning disabled* (pp. 117–138). Rockville, MD: Aspen.

Connolly, A., Nachtman, W., & Prichett, E. M. (1976). *Key Math Diagnostic Arithmetic Test*. Circle Pines, MN: American Guidance Service.

Copeland, R. (1970). *How children learn mathematics*. New York: Macmillan.

Kamii, C. (1985). *Young children reinvent arithmetic*. New York: Teachers College Press.

McLeod, T. M., & Armstrong, S. W. (1982). Learning disabilities in mathematics—Skill deficits and remedial approaches at the intermediate and secondary level. *Learning Disability Quarterly, 5,* 305–311.

Parmar, R. S., Frazita, R., & Cawley, J. F. (1996). Mathematics assessment for students with mild disabilities: An exploration of content validity. *Learning Disability Quarterly, 19*(2), 127–136.

Silbert, J., Carnine, D., & Stein, M. (1981). *Direct instruction in mathematics*. Columbus, OH: Merrill.

Smith, D. D., & Lovitt, T. C. (1976). The differential effects of reinforcement contingencies on arithmetic performance. *Journal of Learning Disabilities, 9,* 32–40.

Thornton, C. A., & Toohey, M. A. (1985). Basic math facts: Guidelines for teaching and learning. *Learning Disabilities Focus, 1,* 44–57.

Voyat, G. E. (1982). *Piaget systematized.* Hillsdale, NJ: Erlbaum.

JOHN F. CAWLEY
JAMES H. MILLER
*University of New Orleans*

ACALCULIA
ARITHMETIC REMEDIATION

# MATHEMATICS, REMEDIAL

Many normal students encounter difficulties in mathematics. Students with disabilities often find the mastery of even rudimentary mathematical skills to be problematic. Concern always has been voiced about these problems, and strides have been taken to improve mathematics instruction in regular education. Yet, relatively little attention has been paid to the improvement of the mathematics skills of children with special needs. There are a variety of reasons for this. One is the availability of inexpensive prosthetics for the mathematically disabled, such as inexpensive hand calculators. Through their use a mathematically incapable student can carry out many of the same calculations and solve many of the problems, providing he or she understands their wording, as their more capable peers. Another reason for the less regard attached to mathematics competencies for special learners is that reading is considered more important for basic learning than mathematics. Furthermore, with technology carrying out fundamental mathematics operations for most people, other language arts (still not managed effectively by technology, with spelling a possible exception) also may presume authority over mathematics for students with special needs. Whatever the reasons, schools neglect corrective and remedial efforts directed at children and youths with disabilities. There has been relatively little literature devoted to these students with regard to mathematics. The advent of the computer, however, promises to improve this situation because it allows the study of mathematics learning and difficulties in ways that appeal to cognitive scientists.

Among those who have studied the mathematics needs and problems of students with disabilities is Cawley (1978, 1984). He points out that failures in mathematics learning may be rooted in mathematics or may grow out of disabilities in other academic skill areas. For example, one student may fail at mathematics because he or she has not mastered its skills and content or has disabilities that prevent such mastery. On the other hand, the student may be capable of such mastery but fail because of poor or impaired cognitive abilities, learning strategies, and study habits (Reisman, 1982). The student also may fail because of inability to master the reading and other language arts required to understand problems and to effectively deploy mathematic applications (Cawley, 1984). Cawley claims that many learning-disabled students would be capable of demonstrating proficiency in mathematics—regardless of the level of content—if their learning disabilities could be removed from their performances. This claim has not been substantiated, mainly because a truly learning-disabled student's disabilities are not readily taken out of the equation. Cawley carefully avoids making extraordinary claims for the approaches that he and his colleagues espouse for improving the mathematics performance of learning-disabled students.

The traditional model of instruction for remedial mathematics has been a diagnostic one; for example, identifying areas of strengths and weaknesses and, traditionally, focusing instructional attention on weak areas, including mathematical skill deficiencies. However, the diagnostic remedial mathematics specialist also might be interested in remediating such dysfunctional learner characteristics as distractibility, inefficient strategies, and poor short- or long-term memory processes (Reisman, 1982). Much of the remedial effort might then go into teaching the mathematically handicapped student strategies appropriate to coping with and overcoming these and other deficiencies related to poor mathematics performance.

In contrast, there are those who recommend a developmental approach, taking the position that good developmental instruction in mathematics represents the best remediation for learners with disabilities. Cawley objects that one of the problems in helping children with learning problems to learn mathematics is that there has been too much emphasis on "how to," to the neglect of the curriculum. He advocates greater emphasis on "what shall we teach, when shall we teach it, and in what sequence is it best taught" (1984, p. ix) in imparting mathematics to learning-disabled children. Nevertheless, he too recommends that the mathematical instruction of learning-disabled children be tailored to their particular strengths and weaknesses. Beyond that, he suggests that mathematics instruction for learning-disabled students should proceed on the premise that the needs of children with learning problems are interrelated and that the activities from skill areas and topics other than mathematics should be used to reinforce positive mathematics behaviors on their part and to encourage application and generalization.

## REFERENCES

Cawley, J. F. (1978). An instructional design in mathematics. In L. Mann, L. Goodman, & J. L. Wiederholt (Eds.), *Teaching the learning-disabled adolescent.* Boston: Houghton-Mifflin.

Cawley, J. F. (1984). Preface. In J. F. Cawley (Ed.), *Developmental teaching of mathematics for the learning disabled*. Rockville, MD: Aspen.

Glennon, V., & Cruickshank, W. (1981). Teaching mathematics to children and youth with perceptual and cognitive processing deficits. In V. Glennon (Ed.), *The mathematical education of exceptional children and youth*. Reston, VA: National Council of Teachers of Mathematics.

Reisman, F. (1982). *A guide to the diagnostic teaching of arithmetic*. Columbus, OH: Merrill.

DON BRASWELL
*Research Foundation, City
University of New York*

## MATHEMATICS, LEARNING DISABILITIES IN

## MATHIAS AMENDMENT

During the 97th Congress (1981–1982) in the U.S. Senate, Honorable Charles McC. Mathias, Jr., from Maryland introduced Senate Bill S.604:

> To amend the Communication Act of 1934 to provide that telephone receivers may not be sold in interstate commerce unless they are manufactured in a manner which permits their use by persons with hearing impairments.

On May 6, 1982, Senator Barry Goldwater, chairman of the Subcommittee on Communications, introduced Senator Mathias, who testified that the bill required no new research or testing and would "provide great assistance for millions of Americans who have some hearing impairment at a relatively small cost and a relatively small effort by the companies" (Senate Hearing, 1982, p. 14). The bill did not call for retrofitting existing incompatible receivers but affected only new telephone receivers to make them compatible with hearing aids. Senator Mathias recalled that the telephone was a by-product of Alexander Graham Bell's search for a device to help the hearing impaired. Ironically, for Americans with hearing aids, one of five existing telephones did not produce electromagnetic signals compatible with magnetic telephone pick-ups built into most hearing aids. Thus hearing impaired people were denied an essential part of independent living. The passage of the Mathias Amendment corrected this problem.

### REFERENCE

Telephone Service for Hearing Impaired. (1982). Hearing Before the Subcommittee on Communications of the Committee on Commerce, Science and Transportation, United States Senate, 97th Congress, Second Session on S.604 and S.2355. Serial No. 97-119. Washington, DC: U.S. Government Printing Office.

C. MILDRED TASHMAN
*College of St. Rose*

## MATTIE T. v. HOLLADAY

In April 1975, *Mattie T.* v. *Holladay* was filed on behalf of all Mississippi school-age children who had disabilities or were regarded by their school as having disabilities, for alleged violations or failure to enforce the children's rights under the Education for All Handicapped Children Act (PL 94-142). The plaintiffs were named as either children with disabilities excluded from school in segregated special programs or ignored in regular classes, or minority students without disabilities who had been misclassified as mentally retarded and hence inappropriately placed.

In 1977, the district court ruled that the defendants were indeed in violation of the plaintiffs' federal rights and ordered a comprehensive compliance plan. On February 22, 1979, the judge approved a comprehensive consent decree, which required that (1) these students be placed in the least restrictive environment (e.g., mainstreamed, put in day programs for institutionalized children, given surrogate parents if parentless); (2) the state must redesign its child evaluation procedures so as to be nondiscriminatory; (3) compensatory education be required for those students who had been misclassified and inappropriately placed; (4) school suspensions of longer than 3 days be discontinued; (5) a statewide complaint procedure service be instituted; (6) the state monitoring system be strengthened to ensure local school district compliance with federal law; and (7) procedural safeguards be put in, as required by the federal statute, to include such features as a parents' rights handbook and community outreach to locate children with special needs.

### REFERENCES

Comprehensive consent decree issued to enforce PL 94-142 in Mississippi. (1979). *Mental Disability Law Reporter, 3*(2), 98–99.

*Mattie T.* v. *Holladay*, 522 F. Supp. 72 (N.D. Mississippi, 1981).

MILTON BUDOFF
*Research Institute for
    Educational Problems*
Second edition

KIMBERLY F. APPLEQUIST
*University of Colorado at
    Colorado Springs*
Third edition

INDIVIDUALS WITH DISABILITIES EDUCATION
  IMPROVEMENT ACT OF 2004 (IDEIA)
LARRY P.
MARSHALL v. GEORGIA

## MATURATIONAL LAG

See DEVELOPMENTAL DELAY.

## MBD SYNDROME

The MBD syndrome, or minimal brain dysfunction syndrome, which is obsolete, has for many years been offered as an explanation for and diagnosis of the cluster of behaviors, including hyperactivity, distractibility, and impulsiveness, commonly found in children with academic and behavior problems (Clements, 1966; Cruickshank, 1966, Strauss & Lehtinen, 1947). The rationale for minimal brain dysfunction as an etiological factor in learning problems has some historical support (although somewhat indirect) from nineteenth-century neuroanatomical findings that certain brain areas appear to be necessary for specific language functions (Wernicke, 1874). The twentieth-century translation into academic problems presumably refers to these neuroanatomical substrates (Myklebust, 1954, 1964). Similar neuroanatomic bases for problems in language, information processing, and praxic functions were also recognized in the earlier half of the twentieth century (Nielson, 1948), and the possible role of multimodal central nervous system problems in academic problems represented a popular explanation (Belmont, Birch, & Karp, 1965; Birch & Belmont, 1964). Related findings suggestive of behavioral problems resulting from cerebral lesions (Teuber, 1959) were seen as lending further scientific support to the etiologic role of brain damage in a variety of maladaptive behaviors in children.

The 1960s represented an era when the MBD syndrome was related to many problems of childhood. In light of interest in the subject, the National Institutes of Health sponsored a major review of research. In 1969 their three-phase project was completed (Chalfant & Scheffelin, 1969). The first phase recommended the use of the term minimal brain dysfunction for children of normal overall intelligence who exhibit characteristics of learning or behavior attributable to a dysfunction of the nervous system. The term was chosen to emphasize that it is the child rather than the environment that is different and that all learning and behavior is a reflection of brain function. The second phase analyzed medical and educational services required for children with MBD. The third phase reviewed the state of scientific knowledge regarding the learning disabilities of these children. With more than 3,000 references considered, it was concluded that "remedial methods are found to rest on varied and shaky hypotheses, and have rarely been subjected to scientific evaluation even on an empirical basis" (Masland, 1969, iv).

Shortly after publication of the U.S. Department of Health, Education, and Welfare report, Reed, Rabe, and Mankinen (1970) reviewed the literature on the subject published during the previous decade. They concluded that the criteria for diagnosing brain damage were generally inadequate or nonexistent, and found little evidence to suggest that children with chronic neurological impairment at the level of the cerebral hemispheres require or benefit from teaching procedures that differ from those used for reading retardates without brain damage.

In recent years there has been comparatively little interest in the use of MBD as either a diagnostic term in medicine or a classificatory term in special education. Recognizing that differential consequences may result from damage to different brain areas, acute versus chronic brain dysfunction can exert different influences on the nature of brain-behavior relationships. The brain contains millions of neurons, with disabilities reflecting both location and numbers of damaged neurons (Hartlage & Hartlage, 1977). It is not surprising, then, that the concept of MBD may be too broad to relate to any meaningful description of a given child or resultant prescription for intervention. Thus the MBD syndrome may represent a term of historic and heuristic value rather than one with specific implications for special education practice.

### REFERENCES

Belmont, I., Birch, H. G., & Karp, E. (1965). The disordering of intersensory and intrasensory integration by brain damage. *Journal of Nervous & Mental Diseases, 141,* 410–418.

Birch, H. G., & Belmont, I. (1964). Auditory-visual integration in normal and retarded readers. *American Journal of Orthopsychiatry, 34,* 852–861.

Chalfant, J. C., & Scheffelin, M. A. (1969). *Central processing disorders in children: A review of research.* Bethesda, MD: U.S. Department of Health, Education, and Welfare.

Clements, S. D. (1966, January). *Minimal brain dysfunction in children* (Public Health Service Publication No. 1415). Washington, DC: U.S. Department of Health, Education, and Welfare.

Cruickshank, W. M. (1966). *The teacher of brain injured children.* Syracuse, NY: Syracuse University Press.

Hartlage, L. C., & Hartlage, P. L. (1977). Application of neuropsychological principles in the diagnosis of learning disabilities. In L. Tarnopol & M. Tarnopol (Eds.), *Brain function and reading disabilities* (pp. 111–146). Baltimore: University Park Press.

Masland, R. L. (1969). In J. Chalfant & M. Scheffelin (Eds.), *Control processing dysfunctions in children: A review of research* (pp. iii–iv). Bethesda, MD: U.S. Department of Health, Education, and Welfare.

Myklebust, H. R. (1954). *Auditory disorders in children: A manual for differential diagnosis.* New York: Grune & Stratton.

Myklebust, H. R. (1964). Learning disorders. Psychoneurological disturbance in children. *Rehabilitation Literature.*

Nielson, J. M. (1948). *Agnosia, aproxia, aphasia: Their value in cerebral localization* (2nd ed.). New York: Hafner.

Reed, J. C., Rabe, E. F., & Mankinen, M. (1970). Teaching reading to brain-damaged children: A review. *Reading Research Quarterly, 5*(3), 379–401.

Strauss, A. A., & Lehtinen, L. U. (1947). *Psychopathology and education of the brain-injured child.* New York: Grune & Stratton.

Teuber, H. L. (1959). Some alterations in behavior after cerebral lesion in man. In *Evolution of nervous control.* Washington, DC: American Association for the Advancement of Science.

Wernicke, C. (1874). *Der aphaisiche symptom komplex.* Breslau: Cohn & Weigart.

LAWRENCE C. HARTLAGE
*Evans, Georgia*

**BRAIN DAMAGE/INJURY**
**LEARNING DISABILITIES**

# McCARTHY, DOROTHEA (1906–1974)

Dorothea McCarthy made her greatest contributions to psychology in the areas of language development and clinical assessment of young children. She earned her PhD in 1928 at the University of Minnesota under the tutelage of Florence Goodenough, who had a strong effect on McCarthy's professional career, convincing her that "cognitive differences among children could be measured at early ages and along several dimensions" (McCarthy, 1972, p. iii). Early in her career, McCarthy contributed two seminal chapters on her pioneering research in the language development of the preschool child and the vocalization of infants; these chapters appeared in Murchison's *Handbook of Child Psychology* and Carmichael's *Manual of Child Psychology,* both prestigious source books at the time.

McCarthy culminated her professional career with the publication in 1972 of the McCarthy Scales of Children's Abilities, a test of the mental and motor abilities of children ages 2½ to 8½ years. This test was developed over a 15-year period and was published one year after her retirement from Fordham University, where she served as associate professor and professor for 40 years (1932–1971).

McCarthy was a fellow of the American Psychological Association (APA), a diplomate in clinical psychology, a former president of both the New York State Psychological Association and APA's Division of Developmental Psychology, and a member of several APA councils and committees. In 1967 she was awarded an honorary degree of doctor of sciences by the College of New Rochelle.

At Fordham University her colleagues considered her most distinctive characteristics to be the soundness and dependability of her research and the high standards she upheld for herself and for the students whose research she directed. Her clinical sense regarding the needs and interests of preschool children is evidenced by the child-oriented tasks she developed for the McCarthy Scales and the clever way these tasks are sequenced within the test to help establish and maintain rapport.

**REFERENCE**

McCarthy, D. (1972). *Manual for the McCarthy Scales of Children's Abilities.* New York: Psychological Corporation.

ALAN S. KAUFMAN
*Yale University Medical School*

**MCCARTHY SCALES OF CHILDREN'S ABILITIES**

# McCARTHY SCALES OF CHILDREN'S ABILITIES

The McCarthy Scales of Children's Abilities (MSCA; McCarthy, 1972) was designed to measure general intellectual ability of children ages 2.5 to 8.5 years. The MSCA consists of 18 subtests that are grouped into five separate scales: Verbal (V), Perceptual-performance (P), Quantitative (Q), Memory, Motor, and General Cognitive (a composite scale). The General Cognitive Index is derived from 15 of the 18 subtests and provides a normative indicator of a child's cognitive level (M = 100, SD = 16). The five MSCA scale indexes each has a mean of 50 and a standard deviation of 15.

The five scale indexes were chosen primarily on the basis of McCarthy's clinical experience, and partially on factor analysis. The Verbal scale is designed to measure verbal expression and maturity of verbal concepts. The Perceptual-performance scale is designed to measure reasoning ability through manipulation of materials. The Quantitative scale measures facility with numbers and understanding of quantitative words. The Memory scale provides a measure of short-term memory for visual and auditory stimuli, and the Motor scale measures fine and gross motor skills.

Kaufman (1982) noted that there is convincing factor-analytic support for all scales except two: the Memory scale, which fluctuates from group to group, and the Quantitative scale, which fails to emerge at all. Caution is advised in the interpretation of these two scales. The factor structure of the McCarthy is similar for different age levels (Kaufman, 1975), different ethnic or racial groups (Kaufman & DiCuio, 1975), for children having low General Cognitive Indexes (Naglieri, Kaufman, & Harrison, 1981), and for children with school-related problems (Keith & Bolen, 1980). The psychometric qualities of the McCarthy have been shown to be strong. However, the norms are now well over two decades old; thus, their usefulness is lessened.

Strengths of the McCarthy are its clearly written format and its well constructed materials that are appealing to children. Weaknesses include excessive clerical work in scoring, a lack of sufficient ceiling or floor, and the limited age range for which the test can be used. Kaufman and Kaufman (1977) provide information on methods of interpreting the McCarthy. However, because of the outdated nature of the McCarthy norms and the availability of more up-to-date measures for assessing young children's cognitive abilities, it is suggested that the McCarthy be administered mainly to gain clinical information and that its scores be interpreted with caution.

## REFERENCES

Kaufman, A. S. (1976). Do normal children have "flat" ability profiles? *Psychology in the Schools, 13,* 284–285.

Kaufman, A. S. (1982). An integrated review of almost a decade of research on the McCarthy scales. In T. R. Kratochwill (Ed.), *Advances in school psychology* (Vol. 2). Hillsdale, NJ: Erlbaum.

Kaufman, A. S., & DiCuio, R. F. (1975). Separate factor analyses of the McCarthy scales for groups of Black and White children. *Journal of School Psychology, 13,* 10–17.

Kaufman, A. S., & Kaufman, N. L. (1977). *Clinical evaluation of young children with the McCarthy Scales.* New York: Grune & Stratton.

Keith, T. Z., & Bolen, L. M. (1980). Factor structure of the McCarthy scales for children experiencing problems in school. *Psychology in the Schools, 17,* 320–326.

McCarthy, D. (1972). *Manual for the McCarthy Scales of Children's Abilities.* New York: Psychological Corporation.

Mishra, S. P. (1981). Factor analysis of the McCarthy scales for groups of White and Mexican American children. *Journal of School Psychology, 19,* 178–182.

Naglieri, J. A., Kaufman, A. S., & Harrison, P. L. (1981). Factor structure of the McCarthy scales for school-age children with low GCIs. *Journal of School Psychology, 19,* 226–232.

ALAN S. KAUFMAN
*Yale University Medical School*

MARY E. STINSON
*University of Alabama*
First edition

ELIZABETH O. LICHTENBERGER
*The Salk Institute*
Second edition

INTELLIGENCE TESTING
KAUFMAN ASSESSMENT BATTERY FOR CHILDREN–II
STANFORD-BINET INTELLIGENCE SCALE–FIFTH EDITION
WECHSLER INTELLIGENCE SCALE FOR CHILDREN–
    FOURTH EDITION

## McGINNIS METHOD

The McGinnis method, also known as the association method, was the recommended teaching approach during the 1950s, 1960s, and early 1970s for children classified as aphasic or diagnosed as suffering from receptive and/or expressive aphasia. Aphasia is defined as an impairment or lesion in the brain causing sensory deprivation.

The association method employs techniques using sight, sound, and kinesthesis as a multisensory teaching approach. The method stresses the importance of attention, recall, and retention. The speech training or oral articulation program emphasizes the kinesthetic sense of movement in the muscular coordination of lip and tongue movements. The student is carefully guided through the training program. The early training establishes the ability to pronounce phonemes in isolation. The memory sequence is established through reading and written form.

The association method further develops language skills through its vertical and horizontal training programs. The vertical program teaches basic language and speech patterns that are to be mastered over a specified period of time. The horizontal training program is the daily teaching paradigm. This program provides for the continuum of grade-level work.

The association method follows seven steps that stress attention, development of specific sounds, the smoothing or combining of sounds into meaningful nouns, the association of appropriate concepts with the noun, the writing of the noun or word using the written word, the development of speech reading, acoustical association, and the association of the meaning of language in both written and oral expression.

### REFERENCE

McGinnis, M. A. (1963). *Aphasic children.* Washington, DC: Alexander Graham Bell Association for the Deaf.

PAUL C. RICHARDSON
*Elwyn Institutes*

## MEASUREMENT

Measurement is the assignment of numbers to observed behaviors or actions. The observation may be made by humans or by machines. The behaviors may be simple and discrete such as movement of a child's head, or may be complex such as a conversation between a therapist and patient. The measurement of simple or complex behaviors is based on a rule for assigning numbers; the degree of inference is important. Inference is the amount of interpretation used by a human observer in assigning the number associated with the behavior. The rule structure of the assignment may vary from one measurement to another, and the defining characteristic is in the quality of the number.

Two major characteristics of importance to measurement in special education are reliability and validity. Reliability has a technical meaning that is somewhat different from the dictionary meaning. Reliability commonly means trustworthiness. To the extent that we can believe the measurement of a behavior is consistent, we can consider it trustworthy. Consistency is defined in terms of psychometrics (the mathematical modeling of measurement) as maintenance of relative position of a score with respect to other scores. For example, if five people are observed and their scores are 1, 3, 4, 4, 6, high reliability in the observation process would occur if the people were ordered exactly the same on another measurement, say 2, 4, 5, 5, 7, even though the scores are all different. Reliability is consistency of measurement of a score with respect to all other scores. That the two sets of scores all differ by one point is an issue of validity.

Reliability can be examined in three ways. One is to make the same measurement twice. In mental testing this means the same test is given with some interval between; this is termed test-retest reliability. If a test consists of parts that are independently measured, the consistency of the parts with respect to the whole can be examined; this is termed internal consistency. Finally, a complete second test may be constructed that is intended to measure the same thing as the first. Reliability for the two scores is termed parallel forms reliability.

Validity is a concept with several different applications. For the example given previously, one might ask which set of scores better indicates the behavior. In measuring children's school learning, we may be most interested in the content validity of the test: To what extent do the questions represent the topics the children were taught and should have learned? In measuring mental processing we are interested in the construct validity of the intelligence test used: To what extent does the test measure the mental processes it is intended to measure? In measuring a prospective college freshman's achievement as an indicator of future success in college, we are interested in predictive validity. Finally, in measuring how well a screening test indicates learning disabilities in comparison with the diagnoses of trained clinicians, we are interested in concurrent validity. Validity of a test must be associated with purpose for the test.

Inference in observation of behavior is a complex mental process. Reliability of measurement of a human observer typically decreases as the degree of inference necessary to the task increases. It is possible to achieve high reliability for high inference observation at a cost of extensive training and frequent retraining or maintenance practice.

VICTOR L. WILSON
*Texas A&M University*

**RELIABILITY**

# MEDIATION

Mediation is an intellectual activity that can be used to direct, control, or regulate one's behavior or responses by thinking before acting (Meichenbaum & Aronson, 1979). Mediation is particularly useful during the initial phases of learning, when one is trying to acquire new facts, establish associations, remember information, or learn sequences of action. Mediation can be used to direct motor behavior, to control emotional and social behavior, to remember information, and to learn academically. Mediation may be verbal or visual in nature and its effects increase with meaningfulness (Peterson, Colavita, Sheanan, & Blattner, 1964).

Verbal mediation has application in many situations. Children can analyze their situations or experiences and plan their responses by literally talking to themselves. Verbal mediation can be used to help children learn physical movements. If a teacher simply counts "One, two, three, four," this mediation helps students to perform each movement in sequence at the correct time. Soon the children count aloud for themselves. Later the children can count silently to themselves until the movement patterns become automatic.

Mediation also can be used to control emotional and social responses. For example, a child who is pushed or knocked down in a lunch line may become very angry. If the child uses verbal mediation, he or she can: (1) focus on the problem—He knocked me down; (2) analyze the emotions—That really makes me mad; (3) analyze the situation—He was playing tag and wasn't looking where he was going; it was accidental. As a result of mediation, the child might conclude that the student should be more careful, but that the situation is not worth getting upset over. The child has controlled his or her own emotions and regulated the social responses. Instead of hitting back, the child might respond by saying, "Hey, be a little more careful." Both Luria (1966) and Vygotsky (1962) suggest that children learn socialization by using language to mediate and regulate their social actions and behaviors.

Mediation has a number of applications in academic learning, as in reading, writing, spelling, and arithmetic. For example, a child might use mediation to remember the steps in computing an addition problem such as

$$\begin{array}{r} 25 \\ +35 \\ \hline \end{array}$$

The child might say, "Five and five are 10. Write the zero and carry the one to the next column. Two and three are five plus the one that was carried—six. Write the six. The answer is 60." In reading, for example, a child who has previously learned to read *cat* and *hat* can use this previous learning to help mediate new but similar words such as *bat* or *fat*. Knowing that the last two letters look alike and sound alike can be used to mediate the rapid learning of the new words.

Mediational strategies can be used for remembering facts, figures, places, and events (Kirk & Chalfant, 1984). For example, a high-school student might use visual mediation to remember a series of errands he or she has to complete on Saturday morning. The student would form a series of visual images of the locations for each errand. The student might visu-alize going to the post office to mail a package, stopping at the store to buy a bottle of milk, and then mowing the yard and washing the car. This kind of visual mediation is useful in remembering the location of each activity. A student may remember the names of the eight planets and their respective distances from the sun by using a verbal code as a mediating device. For example, "Mary's violet eyes make John stay up nights." The first letter in each word will help them remember the name, number, and location of the planet from the sun (Mercury, Venus, Earth, Mars, Jupiter, Saturn, Uranus, Neptune).

During the initial stages of learning, mediation is usually conscious and overt. The child may verbally say things out loud. In time, mediation becomes covert and the child silently speaks to himself or herself. When learning has occurred and the response is nearly automatic, mediation is no longer necessary.

### REFERENCES

Jenkins, J. J. (1963). Mediated associations: Paradigms and situations. In C. N. Cofer & B. S. Musgrave (Eds.), *Verbal behavior and learning* (pp. 210–245). New York: McGraw-Hill.

Kirk, S. A., & Chalfant, J. C. (1984). *Academic and developmental learning disabilities*. Love Publishing.

Luria, A. R. (1966). *Higher cortical functions in man*. New York: Plenum.

Meichenbaum, D., & Aronson, J. (1979). Cognitive behavior modification and metacognition development: Implications for the classroom. In P. Kendall & S. Hollon (Eds.), *Cognitive behavior interventions: Theory, research, and procedures*. New York: Academic.

Peterson, M. J., Colavita, F. J., Sheanan, III, D. B., & Blattner, K. C. (1964). Verbal mediating chains and response availability as a function of the acquisition paradigm. *Journal of Verbal Learning & Verbal Behavior, 3*, 11–18.

Vygotsky, L. S. (1962). *Thought and language* (E. Hanfmann & G. Vakar, Eds. and Trans.). Cambridge, MA: MIT Press.

JAMES C. CHALFANT
*University of Arizona*

**ATTENTION-DEFICIT/HYPERACTIVITY DISORDER**
**BEHAVIOR MODIFICATION**
**LURIA, A. R.**

**THEORY OF ACTIVITY**
**VYGOTSKY, LEV S.**

## MEDIATIONAL DEFICIENCY

Mediational deficiency refers to an inability to use verbal mediators to facilitate learning. Luria (1961) and Vygotsky (1962) proposed that language and thinking are closely related. Progress in one area affects progress in the other. For example, young children use private speech by talking to themselves to direct their activities and formulate their thoughts. This private speech gradually becomes internalized and serves as an effective mediator enabling children to think before they act.

Older children, according to this mediational model, are better learners than young children because they are more likely to use verbal mediators as a learning aid. Consider a concept formation task in which a child is presented with stimuli that combine one of two shapes (triangle, circle) with one of two colors (red, green). The child must choose all instances of the concept, which may be green shapes. Each time the child chooses correctly he or she is reinforced. It has been hypothesized that the older child, using verbal mediators, will label the important features of the situation (in the preceding example, every correct choice is colored green). It has been observed that older children acquire such a concept quicker than younger children. Young children, not using these private labels or mediators, are likely to keep selecting whatever stimulus has been reinforced most often recently.

Younger children have shown that they can perform like older children if they are instructed to use verbal mediators while working on complex concept formation and discrimination problems. (For a review of the role of verbal mediation in discrimination learning, see Kendler & Kendler, 1975.) Because young children are capable of using verbal mediators to improve their performance on learning tasks, they do not have mediational deficiencies. Their difficulty more appropriately reflects a production deficiency. They do not usually produce and use verbal mediators unless instructed to do so.

Mediational research with the mentally retarded began in the early 1960s. Like young children, the retarded were found to have mediational deficiencies. They failed to produce verbal labels that were within their repertoires such as labeling all the responses as instances of a color. A number of studies were carried out to determine whether mentally retarded children and adults could use verbal mediators to facilitate learning if they were instructed to do so. The data indicated that like young children, retarded individuals could use mediational cues to facilitate learning under mediation-prompting conditions. Their problem, then, might be best described as a production deficiency. (For a review of mediational processes in the retarded, see Borkowski and Wanschura, 1974.)

The individual who learns a complex skill and uses it effectively under direct instruction may fail to apply the strategy or skill in other situations. This is especially likely when those situations appropriate for strategy application are not identical to the original situation in which the strategy was learned (Campione & Brown, 1978). Mentally retarded learners experience considerable difficulty when required to transfer their learning to a new situation. After they have been instructed to use mediation and their mediation deficiency has largely disappeared, their performance continues to be characterized by production deficiencies.

The mediational deficiencies so common in the retarded have recently been interpreted in terms of failures of metacognition. Metacognition refers to thinking about one's own thinking. It has two main components. The first is awareness of one's own cognition or thinking (in general, and in relation to the task at hand). The second is regulation of cognition (planning, monitoring, etc.; Flavell & Wellman, 1977). In metacognitive terms, retarded children have a strategy in their cognitive repertoires that is applicable to the task at hand. However, they lack the knowledge of when, how, and why that strategy might be applied or generalized. Recent intervention studies have been designed to increase metacognition and facilitate generalization in the mentally retarded whose learning is characterized by mediational, or more accurately, production deficiencies.

## REFERENCES

Borkowski, J. G., & Wanschura, P. B. (1974). Mediational processes in the retarded. In N. R. Ellis (Ed.), *International review of research in mental retardation* (Vol. 7). New York: Academic.

Campione, J. C., & Brown, A. L. (1978). Toward a theory of intelligence: Contributions from research with retarded children. *Intelligence, 2,* 279–304.

Flavell, J. H., & Wellman, H. M. (1977). Metamemory. In R. V. Kail & J. W. Hagen (Eds.), *Perspectives on the development of memory and cognition*. Hillsdale, NJ: Erlbaum.

Kendler, H. H., & Kendler, T. S. (1975). From discrimination learning to cognitive development: A neobehavioristic odyssey. In W. K. Estes (Ed.), *Handbook of learning and cognitive processes* (Vol. 1). Hillsdale, NJ: Erlbaum.

Luria, A. R. (1961). *The role of speech in the regulation of normal and abnormal behavior.* New York: Liveright.

Vygotsky, L. S. (1962). *Thought and language* (E. Hanfmann & G. Vakaar, Eds. and Trans.). Cambridge, MA: MIT Press.

NANCY L. HUTCHINSON
BERNICE Y. L. WONG
*Simon Fraser University*

LANGUAGE THERAPY
MEDIATION
METACOGNITION
THEORY OF ACTIVITY

# MEDIATION ESSAY

The mediation essay is a series of printed statements that describe specific desirable and undesirable behaviors and the consequences of each. It is used as a behavior change technique that uses cognitive intervention (Blackwood, 1970).

The format of a mediation essay is that of a Socratic dialogue, with a question posed and a response detailed. The content is centered around four specific questions and their answers, using the student's own vocabulary. Generally the four questions are as follows: (1) What did I do wrong? (2) Why shouldn't I do_____ (inappropriate behavior)? (3) What should I do? (4) What will happen if I do _____ (appropriate behavior)? (Blackwood, 1970; Morrow & Morrow, 1985). Responses to the first two questions focus on a description of the student's inappropriate behavior and the negative consequences to the child of that behavior. Responses to the last two questions present the desirable, alternative behavior and its positive, to the child, consequences. An example of a mediation essay composed for a student exhibiting a high rate of talking out is provided in Figure 1.

Mediation essays may be thought of as intermediate management techniques from two perspectives. First, while they act as a form of verbally mediated self-management, imposition of the essay is externally controlled by an adult. This

**What did I do wrong?**
I called out without getting permission. I made funny comments instead of working on my tasks.

**Why shouldn't I talk out during work time?**
When I talk out I disturb the other students, and they get mad at me. When I talk out it slows me down, and I don't finish my work. When I don't finish my work before recess, I don't get to go outside.

**What should I do?**
I should raise my hand and ask for permission to talk. I should talk only about the task and if I need help. I should sit quietly until the teacher comes to help me.

**What will happen if I sit quietly and get permission to talk?**
If I get permission to talk and talk only about the task, I will not disturb the other students. The other students will like me better. Also, if I work quietly, I will get my tasks done sooner, and I will get to have free time.

Figure 1  Sample mediation essay

element of external control is more like traditional behavioral interventions; however, the student's exposure to verbal descriptions of behaviors and consequences is similar to the cognitive-behavioral techniques noted by Meichenbaum (1977). Theoretically, through thinking about the essay's dialogue, the student alters his or her behavior to perform in a more appropriate manner. It has been suggested, too, that the student experiences some gratification from this self-control (Henker, Whalen, & Hinshaw, 1980).

Second, according to Marshall (1981), the mediation essay functions as an intermediate step when working with students who have the desired behavior in their repertoire but fail to use the behavior consistently or at the appropriate time. These students may lack the motivation to change, not recognize internal or external cues, or not respond positively to simple reinforcement programs. It is this group of students with whom mediation essays are thought to be most effective. The technique not only works to eliminate undesirable behavior, it concurrently presents and encourages more desirable alternative behaviors.

Blackwood (1970) and MacPherson, Candee, and Hohman (1974) offer several suggestions about using the mediation essay. The following are the steps in implementing a mediation essay intervention: (1) identify the target behavior, alternative behavior, and consequences for each; (2) compose the essay using vocabulary within the child's repertoire; (3) meet with the student to discuss the need for behavior change, review the essay's content, and explain how the essay will be imposed; and (4) require the student to copy the essay when the student exhibits the target behavior. Marshall (1981) adds that the child should be reinforced for ready compliance with the assignment through a reduction in the number of copies to be made. Furthermore, some backup system is necessary for use in situations of noncompliance.

Research on the efficacy of the mediation essay with both nondisabled (Blackwood, 1970; MacPherson et al., 1974) and disabled (Morrow & Morrow, 1985) students has been promising. The superiority of the mediation essay, with its focus on positive alternative behaviors, over the more traditional punishment essay has been clearly demonstrated in earlier studies.

## REFERENCES

Blackwood, R. O. (1970). The operant conditioning of verbally mediated self-control in the classroom. *Journal of School Psychology, 8,* 251–258.

Henker, B., Whalen, C., & Hinshaw, S. (1980). The attributional contexts of cognitive intervention strategies. *Exceptional Education Quarterly, 1*(1), 17–30.

MacPherson, E. M., Candee, B. L., & Hohman, R. J. (1974). A comparison of three methods for eliminating disruptive lunchroom behavior. *Journal of Applied Behavior Analysis, 7,* 287–297.

Marshall, J. (1981, April). *Mediation essay.* Paper presented at the International Conference of the Council for Exceptional Children, Houston, TX.

Meichenbaum, D. (1977). *Cognitive behavior modification: An integrative approach.* New York: Plenum.

Morrow, L. W., & Morrow, S. A. (1985). Use of verbal mediation procedure to reduce talking-out behaviors. *Teaching: Behaviorally Disordered Youth, 1,* 23–28.

KATHY L. RUHL
*Pennsylvania State University*

**COGNITIVE BEHAVIOR THERAPY
CONTINGENCY CONTRACTING
LIFE SPACE INTERVIEWING
SELF-CONTROL CURRICULUM
SELF-MONITORING**

# MEDICAL CONCERNS OF CHILDREN WITH DISABILITIES

Five percent, roughly 200,000, of school age children are physically disabled. Special education provides for about 150,000 of these children. An increase in certain physical disabilities has been reported in the last two decades (Harkey, 1983; Wilson, 1973). This may be due to improvements in identification, but more likely, medical advances have improved the survival rates of such children. This creates a great need by the schools and their professionals to understand fully the chronically ill, physically handicapped, and sensory-impaired populations, and the problems of these children imposed on the schools. Harkey (1983) feels that at least 1 to 2 percent of the child population, about 1 million children, have severe enough illnesses to require some kind of additional professional services to function adequately in school. Since 80 percent of the children with mild disabilities are included in regular programming for at least a portion of the day, each teacher's chances of interacting with an exceptional student are very high. Many children also have concomitant health problems. Thus it is imperative that school professionals become as knowledgeable as possible about handicapping conditions.

One of the most common causes of physical disabilities is the result of damage to the central nervous system (CNS). The CNS involves the brain and spinal cord. Neurological impairment can be congenital (as with spina bifida), inherited (e.g., muscular dystrophy), or acquired later in life as a result of accident or trauma. Anorexia, infectious diseases like meningitis, poisoning, head injury, and strokes are other causes of CNS damage that result in muscular weakness or paralysis.

Cerebral palsy (CP) is the most common of all physical disabilities (about 50 percent of the physically disabled have CP). Some CP causes are paralysis, weakness, incoordination in the extremities, and possibly visual and hearing impairment, speech defects, behavior disorders, and perceptual disorders (Denhoff, 1976). Hemiplegic and diplegic CP children may have normal intellectual development, but sensory abilities and emotional responsiveness may be affected by loss of motor control (Nolan & Ashcroft, 1969; Thompson, Rubin, & Bilenker, 1983). Children with CP may be spastic (stiff), ataxic (loose), or atetosic (afflicted by involuntary jerky movements). Hemiplegic and diplegic children may have fairly normal life spans but they will need wheelchairs as they advance in age (Denhoff, 1976).

Spina bifida is a congenital midline defect caused when the bony spinal cord does not close entirely during fetal development. There are many forms of spina bifida and with some (acculta and meningocele) relatively little neurological disability is seen. Paralysis of legs, bladder, and bowel, and hydrocephalus (enlargement of the head) caused by excessive pressure of cerebrospinal fluid are not uncommon. Surgery and shunt implantation are needed and IQ levels may vary depending on the early rectification of hydrocephalus. Spina bifida children as a group have low normal intelligence but relatively good verbal skills (Anderson & Spain, 1977).

Multiple sclerosis usually affects adolescents and adults. It is a CNS disease that causes hardening of myelin sheaths of nerves, sensory problems (visual), tremors, muscle weakness, spasticity, dizziness, and difficulty in walking and speaking. There is no known cure. School-aged children usually remain in public school and receive home instruction when school attendance is impossible (Frankel, 1984).

The muscular dystrophies are actually several different diseases (classic, Duchenne, facioscapulohumeral, myotonic, myasthenia gravis, and progressive atrophy). Most are hereditary (myasthenia gravis is not) and affect the muscle fibers of the body causing weakness and wasting away of muscular tissue. The causes of muscular dystrophies are not known and there is no cure. Symptoms may include swayback postures, waddling walks, propping of extremities, and winging of affected extremities. Muscular dystrophies are more common in boys than in girls. Early death and total disability are common.

Juvenile rheumatoid arthritis (Still's disease) causes muscle and joint pain and stiffness. About 1 percent of the children under 17 have the disease and more girls than boys are affected. Complications may include atrophy and joint deformity, heart and respiratory problems, and eye infections (Hallahan & Kauffman, 1986).

Seizure disorders affect 1 out of every 320 children. Matthews and Barabas (1985) found that 85 percent of these children, with the aid of medication, are in ordinary school settings with their disease controlled. About 22 percent, however, are learning disabled (Dickman, Matthews, & Harley, 1975). Children with epilepsy may have convulsions, loss of consciousness, and loss of motor or sensory functions.

Seizures usually fall into three major categories: simple partial, complex partial, and generalized (petit and grand mal). Children with simple petit often have high IQs, while those with mixed type seizures, as a group, have the lowest (Seidenberg, O'Leary, Berent, & Boll, 1981). A wide range of behaviors and inattention can be seen with convulsive disorders. Teachers need to be aware of what to do in situations where seizures occur.

Tic syndromes may affect as many as one out of every four children (American Psychiatric Association, 1980); professionals in an educational setting can expect to encounter them frequently. Tourette syndrome, involving both motor and vocal tics, has been seen with increasing frequency over the past several years. Symptoms may emerge as early as 2 years of age and as late as 15 years. Boys are affected three times more often than girls (Anderson & Abuzzahab, 1976). Training teachers and parents to help the child focus his or her attention and sustain correct responses to situations may help inhibit the behaviors (Golden, 1977). The most effective method for treating tics was developed by Azrin and Nunn (1973).

Congenital defects can include heart and blood vessel damage, as well as abnormalities of the extremities, mouth, and face. These abnormalities can be present at birth (as in the case of Down syndrome), or they can be acquired through accidents or diseases. They may affect the development of speech, language, and cognition. Clefts of the prepalate and palate are most common, occurring in 1 out of 800 births (Leske, 1981). The teacher will need to work closely with the speech pathologist and physician, who may be involved in corrective surgery as lags in language may be seen over a number of early school years. In addition to his or her unusual appearance, the child may suffer brain damage (as with Down, Hurler, Hunter, and Williams syndromes).

Hearing losses will appear in about 6 percent of school-aged children. Only about one-quarter of these children are treated in special education classes (Annals of the Deaf, 1975). The earlier the hearing loss, the more serious the effect, particularly as regards speech development. Meningitis, maternal rubella, and hereditary factors produce the severest deficits. Many hearing-impaired students also have at least one additional disability. These may include visual problems, mental retardation, CP, epilepsy, heart disorders, and orthopedic disorders (Annals of the Deaf, 1975).

Children with visual impairment may also appear in regular classrooms. Nearsightedness, farsightedness, and blurred vision are the most common inherited visual problems (Nolan & Ashcroft, 1969). Glaucoma, cataracts, and diabetes also affect vision and if untreated can cause blindness. Coloboma, a congenital degenerative disease, and retinitis pigmentosa cause damage to the retina. Syphilis and rubella also cause visual problems (Hallahan & Kauffman, 1986). Retrolental fibroplasia (RLF) caused by excessive exposure to oxygen concentrations in prenatal infants in incubators has been on the increase partially because medical breakthroughs enable premature children to survive but only with very high concentrations of oxygen (Chase, 1974). With blind children, muscle tone, midline functioning, rotation, balance, and motor movements may be impaired. Imitative abilities are also developmentally delayed. Blind children also lack facial expressions, have delays in smiling and turning, grasping, and speech acquisition, all of which can retard mental and physical development (Adelson & Frailberg, 1976; Jastrzembska, 1976; Warren, 1977).

Other conditions, which are sometimes referred to as handicaps, include cancer, asthma, hemophilia, scoliosis, and sickle cell anemia. It is important that teachers become aware of the different physical and mental characteristics of their handicapped students and be able to establish a good working relationship with the parents and medical and support personnel involved with the child. In this way an effective educational program can be planned. Public Law 94-142 and subsequent reauthorizations requires that children with disabilities and chronically ill children be served in the least restrictive environment and that they receive an individualized educational program commensurate with their needs. Many of their needed medical accommodations are provided by the school districts in which they reside. These children may need specialized instruction (self-help skills, vocational training, occupational therapy, physical therapy, adaptive physical education), feeding and physical care, and mechanical and manual transportation in addition to regular academic education.

Many teachers have concerns about how best to meet these varied needs in order to provide adequate educational programs for children with disabilities. Recent state, federal, and Supreme Court decisions have substantiated the right of these multihandicapped and chronically ill children to be mainstreamed where possible and to have support services provided by the schools (computer-assisted instruction, mechanical interpreters, extended school year, etc.). Given all these mandates, the teacher needs to develop a good interdisciplinary cooperative program with the many specialists involved with disabled children with medical problems. The teacher must know what other disciplines are involved with the child, and he or she needs to be able to communicate professionally with persons in the medical field about the physical, emotional, cognitive, and social development of the handicapped child. Because of the support services needed, the occupational and physical therapists may be able to give valuable suggestions about working with the child in a regular or resource classroom. Continuing therapeutic management in the classroom will be needed so that the child can have a program that encourages independence and skill development.

Conferences with specialists in prosthetics and orthotics can help the teacher gain a better grasp on the function and operation of devices involved (artificial limbs, mechanical speech devices, life support systems, wheelchairs). Work with the school psychologist, community medical staff, and agencies is necessary to prevent lapses in treatment and to provide vital feedback to medical personnel and parents when new drugs or treatment are initiated. Medical information must be obtained by the teacher regarding the child's condition and the ways in which it may limit his or her participation in the school. Knowledge of hospital school programs needs to be investigated because many of these children will need hospitalization. Cooperative interaction between the sending school and the hospital school is vital if continuity of schooling is to be provided. Itinerant or homebound programs will also be needed and organized augmentation of them should be smooth and timely. Absences are high among these populations and alternative education settings and programs must be available and expediently operated.

Good communication must be maintained with the disabled child's family. Family cooperation and encouragement are necessary for success in school. The most crucial tool for dealing with illness and disabilities is information; thus parents and teachers need to communicate regularly so that information can be shared. Since these children may have erratic attendance, maladaptive social behavior, severe side effects, and isolation owing to equipment needs and geographic location of care facilities, it is important that parents and school personnel work together to make the various transitions as smooth as possible for the child. Hobbs et al. (1984) have pointed out that chronically ill children are often short-changed educationally because teachers and school professionals develop plans for these children based on existing school services instead of what the child needs. Home and hospital programs, though often necessary, can be sketchy, disjointed, and take place in a diversity of settings.

## REFERENCES

Adelson, E., & Frailberg, S. (1976). Sensory deficit and motor development in infants blind from birth. In Z. Jastrzembska (Ed.), *The effects of blindness and other impairments on early development.* New York: American Foundation for the Blind.

American Psychiatric Association. (1980). *Diagnostic and statistical manual of mental disorders* (3rd ed.). Washington, DC: Author.

Anderson, E., & Spain, B. (1977). *The child with spina bifida.* Hampshire, England: Methuen.

Anderson, F., & Abuzzahab, F. (1976). Current knowledge of the syndrome. In F. Abuzzahab & F. Anderson (Eds.), *Gilles de la Tourette's Syndrome: Vol. 1.* St. Paul, MN: Mason.

Annals of the Deaf. (1975). *Demographic studies at Gallaudet College.* Silver Spring, MD: Conference of the American Instructors of the Deaf.

Azrin, N. H., & Nunn, R. G. (1973). Habit reversal: A method of eliminating nervous habits and tics. *Behavior Research & Therapy, 2,* 619–628.

Chase, J. (1974). A retrospective study of retrolental fibroplasia. *New Outlook for the Blind, 68,* 61–71.

Denhoff, E. (1976). Medical aspects. In W. Cruickshank (Ed.), *Cerebral palsy: A developmental disability* (3rd revised ed.). Syracuse, NY: Syracuse University Press.

Dickman, S., Matthews, G., & Harley, J. (1975). The effect of early versus late onset of major motor epilepsy upon cognitive-intellectual performance. *Epilepsy, 16*, 73–81.

Frankel, D. (1984). Long term care issues in multiple sclerosis. *Rehabilitation Literature, 45*, 282–285.

Golden, G. (1977). Tourette syndrome: The pediatric perspective. *American Journal of Diseases in Children, 131*, 531–534.

Hallahan, D., & Kauffman, J. (1986). *Exceptional children* (3rd ed.). Englewood Cliffs, NJ: Prentice Hall.

Harkey, J. (1983). The epidemiology of selected chronic childhood health conditions. *Children's Health Care, 112*, 62–71.

Hobbs, N., Perrin, J., Freys, H., Moynihan, L., & Shayne, M. (1984). Chronically ill children in America. *Rehabilitation Literature, 45*, 206–211.

Jastrzembska, Z. (Ed.). (1976). *The effects of blindness and other impairments on early development.* New York: American Foundation for the Blind.

Leske, M. (1981). Prevalence estimates of communicative disorders in the U.S.: Language, hearing, and vestibular disorders. *ASHA, 23*, 229–237.

Matthews, W., & Barabas, G. (1985). Recent advances in developmental pediatrics related to achievement and social behaviors. *School Psychology Review, 14*(2), 182–189.

Nolan, C., & Ashcroft, S. (1969). The visually handicapped. *Review of Educational Research, 39*, 52–70.

Seidenberg, M., O'Leary, D., Berent, S., & Boll, T. (1981). Changes in seizure frequency and test-retest scores on the Wechsler Adult Intelligence Scale. *Epilepsia, 22*, 75–83.

Thompson, G., Rubin, I., & Bilenker, R. (Eds.). (1983). *Comprehensive management of cerebral palsy.* New York: Grune & Stratton.

U.S. Department of Education. (1984). *Sixth annual report to Congress on the implementation of Public Law 94-142: The Education for All Handicapped Children Act.* Washington, DC: U.S. Government Printing Office.

Warren, D. (1977). *Blindness and early childhood development.* New York: American Foundation for the Blind.

Wilson, M. (1973). Children with crippling and health disabilities. In L. M. Dunn (Ed.), *Exceptional children in the schools* (2nd ed.). New York: Holt, Rinehart, & Winston.

SALLY L. FLAGLER
LOGAN WRIGHT
*University of Oklahoma*

ABNORMALITIES, NEUROPHYSIOLOGICAL
ASTHMA
CHRONIC ILLNESS IN CHILDREN
MEDICAL HISTORY
MEDICAL MANAGEMENT
PHYSICAL ANOMALIES
PHYSICAL DISABILITIES

# MEDICAL HISTORY

When a student has academic or behavioral problems, or does not look physically well, educators often wonder if they should refer the student to a physician or psychologist for further evaluation. There are several areas of inquiry that could help the educator determine the need for one kind of referral or another (Zeltzer & LeBaron, 1984).

An assessment interview with the student should include an inquiry into the student's interests and favorite activities such as hobbies, favorite books, television programs, friends, and pets. The educator should observe whether the student appears unusually shy, defensive, anxious, or depressed. Next, the educator needs to ask about any current academic or interpersonal problems or physical symptoms in general. Questions regarding physical symptoms should include inquiries about pain, fatigue, recent changes in appetite or sleep patterns (including nightmares), activity changes, bodily concerns, or unusual physical sensations. Questions regarding academic and social concerns should include worries about friends, family, teachers, or school performance, or activity in general. Inquiry also should include recent or anticipated problems or changes such as illness in family members, divorce, unemployment, or change of residence.

In obtaining a history of past medical problems such as illnesses, injuries, or hospitalizations special attention should be paid to head injuries, since these may lead to significant changes in school performance, even when minor (Boll, 1983). Bruises or fractures not related to well-documented causes (e.g., automobile accidents or sports injuries) should raise questions in the teacher's mind regarding possible parental abuse. At some point during the interview, the student also should be asked if he or she perceives a problem or wants help. Low self-esteem, fear of parental anger, and other factors may cause a student to be reluctant to volunteer information or ask for help.

The areas of inquiry discussed also should be used in a second interview with parents if no obvious reasons for the problem are immediately evident. Children often are unable to recall important early childhood events that may have a significant impact on them. Also, parents may be willing to talk about family problems that the student feels reluctant to discuss.

A large percentage of visits to general pediatricians are made for nonmedical reasons. In a school setting, one may expect an even greater likelihood that a very large proportion of problems, even when they have a somatic component, are not primarily medical. Somatic complaints are often the manifestation of three types of common problems seen in an educational setting:

1. *Problems Emanating from a Poorly Functioning Family.* Such problems may consist of a poor parent/child relationship, inconsistent parenting, parental dis-

cord, physical or sexual abuse, or parental neglect. In problem families, major psychiatric disorders or alcoholism are frequent findings that require serious attention. Suspicion of abuse or neglect should be reported to the Department of Child Welfare.

2. *Anxiety Regarding Change.* Children are often anxious regarding physical or social change. As children and adolescents grow and develop, they are frequently worried about their ability to match perceived standards set by peers, parents, teachers, or themselves. These anxieties may reflect a distorted view of the child's own abilities, but in other cases may represent a realistic self-assessment of the child's own disabilities.

3. *Medical Problems with an Identifiable Organic Basis.* If the student is not feeling well physically, he or she may not be able to concentrate on school work, and a decline in the student's academic performance may result.

Any of the problems in these first two categories can be manifested as somatic complaints such as headaches, stomach pains, or fatigue. It is important to note that these symptoms are experienced by the student, are distressing to him or her, and are not made up to gain attention. Such problems also may be accompanied by a drop in school grades, chronic absenteeism, or evidence of anxiety or depressed affect.

In general, any somatic complaints or significant changes in appetite or sleep should be cause for referral to a physician for further evaluation. One exception would be when there is an isolated symptom (e.g., abdominal pain) that is clearly related to a specific source of stress and that disappears when the child no longer has that stress. If the physician is unable to find a cause for the complaints and the problems persist, then the child should be seen by a clinical psychologist or other mental health professional associated with the school. Whether or not a mental health referral is made, maintenance of good physician/educator collaboration can prevent further unnecessary medical work-ups for the child and can facilitate a direct line of medical information when needed (LeBaron & Zeltzer, 1985; Marshall, Wuori, & Carlson, 1984; Parette & Bartlett, 1996).

## REFERENCES

Boll, T. J. (1983). Minor head injury in children–Out of sight but not out of mind. *Journal of Clinical Child Psychology, 12*(1), 74–80.

LeBaron, S., & Zeltzer, L. (1985). Pediatrics and psychology: A collaboration that works. *Journal of Developmental & Behavioral Pediatrics, 6*(3), 157–161.

Marshall, R. M., Wuori, D. F., & Carlson, J. R. (1984). Improving physician/teacher collaboration. *Journal of Developmental & Behavioral Pediatrics, 5*(5), 241–245.

Parette, H. P., & Bartlett, C. S. (1996). Collaboration and ecological assessment: Bridging the gap between the medical and educational environments for students who are medically fragile. *Physical Disabilities, 15*(1), 33–47.

Zeltzer, L. K., & LeBaron, S. (1984). Psychosomatic problems in adolescents. *Postgraduate Medicine, 75*(1), 153–164.

SAMUEL LeBARON
LONNIE K. ZELTZER
*University of Texas Health
Science Center*

MEDICAL MANAGEMENT
MENTAL STATUS EXAMS
PREREFERRAL INTERVENTION
TEACHER EXPECTANCIES

## MEDICALLY FRAGILE STUDENT

The medically fragile student requires monitoring by the teacher during the school day in order to ensure that all of the body's physical systems are stable. The student's specific problem may or may not require that the teacher know special intervention techniques in case of emergency.

Medically fragile students are different from each other. They have different needs, energy levels, and potentials. Some children may exhibit a pervasive fragility (a generalized pattern of slow growth and development) but require no specific intervention. More likely, the child will have a chronic illness or experience an acute episode of a condition that requires that specific procedures be available when needed or that the daily routine be modified in order for the child to participate in school activities.

One of the most frequently observed types of medically fragile student is one who requires the use of a ventilator to facilitate breathing. The child may need the ventilator at all times during the school day or for part of the day. Once the medical team has decided the child is stable and no longer requires daily monitoring by medical personnel, the student may attend school. Often the child will be served in a program for physically and health-impaired students.

The teacher has two additional roles in providing education for the child if no health care professional is available. The teacher must be taught to monitor the child and the equipment and must learn about preventing the spread of infection to the child. Any bacteria or virus may be a potential threat to the well-being of the child on a ventilator. School board written policy should be followed as to best practice for the teacher to follow if another child in the room has cytomegalovirus or is a known carrier or exhibitor of any communicable disease.

For each medically fragile child the teacher and school administration should be trained to handle specific procedures that the child may need. For instance, if the student has life-threatening seizures, school personnel need to know exactly what procedures the child's parents and physicians want followed. All directions must be written in detail, signed, dated, and discussed with the principal and teacher before the child attends school.

Other health problems that may label a child medically fragile include chronic diseases, terminal conditions, post-surgery recovery, apnea, severe depression, cardiovascular problems, and kidney dysfunction. For some medically frag-ile children there are periods when they will be hospitalized for a long time, thus requiring hospital-based educational services.

## REFERENCES

Ashcroft, S. (1984, Winter). Education and chronically ill children. *Peabody Journal of Education, 61*, 2.

Dykes, M. K., & Venn, J. (1983). Using health, physical and medi-cal data in the classroom. In J. Umbreit (Ed.), *Physical dis-abilities and health impairments: An introduction.* Columbus, OH: Merrill.

Kleinberg, S. (1982). *Educating the chronically ill child.* Rockville, MD: Aspen.

MARY K. DYKES
*University of Florida*

## HEALTH MAINTENANCE PROCEDURES


## MEDICAL MANAGEMENT

Because of advances made during the past 10 to 15 years in medical diagnosis and treatment, many childhood diseases formerly considered fatal have now become chronic illnesses such as cystic fibrosis and cancer (Zeltzer, 1978). Because of improved medical management, many children who would have been bedridden are now able to attend school. Ex-amples include those with cyanotic heart disease, chronic renal disease, and rheumatologic diseases such as systemic lupus erythematosis and rheumatoid arthritis. Asthma and diabetes mellitus are the most common chronic illnesses of childhood. These and others are discussed in a text by Blum (1984) and a volume edited by Haggerty (1984).

Medical management of these illnesses for some chil-dren involves frequent physician visits, daily medication, and self-monitoring. Some illnesses result in multiple ab-sences or restrictions from normal school-related activities. Some illnesses are associated with pain such as the joint pain found in lupus erythematosis, rheumatoid arthri-tis, hemophilia, or sickle cell disease. Many children who need repeated blood tests or treatment-related injections experience pain and anxiety associated with the needles.

Chronic disease also may cause delayed physical growth and development.

When a chronic illness flares up, children often feel anx-ious or depressed about having to miss out on planned ac-tivities. Some children worry about the possibility of dying. Although chronic illness per se does not invariably lead to increased anxiety or poor self-esteem, such feelings, when they do occur, can lead to chronic school absenteeism and poor relationships with peers. The medications that are required to manage most illnesses often have side effects with psychological consequences. For example, some of the medications taken by children with asthma can lead to hyperactivity or periods of irritability and short attention span.

Chronic illness can restrict the child's independence to varying degrees. Parents usually monitor their ill child's activities more closely than they otherwise would; the child also may be dependent on parents for help with treatment. The achievement of developmental milestones, especially independence, is therefore difficult. The adolescent may try to achieve independence in ways that are destructive and inappropriate such as being noncompliant with medications. Some adolescents engage in risk-taking behaviors or ignore symptoms of the illness. Denial of the chronic illness is not necessarily maladaptive and may help children to engage in age-appropriate activities as long as treatment require-ments are met.

The role of the educator in managing such children in an academic setting is to become as well informed as possible about the particular illness and its treatment. The educa-tor needs to discuss the illness and the treatment with the student and his or her parents and, if possible, with the physician. The educator needs to develop an educational plan that is flexible and highly individualized. This plan needs to be reviewed frequently as the student's needs may change because of variations in the course of the disease. Chronically ill children usually respond well to educators who are personally supportive and interested in them as individuals. It is important for educators to recognize that most children and adolescents are remarkably resilient and that they cope well with illness and its treatment. The most important contribution the educator can make is to become well acquainted with the ill student and to encour-age a normal life as much as possible while responding to the child's individual needs.

## REFERENCES

Blum, R. (Ed.). (1984). *Chronic illness and disabilities in childhood and adolescence.* Orlando, FL: Grune & Stratton.

Haggerty, R. (Ed.). (1984). Chronic disease in children. *Pediatric Clinics of North America, 31*(1), 1–275.

Johnson, I. J., Zeltzer, L., & LeBaron, S. (1981). Chronic disease during adolescence. *Seminars in Family Medicine, 2*(3), 197–200.

Weitzman, M. (1984). School and peer relations. *Pediatric Clinics of North America, 31*(1), 59–69.

Zeltzer, L. (1978). Chronic illness in the adolescent. In I. R. Shenker (Ed.), *Topics in adolescent medicine* (pp. 226–253). New York: Stratton Intercontinental Medical.

SAMUEL LEBARON
LONNIE K. ZELTZER
*University of Texas Health
Science Center*

CHEMOTHERAPY
DIABETES
MEDICAL HISTORY

# MEDICAL MODEL, DEFENSE OF

The medical model describes a theoretical orientation that focuses on the underlying, frequently physical cause of an observed problem, impairment, or disorder (Davis, 1980). Synonyms for the medical model include the disease model and the pathological model. The medical model has its origin in the field of medicine, where the identification of pathology within the individual is an important emphasis. Mercer (1973) describes the medical model as inherently evaluative, in that behaviors or symptoms that disrupt the individual's functioning are negative while those that enhance functioning are positive. In addition, the medical model is bipolar, associated either with sickness or "wellness." In applying the medical model, clinicians use conservative criteria when making diagnostic decisions, because failure to identify pathology when it is present is considered a serious error (Helton, Workman, & Matuszek, 1982).

Within the field of special education, the medical model is most clearly applicable in cases of physical impairment such as visual, hearing, or orthopedic. Assessment techniques are designed to identify signs of such physical disability. Mass screenings in schools for vision or hearing problems, scoliosis, or tuberculosis are conducted within the framework of the medical model. Consistent with the ethical standards of this orientation, conservative decision rules are employed. Children identified as at risk for the disorder as a result of the screening procedure are referred for additional assessment and, if necessary, appropriate treatment (Helton et al., 1982). Application of the medical model in other areas of special education, particularly with the mildly disabled, has been criticized. Mercer (1973), for example, stated that "the medical model for conceptualizing mental retardation in the community was inadequate" (pp. 20–21). Mercer does note, however, that the use of the medical model is more defensible in cases of mental retardation syndromes where there is "clear evidence of biological dysfunction" (p. 8).

In a detailed discussion of the application of the medical model in the interpretation of specific learning disabilities, Gaddes (1985) and Barbour (1995) indicate that many of the most frequent criticisms of the medical model (e.g., that it does not promote change or growth and minimizes the role of psychoeducational intervention) are not inherent in the model itself, but are a result of abuses in its application. Gaddes indicates that use of a neuropsychological model, which is a special orientation within the generic medical model, has a number of important advantages. Neuropsychology, he argues, is a respected, established scientific field. Because all behavior is a byproduct of brain and central nervous system functioning, understanding brain-behavior relationships is critical to knowledge of children's learning and behavior. A neuropsychological or biopsychosocial diagnostic model helps identify the cause of observed disorders, which in turn leads to the development of more effective interventions.

## REFERENCES

Barbour, A. B. (1995). *Caring for patients: A critique of the medical model.* Stanford, CA: Stanford University Press.

Davis, W. E. (1980). *Educator's resource guide to special education.* Boston: Allyn & Bacon.

Engel, J. (1992). The need for a new medical model: A challenge for biomedicine. *Family Systems Medicine, 10*(3), 317–331.

Gaddes, W. H. (1985). *Learning disabilities and brain function: A neuropsychological approach* (2nd ed.). New York: Springer-Verlag.

Helton, G. B., Workman, E. A., & Matuszek, P. A. (1982). *Psychoeducational assessment.* New York: Grune & Stratton.

Mercer, J. R. (1973). *Labeling the mentally retarded.* Berkeley: University of California Press.

CATHY F. TELZROW
*Kent State University*

BIOGENIC MODELS
NEUROPSYCHOLOGY
PSYCHOGENIC MODELS

# MEDICATION

See SPECIFIC MEDICATION.

# MEGAVITAMIN THERAPY

Megadose vitamin therapy (or orthomolecular treatment) is generally defined as the consumption of a vitamin dose greater than ten times the Recommended Dietary Allowance (RDA; Lutz & Przytulski, 1997). Although megavitamin therapy regimes are often prescribed and closely monitored by physicians, controversy remains related to self-administration. Self-dosing with megadoses of vitamins remains popular and may be fraught with numerous adverse effects, even drug-like reactions. Megadoses of vitamins are often consumed by pregnant women who are trying to eat well and mistakenly assume that with vitamin supplementation, more is better (Whitney, Cataldo, & Rolfes, 1998). Such therapy is hazardous during pregnancy and may cause irreversible damage to the unborn fetus. Therapeutic treatments with megadoses of vitamins should be administered only by physicians conversant with both the treatments' risks and side effects.

Documentation regarding the use of megadose vitamins in the treatment of acute schizophrenia (Hoffer, 1994), cancer, and hardening of the arteries (Hoffer, 1995) remains controversial. In terms of megavitamins and children's intelligence, improved performance occurs primarily in children whose diets were low in vitamins and minerals (Benton, 1995).

Evaluation of the controversial megadose-vitamin treatment of individuals with Down syndrome failed to show intellectual improvement (Selikowitz, 1990). Selikowitz cautioned that high-dose vitamins can accumulate in the body causing toxic effects, slowing the child's development, and even causing ill health. Despite inadequate evaluation and negative research findings, elevated doses of vitamins also continue to be frequently prescribed for and taken by individuals affected with pathological conditions such as neurological discomforts, psychosis, alopecia, or inherited metabolic defects (Combs, 1992).

The Council on Scientific Affairs of the American Medical Association (AMA) has stated that support for megadose-vitamin therapy to date is based on anecdotal or nonscientific evidence (Davis & Sherer, 1994). The Council went on to state that use of megadose-vitamin therapies can contribute to false hopes and needless financial expense, as well as produce direct toxic effects or even adverse interactions among vital nutrients (Davis & Sherer, 1994). Research continues on the effects and effectiveness of megadose vitamins. As more is known about the pharmacologic effects of some vitamins, special use of them in larger therapeutic doses is likely to occur.

### REFERENCES

Benton, D. (1995). Vitamin/mineral supplementation and the intelligence of children: A review. *Journal of Orthomolecular Medicine, 7,* 21–29.

Combs, G. E. (1992). *The vitamins: Fundamental aspects in nutrition and health.* New York: Academic Press.

Davis, J., & Sherer, K. (1994). *Applied nutrition and diet therapy for nurses* (2nd ed.). Philadelphia: Saunders.

Hoffer, A. (1994). Follow-up reports on chronic schizophrenic patients. *Journal of Orthomolecular Medicine, 9,* 121–123.

Hoffer, A. (1995). The megavitamin revolution. *Journal of Orthomolecular Medicine, 7,* 3–5.

Lutz, C., & Przytulski, K. (1997). *Nutrition and diet therapy* (2nd ed.). Philadelphia: Davis.

Selikowitz, M. (1990). *Down syndrome: The facts.* New York: Oxford University Press.

Whitney, E., Cataldo, C., & Rolfes, S. (1998). *Understanding normal and clinical nutrition* (5th ed.). Belmont, CA: Wadsworth.

Williams, S. (1997). *Nutrition and diet therapy* (8th ed.). St. Louis, MO: Mosby-Year Book.

BARBARA S. SPEER
*Shaker Heights City School
   District, Shaker Heights, Ohio*
First edition

KARI ANDERSON
*University of North Carolina at
   Wilmington*
Second edition

**MALNUTRITION**
**NUTRITIONAL DISORDERS**

## MEICHENBAUM, DONALD (1940–   )

Donald Meichenbaum earned his BA at the City College of New York in 1962 and his PhD in 1966 from the University of Illinois, Champaign. Meichenbaum is noted as one of the founders of cognitive behavior modification. He is Professor Emeritus from the University of Waterloo, Ontario, Canada, where he has been a professor of clinical psychology since 1966.

**Donald Meichenbaum**

Meichenbaum's major fields of interest include developmental psychopathology, teaching, stress, and coping. His current research centers on how children become self-directive learners. Treatment procedures he developed, such as stress inoculation training with adults and self-instructional training with children, reflect his influential contributions as a researcher and as a psychotherapist. In a survey of North American clinicians, Meichenbaum was voted "one of the ten most influential psychotherapists of the century" as reported in the *American Psychologist*.

Meichenbaum's major publications include *Cognitive Behavior Modification: An Integrative Approach* (1977; considered a classic in the field), *Stress-Inoculation Training* (1985), and most recently, *Nurturing Independent Learners: Helping Students Take Charge of Their Learning* (1988; coauthored with Andrew Biemiller). He has published over 100 journal articles, books, and associated works. In addition, he is an active speaker, presenting workshops and lectures throughout the United States, Canada, Europe, Israel, and Russia.

Donald Meichenbaum is one of the founders of cognitive behavior therapy and he is the author of numerous books, chapters, and articles, including clinical handbooks on treating individuals with anger control and aggressive behavior and assessing and treating adults with Posttraumatic Stress Disorder.

He is the recipient of the Consulting Psychology Research Award given by Division 13 of the American Psychological Association, the Lifetime Achievement Award by the California Psychological Association, and the prestigious Izaak Killam Research Fellowship Award by the Canadian Council. Meichenbaum serves on the editorial board of a dozen journals and is editor of the Plenum Press series on stress and coping. He was one of the founding editors of the *Journal of Cognitive Therapy and Research*. He has received numerous research grants and serves as a consultant to medical, educational, psychiatric, correctional, and business institutions.

## REFERENCES

Meichenbaum, D. (1977). *Cognitive-behavior modification: An integrative approach*. New York: Plenum.

Meichenbaum, D. (1985). *Stress-inoculation training*. New York: Allyn & Bacon.

Meichenbaum, D. (1994). *Treating adults with PTSD*. London, Wiley.

Meichenbaum, D., & Biemiller, A. (1998). *Nurturing independent learners: Helping students take charge of their learning*. Boston: Brookline.

HEATHER S. VANDYKE
*Falcon School District 49,*
*Colorado Springs, Colorado*
Third edition

# MELLARIL

Mellaril is the trade name for the generic phenothiazine, thioridazine. In addition to its general applications for symptomatic relief in psychotic disorders, Mellaril also appears to show some efficacy in psychotic disorders with depressive components. It also has been used in short-term, symptomatic treatment of agitation, depression, sleep disturbance, and fears in elderly patients, and for the short-term symptomatic treatment of hyperactivity, combativeness, attention problems, mood lability, and poor frustration tolerance in children (McEvoy, 1984).

Mellaril has similar dose effectiveness ratios as Thorazine, another phenothiazine that is used in the management of psychotic symptoms (Seiden & Dykstra, 1977). Like all phenothiazines, Mellaril produces some sedation, especially during early administration. In addition, anticholinergic effects (dry mouth, urinary retention, motor incoordination), extrapyramidal symptoms, dystonic reactions, motor restlessness, and parkinsonlike symptoms are among the adverse effects that may be experienced early in treatment or from overdosage. Tardive dyskinesia, which is characterized by rhythmic involuntary movements of the oral musculature and face, and sometimes of the extremities, is also a possible side effect. This is of some concern because tardive dyskinesia is resistant to treatment.

## REFERENCES

McEvoy, G. K. (1984). *American hospital formulary service: Drug information 84*. Bethesda, MD: American Society of Hospital Pharmacists.

Seiden, L. S., & Dykstra, L. A. (1977). *Psychopharmacology: A biochemical and behavioral approach*. New York: Van Nostrand Reinhold.

ROBERT F. SAWICKI
*Lake Erie Institute of*
*Rehabilitation*

THORAZINE
TRANQUILIZERS

# MEMORY DISORDERS

Neuropsychological research suggests that memory disorders may occur with brain injury or neurological disease. Generally speaking, a memory disorder refers to a deficiency in the storage and/or retrieval of information. Impaired memory functioning is one of the most common symptoms of generalized cerebral damage (Straub & Black, 1977).

An understanding of memory disorders is facilitated by an appreciation of the basic memory components. Although a number of memory models have been proposed, three distinct yet interactive memory stores are generally implicated (Shallice, 1979). Incoming sensory information is thought to be held briefly and selected for future processing in a sensory register. Research in this area suggests that information in the sensory register is either transferred to short-term memory or is rapidly replaced by incoming information.

Short-term store, or immediate memory, is portrayed as a temporary working memory of limited capacity. Information in the short-term store has been shown to be accessible for 20 to 30 seconds (Norman, 1973) and limited to approximately five to nine items (Miller, 1956). Information in the short-term memory is rehearsed and subsequently stored in long-term memory or is displaced by incoming information. Thus rehearsal serves to prolong the memory trace as well as to facilitate permanent storage. In sum, information in short-term memory appears to be unstable and lost or inaccessible unless transferred into the more enduring long-term store.

Long-term memory refers to the relatively permanent storage of information. Seen as the result of repeated presentations of information or very salient stimuli, long-term storage involves a relatively permanent structural or biochemical change in the brain (Hillgard & Bower, 1975). The long-term storage of information involves both transfer and consolidation of sensory inputs. Simply stated, transfer refers to the transmission of information from short-term memory to long-term memory or directly to long-term memory from the sensory register. A much more complex process, consolidation involves the progressive strengthening of memory traces over time. Disruption of the consolidation process may impair the ability to learn.

Much of the information in long-term memory has been shown to be stored on the basis of abstract conceptual properties of the stimulus (Craik & Lockhart, 1972). However, a recent investigation by Dean, Gray, and Yekovich (under review) indicates that more superficial stimulus attributes (i.e., visual or auditory components) may also play a prominent role in the storage process. Consistent with the notion of a relatively permanent memory trace, these investigators suggest that under some conditions stimuli may be stored in long-term memory as "literal copy."

Retrieval of a memory trace from the long-term store is seen to involve the reactivation of the same physical structure or biochemical conditions that were responsible for the initial storage or encoding process (Bloch & Laroche, 1984). This reactivation process appears to be triggered by stimuli that are the same or similar to the original encoding event.

The brain has been clearly linked to memory processing. Indeed, convincing data have been offered that closely tie the temporal area of the brain to memory functioning. Primarily involved in audition, the temporal lobe appears to be instrumental in triggering complex memories. In addition, a substantial amount of research has shown that damage to the hippocampus (structure within the limbic system lying just under the temporal flap) serves in the consolidation and transfer of information to long-term store. It has also been shown that bilateral damage to the hippocampus results in the inability to learn other than simple rudimentary motor skills (Barbizet, 1963). On the basis of such data, it has been concluded that the temporal lobe and specifically the limbic system may be the underlying anatomical substrates of the memory system.

Damage to the temporal lobe or its related structures (e.g., hippocampus, fornix, mammillary bodies, thalamus) often results in memory dysfunction. The most prevalent disorder, retrograde amnesia, refers to an impairment in the ability to retrieve information from the period prior to brain pathology. While most often affecting memories stored up to 30 minutes preceding the damage (Lezak, 1983), retrograde amnesia relates to the disturbance of memories from several months to many years prior to onset. However, older, well-ingrained memories are rarely permanently disrupted.

Anterograde amnesia, a much more serious memory disturbance, is characterized by a profound deficit in the ability to retain new information. While immediate (short-term) memory functioning may be intact, the ability to recall day-to-day events over hours is severely impaired. Thus learning new material is difficult, if not impossible. Interestingly, however, a number of investigators have shown that patients suffering from chronic anterograde amnesia generally are able to retrieve information learned prior to the neuropathology (Squire & Slater, 1978). These data suggest that anterograde amnesia stems from a problem in encoding new information rather than from difficulty in retrieving previously stored information.

In addition to affecting memory processes in circumscribed ways, cerebral pathology may also differentially affect the storage and retrieval of specific types of material. For example, depending on the location of the brain dysfunction, a memory deficit may be limited to either verbal or nonverbal material. So, too, a specific memory deficit may be isolated to previously learned motor behaviors (Corkin, 1968).

A further distinction in memory disorders can be made between episodic and semantic memory. As proposed by Tulving (1972), episodic memory refers to the storage of specific temporally dependent information. This type of memory includes contextual information about day-to-day events (e.g., memory for the events of one's day). Semantic memories do not seem dependent on such temporal events, but rather are stored on the basis of abstract conceptual properties. Semantic memory consists of an organized store of symbols, concepts, language, and rules (e.g., the conceptualization that baseball is a game).

Transient global amnesia, a relatively common memory disorder, is characterized by a sudden, seemingly unprovoked onset of anterograde amnesia. In such cases, the individual is temporarily unable to store episodic information. However, there appears to be no loss in other cognitive functions. Interestingly, memories stored hours or even days prior to the attack may also be inaccessible, but retrieval of more remote memories seems to be intact. Typically lasting only several hours, transient global amnesia does not cause permanent memory deficits. Indeed, aside from an inability to remember events that occurred during the amnesic episode, memory functioning is completely restored. Although the etiology is not clear, transient global amnesia has been associated with cerebral vascular problems in the elderly and temporal lobe epilepsy in younger adults (Barbizet, 1970).

Traumatic brain injuries often produce memory impairments (traumatic amnesia). Typically, postconcussion memory loss includes both retrograde and anterograde amnesia. Following a traumatic loss of consciousness, individuals often experience a temporary inability to store and retrieve incoming information. During the posttraumatic period, the individual may appear to behave normally, but may later have little recollection of specific behaviors. A number of investigators have concluded that posttraumatic amnesia is significantly related to the length of coma as well as the severity of the cerebral insult (Evans, 1975).

Older memories usually remain intact after the trauma; however, memories involving the minutes or several hours prior to the cerebral trauma may be inaccessible. Moreover, if the coma lasts for several days or weeks, the retrograde amnesia may be much more pervasive. Over time, however, many of the well-ingrained memories are again accessible. While a number of memory disturbances seem to be concomitant with traumatic head injuries, the specific effects of such trauma are dependent on the severity, age, and site of the damage (Lezak, 1983). There are three basic types of intervention strategies for this population: externally driven interventions aimed at changing the environment, interventions aimed at improving cognitive ability, and interventions that teach compensatory strategies (Mateer, Kerns, & Eso, 1996).

One of the most common memory disorders is dementia. Dementia is characterized by deficits in memory, judgment, abstract reasoning, and cognition in general. Personality disturbances may also be concomitant with dementia. While dementia is often associated with older individuals, it may develop at any age. Although minor memory problems may be concomitant with normal aging, they do not characteristically impede daily functioning. However, the memory deficiencies that accompany dementia may lead to the inability to acquire new information or to use previously stored information. While the etiology of these memory disturbances is not always clear, a number of investigations with demented patients have found reduced cholinesterase levels in those areas of the brain typically associated with memory (Perry et al., 1978).

Congenital anomalies may also lead to problems of memory and learning. Clearly, such congenital abnormalities as cerebral palsy, meningitis, and hydrocephalus have been associated with severe learning and memory difficulties. The memory disorders associated with these congenital conditions tend to be pervasive and may make learning difficult at best. Consistent with this pervasive impairment in learning (Maurer, 1992), severe disruption of the storage and retrieval processes have been shown to be characteristic. Because of this diffuse impairment, patients often require special education services or custodial care. Indeed, there are some that posit many learning disabilities and language disorders as memory disorders (Gathercole & Baddeley, 1990).

## REFERENCES

Baddeley, A. D., & Warrington, E. K. (1970). Amnesia and the distinction between long and short term memory. *Journal of Verbal Learning & Verbal Behavior, 9,* 176–189.

Barbizet, J. (1963). Defect of memorizing of hippocampal-mammillary origin: A review. *Journal of Neurology, Neurosurgery, & Psychiatry, 26,* 127–135.

Barbizet, J. (1970). *Human memory and its pathology.* San Francisco: Freeman.

Bloch, V., & Laroche, S. (1984). Facts and hypotheses related to the search for the engram. In G. Lynch, J. L. McGaugh, & N. M. Weinberger (Eds.), *Neurobiology of learning and memory* (pp. 249–260). New York: Guilford.

Butters, N., & Cermak, L. S. (1980). *Alcoholic Korsakoff's syndrome.* New York: Academic.

Corkin, S. (1968). Acquisition of motor skills after bilateral medial temporal lobe excision. *Neuropsychologia, 6,* 255–266.

Craik, F. I. M., & Lockhart, R. S. (1972). Levels of processing: A framework for memory research. *Journal of Verbal Learning & Verbal Behavior, 11,* 671–684.

Dean, R. S., Gray, J. W., & Yekovich, F. R. (under review). *Modality effects in long-term memory.*

Evans, M. (1975). Discussion of the clinical problem. In *Ciba Foundation Symposium, No. 34 (new series). Symposium on the outcome of severe damage to the CNS.* Amsterdam: Elsevier-Excerpta Medica.

Gathercole, S. E., & Baddeley, A. D. (1990). Phonological memory deficits in language disordered children: Is there a causal connection? *Journal of Memory & Language, 29*(3), 336–360.

Hécaen, H., & Albert, M. L. (1978). *Human neuropsychology.* New York: Wiley.

Hillgard, E. R., & Bower, G. H. (1975). *Theories of learning.* Englewood Cliffs, NJ: Prentice Hall.

Lezak, M. D. (1983). *Neuropsychological assessment.* New York: Oxford University Press.

Mateer, C. A., Kerns, K. A., & Eso, K. L. (1996). Management of attention and memory disorders following traumatic brain injury. *Journal of Learning Disabilities, 29*(6), 618–632.

Maurer, R. G. (1992). Disorders of memory & learning. In S. Segalowitz & I. Rapin (Eds.), *Handbook of neuropsychology* (pp. 241–260). Amsterdam, Netherlands: Elsevier Science.

Miller, G. A. (1956). The magical number seven, plus or minus two: Some limits on our capacity for processing information. *Psychological Review, 63,* 81–97.

Norman, D. A. (1973). What have the animal experiments told us about human memory? In J. A. Deutsch (Ed.), *The physiological basis of memory* (pp. 248–260). New York: Academic.

Perry, E. K., Tomlinson, B. E., Blessed, G., Bergmann, K., Gibson, P. H., & Perry, R. H. (1978). Correlation of cholinertic abnormalities with senile plaques and mental test scores in senile dementia. *British Medical Journal, 2*, 1457–1459.

Ryan, C., Butters, N., & Montgomery, K. (1979). Memory deficits in chronic alcoholics: Continuities between the "intact" alcoholic and the alcoholic Korsakoff patient. In H. Begleiter & B. Kissin (Eds.), *Alcohol intoxication and withdrawal* (pp. 180–196). New York: Plenum.

Shallice, T. (1979). Neuropsychological research and the fractionation of memory systems. In L. G. Nilsson (Ed.), *Perspectives on memory research* (pp. 218–236). Hillsdale, NJ: Erlbaum.

Squire, L. R., & Slater, P. L. (1978). Anterograde and retrograde memory impairment in chronic amnesia. *Neuropsychologia, 16*, 313–322.

Straub, R. L., & Black, F. W. (1977). *The mental status examination in neurology.* Philadelphia: Davis.

Tulving, E. (1972). Episode and semantic memory. In E. Tulving & W. Donaldson (Eds.), *Organization of memory* (pp. 205–218). New York: Academic.

JEFFREY W. GRAY
*Ball State University*

RAYMOND S. DEAN
*Ball State University*
*Indiana University School of Medicine*

AMNESIA
CHOLINESTERASE
DYSNOMIA
LEARNING DISABILITIES
TEST OF MEMORY AND LEARNING

# MENINGITIS

Meningitis is an infection or inflammation of the membranes covering the brain and spinal cord. It may affect the arachnoid, the pia mater, and the cerebrospinal fluid in the subarachnoid space. The infection resulting in meningitis may occur via spinal fluid pathways, directly from a local infection or the bloodstream, or via retrograde thrombophlebitis (*Melloni's,* 1985). Meningitis is classified by the causative agent, and may include bacterial meningitis, meningococcal meningitis, and viral meningitis. A lumbar puncture is conducted to obtain a sample of cerebrospinal fluid in which the causative agent can be identified (Thomson, 1979).

Seventy percent of the cases of bacterial meningitis are caused by Streptococcus pneumoniae, Neisseria meningitidis, and Homophilus influenza type b, collectively (Swartz, 1979). There is a strong age component associated with the etiologic agent in cases of bacterial meningitis. In neonates, gram-negative bacilli are the major bacterial cause of meningitis, with H. influenza type b the most common agent in children under the age of 5 (Swartz, 1979). Neisseria meningitidis is the offending bacterium in meningococcal meningitis, a common form of the disease. Transmission may occur from person to person via hand to hand, hand to mouth, or mouth to mouth contact (Feldman, 1979). Epidemics of meningococcal meningitis may occur in heavily populated areas such as military bases or urban centers (Swartz, 1979).

Bacterial meningitis is characterized by an acute onset of fever, headache, vomiting, and stiff neck. Prior history of upper respiratory infection, acute otitis, or pneumonia may be identified (Swartz, 1979). Drowsiness and lethargy may be evident. Seizures may be present in 20 to 30 percent of affected individuals. Partial or complete sensorineural hearing loss may occur in patients over 3 years of age, and may persist (Swartz, 1979). While rapid recovery from bacterial meningitis typically follows prompt treatment with antibiotics, residual neurologic impairment may be identified in 10 to 20 percent of recovered individuals (Swartz, 1979).

Viral meningitis, in contrast to the bacterial form, is described as "a benign, self-limited illness" (Johnson, 1979, p. 817). The coxsackie and echoviruses are associated with approximately 50 percent of the cases of viral meningitis (Johnson, 1979). Symptoms develop rapidly, and include headache, fever, stiff neck, sore throat, nausea, and vomiting; symptoms may persist from 3 to 14 days. Full recovery is typically within 1 to 2 weeks (Johnson, 1979).

Some children with a history of bacterial meningitis may require special education and related services (Gade, Bohr, Bjerrum, & Udesen, 1992). Hearing loss may be a residual impairment in some individuals, and generalized intellectual deficiency resulting from high fever or seizures may be identified. A multifactored evaluation is essential in planning an educational program for affected children.

## REFERENCES

Feldman, H. A. (1979). Meningococcal disease. In P. B. Beeson, W. McDermott, & J. B. Wyngaarden (Eds.), *Cecil textbook of medicine* (pp. 417–423). Philadelphia: Saunders.

Gade, A., Bohr, V., Bjerrum, J., & Udesen, H. (1992). Neuropsychological sequelae in 91 cases of pneumococcal meningitis. *Developmental Neuropsychology, 8*(4), 447–457.

Johnson, R. T. (1979). Viral meningitis and encephalitis. In P. B. Beeson, W. McDermott, & J. B. Wyngaarden (Eds.), *Cecil textbook of medicine* (pp. 817–821). Philadelphia: Saunders.

*Melloni's illustrated medical dictionary* (2nd ed.). (1985). Baltimore: Williams & Wilkins.

Swartz, M. N. (1979). Bacterial meningitis. In P. B. Beeson, W. McDermott, & J. B. Wyngaarden (Eds.), *Cecil textbook of medicine* (pp. 411–416). Philadelphia: Saunders.

Thomson, W. A. R. (1979). *Black's medical dictionary* (32nd ed.). New York: Barnes & Noble.

CATHY F. TELZROW
*Kent State University*

## BRAIN DAMAGE/INJURY

## MENINGOMYELOCELE

Meningomyelocele is an abnormal outpouching of the spinal cord through an opening in the back of the spine. The term is synonymous with myelomeningocele and is a more common form of spina bifida than a meningocele (an outpouching that includes only the protective membranes but not the spinal cord). The outpouching of the spinal cord and its nerve roots into the meningomyelocele causes a flaccid paralysis and loss of sensation in the lower extremities or trunk. This loss of function depends on the level of the spinal cord defect and the number of nerve roots involved.

The cause of a meningomyelocele is essentially unknown. It occurs when the neural tube (the cells that form the spine and spinal cord) fails to develop and close completely in the first few weeks of pregnancy. A meningomyelocele may be detected using several intrauterine tests, most commonly amniocentesis or ultrasound. Early treatment includes closure of the open sack to prevent infection, a procedure that often requires the removal of some neural elements. Additional surgery also may be required subsequently to repair other conditions that are frequently associated with meningomyelocele. These secondary conditions may include hydrocephalus and orthopedic abnormalities in the legs or spine such as club foot or scoliosis.

Loss of bowel and bladder control is common for persons with a meningomyelocele. Management of bowel and bladder function may include a combination of suppositories, diet, medication, and clean intermittent catheterization. Physical and occupational therapy, bracing, wheelchairs, and other assistive devices often promote increased functional independence and permit a productive and rewarding life.

### REFERENCES

Bleck, E. E. (1985). Myelomeningocele, meningocele, spina bifida. In E. E. Bleck & D. A. Nagel (Eds.), *Physically handicapped children—A medical atlas for teachers* (pp. 181–192). New York: Grune & Stratton.

Burr, H. C. (1970). Classification of myelomeningocele and congenital spinal defects. In *American Academy of Orthopedic Surgeons' Symposium on myelomeningocele* (pp. 1–18). St. Louis, MO: Mosby.

Long, C. (1971). Congenital and traumatic lesions of the spinal cord. In G. H. Krusen, F. J. Kottke, & P. M. Ellwood (Eds.), *Handbook of physical medicine and rehabilitation* (2nd ed., pp. 475–516). Philadelphia: Saunders.

DANIEL D. LIPKA
*Lincoln Way Special Education
Regional Resource Center*

## PHYSICAL DISABILITIES
## SPINA BIFIDA

## MENTAL AGE

Mental age is an age-equivalent score derived from a general test of intellectual skill or aptitude. The mathematical derivation is the same as for other types of age-equivalent scores. A mental age represents the mean level of performance or a group of children at a particular chronological age on the test in question. For example, if the average number of questions answered correctly by children aged 8 years, 2 months on an intelligence test was 33, then, in future administrations of the same test, all children who answer 33 questions correctly would be assigned a mental age of 8 years, 2 months.

This type of score has been often misinterpreted in intelligence and aptitude testing. The mental age does not take into account the dispersion of children's scores about the mean and has a standard deviation that varies considerably across age. Thus a child who is 2 years below chronological age in mental age, may or may not have a significant problem. For a 5-year-old, a mental age of 3 years represents serious retardation in the development of intellectual skills. A 16 year old with a mental age of 14 will fall within the average range of intelligence. It is not true that a 6 year old with a mental age of 9 years has the same intellectual skills or thinks and reasons like a 12 year old with a mental age of 9 years.

Mental ages have been popular for some time and are necessary in the calculation of ratio IQs, a type of IQ scale abandoned many years ago by all major tests of intelligence. Mental ages are regarded by most psychologists and psychometricians as a poor method of score reporting; standard scores are considered superior in all instances (Reynolds, Gutkin, Elliott, & Witt, 1984).

Mental age is usually abbreviated as MA and reported as the year followed by a decimal and the number of months (or in some cases, fraction of a year, though this option is usually confusing), as in MA = 9.4, which means that the child's mental age is 9 years, 4 months.

## REFERENCE

Reynolds, C. R., Gutkin, T. B., Elliott, S. N., & Witt, J. C. (1984). *School psychology: Essentials of theory and practice.* New York: Wiley.

CECIL R. REYNOLDS
*Texas A&M University*

**CENTRAL TENDENCY**
**DEVIATION IQ**
**GRADE EQUIVALENTS**
**RATIO IQ**
**STANDARD DEVIATION**

# MENTAL DEFICIENCY

See MENTAL RETARDATION.

# MENTAL ILLNESS

Mental illness is a disease or condition that is manifested in disruptions of an individual's behavior, thinking, perception, or emotions. Other terms used synonymously are mental, psychiatric, and psychological disorder or disease. The single most important concept in determining whether or not someone is mentally ill is his/her level of adaptive functioning. One area of adaptive functioning, indeed the most critical, is the person's social relations.

Problems in social relations can be viewed in terms of quantity and quality. Does the person shun social contact or the development of close relationships? Social isolation and withdrawal are cardinal manifestations of mental disorder. However, the person's motives for social avoidance must be considered. A motive of intense anxiety or gross indifference, for example, is indicative of a mental disorder. However, social withdrawal may be considered normal under some conditions such as while writing a dissertation or acclimating to a foreign culture.

The quality of social relationships is another dimension of social adaptiveness. Here a diagnostician assesses the degree to which the person manipulates others for his or her own selfish purposes, shows a lack of empathy, or is unable to establish or maintain intimate relationships. Involvements predominantly characterized by excessive hostility, suspiciousness, jealousy, dominance, or undue submissiveness and dependency may also serve as markers of mental disorder. In addition to social adaptation, occu-

pational or academic functioning may also reveal evidence of mental illness.

When evaluating a person's school or job performance, several questions are important. Has there been a decline in functioning? Do emotions, thoughts, or behaviors interfere with performance? Does the person obsessively focus on details to the neglect of the broader perspective? Does the individual report a lack of energy, fatigue, bodily complaints, and pessimism? Is the person's work history characterized by absenteeism, frequent job changes and arguments with bosses and coworkers? Problems in any one of these areas may indicate a psychological disorder.

Use of leisure time may be of concern when it involves excessive drug use, stealing, dangerous impulsive activity, or gambling that disrupts social relations. In the case of children or adolescents, vandalism, unusually premature sexual activity, fighting, delinquency, or arson are all examples of maladaption.

The final area of adaptive functioning that is assessed is self-care. This consists of the basic necessities of feeding, grooming, and hygiene, and is judged within the context of the person's social reference group. One overt manifestation of a mental disorder is a deterioration in self-care, as is found, for example, in chronic schizophrenia.

It is important to note that no single behavior can be used to diagnose mental illness. The circumstances leading to the behavior or cluster of behaviors and their severity in compromising adaptive functioning are taken into account when making a diagnosis of mental disorder.

When a patient complains about his or her behavior, thoughts, perceptions, or emotions, he or she is stating a symptom. Often symptoms are found to cluster together and the term syndrome is applied. For example, sadness, lack of energy, pessimism, and changes in appetite and sleeping are a few of the symptoms that make up the depressive syndrome. The beginning of a syndrome is its onset and the manner in which it unfolds is its course. The individual's level of functioning prior to the onset of the disorder is called premorbid adjustment and is designated along a continuum of good to bad. Just before the onset of the disorder, there may be a transition period that presages the syndrome. This is known as the prodrome or prodromal phase. For example, people who suffer from epilepsy or migraine headaches will notice feeling "different" (called an aura); this feeling signals the seizure or headache. The phase of the disorder that persists after the syndrome has abated but during which problems still exist is called the residual phase. Some disorders seem to develop rapidly and are called acute. If the syndrome persists, the term chronic phase is applicable. Not all disorders show this sequential pattern. For example, simple phobias may be chronic but they have no prodromal or residual phase. Schizophrenia, in contrast, can be meaningfully discussed using all of the mentioned definitions. Clinicians have also found it useful to distinguish disorders based on their cause or etiology.

Those disorders having a biological dysfunction as a basis are referred to as organic. When no known biological cause can be identified, psychological factors are considered the cause and the term functional is applied. One clear example of an organically based mental disorder is delirium. Dependent Personality Disorder represents an example of a functional disorder. The organic/functional dichotomy is not always clear (e.g., schizophrenia), and indeed organic and functional factors may coexist in a single individual (e.g., psychophysiological disorders).

No other term in psychiatry has prompted more heated debate than mental illness. It has been used as a vehicle for politically based, interprofessional fighting, as well as a means of focusing on differences in theoretical approaches to abnormal behavior. Although the current controversies about the usefulness of the concept of mental illness are recent, the term has a long history.

Several arguments have been offered to the effect that the sickness model, embodied in the term mental illness, has outlived its usefulness. One implication of this model is that physician-psychiatrists should hold primary, if not sole, responsibility for the treatment of people labeled as mentally ill. The terms illness, cure, psychiatric hospital, treatment, remission, and relapse are all borrowed from medicine and applied to the psychotherapeutic endeavor. And who best to administer the treatment but someone trained within the medical profession? Thus, some authors have argued that psychiatry is endorsing a view of abnormal behavior that strengthens their professional territorial boundary (Mowrer, 1960).

Other attacks aimed at the sickness model are rooted in alternate theoretical approaches to mental illness such as replacing the term with the phrase "problems in living" (Kanfer & Phillips, 1970; Szasz, 1961). This learning-based framework holds that abnormal behavior is not a manifestation of an underlying psychic disorder, but is a result of a reciprocal interaction between behavior and environment (Bandura, 1969; Davison & Neale, 1982). Within this framework, terms such as mental illness, disease, symptoms, and cure have little meaning. Symptoms are not the outgrowth of an underlying psychic disease process but are the client's problems. They are learned, maladaptive strategies that may have several purposes such as anxiety reduction, avoiding negative social consequences, or evoking positive consequences from others. The implications for diagnosis and treatment are accordingly different from the traditional sickness model (Kanfer & Grimm, 1977, 1980). Recently the debate has become less political, and paradigmatic demarcations are beginning to blur as clinicians strive for a theoretical rapprochement (Wachtel, 1977) and reimbursement for services that are supervised by managed care companies that demand medical model coding.

The purpose of psychological testing is to gather information concerning a person's personality characteristics, psychopathology, strengths, deficits, and interactions with his or her environment. Sometimes testing is conducted to answer a specific question: Does the patient have a thought disorder? At other times, extensive testing is carried out to provide a broad, yet in-depth, picture of the person's functioning. There are virtually hundreds of psychological tests, most of which are used in research settings. The most commonly employed instruments are the Mental Status Exam, the Rorschach Inkblot Test, and the Minnesota Multiphasic Personality Inventory (MMPI).

The Mental Status Exam is administered within an interview format and is qualitative in nature in that no test score is obtained. It provides a general picture of several areas of functioning and is most often used during an intake interview. Some of the dimensions of concern are the person's insight, content of thought, emotional reactions, sensorium, and judgment. The mental status report should address at least the following questions: Is emotional response appropriate? Does the patient comprehend his or her current situation? Is there evidence of delusions or hallucinations? Is there any impairment of retention or recall of information? Is the patient oriented to time, place, and person? What is the patient's physical appearance? Based on the results of the mental status exam, any number of dispositional recommendations follow, including medication, hospitalization, further testing, out-patient therapy, and so on. The mental status examination for children focuses on some of the same areas of functioning as does the exam for adults—appearance, thinking, perception, and emotional reaction. In addition, however, the clinician evaluates the child's activity level and attention span, coordination, speech comprehension and expression, manner of relating, and intellectual functioning (Goodman & Sours, 1967). With younger children, the behavioral facets can be evaluated indirectly through games and role playing. The results of this examination may suggest the need for more formal testing, family therapy, or hospitalization.

The Rorschach is but one of several, albeit the most popular, projective techniques. These projective tests present unstructured or ambiguous stimuli and require the person to identify a picture, tell a story, or complete a sentence, depending on the test. It is assumed that the individual will project or reveal important aspects of his or her personality, such as needs, conflicts, motives, and fears. The Rorschach Test was created in 1911 and consists of 10 inkblots, each of which the person is asked to identify. Several scoring systems are available that code the individual's responses in terms of, for example, level of detail, originality of responses, number of responses to each card, whether or not texture (e.g., "furry") was seen, and reaction to the few cards with color.

Projective tests have been adapted for use with children. They often employ cartoon figures. The Blacky Pictures depict a small dog and his parents and siblings in various scenes for which the child must relate a story. Projective techniques are the subject of controversy because of their questionable reliability and validity. The subjective quality of test interpretation, the high level of inference used in making statements about cognitive and affective functioning, as well as the expense in time needed for administration and scoring have led many psychologists to abandon their use. However, even though the popularity of projectives has waned in the last 20 years, they are still commonly used as part of a diagnostician's battery of tests.

The MMPI-2 and MMPI-A are known as objective tests because they yield quantitative measures of psychopathology. They are rivaled only by the Rorschach in the number of research articles and books concerning the instrument (over 6000). While there are numerous objective measures of personality and mental disorders, none has achieved the degree of popularity afforded the MMPI tests. The tests are comprised of over 500 true-false items that assess several types of disorders, including schizophrenia, depression, hysteria, mania, hypochondriasis, and anxiety, to name a few. The MMPI test was first validated in the 1940s on several groups of patients who were in treatment for various mental disorders. An individual scoring high, for instance, on the depression scale is answering the test items in a manner similar to the way in which the original sample of diagnosed depressives responded on the test.

The *Diagnostic and Statistical Manual,* fourth edition (*DSM-IV*) lists over 30 disorders under the heading "Disorders Usually First Evident in Infancy, Childhood, or Adolescence." The disorders range in severity from infantile autism to Developmental Arithmetic Disorder. It has been charged that knowledge of the *DSM-IV* criteria for neuropsychiatric disorders does not always help diagnosis because children manifest behavior differently than adults (Taylor, 1998).

It is not uncommon for parents to voice concern when their children exhibit what appears to be deviant behavior. Fortunately, most children's problems are time limited. It is typical for 2 year olds to fear strangers, 4 year olds to fear the dark, and 5 year olds to fear dreams and robbers (Gray, 1971). Symptoms occurring before the age of six have little predictive significance for later problems. There are, of course, notable exceptions. A child with many symptoms at one age is likely to have several symptoms at a later age (Robins, 1972). Mental retardation and Infantile Autism are usually evident at an early age and persist through subsequent developmental periods.

An example of a childhood disorder is Attention-Deficit/Hyperactivity Disorder. The main features are short attention span, impulsivity, and excessive motor activity. These children give the impression of not listening and have difficulty in carrying tasks through to completion. Their school work is often sloppy, unorganized, and replete with careless errors of omissions and insertions. Their attention deficit is exaggerated in the classroom and when performing in loosely structured settings. They appear to be perpetually in motion as they run and climb excessively. The disorder is usually evident by age three but may go undiagnosed until

the child enters school. It is typical that the child's behavior fluctuates across situations and time. Thus, the disorder is not invariant and periods of well-organized behavior are to be expected. The child may show personality characteristics of stubbornness, bullying, low frustration tolerance, and outbursts of anger. The disorder may persist into adulthood, disappear at puberty, or show a diminution of excessive motor activity while still revealing attentional deficits. Approximately 3 percent of children have this problem and 90 percent of them are boys.

Another common childhood disorder is Separation Anxiety Disorder. The essential aspect of this disorder is excessive anxiety surrounding separation from major attachment figures, home, or familiar surroundings. The child may become anxious to the point of panic and refuse to sleep at friends' homes, go to school, or play a few blocks from home. Anticipated separation may evoke physical complaints such as headaches or stomachaches. These children are often preoccupied by thoughts of death and horrible fears of harm befalling the family. The ill-defined fears of the younger child may become more focused in later years and center on potential dangers such as kidnapping, burglars, or car accidents. Adolescent boys may deny feeling anxious when away from their mothers, but their propensity to stay at home, and discomfort when forced to leave the house for a day or two, reflect their separation anxiety. Children with this disorder often fear the dark and prefer to sleep with their parents, even if it requires sleeping on the floor outside their mother and father's bedroom door. These children may be described as clinging, demanding, and in need of constant reassurance. The disorder typically begins after some trauma such as a move, death of a pet, illness, or loss of a friend or relative. The disorder may persist for several years with exacerbations and remissions. Further, separation anxiety may continue into adulthood and manifest itself in a person's reluctance to move out of the house or excessive dependency on a spouse.

## REFERENCES

Bandura, A. (1969). *Principles of behavior modification.* New York: Holt, Rinehart, and Winston.

Davison, G. C., & Neale, J. M. (1982). *Abnormal psychology.* New York: Wiley.

Goodman, J. D., & Sours, J. A. (1967). *The child mental status examination.* New York: Basic Books.

Gray, J. (1971). *The psychology of fear and stress.* New York: McGraw-Hill.

Harris, M. (1974). *Cows, pigs, wars, and witches: The riddles of culture.* New York: Random House.

Kanfer, F. H., & Grimm, L. G. (1977). Behavior analysis: Selecting target behaviors in the interview. *Behavior Modification, 1,* 7–28.

Kanfer, F. H., & Grimm, L. G. (1980). Managing clinical change: A process model of therapy. *Behavior Modification, 4,* 419–444.

Kanfer, F. H., & Phillips, J. S. (1970). *Learning foundations of behavior therapy*. New York: Wiley.

Mowrer, O. H. (1960). "Sin," the lesser of two evils. *American Psychologist, 15*, 301–304.

Robins, L. N. (1972). Follow-up studies of behavior disorders in children. In H. C. Quay & J. S. Werry (Eds.), *Psychopathological disorders in childhood*. New York: Wiley.

Sarbin, T. R. (1967). On the futility of the proposition that some people be labeled "mentally ill." *Journal of Consulting Psychology, 31*, 447–453.

Szasz, T. S. (1961). *The myth of mental illness: Foundations of a theory of personal conduct*. New York: Hoeber-Harper.

Taylor, E. H. (1998). Advances in the diagnosis and treatment of children with serious mental illness. *Child Welfare, 77*(3), 311–332.

Wachtel, P. (1977). *Psychoanalysis and behavior therapy: Toward an integration*. New York: Basic Books.

LAURENCE C. GRIMM
*University of Illinois*

## DIAGNOSTIC AND STATISTICAL MANUAL OF MENTAL DISORDERS (DSM-IV-TR)
PROJECTIVE TECHNIQUES

## MENTAL RETARDATION

Mental retardation refers to general cognitive deficits that impair functioning across a wide variety of tasks and situations. It varies in degree, with many specific syndromes associated with more serious impairment. The cause of many cases of mental retardation, particularly milder ones, remains unknown.

### Historical Background

Mental retardation has been known for centuries, and different terms have been used by professionals to refer to individuals having the condition. Among terms used centuries ago are naturals, idiots, and natural fools. From the early- to mid-twentieth century, moron, imbecile, and idiot referred to three levels of retardation (from highest to lowest), and until about 1940, the inclusive term was feeble-minded. More recent terms include mental deficiency, mental subnormality, mental challenge, and developmental disability, the latter implying a long-term severe disability.

Until the twentieth century, when intelligence tests became available, mental retardation was defined in terms of an individual's inability to meet minimal demands of the culture. Around the turn of the century, the French minister of public instruction commissioned Binet to develop a method of identifying Parisian students who could be expected to fail the regular school curriculum and who therefore required special instruction (MacMillan, 1982). In the United States, Goddard initially translated the Binet and used it at the Vineland Training School. Terman later obtained the United States rights to the test, revised it, and provided norms. Terman's 1916 edition of the Stanford Binet Intelligence Scale was quickly adopted as a standardized, objective, norm-referenced way of identifying children as mentally retarded. The IQ became a standard for classification. Indeed, Terman (1916, p. 79) also is apparently responsible for designating an IQ of below 70 (two standard deviations below the mean) as the criterion for mental retardation: "All who test below 70 I.Q. by the Stanford Revision of the Simon-Binet Scale should be considered feebleminded." He further specified levels of IQ for different degrees (moron, imbecile, and idiot) of feeblemindedness. Thus by edict, Terman pronounced that mental retardation should be defined in terms of a particular level of IQ and that all those with retardation, from the mildest to the most severe, are in the same category (Potter, 1964). The belief that all those with mental retardation were of one basic type persisted for many years, but has been persistently questioned by Zigler, his colleagues, and others. Terman's criterion of 70 gained general acceptance and remains today. State laws concerning mental retardation use IQs of no more than 70 or 75 (or occasionally 79) as the criterion for eligibility for special education classes.

### Changing Definitions of Mental Retardation

Prominent psychologists, such as Wechsler, who devised a series of intelligence tests, consistently warned against the rigid use of intelligence test scores as a sole criterion for diagnosing mental retardation. However, not until 1959 did the leading professional organization concerned with mental retardation, the American Association on Mental Deficiency (AAMD), now the American Association on Mental Retardation (AAMR), make a formal change in its definition. Between 1959 and 1983, the AAMD's definition of mental retardation changed from broader to more restrictive and provided criteria that included both measured intelligence and adaptive behavior. The 1983 AAMD definition reads:

> Mental retardation refers to significantly subaverage general intellectual functioning resulting in or associated with concurrent impairments in adaptive behavior and manifested during the developmental period. (Grossman, 1983)

Terms used in the definition were defined as follows:

> *General intellectual functioning* is operationally defined as the results obtained by assessment with one or more of the individually administered standardized general intelligence tests developed for that purpose. [The most frequently used tests at that time were the

Stanford-Binet and the Wechsler Intelligence Scale for Children.]

*Significantly subaverage* is defined as IQ of 70 or below on standardized measures of intelligence. The upper limit is intended as a guideline; it could be extended upward through IQ 75 or more, depending on the reliability of the intelligence test used. This particularly applies in schools and similar settings if behavior is impaired and clinically determined to be due to deficits in reasoning and judgment.

*Impairments in adaptive behavior* are defined as significant limitations in an individual's effectiveness in meeting the standards of maturation, learning, personal independence and/or social responsibility that are expected for his or her age level and cultural group, as determined by clinical assessment and, usually, standardized scales.

*Developmental period* is defined as the period of time between conception and the eighteenth birthday. Developmental deficits may be manifested by slow, arrested, or incomplete development resulting from brain damage; degenerative processes in the central nervous system; or regression from previously normal states due to psychological factors (Grossman, 1983).

The 1983 AAMD definition was adopted, sometimes in slightly modified wording, in the classification systems of the American Psychiatric Association (*Diagnostic and Statistical Manual–III*) and the World Health Organization (*International Classification of Diseases-9*).

Definitions of mental retardation are designed to reflect current thinking about the condition and to represent the status of knowledge of the field (Grossman, 1983). With this in mind, AAMR undertook in 1988 a four-year-long effort under the leadership of Ruth Luckasson to develop a new definition of mental retardation. The resulting 1992 definition is more functional and stresses the interaction among a person's capabilities, the environments in which the individual functions, and the need for supports:

Mental retardation refers to substantial limitations in present functioning. It is characterized by significantly subaverage intellectual functioning, existing concurrently with related limitations in two or more of the following applicable adaptive skill areas: communication, self-care, home living, social skills, community use, self-direction, health and safety, functional academics, leisure and work. Mental retardation manifests before age 18. (AAMR, 1992)

This latest definition is the ninth of the ones formulated by AAMD/AAMR since 1921. While retaining some of the aspects of earlier definitions, this definition and accompanying manual depart from previous editions in four important ways:

1. An attempt to express the changing understanding of what mental retardation is.

2. A formulation of what ought to be classified as well as how to describe the systems of supports required by people with mental retardation.

3. A major shift from a view of mental retardation as an absolute trait expressed solely by an individual to an expression of the interaction between the person with limited intellectual functioning and the environment.

4. An extension of the concept of adaptive behavior from a global description to specific adaptive skill areas.

In adopting this definition and the accompanying classification system, AAMR replaced the mild, moderate, severe, and profound classifications in previous definitions with levels of support needed by an individual: intermittent, limited, extensive, and pervasive. These terms may be summarized as follows:

*Intermittent:* Supports of high or low intensity are provided intermittently as needed. Characterized as episodic or short-term during life-span transitions.

*Limited:* Supports are provided consistently over time, but may not be extensive at any one time. Supports may require fewer staff members and expense than more intense levels of support.

*Extensive:* Supports are provided regularly, perhaps daily, in at least some environments such as work or home. Support may not be intensive but will be needed long term.

*Pervasive:* High intensity supports are provided constantly, across environments, and may be of life-sustaining and intrusive nature. Pervasive supports typically involve a variety of staff members.

Since the 1992 AAMR definition was published, others have been developed in part because of dissatisfaction with it. This dissatisfaction centered around the IQ cutoff level, the adaptive skill areas, and the levels of needed support. The most notable definition is the one proposed by the American Psychological Association (Jackson & Mulick, 1996):

Mental retardation (MR) refers to: (a) significant limitations in general intellectual functioning; (b) significant limitations in adaptive functioning, which exist concurrently; and (c) onset of intellectual and adaptive limitations before the age of 22 years.

This definition essentially restates the 1983 AAMD definition except that it raises the developmental period to age 22, consistent with the federal definition of developmental disabilities.

The American Psychiatric Association in its fourth edition of the *Diagnostic and Statistical Manual of Mental*

*Disorders (DSM-IV; 1994)* also retains the essence of the 1983 AAMD definition of mental retardation as well as the levels of severity of mental retardation. Mental retardation is characterized by significantly subaverage intellectual functioning (an IQ of approximately 70 or below) with onset before age 18 and concurrent deficits or impairments in adaptive functioning. Four degrees of severity are specified reflecting the level of intellectual impairment: mild, moderate, severe, and profound. Furthermore, *DSM-IV* and the *International Statistical Classification of Diseases and Related Health Problems, Tenth Revision (ICD-10)* have coordinated sections on mental and behavioral disorders so that they both have the same definition and classification system for mental retardation. Definitions of mental retardation have changed over time reflecting both social and political forces, and they likely will continue to change in the future. For example, AAMR is reexamining its definition of mental retardation once again.

## Etiology

Individuals classified as mentally retarded represent a heterogeneous group with respect to both etiology and functioning within their environments. A number of predisposing conditions are associated with mental retardation. Hereditary factors include single-gene recessive inborn errors of metabolism, such as Tay-Sachs Disease and tuberous sclerosis, and chromosomal aberrations, of which nondisjunction Down syndrome and Fragile X are the best known. Early alterations of embryonic development include chromosomal changes, such as mosaic Down syndrome, or prenatal damage due to toxins, including maternal alcohol consumption and infections. Fetal malnutrition, prematurity, hypoxia, viral and other infections, and trauma are factors associated with pregnancy and perinatal problems. General medical factors acquired in infancy and childhood include infections, traumas, and poisoning from substances such as lead. Deprivation of nurturance and of social, linguistic, and other stimulation are leading environmental influences associated with mental retardation. Factors associated with other mental disorders, such as autism, are also recognized in medical classification systems.

The two-group approach to mental retardation (e.g., Zigler, 1967; Zigler & Hodapp, 1986) is a useful conceptual framework for describing types of mental retardation and their relation to etiology. The two-group approach suggests that those with mental retardation can be divided into two groups, familial and organic. The familial patients, who comprise the great majority, are generally of relatively mild retardation and have parents and siblings who also have below average levels of intelligence. That is, their intelligence is a familial trait, transmitted from one generation to another as a result of the interaction of many genes with a succession of pre-, peri-, and postnatal environments, as other familial traits such as height. Their intelligence develops through the same general complex of factors as are those of higher intelligence, and they fall on the lower end of the normal distribution of intelligence. The organic patients, on the other hand, have more severe degrees of retardation and form a separate distribution of intelligence at the very low end of the normal distribution. Their retardation is due to some specific organic problem that may be genetic or environmental in origin, and their parents and siblings are likely to have average intelligence. Genetically-based organic conditions include Down and Fragile X syndromes and inborn errors of metabolism; environmentally based ones include fetal alcohol syndrome, effects of prenatal infections such as rubella, and lead poisoning.

Such classification systems are very useful for medical treatments, prevention programs, and research on prevention and treatment, but available psychoeducational research suggests that they offer little aid in the development of educational plans.

## Characteristics of Milder Retardation

Since 1977 when PL 94-142 went into effect, the number of students classified as mentally retarded has significantly decreased, with the group classified as mildly retarded affected the most. This "new" group of students, representing approximately 85 percent of the population classified as mentally retarded, appears to be lower functioning than those called mildly retarded a decade or more ago. For this reason, much of the previous literature on the earlier group may not be true for the current one. Also, not every individual classified as mildly mentally retarded will present all the characteristics described below. This group is heterogeneous, and generally individuals require few or no support systems in most adaptive skill areas. In the past, individuals who were categorized in the mildly retarded range were referred to as educable or trainable, particularly in the school system. In regard to demographic characteristics, more males than females and a disproportionate number of children from minority groups are identified as mildly retarded.

Motivational characteristics include limited self-regulatory behaviors, outerdirectedness (a tendency to look to others for solutions to problems rather than to oneself), expectancy of failure, and an external locus of control. In the area of learning, various cognitive processes may be limited. These include attention, mediation strategies, memory, transfer of training, and generalization. Certain speech, language, and health conditions may occur with greater frequency with this group. These include delayed language and motor development, cerebral palsy, seizure disorders, and sensory deficits.

In terms of education, the predominance of IEP goals in the elementary grades are academic, and many students can succeed in inclusive educational settings. With systematic instruction, skills training, and transition services, these individuals can succeed in integrated, competitive work settings upon completion of formal schooling.

## Characteristics of More Severe Mental Retardation

This group encompasses those individuals previously classified as having severe, profound, or, in some cases, moderate mental retardation. Presently, individuals in this group would be classified as needing more extensive supports. Neither those in the severely retarded (IQ range about 20 to 35) nor profoundly retarded (IQ below 20 or 25) ranges of intelligence were generally considered public-school responsibility until after the passage of PL 94-142 in 1975. Educators usually referred to all children classified as mentally retarded below the moderate level (IQ range about 35–55) as custodial, and most or all of such children would be educated in residential facilities. With the deinstitutionalization movement, this is no longer true. These children are now the responsibility of the public school system, and as such, must be provided an appropriate education in the least restrictive environment.

Current definitions of mental retardation support the use of terms such as severe/profound, persons with extensive support needs, and individuals with severe disabilities. The needs of this group are in many cases directly related to physical or health-related concerns. The extent of support required is influenced by the environment. Environments that encourage independence, productivity, and social interaction can enhance the development of individuals with severe mental retardation. The supports needed differ from those needed by individuals with less severe forms of mental retardation in their frequency, duration, and intensity; and many supplemental supports related to activities of daily living may be required.

In the area of education, IEP goals should be individualized, functional, and age appropriate. Instruction should be community-referenced and delivered in the settings where the skills will be used. The emphasis in transition planning should be on fostering independence, community integration, and supported employment to the maximum extent possible.

In the past, the potential of persons with mental retardation was grossly underestimated and they were subjected to prejudice, fear, and mistreatment. As children with mental retardation are included in public school classrooms, teachers and other school personnel tend to be wary of using the term "retarded." Some believe that the label is stigmatizing. Alternative terms include mentally challenged, cognitive disability, and mental disability. Available research suggests that the label itself is unlikely to stigmatize when teachers and others have opportunities to interact with children. However, in our society, persons classified as mentally retarded seem to be devalued, so any term that identifies the condition tends to become pejorative. As we learn to value others for what they are, rather than for what they are not, the label can become less onerous.

In summary, mental retardation is a condition associated with cognitive disabilities and impairments in adaptive behavior. Students classified as mentally retarded can be provided an appropriate education that will facilitate their leading as productive, independent lives as possible. Although they may have difficulty in learning, all can learn to some extent and profit from well-designed educational programs and systems of support.

### REFERENCES

American Association on Mental Retardation. (1992). *Mental retardation: Definition, classification, and systems of supports* (9th ed.). Washington, DC: American Association on Mental Retardation.

American Psychiatric Association. (1994). *Diagnostic and statistical manual of mental disorders* (4th ed.) Washington, DC: American Psychiatric Association.

Grossman, H. G. (Ed.). (1983). *Classification in mental retardation.* Washington, DC: American Association on Mental Deficiency.

Jackson, J. W., & Mulick, J. A. (1996). *Manual on diagnosis and professional practice in mental retardation.* Washington, DC: American Psychological Association.

MacMillan, D. L. (1982). *Mental retardation in school and society* (2nd ed.). Boston: Little, Brown.

Potter, H. W. (1964). The needs of mentally retarded children for child psychiatry services. *Journal of the American Academy of Child Psychiatry, 3,* 353–363.

Zigler, E. (1967). Familial mental retardation: A continuing dilemma. *Science, 155,* 292–298.

Zigler, E., & Hodapp, R. M. (1986). *Understanding mental retardation.* Cambridge, UK: Cambridge University Press.

SUE ALLEN WARREN
*Boston University*
First edition

ELEANOR BOYD WRIGHT
*University of North Carolina at Wilmington*
Second edition

**AAMR ADAPTIVE BEHAVIOR SCALES**
**ADAPTIVE BEHAVIOR**
**INCLUSION**
**INTELLIGENCE QUOTIENT**
**LABELING**
**VINELAND ADAPTIVE BEHAVIOR SCALES–SECOND EDITION**

# MENTAL RETARDATION: A JOURNAL OF POLICY, PRACTICES, AND PERSPECTIVES

The journal *Mental Retardation* was first published in 1963 by the Boyd Publishing Company. It is now published bimonthly by the American Association on Mental Retardation. Since its inception, the journal has been devoted to meeting the needs of people with mental retardation and providing their families and educators with information about effective ways to help them. As a journal with an applied focus, *Mental Retardation* publishes articles on new teaching approaches, administrative tools, program evaluation studies, new program developments, service utilization studies, community surveys, public policy issues, case studies, and research studies that emphasize the application of new methods. Articles submitted for publication are subject to peer review, with the editor making final publication decisions. Subscription information is available from the American Association on Mental Retardation, 444 N. Capitol St., NW, Suite 846, Washington, DC, 20001-1512.

TERESA K. RICE
*Texas A&M University*
First edition

DONNA WALLACE
*The University of Texas of the
Permian Basin*
Second edition

# MENTAL RETARDATION, SEVERE

The label of severe mental retardation continues to be used to describe persons who receive intelligence testing scores of more than four and up to five standard deviations below the norm (IQ = 20 to 35 on the Stanford-Binet and 25 to 39 on the Wechsler scales). Also, deficits in adaptive behavior (i.e., a lack of behaviors necessary to meet the standards of personal and social responsibility expected for a given chronological age) are considered in the labeling process according to the classification system of the American Association of Mental Deficiency (now AAMR; Grossman, 1977). Adaptive behavior is typically assessed through the administration of the Adaptive Behavior Scale of the AAMD, or a similar instrument that provides a profile of skill levels that can be used to compare an individual's adaptive behavior profile with that of the group of persons who are mentally retarded.

This system of labeling provides a descriptive assessment of the level of functioning that is used for classification of persons; hence it is used for placement into categorical programs. The use of such a categorical approach to labeling emphasizes deviations from a normal developmental sequence and degree of impairment, but it does not reveal the heterogeneity among persons who are labeled severely mentally retarded, or provide prescriptive information pertinent to the development or implementation of individualized habilitative or training programs (Sailor & Guess, 1983).

The inability to perform basic skills suggests a need for labeling that is based on the level and extent of systematic instruction and environmental modification that are required to establish functional skills (Sailor & Guess, 1983). Such an instructional approach to the definition of mental retardation changes the emphasis from that of the limits of learning that are possible to the level of assistance needed in the habilitative or training process (Gold, 1980).

Historically, the care and treatment of persons with severe retardation has largely emphasized deficits in ability. The consequences of such negative attitudes have been neglect, ridicule, segregation in institutional settings, and pessimism regarding habilitative efforts. Kauffman (1981) provides an accounting of the history of mental retardation in the United States since the beginning of the nineteenth century. In the early nineteenth century there was a period of optimism regarding the education of the handicapped. At this time it was assumed that all handicapped persons could be provided with residential care that would make them contributing members of society, or at least greatly improve their skill levels and the conditions under which they lived. This was the period when Dorothea Dix led the movement to institutionalize the handicapped to protect them from abuse, and when successes in teaching the severely retarded were being reported by Samuel Howe and Edouard Seguins. The size of institutions rapidly increased in the late nineteenth century without a corresponding increase in resources. The effect of the cutback in resources relative to the number of persons who were institutionalized resulted in a decline in the quality of care. The focus of institutions changed from that of providing training to that of providing custodial care and permanent segregation from society as pessimism grew in the face of lack of success in curing the condition of mental retardation.

The change from optimism to pessimism regarding educability and the need for segregation in institutional settings continued into the twentieth century and was maintained by H. H. Goddard's theory of eugenics. Goddard believed that mental retardation and criminality were linked together by genetic influences; however, these conclusions were based on the faulty interpretation of family genealogical studies.

In the 1950s an early event was significant for the change in the care of the mentally retarded. That event was the formation of the National Association of Parents and Friends of Retarded Children (which later became the National Association for Retarded Citizens). This organization was influential as an active lobby in securing publicly supported educational programs. Professional organizations such as the American Association for Mental Retardation and the Council for Exceptional Children also were involved in lobbying for the provision of educational services.

In the 1960s and 1970s there was a shift to a more optimistic outlook regarding the provision of services to individuals labeled severely mentally retarded. These persons began to receive skill training services in institutional settings in the 1960s and, to a limited extent, educational services in the public schools in the 1970s. The beginning of deinstitutionalization and the provision of community-based services also appeared. This stands in stark contrast to the preceding decades, in which severely retarded persons were provided food, shelter, and medical care in large institutions.

In the 1960s and 1970s several events were responsible for a change to the provision of habilitative programming. These events included (1) continued advocacy by parents' groups; (2) the enactment of legislation such as PL 94-142, the Education Act for All Handicapped Children of 1975, PL 94-103, the Developmentally Disabled Assistance and Bill of Rights Act of 1975, and PL 93-112, Section 504 of the Rehabilitation Act of 1973, which mandated services and guaranteed the rights of persons with handicaps; (3) litigation such as *Brown* v. *Board of Education* in 1954, in which the Supreme Court struck down segregated education systems, *Wyatt* v. *Stickney* in 1974, in which the Supreme Court decided for a constitutional right to treatment, and the *Pennsylvania Association for Retarded Citizens* v. *Commonwealth of Pennsylvania,* which guaranteed due process in educational placements to prevent exclusion from a free public education; (4) advances in instructional technology by behavioral researchers (Whitman, Sciback, & Reid, 1983); and (5) advocacy for the normalization principle (Wolfensberger, 1969).

During the 1960s and 1970s a number of changes occurred in habilitative programming. The focus of instructional technology changed from basic self-care skills and reduction of inappropriate behaviors in institutional settings to a focus on community living skills for persons working and living in a variety of residential options in the community. These changes were strongly reflective of the instructional approach to the definition of mental retardation (Gold, 1980).

The reforms in treatment models and improvements in instructional technology continued into the 1980s. Models have been developed for the training of vocational and independent living skills. These models actively involve persons with severe retardation in all aspects of community life (Cuvo & Davis, 1983; Rusch, 1986) and represent an optimistic viewpoint that persons with severe retardation can participate more fully in their home communities with appropriate training and support services. To achieve this goal of participation in community life to the fullest extent possible, increased service options in vocational, residential, and community programs need to be developed and expanded to accommodate the needs of persons labeled severely mentally retarded. TASH has emerged as a dynamic coalition of parents and professionals with the purpose of ensuring full integration of people labeled as severely mentally retarded in school, residential, vocational, and other community environments.

## REFERENCES

Cuvo, A. J., & Davis, P. K. (1983). Behavior therapy of community skills. In M. Hersen, R. M. Eisler, & P. M. Miller (Eds.), *Progress in behavior modification* (Vol. 14). New York: Academic.

Gold, M. W. (1980). *Try another way training manual.* Champaign, IL: Research.

Grossman, H. J. (1977). *Manual of terminology and classification in mental retardation.* Washington, DC: American Association on Mental Deficiency.

Kauffman, J. M. (1981). Historical trends and contemporary issues in special education in the United States. In J. M. Kauffman & D. P. Hallahan (Eds.), *Handbook of special education.* Englewood Cliffs, NJ: Prentice Hall.

Rusch, F. R. (Ed.). (1986). *Competitive employment: Issues and strategies.* Baltimore: Brookes.

Sailor, W., & Guess, D. (1983). *Severely handicapped students: An instructional design.* Boston: Houghton Mifflin.

Whitman, T. L., Sciback, J. W., & Reid, D. H. (1983). *Behavior modification with the severely and profoundly retarded: Research and application.* New York: Academic.

Wolfensberger, W. (1969). *Changing patterns in residential services for the mentally retarded.* Washington, DC: President's Commission on Mental Retardation.

HAROLD HANSON
PAUL BATES
*Southern Illinois University*

AAMR
MENTAL RETARDATION

## MENTAL STATUS EXAMS

The mental status examination is an attempt to integrate qualitative observation with standardized assessment in a brief form. An examiner attempts to sample a broad enough representation of mental processes and behavioral performance to decide whether a disorder is present. Additionally, a brief examination also allows hypothesis building in the sense that the pattern of findings may be related to a specific syndrome. Historically, the majority of brief examinations were developed with an eye toward psychopathology; currently, more attention is being placed on the efficient identification of neuropsychological disorders, specifically dementia among the elderly.

In a review of mental state tests, Weintraub and Mesulam (1985) include the following general areas for consideration within an examination:

Wakefulness, arousal, and attention
Mood and emotional responsiveness
Learning and recall

Aspects of language and communication, including pragmatics

Arithmetic manipulation/calculation

Complex perceptual tasks

Constructional tasks

Spatial distribution of attention

Conceptual reasoning

Synthetic reasoning (i.e., translating a problem into plans and action)

Unlike a standardized battery (e.g., Wechsler scales, Halstead-Reitan Neuropsychological Battery, Luria-Nebraska Neuropsychological Battery), mental status evaluation was intended as a flexible approach that could be modified to the needs of a clinical issue. Thus all areas listed generally will not be included in every examination; if all areas are included, the weight given a particular area in terms of the depth of observation is likely to vary with both preliminary findings and the focus of the particular question. The preceding list is more of a menu than a constant procedure. One of the obvious limitations of such a qualitative approach is the expertise of the examiner. Novices are more likely to attend to areas and rely on techniques with which they are familiar than be led by the needs of the question and insightful hypothesis testing.

When selecting procedures and organizing an assessment, the clinician must be prepared to allow assessment items to vary along several dimensions. Assessment techniques must permit observation of both complex performance and very simple performance. Procedures need to vary input and output modalities while attempting to maintain a focus on targeted mental processes. Lateralized performance also must be observed. In creating such an examination, a clinician must not sacrifice depth of observation for brevity. (For applications of mental status examinations, see Weintraub & Mesulam, 1985; Strubb & Black, 1983.) Though these goals sound sensible in terms of a brief diagnostic procedure, the usual mental status exam is a finite set of tasks whose performance generates a score that may be compared with a norm-referenced criterion.

It is interesting to note that if one reviews the development of successive mental status examinations, the usual stimulus for development of a new procedure is that the preceding technique was not extensive enough (Turner, Kreutzer, Lent, & Brockett, 1984). In such an evolutionary process, the distinction between a standardized battery and a brief mental status examination is notably blurred.

### REFERENCES

Strubb, R. L., & Black, F. W. (1983). *The mental status examination in neurology.* Philadelphia: Davis.

Weintraub, S., & Mesulam, M. (1985). Mental state assessment of young and elderly adults in behavioral neurology. In M. Mesulam (Ed.), *Principles of behavioral neurology* (pp. 71–124). Philadelphia: Davis.

ROBERT F. SAWICKI
*Lake Erie Institute of
Rehabilitation*

## CLINICAL INTERVIEW

## MERCER, CECIL D. (1943– )

Cecil D. Mercer received his EdD in special education in 1974 at the University of Virginia. He is currently a professor of special education at the University of Florida at Gainesville, where he was named "Teacher of the Year" (1978, 1990, 1995) of the College of Education and was a finalist (1995) for the University of Florida Distinguished Professor Award of the Alumni Association. In 1992, he was the recipient of the Gordon R. Alley Partnership Award of the University of Kansas Center for Research on Learning.

Mercer is the author or coauthor of 17 books, 10 curriculum materials and numerous journal articles and book chapters in the field of special education. Two of his texts, *Students with Learning Disabilities* (1983) and *Teaching Students with Learning Problems* (1985), have been widely adopted throughout the United States, and his math curriculum, *Strategic Math Series,* is used extensively to teach students basic math facts. His specialty is learning disabilities, with research and interests focusing in the areas of learning strategies, mathematics, reading, effective teaching principles, collaboration, and behavior management. His recent publications address the areas of mnemonics and enhancement of math performance of students with learning problems, teaching methods used to enhance acquisition and understanding of basic math for individuals with learning difficulties, and educational components of mathematics disabilities (Mercer & Miller, 1992; Miller & Mercer, 1993, 1997).

Mercer is a member of the Professional Advisory Board of the Learning Disabilities Association of America and the Board of Directors of the Florida Branch of the Orton Dyslexia Society. A featured speaker at national and state conferences in 34 states, in 1995 he was the General Session Keynote Speaker at the Learning Disabilities Association International Conference in Orlando, Florida. He is currently a consulting editor for *Learning Disability Quarterly* and *Learning Disabilities Research & Practice,* and he has served on conference program committees for the Learning

Disabilities Association and the Division for Learning Disabilities (pers. comm., January 15, 1998).

## REFERENCES

Mercer, C. D. (1983). *Students with learning disabilities*. Columbus, OH: Merrill.

Mercer, C. D., & Mercer, A. R. (1985). *Teaching students with learning problems* (2nd ed.). Columbus, OH: Merrill.

Mercer, C. D., & Miller, S. P. (1992). Teaching students with learning problems in math to acquire, understand, and apply basic math facts. *Remedial & Special Education, 13,* 19–35.

Miller, S. P., & Mercer, C. D. (1993). Mnemonics: Enhancing the math performance of students with learning difficulties. *Intervention in School and Clinic, 29,* 78–82.

Miller, S. P., & Mercer, C. D. (1997). Educational aspects of mathematical disabilities. *Journal of Learning Disabilities, 30,* 47–56.

Tamara J. Martin
*The University of Texas of the
Permian Basin*

## MERCER, JANE R.

See system of multicultural pluralistic assessment.

## MERRILL, MAUD AMANDA (1888–1985)

Maud Amanda Merrill earned her PhD in psychology at Stanford University in 1923 and served on the faculty there until 1947. She was coauthor, with Lewis M. Terman, of the 1937 revision of the Stanford-Binet Tests of Intelligence.

## REFERENCE

Terman, L. M., & Merrill, M. A. (1977). *Measuring intelligence.* Cambridge, MA: Riverside.

Paul Irvine
*Katonah, New York*

## MERRILL-PALMER SCALE

The Merrill-Palmer Scale is an individually administered intelligence test for children ages 18 months to 6 years. The scale was developed by Stutsman in 1931 as an alternative to, or supplement for, the Stanford-Binet. It consists primarily of performance tests measuring fine motor skills, although a few verbal items are included. The specific number and type of items administered varies depending on the age of the child (from 3 to 14 items are administered at each 6-month age period). Each item is scored as a success, a failure, an omission, or a refusal, and the total score can be converted into a mental age, a sigma value, and a percentile rank.

The test is particularly useful for assessing children lacking verbal skills (e.g., very young, developmentally delayed, or disabled). Two excellent reviews of the scale (Honzik, 1975; Loeb, 1985) have identified several problem areas, including an excessive number of timed tests that penalize the slow-moving, thoughtful child and inadequate standardization. In addition, the test is difficult to interpret because the standard deviations of the mental age do not increase in proportion to advancing chronological age beyond 54 months. The test is published by Stoelting Company, Chicago.

## REFERENCES

Honzik, M. P. (1975). The Merrill-Palmer Scale of Mental Tests. In O. K. Buros (Ed.), *Intelligence tests and reviews*. Highland Park, NJ: Gryphon Press.

Loeb, H. W. (1985). Merrill-Palmer Scale. In D. J. Keyser & R. C. Sweetland (Eds.), *Test critiques* (Vol. 2). Kansas City, MO: Test Corporation of America.

Stutsman, R. (1931). *Mental measurement of preschool children.* New York: World Book.

Robert G. Brubaker
*Eastern Kentucky University*

## INTELLIGENCE
## INTELLIGENCE TESTING

## METABOLIC DISORDERS

Metabolic disorders are inherited defects of highly complex disease entities of which there are several general types with more specific and typically rare subtypes. The study of metabolic disorders is expanding rapidly and more than 2000 different types of inborn errors of metabolism and morphology have been identified (Ampola, 1982). Most of these diseases are single recessive gene defects that result in impaired metabolism of fat, protein, amino acids, or carbohydrates because of a deficiency in essential enzymes. Some of the more commonly known of these diseases are cystic fibrosis, diabetes, galactosemia, phenylketonuria (PKU), and Tay-Sachs disease.

Metabolic disorders are of relevance to special education practitioners because of the developmental and behavioral sequelae of these diseases. For example, they have been found to be associated with intellectual deficits (Kanner, 1979), social-behavioral problems (Allen et al., 1984), and childhood psychiatric disorders (Nyhan, 1974). Moreover, the siblings of a child with metabolic disorders may experience psychosocial sequelae (Langdell, 1979). The impact of metabolic diseases on development and behavior varies with such factors as the specific type of medical disorder, age of onset, type and efficacy of medical treatment, social support systems, and premorbid level of functioning (Lehr, 1984). Recent medical advances have resulted in a decline in the morbidity and mortality caused by metabolic disorders with a concomitant rise in the percentage of childhood disabilities attributable to these.

The more common metabolic disorders with known developmental and behavioral sequelae are Cushing's disease, cystic fibrosis, diabetes, galactosemia, and PKU. While cognitive functioning does not appear to be impaired in such diseases as cystic fibrosis, social-emotional adjustment is typically affected owing to associated stressors. There is much still unknown regarding the long-term sequelae of metabolic disorders. For example, while recent advances in the medical treatment of PKU has resulted in decreased mental retardation, hyperactivity, epilepsy, and microcephaly, there is evidence of continued but less severe learning and behavioral problems.

Amniocentesis is effective for identifying only certain metabolic disorders. For example, Tay-Sachs disease can be detected by testing the amniotic fluid, but this is not true for galactosemia and PKU. Genetic counseling, regular education in schools, public education, and planned pregnancy programs are recommended to prevent and minimize developmental disabilities from metabolic disorders (Langdell, 1979). There is presently a lack of effective treatment for most metabolic diseases; the most relevant current emphasis should be directed at prevention through genetic screening and planned parenthood. Practitioners might refer parents to the following two national organizations for reliable information concerning metabolic disorders: Science Information Division, National Foundation–March of Dimes, Box 2000, White Plains, NY, 10602; and National Genetics Foundation, 9 West 57th Street, New York, NY 10019.

## REFERENCES

Allen, D. A., Affleck, G., Tennen, H., McGrade, B. J., & Ratzan, S. (1984). Concerns of children with a chronic illness: A cognitive-developmental study of juvenile diabetes. *Child Care, Health, & Development, 10,* 211–218.

Ampola, M. G. (1982). *Metabolic diseases in pediatric practice.* Boston: Little, Brown.

Kanner, L. (1979). *Child psychiatry.* Springfield, IL: Thomas.

Langdell, J. I. (1979). Working with parents to discover and treat inherited metabolic diseases. In J. D. Nosphitz (Ed.), *Basic handbook of child psychiatry* (Vol. IV, pp. 86–90). New York: Basic Books.

Lehr, E. (1984). Cognitive effects of acute and chronic pediatric medical conditions. In P. R. Magrab (Ed.), *Psychological and behavioral assessment: Impact on pediatric care* (pp. 235–278). New York: Plenum.

Nyhan, W. L. (1974). *Heritable disorders of amino acid metabolism: Patterns of clinical expression and genetic variation.* New York: Wiley.

JOSEPH D. PERRY
*Kent State University*

GALACTOSEMIA
GENETIC COUNSELING
INBORN ERRORS OF METABOLISM
PHENYLKETONURIA
TAY-SACHS SYNDROME

## METACOGNITION

Metacognition refers to one's understanding and knowledge about what one knows and how one learns (Flavell, 1976, 1979). This knowledge and understanding allows individuals to benefit from learning experiences and influences their use of cognitive strategies. Metacognition is developmental in that children's perceptions of what they know and how they learn change as a function of increased age (e.g., Flavell, 1979). For example, if asked how many words they can remember, younger children will likely overestimate their ability. As a result, they will not actively use any strategies to remember the list of words. As they grow older, and realize that they cannot just remember large bits of information without effort, they are more likely to strategize and use strategies to perform tasks. Metacognitive skills include the procedural knowledge (i.e., strategies) needed to gain control over one's learning (Veenman, Kok, & Blote, 2005). Research has consistently indicated that metacognitive abilities moderate and predict learning (e.g., Flavell, 1976, 1979; Glaser, 1990; Schunk & Zimmerman, 1994; Wang, Haertel, & Walberg, 1993). Schunk and Zimmerman argued that metacognition is particularly important in self-regulated learning. For secondary school students, the combination of metacognitive skills and intelligence predicted grade point average (GPA; Veenman et al., 2005). Direct relations between metacognition and problem solving have also been demonstrated. Formal education has been shown to influence how well children can reflect on and understand their own thought processes, particularly in explaining how they solve problems (Rogoff, 2003).

Metacognitive skills can be broad or more specific; for example, metamemory refers to understanding how one remembers information (Cole, Cole, & Lightfoot, 2005). Specific metacognitive skills are critical in reading, math, and for other tasks. Metacognition not only refers to what one knows about acquiring knowledge, but also how to effectively learn from one's mistakes (i.e., error management; Keith & Frese, 2005). What is known about metacognition and metacognitive abilities underlie the use of strategy instruction directed at improving educational outcome. Metacognitive intervention procedures include but are not limited to self-instructional strategy training, strategy instruction, cognitive modeling, self-monitoring, and self-evaluation (Mateer, 1999; Mateer, Kerns, & Eso, 1996). Metacognitive intervention programs commonly involve teaching of systematic problem-solving processes as well as monitoring and regulating of behavior via self-talk. These intervention strategies can incorporate behavioral contingencies (e.g., extrinsic rewards). Strategy instruction and metacognitive research have been done in the area of reading and suggest that good readers identify critical information in text, monitor their comprehension of text, and utilize strategies to aid in comprehension. In the past 5 years, additional research has examined the relation between metacognitive skills and social domains, including risky behavior (e.g., Jaccard, Dodge, & Guilamo-Ramos, 2005).

## REFERENCES

Cole, M., Cole, S. R., & Lightfoot, C. (2005). *The development of children* (5th ed). New York: Worth.

Flavell, J. H. (1976). Metacognitive aspects of problem-solving. In L. B. Resnick (Ed.), *The nature of intelligence* (pp. 231–235). Hillsdale, NJ: Erlbaum.

Flavell, J. H. (1979). Metacognition and cognitive monitoring: A new area of cognitive development inquiry. *American Psychologist, 34,* 906–911.

Glaser, R. (1990). The reemergence of learning theory within instructional research. *American Psychologist, 45,* 29–39.

Jaccard, J., Dodge, T., & Guilamo-Ramos, V. (2005). Metacognition, risk behavior, and risk outcomes: The role of perceived intelligence and perceived knowledge. *Health Psychology, 24,* 161–170.

Keith, N., & Frese, M. (2005). Self-regulation in error management training: Emotion control and metacognition as mediators of performance effects. *Journal of Applied Psychology, 90,* 677–691.

Mateer, C. A. (1999). The rehabilitation of executive disorders. In D. T. Stuss, G. Winocur, & I. H. Robertson (Eds.), *Cognitive rehabilitation* (pp. 314–322). Cambridge, UK: Cambridge University Press.

Mateer, C. A., Kerns, K. A., & Eso, K. L. (1996). Management of attention and memory disorders following traumatic brain injury. *Journal of Learning Disabilities, 29,* 618–632.

Rogoff, B. (2003). *The cultural nature of human development.* Oxford: Oxford University Press.

Schunk, D. H., & Zimmerman, B. J. (1994). *Self-regulation of learning and performance: Issues and educational applications.* Hillsdale, NJ: Erlbaum.

Veenman, M. V., Kok, R., & Blote, A. W. (2005). The relation between intellectual and metacognitive skills in early adolescence. *Instructional Science, 33,* 193–211.

Wang, M. C., Haertel, G. D., & Walberg, H. J. (1993). Toward a knowledge base for school learning. *Review of Educational Research, 63,* 249–294.

CYNTHIA A. RICCIO
*Texas A&M University*

COGNITIVE STRATEGIES
SELF-MANAGEMENT

# MEXICO, SPECIAL EDUCATION IN

The educational system in Mexico has been influenced by a number of international events and has undergone numerous reforms since the early 1980s. Mexico had experienced a long history of high dropout and repetition rates at the elementary school level, and realized the need to restructure the national educational system. In 1990, Mexico attended the World Summit for Infancy. It was at this summit that the objectives of the "Education for All before the year 2000" were approved. This conference resulted in the reaffirmation of the right of every person to an education independent of his or her particular differences. This right to education was interpreted as including children with special needs, but it did not yet mandate special education at the federal level.

Mexico realized that the educational needs of the different states were very diverse and that their educational needs were not being met by a highly centralized system. In 1992, the National Agreement for the Modernization of Basic Education was signed by the federal government, the 31 states of the republic, and the National Syndicate of the Workers for Education. This new education pact attempted to decentralize the national education system (SEN) and permitted each state to operate the basic education services according to the diversity of its population and the unique needs of the people of that state. This pact also created the necessity to make changes to the Constitution and in the educational legislation. In 1993, the General Education Law replaced the Federal Education Law, and modifications were made to the Third Article of the Constitution. The Third Article mandated that every individual had a right to an education, that elementary and secondary education were mandatory, and that public education would be provided at no cost. Article 41 in the new law stated that special education must be provided to individuals with temporary or permanent disabilities, as well as to gifted individuals.

Mexico attended the Education for All (EFA) Summit of Nine High-Population Countries in December of 1993. Other countries who participated in the conference were Bangladesh, Brazil, China, Egypt, India, Indonesia, Nigeria, and Pakistan. A variety of topics were discussed, including a paper by the United Nations Education, Scientific and

Cultural Organization (UNESCO) on education and society. The nine countries agreed to work in collaboration on a distance education initiative, both to enhance training of teachers and other personnel and to better reach marginalized groups.

The Unified Norms for the Equal Opportunity for Handicapped Persons were approved in 1994. This declaration mandated that the educational programs for disabled persons should be developed to meet individual unique needs and integrated with the regular educational system.

Changes in educational legislation initiated changes in the provision of special education services as well. Special education in Mexico has become an integral part of the regular education program and is no longer a separate, segregated service as it had been in previous years. The current theoretical framework for the provision of special education services is to integrate the disabled child with nonhandicapped peers in order to help the child become an independent and productive individual in society. This model is based upon a systems perspective and requires that a multidisciplinary group of professionals work with the child, the teacher, other school staff, and the family (SEP/DEE, 1994).

A variety of types of special education services are available to disabled children, depending upon their individual needs and/or availability of services in the schools. There are active efforts to find disabled children who may be at home and not enrolled in school. In some cities, staff members go from house to house interviewing parents and informing them of the availability of special education and rehabilitation services. Families in rural parts of the country may not receive this type of communication, however, and are often unaware of services available to them.

Special education services are also provided by the psychopedagogical centers that assist students who are having academic difficulties in regular education if the school does not have support services. In this situation, children attend the centers two to three sessions per week in groups of five students. These centers are staffed with a psychologist, regular classroom teachers, a language therapist, a social worker, and a physician. These centers function independently of the public schools (Fletcher et al., 1995).

Mexico also has special education schools that provide services for students who are unable to be integrated with regular peers, and who usually have more serious disabilities such as mental retardation. In 1995, there were 2,158 such schools in the country (Comisión Nacional de Acción en Favor de la Infancia, 1995). Although these schools are still available, the Program for Educational Modernization emphasizes the need to integrate children with special needs rather than segregate them from general education, and thus such schools are used less frequently than in previous years.

In an effort to combat the high incidence of failure and retention of children in first grade, general education adopted the Integrated Groups model of intervention in 1970. The Integrated Groups model constituted Mexico's first attempt at integrating disabled students into the general education program. The main objective of this model was to ensure that all children remained in school through sixth grade. Under this model, a child who failed first grade would be placed in a self-contained special classroom for 1 or 2 years, and then reintegrated into the general classroom when the basic skills were mastered. The Integrated Groups model was followed until 1994 when the Program for Educational Modernization called for a change to a model that would be a complementary service to general education instead of segregating children.

Special education services are provided in the school setting through the Complementary Services for Integration program, which provides support services to disabled children who are being educated in the regular education setting. The principal group in charge of organizing and monitoring the process of integrating disabled children into the regular school program is the Unit of Support Services to Regular Education (USAER). This unit covers two to six schools, depending upon the number of students and schools needing services. Each USAER unit is coordinated by a director and also includes 10 special education teachers, a secretary, and a technical support team. The support team consists of a social worker, a language teacher, and a psychologist. In certain cases, other staff who specialize in mental deficiencies, the blind, physical disabilities, and so on are available to serve students with special educational needs. The director of the USAER is housed at one of the schools it serves, and each school has a special classroom called a support classroom. The children remain in their regular classroom for most of the day, while the general classroom teacher and special education teacher decide which children will receive services in the support classroom and for how long.

The principal functions of the special education teachers in the elementary schools are to serve the disabled students who have been integrated into the regular classroom, students who are repeating a grade, and students who demonstrate considerable delays when compared to their peers. The special education teachers also work with the regular students, school personnel, and parents working toward promoting the understanding and acceptance of the integrated disabled student.

Since 1992, Mexico has recognized a variety of handicapping conditions that require special education intervention and services, which include mental deficiency, visual deficiency, motor impairments, auditory and language delays, learning difficulties, conduct or behavior problems, and autism. Although separate areas of disabilities are recognized, there are no specific criteria for diagnosis or for qualifying for special education services. Under Article 41 of the Mexican General Law of Education, students are identified as needing special education services when they exhibit difficulties relative to their peers when learning grade-level content, and require modifications to the regular curriculum to succeed (Dirección General de Educación Especial, 1994). The point of view of Mexican educators is to assume that the child's difficulties are not within the child, but that they are more likely due to developmental delays based on a Piagetian theoretical framework or inadequate teaching approaches (Fletcher et al., 1995). As a result of this position, intervention efforts are focused more on providing appropriate services than labeling the child.

In 1996, Mexico reported a total of 2,121,365 disabled school-aged children. The state of Mexico, particularly the federal district, reported the highest number of disabled children. The state of Southern Baja California reported the lowest. The disability most often diagnosed was "discapacidad" or general disability including learning disabilities. The records indicate that there were 46,000 children in Mexico identified with autism, and 126,326 children identified as mentally deficient (DIF, 1996).

The identification of the disabled child in Mexico follows the procedures set forth by the General Direction of Special Education. The process begins with a referral made by the general classroom teacher regarding the students who exhibit difficulties in reading, writing, and/or math calculation. The Test of School Knowledge is then administered to assess reading, comprehension, writing, and math calculation. This test will serve as a screen to detect the children who require further assessment. Such further assessment includes administration of the Monterrey Test, which is a more comprehensive test to assess the same areas (Dirección General de Educación Especial, 1984). Mexico has also adapted some of the assessment instruments that are used in the United States, such as the Wechsler Intelligence Scale for Children–Revised Mexican version (WISC-RM), the WISC-R in Spanish, the Kaufman Assessment Battery for Children (KABC) in Spanish, and the System of Multicultural Pluralistic Assessment (SOMPA). To assess psychological functioning, Mexican practitioners sometimes use the Bender-Gestalt Visual Motor Test and the Draw a Person Test.

The lack of trained special education teachers continues to be a critical issue in Mexico. The government sponsors teacher-training institutions called specialized normal schools that train teachers to work with special-needs children. As of 1995, there were 21 states throughout Mexico that have such schools to prepare teachers in the areas of learning disabilities, hearing and language impairment, and mental retardation. Only a few of the state schools prepare teachers in the areas of behavior disorders, visually impaired or blind, or neuromuscular disorders.

Although the special educational system in Mexico has undergone numerous reforms in recent years, there still remain areas of concern. Although Spanish is the native language in

Mexico, there are 56 ethnic groups dispersed throughout the country. Cultural and economic conditions can vary, in some cases significantly, from one state to the other. Even with all of the aforementioned legislation, the educational programs are directly affected by this diversity, which can even prevent the provision of special education services.

The legislative educational reform in Mexico is clearly in place. However, there is still a large discrepancy between the letter of the law and what is actually put into practice. According to a survey of special education administrators from 20 Latin American countries, including Mexico, some of the major difficulties in implementing legislation into practice include a lack of financial resources, resistance to change, lack of coordination between general and special education, and lack of trained personnel who can formulate and implement curricular adaptations (Ministerio de Educación, 1996). Strong resistance to change also exists among some educators. Some general education personnel are opposed to the integration of disabled students in their classrooms, and some special education teachers become overprotective of the disabled students and also do not support integration. Even though the current emphasis for special education is to integrate disabled students with nondisabled peers, some parents still prefer to send their children to special education schools.

In order for any of the special education services to be provided, the school must have physical space available and have enough students who require the services to form a group to be served, or else services will not be provided. Special education services to integrate disabled children are usually not available in rural areas. The quality of the program, services, and facilities vary widely from state to state, and even from school to school within the same city. Very few schools have ramps and other wheelchair-accessible facilities.

Another area of concern is that while it is estimated that 10 percent of the school-aged children in Mexico are in need of special education services, only about 1 percent are actually served (Fletcher et al., 1995). There are still many parents who are unaware that services are available. Some parents are unable to transport their child to the school to receive services, as transportation is not a service provided by the schools.

In the instances where the provisions mandated by law are not followed, the issues have not yet been challenged in the legal system. However, parents of disabled children are beginning to have a voice through advocacy organizations such as the *Asociación de Padres* (Parent Association), which has now gained national status.

In keeping pace with worldwide trends, special education in Mexico is no longer a separate, segregated program, but rather a complementary support service to the general education program. Together, the primary objective is to help disabled students become independent, productive members of society.

## REFERENCES

Cieloha, C. (1996, April). *Special education in the context of national development: The case of Mexico.* Paper presented at the Annual Meeting of the American Educational Research Association, San Francisco, CA.

Comisión Nacional de Acción en Favor de la Infancia. (1995). *Programa nacional de acción en favor de la infancia 1995–2000.* Mexico: Comisión Nacional de Acción en Favor de la Infancia 1995–2000.

Dirección General de Educación Especial. (1994). *Los grupos integrados.* Mexico City, Mexico: SEP.

Fletcher, T., & Kaufman de Lopez, C. (1995). A Mexican perspective on learning disabilities. *Journal of Learning Disabilities, 28*(9), 530–534.

Guajardo Ramos, E. (1996, April). *Hacia una educación básica en México para la diversidad, a finales del siglo XX y principios del XXI.* U.S./Mexico Symposium on Disabilities at the University of Arizona, Tucson, Arizona.

Ministerio de Educación. (1996). *Informe sobre la situación de la región de américa latina y el caribe en relación con la educación especial y la integración de alumnos con necesidades educativas especiales en la escuela regular.* República de Chile: Ministerio de Educación.

National Conference. (1997). *Atención educativa a menores con necesidades educativas especiales: Equidad para la diversidad.* Huatulco, Mexico.

National Coordinating Commission (Comisión Nacional Coordinadora CONVIVE). (1996). *Informe nacional de actividades del programa nacional para el bienestar y la incorporación al desarrollo de las personas con discapacidad.* Mexico: Author.

Secretaría de Educación de Nuevo León. (1997). *Dirección de estadística y control escolar.* Mexico: Author.

Secretaría de Educación Pública (SEP). (1993). *Ley general de educación* (General Education Law). Mexico: Author.

Secretaría de Educación Pública (SEP)-Dirección de Educación Especial (DEE). (1994a). Cuadernos de integración educativa (workbooks on educational integration), #2. *Artículo 41 comentado de la ley general de educación.* Mexico: SEP.

Secretaría de Educación Pública (SEP)-Dirección de Educación Especial (DEE). (1994b). Cuadernos de integración educativa (workbooks on educational integration), #4. Unidad de servicios de apoyo a la educación regular (USAER). Mexico: SEP.

Sistema Nacional para el Desarrollo Integral de la Familia. (DIF). *Menores con discapacidad por entidad federativa de residencia habitual segun tipo de discapacidad.* Published data from the Sistema Nacional para el Desarrollo Integral de la Familia (DIF). Mexico: Author.

Viera Petit-Jean, A. (1994). *La cultura, factor decisivo para la integración del discapacitado.* Monterrey, N.L. Mexico.

Gustavo Abelardo Arredondo
*Monterrey, Mexico*

Kim Ryan-Arredondo
*Texas A&M University*

# MEYERS, C. EDWARD (1912–    )

C. Edward Meyers, born in Chicago, has been a consistent, longstanding contributor to special education and the psychology of exceptional children. He earned his BS in education at the University of Illinois in 1937 and his MA in educational psychology in 1939 also from the University of Illinois. His formal education was completed with the awarding of the PhD in educational psychology by the University of Iowa. Myers also earned the distinction of Professor Emeritus at the University of Southern California in the division of educational psychology, which he formerly chaired, and has served as a research psychologist at the University of California, Los Angeles, Mental Retardation Research Center. He has held many positions in areas related to special education, including service delivery (e.g., psychologist, State Hospital of Iowa, 1941–1944; psychologist, University of Denver Clinic, 1942–1945) and in academic research (mostly in various positions at the University of Southern California).

For 10 years Meyers was editor of the *Monographs of the American Association on Mental Deficiency* (1972–1982). He has served on the editorial boards of most major journals in mental retardation at some time in his career. His academic, scholarly awards are numerous and include the Education Award of the American Association of Mental Deficiency (1977), the Distinguished Service Award of the Division of School Psychology of the American Psychiatric Association (1982), and special citations for research from Phi Delta Kappa in 1965 and 1974.

Meyers is best known and respected for his research in the field of mental retardation. Over his productive career (Meyers directed over 100 doctoral dissertations and has more than 100 journal publications to his credit), Meyers focused on the impact of family and related environmental factors on the cognitive and emotional development of children, particularly those with general cognitive impairments (Meyers et al., 1964; Yoshida & Meyers, 1975). His extensive investigation of the outcomes for children affected by the California "decertification" experience was one of the largest studies of mainstreaming ever conducted (Meyers, MacMillan, & Yoshida, 1978, 1980). Myers continued his research into the lives of those with severe impairments with his more recent research looking at variables related to parental involvement with the schooling of severely impaired students and the predominant places of residence of persons with mental retardation and developmental disabilities (Meyers, 1985; Meyers & Blacher, 1987).

## REFERENCES

Meyers, C. E. (1985). Place of residence by age, ethnicity, and level of retardation of the mentally retarded/developmentally disabled population of California. *American Journal of Mental Deficiency, 90*(3), 266–270.

Meyers, C. E., & Blacher, J. (1987). Parents' perceptions of schooling for severely handicapped children: Home and family variables. *Exceptional Children, 53*(5), 441–449.

Meyers, C. E., Dingham, H. F., Orpet, R. E., Sitkei, E. G., & Watts, C. A. (1964). Four ability factor hypotheses at three preliterate levels in normal and retarded children. *Monographs of the Society for Research in Child Development, 29*(No. 56).

Meyers, C. E., MacMillan, D. L., & Yoshida, R. K. (1978). Validity of school psychologists' work in the light of the California decertification experience. *Journal of School Psychology, 16*, 3–13.

Meyers, C. E., MacMillan, D. L., & Yoshida, R. K. (1980). Regular class education of EMR students: From efficacy to mainstreaming. In J. Gottlieb (Ed.), *Perspectives on handicapping conditions*. Baltimore: University Park Press.

Yoshida, R. K., & Meyers, C. E. (1975). Effects of labeling as EMR on teachers' expectancies for change in a student's performance. *Journal of School Psychology, 67*, 521–527.

CECIL R. REYNOLDS
*Texas A&M University*
First edition

TAMARA J. MARTIN
*The University of Texas of the
Permian Basin*
Second edition

**ADAPTIVE BEHAVIOR SCALE
MAINSTREAMING
MENTAL RETARDATION**

# MICROCEPHALY

Microcephaly, a congenital anomaly, is characterized by an abnormally small head in relationship to the rest of the body and by an underdeveloped brain resulting in some degree of mental retardation. The condition is described by Udang and Swallow (1983) as one in which the cranium of the affected individual is less than two standard deviations below the average circumference size for age, sex, race, and period of gestation. The primary or inherited form of microcephaly is transmitted by a single recessive gene, while the secondary form is the result of environmental factors (Gerald, 1982; Robinson & Robinson, 1965; Telford & Sawrey, 1977; Udang & Swallow, 1983). Factors associated with microcephaly include maternal infections; trauma, especially during the third trimester of pregnancy or in early infancy; anoxia at birth; massive irradiation or indiscriminate use of X-ray; and chemical agents.

Individuals who have the primary form of the disorder are generally more seriously affected (Robinson & Robinson, 1965). In addition to the small, conical-shaped skull, the scalp may be loose and wrinkled. The forehead generally is narrow and receding; the back of the skull is flattened; the facial features can be normal, although frequently the

lower jaw recedes. The stature of the affected individual is very small with a curved spine and stooping posture, flexed knees, and disproportionately long arms and legs. Such individuals almost always are severely retarded and may not develop speech or primary self-help skills.

Individuals with the secondary form of microcephaly are not as severely affected. Although the skull is small, other symptoms are less visible or may not be present at all. The degree of mental retardation is less severe. Occasionally such individuals may be found in day classes for the moderately retarded (Dunn, 1973). There is no treatment for microcephaly. Medical care is primarily supportive and educational. A full range of custodial and educational services is needed (Udang & Swallow, 1983).

## REFERENCES

Dunn, L. M. (1973). Children with moderate, severe and general learning disabilities. In L. M. Dunn (Ed.), *Exceptional children in the schools: Special education transition* (pp. 65–123). New York: Holt, Rinehart, & Winston.

Gerald, P. (1982). Chromosomes and their disorders. In J. Wyngaarden & L. Smith (Eds.), *Cecil 16th edition textbook of medicine* (pp. 17–22). Philadelphia: Saunders.

Robinson, H., & Robinson, N. (1965). *The mentally retarded child: A psychological approach.* New York: McGraw-Hill.

Telford, C., & Sawrey, J. (1977). *The exceptional individual.* Englewood Cliffs, NJ: Prentice Hall.

Udang, L., & Swallow, H. (Eds.). (1983). *Mosby's medical and nursing dictionary.* St. Louis, MO: Mosby.

SALLY E. PISARCHICK
*Cuyahoga Special Education
Service Center*

**CHROMOSOMES, HUMAN ANOMALIES, AND
   CYTOGENETIC ABNORMALITIES
CONGENITAL DISORDERS
PHYSICAL ANOMALIES**

# MICROTRAINING

Microtraining is a practice teaching method used in a majority of teacher education programs. Teacher trainees involved in microtraining typically prepare a brief lesson, present the lesson to a small group of students, observe a videotape of the lesson, modify the lesson based on their own critique or the critique of a supervisor and reteach the lesson. As is apparent from these procedures, microtraining emphasizes the use of objective feedback in improving the teacher's future performance. The term microtraining is used because the teacher trainee is involved in a simulated teaching experience that minimizes the complexities of actual teaching.

Specifically, only a few students are involved in a brief and highly structured lesson (Gregory, 1972).

Microtraining was introduced in the Secondary Teacher Education Program at Stanford University in the early 1960s. Keith Acheson, then a graduate student at Stanford, is frequently credited with its development as a preservice teacher training method. Hundreds of research articles evaluating its effectiveness have been reported and over half of the teacher education programs in the United States have incorporated it as a required preservice clinical experience (Turney, Clift, Durkin, & Traill, 1973).

Allen and Ryan (1969) conceptualized microtraining as including five essential elements. First, although microtraining is conducted in a laboratory setting, and both the students and teacher are aware that the instructional context is fabricated, real teaching and learning take place. Second, as mentioned earlier, the complexities of actual classroom instruction are reduced. From one to five students may be involved in the lesson; the lesson is limited to a single concept or skill; and the length of the lesson may be limited from 5 to 20 minutes. Third, microtraining targets specific instructional competencies. These may include the use of specific materials, teaching procedures, or motivational techniques. Fourth, instructional variables including time, students, feedback, and supervision are controlled to enhance the effectiveness of the practice exercise. Finally, feedback to the teacher is emphasized. In typical microtraining experiences, the teacher observes a videotape of the lesson immediately after the session. He or she, with the assistance of a supervisor, critiques the lesson and identifies objectives for the next microlesson.

Beyond these basic elements, there are a number of variations of the basic microtraining methodology. Jensen (1974) has suggested 24 basic alterations. These result from various combinations of feedback options (e.g., videotapes, audiotapes, peers, critiquer), critique options (e.g., others, self), and reteach options (e.g., teach only, systematic reteach, trials-to-criterion). In addition to these options, microtraining may be conducted with peers versus actual pupils, and with various combinations of feedback modes (e.g., peers using videotape, critiquer using audiotapes, etc.). It is currently being used in culture-specific counseling (Grant, 1991).

## REFERENCES

Allen, D. W., & Ryan, K. A. (1969). *Microteaching.* Cambridge, MA: Addison-Wesley.

Grant, C. A. (1991). *Toward education that is multicultural.* Wisconsin: National Association for Multicultural Education.

Gregory, T. B. (1972). *Encounters with teaching: A microteaching manual.* Englewood Cliffs, NJ: Prentice Hall.

Jensen, R. N. (1974). *Microteaching: Planning and implementing a competency-based training program.* Springfield, IL: Charles Thomas.

Turney, C., Clift, J. C., Durkin, M. J., & Traill, R. D. (1973). *Microteaching: Research theory and practice.* Sydney, Australia: Sydney University Press.

PATRICK J. SCHLOSS
*Pennsylvania State University*

**TEACHER EFFECTIVENESS**
**TEACHING STRATEGIES**

# MIGRANT INDIVIDUALS WITH DISABILITIES

Migratory farmworkers are those individuals who must move their home bases and travel to other locations, usually hundreds of miles away, in search of seasonal farmwork. This mass movement of migratory farmworkers takes place every year during periods that coincide with the planting and/or harvesting of agricultural products; it is commonly referred to as the migrant stream.

There are three major identifiable migrant streams within three broad geographical areas. One stream is found within California, Oregon, and Washington. The other stream begins in the Lower Rio Grande Valley of Texas and farms out into the Midwest, Rocky Mountains, and Red River Valley. The third major stream originates in southern Florida and moves northward along the Atlantic coast as far as New York State (Stoops-King, 1980).

Migrant farmworker families are usually comprised of low socioeconomic ethnic minorities that include Mexicans, Mexican-Americans, Blacks, Native Americans, Indians, and Central and South Americans. The heaviest concentrations of migratory farmworker children reside in the states of Texas, California, Washington, Arizona, Colorado, Florida, and New Mexico (Goldfarb, 1981).

The nature of seasonal migratory labor causes most of the migrant farmworkers to experience considerable deprivation in the basic human needs of nutrition, health, housing, and education. The typical migrant family lives below the poverty level, experiences high infant mortalities, is exposed to the hazards of chemical insecticides and pesticides, and has a low educational level. Children of migrant workers are at high risk for abuse (Larson, Doris, & Alvarez, 1990), mental health disorders such as anxiety (Kupersmidt & Martin, 1997), poor health and nutrition (Leon, 1996), and are rising in numbers of those with disabilities (Interstate Migrant Education Council, 1992). The average life span of a migrant farmworker is thought to be 47 years (Thedinger, 1982). The critical needs of migrant children prompted Congress to amend Title I of the Elementary and Secondary Education Act of 1965 (currently identified as Chapter I of the Consolidated and Improvement Act of 1981) to address the educational and health needs of these children (U.S. Government Accounting Office, 1983).

The federally funded Migrant Education Program was

initiated on the premise that migrant children suffer educational interruptions when forced to move into different school districts. This program provides federal aid for supplementary instructional services, medical and health services, and parent training services provided that the children meet the following specified criteria:

> migratory means a child whose parent or guardian is a migratory agricultural worker or a migratory fisher; and who has moved within the past 12 months from one school district to another to enable the child, the child's guardian or a member of the immediate family to obtain temporary or seasonal employment in an agricultural or fishing activity.

Over 711,000 migratory children have been counted as eligible in approximately 3,100 projects (Interstate Migrant Education Council, 1992; U.S. Government Accounting Office, 1983). In addition, early childhood education and nutrition intervention efforts are available through selected programs in several states.

Characteristically, migrant children are mobile within the educational systems and, as such, pose unique information management concerns. One of the features of the federal migrant education program is an automated telecommunication system, the Migrant Student Record Transfer System (MSRTS), which transmits data regarding the children. This system, headquartered in Little Rock, Arkansas, enables participating school districts to obtain and forward via computer pertinent educational, medical, and demographic information. This system makes it possible to notify a receiving school that a certain migrant student was enrolled in a special education program in the sending school.

While states generally do not have accurate data on numbers of migrant pupils with disabilities, migrant children tend to be underrepresented in special education (Interstate Migrant Education Council, 1992; U.S. Government Accounting Office, 1981). With the national average of 10 to 12 percent of school-aged children identified as disabled, surveys indicate that less than 6 percent of the migrant pupils are identified as disabled. These children are underrepresented despite the presence of a variety of conditions that place this population at risk.

The reasons for this potential underrepresentation of migrant pupils are varied and complex. Many migrant parents have limited information regarding the nature of various handicapping conditions and the variety of special education services that are potentially available. They may view their child's learning or behavior problems as normal adjustment problems or may be completely unaware that the child is experiencing serious learning problems. In addition, as with many parents, they may deny the presence of a problem because of their own perceived guilt that they may have done something that caused the child's problem. These parents may also deny the existence of a handicapping condition if they think that the child will have to be placed in a special residential facility away from the family.

The family also may view their child's participation in an elaborate educational system requiring parental involvement as economically disruptive. Most migrants are employed at daily rates and are not reimbursed for justifiable absences. Typically, all of the adult members in the family are members of the labor crew.

A critical feature of legislation pertaining to the education of pupils with disabilities is that the child's parent or guardian is to be informed about the educational rights and services available. Unfortunately, few migrant parents evidence the knowledge and sophistication required to seek appropriate services for their disabled children. Migrant and special education programs rarely coordinate efforts to guarantee that migrant parents are adequately informed to advocate for the most appropriate interventions for their children with disabilities.

Because of the cultural, economic, and linguistic backgrounds of many migrant pupils, teachers may be hesitant to refer these children for learning or behavioral problems. Teachers may think that the child's severe academic difficulties are due to poverty or the fact that the child's primary language is not English. As a result, teachers may not refer these pupils for special education services. Teachers or administrators may also believe that the child will not remain enrolled long enough to warrant the initiation of costly referral and assessment procedures.

With legislation and litigation, there has been increased concern for the appropriateness of assessment procedures for determining special education eligibility of minority pupils. Since many migrant youngsters are from ethnic minorities, there is some reluctance on the part of school administrators and diagnostic staff to assess and place these children in special education instructional settings.

Providing special education and related services to pupils with disabilities is also an expensive activity. The majority of the costs for special education are covered primarily by local school district and state revenues. Migrant pupils are generally enrolled in small rural school districts with a limited tax base. As a consequence, these schools may have limited financial resources for special education personnel, space, supplies, and other required services for migrant pupils with disabilities. While school districts are required to provide the services the child needs, not merely the services already available in the schools, the quality and range of special education services are, in fact, determined by the financial resources of the schools. Unfortunately, large numbers of migrant youngsters with disabilities may not be served because of the lack of funds that are available within the schools they attend.

Finally, children of migrant workers may not receive special education services because of established bureaucratic policies. For example, migrant pupils with disabilities may receive services for educationally disadvantaged pupils or for limited English-speaking youngsters and as a result of school policy or practices not be eligible for any additional compensatory training programs such as special education. In addition, while there have been efforts such as the MSRTS to more effectively monitor these migrant youngsters as they move from district to district, surveys indicate that when migrant children with disabilities move, only 80 percent of these pupils are provided special education services by receiving schools (U.S. Government Accounting Office, 1981).

Addressing this issue of underrepresentation of migrant youngsters with disabilities in special education will require better informed parents, teachers, and assessment personnel, and closer coordination and monitoring of services by local school districts and state and federal agencies. Reflecting on the history of special education, complex problems such as those associated with migrant children with disabilities may be resolved only through the political and advocacy activities of migrant farmworker organizations.

## REFERENCES

Goldfarb, R. L. (1981). *A caste of despair.* Ames: Iowa State University Press.

Interstate Migrant Education Council. (1992). *Special education: Migrant education policy brief.* Washington, DC: Author.

Kupersmidt, J. B., & Martin, S. L. (1997). Mental health problems of children of migrant and seasonal farm workers: A pilot study. *Journal of the American Academy of Child & Adolescent Psychiatry, 36*(2), 224–232.

Larson, O. W., Doris, J., & Alvarez, W. F. (1990). Migrants and maltreatment: Comparative evidence from central register data. *Child Abuse and Neglect, 14*(3), 375–385.

Leon, E. (1996). *Challenges and solutions for educating migrant students.* (ERIC Clearinghouse No: RC020477)

Stoops-King, J. (1980). *Migrant education: Teaching the wandering ones.* Bloomington, IN: Educational Foundation.

Thedinger, B. (1982, September 14). Testimony in citing U.S. Public Health Service. Subcommittee on Labor Standards of the Committee on Education and Labor, House of Representatives, 97th Congress, HR 7102.

U.S. Government Accounting Office. (1981, September 30). *Disparities still exist in who gets special education.* Report to Subcommittee on Select Education, Committee on Education and Labor, House of Representatives.

U.S. Government Accounting Office. (1983, May). *Analysis of migration characteristics of children served under the migrant education program.* Report to the Congress of the United States.

DIEGO GALLEGOS
*Texas A&M University*

DOUGLAS J. PALMER
*Texas A&M University*

**BILINGUAL SPECIAL EDUCATION**
**CULTURAL BIAS IN TESTS**

## MILD DISABILITIES, TEST-TAKING SKILLS AND

Test-taking skills, or test-wiseness, has been defined by Millman, Bishop, and Ebel (1965) as "a subject's capacity to utilize the characteristics and formats of the test and/or the test-taking situation to receive a high score" (p. 707). Additionally, they state test-wiseness to be "logically independent of the knowledge of the subject matter for which the items are supposedly measured" (p. 707). Test-taking skills can therefore be seen as a set of abilities that can be applied to a variety of tests regardless of their content.

Currently, most students with mild disabilities spend the largest portion of the school day in general education classrooms (Friend & McNutt, 1984; Heller, 1981). Therefore, they are expected to cope with the same academic demands as students without disabilities. A frequent and important demand in the mainstream class is taking teacher-made, objective (e.g., true-false, multiple-choice, matching) tests. Indeed, academic success is largely measured by how well students perform on these tests (Cuthbertson, 1979; Schumaker & Deshler, 1983). For example, Cuthbertson found that 60 percent of a student's grade depends solely on test scores. Apart from prior knowledge and amount of studying, a source of variance affecting test scores is the test-taking skills or test-wiseness of the individual taking the test.

Unfortunately, evidence exists that, when compared as a group with nondisabled peers, mildly disabled students lack test-wiseness (Forness & Duorak, 1982; Keogh, 1971; Scruggs, Bennion, & Lifson, 1985). Some general behaviors considered characteristic of the mildly handicapped that may account for poor test-taking ability include distractibility, impulsivity, and anxiety. Specific behaviors noted by researchers include attending to the wrong part of test directions, making an answer choice before reading all available choices, not reading questions carefully, and not using cues when guessing.

While most related research has investigated the test-taking characteristics of students with disabilities, little research exists on the effectiveness of teaching these students skills or strategies for taking tests. In fact, most available studies have not used subjects with disabilities. Hughes (1985) analyzed test-taking instruction research and noted the most frequently taught skills used in these studies. They are, in order of frequency, efficient use of time, reading directions thoroughly, skipping items when unsure, marking answers appropriately, using available cues when guessing (e.g., choosing the longest options, avoiding absolute words such as always and never), reviewing work, and reading all answer options in a multiple choice question before marking an answer. Test-taking skills can be assessed for individual students with the School Motivation and Learning Strategies Inventory (Stroud & Reynolds, 2006) within the 8 years to 19 years range.

## REFERENCES

Carman, R. A., & Adams, W. R. (1972). *Study skills: A student's guide for survival.* New York: Wiley.

Cuthbertson, E. B. (1979). *An analysis of secondary testing and grading procedures.* Unpublished master's thesis, University of Kansas, Lawrence.

Forness, S. R., & Duorak, R. (1982). Effects of test time limits on achievement scores of behaviorally disordered adolescents. *Behavioral Disorders, 7*(4), 207–212.

Friend, M., & McNutt, G. (1984). Resource room programs: Where are we now? *Exceptional Children, 51*(2), 150–155.

Heller, H. W. (1981). Secondary education for handicapped students: In search of a solution. *Exceptional Children, 47,* 582–583.

Hughes, C. (1985). *A test-taking strategy for emotionally handicapped and learning disabled adolescents.* Unpublished doctoral dissertation, University of Florida, Gainesville.

Hughes, C., Schumaker, J. B., & Deshler, D. D. (in press). *The test-taking strategy.* Lawrence, KS: EXCEL.

Keogh, B. (1971). Hyperactivity and learning disorders: Review and research paradigm. *Developmental Psychology, 10,* 590–600.

Millman, J., Bishop, C. H., & Ebel, R. (1965). An analysis of test-wiseness. *Educational & Psychological Measurement, 25,* 707–726.

Schumaker, J. B., & Deshler, D. D. (1983). *Setting demand variables: A major factor in program planning for the LD adolescent.* Lawrence: University of Kansas, Institute for Research in Learning Disabilities.

Scruggs, T. E., Bennion, K., & Lifson, S. (1985). Learning disabled students' spontaneous use of test-taking skills on reading achievement tests. *Learning Disabilities Quarterly, 8*(3), 205–210.

Stroud, K., & Reynolds, C. R. (2006). *School motivation and learning strategies inventory.* Los Angeles: Western Psychological Services.

CHARLES A. HUGHES
*Pennsylvania State University*

**MEASUREMENT**

**TEST ANXIETY**

# MILLER ASSESSMENT FOR PRESCHOOLERS

The Miller Assessment for Preschoolers (MAP; Miller, 1982) is a comprehensive measure of developmental abilities for children ages 2 years 9 months to 5 years 8 months. The MAP identifies children who show moderate preacademic problems that may affect development. The protocols are clearly labeled for each age group and indicate the child's level of development based on a color-coded system. Twenty-seven performance items create the core of the MAP. The performance indexes are Sensory and Motor, Coordination, Verbal and Nonverbal, Foundations and Coordination, and Complex Abilities. Administration time is approximately 30 minutes. All twenty-seven performance items must be administered to calculate the total MAP score.

Normative data were collected using five different editions of the MAP. The final edition was normed on 1,200 preschoolers. The MAP adequately differentiates children in the lowest 25 percent of abilities but does not adequately identify those in the upper 75 percent. Interrater reliability ranges from .84 to .99 for the performance indexes and is .98 for the total MAP score. Internal consistency reliability is .79. Construct validity was examined between the indexes and the MAP total score and ranges from .65 to .78.

The test materials are clearly organized in marked containers for efficient administration. The examiner's administration binder is also clearly marked with chapter tabs.

## REFERENCES

Daniels, L. E. (1998). The Miller Assessment for Preschoolers: Construct validity and clinical use with children with disabilities. *American Journal of Occupational Therapy, 52,* 857–865.

Humphry, R., & King-Thomas, L. (1993). A response and some facts about the Miller Assessment for Preschoolers. *Occupational Therapy Journal of Research, 13,* 34–49.

Kirkpatrick, L. A., & Schouten, P. G. (1993). Questions and concerns about the Miller Assessment for Preschoolers: Reply. *Occupational Therapy Journal of Research, 13,* 50–61.

Miller, L. J. (1993). Questions and concerns about the Miller Assessment for Preschoolers: Comment. *Occupational Therapy Journal of Research, 13,* 29–33.

Mitchell, J. V., Jr. (Ed.). (1985). *The ninth mental measurements yearbook.* Lincoln, NE: Buros Institute of Mental Measurements.

Parush, S., Winokur, M., & Goldstand, S. (2002). Prediction of school performance using the Miller Assessment for Preschoolers (MAP): A validity study. *American Journal of Occupational Therapy, 56,* 547–555.

Parush, S., Winokur, M., & Goldstand, S. (2002). Long-term predictive validity of the Miller Assessment for Preschoolers. *Perceptual & Motor Skills, 94,* 921–926.

Schouten, P. G., & Kirkpatrick, L. A. (1993). Questions and concerns about the Miller Assessment for Preschoolers. *Occupational Therapy Journal of Research, 13,* 7–28.

RON DUMONT
*Fairleigh Dickinson University*

JOHN O. WILLIS
*Rivier College*

# MILLON CLINICAL MULTIAXIAL INVENTORY–III

Developed by a pioneer in personality assessment, the Millon Clinical Multiaxial Inventory–III (MCMI-III; Millon,

1997) is a 175-item, self-report personality inventory for use with adults 18 years of age or older. The MCMI has undergone two revisions since its inception in 1977; the most recent edition closely parallels the *Diagnostic and Statistical Manual–IV (DSM-IV)*. Given its connection to the current diagnostic system, the MCMI-III may be used in a variety of clinical settings to aid in the assessment and diagnosis of psychiatric disorders.

The test consists of 175 true and false statements worded on the eighth grade reading level that are organized into 24 scales grouped into four categories: Clinical Personality Patterns (14 scales), Severe Personality Pathology (3 scales), Clinical Syndromes (7 scales), and Severe Clinical Syndromes (3 scales). The remaining 4 scales assess atypical response styles and other test-taking behaviors. There is a Validity Scale, and 3 scales are grouped into Modifying Indices–Disclosure, Desirability, and Debasement. The manual provides detailed information about each scale.

The MACI (Millon Adolescent Clinical Inventory), developed with a sixth grade reading level, is the adolescent version of the test for use with children 13 to 19 years old. Given that there is some overlap with the Millon Clinical Multiaxial Inventory–III at ages 18 and 19, clinical judgment should be used to determine which measure is appropriate for an examinee in that age range.

The MCMI-III takes approximately 25 minutes for most respondents to complete. The items are printed in a test booklet and examinees record their responses on a separate sheet, filling in circles corresponding to true or false.

Unlike some of the most popular tests in this category (e.g., MMPI-2), the MCMI-III utilizes base rate transformation scores, which has to do with prevalence of disorders within psychiatric populations (rather than comparisons with a normal population). Obtained scores of 74 or less typically do not indicate the presence of a disorder, scores between 75 and 84 suggest the presence of personality problems and/or psychiatric symptoms, and scores 85 or above indicate the probability of an impairing pathology. The test can be hand scored, although it has been noted that hand scoring may be cumbersome and can take up to an hour to complete (Widiger, 2001). Scoring templates and computer software are available. The publisher also offers mail-in scoring options as well as interpretative software. The two kinds of interpretive reports available are the Profile Report, which provides information about the examinee's scores and profile, and a Narrative Report, which provides information about personality characteristics, symptoms, and possible implications for treatment.

The normative sample for the MCMI-III instrument consists of 998 males and females representing a wide variety of diagnoses. The group includes patients seen in independent practices, clinics, mental health centers, residential settings, and hospitals. Because the norms are based on clinical samples, the instrument is not appropriate for use with nonclinical populations. The standardization sample was primarily White (about 86 percent) and less than 10 percent of the standardization sample consisted of respondents 55 years or older.

The second edition of the MCMI-III manual includes the most current information about the measure's psychometric properties. The validity of the measure has been a source of debate (see Rogers, Salekin, & Sewell, 1999). The measure's ability to discriminate has been called into question, given that so many items overlap scales, yet Retzlaff (2000) notes solid positive and negative predictive power of the MCMI-III. Dyer (1997) asserts that MCMI-III has strong content validity when measured against *DSM-IV* criteria. The manual reports good test-retest reliability (.82 to .95) and includes extensive information about item selection, assignment to scales and analyses. Craig (1999a) commented that, "In general, the scale reliabilities have increased in stability with each edition of the test" (p. 396).

The MCMI is one of the most written about measures of personality. Its strengths are its brevity of administration, and associated with that, the relatively short number of items (when compared to similar instruments such as the MMPI-2). Furthermore, the test is founded on theory. Future research may demonstrate that it has utility in many settings, with diverse populations. It is expected that the "MCMI can be used on a routine basis in outpatient clinics, community agencies, mental health centers, college counseling programs, general and mental hospitals, independent and group practice offices, and in court" (*MCMI-III manual*, p. 5). Yet, these ambitious goals may be hampered by limitations including the expense of scoring tools and the possibility to over-pathologize nonclinical populations. Some authors note that caution should be taken even when using this measure in clinical settings (Boyle & Dean, 2000). The possibility of utilizing the MCMI-III in forensic settings is currently being explored (Dyer & McCann, 2000; Craig, 1999b). When used in conjunction with other psychological assessment measures, the MCMI-III may yield a more complete diagnostic impression that can aid in establishing goals for intervention and treatment.

## REFERENCES

Boyle, G. J., & Dean, L. (2000). Discriminant validity of the illness behavior questionnaire and Millon Clinical Multiaxial Inventory–III in a heterogeneous sample of psychiatric outpatients. *Journal of Clinical Psychology, 56,* 779–791.

Craig, R. J. (1999a). Overview and current status of the Millon Clinical Multiaxial Inventory. *Journal of Personality Assessment, 72,* 390–406.

Craig, R. J. (1999b). Testimony based on the Millon Clinical Multiaxial Inventory: Review, commentary, and guidelines. *Journal of Personality Assessment, 73,* 290–304.

Craig, R. J. (2003). Use of the Millon Clinical Multiaxial Inventory in the psychological assessment of domestic violence: A review. *Aggression & Violent Behavior, 8,* 235–244.

Dyer, F. J. (1997). Application of the Millon inventories in forensic psychology. In T. Millon (Ed.), *The Millon inventories: Clinical and personality assessment* (pp. 124–139). New York: Guilford.

Dyer, F. J., & McCann, J. T. (2000). The Millon Clinical Inventories, research critical of their forensic application and Daubert criteria. *Law & Human Behavior, 24,* 487–497.

Hynan, D. J. (2004). Unsupported gender differences on some personality disorder scales of the Millon Clinical Multiaxial Inventory–III. *Professional Psychology: Research & Practice, 35,* 105–110.

Millon, T. (1997). *The Millon Clinical Multiaxial Inventory–III manual* (2nd ed.). Minneapolis, MN: National Computer Systems.

Retzlaff, P. D. (2000). Comment on the validity of the MCMI-III. *Law and Human Behavior, 24,* 499–500.

Rogers, R., Salekin, R. T., & Sewell, K. W. (1999). Validation of the Millon Clinical Multiaxial Inventory for Axis II disorders: Does it meet the Daubert standard? *Law and Human Behavior, 23,* 425–443.

Widiger, T. A. (2001). Test review of the Millon Clinical Multiaxial Inventory–III. In B. S. Plake & J. C. Impara (Eds.), *The fourteenth mental measurements yearbook* (electronic version). Retrieved June 1, 2004, from http://www.unl.edu/buros

RON DUMONT
*Fairleigh Dickinson University*

JOHN O. WILLIS
*Rivier College*

## MILLS v. BOARD OF EDUCATION OF THE DISTRICT OF COLUMBIA (1972)

In 1972 a class action suit was brought against the District of Columbia Board of Education by the parents of 7 school-aged children with disabilities for failure to provide all such children with a publicly supported education. In December 1971 the court issued a stipulated agreement, an order that required that the plaintiffs be provided a publicly supported education; that the District of Columbia Board of Education provide a list of every school-aged child not receiving a publicly supported education; and that the Board of Education attempt to identify other children with disabilities not previously identified.

In January 1972 the U.S. District Court issued an order establishing the right of all children with disabilities to a publicly supported education. It indicated that the exclusion of children from public school without the provision of a prior hearing and review of placement procedures denied such children the rights of due process and equal protection of the law.

Only 3 years following the *Mills* case, the Education for All Handicapped Children Act of 1975 (PL 94-142) be-came federal law. This act sought to ensure children with disabilities access to a free, appropriate public education and improved educational results. This law was amended and renamed in 1990 as the Individuals with Disabilities Education Act (IDEA). The law has been reauthorized and amended several times since then, with the most recent reauthorization occurring in 2004. The focus of the amendments is directed at improving results for children with disabilities by promoting early identification and provision of services and by ensuring access to the general curriculum. The 2004 reauthorization also seeks to bring certain aspects of the IDEA into compliance with the requirements of the No Child Left Behind Act, which was passed in 2001.

*Mills* v. *Board of Education* has had a strong and lasting impact on how children with disabilities are educated today. Today, every state must ensure the provision of a free appropriate public education to all children with disabilities, and significant progress has been made in addressing many of the educational problems faced by children with disabilities that existed in 1972.

### REFERENCE

The Texas Comprehensive Analysis Process for Special Education Services. (1998). *Aiming high and targeting excellence.* Austin: Texas Education Agency.

JAMES BUTTON
*United States Department of Education*
First edition

DELORES J. HITTINGER
*The University of Texas of the Permian Basin*
Second edition

KIMBERLY F. APPLEQUIST
*University of Colorado at Colorado Springs*
Third edition

## MILWAUKEE PROJECT

The term Milwaukee Project is the popular title of a widely publicized program begun in the mid-1960s as one of many Great Society efforts to improve the intellectual development of low-achieving groups. It was headed by Rick Heber of the University of Wisconsin (UW), Madison, who was also director of the generously funded Waisman Institute in Madison. The Milwaukee Project was a small study with some 20 experimental subjects and 20 control subjects. It was not reported on by the investigators in any refereed scientific journals, yet its cost was some $14 million, mostly in federal funds, and its fame was international, since it claimed to have moved the IQs of its subject children from the dull-normal range of intelligence to the superior range of intelligence.

Enthusiasm, controversy, and scandal subsequently surrounded the history of the project. Its claimed success was hailed by famous psychologists and by the popular media. Later in the project, Heber, the principal investigator, was discharged from UW, Madison, and convicted and imprisoned for large-scale abuse of federal funding for private gain. Two of his colleagues were also convicted of violations of federal laws in connection with misuse of project funds. Almost 2 decades after the beginning of the project, the scientific world had not yet seen the long-promised final report. However, the project received uncritical acceptance in many college textbooks in psychology and education. For this reason, it is an important study to understand.

The first formal report of the Milwaukee Project appears to have been a short oral paper delivered at a conference in Warsaw (Heber & Garber, 1970). The sampling process for selection of children to be studied was later described as follows:

> We surveyed a residential area of the city of Milwaukee characterized by 1960 census data as having the lowest median family income, the greatest rate of dilapidated housing, and the greatest population density per living unit. Over a six-month period, all families residing in this area with a newborn infant, and at least one other child . . . , were selected for study. (Heber et al., 1972, p. 4)

The purpose was to identify families with a high probability of producing retarded offspring. According to reports, among 88 located families, 40 had maternal IQs of 80 or higher, and 48 were below 80.

Earlier work showed an association between child and mother retardation. The Milwaukee Project was designed to treat the whole family to improve the chances for normal child intelligence. The treatment was to consist of two components: (1) the infant, early childhood stimulation program and (2) a maternal rehabilitation program. "Intervention . . . began as soon as was feasible after birth (within 6 months)" (Garber, 1975, p. 289).

According to the experimenters, just 20 children were randomly assigned to the E group and 20 to the C group. Then tests were given frequently to both groups, but only the experimental children received the double treatment of child stimulation and maternal rehabilitation.

From the first reports, there were remarkable claims of treatment effects. A spectacular graphic was displayed: a series of IQ test results beginning at 12 months with scores every 3 to 6 months until the age of 6 years. Both groups, experimental and control, began at about 115 IQ. The control group plummeted to the 90s by 24 months and stayed low throughout the period. But the experimental group actually rose from its high beginning and stayed high. According to Heber et al. (1972):

> The mean IQ of the Experimental group at 66 months is 124 (s.d. = 8.6), compared to the Control group's mean IQ of 94 (s.d. = 10.7): a difference of thirty points. (pp. 48–50)

With such claimed results, the project was widely publicized in the popular press. The President's Commission on Mental Retardation wrote that the intelligence of the parent was indeed "a vital factor in the intelligence of children—mainly because of the environment that the parents create for the young child." And *Time* magazine, apparently taking its cue from the commission, stated flatly that such retardation was environmental in origin. On inquiry, a *Time* staffer explained that this had been proved by the Milwaukee Project (Page, 1972, p. 9). Nor was there more skepticism in the official publications of organized scientific psychology. A former American Psychological Association president described the project as "very exciting" (Trotter, 1976, p. 46).

Furthermore, the message was picked up by writers everywhere. As one scientist later noted:

> Who can forget the great days of the early 1970s when the first reports emerged. . . . The news spread beyond America to the whole English-speaking world. . . . Heber's results quickly found their way into the textbooks: [One] was typically with its references to this 'exciting' study, its 'most encouraging' results, its 'impressive' findings—not the usual language of a text. (Flynn, 1984, p. 40)

The textbook treatment was reviewed by others (Sommer & Sommer, 1983) who saw an actual increase in references (but always in obscure publications) to the project from 1977 to 1982. Their analysis, they noted:

> Yields a picture of research findings becoming widespread in textbooks . . . without ever having been subjected to journal review. Our experience is that textbooks are regarded as authoritative by the students who read them and the faculty who adopt them. (p. 983)

Because the project was not substantially described in refereed journals, and technical reports were of limited circulation, the project did receive extensive technical criticism. Yet there have been sharp exceptions taken to its methodology. There is internal evidence that the randomization was flawed, that replacements in the children were unreported, that the treatments were contaminated by the IQ test material, that the treatments had never been adequately described, and that the IQ testing itself, carried out by friendly project personnel, was cast in doubt by the one outside examiner (Page, 1972, 1986; Page & Grandon, 1981). At no time have project personnel published responses to these criticisms.

Others have written of the violation of scientific practice in the fugitive, unrefereed publications (Sommer & Sommer, 1983, 1984). Flynn (1984) reexamined the data and presented adjusted results that showed a real decline for the experimental group of 16 IQ points (p. 40).

One of the questions remaining is how the experimental children have performed in their later schooling, once away from the control of the project. The goal of such intensive training had been, of course, to prepare them for satisfactory accomplishment in later schooling and life. Reports from the project itself are again cryptic and difficult to find or to interpret. But one source of information (Clarke & Clarke, 1979, pp. 224–225) reported that there was no longer a difference between experimental and control children in measured reading ability. Of course, reading ability is the first goal of elementary education, and comprehension is highly correlated with intelligence tests.

When a study of such symbolic importance deviates so much from any past results and is so inconsistent with other evidence, then it must rely on the reputation of its personnel, or on society's desire to believe in the results. It is therefore relevant that reputations have been severely damaged in federal court. The project's director, Heber, was sentenced and imprisoned for his misuse of federal funds, and two others were also convicted, and one imprisoned (see news stories by Rob Fixmer, *Capital Times*, Madison, Wisconsin, January 1981). Perhaps most relevant has been the project's failure, long before the trials, to bring its sampling, procedures, and data into the light of public scrutiny even after its international publicity and the expenditure of some $14 million, most of it federal, for 20 experimental children and their controls. Several years after his release from prison, Heber died in unusual circumstances that caused many to suspect an act of suicide.

## REFERENCES

Clarke, A. M., & Clarke, A. D. B. (1979). *Early experience: Myth and evidence*. New York: Free Press.

Flynn, J. R. (1984). The mean IQ of Americans: Massive gains 1932 to 1978. *Psychological Bulletin, 95*(1), 29–51.

Garber, H. (1975). Intervention in infancy: A developmental approach. In M. Begab & S. Richardson (Eds.), *The mentally retarded and society*. Baltimore: University Park Press.

Heber, R., & Garber, H. (1970). An experiment in the prevention of cultural-familial retardation. In D. A. Primrose (Ed.), *Proceedings of the Third Congress of the International Association for the Scientific Study of Mental Deficiency* (Vol. 1, pp. 34–43). Warsaw: Polish Medical Publishers.

Heber, R., Garber, H., Harrington, S., Hoffman, C., & Falender, C. (1972, December). *Rehabilitation of families at risk for mental retardation: Progress report*. Madison: University of Wisconsin, Rehabilitation Research and Training Center in Mental Retardation.

Page, E. B. (1972). Miracle in Milwaukee: Raising the I.Q. *Educational Researcher, 1*(10), 8–15.

Page, E. B. (1986). The disturbing case of the Milwaukee Project. In H. H. Spitz (Ed.), *The raising of intelligence*. Hillsdale, NJ: Erlbaum.

Page, E. B., & Grandon, G. M. (1981). Massive intervention and child intelligence: The Milwaukee Project in critical perspective. *Journal of Special Education, 15*(2), 239–256.

Sommer, R., & Sommer, B. A. (1983). Mystery in Milwaukee: Early intervention, IQ, and psychology textbooks. *American Psychologist, 38*, 982–985.

Sommer, R., & Sommer, B. (1984). Reply from Sommer and Sommer. *American Psychologist, 39*, 1318–1319.

Trotter, R. (1976). Environment and behavior: Intensive intervention program prevents retardation. *APA Monitor, 7*, 4–6, 19, 46.

ELLIS B. PAGE
*Duke University*

**HEBER, RICK F.**
**INTELLIGENCE**
**MENTAL RETARDATION**

## MINIMAL BRAIN DYSFUNCTION

See MBD SYNDROME.

## MINIMUM COMPETENCY TESTING

Minimum competency testing is assessment to determine whether students possess skills that have been designated as prerequisites for either grade promotion or graduation with a high school diploma. Minimum competency testing enjoys widespread public and political support as it is seen as a means of raising academic standards and increasing educational achievement (Haney & Madaus, 1978). A majority of the states have instituted minimum competency testing requirements (Pipho, 1978); however, there is no unanimity as to the purpose and content of the tests, which are determined at the state or local school district level.

The inclusion of students with disabilities in minimum competency testing programs is problematic. Some educators are totally opposed to minimum competency testing of the disabled (Chandler, 1982). However, the tide of opinion favors inclusion provided appropriate accommodations are made to ensure fairness and nondiscrimination in the testing process.

Minimum competency testing of the disabled has been challenged on the basis of the Education for All Handicapped Children Act (PL 94-142), Section 504 of the Rehabilitation Act of 1973, and Constitutional grounds. The Constitutionally based objection involves issues of due process and equal protection as set forth in the Fourteenth Amendment. Thus far, the courts have upheld the right of states to establish minimal competency standards. The courts have intervened on behalf of students with disabilities only when academic standards have been clearly arbitrary and unfair, when criteria have been applied in a discriminatory manner, or when students have not been provided with sufficient notice of requirements prior to the imposition of sanctions (McCarthy, 1983).

Section 504 of the Rehabilitation Act of 1973 prohibits discrimination against an "otherwise qualified individual" in any program or activity supported wholly or in part by federal funds. Opponents of minimum competency testing of the disabled have argued that denial of a diploma to a student with disabilities is a violation of Section 504. The courts have not concurred. The courts accept the allegation of discrimination only if an individual with disabilities who is able to meet all requirements of a given program "[i]n spite of his handicap" is denied the benefits of that program. There is no inherent right to a diploma in the absence of the ability to meet academic standards. However, the courts have recognized that Section 504 entitles students with physical disabilities to accommodations of the testing situation (e.g., format, environment, response mode, and so on).

A third challenge to the minimum competency testing stems from the PL 94-142 provision for "appropriate" educational programs for the disabled. Opponents of minimum competency testing have challenged the appropriateness of special education programs that do not prepare students with disabilities to pass minimum competency tests. The Supreme Court addressed the issue in *Board of Education of the Hendrick Hudson Central School District* v. *Rowley* (1982). The majority opinion stated that the entitlement of children with disabilities in PL 94-142 did not guarantee maximization of student potential or guarantee outcomes. Rather, the student is entitled to an individualized educational program "with sufficient supportive services to permit the child to benefit from the instruction" (McCarthy, 1983). Therefore, students who have received special instruction to address their unique deficiency, but were not prepared for minimum competency testing, cannot claim that these programs were "inappropriate" (McCarthy, 1983).

Special educators who condone minimum competency testing for the disabled still face decisions on inclusion and exclusion. Ewing and Smith (1981) found that three general practices prevail: (1) inclusion of all handicapped, (2) exclusion of all handicapped, and (3) selective inclusion or exclusion based on handicapping condition. They suggest that inclusionary or exclusionary decisions can be facilitated by dichotomizing the handicapped into two groups: students who require modification of the learning environment, and students who require modified curricular and instructional goals. Minimum competency testing would be appropriate for the former group, as they share essentially the same educational and curricular goals with nonhandicapped students. Minimum competency testing would not be appropriate for the latter group, which is characterized by lower achievement potential and strives for lower levels of skill development than the curriculum of regular education (Ewing & Smith, 1981).

The exclusion of severely/profoundly impaired students will give rise to few, if any, objections. The appropriate decision for the educable mentally retarded student is less clear-cut. Negative consequences as a result of minimum competency testing, despite testing accommodations, have been reported in at least two studies (McKinney, 1983; Serow & O'Brien, 1983). In contrast, specific modifications in format and presentation reportedly enhanced the performance of students with learning disabilities (Beattie, Grise, & Algozzine, 1983).

The prudent approach is to decide the appropriateness of minimum competency testing on a case-by-case basis as part of the development of the student's individualized educational program (IEP). The IEP can be used as the vehicle for connecting competency testing with the student's overall instructional program (Cressey & Padilla, 1981; Olson, 1980; Schenk, 1981). The minimum competency requirements for which the student will be held accountable and the accommodations to be made can be documented in the IEP, thus ensuring a shared understanding between the school and the family.

Accommodations in minimum competency testing to meet the needs of the disabled can address standards or particulars of the testing situation. Modification of standards involves differential standards for graduation, which can take the form of special competency tests, lowered performance standards, or modifications of testing procedures. Differential standards (with the exception of passage of the regular test with modified procedures) result in the issuance of a special diploma or certificate other than the regular diploma to the student with disabilities at the time of graduation (Cressey & Padilla, 1981).

A variety of possible modifications of testing procedures have been discussed by numerous special educators (Fox & Weaver, 1981; Morrissey, 1978) and the list of recommendations is extensive. The essential goal is to enable the handicapped individual to demonstrate his or her knowledge and accomplishments despite physical or sensory disability.

## REFERENCES

Beattie, S., Grise, P., & Algozzine, B. (1983). Effects of test modification of the minimum competency performance of learning disabled students. *Learning Disabilities Quarterly, 6,* 75–76.

Chandler, H. N. (1982). A modest proposal. *Journal of Learning, Disabilities, 15,* 306–308.

Cressey, J., & Padilla, C. (1981). *Minimal competency testing and special education students: A technical assistance guide.* Menlo Park, CA: SRI International.

Ewing, N. J., & Smith, J. (1981). *Minimum competency testing and the handicapped.* Reston, VA: Council for Exceptional Children.

Fox, C. L., & Weaver, F. L. (1981). Minimal competency testing: Issues and options. *Academic Therapy, 16,* 425–435.

Haney, W., & Madaus, G. F. (1978). Making sense of the competency testing movement. *Harvard Educational Review, 53,* 462–484.

McCarthy, M. M. (1983). The application of competency testing mandates to handicapped children. *Harvard Educational Review, 53,* 146–164.

McKinney, J. D. (1983). Performance of handicapped students on the North Carolina minimum competency test. *Exceptional Children, 49,* 547–550.

Morrissey, P. (1978). Adaptive testing: How and when should handicapped students be accommodated in competency testing programs? In R. M. Jaeger & C. K. Tittle (Eds.), *Minimum competency achievement testing.* Berkeley, CA: McCutchan.

Olsen, K. R. (1980). Minimum competency testing and the IEP process. *Exceptional Children, 47,* 176–183.

Pipho, C. (1978). Minimum competency testing in 1978: A look at state standards. *Phi Delta Kappan, 59,* 585–588.

Schenk, S. J. (1981, April). *Ramifications of the minimum competency movement for special education.* Paper presented at the annual meeting of the American Educational Research Association, Los Angeles, CA.

Serow, R. C., & O'Brien, K. (1983). Performance of handicapped students in a competency testing program. *Journal of Special Education, 17,* 149–155.

LIBBY GOODMAN
*Pennsylvania State University*

**ACHIEVEMENT TESTS**
**COMPETENCY TESTING FOR TEACHERS**

# MINNESOTA MULTIPHASIC PERSONALITY INVENTORY–2 AND ADOLESCENT VERSIONS

## MMPI-2

The Minnesota Multiphasic Personality Inventory–2 (MMPI-2, Hathaway & Charnley) is an objective measure of personality. It is the most widely used and researched objective personality test (Greene, 2000). The MMPI-2 may be utilized with individuals 18 years of age and older, who have at least an eighth grade education. It contains 567 statements to which the individual must respond as "true," "false," or "cannot say." Administration time generally takes between 60 and 90 minutes.

Individual's are scored on 10 clinical scales that measure personality and psychopathology and six scales that measure an individual's test-taking attitudes, including consistency and accuracy of reporting. The clinical scales are: Hypochondriasis (Hy), Depression (D), Hysteria (Hy), Psychopathic Deviate (Pd), Masculinity-Femininity (Mf), Paranoia (Pa), Psychasthenia (Pt), Schizophrenia (Sc), Hypomania (Ma), and Social Introversion (Si). The validity scales are: Lie (L), Infrequency (F), Back Infrequency (Fb), Variable Response Inconsistency (VRIN), True Response Inconsistency (TRIN), and Correction (K).

In addition, the following 15 content scales provide further information that is useful for interpretation: Anxiety (ANX), Fears (FRS), Obsessions (OBS), Depression (DEP), Health Concerns (HEA), Bizarre Mentation (BIZ), Anger (ANG), Cynicism (CYN), Antisocial Practices (ASP), Type A (TPA), Low Self-Esteem (LSE), Social Discomfort (SOD), Family Problems (FAM), Work Interference (WRK), and Negative Treatment Indicators (TRT).

Answers may be scored by hand or with the use of a computer software program. Raw scores are converted to $T$ scores with a mean of 50 and a standard deviation of 10. $T$ scores of 65 or higher are considered to be clinically elevated and scores below 45 are considered depressed. The individual receives a score for each one of the clinical scales. The two most elevated clinical scale scores with a $T$ score of 65 or higher give what is known as the codetype. The codetype is reported using the numbers of these two scales, listing the most elevated one first. Interpretation of the MMPI-2 is based on the codetype of the individual.

The MMPI-2 was standardized on a sample of 1,138 males and 1,462 females who resided in seven states of the United States (California, Minnesota, North Carolina, Ohio, Pennsylvania, Virginia, and Washington). The sample was meant to be consistent with the U.S. census demographics on age, marital status, ethnicity, education, and occupational status. However, the sample has been criticized for not being representative of the general U.S. population on level of education and occupational status.

Two factors have been identified through factor analysis of the MMPI-2: an anxiety factor (A) and a repression factor (R; Welsh, 1956). The MMPI-2 has high predictive validity and high test-retest reliability. Test-retest reliability averages for all of the clinical scales are above .80 over a two-week period.

## MMPI-A

The original MMPI was utilized with adolescents, but it soon became clear that many test items were not appropriate for adolescents. The MMPI-Adolescent version (MMPI-A) is a restandardization of the MMPI, which was developed to be utilized specifically with adolescents. It is for use with adolescents ages 14 through 18 with a reading ability at least at the seventh grade level, although it may also be administered to 12- or 13-year-olds who meet the administration criteria. The MMPI-A manual (Butcher et al., 1992) suggests that the MMPI-A be utilized for 18-year-olds who are in high school, while the MMPI-2 be utilized for those who are in college, working, or otherwise have an independent adult lifestyle.

The MMPI-A contains 478 items and it usually takes about 45 to 60 minutes to complete. The items on the validity and clinical scales of the MMPI have not been changed much on the MMPI-A. However, the validity scales have been renormed for adolescents. The MMPI-A has new items that target adolescent concerns, such as alcohol and drug abuse, family relationships, school and teachers, achievement problems, eating disorders, identity formation, negative peer influences, and sexuality, and lacks items of the original version that were thought to be irrelevant to adolescents.

Fifteen new content scales were developed for the MMPI-A in a similar way as the MMPI-2 scales. These scales are: Anxiety (A-anx), Obsessions (A-obs), Depression (A-dep), Health Concerns (A-hea), Alienation (A-aln), Bizarre Mentation (A-biz), Anger (A-ang), Cynicism (A-cyn), Conduct Problems (A-con), Low Self-Esteem (A-lse), Low Aspiration (A-las), Social Discomfort (A-sod), Family Problems (A-fam), School Problems (A-sch), and Negative Treatment Indicators (A-trt). In addition, the following three new supplementary scales have been added to the MMPI-A: Immaturity (IMM), Alcohol/Drug Problem Acknowledgment (ACK), and Alcohol/Drug Problem Proneness (PRO).

For both tests, raw scores are converted to $T$ scores, with $T$ scores of 65 or higher considered to be clinically elevated. However, marginally elevated $T$ scores between 60 and 64 are of interpretative significance in the MMPI-A.

The MMPI-A was standardized on a sample of 1,610 adolescents who resided in eight states (California, Minnesota, New York, North Carolina, Ohio, Pennsylvania, Virginia, and Washington). The sample had limited representativeness with respect to ethnicity, geographical region, and residence (rural-urban). The normative sample was predominantly white and had parents that were generally well educated and in professional and managerial occupations.

Eight factors have been identified by factor analysis of the MMPI-A (Archer, Belevich, & Elkins, 1994; Archer & Krishnamurthy, 1997). The eight factors are: "general maladjustment, immaturity, disinhibition and excitatory, social discomfort, health concerns, naiveté, familial alienation, and psychoticism" (Maruish, 1999, p. 357). The MMPI-A Structural Summary organizes the scales and subscales within each of these eight factors according to how much they correlate with each factor.

The MMPI-A is a valid and reliable instrument. The MMPI-A manual (Butcher et al., 1992) reports 40 alpha coefficients for the assessment of internal consistencies. Of these coefficients, 17 (43 percent) range from .75 to .91, 18 (45 percent) range from .55 to .68, and 5 (13 percent) range from .35 to .53. Intercorrelations among the clinical scales of the normative sample range from .00 to .85. The validity of the MMPI-A is commensurate to that of the MMPI. The 15 new content scales in the MMPI-A have similar external validity coefficients to those of the original version.

The MMPI-A appears to be an excellent revision of the MMPI for use with adolescents. Its new content scales appear particularly useful for assessing modern adolescent difficulties. Both the MMPI-2 and the MMPI-A are extremely useful for diagnosing, treatment planning, feedback, and personnel selection. Despite the similarities between the MMPI-A and the MMPI-2, there are some differences that must be taken into consideration when interpreting the MMPI-A. A major difficulty in interpreting these tests is that not all of the codetypes are exactly congruent between the MMPI, the MMPI-2, and the MMPI-A. In only 60 percent of the cases would the codetype given by the MMPI-2 and the MMPI-A be the same as that supplied by the MMPI for the same individual. This creates a problem, because much of the empirical research has been carried out on the original MMPI. Until more empirical data has been published on codetype information for the MMPI-2 and the MMPI-A, it is suggested that the clinician replot these later versions back to the original MMPI, utilizing the appropriate tables in the Appendix section of the manuals.

## REFERENCES

Archer, R. P. (1997). *MMPI-A: Assessing adolescent psychology* (2nd ed.). Mahwah, NJ: Erlbaum.

Archer, R. P., Belevich, J. K., & Elkins, D. E. (1994). Item-level and scale-level factor structures of the MMPI-A. *Journal of Personality Assessment, 62,* 332–345.

Archer, R. P., & Krishnamurthy, R. (1997). MMPI-A scale-level factor structure: Replication in a clinical sample. *Assessment, 4,* 337–349.

Ben-Porath, Y. S., & Butcher, J. N. (1989). Psychometric stability of rewritten MMPI items. *Journal of Personality Assessment, 53,* 645–653.

Butcher, J. N., Dahlstrom, W. G., Graham, J. R., Tellegen, A. M., & Kaemmer, B. (1989). *MMPI-2: Manual for administration and scoring.* Minneapolis: University of Minnesota Press.

Butcher, J. N., Graham, J. R., Williams, C. L., & Ben-Porath, Y. S. (1990). *Development and use of the MMPI-2 content scales.* Minneapolis: University of Minnesota Press.

Butcher, J. N., & Williams, C. L. (1992). *Essentials of MMPI-2 and MMPI-A interpretation.* New York: Wiley.

Butcher, J. N., Williams, C. L., Graham, J. R., Archer, R. P., Tellegen, A. M., Ben-Porath, Y. S., & Kaemmer, B. (1992). *MMPI-A (Minnesota Multiphasic Personality Inventory–Adolescent): Manual for administration, scoring and interpretation.* Minneapolis: University of Minnesota Press.

Conoley, J. C., & Impara, J. C. (Eds.). (1995). *The twelfth mental measurements yearbook.* Lincoln, NE: Buros Institute of Mental Measurements.

Greene, R. L. (2000). *The MMPI-2: An interpretive manual* (2nd ed.). Boston: Allyn & Bacon.

Kramer, J. J., & Conoley, J. C. (Eds.). (1992). *The eleventh mental measurements yearbook.* Lincoln, NE: Buros Institute of Mental Measurements.

Lewak, R. W., Marks, P. A., & Nelson, G. E. (1990). *Therapist guide to the MMPI & MMPI-2.* Muncie, IN: Accelerated Development.

Maruish, M. E. (Ed). (1999). *The use of psychological testing for treatment planning and outcomes assessment* (2nd ed.). Mahwah, NJ: Erlbaum.

Welsh, G. S. (1956). Factor dimensions A and R. In G. S. Welsh & W. G. Dahlstrom (Eds.), *Basic readings on the MMPI in psychology and medicine* (pp. 264–281). Minneapolis: University of Minnesota Press.

Williams, C. L., Butcher, J. N., Ben-Porath, Y. S., & Graham, J. R. (1992). *MMPI-A content scales: Assessing psychopathology in adolescents.* Minneapolis: University of Minnesota Press.

RON DUMONT
*Fairleigh Dickinson University*

JOHN O. WILLIS
*Rivier College*

## MINOR PHYSICAL ANOMALIES

A higher than normal number of minor physical anomalies (MPAs) has been linked with various behavioral disorders including schizophrenia, Down syndrome, Mental Retardation, autism, learning disabilities, and Attention-Deficit/Hyperactivity Disorder (Krouse & Kauffman, 1982). MPAs are now being used to determine individuals at an increased risk for adolescent psychopathology. Thus far, MPAs have led to successful predictions of childhood conduct disorder (Pine, Shaffer, Schonfeld, & Davies, (1997).

Examples of MPAs are soft and pliable ears, a tongue with rough and smooth spots, fine electric hair, high-steepled palate, head circumference larger or smaller than normal, curved fifth finger, single crease across the palm of the hand, epicanthus, and a gap between first and second toe (Waldrop & Halverson, 1971).

Recent research has shown a 60 percent increase in occurrence of MPAs in people with schizophrenia over the normal population, which typically exhibits only a 5 percent chance of having MPAs. However, siblings of individuals with schizophrenia also have shown a 38 percent increased occurrence of MPAs. MPAs exhibited in individuals with schizophrenia frequently pertain to eye, mouth, hand, and foot regions (Ismail, Cantor-Graae, & McNeil, 1998). MPAs can often be detected from various events that occur during pregnancy and may lead researchers to a better understanding of the causes of schizophrenia (Waddington et al., 1998).

### REFERENCES

Ismail, B., Cantor-Graae, E., & McNeil, T. F. (1998). Minor physical anomalies in schizophrenic patients and their siblings. *American Journal of Psychiatry, 155,* 1695–1702.

Krouse, J. P., & Kauffman, J. M. (1982). Minor physical anomalies in exceptional children: A review and critique of research. *Journal of Abnormal Child Psychology, 10,* 247–264.

Pine, D. S., Shaffer, D., Schonfeld, I. S., & Davies, M. (1997). Minor physical anomalies: Modifiers of environmental risks for psychiatric impairment? *Journal of the American Academy of Child and Adolescent Psychiatry, 36,* 395–403.

Waddington, J. L., Buckley, P. F., Scully, P. J., Lane, A., O'Callaghan, E., & Larkin, C. (1998). Course of psychopathology, cognition, and neurobiological abnormality in schizophrenia: Developmental origins and amelioration by antipsychotics? *Journal of Psychiatric Research, 32,* 179–189.

Waldrop, M. F., & Halverson, C. F. (1971). Minor physical anomalies and hyperactive behavior in young children. In J. Hellmuth (Ed.), *Exceptional infant: Studies in abnormalities* (Vol. 2, pp. 343–380). New York: Brunner/Mazel.

ROBERT T. BROWN
ELLEN B. MARRIOTT
*University of North Carolina at Wilmington*
First edition

ROBERT T. BROWN
AIMEE R. HUNTER
*University of North Carolina at Wilmington*
Second edition

**DOWN SYNDROME**
**DYSMORPHIC FEATURES**
**PHYSICAL ANOMALIES**
**PHYSICAL DISABILITIES**

## MISCUE ANALYSIS

Miscue analysis is a research technique developed by Kenneth Goodman in 1970 to describe the language and thought processes involved in the act of reading. Based on psycholinguistic theory, Goodman described reading as an interaction between the language of the reader and the language of the author (Goodman & Burke, 1972). To discover how both language and thought processes are involved in reading, children's oral miscues were analyzed as they read unrehearsed passages of text. Miscues were defined as unexpected responses that deviated from the expected responses in the text. Specifically, miscue analysis is used as a means of identifying and evaluating the strategies employed by skilled and unskilled readers as they attempt to construct meaning from written text.

The procedures used in miscue analysis have been simplified for classroom use in a diagnostic instrument called the Reading Miscue Inventory (Goodman & Burke, 1972). Burke (1974) cites procedures that include recording children's oral reading errors and classifying the errors based on the following questions:

1. *Graphic Similarity.* How much does the miscue *look* like the expected response?
2. *Sound Similarity.* How much does the miscue *sound* like the expected response?
3. *Grammatical Function.* Is the grammatical function of the reader's word the same as the grammatical function of the text word?
4. *Syntactic Acceptability.* Is the sentence involving the miscue grammatically acceptable?
5. *Semantic Acceptability.* Is the sentence involving the miscue semantically acceptable?
6. *Meaning Change.* Is there a change in meaning involved in the sentence?
7. *Correction and Semantic Acceptability.* Do corrections by the reader make the sentence semantically acceptable? (p. 23)

These questions are applied to each miscue to determine how readers process three kinds of information from the printed page: grapho-phonic, syntactic, and semantic (Goodman, 1969).

First, grapho-phonic information enables readers to recognize the letters in the text and convert them to sounds. Phonics is the term commonly used to describe this letter-sound matching. Second, syntactic information brings to the act of reading an implicit knowledge of the grammatical rules of the language. With this information readers have the ability to predict linguistic patterns in written materials. Third, semantic information makes it possible for readers to draw on their own experiences and knowledge as they interpret the author's message. This semantic information is crucial as readers attempt to understand the relationship between their personal experiences and the experiences of the author.

Research on miscue analysis is inconclusive because of inconsistencies in classifying and interpreting specific reading miscues. Wixson (1979) points out that miscue procedures are not designed to account for variables such as instructional methods, type of text, passage length and difficulty, and reader's purpose. It has been suggested (Leu, 1982; Wixson, 1979) that miscue patterns may be a function of these variables rather than a reflection of a particular reader's processing strategies.

One of the most significant findings of miscue analysis research is that the reading strategies of proficient readers are different from those of less skilled readers. Because proficient readers have greater language competency, they tend to make errors that are more syntactically and semantically acceptable than less proficient readers (Goodman, 1969; Goodman & Burke, 1972; Goodman, 1995). Readers with a strong language background have already acquired enough semantic and syntactic information to predict the language structures found in many reading materials; they need only a minimal amount of grapho-phonic information to complete the reading process. Conversely, children with deficient language backgrounds or competencies lack the semantic and syntactic information to predict meaningful language patterns in many reading materials. Such children produce miscues that result in meaning changes and alter or obscure the author's message. Lacking the highly developed syntactic and semantic competencies of good readers, poor readers become too dependent on grapho-phonic information.

Teachers can use the results of miscue analysis to improve their instructional strategies. After classifying and interpreting students' miscues, teachers should provide the appropriate language experiences necessary to develop the conceptual understandings needed to comprehend the author's message (Martens, 1995). Once teachers know the type of miscues children make, they can provide experiences that build bridges from the language and thought of the child to the language and thought of the author.

## REFERENCES

Burke, C. (1974). Preparing elementary teachers to teach reading. In K. S. Goodman (Ed.), *Miscue analysis: Applications to reading instruction.* Urbana, IL: National Council of Teachers of English.

Goodman, K. S. (1969). Analysis of reading miscues: Applied psycholinguistics. *Reading Research Quarterly, 5*(1), 9–30.

Goodman, Y. M. (1995). Miscue analysis for classroom teachers: Some history and some procedures. *Primary Voices, 3*(4), 2–9.

Goodman, Y. M., & Burke, C. L. (1972). *Reading miscue inventory: Procedures for diagnosis and evaluation.* New York: Macmillan.

Leu, D. J., Jr. (1982). Oral reading error analysis: A critical review of research and application. *Reading Research Quarterly, 17*(3), 420–437.

Martens, P. (1995). Empowering teachers and empowering students. *Primary Voices, 3*(4), 39–42.

Wixson, K. L. (1979). Miscue analysis: A critical review. *Journal of Reading Behavior, 11*(2), 163–175.

CHRIS CHERRINGTON
*Lycoming College*

**LINGUISTIC READERS**
**READING DISORDERS**
**READING REMEDIATION**

# MNEMONICS

Mnemonics are considered to be strategies and/or devices that aid individuals in their ability to remember and recall information from memory. The primary principle behind mnemonics is that an individual has the ability to create an artificial structure by connecting unfamiliar concepts to previously stored concepts that exist in memory (Encyclopaedia Britannica, 2005). Mnemonic strategies lend themselves to many different uses and can be applied in various learning environments (Mastropieri & Scruggs, 1991; Mastropieri, Sweda, & Scruggs, 2000). Students with learning and behavioral difficulties often have problems in their ability to memorize academic content; therefore, researchers have turned to investigate mnemonic strategies within this population of students.

Moreover, there are many mnemonic strategies known to be effective, although three in particular have been studied and proven to be effective in the instruction of students with learning and behavioral problems: the keyword method, the pegword method, and letter strategies (Scruggs & Mastropieri, 2000a). The keyword method is the most effective and malleable mnemonic strategy, for it allows new information to be connected to prior knowledge and is useful to students when new vocabulary or names for new facts and concepts need to be learned and remembered (Mastropieri & Scruggs, 1991; Scruggs & Mastropieri, 1990, 2000a). Pegwords are short, rhyming proxies for numbers, and although the pegword method is less versatile, it is still a functional strategy that allows for numbered and ordered information to be remembered through interactive pictures that can be connected with numbers (e.g., one is a bun, two is a shoe, three is a tree; Kleinheksel & Summy, 2003; Scruggs & Mastropieri, 2000b). Lastly, letter strategies are likely to be the most familiar type of mnemonic strategy used by students (Mastropieri & Scruggs, 1998). The letter strategy includes acronyms and acrostics (e.g., the acronym HOMES representing the five Great Lakes of North America: Huron, Ontario, Michigan, Erie, and Superior; Kleinheksel & Summy, 2003). "Students and teachers need to work together so students can obtain the maximum academic benefit from mnemonic strategies" (Kleinheksel & Summy, 2003, p. 33).

## REFERENCES

Encyclopaedia Britannica. (2005). *Mnemonics*. Retrieved September 3, 2005, from http://britannica.com/eb/article-9053095

Kleinheksel, K. A., & Summy, S. A. (2003). Enhancing student learning and social behavior through mnemonic strategies. *Teaching Exceptional Children, 36*(2), 30–35.

Mastropieri, M. A., & Scruggs, T. E. (1991). *Teaching students ways to remember: Strategies for learning mnemonically*. Cambridge, MA: Brookline.

Mastropieri, M. A., & Scruggs, T. E. (1998). Enhancing school success with mnemonic strategies. *Intervention in School and Clinic, 33,* 201–208.

Mastropieri, M. A., Sweda, J., & Scruggs, T. E. (2000). Putting mnemonic strategies to work in an inclusive classroom. *Learning Disabilities Research & Practice, 15,* 69–74.

Scruggs, T. E., & Mastropieri, M. A. (1990). Mnemonic instruction for learning disabled students: What it is and what it does. *Learning Disability Quarterly, 13,* 271–281.

Scruggs, T. E., & Mastropieri, M. A. (2000a). The effectiveness of mnemonic instruction for students with learning and behavioral problems: An update and research synthesis. *Journal of Behavioral Education, 10*(2/3), 163–173.

Scruggs, T. E., & Mastropieri, M. A. (2000b). Mnemonic interventions for students with behavior disorders: Memory for learning and behavior. *Beyond Behavior, 10,* 13–17.

NOE RAMOS
*Texas A&M University*

LEARNING DISABILITIES
MEMORY DISORDERS

# MOBAN

Moban is the proprietary name of molindine, a white crystalline powder used as a tranquilizer (Modell, 1985). The drug acts on the ascending reticular activating system to reduce depression, aggressiveness, and spontaneous locomotion. Tranquilizing effects reportedly are achieved without such negative concomitants as incoordination or muscle relaxation. Moban typically is used in the management of schizophrenia.

Common side effects associated with Moban include initial drowsiness, depression, and hyperactivity. Moban has been associated with seizure activity on occasion. Increased activity may occur in some individuals, and hence protective environments may be necessary. Tardive dyskinesia is a possible side effect. Moban has not been shown to be effective in the management of behavior problems associated with mental retardation. Use of Moban in children under 12 years of age is not recommended.

## REFERENCES

Modell, W. (Ed.). (1985). *Drugs in current use and new drugs* (31st ed.). New York: Springer-Verlag.

*Physician's desk reference* (37th ed.). (1983). Oradell, NJ: Medical Economics.

CATHY F. TELZROW
*Kent State University*

THORAZINE
TRANQUILIZERS
STELAZINE

# MOBILE EDUCATION UNITS

As the name implies, mobile education units are vans, buses, recreational vehicles, or trailers that have been converted to house specialized materials, media, and testing equipment to serve handicapped children and youths. They are in use in rural areas primarily, where geographic distances and learner sparsity make the units an efficient means of making special materials and services available to teachers and learners. These units are usually owned by the administrative unit that is responsible for supportive special education services (e.g., BOCES, CESA, Intermediate Unit).

The term mobile special education unit is a generic category of vehicle. The size and purpose of the unit is dependent on the needs of the region being served. Some units are used exclusively for testing. Space is at a premium in many schools and even if space is available, it may not be appropriate for services such as psychological testing or auditory assessments because of noise or distractions. Mobile units that are designed for these purposes have special lighting and noise reduction materials to improve the environment for testing. The unit travels around a geographic region on a schedule and is parked adjacent to a school for an extended period. The psychologist or audiologist may double as the driver of such a unit.

Sometimes a mobile unit will change locations daily and will house an itinerant specialist such as a speech and language specialist, occupational therapist, or physical therapist. Again, because schools may not have the available appropriate space or equipment, these units can become an efficient means of providing services in rural areas. Finally, there are mobile units that move from school to school on a weekly or biweekly schedule. They act like lending libraries, as an extension of a materials resource center. Materials are checked out for a 1- to 2-week period. By using a mobile library, the special education district need not purchase many expensive items for each of its special education classes. Use can be maximized by this system of sharing.

ROBERT A. SEDLAK
*University of Wisconsin at Stout*

**HOMEBOUND INSTRUCTION**
**ITINERANT SERVICES**

# MOBILITY INSTRUCTION

Mobility instruction is a term used to represent specific daily functional living skills that are incorporated into educational programs for moderate and severely disabled populations. The purpose of this instruction is to allow individuals to safely engage in planned movement from one location to another (Merbler & Wood, 1984).

Included in this group of functional skills are activities that promote independent travel within the immediate home environment as well as the local community. Instruction in toileting and meal preparation, and travel training for shopping, employment, or community recreation are examples of the activities included in mobility instruction.

Historically, mobility training has been part of the curriculum for the visually impaired. Only recently has this aspect of instruction been addressed in the curriculum for the mentally retarded. This relatively new focus on mobility training for mentally retarded individuals has resulted from the growing number of disabled persons who are living and working within local communities. These populations must obtain skills that will allow them to function as independently as possible within their communities (Wheeler et al., 1980).

Within the last 10 years there has been growing support for systematically incorporating functional skills into the existing curriculum for the mentally retarded. A variety of programs have been recently developed that focus on the direct teaching of these skills. Mobility training programs such as those reviewed by Martin, Rusch, and Heal (1982), include activities that engage individuals in real-life experiences as well as simulated travel activities conducted within a classroom setting. Basic to any program is the need to provide direct practical instruction in travel as well as related skill development. For example, while it is essential to provide individuals with simulated and real-life experiences in locating and boarding a bus, mobility instruction must also include the development of such related skills as decision making and the ability to adapt to changes in routines. These skills are essential because changes in the environment, as in a bus schedule, are common.

Other considerations for the development of curriculum in this area include the need to analyze the variety of subskills that lead to successful travel. To teach bus travel, it is necessary to teach individuals how to safely cross intersections, locate a bus stop, use a bus ticket, and board a bus.

While there is a need for additional research that will evaluate the effectiveness of mobility instruction, there are preliminary indicators that reveal that real-life experiences are more effective than simulation activities for training mobility skills.

Regardless of how simulation and real-life experiences are combined, it is important that the mobility instruction be systematic. Equally important is that parents and group-home workers allow individuals with disabilities opportunities to practice these skills independently (Certo, Schwartz, & Brown, 1977).

## REFERENCES

Certo, N., Schwartz, R., & Brown, L. (1977). Community transportation: Teaching severely handicapped students to ride a public bus system. In N. G. Haring & L. J. Brown (Eds.), *Teaching the severely handicapped* (Vol. 2, pp. 147–232). New York: Grune & Stratton.

Martin, J., Rusch, F., & Heal, L. (1982). Teaching community survival skills to mentally retarded adults: A review and analysis. *Journal of Special Education, 16*(3), 243–267.

Merbler, J. B., & Wood, T. A. (1984). Predicting orientation and mobility proficiency in mentally retarded visually impaired children. *Education & Training of the Mentally Retarded, 19*(3), 228–230.

Wheeler, J., Ford, A., Nietupski, J., Loomis, R., & Brown, L. (1980). Teaching moderately and severely handicapped adolescents to shop in supermarkets using pocket calculators. *Education & Training of the Mentally Retarded, 15*(2), 105–112.

FRANCINE TOMPKINS
*University of Cincinnati*

**ELECTRONIC TRAVEL AIDS**
**TRAVEL AIDS FOR INDIVIDUALS WITH DISABILITIES**

# MOBILITY TRAINERS

Formal training of the blind to help them move independently had its beginnings in the United States with the founding of the first dog guide school, Seeing Eye, Inc. of Morristown, New Jersey (Bledsoe, 1980). Although many blind individuals had traveled independently for centuries, it was not until the founding of this dog guide school that efforts were made to formalize a sequential approach to independent travel.

However, the formal curriculum for mobility training owes its roots to the cane rather than the dog. Over the years, mobility training for the blind has had many names. Sir Francis Campbell, an American who was naturalized and knighted in Britain, wrote extensively in the 1860s about the need for formal mobility training under the broad term "foot travel." Father Thomas Carroll, founder of the Catholic Guide for All the Blind, coined the term peripatology, which could be loosely defined as the study of travel. The most common term today is orientation and mobility. Orientation in this context is the acquisition of knowledge about one's environment; mobility means one's ability to move freely and safely from one place to another. The individual who teaches orientation and mobility is commonly referred to as a mobility specialist, although the terms peripatologist or orientator are also used.

Richard Hoover, who started his career as a physical education instructor at the Maryland School for the Blind, developed a technique and a cane while he was a sergeant in 1944 with the Army Medical Corps attached to a blind rehabilitation program at Valley Forge Army General Hospital. Hoover recognized the inadequacies of the commonly used white cane, which was in reality an orthopedic aid; he developed a much longer and lighter cane.

The need for teachers to instruct the blind in the use of this new cane and techniques became obvious. Valley Forge Army Hospital, Avon Old Farms Rehabilitation Center, and later Hines Veterans Hospital, trained their own mobility specialists for the instruction of blinded veterans. When the Hoover concept was more widely accepted and applied to the young civilian population, university degree programs were developed, first at Boston College in 1960 and a year later at Western Michigan University.

The training, either at the bachelor's or master's level, consists of course work in the nature and needs of the blind, training in the specific skills and techniques of teaching independence, and a block of hours working under a blindfold. The formal course work is followed by a term of practicum supervised by a qualified mobility specialist. The Mobility Interest Group of the Association for the Education and Rehabilitation of the Blind and Visually Impaired certifies graduates of university training programs.

A sizable number of mobility specialists work in larger school systems, where they provide training to blind students. In addition to direct training of children and youths, they also consult with teachers of younger children in the development of concepts that will later enhance travel independence.

**REFERENCES**

Bledsoe, C. W. (1980). Originators of orientation and mobility training. In R. L. Welsh & B. B. Blasch (Eds.), *Foundation of orientation and mobility*. New York: American Foundation for the Blind.

Muldoon, J. F. (1986, March). Carroll revisited: Inductions in rehabilitation, 1938–1971. *Journal of Visual Impairment & Blindness, 80*(3), 617–626.

GIDEON JONES
*Florida State University*

**BLIND LEARNING APTITUDE TEST**
**DOG GUIDES FOR THE BLIND**
**VISUAL TRAINING**

# MODEL PROGRAMS FOR SEVERELY AND PROFOUNDLY DISABLED INDIVIDUALS

The purpose of model education programs for individuals with severe to profound disabilities is to look at the state of the art in the instruction of such individuals and to continue to innovate by investigating current practices in a variety of ways. Typically receiving funding from outside sources (e.g., Office of Special Education and Rehabilitative Services at the federal level), model programs may include demonstration projects in local school systems, work with nonschool personnel such as parents via parent training projects, or adult vocational and independent living skills training programs.

Common features in model programs use an empirical base to draw conclusions about techniques and services. This database enables investigators to draw accurate conclusions about the best practices for instruction and services for individuals with severe or profound disabilities. In addition, model programs have a consumer orientation in that they involve outcomes that will be of use to service programs, parents, guardians, or advocates who have an interest in the needs of severely and profoundly disabled persons. A variety of research methods are generally used in model programs, including single-subject studies, survey research, and ethnographic investigation (Paine, 1984). Evaluation components of model programs are developed to ensure that all administrative and direct service goals are completed in a timely and satisfactory manner. Finally, dissemination of final products (e.g., specific examples of training programs, assessment manuals, in-service training kits) takes place at the end of the model program's final funding year as well as throughout the years the project is in place. Typically, model programs are funded for 3 to 5 years at the federal level.

Three examples of model programs are the Community-Based Instruction Program (CBIP) in Albemarle County, Virginia (project director, Adelle Renzaglia), the Specialized Training Program (STP) in Eugene, Oregon (program director, G. Thomas Bellamy), and the Inclusive Education Project conducted by Syracuse University and Syracuse Public Schools (Rogan & Davern, 1992). The CBIP (Snell & Renzaglia, 1986) was a federally funded 3-year project that was established to serve school-age students with severe and profound disabilities. Prior to the start of the program, these students were being served inappropriately in preschool classes, in classes for students with mild to moderate disabilities, or in homebound instruction. Three classes were established in integrated settings: a high-school class serving individuals 16 to 21 years of age located in a high school that serves approximately 2,000 nondisabled students; a middle-school class serving students ages 12 to 15 years that was located in a middle school housing approximately 375 nondisabled sixth through eighth grade students; and an elementary classroom serving students ages 6 to 11 years in an elementary school with approximately 225 nondisabled kindergarten through fifth grade students.

Students in the CBIP classrooms had a variety of handicapping conditions. Some had limited expressive language, vision, or hearing impairments. Several students were severely motorically impaired (e.g., severe hypertonic cerebral palsy). Other students exhibited major behavior problems (e.g., aggression, self-stimulation, noncompliance).

Students in the high school class spent most of their day outside of the classroom in vocational, community, leisure/recreational, and domestic skills training. For students ages 20 to 21 years, the major emphasis was on vocational training for future competitive employment. Younger, less skilled students received vocational training in community training sites or in the community sheltered workshops.

Domestic skills training for high school students took place in two sites: a group home in which two students lived and a home in the community where skills could be trained and practiced on a daily basis. Community skill training took place on location (e.g., pedestrian skills taught on a public street, grocery shopping skills taught in grocery stores) or in the classroom (e.g., using vending machines, purchasing food at a restaurant) with generalization assessed and trained at the actual community site. Leisure/recreation skills training also took place in community sites (e.g., using a video machine at a video arcade) as well as in the classroom (e.g., social phone conversations) with generalization assessed and trained in community environments.

Classroom programming in the middle school emphasized (1) providing vocational training on real jobs in a school setting; (2) teaching domestic skills in a school-based apartment setting; (3) teaching community mobility skills; (4) teaching hygienic and grooming skills in the gym locker room before and after physical education class; (5) teaching functional academic skills (e.g., time telling, money skills); and (6) teaching appropriate leisure/recreational activities in the classroom and the community. In addition, behavior management programs were implemented to decrease maladaptive behaviors as needed.

At the elementary level, students received instruction in basic self-care skills (e.g., toileting), appropriate mealtime behaviors, dressing, receptive and expressive language skills, motor skills in the context of functional activities, and appropriate use of leisure time. Several students at this level were taught to partially participate in activities because of severe motor limitations. All elementary students participated in a physical education program daily in which they had a chance to interact with their nondisabled peers.

Extensive contact with parents and ancillary staff (i.e., domestic/home living skills specialist, adaptive physical education instructor) took place in planning educational programs for individual students. A transdisciplinary approach was taken in the CBIP. In addition, trainers looked at the current and future needs of students to ensure the smooth functioning of program goals and to maximize instructional time and student progress.

The STP (Boles, Bellamy, Horner, & Mark, 1984) was implemented to develop, field test, and disseminate a structured employment model emphasizing benchwork assembly tasks for adults with severe disabilities. Initially developed within a university center as an on-campus vocational program for severely and profoundly mentally retarded individuals, the program moved into a field test phase in which community vocational training was offered in three states using the STP model.

The STP provides employment in the area of small parts assembly (e.g., electronic units). Work is procured from local industries and workers are trained on a one-to-one basis until they are able to enter a supported production setting. Applied behavior analysis procedures are used for training and areas of instruction include personal competence in the surrounding community as well as in the work place. Each model site operates as a small not-for-profit business and follows well-defined procedures for management, finance, and commercial operation.

Through careful planning of the site activities and training, as well as support for groups wishing to start replication sites, the STP model has provided multiple work sites for severely to profoundly disabled individuals. Systematic instruction has enabled these individuals, heretofore unserved in competitive employment sites, to have a viable alternative to sheltered work or no-work options.

The Inclusive Education Project was designed to meet special problems of children with severe disabilities in regular education settings. Eight schools participated in building level process, leadership institutes, and community networking. A detailed report can be read in Rogan and Davern (1992).

The three models described indicate the types of programming that are being investigated and disseminated following demonstration of innovative practices. In general, model programs for individuals with severe or profound disabilities should include the following: data-based assessment of current and future needs; ongoing data-based evaluation of progress; integration of severely disabled students/adults with their nondisabled peers; transdisciplinary programming; home-school interaction; chronological age-appropriate programs; objectives that are functional for students'/adults' current or future needs; and systematic instruction in specific domains such as the domestic (e.g., grooming, household chores), leisure/recreation, community (e.g., restaurant use, pedestrian skills, grocery shopping), and vocational (Snell & Renzaglia, 1986).

## REFERENCES

Boles, S. M., Bellamy, G. T., Horner, R. H., & Mark, D. M. (1984). Specialized training program: The structured employment model. In S. C. Paine, G. T. Bellamy, & B. Wilcox (Eds.), *Human services that work* (pp. 181–205). Baltimore: Brookes.

Paine, S. C. (1984). Models revisited. In S. C. Paine, G. T. Bellamy, & B. Wilcox (Eds.), *Human services that work* (pp. 269–276). Baltimore: Brookes.

Rogan, P., & Davern, N. (1992). *Inclusive Education Project: Final report.* Syracuse: New York Division of Special Education and Rehabilitation.

Snell, M. E., & Renzaglia, A. (1986). Moderate, severe, and profound handicaps. In N. G. Haring & L. McCormick (Eds.), *Exceptional children and youth* (4th ed.). Columbus, OH: Merrill.

CORNELIA LIVELY
*University of Illinois, Urbana-
Champaign*

**APPLIED BEHAVIOR ANALYSIS**
**FUNCTIONAL INSTRUCTION**
**TRANSFER OF TRAINING**
**VOCATIONAL EDUCATION**

## MODIFICATIONS

Modifications are similar to accommodations in that they are changes to the way instruction is provided or assessment tasks are administered to students with disabilities. However, modifications are changes that substantially alter the construct being measured. Therefore, a clear and thorough definition of the construct is needed to determine if a change is a modification or accommodation. A common example of a modification is reading aloud a test that is designed to measure reading skills that include processing and comprehending written words. Since the construct implies an ability to decode text, reading the material to the student changes the construct by removing this component of reading. Another example would be providing out-of-level materials or tests.

Modifications are used when the student would not otherwise be able to participate in instruction or assessment with accommodations. Generalizations about student ability are limited due to the changes in the construct. Since the construct is no longer the same as the general education instruction or assessment, the same inferences about student proficiencies are not possible (Thurlow & Wiener, 2000). As such, performance on modified instructional materials or tests are not typically aggregated with scores obtained from standard or accommodated delivery or administration conditions. However, scores can be useful for other decisions made by teachers, parents, or other people involved in providing services to the student.

In testing, modifications and reporting of scores that were obtained under modified conditions are typically identified by state policies on test changes. Terminology, however, may vary considerably from state to state, leading to confusion over what changes are and are not allowed in testing (Thurlow, Lazarus, Thompson, & Robey, 2002). Other terms used to represent test changes that invalidate scores include: nonstandard administration, not-permitted accommodations, and not-allowed accommodations.

Decisions governing the use of modifications are similar to those made for accommodations. Under the Individuals with Disabilities Education Improvement Act, these decisions are made by the Individualized Education Program team.

## REFERENCES

Thurlow, M. L., Lazarus, S., Thompson, S., & Robey, J. (2002). *2001 state policies on assessment participation and accommo-*

*dations* (Synthesis Report 46). Minneapolis: University of Minnesota, National Center on Educational Outcomes. Retrieved from http://education.umn.edu/NCEO/OnlinePubs/Synthesis46 .html

Thurlow, M., & Wiener, D. (2000). *Non-approved accommodations: Recommendations for use and reporting* (Policy Directions No. 11). Minneapolis: University of Minnesota, National Center on Educational Outcomes. Retrieved from http://education.umn .edu/NCEO/OnlinePubs/Policy11.htm

LEANNE KETTERLIN-GELLER
*University of Oregon*

## ACCOMMODATIONS

# MOMENTARY TIME SAMPLING

Momentary time sampling is a data collection method that is used when you want to measure a continuous behavior—that is, a behavior that is displayed over a period of time. Momentary time sampling is a time-based measurement system where the passage of a predetermined amount of time, not each occurrence of a behavior, is the signal for the teacher or researcher to record data (Wolery, Bailey, & Sugai, 1988). Like partial and whole interval recording, momentary time sampling provides a close approximation or sampling of the targeted behavior. Unlike partial and whole interval recording, the intervals for momentary time sampling are usually divided into minutes, not seconds (Alberto & Troutman, 2006). Momentary time sampling is suitable for recording behaviors such as academic engagement, playing, engaging in off-task behaviors such as being out of an assigned seat and/or walking around the classroom, cooperative learning, and self-stimulatory behaviors.

Momentary time sampling first requires an operational definition of the behavior of concern. An operational definition is a written statement that precisely defines the behavior you wish to measure in terms that are observable, measurable, and replicable (Fletcher-Janzen & De Pry, 2003). Next, the observer determines the length of time for each interval. Intervals are predetermined periods of time that are equivalent in length. Interval length is determined by (1) the frequency of the target behavior, (2) the context that elicits the behavior (e.g., times, place, conditions), and (3) the time demands or schedule of the teacher (Wolery et al., 1988).

When the interval length has been determined, a data collection form should be created. The form should have the student's name, the date, the observer's name, the classroom teacher's name, information about the setting or context of the observation (to be completed at each observation session), the start and stop times, and the interval grid.

Teachers who use momentary time sampling need a signal that lets them know when to observe and record data. The signal can be visual (e.g., classroom clock or watch) or auditory (e.g., kitchen timer, countdown timer, or tape player with a recorded tone).

With the above features in place, the observer is now ready to record behavior. For example, a teacher expressed concern about a student who is off-task frequently. She decides to measure the percent of intervals that her student is academically engaged. She operationally defines academic engagement and sets the interval length at 5 minutes. The observation begins at 9:00 AM, and every 5 minutes she hears a tone from an audiocassette player that signals her to look up and determine if the target student is meeting the operational definition for academic engagement. If the student is academically engaged immediately following the signal, the teacher puts a plus mark in the appropriate interval box on the data collection sheet. If the student does not meet the definition of academic engagement, the teacher puts a minus sign in the appropriate interval box on the data collection sheet. This method continues on for the 50-minute observational period (a total of 10 intervals). Later, the teacher reviews her data collection sheet and calculates the percent of intervals that her student was academically engaged for that observation period. For our example, the student had 7 plus marks and 3 minus marks, which means that he was academically engaged 70 percent of the intervals observed. Data is then graphed for future use.

A major benefit of using momentary time sampling is that the teacher or researcher can engage in other instructional tasks and only when signaled does he or she need to observe and record behavior, therefore limiting interference with teaching tasks and other instructional activities (Maag, 1999). However, it is notable that this method may result in an underestimation of behavior if the interval length is too long (Wolery et al., 1988). As with all direct observation systems, collecting interobserver reliability data is critical. The formula for calculating interobserver reliability for momentary time sampling is taking the number of agreement intervals and dividing by the agreements plus disagreement intervals and multiplying by 100. This formula will give you the percent of agreement between the primary observer and an independent observer.

## REFERENCES

Alberto, P. A., & Troutman, A. C. (2006). *Applied behavior analysis for teachers* (7th ed.). Upper Saddle River, NJ: Pearson Merrill Prentice Hall.

Fletcher-Janzen, E., & De Pry, R. L. (2003). *Teaching social competence and character: An IEP planner with goals, objectives, and interventions.* Longmont, CO: Sopris West Educational Services.

Maag, J. W. (1999). *Behavior management: From theoretical implications to practical applications.* San Diego, CA: Singular.

Wolery, M., Bailey, D. B., Jr., & Sugai, G. M. (1988). *Effective teaching: Principles and procedures of applied behavior analysis for exceptional students*. Boston: Allyn & Bacon.

RANDALL L. DE PRY
*University of Colorado at
Colorado Springs*

## BEHAVIORAL ASSESSMENT
## RESEARCH IN SPECIAL EDUCATION

## MONOGRAPHS OF THE SOCIETY FOR RESEARCH IN CHILD DEVELOPMENT

*Monographs of the Society for Research in Child Development* is one of three publications of the Society for Research in Child Development. Published irregularly by the University of Chicago Press, the *Monographs* series is perhaps the longest continuous publication in the field of child development.

In general, the series is intended for the publication of significant research articles that are longer than those normally published in journals. Of particular interest are longitudinal studies and research that appeals to a large number of developmentalists from a variety of fields.

Recent topics for the *Monographs* have been children's friendships, children at risk for developmental disorders, and the lasting effects of early education. In addition to monographs concerning normal child development, the *Monographs* also publish research on special or atypical children, including the hearing and visually impaired. The *Monographs* series is read by psychologists, pediatricians, special educators, anthropologists, social workers, and others, particularly in North America.

MICHAEL J. ASH
JOSE LUIS TORRES
*Texas A&M University*

## MONTESSORI, MARIA (1870–1952)

Maria Montessori, who was Italy's first woman physician, originated the educational system known as the Montessori method. The major features of her method were a nongraded classroom, individualization of instruction, sequential ordering of learning tasks, sensory and motor training, use of concrete materials, abolition of punishment, discovery learning, and freedom of activity and choice. First used in 1899 for the instruction of mentally retarded children. Montessori soon found that her approach was equally effective with nondisabled children. Her influence is evident today in both special classes and preschool and lower elementary programs. Montessori taught and lectured in many countries and her schools sprang up throughout the world. A visit to the United States in 1914 led to the formation of the American Montessori Society, with Alexander Graham Bell as president.

### REFERENCES

Goodman, L. (1974). Montessori education for the handicapped: The methods—The research. In L. Mann & D. A. Sabatino (Eds.), *The second review of special education* (pp. 153–191). Philadelphia: JSE.

Montessori, M. (1964). *The Montessori method*. New York: Schocken.

Orem, R. C. (Ed.). (1970). *Montessori and the special child*. New York: Capricorn.

Standing, E. M. (1962). *Maria Montessori: Her life and work*. New York: New American Library.

PAUL IRVINE
*Katonah, New York*

## MONTESSORI METHOD

## MONTESSORI METHOD

Maria Montessori was born in Chiavalle, Italy, in 1870; after receiving her doctorate she visited asylums, which spurred her interest in retarded children. Using some of the work of Itard and Seguin, she designed materials and an instructional method that was so successful that after one year of instruction, the retarded children had learned enough to pass the state examination given to normal children after one year of schooling. Montessori felt that if a retarded child could accomplish so much through her methods, a normal child should be able to accomplish even more. Gradually she devised materials and equipment to realize her goals and formulated an underlying philosophy based on the dignity and spiritual worth of the child. Between 1912 and 1917 she put her ideas into five key books: *The Montessori Method, Pedagogy and Anthropology, Dr. Montessori's Own Handbook,* and *The Advanced Montessori Method, Volumes I and II* (Gitter, 1970).

Montessori's method has many aspects of relevance to special educators. Because of her background as a physician, Montessori was concerned with the whole child's total development and physical well-being. She believed that children are possessed of an instinctive motivation and potential for psychological development, and that children's natural striving toward intellectual fulfillment is so great that, given the opportunity, they will willingly work toward development of the mind and body (Goodman, 1974).

If the child's role changes in the classroom, the teacher's role also changes. The teacher, or directress, the term Montessori preferred, became a guiding and supporting person in Montessori's classroom. Responsibilities included preparation of the environment, the introduction and demonstration of new materials, the maintenance of order, and the keeping of developmental and anecdotal records on each child (Goodman, 1974). Observation is fundamental to the method; the teacher is trained to observe carefully, so that the classroom becomes a diagnostic environment. The teacher checks the child's physical, perceptual-motor, and speech development, and takes appropriate action when a problem is noted.

The Montessori classroom provides a prepared environment, organized by ground rules, in which the child is able to move and work constructively in relative freedom, without disruption from other children. The engineered classroom resembles this prepared environment, which is organized around activity centers designed to produce order. The centers include the mastery center, where academic tasks are offered; the exploratory center, which contains an array of manipulative materials for the pursuit of scientific exploration; and the order center, which is reserved for specialized supportive one-to-one instruction (Kottler, 1977). The child can work directly with the didactic material he or she has chosen, for as long as desired, creating an individual curriculum paced at an individual rate. This makes it more likely that the child will experience a pattern of success, rather than failure (Orem, 1969).

Montessori believed that the areas in which the child needs assistance are motor function, where balance is secured, walking is learned, and movements are coordinated; and sensory function, from the environment, where the foundations of intelligence are laid for the continued exercise of observation, comparison, and judgment (Livingston-Dunn, 1982). Her curriculum emphasized sensory education, motor education, and language training. The program was, by design, preacademic, and early academic work was included for children only after the more basic skills, gross and fine-motor coordination, and perceptual abilities had been fully developed (Goodman, 1974).

Many educators have turned toward Montessori as a possible solution to the educational problems of children with disabilities. Individuation is central to special education and is attainable using the Montessori system. The nondemanding atmosphere is appropriate for children who cannot deal with pressure, and many children with sensory and perceptual deficits can benefit from the Montessori materials and methods. By applying several senses to a learning task, one sense can substitute for deficits in another sensory channel.

The early entrance age, as young as 3 years, is important in early intervention programs for children who need a head start. However the program's merits are not corroborated by results of objective evaluation, which offer little evidence to support the educational value of the Montessori method (Goodman, 1974). It is indicated that the Montessori environment may help children with disabilities by its nongroup structure to feel more accepted by peers, a prime factor in the development of self-image (Krogh, 1982). However, Montessori does not emphasize transformational thinking, or acknowledge the importance of broad experiences. She does not make use of the unplanned as well as the planned environment and events. She does not place a high value on the early development of symbolic behavior, including language. These are important aspects in childhood development and present serious criticisms of Montessori's method (Bruce, 1984).

## REFERENCES

Bruce, T. (1984). A Froebelian looks at Montessori's work. *Early Child Development and Care, 14*(1–2), 75–83.

Gitter, L. L. (1970). *The Montessori way.* Seattle, WA: Special Child.

Goodman, L. (1974). Montessori education for the handicapped: The methods—The research. In L. Mann & D. A. Sabatino (Eds.), *The second review of special education.* Philadelphia: O.S.E. Press.

Kottler, S. B. (1977, April). *The Montessori approach to the education of the exceptional child—Early childhood through high school.* Paper presented at the Annual International Convention, The Council for Exceptional Children, Atlanta, GA.

Krogh, S. L. (1982, April). Affective and social development. Some ideas from Montessori's prepared environment. *Topics in Early Childhood Special Education, 2*(1), 55–62.

Livingston-Dunn, C. (1982, December). *Functional art therapy for the severely handicapped.* Master's thesis ED229947. Northern Illinois University.

Montessori, M. (1964). *The Montessori method.* New York: Schocken.

Orem, R. C. (1969). *Montessori and the special child.* New York: Putnam.

Taylor-Hershel D., and Webster, R. (1983, January/February). Mainstreaming: A case in point. *Childhood Education, 59,* 175–179.

CATHERINE O. BRUCE
*Hunter College, City University of New York*

**ECOLOGICAL EDUCATION FOR CHILDREN WITH DISABILITIES**
**HUMANISM AND SPECIAL EDUCATION**
**MONTESSORI, MARIA**

## MOORES, DONALD F. (1935–    )

Donald F. Moores obtained his BA in 1958 in psychology from Amherst College in Massachusetts, his MA in 1959 in deaf education from Gallaudet University, and MS in 1963 in school administration from California State University, Northridge. He later earned his PhD in 1967 in educational psychology and psycholinguistics from the University of Illinois. Currently, he is a professor of education at Gallaudet University and editor of the *American Annals of the Deaf.*

Since his early experiences as a teacher of the deaf, Moores has been a professor at the University of Minnesota, Pennsylvania State University, and Gallaudet University, concentrating on research and teacher training in the area of deafness. He has also been a visiting professor at Huazhong University in Wuhan, China, and a participant in the USA/USSR International Research Exchange of Scholars. His textbook, *Educating the Deaf: Psychology, Principles, and Practices* (1996), is in its fourth edition. His approximately 200 other publications include *Educational and Developmental Aspects of Deafness* (1990), edited with Kathryn Meadow-Orlans, and *Meeting Halfway in American Sign Language* (1994), edited by Moores and written by Bernard Bragg and Jack Olson (D. F. Moores, pers. comm., February 24, 1998).

In his research, Moores (1976) found that a child's deafness limits his or her capacity to manipulate and react to the environment, and if nothing is done to help compensate for these difficulties, the child's communication skills deteriorate and overall development is delayed or impoverished. Similarly, he has found that deafness has little direct effect on intellectual and motor development, at least through age eight (Moores, Weiss, & Goodwin, 1978). The harm, according to Moores, comes from delay of either cognitive-academic training or the use of manual communication.

His research has focused on documentation that acquisition of American Sign Language by deaf children (up to 5 years of age) of deaf parents follows the same patterns as acquisition of spoken language by hearing children; assessment of effective preschool programs for young deaf children; identification of factors predictive of literacy in young deaf children; enhancing mathematics achievement; and relationships of school placement and academic achievement in deaf children (D. F. Moores, pers. comm., February 24, 1998).

### REFERENCES

Bragg, B., & Olson, J. (1994). *Meeting halfway in American Sign Language*. Rochester, NY: Deaf Life Press.

Moores, D. (1976). Early childhood special education for the hearing handicapped. In H. Spicker, R. Hodges, & N. Anastasiow (Eds.), *Early education for the handicapped*. Minneapolis: University of Minnesota Press.

Moores, D. (1996). *Educating the deaf: Psychology, principles, and practices* (4th ed.). Boston: Houghton Mifflin.

Moores, D., & Meadow-Orlans, K. (Eds.). (1990). *Educational and developmental aspects of deafness*. Washington, DC: Gallaudet University Press.

Moores, D. F., Weiss, K. L., & Goodwin, M. W. (1978). Early education programs for hearing-impaired children: Major findings. *American Annals of the Deaf, 123*(8), 925–936.

E. Valerie Hewitt
*Texas A&M University*
First edition

Tamara J. Martin
*The University of Texas of the
Permian Basin*
Second edition

## MORAL REASONING

Moral reasoning refers to the manner in which a person cognitively processes information to arrive at a judgment as to whether an act is right or wrong. The research emphasis in this area is not on the factors that influence moral behavior, but rather how increasingly complex levels of moral reason evolve within the context of cognitive development. The prevailing theory of moral judgment is Lawrence Kohlberg's (1976); it has as its underpinnings the work of Jean Piaget (1965).

Piaget and Kohlberg hold that the development of moral reasoning rests on the elaboration of general cognitive development, including, for instance, decreasing egocentrism and the use of concrete and formal operations. For example, a young child will judge a wrongdoer based upon the damage of an act. An older, more cognitively-advanced child will be more capable of abstraction and will judge the immorality of acts based upon intention. It is believed that a child is incapable of reasoning through a moral dilemma at a level more advanced than the overall level of cognitive development at which he or she is functioning.

Kohlberg (1976) proposes three levels of moral reasoning, each with two stages. At the preconventional stage, the child cannot help but solve ethical dilemmas from an egocentric perspective. Thus what is wrong is anything that leads to punishment; the effects of one's actions on others is unappreciated. As egocentrism declines, the child is able to assume the viewpoint of another person, albeit in a concrete, individualistic way. Now an act may be considered right if it is based on an agreement, a deal, or some kind of fair exchange. During the conventional stage, the child begins to consider the perspective of society, yet still within a rather concrete framework. Moral reasoning has an authoritarian flavor in that the child is heavily influenced by adherence to interpersonal expectations and social standards. Notions of "good girl–nice boy" and "law and order" operate as justifications for the resolutions of moral dilemmas. At the postconventional or principled level, the individual is able to engage in more abstract thinking about ethical matters, evidencing the emergence of formal operational thinking. A moral perspective is able to develop that recognizes universal ethical principles that are self-chosen. Laws or social agreements are usually viewed as valid because they are derived from universal principles. If a law is at variance with a principle, behavior should follow the principle. It must be emphasized that the level of moral reasoning displayed is not based on the final answer as to how one should behave or, for that matter, actual conduct. Rather, it is based on the rationale used to justify an action.

As a cognitive-developmental stage theorist, Kohlberg has assumed that his developmental stages were invariant (persons cannot skip a stage or change their order) and universal (stage sequencing and characteristics apply to all persons across all cultures, religions, and gender).

These assumptions generated a great deal of controversy and research (Turiel, 1998). The invariance of stages has been generally confirmed in cross-sectional and longitudinal research that is also cross-cultural (Colby & Kohlberg, 1987; Colby, Kohlberg, Gibbs, & Lieberman, 1983). Those individuals who show moral development do progress systematically through the stages. However, it must be noted that in many cultures, including the United States, most individuals do not advance beyond the fourth stage into the level of postconventional or principled morality.

The universality of the stages has been controversial. Postconventional morality simply does not exist in some societies and may reflect a Western ideal. Many societies do not value individualism and individual rights, and therefore in those societies, the highest morality may be shown in subjugation of individual rights to societal or collective rights (Shweder, Mahapatra, & Miller, 1990). Gilligan (1982) questioned the male bias of Kohlberg's moral reasoning stages. Kohlberg's own male bias and the use of males in his initial studies led him to emphasize a legalistic and individualistic approach to moral reasoning. Gilligan proposed that females would therefore show lower morality by this system because females defined morality in terms of justice (treating others fairly) and care (not turning away someone in need). Concern and care for others within a social network was especially important to females and therefore they would not appear to advance beyond the third stage in the conventionality level of morality. In general, studies have not supported a strong distinction between males and females when they resolve moral reasoning dilemmas. Within Kohlberg's theory there is room for concern about justice and care even at the higher stages of development (Turiel, 1998).

Moral reasoning theory has been applied to many different disciplines including philosophy, anthropology, sociology, criminology, and education (Turiel, 1998). In general, there is a complex but only moderate relationship between moral reasoning and moral conduct. Persons in a higher moral reasoning level tend to act consistently, but situations involving high cost or high punishment may influence behavior consistent with a lower level of morality (Thoma, Rest, & Davison, 1991). Higher education tends to increase the level of moral reasoning, perhaps because of exposure to conflictual problems. Furthermore, nonretarded children and older retarded children with the same mental ages tend to have similar levels of moral reasoning (Weisz & Zigler, 1979). These results demonstrate that cognitive development may underlie moral reasoning but training can affect the level and upper limit of reasoning.

## REFERENCES

Colby, A., & Kohlberg, L. (1987). *The measurement of moral judgment.* (Vol. 1). *Theoretical foundations and research validation.* Cambridge: Cambridge University Press.

Colby, A., Kohlberg, L., Gibbs, J., & Lieberman, M. (1983). A longitudinal study of moral judgment. *Monographs of the Society for Research in Child Development, 48,* Nos. 1–2, Serial No. 200.

Gilligan, C. (1982). *In a different voice: Psychological theory and women's development.* Cambridge, MA: Harvard University Press.

Kohlberg, L. (1976). Moral stages and moralization: The cognitive-developmental approach. In T. Lickona (Ed.), *Moral development and behavior.* New York: Holt, Rinehart, & Winston.

Piaget, J. (1965). *The moral judgment of the child.* New York: Free Press.

Shweder, R. A., Mahapatra, M., & Miller, J. G. (1990). Culture and moral development. In J. W. Stigler, R. A. Shweder, & G. Herdt (Eds.), *Cultural psychology: Essays on comparative human development.* Cambridge, England: Cambridge University Press.

Thoma, S. J., Rest, J. R., & Davison, M. L. (1991). Describing and testing a moderator of the moral judgment and action relationship. *Journal of Personality and Social Psychology, 61,* 659–669.

Turiel, E. (1998). The development of morality. In W. Damon & N. Eisenberg (Eds.), *Handbook of child psychology. Vol. 3, Social, emotional, and personality development* (5th ed., pp. 863–932). New York: Wiley.

Weisz, J. R., & Zigler, E. (1979). Cognitive development in retarded and nonretarded persons: Piagetian tests of the similar-sequence hypotheses. *Psychological Bulletin, 86,* 831–851.

LAURENCE C. GRIMM
*University of Illinois*
First edition

SPENCER K. THOMPSON
*The University of Texas of the Permian Basin*
Second edition

CONSCIENCE, LACK OF IN INDIVIDUALS WITH
  DISABILITIES
PIAGET, JEAN
SOCIAL SKILLS INSTRUCTION

# MORSE, WILLIAM C. (1915–    )

William Morse received his MA in 1939 and his PhD in 1947 in educational psychology from the University of Michigan. From 1945 to 1961, he was the director of the University of Michigan Fresh Air Camp, a group therapy program for disturbed boys and graduate training program for university students. It was here that Morse became an advocate of qualitative and participant-observation methods of research. In addition, with the leadership of Fritz Redl, he worked out a philosophy of residential treatment emphasizing life space interviewing and group dynamics. He has a sustained interest in the training of teachers of the emotionally disturbed.

In 1965 Morse became chairman of the Combined Program in Education and Psychology of the University of Michigan. He is currently professor emeritus of educational psychology and psychology. Since retirement from the University of Michigan in 1985, he taught in California at Northridge (CSUN) for three years, and then at the University of South Florida, until retiring.

His principal and recent publications include *Conflict in the Classroom: The Education of At-Risk and Troubled Students* (1996), *The Education and Treatment of Socio-Emotionally Disturbed Children and Youth* (1985), *Special Education Practice: Applying the Knowledge, Affirming the Values, and Creating the Future* (1997), and *Ethics and Decision Making in Local Schools: Inclusion, Policy, and Reform* (1997; W. C. Morse, pers. comm., October 12, 1998).

## REFERENCES

Long, N. J., Morse, W. C., & Newman, R. G. (1996). *Conflict in the classroom: The education of at-risk and troubled students* (5th ed.). Austin, TX: PRO-ED.

Morse, W. C. (1985). *The education and treatment of socio-emotionally disturbed children and youth.* Syracuse, NY: University Press.

Morse, W. C. (1993). Ecological approaches. In T. R. Kratochwill & R. J. Morris (Eds.), *Handbook of psychotherapy with children and adolescents* (pp. 320–355). Boston: Allyn & Bacon.

Paul, J. L., Berger, N. H., Osnes, P. G., Martinez, Y. G., & Morse, W. C. (Eds.). (1997). *Ethics and decision making in local schools: Inclusion, policy, and reform.* Baltimore: Brookes.

Paul, J. L., Churton, M., Morse, W. C., Duchnowski, A. J., Epanchin, B., Osnes, P., & Smith, R. L. (1997). *Special education practice: Applying the knowledge, affirming the values, and creating the future.* Boston: Brooks/Cole.

ELAINE FLETCHER-JANZEN
*University of Colorado at
Colorado Springs*

## MORSINK, CATHERINE V. (1937–    )

Catherine V. Morsink began her education career in 1959 when she received her BA in elementary education from Western Michigan University. For the next 10 years, she held a variety of teaching positions, in classes for the gifted, remedial reading programs, and the regular classroom. During this period, she also attended Rockford College (Illinois), where she was awarded the MAT in the teaching of reading in 1968. Morsink then went to the University of Kentucky where, while working as a materials specialist and later as training director at the University of Kentucky Regional Special Education Instructional Materials Center, she earned the EdD in special education in 1974.

Catherine V. Morsink

Morsink began her career with an interest in direct service delivery to children. During her various teaching stints, she developed a variety of ideas and materials for working with exceptional children in the context of the regular classroom, long before mainstreaming became popular. Her interests gradually shifted throughout the course of her graduate education, moving toward interests in special education personnel preparation and the evaluation of the various materials and methods she had developed over the years.

Morsink's best known and perhaps most influential work, *Teaching Special Needs Students in Regular Classrooms* (Morsink, 1984a), was an outgrowth of her shifting emphasis. This work reflects Morsink's academic preparation as well as her many years of experience as a front line special education teacher; it came on the heels of a return to the classroom as a grade 3 teacher after a sabbatical leave in 1980. Her research has included examining instructional variables associated with teaching children with various disabilities, developing intervention team models for educating students with learning disabilities, and identifying services needed within the context of the least restrictive environment (Algozzine & Morsink, 1989; Coben, Thomas, Sattler, & Morsink, 1997; Morsink & Lenk, 1992; Thomas, Correa, & Morsink, 1995).

Since earning her PhD in 1974, Morsink's academic ascent has been swift. In 1974, she became an assistant professor of special education at the University of Kentucky. She was promoted to associate rank in 1977, and quickly became chair of the department of special education in 1978. In 1980, Morsink moved to the University of Florida, where she become professor and chair of the department of special education.

Morsink is the author of the DELTA system for teaching decoding skills in reading (Morsink, 1984b). She has served on the editorial board of the *Journal of Teacher Education*, and continues to contribute to the field of special education with her publications concerned with methods of improving education for children with disabilities (Morsink, Thomas, & Correa, 1991; Thomas et al., 1995).

## REFERENCES

Algozzine, B., & Morsink, C. (1989). *A study of instruction in self-contained special education and regular classrooms. Final report.* Washington, DC: U.S. Department of Education.

Coben, S. S., Thomas, C. C., Sattler, R. O., & Morsink, C. V. (1997). Meeting the challenge of consultation and collaboration: Developing interaction teams. *Journal of Learning Disabilities, 30*(4), 427–432.

Morsink, C. V. (1984a). *Teaching special needs students in regular classrooms.* Boston: Little, Brown.

Morsink, C. V. (1984b). *DELTA: A design for word attack* (2nd ed.). Madison, WI: Learning Multi-Systems.

Morsink, C. V., & Lenk, L. L. (1992). The delivery of special education programs and services. *Remedial & Special Education, 13*(6), 33–43.

Morsink, C. V., Thomas, C. C., & Correa, V. I. (1991). *Instructor's manual to accompany interactive teaming: Consultation and collaboration in special programs.* New York: Merrill.

Thomas, C. C., Correa, V. I., & Morsink, C. V. (1995). *Interactive teaming: Consultation and collaboration in special programs* (2nd ed.). Englewood Cliffs, NJ: Merrill.

CECIL R. REYNOLDS
*Texas A&M University*
First edition

TAMARA J. MARTIN
*The University of Texas of the Permian Basin*
Second edition

# MOSAICISM

Mosaicism is a rare type of Down syndrome in which an error in cell division occurs at an early stage of mitosis (cell division). It is the coexistence of cells with different chromosomal counts in one individual. This chromosomal anomaly is not present at conception (Robinson & Robinson, 1965). Individuals who exhibit mosaicism appear to have less pronounced physical features of Down syndrome and their intellectual performance generally is not as impaired. Pueschel (1982) details the three major types of Down syndrome. In all cases of Down syndrome, there is the presence of additional genetic material in the cell. Instead of the usual 46 chromosomes in each cell, an individual with Down syndrome has 47. The extra chromosome may derive from either the egg or the sperm. Nondisjunction, found in 95 percent of individuals with Down syndrome, is rarely familial. In this type of Down syndrome, the two number 21 chromosomes (of the sperm or the egg) do not separate properly during cell division. Thus one cell will have an extra 21 chromosome. When united with a normal cell, trisomy 21 will result. The very first cell at conception will have 47 chromosomes. Translocation, a much less common type of Down syndrome, is inherited. It occurs in only 3 to 4 percent of all Down syndrome cases. It occurs when the additional number 21 chromosome material becomes attached or translocated to another chromosome.

Mosaicism, the least common form of Down syndrome, is found in about 1 percent of all cases. Mosaicism is not familial. Rather, it is thought to be due to an error in early cell division following conception. The first cell resulting from fertilization has the normal number of chromosomes. At some point after the egg is fertilized, the extra chromosome appears. At birth the child has some cells with 46 chromosomes and others with 47, thereby creating a mosaiclike pattern. Cells with 45 or fewer chromosomes usually do not survive.

The extra chromosome 21 is always associated with mental retardation and specific physical characteristics. Gibson and Frank (1961) list the most common features: large fissured tongue; short stubby hands; epicanthal fold at inner corner of the eye; single transverse crease across palm; inward curving little finger; flattened nose; fused ear lobules; cleft between big and second toe; small, flattened skull; short fifth finger; smooth simple outer earlobe; congenital heart problems; and a little finger with one lateral crease rather than two. All traits may not occur in any one individual with Down syndrome. Mosaics may exhibit few if any visible signs. They may have normal intelligence (Koch & Koch, 1974). The number of symptoms present is thought to be dependent on the age of the embryo when the error of cell division occurs. The earlier the division, the more severe the effect.

The reasons that chromosomes do not divide properly are not clearly understood (Smith & Wilson, 1973). Suspect are radiation and X-ray exposure; viral infections; misuse of drugs; or problems of hormone or immunological balance. Mosaics can transmit Down syndrome to the next generation. Some may not know they are mosaics until they produce a child with mosaicism or until cytogenetics reveals their condition. Amniocentesis can be performed during the first 12 to 16 weeks of pregnancy to determine if such chromosomal abnormalities exist (Dorfman, 1972).

## REFERENCES

Dorfman, A. (Ed.). (1972). *Antenatal diagnosis.* Chicago: University of Chicago Press.

Gibson, D., & Frank, H. F. (1961). Dimensions of mongolism: I. Age limits for cardinal mongol stigmata. *American Journal of Mental Deficiency, 66,* 30–34.

Koch, R., & Koch, K. (1974). *Understanding the mentally retarded child: A new approach.* New York: Random House.

Pueschel, S. M. (1982). *A study of the young child with Down syndrome.* New York: Human Science.

Robinson, H. B., & Robinson, N. M. (1965). *The mentally retarded child: A psychological approach.* New York: McGraw-Hill.

Smith, W. D., & Wilson, A. A. (1973). *The child with Down's Syndrome: Causes, characteristics and acceptance.* Philadelphia: Saunders.

SALLY E. PISARCHICK
*Cuyahoga Special Education
Service Center*

## CHROMOSOMES, HUMAN ANOMALIES, AND CYTOGENETIC ABNORMALITIES
## CONGENITAL DISORDERS
## DOWN SYNDROME
## MINOR PHYSICAL ANOMALIES

Moss, J. W. (1974). Trends and issues in special education. In N. G. Harding (Ed.), *Behavior of exceptional children: An introduction to special education.* Columbus, OH: Merrill.

Moss, J. W. (1980). *Postsecondary vocational education for mentally retarded adults.* Reston, VA: Council for Exceptional Children.

Moss, J. W., & Chalfant, J. (1965, November). Research and demonstration programs for handicapped children and youth. *Exceptional Children.*

E. VALERIE HEWITT
*Texas A&M University*
First edition

TAMARA J. MARTIN
*The University of Texas of the
Permian Basin*
Second edition

# MOSS, JAMES W. (1926–    )

Born in Wilmar, California, James W. Moss obtained both his BA in 1952 and MA in 1953 in psychology, with an undergraduate minor in sociology, from San Jose State College. He later earned his PhD in 1958 in clinical psychology (and a minor in special education) from George Peabody College. Moss served as director of the Employment Training Program and research associate at the University of Washington Child Development and Mental Retardation Center.

During most of his career, Moss conducted research related to improving the education of exceptional children and adults (Moss, 1969, 1980). Much of this work centered on the development of training and education programs for individuals with mental retardation (Moss, 1974; Moss & Chalfant, 1965). Believing that diagnostic labels are more harmful than helpful, Moss advocated avoiding their use with children unless the label applied with certainty (Moss, 1973).

Moss has been recognized in *Who's Who in the South and Southwest, Who's Who in the West,* and *American Men and Women of Science.* His contributions to the fields of education and psychology have included his service as associate commissioner of the Office of Developmental Programs, Office of Special Education, and Rehabilitation Services of the U.S. Department of Education, and fellow of the National Institute of Mental Health.

## REFERENCES

Moss, J. W. (1969). *The education of handicapped children: An exploration into instruction materials.* Washington, DC: U.S. Office of Education.

Moss, J. W. (1973). Disabled or disadvantaged: What's the difference? *Journal of Special Education, 7*(4).

# MOTIVATION

Not all students have a positive schooling experience. Indeed, some students are skeptical about the value of school, feel marginalized, disengage from and sometimes even attempt to disrupt the classroom learning process. Students' disaffection from schooling is a great concern for educators (Kumar, Gheen, & Kaplan, 2002), and many educators are at a loss for what they might do to help motivate disengaged and disaffected students. Although there are no easy answers for how to best motivate students, researchers working in the "motivational sciences" (Pintrich, 2003) have started to yield empirically supported insights and considerations for motivating students in classroom settings. And there are several recent summaries available that educators can use to guide their efforts at applying these insights and considerations in their work with students (Stipek, 1998).

What actually motivates a particular student in any given classroom or learning activity will vary as a function of a complex host of personal and social factors. Still, there are general insights and considerations that can be drawn from the past 2 decades of research conducted on motivation in the classroom. Pintrich (2003) has summarized findings from accumulated empirical research into five motivational generalizations and provided accompanying considerations for practice. A brief overview of each of the five motivational generalizations follows.

*Adaptive self-efficacy and competence beliefs motivate students.* When students believe they are capable of being successful they are more likely to exert and sustain effort and ultimately achieve (Bandura, 1997; Pintrich & Schunk, 2002). Unfortunately, there are many students who are fully capable of achieving success but give up too soon or never try because they underestimate their ability to be successful. Of course, there are also students who run into trouble because they have overestimated their current level of competence. It is therefore important that educators provide timely, informative feedback to students so they can gain an accurate estimation of their current level of competence in a particular domain (Pintrich, 2003). This includes helping students understand what competent performance looks like, what they are currently capable of doing, and what they can do to improve their current level of competence. By helping students develop accurate assessments of their ability and providing opportunities that blend challenge and success, educators can help ensure that students develop adaptive competency beliefs and thereby take on challenges, persevere in the face of difficulty, and ultimately develop higher levels of competence.

*Adaptive attributions and control beliefs motivate students.* In general, students who believe they have control over their own learning and behavior are more likely to be engaged in schooling, do well in school, and achieve at higher levels (Pintrich, 2003). Indeed, researchers (see Ryan & Deci, 2000 for review) working in the area of self-determination theory have argued that autonomy (i.e., a sense of control, choice, and ability to determine one's own behavior) is a fundamental human need and is central to healthy and happy human functioning. Educators can help students develop an adaptive sense of control by allowing students to have some choice on assignments and activities. In addition, educators can help students develop more adaptive attributions by helping them realize that they are capable of developing greater levels of competence by exerting effort, using effective learning strategies, and by gaining control over their own learning (Pintrich, 2003).

*Higher levels of interest and intrinsic motivation motivate students.* It should come as no surprise that if students are interested in what is being taught they are more likely to attend to, engage in, and ultimately demonstrate higher levels of achievement than if they were disinterested. Interest is a component of intrinsic motivation. And intrinsic motivation represents an internal, possibly innate, disposition to develop competence, seek out novelty, and engage in self-directed activities (Stipek, 1998). Educators can cultivate interest and intrinsic motivation by incorporating novelty and variety in activities and assignments, ensuring that learning tasks are personally meaningful to students, and by modeling interest in the content of what is being taught (Pintrich, 2003). Given that intrinsic motivation appears to be linked to high levels of engagement, enjoyment, learning, and creativity (Stipek, 1998), educators have good reason to develop learning tasks and activities that appeal to the intrinsic interests of their students rather than relying solely on external rewards and reinforcements.

*Higher levels of value motivate students.* It has been said that if it doesn't matter to students, it simply doesn't matter. Empirical evidence suggests that there may be some truth to this claim, at least with respect to value beliefs influencing students' choice of activities, effort, and persistence (Stipek, 1998). Value beliefs are considered to be a central feature of Expectancy-Value theory, which posits that achievement behaviors (e.g., choice, persistence, engagement, and ultimately performance) result from students' expectations for success and their values for academic tasks (see Pintrich & Schunk, 2002 for an overview). Given that value beliefs have been linked with students' effort, persistence, and choice of learning activities—educators can cultivate adaptive value beliefs by stressing the importance, relevance, and usefulness of learning activities, tasks, and content taught to students (Pintrich, 2003).

*Goals motivate and direct students.* Goals provide students with reasons why they should engage in certain behaviors. Educators can help students develop and pursue a combination of adaptive social and academic goals such that students do their part in establishing a safe and productive learning environment (Pintrich, 2003). In addition, research on Achievement Goal Theory (see Ames, 1992; Pintrich & Schunk, 2002; Urdan, 1997 for reviews) has demonstrated that students who develop a mastery goal orientation demonstrate high levels of engagement, seek out challenges, take intellectual risks, persevere in the face of difficulty, and come to view mistakes as informational rather than something to be avoided. A mastery goal orientation represents a focus on self-improvement, learning, creativity, and understanding. Educators can help students develop a mastery goal orientation by focusing their attention less on comparisons to others and more on self-improvement, understanding, and effort (Pintrich, 2003). In doing so, educators can help students develop adaptive goals that will lead to higher levels of engagement and ultimately a more positive and successful schooling experience.

## REFERENCES

Ames, C. (1992). Classrooms: Goals, structures, and student motivation. *Journal of Educational Psychology, 84,* 261–271.

Bandura, A. (1997). *Self-efficacy: The exercise of control.* New York: Freeman.

Kumar, R., Gheen, M. H., & Kaplan, A. (2002). Goal structures in the learning environment and students' disaffection from learning and schooling. In C. Midgley (Ed.), *Goals, goal structures and patterns of adaptive learning* (pp. 143–174). Mahwah, NJ: Erlbaum.

Pintrich, P. R. (2003). A motivational science perspective on the role of student motivation in learning and teaching contexts. *Journal of Educational Psychology, 95,* 667–686.

Pintrich, P. R., & Schunk, D. H. (2002). *Motivation in education: Theory, research, and applications* (2nd ed.). Upper Saddle River, NJ: Prentice Hall.

Ryan, R. M., & Deci, E. L. (2000). Self-determination theory and the facilitation of intrinsic motivation, social development, and well-being. *American Psychologist, 55,* 68–78.

Stipek, D. (1998). *Motivation to learn: From theory to practice* (3rd ed.). Boston: Allyn & Bacon.

Urdan, T. (1997). Achievement goal theory: Past results, future directions. In P. R. Pintrich & M. L. Maehr (Eds.), *Advances in motivation and achievement* (Vol. 10, pp. 99–142). Greenwich, CT: JAI Press.

RONALD A. BEGHETTO
*University of Oregon*

ACHIEVEMENT NEED
APPLIED BEHAVIOR ANALYSIS
POSITIVE REINFORCEMENT

## MOTOR-FREE VISUAL PERCEPTION TEST–REVISED

The Motor-Free Visual Perception Test–Revised (MVPT-R; Colarusso & Hammill, 1996) is a second edition of a popular test of visual perception first published in 1972. This test measures visual perception without motor involvement. It is designed for use by psychologists, educational diagnosticians, and others trained in individual assessment. The MVPT-R is easily administered in 15 to 20 minutes to children ages 4 through 11½ years. It is divided into five item types intended to measure the following components of visual perception: spatial relationships, visual discrimination, figure-ground, visual closure, and visual memory. The figure illustrates an item from the figure-ground grouping.

As the authors note, most of the tests used to assess visual perception (e.g., Bender Gestalt Test, Developmental Test of Visual-Motor Integration, and the drawing subtests of the McCarthy Scales of Children's Abilities) are actually measures of visual-motor integration skills, which require visual perceptual ability but make major demands on the child's fine motor skills. Children are frequently misdiag-

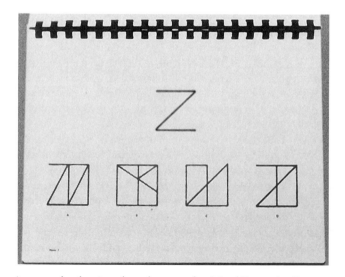

An example of an item from the motor-free Visual Perception Test; can you find the hidden Z?

nosed as having visual-perceptual disorders on the basis of poor performance on tests requiring extensive motor performance. The MVPT-R avoids the confounding of visual perception with motor skills in its assessment.

A good, solid assessment of visual perception independent of motor ability is a useful tool to those who must evaluate handicapped children. However, the MVPT-R manual lacks the necessary information for a proper evaluation of the quality of the scale. The description of the standardization sample is limited, giving little more than the sample size (which at 912 is credibly large). The sample's status regarding race is reported but seems to be different from the United States population statistics. Much of the psychometric data on the MVPT-R as reported in the manual are incomplete and reflect naivete regarding principles of test construction. In fact, in some ways, the 1996 standardization is not as good as the 1972 version (in 1972 the sample was drawn from 22 states; the 1996 sample came from only two states).

Reliability of the scale is moderate (high .70s and low .80s for internal consistency estimates). Surprisingly, no reliability information is provided for children older than eight. Validity information is dated; only studies pertaining to the 1972 edition are provided.

The MVPT-R is useful principally because of the lack of other instruments from which to choose. It is easy to administer and score and has considerable intuitive appeal. In fairness to the test's authors, the current edition was prepared by the publisher's staff; the authors were not intimately involved in designing the revision, writing the manual, or collecting the sample.

### REFERENCE

Colarusso, R. P., & Hammill, D. D. (1996). *Motor-Free Visual Perception Test–Revised*. Novato, CA: Academic Therapy Publications.

CECIL R. REYNOLDS
*Texas A&M University*

## DEVELOPMENTAL TEST OF VISUAL PERCEPTION–SECOND EDITION
VISUAL-MOTOR AND VISUAL-PERCEPTUAL PROBLEMS

## MOTOR LEARNING

Motor learning is necessary to acquire the skills required for effective movement of the body. Although some authors have distinguished between motor and movement activities, the terms are often interchangeable (Harrow, 1972). Oxendine (1984) has noted three types of motor (or perceptual motor) learning. First is the maturationally related behavior that typically is developed early in life. Walking, speaking, and general body coordination are in this category. The second group of skills is high in perceptual components and includes communicative behaviors such as handwriting. These activities are necessary for continued educational progress. A final set of motor behaviors is learned because the performance of these activities results in direct benefits to the actor. Much of vocational and recreational accomplishment is built on motor learning.

The motor learning process involves progress from a cognitive phase, where the learner tries to understand the process involved, to an associative or practice phase, where the learner perfects the skill. Finally, the learner enters an autonomous phase, where the activity becomes habitual (Oxendine, 1984). Once the activity is habitual, it does not require conscious control and may operate under a different memory system from that used for other activities (Tulving, 1985). It is difficult for individuals for whom many motor tasks are routine to separate and verbally label the components of these activities. An individual who has reached the autonomous phase may thus find it difficult to communicate with someone in the cognitive phase of motor learning. Many special education students may be in the cognitive phase on tasks that most people have mastered and take as a matter of course.

The sensorimotor deficits faced by many special education students make the issue of motor performance objectives particularly central in the design of education for those students. Motor learning is not only important for its own sake, but as a component of cognitive and affective development. Activities learned in physical-education programs for the handicapped increase self-esteem and allow for social interaction in games (Moon & Renzaglia, 1982). Basic motor skills are necessary for the activities of daily living. Learning the motor behaviors required for communication is crucial for cognitive development.

Harrow (1972) has developed a taxonomy of tasks in the psychomotor domain. As with classification systems in the cognitive and affective domains, this taxonomy is designed to allow the teacher to specify educational objectives. Often the special education teacher must produce objectives aimed at needs of a given disability group. Motor learning behavioral objectives typically include motor skills of daily living and fine and gross motor performance (Fredericks et al., 1976; Hawkins et al., 1983).

Motor learning objectives for moderately and severely disabled students may involve behaviors that can be taught to most nondisabled individuals without any carefully constructed plan or method. The Hawkins et al. (1983) project is an example of the use of motor performance objectives to produce detailed activity programs for an enriched home and school environment. Such planning may be necessary to produce desired levels of simple motor learning. In general, motor learning has better outcomes the earlier it is initiated (Sanz & Melendez, 1992).

## REFERENCES

Fredericks, H. D., Riggs, C., Furey, J., Grove, D., Moore, W., McDonnell, J., Jordan, E., Hanson, W., Baldwin, V., & Wadlow, M. (1976). *The teaching research curriculum for moderately and severely handicapped.* Springfield, IL: Thomas.

Harrow, A. J. (1972). *Taxonomy of the psychomotor domain.* New York: McKay.

Hawkins, R. P., McGinnis, L. D., Bieniek, B. J., Timmons, D. M., Eddy, D. B., & Cone, J. D. (1983). *The school and home enrichment program for severely handicapped children.* Champaign, IL: Research.

Moon, M. S., & Renzaglia, A. (1982). Physical fitness and the mentally retarded: A critical review of the literature. *Journal of Special Education, 16,* 269–287.

Oxendine, J. B. (1984). *Motor learning* (2nd ed.). Englewood Cliffs, NJ: Prentice Hall.

Sanz, M. T., & Melendez, F. J. (1992). Early motor training in Down syndrome babies: Results of an intervention program. (ERIC Clearinghouse No. EC 301660)

Tulving, E. (1985). How many memory systems are there? *American Psychologist, 40,* 385–398.

Lee Anderson Jackson, Jr.
*University of North Carolina at Wilmington*

MOVEMENT THERAPY
PERCEPTUAL TRAINING
VISUAL-MOTOR AND VISUAL-PERCEPTUAL PROBLEMS

## MOTOR SPEECH DISORDERS

Motor speech disorders are caused by a neuropathology that affects a person's ability to plan a program of motor activity (apraxia) or impairs their ability to carry out the movements which produce speech sounds (dysarthria). Motor speech disorders comprise more than 36 percent of all acquired communication disorders (Duffy, 1995). A motor speech disorder can be acquired or congenital, and may occur in both children and adults. Any type of language disorder is excluded from the category of motor speech disorder. Speech disorders caused by deficits or deviation in speech structures, such as laryngectomy, or delays in development, such as phonological processes, are also not classified as motor speech disorders.

Dysarthria describes a group of disorders in which speech movement errors are due to muscle weakness, incoordination, neural disinhibition, and sensory deficits. While problems can be focused on a single component of the speech system (i.e., respiration, phonation, articulation, or resonation), most dysarthrias impact all systems to some degree. The speech symptoms of different dysarthrias can be evaluated perceptually and these characteristics can be reliably related to distinct neuropathologic substrates. Therefore, dysarthric speech can be used to differentially diagnose certain types of neurological disorders. Treatment for dysarthria requires both behavioral and medical treatment.

In apraxia of speech, speech muscles and their neural supply are intact. However, the person demonstrates an impaired ability to map out a sensorimotor program—or plan of action—that determines the correct number and type of motor movements needed and the sequence in which they should occur. In speech apraxia, a person who produces involuntary movements of articulators effortlessly often cannot reproduce these same movements on command for speech production. Apraxia of speech can co-occur with apraxic dysfunction in other systems, such as nonspeech oral movements, oculomotor function, and limb movement. Treatment for speech apraxia is behaviorally based. Very little evidence can be found for efficacy of medical treatments applied to speech apraxia.

Motor speech problems can be caused by vascular accidents, neoplasms, degenerative diseases, trauma, infection, allergic reaction, and metabolic abnormalities. Appearance of motor speech symptomology concomitant with the beginning of speech development is problematic for differential diagnosis unless a known neurologic etiology is present. Often, a motor speech disorder is found to coexist with other communication disorders that may result from neurologic (e.g., aphasia), developmental (e.g., delayed language), or musculoskeletal (e.g., cleft palate) disorders. Careful evaluation is needed to differentiate between multiple communication disorders in order to devise an effective treatment plan.

### REFERENCES

Duffy, J. R. (1995). *Motor speech disorders.* St. Louis, MO: Mosby.

Dworkin, J. P. (1991). *Motor speech disorders: A treatment guide.* St. Louis, MO: Mosby Year Book.

LINDA H. LEEPER
*New Mexico State University*

## MOVE INTERNATIONAL

The Mobility Opportunities via Education (MOVE®) curriculum is a dedicated functional mobility curriculum specifically designed for individuals who experience severe disabilities. The curriculum is activity based and is a naturalistic approach to teaching students with physical disabilities functional motor skills necessary for successful integration into school and community environments (Blanton, 1990).

MOVE is a top-down, activity-based curriculum designed to teach children and adults with physical disabilities basic, functional motor skills needed within home, school, and community environments (Kern County Superintendent of Schools, 1999). The curriculum was developed in the early 1980s by D. Linda Bidabe. Linda refused to accept that some of her students with severe disabilities were not learning to sit, stand, or walk. She held the belief that all people can learn, and that if her students were provided the needed instruction, training, and adaptive equipment, they could learn and benefit from their new-found skills. She desired to disengage herself and her students from a deficit model widely practiced in education for students with developmental disabilities, in which the individual's limitations are emphasized, and replace it with a support model where future potentials are emphasized. She believed that educational programs that incorporate the support model provide many more opportunities for persons with severe disabilities to become active participants in life activities (Bidabe, Barnes, & Whinnery, 2001).

The MOVE curriculum is a natural approach to teaching functional mobility skills that focus on increased participation in normal activities of daily living. Individuals using the MOVE curriculum follow a top-down approach to program planning. Instructional activities and basic skills needed by an individual are selected based on functional outcomes. Instruction is incorporated into routinely occurring events that take place during the day. MOVE is successfully implemented by a transdisciplinary team that includes educators, therapists, parents, paraprofessionals, and anyone else who interacts with the individual. The team works collaboratively to assess the student's present skills, design an individualized program specific for the individual, and teach those necessary skills while the student engages in school, home, and community activities. Every team member involved with the student is encouraged to take an active role in teaching the skills needed for sitting, standing, and walking (Bidabe et al., 2001).

There are six steps in using the MOVE curriculum: testing, setting goals, task analysis, measuring prompts, reducing prompts, and teaching skills. The first three steps of the MOVE curriculum form the foundation for deciding what to teach. Critical to these first steps is the administration of the Top-Down Motor Milestone Test (TDMMT) that identifies strengths and weaknesses in functional motor skill development. In steps 2 and 3 the student's immediate and long-term goals are identified, based on a family interview. Once needs have been determined, the transdisciplinary team selects priority activities to be focused on in the student's program. A task analysis to identify critical skills necessary for participation in identified activities is conducted by those persons working with the individual. While the first three steps of the curriculum addresses what to teach, steps 4, 5, and 6 determine the interventions necessary or how to teach the desired skills.

The MOVE curriculum can be implemented in a home, at a school, in a facility, or in the community, and it is easily adapted for a person who might be fully included as a student in a general education classroom. Wherever the individual might be they can enjoy opportunities for sitting, standing, or walking as a natural part of the setting or the activity. Wheelchairs are only used in bus transportation and for long walking distances. Equipment may be standard chairs, adapted chairs, standers, and walkers. Specialized adaptive equipment specific to the purposes of the MOVE curriculum has been produced during recent years and will likely continue to evolve in use and availability as the curriculum model is adopted in various regions and countries throughout the world. MOVE is integrated across the environments of an individual's life; abilities become the focal point rather than deficits, which generalizes to increased opportunities and the very real likelihood of improvement in the quality of life. For additional information on MOVE International, please visit their web site at http://www.move-international.org.

## REFERENCES

Bidabe, D., Barnes, S., & Whinnery, K. (2001). MOVE: Raising expectations for individuals with severe disabilities. *Physical Disabilities: Education and Related Services, 19*(2), 31–48.

Blanton, K. F. (1990). *MOVE: Mobility opportunities via education.* Bakersfield, CA: Kern County Superintendent of Schools.

Kern County Superintendent of Schools. (1999). *MOVE: Mobility opportunities via education.* Bakersfield, CA: Author.

PETER KOPRIVA
*Fresno Pacific University*

## MOTOR LEARNING
## MOTOR SPEECH DISORDERS

## MOVEMENT THERAPY

Movement therapy, creative movement therapy, body movement therapy, and dance therapy are all terms used interchangeably in the literature to describe a psychoanalytic, therapeutic approach that assists the disabled individual in the expression of his or her feelings and emotions in an acceptable manner through movement. Body movement therapy was described by Weisbrod (1972) as "the planned use of any aspect of dance, movement, and sensory experience to further the physical and psychic integration of the individual" (p. 66). It has been used successfully with the learning disabled, emotionally disturbed (e.g., schizophrenics and inhibited neurotics), deaf or hearing impaired, blind, aphasic, and retarded, as well as normal children and adults, to assist in language development and/or nonverbal communication skills (Chace, 1971; Weisbrod, 1972; Zumberg & Zumberg, 1979).

Movement therapy was greatly influenced by the psychoanalytic theories of Reich (1942), Jung (Hochheimer, 1969), and Sullivan (1953). Their contributions related to the expressiveness of body language, the therapeutic value of artistic experiences, and the interactive nature of personality. Influence was also exhibited by Laban's (1950) analysis of movement behaviors, Burton's (1974) improvision techniques, and Jacobson's (1958) and Schultz and Luthe's (1959) relaxation techniques.

The goal of movement therapy for childhood schizophrenics, who may be nonverbal or confused verbally, is to assist them to communicate and relate through movement. The goal for inhibited neurotics, who may be verbal but unable to clearly express certain ideas, notions, or convictions about themselves, the world, or others, is to confront blocked areas through the use of the body (Long, Morse, & Newman, 1971). The goal for all individuals is to present experiences that have underlying value to assist them in confronting their emotions (Weisbrod, 1972). This can be accomplished through activities that include imitation of nature or animals, expression of past, present, or future feelings of self or others, and use of music, voice, hand clapping, feet stamping, or environmental sounds in rhythm instruments (Shea, 1978). For example, having a child demonstrate the movement related to the loss of a toy may help him or her to express sadness or pain. Emotions such as anger, joy, and depression may be expressed by having the child perform the rhythm attached to rhythmic bases. Individuals with eating disorders may acknowledge body sensations and body image in creative movement (Williams, 1993).

Chace (1971) described differences between goals for normal children and disturbed individuals. For normal children, who are constantly, conscientiously, reaching out for knowledge, and using movement to explore the world, movement goals are established that allow them to develop a heightened awareness of body coordination, a sensitivity to musical tones and rhythms, and an alertness to new ways of using the body in dance patterns. For disturbed adults, on the other hand, the goals must be to reeducate them to use their bodies for more than expressing immediate emotions. They must learn to reach out to the world around them. "With both children and mental patients, it is important to remember that dance (movement) sessions . . . are for the purpose of building sufficient awareness of self through expressive movement" (Chace, 1971, p. 218). The final goal of all movement therapy is the development of more confidence in functioning in the world of reality.

Although movement therapeutic techniques must have defined limits of expected behavior and organized instruction in the use of the body, they must also be structured to allow for experimentation and the development of self-confidence. Chace (1971) stated that with children, this is accomplished by holding firm limits while allowing the child to widen them as he or she develops naturally, but with mental patients, the limits must not only be clearly defined, but often help must be given to the patient to expand and push outward from the limits into the real world. "Demonstration followed by guided exploration facilitates the development of creative movement" (Weisbrod, 1972, p. 68).

## REFERENCES

Burton, C. (1974). Movement as group therapy in the psychiatric hospital. In *Dance therapy—Focus on dance.* Washington, DC: American Association for Health, Physical Education and Recreation.

Chace, M. (1971). Dance in growth or treatment settings. In N. J. Long, W. C. Morse, & R. G. Newman (Eds.), *Conflict in the classroom: The education of children with problems* (2nd ed.). Belmont, CA: Wadsworth.

Hochheimer, W. (1969). *The psychotherapy of C. G. Jung.* New York: Putnam.

Jacobson, E. (1958). *Progressive relaxation.* Chicago: University of Chicago Press.

Laban, R. (1950). *The mastery of movement.* London: MacDonald & Evans.

Long, N. J., Morse, W. C., & Newman, R. G. (Eds.). (1971). *Conflict in the classroom: The education of children with problems* (2nd ed.). Belmont, CA: Wadsworth.

Reich, W. (1942). *Character analysis.* New York: Farrar, Straus & Giroux.

Schultz, J. H., & Luthe, W. (1959). *Autogenic training: A psychophysiological approach in psychotherapy.* New York: Grune & Stratton.

Shea, T. M. (1978). *Teaching children and youth with behavior disorders.* St. Louis, MO: Mosby.

Siegel, E. V. (1984). *Dance-movement therapy: The mirror of ourselves: A psychoanalytic approach.* New York: Human Services.

Sullivan, H. S. (1953). *The interpersonal theory of psychiatry.* New York: Norton.

Weisbrod, J. A. (1972). Shaping a body image through movement therapy. *Musical Education Journal, 58*(8), 66–69.

Williams, J. (1993). *Anorexia nervosa: Sociocultural factors and treatment.* (ERIC Clearinghouse No. CG 025009)

Zumberg, C., & Zumberg, M. (1979). Movement: A therapeutic technique for use with the learning disabled. *Academic Therapy, 14*(3), 347–352.

SUSANNE BLOUGH ABBOTT
*Bedford Central School District,
Mt. Kisco, New York*

## DANCE THERAPY

# MOVIGENICS

Movigenics is a theory of learning disabilities developed by Raymond H. Barsch (1965, 1967), in which he postulated that learning difficulties are related to an individual's in-ability to interact effectively with space. The word movigenics was derived from two Latin words, *movere,* meaning to move, and *genesis,* meaning origin and development. "It is, therefore, the study of the origin and development of patterns of movement in man and the relationship of these movements to his learning efficiency" (Barsch, 1967, p. 33). The theory is based on Barsch's premise that human learning is related to movement efficiency. As a child adapts to his or her environment and learns to move effectively through it, he or she also develops language as a means of defining experience in connection with space (Lerner, 1971). Movigenics is based on 10 constructs of human behavior (Barsch, 1967, pp. 35–64):

1. The fundamental principle underlying the design of the human organism is movement efficiency.

2. The primary objective of movement efficiency is to economically promote the survival of the organism.

3. Movement efficiency is derived from the information the organism is able to process from an energy surround.

4. The human mechanism for transducing energy forms into information is the percepto-cognitive system.

5. The terrain of movement is space.

6. Developmental momentum provides a constant forward thrust toward maturity and demands an equilibrium to maintain direction.

7. Movement efficiency is developed in a climate of stress.

8. The adequacy of the feedback system is critical in the development of movement efficiency.

9. Development of movement efficiency occurs in segments of sequential expansion.

10. Movement efficiency is symbolically communicated through the visual-spatial phenomenon called language.

These constructs form the theory from which Barsch developed a curriculum that allows a child to explore and experience himself or herself in space. The classroom stimuli is well structured and kept to a minimum; there are no desks or books, lighting is artificially controlled, and a designated space is carpeted for crawling. Although activities are well planned, they are presented randomly to assist children in becoming less rigid (McCarthy & McCarthy, 1969). Hart and Jones (1968) describe the way in which Barsch's curriculum can be used as a social model for guiding parents in child-rearing practices.

Barsch was highly influenced by Werner, Strauss, and Getman. He is one of the four main perceptual-motor theorists who are well known for their work with learning-disabled children. The other three theorists are Kephart, Getman, and Frostig (Hallahan & Cruickshank, 1973).

## REFERENCES

Barsch, R. H. (1965). *A movigenic curriculum.* Madison, WI: Bureau for Handicapped Children.

Barsch, R. H. (1967). *Achieving perceptual-motor efficiency. A space-oriented approach to learning* (Vol. 1). Seattle, WA: Special Child Publications.

Hallahan, D. P., & Cruickshank, W. M. (1973). *Psycho-educational foundations of learning disabilities.* Englewood Cliffs, NJ: Prentice Hall.

Hart, J., & Jones, B. (1968). *Where's Hannah? A handbook for parents and teachers of children with learning disorders.* New York: Hart.

Lerner, J. W. (1971). *Children with learning disabilities* (2nd ed.). New York: Houghton Mifflin.

McCarthy, J. J., & McCarthy, J. F. (1969). *Learning disabilities.* Boston: Allyn & Bacon.

SUSANNE BLOUGH ABBOTT
*Bedford Central School District,*
*Mt. Kisco, New York*

## BARSCH, RAY H.
## PERCEPTUAL-MOTOR DIFFICULTIES
## SENSORY INTEGRATIVE THERAPY

## MULLEN SCALES OF EARLY LEARNING: AGS EDITION

The Mullen Scales of Early Learning: AGS Edition (MSEL: AGS; Mullen, 1995) is an individually administered test of cognitive functioning that may be used with children from birth to 68 months. The MSEL:AGS consists of four cognitive scales: Visual Reception, Receptive Language, Expressive Language, and Fine Motor, as well as a Gross Motor Scale. Scores on the four cognitive scales are combined to yield the Early Learning Composite (ELC).

The Visual Reception Scale attempts to measure visual processing, visual discrimination, and visual memory, by requiring the child to respond by pointing to objects or pictures or by manipulating objects. Item examples include fixating on and tracking a silver triangle, looking for a toy when covered and then displaced, and sorting blocks and spoons by category.

The Receptive Language Scale purports to assess a child's auditory comprehension and auditory memory skills. This scale places the emphasis on a child's ability to decode verbal input while reducing output requirements. Examples of questions on this item include "What is your name?" and "What do we wash our hands with?"

The Expressive Language Scale was constructed to measure speaking ability and language formation. This scale assesses a child's spontaneous utterances, verbal responses to items, and concept formation. Children can receive points for jabbering with inflection, naming objects, or repeating numbers or sentences back to the examiner.

The Fine Motor Scale purports to measure a child's ability to manipulate small objects and use control and coordination skills. As on the Visual Reception Scale, vocalization is not required. This scale requires the child to manipulate objects using one hand (unilaterally) and two hands (bilaterally).

The Gross Motor Scale attempts to assess the range of gross motor abilities from 0 to 33 months, with 35 items. Given that the data for the Gross Motor Scale are available only for children aged 34 months to 68 months, this scale is not included in the ELC. The scale asks the child to perform such tasks as support oneself on forearms, walk with one hand held, and walk on a line with arms at side.

The raw scores for each scale can be converted into age-adjusted normalized scores. The $T$ score for the four cognitive skills can be further converted into a normalized ELC score (M = 100, SD = 15). In addition, the scores can be used to obtain the child's percentile rank and age equivalent score, the age at which the child's raw score is the median score.

The MSEL:AGS was standardized on a nationally representative sample of 1,849 children aged 2 days to 69 months with no known physical and mental disabilities and parents who spoke primarily English. Data on children were collected during two different periods—1981 to 1986 and 1987 to 1989—for the south, west, north, and north central regions. Approximately 40 percent of the sample came from the earlier norming period and included children only in the northeast region. Although the standardization sample included 1,849 individuals, with at least 200 individuals per 1-year interval, the sample approximated the U.S. population, as indicated by 1990 census data, only on gender. There was limited correspondence between U.S. population estimates and the standardization sample on race/ethnicity, community size, and socioeconomic status (i.e., fathers' occupation). Users should be extremely cautious in interpreting an individual's performance using the MSEL:AGS norms, given that the data were collected during two different time periods and later combined to form the current standardization sample data.

The total test (i.e., ELC) internal consistency reliability coefficients of the MSEL:AGS range from .83 to .95 (median = .91) and are considered at least adequate. However, the test-retest reliability coefficients for the ELC cannot be assessed because they are not available. That is, test-retest reliability data are based on an earlier version of the scales that did not contain the ELC. Specific construct validity evidence consists of the developmental trend of the raw scores, intercorrelations of the scales, and factor analysis. Although this analysis provides some evidence for the ELC approximation of *g,* there is limited empirical evidence to support the placement of items on their respective scales or for the inclusion of the scales themselves. In addition, no confirmatory factor analyses were conducted with the

AGS version of the MSEL. The limited construct validity evidence of the MSEL:AGS may be a major quantitative weakness of this instrument because interpretation of an individual's performance on the various scales is rendered tentative at best.

## REFERENCES

Bradley-Johnson, S. (2001). Cognitive assessment for the youngest children: A critical review of tests. *Journal of Psychoeducational Assessment, 19,* 19–44.

Dumont, R., Cruse, C., Alfonso, V., & Levine, C. (2000). A test review: The Mullen Scale of Early Learning: AGS Edition (MSEL:AGS). *Journal of Psychoeducational Assessment, 18,* 125–132.

Plake, B. S., & Impara, J. C. (Eds.). (2001). *The fourteenth mental measurements yearbook.* Lincoln, NE: Buros Institute of Mental Measurements.

RON DUMONT
*Fairleigh Dickinson University*

JOHN O. WILLIS
*Rivier College*

# MULTICULTURAL SPECIAL EDUCATION

Poplin and Wright (1983) have indicated that the topic of cultural pluralism is necessary to special education literature and practice for three reasons: (1) many culturally and linguistically diverse children are placed in special education because of cultural, linguistic, or racial differences; (2) of those minority-culture students who do not have disabilities, some have specific learning disabilities, and (3) special educators are often vanguards of new ideas in the schools. In addition, there appears to exist a continued overrepresentation of minority students in special education programs.

The concept of multicultural special education abounds with controversies, one of which is the issue of overrepresentation of minority children in special education classes. However, there are other issues that demand even greater attention, such as linguistic differences versus linguistic difficulties, minority-culture norms versus expected classroom behavior, and biases on assessment procedures as well in instrumentation.

Plata and Santos (1981) state that the purpose of bilingual special education "is to meet the academic, sociocultural, and psychological needs of non-English speaking handicapped pupils who cannot meet performance standards normally expected of a comparable group of English speaking handicapped pupils" (p. 98). Chan and Rueda (1979) refer to a "hidden curriculum" that interferes with learning and social adaptations by many children who come from a culturally deprived environment. Cartwright, Cartwright, and Ward (1984) suggest that educators must address the role of the school in socializing culturally different students in terms of expectation and accommodate greater diversity within the schools.

In addition to the hidden curriculum (Chan & Rueda, 1979), consideration should be given to the language variables, sometimes referred to as a double handicap (Megan, 1982). Many times the language used by minority children is somewhat different; this should not be perceived as negative but should be appreciated and respected. In fact, most experts suggest that schools should not try to change a child's dialect in the hopes of improving academic skills.

The concept of nondiscriminatory testing is a major concern regarding multicultural special education. Assessment of students referred for special education services, especially the mentally retarded and learning disabled, has been an intensely debated topic; a major issue is the fairness and usefulness of conventional practices (Reschly, 1982). However, this issue is far from simple. As Sattler (1984) points out, there are many different types of biases in assessment. Reschly (1982) indicates that there are many different ways to define the concept of test biases. Compounded by strong emotional feelings and the complexity of the assessment process, Reynolds (1982) suggests that the controversy over nondiscriminatory assessment will probably continue. Test developers, test authors, and test users (teachers, psychologists) must be sensitive to the many differences children from various cultures bring to assessment procedures. These factors, along with a commitment to interpreting test scores cautiously and objectively and in accordance with economic and cultural factors, may enhance efforts to meet the educational needs of multicultural students.

The issues concerning multicultural education have received serious consideration by those in special education because of the overrepresentation of minorities in classes for the mildly disabled. The major challenge faced by educators is the ability to appreciate and understand the abilities of culturally and linguistically diverse children. Multicultural education and inclusion share a common goal: integrating the disabled and the culturally different student and adult into the mainstream of school and society. We must insist on sound and effective instructional programs that are relevant to the students who come from different cultures (Garcia & Malkin, 1993).

## REFERENCES

Cartwright, G. P., Cartwright, C. A., & Ward, M. E. (1984). *Educating special learners* (2nd ed.). Belmont, CA: Wadsworth.

Chan, K. S., & Rueda, R. (1979). Poverty and children in education: Separate but equal. *Exceptional Children, 45*(6), 422–428.

Garcia, S. B., & Malkin, D. H. (1993). Toward defining programs and services for culturally and linguistically diverse learners in special education. *Teaching Exceptional Children, 26*(1), 52–58.

Megan, E. L. (1982). *Exceptional children in today's schools: An alternative resource book.* Denver, CO: Love.

Plata, M., & Santos, S. L. (1981). Bilingual special education: A challenge for the future. *Teaching Exceptional Children, 14*(3), 97–100.

Poplin, M. S., & Wright, P. W. (1983). The concept of cultural pluralism: Issues in special education. *Learning Disability Quarterly, 6*(4), 267–272.

Reschly, D. J. (1982). Assessing mild mental retardation: The influence of adaptive behavior, sociocultural status, and prospects for nonbiased assessment. In C. R. Reynolds & T. B. Gutkin (Eds.), *The handbook of school psychology.* New York: Wiley.

Reynolds, C. R. (1982). The problem of bias in psychological assessment. In C. R. Reynolds & T. B. Gutkin (Eds.), *The handbook of school psychology.* New York: Wiley.

Sattler, J. M. (1984). *The assessment of children's intelligence and special abilities* (2nd ed.). Boston: Allyn & Bacon.

HUBERT R. VANCE
*East Tennessee State University*

## CULTURALLY/LINGUISTICALLY DIVERSE STUDENTS AND LEARNING DISABILITIES
## CULTURE FAIR TESTS
## MAINSTREAMING
## NONDISCRIMINATORY ASSESSMENT

## MULTIDISCIPLINARY TEAM

Multidisciplinary team (MDT) is defined by Golin and Ducanis (1981, p. 2) as "a functioning unit composed of individuals with varied and specialized training who coordinate their activities to provide services to children." The term MDT is often used interchangeably with the term interdisciplinary team. Teamwork in child guidance has been prominent since the early 1900s; it became even more evident in education in the 1950s. The use of the MDT with exceptional children increased because of the whole child concept and because of the legislative mandates passed by various states and, later, by the federal government. The whole child concept was developed by Whitehouse when he described a human being as an "interacting, integrated, whole" (1951, p. 45). Problems of exceptional children are interrelated and cannot be adequately treated in isolation. The various services needed by the exceptional child must be coordinated; therefore, the team approach was developed.

In 1975, the Education for All Handicapped Children Act (PL 94-142) was passed. Both it and its successor legislation, the Individuals with Disabilities Education Act (IDEA) require that all children with disabilities be provided with an appropriate individualized educational program (IEP) in the least restrictive environment. Regulations implementing the statutory provision state that the IEP team includes "a representative of the public agency who is qualified to provide, or supervise the provision of, specially designed instruction to meet the unique needs of children with disabilities" (34 CFR §300.321). "The child is assessed in all areas related to the suspected disability, including where appropriate, health, vision, hearing, social and emotional status, general intelligence, academic performance, communicative status, and motor abilities" (Golin & Ducanis, 1981, pp. 86–87).

Since the time of PL 94-142, requirements for the makeup of the MDT have expanded to include a variety of possible team members, including school administrators, school psychologists, special educators, physicians, parents, social workers, both regular and special education teachers, student teachers, diagnosticians, speech therapists, physical therapists, occupational therapists, audiologists, nurse counselors, curriculum specialists, optometrists, and vocational rehabilitation counselors (Jones, 1978). The role of the school psychologist can be augmented or supplemented by a psychiatrist, a neuropsychologist, or an ophthalmologist, as appropriate. This will depend on the needs of the student and school experiences with local professionals. The physician, in many instances, will be either the family physician or the student's pediatrician. An occupational therapist can provide insight as to needed therapy concerning fine motor control. The student's regular classroom teacher will probably be the most reliable reference for components of the student's classroom performance beyond that indicated by formal tests.

The MDT is responsible for the individual evaluation and educational planning for public school disabled children. The team decides if the student is eligible for special services. Through the IEP planning process, a written program is developed for the student. The intervention of the MDT must be evaluated periodically so the program can be adjusted if necessary for the child's best interests. The service can be only as good as the composition and functioning of the team.

Communication, both written and oral, is essential for understanding and for progress within the parameters of the IEP. Teams function within and among organizations. For example, members to serve one client might represent a group home, a mental health center, or a vocational school. Roles of team members are usually defined by the professional roles they have in the school system. Diverse knowledge and skills are combined to provide solutions to specific problems. This is the basic reason for involving an MDT. The child is the center, the focus of the team. If the team is sidetracked or weakened by conflicts and misunderstandings, the child will suffer.

The parents are important members of the team, yet many researchers report a breakdown of communication between parents and professionals. Professionals complain that parents are overprotective, interfering, and not understanding. Parents complain that professionals are intimidating and do not allow them to be active in the decision-making process (Golin & Ducanis, 1981). Many of the issues are culturally based and, with appropriate cultural competency training, can be avoided.

Determining the professional structure of the MDT is often easier than determining the best course of study for the student with a disability. The purpose of the MDT is to develop a plan of instructional remediation to obviate a given child's academic deficits, and thereby assist the student with a disability to succeed in school. Kavale and Forness (1985, p. 138) state, "The basic nature of LD intervention has proven to be an elusive and vexing problem for the field. The many proposed hypotheses regarding the essence of LD have generally failed to provide a comprehensive and definitive statement regarding its essence."

If MDTs are to serve the purpose for which they are intended, there must be a concerted effort by all members of the MDT to keep communication and participation at the highest possible level.

## REFERENCES

Coalition for Literacy. (1984). *Volunteer against illiteracy*. New York: Advertising Council.

Golin, A. D., & Ducanis, A. J. (1981). *The interdisciplinary team: A handbook for the education of exceptional children*. Rockville, MD: Aspen.

Jones, R. L. (1978). Protection in evaluation procedures criteria and recommendation. In *Developing criteria for evaluation of the protection in evaluation procedure provisions of Public Law 94-142*. Washington, DC: U.S. Office of Education, Bureau of Education for the Handicapped.

Kavale, K., & Forness, S. (1985). *Science of learning disabilities*. San Diego: College Hill Press.

Kirk, S. A., & Chalfant, J. C. (1984). *Academic and developmental learning disabilities*. Denver, CO: Love.

Popham, W. J., & Baker, E. (1970). *Systematic instruction*. Englewood Cliffs, NJ: Prentice Hall.

Whitehouse, F. A. (1951). Teamwork: A democracy of professions. *Exceptional Children, 18*, 45–52.

ROBERT T. NASH
*University of Wisconsin at Oshkosh*
Second edition

KIMBERLY F. APPLEQUIST
*University of Colorado at Colorado Springs*
Third edition

**INDIVIDUAL EDUCATIONAL PLAN
INDIVIDUALS WITH DISABILITIES EDUCATION
IMPROVEMENT ACT OF 2004 (IDEIA)
LEAST RESTRICTIVE ENVIRONMENT**

# MULTIELEMENT DESIGN

The multielement design is used to compare the effect of two or more conditions (treatments) on a dependent variable (Alberto & Troutman, 1999; Barlow & Hayes, 1979). This experimental design is also known as a multiple-schedule design, multitreatment design, and simultaneous treatment design (Barlow & Hayes, 1979; Kennedy, 2005; Tawney & Gast, 1984; Wolery, Bailey, & Sugai, 1988). The multielement research design allows the researcher to present two or more conditions in a rapid and interspersed pattern over a relatively short period of time in order to identify possible functional relationships between two or more conditions and a targeted student's behavior (see sample graph). This design can be used by teachers and researchers to efficiently determine which treatment is most effective for an individual student (Cooper, Heron, & Heward, 1987) or which condition predicts when a targeted problem behavior may or may not occur in a particular setting or context. The latter is referred to as a functional analysis (O'Neill et al., 1997). Multielement designs have been used to examine the effect of interspersal training on spelling word acquisition (Neef, Iwata, & Page, 1980); to generate and verify hypotheses of the function or purpose of problem behavior across a variety of settings and populations (Iwata et al., 1994; O'Neill et al., 1997; Taylor & Romanczyk, 1994); to investigate the effect of instructional strategies for increasing reading fluency (Daly & Martens, 1994); and to examine the effect of low and high preference tasks on rates of problem behavior (Vaughn & Horner, 1997).

Guidelines for using the multielement design include operationally defining all intervention procedures; developing a schedule for the rapid and interspersed presentation of conditions/treatments that allows for counterbalancing across time, teachers, and settings; and the systematic introduction of rapidly alternating conditions/treatments (Tawney & Gast, 1984). Multielement designs have several advantages over other research designs that are used in applied settings. For example, this type of design reduces the likelihood that the results will be influenced by sequence effects; does not require the withdrawal or reversal of behavior in order to establish a functional relationship; allows for a rapid and effective comparison of treatments and/or conditions; allows the researcher to randomly present conditions/treatments within a single session, at different times of the day, or on successive days; and can be used without an initial baseline phase (Alberto & Troutman, 1999; Cooper, Heron, & Heward, 1987; Tawney & Gast, 1984). When using the multielement design, educators should attempt to identify and control for any interaction effects that may occur when the effect of one condition influences subsequent conditions (Vollmer & Van Camp, 1998).

## REFERENCES

Alberto, P. A., & Troutman, A. C. (1999). *Applied behavior analysis for teachers* (5th ed.). Upper Saddle River, NJ: Merrill.

Barlow, D., & Hayes, S. (1979). Alternating treatments design: One strategy for comparing the effects of two treatments in a single subject. *Journal of Applied Behavior Analysis, 12,* 199–210.

Cooper, J. O., Heron, T. E., & Heward, W. L. (1987). *Applied behavior analysis.* New York: Macmillan.

Daly, E. J., III, & Martens, B. K. (1994). A comparison of three interventions for increasing oral reading performance: Application of the instructional hierarchy. *Journal of Applied Behavior Analysis, 27,* 459–469.

Iwata, B. A., Pace, G. M., Dorsey, M. F., Zarcone, J. R., Vollmer, T. R., Smith, R. G., et al. (1994). The functions of self-injurious behavior: An experimental-epidemiological analysis. *Journal of Applied Behavior Analysis, 27,* 215–240.

Kennedy, C. H. (2005). *Single-case designs for educational research.* Boston: Allyn & Bacon.

Neef, N. A., Iwata, B. A., & Page, T. J. (1980). The effects of interspersal training versus high density reinforcement on spelling acquisition and retention. *Journal of Applied Behavior Analysis, 13,* 153–158.

O'Neill, R. E., Horner, R. H., Albin, R. W., Sprague, J. R., Storey, K., & Newton, J. S. (1997). *Functional assessment and program development for problem behavior: A practical handbook* (2nd ed.). Pacific Grove, CA: Brooks/Cole.

Tawney, J. W., & Gast, D. L. (1984). *Single subject research in special education.* New York: Merrill.

Taylor, J. C., & Romanczyk, R. G. (1994). Generating hypotheses about the function of student problem behavior by observing teacher behavior. *Journal of Applied Behavior Analysis, 27,* 251–265.

Vaughn, B. J., & Horner, R. H. (1997). Identifying instructional tasks that occasion problem behaviors and assessing the effects of student versus teacher choice among these tasks. *Journal of Applied Behavior Analysis, 30,* 299–312.

Vollmer, T. R., & Van Camp, C. M. (1998). Experimental designs to evaluate antecedent control. In J. K. Luiselli & M. J. Cameron (Eds.), *Antecedent control: Innovative approaches to behavioral support* (pp. 47–65). Baltimore: Paul H. Brooks.

Wolery, M., Bailey, D., Jr., & Sugai, G. (1988). *Effective teaching: Principles and procedures of applied behavior analysis with exceptional students.* Boston: Allyn & Bacon.

RANDALL L. DE PRY
*University of Colorado at
Colorado Springs*

**BEHAVIORAL ASSESSMENT RESEARCH IN SPECIAL EDUCATION**

## MULTIPLE BASELINE DESIGN

The multiple baseline design is one of several single-subject applied behavior analysis research designs for evaluating the effects of interventions on the behaviors of children and youths with disabilities. While intervention withdrawal or reversal designs are the most frequently used of the single-subject designs, there are instances in behavioral research where a return to baseline phase is not an appropriate alternative for evaluation purposes. Zucker, Rutherford, and Prieto (1978), Kazdin (1982), and Barlow and Hersen (1984) identify several situations where a return to baseline is not appropriate for either ethical or scientific reasons.

First, once some behaviors are acquired, they may no longer be dependent on the intervention and thus will be maintained by naturally occurring reinforcers in the environment. For example, if an intervention is initiated to increase an isolate child's cooperative behavior with peers on the playground, the child may continue cooperative behavior through acquired peer social reinforcement despite the fact that the teacher intervention is reversed.

A second situation where the reversal design may be inappropriate occurs with behaviors that, once they are acquired, are essentially nonreversible. For example, if a behavioral intervention program is initiated to teach a child the letters of the alphabet, once the child has acquired this skill, it is unlikely that withdrawal or reversal of the intervention will result in a loss of ability to repeat the alphabet. Rate of response may decrease, but probably not the basic skill itself.

A third instance is when the teacher cannot accurately reverse the intervention procedures to return to baseline levels of functioning. For example, if the intervention involves systematic attention to student on-task behavior and ignoring of off-task behavior, the teacher may find it impossible to replicate baseline rates of attention and ignoring during the reversal phase.

The fourth situation involves children's behaviors that may be so dangerous or noxious that further instances of the behavior cannot be tolerated, even for a brief reversal period. If, for example, an intervention is effective in stopping a child's self-destructive behaviors, few teachers would want to withdraw the intervention and count the number of self-destructive behaviors.

The multiple baseline design (see Figure) is used in situations where the reversal design may not be appropriate for evaluating intervention effects. This design involves establishing baselines on several different behaviors concurrently, and then systematically applying the intervention to one of the targeted behaviors. If this behavior changes in the desired direction, then the same intervention is applied to the second behavior. If the second behavior also changes in the direction desired, the intervention is then applied to the third target behavior, and so on. If each behavior changes when, and only when, intervention is applied to it, experimental control is demonstrated.

There are three types of multiple baseline designs. The first of these involves evaluating the effects of the intervention on the same behavior of the same child in two or more settings. For example, the teacher may be interested in stopping a child's hitting other students during recess, lunchtime, and classtime. Response contingent time-out

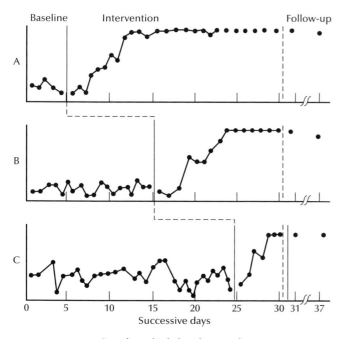

Sample multiple baseline graph

may be applied to hitting during recess; if successful, then during lunchtime; if successful, then during classtime.

The second type of multiple baseline design involves measuring and evaluating the effects of a particular intervention on two or more behaviors of the same child in the same setting. For example, an overcorrection procedure might be made contingent on various self-stimulatory behaviors of an autistic student. Following a period of baseline on finger flicking, clapping, and hand gazing episodes, overcorrection would be made contingent on finger flicking while baseline was continued on clapping and hand gazing. If finger flicking decreased significantly, the overcorrection procedure would then be applied to clapping and so on.

The third variation of the baseline design involves evaluating intervention effects across several children who exhibit a similar behavior in the same setting. The example here might be to begin simultaneous baselines on the rate per minute of two or more children's summing of two-digit addition facts. Intervention, perhaps in the form of a contract for increased rate, would be initiated first with one child while baseline data were continued to be collected for the other two children. If the first child's rate increased contingent on the intervention, a contract would then be initiated with the second child and so on.

The most important factors in research using multiple baseline designs are that baselines for all behaviors are begun at the same time and that ongoing measurement and recording of all behaviors is continuous throughout the procedure. Subsequent applications of the intervention are determined by their effects on the immediately preceding behavior. The most powerful conclusions regarding the effectiveness of the interventions can be drawn when there are closely related or functional behavior changes following repeated applications of the intervention across settings, behaviors, or subjects.

### REFERENCES

Barlow, D. H., & Hersen, M. (1984). *Singlecase experimental designs: Strategies for studying behavior change.* New York: Pergamon.

Kazdin, A. E. (1982). *Single-case research design: Methods for clinical and applied settings.* New York: Oxford University Press.

Zucker, S. H., Rutherford, R. B., & Prieto, A. G. (1979). Teacher directed interventions with behaviorally disordered children. In R. B. Rutherford & A. G. Prieto (Eds.), *Monograph in behavior disorders: Severe behavior disorders of children and youth* (Vol. 2, pp. 49–61). Reston, VA: CCBD.

Robert B. Rutherford, Jr.
*Arizona State University*

BEHAVIORAL MODIFICATION
BEHAVIOR OBJECTIVES
BEHAVIORAL OBSERVATION

## MULTIPLE HANDICAPPING CONDITIONS

Students with multiple handicapping conditions are persons with two or more disabilities that result in handicaps within functional living experiences. Also called persons with severe handicapping conditions, dual diagnosis, and orthopedic disabilities, persons with multiple handicapping conditions include individuals who are deaf-blind, autistic, cerebral palsied, neurologically impaired, brain damaged, schizophrenic, or mentally retarded (Fewell & Cone, 1983). Labeling individuals as multiply handicapped should be done with caution and with particular focus on outcomes. Accordingly, the World Health Organization (1978) urges the adoption of a three-tier classification system including the terms impairment, disability, and handicap. Impairment refers to a physiological or anatomical loss or other abnormality or both. Disability is the limitation of an individual's capacity to perform some key life function because of an impairment. Handicap describes the limitation imposed by a disability on an individual's ability to carry on his or her usual activities.

According to these definitions, a student with multiple handicapping conditions would have limitations in educational development as a result of two or more disabilities. Thus the definition of children with severe handicaps of the U.S. Office of Education describes children

who, because of the intensity of their physical, mental, or emotional problems, need educational, social, psychological, and medical service, beyond those which are traditionally offered by regular and special education programs, in order to maximize their full potential for useful and meaningful participation in society and for self-fulfillment. (U.S. Office of Education, 1974)

From another perspective, Baker (1979) provides a definition that includes an individual

whose ability to provide for his or her own basic life-sustaining and safety needs is so limited, relative to the proficiency expected on the basis of chronological age, that it could pose a serious threat to his or her survival.

Numerous specialists are involved in educational programming for students with multiple handicaps, including therapists in speech, language, communication, occupational, physical, adapted physical education, and recreation areas. Together these specialists form a multidisciplinary team for the development of an individualized education plan. A sharing of roles should be emphasized, with the classroom teacher assuming the position of coordinator. The educational curriculum focuses on chronological-age-appropriate programs, functional activities, implementation of precise daily schedules, and the development of curricular domains within domestic living, general community functioning, recreation/leisure, and vocational areas (Snell & Renzaglia, 1986). An important component within the curriculum is the provision for integration with students without identifiable handicaps. Although physical integration is a first step, strategies to promote reciprocal social interactions among students with multiple handicaps and their peers is an essential component for preparing students to function within home community settings.

## REFERENCES

Baker, D. B. (1979). Severely handicapped: Toward an inclusive definition. *AAESPH Review, 4,* 52–65.

Fewell, D., & Cone, J. (1983). Identification and placement of severely handicapped children. In M. Snell (Ed.), *Systematic instruction of the moderately and severely handicapped* (2nd ed., pp. 46–73). Columbus, OH: Merrill.

Snell, M. E., & Renzaglia, A. M. (1986). Moderate, severe, and profound handicaps. In N. G. Haring & L. McCormick (Eds.), *Exceptional children and youth* (4th ed., pp. 271–310). Columbus, OH: Merrill.

U.S. Office of Education. (1974). *Code of federal regulations, Title 45, Section 121.2.* Washington, DC: Bureau of Education for the Handicapped.

World Health Organization. (1978). *International classification of diseases* (9th rev.). Washington, DC: Author.

ERNEST L. PANCSOFAR
*University of Connecticut*

**CHILDHOOD SCHIZOPHRENIA**
**DEAF-BLIND**
**LABELING**
**MENTAL RETARDATION**
**OTHER HEALTH IMPAIRED**

## MULTIPLE REGRESSION

Multiple regression is a statistical procedure in which a single continuous dependent variable is regressed on several continuous independent variables. Typical purposes are to predict dependent variable scores from the independent variables, model real world variable relationships, and explain dependent variable variation concisely.

There are two conditions in multiple regression that determine analysis and interpretation. In the first condition, all independent variables are statistically independent of each other. While this does not occur naturally very often, it can be occasionally obtained from theory or from judicious selection of independent variables. In this case, each independent variable is related to the dependent variable in magnitude equal to Pearson's correlation; the Pearson correlation squared equals the proportion of dependent variable variance accounted for. The sum of all the squared correlations for independent variables is equal to the squared multiple correlation, a measure of the total variance proportion accounted for by all independent variables. In a Venn diagram of these circles, the two independent variables intersect the dependent variable circle but do not intersect each other between independent variables.

The more usually observed condition is one in which one or more of the independent variables are not statistically independent of each other. This implies that the independent variables will be correlated with each other and with the dependent variable. In this case, there is overlap in the amount of variance accounted for in the dependent variable by two or more independent variables. In a Venn diagram, the circles representing independent variables intersect each other as well as the circle representing the dependent variable. The squared multiple correlation is still defined as the total proportion of variance in dependent variable accounted for. However, now the contributions of the individual independent variables are more difficult to discern because they overlap. The partial correlation between an independent variable $X1$ and dependent variable $Y$ is defined as the Pearson correlation between two errors of regression. $X1$ is regressed on all the other independent variables and for each subject a predicted score is subtracted from the observed score to create one error score, $E1$. Similarly, the dependent variable is regressed on the other independent variables and an error score $Ey$ is computed. The partial correlation is the correlation between $E1$ and $Ey$. Its square represents the unique or independent contribution of $X1$ to the variance in $Y$. The total squared multiple correlation is a function of the partial correlations but it cannot be simply stated (Darlington, 1978).

Uses of multiple regression in prediction are usually to make decisions based on past performance. For example, colleges make first-year selection decisions based on high school percentile rank and Scholastic Aptitude Test (SAT) scores' prediction of the first year's college grade point average (GPA). High-school rank and SAT score are independent variables, termed predictors; college GPA is the dependent variable. Typical multiple correlation is about .5, with about 25 percent of freshman GPAs predictable. The SAT score might add about 5 percent to the prediction based on high school rank alone.

The use of multiple regression in modeling or theory building is based on specifying the order of including independent variables in the multiple regression. Thus contributions of the independent variables to dependent variable variance is dependent on the order of entry. This is sometimes called hierarchical regression or ordered regression. A special case is termed path analysis, in which the partial correlations are computed in specified order. They are interpreted as path coefficients, the direct influence of one variable on another (Pedhazur, 1982).

Often the purpose for multiple regression is parsimonious prediction when there are many possible predictors or independent variables. Not all are necessary or desirable owing to the expense of data collection, so a smaller subset of predictors that will perform nearly as well as all predictors available is sought. There are several strategies available to find this parsimonious subset: forward, backward, and stepwise regression. There are several variants available with each. Forward multiple regression begins with the best single predictor, the greatest magnitude Pearson correlation with the dependent variable. It adds new predictors according to some criteria for improving prediction or increasing squared multiple correlation with the dependent variable. When there is little change after adding a new variable, the procedure ends. Backward regression begins with all predictors and drops them out until there are large drops in the predictive criteria. For example, with both forward and backward regression, a criterion might be used that additional predictors must improve the squared multiple correlation by .05 (Draper & Smith, 1982). Stepwise multiple regression is a variant on either forward or backward regression in which variables previously entered are tested to see whether they are no longer needed after new variables have been included. This means that a new combination of predictors are now able to predict along with the previous set. Thus the first predictor entered might eventually be dropped. Multiple regression is widely used in the behavioral sciences. In its most general form, it encompasses most statistical techniques, including the analysis of variance, as the general linear model.

## REFERENCES

Darlington, R. B. (1978). Reduced variance regression. *Psychological Bulletin, 85,* 1238–1255.

Draper, N. R., & Smith, H. (1982). *Applied regression analysis* (2nd ed.). New York: Wiley.

Pedhazur, E. (1982). *Multiple regression in behavioral research* (2nd ed.). New York: Holt, Rinehart, Winston.

Victor L. Willson
*Texas A&M University*

## DISCRIMINANT ANALYSIS
## RESEARCH IN SPECIAL EDUCATION

## MULTIPLE SCLEROSIS

Multiple sclerosis (MS) is a progressive neurologic disease affecting the brain and spinal cord. It generally is considered a disease of young adults, with symptoms rarely occurring before adolescence or after age 40 (Brown, 1971); mean age of onset is 30 years (Kaufman, 1981). Females are affected more than males (Kaufman, 1981; Magalini, 1971), and although no clear-cut hereditary component has been identified, the incidence is much higher in close relatives of afflicted persons (Kaufman, 1981; Thompson, 1979).

Multiple sclerosis is considered a demyelinating disease, in that the myelin (fatty sheaths surrounding nerve fibers) in the central nervous system is disseminated. Plaques or hardened patches of scarred nerve fibers are evident in the central nervous system of MS patients. The name multiple sclerosis derives from these scarred (sclerosed) masses, together with the multiple episodic nature of the disease (Kaufman, 1981; *Melloni's,* 1985). Multiple sclerosis is also known as *disseminated sclerosis* (Brown, 1971; Magalini, 1971).

Early symptoms of MS may be mild and vague, and hence may be dismissed by affected individuals or their families. Such symptoms include blurred vision, tingling or numbness in the trunk or extremities, vertigo, intention tremor, and clumsiness. Episodes of symptoms characteristically are followed by periods of remission, a pattern that may persist for several years. Despite the intermittent nature of the disease, MS is a progressive condition, and afflicted individuals demonstrate increasing neurologic impairment. Advanced symptoms of MS include ataxia (a gait disturbance characterized by a broad-based stance and lurching movements), scanning speech (evidenced by monotonous, staccato speech with slurring adjacent sounds), and nystagmus (tremor of eye movements). Other signs associated with the disease include bladder and bowel disturbances, partial or complete blindness (retrobulbar neuritis), and hyper-reflexive movements (e.g., Babinski sign). While a number of experts report affective disturbances in MS patients, particularly emotional lability and euphoria (Kaufman, 1981; Magalini, 1971; *Mosby's*, 1983), Lechtenberg (1982) takes issue with such reports. He cites studies that indicate a high incidence of depression in MS patients, and suggests the symptom of euphoria may be better described as "a masked depression manifested by unrealistic or excessively optimistic attitudes" (p. 216).

The cause of MS is unknown, although commonalities have been identified among afflicted patients. Multiple sclerosis is considered a disease of temperate climates (Brown, 1971; Kaufman, 1981). While their role in transmission of the disease is unknown, many MS patients had small, indoor pets as children (Kaufman, 1981). Toxic viral and allergic metabolic etiologies have been hypothesized (Magalini, 1971). Diagnosis of MS relies largely on clinical symptoms and the multiple episodic nature of the disease. Few laboratory tests are pathognomonic of MS, although elevated gamma globulin in conjunction with normal protein levels in cerebrospinal fluid may suggest the presence of the disease (Kaufman, 1981). Numerous medical and psychological conditions may mimic MS, including Guillain-Barre syndrome, tumors of the brain or spinal cord, and hysteria.

Few beneficial therapeutic interventions have been identified in the treatment of MS. Physical or occupational therapy may facilitate optimal range of motion and may provide for environmental adaptations when necessary. Corticosteroid treatments may shorten symptomatic episodes (Kaufman, 1981). Diets designed to reduce exposure to allergy-related foods reportedly have been associated with remissions of symptoms in some MS patients (*MS and diet*, 1984). Advances in pharmaceutical treatment are believed to be on the verge of development.

## REFERENCES

Brown, J. A. C. (1971). *The Stein and Day international medical encyclopedia*. New York: Stein & Day.

Kaufman, D. M. (1981). *Clinical neurology for psychiatrists*. New York: Grune & Stratton.

Lechtenberg, R. (1982). *The psychiatrist's guide to diseases of the nervous system*. New York: Wiley.

Magalini, S. (1971). *Dictionary of medical syndromes*. Philadelphia: Lippincott.

*Melloni's illustrated medical dictionary* (2nd ed.). (1985). Baltimore: Williams & Wilkins.

*Mosby's medical and nursing dictionary*. (1983). St. Louis, MO: Mosby.

MS and diet. (1984). *Programs for the handicapped* (ISSN 0565-2804), *5*, 12.

Thompson, W. A. R. (1979). *Black's medical dictionary* (32nd ed.). New York: Barnes & Noble.

CATHY F. TELZROW
*Kent State University*

GAIT DISTURBANCES
PHYSICAL DISABILITY

## MULTISENSORY INSTRUCTION

A multisensory approach to instruction involves presenting instructional content through several modalities such as the visual, auditory, kinesetic, and tactile modalities. The rationale underlying this instructional approach is that learning may be enhanced if the content to be learned is presented through several sensory modalities. The Fernald (1943) method and the Gillingham-Stillman (1960) method typify the multisensory approach to teaching reading. However, the two methods differ in emphasis. While the Fernald method emphasizes whole-word learning, the Gillingham-Stillman method emphasizes the teaching of phonics, specifically individual phonemes and sound blending.

Recently "multisensory" terms have evolved into "holistic" methods that infuse a wide range of activities into the teaching of academic subjects and the classroom (Fox & Thompson, 1994). The definition has evolved from a concrete delivery to a more interactive and integrated learner experience (Enz & Searfoss, 1993; McKeon, 1995).

## REFERENCES

Bryan, T. H., & Bryan, J. H. (1979). *Understanding learning disabilities* (2nd ed.). Sherman Oaks, CA: Alfred.

Enz, B. J., & Searfoss, L. W. (1993). Who evaluates teacher performance? Mismatched paradigms, the status quo, the missed opportunities. (ERIC Clearinghouse No. EA 025322)

Fernald, G. M. (1943). *Remedial techniques in school subject*. New York: McGraw-Hill.

Fox, L. H., & Thompson, D. L. (1994). *Bringing the lab school method to an inner city school*. Washington, DC: American University, School of Education.

Gillingham, A., & Stillman, B. (1960). *Remedial training for children with specific disability in reading, spelling, penmanship*. Cambridge MA: Educators Publishing Service.

McKeon, K. J. (1995). What is this thing called accelerated learning? *Training and Development, 49*(6), 64–66.

Myers, P. I., & Hammill, D. D. (1982). *Learning disabilities: Basic concepts, assessment practices, and instructional strategies*. Austin, TX: PRO-ED.

Silberberg, N., Iverson, I., & Goins, J. (1973). Which remedial method works best? *Journal of Learning Disabilities, 6*, 547–556.

BERNICE Y. L. WONG
*Simon Fraser University*

READING
READING REMEDIATION
TEACHING STRATEGIES

## MUNSON, GRACE E. (1883–1980)

Born in a sod house near Orleans, Nebraska, Grace Munson believed in self-growth and advancement through educational attainment. From one-room schools on the prairie, she moved through Peru (Nebraska) Normal School in 1905 and the University of Nebraska (Phi Beta Kappa) for a BA in 1911 and a PhD in 1916 with time out for an MA from Wellesley College in 1912, where she was an alumnae fellow.

Professionally, she was a rural Nebraska teacher near Geneva (1899–1903), teacher and principal in Harlan County (1905–1909), and instructor in education at the University of Nebraska (1912–1918) before moving to Chicago, where she was a school psychologist and teacher (1918–1935), director of the Bureau of Child Study (1935–1946), and assistant superintendent in charge of special education (1946–1949).

While she was director of the bureau, the staff moved beyond serving the mentally retarded to improving programs and services for the gifted, maladjusted, truants, and others whose achievement was not as expected on the basis of their intellectual ability. As a psychologist and educator, her work was guided by an interpretation of Rousseau's *Emile* in light of contemporary child study methods. She continually sought ways of moving children through the basic skills at their own rates regardless of grade placement. As bureau director she initiated throughout Chicago an adjustment teacher program, which involved releasing teachers from classroom duties to work with individuals needing help, a reading readiness program for children in first grade who were not ready to read, a reading improvement program for students entering high school, and self-appraisal and careers courses for juniors in high school. In addition, she expanded and standardized the citywide testing program in reading readiness, achievement, and intellectual assessment.

An innovative leader who welcomed suggestions, her criticism of others and of ideas was both trenchant and effective. Although her professional activity and leadership was usually limited to greater Chicago, she helped organize the Chicago Psychological Club in 1924 for psychologists in the bureau and the Institute for Juvenile Research, a group serving mental health needs. Through the club she was instrumental in bringing some of the great names from across the United States into dialogue with Chicago professionals.

JOSEPH L. FRENCH
*Pennsylvania State University*

## MUSCULAR DYSTROPHY

Muscular dystrophy (MD) describes a group of inherited disorders characterized by severe, progressive weakness associated with atrophy of the skeletal muscles bilaterally. The most common forms of the disease typically have an early onset and produce increased wasting and eventual death. Because of the shortened life of afflicted persons, approximately two-thirds of muscular dystrophy patients are children ages 3 to 15 (Weiner, 1973).

Although classification systems for muscular dystrophy vary, there is general agreement that Duchenne's dystrophy (pseudohypertrophic type) is the most common variant. Other categories include faciocapulohumoral dystrophy (affects facial and shoulder muscles; onset in second decade) and limb-girdle muscular dystrophy (typically does not affect children; Bleck, 1975; Buda, 1981; Rowland, 1979). Incidence figures vary widely by type, from 5 per million births for faciocapulohumoral type to 250 per million births for Duchenne's (Rowland, 1979). Duchenne's dystrophy is inherited via an x-linked mode of transmission, although spontaneous genetic mutation is reported to be fairly common, with perhaps two-thirds of afflicted children having no family history of the disorder (Rowland, 1979). It is by definition a condition that affects males exclusively, although female carriers have been reported to show mild clinical symptoms (Buda, 1981). In late 1985, researchers reported the ability to identify carriers of the Duchenne's gene with 98 percent accuracy; significant progress was also being made in the effort to identify the exact location of the gene (Kolata, 1985). Other forms of muscular dystrophy are transmitted as autosomal dominant or recessive traits (Rowland, 1985).

The onset of Duchenne's dystrophy generally occurs during the preschool period. Walking may be delayed, and early signs of the disorder may include difficulty in raising from a supine or sitting position or difficulty in climbing stairs. As the disease progresses and muscles in the pelvic girdle become affected, a characteristic waddling gait, with a sway back and protruding pelvis, may be observed (Bleck, 1975). Progressive weakness is characteristic of Duchenne's dystrophy, and children may be wheelchair bound by age 10 or 12 (Bleck, 1975; Kolata, 1985). Death typically occurs in the third decade, as a result of respiratory failure or involvement of the heart muscles. (Weiner, 1973).

A number of early studies reported an increased incidence of mental retardation in boys afflicted with Duchenne's dystrophy; the mean IQ was reported to be approximately one standard deviation below the mean. Other studies have revealed a verbal < nonverbal discrepancy in boys with Duchenne's dystrophy, although there is no consensus among the experts (Mearig, 1983). A recent study of older and younger Duchenne's victims reported an age effect, with younger boys exhibiting greater deficits in verbal and attentional-organizational skills than older subjects (Sollee, Latham, Kindlon, & Bresnan, 1985).

Children with MD may require special education and related services. Adaptive equipment, attendant services, and appropriate therapies may be necessary for MD children. While a typical profile of neuropsychological strengths and weaknesses has not been established for boys with Duchenne's dystrophy, converging data suggest individual differences may be present that warrant a modified instructional program. Indeed, Kendall (1991) and Nielsen (1997) identify modified programs that call for trained educational personnel, flexible scheduling, continuum of services, parent support and training, and trained personnel in technological advances.

## REFERENCES

Bleck, E. E. (1975). Muscular dystrophy-Duchenne type. In E. E. Bleck & D. A. Nagel (Eds.), *Physically handicapped children: A medical atlas for teachers* (pp. 173–179). New York: Grune & Stratton.

Buda, F. B. (1981). *The neurology of developmental disabilities.* Springfield, IL: Thomas.

Kendall, R. M. (1991). Unique educational needs of learners with physical and other health impairments. (ERIC Clearinghouse No. EC 300945)

Kolata, G. (1985). Closing in on the muscular dystrophy gene. *Science, 230,* 307–308.

Mearig, J. S. (1983). Evaluation of cognitive functioning in children with neuromuscular and related physical disabilities. In C. R. Reynolds & J. H. Clark (Eds.), *Assessment and programming for young children with low-incidence handicaps* (pp. 157–199). New York: Plenum.

Nielsen, L. B. (1997). *The exceptional child in the regular classroom: An educator's guide.* Thousand Oaks, CA: Sage.

Rowland, L. P. (1979). Diseases of muscle and neuromuscular junction. In P. B. Beeson, W. McDermott, & J. B. Wyngaarden (Eds.), *Cecil textbook of medicine* (15th ed., pp. 914-930). Philadelphia: Saunders.

Sollee, N. D., Latham, E. E., Kindlon, D. J., & Bresnan, M. J. (1985). Neuropsychological impairment in Duchenne muscular dystrophy. *Journal of Clinical & Experimental Neuropsychology, 7,* 486–496.

Weiner, F. (1973). *Help for the handicapped child.* New York: McGraw-Hill.

CATHY F. TELZROW
*Kent State University*

**MUSCULAR DYSTROPHY ASSOCIATION**
**PHYSICAL DISABILITIES**

# MUSCULAR DYSTROPHY ASSOCIATION

MDA is a national voluntary health agency—a dedicated partnership between scientists and concerned citizens aimed at conquering neuromuscular diseases. MDA is one of the world's leading voluntary health agencies, fostering research and patient care funded almost entirely by individual private contributors.

MDA combats 40 neuromuscular diseases through a worldwide research effort, a nationwide program of services to individuals, and far-reaching professional and public health education. Individual MDA research grants to scientific and clinical investigators in the United States and abroad number some 400. MDA's patient services program offers diagnostic services and rehabilitative follow-up care to children and adults with neuromuscular diseases through a nationwide network of some 240 MDA hospital-affiliated clinics. The association offers financial assistance toward the purchase and repair of selected orthopedic appliances, physical therapy, and transportation to and from clinics. MDA also offers a nationwide summer camping program for young people and sponsors ongoing self-help support groups and educational seminars. Educational literature and videos are available upon request. There are some 160 local chapters of the Muscular Dystrophy Association in the 50 states, Washington, DC, and Puerto Rico.

STAFF

# MUSCULAR IMBALANCE

Muscular imbalance occurs when there is difficulty or lack of integration in the interaction of opposing muscle groups. Normally there is a finely graded interaction of opposing muscle groups facilitated by reciprocal innervation of the muscles. Paralysis, weakness, or interruption in innervation may result in an imbalance. Depending on the location and severity of the muscle imbalance, the individual may not be able to remain upright, extend the arm, focus the eyes, or hop on one foot. Motor skills performance may be severely impaired or minimally affected. A muscle imbalance may lead to fatigue, difficulty in respiration, impaired oral-motor skills, pain, impaired visual focus, or numerous other conditions depending on the nature, location, and pervasiveness of the imbalance.

Signs of muscle imbalance may be observed in the classroom. Actions such as tilting the head to read, leaning to one side after being seated for a period of time, slumping, or significant deterioration of handwriting toward the end of a writing period may all be signs of a muscle imbalance or weakness.

## REFERENCES

Fraser, B., & Hensinger, R. (1980). *Managing physical handicaps.* Baltimore: Brookes.

Heiniger, M., & Randolph, S. (1981). *Neurophysiological concepts of human behavior.* St. Louis, MO: Mosby.

Ward, D. (1984). *Positioning the handicapped child for functions.* St. Louis, MO: Phoenix.

MARY K. DYKES
*University of Florida*

MOVEMENT THERAPY
MUSCULAR DYSTROPHY
PHYSICAL DISABILITIES
VISUAL-MOTOR AND VISUAL-PERCEPTUAL PROBLEMS

# MUSEUMS AND INDIVIDUALS WITH DISABILITIES

Access of individuals with disabilities not only to museums but to fuller appreciation of art itself was vastly extended with the passing of the Vocational Rehabilitation Act of 1973. Section 504 of the law prohibits discrimination against the disabled by government-funded organizations; this has had a significant impact on the way museums plan and implement their exhibits and educational programs. This is not to say that there were no programs for the handicapped prior to Section 504. The Mary Duke Biddle Gallery in Raleigh, North Carolina, pioneered the tactile approach for blind and visually impaired patrons as early as 1966, and the Lions Gallery of the Senses was established in Hartford, Connecticut, in 1972. These early efforts were exceptional, however, and they were not without their critics (Kenny, 1983). One important criticism stemmed from the fact that galleries and museums specifically for individuals with disabilities, while admirable in their motivation, were unintentionally segregationist in their effect.

Museums responded in a variety of ways. To avoid segregation, the efforts generally revolved around an expansion of services and multisensory experiences for all visitors. But the museums had little experience with nonvisual efforts. Steiner (1983) points out some of the misapprehensions that surfaced as sighted curators began to plan for the visually impaired: that the legally blind have no sight at all; that most blind people read braille; and that the blind are automatically more sensitive to touch and sound than the sighted. Without conscious effort, it is also very easy to underestimate (or overlook altogether) the amount of background knowledge that the sighted pick up unconsciously from their environment and apply to the appreciation of art. In an effort to avoid mistakes that might easily result from such misunderstandings, museums across the country began organizing advisory boards made up of individuals with disabilities to help guide and plan the new efforts.

Since then, tactile exhibits have become much more common. Conservation experts found ways to avoid some of the worst dangers of human touch: coating objects with lacquer or wax, for example, or requiring that visitors wear gloves or wash their hands and remove jewelry before enjoying the exhibit. Sometimes, when objects are too valuable or perhaps too large for touching, reproductions are created. There have been cases in which the reproductions were constructed so that they could be taken apart to show their inner structure as well. Occasionally, paintings have been specially reproduced with a variety of textures replacing the colors of the original. Black and white photographs often accompany objects on display. This has helped the partially sighted by enlarging details, simplifying the visual information by reducing it to two dimensions, and increasing contrast for better comprehension (Smithsonian Institute, 1977).

Museums have also become much more sensitive to the special problems people with disabilities face when trying to move through exhibit areas (Hunt, 1979). Barriers have been removed for those in wheelchairs. Tactile maps, three-dimensional models of exhibit spaces, and specially designed carpet trails help the visually impaired find their way around. Staff training has helped museum personnel be sensitive to those patrons who need extra help and those who prefer more independence. Training has also been aimed at improving the clarity and precision of oral directions. Other services geared specifically to individuals with disabilities have also been introduced (Mims, 1982). These include regularly scheduled tours conducted by staff and volunteers who can communicate with the deaf, braille and large-print labels, subtitled and captioned films, large-print newsletters and announcements of coming attractions, and the inclusion of art education and special tours on radio reading services and in talking-book projects. For those who are institutionalized or homebound, there are suitcase exhibits that can be borrowed from museums. These often include slides and audio tapes, along with reproductions of art objects.

Some museums across the country have been able to implement exemplary programs, maintaining continuous gallery experiences for individuals with disabilities and interweaving them with other aspects of the art education program. The New York Metropolitan Museum in New York City, the De Young Memorial Museum in San Francisco, the Plimouth Plantation, a living history museum in Plymouth, Massachusetts, the Smithsonian Institute in Washington, DC, and the Wadsworth Antheneum in Hartford, Connecticut, are only a few examples. Horizons for the Blind of Chicago is a good source of further information on accessibility and special programs for individuals with disabilities in museums, galleries, and art and science centers.

## REFERENCES

Hunt, S. (1979). An exhibit for touching. *Journal of Visual Impairment & Blindness, 73*(9), 364–366.

Kenny, A. P. (1983). A range of vision: Museum accommodations for visually impaired people. *Journal of Visual Impairment & Blindness, 77*(7), 325–329.

Mims, S. K. (1982). Art museums and special audiences. *School Arts, 81*(7), 32–33.

Smithsonian Institute National Air and Space Museum. (1977). *Museums and handicapped students: Guidelines for educators.* (ERIC Document Reproduction Service No. ED 152 062) Washington, DC: Smithsonian Institute.

Steiner, C. (1983). Art museums and the visually handicapped consumer: Some issues in approach and design. *Journal of Visual Impairment & Blindness, 77*(7), 330–333.

JANET S. BRAND
*Hunter College, City University
of New York*

**AMERICANS WITH DISABILITIES ACT**

# MUSIC THERAPY

Music therapy is the use of music in all of its forms to modify nonmusical behavior (Lathom & Eagle, 1982) and to promote mental health, social development and adjustment, and motor coordination. At times it is used as a therapeutic tool in rehabilitation and for recreational or educational purposes. Perhaps the most important contribution of music to special education is that it can promote learning through activities that are enjoyable.

Therapeutically, music has been known to have a significant psychological and physiological effect on disabled students' personality (Nordoff & Robbins, 1971). Behaviorists have used music to alter overt behavior (Warren, 1984). Freudians have recommended the use of music to reduce anxiety, catharsis, and sublimation, and to change affective states. Humanists view the use of music as a vehicle to stimulate the process of self-actualization (Harvey, 1980).

Music therapy in a variety of applications has been practiced in hospitals, schools, institutions, and private settings in a one-to-one or group approach. It includes moving to music, playing instruments, presenting musicals, attending concerts, dancing, creating music, singing, and listening.

The role of the music therapy should be distinguished from the role of music education in special education. Music therapy has remedial goals. Music education teaches the knowledge and skills of music as an aesthetic, enriching, and pleasurable experience for all children, including those with disabilities (Alley, 1979). In special education, music therapy has been used to increase students' ability to follow directions and to attend to and respond to logical sequences of movement, voice, and music. Task analysis has assisted in these purposes (Alley, 1979). It is advised that in special education, the music therapist select musical activities that are within the students' skill levels; thus tasks may be as simple as listening to rock music or playing in the school orchestra.

Lathom and Eagle (1982) found that the majority of music therapists focus on improving gross and motor skills. This is accomplished by movement activities to music and the coordinated use of the hands, arms, and body while playing a musical instrument. Music therapists have sought to encourage cooperation between children with disabilities and adults in producing musical effects. They have also used music to reinforce correct performance in group behavior.

After the passage of PL 94-142, music educators turned to music therapists, who had already established a tradition of success in teaching music to populations with disabilities. As a result, many of the music materials and teaching procedures for the disabled have their basis in music therapy. From 1975 to the present, music education and music therapy for individuals with disabilities have spread from private or residential programs to all aspects of special education under the aegis of IDEA. In fact, the CEC's Teacher of the Year in 1995 was Brenda Robbins, a music teacher and therapist.

**REFERENCES**

Alley, J. (1979). Music in the IEP: Therapy education. *Journal of Music Therapy, 16*(3), 111–127.

Boxill, E. (1985). *Music therapy for the developmentally disabled.* Rockville, MD: Aspen.

Harvey, P. (1980). The therapeutic role of music in special education: Historical perspectives. *Creative Child & Adult Quarterly, 5*(3), 196–203.

Lathom, W., & Eagle, C. (1982). Music for the severely disabled child. *Music Education Journal, 38*(49), 30–31.

Nordoff, P., & Robbins, C. (1971). *Therapy in music for handicapped children.* New York: St. Martins.

Voyles, L. (1995). CEC Teacher of the Year. *Teaching Exceptional Children, 28*(1), 32–33.

Warren, B. (Ed.). (1984). *Using the creative arts in therapy.* Cambridge, MA: Brookline.

THOMAS R. BURKE
*Hunter College, City University
of New York*

**DANCE THERAPY**
**RECREATIONAL THERAPY**

# MUTISM

Mutism is defined as the lack of articulate speech (Kanner, 1975). According to Kolvin and Fundudis (1981), there are many forms of mutism. They may be divided into those with a presumed biological basis and those considered psychological in nature. Mutism with a biological basis is typically associated with profound deafness, serious mental handicap, infantile autism, or akinetic mutism. As a symptom of psychological disturbance, two further types are delineated.

Traumatic mutism is identified as having a sudden onset immediately following a psychological or physical shock and is thus considered a hysterical reaction. Selective mutism is a condition in which speech is confined to a familiar situation or a small group of select others.

Kanner (1948) was among the first to discuss mutism in the psychiatric literature. He identified lack of sound perception as the most frequent cause and differentiated deaf mutism into congenital and acquired forms. Deafness existing at birth or acquired at a very early age usually prevents the development of speech. Congenital mutism can be due to physical anomalies of speech or auditory mechanisms; acquired mutism may be the result of illnesses such as meningitis or congenital syphilis. The congenital form is more common in boys than girls. Kanner estimated approximately .07 percent deaf mutes in the population.

Other forms of mutism are also described by Kanner. Mutism without deafness may be identified in cases of severe and profound mental retardation when the capacity for verbal expression and comprehension is severely delayed. Mutism as a symptom of childhood schizophrenia and early infantile autism is also common and has been observed in older children with autism (Bryson, 1994). Temporary mutism as an occasional symptom of hysteria was suggested by Kanner as a result of emotional conflict.

Kanner also described cases of voluntary silence associated with aphasia. "Comprehension of language and motor ability are intact. Some of the patients speak to certain people and on certain occasions only. Their responses in areas other than speech are adequate" (p. 492). This description is strikingly similar to current conceptions of elective or selective mutism.

A variety of terms can be found in traditional classifications of childhood mutism. For example, speech avoidance (Lerea & Ward, 1965), speech inhibition (Treuper, 1897), speech phobia (Mora, Devault, & Schopler, 1962), thymogenic mutism (Waternik & Vedder, 1936), and traumatic mutism (Hayden, 1980) are among the terms used to describe and classify children displaying similar symptomatology.

Early writers commonly defined mutism by exclusion (Kratochwill, 1981). Tramer (1934) distinguished selective mutism from language retardation and schizophrenic mutism. Some writers perceived mutism as being closely tied to other forms of intrapsychic personality patterns. Weber (1950) stressed a specific disposition to reactions of stupor and depression in mute children. An abnormal dependence on the mother was noted, which was hypothesized to be related to oral dependency needs and a regression to early infantile social relations. Heuger and Morgenstern (1927) related a case in which partial mutism developed into total mutism. The authors reported that the child continued to communicate through drawings, and they proposed that the disorder was caused by castration anxiety.

In an extensive discussion of mutism among psychotic children, Etemad and Szurek (1973) reported that 30 percent of the 264 psychotic children seen at the Langley Porter Neuropsychiatric Institute Children's Service between 1946 and 1961 were totally mute or showed a marked paucity of verbal expression relative to expected age norms. The terms hysterical aphonia, childhood aphasia, and developmental aphasia have been used to describe failure to develop or extreme difficulty in using language and speech as symptomatic of psychoses (Schroeder, Gordon, & Hawk, 1983). Other writers suggest that mutism occurs in childhood schizophrenia and early infantile autism (Kanner, 1975; Shirley, 1963).

Differential diagnosis is important in distinguishing between elective mutism and mutism owed to other disorders. In severe and profound mental retardation there may be a general inability to speak reflective of a pervasive developmental disorder and developmental language disorder. Rutter (1977) notes that where elective mutism is typically a "pure" emotional disorder, mutism may develop as a reaction to an underlying speech or language handicap. Kolvin and Fundudis (1981) report that 50 percent of the elective mute children identified in the Newcastle Epidemiological Study displayed immaturities of speech or other speech difficulties.

Several considerations are important in distinguishing elective mutism from the mutism of the child with a language disorder. The chronicity of the symptom and premorbid verbal facility are important in the differential diagnosis. The child with a developmental or congenital language disorder is more likely to have a history of atypical speech and language development, whereas the elective mute child frequently has normal speech and language development during preschool years (Richman & Eliason, 1983).

Another group of children who may appear to be selective mutes are children of families who have emigrated to a new country and who refuse to speak the new language (Bradley & Sloman, 1975). Selective mutism should usually be diagnosed only in those cases where comprehension of the new language is adequate but the refusal to speak persists.

According to the fourth edition of the *Diagnostic and Statistical Manual of Mental Disorders* (*DSM-IV;* 1994), only in selective mutism is lack of speaking the predominant disturbance. General refusal to speak, as seen in some cases of major depression, avoidant disorder of childhood or adolescence, overanxious disorder, oppositional disorder, and social phobia, should not be diagnosed as such.

Elective or selective mutism as a childhood disorder was first described by Kussmaul in 1877 and later formally identified by Tramer (1934). The disorder is currently conceptualized as having the following features by the American Psychiatric Association (*DSM-IV,* 1994):

A. Consistent failure to speak in specific social situations (in which there is an expectation for speaking, e.g., at school) despite speaking in other situations.

B. The disturbance interferes with education or occupational achievement or with social communication.

C. The duration of the disturbance is at least 1 month (not limited to the first month of school).

D. The failure to speak is not due to a lack of knowledge of, or comfort with, the spoken language required in the social situation.

E. The disturbance is not better accounted for by a communication disorder (e.g., stuttering) and does not occur exclusively during the course of a pervasive developmental disorder, schizophrenia, or other psychotic disorder.

Hayden (1980) created four diagnostic categories of elective mutism based on a study of 68 children. These types include (1) symbiotic, characterized by a symbiotic relationship with a caretaker and a submissive but manipulative relationship with others; (2) speech phobia, characterized by fear of hearing one's own voice often accompanied by ritualistic behaviors; (3) reactive, characterized by withdrawal and depression possibly resulting from trauma; and (4) passive aggressive, characterized by hostile use of silence as a weapon. Although the information obtained in this study was not well standardized, an important finding was that there was a high prevalence of child physical and sexual abuse in all four groups.

Although there are few prevalence studies of this childhood disorder, some data currently available suggest that it is relatively rare. Morris (1963) reported an incidence of .4 percent of clinic cases and Salfield (1950) reported 1 percent. Existing incidence studies are not of the highest quality and these reported data cannot be trusted at this time. The number of treatment reports in the applied and clinical literature suggest that the disorder may be more prevalent than incidence data suggest. For example, Hayden (1980) and Sanok and Ascione (1979) suggest that many cases of elective mutism may go unreported because of the self-isolating nature of families of elective mute children, lack of acknowledgment of its severity, and general occurrence only in school situations. There is agreement that the disorder occurs most often in early childhood (5–7 years of age), is difficult to treat, and tends to be intractible over time (Kratochwill, 1981; Labbe & Williamson, 1984). The disorder is often accompanied by social withdrawal and even social skill deficits, but little research has focused on this aspect of the disorder.

There is a good deal of clinical literature in which there are reports of successful treatment; these studies have been reviewed in detail elsewhere (Friedman & Karagon, 1973; Kratochwill, 1981; Kratochwill, Brody, & Piersel, 1979; Labbe & Williamson, 1984; Sanok & Ascione, 1979). Both traditional dynamic therapy and behavior therapy treatment procedures have been employed with elective mute children.

Dynamic therapies have concentrated on the neurotic characteristics of elective mutism and usually involve insight-oriented therapy focusing on the child's personality structure. Traditional research and treatment programs have been in the form of descriptive and/or treatment case studies; they generally suggest a heterogeneous group of children (Koch & Goodlund, 1973). Common features include neurotic behaviors related to trauma experienced at critical times during speech development, with fixation occurring within the oral stage (Parker, Olsen, & Throckmorton, 1960; Salfield, 1950). Anxiety-related reactions to unfamiliar people or situations, including school and separation, suggest a fear-reduction function of mutism (Von Misch, 1952). Negative, insecure home environments also appear highly related to mutism, with the child engaged in a highly controlling, ambivalent, dependent relationship with his or her mother (Wright, 1968).

Diverse psychodynamic therapeutic interventions have been employed with electively mute children. Unfortunately, lack of specificity in treatment content and long-term therapeutic effectiveness make conclusive statements impossible. Clinically based individual therapies are documented in the literature with varying degrees of success (Arajarvi, 1965; Chetnik, 1973). Adams and Glasner (1954) described separate treatments using play and speech therapy with some concomitant psychotherapy. However, the course of treatment and follow-up were nonspecific and appeared ineffective.

In general, dynamically oriented therapists view mutism as symptomatic of family conflict (Von Misch, 1952; Weber, 1950). Long-term family therapies have been employed with some success (Browne, Wilson, & Laybourne, 1963; Elson, Pearson, Jones, & Schumacher, 1965; Pustrom & Speers, 1964). Similarly, individual psychotherapy with concurrent parental counseling has been the focus of treatment (Mora, Devault, & Schopler, 1962; Koch & Goodlund, 1973).

Although it remains difficult to identify the specific psychodynamic strategies that appear most effective in the treatment of elective mutism, a consistently identified theme is difficulty in treatment. This is especially reflected in the overall length of treatment (several months to several years), lack of generalization from the treatment setting (e.g., clinic) to the problem areas in the natural environment where the mutism occurs (e.g., school), and lack of consistent follow-up and maintenance of results (Kratochwill, 1981; Kratochwill, Brody, & Piersel, 1979).

Behavior therapy treatment procedures have been divided into neomediational S-R or applied behavior analytic techniques. Although neomediational S-R procedures (e.g., systematic desensitization) have focused on purported anxiety components of the disorder, most specific treatment components within this area are operant treatment techniques (Kratochwill, 1981; Labbe & Williamson, 1984). The operant procedures can be broken down into the following categories: contingency management, stimulus fading with positive reinforcement, response initiation procedures including shaping, response cost, escape avoidance, and

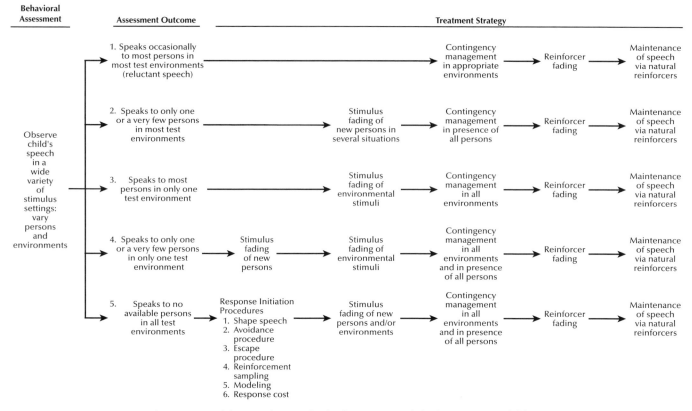

Assessment and therapeutic strategies for the treatment of elective mutism in children

reinforcer sampling. Most studies have involved treatment packages in which several of these independent treatment techniques have been used in combination or successively across a treatment program.

Behavioral interventions used in the treatment of elective mutism generally have been shown to have positive results. However, a number of conceptual and methodological issues have been raised in the empirical research literature in this area. First, there has typically been little work focusing on the systematic link between assessment tactics and development of a treatment program. Second, there have been few standardized (in the procedural rather than psychometric sense) assessment and treatment procedures for dealing with elective mutism. In addition, many of the clinical outcome studies have a number of methodological limitations including inadequate experimental controls, definition of outcomes, and criteria that meet contemporary standards of good clinical research (Kratochwill, 1981).

Labbe and Williamson (1984) developed a conceptual framework for linking assessment and treatment (see Figure). Assessment involves direct measures of the child's speech in numerous settings (e.g., school, home, community) in the presence of various individuals (parents, teachers, peers). Treatment procedures are then linked to a possible assessment outcome. Five outcomes are possible: (1) the child speaks to most people in most situations, but with low frequency; (2) the child speaks to at least one person

in all situations; (3) the child speaks to most persons, but only in one environment, (4) the child speaks to only one or a very few persons in only one environment, and (5) the child speaks to no one who is available for participation in a treatment program. As noted in the figure, various treatment procedures that have been developed in the operant literature are matched to the assessment outcomes that characterize the disorder.

## REFERENCES

Adams, H. M., & Glasner, P. J. (1954). Emotional involvement in some form of mutism. *Journal of Speech & Hearing Disorders, 19,* 59–69.

American Psychiatric Association. (1994). *Diagnostic and Statistical Manual of Mental Disorders* (4th ed.). Washington, DC: Author.

Arajarvi, T. (1965). Elective mutism in children. *Annals of Clinical Research of the Finnish Medical Society, 11,* 46–52.

Bradley, S., & Sloman, L. (1975). Elective mutism in immigrant families. *Journal of the American Academy of Child Psychiatry, 14,* 510–514.

Browne, E., Wilson, V., & Laybourne, P. (1963). Diagnosis and treatment of elective mutism in children. *Journal of the American Academy of Child Psychiatry, 2,* 605–617.

Bryson, S. E. (1994). A case study of literacy and socioemotional development in a mute autistic female. *Journal of Autism and Developmental Disorders, 24*(2), 255–231.

Chetnik, M. (1973). Amy: The intensive treatment of an elective mute. *Journal of the American Academy of Child Psychiatry, 12,* 482–498.

Elson, A., Pearson, C., Jones, C. D., & Schumacher, E. (1965). Follow-up study of childhood elective mutism. *Archives of General Psychiatry, 13,* 182–187.

Etemad, J. G., & Szurek, S. A. (1973). Mutism among psychotic children. In S. A. Szurek & I. N. Berlin (Eds.), *Clinical studies in childhood psychoses: 25 years in collaborative treatment and research, the Langley Porter Children's Service.* New York: Brunner/Mazel.

Friedman, R., & Karagon, N. (1973). Characteristics and management of elective mutism in children. *Psychology in the Schools, 10,* 249–252.

Hayden, T. L. (1980). Classification of elective mutism. *Journal of the American Academy of Child Psychiatry, 19,* 118–133.

Heuger, M. G., & Morgenstern, M. (1927). Un cas to mutisme chez un enfant myopathique ancieu convulsif. Gverion dn. muttisme par la psychoanalyse. *L'Encephale, 22,* 478–481.

Kanner, L. (1975). *Child psychiatry* (3rd ed.). Springfield, IL: Thomas.

Koch, M., & Goodlund, L. (1973). Children who refuse to talk: A follow-up study. *Bulletin of the Bell Museum of Pathology, 2,* 30–32.

Kolvin, I., & Fundudis, T. (1981). Elective mute children: Psychological development and background factors. *Journal of Child Psychology & Psychiatry, 22,* 219–232.

Kratochwill, T. R. (1981). *Selective mutism: Implications for research and treatment.* Hillsdale, NJ: Erlbaum.

Kratochwill, T. R., Brody, G. H., & Piersel, W. C. (1979). Elective mutism in children: A review of treatment and research. In B. B. Lahey & A. E. Kazdin (Eds.), *Advances in clinical child psychology* (Vol. 2, pp. 193–240). New York: Plenum.

Labbe, E. E., & Williamson, D. A. (1984). Behavioral treatment of elective mutism: A review of the literature. *Clinical Psychology Review, 4,* 273–292.

Lerea, L., & Ward, B. (1965). Speech avoidance among children with oral-communication defects. *Journal of Psychology, 60,* 265–270.

Mora, G., Devault, S., & Schopler, E. (1962). Dynamics and psychotherapy of identical twins with elective mutism. *Journal of Child Psychology & Psychiatry, 3,* 41–52.

Morris, J. V. (1963). Cases of elective mutism. *American Journal of Mental Deficiency, 57,* 661–668.

Parker, E. B., Olsen, T. F., & Throckmorton, M. C. (1960). Social case work with elementary school children who do not talk in school. *Social Work, 5,* 64–70.

Piersel, W. C., & Kratochwill, T. R. (1981). A teacher-implemented contingency management package to assess and treat selective mutism. *Behavioral Assessment, 3,* 371–382.

Pustrom, E., & Spears, R. W. (1964). Elective mutism in children. *Journal of the American Academy of Child Psychiatry, 3,* 287–297.

Richman, L. C., & Eliason, M. (1983). Communication disorders of children. In C. E. Walker & M. C. Roberts (Eds.), *Handbook of clinical child psychology* (pp. 697–722). New York: Wiley.

Rutter, M. (1977). Delayed speech. In M. Rutter & L. Hersov (Eds.), *Child psychiatry: Modern approaches* (pp. 688–716). Oxford, England: Blackwell Scientific.

Salfield, D. J. (1950). Observations in elective mutism in children. *Journal of Mental Science, 96,* 1024–1032.

Sanok, R. L., & Ascione, F. R. (1979). Behavioral interventions for childhood elective mutism: An evaluative review. *Child Behavior Therapy, 1,* 49–68.

Schroeder, C. S., Gordon, B. N., & Hawk, B. (1983). Clinical problems of the preschool child. In C. E. Walker & M. C. Roberts (Eds.), *Handbook of clinical child psychology* (pp. 296–334). New York: Wiley.

Scott, E. (1977). A desensitization program for the treatment of mutism in a 7-year-old girl: A case report. *Journal of Child Psychology & Psychiatry, 18,* 263–270.

Shirley, H. F. (1963). *Pediatric psychiatry.* Cambridge, MA: Harvard University Press.

Tramer, M. (1934). Electiver mutismus bei Kindern. Z. *Kinderpsychiatric, 1,* 30–55. In E. Postrum & R. W. Speers (1964). Elective mutism in children. *Journal of American Academy of Child Psychiatry, 3,* 287–297.

Treuper, J. (1897). Ein knabe mit sprechhemmunger auf psychopathischer grundlage. *Zeitschrift fur Kinderfehler, 5,* 138–143.

Von Misch, A. (1952). Elektiver mutismus in kindersalter. *Zeitschrift fuer Kinderpsychiatrie, 19,* 49–87.

Waternik, J., & Vedder, R. (1936). Einige faelle von thymogenem nutismus bu sehr jungen kindern und seine behandlung. *Zeitschrift Kinderforsch, 45*(Suppl.), 368–369.

Weber, A. (1950). Zum elektiven mutisums der kinder. *Zeitschrift fuer Kinderpsychiatrie, 17,* 1–15.

Wright, H. L. (1968). A clinical study of children who refuse to talk in school. *Journal of the American Academy of Child Psychiatry, 7,* 603–617.

SYLVIA Z. RAMIREZ
*University of Texas*

THOMAS R. KRATOCHWILL
SUSAN M. SHERIDAN
*University of Wisconsin at
Madison*

ELECTIVE MUTISM
LANGUAGE DISORDERS
SPEECH, ABSENCE OF

## MUTISM, ELECTIVE

See ELECTIVE MUTISM; COMMUNICATION DISORDERS.

## MYKLEBUST, HELMER R. (1910–    )

Helmer Myklebust received his BA in 1933 from Augusta College, MA in the psychology of deafness in 1935 from Gal-

Helmer R. Myklebust

laudet College, and an MA in clinical psychology in 1942 from Temple University in Philadelphia. He then went on to receive his EdD in psychology and guidance in 1945 from Rutgers University. Myklebust also completed several postdoctoral studies in mental retardation and clinical psychology, neurology, and psychoanalysis.

In 1948 Myklebust developed the Institute for Language Disorders at Northwestern University. With an interdisciplinary staff of ophthalmologists, pediatricians, neurologists, and otolaryngologists, research was conducted on the diagnosis and definition of language disorders in children. Myklebust coined the term language pathology, which gave emphasis to the aphasias and dyslexias, which, in turn, served as a foundation for the development of the concept of learning disabilities.

Myklebust also developed the first graduate training program in learning disabilities and organized a systematic approach to observing the behavioral impact (behavioral symptomatology) of deafness, brain dysfunction, mental retardation, and emotional disturbance.

His principal publications include *Auditory Disorders in Children: A Manual for Differential Diagnosis* (1954) (the most complete statement of his behavioral symptomatological approach to the differential diagnosis of handicaps in young children) and *The Psychology of Deafness: Sensory Deprivation, Learning and Adjustment* (1967), which addressed evidence of the psychological consequences of early life deafness (cognitive, personality, social, language, and motor).

Myklebust was editor of and contributor to *Progress in Learning Disabilities* (1968–1983), five volumes that address the relationship between brain dysfunctions and learning—neurologic, psychologic, and educational. He has written numerous book chapters and over 130 journal articles, and has received many awards and honorary degrees. He continues to work on a third volume on development and disorders of writing in children because he believes "that we have only begun to think about the importance of ability to write, normal and abnormal, and its role in intellectual development, illiteracy, and in all aspects of special education" (personal communication, August 1985). His most recent book is entitled *Conscience—Knowing Right from Wrong* (1997). Myklebust is a member of *Who's Who in America.*

## REFERENCES

Myklebust, H. R. (1954). *Auditory disorders in children: A manual for differential diagnosis.* New York: Grune & Stratton.

Myklebust, H. R. (1967). *Psychology of deafness: Sensory deprivation, learning and adjustment.* New York: Grune & Stratton.

Myklebust, H. R. (Ed.). (1968–1983). *Progress in learning disabilities* (Vols. 1–5). New York: Grune & Stratton.

Myklebust, H. R. (1997). *Conscience—Knowing right from wrong.* Monograph Service # 7. Sioux Falls, SD: Augustana College Press.

ELAINE FLETCHER-JANZEN
*University of Colorado at Colorado Springs*
First edition

TAMARA J. MARTIN
*The University of Texas of the Permian Basin*
Second edition

## MYOPIA

See VISUAL IMPAIRMENT.

## MYOTONIC DYSTROPHY (STEINERT'S DISEASE)

Myotonic dystrophy, which is also called Steinert's disease, dystrophia myotonica, DM1, and DM2, is a type of muscular dystrophy caused by an inherited anomaly on Chromosome 19. Prevalence rate is approximately 1:20,000 worldwide. Based on the type of Chromosome 19 anomaly, there are two types of myotonic dystrophy: type 1 (DM1), which is most commonly diagnosed, and type 2 (DM2). DM1 typically has the full range of symptoms, including weakness in the limbs. DM2 does not appear to cause congenital myotonic dystrophy, and is characterized by fewer or less severe symptoms, and by weakness in the trunk of the body rather than the limbs.

DM1 is classified as mild, classic, and congenital based on symptoms. Mild DM1 symptoms include muscle weakness, low energy levels, development of cataracts, and/or diabetes mellitus. Life span tends to be normal or minimally shortened. Classic DM1 includes the symptoms associated with mild DM1, along with balding, cardiac arrhythmia, digestive problems, and limb weaknesses such as foot drop. Symptoms can worsen over time, and life span may be shortened. Congenital DM1 (also called CMyD) is a rare variant of the disorder. Symptoms are evident at birth. Congenital DM1 symptoms are seen in infancy and typically include extreme muscle weaknesses manifested by sucking and swallowing problems, respiratory weaknesses, delayed motor development, and cognitive delays. The other symptoms seen in mild and classic forms will typically also be seen as the child develops. Infant mortality related to respiratory failure does occur. For the infants that survive, some gains in motor can be seen; however, these gains may be lost as the disorder progresses. Mental retardation is present in 50–60 percent of the affected individuals. The symptoms associated with congenital DM1 can worsen in late childhood or early adolescence, and a shortened life span is typical.

Onset of DM1 is categorized as congenital, juvenile, adult, and late onset. Congenital DM1 is the most severe and is seen at birth. Educational intervention will likely include occupational and physical therapy as well as support for cognitive development. Since deterioration of motor skills is typical as a child with congenital DM1 enters late childhood, ongoing assessment of skills and abilities will be vital for safety and for maintaining daily living functioning as much as possible. Additional intervention may be needed for general health functioning, such as feeding and toileting needs. Juvenile onset symptoms appear after birth, typically first seen in the teen years. Health issues like respiratory problems, as well as possible deterioration of motor skills, must be continually assessed, with adjustments made as needed. Initial occurrence of symptoms at ages 20 to 40 is called Adult Onset. Late Onset is when symptoms occur after age 40. Intervention for all types of myotonic dystrophy depends on the manifestation and the severity of symptoms.

## REFERENCES

Bird, T. D. (2004). *Myotonic dystrophy type 1. NIH gene reviews.* Retrieved August 31, 2005, from http://www.geneclinics.org

International Myotonic Dystrophy Organization. (2005). *General information about myotonic dystrophy.* Retrieved August 31, 2005, from http://www.mda.org.au/specific/mdamyt.html

Modoni, A., Silvestri, G., Pomponi, M. G., Mangiola, F., Tonali, P. A., & Marra, C. (2004). Characterization of the pattern of cognitive impairment in Myotonic Dystrophy Type 1. *Archives of Neurology, 61*(12), 1943–1947.

Muscular Dystrophy Association. (2005). *Fact sheet: Myotonic dystrophy.* Retrieved August 31, 2005, from http://www.mda.org.au/specific/mdamyt.html

Constance J. Fournier
*Texas A&M University*

## CHROMOSOMES, HUMAN ANOMALIES, AND CYTOGENIC ABNORMALITIES
## MUSCULAR DYSTROPHY

# N

## NAGLIERI NONVERBAL ABILITY TEST

The Naglieri Nonverbal Ability Test (NNAT; Naglieri, 1997) is a test of ability that can be used to predict academic achievement for children ages 5 through 17 years. The test, based on earlier forms of the Matrix Analogies Tests (MAT-SF, 1985b and MAT-EF, 1985a), has two forms: one that can be administered individually (NNAT-I), and a group-administered measure (the NNAT-MLF). The nonverbal nature of the test means that the examinee is not required to speak, read, or write, which may be especially appropriate for children with diverse linguistic and educational backgrounds. Administration time is approximately 30 minutes and test booklets may be hand scored or scored by machine.

The NNAT-I has two parallel forms consisting of 75 items each, while the multilevel group-administered test (NNAT-MLF) is organized into 38 items in each of seven levels. Item levels demarcate corresponding grades, starting with A = kindergarten and ending with G = grades 10–12. Examinees are presented with visual stimuli in the form of shapes and geometric designs and may respond by filling in a circle corresponding to the selected answer. The items are divided into four types: Pattern Completion, Reasoning by Analogy, Serial Reasoning, and Spatial Visualization. For each item category, examinees are required to use logic and reasoning to determine relationships between the stimuli. The Nonverbal Ability Index (NAI) reflects overall general ability and utilizes scaled scores with a mean of 100 and a standard deviation of 10 and can yield age- or grade-based scores. Percentile ranks, stanine scores, and normal curve equivalent scores may also be obtained.

A strength of the NNAT is the large and representative sample on which it was standardized. Fall (in 1995) samples included 22,600 children, and spring (in 1996) samples consisted of 67,000 students from kindergarten to twelfth grade. Based on 1994 National Center for Education Statistics, stratified, random sampling was employed to ensure adequate geographic, socioeconomic, and ethnic representation. However, Midwestern, suburban, and rural students were slightly overrepresented.

The psychometric properties of the test are adequate, with internal consistency of grade-based and age-based cluster scores ranging from .83 to .93 and .81 to .88 (KR-20). Yet cluster score internal consistency reliability yielded more variability and lower coefficients. The test was standardized concurrently with the established Stanford Achievement Test Series, Ninth edition (SAT-9). Consistent with data reported in the manual, Naglieri and Ronning (2000) found strong correlations between the SAT-9 and the NNAT. The manual also reports minimal correlations (.07–.51) to the Aprenda2, a Spanish normed test of achievement. The authors controlled for bias by subjecting items to statistical analyses, whereby statistical differences between groups determined an item's elimination.

Given the growing diversity of the United States, culturally fair measures of ability and intelligence are a necessity. It has been noted that Black and Hispanic students typically score lower on traditional tests and while some of these students may lack academic skills, there may be strengths that the most popular tests do not assess. Recent work by Naglieri and Ford (2003) highlights a potential important use of the NNAT. The authors demonstrate that the NNAT may be an effective tool in the identification of gifted ethnic minority children. Furthermore, it is suggested that the nonverbal nature of the test provides children with the opportunity to demonstrate abilities when other measures relying more heavily on verbal abilities may place these groups at a disadvantage.

### REFERENCES

Naglieri, J. A. (1985a). *Matrix Analogies Test–Expanded Form.* San Antonio, TX: Psychological Corporation.

Naglieri, J. A. (1985b). *Matrix Analogies Test–Short Form.* San Antonio, TX: Psychological Corporation.

Naglieri, J. A. (1997). *Naglieri Nonverbal Ability Test.* San Antonio, TX: Psychological Corporation.

Naglieri, J. A., & Ford, D. Y. (2003). Addressing underrepresentation of gifted minority children using the Naglieri Nonverbal Ability Test (NNAT). *Gifted Child Quarterly, 47,* 155–160.

Naglieri, J. A., & Ronning, M. E. (2000). The relationship between general ability using the Naglieri Nonverbal Ability Test (NNAT) and Standard Achievement Test (SAT) Reading Achievement. *Journal of Psychoeducational Assessment, 18,* 230–239.

Plake, B. S., & Impara, J. C. (Eds.). (2001). *The fourteenth mental measurements yearbook.* Lincoln, NE: Buros Institute of Mental Measurements.

RON DUMONT
*Fairleigh Dickinson University*

JOHN O. WILLIS
*Rivier College*

# NARCOLEPSY

Narcolepsy is a psychiatric disorder characterized by an abnormal need to sleep during the day along with pathological episodic attacks of REM sleep. Symptoms include sleep paralysis, cataplexy, and hypnogogic hallucinations. In the past, this disorder also has been referred to as Friedmann's disease and as Gelineau syndrome.

Narcoleptic attacks typically come at predictable times during the day; for example, postprandial drowsiness is especially common among narcoleptics after they have ingested meals high in protein. The narcoleptic attacks are typically irresistible. The patient with narcolepsy is an individual who will usually be able to fall asleep easily at night but who may have trouble remaining asleep.

Age of onset for narcolepsy is typically in the late teens or early twenties. The symptoms may be controlled with medication, but the condition usually persists throughout adult life. The prevalence of the disorder is estimated to be 4/10,000, with males and females equally affected (Kaplan & Sadock, 1981).

Cataplexy occurs in the majority of cases of narcolepsy. Cataplexy refers to sudden transient loss of muscle tone in the trunk or extremities. It is often triggered by strong emotions, either positive or negative. During cataplexy, the afflicted individual is still conscious but is rendered totally immobile. Most narcoleptics can remember the events that occurred during the period of cataplexy.

Sleep paralysis also occurs in many cases of narcolepsy. It is somewhat rarer than cataplexy and typically occurs as the narcoleptic individual falls off to sleep or just as he or she is emerging from sleep. It is a frightening experience in which the individual finds himself or herself awake but unable to move.

The diagnosis of narcolepsy is typically established by documenting sleep-onset REM periods in an all-night polysomnogram or by multiple sleep latency testing. The polysomnograms of some narcoleptics will reveal significant sleep apnea and sleep related myoclonus (Gregory & Smeltzer, 1983).

Genetic studies have demonstrated a strong genetic loading for this disorder (Mignot, 1998). The etiology is still not fully understood. However, more than 85 percent of all narcoleptic patients with cataplexy share a human leukocyte antigen (HLA) allele, compared with 12–38 percent of the general population (Mignot, 1998). Treatment with tricyclic antidepressants may sometimes be useful. Imipramine is the tricyclic that has been most studied. In addition, amphetamines and methylphenidate have been used in the treatment of narcolepsy (Wise, 1998). In the treatment of youth with narcolepsy, management is educational and supportive with consistent follow-up (Wise, 1998).

## REFERENCES

Gregory, I., & Smeltzer, D. J. (1983). *Psychiatry*. Boston; Little, Brown.

Kaplan, H. I., & Sadock, D. J. (1981). *Modern synopsis of comprehensive textbook of psychiatry*. Baltimore: Williams & Wilkins.

Mignot, E. (1998). Genetic and familial aspects of narcolepsy. *Neurology, 50*(2), 16–22.

Wise, M. S. (1998). Childhood narcolepsy. *Neurology, 50*(2), 37–42.

DANNY WEDDING
*Marshall University*

# NASH, CHARLES E. (1875–1953)

Charles Emerson (Ted) Nash served as a teacher at the Training School at Vineland, New Jersey, from 1898 to 1923, and as the institution's superintendent from 1923 until his death in 1953. A talented teacher and inspirational leader, Nash was a mainstay of the Training School during the years of growth to its preeminent position in the field of mental retardation.

## REFERENCES

Commemorative issue: Charles Emerson Nash. (1948). *Training School Bulletin, 45*, 134–153.

Honoring Charles Emerson Nash. (1953). *Training School Bulletin, 50*, 31–37.

PAUL IRVINE
*Katonah, New York*

**Charles E. Nash**

## NASH, WILLIAM R. (1943–      )

William R. Nash, a native of Cincinnati, earned his BA in psychology in 1965 and MEd in education in 1967 at Georgia Southern College. He went on to the University of Georgia, where his mentor was E. Paul Torrance, earning the EdD in educational psychology in 1971. He joined the faculty of the Department of Educational Psychology at Texas A&M University (TAMU) in 1972. Nash is now a professor in that department, where he has also served as director of the TAMU Institute for the Gifted and Talented.

Nash's professional interests and most significant writings have centered around education for the gifted and talented and creative thinking skills (Alexander, Parsons, & Nash, 1996; Scobee & Nash, 1983). His work has not only provided conceptual guidance to the field, but also has significantly contributed to advocacy and political activity on behalf of gifted children. Nash has served the National Association for Gifted Children (NAGC) in nearly every available elective office, including each of the vice presidencies and the presidency. Additionally, he has been a consultant to numerous school districts on matters related to educational programs for the gifted and talented and also to other noteworthy organizations such as the Sid W. Richardson Foundation and the Texas Scottish Rite Hospital. Nash is a frequently sought speaker for state meetings and conferences on the gifted.

In addition to these activities, Nash has acted as mentor to a number of gifted adolescents. Many of his doctoral students have gone on to become leaders in their fields, often aspiring to leadership positions in NAGC, taking faculty positions at a variety of universities, and establishing other institutes for the gifted and talented throughout the country.

### REFERENCES

Alexander, P. A., Parsons, J. L., & Nash, W. R. (1996). *Toward a theory of creativity*. Washington, DC: National Association for Gifted Children.

Haensly, P., Reynolds, C. R., & Nash, W. R. (1986). Giftedness: Coalescence, context, conflict, and commitment. In R. J. Sternberg & J. Davidson (Eds.), *Conceptions of giftedness*. New York: Cambridge University Press.

Scobee, J., & Nash, W. R. (1983). A survey of highly successful space scientists concerning education for gifted and talented students. *Gifted Child Quarterly, 27*(4), 147–151.

CECIL R. REYNOLDS
*Texas A&M University*
First edition

TAMARA J. MARTIN
*The University of Texas of the
Permian Basin*
Second edition

## NATIONAL ASSOCIATION FOR GIFTED CHILDREN
## TORRANCE, E. PAUL

## NATIONAL ADVISORY COMMITTEE ON HANDICAPPED CHILDREN AND YOUTH

The National Advisory Committee on Handicapped Children and Youth was authorized in Section 604 of Public Law 98-199:

> Amendments with respect to the Advisory Committee on the Education of Handicapped Children and Youth, National Advisory Committee on Handicapped Children and Youth
>
> Sec., 4. Section 604 of the act is amended to read as follows: National Advisory Committee on the Education of Handicapped Children and Youth.
>
> Sec. 604.(a) The secretary shall establish in the Department of Education a national advisory committee on the education of handicapped children and youth, consisting of 15 members, appointed by the secretary. Not less than five such members shall be parents of handicapped children and the remainder shall be handicapped persons (including students), persons affiliated with education, training, or research programs for the handicapped, and those having demonstrated a commitment to the education of handicapped children.
>
> (b) The advisory committee shall review the administration and operation of the programs authorized by this act and other provisions of the law administered by the secretary with respect to handicapped children (including the effect of such programs on improving the educational attainment of such children) and make recommendations for the improvement of such programs. Such recommendations shall take into consideration experience gained under this and other federal programs for handicapped children and, to the extent appropriate, experience gained under other public and private programs for handicapped children. The advisory committee may make such recommendations to the secretary as the committee considers appropriate and shall make an annual report of its findings and recommendations to the secretary not later than June 30 of each year. The Secretary shall transmit each such report, together with comments and recommendations, to the Congress.
>
> (c) There are authorized to be appropriated for the purpose of this section $200,000 for fiscal year 1984, and for each of the two succeeding fiscal years.

Although funds were authorized to provide for the establishment of this committee, funds have never been appropriated. Consequently, this committee has never met and its membership has not been noted. It is possible that the administration has not used existing funds to create this committee out of concern that the committee would assume oversight responsibility for the programs operated by the department.

MARTY ABRAMSON
*University of Wisconsin at Stout*

# NATIONAL ASSOCIATION FOR GIFTED CHILDREN

The National Association for Gifted Children (NAGC) is an organization of parents, educators, and other professionals united to address the unique needs of children and youth with demonstrated gifts and talents as well as those children who may develop their talents with appropriate educational experiences. The association supports and develops policies and practices that encourage and respond to the diverse expressions of gifts and talents in children and youth from all cultures, racial and ethnic backgrounds, and socioeconomic groups. To this end, NAGC supports and engages in advocacy, communication, personnel preparation, collaboration with other organizations, and research and development.

NAGC purports that, as a society, we have failed to recognize the special needs of the gifted and talented, thus resulting in loss of talent in the brightest and most creative youth. The association envisions its goals as (1) society valuing the diverse expressions of the gifts and talents of all individuals; (2) families, schools, and communities accepting and sharing the responsibility for nurturing, encouraging, and supporting the full development of potential in children; and (3) universal celebration of their accomplishments and contributions to self and society.

Among the special services offered by NAGC in support of this vision are: active public advocacy; dissemination of information on effective practices and policies to legislative and educational leaders; assistance to state and local gifted-education organizations in their advocacy efforts; and an annual convention on current trends in theory, research, and practice in the education of gifted and talented learners. Publications in furtherance of these goals include *Gifted Child Quarterly,* a professional journal for teachers and researchers, and *Parenting for High Potential,* devoted to helping families develop their children's full potential. *Teaching for High Potential* is a new quarterly publication for educators, incorporating classroom materials and practical guidance. In addition, NAGC publishes monographs, pamphlets, and support materials for parents, teachers, and policy makers.

Since its establishment in 1954, NAGC has become internationally recognized as an effective advocacy organization for gifted children, answering questions and providing expert information on gifted education. Affiliated groups are located in practically every state, and parents, educators, and policy makers are often referred to association contacts in Canada and Europe. Support generated by NAGC at the state and federal level is exemplified in the passage of the Jacob K. Javits Gifted and Talented Students Education Act, which provides funding for research and demonstration projects and which targets high-potential young people who may not be readily identifiable as gifted by conventional means (e.g., the economically disadvantaged, those limited in English proficiency, the disabled).

NAGC welcomes participation through membership, attendance at conferences and regional meetings, and communication with elected leaders and professional staff. Headquarters are located at 1707 L Street, NW, Suite 550, Washington, DC, 20036.

NATIONAL ASSOCIATION FOR
GIFTED CHILDREN
*Washington, DC*

# NATIONAL ASSOCIATION FOR RETARDED CITIZENS

See ARC, THE.

# NATIONAL ASSOCIATION FOR THE DEAF

The National Association for the Deaf (NAD), celebrated its 125th anniversary in the spring of 2005. Year-long celebrations included galas and community initiated activities to acknowledge NAD's successes to date. Founded in 1880, NAD is a private, nonprofit federation of 51 state association affiliates, sponsoring and organizational affiliates, and direct members. Washington, D.C. and U.S. territories are considered state affiliates. Organizational affiliates may be nonprofit or for-profit. Direct members are classified as regular, senior, student, junior, or international. The NAD is a member of the World Federation of the Deaf.

The NAD promotes the accessibility and civil rights of deaf and hard of hearing Americans in education, employment, health care, social services, and telecommunications. It serves as a clearinghouse for information about the deaf community, culture, heritage, and language, as well as information about the programs and services that it provides. Those services include captioned media and certification of American Sign Language and Deaf Studies professionals and interpreters. In addition, it offers free legal representation to deaf and hard of hearing constituents in areas related to civil, employment, and education rights, and equal access as mandated by law. The NAD also provides programs to prepare deaf and hard of hearing youth for positions of leadership.

Publications of the NAD include *The NAD Broadcaster,* printed 11 times a year since 1979, the *Deaf American Monograph,* an annual journal, and books concerning various aspects of deafness. The organization's bylaws and other information can also be accessed on the World Wide Web.

## REFERENCE

National Association for the Deaf. *Inside NAD*. Retrieved February 18, 2006, from http://www.nad.org

DONNA WALLACE
*The University of Texas of the
Permian Basin*

RACHEL TOPLIS
*Falcon School District 49,
Colorado Springs, Colorado*

# NATIONAL ASSOCIATION OF SCHOOL PSYCHOLOGISTS

Formed in 1969, the National Association of School Psychologists (NASP) is a 21,000-member professional association. The NASP was formed because many practicing school psychologists saw a need for uniform credentialing of school psychologists, a national identity for the profession of school psychology, a vehicle for communication among school psychologists, and a means for influencing legislation and regulations related to the delivery of school psychological services. The founding members of NASP believed the American Psychological Association (APA) to be unresponsive to the needs of practicing school psychologists, most of whom possessed degrees beneath the doctoral level and who were, therefore, not eligible for membership in APA. In addition, the NASP members believed APA emphasized scientific/academic issues and wanted a national organization that emphasized issues of more immediate concern to practitioners. The four stated purposes of the new organization were (1) to actively promote the interests of school psychology; (2) to advance the standards of the profession; (3) to help secure the conditions necessary to the greatest effectiveness of its practice; and (4) to serve the mental health and educational interests of all children and youths (Farling & Agner, 1979).

The NASP showed phenomenal growth during its first 15 years. True to its name, membership today is overwhelmingly composed of practicing school psychologists and is open to anyone working or credentialed as a school psychologist, trained as a school psychologist and working as a consultant or supervisor of psychological services, those primarily engaged in the training of school psychologists at a college or university, and others. In addition, a nonvoting associate membership is offered for those who support organizational goals but are not eligible for other categories (NASP, 1998).

The NASP has been at the forefront of many issues affecting handicapped students. Its input has shaped numerous federal and state laws, including PL 94-142 (Rights of All Handicapped Children Act of 1975). It works in partnership with national education and special education groups to influence legislation and regulations affecting schoolchildren. The NASP has published position papers and adopted resolutions relating to nondiscriminatory assessment, parental rights in child evaluations, corporal punishment, and other issues relevant to the education of all students. The organization has a governmental and professional relations committee that provides information and technical assistance to a network of affiliated state school psychology associations. Its Social Issues Committee vigorously advocates for children's rights, cosponsoring a major international conference on the psychological abuse of children in 1983.

A primary objective of the NASP has been the promotion of high-quality professional practice. Toward this objective, the NASP, as a constituent member of the National Council for Accreditation of Teacher Education (NCATE), accredits school psychology training programs at the specialist and doctoral levels. Also, the NASP strives to meet its members' professional development needs. Members receive the *Communiqué* eight times a year and a highly regarded professional journal, *School Psychology Review*, containing theory, research, and opinions related to the profession. The NASP's publication committee is responsible for disseminating many additional NASP publications, including books, monographs, pamphlets, videos, position papers, and fact sheets. The 38th Annual Convention was held in Anaheim, California (March 2006).

In its short history, the NASP has had a substantial impact on the delivery of school psychology services. In partnership with other professional groups, including the Council for Exceptional Children and the APA, it strives to "promote educationally and psychologically healthy environments for all children and youth by implementing research-based, effective programs that prevent problems, enhance independence, and promote optimal learning" (NASP, 1998).

## REFERENCES

Farling, W. H., & Agner, J. (1979). History of the National Association of School Psychologists: The first decade. *School Psychology Digest, 8,* 140–152.

National Association of School Psychologists (NASP). (1998, September 12). *The National Association of School Psychologists: Serving children and the profession.* Retrieved December 29, 1998, from http://www.naspweb.org/about_nasp.html

Reschly, D. J., & Genshaft, J. (1986, April). *Preliminary report: Survey of NASP leadership and practitioner members on selected issues.* Ames: Iowa State University.

JAN N. HUGHES
*Texas A&M University*
First edition

TAMARA J. MARTIN
*The University of Texas of the
Permian Basin*
Second edition

**AMERICAN PSYCHOLOGICAL ASSOCIATION**

## NATIONAL ASSOCIATION OF STATE BOARDS OF EDUCATION

The National Association of State Boards of Education (NASBE) is a nonprofit, private association that represents state and territorial boards of education. The principal objectives of the association include strengthening state leadership in educational policymaking; promoting excellence in the education of all students; advocating equality of access to educational opportunity; and assuring continued citizen support for public education.

The association serves over 600 individuals, including members of state boards, state board attorneys, and state board executives. These members are responsible for the educational interests of more than 40 million students in public schools and more than three million students in postsecondary institutions.

As the single organization representing state boards nationwide, NASBE seeks to further its goals by providing high-quality training and technical assistance to members and the larger education community, sponsoring regional and national conferences on critical policy issues, and publishing resource materials tailored to policymakers' needs. Communicating with Congress, federal executive agencies, business and industry, national associations, and other state decisionmakers is another important service provided by the association.

NASBE offers several free e-mail updates of education-related information; for example legal and legislative briefs. Legislative conferences and study groups are also offered through NASBE; for example, 2006 study group on early childhood: creating high-quality early childhood learning environments (March 17, 2006).

Boardsmanship training institutes, state board retreats, and study groups on critical education topics are sponsored by NASBE to help state boards maintain the highest level of discussion and arrive at the wisest possible decisions for the benefit of all students. The Policy Information Clearinghouse provides members with current information on emerging education policy, research, and governance issues; and the Governmental Affairs Committee (GAC) assists state board members in understanding, influencing, and planning for federal education policies. Over the years, NASBE has worked closely with legislators in crafting important legislation such as Goals 2000, the School-to-Work Opportunities Act, and reauthorization of the Elementary and Secondary Education Act.

Located in Alexandria, Virginia, NASBE has two affiliated bodies that provide the unique informational and training needs of related professionals who serve as state board members: the National Council of State Board of Education Executives and the National Council of State Education Attorneys.

### REFERENCE

National Association of State Boards of Education (NASBE). (1997). *Annual report.* Alexandria, VA: Author.

STAFF

## NATIONAL ASSOCIATION OF STATE DIRECTORS OF SPECIAL EDUCATION

The National Association of State Directors of Special Education (NASDSE) is an independent, nonprofit membership organization designed to serve the informational and professional needs of the chief administrators of special education at the state level.

Founded in 1938, NASDSE provides state directors of special education and related state education agency staff with information on national trends and activities; in-service training in program administration and policy development; and technical assistance in implementing programs at the state and local levels. Additionally, the association serves as the national representative for state directors of special education and their state agency colleagues, advocating on behalf of NASDSE membership before federal and state-level deliberative bodies and decision makers (including legislative and executive branch officials and commissions). NASDSE maintains a close affiliation with other national professional and advocacy organizations in order to effectively represent the positions and interests of the association members and to address the broader needs and interests of the special education community.

Members of NASDSE can subscribe to *Counterpoint,* a quarterly publication that reports the latest news related to the education of students with disabilities.

NASDSE is governed by a board of directors elected from the general membership of 57 state directors of special education (representing the states, territories, Bureau of Indian Affairs, and the Department of Defense Dependents Schools). With its offices located in Alexandria, Virginia, NASDSE serves as an important resource for improving state capabilities in administering the array of federal special education program and funding requirements. The organization also serves as a central vehicle for state administrators of special education programs to identify collectively and address, in a national forum, current and emerging issues and concerns.

REFERENCE

National Association of State Directors of Special Education (NASBE). (1986). *NASDSE: Its mission, programs and activities.* Washington, DC: Author.

GEORGE JAMES HAGERTY
*Stonehill College*

ADMINISTRATION OF SPECIAL EDUCATION
SUPERVISION IN SPECIAL EDUCATION

# NATIONAL CENTER, EDUCATIONAL MEDIA AND MATERIALS FOR THE HANDICAPPED

The National Center, Educational Media and Materials for the Handicapped facilitated the production and distribution of instructional media and materials designed for use in the special education of handicapped students. The center was founded in 1972 and had a staff of seven under the direction of Thomas M. Stephens. The center developed instructional management systems, conducted in-service training workshops and conferences, and provided individualized instruction to teachers on media and materials for handicapped students. The center also published the journal *The Directive Teacher* semiannually along with texts, teacher materials, and bibliographies. The journal was discontinued in 1986, as well as the project's funding. The National Center, Educational Media and Materials for the Handicapped is now defunct.

DANIEL R. PAULSON
*University of Wisconsin at Stout*
First edition

MARIE ALMOND
*The University of Texas of the
    Permian Basin*
Second edition

# NATIONAL CENTER ON EDUCATIONAL OUTCOMES

## Overview

The National Center on Educational Outcomes (NCEO) was established in 1990 by the Office of Special Education Programs (OSEP) of the U.S. Department of Education. NCEO was the only national center at the time that focused its efforts on educational outcomes for all students, including students with disabilities (NCEO, 1999). In order to monitor educational results for students with disabilities, NCEO's mission was to provide leadership in identifying outcomes, indicators, and assessments that could be developed and used by state and federal agencies. NCEO's work is grounded in the belief that identifying indicators of educational outcomes and using them effectively and responsibly will allow students with disabilities to achieve better results from their educational experiences. Through the process of monitoring the educational results of students with disabilities, NCEO works to increase educational accountability for all students at both state and national levels.

Some of the major activities of NCEO include the development of a conceptual framework of educational outcomes to guide future efforts in collecting data, particularly data on students with disabilities. Surveys are conducted in order to gather information from states regarding their current methods of collecting data on students with disabilities. Other efforts include collecting and analyzing information from states related to educational outcome data on students with disabilities.

## Research

Since its establishment, the NCEO staff has collected and analyzed a vast array of information from state and federal agencies. By examining efforts regarding the implementation of standards, goals, and assessment systems, NCEO has been able to identify important outcomes for students with disabilities. Information has also been gathered by holding consensus-building working meetings with state directors, educators, parents, and others on the domains of educational outcomes for all students. Similarly, current state outcome policies and accountability practices have been studied thoroughly by NCEO (NCEO, 1999).

Another line of research has focused on examining the extent to which students with disabilities are participating in and using accommodations for national or statewide assessments. Using the educational outcome framework developed by NCEO, the staff has examined state practices related to the inclusion and exclusion of students with disabilities in state and national data collection programs (NCEO, 1999). The center has further examined the availability and use of statewide assessments for students with disabilities.

NCEO has extensively reviewed and studied the implementation of testing accommodations and adaptations for students with disabilities. Other efforts have been focused on evaluating the extent to which assessment information on students with disabilities is provided in national and state reports.

Recently NCEO has collected and reported numerous studies addressing the needs of English language learners with disabilities. These include policy and procedures of ELL students on statewide assessments, and English Language learners and large scale assessments. On their web site (http://education.umn.edu/NCEO/OnlinePubs) there is access to research on a variety of special topics such as accountability, accommodations, out-of-level testing, and LEP students.

As well as its research activities, NCEO also actively disseminates information through publications, presentations, and technical assistance and other net working activities.

NCEO personnel have produced a large number of publications describing the data that have been collected from states; These include syntheses of state standards, policy briefs on important topics like alternate assessments, and technical reports. NCEO regularly publishes a summary of state assessment activities, and reports on state practices in providing testing accommodations. Self-study guides are also available for use by states in developing inclusive assessments and accountability systems.

NCEO is also committed to developing collaboration and leadership, to build on the expertise of others, and to develop leaders who can conduct research and provide additional technical assistance.

According to NCEO, current and emerging issues being addressed at this time are, accommodations, achievement gap, alternate assessment, graduation tests, reporting and/or monitoring students with disabilities in state accountability systems, test design, and content.

**REFERENCE**

National Center on Educational Outcomes (NCEO). (2006). Retrieved from http://education.umn.edu.nceo/default.htm

ELLEN A. TEELUCKSINGH
JAMES E. YSSELDYKE
*University of Minnesota*

RACHEL TOPLIS
*Falcon School District 49,*
*Colorado Springs, Colorado*

# NATIONAL COUNCIL FOR ACCREDITATION OF TEACHER EDUCATION

The National Council for Accreditation of Teacher Education (NCATE) was founded in 1954 to establish a national body for uniform application of standards in teacher preparation. The primary activities of the NCATE are at present the development and promulgation of standards for and review and accreditation of college and university programs for the preparation of all teachers and other professional school personnel at the elementary and secondary levels. The NCATE is the only appropriately credentialed organization to conduct such activities on a national level. It is authorized by the Council on Postsecondary Accreditation (COPA) to adopt standards and procedures for accreditation

and to determine the accreditation status of institutional programs engaged in the basic and advanced preparation of professional school personnel. The NCATE is also recognized as the appropriate accrediting body in educational preparation by the U.S. Department of Education.

Thirty-three professional associations make up the NCATE coalition of teachers, teacher educators, content specialists, and local and state policy makers who represent over three million individuals. The professional associations appoint representatives to NCATE's boards, provide financial support, and aid in the development of standards, policies and procedures within four categories, including design of professional education, candidates in professional education, professional education faculty, and the unit for professional accreditation. The four categories "emphasize prospective teacher performance in the context of solid preparation in professional and liberal arts studies" (NCATE, 1998).

The purpose of NCATE accreditation is fourfold:

1. To assure the public that particular institutions offer programs for teachers and professional school personnel that meet national standards of quality.

2. To ensure that children and youths attending school are served by well and appropriately trained personnel.

3. To advance the teaching profession through the improvement of preparation programs.

4. To provide a practical basis for reciprocity among the states in certifying professional school personnel.

The NCATE's efforts have been largely successful to this point. Most major institutions of higher learning that offer teacher and related personnel programs adhere to the NCATE standards.

The NCATE offers accreditation in special education and in most of the related service categories as well, including school psychology, educational diagnosis, and school counseling. Any school that offers a 4-year or more degree in education or a related field is eligible for an evaluation for accreditation by the NCATE provided the school is approved by its appropriate state agency, has obtained the appropriate regional accreditation, is an equal opportunity, nondiscriminatory employer, and has graduated a sufficient number of students from its program to allow for an evaluation of the quality of the preparation. The specific standards for NCATE accreditations are revised frequently as are application procedures. Institutions, associations, societies, or individuals seeking to obtain more detailed information about the NCATE, its standards, or the accreditation process should contact the director at NCATE, 2010 Massachusetts Ave., N.W., Suite 500, Washington, DC, 20036-1023. As of 2005, 691 institutions are part of the NCATE accreditation system. This is an increase of 110 institutions since 1999.

## REFERENCE

National Council for Accreditation of Teacher Education(NCATE). (1998, August 16). *About NCATE.* Retrieved from http://www.ncate.org/

CECIL R. REYNOLDS
*Texas A&M University*
First edition

TAMARA J. MARTIN
*The University of Texas of the
Permian Basin*
Second edition

national headquarters of the organization are located at 1350 New York Avenue, Washington, DC.

## REFERENCE

National Easter Seal Society. (1998, August 3). *What's new?* Retrieved from http://www.seals.com/html/the_easter_seal.html

PHILIP R. JONES
*Virginia Polytechnic Institute
and State University*
First edition

TAMARA J. MARTIN
*The University of Texas of the
Permian Basin*
Second edition

## NATIONAL EASTER SEAL SOCIETY

Founded in 1919 by a concerned Ohio businessman in cooperation with Rotary Clubs, the National Easter Seal Society, originally the Ohio Society for Crippled Children, became the first organization established for the purpose of helping children with physical disabilities. The movement spread gradually until, in 1934, Easter Seals introduced a small, colorful stamp to attract attention and support for the organization. This successful endeavor launched an unprecedented growth of the organization, as well as a nationwide movement on behalf of people with disabilities. Although Easter Seals currently utilizes other fundraising techniques, direct mail, with the Easter seal as its foundation, continues to be the largest single source of revenue for the society.

For more than 80 years, this national volunteer health-care organization has provided 1.5 million children and adults with disabilities and their families with services such as early intervention programs to help children with disabilities adapt and succeed in school, preschool and daycare programs for children with and without disabilities, adult vocational training and employment, and medical rehabilitation services. An advocacy role, ensuring equal rights for all disabled persons, is also assumed by the society and includes emphasis on elimination of environmental barriers, enhancement of positive attitudes, and increased recognition of individual abilities. Direct services are available to all persons with a disability resulting from any cause, including disease, illness, injury, or accident.

Easter Seals service sites are maintained in each of the 50 states, the District of Columbia, and Puerto Rico. The

## NATIONAL EDUCATION ASSOCIATION

Founded in 1857 as the National Teacher Association, the name National Education Association (NEA) was adopted in 1876. The NEA is the largest and oldest organization of teachers. NEA has 2.7 million members who work at every level of education, from preschool to university graduate programs. NEA has affiliate organizations in every state, as well as in more than 14,000 local communities across the United States.

As its mission, NEA advocates for the cause of public education, but also has a primary interest in the rights and welfare of teachers. Governmental relations, political action, and professional development are key components in the achievement of NEA goals. At the local level, the organization conducts workshops on topics relevant to school faculty and support staff, and is involved in negotiating contracts for school district employees; while at the state level, affiliates lobby government representatives for needed school resources and file legal actions protecting academic freedom. Work at the national level is wide-ranging and includes formulating inventive projects, restructuring how learning is achieved, and lobbying to prevent privatization of public education (NEA, 1998).

NEA policy is determined by its members, primarily through the annual Representative Assembly (RA) held each July and attended by more than 9,000 delegates who elect officers, debate issues, and set policy. In the interim, the Board of Directors and the Executive Committee make important decisions affecting education. NEA headquarters is located at 1201 16th Street, NW, Washington, DC, 20036 (NEA, 1998).

**REFERENCE**

National Education Association (NEA). (1998). *About NEA.* Retrieved from http://www.nea.org/

PHILIP R. JONES
*Virginia Polytechnic Institute
and State University*
First edition

TAMARA J. MARTIN
*The University of Texas of the
Permian Basin*
Second edition

# NATIONAL ENDOWMENT FOR THE HUMANITIES

The National Endowment for the Humanities (NEH) was created by the National Foundation on the Arts and Humanities Act in 1965 for the advancement of scholarship and progress in the arts and humanities. NEH is a grant-making agency of the federal government supporting research in the humanities, educational opportunities for teachers, preservation of texts and materials, translations of various works, museum exhibitions, television and radio programs, and public discussion and studies. According to the 1965 act, the humanities broadly embraces such disciplines as archaeology; comparative religion; theory, history, and criticism of the arts; modern and classical languages; literature; the social sciences; and history, as well as other areas that study and apply the humanities to the present conditions of national life. Thus, NEH supports work promoting knowledge in all subject areas encompassing the humanities while complementing local and private efforts by increasing nonfederal aid for high-quality projects.

NEH grants are awarded on a competitive basis according to the merit and significance of the project, with funding requiring importance to learning in the humanities, exemplary theory and concept, and the likelihood of success. Support is expressed in many forms, including fellowships and stipends for research, seminars and institutes for high school and college teachers, symposiums led by distinguished scholars, scholarly publications, and promotional liberal arts materials. Bibliographies, encyclopedias, and textbooks are examples of publications receiving awards from the agency. NEH generally excludes study or research in pursuit of an academic degree (with some exceptions); political, ideological, religious, or partisan works; training in the arts; and works of art.

The council also recognizes the highest official honor for intellectual achievement in the humanities bestowed by the federal government, the Jefferson Lecture. The lecture, open to scholars, professionals, and the general public, is delivered in the spring and addresses important issues relevant to the humanities. Past Jefferson lecturers have included Saul Bellow, Erik Eriksen, Barbara Tuchman, and Jaroslav Pelikan.

In 2005, NEH funded 346 successful grants for a variety of projects, such as NEH special initiative "Recovering Iraq's Past," fellowship and faculty research awards, and cultural institutions to protect and preserve their collections. Fifty of the successful grants were designated as *We the People* projects, which supports the study, teaching, and understanding of American history and culture. The *We the People* project developed after the attacks of September 11th, 2001. Numerous polls and surveys support the fact that many Americans lack even a basic knowledge about their nation's history. Therefore, on Constitution Day 2002, President George W. Bush announced *We the People,* an NEH initiative to explore significant events and themes in the nation's history, and to share these lessons with all Americans.

From its inception in 1965 NEH has awarded more than $3 billion for more than 54,000 fellowships and grants, with some grants requiring one-to-one matching funds from private-sector donations generating more than $333 million in additional capital. The NEH Challenge Grants Program, begun in 1977, has resulted in some $1.15 billion in nonfederal support for America's libraries, colleges, museums, and other institutions.

Through its Public Information Office, the NEH publishes a variety of materials, including *Humanities,* a magazine reviewing current work and theory in the humanities, as well as an annual report, *NEH in the Digital Age,* The Media Log, Exhibitions Today, Timeless Classics, *NEH Connect!* which is delivered monthly publishes the latest news, projects, upcoming events, and grant deadlines from NEH. Copies of these publications and application materials may be requested via email at info@neh.gov.

**REFERENCE**

National Endowment for the Humanities (NEH). (1997). *Welcome to the National Endowment for the Humanities.* Retrieved from http://www.neh.fed.us/

MARY LEON PEERY
*Texas A&M University*
First edition

TAMARA J. MARTIN
*The University of Texas of the
Permian Basin*
Second edition

RACHEL TOPLIS
*Falcon School District 49,
Colorado Springs, Colorado*
Third edition

## NATIONAL FEDERATION OF THE BLIND

Founded in 1940, the National Federation of the Blind (NFB) is a consumer organization that provides a vehicle for joint action and advocacy for blind people to improve their opportunities and increase public understanding of blindness. The largest organization of the blind in America, affiliates exist in all 50 states, the District of Columbia, and Puerto Rico, and chapters are located in most major cities. NFB currently has over 50,000 members nationwide.

Since its beginning, NFB has worked to help blind persons achieve self-confidence and self-respect as well as complete integration into society on the basis of equality. Objectives include removal of legal, economic, and social discrimination, education of the public, and achievement by all blind individuals of the right to exercise to the fullest their talents and capacities. These objectives are accomplished by providing public education about blindness; information and referral services on blindness for the blind, the newly blinded, and the public at large; advocacy services; scholarships; protection of civil rights; development and evaluation of technology; aids, appliances, and other adaptive equipment for the blind; literature and publications about blindness; support for blind persons and their families; and Job Opportunities for the Blind (JOB). Major emphasis is devoted to legislative affairs at the state and federal level, both in lobbying and subsequent dissemination of information regarding programs and services available to the blind. The organization provides for joint action by the blind and provides an avenue for the blind to advocate on behalf of themselves.

Services offered by the NFB include JOB, a highly successful program begun in 1979 and operated in conjunction with the United States Department of Labor to assist blind persons in finding competitive employment, and the International Braille and Technology Center for the Blind (IBTC), which provides evaluation and demonstration of adaptive technology used by the blind. Additional services include *Newsline®,* the first digital talking newspaper, and the Materials Center, offering over 1,200 publications dealing with issues about blindness.

NFB publications provide information to parents and educators of blind children, address the problems and concerns of blind diabetics, answer common questions about blindness, provide information about services and programs for the blind, and help to educate the blind and the sighted about a positive philosophy regarding blindness. *The Braille Monitor,* published monthly in braille, in print, and on cassette, is the voice of the National Federation of the Blind. With over 3,000 in attendance, the organization's annual convention is the largest gathering of the blind in the world. NFB national headquarters are located at 1800 Johnson Street, Baltimore, MD, 21230.

PHILIP R. JONES
*Virginia Polytechnic Institute*
First edition

TAMARA J. MARTIN
*The University of Texas of the
    Permian Basin*
Second edition

## NATIONAL HEAD INJURY FOUNDATION

See BRAIN INJURY ASSOCIATION.

## NATIONAL INFORMATION CENTER FOR CHILDREN AND YOUTH WITH DISABILITIES

Founded in 1970 as the National Special Education Information Center and undergoing four name changes since its inception, the National Information Center for Children and Youth with Disabilities (NICHCY) is a project of the Academy for Educational Development within the Disabilities Studies and Services Center operated through a cooperative agreement with the Office of Special Education Programs of the U.S. Department of Education. NICHCY provides information and makes referrals on disabilities and disability-related issues for families, educators, and other professionals. Some of the numerous topics addressed through NICHCY include special education, individualized education programs, education rights, family issues, and specific disabilities. A wide array of services is available through NICHCY, and among them are personal responses to specific questions; referrals to disability organizations, parent groups, and professional organizations; information from the center's databases and library; and disk and camera-ready originals in Spanish.

NICHCY also provides a variety of publications, including fact sheets on specific disabilities, state resource sheets, parent guides, and bibliographies. Most publications are available in two formats, text-only and portable document format, on the organization's web site at http://nichcy .org/.

### REFERENCES

National Information Center for Children and Youth with Disabilities (NICHCY). (1998, June 11). *About NICHCY.* Retrieved from http://nichcy.org/

National Information Center for Handicapped Children and Youth (NICHCY). (Undated brochure). *National Information Center for Handicapped Children and Youth.* Washington, DC: Author.

DOUGLAS L. FRIEDMAN
*Fordham University*
First edition

TAMARA J. MARTIN
*The University of Texas of the Permian Basin*
Second edition

## SPECIAL NET

## NATIONAL INSTITUTE OF EDUCATION

Founded in 1972, the National Institute of Education's (NIE) mission was to promote educational equity and to improve the quality of educational practice. In carrying out this mission, the NIE supported research and dissemination activities that were designed to help individuals regardless of race, age, sex, economic status, ethnic origin, or handicapping condition, and to realize their full potential through education.

Support for research was organized in three main program areas: (1) teaching and learning, (2) educational policy and organization, and (3) dissemination and improvement of practice. The NIE was charged by the U.S. Congress with critically examining such features of the educational system as vocational education, the benefits of supportive programs for failing low income students, and sex equity issues. Another major activity of the NIE was funding the efforts in research and development of improved practices. The NIE also provided support for, and monitored the activities of, a number of independent educational research laboratories and centers located throughout the United States.

When the Department of Education was established in 1980, the NIE was placed within the DOE's Office of Educational Research and Improvement (OERI). A 1985 reorganization of OERI abolished the NIE as a separate agency, and its programs were spread throughout the rest of OERI.

MILTON BUDOFF
*Research Institute for Educational Problems*

## NATIONAL INSTITUTES OF MENTAL HEALTH

The National Institutes of Mental Health (NIMH), founded in 1946, is the federal agency responsible for supporting and conducting research into the causes, diagnosis, treatment, and prevention of mental disorders. To understand the causes and improve the treatment and prevention of mental illness, NIMH research utilizes a multidisciplinary approach to research on the human brain in health and in illness by integrating findings from the neurosciences, basic behavioral sciences, clinical research, epidemiology, prevention research, and mental health services research. With this overall approach, the Institute supports basic research and studies addressing the causes and treatments for specific mental disorders such as schizophrenia, mood disorders, anxiety disorders, eating disorders, Alzheimer's Disease, and childhood mental illness. NIMH research also focuses on the mental health needs of special populations including racial and ethnic minority populations, women, and residents of rural areas.

The Institute publishes *Schizophrenia Bulletin* and *Psychopharmacology Bulletin* as well as printed materials regarding basic behavioral research, neuroscience of mental health, and the diagnosis and treatment of mental disorders. Public and professional education campaigns include The Depression/Awareness, Recognition, and Treatment Program (1-800-421-4211); Anxiety Disorders Education Program (1-88-88-ANXIETY or 1-800-64-PANIC); and Eating Disorders. In addition, the Institute sponsors The Mental Health FAX4U (301-443-5158), a fax-back system containing a list of publications, order form, complete texts of PAs and RFAs, and other items of interest. The Resources and Inquiries Branch of NIMH may be contacted by calling (301) 443-4513, or by emailing nimhinfo@nih.gov. The Institute's offices are located at 6001 Executive Blvd. Room 8184, MSc 9663 Bethesda MD 20892

NATIONAL INSTITUTES OF MENTAL
HEALTH
*Rockville, Maryland*

## NATIONAL INSTITUTE OF NEUROLOGICAL DISORDERS AND STROKE

The National Institute of Neurological Disorders and Stroke (NINDS) conducts and supports fundamental and applied research on human neurological disorders such as Parkinson's disease, epilepsy, multiple sclerosis, muscular dystrophy, head and spinal cord injuries, stroke, and neurogenetic disorders. The institute also conducts and supports research on the development and function of the normal brain and nervous system in order to better understand normal processes relating to disease states.

MILTON BUDOFF
*Research Institute for Educational Problems*
First edition

TAMARA J. MARTIN
*The University of Texas of the
Permian Basin*
Second edition

# NATIONAL JOINT COMMITTEE ON LEARNING DISABILITIES

The National Joint Committee on Learning Disabilities (NJCLD), founded in 1975, is a national committee of representatives of organizations concerned about the education and welfare of individuals with learning disabilities. Those organizations include the American Speech-Language-Hearing Association (ASHA), the Council for Learning Disabilities (CLD), the Division for Learning Disabilities (DLD) of the Council for Exceptional Children, the International Reading Association (IRA), the National Association of School Psychologists (NASP), the Association for Higher Education and Disability (AHEAD), the Division for Children's Communication Development (DCCD) of the Council for Exceptional Children, the International Dyslexia Association (IDA), the Learning Disabilities Association of America (LDA), and the National Center for Learning Disabilities (NCLD). Over 350,000 members of the various organizations are represented by the NJCLD, whose funding is provided by their contributions.

The primary purposes of the NJCLD are facilitating communication and cooperation among the member organizations; providing an interdisciplinary forum for the review of issues for educational and governmental agencies, as well as acting as a resource committee for those agencies; providing a response to national issues in the area of learning disabilities; preparing and disseminating statements to various organizations to clarify learning disability issues; and identifying research and service delivery needs in learning abilities. Numerous publications on issues relating to learning disabilities are available from NJCLD, 10801 Rockville Pike, Rockville, MD, 20852.

## REFERENCE

National Joint Committee on Learning Disabilities (NJCLD). *Fact sheet.* Retrieved from http://www.ldonline.org/njcld/fact_sheet.html

SHIRLEY A. JONES
*Virginia Polytechnic Institute
and State University*
First edition

DONNA WALLACE
*The University of Texas of the
Permian Basin*
Second edition

# NATIONAL LEARNING DISABILITIES ASSISTANCE PROGRAM

Public Law 91-230, the Elementary and Secondary Education Act Amendments of 1970, repealed Title VI of the Elementary and Secondary Education Act as of July 1, 1971. The act consolidated a number of previously separate federal grant programs relating to handicapped children under a new authority, the Education of the Handicapped Act (EHA). The 1970 EHA also added Part G, a new authorization for funding programs for children with specific learning disabilities.

The purpose of the program under Part G of the EHA was to assist states in identifying, diagnosing, and serving children with specific learning disabilities. This discretionary grant program provided support for research efforts, training for teachers and supervisors of teachers of children with specific learning disabilities, and model demonstration service centers aimed at stimulating increased statewide services for the target population.

Public Law 94-142 amended the definition of handicapped children to include the category of specific learning disabilities. With that statutory change, funds under any of the other EHA programs could be used for children with specific learning disabilities. Part G was repealed in 1983 by PL 98-199.

SHIRLEY A. JONES
*Virginia Polytechnic Institute
and State University*

# NATIONAL MERIT SCHOLARSHIP CORPORATION

Founded in 1955, this independent organization is devoted to scholarship activities for intellectually talented young people. Organizations and businesses are solicited to support scholarships through the merit program. Annual testing by some 18,000 high schools for eligible juniors results in the naming of semifinalists. Semifinalists represent the top half of 1 percent tested in each state. Semifinalists compete for nonrenewable and renewable awards ranging from $1000 to $8000. Approximately 6500 awards are made annually.

Over 600 corporate foundations, professional associations, unions, trusts, and universities underwrite grants to support the program. Recipients must be U.S. citizens. The corporation has also administered since 1964 the Achievement Scholarship Program for Outstanding Negro Students. This separate program is devoted to increasing educational opportunities for promising black students. Over 650 black undergraduate scholarships are awarded annually. The corporation publishes booklets and other information for secondary students and interested individuals. Headquarters are located at One American Plaza, Evanston, IL 60201.

PHILIP R. JONES
*Virginia Polytechnic Institute
and State University*

## NATIONAL ORGANIZATION FOR RARE DISORDERS

The National Organization for Rare Disorders (NORD) is a federation of voluntary health organizations dedicated to helping people with rare "orphan" diseases and assisting the organizations that serve them. NORD is committed to the identification, treatment, and cure of rare disorders through programs of education, advocacy, research, and service.

Members of NORD receive:

- NORD's newsletter, *Orphan Disease Update,* published three times a year
- Entry into the Family Networking Program
- Reduced registration fee for the annual Patient Family Conference
- Online search session(s) at no charge.

Basic membership fees are $30, which includes one free on-line session.

NORD has developed its own Rare Disease Database (RDB) Subscription Service. The RDB is a unique copyrighted consumer-based compendium of information on more than 1,150 rare orphan diseases. Selected portions (abstracts) of the RDB are currently available on the internet web site and can be accessed for free. Subscribers can access the full text versions of the *Rare Disease Database* entries. Subscribers receive a user name and password that will provide them with unlimited access to the full text versions. In addition, two other databases are searched simultaneously. These include NORD's *Organizational Database* (containing information on over 1,400 organizations that serve people with rare disorders) and NORD's *Orphan Drug Designation Database* (containing information from the Food & Drug Administration [FDA] on newly designated orphan drugs). NORD can be contacted at The National Organization for Rare Disorders, Inc., P.O. Box 8923, New Fairfield, CT, 06812-8923. NORD's telephone number is 1-800-999-6673, and their internet site is located at http://www.rarediseases .org. Information for this entry was obtained from the NORD web site.

STAFF

## NATIONAL REHABILITATION ASSOCIATION

The National Rehabilitation Association (NRA) was founded in 1925. It consists of 15,000 members constituting 70 local groups. With its headquarters in Alexandria, Virginia, the NRA is a consolidation of counselors, therapists, physicians, disability examiners, vocational evaluators, and other individuals interested in the rehabilitation of people with disabilities.

Among its activities, the NRA sponsors the Graduate Literary Award Contest, is involved in legislation, develops accessibility guidelines, and offers specialized education. Its newsletter is published six times annually; its *Journal of Rehabilitation* is published quarterly; and there is a Monograph of the Annual Mary E. Surtzer Memorial Seminar.

The NRA holds its annual convention in the fall, usually during the period of August to October.

MARY LEON PEERY
*Texas A&M University*

## NATIONAL SOCIETY FOR AUTISTIC CHILDREN

The National Society for Autistic Children (NSAC) was incorporated into the Autism Society of America in 1981. It no longer exists as a separate organization.

STAFF

## NATIONAL SOCIETY FOR CHILDREN AND ADULTS WITH AUTISM

The National Society for Children and Adults with Autism was founded in 1965 and incorporated into the Autism Society of America in 1987. It no longer exists as a separate organization.

STAFF

## NATIONAL SOCIETY FOR CRIPPLED CHILDREN AND ADULTS

See NATIONAL EASTER SEAL SOCIETY.

## NATIONAL SOCIETY FOR THE PREVENTION OF BLINDNESS

Founded in 1908, the National Society for the Prevention of Blindness (NSPB) has as its primary purpose preventing blindness and conserving sight. This purpose is addressed through nationwide programs of public and professional education, research, and industrial and community services. Services include promotion and support of local glaucoma screening, preschool vision testing, industrial eye safety, and collection of data on the nature and extent of the causes of blindness and defective vision. Funding is entirely from contributions, memorial gifts, bequests, and legacies. Corporate and foundation support is extensive.

Grants for medical research and research fellowships in ophthalmology are available through NSPB. The society publishes a quarterly journal and a newsletter. Pamphlets on eye diseases, children's eye care, and industrial, sports, and school eye safety are available. The NSPB distributes home eye tests for preschoolers and adults and issues testing charts, posters, films, and radio/TV material. A major thrust of the organization has been the promotion of safety eyewear for various occupations and athletics. Offices are located at 500 E. Remington Road, Schaumburg, Illinois, 60173.

PHILIP R. JONES
*Virginia Polytechnic Institute
and State University*

## NATIONAL TECHNICAL INSTITUTE FOR THE DEAF

The National Technical Institute for the Deaf (NTID) was established in June 1965 by Congress and signed into law (PL 89-36) by President Lyndon B. Johnson. The law specifically included provisions relating to program size, program objectives, location, administration, curriculum, admission standards, duration of course study, and research. The bill also mandated that a national advisory board on the establishment of NTID be appointed. This board consisted of 12 members with the commissioner of education and the commissioner of vocational rehabilitation specified as ex officio members.

The board was to review proposals from institutions of higher education for the construction and operation of NTID. Further, the board was to make other recommendations to the secretary of health, education, and welfare as appropriate regarding the establishment and operation of NTID. Under PL 89-36, the board ceased to exist once the secretary entered into an agreement with an institution of higher education.

In November 1966 the Rochester Institute of Technology (RIT) in Rochester, New York, was announced as the site for the NTID. The following January, D. Robert Frisina was selected to head NTID with the title of RIT vice president for NTID. A pilot group of students enrolled in September 1968.

Today NTID is the world's largest technical college for the deaf on a campus of primarily hearing students. NTID serves about 1,100 deaf students from across the United States and foreign countries. Students can enroll in diploma, associate, baccalaureate, and master's degree programs in a variety of career fields. NTID is one of the eight colleges of Rochester Institute of Technology (RIT). Approximately 94 percent of deaf RIT graduates have found jobs upon graduation. They are employed across the United States in business, industry, government, and education.

Students at NTID must have good high school grades, at least an overall grade 8 achievement level on a standardized test, and a hearing loss of about 70 dBs or greater (without a hearing aid) in the better ear. Appropriate support services are available for students who need them. Further information may be obtained by writing NTID, P.O. Box 9887, Rochester, NY 14623, or by calling (716) 475-6219.

### REFERENCES

Brill, R. G. (1974). *The education of the deaf,* Washington, DC: Gallaudet College Press.

Culhane, B., & Clarcq, J. (1994). Deaf and capable. *HR Magazine, 39,* 81–83.

National Technical Institute for the Deaf (NTID). (undated). *Your college for careers.* Rochester, NY: Rochester Institute of Technology.

PHILIP E. LYON
*College of St. Rose*
First edition

MARIE ALMOND
*The University of Texas of the
Permian Basin*
Second edition

## NATURE VERSUS NURTURE

The source of various traits has been debated throughout history. Some attribute honesty to genetic inheritance while others emphasize the modeling of family members, the influence of peers, or perhaps the mores held within a sector of society (Weinberg, 1983).

No area of human achievement has spurred greater controversy concerning the contributions of heredity and environment than the study of intelligence (Hallahan & Kauffman, 1986). Owing to the longstanding controversy and its social and political ramifications, it is vital that key issues be kept clear. Two issues are disputed: the validity of intelligence tests and the extent to which intelligence can be attributed to genetic inheritance. Intelligence tests, in particular the IQ test, contain items that probe an individual's ability to solve problems, comprehend words and passages, complete puzzles, and so forth. Such tests have been used in Europe and the United States for years, but have been under attack for being culturally biased. That is, the knowledge needed to do well on these tests is of value in some sections of society but not others.

The second major issue, the degree to which intelligence is inherited, is even more controversial. Some authorities (e.g., Jensen, 1969; Scarr & McCartney, 1983) have held that most of a person's intelligence is genetically determined. A majority of scholars in the field, however, have taken the position that intelligence is influenced mostly by environmental factors, or that the relative contributions of the two factors cannot be separated. (Block & Dworkin, 1976; Bouchard & McGue, 1981). Today, there is general agreement among geneticists that at least fifty percent of variance in IQ is genetic in origin (Carroll, 1992).

Nature does provide a promising method for evaluating the relative effects of heredity and environment. The crucial factor is to keep heredity constant. To study the offspring of the same parents is not sufficient, for each child has his or her own unique genetic makeup. It is only identical or monozygotic twins who share identical heredity; consequently, differences between these twins can be safely attributed to environmental factors.

In order to control for the effects of the environment, a number of comparisons need to be made. One comparison can be made between identical twins and between identical twins and their siblings. Another comparison can be made between the degree of difference between fraternal or dizygotic twins. Although fraternal twins are products of separate ova and sperm, they should otherwise be treated similarly to identical twins. Studies reveal that identical twins are consistently similar across a variety of measures. It is therefore reasonable to conclude that heredity does significantly influence children's development (Weinberg, 1983). However, the influence differs across traits: identical as well as fraternal twins resemble each other most in their physical traits, somewhat less in intelligence, and still less in personality and emotions.

Research on identical twins raised in different environments studies the extent of the contribution of the environment. A review of the literature on this topic by Farber (1981) reveals that identical twins who were separated but raised in similar environments had negligible differences in intelligence. However, identical twins' performances on intelligence tests could differ markedly if their environments were very different.

It is not possible to directly assess hereditary factors where there are no twins. Because some people have made unsubstantiated inferences about racial differences in intelligence, many psychologists are extremely cautious about speculating on the inheritability of intelligence (Block & Dworkin, 1976). Consequently, psychologists have favored the study of environmental factors, trying to determine how family factors, as well as the persons, institutions, and norms of the larger society, influence children's behavior, and how children themselves may affect their environments (McEwen & Schmeck, 1994).

Most socialization studies take a broad view of the context in which the human develops. Research into the effects of malnutrition on intelligence is difficult to conduct for ethical reasons, yet evidence does exist, from animal and human studies, to lead to the conclusion that early malnutrition contributes to the incidence of mental retardation. Offspring of high socioeconomic groups, on the average, earn higher IQs than those of low socioeconomic parents. Poor performance on infant developmental scales are more likely to result in poor intellectual performance at later ages (4 and 10 years) in the context of low socioeconomic status than in the context of high socioeconomic status (Scarr & Weinberg, 1981).

The research clearly reveals that intelligence is influenced by both hereditary and environmental factors. Environmental influences come from birth weight, nutrition, and various familial sources. Consequently, hereditary and environmental factors continually interact to influence the child's development.

## REFERENCES

Block, N., & Dworkin, G. (Eds.). (1976). *The IQ controversy.* New York: Pantheon.

Bouchard, T. J., Jr. (1983). Do environmental similarities explain the similarity in intelligence of identical twins reared apart? *Intelligence, 7,* 175–184.

Bouchard, T. J., Jr., & McGue, M. (1981). Familial studies of intelligence: A review. *Science, 212,* 1055–1059.

Carroll, J. B. (1992). Cognitive abilities: The state of the art. *Psychological Science, 3*(5), 266–270.

Farber, S. L. (1981). *Identical twins reared apart: A reanalysis.* New York: Basic Books.

Hallahan, D. P., & Kauffman, J. M. (1986). *Exceptional children.* Englewood Cliffs, NJ: Prentice Hall.

Jensen, A. R. (1969). How much can we boost I.Q. and scholastic achievement? *Harvard Educational Review, 39,* 1–123.

McEwen, B. S., & Schmeck, H. M. (1994). *The hostage brain.* New York: Rockefeller University Press.

Scarr, S., & McCartney, K. (1983). How people make their own environments: A theory of genotype-environmental effects. *Child Development, 54,* 424–435.

Scarr, S., & Weinberg, R. A. (1981). The transmission of authoritarianism in families: Genetic resemblance in social-political attitudes? In S. Scarr (Ed.), *Race, social class, and individual differences in I.Q.* Hillsdale, NJ: Erlbaum.

Weinberg, R. A. (1983). A case of a misplaced conjunction: Nature or nurture? *Journal of School Psychology, 21,* 9–12.

JOSEPH M. RUSSO
*Hunter College, City University
of New York*

INTELLIGENCE
INTELLIGENCE TESTING
SOCIOECONOMIC STATUS

## NAVANE

Navane (thiothixene hydrochloride) is a psychotropic drug used in the management of manifestations of psychotic disorders. It is not recommended for use in children under 12 years of age. Side effects can include drowsiness, especially on initiation of drug therapy, as well as agitation, restlessness, insomnia, and occasional instances of seizures and paradoxical exacerbation of psychotic symptoms. Overdosage symptoms can include muscular twitching, drowsiness, and dizziness, with gross overdose potentially resulting in gait disturbance and coma.

A brand name of Roerig Pharmaceuticals, Navane is available in capsules containing 1, 2, 5, and 10 mg, as a concentrate, and as an injection (intramuscular) vial. Dosages are individually adjusted, generally beginning with small doses of 2 mg three times a day, with increases up to 60 mg per day as needed.

### REFERENCE

*Physicians' desk reference.* (1984). (pp. 1685–1688). Oradell, NJ: Medical Economics.

LAWRENCE C. HARTLAGE
*Evans, Georgia*

ATARAX
BENADRYL
COMPAZINE

## NCATE

See NATIONAL COUNCIL FOR ACCREDITATION OF TEACHER EDUCATION.

## NEAR INFRARED SPECTROSCOPY

Based on advances in understanding means by which light migrates through living tissue, Near Infrared Spectroscopy (NIRS) and Diffuse Optical Tomography have been developed. If you shine a flashlight onto your hand you can clearly see the light travel through centimeters of tissue and still be detected. Light can be used to image or see inside the body. Optical imaging at centimeter depths is afforded by the relationships of the absorption spectra of water, oxygenated hemoglobin and deoxygenated hemoglobin, the three primary absorbers in tissue at near-infrared wave lengths. The water spectrum at those wave lengths permits a sort of spectral window in the background absorption, allowing researchers to view the hemoglobin. Moreover, within this window the spectra of oxy and de-oxy hemoglobin are distinct enough to allow spectroscopy and recovery of separate concentrations of both types of molecules. Scattering properties of different tissue types are also distinct enough to be recorded. NIRS offers the opportunity to image three-dimensional, spatial variations in blood parameters, particularly hemoglobin concentration and oxygen saturation and therefore the metabolic factors that these concentrations reflect, as well as tissue scattering characteristics. NIRS has been used in brain mapping to identify visual, auditory, and somatosensory stimuli associated with certain cognitive functions. NIRS also shows promise as a clinical tool, particularly as it relates to the brain. NIRS has been used in efforts to prevent and treat seizures, understand depression, and diagnose Alzheimer's disease and schizophrenia. NIRS equipment is now available commercially. However, in comparison to other functional neuroimaging methods, such as PET or fMRI, NIRS lacks spatial resolution and depth penetration. NIRS, however, has some advantages. It offers biochemical specificity by directly measuring concentration of molecules. The data obtained provides information not only about vascular response, consequent upon neuroactivation, but also intracellular events. NIRS is increasingly finding its way into clinical practice as a noninvasive diagnostic tool.

SAM GOLDSTEIN
*University of Utah*

DIFFUSION TENSOR IMAGING
MAGNETIC RESONANCE IMAGING
SPECT

## NEGATIVE PUNISHMENT

The removal of a stimulus to decrease inappropriate/interfering behaviors is referred to as negative punishment. Time-out from positive reinforcement and response cost procedures are commonly employed strategies for decreasing the future probability of targeted behaviors. When employing these strategies, the obtrusiveness with which the environment is altered deserves special attention. For example, a tantrum during a meal can be handled by removing the child from the room, removing the child to a short distance from the table so direct observation of peers is still present, or removing the food from the child for a specified number of minutes. A recommendation for teachers is to provide the least amount of change in the environment that is most effective in reducing future occurrences of inappropriate behaviors. In a similar manner, the removal of previously earned points/tokens (response cost) can vary in intensity relative to the severity of the targeted activity to be decreased. For further information and examples the references below may be consulted.

### REFERENCES

Bellack, A. S., & Hersen, M. (Eds.). (1985). *Dictionary of behavior therapy techniques* (p. 155). New York: Pergamon.

Kazdin, A. E. (1984). *Behavior modification in applied settings* (3rd ed., pp. 125–153). Homewood, IL: Dorsey.

ERNEST L. PANCSOFAR
*University of Connecticut*

## NEGATIVE REINFORCEMENT

Negative reinforcement is the removal or avoidance of an aversive stimulus from the environment that increases the future occurrence of the behavior immediately preceding the removal. Examples from everyday situations include buckling a seat belt to remove the aversive sound of the buzzer, bringing an umbrella outside on a rainy day to escape being wet, and ingesting a pain reliever to reduce the intensity of a headache. Negative reinforcement includes both escape and avoidance components. In a classroom situation, escape from the loud sound of a fire alarm increases the future likelihood of vacating a room during a fire drill. Similarly, avoiding a verbal reprimand from a teacher by remaining on task during a math assignment is an example of negative reinforcement.

Negative reinforcement is often confused with and mislabeled as punishment. In negative reinforcement, the future probability of a behavior that is followed by the removal of an aversive stimulus increases. However, the future probability of the occurrence of a behavior followed by the removal of a positive stimulus (negative punishment) or the presentation of an aversive event (positive punishment) decreases. Further reading references are cited below.

### REFERENCES

Kazdin, A. E. (1984). *Behavior modification in applied settings* (3rd ed., pp. 31–33). Homewood, IL: Dorsey.

Sulzer-Azaroff, B., & Mayer, G. R. (1977). *Applying behavior-analysis procedures with children and youth* (pp. 140–141). New York: Holt, Rinehart, & Winston.

ERNEST L. PANCSOFAR
*University of Connecticut*

**BEHAVIOR ANALYSIS, APPLIED**
**BEHAVIOR MODIFICATION**
**NEGATIVE PUNISHMENT**

## NEISWORTH, JOHN T. (1937–    )

Born in Pittsburgh, Pennsylvania, John T. Neisworth received his BS (1959) in psychology, his MEd (1961) in special education, and his PhD (1967) in special education and educational psychology from the University of Pittsburgh. He is currently a professor of special education in the educational and school psychology and special education departments at Pennsylvania State University.

Neisworth has focused on a wide range of issues related to early childhood education. As an advocate for individuals with mental retardation, he holds that persons with mental retardation have the capacity to accomplish more than most people assume and recommends abandoning the use of IQ labels, believing that the label of mentally retarded is more likely to be harmful to a child than to assist her or him in obtaining appropriate services (Neisworth, 1969). In his earlier work, Neisworth wrote on multidisciplinary concerns regarding mental retardation, specifically addressing the education of these students while elaborating on the definition, causes, and appropriate interventions for those with mental retardation (Neisworth & Smith, 1978).

Neisworth's work in the area of assessments and interventions for young children, particularly as related to eligibility for services in special education, is prolific (Bagnato & Neisworth, 1994; Bagnato, Neisworth, & Munson, 1997; Banks & Neisworth, 1995). His investigations have ranged from intelligence testing for use with young children to dynamic assessment as a tool for assessment of infants and youth with sensory, motor, affective, and cultural differences not represented in norms of typical instruments. Neisworth continues to make important contributions to the field of education, advocating a united effort among professionals in objecting to the use of intelligence testing in early intervention (Neisworth & Bagnato, 1992).

### REFERENCES

Bagnato, S. J., & Neisworth, J. T. (1994). A national study of the social and treatment "invalidity" of intelligence testing for early intervention. *School Psychology Quarterly, 9*(2), 81–102.

Bagnato, S. J., Neisworth, J. T., & Munson, S. M. (1997). *Linking assessment and early intervention: An authentic curriculum-based approach.* Baltimore: Brookes.

Banks, S. R., & Neisworth, J. T. (1995). Dynamic assessment in early intervention: Implications for serving American Indian/Alaska Native Families. *Journal of American Indian Education, 34*(2), 27–43.

Neisworth, J. T. (1969). Educational irrelevance of "intelligence." In R. M. Smith (Ed.), *Diagnosis of educational differences.* Columbus, OH: Merrill.

Neisworth, J. T., & Smith, R. M. (Eds.). (1978). *Retardation: Issues, assessment, and intervention.* New York: McGraw-Hill.

Neisworth, J. T., & Bagnato, S. J. (1992). The case against intelligence testing in early intervention. *Topics in early childhood special education, 12*(1), 1–20.

E. VALERIE HEWITT
*Texas A&M University*
First edition

TAMARA J. MARTIN
*The University of Texas of the Permian Basin*
Second edition

## NEONATAL BEHAVIORAL ASSESSMENT SCALE

The Neonatal Behavioral Assessment Scale (NBAS; Brazelton, 1973, 1984) is designed to examine the behavior of neonates at not less than 37 weeks gestation or more than 30 days after birth. Characteristics of the normal, healthy, full-term newborn are measured, such as his or her adjustment to labor, delivery, and new environment. The sociability with caregivers and management of homeostasis are also assessed. How well a neonate adapts is primarily examined by looking at the newborn's states of consciousness.

The 1984 NBAS contains a test manual, an audiovisual tape, and a case of necessary equipment (shiny red ball, flashlight, rattle, bell, and tactile probe in a carrying case). There are 20 reflex items on the NBAS, and each are scored on a 4-point scale. The two global behavioral scales on the NBAS are (1) attractiveness (measuring the infant's organized response capacity, integration of behavior, and positive feedback to examiner), and (2) need for stimulation (infant's need for stimulation to organize responses). There are a total of 28 behavioral items that are scored on a 9-point scale. The exam itself takes approximately 20 to 30 minutes to complete. It is recommended that the exam be done on at least two different days to avoid making erroneous conclusions based on a single day.

Interpretation of scoring on the NBAS can be problematic (Silverman, Killian, & Burns, 1994) because some scales have varying "optimal" scores. For example, some items are considered optimal at a score of 9, while others are optimal at 5. An overall summary score cannot be obtained, but score clusters are available for the following: habituation, orientation, motor performance, range of states, regulation of state, autonomic regulation, and reflexes.

Comprehensive standardization data are not available on the NBAS, but the author warns that the NBAS is not a normative test for infant development. However, several studies have been conducted using the NBAS. The scales have been found to be sensitive to many signs of narcotic withdrawal in newborns (Silverman et al., 1994). The NBAS has also been suggested to be useful as a tool to provide educational information to parents about abilities of newborns. The NBAS has been used as a teaching technique for neonatal nurses, who then can educate parents regarding their newborn's capacities (Gibbs, 1981).

It is recommended that researchers and clinicians who plan to use the NBAS attend a training seminar to ensure interrater reliability. Because the score is based on clinical judgment, precise methods for administration are crucial, in addition to clinical experience with babies and a knowledge of infant development. The NBAS is quite time-consuming to learn to administer (Silverman et al., 1994). However, it is one of the most widely used scales in research. Silverman et al. (1994, pp. 474–475) state that the NBAS "appears to meet acceptable standards for basic research at this time, although it is not a clinically tested tool, as Brazelton will confirm." Caution must be used when administering the NBAS for clinical purposes, and generalizations to the general population cannot be made at this time.

### REFERENCES

Brazelton, T. B. (Ed.). (1973). Neonatal Behavioral Assessment Scale [Special issue]. *Clinics in Developmental Medicine, 50.*

Brazelton, T. B. (Ed.). (1984). *Neonatal Behavioral Assessment Scale* (2nd ed.). London: Spastics International.

Gibbs, R. M. (1981). *Clinical uses of the Brazelton Neonatal Behavioral Assessment Scales in nursing practice* (Adapted from a presentation sponsored by the Johnson & Johnson Baby Products Co. and given at the NAPNAP First Annual Nursing Conference on Pediatric Primary Care, Feb. 27–Mar. 1, 1980, Washington, DC). Washington, DC: NAPNAP.

Silverman, C. R., Killian, G. A., & Burns, W. J. (1994). The Neonatal Behavioral Assessment Scale. In D. Keyser & R. Sweetland (Eds.), *Test critiques, Volume X.* Austin, TX: PRO-ED.

ELIZABETH O. LICHTENBERGER
*The Salk Institute*

## INFANT ASSESSMENT

## NEPSY: A DEVELOPMENTAL NEUROPSYCHOLOGICAL ASSESSMENT

The NEPSY: A Developmental Neuropsychological Assessment (Kemp, Kirk, & Korkman, 1998) was designed to assess the neuropsychological development of children between the ages of 3 and 12. Its name NEPSY is derived from the NE in neuro and the PSY in psychological. After administration, a Core Assessment of the child is obtained, presenting an overview of the child's neuropsychological functioning. An

Expanded Assessment can also be obtained, giving a more thorough assessment of the child's capabilities. This consists of pools of tests from five different domains:

*Attention and Executive Functions*—assesses inhibition, self-regulation, monitoring, vigilance, selective and sustained attention, maintenance of response set, planning, flexibility in thinking, and figural fluency.

*Language*—assesses phonological processing abilities, receptive language comprehension, expressive naming under confrontation and speeded naming conditions, verbal fluency, and the ability to produce rhythmic oral motor sequences.

*Sensorimotor Functions*—assesses sensory input at the tactile level, fine motor speed for simple and complex movements, the ability to imitate hand positions, rhythmic and visuospatial processing—assesses the ability to judge position and directionality and the ability to copy two-dimensional geometric figures and reconstruct three-dimensional designs from a model or picture.

*Memory and Learning*—assesses immediate memory for sentences, immediate and delayed memory for faces, names, and list learning, and narrative memory under free and cued recall conditions.

The core battery takes approximately 1 hour to administer and the expanded battery takes about 3 hours. Supplemental scores can also be obtained by exploring the subcomponents of the subtests. Qualitative observations can be made about the presence or absence of specific behavior, comparing them to a standardization sample. Each subtest is given a scaled score with a mean of 10 and a standard deviation of 3. Each domain receives a standard score with a mean of 100 and a standard deviation of 15.

The NEPSY was normed on a sample of 1,000 children that was representative of the U.S. population of children. There were 50 males and 50 females in each of the 10 age groups ranging from 3 to 12. The proportion of Whites, African Americans, Hispanics, and other race and ethnic groups was based on the proportions according to the 1995 census survey.

Reliability coefficients range from .72 to .87 for the core domain for ages 5 to 12. The NEPSY has been found to have good content and construct validity after being reviewed by panels consisting of expert pediatric neuropsychologists and school psychologists. Low to moderate correlation correlations have been found, ranging from .34 to .85, between the NEPSY subtest scores and core domain scores for children ages 5 to 12. Subtests within domains are more highly correlated than subtests across domains. The NEPSY has also shown good convergent and discriminant validity.

Some of the subtests are difficult to administer, so it is recommended that the examiner practice the subtests prior to administration. However, once the examiner becomes familiar with the test, it is useful in providing a great deal of information about a child's cognitive abilities and behaviors. A major advantage of the NEPSY is the flexible nature of its administration, allowing the examiner to individualize the test to the subject (Ahmad & Warriner, 2001). Stinnett, Oehler-Stinnett, and Fuqua (2002) found that for children ages 5 to 12, a one-factor solution best describes the NEPSY core domain structure and that the five core domains specified in the test manual may significantly over-define the NEPSY structure. They also noted that the subtest data should not be interpreted as if they reflect unique neuropsychological processing skills.

## REFERENCES

Ahmad, S. A., & Warriner, E. M. (2001). Review of the NEPSY: A developmental neuropsychological assessment. *The Clinical Neuropsychologist, 15,* 240–249.

Kemp, S., Kirk, U., & Korkman, M. (2001). *Essentials of NEPSY assessment.* New York: Wiley.

Korkman, M., Kirk, U., & Kemp, S. (1998). *NEPSY: A developmental neuropsychological assessment.* San Antonio, TX: Psychological Corporation.

Plake, B. S., & Impara, J. C. (Eds.). (2001). *The fourteenth mental measurements yearbook.* Lincoln, NE: Buros Institute of Mental Measurements.

Stinnett, T. A., Oehler-Stinnett, J., & Fuqua, D. R. (2002). Examination of the underlying structure of the NEPSY: A developmental neuropsychological assessment. *Journal of Psychoeducational Assessment, 20,* 66–82.

RON DUMONT
*Fairleigh Dickenson University*

JOHN O. WILLIS
*Rivier College*

# NETHERLANDS, SPECIAL EDUCATION IN THE

## History of Special Education Services

The first schools for blind and deaf pupils were founded at the beginning of the nineteenth century. From 1900, special schools for various groups of children gradually evolved on a small scale. Special education was originally regulated via specific legislation of the 1920 Primary Education Act. In 1967, a Special Education Act came into force. In 1985, this was replaced by the Interim Act for Special Education and Special Secondary Education.

## Legal Rights and Safeguards

With the passing of the Elementary Education Act in 1801, Dutch education acquired its first legal framework. A few years later, in 1806, the Third Schools Act followed, which made arrangements for teaching qualifications, the curriculum, and the government inspection of schools. The government funded all public schools, while private schools were maintained by private organizations. In subsequent decades, the education agenda was dominated by the so-called "school battle." Several religious organizations and, in particular, religion-based political parties, demanded freedom of education and equal funding for public and private schools. This was finally enshrined in the Elementary Education Acts of 1889 and 1917. Currently, there are nearly twice as many denominational schools as public ones.

## Public Policy and Financing

The 1985 Primary Education Act states as an overall goal that education should offer pupils "appropriate instruction and guarantee them an uninterrupted school career." Education should meet the (special) educational needs of pupils and "teaching should be aimed at promoting the emotional and intellectual development as well as the creativity of each individual pupil."

Recent policy initiatives have focused on integrating special needs pupils in regular education. This has resulted in new legislation (the Primary Education Act and the Act on the Expertise Centers) and regulations, in new methods of funding, and in changes to the organization of regular and special education. The government increasingly leaves the decisions on placing pupils to parents and enables regular schools to provide special services without forcing them to integrate every special needs student.

The Dutch government funds virtually all special needs education, while local authorities are responsible for the costs of transporting pupils with special needs to schools and for making school buildings physically accessible for these pupils. The amount of governmental funding for a school depends on the total number of pupils, their types of special needs, age, and other characteristics (ethnic background, level of schooling of parents). Budgets are forwarded directly to the school board. The government also provides an additional budget for peripatetic teaching (the support provided by the special school for students returning into regular education).

## Organization of Special Education Services

Special education services in the Netherlands are in a state of flux. Currently special education consists of ten types of special schools, including those for the deaf, the visually impaired, the physically impaired, the behaviorally disturbed or the severely mentally impaired pupils. Such schools are either located separately or attached in a department to another type of special education (e.g., a department for children with severe speech disorders in a school for hearing impaired children). As a result of recent legislation, two former types of special schools, those for the learning

Table 1  Special education in the Netherlands[a]

| School types/departments | Schools | Pupils |
|---|---|---|
| Learning disabled (LOM schools)[b] | 334 | 44,445 |
| Mildly mentally impaired (MLK schools)[b] | 328 | 40,426 |
| Deaf | 9 | 719 |
| Hearing impaired | 31 | 4,614 |
| Children with severe speech disorders | 2 | 410 |
| Blind and partially sighted | 4 | 743 |
| Physically impaired | 29 | 3,804 |
| Chronically ill | 36 | 3,928 |
| Behavior disorders (ZMOK schools) | 69 | 7,327 |
| Multiply impaired | 19 | 1,972 |
| Children in schools attached to paedological institutes[c] | 11 | 1,356 |
| Severely mentally impaired children | 103 | 9,229 |
| Total | 975 | 118,973 |

[a]Data are based on Central Bureau for Statistics, 1996; Min. OC & W, 1996.
[b]No longer part of special education legislation.
[c]These institutes are affiliated with a university.

disabled and the mildly mentally impaired, have been renamed special schools for primary education and are no longer part of special education legislation. Although most of these schools currently operate as segregated schools, it is expected that in the near future they will merge with regular schools (see "future trends").

Special school students re-entering regular education are entitled to certain facilities, as are students with sensory, physical, or multiple impairments, who, although eligible for special education, have not been referred to a special school. This so-called preventive peripatetic teaching is becoming increasingly widespread. In 1998, some .002 and .003 percent of all pupils received peripatetic teaching in primary and secondary schools, respectively.

Pupils eligible for special education may or may not have already been following regular education for some years. Although pupils are formally referred to special education by parents, the majority of referrals are initiated by regular school teachers in consultation with the school principal, the school support service, and parents. The placement decision is taken by the admission board of the proposed special school (comprised of psychologist, physician, social worker, and school principal).

Compared to many other European countries, Dutch special education is extensive, differentiated, and segregated, and since the 1960s has evolved into a wide-ranging system for pupils who cannot keep up in regular schools. Almost 4 percent of all primary and secondary school-age pupils attend separate special schools, and over the past decades there has been a dramatic increase in their numbers. In October 1998, 4.3 percent of pupils between 4 and 11 (Dutch primary school age) attended a special school. In 1972, this was a mere 2.2 percent. The number of special education pupils depends on specific age groups. For example, almost

Table 2  Increase in special education attendance

| Year | 1975 | 1980 | 1985 | 1990 | 1995 |
|---|---|---|---|---|---|
| Total number of pupils aged 4–19 | 3,828,708 | 3,729,826 | 3,392,496 | 3,072,116 | 2,988,610 |
| Mildly mentally impaired | .86 | .87 | .95 | 1.10 | 1.49 |
| Learning disabled | .62 | .81 | 1.13 | 1.40 | 1.35 |
| Severely mentally impaired | .22 | .22 | .23 | .24 | .31 |
| Behaviorally disturbed | .09 | .11 | .14 | .20 | .25 |
| Remaining special education | .31 | .33 | .37 | .49 | .58 |
| Total | 2.09 | 2.34 | 2.82 | 3.44 | 3.98 |

*Source:* Pijl, 1997

8 percent of eleven-year-olds are in separate schools. In general, boys and ethnic minority pupils are overrepresented. The growth has not been equal in each type of school.

## Relationship to General Education

For several decades, Dutch educational policy has been described as a "two track" policy: one track being regular education and the other special education. It was widely accepted that handicapped pupils and those with learning and/or behavior problems were referred to separate special schools. The special system was seen as reflecting concern for special needs pupils. However, a growing group of policymakers, educators, and parents have voiced their concern that the growing number of special education placements is socially unacceptable. An increasing number of parents want their special needs child to be in a regular school because of their wish for their child to attend a local school or the same school as siblings, and for it to be educated with non–special needs children. They also consider segregation to be in conflict with widely accepted human rights.

A separate special education system has long been maintained through a combination of educational factors, system characteristics, legislation, and funding. Regular schools, for instance, find it difficult to cope with special needs pupils in the classroom. The available support is located outside the school building, in special schools and school counseling services. Thus, the way out for teachers is to refer such children to these special schools that have more time and expertise available.

Special and regular education have long worked independently of each other, and it is this independent aspect, among other things, which stimulates special education referral. Collaboration has always been hindered, because each school had its own financial, administrative, and staffing systems. Special help was only available when pupils attended a special school. Even if support in regular education was available, in practice it was difficult to obtain. This always meant that pupils with special needs had to be taken to the facilities instead of vice versa.

The regulations for peripatetic teaching introduced since 1985 have resulted in a growing number of special needs pupils attending regular schools. However, these regulations are complex, and funding is only available under strict conditions, which makes it difficult to implement them flexibly.

Finally, separate legislation for regular and special education is a key factor in creating a segregated system. The specific rulings tend to limit the money available in regular schools to meet pupils' special needs compared to that which is spent on pupils once they have been admitted to special education. This mechanism is in itself a tremendous incentive to refer pupils to special schools.

## Trends for the Future

Recent developments in the Netherlands have been influenced by two policy papers published in 1990 and 1996. The first, *Together to School Again,* aims to support the integration of pupils with learning difficulties (so-called LOM pupils) and mildly mentally disabled pupils (so-called MLK pupils). The implementation of this policy has resulted in all primary schools and special schools for these types of pupils being grouped into regional clusters; each cluster generally consists of one or more special schools working with 27 primary schools. Next to the forming of clusters of cooperating schools, a new funding system has been introduced, whereby about 50 percent of the additional costs for special education will be allocated jointly to the school clusters. This allows for variation in the way integration is implemented. School clusters may decide to maintain special needs provision in special schools or decide to transfer parts of that provision to regular schools. The key factor is that regular schools participate in the decision-making process concerning the structure of special education provision. Each of the 250 school clusters is funded equally, based on the total enrollment in primary education. This was first implemented in 1998, and by 2002 the new funding structure was fully operational.

Plans to restructure parts of special secondary education into lower regular secondary education are fairly new. Special secondary education for pupils with learning difficulties (LOM) and mild mentally retarded (MLK) will no longer be part of separate special education legislation, but will become an integral part of new secondary education law. In keeping with integration policy for primary education, schools for secondary education and schools for secondary special education will also have to work together in clusters. In the near future, these clusters will also be funded equally according to the total enrollment in this sector. This reform was initially implemented on August 1, 1998 in the form of a number of pilot-projects nationwide in order to gain experience with several aspects of the new structure.

In 1996 the second policy paper, *The Back-Pack*, appeared, outlining separate plans for educating pupils with sensory, physical, and mental impairments and/or behavioral problems. The basic idea is that financing special school places for these pupils should be stopped in favor of linking the funding of special services to the pupil involved, regardless of the school type. The pupil does not follow the funding, but funding follows the pupil. An important characteristic of demand-oriented funding is that parents have an important voice in choosing a school for their child. If a pupil meets the criteria for a pupil-bound budget, parents and pupil can choose a school and decide together with the school on how to use the funding. Only in cases where a school could clearly demonstrate that it is incapable of providing suitable schooling for a special needs pupil would placement be denied. Directly linked to this new funding system is a reorganization of special (secondary) education. The number of different school types will be reduced to four; schools for the visually impaired, for pupils with communication disorders, for the physically and mentally impaired, and for pupils with behavior problems. In 1997, Parliament approved this new funding system and the changes are currently being implemented.

## REFERENCES

CBS. (1996). *Statistiek van het basisonderwijs, het speciaal onderwijs en het voortgezet speciaal onderwijs 1995 / 1996; Scholen en leerlingen.* Unpublished tables,Voorburg.

Ministerie van Onderwijs, Cultuur, & Wetenschappen. (1996). *De rugzak, Beleidsplan voor het onderwijs aan kinderen met een handicap.* Den Haag: SDU.

Pijl, S. J. (1997). *Twintig jaar groei van het speciaal onderwijs.* De Lier: ABC.

SIP JAN PIJL
*University of Groningen*

# NEURAL EFFICIENCY ANALYZER

During the past 40 years, a number of psychologists have argued that traditional intelligence tests (e.g., Stanford-Binet, Wechsler) are often inappropriate because they are culturally biased. In response to such criticism, many attempts have been made to develop measures of cognitive functioning that are both objective and culturally free.

A unique approach to culture-free assessment of cognitive functioning came in the late 1960s and early 1970s with Ertl's (1968) work with the Neural Efficiency Analyzer (NEA; Tracy, 1972). Seen as providing an unbiased view of intelligence, the NEA was purported to measure the efficiency and speed of neuronal transmission. Specifically, the instrument measures the latency in milliseconds from the onset of a flash of light to the appropriate change in electrical activity in the brain. Ertl (1968) argued that tachistoscopically presented light flashes evoke a change in the electrical activity in the brain that could be detected by an electroencephalogram (EEG). Following the presentation of 100 flashes of light (presented at random intervals), the latency data were subjected to a computer analysis that provided both an average evoked potential and a predicted intelligence quotient (Ertl Index).

Although Ertl and Douglas (1970) reported that scores on the NEA correlate significantly with a number of standardized intelligence tests (e.g., Wechsler Intelligence Scale for Children, Primary Mental Abilities Test), later investigations failed to replicate Ertl's claims (Sturgis, Lemke, & Johnson, 1977). Indeed, contrary to the earlier investigation by Ertl and Douglas (1970), NEA scores did not prove useful in discriminating among children with different levels of academic abilities (Evans, Martin, & Hatchette, 1976).

While the NEA appeared to be an innovative attempt to minimize the presumed cultural bias in intelligence testing, little empirical evidence exists to support the use of this measure on a clinical basis. Moreover, with the major goals of intellectual assessment being to portray an individual's functioning in a number of separate yet related cognitive areas as well as to predict potential for future development, any unitary measure of cognitive functioning would have questionable use.

## REFERENCES

Ertl, J. (1968). Evoked potential and human intelligence. Final Report, VSOE, Project No. 6-1454.

Ertl, J., & Douglas, V. (1970). Evoked potentials and dyslexia. Internal Report No. 32, Neural Modals, LTD.

Evans, J. R., Martin, D., & Hatchette, R. (1976). Neural Efficiency Analyzer scores of reading disabled, normally reading and academically superior children. *Perceptual & Motor Skills, 43,* 1248–1250.

Sturgis, R., Lemke, E. A., & Johnson, J. J. (1977). A validity study of the Neural Efficiency Analyzer in relation to selected measures of intelligence. *Perceptual & Motor Skills, 45,* 475–478.

Tracy, W. (1972). Goodbye IQ, hello EI (Ertl Index). *Phi Delta Kappan, 54,* 89–94.

JEFFREY W. GRAY
*Ball State University*

RAYMOND S. DEAN
*Ball State University*
*Indiana University School of Medicine*

ERTL INDEX
INTELLIGENCE

## NEURODEVELOPMENTAL THERAPY

Neurodevelopmental therapy (NDT) is an approach toward working with individuals who have cerebral palsy and other neuromuscular disorders. Originating in England with the work of Berta and Karl Bobath in the 1940s (Bobath, 1980), NDT was presented to professionals in the United States in 1959 (Campbell, 1982). A number of basic and advanced courses in principles and techniques of NDT are offered in the United States; they lead to certification in neurodevelopmental therapy for teachers and therapists (speech, occupational, and physical). These courses are presented by the Neurodevelopmental Treatment Association, headquartered in Chicago, Illinois.

Several key aspects are considered to be important when providing NDT. Children with movement disorders may have an underlying basis of atypical postural tone (e.g., hypertonia, hypotonia) that needs to be normalized. Failure to develop normal tone may lead to an abnormal sequence of motor development that could result in postural fixations or blocks and compensatory movement patterns. This abnormal sequence may ultimately lead to contractures and orthopedic deformities (Campbell, 1983). A problem-oriented approach is used in NDT, and assessment of tone and movement patterns is completed prior to intervention. Intervention includes providing support at key points of control (i.e., head/neck, shoulders, hips/pelvis) and normalizing tone through positioning and handling techniques that sometimes make use of adaptive equipment (Finnie, 1975). Major emphasis in this treatment technique is on goal-directed movement leading to normalized movement patterns within the context of functional activities.

The main goals for NDT in the classroom are to analyze movement dysfunction accurately, to implement facilitation/inhibition procedures (to increase normal movement), to teach others necessary procedures for consistent management of the motor-impaired student across people and situations, to use adaptive equipment to the extent that equipment replaces unattainable functions, and to prevent the sequence of abnormal motor development from progressing to the point of formation of contractures and orthopedic deformities (Campbell, 1982). Studies on NDT have equivocal results (Degangi, 1994; Law et al., 1997).

### REFERENCES

Bobath, K. (1980). *A neurophysiological basis for treatment of cerebral palsy.* London: Heinemann.

Campbell, P. H. (1982). *Introduction to neurodevelopmental treatment.* Akron, OH: Children's Hospital Medical Center.

Campbell, P. H. (1983). Students with movement difficulties. In M. E. Snell (Ed.), *Systematic instruction of the moderately and severely handicapped* (pp. 169–202). Columbus, OH: Merrill.

Degangi, G. A. (1994). Examining the efficacy of short-term NDT intervention using a case study design. *Physical & Occupational Therapy, 14*(2), 21–61.

Finnie, N. (1975). *Handling the young cerebral palsied child at home.* New York: Dutton.

Law, M., Russell, D., Pollock, N., Rosenbaum, P., Walter, S., & King, G. (1997). A comparison of intensive neurodevelopmental therapy plus casting and a regular occupational therapy program for children with cerebral palsy. *Developmental Medicine & Child Neurology, 39*(10), 664–670.

CORNELIA LIVELY
*University of Illinois, Urbana-Champaign*

CEREBRAL PALSY
PHYSICAL THERAPY

## NEUROFIBROMATOSIS

The neurofibromatoses are genetic disorders of the nervous system that primarily affect the development and growth of neural (nerve) cell tissues. They are inherited as dominant disorders, which means that if either parent has the defective gene, each child born to that parent has a 50 percent chance of inheriting the defective gene. These disorders cause tumors to grow on nerves and produce other abnormalities, such as skin changes and bone deformities. Although many affected persons inherit the disorder, between 30 and 50 percent of new cases arise spontaneously through a change (mutation) in an individual's genes. Once this change has taken place, the mutant gene can be passed on to succeeding generations. Scientists have classified the disorders as neurofibromatosis type 1 (NF1) and neurofibromatosis type 2 (NF2).

NF1 is the more common type of the neurofibromatosis; NF2 is rare, occurring in 1 out of 40,000 individuals (NINDS, 2005). Symptoms of NF1 include tumors, bone abnormalities, and light brown spots on the skin (cafe-au-lait macules). These are often seen at birth or during infancy, and almost always by the time a child is about 10 years old. In most cases, symptoms are mild and patients live normal and productive lives. In some cases, however, NF1 can be severely debilitating.

NF2 is characterized by bilateral (occurring on both sides of the body) tumors on the eighth cranial nerve. The tumors cause pressure damage to surrounding nerves. Symptoms of NF2 include early hearing loss, tinnitus (ringing noise in the ear) and poor balance. Headache, facial pain, or facial numbness, caused by pressure from the tumors, may also occur.

Treatment for neurofibromatoses is presently aimed at controlling symptoms. Improved diagnostic technologies, such as magnetic resonance imaging (MRI), can reveal tumors as small as a few millimeters in diameter, thus allowing for early treatment. Surgery can help remove painful or disfiguring tumors; however, there is a chance that the tumors may grow back and in greater numbers. In rare instances, when tumors become malignant (3 to 5 percent of all cases), treatment may include surgery, radiation, or chemotherapy (NINDS, 2005).

Genetic testing is available for families with documented cases of NF1 and NF2. Genetic analysis can be used to confirm clinical diagnosis if the disease is a result of familial inheritance; however, new mutations cannot be genetically confirmed. Prenatal diagnosis of familial NF1 or NF2 is also possible through the use of amniocentesis or chorionic villus sampling procedures (NINDS, 2005). Genetic counselors can provide information about these procedures and offer guidance in coping with the neurofibromatoses.

Cognitive impairment is the most common neurological complication of neurofibromatosis 1 in childhood, and often the major concern of the parent of a child with the disorder (North, Hyman, & Barton, 2002). Although mental retardation is not a common feature of neurofibromatosis 1, there is a high frequency of associated learning disabilities and psychosocial problems linked to academic underachievement, failure to complete higher education, and limitation of career choice (North et al., 2002). The presence of comorbidity, particularly with Attention-Deficit Hyperactivity Disorder, is the major risk factor for poor social skills in children with NF1 (Barton & North, 2004). In addition, research suggests that children with more severe and visible NF symptoms may be at risk for a myriad of psychological difficulties, including low self-esteem (Counterman, Conway, Saylor & Pai, 1995). This is because children with physical deformities, including neurofibromatosis, have difficulties in forming friendships and are often rejected by their peers. For these children, parent and teacher support are important for healthy adjustment; however, it may be difficult to persuade some parents that their youngsters need special attention. In an effort to maximize a child's sense of normalcy and adequacy, parents and teachers may inadvertently ignore a child's emotional distress. Therefore, psychologists, physicians, and other professionals who work with children should consider assessing the need for supportive and preventive services, particularly at ages where appearance and competence are crucial developmental issues.

## REFERENCES

Barton, B., & North, K. (2004). Social skills and neurofibromatosis 1. *Developmental Medicine and Child Neurology, 46,* 553–563.

Counterman, A. P., Saylor, C. F., & Pai, S. (1995). Psychological adjustment of children and adolescents with neurofibromatosis. *Children's Health Care, 24*(4), 223–234.

Electronic reference formats recommended by the National Institute of Neurological Disorders and Stroke. Retrieved August 29, 2005, from http:/ninds.nih.gov/healinfo/disorder

North, K., Hyman, S., & Barton, B., (2002). Cognitive deficits in neurofibromatosis 1. *Journal of Child Neurology, 17*(8), 605–703.

ESMERELDA LÓPEZ
*Texas A&M University*

**PHYSICAL DISABILITIES**
**ELEPHANT MAN, THE**
**CAFÉ AU LAIT SPOTS**

## NEUROLINGUISTIC PROGRAMMING

Neurolinguistic programming (NLP) is a model for effective interpersonal communication introduced by Bandler and Grinder (1975, 1976) for use in counseling and psychotherapy. The model is based on the belief that humans receive, store, and process information through their senses, or representational systems. Each individual has a preferred or primary representational system (PRS), either visual, auditory, or kinesthetic, through which information is most effectively processed. Interpersonal communication is enhanced, according to the theory of NLP, when dialogue reflects a match of preferred representational systems.

According to Bandler and Grinder, there are three ways PRS can be identified. One method is through analysis of language patterns. The predicates used in natural language (verbs, adjectives, and adverbs) relate to the three representational systems. One person "sees" the point; another "hears" what is meant; still another "grasps" a situation. Lankton (1980) found that matched predicates between counselor and client resulted in greater therapeutic rapport.

Observation of eye movements is another method proposed by Bandler and Grinder (1979) for determining PRS. They suggest that the direction of eye movements indicates the specific part of the brain in which information is stored, and, therefore, the representational system being used. For most right-handed people, upward eye movements indicate visual images, lateral movements indicate auditory images, downward movements to the left show internal dialogue or auditory representation, and downward movements to the right reflect kinesthetic representation. The third method proposed is direct questioning regarding preferred modality.

In addition to matching speech patterns, Bandler and Grinder highlight other nonverbal behaviors that result in enhanced rapport and communication. These include matching of body postures, facial expressions, hand gestures, and speech rate. Once rapport is established, leading is employed: the counselor slowly changes the language and gestures used in an effort to move the client to a more productive state. Anchoring refers to the use of a verbal or kinesthetic signal to return the client to a productive state.

The NLP has recently been applied to the field of education. Torres and Katz (1983) suggest that if teachers are aware of their own PRS and the PRS of their students, and if the channels of communication are matched, learning is facilitated. Teachers who are aware of the multiplicity of receptive modes present within a group may develop greater flexibility and teach more effectively through a variety of communication channels.

Neurolinguistic programming and the implications derived from it remain controversial. Studies have shown that neither predicate analysis nor eye movement observations are reliable methods of determining PRS (Badderley & Predebon, 1991; Beyerstein, 1990; Dorn, Atwater, Jereb, & Russell, 1983; Shaw, 1977). Further evaluation in classrooms and clinics will be necessary to determine the full value of these theories.

## REFERENCES

Badderley, M., & Predebon, J. (1991). "Do the eyes have it?": A test of neurolinguistic programming's eye movement hypothesis. *Australian Journal of Clinical Hypnotherapy & Hypnosis, 12*(1), 1–23.

Bandler, R., & Grinder, J. (1975). *The structure of magic I.* Palo Alto, CA: Science and Behavior.

Bandler, R., & Grinder, J. (1976). *The structure of magic II.* Palo Alto, CA: Science and Behavior.

Bandler, R., & Grinder, J. (1979). *Frogs into princes: Neurolinguistic programming.* Moab, Utah: Real People Press.

Beyerstein, B. L. (1990). Brain scams: Neuromythologies of the new age. *International Journal of Mental Health, 19*(3), 27–36.

Dorn, F. J., Atwater, M., Jereb, R., & Russell, R. (1983). Determining the reliability of the NLP eye-movement procedure. *American Mental Health Counselors Association Journal, 5*(3), 105–110.

Lankton, S. (1980). *Practical magic.* Cupertino, CA: Meta Publications.

Shaw, D. L. (1977). *Recall as effected by the interaction of presentation representational system and primary representational system.* Unpublished doctoral dissertation, Ball State University.

Torres, C., & Katz, J. (1983). Neuro-linguistic programming: Developing effective communication in the classroom. *Teacher Educator, 19*(2), 25–32.

BARBARA S. SPEER
*Shaker Heights City School District, Shaker Heights, Ohio*

## ABILITY TRAINING, EARLY EFFORTS IN
## CEREBRAL DOMINANCE
## HYPNOSIS
## PSYCHOTHERAPY WITH INDIVIDUALS WITH DISABILITIES
## TEACHING STRATEGIES

# NEUROLOGICAL IMPRESS METHOD

The neurological impress method was developed to facilitate reading among children with severe reading disabilities (Hecklman, 1969; Langford, Slade, & Barnett, 1974). It may be most effective with students beyond 10 years of age. In this approach, teacher and student read aloud at a rapid pace, with the teacher sitting slightly behind and directing his or her voice into the student's ear. At first, the teacher may read somewhat louder and faster, encouraging the student to maintain pace and not to worry about faltering or misreading. The teacher's finger slides along the print, underscoring the words as they are read. As the student becomes more comfortable, he or she may assume the vocal and pointing lead. Continuing through the passage, teacher and student alternate leading and following.

While initially easier material is selected, the level of difficulty is gradually increased. Other than this selection process, there is no particular preparation of material prior to the oral unison reading. The approach is not specifically concerned with word recognition, word analysis, or comprehension; its focus is on fluency and on phrasing. The aim is to develop and maintain reading fluency over as many pages as possible, stopping before fatigue sets in.

In a study using the neurological impress method, Lorenz and Vockell (1979) and Skinner, Logan, & Robinson (1997) found no significant gains in either word recognition or reading comprehension. On the other hand, improvement was noted in reading expressiveness, in fluency, and in students' confidence in their reading ability. Students' perceptions of gains using this method, however, have been subsequently refuted (Reetz & Hoover, 1992). Kann (1983) has suggested that the neurological impress method may be profitably combined with repeated readings, another approach that promotes fluency and syntactic competence (Samuels, 1979). Clearly, the neurological impress method does not represent a full reading program for disabled readers. It may, however, provide a valuable adjunct to other approaches. It may facilitate the chunking of phrases and the smoothing out of slow or choppy reading habits in some poor readers.

## REFERENCES

Hecklman, R. G. (1969). The neurological impress method of remedial reading instruction. *Academic Therapy, 4,* 277–282.

Kann, R. (1983). The method of repeated readings: Expanding the neurological impress method for use with disabled readers. *Journal of Learning Disabilities, 16,* 90–92.

Langford, K., Slade, K., & Barnett, A. (1974). An explanation of impress techniques in remedial reading. *Academic Therapy, 9,* 309–319.

Lorenz, L., & Vockell, E. (1979). Using the neurological impress method with learning disabled readers. *Journal of Learning Disabilities, 12,* 420–422.

Reetz, L. J., & Hoover, J. H. (1992). The acceptability and utility of five reading approaches as judged by middle school LD students. *Learning Disabilities Research & Practice, 7*(1), 11–15.

Samuels, S. J. (1979). The method of repeated readings. *Reading Teacher, 32,* 403–408.

Skinner, C. H., Logan, P., & Robinson, S. L. (1997). Demonstration as a reading intervention for exceptional learners. *School Psychology Review, 26*(3), 437–447.

KATHERINE GARNETT
*Hunter College, City University of New York*

## NEUROLOGICAL ORGANIZATION

Used generically, neurological organization refers to the functional organization of the brain, including the brain stem, the midbrain, and the neocortex. It is frequently encountered in neuropsychological research, a large portion of which is devoted to the investigation of individual differences in neurological organization and to the development of comprehensive theories of the functional organization of the brain. The term also has a more specific usage, as it is most often encountered in special education.

Special education and related services personnel are most likely to see the term used in the context of the Doman and Delacato approach to remediation of learning disorders. The Doman and Delacato theory and the subsequently derived treatment methods rely on a systematic vertical and horizontal development and organization of function within the human brain. The neuropsychological theory that underlies the work of Doman and Delacato is based on the biogenetic principle that "ontogeny recapitulates phylogeny;" this principle contends that if an individual does not follow this sequential continuum of development, as prescribed by Doman and Delacato, problems of mobility and/or communication will develop. The therapeutic methods of Doman and Delacato are designed to overcome early deficiencies in development and to restore proper neurological organization.

Doman and Delacato maintain that there are six major functional attainments of humans: motor skills, speech, writing, reading, understanding, and stereognosis (recognition of objects by touch). The attainment of these skills is believed to be dependent on the uninterrupted and successful neuroanatomical progress toward neurological organization. Delacato (1959) defines neurological organization as

> that physiologically optimum condition which (sic) exists uniquely and most completely in man and is the result of a total uninterrupted ontogenetic neural development. This development recapitulates the phylogenetic neural development of man and begins during the first trimester of gestation and ends at about six and one-half years of age in normal humans.

> This orderly development progresses *vertically* through the spinal cord and all other areas of the cortex, as it does with all mammals. Man's final and unique developmental progression takes place at the level of the cortex and is *lateral* (from left to right or from right to left). (p. 19)

Each higher level of functioning is dependent on successful movement through each of the lower levels of development. Doman and Delacato argue that if the highest level of function (cerebral dominance) is incomplete or unfunctioning, then a lower level of neurological organization will dominate the individual's intellectual behavior. The highest level of neurological organization, complete cerebral dominance, is, according to the theories of Doman and Delacato, what gives humans their great capacity for communication and sets them apart from other animals.

Unfortunately, there has been virtually no research supportive of either the Doman and Delacato theory of neurological organization or its derived treatment programs. The developmental milestones appear to have been misplaced as well. Forty percent of normal five- to nine-year-olds have mixed dominance (eye-hand preference), showing that complete dominance is not typically established by age six and one-half, as Doman and Delacato claim. The treatment programs of Doman and Delacato have been condemned by resolution by many major health organizations in the United States and Canada. It is unlikely that the Doman and Delacato concept of neurological organization will prove useful in working with individuals with disabilities. A longer review of the approach is available in Reynolds (1981).

### REFERENCES

Delacato, C. H. (1959). *The treatment and prevention of reading problems: The neuropsychological approach.* Springfield, IL: Thomas.

Reynolds, C. R. (1981). The neuropsychological basis of intelligence. In G. Hynd & J. Obrzut (Eds.), *Neuropsychological assessment and the school age child: Issues and procedures.* New York: Grune & Stratton.

CECIL R. REYNOLDS
*Texas A&M University*

DELACATO, CARL H.
DOMAN, GLEN
PATTERNING
READING DISORDERS

## NEUROPSYCHOLOGY

Neuropsychology is the study of the relationships between behavior and the brain. Its emphasis is on understanding the mechanisms of the brain responsible for both simple and complex patterns of functioning (e.g., auditory discrimination, reading, memory). Since the mid-twentieth century, a good deal of professional attention has been directed to the understanding of specific loci of functioning in the brain. Indeed, Broca (1861) and Jackson (1874) observed a relationship between patients' behavior and specific areas of damage to the brain. In fact, some credit these observations of brain-behavior relationships as the birth of neuropsychology (Dean, 1986).

The clinical neuropsychologist's role has both diagnostic and therapeutic elements. Diagnosis concerns the identification of impaired neurological processes and the area of the brain implicated. Through therapeutic interventions, the neuropsychologist often works to structure experiences that maximize strengths and minimize weaknesses, in an attempt to remediate processing disorders (Pfeiffer, Dean, & Shellenberger, 1986). In child neuropsychology, an increasing interest has been shown in the use of neuropsychological methods that use children's cognitive strengths to structure educational experiences for the remediation of learning and behavior problems.

Clinical neuropsychology continues to be concerned with functional assessments and the mapping of specific behaviors to areas of the brain. A number of assessment measures have been specifically designed by neuropsychologists to make inferences about the brain. These measures provide information concerning the integrity of patients' brain functioning in both cognitive processing and affective dimensions of behavior. The assessment of cognitive processing may include measures of general ability, verbal and nonverbal functions, perceptual-motor functioning, and academic achievement. Affective dimensions of behavior may include measures of personality, emotional functioning, and interpersonal/social skills. These measures allow one to describe brain functioning on a continuum, ranging from brain damage involving trauma to the brain (e.g., head injury or stroke) to the opposite end of the continuum, in which the individual is neurologically intact with no signs of dysfunction. Moreover, the search for a single measure of brain damage or organicity (e.g., Bender-Gestalt Test) has been abandoned by most neuropsychologists because of the complex nature of brain functioning (Dean, 1986).

The hemispheres of the brain can be viewed as processing information using different modes. The right hemisphere seems to use a more visual, spatial, simultaneous processing style, whereas the left seems to use a more analytical, verbal, sequential style. The application of these processing differences recently has been attempted with some success in both educational assessment and remediation (Dean, 1981, 1984; Reynolds, 1984).

A number of neuropsychologists have begun to isolate the biological or organic factors involved in many of the emotional (behavioral) disorders (e.g., some forms of depression, hyperactivity, schizophrenia) that previously were thought to be functionally related to stress in the environment (Dean, 1985). These findings are important because they begin to tie brain functioning more clearly to human emotions and psychopathology. Additionally, these findings indicate that some disorders, or even subgroups of certain disorders, once considered environmentally caused actually may be biologically based. Therefore, in school remedial planning, an evaluation of the neuropsychological components of functioning may be as important as an evaluation of the child's current environment. In sum, neuropsychology has made significant contributions in the understanding of brain-behavior relationships and in providing distinct direction for the education and rehabilitation of children and adults with brain dysfunctions. Neuropsychology has become a major link between medicine, education, and the psychological sciences (D'Amato, Fletcher-Janzen, & Reynolds, 2005).

## REFERENCES

Broca, P. (1861/1960). Remarks on the seat of the faculty of articulate language, followed by an observation of aphasia. In G. von Bonin (Trans.), *Some papers on the cerebral cortex.* Springfield, IL: Thomas.

D'Amato, R., Fletcher-Janzen, E., & Reynolds, C. R. (Eds.). *Handbook of school neuropsychology.* New York: Wiley.

Dean, R. S. (1981). Cerebral dominance and childhood learning disorders: Theoretical perspectives. *School Psychology Review, 10,* 373–388.

Dean, R. S. (1984). Functional lateralization of the brain. *Journal of Special Education, 18,* 239–256.

Dean, R. S. (1985). Neuropsychological assessment. In J. D. Cavenar, R. Michels, H. K. H. Brodie, A. M. Cooper, S. B. Guze, L. L. Judd, G. L. Klerman, & A. J. Solnit (Eds.), *Psychiatry* (pp. 1–16). Philadelphia: Lippincott.

Dean, R. S. (1986). Perspectives on the future of neuropsychological assessment. In B. S. Plake & J. C. Witt (Eds.), *Buros–Nebraska series on measurement and testing: Future of testing and measurement* (pp. 203–244). Hillsdale, NJ: Erlbaum.

Jackson, J. H. (1874/1932). On the duality of the brain. In J. Taylor (Ed.), *Selected writings of John Hughlings Jackson* (Vol. 2). London: Hodder & Stoughton.

Pfeiffer, S. I., Dean, R. S., & Shellenberger, S. (1986). The school psychologists in medical settings: Neurology section. In T. Kratochwill (Ed.), *Advances in school psychology* (pp. 177–202, Vol. 5). Hillsdale, NJ: Erlbaum.

Reynolds, C. R. (Ed.). (1984). The Kaufman Assessment Battery for Children. *Journal of Special Education, 18*(3).

RIK CARL D'AMATO
*University of Northern Colorado*

RAYMOND S. DEAN
*Ball State University*
*Indiana University School of*
*Medicine*

## CEREBRAL DOMINANCE
## HEMISPHERIC FUNCTIONING

LEFT BRAIN/RIGHT BRAIN
NEUROLOGICAL ORGANIZATION
SPLIT-BRAIN RESEARCH

## NEWLAND, T. ERNEST (1903–1992)

T. Ernest Newland earned his BA from Wittenberg College in 1925 and his PhD under Sidney Pressey at Ohio State in 1931. After 7 years at Bucknell University, Newland became chief of the Division of Special Education in the Pennsylvania Department of Public Instruction; he served from 1938 to 1942, while services to exceptional children were rapidly developing in both number of children served and quality of programming. For 20 years he was a professor in the College of Education at the University of Illinois.

Newland authored over 200 articles, editorials, reviews, and abstracts, most on topics relevant to special education. He is most noted for increasing educators' understanding of testing as one part of the assessment process, furthering psychologists' understanding of intelligence as involving both product and process, developing the Blind Learning Aptitude Test (1980), and writing *The Gifted in Socioeducational Perspective* (1976).

In addition, Newland is responsible for many "firsts" in the field of special education. He implemented the first statewide county supervisor of special education programs; inaugurated the first mandated state hearing test program for public school children; caused the first legal state definition of exceptional children to include the gifted; and facilitated the establishment and functioning of the first fully committed doctoral program in school psychology at the University of Illinois (Urbana).

During his lifetime, Newland served the profession in numerous ways, including chairing committees of the Council for Exceptional Children (and its predecessor)

T. Ernest Newland

and the American Psychological Association. He was honored with awards from the Association for the Gifted, the Illinois Psychological Association, and the Division of School Psychology of the American Psychological Association.

### REFERENCES

Newland, T. E. (1976). *The gifted in socioeducational perspective.* Englewood Cliffs, NJ: Prentice Hall.

Newland, T. E. (1980). *Blind Learning Aptitude Test.* Champaign: University of Illinois.

JOSEPH L. FRENCH
*Pennsylvania State University*
First edition

TAMARA J. MARTIN
*The University of Texas of the Permian Basin*
Second edition

## NEW YORK STATE ASSOCIATION FOR RETARDED CHILDREN v. CAREY

See WILLOWBROOK CASE.

## NEW ZEALAND, SPECIAL EDUCATION IN

The New Zealand government attempts to improve learning outcomes for all children at their local school, early childhood centers, and other locations where they are educated. Special education is concerned with the coordination and integration of the multidisciplinary services that support the inclusion of every child from birth to 21.

New Zealand has long recognized the need to provide education for all students. The Education Act of 1877 specified that education should be free, secular, and compulsory for all children of primary school age. However, without structures in place to support the act, this ideal could not be realized. Over 40 years later, in 1920, special education classes were established to support the learning of students whose needs were not met in the general education system. Gradually, over time, special education services were established. For example, in 1940, speech language therapists were prepared for service in education. In 1949, psychological services were established, and in 1962 a visiting teacher service was introduced to strengthen links between schools and families. Until 1989, such services operated somewhat independently.

The Education Act (1989) reiterated New Zealand's commitment to the education of all children. On the recommendation of the *Picot Report,* delivered by the *Taskforce to Review Education Administration* (1988), the government carried out changes in education to accommodate the learning needs of all children. The provision of education was largely decentralized, and many decisions, once made at a national level, were now the concerns of locally elected school boards. The Department of Education was reformed into the new Ministry of Education, resulting in the amalgamation of the various special education support systems. These services comprised a single agency, the Special Education Service, an agency that was nominally independent of but largely funded by the New Zealand government. This amalgamation resulted in the delivery of services in coordinated multidisciplinary teams. More recently, the special education agency has been reinstated within the New Zealand government, but continues to operate as a separate division.

The philosophy of special education in New Zealand is strongly inclusionary and ecological (Cullen & Carroll-Lind, 2005; Mentis, Quinn, & Ryba, 2005; Ministry of Education, 2000, 2004a). Special education policy guidelines state that all children have the same rights, freedoms, and responsibilities. All children with special needs must have a fair share of available resources and access to a seamless education. The focus of education is to meet the individual needs of each child, taking into account the language and culture of each. The New Zealand government views partnerships between parents and education providers as essential in developing the most efficient and most effective ways of utilizing the resources available to children with special needs (Ministry of Education, 2004b). All special educators in New Zealand are obliged to work consistently with the principles of the Treaty of Waitangi (1840), the nation's founding document that represents a covenant between Māori and the Crown. New Zealand law requires that, in the delivery of special education services, the Māori worldview, or Te Ao Māori, must be considered. All education services must ensure Maori-determination and ownership of the service delivery process

Services to learners with special needs are provided largely by the Ministry of Education, although there are some independent providers. The Ministry of Education services are delivered in three groups to support children: services in early childhood, services to children with moderate needs, and services to children with high needs.

Early intervention support is available for children until the time they transition to school, irrespective of the settings in which they receive their education or the nature of their needs. Early intervention teams collaborate with families and early childhood center staff to coordinate access to occupational therapy, physiotherapy, psychological services, specialist teaching, and support for communication. The services of the early intervention teams are delivered in the children's regular contexts and provide both direct and indirect assistance.

Services to students with moderate special education needs involve a variety of groups that, where necessary, work in conjunction with one another. These include resource teachers of behavior and learning and literacy. Students with moderate sensory needs are supported by resource teachers of visual impairment, advisors on deaf children, and itinerant teachers of the deaf. Schools in New Zealand also receive a special education grant to make the adaptations necessary to assist students with moderate needs.

Children with high needs are supported in schools by the Ongoing Reviewable Resourcing Scheme. Students who are verified for the scheme generate funding and additional teacher time in the schools they attend. In most cases, this fund is managed by the Ministry of Education. Schools with large numbers of children who have been verified can apply to be fundholders and manage the use of the resource. The Ministry of Education supports children with behavioral and communication needs through the work of their multidisciplinary teams in collaboration with children, teachers, families, and other agencies.

Despite the extensive systems developed to meet the special education needs of all children and the many successes evident in educational facilities throughout the country, practitioners continue to report problems in delivering services. The resources available are finite, and debates about eligibility of individuals for funding and availability of special education services to educational facilities are not uncommon. Decisions regarding eligibility for the previously noted services involve some categorization, although these judgments take into account the contextual factors associated with the particular learning environments of the children. Practitioners report that they take a strength-based approach to their work, meeting the needs of children with special needs while collaboratively building interventions on the positive foundations of educational contexts. Special educators attribute their effectiveness to their respect for the uniqueness of each context, the valuing of people, and the acknowledgment of the views of others (Ministry of Education, 2004a), illustrating the ecological, inclusive beliefs that underlie special education practice.

## REFERENCES

Cullen, J., & Carrol-Lind, J. (2005). An inclusive approach to early intervention. In D. Fraser, R. Moltzen, & K. Ryba (Eds.), *Learners with special needs in Aotearoa New Zealand* (3rd ed.). Southbank Victoria, AUS: Thomson, Dunmore.

Mentis, M., Quinn, S., & Ryba, K. (2005). Linking inclusive policies with effective teaching practices. In D. Fraser, R. Moltzen, & K. Ryba (Eds.), *Learners with special needs in Aotearoa New Zealand* (3rd ed.). Southbank Victoria, AUS: Thomson, Dunmore.

Ministry of Education. (2000). *Including everyone; Te Reo tātake.* Wellington, AUS: Learning Media.

New Zealand Ministry of Education. (2004a). *Professional practice in special education.* Wellington, AUS: Ministry of Education, Group Special Education.

New Zealand Ministry of Education. (2004b). *Special education aims and policies.* Retrieved July 5, 2005, from http://www .minedu.govt.nz/index

Taskforce to Review Educational Administration. (1988). *Administering for excellence: Effective administration in New Zealand* (Chair. B. Picot). Wellington, AUS: Government Printer.

JEAN ANNAN
*Massey University, New Zealand*

# NIGERIA, SPECIAL EDUCATION IN

Some special education services in Nigeria were established during the premissionary period (i.e., prior to the twentieth century) when some persons with disabilities (physical and/or mental disabilities) were placed under the care of a native doctor who assumed the roles of a healer and a trainer. During the missionary era, some voluntary organizations—mainly religious agencies (e.g., the Catholic, Methodist, and Sudan missions)—established a few special centers, notably for the blind and the deaf (Eniola, 2000). The first school for the blind was established in 1940 in Kano to provide social welfare and education services (Abosi & Ozoji, 1985). Between 1950 and 1960, some missionaries, together with charitable and philanthropic organizations, established homes for children with severe physical disabilities or mental retardation.

From the mid-1970s onward, the federal government assumed responsibility for schools for children with disabilities through its Universal Primary Education program. The federal government's involvement in special education became formalized with the passage of section 8 in the National Policy on Education (1977, revised in 1981) called for the integration of the disabled with normal students.

The national policy on education, established by the federal government of Nigeria, defines special education as formal educational training provided to special needs children and adults who may be classified as disabled, disadvantaged (e.g., nomads), or gifted/talented. The national policy on education classified all of them (with the exception of the intellectually gifted) as disabled. Some adults with disabilities (e.g., persons with visual impairments or deformed limbs—the physically and health impaired) attend universities.

Disabilities generally are thought to emanate from circumstances of birth, inheritance, social position, mental and physical health, or accident in later life (Federal Republic of Nigeria, 2004). Special educational services are offered to those who are intellectually gifted, physically handicapped (e.g., crippled), mentally retarded, emotionally disturbed, speech disordered, or who have multiple handicaps, brain-injuries, hearing or visual impairments, or are hospital bound. The terms *handicap, disability,* and *exceptionality* are used interchangeably to describe individuals with various defects (Eniola, 2000).

Before 1976, most children with disabilities did not attend school because schooling was not free and parents were unable to pay needed fees (Eniola, 2000). Legislation establishing universal primary education removed the fee-paying system and ushered in a new era of hope for children with disabilities. With universal primary education, all children, including those with disabilities, could attend school.

Many children with learning difficulties entered school for the first time. Their presence generated the need to establish special education programs, locations for these programs, specialists to serve them, and institutions of higher learning to prepare specialists. Special education schools have been established in some states to train and educate children with specific types of disabilities. Ibadan University and Jos University established departments of special education to prepare special education teachers. In 1977, the federal government established the Federal College of Education (Special) in Oyo to prepare middle-level managers. Each of these three institutions has a unit for all the categories of children with disabilities for those who wish to specialize.

The 1976 national policy on education favored equalizing educational opportunities for all categories of handicapped children, and emphasized that education should adequately prepare persons with disabilities to become fully engaged citizens. After 1977, the federal ministry of education established a committee to promote collaboration among the ministries of health, social welfare, and labor to better address the needs of persons with disabilities. A census of all children and adults with disabilities was taken by age, sex, locality, and disability type. Teacher colleges were required to provide courses to help prospective normal school teachers identify and address the needs of children with disabilities. The adoption of this policy helped with efforts to integrate special needs students into regular classrooms, including the creation of special classes and units within the regular schools. These and other efforts attempted to emphasize the special needs of children, not their disability categories (Akinpelu, 1994). The Nigerian Educational Research Council, British Council, Nigerian National Advisory Council for the Blind and the Deaf, Royal Commonwealth Society for the Blind, and the Department of Special and Rehabilitation Centre at Kaduna Polytechnic have contributed importantly to the advancement of special education services.

Services for special needs children are provided in three

types of administrative units: schools for children with one type of disability (e.g., school for the blind or the deaf), integrated schools for two or more categories of disability, and regular schools in which disabled and normal children learn together. Four major types of special education services that are often provided (Eniola, 2000) are through specially trained professional educators (i.e., educators who possess additional competencies for serving a certain type or types of exceptional children beyond that possessed by regular classroom teachers), special curricular content that differs from that commonly offered in the regular school setting (e.g., speech therapy or training in the use of hearing aids for deaf students and Braille for blind students), special methodology (e.g., a special refinement in behavior modification techniques for those with severe behavior problem), and special instructional materials (e.g., specially designed electric typewriters for the uncoordinated cerebral palsied children, Braille and large-type books for the visually impaired, inquiry-oriented teaching materials for the gifted, and programmed and more highly detailed materials for those with mental retardation).

Local, state, and federal governments fund the education of children with disabilities. Using UNESCO's formula that 10 percent of school-aged children are handicapped, Nigeria may have about two million school-aged children with disabilities (Akinpelu, 1994). Using these estimates as the basis for funding, between 5 to 10 percent of the total annual education budget should be set aside by governments at all levels for the education of children with disabilities.

In virtually all countries, special education services are fully implemented only after illiteracy is eradicated and schooling is compulsory. The federal government is committed to eradicating illiteracy and attaining 100 percent school enrollment by the year 2010. Thus, as can be expected, efforts to establish universal special education services will occur some years later. The federal government has not created separate budgetary lines for regular and special education. The percent of the total federal budget allocated to education was 8.7 percent in 2000 and 9.3 percent in 2005. These allocations have been lower than the 25 percent suggested by UNESCO. The federal government subsidizes education at the primary level through the universal basic education program at about $180 million. At the university level, each student enjoys a subsidy of about $1,120. Handicapped persons receive a free education up to the tertiary level by some states and receive a scholarship by the federal ministry of education.

## REFERENCES

Abosi, C. O. & Ozoji, E. D. (1985). *Educating the blind.* Ibadan: Spectrum Books.

Akinpelu, J. A. (1994). Education for special groups. In O. O. Akinkugbe (Ed.), *Nigeria and education: The challenges ahead.* Ibadan: Spectrum Books.

Eniola, N. S. (2000). *General introduction to special education: Professional practice I.* Ibadan: The Centre for External Studies, University of Ibadan.

Federal Republic of Nigeria (2004). *National Policy on Education.* Lagos: NERDC Press.

ANDREW A. MOGAJI
*University of Lagos*

## AFRICA, SPECIAL EDUCATION IN

## NIMH

See NATIONAL INSTITUTES OF MENTAL HEALTH.

## NIND

See NATIONAL INSTITUTE OF NEUROLOGICAL AND COMMUNICATIVE DISORDERS AND STROKE.

## NMR

See NUCLEAR MAGNETIC RESONANCE.

## NO CHILD LEFT BEHIND ACT (2001)

The No Child Left Behind Act of 2001 (NCLB; PL 107-110) was signed into law by President George W. Bush on January 8, 2002. The law was designed to implement many of the education reforms proposed during the president's first presidential campaign, though whether the changes made by the statute constitute actual improvements remains the subject of much heated debate. According to one government source, the statute is designed to improve schools by mandating "accountability for results; an emphasis on doing what works based on scientific research; expanded parental options; and expanded local control and flexibility" (U.S. Department of Education, n.d.)

NCLB reauthorizes but significantly revises the provisions of the Elementary and Secondary Education Act of 1965 (ESEA; 20 U.S.C. 6301 et seq.). Indeed, since it would be a mammoth undertaking to revise all other statutes and regulations that refer to the previous statute (e.g., the Individuals with Disabilities Education Act), the prior designation is still used to refer to the relevant sections of the U. S. Code (which is a compendium of all statutes currently in effect). In practice, ESEA is often used to refer to the relevant code sections, while NCLB refers primarily to the changes made by the new statute, which are later discussed in some detail.

NCLB represents a major philosophical shift from the original policies and goals under the ESEA. Where the ESEA emphasized providing federal financial assistance to local school districts based upon the number of students living at or below the federal poverty level, the focus of NCLB is on improving underperforming schools through a variety of incentives and penalties, without regard to the socioeconomic status of the students attending a particular school, although funding to schools that previously received funding under Title I of the ESEA is authorized through 2007.

## Adequate Yearly Progress

Under NCLB, schools are required to demonstrate *adequate yearly progress* toward academic proficiency goals established by each state, with an emphasis on math, reading, and science. Under the statute, adequate yearly progress is defined by each state individually, in a manner that:

(1) Applies the same high standards of academic achievement to all public elementary school and secondary school students in the State;

(2) Is statistically valid and reliable;

(3) Results in continuous and substantial academic improvement for all students;

(4) Measures the progress of public elementary schools, secondary schools, and local educational agencies and the State based primarily on the academic assessments described in [20 U.S.C. §6311(b)(3)];

(5) Includes separate, measurable annual objectives for continuous and substantial improvement for each of the following:

(A) The achievement of all public elementary school and secondary school students.

(B) The achievement of

(i) economically disadvantaged students;

(ii) students from major racial and ethnic groups;

(iii) students with disabilities;

(iv) students with limited English proficiency; except that disaggregation of data under subclause (B) shall not be required in a case in which the number of students in a category is insufficient to yield statistically reliable information or the results would reveal personally identifiable information about an individual student;

(6) in accordance with [20 U.S.C. § 6311(b)(2)(D)], includes graduation rates for public secondary school students (defined as the percentage of students who

graduate from secondary school with a regular diploma in the standard number of years) and at least one other academic indicator, as determined by the State, for all public elementary school students; and

(7) in accordance with [20 U.S.C. § 6311(b)(2)(D)], at the State's discretion, may also include other academic indicators, as determined by the State for all public school students, measured separately for each group described in clause (5), such as achievement on additional State or locally administered assessments, decreases in grade-to-grade retention rates, attendance rates, and changes in the percentages of students completing gifted and talented, advanced placement, and college preparatory classes.

## 20 U.S.C. § 6311(b)(2)(C).

States must indicate how they define adequate yearly progress, and document their actual yearly progress toward their ultimate goal of 100 percent academic proficiency in reading, math, and science within 12 years in annual reports to the federal government. Schools receiving funding under NCLB that fail to demonstrate adequate yearly progress may receive additional funds to help bring them into compliance with this requirement, but also face additional legal requirements, which some feel are more punitive than beneficial in nature, including requirements for supplemental instructional services, corrective actions, and even restructuring activities.

## Annual Testing

As part of their documentation of adequate yearly progress, states are required to test all students in grades three through eight annually in reading and math, with periodic testing of a sample of children in grades four through eight using the National Assessment of Educational Progress test, to serve as a benchmark for comparison of states against each other. Of particular interest to special educators is that this requirement applies to *all* students, including students receiving special education and related services. Although Department of Education guidelines indicate that schools may assess up to 1 percent of the total student population using alternative assessment methods, students must otherwise be included with the general student population in testing, regardless of the provisions of such students' individualized assessment programs regarding appropriate assessment for the individual student (Applequist, 2005). Although schools may petition for a waiver of the 1 percent limitation, this requirement has the potential to adversely impact schools with a higher-than-average percentage of students receiving special education services.

## School Choice

If a school fails to demonstrate adequate yearly progress for 2 or more consecutive years, it must offer students the option of transferring to another public school unless existing state law prohibits public school choice, with the student's home district paying the cost of transporting students to the chosen school (Council for Exceptional Children, 2004).

## Supplemental Instructional Services

Schools that fail to demonstrate adequate yearly progress for 3 or more consecutive years are required to provide supplemental instructional services, which may include tutoring, after-school classes, and/or summer school, to low achieving and disadvantaged students (Council for Exceptional Children, 2004).

## Corrective Actions

In addition to the preceding requirements, if a school fails to demonstrate adequate yearly progress for a fourth consecutive year, the applicable school district is required to take certain corrective actions, which may include replacement of teachers or staff members, alteration of the curriculum, or similar measures. Failure to meet the requirements for a fifth consecutive year can lead to restructuring activities, which could include state takeover of the underperforming school, appointment of a private contractor to manage the school, or a broader restructuring of the staff (Council for Exceptional Children, 2004).

## "Highly Qualified" Teachers

In addition to its requirements relating to testing and adequate yearly progress, NCLB also imposes new requirements for teacher qualifications. States are required, as part of their state plan, to develop a method for ensuring that by the end of the 2005–2006 academic year, all teachers will be "highly qualified" within the meaning of the statute (Council for Exceptional Children, 2004). Similar standards apply to teachers' aides and other members of the academic faculty.

## Other Provisions

The statute contains numerous other provisions relating to education, including fiscal flexibility provisions, which allow a certain amount of flexibility in the use of federal funds at both the state and local levels for certain activities, demonstration projects, report cards to parents documenting aggregate student performance and teacher qualifications, funds for testing, and special grants for a variety of education improvement activities. As noted previously, NCLB amends and restates the older ESEA, and it is truly a mammoth statute, with the official printed version of the statute running approximately 670 pages. Its implementing regulations, which provide greater guidance on the requirements of the statute, are similarly lengthy, and a full discussion of these provisions is beyond the scope of this article.

## Controversies Relating to NCLB

The No Child Left Behind Act remains highly controversial in educational circles for a variety of reasons. In addition to the problems noted elsewhere in this entry, at least one organization has argued that NCLB creates barriers to helping students and schools because of its focus on "punishments rather than assistance, mandates rather than support for effective programs, [and] privatization rather than teacher-led, family-oriented solutions" (National Education Association, n.d.). At the time this article went to press, a number of individual school districts had decided to reject NCLB funding rather than comply with its assessment requirements, and at least one state, Utah, was reported to be considering doing so as well. A second state, Connecticut, filed suit in August of 2005 against the federal government, arguing that the statute amounted to "an unfunded mandate from the federal court (Gillespie, 2005). Four years after the enactment of NCLB, the ultimate effect of this law remains unclear. Indeed, it may be many years before its full impact, in terms of educational outcomes, is known.

### REFERENCES

Applequist, K. F. (2005). Special education legislation. In E. Fletcher-Janzen & C. R. Reynolds (Eds.), *Special educators' almanac.* New York: Wiley.

Council for Exceptional Children. (2004). *No Child Left Behind Act of 2001: Reauthorization of the Elementary and Secondary Education Act—A technical assistance resource.* Retrieved July 28, 2005, from http://www.cec.sped.org/Content/NavigationMenu/PolicyAdvocacy/CECPolicyResources/OverviewNCLB.pdf

Gillespie, N. (2005). *Connecticut challenges No Child Left Behind.* Retrieved August 22, 2005, from http://news.yahoo.com/s/ap/20050822/ap_ib_re_us/no_child_lawsuit

National Education Association (n.d.). 'No Child Left Behind' Act / ESEA. Retrieved September 30, 2004, from http://www.nea.org/esea/

U.S. Department of Education. (n.d.). *Introduction: No Child Left Behind.* Retrieved August 20, 2005, from http://www.ed.gov/nclb/overview/intro/index.html

KIMBERLY F. APPLEQUIST
*University of Colorado at Colorado Springs*

## INDIVIDUALS WITH DISABILITIES EDUCATION IMPROVEMENT ACT OF 2004 (IDEIA)
## RESPONSE TO INTERVENTION

# NONCOMPLIANT CHILDREN

Noncompliant children are those who fail to comply with the desires, rules, or policies established by others. They are norm-violating and frequently chronically disruptive. The term noncompliant is used in some states to describe youths who have come to the attention of the courts or the authorities. A noncompliant child is not necessarily emotionally disturbed or behaviorally disordered. Frequently, noncompliant children are socially different but not necessarily socially deviant.

What can be done to assist noncompliant children in the classroom? Unfortunately, special educators often neglect to inform their pupils of what is expected of them in terms of acceptable classroom behavior. Initial class periods should be used to orient students to student/teacher (jointly established) classroom rules that will provide a solid learning atmosphere. If the teacher permits a loose structure to being with, it will become more difficult to establish rules later. Time should be allowed in the classroom to regularly rehearse and review the rules. Students should be reminded of the rules periodically. The teacher and the students can identify which rules are not working or need further clarification.

Pupils should become part of the rule-making process. If the teacher and students cooperate in developing rules, students will learn courtesy, respect for authority, and acceptance of responsibility in the process. The teacher must actively involve students, requesting input and providing feedback about classroom procedures and policies as they are developed and administered. The purpose is to create a healthy climate in the classroom. Such a climate exists when there are known and shared expectations for both teachers and students as they work cooperatively to help students with the learning of social skills.

A first step in selecting appropriate classroom rules is to ask what students need to accomplish in social learning to create an effective teaching/learning environment. Thus the rules focus on social learning and not discipline, facilitating instruction and learning. This point is particularly important for children placed in least restrictive environments.

The second step in developing rules is to identify and explicitly state them (Canter & Canter, 1979). The rules need to be precise, practical, and understood by all. Rules should be clear to all teachers working with a child, to the child, and to any observers. It is useful to post rules so that children will see them, use them, and not forget them. It should be made clear when a rule has been observed or broken, especially with mentally retarded and behaviorally disordered students.

Students should be given a clear rationale for the rules to help them understand that good behavior generates a positive classroom environment. Inappropriate behavior, on the other hand, disrupts the classroom, causes tension, and makes learning and development difficult or even impossible. Mainstreamed students may be tempted to act out frustrations if they fail to understand the reasons for their frustrations.

It is also important to establish an appropriate learning climate. A number of teacher role behaviors are prerequisite to the elimination of noncompliant behaviors. Pupils seem to respect a teacher who is firm, decisive, and at the same time kind and patient. Through consistency, the child learns that certain behaviors are not acceptable and that others must be learned. Inconsistency, however, leaves a student unable to predict what will happen as the consequence of an act.

A positive attitude is necessary to project an atmosphere of optimism regarding students' academic accomplishments. A planned instructional approach is required if the teacher is to enable the students to learn academic material. Flexibility in teacher expectations and resulting student behavior is needed in the classroom; without it, there is the possibility that students will become stereotyped by the teacher. Consistency is necessary if students are to accurately identify and predict the important rules of the classroom. Understanding between human beings (i.e., empathy, concern, or appreciation) goes a long way in promoting preventive discipline with handicapped students.

Pupils may become dissatisfied with poor learning conditions in the classroom and frustrated because of pressure stemming from inappropriate teacher control techniques. How we teach is critical to maintaining preventive discipline. Teaching behaviors that enhance achievement tend to reduce deviant behaviors and vice versa. Teaching behaviors that do not promote achievement, positive attitudes, or student involvement are linked with higher rates of deviant behavior.

Teachers should seek to provide meaningful learning experiences. If learning is to be meaningful, it must be related to an individual's concerns, meet social and personal needs, and promote interaction with the environment.

Even adults respond to the requests of authority figures readily and willingly when the task appears meaningful to them personally. Certainly, meaningfulness is important to youngsters who may have difficulty in understanding long-term reinforcements of successful memory exercises, rote learning, and busy work.

Traditional disciplinary practices require school officials to make rules; students are to obey them. School officials enforce rules; students are the recipients of that enforcement. School officials establish punishment; students are to accept the punishment. In short, historic punishment practices place teacher and student into adversarial relationships. Positive discipline brings the student and teacher into a planned social learning environment where the classroom, the playground, the corridor, the bus, or the walk to and from school become the curriculum. This social learning curriculum is just as important as any academic, vocational, or remedial instruction.

The quality of teacher/student interactions is a useful indicator of behavior control in the classroom. These interactions can be either positive or negative. In an ideal classroom, positive interactions should be a major goal and should be achieved frequently.

Teacher-initiated interactions generally require compliance from the student. If the student complies, the teacher provides positive consequences. If the student does not comply, the teacher provides negative consequences first and then repeats the original direction. If the student then complies, the teacher provides positive consequences. If the student does not comply again, the teacher provides stronger negative consequences and the cycle continues until the student complies. The teacher then provides positive consequences.

Student-initiated interactions can be either appropriate or inappropriate behaviors. If behavior is appropriate, the teacher provides positive consequences. If behavior is inappropriate, the teacher provides negative consequences first and directs the student toward appropriate behavior. If the student then exhibits appropriate behavior, the teacher provides positive consequences. In all cases of teacher/student interactions, the end result should be the teacher's providing positive consequences. These consequences should also be communicated to the parents, who can then support the positive process (Alborz, 1993).

### REFERENCES

Alborz, A. (1993). Parent input in education: An illustration. *Mental Handicap, 21*(4), 142–146.

Canter, L., & Canter, M. (1979). *Assertive discipline workbook: Competency based guidelines and resource materials.* Los Angeles: Lee Carter Associates.

STAN KARCZ
*University of Wisconsin at Stout*

APPLIED BEHAVIOR ANALYSIS
CLASSROOM MANAGEMENT
CONDUCT DISORDERS

# NONDISCRIMINATORY ASSESSMENT

Millions of tests are used yearly in schools for many purposes (e.g., grading, screening, placement, guidance, diagnosis, advancement, retention, formative and summative evaluation). While the public's attitudes toward testing are positive (Lerner, 1981), a number of authors (Black, 1963; Gross, 1963; Kamin, 1974; Mercer, 1972) have criticized testing generally; criticisms directed toward the uses of tests with minority students have identified additional abuses (Williams, 1974; Samuda, Kong, Cummins, Pascual-Leon, & Lewis, 1991). These abuses include assessing students in their nondominant language; using tests that reflect only white middle-class values and abilities; using inadequately prepared and culturally insensitive assessment personnel; overidentifying and placing minority students in mentally retarded classes and lower ability groups; allowing minority students to remain in inferior classes for years; restricting minorities' educational opportunities; not informing parents when important educational decisions are made; basing important educational decisions on meager and unvalidated information; and denigrating the dignity of racial groups in light of low test performance (Oakland, 1977; Oakland & Parmalee, 1985).

Once aware of these issues, educators, psychologists (Reynolds, 1982), politicians (Bersoff, 1981), judges (Sattler, 1981), and others sought different but often complementary ways of clarifying the issues and improving the assessment of minority children. For example, in their quest to obtain suitable measures, psychologists have developed culture-fair and culture-specific measures, criterion-referenced measures, and behavioral assessment devices; translated tests from English to other languages; normed tests to include more minority children, developed ethnic and pluralistic norms; and developed statistical models to use tests fairly (Oakland & Parmalee, 1985; Jensen, 1980).

Attempts to resolve questions of test bias are confused by differing definitions of bias. Some of the more prominent definitions follow. Readers are encouraged to see Reynolds (1982, 1995), Li (1994), Scheuneman (1981), Jensen (1980, 1981), Flaugher (1978), Humphreys (1973), Darlington (1971), Lord (1980), and Berk (1982) for extensive reviews of methods to detect test bias.

Traditional definitions of bias rely largely on the three conceptions of validity: content, criterion related (including concurrent and predictive), and construct (including internal and external). Statisticians seemingly favor those methods that combine judgment and statistics. For example, logical analysis may be employed to establish the relevance of items to the trait being assessed and to identify items that may offend members of particular groups. Statistical techniques then can be used to identify aberrant items—those operating inconsistently with other items presumably measuring the same trait. Judgment again may be used to examine possible patterns among the statistically biased items and to further refine one's understanding of the trait (Shepard, 1982). Methods using item bias (as opposed to criterion-related validity) may be preferred because they can be incorporated into the first stages of test construction, thus leading to the early elimination of biases that may eventually compromise the test's validity. Furthermore, regression methods to detect criterion-related bias and factor-analytic methods to detect construct bias may be employed later with greater ease and confidence following the use of item methods.

Psychometrists often define bias through definitions that emphasize the relation between test items and the total test (e.g., item-total correlations). However, others prefer definitions that emphasize the entire test and focus on possible bias in selection or placement decisions.

Three definitions of bias appear prominently. The regression approach holds that bias is present when a test predicts differently for one group than another. Thus, bias is defined in terms of differences in the regression of a criterion measure on an independent variable (Cleary, 1968).

A second model frequently used is the quota system. Using this model, persons are selected in the same proportion as they are found in the population. If a community's population is 80 percent white and 20 percent black, one black person will be selected for every four white persons. Two separate cutoff scores are set to allow this selection ratio when between-group differences in mean scores exist.

A third model, the corrected-criterion model (Darlington, 1971), allows social and political implications using various culture-fair models to be weighed. A choice of models depends on the relative importance attributed to selecting persons with the highest scores versus giving members of minority groups more opportunities to be selected. A practical effect of this model is to add bonus points to scores of members of certain groups to help ensure a larger selection ratio for them.

In terms of a functional definition of bias, the testing process with students typically has two major activities: the collection and interpretation of information and the use of it. Oakland (1981) has suggested that a definition of bias should address both components and proposed the following broad definition for nonbiased assessment:

> Nonbiased assessment provides a quality assessment that eliminates, minimizes, or at least recognizes the presence of biasing conditions. Bias is apparent from predilections and procedures that prevent or obscure either (1) the full and accurate appraisal of conditions influencing a child's development or (2) the use of information to help maximize a child's development. (p. 2)

Thus multiple sources of bias need to be considered without focusing attention exclusively on narrow psychometric issues.

Biases can emanate from many sources: children, parents, educational personnel, assessment and intervention processes, and school system policies and practices. Possible child-related characteristics that can contribute to bias include linguistic dominance and competence, test-taking skills and attitudes, motivations, expectations, cultural values, lifestyles, and personality characteristics. Parental characteristics that can contribute to bias include attentiveness to factors important to their children's growth and development, interest in and support for educators and education, use of time and motivation to attend to children's needs, adequate information about their children's school and social activities, values, lifestyles, and linguistic and communication abilities. Characteristics of educational personnel that can contribute to bias include attitudes toward persons based on age, gender, race, social class, and religion, language and dialects, commitments and values, and professional competence. Assessment and intervention strategies that can affect bias include the validity and comprehensiveness of information acquired, the technical adequacy of the measures used, the attitudes and competencies of the appraisal staff, the standards used to evaluate pupil performance, and the availability of viable interventions. Policies and practices of school systems that can contribute to bias include willingness to use financial and professional resources appropriately, responsiveness to the needs of individual pupils, commitment to high professional standards, compliance with state and national legislation and litigation, diversity and quality of personnel and services, and morale of the staff. Each of these areas can affect the accuracy of the appraisal and the use of appraisal information to maximize a child's development (Trent & Artiles, 1995).

Numerous sets of guidelines exist for designing and delivering nonbiased assessment programs. Professional associations together with federal and state agencies have proposed strategies intended to be both professionally sound and educationally relevant.

National associations such as the American Personnel and Guidance Association (APGA) and the American Psychological Association (APA) have tried to steer a steady course by providing guidelines for the development and use of tests (e.g., APA's Standards for Educational and Psychological Testing, 1985) and position papers that address specific issues.

The federal government has responded in various ways (Oakland, 1977). The Individuals with Disabilities Education Act (IDEA) has had the most significant and far-reaching influence on determining nonbiased assessment policies and practices in the schools. The legislation contains six key features that affect assessment.

An individual educational plan (IEP) is written annually and specifies desirable educational goals and methods. Parents are encouraged to participate on the team that develops the IEP and to exercise their right to receive and consider all pertinent information the school has about their child. Due process provisions of the bill help to ensure that parents may examine all documents concerning their child, receive written notices in their native language when their child is being evaluated, question and object to information they think is incorrect or injurious, submit evidence and obtain legal council and other professional advice, request that their case be reviewed by an impartial hearing officer, and appeal any decision through other courts.

Tests are described as being culturally nondiscriminatory when they have been validated for the specific purposes for which they are being used, are administered by trained and competent examiners using standardized procedures, and assess multiple yet specific areas of education need. Information about the pupil's medical, social, psychological, and educational development should be collected and interpreted by trained professionals. When assessing pupils with sensory or other physical impairments, the tests must assess their capabilities unattenuated by their impairments. Submitting all information to a multidisciplinary team for evaluation and decisions constitutes a key feature of a nonbiased program. Specialists also are encouraged to propose helpful interventions (Heller, Holtzman, & Messick, 1982). School systems must fully reassess pupils every 3 years in order to note progress toward goals specified in the IEP and to determine continued eligibility for special education.

## REFERENCES

American Personnel and Guidance Association. (1972). The responsible use of tests: A position paper of MEG, APGA, and NCME. *Measurement and Evaluation in Guidance, 5,* 385–388.

American Psychological Association. (1985). *Standards for educational and psychological testing.* Washington, DC: Author.

Berk, R. A. (Ed.) (1982). *Handbook of methods for detecting test bias.* Baltimore: Johns Hopkins University Press.

Bersoff, D. (1981). Legal principles in the nondiscriminatory assessment of minority children. In T. Oakland (Ed.), *Nonbiased assessment.* Minneapolis: University of Minnesota.

Black, H. (1963). *They shall not pass.* New York: Morrow.

Cleary, T. A. (1968). Test bias: Prediction of grades of Negro and white students in integrated colleges. *Journal of Educational Measurement, 5,* 115–124.

Darlington, R. B. (1971). Another look at "culture fairness." *Journal of Educational Measurement, 8,* 71–72.

Flaugher, R. L. (1978). The many definitions of test bias. *American Psychologist, 33,* 671–679.

Gross, M. (1963). *The brain watchers.* New York: New American Library.

Heller, K. A., Holtzman, W. H., & Messick, S. (Eds.). (1982). *Placing children in special education: A strategy for equity.* Washington, DC: National Academy.

Humphreys, L. G. (1973). Statistical definitions of test validity for minority groups. *Journal of Applied Psychology, 58*(1), 1–4.

Jensen, A. R. (1980). *Bias in mental testing.* New York: Free Press.

Jensen, A. R. (1981). *Straight talk about mental tests.* New York: Free Press.

Kamin, L. (1974). *The science and politics of IQ.* Hillsdale, NJ: Erlbaum.

Lerner, B. (1981). Representative democracy, "men of zeal," and testing legislation. *American Psychologist, 36,* 270–275.

Li, A. K. F., (1994). Equity in assessment: From the perspective of new immigrant students. *Canadian Journal of School Psychology, 10*(2), 131–137.

Lord, F. M. (1980). *Application of item response theory to practical testing problems.* Hillsdale, NJ: Erlbaum.

Mercer, J. R. (1972). IQ: The lethal label. *Psychology Today, 6,* 44–47, 95–97.

Oakland, T. D. (Ed.). (1977). *Psychological and educational assessment of minority children.* New York: Brunner/Mazel.

Oakland, T. D. (Ed.). (1981). *Nonbiased assessment* (a project of the National School Psychology Inservice Training Network). Minneapolis, MN: Upper Midwest Regional Resource Center.

Oakland, T., & Parmalee, R. (1985). Mental measurement of minority-group children. In B. Wolman (Ed.), *Handbook of intelligence.* New York: Wiley.

Reynolds, C. R. (1982). The problem of bias in psychological assessment. In C. R. Reynolds & T. B. Gutkin (Eds.), *The handbook of school psychology.* New York: Wiley.

Reynolds, C. R. (1995). Test bias and the assessment of intelligence and personality. In D. Saklofske & M. Zeidner (Eds.) *International handbook of personality and intelligence* (pp. 545–573). New York: Plenum.

Samuda, R. J., Kong, S. L., Cummins, J., Pascual-Leone, J., & Lewis, J. (1991). *Assessment and placement of minority students.* Toronto, Canada: Hogrefe & Huber.

Sattler, J. M. (1981). Intelligence tests on trial: An "interview" with judges Robert F. Peckham and John F. Grady. *Journal of School Psychology, 19*(4), 359–369.

Scheuneman, J. D. (1981). A new look at bias in aptitude tests. In P. Merrifield (Ed.), *Measuring human abilities (New Directions in Testing and Measurement,* No. 12). San Francisco: Jossey-Bass.

Shepard, L. A. (1982). Definitions of bias. In R. A. Berk (Ed.), *Handbook of methods for detecting test bias.* Baltimore: Johns Hopkins University Press.

Trent, S. C., & Artiles, A. J. (1995). Serving culturally diverse students with emotional or behavioral disorders. In J. Kaufman, J. Lloyd, & J. Will (Eds.), *Issues in educational placement* (pp. 215–249). Hillsdale, NJ: Erlbaum.

Williams, R. L. (1974). Scientific racism and IQ: The silent mugging of the black community. *Psychology Today, 7*(12), 32–41.

THOMAS OAKLAND
*University of Florida*

**CULTURAL BIAS IN TESTING**
**INDIVIDUAL EDUCATION PLAN**
**RACIAL DISCRIMINATION IN SPECIAL EDUCATION**

## NONLITERAL LANGUAGE

Literal language is the ordinary, common construction or primary meaning of terms or expressions. *Nonliteral language* is the extraordinary construction or primary meaning of terms or expressions, i.e., going beneath the conventional code of language to interpret the intentions and attitudes of words, phrases, or sentences. The literal/nonliteral distinction is often a matter of degree; therefore, the notion of a continuum is used when discussing literal or nonliteral oral and written communication (Adamson & Romski, 1997; Kudor, 1997; Milosky, 1994; Nippold, 1998). Twelve categories of language that are important in social, academic, and employment situations are included in the continuum.

1. Figurative language
   - proverbs ("A rolling stone gathers no moss;" "Every cloud has a silver lining.")
   - similes ("Gandhi was like a magician"; "The giraffe was like a flagpole.")
   - metaphors ("Gandhi was a magician"; "The giraffe was a flagpole.")
   - idioms ("Keep your nose clean"; "Keep your shirt on.")
2. Humor (cartoons, riddles, jokes, puns)
3. Advertisements ("Built to move you"—advertising a sports car)
4. Headlines ("Chicago Cubs Lead"—are they playing ball well or are they sluggish?)
5. Multiple-meaning words (the word "set" has more than 200 meanings)
6. Ambiguous words ("The turkey is ready to eat"; "She fed her dog biscuits.")
7. Sarcasm ("Oh yeah, cool hair"; "I've seen everything.")
8. Verbal aggression (ritualistic insults, dissing, play the dozens) ("Your old lady wears combat boots.")
9. Teasing ("I'm going to kick your butt"; "Johnny luvs Suzie!")
10. Slang ("Rad dress, man!", "funky!", "cool!", "cheesy!")
11. Deception (dependent on the intent of the speaker's statement)
    - lying (the speaker wants the listener to believe the statement)
    - irony (the speaker does not want the listener to believe the statement)
12. Fantasy (imaginative fiction; unrealistic or improbable mental images such as daydreams).

Nonliteral communication varies from culture to culture. Nonliteral language problems are common with speakers of English as a second language (ESL) and with individuals who have developmental or acquired communication-learning disorders. For the mainstream culture, the ability to understand and use nonliteral language forms begins to develop around age 5 and continues through life (Lane & Molyneaux, 1992). Being able to understand and use figurative language, humor, teasing, sarcasm, deceit, verbal aggression, and slang is necessary for social development. Comprehension and production of figurative language, deceit, advertising, headlines, multiple meanings, and ambiguity is important in academic settings. Knowing scripts and schemas, advertising language, and forms of deception are critical for employment and careers (Kudor, 1997; Lane & Molyneaux, 1992; Milosky, 1994; Nippold, 1998).

## REFERENCES

Adamson, L. B., & Romski, M. A. (Eds.). (1997). *Communication and language acquisition: Discoveries from atypical development.* Baltimore: Brookes.

Kudor, S. J. (1997). *Teaching students with language and communication disabilities.* Needham Heights, MA: Allyn & Bacon.

Lane, V. W., & Molyneaux, D. (1992). *The dynamics of communicative development.* Englewood Cliffs, NJ: Prentice Hall.

Milosky, L. A. (1994). Nonliteral language abilities: Seeing the forest for the trees. In G. P. Wallach and K. G. Butler, (Eds.), *Language learning disabilities in school-age children and adolescents: Some principles and applications* (2nd ed., pp. 275–304). New York: Merrill/Macmillan College.

Nippold, M. A. (1998). *Later language development: The school-age and adolescent years.* Austin, TX: PRO-ED.

STEPHEN S. FARMER
*New Mexico State University*

# NONSHELTERED EMPLOYMENT

Diverse employment options are available for graduates of special education programs. In the past, sheltered employment was a highly probable adult work setting for individuals with mental retardation. Today, several alternative employment options provide graduates with opportunities to experience work conditions in the mainstream of society (Rusch & Hughes, 1990). Nonsheltered employment comprises a range of work situations, including mobile work crews, enclaves within industry, competitive employment, and a supported work approach. These outcomes are enhanced through a commitment to a longitudinal progression of functional vocational curricular activities. The activities provide the mentally retarded with the requisite skills to function within integrated, community employment settings. The sequence of activities that follows results in nonsheltered employment options for individuals graduating from special education programs.

The first of these activities is a survey of nonsheltered community employment opportunities. Local market conditions, as well as future trends in employment, are carefully analyzed by vocational development specialists. Advisory committees comprised of representatives from the chamber of commerce, local manufacturing companies, government agencies, industries, nonprofit agencies, and other major sources of employment in the local community convene to provide feedback relative to local community employment opportunities.

The second step is to analyze requisite skills from targeted employment opportunities. Detailed job skill inventories are collected by job development specialists as they observe currently employed workers performing activities within selected occupations. Socialization, academic, strength/stamina, transportation, orientation, and other critical skills are detailed. Two outcomes emerge from this analysis. First, for transition plans, priority individual educational plan objectives are directly related to requisite skills within anticipated future work settings. Second, a longitudinal sequence of activities is integrated into the curriculum to provide ample exposure and opportunities for acquiring requisite skills.

A criterion-referenced assessment of the trainee is the third step in the sequence of activities. Once the requisite employment skills have been delineated through local job skill inventories, students/adults are assessed in natural, community work environments to evaluate current proficiencies relative to job demands. Norm-referenced, simulated assessments should be deemphasized when readying individuals for nonsheltered employment. The focus of assessment is to match as closely as possible currently available jobs with proficiency strengths of individuals. When deficiencies occur, trainers use systematic training strategies to teach new skills.

With systematic training strategies, trainers are paired with students/adults at an employment site and act as job coaches for the trainees. Acquisition strategies include varying the intensity of prompts prior to the occurrence of a behavior or providing varying intensities of feedback/reinforcement. Additionally, modification of the task itself may include altering the sequence of steps, modifying the physical nature of the materials, allowing the trainee to independently complete parts of the task, and rearranging duties of the trainee so that coworkers complete the more difficult steps of an activity.

Follow-along services are supplied in the final activity of the nonsheltered employment options. A critical dimension of nonsheltered employment is the fading of assistance from the trainer to allow the site supervisor of nondisabled workers to assume the same duties with the trainee. This fading process includes the analysis of supervisory feedback forms, the collection of data for rate and quality of work, the interviewing of parents to clarify incentives for long-term employment, and the willingness of a school/agency to be on call for crisis situations that, if not immediately handled, could result in termination of the trainee.

## REFERENCES

Rusch, F. R. (Ed.). (1986). *Competitive employment: Service delivery models, methods, and issues.* Baltimore: Brookes.

Rusch, F. R., & Hughes, C. (1990). Historical overview of supported employment. In F. R. Rusch (Ed), *Supported employment: Models, methods, and issues* (pp. 5–14). Sycamore, IL: Sycamore Publishing.

Wehman, P., & Hill, J. (1985). *Competitive employment for persons with mental retardation: From research to practice.* Richmond, VA: Commonwealth University, Research Training Center.

Wehman, P., Kregel, J., & Barcus, J. M. (1985). From school to work: A vocational transition model for handicapped students. *Exceptional Children, 52,* 25–37.

ERNEST PANCSOFAR
*Bowling Green State University*

**SHELTERED WORKSHOPS**
**VOCATIONAL EDUCATION**
**VOCATIONAL REHABILITATION COUNSELING**

# NONVERBAL LANGUAGE

Nonverbal language is commonly used to describe all human communication events which transcend spoken or written words (Knapp, 1980; Lane & Molyneaux, 1994; Wood, 1981). Nonverbal communication begins at birth and continues throughout life (Bretherton, 1991). The early development of nonverbal communication skills occurs in three phases (Mundy & Gomes, 1997); (1) the birth to 5-month dyadic phase where communication often involves face-to-face exchanges of affective signals between the infant and caregiver; (2) the 6- to 18-month phase where triadic exchanges occur more frequently (e.g., an infant points to a toy while making eye contact with a caregiver); and (3) the third phase, which overlaps with phase two (12–24 months) and involves the child's increasing utilization of verbal communication in conjunction with nonverbal signals. The third phase continues to be developed so that nonverbal communication serves at least four important functions:

- Taking the place of verbal communication (when verbal communication is unnecessary or impossible).
- Adding clarity to the meaning of verbal communication (by inflection, stress, tone of voice, intensity, gestures, and so forth).
- Revealing the general emotional state of the participants (e.g., comfort or anxiety; relaxed or fearful).
- Revealing specific feelings regarding topics under discussion (not only the nature of the emotion but its relative intensity).

Thirteen aspects of nonverbal language are important when negotiating meaning in social, academic, and employment contexts (Devito, 1997; Knapp, 1980; Lane & Molyneaux, 1994; McKay, Davis, & Fanning, 1983; Neill, 1991; Trenholm & Jensen, 1997; Wood, 1981):

1. Paralinguistics: symbols communicated in variations of vocal quality; auditory nonverbal signals. Includes prosodic features of vocal effects, such as variations of pitch, loudness, duration, quality, and timing; noticeable changes in intonation, such as teasing, whining, sarcasm; sounds of yawning, crying, laughing.

2. Kinesics: use of movements to convey messages. Includes body movements and postures, gestures, facial expressions, and eye movements (Ekman & Friesen, 1975; Morris, 1994).

3. Tactile communication: communication through touching; developmentally the most primary sense. Touch can be used as a modality inroad in therapy; as a relaxing, calming stimulus; for support, as in a pat on the back; to convey warmth, anxiety, protection, friendliness, or fear; to show desire to touch and be touched, or not to touch or be touched. Includes touching oneself and touching others.

4. Proxemics: the manipulation of space to send messages between individuals. Includes size and arrangement of setting or room; size and shape of furniture; proximity of individuals (intimate, social, or public distances); combination of seating arrangements; respect for personal space; crowded versus open spacing.

5. Chronemics: time as a conveyer of messages. Includes time orientation, understanding and organization; use of and reaction to time pressures; our innate and learned awareness of time; wearing or not wearing a watch; arriving, starting, and ending late or on time.

6. Color: the use of color in the setting (walls, floor, furniture), in clothing, or in other materials to convey messages.

7. Olfactory sense: smells used to transfer messages. Includes aromas or odors within the environment, of foods, and of seasons; olfactory memory; personal aromas such as body smells, perfumes and deodorants, odors from certain diseases. Smell is used as a sensory inroad in intervention approaches; the accuracy of the sense may decrease with aging.

8. Gustatory sense: signals sent via taste. Includes increased or decreased nutritional intake; gustatory memory; pleasant and unpleasant interpretations. Accuracy of gustatory sense may decrease with aging.

9. Objects and artifacts: message carriers such as clothing, jewelry, eyeglasses and hearing aids, personal possessions, items a student brings to school, or professional markers such as name plates or uniforms. May function as supports or distractions.

10. Atmosphere or ambience: overall communication in a setting; combines the perceived attitudes of the occupants with proxemics, colors, sounds or silence, olfactory messages, and object messages.

11. Silence: use of oral quiet and body inactivity to transmit messages. May be for listening, waiting, observing, gaining attention, thinking; may express anger, frustration, signal inability to talk or respond; may be used as a counseling response; may convey boredom, discomfort, hostility, reverence, agreement, grief; may be appropriate or inappropriate.

12. Organismics: the effects of relatively unalterable physical attributes on communication. Includes physical characteristics such as height, weight, eye and skin color, body dimensions, sex, race, age; physically apparent disabilities such as various syndrome characteristics, neurological and orthopedic handicaps, or physical deformities.

13. Situation or environment: the effects the immediate setting has on communication. Individuals behave differently in different settings; the perceived expectations in a particular setting (home, school, or work) produce characteristic communication patterns.

Easily taken for granted, and often more difficult to observe and record systematically than verbal or linguistic behavior, nonverbal communication may convey as much as 80 percent of a message (Devito, 1997; Trenholm & Jensen, 1997). Although nonverbal communication is important in all social and academic communication-learning interactions, it is critical when negotiating meaning with prelinguistic infants and individuals with severe disabilities (Bretherton, 1991; Mundy & Gomes, 1997). Nonverbal communication varies from culture to culture and needs to be interpreted relative to the illocutionary (intent), locutionary (actual signals), and perlocutionary (interpretation by receiver) aspects of a situation.

## REFERENCES

Bretherton, I. (1991). Intentional communication and the development of an understanding of mind. In D. Frye & C. Moore (Eds.), *Children's theories of mind: Mental states and social understanding* (pp. 271–289). Hillsdale, NJ: Erlbaum.

Devito, J. A. (1997). *Human communication.* New York: Addison Wesley Longman.

Ekman, P., & Friesen, W. V. (1975). *Unmasking the face: A guide to recognizing emotions from facial clues.* Englewood Cliffs, NJ: Prentice Hall.

Knapp, M. L. (1980). *Essentials of nonverbal communication.* New York: Holt, Rinehart & Winston.

Lane, V. W., & Molyneaux, D. (1994). *The dynamics of communicative development.* Englewood Cliffs, NJ: Prentice Hall.

McKay, M., Davis, M., & Fanning, P. (1983). *Messages: The communication skills book.* Oakland, CA: New Harbinger.

Morris, D. (1994). *Bodytalk: The meaning of human gestures.* New York: Crown.

Mundy, P., & Gomes, A. (1997). A skills approach to early language development. In L. B. Adamson and M. A. Romski (Eds.), *Communication and language acquisition: Discoveries from atypical development* (pp. 107–133). Baltimore: Brookes.

Neill, S. R. St. J. (1991). *Classroom nonverbal communication.* New York: Routledge.

Trenholm, S., & Jensen, A. (1997). *Interpersonal communication* (3rd ed.). New York: Wadsworth.

Wood, B. S. (1981). *Children and communication: Verbal and nonverbal language development* (2nd ed.). Englewood Cliffs, NJ: Prentice Hall.

STEPHEN S. FARMER
JUDITH L. FARMER
*New Mexico State University*

NONVERBAL LEARNING DISABILITY SYNDROME

# NONVERBAL LEARNING DISABILITY SYNDROME

A nonverbal learning disability (NLD) is a neuropsychological disorder composed of a specific pattern of assets and deficits related to right hemispheric dysfunction. Nonverbal learning disabilities manifest as a cluster of deficits affecting the nonverbal aspects of a child's functioning, such as visual-spatial skills, psychomotor coordination, tactile perception, nonverbal problem solving, and social skills. Children with NLD typically have normal general intelligence. Cognitive deficits may be apparent in executive functioning, visual attention and memory, novel problem solving, and concept formation. Academic deficits commonly occur in writing, reading comprehension, written expression, mechanical arithmetic, and mathematical application. Common psychosocial deficits seen in children with NLD include inadequate social skills, difficulty with speech prosody and pragmatic language, emotional lability, and difficulty adapting to novel situations. Children with NLD display relative strengths in verbal rote memory, vocabulary, sight word reading, decoding, phonetic spelling, basic mathematical concepts, and auditory skills (Drummond, Ahmad, & Rourke, 2005; Harnadek & Rourke, 1994).

Symptoms associated with NLD syndrome were first described by Myklebust in 1968. The syndrome later was more clearly defined and delineated by Rourke (1989), who remains one of the leading experts on NLD. Although the prevalence of nonverbal learning disabilities is unknown, Rourke (1995) estimates that as many as ten percent of learning disabled children may display this syndrome. Although the etiology of the developmental form of NLD is unclear, it is often diagnosed in patients suffering from conditions that have affected the white matter in the right hemisphere of the brain. Such conditions may include closed head injury, congenital hypothyroidism, brain lesions, callosal agenisis, and hydrocephalus.

Roman (1998) gives a sound description of the developmental progression of NLD. Young children who will later develop NLD frequently lack exploratory play and are less interactive with adults than other children. As toddlers, they display immature motor coordination and often exhibit delays in the development of self-help skills. Speech and vocabulary development usually progress normally. Preschoolers who later develop NLD often are misdiagnosed with Attention-Deficit Hyperactivity Disorder. This may be due to disruptive behaviors stemming from frustrations experienced as a result of poor social judgment and/or visual-spatial and tactile perceptual deficits. These children may also be misdiagnosed as having a mild form of Aspergers syndrome due to increasingly apparent difficulties with social interaction and poor adjustment to novel situations. The acquisition of pre-academic skills typically is delayed. These children have difficulty recognizing and copying letters and exhibit delays in the development of age-appropriate fine motor skills. With repeated practice, skills related to writing letters and numbers and other fine motor skills required in academic settings can develop to a normal level of proficiency. After acquiring these basic skills the NLD child may display relatively normal academic achievement through the early elementary school years. However, as academic demands increase with grade level and require more abstract, higher order reasoning skills, NLD children find the maintenance of an adequate level of academic achievement increasingly difficult. Those with higher intellectual abilities may complete college or obtain higher degrees (Johnson, 1987; Roman, 1998; Rourke, 1995).

The assessment and diagnosis of nonverbal learning disabilities requires the use of a comprehensive, multidisciplinary neuropsychological assessment battery. Psychoeducational assessment results usually show verbal cognitive abilities well in excess of visual-perceptual cognitive abilities, poor visual-motor integration skills, basic reading skills considerably better than reading comprehension, poor writing quality, poor written composition, and reading skills that are superior to mathematics skills. Language assessment results indicate sufficient concrete language skills, whereas abstract language is deficient. Auditory skills, including auditory memory and phonological awareness, are usually strengths (Foss, 2001; Roman, 1998). Psychosocial difficulties such as anxiety, depression, withdrawal, attention difficulties, poor social and adaptive skills and behaviors may become more problematic with advancing age (Little, 1993; Rourke, 2005). Drummond et al.

(2005) and Pelletier, Ahmad, and Rourke (2001) provide a more detailed description of potential diagnostic criteria for NLD in children.

Interventions for those with nonverbal learning disabilities must be multidisciplinary in nature and should be highly individualized. A thorough intervention plan should include academic accommodations as necessary, language therapy, occupational therapy, social skills training, and psychotherapy to assist with emotional difficulties, organizational skills, behavioral difficulties, and adaptive skills. Federal law and the *Diagnostic and Statistical Manual for Mental Disorders* do not officially recognize NLD as a separate disability that negatively impacts learning. In addition, NLD is unrecognized under federal special education law. The Individuals with Disabilities Education Act (IDEA) classifications may include specific learning disability, other health impaired, language impaired, and others as needed. Regardless of the classification, the specific pattern of deficits and assets should be considered when developing intervention plans. For more information on intervention strategies, see Tanguay (2002), Foss (2001), and Thompson (1997).

## REFERENCES

Drummond, C. R., Ahmad, S., & Rourke, B. P. (2005). Rules for the classification of younger children with nonverbal learning disabilities and basic phonological processing disabilities. *Archives of Clinical Neuropsychology, 20,* 171–182.

Foss, J. M. (2001). Nonverbal learning disability: How to recognize it and minimize its effects. (ERIC #E619)

Harnadeck, M. C. S., & Rourke, B. P. (1994). Principal identifying features of the syndrome of nonverbal learning disabilities in children. *Journal of Learning Disabilities, 27,* 144–155.

Johnson, D. J. (1987). Nonverbal learning disabilities. *Pediatric Annals, 16,* 133–141.

Liddell, G. A., & Rasmussen, C. (2005). Memory profile of children with nonverbal learning disability. *Learning Disabilities Research & Practice, 20,* 137–141.

Little, S. S. (1993). Nonverbal learning disabilities and socioemotional functioning: A review of the recent literature. *Journal of Learning Disabilities, 26,* 653–666.

Pelletier, P., Ahmad, S., & Rourke, B. P. (2001). Classification rules for basic phonological processing disabilities and nonverbal learning disabilities: Formulation and external validity. *Child Neuropsychology, 7,* 84–98.

Roman, M. A. (1998). The syndrome of nonverbal learning disabilities: Clinical description and applied aspects. *Current Issues in Education, 1.* Retrieved from http://cie.ed.asu.edu/volume1/number7/

Rourke, B. P. (1989). *Nonverbal learning disabilities: The syndrome and the model.* New York: Guilford.

Rourke, B. P. (1995). *Syndrome of Nonverbal Learning Disabilities: Neurodevelopmental manifestations.* New York: Guilford.

Tanguay, P. B. (2002). *Nonverbal Learning Disabilities at school.* Philadelphia: Jessica Kingsley.

Thompson, S. (1997). *The source for nonverbal learning disorders.* Illinois: Linguisystems.

JULIE ELLIS
*University of Florida*

# NOONAN'S SYNDROME (MALE TURNER SYNDROME)

Noonan's syndrome, which closely resembles Turner syndrome phenotypically, primarily affects males; it may be a sex-linked chromosomal abnormality, but the specific cause is uncertain. Characteristics are similar to those of females with Turner syndrome (Bergsma, 1979). Children with Noonan's syndrome usually are short in stature, have webbed necks or short broad necks with excessive skin folds, and swelling and puffiness of the extremities, especially the hands and feet. Swelling, present at birth, may disappear as the child develops. Testicular underdevelopment and missing secondary sexual development are often seen. Eyes are widely spaced, may slant, squint, or have epicanthal folds, and nearsightedness is often noted (Collins & Turner, 1973). Low-set ears are prominent and slanted. Hair is coarse and teeth may be misshapen. Fingers and toes may be shortened and nails will be short and poorly developed. Occasionally loss of muscle tone may be reported, as will visual and hearing deficits. Congenital heart disease is a common finding. Mild mental retardation is fairly common, although some children with Noonan's syndrome will have normal intelligence (Lemeshaw, 1982).

Educational placement should consider the degree of cognitive developmental disability that exists in the child although educable or trainable classes may often be necessary because of additional disabilities that may accompany this syndrome. Related services will be necessary if hearing and vision losses are documented. Secondary sexual characteristics may be lacking; therefore, psychological and guidance counseling may be necessary to remediate for self-image and adjustment conflicts that may arise as the male reaches puberty. This will be more necessary if the child is included in the general classroom. Medical care may often be necessary because of heart problems, as well as an adaptive physical education program. It is important to work with the student to make sure that academic and social goals are appropriate (Besag, Fowler, Watson, & Bostock, 1993).

## REFERENCES

Bergsma, D. (1979). *Birth defects compendium* (2nd ed.). New York: National Foundation, March of Dimes.

Besag, F. M., Fowler, M., Watson, J., & Bostock, R. (1993). The practical management of specific learning disabilities. *Educational and Child Psychology, 10*(1), 23–27.

Collins, E., & Turner, G. (1973). The Noonan syndrome: A review of the clinical and genetic features of 27 cases. *Journal of Pediatrics, 83,* 941–950.

Lemeshaw, S. (1982). *The handbook of clinical types in mental retardation.* Boston: Allyn & Bacon.

SALLY L. FLAGLER
*University of Oklahoma*

**CROUZON'S SYNDROME
HUNTER SYNDROME
MENTAL RETARDATION
PHYSICAL ANOMALIES**

## NORMAL CURVE EQUIVALENT

Normal Curve Equivalent (NCE) scores are standardized scores required in reporting to many federal agencies by school systems (Hopkins 1998). The original scores from a test or assessment are transformed to a mean of 50 and standard deviation of 21.06, intended to mirror the percentile ranks associated with the normal distribution. That is, NCE scores are intended to approximate the percentile rank scores of a normal distribution assumed to underlie the original scores. Unfortunately, the two distributions coincide only at the 1st, 50th, and 99th percentile (and NCE) scores. Since NCE scores are a linear transformation of the original scores and thus an equal interval distribution, they must necessarily depart from the normal curve percentiles, since the normal curve probability distribution is not equal interval in nature. That is, a 1-point change in the normal curve percentile distribution is equivalent to different score points, depending on the score. For a test score 2 standard deviations below the mean, which is at the 2.28 percentile point (.0228), moving to 3.28th percentile point (.0328) changes the test score approximately to 1.84 standard deviations below the mean. For a score at the mean (0 standard deviations above/below), which has a percentile score of 50 (.50), moving to the 51st percentile score (.51) changes the test score to about .025, seven times less than for the low score. The distribution of differences between probability score under the normal distribution and NCE is illustrated with 10,000 sample scores generated randomly to approximate a normal distribution.

Notice that the scores are well over 10 points apart at some score ranges. The extremes, well beyond 2 standard deviations from the mean, exhibit even greater differences between percentile score under the normal distribution and NCE score.

The use of a standard score is not controversial, and as long as the NCE is treated simply as a standard score there is no problem in interpretation. Linking it to percentile ranks, however, is not appropriate, and the confusion that may arise with practitioners and their reports to parents can be significant.

### REFERENCE

Hopkins, K. D. (1998). *Educational and Psychological Measurement and Evaluation.* Boston: Allyn & Bacon.

VICTOR L. WILLSON
*Texas A&M University*

**PERCENTILE SCORES
Z-SCORES, IN DETERMINATION OF DISCREPANCIES**

## NORMALIZATION

The strong belief of parents and advocates that individuals with mental retardation have a right to live and function in what is considered a normal environment led to the concept of normalization. These advocates stressed the fact that the disabled are citizens and should be provided with opportunities and programs similar to those provided to nondisabled children and adults. The term normalization originated in Denmark and was first implemented successfully in Scandinavian countries (Wolfensberger, 1972). Nirje (1979) introduced the term to America and defined it as "making available to all mentally retarded people patterns of life and conditions of everyday living which are close as possible to the regular circumstances of society" (p. 173).

During the 1970s there were many publications that listed suggestions for implementing the normalization principles. A collection of some popular comments were made by Bruininks and Warfield (1979), including the following:

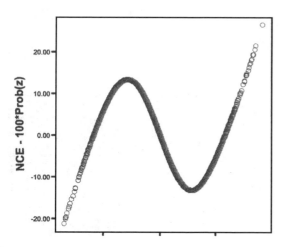

Difference between NCE score and 100 x probability of normal distribution z-score

Planning and managing for retarded people services that require attention to normative cultural patterns.

Allowing retarded people to experience normal routines of the day (e.g., dressing, eating in normal-sized groups) and normal routines of the life cycle (e.g., activities appropriate to one's age) that generally accompany increasing maturity.

Respecting choices and desires, and providing normal economic and civic privileges.

Providing education, training, care, and residential living facilities of normal size and appearance.

Using generic services whenever possible rather than separate ones. (pp. 191–192)

Recently, the term has been used to refer not only to the mentally retarded but to all individuals with disabilities. Regardless of the type of disability, the individual should be included as much as possible in the community and society. This involves participation in what is considered normal daily living activities such as attending school (education), working at a job, or sheltered workshop (employment), and attending movies and participating in activities at parks and YMCAs (recreation and leisure activities). Hallahan and Kauffman (1986) state that there are three major ways professionals have tried to implement the normalization principle. They are antilabeling, mainstreaming, and deinstitutionalization. The antilabeling movement focuses on eliminating labels and categories such as mental retardation, emotionally disturbed, and learning disabled. There are many disadvantages to labeling, which numerous educators believe strongly outnumber the advantages. It has been suggested and supported by research that labels bias expectations and views of individuals with disabilities. The mainstreaming movement involves placing a child with disabilities in an educational setting that is in the least restrictive environment; this means that, based on educational and related service needs, the child should be placed with children without disabilities as much as possible. Deinstitutionalization is the process of removing disabled individuals from the institution to community-based living quarters. During the late 1960s, there was a great deal of attention placed on the inadequate care provided by many institutions. The institution was considered the dumping ground for the helpless individuals, regardless of the level of severity of the handicapping condition. The current trend is to place the disabled closer to their families and communities. These environments include community residential facilities, group homes, and halfway houses.

## REFERENCES

Bruininks, R. H., & Warfield, G. (1979). The mentally retarded. In E. L. Meyen (Ed.), *Exceptional children and youth: An introduction*. Denver: Love.

Hallahan, D. P., & Kauffman, J. M. (1986). *Exceptional children: Introduction to special education*. Englewood Cliffs, NJ: Prentice Hall.

Nirje, B. (1979). Changing patterns in residential services for the mentally retarded. In E. L. Meyen (Ed.), *Exceptional children and youth: An introduction*. Denver: Love.

Wolfensberger, W. (1972). *The principle of normalization in human services*. Toronto, Canada: National Institute on Mental Retardation.

JANICE HARPER
*North Carolina Central University*

**COMMUNITY RESIDENTIAL PROGRAMS**
**DEINSTITUTIONALIZATION**
**INDEPENDENT LIVING CENTERS**

## NORM-REFERENCED TESTING

Norm-referenced tests (NRT) refer to a broad array of standardized tests, the results of which are interpreted by comparing the performance of examinees with that of a specified population of individuals, or norm group. In a broader sense, NRT often refers to a type of test frequently defined by contrasting it with criterion-referenced tests (CRT), where test results are referenced to a particular content domain and provide information about the skills an examinee has acquired, not the rank of an examinee in a norm group (Anastasi, 1982).

Most standardized tests are norm referenced. They are designed to be administered under standard conditions, according to carefully specified directions, and scored in an objective manner so that the results may be referenced to norms based on a representative sample of the population who took the test under similar conditions during standardization. The normative frame of reference for most standardized tests used in schools is usually a national (U.S.) age or grade group such as eight-year-old children, sixth-grade pupils, or college-bound high-school seniors.

A variety of norm-referenced tests are used in psychology and education. Intelligence tests, aptitude tests, achievement tests, and interest and personality tests all rely mainly on norm group comparisons for their interpretation. The contrast between NRT and CRT refers specifically to achievement tests and, even more specifically, to those at the elementary school level that assess basic reading, arithmetic, and language skills (Anastasi, 1982; Mehrens & Lehmann, 1984). Even though the items used in NRT and CRT may appear to be indistinguishable, norm-referenced tests are almost always broader in their content coverage than the narrowly focused criterion-referenced tests.

With NRT, the interpretive process typically consists of

consulting various types of norms, of which standard scores and percentile ranks have the greatest utility. Intelligence and scholastic aptitude test results are usually reported in terms of age-based standard scores and percentile ranks, while achievement test results are commonly reported in terms of grade-based standard scores and percentile ranks. Grade equivalents are also frequently reported for achievement tests, despite the fact that there are logical and statistical problems that obfuscate their meaning (Thorndike & Hagen, 1977). A typical norm-referenced interpretation for a 10-year-old child who obtained a standard score of 110 and a percentile rank of 74 on a verbal intelligence test would emphasize the fact that this child's standard score in verbal intelligence of 110 equaled or exceeded 74 percent of 10-year-old children tested in the norming sample. Standard scores frequently reference performance to the curve of normal distribution, a mathematical function that underlies much of NRT test construction and norming procedures.

The current pedagogic emphasis on individualized instruction, especially computer-assisted instruction, with its reliance on mastery of a carefully sequenced curriculum, has advanced the cause of CRT. In fact, Cronbach (1984) has observed that enthusiasm for criterion reference and domain reference is chiefly a reaction against a competitive, comparative emphasis in education: an emphasis fostered by NRT.

Measurement experts seem to agree that too much attention has been focused on the apparent differences between norm-referenced and criterion-referenced tests, while too little attention has been given to their similarities, especially the fact that a normative frame of reference is implicit in all testing regardless of the interpretive system used to reference the scores. The construction of criterion-referenced tests requires information about the skills and capabilities of the intended examinees. In addition, normative information of a sort is needed when criterion-referenced mastery tests are used to regulate progress through a curriculum. In the latter instance, questions inevitably arise about the typical, or expected, rate of progress through the sequenced curricular units or content strands (Anastasi, 1982; Thorndike & Hagen, 1977).

The ultimate justification for any test is the use to be made of the results. While at one time a considerable difference of opinion existed between proponents of NRT and CRT, the chasm seems to have been narrowed by the recognition that both types of measures provide useful information. Choice of one or the other depends on the decisions that need to be made by the test user. The NRT is most appropriate for educational and employment selection. As stated earlier, aptitude, interest, and personality assessment are all norm-referenced because an external, comparative frame of reference provides the most useful sort of interpretation. Achievement testing may employ both NRT and CRT. If information is needed, for example, about which curriculum objectives a student has mastered, then CRT will provide the most useful information. If, on the other hand, a survey of pupil achievement in several areas is needed, or if a school district wants to know how its pupils compare with those in other districts, then NRT provides more useful information (Mehrens & Lehmann, 1984). Current elementary achievement batteries, which provide both norm-referenced and criterion-referenced interpretive data, attest to the utility of having both types of information available. Such tests frequently provide standard norm-referenced information for broad content domains such as reading, mathematics, and language (Merrell & Plante, 1997). They also provide information on content objectives, or clusters, and sometimes on the test items.

Benefits of both NRT and CRT come closest to realization when users exercise caution and sound judgment in the selection and interpretation of either type of measure. Since its introduction around 1920, NRT has undergone periodic episodes of both unrestrained use and enthusiasm followed by disenchantment and disillusionment. When introduced in mastery testing in the 1920s, CRT was subsequently abandoned because of its narrow focus and inability to capture the full extent of individual differences. Readers are urged to keep this historical perspective in mind when assessing the merits of NRT and CRT. A balanced view of both types of measurement procedures will undoubtedly yield the most benefits to test users and test takers.

## REFERENCES

Anastasi, A. (1982). *Psychological testing*. New York: Macmillan.

Cronbach, L. J. (1984). *Essentials of psychological testing*. New York: Harper & Row.

Mehrens, W. A., & Lehmann, I. J. (1984). *Measurement and evaluation in education and psychology*. New York: CBS College.

Merrill, A. W., & Plante, E. (1997). Norm-referenced test interpretation in the diagnostic process. *Language, Speech, and Hearing in the Schools, 28*(1), 50–58.

Thorndike, R. L., & Hagen, E. P. (1977). *Measurement and evaluation in psychology and education*. New York: Wiley.

GARY J. ROBERTSON
*American Guidance Service*

CRITERION-REFERENCED TESTING
MEASUREMENT

## NORTHWESTERN SYNTAX SCREENING TEST

The Northwestern Syntax Screening Test, developed by Laura L. Lee, is purported to measure the syntactical language structure of students ages 3 to 8. This instrument was developed as a screening device and was not intended to be used as a measure of a student's overall language skills. It consists of 20 identical linguistic structures that compose the instrument's receptive and expressive portions (Lee, 1979).

The developers suggest that when using the test as a screening device for a kindergarten class, the examiner cease testing when it is determined that the student is at or above the 10 percent level for his or her age group. If the instrument is being used to obtain supplemental information on a student's syntactical language ability, it is suggested that the test be completed. Although the paired sentences are ordered by increasing difficulty, the test is too short to establish basal or ceiling scores (Lee, 1979).

This test has been criticized because of a lack of reliability data. Klein (1980) attempted to establish reliability data, but the time period between test-retest was 7 months. Based on this extended time period and the lack of reliability data, Pearson and Stick (1985) concluded that a need for these data still exists.

In addition, researchers have expressed concern over the lack of validity data. Most researchers reported that this screening instrument has been effective in identifying students with delayed syntactical language abilities, but there have also been reports of false positives (Pearson & Stick, 1985).

Normative data have been criticized based on the limitations of geographic area, economic class, and age intervals of 1 year. Norms were established on 344 students between the ages of 0–3 and 7–11. These students attended nursery or public school, were from middle- or upper-income families in which standard American dialect was spoken, and were judged by their teachers as not having handicapping conditions that would inhibit normal language development (Pearson & Stick, 1985).

Lee acknowledges these criticisms and recommends that the clinician use the instrument for its intended purpose, as a screening device for students speaking standard English. Lee also recommends that clinicians establish their own norms dependent on their local population (Lee, 1979).

## REFERENCES

Klein, A. E. (1980). Test-retest reliability and predictive validity of the Northwestern Syntax Screening Test. *Educational & Psychological Measurement, 40,* 1167–1172.

Lee, L. L. (1979). *Northwestern Syntax Screening Test.* Evanston, IL: Northwestern University Press.

Pearson, M. E., & Stick, S. L. (1985). Review of Northwestern Syntax Screening Test. In J. V. Mitchell, Jr. (Ed.), *The ninth mental measurements yearbook* (pp. 1059–1063). Lincoln: University of Nebraska Press.

ETTA LEE NURICK
*Montgomery County
Intermediate Unit,
Norristown, Pennsylvania*

# NUCLEAR MAGNETIC RESONANCE OR MAGNETIC RESONANCE IMAGING

Nuclear magnetic resonance (NMR) or magnetic resonance imaging (MRI) is a technique for imaging the brain and body parts. This technique is based on the premise that atomic nuclei with odd numbers of either protons or neutrons possess a small magnetic field that is dependent on the spin of these nuclear particles. With the application of a strong external magnetic source, there is a weak torque that is exerted on the nuclei; the nuclear particles orient to the applied magnetic field. During this alignment process, the nuclei oscillate about the magnetic field like a compass needle aligning with Earth's magnetic field. The degree of oscillation is directly related to the strength of the magnetic field. The degree of magnetic field resonance emitted can be detected by measuring the magnetic field changes, which in turn relate to the density of the tissue or structure being examined. At this point, the process becomes similar to computerized axial tomography (CAT scanning) in that a density coding system is used to create the image. In CAT scanning this is based on the number of X-ray particles that pass through tissue. In NMR or MRI the density is dependent on the resonance of atomic nuclear particles to different magnetic fields. The physics of this procedure are outlined in the works by Bottomley (1984) and Pykett, Newhouse, and Buonanno (1982).

The NMR technique provides an image that approximates anatomical appearance of the structure being imaged (see Figure 1). In comparison with CAT scanning, there are

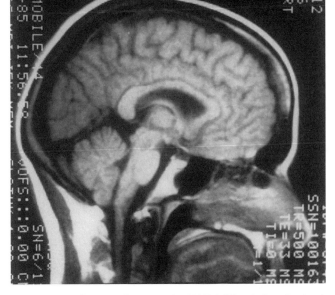

Figure 1 Sagittal section demonstrating NMR-MRI technique in visualizing cerebral structures. The detail obtained with NMR-MRI techniques approaches what would be observed with an actual anatomic specimen.

some major advantages. Since no ionizing radiation is used, there is no hazard from X-ray irradiation. The NMR image better differentiates certain tissue differences, so that in NMR brain sections there is a clearer image between brain and bone and white and gray matter (see Figure 1). The NMR also allows the detection of subtle tissue changes that cannot be detected with CAT scanning, and permits the topographic demonstration of the anatomic changes underlying neurobehavioral syndromes (DeMyer, Hendrie, Gilmor, & DeMyer, 1985; DeWitt, Grek, Buonanno, Levine, & Kistler, 1985). Current drawbacks to NMR include its cost, the fact that clinical studies are lacking, and the inability to scan patients with any type of metallic implants (i.e., pacemakers, artificial joints, aneurysm, clips, etc.) because of the strength of the magnetic field. Recent research has utilized this technology to visualize the development of perceptual and cognitive functioning (Thatcher, Lyon, Reid, Rumsey, & Krasnegor, 1996); to demonstrate the structural changes in psychiatric disorders such as schizophrenia (Potts, Davidson, & Krishnan, 1993); and to investigate higher cortical functions (Shaywitz, Shaywitz, Pugh, & Skudlarski, 1996) and epilepsy (Cascino, 1998).

## REFERENCES

Bottomley, P. A. (1984). NMR in medicine. *Computerized Radiology, 8,* 57–77.

Cascino, G. D. (1998). Neuroimaging in partial epilepsy: Structural magnetic resonance imaging. *Journal of Epilepsy, 11*(3), 121–129.

DeMyer, M. K., Hendrie, H. C., Gilmor, R. L., & DeMyer, W. E. (1985). Magnetic resonance imaging in psychiatry. *Psychiatric Annals, 15,* 262–267.

DeWitt, L. D., Grek, A. J., Buonanno, F. S., Levine, D. N., & Kistler, J. P. (1985). MRI and the study of aphasia. *Neurology, 35,* 861–865.

Potts, N. L. S., Davidson, J. R. T., & Krishnan, K. R. R. (1993). The role of nuclear magnetic resonance imaging in psychiatric research. *Journal of Clinical Psychiatry, 54*(12), 13–18.

Pykett, I. L., Newhouse, J. H., & Buonanno, F. S. (1982). Principles of nuclear magnetic resonance imaging. *Radiology, 143,* 157–163.

Shaywitz, B. A., Shaywitz, S. E., Pugh, K. R., & Skudlarski, P. (1996). Functional magnetic resonance imaging as a tool to understand reading and reading disability. In R. W. Thatcher, G. R. Lyon, J. Rumsey, & N. Krasnegor (Eds.), *Developmental neuroimaging: Mapping the development of brain and behavior* (pp. 157–167). San Diego, CA: Academic Press.

Thatcher, R. W., Lyon, G. R., Rumsey, J., & Krasnegor, N. (Eds.). (1996). *Developmental neuroimaging: Mapping the development of brain and behavior.* San Diego, CA: Academic Press.

ERIN D. BIGLER
*Bringham Young University*

CAT SCAN
DIFFUSION TENSOR IMAGING
X-RAY SCANNING TECHNIQUES

# NUTRITIONAL DISORDERS

See MALNUTRITION; EATING DISORDERS; PICA.

# O

## OBESITY

Obesity refers to excess adiposity or body fat. Adiposity is commonly calculated by the use of a body mass index. This index is a measure of one's weight in kilograms divided by the square of one's height in meters (kg/m$^2$; World Health Organization [WHO], 2005). For children, overweight can be defined as a body mass index greater than the 85th percentile for children of the same age and sex, and obesity can be defined as a body mass index of greater than the 95th percentile for children of the same age and gender (Centers for Disease Control and Prevention, 2005).

Body mass index displays natural fluctuations during childhood. The first critical period of elevated body mass is the prenatal period. Infants with high birth weights appear to have an increased risk of being overweight in childhood. Body mass generally reaches a low point during early childhood and then begins to increase during the period known as adiposity rebound. Adolescence constitutes the third critical period, when the onset of overweight may occur. Overweight in adolescence can increase the risk of obesity in adulthood. Up to 80 percent of overweight adolescents will become obese adults (Dietz 2004).

The prevalence of obesity is increasing at a staggering rate worldwide in both developing and developed countries. In low-income countries, obesity is more prevalent among people of higher socioeconomic status, middle-aged women, and persons residing in urban communities. In more affluent nations, obesity is more prevalent among children, younger adults, and the middle-aged population, especially in persons of lower socioeconomic status in rural settings (WHO Western Pacific Regional Office, 2005).

Childhood obesity is an ongoing epidemic in the United States. Approximately 15 percent of U.S. children, ages 6–11, and 16 percent of U.S. adolescents, ages 12–19, are obese (American Obesity Association, 2000). These numbers have been steadily increasing over the years. The rate of obesity in the United States has more than doubled for preschoolers and adolescents and has more than tripled for children ages 6–11 (Mayo Clinic, 2005).

Obesity in childhood has both fixed and modifiable causes. A fixed cause is genetics. Overweight and obese parents are at greater risk of producing offspring who also become overweight or obese. The modifiable causes include physi-cal activity (e.g., lack of regular exercise), high frequency of sedentary behavior, food preferences, eating habits (e.g., over-consumption of high calorie foods), and environmental factors (e.g., overexposure to advertisements promoting high calorie foods; American Obesity Association, 2002). Children's initial food preferences are biologically driven. They prefer sweets and salts, fear new and unfamiliar foods, and are predisposed to learn to prefer energy-dense foods. Parenting factors may play a role in children's food preferences. It has been demonstrated that children require approximately 10 exposures to accept new foods (Schwartz & Puhl, 2003).

Socioeconomic status influences the risk for obesity for several reasons. People of lower income may have physical and economic barriers to obtaining healthy foods (Cummins, 2002). Children from lower socioeconomic families consume more foods out of the home, consume more processed foods, and have diets that include a greater proportion of snack foods than do children of higher socioeconomic status (British Medical Association, 1999). Families of lower socioeconomic status may not have access to safe facilities for exercise and may not have funds to use these kinds of after-school activities.

Childhood obesity has many health consequences. Obesity in childhood may be predictive of obesity in adulthood. Despite the fact that only 25 to 30 percent of obese adults were also obese during childhood or adolescence, early childhood overweight that is maintained into adulthood is associated with more severe obesity among adults (Deitz, 2004). Children express the same comorbidities with overweight and obesity as adults. The associated medical problems affect various systems in the body, including the cardiovascular system, which results in high cholesterol, high blood pressure, and cardiovascular disease, and the endocrine system, producing insulin resistance, impaired glucose tolerance, type 2 diabetes mellitus, and menstrual irregularity (American Academy of Pediatrics, 2003). Gallbladder disease is another life-threatening condition associated with obesity. Debilitating but nonthreatening associated conditions include respiratory difficulties such as asthma and sleep apnea, chronic musculoskeletal problems, skin problems, and infertility. Elevated body mass index increases the risk for cancer of the breast, colon, prostate, endrometrolum, kidney, and gallbladder. Chronic overweight and obesity also significantly contribute to osteoarthritis, which is a significant cause for disability among adults (WHO, 2005).

Obesity also has social and psychological consequences. Children and adolescents who are overweight and obese are often stigmatized by society and rejected by their peers. This stigmatization may hinder social development, thus producing adverse secondary effects. For example, overweight adolescents are less likely to marry as adults than their average-weight peers, and obese adolescent girls complete less schooling and, as adults, have lower household incomes than cohorts who are not obese (Gortmaker, Must, Perrin, Sobol, Arthur, & Dietz, 1993). Obesity in children is often inversely related to self-esteem and body esteem, and a positive relationship exists between overweight and depression in children and adolescents. Parents may also unknowingly stigmatize their overweight and obese children. They play a critical role in influencing how their children believe they should look, and children can predict parental responses about their body sizes fairly accurately (Schwartz & Puhl, 2003).

Methods for obesity prevention should begin at a young age, in order to avoid the numerous associated health problems in overweight and obese adults. During the prenatal period, mothers should have proper nutrition and should avoid excessive weight gain (Deckelbaum & Williams, 2001). During infancy and early childhood, parents should maintain breastfeeding until at least 6 months of age, avoid the use of added sugars and starches in formulas, accept the child's ability to regulate energy intake, and provide the appropriate nutritional intake to promote optimal linear growth. During childhood and adolescence, parents should endorse an active lifestyle, limit television viewing, encourage the intake of fruits and vegetables, restrict the intake of energy-dense, micronutrient-poor foods (such as packaged snacks), and restrict the intake of sugared soft drinks. Additional preventive measures include ensuring that the school and community environment provide suitable physical activity, increasing opportunities for family interaction (such as family meals), restricting children's exposure to advertisements for energy-dense, micronutrient-poor foods, and supplying the necessary information and abilities to make healthy food choices (WHO, 2003).

The treatment of existing childhood obesity is varied. Obstacles include children's relative intellectual and psychological immaturity compared to adults and their susceptibility to peer pressure. Therefore, many techniques to reduce obesity in children have utilized either family-based or school-based approaches. Family intervention is based on the premise that family functioning, home environment, and parental support are crucial determinants of treatment outcome. School-based approaches have often been oriented toward prevention, targeting all students to avoid stigmatizing obese children (Ebbeling, Pawlak, & Ludwig, 2002).

Other intervention methods for childhood obesity are summer weight-loss camps and behavior modification techniques for families. Participants in summer weight-loss camps have reduced their body mass and have derived benefits in blood pressure, aerobic fitness, and self-esteem (Gately, Cooke, Barth, Bewick, Radley, & Hill, 2005). The four main behavioral strategies are controlling the environment, monitoring behavior, setting goals, and rewarding successful behavioral changes. Modifications to diet and activity level for pediatric patients have included caloric and fat reduction, low carbohydrates, the integration of physical activity into daily lifestyles, participation in controlled and vigorous physical activities, and reduction in sedentary behaviors. Consensus is lacking on the best way to achieve long-term weight control. Therefore, the clinician, child, and family should collaborate to select achievable goals (Dietz & Robinson, 2005).

## REFERENCES

American Academy of Pediatrics. (2003). Prevention of pediatric overweight and obesity. *Pediatrics, 112,* 2, 424–430.

American Obesity Association. (2002). *Childhood obesity.* Retrieved September 12, 2005, from http://obesity.org/subs/childhood/

British Medical Association. (2005). *Preventing childhood obesity.* Retrieved September 10, 2005, from http://www.bma.org.uk/ap .nsf/content/childhoodobesity

British Medical Association. *Growing up in Britain: Ensuring a healthy future for our children.* (1999). London: BMA.

Centers for Disease Control and Prevention. (2005). *BMI for children and teens.* Retrieved September 17, 2005, from http://www .cdc.gov/nccdphp/dnpa/bmi/bmi-for-age.htm

Cummins, S., & Macintyre, S. (2002). Food deserts—Evidence and assumption in health policy making. *British Medical Journal, 325,* 436–438.

Dietz, W. H. (2004). Overweight in childhood and adolescence. *New England Journal of Medicine, 350,* 855–857.

Dietz, W. H., & Robinson, T. N. (2005). Overweight children and adolescents. *New England Journal of Medicine, 352,* 2100–2109.

Ebbeling, C. B., Pawlak, D. B., & Ludwig, D. S. (2002). Childhood obesity: Public-health crisis, common-sense cure. *The Lancet, 360,* 473–482.

Gately, P. J., Cooke, C. B., Barth, J. H., Bewick, B. M., Radley, D., & Hill, A. J. (2005). Children's residential weight-loss programs can work: A prospective cohort study of short-term outcomes for overweight and obese children. *Pediatrics, 11,* 73–77.

Gortmaker, S. L., Must, A., Perrin, J., Sobol, A. M., Arthur, M., & Dietz, W. H. (1993). Social and economic consequences of overweight in childhood and adolescence. *New England Journal of Medicine, 329,* 1008–1012.

Mayo Clinic. (2005). *Childhood obesity: What parents can do.* Retrieved September 15, 2005, from http://www.mayoclinic .com/invoke.cfm?objectid=40439628-A901-4432-A088B7 DA0721BEC7

Schwartz, M. B., & Puhl, R. (2003). Childhood obesity: A societal problem to solve. *Obesity Reviews, 4,* 57–71.

World Health Organization (WHO). (2005). *Obesity and overweight*. Retrieved September 13, 2005, from http://www.who.int/dietphysical activity/media/en/gsfs_obesity.pdf

World Health Organization (WHO), Regional Office for the Western Pacific. (2005). *Obesity*. Retrieved September 13, 2005, from http://www.wpro.who.int/health_topics/obesity/

World Health Organization (WHO) Technical Report Series. (2003). *Diet, nutrition, and the prevention of chronic diseases*. Retrieved September 13, 2005, from http://www.who.int/nut/documents/trs_916.pdf

MARNI R. FINBERG
*University of Florida*

## ANOREXIA NERVOSA
## BULIMIA NERVOSA
## EATING DISORDERS

## OBJECTIVE PERSONALITY TESTS

See PERSONALITY TESTS, OBJECTIVE.

## OBSERVATIONAL LEARNING

Observational learning, the currently preferred term for imitation, is a basic process in the development of normal and abnormal behavior. As Bandura (1986) has said, "Through the years, modeling has always been acknowledged to be one of the most powerful means of transmitting values, attitudes, and patterns of thought and behavior" (p. 47). But that acknowledgment has not been explicit in many theories of learning, and only in recent decades has observational learning itself been extensively studied. The current status of observational learning is due in large part to the pioneering work of two groups of researchers. Miller and Dollard (1941) emphasized the role of imitation in both the acquisition of new behaviors and the facilitation or disinhibition of previously learned behaviors. Bandura (1962) and Bandura and Walters (1963) provided evidence on the way in which imitation influences the development of behavior, the role of imitation in identification, and the extent to which children imitate behavior modeled by others. Observational learning is a basic concept in social learning theory. Further, imitation, particularly delayed imitation, is for Piaget an important aspect of development during the sensorimotor period.

Although behaviorists (Gewirtz, 1971) have attempted to explain imitation on the basis of reinforcement of stimulus-response associations, such an explanation appears unable to easily handle a variety of phenomena, including initial imitation and delayed imitation. Therefore, this entry will generally follow the cognitive model of observational learning proposed by Bandura (1986).

## Types of Modeling Effects

A model can affect an observer's behavior in a variety of ways.

### Acquisition of Novel Responses

Strictly speaking, observational learning refers to the acquisition of novel responses. Indeed, observing a model can result in a child's performing a response that had virtually zero probability before the observation. For example, to evaluate different theories of identificatory learning, Bandura, Ross, and Ross (1963) exposed nursery-school children to adult models who exhibited a number of novel—and bizarre—behaviors such as exclaiming "A stickero" on picking up a sticker picture and "Weto-smacko" on licking it. The children later imitated a number of these behaviors. Further, children exposed to aggressive models tended to imitate the specific aggressive responses displayed.

### Inhibition and Disinhibition

Modeling may also decrease (inhibit) or increase (disinhibit) previously learned responses. In many studies of modeled aggression, subjects emit a variety of aggressive behaviors, not just those modeled, in testing (Steuer, Applefield, & Smith, 1971). Further, the consequences to models of their behavior may influence observers. In one study, children who saw a model punished for aggressive behavior subsequently showed lower aggression than those who saw a model who received no consequences. In that particular study, however, children who saw a model rewarded for aggressive behavior did not show higher aggression (Bandura, 1965). Thus disinhibition may occur when observers see models perform prohibited responses without suffering adverse consequences, and inhibition may occur when observers see models punished for their behavior (Bandura, 1986).

### Response Facilitation

Response, or social, facilitation occurs when models cue particular behaviors. Thus models can activate, channel, or support the behavior of others (Bandura, 1986). A common example is looking up when one sees a group of people looking up.

### Environmental Enhancement

In this case, the model's behavior directs the observer to specific stimuli rather than specific responses. Thus a child watching a group of children eating a particular food may start eating that food instead of another food.

## Arousal Effects

Models who express emotional reactions may arouse those emotions in observers. In some studies of modeling of aggressive behavior, the observers not only showed more aggressive behavior, but appeared to be experiencing a heightened state of aggression.

## Processes in Observational Learning

In Bandura's (1986) social cognitive analysis of observational learning, modeling is presumed to operate mainly by providing information. Bandura (1986) proposes a four-component model to account for observational learning. Because these processes become more sophisticated with age, observational learning shows important developmental trends. The processes may be briefly summarized:

### Attentional Processes

In order to learn, one must attend to the modeled activities. Given the variety of models and other stimuli generally available, a child will selectively attend to relatively few. Observer factors that influence attention include perceptual capabilities and arousal level. Characteristics of the modeled activity such as conspicuousness and functional value also influence attention. Model characteristics and past experiences of the observer with the model are additional factors.

### Retention

For delayed imitation to occur, the observer must be able to remember the modeled activity. Retention entails symbolic transformation into images and words. As with verbal material, transformation into meaningful terms and elaborated rehearsal facilitate retention of observed activities. Bandura (1986) stresses the importance of immediate and intermittent actual and cognitive rehearsal of observed activities.

### Production Processes

Bandura (1986) suggests that "most modeled activities are abstractly represented as conceptions and rules of action which specify what to do" (p. 63). To produce the activity, responses must be organized in accordance with those conceptions and rules. A variety of evidence using verbal reports and recognition tests indicate that both children and adults can learn modeled activities without actually having performed them. Motor deficits may limit accurate imitation, and improvement may result from improvement in motor skills. Feedback is important in improving such skills. In complex motor skills such as those involved in playing a musical instrument, corrective modeling may be the most valuable. In corrective feedback, a skilled individual models the activity correctly; students then attempt to match it.

### Motivational Processes

Behavior may be acquired through observational learning but not performed in the absence of appropriate incentive. Direct, vicarious, and self-produced rewards are all important in the actual production of learned responses, as is the observer's own motivation.

## Reducing Children's Fears

Exposure to a fearless model is an effective way of reducing severe fears and anxiety in both children and adults. The general procedure involves having the anxious or fearful person observe a model (sometimes multiple models) coping with a situation that arouses anxiety in the observer. After several such observations, reduction in fear or anxiety frequently occurs.

To consider one classic example, Bandura, Grusec, and Menlove (1967) randomly assigned nursery-school children who were severely afraid of dogs to watch one of several films. Two treatment films showed a 4 year old coming into increasingly close contact with a dog. Across eight brief sessions, the child went from initially standing near the dog while it was in a pen to finally being in the pen playing with the dog. The two films differed only in that one was conducted in a party atmosphere and the other in a neutral atmosphere. Control groups watched films that showed the dog and the party, but no model, in order to control for effects of mere exposure to the feared object or a playful setting. In a series of graded tests, the children were asked to approach and pet a novel dog and even to climb into a pen and remain alone with a dog. Children who had watched either treatment film showed less fear of and more interaction with the dogs in testing relative both to pretest scores and the control groups. Follow-up tests showed that the reduction in fear lasted at least 1 month.

Modeling techniques, using live, filmed, or even cognitive (imagined) models, have been used to reduce fears of a variety of settings, including the dentist's office and the hospital (Bandura, 1986).

Modeled information can be acquired and retained without being immediately performed in the absence of appropriate incentives. For example, Bandura (1965) had groups of children watch a film in which a model displayed a high level of aggressive behavior toward another character. Different groups of children saw different endings to the film; the model was rewarded, punished, or suffered no consequences for aggressive behavior. In immediate testing, children who saw the model punished showed much less aggressive behavior; girls were less aggressive than boys. However, when offered reinforcement for producing the modeled aggressive behavior, both boys and girls who saw all films reproduced a large number of the modeled behaviors. Thus, consequences to a model influence performance of modeled behaviors much more than learning of the behaviors.

Different models induce different degrees of imitation. Two factors that consistently appear as important in both experimental (Bandura, Ross, & Ross, 1963) and correlational (Hetherington & Frankie, 1967) research are power and warmth. Models are particularly likely to be imitated if they behave in an authoritative way, exerting control but showing care and concern.

An observer who is reinforced for imitating some modeled responses will also imitate other responses of the same model; this is important for the application of modeling techniques (Baer & Sherman, 1964). Thus a child who does not initially show high levels of imitation may be conditioned by appropriate reinforcement techniques to imitate in general.

Imitation begins to develop in infancy and becomes more exact during early childhood, with imitation of some responses developing earlier than others. For example, imitation of simple motor and social behaviors increases regularly from 12 to 24 months, whereas imitation of more complicated sequences may begin to occur only at 24 months or later (McCall, Parke, & Kavanaugh, 1977). Motor tasks not only use observation of the model, but self-observation as well (Ferrari, 1996).

Although most theories suggest that infants should not begin to imitate until several months of age, Meltzoff and Moore (1977) have reported that 12- to 20-day-old infants imitate simple facial expressions such as sticking out the tongue and gaping. Some subsequent studies failed to find any evidence for newborn imitation (McKenzie & Over, 1982), while others reported imitation in even younger infants (Field et al., 1982), leaving the phenomenon in considerable doubt.

Television has a variety of effects on children. Considerable experimental and correlational evidence indicates that televised violence increases the aggressive behavior of some children, particularly boys and those who were already aggressive. On the other hand, viewing of programs such as "Mr. Rogers' Neighborhood" increases prosocial behavior. The research literature is voluminous (Liebert, Sprakin, & Davidson, 1982).

A common recommendation to parents and teachers is to avoid using physical punishment with children because the punisher is providing a model of aggressive behavior that may be imitated by the child. Laboratory research (Gelfand et al., 1974) supports this recommendation. Young children imitate both punitive and reward control techniques, and the imitation persists over time.

Most children do imitate; others can be trained to imitate. Formal observational learning and reinforcement programs can be used to increase a variety of prosocial behaviors and to decrease antisocial or maladaptive ones. Additionally, children will imitate under informal circumstances.

Teachers should remember that they generally have the characteristics that further imitation. If their behaviors are discrepant with their words, children are likely to follow the behaviors. "Do as I say and not as I do" is not likely to be successful. Finally, all who work with children would do well to remember that power and warmth, not power alone, are important characteristics of successful models.

## REFERENCES

Baer, D. M., & Sherman, J. A. (1964). Reinforcement control of generalized imitation in young children. *Journal of Experimental Child Psychology, 1,* 37–49.

Bandura, A. (1962). Social learning through imitation. In M. R. Jones (Ed.), *Nebraska symposium on motivation* (Vol. 10, pp. 211–274). Lincoln: University of Nebraska Press.

Bandura, A., & Walters, R. H. (1963). *Social Learning and Personality Development.* New York: Holt, Rinehart, & Winston.

Bandura, A. (1965). Influence of models' reinforcement contingencies on the acquisition of imitative responses. *Journal of Personality & Social Psychology, 1,* 589–595.

Bandura, A. (1986). *Social foundations of thought and action: A social cognitive theory.* Englewood Cliffs, NJ: Prentice Hall.

Bandura, A., Grusec, J. E., & Menlove, F. L. (1967). Vicarious extinction of avoidance behavior. *Journal of Personality & Social Psychology, 5,* 16–23.

Bandura, A., Ross, D., & Ross, S. A. (1963). A comparative test of the status envy, social power, and secondary reinforcement theories of identificatory learning. *Journal of Abnormal & Social Psychology, 67,* 527–534.

Ferrari, M. (1996). Observing the observer: Self-regulation in the observational learning of motor skills. *Developmental Review, 16*(2), 203–240.

Field, T. M., Goodson, R., Greenberg, R., & Cohen, D. (1982). Discrimination and imitation of facial expressions by neonates. *Science, 28,* 179–181.

Gelfano, D. M., Hartmann, D. P., Lamb, A. K., Smith, C. L., Mahan, M. A., & Paul, S. C. (1974). The effects of adult models and described alternatives on children's choice of behavior management techniques. *Child Development, 45,* 585–593.

Gewirtz, J. L. (1971). Conditioned responding as a paradigm for observational, imitative learning and vicarious reinforcement. In H. W. Reese (Ed.), *Advances in child development and behavior* (Vol. 6, pp. 273–304). New York: Academic.

Hetherington, E. M., & Frankie, G. (1967). Effects of parental dominance, warmth, and conflict on imitation in children. *Journal of Personality & Social Psychology, 6,* 119–125.

Liebert, R. M., Sprakin, J. N., & Davidson, E. S. (1982). *The early window: Effects of television on children and youth* (2nd ed.). Elmsford, NY: Pergamon.

McCall, R. B., Parke, R. D., & Kavanaugh, R. D. (1977). Imitation of live and televised models by children one to three years of age. *Monographs of the Society for Research in Child Development, 42*(5, Serial No. 173).

McKenzie, B., & Over, R. (1982). Young infants fail to imitate facial and manual gestures. *Infant Behavior & Development, 6,* 85–95.

Meltzoff, A., & Moore, M. K. (1977). Imitation of facile and manual gestures by human neonates. *Science, 198,* 75–78.

Miller, N. E., & Dollard, J. (1941). *Social learning and imitation.* New Haven, CT: Yale University Press.

Steuer, F. B., Applefield, J. M., & Smith, R. (1971). Televised aggression and the interpersonal aggression of preschool children. *Journal of Experimental Child Psychology, 11,* 442–447.

ROBERT T. BROWN
*University of North Carolina at Wilmington*

BEHAVIOR MODELING
LEARNING STYLES
PHOBIAS AND FEARS
SOCIAL LEARNING THEORY
THEORY OF ACTIVITY

## OBSESSIVE COMPULSIVE DISORDERS

Obsession is defined by the American Psychiatric Association (1994) as, "A persistent, unwanted idea or impulse that cannot be eliminated by logic or reasoning" (p. 98). A compulsion is, "An insistent, repetitive, intrusive, and unwanted urge to perform an act that is contrary to one's ordinary wishes or standards. . . . Failure to perform the compulsive act leads to overt anxiety. Compulsions are obsessions that are still felt as impulses" (American Psychiatric Association, 1994, p. 20). In addition to the major attributes of obsession and compulsion, a number of additional responses are often present. Yaryura-Tobias and Nezirogly (1983) report that individuals who exhibit obsessive compulsive responses are also likely to be depressed (94 percent), anxious (90 percent), aggressive (65 percent), and dysperceptive (60 percent). Though occurring less frequently, individuals with obsessive compulsive disorders may also have sleep disorders (49 percent), family disturbances (45 percent), sexual dysfunctions (34 percent), or appetite disorders (33 percent); they may also be self-abusive (16 percent). Obsessive-compulsive disorder has been linked to pediatric autoimmune neuropsychiatric disorders related to rheumatic fever (Swedo, Leonard, Mittleman, & Allen, 1997).

The disorder has an extensive history in the psychological literature, with reports of obsessive compulsive behavior even appearing in ancient writings (Yaryura-Tobias & Nezirogly, 1983). It has also produced a substantial body of applied treatment research as illustrated in a review by Foa and Steketee (1980). Despite substantial professional interest, the incidence of obsessive-compulsive disorders is relatively low. Beech and Vaughan (1978) report that the incidence in psychiatric patient populations is between 0.1 and 4 percent. Among the general population, an incidence of approximately .05 percent has been reported (Black, 1974).

Although there is some disagreement, many authorities believe that individuals are constitutionally predisposed to developing obsessive compulsive behavior and that life events eventually trigger the responses (Vila & Beech, 1978). Supporting this view is an increased rate of occurrence among relatives of people with obsessional disorder (Kringlen, 1965). Also, onset of the disorder typically occurs in association with difficult events occurring in the teens or early twenties (Lo, 1967).

Obsessive compulsive reactions have been described as conforming to four major courses: progressive deterioration, variable severity but never symptom free, phasic with remissions, and constant. Regardless of the course, the disorder is typically considered to be serious and the prognosis for a majority of affected persons is poor (Kringlen, 1965). Common treatments have included psychotherapy, behavior therapy, pharmacological intervention, vitamin and diet therapy, and psychosurgery (Grados, Labuda, Riddle, & Walkup, 1997). Each approach has been demonstrated to be variably effective, and is more likely to be prescribed based on the orientation of the therapist rather than the clinical features of the individual.

### REFERENCES

American Psychiatric Association. (1994). *A psychiatric glossary* (5th ed.). New York: Author.

Beech, H. R., & Vaughan, M. (1978). *Behavioral treatment of obsessional states.* New York: Wiley.

Black, A. (1974). The natural history of obsessional neurosis. In H. R. Beech (Ed.), *Obsessional states* (pp. 19–54). London: Methuen.

Foa, E. B., & Steketee, G. S. (1980). Obsessive compulsives: Conceptual issues and treatment interventions. In M. Hersen, R. M. Eisler, & P. M. Miller (Eds.), *Progress in behavior modification* (Vol. 8). New York: Academic.

Grados, M. A., Labuda, M. C., Riddle, M. A., & Walkup, J. T. (1997). Obsessive-compulsive disorder in children and adolescents. *International Review of Psychiatry, 9*(1), 83–98.

Kringlen, E. (1965). Obsessional neurotics. *British Journal of Psychiatry, 11,* 709–722.

Lo, W. H. (1967). A follow-up study of obsessional neurotics in Hong Kong Chinese. *British Journal of Psychiatry, 113,* 823–832.

Swedo, S. E., Leonard, H. L., Mittleman, B. B., & Allen, A. J. (1997). Identification of children with pediatric autoimmune neuropsychiatric disorders associated with streptococcal infections by a marker associated with rheumatic fever. *American Journal of Psychiatry, 154*(1), 110–112.

Vila, J., Beech, H. R. (1978). Vulnerability and defensive reactions in relation to the human menstrual cycle. *British Journal of Social & Clinical Psychology, 16,* 69–75.

Yaryura-Tobias, J. A., & Nezirogly, F. A. (1983). *Obsessive-compulsive disorders.* New York: Marcel Dekker.

PATRICK J. SCHLOSS
*Pennsylvania State University*

**EMOTIONAL DISORDERS**
**MENTAL ILLNESS**

## OCCUPATIONAL THERAPY

Occupational therapy is the art and science of directing man's participation in selected tasks to restore, reinforce, and enhance performance, facilitate learning those skills and functions essential for adaptation and productivity, diminish or correct pathology, and to promote and maintain health. (Council on Standards, 1972, pp. 204–205)

The primary concern of occupational therapy is response to activity. Special activities rather than exercise are used to increase function. These activities are purposeful and often medically prescribed. They may include manual, creative, or industrial arts. Occupational therapy activities are often part of the treatment plans for persons with physical, mental, and/or psychiatric disorders or disabilities. Although functional activity is the primary goal, the occupational therapist is equally concerned with the social, psychological, and communicative development of the patient.

In the early years, occupational therapy was primarily a service-oriented field with practice occurring mainly in hospitals and rehabilitation facilities. Today, occupational therapists have added research and the investigation and perfection of improved treatment methodology to their professional obligations. The field has broadened dramatically. Occupational therapists are members of multidisciplinary teams wherever their services are needed, as consultants, supervisors, or direct-service givers.

Along with the implementation of PL 94-142 came the critical need for occupational therapists in public school settings. Here they became involved in direct services (e.g., screening, referral, evaluation, program planning and implementation, reevaluation, and formulation of individual education plans) and indirect services (e.g., administration and management and consultation; American Occupational Therapy Association, 1980). This service continues today under IDEA (American Occupational Therapy Association, 1997). Many services that are critical to the development of severely disabled children are provided by occupational therapists. The most important of these include the improvement of sensory integration, handling, and positioning. In many instances, it is necessary for the occupational therapist to adapt equipment for individuals. It is not uncommon for the occupational therapist to work with the physical therapist to provide services.

Increasing patients' daily living is another area for which occupational therapists assume responsibility. Patients may be physically disabled or developmentally delayed, young or old. Occupational therapists also may work with speech and language pathologists to develop strategies for improving oral motor functioning, thereby improving feeding and eating skills.

In 1984 W. L. West reaffirmed the philosophy and practice of occupational therapy today. A few of the important points follow:

Activity is the essence of living and is significantly interrelated with high morale.

To some degree, life itself is seen as purposeful occupation.

It is the purposefulness of behavior and activity that gives human life order.

Occupational therapy's body of knowledge lies in human behavior and activity as well as in the effect of pathology on behavior and the effect of activity on pathology (p. 16).

These statements reiterate the importance of functionality within the field of occupational therapy. The occupational therapist's task is to help each individual served achieve the fullest potential for a productive, satisfying, and self-sufficient life.

Two levels of assistants are available to work under the supervision of a registered occupational therapist: the certified occupational therapy assistant (COTA) and the occupational therapy aide (OTA).

### REFERENCES

American Occupational Therapy Association. (1980). Standards of practice for occupational therapists in schools. *American Journal of Occupational Therapy, 34,* 900–905.

American Occupational Therapy Association. (1997). *Occupational therapy services for children and youth under the Individuals with Disabilities Education Act (IDEA).* Bethesda, MD: Author.

Council on Standards, American Occupational Therapy Association. (1972). Occupational therapy: Its definition and functions. *American Journal of Occupational Therapy, 26,* 204–205.

West, W. L. (1984). A reaffirmed philosophy and practice of occupational therapy for the 1980s. *American Journal of Occupational Therapy, 38,* 15–24.

ANNE CAMPBELL
*Purdue University*

**CAREER EDUCATION FOR STUDENTS RECEIVING SPECIAL**
  **EDUCATION SERVICES**
**PHYSICAL THERAPY**
**REHABILITATION**

## OFFICE OF RARE DISEASES

The Office of Rare Diseases (ORD) is under the supervision of the National Institutes of Health. ORD offers information on more than 6,000 rare diseases, including research, publications, research resources, genetics information, patient support groups, reports on progress in research studies, and news and events. ORD has an extensive web site on the Internet that allows easy access to both the information that ORD disseminates and ORD itself. ORD can be reached at Office of Rare Diseases, National Institutes of Health, 31 Center Drive, MSC 2082, Room 1B03, Bethesda, MD, 20892-2082; telephone: 301-402-4336; fax: 301-402-0420; e-mail: sg18b@nih.gov; URL: http://rarediseases.info.nih.gov/ord.

STAFF

## OFFICE OF SPECIAL EDUCATION AND REHABILITATIVE SERVICES

The Office of Special Education and Rehabilitative Services (OSERS) supports programs that assist in educating children with special needs, provides for the rehabilitation of youth and adults with disabilities, and supports research to improve the lives of individuals with disabilities. To carry out these functions, OSERS consists of three program-related components:

- the Office of Special Education Programs (OSEP);
- the Rehabilitation Services Administration (RSA); and
- the National Institute on Disability and Rehabilitation Research (NIDRR).

The Office of Special Education Programs (OSEP) has primary responsibility for administering programs and projects relating to the free, appropriate public education of all children, youth, and adults with disabilities, from birth through age 21. The bulk of special education funds is administered by OSEP's Division of Assistance to States, which provides grants to states and territories to assist them in providing a free, appropriate public education to all children with disabilities. The early intervention and preschool grant programs provide grants to each state for children with disabilities, ages birth through five.

The Rehabilitation Services Administration (RSA) oversees programs that help individuals with physical or mental disabilities to obtain employment through the provision of such supports as counseling, medical and psychological services, job training, and other individualized services. RSA's major formula grant program provides funds to state vocational rehabilitation agencies to provide employment-related services for individuals with disabilities, giving priority to individuals who are severely disabled.

OSERS' third component, the National Institute on

Disability and Rehabilitation Research (NIDRR) provides leadership and support for a comprehensive program of research related to the rehabilitation of individuals with disabilities.

All of the programmatic efforts are aimed at improving the lives of individuals with disabilities from birth through adulthood. The Office of Special Education and Rehabilitation Services maintains an extensive web site at http://www.ed.gov/offices/OSERS/.

STAFF

## SPECIAL EDUCATION PROGRAMS

## OLYMPICS, SPECIAL

The Special Olympics is the world's largest training and sports competition for the mentally retarded (Cipriano, 1980). Since its inception in 1968, over 2 million participants and volunteers have been involved in its local, regional, national, and international programs.

The development of the Special Olympics can be traced to the establishment of the Joseph P. Kennedy, Jr., Foundation in 1946. The foundation's goal was "to seek the prevention of mental retardation by identifying its causes and to improve the means by which society deals with its citizens who are mentally retarded" (Fact Sheet). The foundation subsequently sought to develop programs that foster public awareness of mental retardation; the Special Olympics is one of these programs.

The goal of the Special Olympics is to train its participants to compete in individual and team sports. The Olympics emphasizes sportsmanship, skill development, cooperation through teamwork, working toward achieving athletic goals, competing for self-fulfillment. As is the case in the other Olympic Games, the importance of the Special Olympics lies in the training and preparation of individuals to compete, not in the games themselves. The games are intended to demonstrate the results of training progress (Henroid, 1979).

The first International Special Olympics was held in Chicago in 1968. There were 1000 competitors from 20 states and Canada on that occasion. By 1985 every state and 33 countries had organized Special Olympics training and competition programs. In the United States, over one million persons with mental retardation participate each year in local and state training and competition efforts in over 20,000 communities.

The International Special Olympic Games are held every 4 years. There are 16 different sports conducted during the summer and winter phases of the games. These include track and field, pentathlon, frisbee, swimming, diving, bowling, floor hockey, poly hockey, volleyball, team basketball, cheerleading, run-dribble and shoot, cross-country, soccer, equestrian, race walking, figure skating, alpine skiing, Nordic skiing, and snowshoeing.

A significant feature of the Special Olympics program is the large (now over 450,000 in number) volunteer force that organizes and administers the training and conditioning programs from local to international levels. The volunteers' tasks include fundraising at the local and regional levels, transportation, and administrating local training clubs, as well as coaching and conducting competitions. Special Olympics volunteers come from schools, colleges, churches, social groups, and civil organizations such as the Rotary Club. They also come from the National Basketball and National Hockey professional sports leagues.

The International Special Olympic Games are fully sponsored by the Joseph P. Kennedy, Jr., Foundation. Local and regional programs and competitions preparing participants for the Special Olympics are funded through fund-raising efforts by the volunteer force. Contributions are secured from individual, group, and sources. The funds so raised are administered by a professional staff at regional and state Special Olympics offices.

State Special Olympics organizations conduct Special Olympics training schools in 16 sports. They use volunteer coaches that are certified by the training schools to coach mentally retarded participants. A participant must belong to a local training club for a specified period of time and be trained by the certified coaches.

An evaluation conducted by Orelove, Wahman, and Wood (1982) indicates the following advantages derived from participation in the Special Olympics program: development of sports skills; participation in activities endorsed and supported by society; a high degree of parental involvement and relationships with school and community groups; and the opportunity for mentally retarded persons to engage in age-, sex-, and ability-related competition. Nevertheless, Orelove, Wahman, and Wood (1982) state that the Special Olympics program does not espouse the principle of normalization. The program is only for individuals with disabilities. In contrast, proponents of normalization advise that athletic competition should be integrated so as to include both disabled and nondisabled persons. They also advise that the Special Olympics be expanded to include recreational activities and to minimize the overemphasis on competition and athletic training (Orelove, Wahman, & Wood, 1982). Studies in the 1990s have suggested that long-term participation in the Special Olympics improves social competence and helps individuals with mental retardation deal with their own lives in terms of teamwork and cooperation (Munson, 1997).

**REFERENCES**

Cipriano, R. (1980). *Readings in Special Olympics*. Guilford, CT: Special Learning Corporation.

Fact sheet. (Undated). Washington DC: Joseph P. Kennedy, Jr., Foundation.

Henroid, L. (1979). *Special Olympics and Paraolympics*. New York: Watts.

Munson, D. (1997). The current research efforts of Special Olympics International. (ERIC Clearinghouse No. RCO20999)

Orelove, F., Wahman, T., & Wood, J. (1982). An evaluative review of Special Olympics: Implications for community recreation. *Education & Training for the Mentally Retarded, 17*(5), 325–329.

THOMAS R. BURKE
*Hunter College, City University
of New York*

**EQUINE THERAPY
RECREATION FOR INDIVIDUALS WITH DISABILITIES
THERAPEUTIC RECREATION**

## ONLINE SPECIAL EDUCATION

Technological innovations are transforming the face of education, and simultaneously, special education. With the advent of online public education, and its rapid growth in recent years, it is not surprising that special education has found its place in cyberspace learning. Although online special education is not for everyone, it is successful for many students with special needs.

An example of one particular online program is Branson School Online (BSO), from Branson, Colorado. This virtual school was founded in 2001, and the evolution of special education services within the online school environment has been dramatic. The extant service delivery model at BSO is generally full inclusion, with special education playing a consultative role. The regular education teachers work to meet the goals of the individualized educational plan (IEP), while collaboratively providing the necessary modifications and accommodations to the curriculum to meet students' needs. The special education staff works primarily with regular education teachers to ensure that the IEP is being followed. Branson collaborates with other school districts to provide direct services for those students for whom that support is essential. (e.g., speech therapy, occupational therapy). Additionally, the virtual school utilizes several online programs to assist students with moderate educational accommodations and modifications.

Since staff and students in an online program are spread throughout the state, IEP meetings at BSO are conducted via conference call. State rules and regulations are closely followed and state IEP documents are used. Appropriate Branson staff, direct service staff, and staff from the student's district of residence are invited and attend the IEP meetings, along with parents and the student (when appropriate). In order to meet family needs and ensure confidentiality, parents are given a choice of avenues for receiving the IEP and related documents, such as by e-mail, postal mail, and fax.

Students with IEP's benefit from the individualization cyberlearning offers. For example, a student in tenth grade who reads at a fourth grade level can access age-appropriate textbooks and novels, read aloud to the student by audio-enabled reading programs on the computer. Other online resources provide larger print, voice recognition typing, and even "blackboard" sessions live with a teacher for direct instruction. At BSO, curriculum is aligned to state standards. It is designed by staff or purchased through a myriad of online programs and publishers. This allows for more remedial curriculum and individualization of lessons.

Close communication with the teacher is a hallmark of online special education services. At BSO, teachers regularly communicate with students by e-mail and telephone. Instant messaging is also a great communication tool for students. They can engage in live chat sessions (e.g., Instant Messenger) with their teacher(s) when they need help with an assignment, and often receive immediate one-on-one assistance. Although they are not in a traditional classroom, online students are not isolated. Teachers can conduct group lessons through interactive, virtual whiteboard sessions with several students at once via the students' computers and a conference call. The advances of technological innovations are so rapid that those mentioned here may likely be outdated by the time this article goes to print!

Parental involvement is essential in an online school environment. Although each child is assigned highly qualified teachers, parent involvement is pertinent. This proves to be even more essential for a student with special needs. Parents are responsible for providing a school environment in the home that can be specifically tailored to their child's level of educational support, whether the needs are physical, emotional, or academic. Parents are also key to helping their child stay organized and assuring that assignments are completed. The parent is often a teacher's best line of communication, especially for young elementary children. Many parents report not realizing the true depth of their child's specific disability and academic needs until they have had the opportunity to watch and assist them with their classes. Stronger bonds are often forged through this opportunity. Parental involvement is the linchpin to success with online schooling.

In summary, online special education provides tremendous individualized educational support that opens up a myriad of new doors and opportunities for many students with special needs. The collaboration between regular education teachers, special education staff, and parents is integral to the academic success of students with IEPs in an online environment. The advances of technology are continuously augmenting instruction and educational tools to assist students' academic growth. In the future, online special education services are anticipated to continue evolving at a pace commensurate with that of technology.

Kathryn A. Sullivan
Shannon Atwater
*Branson School Online*

# OPERANT CONDITIONING

As conceived by Skinner (1938), operant conditioning is essentially learning in which behavior is affected by its consequences, as in the simple paradigm for positive reinforcement:

$$R \to S^R$$

A contingency exists such that reinforcement ($S^R$) occurs only if a particular response ($R$) has occurred. The contingent relationship between response and reinforcement is one of the factors that most differentiates operant from Pavlovian conditioning. The response becomes more frequent (increases in probability) when followed by a reinforcing stimulus. The paradigm is clearly related to Thorndike's (1911) Law of Effect, which says, in essence, that responses followed by satisfying consequences become more firmly connected to the situation. The classic example of operant conditioning is a rat in an operant chamber containing a lever. If the rat is deprived of food, presses the lever, and is reinforced with food, then lever presses increase. If the response is reinforced only in the presence of a specific stimulus, $S^D$ or discriminative stimulus, then the paradigm becomes:

$$S^D \to R \to S^R$$

For example, the rat may be reinforced ($S^R$) for bar pressing ($R$) only when a light ($S^D$) is on.

Skinner has proposed that the main task of psychology should be the functional analysis of behavior. That is, psychologists should determine of what antecedents and consequences behavior is a function. This approach has led to a model of behavior widely used by those who apply the operant approach to human behavior:

$$A \to B \to C$$

(Antecedents) (Behavior) (Consequences)

Operant conditioning is an important factor in the development of a wide variety of children's social and play behavior and also is important in the development of self-esteem and self-control (Bijou & Baer, 1967). Skinner has applied operant concepts to an understanding of everyday life (1953) and the development of a utopian society (1948).

## Basic Aspects

The basics of operant conditioning can be briefly described.

**Acquisition.** As more responses are followed by reinforcement and response strength increases up to some maximum.

**Extinction Occurs.** If the response is no longer followed by reinforcement, its probability decreases, and it occurs less often.

**Spontaneous Recovery.** When put in the situation some time after extinction, the organism responds again, but at a lower rate.

**Generalization and Discrimination.** When responses are conditioned to occur to one discriminative stimulus, the child or animal will respond to similar stimuli; but if explicitly nonreinforced for responding to a second stimulus, the organism generally will learn to respond only to the first.

**Punishment.** A response will become less likely if followed by either presentation of an aversive stimulus (positive punishment) or removal of a desired stimulus (negative punishment). Because punishment, particularly positive punishment, may have a variety of undesirable consequences, operant psychologists generally recommend other means of behavioral control.

## Important Issues and Concepts

**Nature of the Operant.** Although we frequently talk about responses, Skinner's (1988) concept of the operant emphasizes a specified outcome rather than an actual response in terms of specific muscle movements. Thus if a child is reinforced for pushing a panel, panel-pushing is the operant. It does not matter whether the child presses with his or her left or right hand, left or right foot, or even the nose. The effects of behavior rather than the structure of the response itself are stressed.

**Timing of Reinforcement and Punishment.** Generally, reinforcing and punishing stimuli affect performance most if presented as soon as possible after the specified response. A reinforcing stimulus reinforces whatever response it immediately follows, such that a response that occurs between the target response and the reinforcement will be most reinforced. Punishment is actually most effective if delivered as the child just begins to make the undesirable response (Aronfreed, 1968).

In older children, time between response and reinforcement or punishment can be bridged by verbal mediators. At the time reinforcement or punishment is presented, words are used to reinstate the original situation where the child's behavior occurred. Aronfreed (1968) has demonstrated that such mediators increase the effectiveness of delayed punishment in inhibiting children's undesirable behavior.

**Schedules of Reinforcement.** Responses can be reinforced only intermittently rather then continuously (e.g., after every fourth response rather than after every response). One of Skinner's most important discoveries was that these partially reinforced responses are far more resistant to extinction than are 100 percent reinforced responses. Thus intermittent and unsystematic reinforcement increases the persistence of behavior. More detail on schedules and partial reinforcement can be found in most introductory or child psychology texts.

**Primary vs. Conditioned (Secondary) Reinforcers.** Primary reinforcers are stimuli that are intrinsically reinforcing such as food, water, and some kinds of tactile stimulation. Conditioned reinforcers are those stimuli that have acquired reinforcing power by being paired with another reinforcer. Thus money, grades, praise, and recognition are conditioned reinforcers. Conditioned reinforcers such as money can be very powerful because they are generalized reinforcers—they can be used to obtain a variety of other reinforcers.

**Reinforcement History and Hierarchy.** Different stimuli are reinforcing for different children and adults, making universal reinforcements hard to identify. Children will, partly as a result of their own histories, have different hierarchies of preferred reinforcers, although some items such as bubble gum are highly preferred by many young children. Further, reinforcement hierarchy generally changes with age: young children prefer tangible rewards, older children prefer social approval, and still older children prefer the intrinsic reinforcement from being correct (Witryol, 1971). However, tangible rewards may be more important for older low socioeconomic status children and for retarded children (Zigler, 1984), indicating that individual reinforcement hierarchies need to be considered in working with children.

Idiosyncrasies in reinforcer value led Premack (1965) to formulate a heuristic principle: preferred activities may be used to reinforce nonpreferred activities.

**Positive and Negative Reinforcement.** Reinforcement, by definition, increases behavior. Positive reinforcement occurs when a response is followed by presentation of a preferred event; negative reinforcement occurs when a response is followed by termination of an aversive event.

**Shaping.** Occasionally, a desired response may not be in the child's behavioral repertoire, in which case no response occurs that can be reinforced. In such cases, operant psychologists use shaping, or the method of successive approximations, to reinforce behaviors that increasingly resemble the target response. For example, Harris, Wolf, and Baer (1964) observed that a young boy spent virtually all of his time playing alone. Concerned about the child's subsequent social development, they established a target behavior of interactive play with other children and instructed the boy's preschool teacher to reinforce, with attention and approval, successive approximations to interactive play. The teacher ignored the boy when he played alone, but reinforced him initially when he just looked at other children playing, then when he began to move toward other children, and finally only when he interacted with other children. In a limited number of sessions, interactive play was successfully shaped.

## Implications for Educators

Educators and others working with children should be sensitive to the effects of their behavior on children with whom they interact. Their behavior will frequently reinforce or punish children, sometimes inadvertently. Further, the child's perception determines whether a given event is rewarding or punishing. Using a common example, a teacher who yells at a misbehaving child views the yelling as a punisher, but to the child the attention may be reinforcing. On the other hand, to a very shy child, public recognition may be punishing. Of concern also is the possibility that adults will intermittently reinforce a child's undesirable response, therefore increasing its persistence and resistance to extinction.

In dealing with handicapped, particularly retarded, children, we need to consider that more tangible reinforcers and praise may be required to maintain performance than is the case with normal children.

### REFERENCES

Aronfreed, J. (1968). Aversive control of socialization. In W. J. Arnold (Ed.), *Nebraska symposium on motivation* (pp. 271–320). Lincoln: University of Nebraska Press.

Bijou, S. W., & Baer, D. M. (Eds.). (1967). *Child development: Readings in experimental analysis.* New York: Appleton-Century-Crofts.

Bijou, S. W., & Baer, D. M. (1978). *Behavior analysis of child development.* Englewood-Cliffs, NJ: Prentice Hall.

Harris, F. R., Wolf, M. M., & Baer, D. M. (1964). Effects of adult social reinforcement on child behavior. *Young Children, 20,* 8–17.

Premack, D. (1965). Reinforcement theory. In D. Levine (Ed.), *Nebraska symposium on motivation* (pp. 123–180). Lincoln: University of Nebraska Press.

Skinner, B. F. (1938). *The behavior of organisms: An experimental analysis.* New York: Appleton-Century-Crofts.

Skinner, B. F. (1948). *Walden two.* New York: Macmillan.

Skinner, B. F. (1953). *Science and human behavior.* New York: Macmillan.

Thorndike, A. E. L. (1911). *Animal intelligence.* New York: Macmillan.

Witryol, S. I. (1971). Incentives and learning in children. In H. W. Reese (Ed.), *Advances in child development and behavior* (Vol. 6). New York: Academic.

Zigler, E. (1984). A developmental theory on mental retardation. In B. Blatt & R. J. Morris (Eds.), *Perspectives in special education: Personal orientations* (pp. 173–209). Glenview, IL: Scott, Foresman.

ROBERT T. BROWN
*University of North Carolina at Wilmington*

**BEHAVIOR MODIFICATION
CONDITIONING
GENERALIZATION
SKINNER, B. F.**

# OPHTHALMOLOGIST

An ophthalmologist, sometimes called an oculist, is a medical doctor who specializes in the diagnosis and treatment of defects and diseases of the eye by prescribing lenses and, in some cases, drugs, performing eye surgery, and carrying out other types of medical treatment (Cartwright, Cartwright, & Ward, 1981, p. 71). Ocular disorders are of special significance because they often provide clues to the presence of systemic diseases and to other congenital malformations present in many handicapped children. Congenital rubella, Down syndrome, and Marfan's syndrome are three conditions that are commonly associated with or are causes of visual impairments. Lists of ocular diseases and disorders are available in several resources (Goble, 1984; Jose, 1983; Nelson, 1984).

An important responsibility of the ophthalmologist related to serving visually impaired children and youths (which can also be performed by the optometrist) is a complete eye examination. This should include the following: developmental history, distance visual acuity, inspection of the eyes for evident physical problems, evaluation of ocular motility, determination of basic refractive status of the eyes, evaluation of accommodation of the eyes for near vision; visual field studies; testing of intraocular pressure; testing of color vision; and examination of the interior of the eye including the retina and vitreous (Goble, 1984; Nelson, 1984).

One of the subspecialists within the field of ophthalmology is a pediatric ophthalmologist, who focuses on the recognition, understanding, early treatment, and ultimately, prevention of ocular disease in childhood. This specialist is particularly skilled in areas such as visual development in the preverbal child, ocular genetics, amblyopia, and congenital cataracts (Nelson, 1984). He or she may be of particular value on multidisciplinary teams with special educators and parents to provide resources to meet the visually impaired child's developmental and educational needs.

### REFERENCES

Cartwright, G. P., Cartwright, C. A., & Ward, M. E. (1981). *Educating special learners.* Belmont, CA: Wadsworth.

Goble, J. L. (1984). *Visual disorders in the handicapped child.* New York: Marcel Dekker.

Jose, R. (1983). *Understanding low vision.* New York: American Foundation for the Blind.

Nelson, L. B. (1984). *Pediatric ophthalmology.* Philadelphia: Saunders.

ROSANNE K. SILBERMAN
*Hunter College, City University of New York*

DEVELOPMENT OPTOMETRY
MULTIDISCIPLINARY TEAMS
OPTOMETRIST
VISUAL ACUITY
VISUAL IMPAIRMENT

# OPPOSITIONAL DEFIANT DISORDER

Oppositional Defiant Disorder (ODD, along with Conduct Disorder, CD) is considered the predominant juvenile disorder seen in community mental health and juvenile correction facilities (Loeber, Burke, Lahey, Winters, & Zera, 2000). While there is ample empirical support for the distinction between ODD and CD, they are commonly grouped together in reviews of the literature due to their similar characteristics, but more so because of the developmental progression often seen from ODD to CD to Adult Antisocial Personality Disorder (ASPD; cf. Hinshaw & Lee, 2003; Loeber et al., 2000). Because children with moderate to severe ODD are often diagnosed with CD later on, many research studies have simply combined ODD and CD (Angold, Costello, & Erkanli, 1999). In fact, because of the strong association with CD, there is still some controversy in the literature about whether ODD constitutes a viable category on its own (Hinshaw & Lee, 2003). Concerning ODD/CD, readers will encounter the descriptive, while synonymous, use of words like "antisocial behavior" (ASB) or "disruptive behavior disorder" (DBD) to refer to the voluminous information and research on these two diagnostic groups in a more broad and concise way (cf., Hinshaw & Lee, 2003; Loeber et al., 2000).

With as many as 2 to 6 percent of youth described as displaying serious ASB (Kazdin, 1993), public school systems are destined to encounter children with ODD on a daily basis. Currently, about 1 percent of students displaying DBD are actually certified to receive comprehensive special education services, a figure that some feel is well below the actual numbers of students who could or should receive services; moreover, researchers believe this issue demonstrates (1) a political and professional unwillingness of public school systems to address their needs, and (2) a major problem with the current federal definition (i.e., IDEA), which excludes many children who would ordinarily need and qualify for special education and mental health services (Kauffman, 2000; Merrell & Walker, 2004; Nelson, Rutherford, Center, & Walker, 1991; Walker, Nishioka, Zeller, Severson, & Feil, 2000). As mentioned previously, the essential dimension associated with ODD is aggressive, antisocial behavior. These troubled children (and by implication, their families) are very troubling to everyone and every system they encounter. Children with ODD often end up on the pathway to delinquency and jail; they fare worse than any other class of student with disabilities in the public school system, and their quality of life as adults can best be described as abysmal (cf. Walker, 1995; Walker, Colvin, & Ramsey, 1995).

## DSM-IV Criteria and Features of ODD

According to the *Diagnostic and Statistical Manual of Mental Disorders,* fourth edition (*DSM-IV;* American Psychiatric Association, 1994), the hallmark of ODD is the recurrent pattern of negativistic, defiant, disobedient, and hostile behavior toward authority figures, which leads to major life impairment. This recurrent pattern must last at least 6 months, with four (or more) of the following qualifying behaviors being exhibited before a diagnosis can be made: (1) often loses temper; (2) often argues with adults; (3) often actively defies or refuses to comply with adults' requests or rules; (4) often deliberately annoys people; (5) often blames others for his or her mistakes or misbehavior; (6) is often touchy or easily annoyed by others; (7) is often angry and resentful; and (8) is often spiteful or vindictive. This pattern criterion can only be met if the behavior(s) occur more frequently than is typically observed in children of comparable age and developmental level. Moreover, these behavioral patterns must lead to significant impairment in social, academic, or adaptive functioning; otherwise, a diagnosis of ODD cannot be made (American Psychiatric Association, 1994). If symptoms occur exclusively during episodes of documented mood or psychotic disorders, or if criteria are met for CD, then ODD is not warranted.

ODD is usually evident before age 8 and emerges no later than early adolescence, as this might be associated with the process of normal developmental individuation (American Psychiatric Association, 1994). Typically, ODD is considered less severe in nature than CD, but in severe cases, a diagnosis of CD is warranted when behaviors escalate to unprovoked aggression toward people, animals, destruction of property, or there is documented patterns of theft or deceit. If a child is given the diagnosis of CD before age 10, it is regarded as "childhood-onset type" and is considered to be a more persistent form of CD and is more likely to lead to a diagnosis of adult ASPD than if CD is diagnosed after age 10 (American Psychiatric Association, 1994; Hinshaw & Lee, 2003).

The majority of evidence supports a basic distinction between ODD and CD, as well as between ADHD and both ODD and CD (Hinshaw & Lee, 2003; Loeber et al., 2000). One difficulty with the *DSM-IV* (and previous editions) diagnosis of ODD is that it does not seem to accurately identify preadolescent girls with early-onset antisocial behavior (i.e., before age 8), because rather than being overtly aggressive, females tend to use indirect, verbal, and relational aggression toward friends (Crick & Grotpeter, 1995). The *DSM-IV* criteria focuses more on overt aggression, forcing some to call for a modification in the diagnostic criteria for girls (e.g., Loeber et al., 2000).

Adding to the diagnostic validity of ODD is its stability over time. Generally, the more severe the symptoms of ODD, the more stable or persistent it is over time (Loeber, 1991). What researchers have learned is that the stability of ODD/CD over a decade is about equal to the stability for intelligence. The correlation for IQ over 10 years is .70, whereas for children/youth displaying aggressive behavior, it is .80 (Walker et al., 1995). ODD/CD in girls is at least as stable as it is for boys, especially when girls become more overtly aggressive by adolescence (Loeber et al., 2000). In order to identify which children will persist in ASB (i.e., a diagnosis of CD and later ASPD) as opposed to those who will outgrow the behavior, prognostic subtypes such as early versus late onset, severity level of symptoms, overt versus covert disruptive behavior, CD with and without ADHD, and early ASPD symptoms have been investigated. The best evidence for prognostic utility and relevance for practitioners is with age and gender atypicality (e.g., running away, cruelty, breaking into buildings), overt versus covert disruptive behaviors, the nature of any aggression (i.e., proactive/unprovoked as opposed to reactive aggression/fighting), and early presence of ASPD symptoms (e.g., reckless disregard, encompassing impulsivity, lack of remorse; Loeber et al, 2000). Because boys with CD and ADHD have worse outcomes than for boys with CD but without ADHD, it is quite possible that for children with ODD, having a diagnosis of ADHD appears to be a marker for early onset of CD symptoms (Hinshaw, 1994; Loeber et al., 2000).

Epidemiological, or prevalence, information is critical for understanding disorders such as ODD, so that effective planning and administration of mental and public health and school-based intervention services can occur. Prevalence data are affected by such things as the measurement used, which *DSM* criteria are used (e.g., *DSM-III-R* versus *DSM-IV*), the number of informants, and the location of the study sample. As a case in point, a diagnostic comparison of the *DSM-III* with the *DSM-III-R* on the same sample of ODD children showed a drop in prevalence by 25 percent; children with CD became 44 percent less prevalent using the *DSM-III-R* (Lahey et al., 1990). When the prevalence of ASB (encompassing ODD and CD) is examined across age, generation, gender, urban versus rural location, and socioeconomic levels, the results are quite mixed, suggesting that the field of psychology should continue to incorporate notions of flux and developmental pathways as opposed to viewing ODD and the subsequently more serious form of CD as being static clinical categories (Hinshaw & Lee, 2003). What some of the epidemiological data do suggest is that, for the most part, boys are more likely to meet *DSM* definitions of ODD and CD and display a higher frequency of such symptoms; ODD and CD are more prevalent among youths from families of low socioeconomic status, and interestingly, some data suggest that sex differences in delinquency have narrowed over the years, quite likely owing to the increased prevalence of girl gangs (Loeber et al., 2000).

Researchers in the field of DBD report that when children with ODD receive additional psychiatric diagnoses, known as *comorbidity*, it signals higher degrees of impairment that must be understood more clearly if effective prevention and treatment is to be offered. *Comorbidity* refers to the greater-than-chance rate of overlap between two or more independent disorders (for an in-depth discussion of this topic, see Angold et al., 1999; Hinshaw & Lee, 2003; and Loeber et al., 2000). Of the studies investigating this phenomenon, few have examined ODD itself with other psychiatric disorders, because many researchers combine ODD and CD samples (Angold et al., 1999). What little is known about ODD and its comorbidity with other psychiatric diagnoses is that low levels of comorbid conditions exist in community samples of ODD and ADHD (14 percent), ODD and anxiety disorder (14 percent), and ODD and Depressive Disorder (9 percent; Angold & Costello, 1996). When children and youth meet criteria for CD, however, increased rates of psychiatric disorders appear, such as symptoms of ASPD (even though this is not formally diagnosed until age 18), substance abuse, mania, schizophrenia, obsessive-compulsive disorder, and ADHD; the latter disorder of which increases the risk of depression and anxiety in children with CD (Hinshaw, 1994; Loeber et al., 2000).

## ODD in the Public School Setting

The fact that children with ODD are present in the public school system is without argument (cf. Forness, Kavale, & Lopez, 1993; Walker, Horner, Sugai, Bullis, Sprague, Bricker, et al., 1996). Public school systems have had to deal with children with ASB ever since public school attendance became mandatory in the United States (Kauffman, 1976). What is different is that the public education system does not, and is not supposed to, rely on the mental health approach to diagnosing psychiatric disorders typically seen in the traditional fields of clinical psychology, psychiatry, and clinical social work, all of which rely on the use of the *DSM* system for medical and insurance tracking and billing purposes. In public schools, the referral, identification, and placement for services process relies on procedures set forth in the federal law known as the *Individuals with Disabilities Education Act* of 1997 (or IDEA). Children who qualify receive an *Individualized Education Program* (IEP) and any other related service that might be necessary or appropriate to ensure adequate educational progress (e.g., specialized transportation, occupational therapy). Children with ODD would most likely qualify under the IDEA category of *Emotionally Disturbed* (ED), but there is no absolute guarantee. A child may come to school with a mental health diagnosis of ODD, but whether they are officially certified as ED is decided by a school-based multidisciplinary team and the parent(s).

To be considered for services (upon a referral), careful assessment is conducted to determine eligibility, which includes gathering data such as academic achievement, peer interaction, and classroom observations, behavior ratings, functional assessments, developmental history, file reviews, health assessment, and any other testing, such as for language processing, if a difficulty in this area is suspected by the multidisciplinary team. A child with ODD would qualify for services if one or more of the five following characteristics is exhibited over a long period of time (i.e., 6 months or more) and to a marked degree: (1) an inability to learn that cannot be explained by intellectual, sensory, or health factors; (2) an inability to build or maintain satisfactory interpersonal relationships with peers and adults; (3) inappropriate types of behavior or feelings under normal circumstances; (4) a general, pervasive mood of unhappiness or depression; and (5) a tendency to develop physical symptoms or fears associated with personal or school problems. Based on this, a child with ODD would ordinarily seem to qualify as ED and have an IEP developed for him or her to address their educational and/or behavioral needs. Similar to the *DSM-IV* criteria for ODD, however, there must be evidence that the ODD child's disruptive behaviors are truly *adversely* affecting or impacting their educational performance to the degree that they would need intensive, specially designed instructional services to succeed in school. It is possible that their needs could be adequately addressed by proactive schoolwide behavior management programs that target such behavior (e.g., through prereferral, targeted, or universal intervention strategies that might effectively abate problem behaviors). Achieving such results is feasible, but is more than likely for children who display more moderate to low levels of ODD and in schools with effectively trained staff.

Children with ODD (including those who progress to CD) present enormous challenges to educational practitioners, such as contributing to the problem of professional burnout and requests for reassignment (Bibou-Nakou, Stogiannidou, & Kiosseoglou, 1999). In an 8-year followup of an ongoing longitudinal sample of antisocial boys (reported in Walker et al., 1995), half reported using drugs, alcohol, and tobacco; 80 percent said they often came to school stoned. Between grade 4 and grade 12, the antisocial boys in the sample experienced 350 arrests between them. The dropout rate for these antisocial boys during high school was 62 percent. In another study, Walker et al. (1995) report that 3 years after leaving school, 70 percent of antisocial boys are arrested at least once; sadly, about half of all antisocial children with ODD/CD or ED go on to become adolescent delinquent offenders, and about one-half to three-quarters of these adolescent offenders become adult criminals. When an antisocial child with ODD is put into a play group with same-age children who are all unfamiliar with each other, the ODD child can be socially rejected and ostracized within minutes (Coie & Kupersmidt, 1983). Children with ODD often misinterpret even the simplest of social cues from peers and adults, have quite abnormal expectations of their own behavior, possess sophisticated repertoires of bullying oth-

ers, and often experience moderate to severe academic skill deficits and overall low achievement. Academic engagement in the classroom for children with ODD averages between 60 and 70 percent, as compared to the more normative academic engagement standard of between 90 and 95 percent; what exacerbates the problem, too, is that these same children with ODD/ED also exhibit higher rates of aggression, noncompliance, noise-making, and out-of-seat behavior in the classroom than normal peers (Walker et al., 1995). Out on the playground, it is interesting to note that children with ODD/ED display nearly matching levels of positive behavior with normal peers; however, ODD children's rate of negative social behavior is dramatically higher than is normal for the playground. Unfortunately, normal peers tend to react to ODD children's negative behavior in kind. As Walker et al. (1995) explain, their reaction is probably because normal peers have an unpleasant history of aversive, negative interactions with them and are quite exasperated, even to the point where the most neutral social actions of ODD children are attributed by normal peers as malevolent behavior.

Given these characteristics and long-term outcomes for children with ODD/ED, one is not necessarily shocked by the mismatch between the goals and expectations of the public educational system and the antisocial behavior that children with ODD/ED bring with them to the schoolhouse door. In fact, if one looks closely on the ED eligibility forms generated for public schools by state-level educational authorities, an incomprehensible (Kauffman, 2000) addendum has been added, which reads: "The term [ED] does not include children who are socially maladjusted, unless it is determined that they are seriously emotionally disturbed." This clause was not part of the original ED definition developed by Eli Bower and presented to Congress in 1977 when the original special education act was placed into law, nor did Bower ever intend for such a clause to be introduced (Merrell, 2004). The social maladjustment (SM) controversy was thus born and has been a source of professional contention ever since. Although the assertion has no actual smoking gun documentation, leaders in the field of behavior disorders believe that the SM clause was probably introduced to assuage the concerns of certain legislators and educational administrators who were not happy about mandating services to delinquent and antisocial youth (Merrill, 2004). Furthermore, it is noted that the SM clause was never defined in the federal statutes, nor was a valid process described about how to differentiate between children with ED (ODD/CD) and SM. Merrill (2004) suggests that when presented with the most basic operationalization of SM, it appears the SM clause was meant to weed out children/youth who display a more *socialized-aggressive* form of ODD/CD, whose actions are more in line with willful/purposeful antisocial behavior, who belong to a deviant peer group, who do not have any emotionally based mental health problems, and who are streetwise and callous.

To date, no data exist to show that SM (i.e., ODD/CD) can be reliably differentiated from ED, nor does it appear that such differentiation is actually needed, because no matter how SM is conceptualized, children/youth who fall into such a category still manage to exhibit one of the five behavioral characters of ED to a marked degree and over a long period of time (Kauffman, 2000), and are thus still eligible for special education services. Ironically, as much as this issue has been a bone of contention since the 1970's, Forness (1992) reports that nearly half of state and local educational agencies simply ignore the SM clause altogether! Readers who are interested in the SM issue as it pertains to ODD/ED are encouraged to obtain the 1992 special publication of *School Psychology Review* (volume 21, issue 1), Merrill's (2004) article, as well as Forness and Kavale's (2000) fascinating article in *Behavioral Disorders*. As far as the treatment of ODD and its educational diagnostic counterpart of ED are concerned, there is movement to codify the more descriptive and less stigmatizing label of *Emotional or Behavioral Disorder* (i.e., E/BD) into IDEA (Forness & Kavale, 2000).

Intervening to successfully prevent and treat ODD/ED is possible, with the most cost efficient and effective treatments being multimodal in nature, addressing multiple domains of risk factors (Burke et al., 2002; Offord, Kraemer, Kazdin, Jensen, & Harrington, 1998; Walker, 1995; Walker et al., 1995), but it is also a daunting task that can sometimes be undermined by the very system that is supposed to address their needs (Kauffman, 2004). Moreover, the cost of using public services for intervening with and treating ODD/ED (e.g., special education, foster/residential care) is ten times that of treating children with no CD (Burke et al., 2002), which can make public school systems or other agencies balk at the price tag. Intervention and treatment programs in the school system often lack potency because systematic procedures and structures are typically not in place for changing behavior. What is often substituted for empirically supported programs is either drug therapy and/or counseling/psychotherapy. While drug therapy may suppress ODD/CD symptoms, it is often at the expense of academic achievement, since these powerful drugs may actually impair performance on cognitive and academic tests. And as appealing as counseling is to teachers, it is perhaps the least effective option in schools as it primarily involves trying to change ODD/ED children's "awareness" as opposed to directly and explicitly teaching adaptive/functional replacement behaviors; as Walker (1995) and Dryfoos (1990) point out, there is no evidence to show that an acting-out child's awareness of the probable causes of his or her behavior has any effect on improving actual classroom/school behavior. Quite simply, the best available means for addressing the issue of ODD/ED is early identification and prevention of academic and social failure, as well as ensuring that proactive, schoolwide

positive behavioral support and intervention systems are in place (Anderson & Kincaid, 2005; Walker et al., 1995; Walker et al., 1996)

## Informational Resources on ODD Seen in School and Clinic Settings

The present knowledge and research base on ODD is voluminous, making it a challenge to present in any definitive or exhaustive fashion. For that reason, the reader is directed to the various (albeit limited) following sources, so that they may engage in a program of personal professional development or self-study. Many of these resources themselves have outstanding references and leads to more material on ODD and anything related to it in clinical or educational settings.

Recommended articles, reviews, chapters, and monographs include Burke, Loeber, and Birmaher (2002), Hinshaw (1994), Hinshaw and Lee (2000), Moffitt (1993), and Patterson, Reid, and Dishion (1992). Stoff, Breiling, and Maser's (1997) edited book, and the special issue in *Development and Psychopathology* (Cicchetti & Nurcombe, 1993) are essential reading on the topic, as are Angold and Costello (1996) and Zoccolillo (1993), if one wants an understanding of the empirical basis for the diagnosis of ODD, as well as insight into the role of gender and the development of CD, respectively. Loeber (1991) examines the stability of antisocial behavior, and Loeber and Hay (1994) discuss developmental approaches to aggression and CD. It should be noted that Burke et al. (2002) also provide a concise overview of effective treatment strategies and programs for ODD/CD. For issues concerning the assessment and treatment of ODD, the reader is directed to Hinshaw and Zupan (1997), and Quay and Hogan (1999).

Within the realm of special education, material by Forness and Kavale (2000), Kauffman (2000, 2003, 2004), Walker (1995), and Walker et al. (1995), provide comprehensive coverage of E/BD, including diagnostic issues, prevention, and assessment and intervention strategies/packages. For further coverage of assessment of antisocial children in school settings, see Merrell (2003). The controversy surrounding the under identification and underserved nature of children with ODD or E/BD in schools is an issue that readers should be cognizant of, since it will probably go unresolved for some time: see the Peacock Hill Working Group (1991) and United States Department of Education's (1994) discussion about this disconcerting topic.

The internet now provides a number of resourceful links to information concerning antisocial behavior and its treatment. For example, http://www.colorado.edu/cspv/blueprints helps disseminate well-evaluated programs to agencies for implementation in their own community. Along this line, a proactive, schoolwide systems approach known as Effective Behavior Support helps schools to deal effectively with antisocial behaviors within the school context (Anderson & Kincaid, 2005; Sugai, Horner, Dunlap, Hieneman, Lewis, Nelson, et al., 2000). Now referred to as Positive Behavioral Interventions and Supports, this research-based systems approach currently has an internet-based national technical assistance center, established with support from the U.S. Department of Education's Office of Special Education Programs. The Center can be found at http://www.pbis.org.

Probably the best way for individuals to stay current with ODD or E/BD would be to join a professional organization such as the National Association of School Psychologists (NASP), Council for Exceptional Children (CEC), or the American Psychological Association (APA), and participate in a relevant special interest group, subdivision, or council that focuses on issues and research related to ODD or E/BD. The CEC site is http://www.cec.sped.org, with the relevant division being the Council for Children with Behavioral Disorders (CCBD), at http://www.ccbd.net. NASP is located at http://www.nasponline.org, and the APA can be found at http://www.apa.org. Within the APA are upward of 55 separate divisions or societies that one can research for information related to ODD. An excellent peer-refereed journal that specifically discusses issues and related research findings on children with ODD/ED is CCBD's *Behavioral Disorders*.

## REFERENCES

American Psychiatric Association. (1994). *Diagnostic and statistical manual of mental disorders* (4th ed.). Washington, DC: Author.

Anderson, C. M., & Kincaid, D. (2005). Applying behavior analysis to school violence and discipline problems: Schoolwide positive behavior support. *The Behavior Analyst, 28*, 49–63.

Angold, A., & Costello, E. J. (1996). Toward establishing an empirical basis for the diagnosis of oppositional defiant disorder. *Journal of the American Academy of Child and Adolescent Psychiatry, 35*, 1205–1212.

Angold, A., & Costello, E. J., & Erkanli, A. (1999). Comorbidity. *Journal of Child Psychology and Psychiatry, 40*, 57–87.

Bibou-Nakou, I., Stogiannidou, A., & Kiosseoglou, G. (1999). The relation between teacher burnout and teachers' attributions and practices regarding school behaviour problems. *School Psychology International, 20*, 209–217.

Burke, J. D., Loeber, R., & Birmaher, B. (2002). Oppositional defiant disorder and conduct disorder: A review of the past 10 years, part II. *Journal of the American Academy of Child and Adolescent Psychiatry, 41*, 1275–1293.

Cicchetti, D., & Nurcombe, B. (Eds.). (1993). Towards a developmental perspective on conduct disorder (special issue). *Development and Psychopathology, 5*.

Coie, J., & Kupersmidt, J. (1983). A behavioral analysis of emerging social status in boys' groups. *Child Development, 54*, 1400–1416.

Crick, N. R., & Gropeter, J. K. (1995). Relational aggression, gender, and social-psychological adjustment. *Child Development, 66*, 710–722.

Dryfoos, J. (1990). *Adolescents at risk*. New York: Oxford University Press.

Forness, S. R. (1992). Legalism vs. professionalism in diagnosing SED in the public schools. *School Psychology Review, 21*, 29–34.

Forness, S. R., & Kavale, K. A. (2000). Emotional and behavioral disorders: Background and current status of the E/BD terminology and definition. *Behavioral Disorders, 25*, 264–269.

Forness, S. R., & Kavale, K. A., & Lopez, M. (1993). Conduct disorders in school: Special education eligibility and comorbidity. *Journal of Emotional and Behavioral Disorders, 1*, 101–108.

Hinshaw, S. P. (1994). Conduct disorder in childhood: Conceptualization, diagnosis, comorbidity, and risk status for antisocial functioning in adulthood. In D. C. Fowles, P. Sutker, & S. H. Goodman (Eds.), *Progress in experimental personality and psychopathology research* (pp. 3–44). New York: Springer.

Hinshaw, S. P., & Lee, S. S. (2003). Conduct and oppositional defiant disorders. In E. J. Mash & R. A. Barkley (Eds.), *Child psychopathology* (2nd ed.). New York: Guilford.

Hinshaw, S. P., & Zupan, B. A. (1997). Assessment of antisocial behavior and conduct disorder in children. In D. Stoff, J. Breiling, & J. D. Maser (Eds.), *Handbook of antisocial behavior* (pp. 36–50). New York: Wiley.

Kauffman, J. M. (1976). Nineteenth-century views of children's behavior disorders: Historical contributions and continuing issues. *Journal of Special Education, 10*, 335–349.

Kauffman, J. M. (2000). *Characteristics of emotional and behavioral disorders of children and youth* (7th ed.). Upper Saddle River, NJ: Pearson Prentice Hall.

Kauffman, J. M. (2003). Appearances, stigma, and prevention. *Remedial and Special Education, 24*, 195–198.

Kauffman, J. M. (2004). How we prevent the prevention of emotional and behavioral difficulties in education. In P. Gardner, F. Yuen, P. Clough, & T. Pardeck (Eds.), *Handbook of emotional and behavioral difficulties in education*. London: Sage.

Kazdin, A. E. (1993). Treatment of conduct disorder: Progress and directions in psychotherapy research. *Development and Psychopathology, 5*, 277–310.

Lahey, B. B., Loeber, R., Stouthamer-Loeber, M., et al., (1990). Comparison of *DSM-III* and *DSM-III-R* diagnoses for prepubertal children: Changes in prevalence and utility. *Journal of the American Academy of Child and Adolescent Psychiatry, 29*, 620–626.

Lewis, T. J., & Sugai, G. (1999). Effective behavior support: A systems approach to proactive school wide management. *Focus on Exceptional Children, 31*(6), 1–24.

Loeber, R. (1991). Antisocial behavior: More enduring than changeable? *Journal of the American Academy of Child and Adolescent Psychiatry, 30*, 393–397.

Loeber, R., Burke, J. D., Lahey, B. B., Winters, A., & Zera, M. (2000). Oppositional defiant and conduct disorder: A review of the past 10 years, part I. *Journal of the American Academy of Child and Adolescent Psychiatry, 39*, 1468–1484.

Loeber, R., & Hay, D. F. (1994). Developmental approaches to aggression and conduct problems. In M. Rutter & D. F. Hay (Eds.), *Development through life: A handbook for clinicians* (pp. 485–515). London: Blackwell.

Merrell, K. W., & Walker, H. M. (2004). Deconstructing a definition: Social maladjustment versus emotional disturbance and moving the EBD field forward. *Psychology in the Schools, 41,* 899–910.

Moffitt, T. E. (1993). Adolescence-limited and life-course-persistent antisocial behavior: A developmental taxonomy. *Psychological Review, 100,* 674–701.

Nelson, C. M., Rutherford, R. B., Center, D. B., & Walker, H. M. (1991). Do public schools have an obligation to serve troubled children and youth? *Exceptional Children, 57,* 406–415.

Offord, D. R., Kraemer, H. C., Kazdin, A. E., Jensen, P. S., & Harrington, R. (1998). Lowering the burden of suffering from child psychiatric disorder: Trade-offs among clinical, targeted and universal interventions. *Journal of the American Academy of Child and Adolescent Psychiatry, 37,* 686–694.

Patterson, G. R., Reid, J. B., & Dishion, T. J. (1992). *A social interactional approach (vol. 4): Antisocial boys.* Eugene, OR: Castalia.

Peacock Hill Working Group (1991). Problems and promises in special education and related services for children and youth with emotional or behavioral disorders. *Behavioral Disorders, 16,* 299–313.

Quay, H. C., & Hogan, A. E. (Eds.). (1999). *Handbook of disruptive behavior disorders.* New York: Plenum.

Stoff, D. M., Breiling, J., & Maser, J. D. (1997). *Handbook of antisocial behavior.* New York: Wiley.

Sugai, G., Horner, R. H., Dunlap, G., Hieneman, M., Lewis, T. J., Nelson, C. M., et al. (2000). Applying positive behavior support and functional behavioral assessment in schools. *Journal of Positive Behavior Interventions, 2,* 131–143.

Swanson, J., Cantwell, D., Lerner, M., McBurnett, K., Pfiffner, L., & Kotkin, R. (1992). Treatment of ADHD: Beyond medication. *Beyond Behavior, 41,* 13–22.

United States Department of Education (1994). *National Agenda for Achieving Better Results for Children and Youth with Serious Emotional Disturbance.* Retrieved August 8, 2005, from http://cecp.air.org/help/contents.asp

Walker, H. M. (1995). *The acting-out child: Coping with classroom disruption* (2nd ed.). Longmont, CO: Sopris West.

Walker, H. M., Colvin, G., & Ramsey, E. (1995). *Antisocial behavior in school: Strategies and best practices.* Pacific Grove, CA: Brooks/Cole.

Walker, H. M., Horner, R. H., Sugai, G., Bullis, M., Sprague, J. R., Bricker, D., et al. (1996). Integrated approaches to preventing antisocial behavior patterns among school-aged children and youth. *Journal of Emotional and Behavioral Disorders, 4,* 193–256.

Walker, H. M., Nishioka, V. M., Zeller, R., Severson, H. H., & Feil, E. G. (2000). Causal factors and potential solutions for the persistent under-identification of students having emotional or behavioral disorders in the context of school. *Assessment for Effective Intervention, 26,* 29–40.

Zoccolillo, M. (1993). Gender and the development of conduct disorder. *Development and Psychopathology, 5,* 65–97.

Rollen C. Fowler
*Eugene 4J School District,
Eugene, Oregon*

**CONDUCT DISORDER
JUVENILE DELINQUENCY**

# OPTACON

The optacon (optical-to-tactile converter) is a small electronic device that converts regular print into a readable vibrating form for blind people. When its tiny camera, containing a transistorized retina lens module, moves over print symbols, the image is converted to a tactual representation of the letter shape through vibrating pins. The machine is divided into three subsystems: the camera, which converts images of print into corresponding electrical impulses; the electronics section, which processes the electrical impulses; and the tactile array, which displays in vibrating form the information transmitted by the electronics from the camera. The blind person tracks the printed material using the camera with his or her right hand and reads the tactile image with the forefinger of the left hand, which is resting on the tactile array (Telesensory Systems, 1977).

Learning to read with the optacon requires extensive training, practice, and motivation. The blind learner is taught letter recognition through associating tactile sensations with letter shapes and their corresponding names. To recognize a letter, the student must be able to discriminate the characteristics or critical features of the letter from a moving image, and then match the features to the correct name of the letter. In addition to good tactile discrimination, the successful user has to have excellent language skills and knowledge of spelling rules (orthography), grammar rules (syntax), and sentence meaning (semantics).

Reading with the optacon is a slow process because the machine displays only one letter of a word at a time. It is not intended to replace braille. However, it provides the blind reader with instant access to printed matter such as personal mail, greeting cards, recipes, catalogs, applications for college or jobs, banking statements, bills, musical notation, and phone numbers. It also enables the blind student to read graphs and charts. In addition, there are special lens attachments that enable the blind user to read cathode-ray tubes and find employment using computers. Optacon use is not being taught in school programs as extensively as possible because of the time required and the wide variety of other skills needed by the visually impaired student. In addition, braille translating computer programs are rapidly performing translation of data in multiple formats (Kapperman, 1997).

## REFERENCES

Howell, M. (1984). A tingle of print. *New Beacon, 63,* 208–210.

Kapperman, G. (1997). *Project VISION: Visually impaired students and internet opportunities now.* Sycamore, IL: Research and Development Institute.

Telesensory Systems. (1977). *Optacon training: Teaching guidelines.* Palo Alto, CA: Author.

ROSANNE K. SILBERMAN
*Hunter College, City University
of New York*

**BLIND
BRAILLE
VISUAL IMPAIRMENT
VISUAL TRAINING**

## OPTOMETRIST

An optometrist (OD) is a licensed doctor of optometry who is trained to measure the refractive errors of the human eye and prescribe lenses to correct those refractive errors (Chalkley, 1982). Some optometrists specialize in prescribing lenses and other types of optical aids for low-vision students and spend a major portion of their professional time in low-vision clinics. These eye specialists work closely with special educators and base their decisions on information given and recommendations made by parents and other professionals on a multidisciplinary team. It is critical for the special educator and the optometrist to establish good communication to be sure that the student's corrective lenses are providing maximum vision for school activities. The aid of choice will vary, depending on the strength of the power needed, the visual fields and working distances required, and the low-vision student's motivation (Jose, 1983).

The categories of low-vision aids that can be prescribed by the optometrist are:

Telescopes (including binoculars), which assist with distance tasks

Telemicroscopes (near-point telescopes), which incorporate a reading cap into the front lens for near tasks

Microscopes (any spectacle-mounted device such as a reading lens, a loupe, or a clip-on), to increase magnification for long-term near-distance tasks

Magnifiers (stand and hand-held), to assist in short-term spotting tasks at near distance

Field-utilization aides (prisms, minification), to assist in increasing field of vision (Jose, 1983)

Some optometrists are involved in doing perceptual-motor training. The appropriateness of this role for the optometrist is questioned by many special educators.

## REFERENCES

Chalkley, T. (1982). *Your eyes* (2nd ed.). Springfield, IL: Thomas.

Jose, R. (1983). *Understanding low vision.* New York: American Foundation for the Blind.

ROSANNE K. SILBERMAN
*Hunter College, City University
of New York*

**DEVELOPMENTAL OPTOMETRY
LOW VISION
MULTIDISCIPLINARY TEAMS
OPHTHALMOLOGIST
VISUAL IMPAIRMENT
VISION TRAINING**

## ORAL AND WRITTEN LANGUAGE SCALES

The Oral and Written Language Scales (OWLS; Carrow-Woolfolk, 1996) are an individually administered assessment of receptive and expressive (oral and written) language for children and young adults. The OWLS Listening Comprehension and Oral Expression Scales and the Written Expression Scale can be purchased and used alone. The OWLS are intended for children aged 3 years to 21 years 11 months on the Listening Comprehension and Oral Expression scales and for children 5 years to 21 years 11 months on the Written Expression scale. Neither Oral Language scale requires reading; in Listening Comprehension, responding verbally is not required—the child may point to the correct answer.

The Listening Comprehension Scale (LCS) of the OWLS is a measure of receptive language. It contains three examples and 111 items and takes approximately 5 to 15 minutes to administer, depending upon the examinee's age. The examiner reads a verbal stimulus aloud. The examinee responds by indicating a picture on the examinee's side of the easel. Correct responses are indicated on the examiner's side of the easel and on the record form.

The Oral Expression Scale (OES) is a measure of expressive language. It consists of two examples and 96 items and takes approximately 10 to 25 minutes to administer, depending upon the examinee's age. The examinee answers a question, completes a sentence, or generates one or more sentences in response to a visual or verbal stimulus. Common correct and incorrect responses are included on the record form.

The Written Expression Scale (WES) is designed to assess writing skills. It consists of 39 items divided into four overlapping item sets, each designed for a specified age level, and takes approximately 10 to 40 minutes to administer, depending upon the examinee's age. There is a variety of item types, including copying printed words and sentences; writing letters, words, and sentences from dictation; and writing sentences and paragraphs according to specific oral instructions. The OWLS Written Expression scale may be administered in small groups "with examinees 8 years and older who are being assessed for reasons other than placement decisions" (Carrow-Woolfolk, 1996, p. 33), as was done in some cases during the standardization. The OWLS Written Expression Scale does not have subtests but does provide reproducible Descriptive Analysis Worksheets, which permit calculation of percentile ranks and determination of strengths and weaknesses for 9 of the 15 Skills Areas at each year of age.

For each OWLS Scale, age-based standard scores (M = 100, SD = 15), grade-based standard scores (WE only), percentiles, normal curve equivalents (NCEs), stanines, test-age equivalents, and grade equivalents (WE only) are provided.

The standardization group contained a representative national sample of 1,373 students stratified to match the U.S. Census data for 1991 on the basis of age, sex, and four categories each of mother's education, race/ethnicity, and geographic region.

Internal consistency reliabilities range from .84 to .93. Test-retest reliabilities were .73 and .90. Interrater reliability averaged .95. Construct validity of the OWLS is based on extensive development efforts to match the content and format of the test to language theory (e.g., Carrow-Woolfolk, 1988, 1996; Carrow-Woolfolk & Lynch, 1981).

The OWLS offers a brief but comprehensive assessment of receptive and expressive language. The manuals for the tests are clear, explicit, and helpful. After a little practice, scoring and interpretation quickly become efficient. The OWLS manuals include data on statistical significance and base rates of differences among the three scales.

## REFERENCES

Carrow-Woolfolk, E. (1988). *Theory, assessment and intervention in language disorders: An integrative approach.* Philadelphia: Grune & Stratton.

Carrow-Woolfolk, E. (1996a). *Oral and Written Language Scales: Listening Comprehension and Oral Expression Scales manual.* Circle Pines, MN: American Guidance Service.

Carrow-Woolfolk, E. (1996b). *Oral and Written Language Scales: Written Expression Scale manual.* Circle Pines, MN: American Guidance Service.

Carrow-Woolfolk, E., & Lynch, J. I. (1981). *An integrative approach to language disorders in children.* San Antonio, TX: Psychological Corporation.

Goldblatt, J., & Friedman, F. (1998–1999). Oral and Written Language Scales (OWLS). *Diagnostique, 24,* 197–209.

Oral and Written Language Scales. Retrieved May 22, 2006, from http://alpha.fdu.edu/psychology/oral_and_written_language _scales.htm

OWLS descriptive analysis worksheets. Retrieved May 22, 2006, from http://www.agsnet.com/assessments/owls_worksheets .asp

OWLS frequently asked questions. Retrieved May 22, 2006, at http://www.slpforum.com/faq/owls.asp

Plake, B. S., & Impara, J. C. (Eds.). (2001). *The fourteenth mental measurements yearbook.* Lincoln, NE: Buros Institute of Mental Measurements.

RON DUMONT
*Fairleigh Dickinson University*

JOHN O. WILLIS
*Rivier College*

## ORAL FACIAL DIGITAL SYNDROME

Oral facial digital syndrome (OFDS) appears to be a result of an X-linked chromosome that affects both males and females but that is said to be lethal in males. It is characterized by a midline cleft of the face with visibly abnormal structural defects of the mouth, teeth, tongue, and hands. Prominent clefting of the lips and palate and a marked lobulated tongue are highly visible; these may result in speech dysfunction. Teeth are abnormal. The nose tends to be broad and lacks demarcation from the skull. Growths may appear on the face and scalp hair may be sparse (Goodman & Gorlin, 1977). Fingers are broad, fused, and abnormal and extra fingers are often seen. Extremities may also have abnormal growth. No significant posture or neurological or motor problems are noted, although finger abnormalities may be apparent in fine motor development. In half of the cases, mild mental retardation is reported. No significant health problems are seen with this syndrome (Katzman, 1979; Lemeshaw, 1982).

In nearly half of the cases of OFDS, mental retardation will probably result in placement in an educable class. Speech may be affected by clefting and related services will probably be necessary. Digital abnormalities will definitely affect fine motor development so special training and materials will be required to help the child develop appropriate skills. Physical and occupational therapy may be required, as will adaptive physical education. Because deficits are so visible, counseling may be required and long-term emotional problems (particularly poor self-image) may be a result of this syndrome. For this reason, mainstreamed settings, while cognitively appropriate, may not be the optimal setting for a child with this syndrome. Team management of this child's educational plan will be necessary.

**REFERENCES**

Goodman, R., & Gorlin, R. (1977). *Medical aspects of mental retardation* (2nd ed.). Springfield, IL: Thomas.

Katzman, R. (Ed.). (1979). *Congenital and acquired cognitive disorders.* New York: Power.

Lemeshaw, S. (1982). *The handbook of clinical types in mental retardation.* Boston: Allyn & Bacon.

SALLY L. FLAGLER
*University of Oklahoma*

**HURLER SYNDROME**
**MENTAL RETARDATION**
**PHYSICAL ANOMALIES**

# ORAL LANGUAGE AND INDIVIDUALS WITH DISABILITIES

Language is defined as a coded set of rule-governed, arbitrary symbols, universally understood by a particular set of people and used to catalog or express ideas, objects, and events. There are five distinct but interlinked components of language: phonology, morphology, semantics, syntax, and pragmatics. Phonology refers to the rules associated with the ordering of phonemes. Phonemes are speech sounds that distinguish meaning in a language. For example, /m/ and /p/ are phonemes in English; if they are interchanged in words, there is a corresponding change in meaning. Morphology refers to the rules governing morphemes, the smallest meaningful units in language. There are free morphemes that can stand by themselves such as "happy" and "the," and bound morphemes that carry meaning but cannot stand by themselves. Prefixes such as un- and suffixes such as -ly are bound morphemes.

Semantics refers to the meaning of words in a language. Syntax describes the manner in which words are arranged in sentences. Pragmatics refers to the rules of communication in social interactions. The basic unit of pragmatics is a speech act; a behavior that communicates a single message. Speech acts include a locutionary act, an illocutionary act, and a perlocutionary act. A locutionary act is the actual surface form of the utterance and includes syntax, semantics, and phonology. The illocutionary act is the actual intent of the utterance. The perlocutionary act is the effect of the utterance on the listener.

While much is known about the components of language, researchers are less sure how children acquire language.

However, numerous investigators have established major milestones in the development of language in children (Eisenson, 1972; Menyuk, 1972). Although the rate of acquisition varies from child to child, major changes occur between the ages of 2 and 4 years, with development continuing through the elementary school years (Carrow-Woolfolk & Lynch, 1982). Between birth and 2 months of age the infant's cry is similar to an animal sound and represents an instinctive means of expressing cold, hunger, discomfort, and other physical sensations. Babbling begins around 2 months, and continues until the baby is approximately 6 months old. The baby produces playful sounds with his or her speech organs, using the upper food-ways for secondary, expressive purposes rather than for the primary purpose of food intake. Much of this babbling occurs when the baby is alone.

Around the age of 6 months, the baby begins to use vocalizations to get attention or express demands. Inflection becomes prominent around 8 months of age, giving the baby's vocal play the tonal characteristics of adult speech. Somewhere between 10 and 18 months of age, the child's first true words appear, although gestures are very important in stabilizing their meaning. Talking continues to be largely a form of play or an accompaniment to action. Spoken words gradually assume communication functions between 18 months and 24 months. During this time, vocalizations increase in variety and inflection, assuming a conversational character so strongly marked that the child seems to be conducting a long, meaningful conversation in a foreign language.

Between 24 and 30 months, the child begins to display holophrastic speech. Holophrastic speech refers to the possibility that a single word utterance expresses a complex idea. For example, the word "milk" may mean, "I want some milk," "the milk is gone," or "I spilled the milk." Often, a child's one-word utterance is closely linked with action, emotion, or things and their names. During this time, longer and more varied combinations of words develop. Earliest combinations are verbs with nouns such as "Daddy go" followed by adjective-noun combinations. First- and second-person pronouns are also common. The speaking vocabulary shows a sharp increase and ranges from between 200 and 300 words.

By approximately 3 years of age, the child's vocabulary is extensive and sentences are longer and more complex. Language behavior progresses toward a functional integration with the total behavior of the child. At 4 years of age, the child talks about everything, playing with words and questioning persistently. By 5 years of age, the child has acquired the rules of grammar and syntax governing tense, mood, number, word order, and construction of compound and complex sentences. In addition, the child has learned intonation patterns. Language continues to develop throughout the elementary school years, with some aspects such as vocabulary expanding throughout life.

Although normal children vary in their acquisition of

language structure, they typically speak and comprehend standard English by the time they enter first grade. However, children displaying a handicapping condition may be at risk for delayed or deviant language development. A language disability may be concomitant in children displaying any of the following handicapping conditions: learning disability, mental retardation, hearing impairment, autism, or emotional disturbance.

Children with learning disabilities may display deficits in one or more of the following areas: oral expression, listening comprehension, written expression, basic reading skills, reading comprehension, mathematics calculation, or mathematics reasoning (Federal Register, 1977). Although language is one of many areas in which a child may evidence a learning disability, the ramifications are tremendous with language, as they may be associated with problems in reading, spelling, writing, and arithmetic. Preschool learning-disabled children are frequently not interested in verbal activities and may be delayed in their language development. Their syntax is primitive and may be accompanied by delays in the acquisition of morphological patterns. They may be unable to name pictures rapidly or identify colors, letters of the alphabet, days of the week, months of the year, and seasons (Bryen, 1981). School-aged learning-disabled children have an overall vocabulary that is within normal limits; however, they may have difficulty understanding that one object can be represented by several symbols. In addition, they may be unable to comprehend pronouns and the passive voice or to express comparative, spatial, and temporal relationships (Wiig & Semel, 1976).

Language impairment in an individual who is mentally retarded may reflect the degree of retardation. Investigators report that 45 percent of the mildly retarded, 90 percent of the severely retarded, and nearly 100 percent of the profoundly retarded have a language disability (Gomez & Podhajski, 1978; Schlanger, 1973; Spreen, 1965). Investigations of the language of the mentally retarded have yielded conflicting results. Lackner (1968) reported that retardation does not result in a different form of language; rather, language develops more slowly and terminates at a stage below that of a nonhandicapped child. Coggins (1979) and Miller and Yoder (1974) report similar findings. In contrast, Menyuk (1971) and Schiefelbusch (1972) report that retarded individuals use morphemes differently than their nonhandicapped peers. They do not generate rules of inflection; rather, they use only those inflections they have memorized through repeated use. Bliss, Allen, and Walker (1978) report limited use of the future tense, embedded sentences, and double-adjectival noun phrases.

Many researchers have demonstrated that hearing-impaired individuals are delayed in language acquisition (Goda, 1959; Myklebust, 1960; Pugh, 1946). However, it is still not clear whether hearing-impaired individuals develop language at a slower rate or whether their language is deviant. Investigators report that deaf children have smaller vocabularies than hearing peers and have difficulty with analogies, synonyms, and multiple meanings (Templin, 1963). Deaf children use more noun and verbs but fewer conjunctions and auxiliaries than hearing peers (Goda, 1964; Simmons, 1962). Results of studies of grammatical structure indicate difficulty with use of the passive voice (Power & Quigley, 1973), gerunds and infinitives (Quigley, Wilbur, & Montanelli, 1976), relative pronouns (Wilbur, Montanelli, & Quigley, 1976), and verb constructions (Swisher, 1976). Pragmatic growth is also affected by hearing impairment. Deaf children have difficulty understanding how to communicate information to others, interact less frequently, and are less comfortable in social interchanges (Hoemann, 1972).

Although very little descriptive data exist, emotionally disturbed children are often characterized as having problems in language (Lovaas, 1968; Werry, 1979). In fact, a child's inability to use language is often a factor in the diagnosis of emotional disturbance. Rich, Beck, and Coleman (1982) noted sporadic and usually inappropriate imitation of words and phrases by behaviorally disordered children. The language of children suffering from infantile psychosis has been described as lacking true meaningful verbal interaction (Lovaas, 1977). Schizophrenic children exhibit wide variations in the meaningfulness of the language they display (Swanson & Reinert, 1984). More extensive research has been conducted on the language displayed by children diagnosed as autistic. Almost half of all autistic children are mute (Rutter, 1965), while those who are verbal display atypical language. Many are echolalic, repeating the last word of a phrase or an entire sentence spoken to them with no apparent comprehension of their meaning (Baltaxe & Simmons, 1975; Fay, 1969). Autistic children sometimes display delayed echolalia, repeating utterances in new, inappropriate contexts. Vocabulary acquired by some autistic children may consist of memorized lists (such as capital cities) or may focus on a single topic (such as dates); however, this vocabulary is rarely used to communicate in a functional manner (Fay, 1980). In addition to unusual vocabulary development, verbal autistic children may display pronoun reversal, using you instead of I to refer to themselves. They may also omit prepositions and conjunctions from phrases (Wing, 1969). Verbal autistic children may display pragmatic errors. They are unaware of the rules of conversation, do not judge the appropriateness of their comments, and may talk about topics of interest only to themselves (Ricks & Wing, 1976).

It is important to consider the interaction between the handicapping condition and delayed or deviant language development. For example, a child who evidences a language disorder may be unable to express feelings and concerns in a socially acceptable manner and may resort to disruptive and violent behaviors. Such a child may subsequently be labeled emotionally disturbed when, in fact, the language disability may be the primary handicapping condition. Conversely, a child evidencing Down syndrome may be unable to respond appropriately to parental overtures of love and affection. Parents may find a lack of smiling and cooing discouraging and may inadvertently provide less verbal stimulation to their child. The child may subsequently be labeled mentally retarded but may also evidence a language disability. Educators are advised to consider the relationship between a handicap and a language disability when designing and implementing intervention strategies for exceptional children.

## REFERENCES

Baltaxe, C., & Simmons, J. (1975). Language in childhood psychosis: A review. *Journal of Speech & Hearing Disorders, 40,* 439–458.

Bliss, L., Allen, D., & Walker, G. (1978). Sentence structures of trainable and educable mentally retarded subjects. *Journal of Speech & Hearing Research, 20,* 722–731.

Bryen, D. N. (1981). Language and language problems. In A. Gerber & D. N. Bryen (Eds.), *Language and learning disabilities* (pp. 27–60). Baltimore: University Park Press.

Carrow-Woolfolk, E., & Lynch, J. I. (1982). *An integrative approach to language disorders in children.* New York: Grune & Stratton.

Coggins, T. (1979). Relationship meaning encoded in the two-word utterance of Stage I Down's syndrome children. *Journal of Speech & Hearing Research, 22,* 166–178.

Eisenson, J. (1972). *Aphasia in children.* New York: Harper & Row.

Fay, W. H. (1969). On the basis of autistic echolalia. *Journal of Communication Disorders, 2,* 38–47.

Fay, W. H. (1980). Aspects of language. In W. H. Fay & A. L. Schuler (Eds.), *Emerging language in autistic children* (pp. 21–50). Baltimore: University Park Press.

*Federal Register.* (1977, Dec. 29). (65082–65085.) Washington, DC.

Goda, S. (1959). Language skills of profoundly deaf adolescent children. *Journal of Speech & Hearing Research, 2,* 369–376.

Goda, S. (1964). Spoken syntax of normal, deaf, and retarded adolescents. *Journal of Verbal Learning & Verbal Behavior, 3,* 401–405.

Gomez, A., & Podhajski, B. (1978). Language and mental retardation. In C. H. Carter (Ed.), *Medical aspects of mental retardation* (pp. 51–65). Springfield, IL: Thomas.

Hoemann, H. (1972). The development of communication skills in deaf and hearing children. *Child Development, 43,* 990–1103.

Lackner, J. R. (1968). A developmental study of language behavior in retarded children. *Neuropsychologia, 6,* 301–320.

Lovaas, O. (1968). A program for the establishment of speech in psychotic children. In H. Sloan & B. MacAulay (Eds.), *Operant procedures in remedial speech and language-training* (pp. 125–156). Boston: Houghton Mifflin.

Lovaas, O. (1977). *The autistic child.* New York: Halsted.

Menyuk, P. (1971). *The acquisition and development of language.* Englewood Cliffs, NJ: Prentice Hall.

Menyuk, P. (1972). *The development of speech.* New York: Bobbs-Merrill.

Miller, J. F., & Yoder, D. E. (1974). An orthogenetic language teaching strategy for retarded children. In R. L. Schiefelbusch & L. L. Lloyd (Eds.), *Language perspectives-acquisition retardation, and intervention* (pp. 505–528). Baltimore: University Park Press.

Myklebust, H. (1960). *The psychology of deafness.* New York: Grune & Stratton.

Power, D. J., & Quigley, S. P. (1973). Deaf children's acquisition of the passive voice. *Journal of Speech & Hearing Research, 16,* 5–11.

Pugh, G. (1946). Appraisal of the silent reading abilities of acoustically handicapped children. *American Annals of the Deaf, 91,* 331–335.

Quigley, S. P., Wilbur, R. B., & Montanelli, D. S. (1976). Complement structures in the language of deaf students. *Journal of Speech & Hearing Research, 19,* 448–466.

Rich, H., Beck, M., & Coleman, T. (1982). Behavior management: The psychoeducational model. In R. McDowell, G. Adamson, & F. Wood (Eds.), *Teaching emotionally disturbed children* (pp. 131–166). Boston: Little, Brown.

Ricks, D. M., & Wing, L. (1976). Language communication and the use of symbols in normal and autistic children. In L. Wing (Ed.), *Early childhood autism* (pp. 93–134). Oxford, England: Pergamon.

Rutter, M. (1965). Speech disorders in a series of autistic children. In A. W. Franklin (Ed.), *Children with communication problems.* London: Pitman.

Schiefelbusch, R. L. (1972). Language disabilities of cognitively involved children. In J. Irwin & M. Marge (Eds.), *Principles of childhood language disabilities.* Englewood, NJ: Prentice Hall.

Schlanger, B. S. (1973). *Mental retardation.* Indianapolis, IN: Bobbs-Merrill.

Simmons, A. A. (1962). A comparison of the type-token ratio of spoken and written language of deaf children. *Volta Review, 64,* 417–421.

Spreen, O. (1965). Language function in mental retardation. *Journal of Mental Deficiency, 69,* 482–489.

Swanson, H. L., & Reinert, H. R. (1984). *Teaching strategies for children in conflict* (2nd ed.). St. Louis, MO: Times Mirror/Mosby.

Swisher, L. P. (1976). The language performance of the oral deaf. In H. Whitaker & H. A. Whitaker (Eds.), *Studies in neurolinguistics* (pp. 53–93). New York: Academic.

Templin, M. C. (1963). Vocabulary knowledge and usage among deaf and learning children. *Proceedings of the International Congress on Education of the Deaf.* Washington, DC: U.S. Government Printing Office.

Werry, J. (1979). The childhood psychoses. In H. Quay & J. Werry (Eds.), *Psychopathological disorders of childhood* (pp. 43–89). New York: Wiley.

Wiig, E., & Semel, E. M. (1976). *Language disabilities in children and adolescents.* Columbus, OH: Merrill.

Wilbur, R. B., Montanelli, D. S., & Quigley, S. P. (1976). Pronominalization in the language of deaf students. *Journal of Speech & Hearing Research, 19,* 120–140.

Wing, L. (1969). The handicaps of autistic children: A comparative study. *Journal of Child Psychology and Psychiatry, 10,* 1–40.

MAUREEN A. SMITH
*Pennsylvania State University*

**LANGUAGE DELAYS**
**LANGUAGE DISORDERS**

## ORAL-MOTOR DEVELOPMENT IN INFANTS

The term oral-motor development in infants encompasses the development of the areas of chewing and swallowing, oral exploration, and sound play (Morris & Klein, 1987). Oral-motor development progresses at a rapid rate in the typically developing infant. In the first year of life, the child advances from a being whose early motor movements that are largely controlled by primitive reflexes (subcortical) to the ability of purposeful movement that is controlled by higher levels of the brain.

Typically developing newborns begin life with a collection of movement patterns known as primitive reflexes. These complex patterns of movement responses are observed in numerous situations as the child reacts to various forms of sensory stimuli. Most of the early movements of newborns, however, are not purposeful. These movements are predictable reactions to the stimuli in the child's environment (Schor, 1990).

Primitive reflexes emerge as a part of the child's movement repertoire and are suppressed on a predictable timetable during the first year of the normally developing infant's life. Reflexes that fail to appear or that are not inhibited until long after they should have been are considered to be abnormally present. Infants with cerebral palsy or other disorders affecting motor development may retain primitive reflexes long after they normally disappear. Such abnormal movement patterns, over which the child lacks intentional control, negatively affect oral-motor development and often lead to dysphagia. The term disphagia refers to eating, drinking, and swallowing difficulties.

Oral-motor development is related to early speech development and is an important aspect of the development of eating and drinking skills in the young child. Eicher (1998, p. 261) states that: "The act of feeding requires a high level of oral-motor control and coordination superimposed on adequate trunk alignment and support. Atypical muscle tone and persistent primitive reflex activity frequently interfere with body alignment and trunk support."

The growth of oral-motor skills by the young child follows a sequence similar to other motor skills (Eicher, 1998). The oral-motor skills needed for eating and drinking continue to mature from birth through the first year. During this period, the child progresses from the reflexive actions of uncontrollable responses such as the automatic phasic bite-release pattern that looks as though the baby were chewing to actual, purposeful chewing of solid and semisolid foods. Infants also advance from suckling, in which the tongue moves back and forth in a licking-like manner while the jaw moves up and down rhythmically in an uncontrolled reflexive movement, to being able to purposefully suck to take in nourishment by building a negative pressure between the mouth and the nipple of the bottle or breast (Alexander, 2005). However, Orelove and Sobsey (1996) point out that research indicates that much of the oral-motor activity involved in eating and drinking is rhythmic, with one action creating sensory input that signals the next action to begin. These movements, such as chewing, are reflexive to a great extent, even though the individual can extend some voluntary control. Thus, feeding involves actions that are reflexes, reflex-like patterns, and voluntary.

Many of the same oral-motor movements that make eating and drinking possible are also utilized in oral communication. The anatomical areas of the mouth, tongue, jaws, and lips are integral in the speech process as well as in chewing and swallowing. The level of development of oral-motor control directly affects the ability of the child to learn to speak. Oral-motor difficulties may affect the child's ability to form sounds required to produce understandable oral language. Speech and language specialists are equipped with the training and qualifications to address such disorders in the child's language.

Historically, the professionals most often involved in the child's oral-motor development have been speech and language specialists and occupational therapists. Lowman (2000) points out that in the schools, the primary responsibility for daily feeding the child with disabilities belongs to the educator. The educator must assume the responsibility of team leader in coordinating the creation of a comprehensive feeding plan. Special educators, in order to meet these responsibilities, must be knowledgeable of oral motor development and interventions that will assist the child with special needs in and out of the classroom and in working as a member of a collaborative team.

### REFERENCES

Alexander, R. (2005). Feeding and swallowing. In S. J. Best, K. W. Heller, & J. Bigge (Eds.), *Teaching individuals with physical or multiple disabilities.* Upper Saddle River, NJ: Pearson Prentice Hall.

Eicher, P. S. (1998). Nutrition and feeding. In J. P. Dormans, & L. Pelligrino (Eds.), *Caring for children with cerebral palsy: A team approach.* Baltimore: Brookes.

Lowman, D. K. (2000). *Feeding students with disabilities: An holistic approach for educators. Physical Disabilities: Education and Related Services, 18,* 75–88.

Morris, S. E., & Klein, M. D. (1987). *Pre-feeding skills: A comprehensive resource for feeding development.* Tucson, AZ: Therapy Skill Builders.

Orelove, F. P., & Sobsey, D. (1996). *Educating children with multiple disabilities: A transdisciplinary approach.* Baltimore: Brooks.

Schor, D. P. (1990). Neurological examination. In J. A. Blackman (Ed.), *Medical aspects of developmental disabilities in children birth to three* (pp. 205–209). Rockville, MD: Aspen.

JOSEPH R. TAYLOR
*Fresno Pacific University*

# ORAL READING

Oral reading, or reading aloud, is a technique that is used frequently during reading instruction, especially in the early elementary school grades. Oral reading often occurs in small groups in which each child takes a turn reading aloud sections of text. Allington (1984) reports a general decline in the amount of oral reading across grade levels. The decline is more dramatic for good reader groups; poor readers spend proportionately more time reading orally than do good readers.

Oral reading has been used as a technique for reading practice, as an assessment technique, and as intervention for improving student reading motivation (Carr, 1995). Errors in reading aloud can be analyzed to determine what kind of instruction is needed. Much attention also has been given to the best procedures for handling oral reading errors.

Several error correction procedures have been associated with greater than average reading gains (Anderson, Hiebert, Scott & Wilkinson, 1985). Most research suggests that if large numbers of errors are made, the selection may be too difficult and an easier one should be provided. Generally, errors should be ignored unless they disrupt the meaning of the text; frequent corrections will interrupt the child's train of thought and comprehension and may encourage the child to wait passively for help. For errors that affect meaning, an initial strategy is to see whether the child self-corrects without help. If that does not happen, the teacher should direct the child to clues about the word's meaning or pronunciation, depending on the error made. Once the correct word has been identified, the child should reread the sentence to help preserve the meaning.

As an assessment technique, oral reading in small groups is largely impressionistic, since teachers rarely make written records of oral reading strategies and behaviors (Allington, 1984). Both qualitative and quantitative systems for noting the nature and number of errors have been developed. Yet an analysis of oral reading errors may have limited generalizability to errors in other contexts, i.e., errors in isolation may not be comparable to those in context or to silent reading.

Much debate has occurred over the relative merits and disadvantages of oral and silent reading. Some studies have suggested that the merits and disadvantages may vary as a function of the child's skill level. For example, Miller and Smith (1985) found that poor readers had higher comprehension scores when reading grade-level passages orally than when reading them silently, although performance levels were relatively low for both reading formats. Readers at a medium level of competence had higher comprehension scores when reading silently than orally; no differences were found for the best readers in the study. The researchers hypothesized that oral reading may improve the performance of poor readers by demanding attention to individual words.

Oral reading has been used frequently with handicapped children exhibiting difficulties. It provides practice for students who might otherwise not read; a method for teachers to determine the effects of their instruction; and a diagnostic function that indicates sources of difficulty for particular students (Jenkins, Larson, & Fleisher, 1983).

Several studies have been conducted on the effects of error correction procedures with handicapped students. In an investigation of the effects of two such procedures (word supply and phonic analysis) on elementary learning-disabled (LD) students' oral reading rates, Rose, McEntire, and Dowdy (1982) found both procedures generally more effective than no error corrections. The word supply procedure was found to be relatively more effective than the phonic analysis procedure. In contrast, delayed teacher attention to oral reading errors was more effective than immediate attention or no attention in reducing the number of uncorrected oral reading errors and increasing the number of self-corrections by moderately mentally retarded children (Singh, Winton, & Singh, 1985).

Allington (1984) notes that poor readers tend to receive instruction emphasizing accuracy over rate, fluency, or sensitivity to syntactic elements. Poor readers are corrected more quickly and more often than good readers, and are more often directed to surface level features of text. Poor readers have been found to make fewer self-corrections than good readers.

One way to diminish the problem of poor fluency or comprehension with oral reading by small groups of poor readers is to have the children repeatedly read the same passage until attaining acceptable level of fluency. Repeated reading can occur with the assistance of a tape recorder, a teacher aide, or peers.

Another method to improve oral reading fluency is to have children read a passage silently before reading it aloud. However, classroom observations indicate that previewing is the exception, rather than the rule (Anderson, Hiebert, Scott, & Wilkinson, 1985).

Rose (1984; Rose & Sherry, 1984) and Sutton (1991)

found previewing procedures (allowing the learner to read or listen to a passage prior to instruction and/or testing) to be effective in increasing oral reading rates of both elementary and secondary LD students.

## REFERENCES

Allington, R. L. (1984). Oral reading. In P. D. Pearson (Ed.), *Handbook of reading research* (pp. 829–864). New York: Longman.

Anderson, R. C., Hiebert, E. H., Scott, J. A., & Wilkinson, I. A. G. (1985). *Becoming a nation of readers: The report of the Commission on Reading.* Champaign, IL: Center for the Study of Reading.

Carr, D. (1995). Improving student reading motivation through the use of oral reading strategies. (ERIC Clearinghouse No. CS012245)

Jenkins, J. R., Larson, K., & Fleisher, L. (1983). Effects of error correction on word recognition and reading comprehension. *Learning Disability Quarterly, 6*(2), 139–145.

Miller, S. D., & Smith, D. E. P. (1985). Differences in literal and inferential comprehension after reading orally and silently. *Journal of Educational Psychology, 77*(3), 341–348.

Rose, T. L. (1984). The effects of two prepractice procedures on oral reading. *Journal of Learning Disabilities, 17*(9), 544–548.

Rose, T. L., McEntire, E., & Dowdy, C. (1982). Effects of two error-correction procedures on oral reading. *Learning Disability Quarterly, 5*(2), 100–105.

Rose, T. L., & Sherry, L. (1984). Relative effects of two previewing procedures on LD adolescents' oral reading performance. *Learning Disability Quarterly, 7*(1), 39–44.

Singh, N. N., Winton, A. S. W., & Singh, J. (1985). Effects of delayed versus immediate attention to oral reading errors on the reading proficiency of mentally retarded children. *Applied Research in Mental Retardation, 6*(3), 283–293.

Sutton, P. A. (1991). Strategies to increase oral reading fluency of primary resource students. (ERIC Clearinghouse No. CS010683)

LINDA J. STEVENS
*University of Minnesota*

## ORAL VERSUS MANUAL COMMUNICATION

Oral versus manual communication refers to the debate surrounding the methodology used to educate individuals with hearing impairments. The oral method consists of speech reading, auditory training, speech, written expression, reading, and the use of common gestures (Chasen & Zuckerman, 1976). This method emphasizes maximum use of audition to develop the oral communication skills necessary for successful integration of hearing-impaired persons into society. The oral method has also been referred to as the auditory-oral, acoupedic, natural, and unisensory method (Bender, 1981). Strictly interpreted, the manual method includes the use of sign language, finger spelling, and common gestures. Rarely, however, do supporters of manual communication advocate exclusion of speech and speech reading; rather, they encourage simultaneous use of these methods (Pahz & Pahz, 1978).

Manual communication has been used interchangeably with total communication, a phrase coined in the late 1960s and formally adopted in 1976. Total communication actually refers to a philosophy of communication with and among hearing-impaired people. Deaf individuals select communication methods from a variety options including speech, speech reading, audition, finger spelling, sign language, reading, and written expression (Convention of Executives of American Schools for the Deaf, 1976).

Much of the debate surrounding oral and manual communication has focused on the merits of each. Advocates of oral communication express the following beliefs:

1. Maximum development of speech and speech-reading skills can be achieved only through maximum dependence on speech and speech reading. Using sign language interferes with the development of these skills.

2. Oral communication enhances integration into the mainstream of society. Use of sign language separates the child from family and friends (Berger, 1972).

3. A deaf child should be exclusively oral until it is established through repeated attempts that he or she cannot progress without some means of manual communication.

In contrast, advocates of manual communication express the following beliefs:

1. Oral communication gives the development of language a low priority after speech, speech reading, and auditory training.

2. Use of manual communication facilitates the development of language and other concepts and knowledge vital to normal mental development. Use of oral communication to learn language is a painfully slow process for most children and may waste many of the formative years necessary for language acquisition.

3. Reliance on speech reading to gain information is unreasonable as many speech sounds are not visible on the lips. Use of manual communication provides complete, accurate information that requires no educated guesses to fill in gaps.

Each of these methods has enjoyed a period of popularity only to be discarded in favor of the other in light of changes in public opinion or medical and technological advances. Participants in the oral/manual controversy have debated these methods for over 200 years. The first debate occurred between Abbe Charles, Michel de l'Epée, the "father of sign language," and Samuel Heinicke, the "father of oralism."

In 1760 de l'Epée opened a school in Paris, France, the first school anywhere in which deaf children could receive an education. Epée believed deaf people could communicate more effectively by using visual symbols rather than speech. Therefore, students attending the school were instructed by teachers communicating with signs collected by de l'Epée from populations large enough to include deaf people. He believed these signs constituted a mother tongue for the deaf and supplemented them with grammatical markers to indicate gender, tense, and number. Eighteen years later, in 1798, Heinicke opened Germany's first school for the deaf, in which students were educated through speech and lip reading. Heinicke maintained his approach facilitated integration of the deaf into general society. Word of de l'Epée's success reached Heinicke and in 1782 both men asked scholars at the Zurich Academy to settle their dispute. Although academy members found in favor of de l'Epée's methods, Heinicke and his supporters remained unconvinced and continued to argue vigorously for the oral method.

De l'Epée's method of manual communication was brought to the United States by Thomas Hopkins Gallaudet. Gallaudet had been sent to Europe by Mason Cogswell and a group of influential friends to study techniques for educating hearing-impaired individuals. Gallaudet traveled to Paris to study the manual methods of Abbe Roch Ambrose Cucurron Sicard, who had trained as a teacher under Epée. He returned to America in 1816 and, in 1817, assisted in the establishment of the American Asylum for the Deaf in Hartford, Connecticut. Assisted by Larent Clerc, a former pupil of Sicard, Gallaudet succeeded in adapting French sign language in order to teach English. Thus, manual communication was established as a method for educating hearing-impaired students in America.

By the middle of the nineteenth century, prominent educators had become dissatisfied with manual communication. In 1843 Horace Mann and Samuel Gridley Howe traveled to Germany to visit the oral schools there and returned to the United States convinced of the superiority of oral communication. Interest in this method of communication led to the establishment of the New York Institute for Impaired Instruction (now the Lexington School) in 1874 and the Clarke School for the Deaf in Chelmsford, Massachusetts, in 1867. Thus proponents of each method of communication had firmly established schools for hearing-impaired students that used their preferred methods.

By the end of the nineteenth century, each side of the oral/manual controversy was represented by prominent, highly educated men. Edward Miner Gallaudet, president of the National College for the Deaf and Dumb (predecessor to Gallaudet College), sided with advocates of manual communication. Alexander Graham Bell, an oral teacher of the deaf and future inventor of the telephone, sided with advocates of oral communication. Both were strong-willed and opinionated and disagreed over the goals of educating hearing-impaired people as well as the methods by which to accomplish those goals (Benderly, 1980). Gallaudet believed manual communication encouraged the development of a deaf culture and community. Bell maintained that deaf people should be absorbed into the mainstream of society and that oral communication was the best way to ensure this process. His position received far-reaching support. In 1880 delegates to the Congress of Teachers of the Deaf in Milan voted overwhelmingly in favor of oral communication as the preferred method of educating hearing-impaired children. By the close of the nineteenth century, every country except the United States made the oral method a national policy. Although still used in the United States, manual communication was reserved for use with slower students in upper grades.

During the twentieth century, interest in the oral method continued as a result of technological advances. Improvements in hearing-aid technology and the development of auditory training programs allowed many deaf children to use their residual hearing and maximize the benefits received from an oral education. However, many improvements also occurred in medicine during the twentieth century. Widespread use of antibiotics and vaccinations eliminated many of the causes of hearing impairments. These medical advances saved the lives of children born prematurely or suffering from infections but at the same time left many of these children hearing impaired. Thus during the 1940s and 1950s, hearing-impaired students being served in programs for the deaf were more likely to be suffering from prelingual losses and multiple handicaps (Benderly, 1980). By the 1960s, professionals' concern for the welfare of these students, coupled with an increased sensitivity to minority groups and an appreciation of their distinct characteristics, resulted in a revived interest in the use of manual communication (Pahz & Pahz, 1978). Schools in Louisiana, North Carolina, and California began experimenting with manual methods of communication (Benderly, 1980). Once again, the controversy between supporters of each method surfaced. To settle the issue once and for all, supporters on each side began to gather empirical data to demonstrate the superiority of their methods. Unfortunately, the evidence failed to decide definitively in favor of either oral or manual communication.

Berger (1972) reported orally trained deaf students demonstrated speech-reading skills superior to those demonstrated by manually trained deaf students. Lavos (1944), in an early study, reported that orally trained students scored higher than their manually trained peers on language usage, arithmetic reasoning, and computation. Other studies have supported the use of manual communication.

Manually trained deaf students have demonstrated superior performance on measures of word recognition (DiCarlo, 1964), reading (Delaney, Stuckless, & Walter, 1984; DiCarlo, 1964; Meadow; 1968; Orwid, 1970), speech reading (Delaney, Stuckless, & Walter, 1984; DiCarlo, 1964; Orwid, 1971), written language (Meadow, 1978; Orwid, 1971), and math (Chasen & Zuckerman, 1976; Delaney, Stuckless, & Walter, 1981; Meadow, 1968). It should be noted, however, that many of the manually trained students included in those investigations were educated in programs incorporating a philosophy of total communication. Therefore, they were encouraged to develop speech and speech-reading skills and to use any residual hearing.

It is apparent that no clear winner of the oral/manual debate has emerged as supporters on either side can easily document the superiority of their methods. This has led some school systems to offer a choice of communication options to hearing impaired students (Hawkins & Brawner, 1997). The trend appears to be toward manual methods as provided in programs embracing a philosophy of total communication. Whatever system the school system and educators propose, the future is colored by the growth and adherence to deaf culture (Gustason, 1997).

**REFERENCES**

Bender, R. (1981). *Conquest of deafness* (3rd ed.). Danville, IL: Interstate Printers.

Benderly, B. L. (1980). *Dancing without music: Deafness in America.* Garden City, NY: Anchor/Doubleday.

Berger, K. (1972). *Speech reading: Principals and methods.* Baltimore: National Education Press.

Chasen, B., & Zuckerman, W. (1976). The effects of total communication and oralism in deaf third-grade "rubella" students. *American Annals of the Deaf, 121,* 394–402.

Convention of Executives of American Schools for the Deaf (1976). *Defining total communication.* Rochester, NY.

Delaney, M., Stuckless, E. R., & Walter, G. G. (1984). Total communication effects—A longitudinal study of a school for the deaf in transition. *American Annals of the Deaf, 129,* 481–486.

DiCarlo, L. (1964). *The deaf.* Englewood Cliffs, NJ: Prentice Hall.

Gustason, G. (1997). Educating children who are deaf or hard of hearing: English-based sign systems. *ERIC Digest # E556.* Reston, VA: ERIC Clearinghouse on Disabilities and Gifted Education.

Hawkins, L., & Brawner, J. (1997). Educating children who are deaf or hard of hearing: Total communication. *ERIC Digest #559.* Reston, VA: ERIC Clearinghouse on Disabilities and Gifted Education.

Jordan, I. K., Gustason, G., & Rosen, R. (1979). An update on communication trends at programs for the deaf. *American Annals of the Deaf, 124,* 350–357.

Lavos, G. (1944). The reliability of an educational achieved test administered to the deaf. *American Annals of the Deaf, 89,* 226–232.

Meadow, E. (1968). Early manual communication in relation to the deaf child's intellectual, social, and communication functioning. *American Annals of the Deaf, 113,* 29–41.

Orwid, H. L. (1971). Studies in manual communication with hearing impaired children. *Volta Review, 73,* 428–438.

Pahz, J. A., & Pahz, S. P. (1978). *Total communication.* Springfield, IL: Thomas.

MAUREEN A. SMITH
*Pennsylvania State University*

DEAF EDUCATION
SIGN LANGUAGE
TOTAL COMMUNICATION

# ORDINAL SCALES OF PSYCHOLOGICAL DEVELOPMENT

The Ordinal Scales of Psychological Development (Uzgiris & Hunt, 1975) were designed to assess development abilities in infants up to 2 years of age. The scales were developed from a Piagetian principle that there is an invariant sequence of developmental landmarks, not linked to a specific age, that are characteristic of an infant's ability to manipulate and organize interactions with the environment (Gorrell, 1985). There are six basic abilities measured: (1) the development of visual pursuit; (2) the development of means for obtaining desired environmental events; (3) the development of vocal and gestural imitation; (4) the development of operational causality; (5) the construction of object relations in space, and (6) the development of schemes for relating to others.

Scoring is done by checking possible actions from a sample list. Interpretation is objective; therefore, for more reliable results, the tester should be familiar with the test procedure. The obtained information is compared in terms of the developmental advancement or retardation exhibited by the testee. Rosenthal (1985) has found the ordinal scales to have good reliabilities. Percentage of interrater agreement was found to be 96.1 percent, and agreement between sessions was 79.9 percent. The test was praised because it narrowed its focus for assessment, unlike its broad-ranged predecessors.

**REFERENCES**

Gorrell, J. (1985). *Test critiques* (Vol. 2). Kansas City: Test Corporation of America.

Rosenthal, A. C. (1985). Review of assessment in infancy: Ordinal Scales of Psychological Development. In J. H. Mitchell, Jr. (Ed.), *The ninth mental measurements yearbook* (Vol. 2). Lincoln: University of Nebraska Press.

Uzgirus, T. C., & Hunt, J. (1975). *Assessment in infancy: Ordinal Scales of Psychological Development.* Urbana: University of Illinois Press.

LISA J. SAMPSON
*Eastern Kentucky University*

# ORGANIZATIONAL CHANGE

During the remainder of this century, organizational change will be an important issue in special education. Organizational change refers to the process that any organizational unit (e.g., work group, department, school, school district) adapts to client needs, rules, regulations, and other factors. Organizational change acknowledges the fact that all organizational units are in flux and that they adapt to demands in either functional or dysfunctional ways. Currently, concern exists nationwide for effective, efficient, and responsive service delivery systems (National Coalition of Advocates for Students, 1985). Furthermore, it is important for special education systems to be compatible and well-coordinated with regular education systems. Functional organizational change in special education, therefore, should take into account these important issues.

To accomplish functional organizational change, it is fundamental that a planned, systematic approach be employed by local level professionals. A planned, systematic approach is one that includes the following phases and constituent activities (Maher & Bennett, 1984):

## Clarifying the Organizational Problem

1. Assessing the organizational problem
2. Assessing organization readiness for change
3. Defining the problem in measurable terms

## Designing the Organizational Intervention

1. Describing purpose, goals, and objectives
2. Generating and selecting interventions to implement
3. Developing a written intervention design

## Implementing the Organizational Intervention

1. Maximizing the degree to which the intervention is implemented in technically adequate, ethical, useful, and practical ways

## Assessing the Organizational Intervention

1. Assessing the extent to which design elements were implemented
2. Assessing the extent to which goals of the interventions were attained

The first phase, clarifying the organizational problem, is an often neglected but important activity. It assesses an organization's readiness for change. One framework that has seemed useful for assessing organizational readiness for change is Davis and Salasin's (1975) A-VICTORY framework. The A-VICTORY is an acronym of eight factors believed to be related to organizational readiness for change (see Illback & Hargan, 1984 for an example of how the A-VICTORY framework can be used in special education). These eight factors are:

*Ability.* Resources available to carry out implementation of the intervention, including human, financial, material, technological, and physical ones.

*Values.* Attitudes and beliefs of organizational members concerning what comprises acceptable organizational behaviors.

*Idea.* Degree to which organizational members have a clear and comprehensive understanding of a proposed intervention.

*Circumstances.* Current organizational factors that may either inhibit or facilitate an organization's accommodation of an intervention.

*Timing.* Degree that implementation of intervention is compatible with important events occurring within the organization.

*Obligation.* Organizational members' perceptions of the extent to which an intervention is needed.

*Resistance.* Extent that organizational members have misgivings or concerns about adopting the intervention.

*Yield.* Extent that organizational members believe that there will be important benefits from the intervention.

In regard to the second phase, designing the organizational intervention, five criteria can be used in developing the intervention's design. These criteria have been adapted from Provus (1972). The first criterion, clarity, refers to the degree to which the design is understandable and clear. Comprehensiveness, the second criterion, concerns the extent to which the design includes details relative to the purpose, implementation, and expected outcomes of the intervention. The third criterion, internal consistency, denotes the extent that components of the design are logically interrelated. Compatibility is the fourth criterion and refers to the degree to which the design is compatible with both the need for the intervention and with ongoing routines within the organization. The final criterion, theoretical soundness, denotes the extent that the components of the design are consistent with good professional practice as indicated by expert opinion and empirical research.

An often neglected aspect of the third phase, implementing the organizational intervention, is systematically facilitating the implementation of the intervention. Recent research (e.g., Maher, 1984) identified six activities that appear to be related to facilitating the implementation of organizational interventions. First, implementors of the intervention should discuss with one another the purpose, implementation, and expected outcomes of the intervention. Second, intervention implementors should have the opportunity to understand each other's concerns and misgivings about the intervention. Third, intervention implementors should be encouraged, given positive feedback, and otherwise reinforced for their contributions. Fourth, the intervention should be adapted as a result from feedback from relevant organization members. Fifth, positive expectations about the intervention's success should be fostered and maintained among the intervention's implementors. Finally, learning should occur about potential obstacles to implementing the intervention.

During the fourth phase, assessing the organizational intervention, at least two types of assessment questions should be addressed: (1) what components of the intervention were implemented? and (2) Were the stated goals of the intervention attained? These two questions seem to be particularly germane to developing and improving special education service delivery systems (Maher & Bennett, 1984). However, other assessment questions can also be addressed: (1) did the intervention cause the observed outcomes? (2) What were the related or unintended effects (either positive or negative) of the intervention? (3) What were an individual's reactions to the intervention?

Beer (1980) has identified four general categories of approaches to organizational change. They are diagnostic, process, technostructural, and individual. The purpose of a diagnostic intervention is to collect information that might help define the nature and scope of the organizational problem. Often, a diagnostic intervention is followed by other organizational interventions. One or more of four data collection methods can be used in diagnostic intervention: direct observation, review of permanent products or written records, interviews, and questionnaires or rating forms.

Process approaches to organizational intervention target relationships among organizational members for change. One approach to process intervention, survey feedback, encompasses both the collection of survey data and the communication of the survey's results to selected organizational members. Another process approach, team development, involves team members in a collaborative effort to improve their teams' effectiveness and efficiency. The system development process approach is intended to improve relationships between interdependent work teams. The final process approach is process consultation. Though process consultation can overlap with the other process approaches, it is chiefly concerned with a consultant helping selected organizational members to understand and change problematic organizational processes.

Technostructural approaches to organizational change entail altering organizational structures as a means to improving worker satisfaction or productivity. One technostructural approach involves altering systems of reward, such as the manner in which wages or verbal praise are delivered to staff. The second technostructural approach is managing job performance. This approach may involve management by objectives (MBO), goal setting, performance appraisal, or performance review and development. Job design, also a technostructural approach, entails altering characteristics of work tasks or working conditions so that workers are more satisfied or productive. The fourth technostructural approach to intervention, organizational design, concerns making global structural changes such as decentralizing the decision-making process within an organization.

The fourth category of approaches to organizational change focuses on the individual staff. An example of this approach, recruitment and selection, is concerned with matching the job role demands with abilities and skills of the individual. Another individual approach attempts to further organizational change by engaging individuals in continuing professional development activities. Finally, individual counseling can be used to reduce or alleviate interpersonal or personal problems that may be interfering with a staff's productivity (for a more extensive discussion of approaches to changing school organizations, see Maher, Illback, & Zins, 1984).

## REFERENCES

Beer, M. (1980). *Organization change and development: A systems view.* Santa Monica, CA: Goodyear.

Davis, H. T., & Salasin, S. E. (1975). The utilization of evaluation. In E. L. Struening & M. Guttentag (Eds.), *Handbook of evaluation research* (Vol. 1). Beverly Hills, CA: Sage.

Illback, R. J., & Hargan, L. (1984). Assessing and facilitating school readiness for microcomputers. *Special Services in the Schools, 1,* 91–105.

Maher, C. A. (1984). Implementing programs and systems in organizational settings: The DURABLE approach. *Journal of Organizational Behavior Management, 6,* 69–98.

Maher, C. A., & Bennett, R. E. (1984). *Planning and evaluating special education services.* Englewood Cliffs, NJ: Prentice Hall.

Maher, C. A., Illback, R. J., & Zins, J. E. (1984). *Organizational psychology in the schools: A handbook for professionals.* Springfield, IL: Thomas.

National Coalition of Advocates for Students. (1985). *Barriers to excellence: Our children at risk.* Boston: Author.

Provus, M. (1972). *Discrepancy evaluation.* Berkeley, CA: McCutchan.

CHARLES A. MAHER
*Rutgers University*

LOUIS J. KRUGER
*Tufts University*

## HUMAN RESOURCE DEVELOPMENT SUPERVISION IN SPECIAL EDUCATION

## ORPHAN DISEASES

See NATIONAL ORGANIZATION OF RARE DISORDERS.

## ORTHOGENIC SCHOOL

The Orthogenic School was established by Bettelheim (1950) to promote the application of Freudian principles of psychoanalysis to the treatment of behaviorally disordered children and youths. Adherents to psychoanalysis and the Orthogenic School approach believe that each individual's thoughts and behaviors are determined by unconscious motivations, formed during earlier stages of development. Disorders of behavior (overt and covert) are the result of early conflicts left primarily unresolved; these conflicts can result in a fixation of development at a particular Freudian stage. In the Orthogenic School of Bettelheim, teachers would create a permissive environment in which children could act on their impulses. Rather than correct behavior problems, teachers would work to help students achieve insight into their behavior through interpreting the symbolism of their actions. The Orthogenic School created a therapeutic milieu where the intrapsychic anxieties of troubled youths need not be contained. The Orthogenic School movement did not achieve widespread acceptance or implementation in special education circles although psychodynamic thought has influenced the development of various psychoeducational models of treatment in the schools.

### REFERENCE

Bettelheim, B. (1950). *Love is not enough.* New York: Macmillan.

CECIL R. REYNOLDS
*Texas A&M University*

## ORTHOPEDIC DISABILITY

With advances in legislation for individuals with disabilities (e.g., IDEA, its reauthorizations Section 504 of the Rehabilitation Act), a greater number of students with orthopedic disabilities are being included into regular or general education classes. In addition, students with multiple disabilities (e.g., severe mental retardation and cerebral palsy) are being served in public school settings with increasing frequency. The classroom teacher must take into account the specific needs of students with orthopedic disabilities when planning instruction. An awareness of the types of orthopedic disabilities as well as intervention methods is useful for teachers of students with such disabilities.

Orthopedic disabilities may be congenital (present from birth) or acquired (from trauma or injury). Certain conditions such as cerebral palsy involve one or all of the extremities. Cerebral palsy is a nonprogressive disorder caused by damage to the brain that results in disturbance of voluntary motor function. Individuals with cerebral palsy may be affected in one (monoplegia) to all of their limbs (quadriplegia; Jones, 1983). Other students may have disabilities in just one area of the body (Fraser & Hensinger, 1983). Common spinal deformities that affect voluntary movement include scoliosis (curvature of the spine) and spina bifida. Spina bifida may have associated hydrocephalus (fluid accumulation in or around the brain) and may cause various levels of disturbance of voluntary limb function depending on the degree and location of the spinal deformity.

Common disabilities in the legs and feet include hip dislocation or subluxation (separation of the femur and acetabulum that does not entail complete dislocation), knee flexion and extension deformities, and foot deformities such as equinus (foot pointed down) and calcaneus (foot pointed up). Wrist, hand, and arm deformities may include contractures of the elbow flexors (in which the elbow stays stiffly bent), ulnar deviation of the wrist (in which the wrist is flexed and the hand deviates to one side), thumb-in-hand deformity, or finger flexion deformity.

Surgical treatment of these deformities is sometimes the option chosen by parents or guardians, specialists, or the physically disabled person. In addition, various types of braces, prosthetic, and orthotic devices may be used prior to the decision to have surgery or following surgery as a method of preventing further deformities. The classroom teacher should be familiar with prosthetic and orthotic devices and positioning equipment (e.g., adapted wheelchairs) that are used by students with orthopedic disabilities. Close consultation with ancillary staff (e.g., occupational therapists, physical therapists) should occur on a regular basis to facilitate appropriate management techniques.

Because the classroom teacher often has students with orthopedic disabilities in class for most of the day, carry over of techniques used in special therapy sessions should occur in the classroom (Dykes & Venn, 1983). Classroom teachers should closely observe the general health and changes in health status of their students and make referrals as needed. Teachers should also be sensitive to and aware of negative attitudes of normal peers toward the child with orthopedic disabilities and adjust accordingly (Cohen, 1994). Knowledge of physical adaptations through consultations with specialists and attendance at in-service or preservice classes on management of the orthopedically disabled will be necessary for the classroom teacher. Modification of instructional strategies and materials may be required to meet students' physical needs. Finally, awareness of the psychosocial aspects of physical disabilities (Carpignano, Sirvis, & Bigge, 1982) will be necessary in order to address the social and emotional needs of students with orthopedic disabilities. Indeed extracurricular activities should be encouraged to support social inclusion (Niva, 1994).

As technological advances in electronics and computers continue, increased adaptation of seating, communication devices, and replacements for bracing equipment (e.g., the use of electronic stimulation) will be seen. Advances in medical care (e.g., computerized tomography [CT] scanners, position emission tomography [PET] scanners, computerized gait laboratories) will continue to allow doctors and physical therapists to make better use of their resources in managing neuromuscular problems in persons with disabilities. In addition, advances in surgical care will allow for more sophisticated analyses of pre- and post-operative conditions. In addition, prevention of deformities through surgery will continue to have successful results in coming years (Fraser & Hensinger, 1983). These advances will surely have an effect on students with orthopedic disabilities entering public school classrooms.

The teacher of students with orthopedic disabilities can provide appropriate instruction by working closely with specialists and providing carry over of techniques and adaptations suggested by specialists into the classroom. With a team approach in which all members of the staff, as well as the student where appropriate, have a share in program planning, education for students with orthopedic disabilities will allow such students to function as independently as possible.

**REFERENCES**

Carpignano, J., Sirvis, B., & Bigge, J. (1982). Psychosocial aspects of physical disability. In J. L. Bigge (Ed.), *Teaching individuals with physical and multiple disabilities* (2nd ed., pp. 110–137). Columbus, OH: Merrill.

Cohen, R. (1994). Preschoolers' evaluations of physical disabilities: A consideration of attitudes and behavior. *Journal of Pediatric Psychology, 19*(1), 103–111.

Dykes, M. K., & Venn, J. (1983). Using health, physical, and medical data in the classroom. In J. Umbreit (Ed.), *Physical disabilities and health impairments: An introduction* (pp. 259–280). Columbus, OH: Merrill.

Fraser, B. A., & Hensinger, R. N. (1983). *Managing physical handicaps: A practical guide for parents, care providers, and educators.* Baltimore: Brookes.

Jones, M. H. (1983). Cerebral palsy. In J. Umbreit (Ed.), *Physical disabilities and health impairments: An introduction* (pp. 41–58). Columbus, OH: Merrill.

Niva, W. L. (1994, July 8–11). *The extent of participation in extracurricular activities at the secondary level of students with different exceptionalities in an urban school district.* Paper presented at the International Conference of the Association for the Study of Cooperation in Education, Portland, OR.

CORNELIA LIVELY
*University of Illinois, Urbana-Champaign*

**CEREBRAL PALSY**
**SPINA BIFIDA**

# ORTHOPSYCHIATRY

Orthopsychiatry is perhaps best described as a collaborative or interdisciplinary approach to the promotion of mental health and the study of human development. Psychiatrists, psychologists, educators, social workers, pediatricians, nurses, lawyers, and other professionals constitute the American Orthopsychiatric Association, founded in 1924. From its earliest years, orthopsychiatry as a field has served as a forum for uniting the contributions from many disciplines and attacking mental health problems with a unified approach (Levy, 1931). Orthopsychiatry addresses issues affecting adolescents, adults, families, and, especially, children. Based on the assumption that an individual's problems are the result of the interplay of one's psychic and organic capabilities with the social milieu, orthopsychiatry focuses on both prevention and treatment of the individual in societal and environmental contexts. Extending the scope of health care beyond the consultation room and clinic has also been an historical emphasis in orthopsychiatry.

In recent years, orthopsychiatry has become widely known as the field where the roles of professionals from numerous disciplines are integrated in the prevention of illness and the promotion of mental health. The American Orthopsychiatric Association has actively promoted the elimination of rivalries and competition among professionals, and has become involved with issues of civil liberty, behavioral illnesses, fetal mental health, and genetic engineering (Pierce, 1984).

Membership in the American Orthopsychiatric Association is open to all those working in the mental health fields who meet certain educational, or employment criteria. The association publishes the *American Journal of Orthopsychiatry,* a quarterly publication of selected theoretical, research, administrative and clinical articles; *Readings,* a journal of reviews and commentary; and the *Ortho Newsletter.* The American Orthopsychiatric Association is headquartered in New York City; it sponsors an annual meeting each spring.

**REFERENCES**

Levy, D. M. (1931). Psychiatry, and orthopsychiatry. *American Journal of Orthopsychiatry, 1,* 239–244.

Pierce, C. M. (1984). Twenty-first century orthopsychiatry. *American Journal of Orthopsychiatry, 54,* 364–368.

GREG VALCANTE
*University of Florida*

ECOLOGICAL ASSESSMENT
PSYCHOLOGICAL CLINICS
PSYCHOLOGY IN THE SCHOOLS

# ORTHOPSYCHIATRY MOVEMENT

Orthopsychiatry is a term that was adopted by a group of nine psychiatrists who first met in January 1924. The prefix ortho is a derivation of the Greek word for straight. Orthopsychiatry, therefore, literally means straight psychiatry. It was originally defined by the founding members as the "endeavor to obtain straightness of mind and spirit" (American Orthopsychiatric Association, 1985). By 1949 the American Orthopsychiatric Association (AOA) stated that "Orthopsychiatry connotes a philosophy . . . of interrelationships of various professions interested in learning about and shaping human behavior" (AOA, 1985). Since that time, it has "evolved to include the concepts of a preventive interdisciplinary approach and the interrelationship of social policy and mental health" (AOA, 1985).

The impetus to found the orthopsychiatry movement came from a group of psychiatrists, but it quickly moved to include psychologists and social workers (Lowrey, 1957). The initial meeting of the AOA, held in Chicago in June 1924, had the topic of prevention as its major theme (Mohr, 1938). This interest in prevention became a primary focus of the movement, and was expanded on to include three types of prevention. "Primary prevention refers to preventing the disease before it begins. Secondary prevention involves diagnosing the disease and instituting immediate treatment. Tertiary prevention concerns itself with treatment efforts to prevent or minimize further progression of a chronic condition" (Wolman, 1977, p. 161). From the standpoint of prevention as well as of treatment, it soon became apparent that a need existed for services from more than one specialty or discipline. This need for teamwork among professionals was recognized and encouraged by the orthopsychiatry movement. Initially this teamwork was seen as being the strict domain of psychiatrists, psychologists, and social workers. The anticipated roles were for the psychiatrist to see the child, the social worker to counsel the parent, and the psychologist to perform needed testing. During the 1960s, as other disciplines became more involved in the counseling field, the movement expanded to include many other professionals.

In 1985 the AOA had over 10,000 members, including psychiatrists, psychologists, social workers, nurses, educators, pediatricians, sociologists, lawyers, anthropologists, and other mental health professionals and paraprofessionals.

The AOA has published the *American Journal of Orthopsychiatry* since 1930. The goal of the journal is to synthesize and apply the

knowledge base of psychiatry, psychology, social work, and related medical, behavioral, educational, and social sciences. The relationship of clinical concerns to broader issues—environmental, familial, societal—that affect individual development . . . as well as the journal's dedication to promoting a preventive approach to problems of mental illness

have been consistent themes since its inception (AOA, 1985).

Membership in the organization as of 1985 is open to anyone working in the mental health or a related field who meets one of the following conditions: has a master's degree, a postgraduate degree, 2 years' employment in a mental health setting, 2 years in private practice, 4 years of active involvement in community mental health work, or full-time graduate work.

Members of the organization receive the *American Journal of Orthopsychiatry;* are exempt from general registration fees at the annual meeting; have priority registration for all meetings and workshops; are encouraged to submit proposals for presentation at meetings; receive *Ortho Newsletter;* participate in the association's governance, committees, and task forces; receive annual book discounts; are listed in and receive the *Ortho Membership Directory;* and have free use of the employment services at the annual meeting. As membership expanded, the movement's emphasis also began to change from one of concern about theoretical constructs and techniques of therapy to one of broader sociological and political problems and their relationship to mental health. The orthopsychiatry movement led the way for the concept of child guidance clinics and the subsequent passage by Congress of the Community Mental Retardation and Mental Health Centers Act of 1963. It also assisted in assuring that the educational system provide appropriate educational services to children in the area of mental health (Trippe, 1958). An excellent compilation of articles related to orthopsychiatry and education demonstrated the diversity of the roles of members of the movement (Krugman & Gardner, 1958).

The orthopsychiatric movement was a leader in the interdisciplinary approach to clinical practice, theory, research, and the study of social factors as they affect mental health.

Ortho has applied an interdisciplinary perspective to a wide range of issues affecting children, adolescents, adults, families, schools, and community mental health. Since the beginning, orthopsychiatry's philosophy has included an emphasis on prevention as well as treatment and has focused on the individual within the context of society. This broad-based interdisciplinary concept best characterizes orthopsychiatry and distinguishes it from the more specifically focused professional membership organization. (*Ortho: Interdisciplinary approaches to mental health,* 1985, p. 4)

## REFERENCES

American Orthopsychiatric Association (AOA). (1985). New York: Author.

Krugman, M., & Gardner, G. E. (Eds.). (1958). *Orthopsychiatry and the schools.* New York: American Orthopsychiatric Association.

Lowrey, L. G. (1957). Historical perspective. *American Journal of Orthopsychiatry, 27,* 223.

Mohr, G. J. (1938). Orthopsychiatry—fifteenth year. *American Journal of Orthopsychiatry, 8,* 185.

*Ortho: Interdisciplinary approaches to mental health.* (1985, April). Paper presented at 62nd annual meeting of the American Orthopsychiatric Association, New York.

Trippe, M. J. (1958). Mental health and the education of the exceptional child. In M. Krugman & G. E. Gardner (Eds.), *Orthopsychiatry and the schools.* New York: American Orthopsychiatry Association.

Wolman, B. B. (Eds.). (1977). *International encyclopedia of psychiatry, psychology, psychoanalysis, and neurology* (Vol. 8). New York: Aesculapius.

SUSANNE BLOUGH ABBOTT
*Bedford Central School District,
Mt. Kisco, New York*

**CHILD PSYCHIATRY**
**CLINICAL PSYCHOLOGY**

## ORTON, SAMUEL T. (1879–1948)

Samuel T. Orton, a physician, is best known for his studies of children with severe reading disabilities. The children with whom he worked, although not otherwise impaired, experienced extreme difficulty in acquiring the skills of reading, writing, spelling, or speech. Orton found that these language difficulties were constitutional and were often associated with confusion in direction, time, and sequence.

**Samuel T. Orton**

Orton called this syndrome word blindness and set forth principles for its remediation. Teaching procedures developed by his associates, Anna Gillingham and Bessie W. Stillman, are widely used today in special education. The Orton Society, formed a year after Orton's death, carries forward the work that be began.

**REFERENCES**

*Bulletin of the Orton Society.* Pomfret, CT: Orton Society.

Orton, S. T. (1937). *Reading, writing and speech problems in children.* New York: Norton.

PAUL IRVINE
*Katonah, New York*

## ORTON DYSLEXIA SOCIETY

See INTERNATIONAL DYSLEXIA ASSOCIATION.

## ORTON-GILLINGHAM METHOD

The Orton-Gillingham method of teaching reading was developed by Anna Gillingham (Gillingham & Stillman, 1968) and is based on the theoretical work of the American neurologist Samuel Orton. Orton (1937) cultivated a special interest in dyslexic children (children of normal intelligence with a severe reading disability). He believed that weak associative power was central to these children's difficulties, stemming from incomplete suppression of the nondominant cerebral hemisphere. Gillingham translated these theories into a highly structured reading method that stresses the repeated association of individual phonemes with their sound, name, and cursive formation.

Initially, individual letters are taught using drill cards and a carefully structured question-answer format focused on the letter sound (introduced by key words), the letter name, and the letter formation (first traced, then copied, and finally written from memory). After mastering all these aspects of the first group of letters (a, b, h, i, j, k, m, p, t), the student is taught to blend them into simple consonant-vowel-consonant words (e.g., map, hit, Tim). Instruction then focuses on the spelling of these same simple words, again in a structured format that requires repeating the word, naming and simultaneously writing the letters, and reading the word after it is written.

The similarly structured introduction of subsequent single letters, blends (e.g., st, cl, tr) and other letter combinations (e.g., sh, ea, tion) is meticulously sequenced. Later stages in the sequence include sentence and story writing, syllabification, dictionary skills, and advanced spelling rules.

Often referred to as a multisensory approach (Oakland, Black, Stanford, Nussbaum, & Balise, 1998), the Orton-Gillingham method is one of several reading methods that emphasizes the phonetic regularities of English in its instructional sequence. It differs from other code-emphasis approaches by teaching letter sounds in isolation and requiring a considerable amount of individual letter blending (e.g., m-a-p = map). Its instructional format is highly repetitious. Within this method the teacher repeatedly combines reading with writing activities and relies heavily on drill techniques. The instructional materials include phoneme drill cards, phonetically regular word cards, syllable concept cards, little stories, and a detailed manual (Gillingham & Stillman, 1968).

The Orton-Gillingham method assumes a tutorial setting. Two adaptations of the method, which are conceived for small groups and classrooms as well as a tutorial arrangement, are *Recipe for Reading* (Traub & Bloom, 1970) and *Multisensory Approach to Language Arts* (Slingerland, 1974). Recent studies have found that students taught by this method for two years demonstrated significantly higher reading recognition and comprehension than control counterparts (Oakland et al., 1998). It has also been adapted for at-risk students learning a second language (Sparks, 1991).

## REFERENCES

Gillingham, A., & Stillman, B. (1968). *Remedial teaching for children with disability in reading, spelling, and penmanship.* Cambridge, MA: Educator's Publishing Service.

Oakland, T., Black, J. L., Stanford, G., Nussbaum, N. L., & Balise, R. (1998). An evaluation of the dyslexia training program: A multisensory method for promoting reading in students with reading disabilities. *Journal of Learning Disabilities, 31,* (2), 140–147.

Orton, S. T. (1937). *Reading, writing, and speech problems in children.* New York: Norton.

Slingerland, B. H. (1974). *A multisensory approach to language arts for specific language disability children.* Cambridge, MA: Educator's Publishing Service.

Sparks, R. L. (1991). Use of the Orton-Gillingham approach to teach a foreign language to Dyslexic learning disabled students. *Annals of Dyslexia, 41,* 96–118.

Traub, N., & Bloom, F. (1970). *Recipe for reading.* Cambridge, MA: Educator's Publishing Service.

KATHERINE GARNETT
*Hunter College, City University of New York*

## OSBORN, ALEXANDER FAICKNEY (1888–1966)

Alexander Faickney Osborn, an advertising executive, financier, civic leader, author, and educator, was widely known for his emphasis on creativity as a teachable skill. He has been described as "a seminal thinker and gifted writer, whose clear and practical explanation of the basic concepts of creative thinking and problem solving would influence the thinking, teaching, and research of tens of thousands of others over at least a half-century" (Isaksen & Treffinger, 1985, p. 4). Among Osborn's accomplishments are his introduction and promotion of a technique of organized ideation called brainstorming and the development of a system for teaching creative problem solving.

He authored several books on creativity including *How to Think Up* (1942), *Your Creative Power* (1948), and *Wake Up Your Mind* (1952). His most popular book, *Applied Imagination: Principles and Procedures of Creative Thinking* (1953), now in its third revision and eighteenth printing, is a classic. Osborn's dedication to the power of imagination has had a significant impact on the development and training of creative potential. His firm belief in the idea that people can be taught to become better creative thinkers led to the establishment of the Creative Education Foundation in Buffalo, New York in 1954. The foundation was developed to disseminate information on the development of creative thinking skills and to sponsor the annual week-long Creative Problem Solving Institute. In 1967 the first issue of the *Journal of Creative Behavior,* a quarterly on creative development, was published by the foundation.

## REFERENCES

Dodge, E. N. (Ed.). (1968). *Encyclopedia of American biography.* (Vol. 38). New York: American Historical.

Isaksen, S. G., & Treffinger, D. J. (1985). *Creative problem solving: The basic course.* New York: Bearly.

Osborn, A. F. (1957). *Applied imagination: Principles and procedures of creative thinking.* New York: Scribner.

Staff. (1971). *The national cyclopedia of American biography* (Vol. 53). New York: James T. White.

MARY M. FRASIER
*University of Georgia*

## CREATIVE PROBLEM SOLVING INSTITUTE

## OSGOOD, CHARLES E. (1916–1991)

Charles E. Osgood was born in Brookline, Massachusetts on November 20, 1916. He was a noted linguist, researcher, and Guggenheim fellow. He obtained his BA at Dartmouth College in 1939 and his PhD in psychology at Yale University in 1945. Osgood was an instructor at Yale from 1942 to 1945, conducted psychological research for the U.S. Air Force and Navy from 1946 to 1947, and was an assistant professor from 1946 to 1949. Beginning in 1950, Osgood was associated with the University of Illinois in Urbana as an associate professor (1950–1955), professor (1955–1981), and professor emeritus from 1981. Osgood also served as director of the Institute of Communication Research during his tenure there.

During his distinguished career, Osgood conducted research on a variety of topics related to semantics, with particular interest in cultural differences in the meaning of language (Adams & Osgood, 1973; Osgood, 1969, 1975). His 23-culture investigation of the concept of color revealed similar cross-cultural feelings about colors, with black and gray being perceived as bad, while blue and green were seen as good. Osgood's work in this area is detailed in his book, *Language, Meaning and Culture* (1990), published prior to his death in 1991.

Osgood's model of verbal interaction provided the theoretical basis for the construction of ITPA (Illinois Test of Psycholinguistic Abilities), which was widely used in the late 1960s and 1970s for the assessment of children with learning disabilities. During his lifetime, Osgood authored or coauthored numerous publications, including *Measurement of Meaning* (1975) and *Lectures on Language Performance* (1980).

**REFERENCES**

Adams, F. M., & Osgood, C. E. (1973). A cross-cultural study of the affective meanings of color. *Journal of Cross-Cultural Psychology, 4*(2), 135–156.

Osgood, C. E. (1969). On the whys and wherefores of E, P, and A. *Journal of Personality and Social Psychology, 12*(3), 194–199.

Osgood, C. E. (1980). *Lectures on language performance.* New York: Springer-Verlag.

Osgood, C. E., Suci, G. J., & Tannenbaum, P. (1975). *Measurement of meaning.* Urbana, IL: University of Illinois.

Osgood, C. E., & Tzeng, O. C. (1990). *Language, meaning and culture: The selected papers of C. E. Osgood.* New York: Praeger.

IVAN Z. HOLOWINSKY
*Rutgers University*
First edition

TAMARA J. MARTIN
*The University of Texas of the
Permian Basin*
Second edition

# OSTEOPOROSIS

Osteoporosis is the manifestation of the disorder known as osteopenia, meaning a reduction of bone mass (Behrman & Vaughan, 1983). Primary osteoporosis is most common in elderly postmenopausal women. Secondary osteoporosis is more common in inactive younger people such as hemiplegics, alcoholics, or those suffering from malnutrition. Adolescents possess several modifiable risk factors for osteoporosis (Lysen & Walker, 1997). Treatment with steroids and heparin may also cause the condition. It is generally asymptomatic until a fracture or cracking of a vertebrae has occurred while lifting a heavy object or from an unexpected jolt (Wandel, 1981).

Treatment of the condition may include dietary alteration, administration of sex hormones, and minerals to aid in calcification (Cooley, 1977; Rubin, 1985). Safeguards must be taught to both the individual and the family, including instruction on how to lift heavy objects safely. First-aid instruction for fractures is also essential (Wandel, 1981).

**REFERENCES**

Behrman, R., & Vaughan, V. (1983). *Nelson textbook of pediatrics* (12th ed.). Philadelphia: Saunders.

Cooley, D. (Ed.). (1977). *Family medical guide.* New York: Better Homes and Gardens.

Lysen, V. C., & Walker, R. (1997). Osteoporosis risk factors in eighth grade students. *Journal of School Health, 67*(8), 317–321.

Rubin, K. (1985). *Osteoporosis in Prader-Willi syndrome.* Presentation at Prader-Willi Association National Conference, Windsor Locks, CT.

Wandel, C. (1981). *Diseases, the nurses' reference library series.* Philadelphia: Informed Communications.

JOHN E. PORCELLA
*Rhinebeck Country School*

**BRITTLE BONE DISEASE
PRADER-WILLI SYNDROME**

# OTHER HEALTH IMPAIRED

Other health-impaired children include those pupils whose health problems severely affect learning. Federal law designates this group as including children with severe orthopedic impairments, illnesses of a chronic or acute nature that require a prolonged convalescence or that limit that child's vitality and strength (Acquired Immune Deficiency Syndrome), congenital anomalies (e.g., spina bifida or clubfoot), other physical causes (e.g., amputation or cerebral palsy), and other health problems including, but not limited to, hemophilia, asthma, severe anemia, and diabetes. This category constitutes about 4 percent of those children classified as handicapped (Ysseldyke & Algozzine, 1984). Unfortunately, the terminology used for children suffering other health impairments does not indicate any commonality in student need as the categorization is based on recognizable differences in condition and not on necessary educational interventions (Reynolds & Birch, 1982). In addition, the overrepresentation of ethnic minorities in this category is much smaller than other categories, such as learning disabilities (Coulter, 1996).

Other health impairments may the be result of congenital defects or adventitious (acquired) disabilities. The tremendous heterogeneity associated with the term requires attention to the one obvious common factor of such children, a physical condition that interferes with normal functioning by limiting the child's opportunity to participate fully in learning activities by affecting the body's supply of strength and energy or the removal of wastes; by reducing mobility; and by creating severe problems in growth and development (Kneedler, Hallahan, & Kauffman, 1984).

Although the continuum may range from mild to severe impairments, educational principles for other health-impaired children include:

1. Placement and education within the mainstream of the public school to the maximum capability of the child. For those children requiring special classes, special schools, or home/hospital instruction, direct efforts to return them as soon as possible to regular education (Heron & Harris, 1982).

2. Architectural modifications including the removal of all architectural barriers to full school integration and the modification of classroom structure and environment to allow optimal mobility and exploration.

3. Parent and family education (assumed by the school) to provide for coordination of effort, resources, and services.

4. Trained teachers and paraprofessionals who will assist other health-impaired children within the school setting.

5. Coordination and use of all necessary support and resource personnel by school districts serving such children, including transportation modifications, physical and occupational therapy, adaptive physical education, and vocational education and counseling (Gearheart & Weishahn, 1980).

## REFERENCES

Coulter, A. (1996, April 1–5). *Alarming or disarming: The status of ethnic differences within exceptionalities.* Paper presented at the Annual Convention of the Council for Exceptional Children, Orlando, Florida.

Gearheart, B. R., & Weishahn, M. W. (1980). *The handicapped child in the regular classroom* (2nd ed.). St. Louis, MO: Mosby.

Heron, T. E., & Harris, K. C. (1982). *The educational consultant: Helping professionals, parents, and mainstreamed students.* Boston: Allyn & Bacon.

Kneedler, R. D., Hallahan, D. P., & Kauffman, J. M. (1984). *Special education for today.* Englewood Cliffs, NJ: Prentice Hall.

Reynolds, M. C., & Birch, J. W. (1982). *Teaching exceptional children in all America's schools.* Reston, VA: Council for Exceptional Children.

Ysseldyke, J. E., & Algozzine, B. (1984). *Introduction to special education.* Boston: Houghton Mifflin.

RONALD S. LENKOWSKY
*Hunter College, City University
of New York*

ASTHMA
CHRONIC ILLNESS IN CHILDREN
DIABETES
PHYSICAL DISABILITIES
SPINA BIFIDA

## OTIS-LENNON SCHOOL ABILITY TEST– SIXTH EDITION

The sixth edition of Otis-Lennon School Ability Test (OL-SAT; Otis & Lennon, 1990) is the most recent in a series that began over a half-century ago with the publication of the Otis Group Intelligence Scale. The OLSAT is designed to assess individuals' abilities to cope with school learning tasks and to suggest their possible placement for school learning functions. The test may be administered to those in kindergarten through the twelfth grade.

All items in the OLSAT–Sixth Edition are new. The items are grouped into five clusters: Verbal Comprehension, Verbal Reasoning, Pictorial Reasoning, Figural Reasoning, and Quantitative Reasoning. There are seven different levels of the OLSAT, which are administered according to the examinee's grade level. All levels of the test are preceded by a practice test, and the four lower levels have full oral administration. Self-administration is gradually introduced in the third and fourth levels, and the upper three levels (for grades 4 to 12) are completely self-administered. Total raw scores on the test are converted to School Ability Indexes that are standard scores (M = 100, SD = 16). Scores are also available for the verbal and nonverbal parts of the test.

The OLSAT was standardized on a sample of approximately 175,000 students. Internal consistency estimates of reliability for the Total, Verbal, and Nonverbal scores range from the .70s to the low .90s across all grade levels. The reliability estimates for the clusters are lower with one as low as .24 and some in the .60s. Swerdlik (1992) noted that no data on the stability of scores are available. Anastasi (1992) noted that the treatment of the validity data uses an outdated approach, and that it would be beneficial to have an integrated, comprehensive discussion of validation procedures. Although there are limitations of this group-administered school ability test, the OLSAT represents a technically adequate test for screening purposes with a variety of strengths (Swerdlik, 1992).

**REFERENCES**

Anastasi, A. (1992). Review of the Otis-Lennon School Ability Test, Sixth Edition. In J. J. Kramer & J. C. Conoley (Eds.), *The eleventh mental measurements yearbook* (pp. 623–635). Lincoln, NE: Buros Institute of Mental Measurements.

Otis, A. S., & Lennon, R. T. (1990). *Otis-Lennon School Ability Test, Sixth Edition*. San Antonio, TX: Psychological Corporation.

Swerdlik, M. E. (1992). Review of the Otis-Lennon School Ability Test, Sixth Edition. In J. J. Kramer & J. C. Conoley (Eds.), *The eleventh mental measurements yearbook* (pp. 635–639). Lincoln, NE: Buros Institute of Mental Measurements.

ELIZABETH O. LICHTENBERGER
*The Salk Institute*

ACHIEVEMENT TESTS
DEVIATION IQ
INTELLIGENCE TESTING

# OTITIS MEDIA

Otitis media is an inflammation or infection of the middle ear. Nasal secretions back up and infect the Eustachian tube so that the air pressure in the middle ear is no longer equalized and a partial vacuum is created, causing an impairment in hearing. The infection can also be caused by the puncturing of the eardrum. There are three types of otitis media—acute, serous, and chronic.

Acute otitis media and serous otitis media are the most prominent causes of conductive hearing loss in children. The symptoms of acute otitis media include ear pain, hearing loss, aural discharge, and a sensation of fullness in the ear. While commonly occurring in infants and children, it may occur at any age. The onset usually follows an upper respiratory tract infection. Fever is usually present. The common treatment is bed rest, analgesics, and antibiotics. Ear drops are usually of limited value but local heat is helpful. Oral decongestants may also hasten relief. Acute otitis media, if properly treated with antibiotics, usually is resolved. If treatment is terminated prematurely, resolution of the infection may be incomplete and a conductive hearing loss may persist. Studies suggest that chronic conditions, regardless of onset, can significantly interfere with language/speech acquisition.

Serous otitis media is characterized by the accumulation of fluid in the middle ear that results in a temporary hearing loss. The absence of fever and pain distinguish it from acute otitis media. The hearing loss is characterized by a plugged feeling in the ear and a reverberation of the patient's voice. Treatment consists of nasal decongestants. Antihistamines may be given if a nasal allergy is suspected as the cause.

Tonsillectomy and adenoidectomy may be necessary to permanently correct the condition (Bluestone, 1982).

Chronic otitis media is nearly always associated with perforation of the eardrum. There are two types of chronic otitis media: benign and that which is associated with mastoid disease (Shaffer, 1978). The latter is more serious by far and is characterized by a foul smelling drainage from the ear as well as impaired hearing. If chronic mastoiditis occurs in infancy, the mastoid bone does not develop a good cellular structure. Antibiotic drugs are usually of limited use in combating the infection, but they may be useful in treating complications. Local cleansing of the ear with antibiotic powders and solutions is one method of treatment. Surgery may be needed in other cases. The complications of chronic otitis media and mastoiditis may be meningitis and sinus thrombosis.

**REFERENCES**

Bluestone, C. D. (1982). Otitis media in children: To treat or not to treat? *New England Journal of Medicine, 306,* 1399.

Shaffer, H. L. (1978). Acute mastoiditis and cholesteatoma. *Otolaryngology, 86,* 394.

ROBERT A. SEDLAK
*University of Wisconsin at Stout*

DEAF
LANGUAGE DELAYS

# OTOLARYNGOLOGIST

An otolaryngologist is a specialist who can treat diseases of and perform surgery on the ear, nose, and throat. An otolaryngologist may be consulted for disorders that might manifest themselves as speech or hearing disorders. An examination by an otolaryngologist will require an inspection of the nose, neck, throat, head, and ears. The otolaryngologist will locally anesthetize the area of the nose and use a series of probes to check for blockages and mucus. The Eustachian tubes are then checked for their functional efficiency. The physician checks for thick bands of adhesions or growths of adenoid tissue in the fossae of Rosenmueller behind the tubal openings. Using a tongue depressor and a mirror these can be seen by looking up the nasopharynx. The entire interior of the mouth is examined, including the teeth and tongue. Finally, the ears are examined using an otoscope (Sataloff, 1966).

The otolaryngologist may work in cooperation with other specialists. An audiologist may be consulted to do a hearing examination and consider nonsurgical remedies for a hearing problem or postsurgical services. A speech pathologist may work with an otolaryngologist for nonsurgical remedies for speech difficulties or for postsurgical services (Northern & Downs, 1974).

## REFERENCES

Cowley, J. (1996). Longitudinal studies—Are they worth it? *Australian Research in Early Childhood Education, 1,* 225–226.

Northern, J. L., & Downs, M. P. (1974). *Hearing in children.* Baltimore: Williams & Wilkins.

Johnson, D. L. (1997, April, 3–6). *The effects of early otitis media with effusion on child cognitive and language development at ages three and five.* Paper presented at the Biennial Meeting of the Society for Research in Child Development, Washington, DC.

Sataloff, J. (1966). *Hearing loss.* Philadelphia: Lippincott.

ROBERT A. SEDLAK
*University of Wisconsin at Stout*

DEAF
OTITIS MEDIA
SPEECH-LANGUAGE PATHOLOGIST

## OTOLOGY

Otology is the study of diseases of the ear. This includes deafness and other hearing defects as well as earaches, discharges, and infections of the mastoid. An otologist is a medical doctor who specializes in the treatment of these diseases and problems. An otologist can diagnose causes of hearing problems and recommend medical and surgical treatments. An otologist may have an MD (doctor of medicine) or a DO (doctor of osteopathy) degree.

An otologic examination will involve far more than just an examination of the ear because the cause of some symptoms may lie in the nose, neck, or throat. An initial examination begins with a case history. Surgery for correction of otosclerosis and ossicular defects leaves no detectable scars; therefore questions regarding such surgery are necessary in taking a health history. Since otology deals with diseases of the ear, an otologist may call in an otolaryngologist to assist with a case when the source of the condition might originate in the nose or throat. An otolaryngologist deals with symptoms and diseases in which there is some relationship among the ear, nose, and throat.

ROBERT A. SEDLAK
*University of Wisconsin at Stout*

DEAF
OTITIS MEDIA
OTOLARYNGOLOGIST

## OTOSCLEROSIS

Otosclerosis is a common conductive hearing loss that occurs with the onset of middle age. The eardrum and middle ear appear to be normal through an otoscope. What develops, however, is the formation of spongy bone in the cochlear bone. The cause is unknown. The name otosclerosis is misleading for the process is really not a sclerotic one but more like a vascularization in the bone. There are more people with otosclerosis than have sought medical attention for the condition. Evidence of this fact is the result of autopsies that have been done on persons without any known history of hearing impairment. Otosclerosis can occur without a resultant hearing loss. This occurs when otosclerotic changes affect areas of the bony labyrinth other than the oval window. When a hearing loss is associated with otosclerosis, it is referred to as clinical otosclerosis. The condition develops over a period of months or even years. The hearing gradually diminishes as the footplate becomes more fixed. In some cases, the hearing loss stops after reaching only a mild level. More frequently, the hearing loss stabilizes at 50 to 60 dB. The hearing deficit starts in the lower frequencies and progresses to the higher ones (Davis & Silverman, 1974).

Otosclerosis is a condition more common in females than in males and the symptoms may be aggravated by pregnancy. The condition is often found in several people in the same family. While there may be a genetic linkage to the condition in some cases, prediction based on genetic theory is not refined. Offspring of two people with otosclerosis have been found to have normal hearing. The condition could occur in just one ear. Surgery may help to restore some of the hearing loss (Sataloff, 1966).

## REFERENCES

Davis, H., & Silverman, S. R. (1974). *Hearing and deafness.* New York: Holt, Rinehart, & Winston.

Sataloff, J. (1966). *Hearing loss.* Philadelphia: Lippincott.

ROBERT A. SEDLAK
*University of Wisconsin at Stout*

DEAF
DEAF EDUCATION
OTITIS MEDIA

## OVERACHIEVEMENT AND SPECIAL EDUCATION

Typically, overachievement is not an area considered in association with special education. However, there are areas within special education where children exhibit superior abilities. For example, gifted and talented children possess skills or abilities that are considered to be superior to those found in the normal population. This is the area of special education where overachievement is prevalent. Another example of a group of children who exhibit extraordinary abilities are idiot savants. These children are markedly retarded except for some highly developed skill that is grossly discrepant with their functioning in other areas (Knopf, 1984). These unusual abilities within the context of delayed development are also found in autistic children (Rimland, 1964). There is no satisfactory explanation for these rare occurrences of isolated areas of outstanding abilities in individuals who show delayed development in all other areas. Nevertheless, idiot savants have been noted with special abilities that are, by far, superior to those found in the normal population in art, music, mechanics, calculation, mental calendar manipulation, and memory (Rimland, 1964).

Aside from those areas where children possess superior skills or abilities, overachievement would not usually be considered associated with special education. Achievement below normal performance, or underachievement, is more common, and most areas of special education focus on the inability to learn. For example, the mentally retarded, learning disabled, and emotionally disturbed manifest conditions that adversely affect educational performance; children with speech and language problems who are unable to comprehend language or express themselves adequately have difficulties in learning; and the physically impaired (e.g., those with hearing impairments, visual impairments, and health impairments) exhibit disabilities that affect achievement.

Special education has generally focused on these children's deficiencies, but in addition to weaknesses, these children also have strengths. It is these strengths that allow the special child to overachieve in some areas. For example, moderately retarded children generally do not learn to read beyond a first-grade level (Kirk & Gallagher, 1983). However, some of these children do read at higher levels. This ability to read at higher levels is probably owed to individual strengths in reading ability. In all likelihood, this reading ability would not demonstrate overachievement when compared with the normal population, but when compared with these children's other abilities, it may well demonstrate overachievement. Therefore, overachievement in special education must be considered in relation to each child's abilities and disabilities.

It appears that the key to understanding overachievement in special education is to focus on intraindividual differences (i.e., differences within individual children). If we focus on the individual strengths of each child, it then becomes possible to discover areas of skill development where the child is overachieving. By considering overachievement in this manner, it becomes clear that a child in any area of special education can demonstrate overachievement in a wide variety of skills. Furthermore, in many instances these children can also demonstrate overachievement in those areas restricted by their disabilities if some compensation or modification is made to the learning environment that will allow them the opportunity to learn and/or display those skills.

## REFERENCES

Kirk, S. A., & Gallagher, J. J. (1983). *Educating exceptional children* (4th ed.). Boston: Houghton Mifflin.

Knopf, I. J. (1984). *Childhood psychopathology: A developmental approach* (2nd ed.). Englewood Cliffs, NJ: Prentice Hall.

Rimland, B. (1964). *Infantile autism.* Englewood Cliffs, NJ: Prentice Hall.

LARRY J. WHEELER
*Southwest Texas State
University*

## OVERCORRECTION

Overcorrection refers to a punishment procedure and includes the systematic application of prescribed strategies to decrease the future occurrence of targeted behaviors. An overcorrection package may include verbal reprimands, time-out from positive reinforcement, short verbal instructions, and graduated guidance. The two major procedures of overcorrection are restitution and positive practice. Restitution means restoring the environment or oneself to a state that is vastly improved relative to the prior condition. Positive practice involves the repeated practice of certain forms of behaviors relevant to the content in which the behavior occurred (Hobbs, 1985).

Foxx (1982) describes three characteristics of overcorrection acts, including the existence of a direct relationship to the student's misbehavior; implementation immediately following the misbehavior; and rapid administration of overcorrection acts. While administering overcorrection acts, the teacher employs a full or partial graduated guidance form of assistance followed by a shadowing procedure as the program develops. In a full graduated guidance technique, the teacher maintains full contact with the student's hands. In partial graduated guidance, the teacher uses a thumb and forefinger to gently guide the movements of the student. Eventually, the teacher shadows the student by placing a hand in close proximity to the student's hand and initiating contact only when the student fails to complete the movements of the overcorrection act.

A sample behavior that could result in an overcorrection consequence is excessive spillage of food during meals. A simple, correction procedure would require the student to clean only the immediate area of the spillage. Overcorrection would extend this requirement to cleaning additional areas in the cafeteria as well. Additionally, the teacher may require the student to overly clean designated areas even though these areas may not need attention.

In a review of behaviors that have been targeted for overcorrection acts, Ferretti and Cavalier (1983) summarized the reported effectiveness with eating skills, toileting skills, aggressive-disruptive behaviors, stereotype behaviors, and self-injurious behaviors. In these research reports, the individual components of each overcorrection package of strategies were not evaluated. However, general observations of the effectiveness of overcorrection procedures were favorable. Overcorrection acts have been successfully implemented with individuals with mental retardation, autism, emotional and/or behavioral disorders (Tyson & Spooner, 1991).

Caution must be exercised during the formulation and implementation of the components of an overcorrection package. A minimum intensity level of intrusiveness should be maintained that affects the desired behavioral reduction of the targeted behavior. From a practical standpoint, overcorrection requires the investment of close teacher to student contact throughout the implementation of the procedures. Additionally, the physical strength of a strong student must be considered relative to a teacher's ability to guide the movements of the overcorrection acts. A different reductive procedure may be necessary if the teacher is unable to complete the required full graduated guidance.

The appeal of overcorrection is the educative component of teaching the student a correct way of behaving to replace the targeted negative behavior. The implementation of aversive consequences that resemble overcorrection acts, but fail to include this educative component, are mislabeled as overcorrection. Careful monitoring of all aspects of this reductive procedure needs to be included to provide adequate safeguards against potentially abusive situations. As a punishment alternative, overcorrection requires additional investigations to substantiate previous claims of rapid reduction of undesirable behaviors.

## REFERENCES

Axelrod, S., Brantner, J. P., & Meddock, T. D. (1978). Overcorrection: A review and critical analysis. *Journal of Special Education, 12,* 367–391.

Ferretti, R. P., & Cavalier, A. R. (1983). A critical assessment of overcorrection procedures with mentally retarded persons. In J. L. Matson & F. Andrasik (Eds.), *Treatment issues and innovations in mental retardation* (pp. 241–301). New York: Plenum.

Foxx, R. M. (1982). *Decreasing behaviors of severely retarded and autistic persons* (pp. 91–111). Champaign, IL: Research Press.

Hobbs, S. A. (1985). Overcorrection. In A. S. Bellack & M. Hersen (Eds.), *Dictionary of behavior therapy techniques* (pp. 158–160). New York: Pergamon.

Kazdin, A. E. (1984). *Behavior modification in applied settings* (3rd ed.) (pp. 136–139). Homewood, IL: Dorsey.

Ollendick, T. H., & Matson, J. L. (1978). Overcorrection: An overview. *Behavior Therapy, 9,* 830–842.

Tyson, M. E., & Spooner, F. (1991). A retrospective evaluation of behavioral programming in an institutional setting. *Education and Training in Mental Retardation, 26*(2), 179–189.

ERNEST L. PANCSOFAR
*University of Connecticut*

**BEHAVIOR MODELING**
**BEHAVIOR MODIFICATION**
**DESTRUCTIVE BEHAVIORS**